INFORMATION FOR SCHOOL NEEDS

ENGLISH LITERATURE	AFRICA	SPACE EXPLORATION
UNITED NATIONS	DEBATE	MAN
ECONOMICS	TRANSPORTATION	COMMUNICATION

CAREER PLANNING

EDUCATION	BOOK PUBLISHING	LIBRARY SERVICE
BROADCASTING	ADVERTISING	NURSING
LAW	SOCIAL WORK	ACCOUNTING

ATHLETICS

TENNIS	BOXING	FOOTBALL
LITTLE LEAGUE BASEBALL	WATER SKIING	GOLF
	BASKETBALL	BOWLING

EVERYDAY LIFE

HOME and FAMILY

INFANT CARE	COOKERY	COSMETICS
HOME MANAGEMENT	INTERIOR DECORATION AND DESIGN	CLOTHING FOR THE FAMILY
ADOLESCENCE		DISEASE

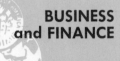

BUSINESS and FINANCE

PUBLIC FINANCE	TAXATION	MORTGAGE
MARKETING	AUTOMATION	DATA PROCESSING
RETAILING	BUSINESS	STOCK MARKETS

HOBBIES and RECREATION

VACATION	BIRD	DOG AND DOG SHOWS
STAMP COLLECTING	GARDENS AND GARDENING	SAILBOAT AND SAILING
BRIDGE		SKIN DIVING

ENCYCLOPEDIA
INTERNATIONAL

Grolier
INCORPORATED
New York

6

E

I

DIATOM
—
EXPLOSION

DRESS color plates following page 118:
Costumes 2600 B.C. through 1870 adapted from A PICTORIAL
HISTORY OF COSTUME by Wolfgang Bruhn and Max Tilke; publisher, Frederick A. Praeger Inc. Costumes 1890 through 1950's
from WESTERN WORLD COSTUME by Carolyn G. Bradley; copy-
right 1954, Appleton-Century-Crofts, Inc.; adapted by permission
of the publisher Appleton-Century-Crofts.

Standard Book Number: 7172-0700-5
Library of Congress Catalog Card Number: 69–10050

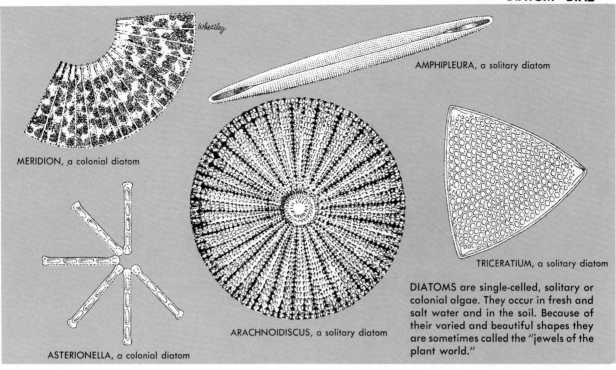

MERIDION, a colonial diatom

AMPHIPLEURA, a solitary diatom

TRICERATIUM, a solitary diatom

ARACHNOIDISCUS, a solitary diatom

ASTERIONELLA, a colonial diatom

DIATOMS are single-celled, solitary or colonial algae. They occur in fresh and salt water and in the soil. Because of their varied and beautiful shapes they are sometimes called the "jewels of the plant world."

DIATOM [dī'ə-tŏm], one-celled algae. The cell wall consists of two valves which fit over each other. The valves are often beautifully sculptured, but this can only be seen through a very good microscope. Diatoms were undoubtedly observed in the 17th century, but they were really studied in earnest only toward the end of the 18th century. This research had much to do with the improvement of the microscope, for it was impossible to observe these minute forms of plant life with the naked eye. Diatoms inhabit stagnant water, wet rocks, and the sea. A large part of the oceanic plankton is composed of diatoms, either free-floating or attached by threads. Directly or indirectly, they are among the most important foods of fresh-water and marine fish. Deposits of diatom shells are found in many parts of the world. They are the basis of powders and soaps for polishing metals and, since the cell walls resist burning, the deposits are also valuable in the manufacture of fireproof linings and walls.

ALYS SUTCLIFFE, Horticulturist, Brooklyn Botanic Garden

DIATOMACEOUS [dī-ə-tə-mā'shəs] **EARTH,** also known as diatomite or kieselguhr, is a siliceous rock of sedimentary origin, made up of fossilized remains of diatoms (microscopic algae). Mineralogically, diatomaceous earth is a variety of opal, or hydrated silica, $SiO_2 \cdot nH_2O$. White and chalklike, it is generally so porous that it will float in water. The world's important deposits are of either marine or fresh-water origin, and they are of Cenozoic Age (less than about 65 million years old). Diatomaceous earth has many industrial uses based largely on its unique microscopic structure, which gives it high porosity and low density. It is used mainly for insulation or as a filtering agent, a mineral filler, an absorbent, a mild abrasive, or a source of reactive silica. About 1,000,000 tons are mined annually throughout the world; half of this is produced in the

United States, much of it from a single large deposit at Lompoc, Calif.

BRIAN MASON, American Museum of Natural History
See also OPAL.

DIATRYMA [dī-ə-trī″mə], large, flightless bird, now extinct. It was about 7 ft. high, had extremely reduced wings, and walked with long, massive legs. Its neck was long and its head large, with a powerful beak. Fossil remains of *Diatryma* are found in rocks of early Eocene Age (more than 50 million years old) in North America and Europe. *Diatryma* must have been a dangerous enemy to the small mammals of its time.

DÍAZ [dē'äs], **(JOSÉ DE LA CRUZ) PORFIRIO** (1830–1915), Mexican President, dictator, and soldier. Díaz, a mestizo of poor parentage, was first educated for the priesthood but, under the influence of the Indian leader Benito Juárez, changed to the law. For some years he remained under Juárez' influence and supported the reform movement headed by him. During the Mexican War (1846–48) he entered the army and thereafter, even though engaged in politics, remained closely associated with it. During the French invasion (1862–67), Díaz bravely and brilliantly opposed the invaders and was able in 1867 to capture and control Mexico City until Juárez could resume the presidency there. Díaz then went into retirement for several years until his growing dissatisfaction with Juárez led him into an unsuccessful army-backed race for the presidency in 1871. In 1876 Díaz revolted against President Sebastián Lerdo de Tejada, forced him out of office, and in 1877 was elected President. From then on until 1911, except for a puppet regime from 1880 to 1884, Díaz occupied the presidency.

Even though he had earlier been anticlerical, Díaz

3

Brown Brothers

Porfirio Díaz, the dictatorial Mexican President who died in exile in Paris in 1915.

quickly and successfully cultivated support from the Roman Catholic Church, largely by giving only lip service to anticlerical legislation continuing on the statute books while he quietly allowed the church to regain much of its former influence and property. He took prompt steps to restore order, chiefly through the well-disciplined *rurales*, a sort of rural militia, some of whom had previously been bandits. Even remote parts of the country became entirely safe for travelers.

Díaz also allied himself with the large landowners, and concentration of land in a few hands increased greatly during his rule. It was estimated that by 1910 the percentage of landless heads of families in eight of the most important agricultural states of Mexico ranged from 96.2% to 99.8%. Investment of foreign capital was also encouraged and large amounts flowed into Mexico from the United States, Britain, France, Germany, and elsewhere.

Chief counsel for his policies came from a small group of well-educated upper-class intimates known as the *científicos*. Some attempt to organize political parties was made in the 1890's, but no effective party competition ever resulted. Díaz gave some indication in 1908 that he would retire in 1910 but he ran for re-election and, after the temporary jailing of his principal opponent, Francisco Madero, was easily re-elected. General revolt soon broke out against him, however, and in May, 1911, he resigned and departed for Europe.

Mexico's fiscal and political credit was excellent during Díaz' rule, but education, land reform, basic living conditions, and cultural life were woefully neglected. The excesses of the first years of the Revolution beginning in 1910 were largely due to earlier repressions by the Díaz regime.

Consult Beals, Carleton, *Porfirio Díaz, Dictator of Mexico* (1932).

Russell H. Fitzgibbon, University of California

DÍAZ DEL CASTILLO [dē'äth thĕl käs-tē'lyō], **BERNAL** (c.1492–1581), Spanish explorer and historian of the New World. Bernal, who was born in Medina del Campo, Spain, accompanied (1514) the Pedrarias Dávila expedition to Panama. Afterward, he served under Diego de Velázquez in Cuba, Francisco Fernández de Córdoba in Yucatán (1517), and then (1519) joined Hernán Cortés in his conquest of Mexico. Many years later, after settling in Guatemala, Bernal wrote *The True History of the Conquest of New Spain* (1632), a vivid, detailed memoir of the venture, of Aztec society, and of the early colonization in Mexico.

DIAZO [dī-ăz'ō] **COMPOUNDS,** substances with two nitrogen atoms linked to one hydrocarbon radical. Dry diazonium salts are explosive. Several important classes of compounds, including dyes, are prepared commercially, using these salts. Diazotype printing depends on the light-sensitivity of these compounds.

DÍAZ ORDAZ [dē'äs ôr-däs'], **GUSTAVO** (1911–), Mexican President. He studied law in the Puebla state college, was admitted to the bar in 1937, and later served on the bench. Entering politics in 1946, he was a deputy in the National Assembly and then a senator unt'l 1952, when he was appointed director general of judicial affairs in the Ministry of the Interior. He was made Interior Minister in 1958, a post he resigned, according to Mexican tradition, when he became officially a candidate for the presidency in 1963. Receiving over 90% of the vote in the elections of July, 1964, he was inaugurated as President on Dec. 1.

DICE GAMES are played with small cubes, whose faces are marked with dots numbering from one to six. The sum of the dots on opposite faces equals seven. Dice games date back at least as far as ancient Greek, Roman, and Egyptian civilizations. Dice also are used incidentally in a number of games, including backgammon; they have a basic role in the following:

Bird Cage (also called Chuck-a-Luck). This game is played in casinos and involves betting against the house (game's management). Three dice are placed in a wire cage shaped like an hourglass, and bets are made on the numbers appearing on the top surfaces of the dice when the cage is turned over and the dice fall to the other end. The simplest wager is one based on the appearance of a selected number. If the number appears once, the bettor collects the amount of his bet; if it appears on two dice, he collects double the amount of his bet; if it appears on all three dice, the amount is tripled. Most casinos also provide for bets on various combinations of numbers, on high and low numbers, and on even and odd. In betting involving single numbers, the house's average take is 8%; the percentage is higher when combinations are involved.

Craps. This is the most widely played dice game in the United States. Any number can play, and two dice are used. The total number of dots showing on the top surfaces after the dice have been thrown determines the value of the throw. The shooter wins immediately if he rolls a 7 or 11 ("natural"), and throws again to begin a new series. He loses if he rolls 2, 3, or 12 (craps), but retains the dice. If his first roll produces 4, 5, 6, 8, 9, or 10, he neither wins nor loses; that number then becomes his point, and he continues to throw until he repeats his original number (makes his point), in which case he wins; or he rolls a 7, in which case he loses both his bet and possession of the dice, which pass to the next player.

Before each series of rolls, bets are made. The shooter first puts the amount of his bet on the playing surface, and other players may fade, or accept, all or any part of it. To fade is to bet that the caster will not pass—that is, win by rolling a natural or making his point before throwing a 7. In wagering, the caster obviously bets that he will win, or pass. In addition to these original bets, there are many others in most games; these are known as "come bets," "side bets," and "hard-way bets," and are based on the almost infinite combinations provided by a cast of the dice.

The odds are 251–244 against the shooter before he rolls. When he has established a point, the odds are 6–5 against his making a 6 or 8, 3–2 against a 5 or 9, and 2–1 against a 4 or 10. "Wise" players specialize in side bets at favorable odds.

When craps is played in casinos, betting is against the house only, and includes many possibilities not found in informal games. The house percentage on combinations is often exorbitant.

Poker Dice. In this game five dice are cast from a cup; the object is to build a winning poker "hand" in three rolls or less. The value of faces descends in this order: 1, 6, 5, 4, 3, 2. The player can set aside as many dice as he wishes in each of his first two rolls. The best "hand" is produced by having all five faces show the same number (five of a kind). In descending order, the others are four of a kind, full house (three of one rank and two of another), three of a kind, two pairs, and one pair. Sometimes the game is played with deuces "wild," that is, a 2 (deuce) has any value the caster specifies.

FRANK K. PERKINS, Games Columnist, Boston *Herald*

DICKENS, CHARLES (JOHN HUFFAM) (1812–70), one of the best-known, most successful, and greatest English novelists. Dickens was born in Portsmouth to parents clinging precariously to the bottom edge of the middle class. When Dickens was only 12 his father went to prison for debt and the boy went to work in a blacking warehouse, a brief but agonizing experience that affected his life and writings in many ways. After some schooling he became a legal clerk and then a legal and Parliamentary shorthand reporter. From these activities and from his acute observation of the London around him, he got his real education. He had an unhappy romance with Maria Beadnell, the Dora Spenlow of *David Copperfield* and the Flora of *Little Dorrit*.

Dickens' first imaginative writings were the *Sketches by Boz*, short sketches of characters and life in the England and London of his day. His first major work, and one that made him famous, was *Pickwick Papers*, first published in monthly paper-bound sections from Apr., 1836, to Nov., 1837. All of Dickens' novels were published serially, either in sections or in periodicals he edited.

In 1836 he married Catherine Hogarth, by whom he had ten children. He was separated from her in 1858 under complex circumstances involving a young actress, Ellen Lawless Ternan, who apparently became his mistress. From 1837 to 1839 he edited *Bentley's Miscellany*, and in 1846 he helped found the *Daily News*. From 1850 until his death he edited, and wrote extensively for, *Household Words* (1850–58) and *All the Year Round* (1858–70). In 1842 he visited America and aroused anger by his frank comments not only during his trip, but afterward in the travel book *American Notes* (1842) and in *Martin Chuzzlewit*. On his second visit in 1867–68 he toured triumphantly, giving the dramatic readings from his works that had already succeeded so well in England. Partly from the extra strain of these public readings, he

George Cruikshank   *Culver Pictures, Inc.*

Drawing by George Cruikshank from Dickens' *Oliver Twist* shows Oliver asking for food.

National Portrait Gallery, London

Charles Dickens, as portrayed by Ary Scheffer in 1855.

The Bettmann Archive

Fagin, the villain, in prison. Illustration from *Oliver Twist* by George Cruikshank.

died of a stroke. He was buried in the Poets' Corner of Westminster Abbey.

Dickens wrote 14 novels as well as many shorter works; among the latter are his five Christmas stories, the best-known of which is *A Christmas Carol*. His early novels, *Pickwick Papers, Oliver Twist, Nicholas Nickleby*, and *The Old Curiosity Shop*, written in rapid succession from 1836 to 1840, brought him fame at once, and are still among his most popular works. After this date he wrote more slowly, and in books such as *Martin Chuzzlewit* and *Dombey and Son* worked toward the unified treatment of a single problem. The most popular of his later novels is the historical romance *A Tale of Two Cities*. But critics such as Edmund Wilson and Lionel Trilling recognize more complex, more sombre novels such as *Bleak House, Little Dorrit, Great Expectations*, and *Our Mutual Friend* as Dickens' greatest work. How his last novel, *The Mystery of Edwin Drood*, would have ended is an enigma.

Many of the more grotesque characters in Dickens' novels, such as Fagin, Scrooge, and Sam Weller, have become as proverbial as Chaucer's Wife of Bath or Shakespeare's Bottom and Falstaff. The characters in Dickens' later novels are less purely comic and fantastic and often take on fuller, symbolic identities. The settings of his novels evoke the London of his day and earlier with realistic authenticity and at the same time surrealistic intensity. Not only do his novels have exciting and memorable plots, but they are also angry exposures of social and moral injustices as well as rich symbolic visions of life as Dickens, morally sensitive and courageous and artistically imaginative, saw it.

Consult Johnson, Edgar, *Charles Dickens, His Tragedy and Triumph* (1952); Ford, G. H., *Dickens and His Readers* (1955); *The Dickens Critics*, ed. by G. H. Ford and Lauriat Lane, Jr. (1961).

LAURIAT LANE, JR., University of New Brunswick, Canada
See also articles on individual works and characters.

DICKEY, JAMES (1923–   ), American poet, born in Atlanta, Ga. Awarded a number of prizes, his verse has a wide variety of subject and tone, from sensitive concentration on nature, as in *Drowning With Others* (1962), to the social concerns of *Buckdancer's Choice* (1965). With diction and rhythms close to common speech, the poems are quiet but firm in contemplation of ordinary sights and events. Other volumes of his poetry are *Into the Stone* (1960), *Interpreter's House* (1963), *Helmets* (1964), and *Two Poems of the Air* (1964). Dickey was a Guggenheim fellow in 1962–63.

DICKINSON, EMILY (1830–86), American poet. Though she seldom left her native Amherst, Mass., her poems were not devoted to the local scene, but to speculation and lightly philosophic observation. Well-educated and better read, with a year at Mount Holyoke Female Seminary in nearby South Hadley, she drew less upon books than upon her relationships with people and on candid intuitions concerning love, death, and eternity. Only seven of her poems were printed during her lifetime. The rest, collected after her death, were first edited by Mabel Loomis Todd and T. W. Higginson in 1890 and 1891, and most accurately by T. H. Johnson as *The Poems of Emily Dick-*

Emily Dickinson, American poet. (BROWN BROTHERS)

inson (3 vols., 1955). Johnson also edited *The Prose of Emily Dickinson* (3 vols., 1958).

Usually brief and in simple ballad meter, with faintly articulated rhymes, her poems combine vivid imagery with subtle choice of words. But if her poems are small, her subjects are large: her often compressed, elliptical language evokes the power of love, the awesomeness of death, and the value of aspiration, all of which weight her fragile lines with solid insights.

Consult Whicher, G. F., *This Was a Poet* (1938); Johnson, T. H., *Emily Dickinson* (1955).

LEWIS LEARY, Columbia University

DICKINSON, JOHN (1732–1808), American political essayist and statesman. Dickinson, who was born in Talbot County, Md., and reared in Delaware, studied law in Philadelphia and London and in 1757 opened a lucrative practice in Philadelphia. After sitting (1760–62) in the Assembly of the Lower Counties (Delaware), he served (1762–64) in the Pennsylvania legislature. In challenging Benjamin Franklin's movement to change the colony from proprietary to royal government, Dickinson failed of reelection. But his writings against the Sugar Act and the Stamp Act prompted the legislature to send him to the Stamp Act Congress (1765) where he exerted a moderating influence.

In response to the Townshend Acts (1767), Dickinson made his greatest contribution to the colonial definition of parliamentary power in his *Letters from a Farmer in Pennsylvania to the Inhabitants of the British Colonies*. Appearing first in the *Pennsylvania Chronicle*, these essays conceded Parliament's right to regulate trade but denied its taxing authority. Dickinson, however, opposed the use of force, and as a delegate to the Continental Congress (1774–76), he urged conciliation and voted against the Declaration of Independence. Nevertheless, he supported the Revolution, serving as a brigadier of militia.

He was the President of Delaware (1781–82) and the Governor of Pennsylvania (1782–85). After presiding over the Annapolis Convention (1786), he made his final important political contribution by representing Delaware and championing the small states at the federal Constitutional Convention (1787). There he professed admiration for a limited monarchy, but conceded it was unsuitable in a republic. Several of his less conservative ideas were reflected in the Constitution, which he supported in his writings.

ROBERT MIDDLEKAUFF, Yale University

DICKINSON, city of southwestern North Dakota, and seat of Stark County. It is an important livestock- and wheat-shipping center. As a gateway to the scenic Badlands, it is a tourist center. Dickinson State Teachers College is located here. Pop. (1950) 7,469; (1960) 9,971.

DICKSON, town of west-central Tennessee located on the western Highland Rim, about 40 mi. west-southwest of Nashville. Situated in an agricultural region devoted to general farming and grazing, the town also has manufactures of work clothing, Fiberglas outboard boats, missile parts, and a wide range of wood products based on local hardwood-lumber supplies. Inc., 1899; pop. (1950) 3,348; (1960) 5,028.

DICKSON CITY, coal-mining borough near Scranton, in northeastern Pennsylvania. The town was named for a president of the Delaware and Hudson Railroad. Inc., 1875; pop. (1950) 8,948; (1960) 7,738.

DICOTYLEDON [dī-kŏt-ə-lē′dən], plants with two seed leaves, or cotyledons, which can be easily identified when the seed germinates. The plants have net-veined leaves, as found in oaks, maples, sunflowers, asters, and clovers. The stems are herbaceous or woody with vascular bundles arranged in circles. Inside the circles is the pith, outside the bundles is the cortex, and covering that is the epidermis, which in trees and shrubs is eventually replaced by bark. In the dicotyledon group there are more than 100,000 species. The stems of plants are usually much-branched. The primary root remains until the plant is full grown, then sometimes forms a taproot.

Some well-known families are the birch family (birch, alder, hazel); the beech family (beech, chestnut, oak), which is the largest group; the elm family, with over 140 species of ornamental trees and shrubs; the rose family, which includes nearly all the edible fruits grown in the temperate zone, as well as species and garden varieties of roses; and the pea family, which includes many crop plants and ornamental trees and shrubs.

ALYS SUTCLIFFE, Horticulturist, Brooklyn Botanic Garden
See also ANGIOSPERMS; FLOWER; LEAF; PLANT; SEED.

DICTATORSHIP, a form of political rule. Dictatorship is a kind of autocracy, which to the Greeks signified a regime where the ruler was not responsible to anyone but himself for his actions. Both dictatorship and autocracy have been equated at various times with despotism, absolutism, tyranny, authoritarianism, and totalitarianism. Important distinctions involving these terms have been drawn by the great political philosophers in the West, which should be considered. Tyranny, in Aristotle's

classic definition in the *Politics*, was a form of government carried on in the interest of the rulers instead of the ruled. But in this connection it should be pointed out that the dictatorship established by Nikolai Lenin in Russia was not administered for the private advantage of Lenin. This term has always had certain emotional connotations, as Thomas Hobbes indicated in his *Leviathan*, when he said that tyranny is a form of government "misliked." But even the attribution of unlimited or willful power to all dictatorship needs qualification, in view of the constitutional dictatorship in the Roman Republic.

Constitutional Dictatorship. From 501 to 216 B.C. there were 88 constitutional dictators appointed by the Roman Republic. The most famous was Cincinnatus, a member of the Roman aristocracy. According to tradition, after saving the Roman state from the menace of the Aequians in 458 B.C., he returned to a private life of farming on his country estate. His career thus dramatically illustrates the nature of Roman constitutional dictatorship. It was only employed to save the commonwealth in an emergency. It could not change the constitution; it was temporary in duration, six months, at most; and it provided for the accountability of the dictator for his actions. With the dictator being chosen by one of the two Roman consuls, his authority was really, therefore, a form of legitimate rule, a type of crisis government.

In modern times Niccolò Machiavelli and Jean Jacques Rousseau, who both admired Republican Rome, thought that under conditions of crisis or emergency "let the safety of the people be the supreme law." According to Machiavelli, "those republics which in times of danger cannot resort to dictatorship will generally be ruined when grave occasions occur." To the proud citizen of Geneva "the people's first intention is that the state shall not perish" but "in the crises which lead to [the] adoption [of dictatorship] the state is either soon lost or soon saved." The most recent historical examples of constitutional provisions for temporary dictatorship are to be found in the constitution of the Weimar Republic in Germany (1919–33)—Article 48—and in the constitution of the Fifth Republic in France (1958–)—Article 16.

Modern Dictatorship. The Roman generals Lucius Cornelius Sulla, appointed dictator in 81 B.C., and Gaius Julius Caesar, made dictator for life in 44 B.C., were the forerunners of the modern dictator, dedicated to permanent rule. Oliver Cromwell, the English Lord Protector, emerged from the English Revolution of the 17th century as the first modern dictator, and Napoleon Bonaparte rose from the French Revolution as the second. Napoleon rationalized and justified his unlimited authority on the basis of the French revolutionary principle of popular sovereignty, to which he always appealed through the technique of the plebiscite to ratify his acts.

If this perversion of democracy gave rise to Napoleon's military dictatorship at the beginning of the 19th century, Marxian Communism gave birth to the famous "dictatorship of the proletariat" before the end. Lenin applied this theory in the 20th century in the Soviet Union. "We have created," he said, "a new type of state . . . the epoch of bourgeois-democratic parliamentarism is ended; a new chapter in world history begun; the epoch of the proletarian dictatorship."

In the early centuries of the ancient Roman Republic "dictator" was often a term of honor. Absolute rule by one man during a time of crisis was permitted by Roman law. In the 20th century "dictator" has become a term of vilification, applied to one who flouts law and basic liberties and rules by violence. These different meanings of the term are explained in the article on these pages. The first section deals with the Roman Republic. The constitution allowed a dictator to head the state during a war or similar crisis. Some — like Cincinnatus, who led the Republic to victory and then resumed his farming — became heroes of Roman tradition. In later years dictators like Sulla showed the danger of absolute power being used against the public welfare rather than for it.

The second major section of the article is concerned with the 20th century and discusses totalitarian dictatorships established after World War I: the Fascist regime of Mussolini in Italy, the Nazi state under Hitler in Germany, and the Communist rule of Stalin in the U.S.S.R. Although these men often pretended to follow constitutional procedures, they ruled, in fact, by force and fear. Whereas the early Roman dictators gave up their powers as soon as a crisis was past, these modern strong men sought to make their rule permanent.

The explanation given in this present article is extended in articles elsewhere in the **ENCYCLOPEDIA INTERNATIONAL**. For example, GOVERNMENT deals with the various major political theories. ABSOLUTISM treats the theory basic to dictatorship, that one individual or group should hold all the powers of government. The workings of dictatorships in ancient Rome are covered in ROME: *Republic and Empire* and in the biographic entries on Lucius Cornelius SULLA and Gaius Julius CAESAR.

Examples of absolute rule are numerous in the Orient — the regimes of GENGHIS KHAN and KUBLAI KHAN, for example. More recent European monarchs such as PETER I (or Peter the Great) of Russia and LOUIS XIV of France were also despotic rulers. The same is true of Oliver CROMWELL, who briefly governed England after the Civil War overthrew King Charles I.

Sometimes absolute power was used in part for the benefit of the country and people. Frederick the Great of Prussia is called a "benevolent despot" because, though a man of absolute power, he was interested in human welfare (see FREDERICK II OR FREDERICK THE GREAT).

Although such rulers — and other figures like NAPOLEON I and NAPOLEON III of France — seem to qualify for the label "dictator," the term is most often applied to Mussolini, Hitler, Stalin, and lesser despots of recent times. The Italian dictatorship is described in FASCISM, in ITALY: *History,* and in the article on Benito MUSSOLINI. The German variety is covered in NATIONAL SOCIALISM OR NAZISM, in GERMANY: *History,* and in the biographic article on Adolf HITLER. Although the Soviet Union professed to have a different form of government, the rule of Joseph STALIN was absolute and ruthless. A detailed discussion is in COMMUNISM and in UNION OF SOVIET SOCIALIST REPUBLICS: *History.*

Among other dictators of the present century have been Francisco FRANCO of Spain, Antonio de Oliveira SALAZAR of Portugal, and a number of Latin-American rulers. Juan Domingo PERON of Argentina, Juan Vicente GOMEZ of Venezuela, and Rafael Leónidas TRUJILLO MOLINA of the Dominican Republic are examples.

One way to gain an appreciation of the meaning of dictatorship is to consider the individual rights and liberties that are lost when a dictator seizes power. These cherished possessions are covered in DEMOCRACY, CIVIL RIGHTS AND LIBERTIES, and such related articles as SPEECH, FREEDOM OF. In a democracy these rights, as well as the form of government, are embodied in laws that can be changed only by lawful processes. (See, for example, CONSTITUTION OF THE UNITED STATES.) A dictatorship is typically a government of men, not of laws.

Many books in the library provide material for still further study of the workings of government and· the rise and fall of dictators. Selected books are listed at the ends of many articles.

Totalitarian Dictatorship. In the Bolshevik Revolution of Nov., 1917 in Russia, the groundwork was laid for the development of an historically unique form of dictatorship—the totalitarian type. As early as 1902 Lenin had outlined the nature of the Communist party, which, as the vanguard of the proletariat, seized power 15 years later as it called for "Peace, Land, and Bread" and "All power to the Soviets," proposals having far more appeal than anything offered by Russia's short-lived Duma or provisional government. In backward agrarian countries like Czarist Russia and China, first Lenin and Stalin and, later, Mao Tse-tung successfully led Marxist revolutions and established totalitarian dictatorships.

The Fascist variety of dictatorship evolved in Italy and Germany (in a period between the Russian and Chinese dictatorships) under a revolutionary *Duce* and *Führer* of the Right—Benito Mussolini and Adolf Hitler. They promised to solve the grave political, social, and economic problems with which weak and unstable parliamentary governments in the two countries had been unable to cope. Manipulating the myth of the nation in Italy, Mussolini held out the prospect of a Third Rome. Hitler, utilizing the myth of race, envisaged his regime as the Third Reich, which was to have lasted 1,000 years.

Although violently anti-Marxist, these Fascist dictatorships were very similar in nature to their Communist

counterparts. A major innovation of Hitler's dictatorship was the use of science and technology to bolster the regime. Control of radio, press, and films allowed him to manipulate and dominate the minds of 80,000,000 people. Hitler's definition of political leadership, "To be a leader, means to be able to move masses," illustrates how a totalitarian dictatorship is related to mass participation in politics, which is a 20th century development of democracy. He proceeded to effect his theory with great skill, by means of his charismatic, messianic, and demoniac political style.

Through a combination of mass support through propaganda and mass coercion through terror, four totalitarian dictators—Mussolini, Stalin, Hitler, and Mao Tse-tung—acquired more power than any previous rulers in history and established regimes which must be differentiated from other types of dictatorship in the past. The distinguishing characteristics of these totalitarian dictatorships include an official ideology, a single mass party, terrorist police control, governmental monopoly of communications and weapons, and a state-directed economy.

The Continuing Attraction of· Dictatorship. In 1938 French philosopher Paul Valéry stated that "dictatorship is at present as contagious as liberty was formerly." More than a generation later the trend toward some kind of dictatorship is still to be observed. In Europe varying forms of dictatorial regimes control governments in both eastern and western nations. In Latin America, military dictators with a long tradition of rule by *caudillo* govern many countries. The Middle East and Asia also have many governments based upon dictatorship of varying forms and degrees of control. Finally, in some of the emerging states of Africa, military men are running countries that have had little experience with democracy.

In spite of these developments, it is important to note that even a totalitarian dictatorship is always presented as either a "people's democracy," a "perfect democracy," or as an "organized, centralized, authoritarian democracy." Whether they are anticapitalist or antisocialist or antiliberal, modern dictatorships do not ever claim to be antidemocratic. This practice demonstrates the accuracy of the 19th-century French statesman François Guizot's observation that "such is the power of the word democracy that no government or party dares to exist or believes it can exist without inscribing that word on its banner."

Consult Rossiter, Clinton, *Constitutional Dictatorship* (1948); Neumann, Franz, "The Theory of Dictatorship" in *The Democratic and the Authoritarian State* (1957); Hallgarten, George, *Devils or Saviours: A History of Dictatorship Since 600 B.C.* (1960); Ebenstein, William, *Totalitarianism: New Perspectives* (1962); Friedrich, C. J. and Brzezinski, Z. K., *Totalitarian Dictatorship and Autocracy* (1965); Arendt, Hannah, *The Origins of Totalitarianism* (1966); Bainville, Jacques, *Dictators* (1967); *Totalitarianism*, ed. by Mason, P. T. (1967).

GUY H. DODGE, Brown University
See also ABSOLUTISM; COMMUNISM; COUP D'ETAT; FASCISM; NATIONAL SOCIALISM OR NAZISM.

DICTIONARY, an ordered list of the words of a language or a part of a language, supplying meanings and related information for each entry. For each entry most modern-language dictionaries include such information as alternate or variant spellings; part of speech; the most common pronunciation or pronunciations; etymology, including the history of the form before it became a part of the language being defined and changes in form that occurred afterward; and a numbered list of definitions of all but the most uncommon meanings. In addition, certain words or meanings may be labeled to indicate the special fields or contexts in which they most commonly appear, or to indicate their status or the style to which they are appropriate ("substandard," "slang," for example). Most large dictionaries also provide synonyms and antonyms.

The order of entries is usually alphabetical, though in many instances (as in dictionaries of synonyms or of particular subject areas) entries may be classified and presented in related groups.

Specialized dictionaries exist in great variety, ranging

Title page of the second volume of Johnson's Dictionary (1755). (ART REFERENCE BUREAU)

Samuel Johnson, portrayed by Sir Joshua Reynolds. Johnson's *Dictionary* is shown on the table. (NATIONAL PORTRAIT GALLERY)

Portrait of Noah Webster, who in 1828 produced *An American Dictionary of the English Language*. (G. & C. MERRIAM CO.)

from dictionaries of particular dialects and slang to the technical language of particular occupations, pronunciation, etymology, names, places, biography, literature, history, science, and many other subjects.

In the view of modern lexicographers, a language dictionary provides a description of the vocabulary and idiom of a language. As a description, a dictionary is valuable to the degree that it is accurate and complete. These qualities are achieved, not by setting forth the opinions of any group of editors, but by examining and describing the language as it is spoken and written by a large number of representative users.

Thus, making a dictionary that proposes to be more than a rewriting of its predecessors involves extensive research into the nature of the vocabulary and the idiom. There must be established a program of reading and excerpting representative quotations from a very wide variety of printed matter. All of the best dictionaries of both past and present have been based upon extensive reading programs.

Early Dictionaries. Throughout their history, dictionaries have closely reflected the varying attitudes of their makers toward language. The earliest English dictionaries were bilingual, consisting most commonly of lists of English words with Latin equivalents. In the 16th and 17th centuries the growing fondness of English writers for using large numbers of words borrowed from foreign languages was directly responsible for the appearance of the first purely English-language dictionaries. These were the works of Robert Cawdrey (1604) and Henry Cockeram (1623), both of whom were concerned chiefly with defining these new and unusual words. The subtitle of Cockeram's book is indicative of its purpose: *A New Interpreter of Hard English Words.*

Also during the 17th century there developed on the Continent an attitude toward language which was to have so profound an effect on dictionaries and on linguistic thought that it is still felt by perhaps the majority of users of European languages. This was the concept that it is possible and desirable for men of learning and taste to purify a language of its undesirable elements and then to fix that language in a more or less permanent form. To carry out this process the Accademia della Crusca was formed in Italy to produce in 1612 a dictionary of Italian designed to establish a literary standard from which that language should not be permitted to depart. In 1694 the French Academy followed with a dictionary of "standard" French intended to achieve the same purpose.

These ideas were quick to be felt in England, and in 1721 they were reflected in Nathaniel Bailey's *An Universal Etymological English Dictionary*, the first book that professed to include all the words proper to English. Though Bailey's dictionary was, in general, well received, it was not felt that it adequately performed for English the purpose served by the great dictionaries of the French and Italian academies. It was to remedy this lack that Samuel Johnson produced in 1755 his *Dictionary of the English Language.*

Johnson and Webster. Johnson's *Dictionary* is the first great landmark in English lexicography. It supplied greatly improved etymologies, and, though it did not provide pronunciations, it was the first English dictionary to indicate

the place of accent for the word entered. It was probably the most influential force in fixing English spelling, which at that time still exhibited much confusing variety. Its most important innovation, however, was the inclusion of quotations drawn from literary works and inserted into the definitions to illustrate the use of the word being defined. Though the book did not, of course, fix the language for all time, nevertheless for many years it was enormously influential and served as an authoritative court of appeal in matters of language. It was revised and re-edited many times and for more than a century was an acknowledged basis for many subsequent dictionaries.

Of the numerous supplements, revisions, and improvements of Johnson appearing in the 19th century, those of Noah Webster were the most important. In the United States the prestige of Johnson's work had been at least as great as it was in England, but by the early years of the new century it was evident to Webster that the book was an increasingly inadequate guide to the language. Not only had the natural growth and change of English made extensive revision necessary, but to Webster's patriotic eye the changes and additions peculiar to the use of English on a new continent and in a new nation demanded the production of a specifically American dictionary. Accordingly, in 1828 he produced his great two-volume work *An American Dictionary of the English Language.* After Johnson's, this book is the next great monument of English dictionary making. It greatly expanded the vocabulary of the earlier book, improved numerous definitions, and corrected many of the etymologies. But it is most interesting for its espousal of two of Webster's favorite causes. It entered pronunciations that were common in the United States but had not previously been recognized in dictionaries of standard English, and it embraced the cause of spelling reform. The greater number of its reformed spellings did not survive, but those that did so account for much of the present-day differences between American and British spelling (for example, words with final "-or," "-er," where British English has "-our," "re"). Webster's book was widely recognized both in the United States and abroad, being regarded even by many Englishmen as the best dictionary of the language. It was extensively revised during Webster's lifetime and has since been revised and brought up to date many times by its present publishers, the G. & C. Merriam Company.

Rise of Historical Dictionaries. In the meantime there emerged in Europe a second great change in linguistic theory which was early reflected in lexicographic practice. This was the development of modern historical philology, which sought to ascertain the facts of linguistic growth and change and, insofar as possible, to rationalize and explain that change. The first lexical products of this new school were the great dictionaries of the German scholars Jacob and Wilhelm Grimm, *Deutsches Wörterbuch* (1854), and of the French scholar Émile Littré, *Dictionnaire de la Langue Française* (1863–72).

These historical dictionaries incorporated in their etymologies the results of the new scientific study of sound change in language history and, for the first time, employed quotations for historical purposes. The dated quotations included in these books were chosen not merely to present the authority of the best writers for a particular usage, but to illustrate the historical record. Frequently, though with some inconsistency, they demonstrated and identified the dates of the earliest known use of each word, the change and development of its meanings, and the decline and obsolescence of such meanings and words as had dropped from the language.

In 1857 the Philological Society of Great Britain began a program for the collection of quotations for a historical dictionary. The final collection of quotations, contributed by approximately 1,300 volunteer readers, numbered 3,500,000. Editing did not begin until 1879, after James A. H. Murray had been appointed editor; the first part appeared in 1884, and the last in 1928. This book, the *Oxford English Dictionary*, is an indispensable source of information about the English language, and largely because of its detailed presentation, the history of the English vocabulary is clearer than that of any other language.

Since the completion of the *Oxford English Dictionary*, several other historical dictionaries of English have been undertaken. Two which have been completed are *A Dictionary of American English on Historical Principles* (1938–44), edited by Sir William Craigie and James Root Hulbert, and *A Dictionary of Americanisms on Historical Principles* (1951), edited by Mitford M. Mathews. These two books supplement the *Oxford* by setting forth the history of English words of American origin or those that have undergone special development in America.

Publication of the *Grand dictionnaire universel du XIXe siècle* (1866–76), by the French lexicographer Pierre Larousse, gave primary impetus to the idea of including in language dictionaries material that is auxiliary to the true vocabulary of the language—encyclopedic rather than lexical: biographical, geographical, historical, technical, and statistical, to which may be added such contemporary dictionary features as illustrations and color plates.

In the United States the *Century Dictionary and Cyclopedia* appeared in 1889, combining a relatively generous use of historical and illustrative quotations with a considerable quantity of encyclopedic material. At the same time, of course, other books such as the Merriam-Webster and the Funk and Wagnalls' *Standard* were being liberally augmented with this kind of matter.

20th-Century Developments. In the 20th century, painstaking examination and comparison of earlier stages of language by means of its written records has led to a more careful study of present-day languages both in their fundamental form as speech and in their representation in writing. Students of present-day English, for example, have learned that there exists in the writing and even more in the speech of educated persons a far greater diversity of linguistic forms than was formerly imagined. Accordingly, it has been necessary to revise descriptions of the standard language to fit these facts.

The best dictionaries have for many years been regarded as recorders of language, not legislators. The good dictionary tries to record the language as it is, to determine the facts of usage and report them as completely as knowledge and space permit; it does not prescribe what ought to be.

With the notable exception of the third edition of *Webster's New International Dictionary* (1961), the so-called "unabridged," current dictionary publication in the United States has been concerned with smaller, abridged, "desk" or "college" dictionaries, usually containing about 150,000 entries. The best known of these are probably the Merriam Company's *Webster's New Collegiate Dictionary*, *The American College Dictionary*, *Webster's New World Dictionary*, *The Standard College Dictionary*, the various Thorndike-Barnhart dictionaries, the *Winston Dictionary, College Edition*, and the *Random House Dictionary of the English Language*. Though differing considerably in their originality, all of these profit greatly from the contributions made to our knowledge of English by the *Oxford English Dictionary*, and most reflect, in varying degrees, modern concepts of the nature of language.

Consult Starnes, D. T., and Noyes, G. E., *The English Dictionary from Cawdrey to Johnson* (1946); Hulbert, J. R., *Dictionaries British and American* (1955); Sledd, J. H., and Kolb, G. J., *Dr. Johnson's Dictionary* (1955); Sledd, J. H., and Ebbitt, W. R., *Dictionaries and That Dictionary* (1962)

DANIEL COOK, American University of Beirut
See also AMERICAN ENGLISH; ENGLISH; LANGUAGE.

DICTIONARY CATALOG. *See* LIBRARY CATALOGING.

DICTUM (Lat., "something said"), or obiter dictum (Lat., "spoken by the way"), in law, refers to a collateral comment, such as, for example, a hypothetical illustration by the court on how it would decide a factual situation different from the one before it.

Dictum is distinguishable from the *ratio decidendi* (Lat., "reason for decision") of a case. The latter establishes a precedent or rule of law to be followed by other courts as mandatory under certain circumstances. The former, however, is never binding on the courts, although it can be highly persuasive as authority, if well reasoned, or stated by a judge of important stature.

DICUMAROL [dī-kōō'mə-rôl], also known as bishydroxy-coumarin, a drug used to prevent the formation of blood clots in veins and arteries. Dicumarol was first isolated from spoiled sweet clover hay, which was found to be responsible for excessive and sometimes fatal bleeding in cattle. The drug decreases the clotting power of the blood by inhibiting the formation of an essential clotting agent (prothrombin) in the liver. Dicumarol is used in certain types of heart disease and to prevent clotting in blood vessels throughout the body.
See also ANTICOAGULANTS.

DIDACHE [dĭd'ə-kē], **THE**, or "Teaching of the Twelve Apostles to the Gentiles," a manual of church orders from the mid-1st century. This document, first published in 1883, revolutionized early church history, since it contains not only a kind of catechism, a description of early Christian worship, and instructions for dealing with wandering apostles and prophets, but also the counsel to appoint bishops and deacons as equivalents of apostles and prophets. The work either comes from a very early period or is a forgery intended to give an impression of antiquity. Used by Christians by 180, it is probably early and shows that church orders were a concern of the early postapostolic age. It is based on Jewish models and makes use of the Gospel of Matthew.

DIDEROT [dē-drō'], **DENIS** (1713–84), French philosopher and writer, editor of the *Encyclopédie*. His *Lettre sur les aveugles* (Letter on the Blind), 1749, and *Lettre sur les sourds et muets* (Letter on the Deaf and Dumb), 1751, are significant in their anticipation of scientific naturalism and relativism. Thought to be a dangerous writer, he was imprisoned for three months in the château of Vincennes in 1749. In 1747 Diderot undertook to translate Ephraim Chambers' two-volume *Cyclopaedia* for the publisher Le Breton, but he soon proposed a more ambitious work that would reflect contemporary learning and ideas. Jean Le Rond d'Alembert, a leading mathematician and physicist, joined this enterprise as coeditor. In 1751 the first volume was published; with nearly 4,000 subscribers, the work soon became a best seller. The text was complete in 17 volumes in 1765, and by 1772 Diderot had finished editing 11 more volumes of illustrations. The leaders of the Enlightenment contributed many of the major articles, their liberal, tolerant attitudes provoking the opposition of the traditionalists. In 1759 the *Encyclopédie* was officially banned, though high officials allowed it to be printed secretly.

Without the help of d'Alembert and other valuable coworkers, who were frightened into withdrawing from the staff, the writing was continued by Diderot, who alone wrote several hundred articles, many of them based on first-hand research and observation of artisans at their work. The discovery, when all of the volumes had been printed, that the over-timid publisher had been omitting certain passages which he thought might prove offensive, was Diderot's greatest disappointment: he feared—wrongly, as it turned out—that 20 years of untiring labor had been ruined. *Le Fils Naturel* (The Natural Son), 1757, and *Le Père de Famille* (The Father of a Family), 1758, are examples of the "bourgeois" drama of morality and sensibility advocated by Diderot in his *Paradoxe sur le comédien* (Paradox on Acting), 1770. He wrote for his friend Friedrich Melchior von Grimm brilliant criticisms of art in his *Salons* (1759–81). A sentimental novel, *Jacques le Fataliste* (Jacques the Fatalist), first published 1796, shows Diderot's admiration for Sterne and Richardson. His most famous piece is the witty, satirical *Le Neveu de Rameau* (Rameau's Nephew), probably written between 1764 and 1769 and first published in German by Johann Wolfgang von Goethe, 1805. His letters to his mistress, Sophie Volland, contain a brilliant evocation of Diderot's lively and fertile mind, as well as vivid portrayals of leading figures of the age.

RALPH H. BOWEN, Northern Illinois University

DIDIUS JULIANUS [dĭd'ē-əs jōō-lē-ā'nəs], **MARCUS,** Roman Emperor (reigned 193 A.D.). Upon the murder of the Emperor Pertinax he is said to have bribed the Praetorian Guard to proclaim him Emperor, though he was a Senator of no particular distinction. His reign lasted only a few weeks. He was deposed and murdered on the approach of Septimius Severus with the army of the Danube.

DIDO [dī'dō], legendary founder and Queen of Carthage. She had fled from her brother, King Pygmalion of Tyre, who had murdered her husband. In Vergil's *Aeneid*, Dido became the mistress of Aeneas.

DIDO AND AENEAS, opera in three acts by Henry Purcell, libretto by Nahum Tate; first performance at Josias Priest's school for young ladies, Chelsea, England, c.1689; first American performance, New York, Town Hall (in concert form) Jan. 13, 1924.

The story concerns the love of Dido, Queen of Carthage, and the Trojan hero Aeneas. Obedient to the command of a witch disguised as Mercury, Aeneas tells Dido of his necessary departure from Carthage and she, crushed by his seeming disloyalty to her, stabs herself and dies.

The opera achieves moments of great dramatic effect and emotional expression. Purcell's style combines elements from the English masque, the Italian cantata, and French opera, the latter especially apparent in the treatment of the chorus and ballet. Of well-deserved fame is Dido's final lament in an expressive recitative and aria in the form of a chaconne (melodic development over a constantly reiterated bass phrase).

WILLIAM KIMMEL, Hunter College

CASTING PROCESS

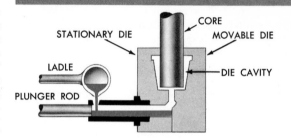

METAL POURED INTO SLEEVE

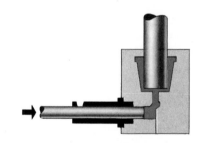

PLUNGER FORCES METAL INTO DIE

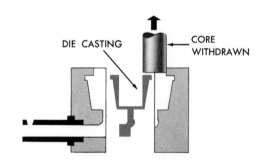

DIE SEPARATED AND METAL EJECTED

In the die-casting process illustrated above, the molten metal is introduced by hand ladle or automatic feed for each casting. This process is used in the casting of aluminum- and copper-base alloys where very high pressures are needed.

DIDOT [dē-dō'], French publishers, printers, and type-founders. The Didot firm was founded by **FRANÇOIS DIDOT** (1689–1757), whose son, **FRANÇOIS AMBROISE** (1730–1804), created the first Didot types about 1770 and devised the Didot point system of type measurement. Characteristic productions of the firm were monumental editions of the classics, using the "modern" types. Other members of the family contributed to printing and scholarly publishing down through the 19th century.

DIDYMIUM [dĭ-dĭm'ē-əm], supposed element of the lanthanide series, first isolated by C. G. Mosander in 1841. It was named from a Greek word meaning "twin" because it was so similar in properties to lanthanum. However, in 1885, didymium proved to be twins, for C. A. von Welsbach showed it to be a mixture of two lanthanide elements, praseodymium and neodymium. Special optical glasses, didymium glass, are prepared containing praseodymium and neodymium. These absorb narrow-wavelength bands of light, the yellow light of sodium, for instance, and can therefore be used as specialized filters. *See also* LANTHANIDE SERIES.

DIE-CASTING, process for casting alloys into dies. There are two basic methods. One, called the "hot chamber," is used for relatively low-melting alloys of tin, lead, and zinc. A cylinder-piston assembly, submerged in a pot of molten metal, forces the metal through a tube into the die at pressures of about 1,500 lb. per square inch. A familiar example of this method is the linotype machine.

The other method is used to cast alloys with a higher melting point, such as magnesium, aluminum, and copper. The molten metal is ladled into a cylinder, then forced by a piston into the die assembly at pressures of 6,000 to 12,-000 lb. per square inch, and in some instances, 100,000 lb. per square inch. Typical examples of die-cast parts are slide fastener elements, sleeve bearings, cooking utensils, and components for automobiles, typewriters, radio and television equipment, sewing machines, and refrigerators.
PAUL B. EATON, Purdue University
See also DIES AND DIEMAKING.

DIEFENBAKER [dē-fən-bā-kər], **JOHN GEORGE** (1895–), Prime Minister of Canada (1957–63). A native of Grey County, Ontario, he came of third-generation Canadian stock on both sides. His mother's grandfather, George Bannerman, was one of Lord Selkirk's settlers on the Red River. Diefenbaker spent his boyhood and youth on the Saskatchewan prairies. At 20 he graduated in arts from the University of Saskatchewan. After overseas service in World War I he obtained his law degree from the same university and began law practice. He won a wide reputation as a trial lawyer, specializing in criminal cases.

Although his political ambitions appeared early, his path to the prime ministership was strewn with failures. In 1925 and 1926 he was defeated in federal elections. In 1929 and 1938 he failed in bids for a provincial seat. From 1937 to 1940 he led the Saskatchewan Conservatives during a barren period. He tried again for the House of Commons in the general election of 1940. This time he succeeded, and he represented Lake Centre until 1953 and then represented Prince Albert. In 1942 and 1948 he

John G. Diefenbaker, Canadian statesman.   (NATIONAL FILM BOARD)

unsuccessfully sought the national leadership of his party. A third attempt, in 1956, was successful.

During 17 years in opposition in the House of Commons, Diefenbaker became an outstanding parliamentarian, and he acquired a reputation as the most scathing critic in his party of the long-entrenched Liberal government. A lean, tall, angular man with flashing gray-blue eyes beneath a high forehead and dark, curly hair, he was noted for frequently pointing a long, accusing finger at the government. He associated himself with many crusades and reforms, among them protection of civil liberties, penal reforms, and the cause of a free press. As a guardian of the rights of Parliament, he attacked the encroachments of the executive and indicted the government for being in power too long and for displaying an autocratic temper. In the general election of 1957, holding out a new "vision of the north" and promising extensive social welfare benefits, he led his Progressive Conservative party to victory and became Prime Minister, ending the 22-year tenure of office of the Liberal party. A second general election in 1958, gave his party 208 out of 265 seats in the House of Commons and the largest majority in Canadian history. His party lost this majority in 1962 and following a vote of no confidence in 1963, Diefenbaker was forced to call for new elections. The Liberal party won a plurality in these elections (Apr., 1963), and Lester B. Pearson succeeded

John G. Diefenbaker (*left*) talks with Premier Charles de Gaulle in Paris late in 1958.

Robert Cohen—Black Star

Diefenbaker as Prime Minister. The integration of U.S. and Canadian defenses was a major issue, and Canadians were highly sensitive to their economic dependence on their neighbor. U.S. tariffs and the U.S. policy of disposing of farm surpluses were important factors in Canada's unfavorable balance of trade. In 1957 Diefenbaker proposed to transfer 15% of Canada's trade from the United States to Great Britain. In 1961 he expressed concern at the possible consequences to Canada of Britain's joining the European Common Market, which would end Canada's preferential position in the British market. Diefenbaker, like other Canadians, was also concerned with the dominance of U.S. investors in many Canadian industries. In 1960 he made it clear that he expected foreign companies operating in Canada to conduct themselves as Canadian businesses by making their securities available to Canadian purchasers, by including Canadians on their boards of directors, and by buying their supplies whenever possible in Canada.

In June, 1929, Diefenbaker married Edna M. Brower of Saskatoon; she died in 1951. In Dec., 1953, he married Olive E. Freeman Palmer of Toronto.

WILFRID EGGLESTON, Carleton University

DIEFFENBACHIA [děf-ən-băk′ē-ə], a genus of shrubby plants in the Araceae, or arum family, native to Central and South America. Dieffenbachias thrive in warm, humid climates and require ample moisture for their vigorous growth of luxurious foliage. The plants are sturdy and of a low, erect growing habit. The leathery, oval-shaped leaves emerge from a single, thick stem. The foliage may be light- or dark-green and is often marked with creamy-white blotches. Dieffenbachia flowers are not very striking and consist of a sheathlike spathe surrounding an erect spadix. In cool and temperate climates dieffenbachias are popular greenhouse and house plants. The best-known species are *Dieffenbachia picta* and *D. amonea* from which many hybrid varieties have been derived.

DIÉGO-SUAREZ [dyā′gō-swä′räs], town of the Malagasy Republic, a port located on Diégo-Suarez Bay, an inlet of the Indian Ocean. It has large drydocks, fuel depots, warehouses, and an important corn and livestock export trade. The bay was named by the Portuguese in 1543, and the city developed in the 19th century. It is the site of a strategic naval base occupied by the British during World War II. Pop., 38,142.

DIELECTRIC [dī-ĭ-lĕk′trĭk], material used as an insulator in many forms of electric equipment. Dielectrics include glass, paper, and other fibrous products, as well as liquids such as mineral oil, which can be impregnated in cable insulation. Ceramic, mica, quartz, and magnesia dielectrics are strong mechanically and have high temperature resistance; the flexibility of rubber and some plastics is useful in other types of electric parts. One of the main applications of dielectrics is in the capacitor, which uses a dielectric to store electric energy. Dielectric strength is determined by the voltage (per cm.) required to rupture the dielectric.

DIELS [dēls], **OTTO PAUL HERMANN** (1876–1954), German chemist who, with his student Kurt Alder, discovered a method of synthesizing organic compounds; the method is of great value in preparing many important substances. His chief discovery, the diene synthesis, won him the Nobel Prize jointly with Alder in 1950.

DIEMEN, ANTON VAN. *See* VAN DIEMEN, ANTON.

DIEPPE [dē-ĕp], town and residential suburb of Moncton, New Brunswick, Canada, in Westmorland County. Nearly the entire population is French-speaking. Pop., 4,032.

DIEPPE, resort, fishing port, and ferry port of northern France, on the coast of the English Channel, about 100 mi. northwest of Paris. There is regular ferry service to England, and a harbor and market for small fishing boats. Dieppe dates from the 12th century and was a Huguenot center in the 17th century. In Aug., 1942, German troops repulsed a large-scale commando raid on Dieppe after bloody fighting. Pop., 30,327.

DIES [dīz], **MARTIN** (1900–   ), American Congressman, chairman of the House Committee to Investigate Un-American Activities that was created in 1938. A native Texan, Dies served as a Democrat in the U.S. House of Representatives from 1931 until 1945, and again from 1953 to 1959. He was at first a strong supporter of the New Deal, but after 1937 he became one of the recognized anti-Roosevelt Democrats. His direction of the House Committee aroused considerable controversy.

DIES AND DIEMAKING. A die is a tool used in conjunction with a press to shape or cut metal into usable parts or products called stampings. A punch in the die corresponds with the cavity of the die block. In operation the metal, or hard plastic, is introduced between the punch and the die block and the two are brought together under pressure to cause the material to acquire the desired shape. Dies provide stampings in quantity and with exact duplication between the pieces; die-stamped parts range from tiny watch and instrument components to larger parts such as automobile doors, fenders, and tops.

The three major classes of die tools are: cutting, forming, and assembling. Cutting dies, as the name implies, cut and trim metal strip into workpieces or cut internal openings or holes. Other cutting die types trim irregular edges of shells, shave workpiece edges to improve the finish and dimensional accuracy, or emboss irregular surfaces onto flat plates.

Forming dies bend flat pieces of metal. The drawing type of forming die produces cup and shell forms, and the bulging type expands portions of shells, for example the flared bottoms of coffee pots. Another type curls the edges of drawn or flat material to produce, for example, hinges or the tops of cooking pots. Swaging dies change the shape of workpieces by the application of heavy pressure while the piece is partly confined in the die.

Separate parts can be assembled by dies that force parts into each other; reshape a portion of one after assembly into the other; or hammer rivets to join parts.

Progressive dies may combine any of the foregoing operations. The work is done at a number of stations in series and the completed part or assembly is produced at the final station.

Diemaking. Diesinking is the art of building dies. Before one is built complete drawings and specifications are made to guide the diemaker. Each component must be machined, then fitted together, before testing for proper functioning to find that stampings are produced in quantity at the required tolerances. Diemaking requires extremely skilled and precise workmanship because of the great accuracy required and the intricacy of many of the components. The diemaker must be an expert in the operation of all tool-room machines such as lathes, milling machines, shapers, planers, and grinders.

J. R. PAQUIN, SUPERVISOR, Tool & Die Design
Department, Cleveland Engineering Institute
See also DIE-CASTING; FORGING; PRESS.

PUNCH PRESS DIE

A small punch press and progressive die. The block in the upper right-hand corner of the photograph fits over the block to the left. The metal strip that the operator holds is introduced and the blocks brought together. The die pierces the holes, shapes the link, and cuts out the part. Each completed part exactly duplicates the others.

DIESEL [dē'zəl], **RUDOLF** (1858–1913), inventor of the diesel engine. A German, born in Paris, he was educated at the Polytechnic Institute at Munich. After joining Sulzer Bros., Swiss builders, he developed the first effective internal combustion engine to use heavy fuel oil, patented in 1892. Diesel did not live to witness the remarkable applications of his engine; he disappeared from a Channel steamer in 1913 while returning from England to Belgium.

DIESEL ENGINE. Considered the heavy duty engine of industry and transportation, the diesel has greater economy of operation than the gasoline engine. It uses lower cost fuel and converts more of the energy into useful work. Although both the gasoline and the diesel are internal-combustion engines, the main difference lies in the nature of the combustion process. The gasoline engine needs a spark to ignite the fuel-air mixture, but the diesel does not. Instead, the air, drawn into the cylinder and compressed to a high pressure by a moving piston, becomes so hot that the fuel sprayed into the cylinder burns without the need for another ignition source. The process requires the diesel engine to have a much higher compression ratio than the gasoline engine.

Although most diesel engines burn low-octane oil, similar to kerosene or furnace oil, some are designed to burn gaseous fuel as well. With this, a small amount of regular diesel fuel oil, called a pilot charge, is injected into the air-gas mixture at the proper time to initiate combustion.

Engine Cycle. Both four-stroke cycle and two-stroke cycle diesel engines are built. The four-stroke cycle operates as follows: after the piston moves downward, sucking air in through a valve (intake stroke), the valve closes and the piston moves up (compression stroke). Trapped air is squeezed to about 1/16 of its initial volume, which corresponds to a compression ratio of about 16. During compression the temperature also rises rapidly. Near the end of the stroke, fuel is sprayed into the cylinder through the fuel nozzle, in amounts controlled to suit the load on the engine. The burning fuel pushes the piston downward (power stroke) and the connecting rod changes the straight-line motion of the piston into rotation of the crankshaft, which drives a generator, truck, locomotive, or other load. When the piston reaches the end of its downward stroke, the exhaust valve opens. On the next upward (exhaust) stroke the burned gas is expelled from the cylinder. The exhaust valve closes, the air inlet opens, and the piston descends again on the intake stroke.

In the two-stroke cycle, only two piston strokes are required to complete the operation. Fuel is sprayed in, as in the first process, to burn and drive the piston downward. Near the end of this power stroke, a valve opens or an opening, called a port, in the cylinder wall is uncovered by the piston, allowing burned gas to escape to the atmosphere. A short time later, as the piston is nearly at the bottom, another valve or port opens to admit fresh air which has been compressed elsewhere in the engine during the previous power stroke. Then as the piston rises, the ports or valves are closed, the fresh air is trapped in the cylinder, and the air is squeezed on the compression stroke. Near the end of this stroke the fuel is sprayed in and the cycle begun again.

Supercharging. Before delivery to the cylinder, the fresh air must be compressed slightly, either in the crankcase or by a blower geared to the engine, for two-stroke engines. Normal pressure is only enough to insure positive flow into the cylinder to help clean it of burned gas which can no longer support combustion. But when air is trapped in the cylinder at above-atmospheric pressure, in either the two-stroke or four-stroke types, the engine is supercharged and extra fuel can be burned with the extra air to produce more power. A supercharging blower which is connected to a gas turbine driven by the hot engine exhaust gases is called a turbo-blower, and the engine using it is said to be turbo-charged. Many diesel engines are supercharged, but the amount is limited because of the higher pressures and temperatures developed.

Fueling. The fuel-injection system must meter and deliver rather small amounts of fuel at the proper time in the engine cycle and in the proper condition to mix and burn rapidly with the air in the cylinder. The high pressure required to push the fuel in against cylinder pressure and to produce a satisfactory spray is usually produced by motion of plungers in precision-fitted mating cylinders.

The fuel is not mixed with air before entering the cylinder as in the gasoline engine. It enters in special spray patterns into combustion chambers shaped to promote rapid swirling and mixing with air. The spraying continues during the delay time, defined as the time from the moment the fuel enters to the time it becomes heated, vaporizes, finds oxygen, and burns. Engine knock results after a long delay time when a considerable fraction of the fuel charge accumulates in the cylinder before combustion finally takes place. Then, at the start of combustion, a large amount of fuel burns suddenly, giving a sharp increase in cylinder pressure and causing the knock. Diesel knock occurs near the beginning of the combustion process, whereas gasoline-engine knock occurs near the end of the combustion process.

Diesel knock is reduced by a fuel with short ignition-delay characteristics, meaning it has a higher cetane number than for a gasoline engine (cetane number is a measure of the ignition delay of a fuel in a standard laboratory test; a high cetane number fuel gives less knock). A certain amount of knock in a diesel engine is almost unavoidable and, in some respects, is desirable. It promotes rapid mixing of the remaining fuel and air to give more complete combustion. It also allows fuller use of the expansion stroke of the engine to produce more power by causing the combustion pressure rise to occur more nearly at one time near the beginning of the expansion stroke. Heavy knock obviously is hard on the engine, and diesel engines generally must be more heavily constructed than gasoline engines.

A diesel engine may have from 1 or 2 to 12 or 16 or more cylinders. They may be arranged in a line on one side of the crankshaft, along two banks of a V, radially, or be horizontally opposed. Factors of cost, total power that must be developed, and space into which the engine must fit, influence the choice of the arrangement of the cylinders.

Applications. The higher cylinder pressures of a diesel engine require heavy and sometimes costly construction. Thus the natural place for the diesel engine is in heavy duty work. Diesel locomotives have replaced old "iron horses," or steam locomotives. Diesel engines are used also in electric-power generating stations, bulldozers, heavy trucks and buses, boats, ships, submarines, and heavy-power equipment like draglines, power shovels, and mining machinery. They have been used in passenger automobiles, though not commonly.

Special diesel engines with cylinders of more than 3 ft. diameter have been built and there are standard types with cylinders of about 2½ ft. in diameter. On the other hand, tiny diesel engines power model airplanes and boats. For large engines with high cylinder pressures of 500 to 1,000 lb. per square inch, engine rotational speeds are low. These may turn from less than a hundred to a few hundred revolutions per minute. In smaller sizes, two or three thousand rpm are possible. The tiniest diesel engines made for model airplanes rotate much faster, at many thousand rpm.

WILLARD L. ROGERS, University of Arizona
See also DIESEL, RUDOLF; ENGINE; GASOLINE ENGINE.

DIESEL LOCOMOTIVE. *See* LOCOMOTIVE.

DIETETIC FOODS. There are six principal types of dietetic foods: low-calorie, or reducing; low-sodium, or salt-free; sugar-restricted (principally for diabetics); foods for persons with specific allergies; vegetarian, and so-called health foods, featuring coarse or stone-ground grains, blackstrap molasses, and similar products.

Most important are the low-calorie foods. Canned, water-packed fruits with non-nutritive sweetening are the most popular. Other widely distributed reducing foods include dietetic, sugar-free carbonated beverages; low-calorie salad dressings; sugar-free preserves; sugar- and salt-free baking mixes and frostings; and noncaloric sweeteners available in tablet, crystal, powdered, and liquid form. Some artificial sweeteners are made from saccharin; others are of the cyclamate types which do not leave a bitter aftertaste.

Also available on the market are breads, toast, and breadsticks made from gluten, soy, artichoke, and rice flour; low-sodium cheeses; vegetarian brown gravy; soy and low-sodium milk; and salt substitutes.

POPPY CANNON, Author, *Unforbidden Sweets*

DIETRICH [dē'trĭk], **MARLENE** (1904–), German-born film actress. She first achieved popularity as the amoral music-hall singer in the German motion picture *The Blue Angel* (1930). She became an international symbol of feminine glamor in a series of Hollywood films directed by Josef von Sternberg, notably *Morocco* (1930) and *Shanghai Express* (1932). Miss Dietrich, who became an American citizen in 1937, had a starring part in the satiric western *Destry Rides Again* (1940). She was active in government-sponsored entertainment for American troops during World War II and established a reputation as a night-club singer and recording artist.

DIETS AND WEIGHT LOSS. *See* NUTRITION.

DIETZ [dēts], **HOWARD** (1896–), American lyricist, librettist, and publicist. Born in New York City, he wrote his first Broadway score with Jerome Kern for *Dear Sir* in 1923. With composer Arthur Schwartz, he created songs for *The Little Show* (1929), *Three's a Crowd* (1930), *The Band Wagon* (1931), *Flying Colors* (1932), *At Home Abroad* (1935), and *Inside U.S.A.* (1948). Others with whom he has collaborated have been Walter Donaldson, George Gershwin, Vernon Duke, and Jimmy McHugh. He also wrote English versions of *Die Fledermaus* and *La Bohème* for the Metropolitan Opera, New York City. During the greater part of his career, Dietz was in charge of advertising and publicity for Metro-Goldwyn-Mayer Pictures.

DIEZ [dēts], **FRIEDRICH CHRISTIAN** (1794–1876), German philologist. Upon Goethe's suggestion, Diez turned his attention to the Provençal language and literature. As a professor at the university of Bonn, he became the initiator of Romance philology as a scholarly discipline, applying the comparative method to the study of the Romance languages.

DIFFRACTION, in light or other wave phenomena, variations in space distribution of the wave energy, caused by interference among different portions of the wave front. Diffraction effects are not prominent in ordinary situations, but are an important factor in many optical instruments.

Light is commonly said to travel in straight lines; this is not strictly true, and in some circumstances is not even approximately so. The principles of diffraction of light waves can be understood by an analogy to water waves. When waves on water encounter an obstacle such as a post, a shadow area of quiet water is formed behind the post. However, the waves bend into the quiet area, and close ranks a short distance beyond the post. The amount of such bending, or diffraction, depends mainly upon the wave length, or distance from crest to crest of the waves, in relation to the size of the obstacle. The longer the waves, the less an obstacle affects their regular pattern. Light waves are short compared to ordinary objects; therefore, the objects are easily shadowed. Nevertheless, light waves bend enough so that the edge of the shadow of a sharp-edged object is blurred, even when the source of light is extremely small.

If a small circular object is placed in the path of light from a small source, such as an illuminated pinhole, its shadow on a screen at a suitable distance will be a dark circular area with a bright spot at the center. This striking demonstration results from the overlapping at the center of the shadow of light diffracted around the entire edge of the circular object.

The moon or other distant light source viewed through a window screen is attended by bright horizontal and vertical "rays" or streaks of light. A binocular or small telescope will show that each streak is actually a series of spectra, each appearing as a short series of colors from red to violet. This is a diffraction effect of the series of uniformly spaced wires in the screen. This principle is used in the diffraction grating.

Diffraction is an important limiting factor in the performance of a telescope or microscope. Because of diffraction effects, the ability of the instrument to distinguish

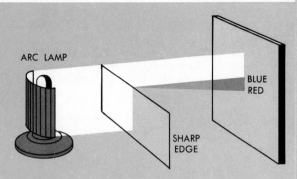

Light waves encountering an obstacle (sharp edge) bend around it. Amount of bending depends on wave length. Thus blue light bends less than red.

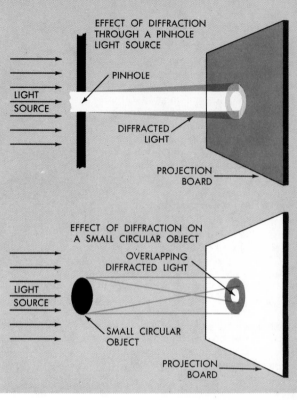

Light projected through a pinhole onto a board in a dark room forms a bright spot surrounded by a hazy area, caused by diffraction. Light passing around a small circular object gives, at a certain distance, a circular dark area with a center bright spot.

closely spaced details is proportional to the diameter of the telescope lens or mirror, or to the angular width of the cone of light entering the microscope.

JOSEPH H. RUSH, National Center for Atmospheric Research
See also DIFFRACTION GRATING; LIGHT.

DIFFRACTION GRATING, an optical device that produces orderly diffraction of light, usually for use in spectroscopy. Precision optical gratings are made by ruling many thousands of fine, uniformly spaced grooves with a diamond point on a flat glass plate. The glass may be used directly as a transmission grating or coated with aluminum or silver for use as a reflection grating. A spectrograph consists of a reflection grating ruled on a concave spherical surface; it requires no other optical parts.
See also DIFFRACTION; SPECTROSCOPY.

DIFFUSION, process by which molecules, atoms, and ions tend to spread out to establish a uniform concentration. Gas molecules are free of one another's attractive force and diffuse rapidly through the open spaces between them. In liquids, the molecules are still free to slide and tumble about, but forces of attraction keep them close together and the diffusion is moderately fast. In solids, molecules are largely restricted to vibration in a rigid structure, but some movement between them, and therefore diffusion, of individual molecules occurs slowly.

All motion, or kinetic energy, of molecules is directly proportional to the absolute temperature; the higher the temperature, the faster the motion. The rate of diffusion, therefore, increases with rising temperature.

Diffusion proceeds uniformly in all directions from a region of high concentration to a region of lower concentration. The molecules in a spoonful of sugar dropped into a glass of cold water will slowly spread until the concentration of sugar is the same all through the glass. In hot water, uniform sweetness is achieved much more quickly.

Graham's law of diffusion states that at constant temperature the rate of diffusion of a gas is inversely proportional to the square root of its molecular weight. This law follows from the fact that, at a given temperature, the average kinetic energy of the molecules of all gases is the same. The kinetic energy of a molecule equals $\frac{1}{2} mv^2$, where m is its mass and v its velocity. If m_1 and m_2 are the molecular weights and v_1 and v_2 are the average molecular velocities of two different gases, then at the same temperature and pressure, $\frac{1}{2} m_1 v_1{}^2 = \frac{1}{2} m_2 v_2{}^2$. The relative diffusion rates are in the ratio of the velocities of the molecules, or v_2/v_1, which is equal to $\sqrt{m_1/m_2}$ as stated in Graham's law.

An important application of gaseous diffusion is in the separation of isotopes. Isotopes have identical chemical properties but their masses, and therefore their rates of diffusion, vary. This method of separation is especially useful in concentrating fissionable uranium from a mixture of uranium salts.

Distinction should be made between diffusion, which always concerns the independent motion of individual molecules, and convection, or bulk mixing due to gravity.

H. A. LAITINEN, University of Illinois

DIFFUSION, CULTURAL. *See* CULTURE.

DIGBY, fishing port and summer resort of western Nova Scotia, Canada, and seat of Digby County, on the Bay of Fundy. Digby is the terminus for steamship service to Saint John, New Brunswick. The Royal Canadian Navy has a training base nearby. The town was founded by Loyalists who left New York in 1783 with the fleet of Adm. Robert Digby. Inc., 1890; pop., 2,308.

DIGESTION, the process by which food is changed from a complex to a simple form so that it can be absorbed and utilized by the body. Foods consist principally of carbohydrates (starches and sugars), proteins (in meats, eggs, and fish), and fats (cream, animal fat, butter, and vegetable fat). During the course of digestion each of these foods is broken down into its constituents: carbohydrates are changed into simple sugars, proteins are broken down into their component amino acids, and fats are changed into fatty acids and glycerol. These changes occur during the passage of food through the digestive tract, a hollow tube which extends from the mouth to the anus. Food is moved along the tract by muscular action while chemicals (enzymes) poured into the tube break down the food substances into successively finer form, until they can be taken into the blood and lymph streams.

Digestion begins in the mouth, where the teeth grind and tear the food, reducing it to a semisolid mass. Three pairs of salivary glands located under the jaw (submaxillary), under the tongue (sublingual), and next to the ear (parotid), continually pour out a watery secretion which bathes the teeth and moistens the mouth and throat. The presence of food in the mouth stimulates these glands to secrete an enzyme (salivary amylase), which breaks down complex starches into simpler units.

Food leaves the mouth and enters the stomach via a long passageway, the gullet, or esophagus. In the stomach, proteins are broken down into simpler forms (proteoses and peptones) by the enzyme pepsin. The stomach juice also contains hydrochloric acid, which maintains the proper acid level necessary for the action of pepsin. The muscles of the stomach wall facilitate the action of the enzymes by churning the food and stomach juices into a thoroughly mixed liquid, called chyme. Certain stomach cells secrete mucus, which coats the lining of the stomach, thereby preventing it from being digested by its own enzymes. The stomach of infants secretes the enzyme rennin, which curdles milk, keeping it in the stomach longer and permitting pepsin to digest it more thoroughly.

When the pressure in the stomach becomes sufficiently great, a muscular valve (the pyloric sphincter) situated in the lower portion of the stomach is pushed open, allowing some liquid chyme to pass into the small intestine. The pyloric sphincter is one of many valves found along the digestive tract. These include a valve in the esophagus (the esophageal sphincter), and one in the small intestine (ileo-cecal valve). These structures prevent material from being regurgitated and from being passed too rapidly forward along the digestive tract.

The small intestine is the most active site of digestion. Large quantities of enzyme-containing digestive juices enter the small intestine from the pancreas and from glands in the intestinal lining. The intestinal juices are alkaline in contrast to the acidic stomach contents, so that the hydrochloric acid from the stomach is neutralized in the small intestine. The final stage of protein breakdown is achieved here as the intestinal enzymes break down the peptones and proteoses to simple amino acids. Large fat globules are broken up into smaller particles by the bile salts and are changed into fatty acids by another pancreatic enzyme—lipase.

The food has now been broken down into its basic components: carbohydrates into simple sugars, proteins into amino acids, and fats into fatty acids and glycerol. In these forms food is absorbed into the blood stream, primarily from the midportion of the small intestine. While sugars and amino acids are absorbed directly into the blood stream from the intestine, most fat enters the lymph vessels and reaches the blood stream at the point where the large lymph channel, the thoracic duct, empties into a large vein in the lower part of the neck.

In the large intestine fluid is absorbed from the undigested residue which leaves the small intestine. Rhythmic muscular contractions of the intestinal wall propel this waste to the rectum, from where it is excreted.

Nervous and Hormonal Control of Digestion

The digestive apparatus is richly supplied with nerves which control the activity of the muscles and glands of the digestive organs. These nerves are not under conscious control, but form part of the vast automatic, or autonomic nervous system, which has its centers of control in the more primitive parts of the brain. The system is divided into two parts: one division stimulates digestive function, while the other inhibits digestion and prepares the body for vigorous exertion. These effects result from the action of the two basic types of nerves found in the autonomic nervous system, the cholinergic and the adrenergic. The cholinergic fibers stimulate the flow of digestive juices and increase muscular activity in the digestive organs. The adrenergic fibers are activated by strong emotions such as fear and anger. They mobilize the body's resources for intense exertion by inhibiting digestion and by shunting blood from the skin and abdominal organs to the muscles of the arms, legs, and brain.

The secretions of the digestive tract are also regulated by hormones given off by the small intestine. Various foods stimulate the intestine to secrete hormones which travel through the blood stream to act upon the stomach, pancreas, liver, and on the intestinal lining itself.

Digestive Disorders

Digestive disturbances may be brought about by abnormal changes in the digestive organs, by diseases in other organs which result in poor digestive functioning, or by emotional problems which produce digestive symptoms in the absence of actual disease of the digestive organs. For example lack of appetite (anorexia) may result from an inflamed stomach lining (gastritis), from a common cold, or from a psychic disorder—such as anorexia nervosa, which appears in young women.

Disease of the organs of digestion may be present from birth, as in cystic fibrosis, in which the obstruction of certain ducts in the pancreas prevents essential fat and protein digesting enzymes from reaching the intestine. Other conditions arise later in life, such as gallstones which may block the normal flow of bile, causing severe abdominal pains and jaundice. Intestinal parasites which rob the body of nutrients are common in some tropical regions. Bacterial toxins are responsible for the violent digestive upsets associated with certain types of food poisoning.

Symptoms of digestive disorders may be produced by disease of the heart, lungs, kidneys, or other organs. A heart attack may be mistaken for an upset stomach, pneu-

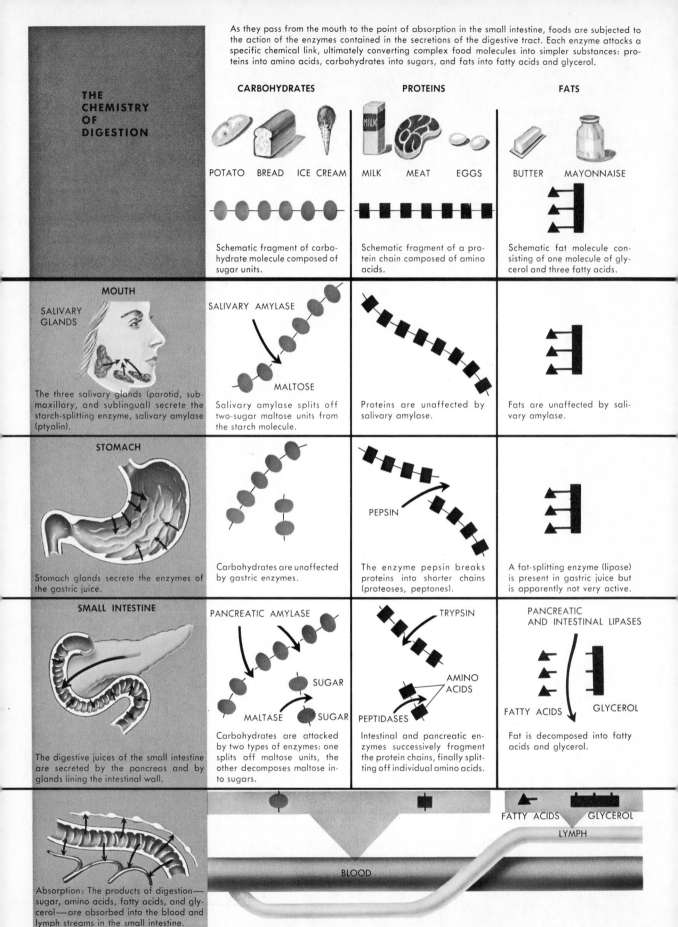

As they pass from the mouth to the point of absorption in the small intestine, foods are subjected to the action of the enzymes contained in the secretions of the digestive tract. Each enzyme attacks a specific chemical link, ultimately converting complex food molecules into simpler substances: proteins into amino acids, carbohydrates into sugars, and fats into fatty acids and glycerol.

THE CHEMISTRY OF DIGESTION

CARBOHYDRATES

POTATO   BREAD   ICE CREAM

Schematic fragment of carbohydrate molecule composed of sugar units.

PROTEINS

MILK   MEAT   EGGS

Schematic fragment of a protein chain composed of amino acids.

FATS

BUTTER   MAYONNAISE

Schematic fat molecule consisting of one molecule of glycerol and three fatty acids.

MOUTH

SALIVARY GLANDS

The three salivary glands (parotid, submaxillary, and sublingual) secrete the starch-splitting enzyme, salivary amylase (ptyalin).

SALIVARY AMYLASE

MALTOSE

Salivary amylase splits off two-sugar maltose units from the starch molecule.

Proteins are unaffected by salivary amylase.

Fats are unaffected by salivary amylase.

STOMACH

Stomach glands secrete the enzymes of the gastric juice.

Carbohydrates are unaffected by gastric enzymes.

PEPSIN

The enzyme pepsin breaks proteins into shorter chains (proteoses, peptones).

A fat-splitting enzyme (lipase) is present in gastric juice but is apparently not very active.

SMALL INTESTINE

The digestive juices of the small intestine are secreted by the pancreas and by glands lining the intestinal wall.

PANCREATIC AMYLASE

SUGAR

MALTASE   SUGAR

Carbohydrates are attacked by two types of enzymes: one splits off maltose units, the other decomposes maltose into sugars.

TRYPSIN

AMINO ACIDS

PEPTIDASES

Intestinal and pancreatic enzymes successively fragment the protein chains, finally splitting off individual amino acids.

PANCREATIC AND INTESTINAL LIPASES

FATTY ACIDS   GLYCEROL

Fat is decomposed into fatty acids and glycerol.

FATTY ACIDS   GLYCEROL

LYMPH

BLOOD

Absorption: The products of digestion—sugar, amino acids, fatty acids, and glycerol—are absorbed into the blood and lymph streams in the small intestine.

THE MOVEMENT OF FOOD THROUGH THE DIGESTIVE TRACT

Food is propelled through the digestive tract by contractions of the smooth muscles which line the walls of the digestive organs. These contractions also mechanically grind the food and mix it with the digestive juices.

LONGITUDINAL MUSCLE
CIRCULAR MUSCLE

Section of esophagus showing characteristic musculature of digestive tract: an inner layer of circular muscle and an outer layer of longitudinal muscle.

THE SPHINCTERS are muscular rings that maintain a one-way flow of digestion by closing off segments of the digestive tract so that food masses can be mixed without spilling back into other sections of the tract.

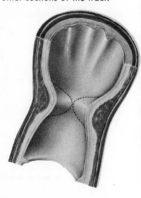

THE LARGE INTESTINE. The large intestine undergoes peristaltic waves similar to those of the small intestine.

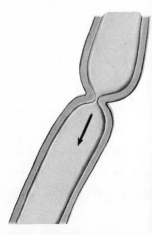

THE DIGESTIVE TRACT

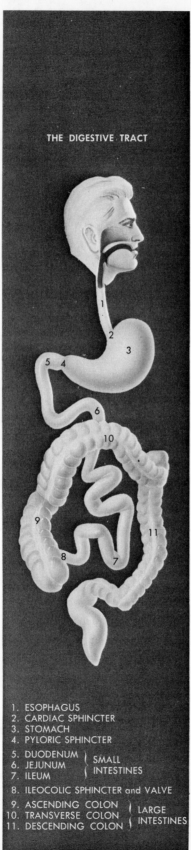

1. ESOPHAGUS
2. CARDIAC SPHINCTER
3. STOMACH
4. PYLORIC SPHINCTER
5. DUODENUM ⎫
6. JEJUNUM ⎬ SMALL INTESTINES
7. ILEUM ⎭
8. ILEOCOLIC SPHINCTER and VALVE
9. ASCENDING COLON ⎫
10. TRANSVERSE COLON ⎬ LARGE INTESTINES
11. DESCENDING COLON ⎭

THE ESOPHAGUS. Food is carried to the stomach by wave-like (peristaltic) contractions.

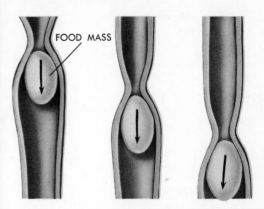

FOOD MASS

Peristaltic wave moves along esophagus.

THE STOMACH. Peristaltic waves sweep toward the pylorus, mixing and grinding the stomach contents. Two or more such waves may grip the stomach simultaneously.

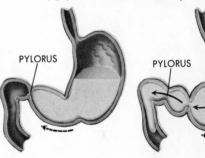

PYLORUS

PYLORUS

(A) Peristaltic wave begins moving toward pylorus.

(B) Second wave begins on heels of first.

The small intestine undergoes two basic types of movement: (1) a rhythmic contraction of intestinal segments and (2) peristaltic contractions.

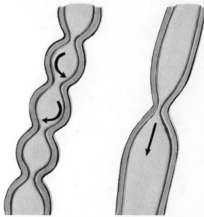

(1) Segmental contractions

(2) Peristaltic waves

21

THE CONTROL OF THE DIGESTIVE SECRETIONS

STIMULATION BEFORE EATING

The secretions of the digestive glands are controlled by nerve impulses and hormones. Stimulation first begins at the sight, smell, or taste of food, which through reflex action generates nerve impulses to the salivary glands, stomach, and pancreas.

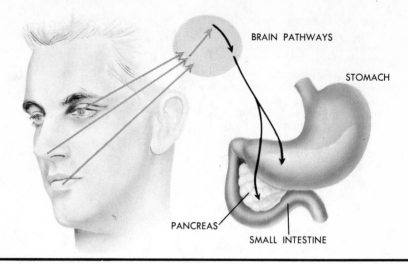

BRAIN PATHWAYS

STOMACH

PANCREAS

SMALL INTESTINE

FOOD IN THE STOMACH

Food in the stomach stimulates the release of GASTRIN, which travels to the stomach glands via the blood stream and induces the secretion of gastric juice. Nerve mechanisms are apparently important in this process.

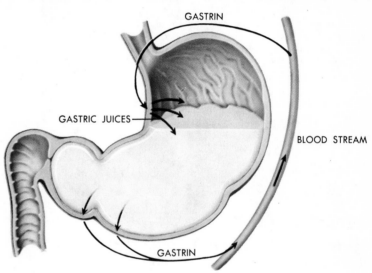

GASTRIN

GASTRIC JUICES

BLOOD STREAM

GASTRIN

FOOD IN THE INTESTINE

(A) STIMULATION. In the intestine certain foods increase gastric secretion, probably by the action of a chemical which is liberated from the intestine and travels to the stomach. Two pancreas-stimulating substances, SECRETIN and PANCREOZYMIN, are known to be released from the intestine by the action of foods and gastric juice.

(B) INHIBITION. Fats in the intestine stimulate the release of intestinal hormone enterogastrone, which inhibits gastric secretion.

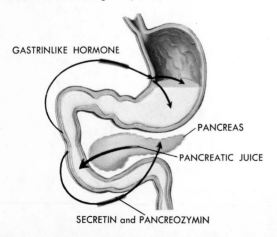

GASTRINLIKE HORMONE

PANCREAS

PANCREATIC JUICE

SECRETIN and PANCREOZYMIN

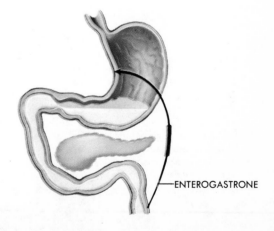

ENTEROGASTRONE

monia may be responsible for abdominal pains, inflammation of the fallopian tubes which carry the egg from the ovary to the womb may result in pains which mimic acute appendicitis.

Emotional distress may produce peptic ulcers, and possibly ulcerations of the colon (ulcerative colitis). Chronic constipation, belching, and heartburn may also be produced by emotional difficulties.

The frequently misleading nature of abdominal pains and digestive difficulties makes the problem of diagnosis particularly difficult.

IRVING SOLOMON, M.D.

See also INTESTINE; LIVER; PANCREAS; STOMACH.

DIGESTIVE SYSTEM. *See* DIGESTION; HUMAN ANATOMY.

DIGGERS, in English history, one of the more extreme radical movements that developed during the course of the English Civil War. The True Levellers, or Diggers, led by Gerrard Winstanley (1609–52), were convinced of the inadequacy of political reform without economic reform, and advocated the peaceful establishment of communal ownership of property. Assuming that God had provided land as a common resource from which all were entitled to draw their sustenance, they held that communal ownership was the natural state of men. They likewise maintained that since most social ills and human vices derived from private property, its abolition would effect the improvement of society. Inspired by these convictions, a small group of them occupied (1649–50) land on St. George's Hill, Surrey, and tilled it in common as the first step toward setting up a better social order. But after a few months they were dispersed by force.
See also CIVIL WAR, ENGLISH.

DIGITAL COMPUTER. *See* COMPUTER.

DIGITALIS [dĭj-ə-tăl′ĭs], name given to a group of chemically related drugs obtained from the dried leaves of certain flowering plants (*Digitalis purpurea* and *D. lanata*). Digitalis was mentioned in the writings of Welsh physicians as early as 1250 and for some time it was indiscriminately used to treat a wide variety of unrelated disorders. It is now recognized that the therapeutic benefits of digitalis can be traced to its action on the heart. It is used today to treat heart failure and certain irregularities of the heartbeat.

DIJON [dē-zhôn′], tourist, wine-marketing, industrial, communications, and university center of eastern France, prefecture of the department of Côte-d'Or, on the Ouche River, about 200 mi. southeast of Paris. The community existed in Roman times and became the capital of the Duchy of Burgundy in the 13th century. At its zenith in the 15th century, when it was capital of the French province of Burgundy, Dijon rivaled Paris, and the city has many Burgundian Gothic churches, medieval public buildings, and fine old mansions. The former palace of the Dukes of Burgundy is now the town hall, and contains a museum of fine arts which is one of the richest in France. With the establishment of its university in 1722 and its bishopric in 1731, Dijon began a new period of prosperity.

It was the scene of bitter fighting in 1870. Dijon is one of the most important railroad and highway centers in France, and has factories producing cycles, machinery, shoes, and chemicals. The town is famous for its food products, including Burgundy wine, strong mustard, and confectionery, which are displayed at its renowned annual Gastronomic Fair. Pop., 106,267.

JOHN FRASER HART, Indiana University

DIK-DIK, a tiny antelope native to semiarid grassland habitats in many parts of Africa. Dik-diks rarely exceed a shoulder height of 14 in. and weigh about 7 lb. The males have short, spikelike horns. Among the several species are the Damara dik-dik, *Rhynchotragus damarensis*, native to southwestern Africa, and Salt's dik-dik, *Madogua saltiana*, of northeastern Africa. Dik-diks are hunted for their hides, which are made into fine glove leather.

DIKE, an embankment or wall constructed to exclude the sea or to confine flood waters of rivers; in the latter use it is often termed a levee. Spur dikes, or groins, are built away from the shore, toward the bed of a stream, to concentrate water currents for the protection of the banks or for deepening the channel by water erosion. A secondary use for dikes is to retain fill deposited by hydraulic dredges. In geology, a dike is a narrow inclined formation of igneous rock.

DIKE, in Greek myth, the personified goddess of justice, also called Astraea, daughter of Zeus and Themis. In the wicked Bronze Age she withdrew to heaven and became the constellation Virgo.

DIKE, IGNEOUS, tabular body of igneous rock that cuts through the structure or layering of another body of rock. A dike is produced when molten rock fills a crack, then hardens. If the dike is nearly vertical it may remain standing as a narrow wall after the enclosing rock has been eroded.
See also SILL, IGNEOUS.

DILL, SIR JOHN GREER (1881–1944), British army officer. He was born in Lurgan, Northern Ireland and graduated (1901) from the Royal Military College, Sandhurst. Between 1934 and 1936 he directed military operations and intelligence for the War Office. He was promoted to general in 1939, commanded (1939–40) the First Army Corps in France, and served (1940–41) as Chief of the Imperial General Staff. Dill accompanied Prime Minister Winston Churchill to Washington, D.C., in Dec., 1941, and remained there on the Allied Board of Strategy. After his death he was awarded the Distinguished Service Medal by President Franklin D. Roosevelt and was buried in Arlington National Cemetery.

DILL, annual or biennial herb, *Anethum graveolens*, in the carrot family, Umbelliferae, native to southeastern Europe. Dill plants grow to a height of about 3 ft., have feathery, finely divided leaves, and produce flat heads of small, yellowish flowers. The seeds are used medicinally and both the seeds and leaves are employed as a culinary spice.

DILLINGHAM, CHARLES BANCROFT (1868–1934), American theatrical producer and manager, especially of musicals. He was born in Hartford, Conn. His productions, which included *Mlle. Modiste, Sunny, Blossom Time*, and *A Bill of Divorcement*, reflected urbanity, charm, and gaiety. Marilyn Miller, Maxine Elliott, Will Rogers, and others appeared under his management.

DILLON, C(LARENCE) DOUGLAS (1909–), American government official and investment banker. Born in Switzerland to American parents and educated at Harvard, he entered his father's New York investment firm and, after serving in the Navy, was its board chairman (1945–53). One of several foreign policy advisers to Republican presidential candidate (1948) Thomas E. Dewey and a "draft Eisenhower" leader (1952) in New Jersey, he was ambassador to France (1953–57), deputy under secretary of state for economic affairs (1957–59), and under secretary of state (1959–61). He served as Secretary of the Treasury under presidents John F. Kennedy and Lyndon B. Johnson (1961–65).

DILLON, town of eastern South Carolina, and seat of Dillon County, 27 mi. northeast of Florence. It is well known for its tobacco market, and also has manufactures of cotton textiles, wood products, carpets, and yarn. Pop. (1950) 5,171; (1960) 6,173.

DILUVIALISM [dĭ-loō'vē-əl-ĭz-əm], obsolete geological theory, according to which surficial deposits and physiographic features resulted from a world-wide flood, usually the Biblical deluge. The presence of great boulders and gravel deposits, beyond the power of present streams to transport, seemed to support the theory. Deep valleys were believed to have been cut by the deluge. Fossils of extinct mammals were thought to be remains of animals caught in the flood. Diluvial theory was best expressed by the English geologist William Buckland in *Reliquiae Diluvianae* (Diluvial Relics), 1823. It was the strongest feature of the religious interpretation of geologic history. After 1850 the recognition of widespread ancient glaciation gradually discredited diluvialism because anomalous phenomena were explained by glacial action instead of a deluge.

DIMAGGIO [dĭ-măj'ē-ō], **JOSEPH PAUL** (1914–), American baseball player, born in Martinez, Calif. He spent his entire major-league career (1936–51) with New York of the American League, but missed three seasons (1943–45) because of Army service. A fine defensive center fielder and a powerful right-handed hitter, he won the league batting championship in 1939, with .381, and in 1940 with .352. He was voted the league's most valuable player in 1939, 1941, and 1947. His feat of hitting safely in 56 consecutive games, in 1941, still stands as a major-league record. He was elected to the National Baseball Hall of Fame in 1955.

DIMASHQ. *See* DAMASCUS.

DIME NOVEL, a fast-moving, incident-packed adventure story, published from 1860 to the early 1900's on cheap

Sy Seidman

Cover of a dime novel by William F. Cody.

newsprint paper, provided with a colored pictorial cover, and sold for ten cents a copy. The first one, *Malaeska, or the Indian Wife of the White Hunter* (1860) by Anne Stephens, was such a success that hundreds more followed, portraying romantic incidents of the Revolution, Indian warfare on the frontier, and the Civil War. Among early authors were Edward Z. C. Judson ("Ned Buntline"), William F. Cody ("Buffalo Bill") and Mayne Reid. Especially popular were series about the Liberty Boys of 1776; about Deadwood Dick, an Indian fighter in the Sioux country of South Dakota; and about the detective Nick Carter.

DIMENSION, in mathematics, the magnitude of a figure in a given direction; for example, the length and width of a plot of ground; or the length, width, and thickness of a box. Euclid defined a one-dimensional figure as one whose boundary consists of points; a two-dimensional figure, one whose boundary consists of curves; and a three-dimensional figure, one whose boundary consists of surfaces. In analytic geometry, the number of co-ordinates needed to fix a point in space is called the dimension of the space. Thus, a line is one-dimensional; the plane, two-dimensional; and the ordinary space of experience, three-dimensional.

DIMERCAPROL. *See* BAL.

DIMITROV [dĭ-mē′trôf], **GEORGI** (1882–1949), Bulgarian Communist leader. Following an unsuccessful Communist insurrection in Bulgaria (1923), Dimitrov lived in Germany, where he was tried (1933) for setting fire to the Reichstag. His effective self-defense gained him international prominence. Dimitrov went to the Soviet Union after his acquittal, acquired Soviet citizenship, and was secretary general (1934–43) of the Comintern. Returning (1944) to Bulgaria, Dimitrov violently suppressed democratic opposition, disregarded peace-treaty provisions, and disrupted U.S.-Bulgarian diplomatic relations. As Premier (1946–49) he established the Communist regime in Bulgaria. Dimitrov died in the Soviet Union, where he had gone for medical care.

DIMITROVGRAD, town of southern Bulgaria, situated on the Maritsa River, midway between Plovdiv and the Turkish border. It was founded in the late 1940's and includes the former village of Rakovski with its important railroad junction. Pop., 41,612.

DIMITROVO, town of western Bulgaria, formerly called Pernik. It is situated in an upland basin on the Struma River, about 15 mi. southwest of Sofia, to which it is connected by railroad. At Dimitrovo are cement, ceramic, coal-processing, mining-machinery, and thermoelectric plants, and also the Lenin steel mill. Pop., 59,721.

DIMITY. *See* TEXTILES: *Glossary.*

DIMONA, new mining town of Israel, in the Negev, on a junction of the road southeast from Beersheba. Most of its inhabitants are employed by the potash works at Sdom, on the shore of the Dead Sea, and in the phosphate mines in the area. Dimona is named after one of the southern towns of the tribe of Judah. Nearby are the ruins of Mamshit (Arab. *Kurnub*), site of an ancient Greek city. In the deep gorge at the foot of Mamshit rise three successive dams of the 5th and 6th centuries, the golden era of the town. On the surrounding hills are the remains of small forts that were erected to guard the ancient reservoirs. Pop., 4,500.

DINARIC [dĭ-năr′ĭk] **ALPS** (Serbo-Croat., **DINARA PLANINA**), a continuation of the Alps, extending from the Ljubljana Basin in northwestern Yugoslavia through Albania to Greece, where they are known as the Pindus Mountains. Dinaric Alps usually refers to the ranges in western Yugoslavia. They form a barrier between the Adriatic coast and the interior Carpathian Basin. They vary from 60 to 100 mi. wide and reach heights of 5,000 to 8,000 ft. Durmitor, in Montenegro, is the loftiest peak (8,275 ft.). The Dinaric Alps consist of limestone plateaus and flat ridges, and vary from the barren, dissected, and waterless high Karst in the west to a series of parallel forested mountains and hills in the north and northeast. The Dinaric Alps include the narrow coastal zone with its many islands and depressions. The fortress-like high Karst, a barren, mainly Mesozoic limestone zone extending for some 350 mi., has no good passes. Because precipitation falling upon the exposed rocks quickly sinks underground, the river valleys are short. The plateaus and ridges (*planine*) alternate with longitudinal troughs or fields (*polja*). The latter are relatively fertile. The inner part of the Dinaric Alps is less barren and rugged, with narrow, open valleys. There is extensive mining and logging throughout this area.

GEORGE W. HOFFMAN, The University of Texas

D'INDY, VINCENT. *See* INDY, VINCENT D'.

DINESEN [dē′nə-sən], **ISAK,** pseudonym of Baroness Karen Christence Dinesen Blixen-Finecke (1885–1962), Danish writer. In 1914 she went to Kenya with her husband (whom she divorced in 1921); she operated a coffee plantation until 1931, when she returned to Denmark and settled in her native town of Rungsted. She won world recognition with her *Seven Gothic Tales* (1934), brilliant stories of love and fantasy contrasting sharply with the earthbound realism of the 1930's. In *Out of Africa* (1937) she wrote about her life in Kenya, but she returned to her former theme in *Winter's Tales* (1942). Her later books, in which she revealed herself as one of the world's greatest storytellers, include *Last Tales* (1957), *Anecdotes of Destiny* (1958), and *Shadows on the Grass* (1960). Isak Dinesen wrote both Danish and English versions of all her books.

DINGLEY, NELSON (1832–99), U.S. Representative. Born in Maine, Dingley graduated (1855) from Dartmouth, edited the Lewiston *Evening Journal* for several years, and served (1862–65, 1868, 1873) in the state house of representatives. He was Governor of Maine (1874–75) and was elected (1881) as a Republican to the U.S. House of Representatives, where he soon became known for his strong protectionist views. Appointed (1889) to the Ways and Means Committee, Dingley became (1895) its chairman and drafted the high-protection tariff law—known as the Dingley Act—that replaced (1897) the low-rate Wilson-Gorman Act. Dingley remained in the House until his death.

Consult Dingley, E. N., *Nelson Dingley* (1902).

DINGO, a wolflike wild dog, *Canis dingo*, native to Australia. Dingos are about 2 ft. tall at the shoulder, have soft fur of a tawny, rusty, or almost black color, and a bushy tail. Unlike domesticated dogs dingos do not bark but make howling or yelping sounds like coyotes. Dingos have been outlawed because they are sheep killers. But although they are despised for this activity, they are useful in keeping down the rabbit population which at times threatens to overrun Australia.
See also DOG.

DINOCERATA [dĭ-nō-sĕr′ə-tə], extinct, heavy-bodied mammals with strong legs and broad, spreading, five-toed feet with hooflike toe nails. The massive, elongated skull bore two or three pairs of horns, and the canine teeth were long and sharp. Dinocerata, some of which have been called amblypods, lived in North America and Asia during Paleocene and Eocene time (about 65 million to 35 million years ago). They were among the largest early mammals; one group, the Uintatheres, resembled large rhinoceroses.

Among the largest of land animals, herbivorous *Brontosaurus* is seen in the mural. His skeleton is contrasted to man's.

Dinosaurs, prevailing land animals for over 130 million years, became extinct during the last period of the Mesozoic Era, which ended about 63 million years ago.

Trachodon (left) had a long spatulate snout, small forelegs, and a heavy tail that probably was an aid in standing upright.

DINOSAUR [dī′nə-sôr], meaning "terrible lizard," any of the reptiles that were the dominant land animals for more than 130 million years during the Mesozoic Era. Mesozoic time ended almost 65 million years ago, and it included the Triassic, Jurassic, and Cretaceous periods. There were two great orders of dinosaurs, the Saurischia and Ornithischia, within which many specialized forms evolved.

Saurischia

The saurischians appeared first, the earliest fossil remains having been found in rocks of late Triassic age (about 200 million years old). Saurischia were characterized by a three-pronged pelvic structure similar to that of modern reptiles. Generally the toes bore strong claws, and the teeth were either limited to the front of the jaw or they extended around the margins. Saurischia are divided into two suborders, the Theropoda and Sauropoda.

Theropoda. The theropods were the only carnivorous (meat-eating) dinosaurs. All forms walked with two strong hind limbs, with the body pivoted at the hips. Most early theropods were swift runners, with long, grasping fingers

on the forelimbs. Many were about the size of the modern ostrich. *Ornithomimus*, with its long, sinuous neck and small, beaked head, must have looked much like a featherless, long-tailed ostrich. Late in the Mesozoic Era there developed a group of giant theropods with tremendous hind limbs, and with forelimbs that were greatly reduced. Among these *Allosaurus*, which lived during late Jurassic time (about 140 million years ago), had clawed hands that probably were used for holding prey. In contrast another genus, *Tyrannosaurus*, had hands that were so small that they must have been quite useless. *Tyrannosaurus* lived during the Cretaceous Period (between about 135 million and 65 million years ago). It was about 40 ft. long and 20 ft. high, weighing six or eight tons. Its huge head had long jaws armed with large, daggerlike teeth, the only offensive weapons of the largest carnivore of all time.

Sauropoda. The sauropods were giant, herbivorous (plant-eating), semiaquatic creatures, and most had four legs. They all had small heads, long necks and tails, and elongated bodies supported by heavy, pillarlike legs and broad feet. The hindquarters were more massive than the forequarters. Three genera, *Brontosaurus*, *Diplodocus*, and *Brachiosaurus*, were the largest animals ever to live on land. They were 60 to 80 ft. long and they weighed 30 to 50 tons. To help support their great weight these giant reptiles must have spent much time wading in swamps and lakes, feeding upon the lush vegetation.

Ornithischia

The second major group of dinosaurs, the Ornithischia, had a four-pronged pelvic structure similar to that of birds. The teeth were limited to the sides of the jaw, and the front of the skull resembled a beak. The toes had flat nails rather than claws. Most ornithischians walked with four feet, and all were herbivorous. Ornithischia are divided into the suborders Ornithopoda, Stegosauria, Ankylosauria, and Ceratopsia.

Ornithopoda. The ornithopods, which lived during the Jurassic and Cretaceous periods (between about 180 million and 65 million years ago), were the most primitive of the ornithischians. Usually they walked with their hind limbs only, but most had strong forelimbs, that could also be used for locomotion. One of the earliest members of this semiaquatic group was *Camptosaurus*, a medium-sized dinosaur with a long, low skull, leaf-shaped teeth, and a flattened beak. The most spectacular of the ornithopods were the duck-billed trachodonts of late Cretaceous age. One of the largest, *Trachodon*, was 30 or 40 ft. long, weighing several tons. It had a ducklike bill-behind which elongated jaws bore about 2,000 lozenge-shaped teeth. Some of the trachodonts, such as *Corythosaurus*, had a high, bony crest at the top of the skull.

Stegosauria. The stegosaurs appeared early in Jurassic time, and they were the first dinosaurs to become extinct, dying out early in the Cretaceous Period. *Stegosaurus* was 20 or more ft. long, with four feet and heavy hindquarters. The pelvic region was the highest part of its body. The skull was extremely small, with room for only a tiny brain. Probably for protection, a double row of triangular, bony plates stood vertically along the backbone, and four long, bony spikes made a weapon of the tail.

Ankylosauria. The ankylosaurs were broad, bulky reptiles of Cretaceous age. The genus *Ankylosaurus* was about 20 ft. long, with the top of its head and its back protected by a continuous armor of bony plates. Spikes ranged along the sides of the body, and the tail ended in a massive club of bone. Such protection was undoubtedly necessary when *Tyrannosaurus* was abroad.

Ceratopsia. The ceratopsians were the last dinosaur group to evolve. They lived only during late Cretaceous time but they were represented by a diversity of genera. Ceratopsians were thick-bodied, four-footed animals with a hooked beak and bony frills at the rear of the skull. All but the most primitive had one or more horns. *Protoceratops*, a genus that lived in Mongolia, is the best known of all dinosaurs. Fossilized eggs have revealed its prenatal development, and skeletons have been assembled of all growth stages from the newly hatched infant to the adult. *Triceratops*, a large, three-horned ceratopsian, roamed the uplands of North America in large numbers.

The dinosaurs lived during an era of relatively mild, uniform climate throughout the world. There were extensive, low-lying lands and shallow seas. Conditions were optimal for reptiles, and it is not surprising that they developed in such a profuse and bizarre array. However, the close of the Cretaceous Period, at the end of the Mesozoic Era, saw the last of the dinosaurs, a sudden extinction in terms of geologic time. It has been thought that they died out because they lacked adaptability, but this is now considered a minor factor. During Cretaceous time the dinosaurs adjusted to many changes, caused both by the uplift of mountain chains and by the appearance of new kinds of vegetation. Moreover, climatic changes were neither sudden nor drastic at the close of the Mesozoic Era. Possibly the depredation of dinosaur eggs by primitive mammals and birds contributed to the extinction of these great reptiles, but the true combination of factors that caused them to die out remains a mystery.

Consult Colbert, E. H., *Dinosaurs, Their Discovery and Their World* (1961).

DONALD F. SQUIRES, American Museum of Natural History

The plant-eating *Triceratops* (right) had three horns and a rufflike plate of bony armor. *Tyrannosaurus* (below), about 20 ft. high, was the largest-known flesh-eating land animal.
American Museum of Natural History

Stegosaurus (right) had a spiked tail for defense, and the finlike, bony plates probably helped ward off attackers.
© Chicago Natural History Museum and Charles R. Knight

DINUBA [dǐ-nū′bə], city of south-central California in the San Joaquin Valley. The leading industry is the packing and shipping of grapes and other fruits, and turkeys. Pop. (1950) 4,971; (1960) 6,103.

DINWIDDIE, ROBERT (1693–1770), British colonial administrator, acting Governor of Virginia (1751–58). Dinwiddie's efforts to check French expansion in the Ohio region often had the aspect of a one-man war. Dinwiddie went to Virginia after service as collector of customs (1727–38) for Bermuda and surveyor-general (1738–51) for the southern colonies, which included jurisdiction over all English settlements from Jamaica and the Bahamas to Pennsylvania. Since his commission entitled him to sit on any colonial council within his jurisdiction, he chose that of Virginia in 1741. In 1751 the Home Office appointed him Lieutenant, or acting, Governor in the absence of the sinecure holder resident in England.

Dinwiddie's principal preoccupation was with raising the military power of the colonies to resist French expansion. Personally interested in the Ohio Company, Dinwiddie recruited troops and dispatched them beyond the Alleghenies to thwart the French. He sent young George Washington on one such mission in 1753; in 1754 Washington's hastily constructed Fort Necessity was overrun by French troops. A foray by British Gen. Edward Braddock against the French stronghold, Fort Duquesne, in 1755 ended in disaster. But despite the danger, Dinwiddie could not rouse the colonists to raise the necessary funds or men, or even to unite their commands. "I was never among People," he wrote in despair, "who have so little regard to their own safety." Dinwiddie finally gave up; he left Virginia early in 1758, shortly before the British army came to the colonies' rescue and expelled the French from North America.

RICHARD M. ABRAMS, Columbia University

DINWIDDIE COURTHOUSE AND WHITE OAK ROAD, BATTLE OF. *See* APPOMATTOX CAMPAIGN.

DIO CASSIUS [dī′ō kǎsh′ē-əs] (c.155–after 230 A.D.), Roman historian. Engaged under the emperors Commodus and Alexander Severus in the administration of Roman provincial government, Dio undertook the composition of a history of Rome from its beginnings. Originally numbering 80 books, the work survives in somewhat less than one third its original size. Treating history not only in the manner of the chronicler, but also, like Thucydides, underlining important events by the insertion of dramatic speeches, Dio divided his work into three large epochs: the first covers the history of the Republic; the second, ending with the reign of Marcus Aurelius, gives an account of the Roman Empire at its height; the last relates the story of Rome during Dio's own lifetime.

DIOCESE [dī′ə-sēs] (Gr. *dioikesis*, "administrative district"), an ecclesiastical territory under a Bishop's jurisdiction. In the Eastern Roman Empire a diocese was a district subject to a city. Under Diocletian (reigned 284–305) the Empire was divided into four prefectures, which were subdivided into dioceses. In the 4th century the word was applied to the area within a Bishop's or Patri-arch's jurisdiction. By the 5th century the territorial limits of dioceses conformed to the civil divisions of large towns and population centers. New ecclesiastical dioceses were often formed independent of papal authority. But since the 10th to 11th centuries the Roman Catholic Church has considered the creation of new dioceses a papal prerogative, and details of this work are handled by special congregations of the Roman Curia. Once established, the diocese is governed by the Bishop through his vicar-general, chancellor, synod, and cathedral chapter (or clerical consultors in the United States).

In churches of the Anglican Communion new dioceses are organized by the local clergy and laity, and are governed by the Bishop and diocesan convention of clerical and lay delegates. Ordinarily the diocese is named after the principal city or state of the area.

In Eastern Churches not affiliated with Rome the formation of dioceses belongs to the Patriarch and Archbishop, who appoint the Bishop and vicar-general.

JOHN P. MARSCHALL, C.S.V., Viatorian Seminary, Washington, D.C.

DIOCLETIAN [dī-ə-klē′shən] (c.243–313), Roman emperor (reigned 284–305), born in Salonae in Dalmatia. He was responsible for the recovery of the Roman Empire from the near collapse of the mid-3d century and was the author of the military and administrative system of the later Roman Empire, which developed into the Byzantine state. Rising in a military career by his ability, Diocletian was chosen by the army to succeed Numerian. He took Maximian I as his colleague, and the two in a series of wars with the barbarians rescued the Empire from the external dangers through which it had been passing. To assure the defense of the Empire and make the government more efficient, Diocletian instituted (293) the system of the Tetrarchy (rule of four), by which the Empire was divided into two parts, east and west, each half being ruled by a senior Emperor, the "Augustus," assisted by a junior ruler, the "Caesar," who was his heir-designate.

The administration was completely overhauled. The provinces were reduced in size and increased in number, and were grouped into 12 dioceses, each administered by a *vicarius*, who was responsible to the praetorian prefect. Military and civil commands were separated, as they had not been previously. The army, which had become demoralized, was strengthened and reorganized. The currency, which had been inflated and unstable, was completely reformed, though an edict of price control (301) proved unsuccessful. A new system of taxation, based on units of agricultural land, was introduced, and payments were collected in kind as well as in money. To increase the dignity of the Emperor's position, Diocletian introduced the costume and ceremonial of the Persian royal court and made the Emperor a remote figure. His political principles led him to initiate a severe persecution of the Christians (303). After a serious illness (304) Diocletian abdicated and retired, being succeeded by Galerius. His policies were continued and developed by Constantine I.

GLANVILLE DOWNEY, Dumbarton Oaks Research Library and Collection of Harvard University

See also ROME: *Republic and Empire.*

DIOCLETIAN, BATHS OF. *See* BATHS, ROMAN.

DIOGENES LAERTIUS [*dī-ŏj′ə-nēz lā-ūr′shē-əs*], author of a work *On the Lives and Opinions of Famous Philosophers*, probably in the early 3d century A.D. Though himself a compiler of little talent, he had access to many earlier authorities now lost, and the work is an important source of our knowledge of earlier philosophers.

DIOGENES OF APOLLONIA [*ăp-ə-lō′nē-ə*] (5th century B.C.), Greek philosopher. He followed Anaximenes in naming air as primary substance from which everything else comes by condensation or rarefaction. It is also the vehicle of life and intelligence, both in man and in the universe, these attributes depending on its degree of warmth.

DIOGENES OF SINOPE [*sĭ-nō′pē*] (c.400–325 B.C.), Greek philosopher, founder of the Cynic school. He scorned all convention and taught that happiness consists in satisfying only natural needs in the simplest and cheapest way. They should also be satisfied publicly, since nothing natural could be shameful. His shameless behavior earned him the nickname "dog," which his school inherited (*cynicus*, "doglike"). His goal was an ascetic self-sufficiency achieved by training the body to reject all possessions. It is illustrated by the story that he threw away his one cup on seeing a child drinking from its hands, and by the famous account of his meeting with Alexander the Great, who, on finding him sitting in the wooden tub in which he lived, asked him what he could do for him; to which Diogenes replied, "Get out of the light." He is also reported to have gone about the streets of Athens with a lantern in broad daylight looking, as he said, "for an honest man."

W. K. C. GUTHRIE, Cambridge University

DIOMEDES [*dī-ə-mē′dēz*], legendary Greek hero. He participated in the expedition of the Epigoni against Thebes and later fought bravely at Troy. He aided Odysseus in taking Rhesus' horses, and, in a post-Homeric account, he and Odysseus carried off the Palladium.

DION [*dī′ŏn*] (c.408–354 B.C.], Greek political leader of Syracuse. He was stern and autocratic like his kinsman Dionysius I, whose minister he was. Deeply impressed by Plato's first visit to the Syracusan court in 387 B.C., Dion persuaded him to return after the death of Dionysius I (367) to try to educate the new ruler Dionysius II as a philosopher-king. They failed completely in this effort, and Dion, exiled, went to Athens to study at the Academy. Provoked by Dionysius' continued hostility, Dion attempted an armed coup in 357. He gained, lost, and regained control in Syracuse. But being unable to reconcile his philosophical principles with political expediency, he eventually lost popularity and was assassinated in 354.

DIONE [*dī-ō′nē*], in Greek legend, a Titaness who was consort of Zeus at his great oracular shrine of Dodona. Often called the mother of Aphrodite, she was probably Zeus's wife in earliest Greek mythology.

DIONNE [*dē-ŏn′, dē-ōn′*] **QUINTUPLETS,** five daughters of Oliva and Elzire Dionne. Born in Callander, near North Bay, Ontario, Canada, on May 28, 1934, they were named Cécile, Annette, Marie, Yvonne, and Émilie. Primary credit for their survival went to the local country doctor, Allan Roy Dafoe, after whom a hospital, built by public subscription for the care of the children, was named. The birth of quintuplets is extremely rare, and this was the first known case of survival of all five beyond a few hours. To protect them against both disease and exploitation during their infancy, the provincial government appointed guardians. Their father later resumed jurisdiction over them. Émilie died in 1954; the four surviving quintuplets were then living in Montreal. Cécile and Annette married and had children of their own. Marie, abandoning her intention of becoming a nun, married in 1958. Their parents continued to live in Callander, raising a larger family.

W. MENZIES WHITELAW, American International College

DIONYSIA [*dī-ə-nĭs′ē-ə*], ancient Greek festivals celebrated in honor of the god Dionysus. In Athens there were, besides the Anthesteria, three distinct festivals called the Dionysia. (1) The Rural Dionysia was celebrated in the local townships of Attica in the month Poseideon (Dec.-Jan.). The rites comprised a phallic procession, a sacrifice, and a *komos*, or masked revel, out of which Athenian comedy probably developed. (2) The Epilenaea Dionysia, or Lenaea, was held a month later in Athens. The name (from *lenai*, "madwoman") suggests that the rites were emotional, concerned with Dionysus as the god of ecstasy. (3) The City Dionysia, a relatively late creation (6th century B.C.), was held in spring. The five-day celebration included, on a grander scale, the elements of the ancient rural festival, but is chiefly famous as the major occasion for dramatic performances. Both tragedy and comedy arose in Athens as part of the cult of Dionysus and were always regarded not as mere entertainment, but as religious ceremonies in his honor. Plays were also presented at the Lenaea, and at least in later times at the Rural Dionysia as well.

FRANCIS R. WALTON, Gennadius Library, Athens
See also COMEDY; GREECE: *Greek Religion.*

DIONYSIUS [*dī-ə-nĭsh′ē-əs*] **OF ALEXANDRIA** (c.200–64), Bishop of Alexandria (from 247) and pupil of Origen. He was (from c.233) head of the Catechetical School at Alexandria and was one of the first higher critics of the Bible, arguing on grounds of style and content that the St. John of Revelation was different from the author of the Fourth Gospel. His letters are extensively quoted in the *Church History* of Eusebius and reflect his conciliatory spirit.

DIONYSIUS OF HALICARNASSUS [*hăl-ĭ-kär-năs′əs*] (fl.1st century B.C.), Greek literary critic and antiquarian, resident in Rome during the reign of Augustus. Although Dionysius composed an account of early Roman history, the *Roman Antiquities*, it is chiefly as a literary critic that he is studied today. Dionysius clearly lacked the qualifications of a historian, but as a student of literary history and, more particularly, of the elements of fine style, he occupies a high place in the history of ancient literary criticism. Dionysius wrote studies of the Athenian orators, among them Demosthenes, and of the historian Thucydides; but a fine essay *On the Arrangement of Words* is undoubtedly his masterpiece.

DIONYSIUS OF ROME, Pope (259–68 A.D.), known mainly by his letter to Dionysius of Alexandria, expounding the doctrine of the Trinity on lines similar to those of later orthodoxy—an early exercise of papal authority in dogma, reflecting also the special relation which existed between the churches of Rome and Alexandria.

DIONYSIUS THE AREOPAGITE [ăr-ĕ-ŏp'ə-jīt], one of the few Greeks whom Paul converted at Athens (Acts 17:34). In Christian tradition, he has been erroneously identified with St. Denis, first Bishop of Paris, who lived in the 3d century, and with the author of an influential mystical writing of the 5th century.

DIONYSIUS THE ELDER (c.430–367 B.C.), Greek Tyrant of Syracuse. Elected one of the city's generals in 406 B.C., Dionysius soon superseded his colleagues and became sole ruler. Relying on mercenary troops, he began a program of expansion over both Greek and Carthaginian territory in Sicily. He made Syracuse the strongest fortified city in the western Mediterranean and employed advanced military techniques. When Carthaginian resistance in the west of the island proved formidable, Dionysius undertook the conquest of southern Italy. His fleet ranged as far as the Etruscan coast, and he twice sent aid to Sparta. Dionysius was not only politically ambitious but fancied himself as a poet and patron of literary men and philosophers. His tragedy was expediently granted first prize at the Lenaean Festival in Athens in 367. Toward Plato he displayed his customary haughtiness. Yet in spite of notorious cruelty, impiety, and greed, Dionysius enjoyed a relatively stable reign and made of Syracuse a considerable power in contemporary world politics.

WILLIAM A. McDONALD, University of Minnesota

DIONYSIUS THE YOUNGER, Tyrant of Syracuse (reigned 367–357 B.C.). Succeeding his father, Dionysius the Elder, in 367 B.C., Dionysius resisted the efforts of Dion and Plato to educate him as a philosopher-king. Succumbing to the flattery of courtiers, he soon dismissed his mentors and yielded to dissipation. Like his father, Dionysius cultivated philosophers and writers, but, unlike his father, he was weak, vacillating, and unstable. He lost Syracuse to Dion in 357 B.C., then retired to Locri, where he ruled despotically for 10 years. He regained Syracuse by treachery in 347, but was finally forced by Timoleon of Corinth to abdicate in 343.

DIONYSUS [dī-ə-nī'səs], also known as Bacchus, Greek god of fertility and vegetation, especially of the vine. His Roman name was Liber. Until recently scholars believed that he was originally Thracian, but it now seems probable that he was an early Greek deity. The historic Dionysus, however, was a composite of various origins—Greek, Cretan, Thracian, and Anatolian. His worship, accompanied by wine drinking, was often ecstatic and orgiastic. The great Greek dramas were presented at the Dionysiac

Dionysus with Satyrs and maenads as depicted on a Greek vase (5th century B.C.). (THE METROPOLITAN MUSEUM OF ART, ROGERS FUND, 1907)

festivals of Athens. He also had important cults in Thebes and Delphi, and, in fact, was worshiped nearly everywhere. His favorite plants were the grapevine and ivy; his sacred animals, whose shapes he could assume, the goat, bull, snake, panther, and lion.

Many Dionysiac myths were told in varying versions. In a widespread tradition he was the son of Zeus and Semele, and the nursling of Ino. Attended by Satyrs (Sileni) and maenads, he wandered over the earth as far as India, teaching men viticulture and wine-making. Several myths tell of his opponents—Lycurgus of Thrace, the daughters of Minyas in Orchomenus, Proetus in Argos, the Lydian pirates, and Pentheus of Thebes. All his enemies were driven mad, transformed into animals, or torn to pieces. In other myths he recovered his mother from Hades, married Ariadne, and fought the Giants. He was a dying-and-rising god. In one story the Titans tore him to pieces; and at Delphi one could see the tomb from which he rose to reign through the winter months. He was later an important figure in the doctrines of the mystery religions.

Consult Farnell, L. R., *Cults of the Greek States* (Vol. 5, 1909); Guthrie, W. K. C., *The Greeks and Their Gods* (1950); Seltman, Charles, *The Twelve Olympians* (1956).

JOSEPH FONTENROSE, University of California, Berkeley

DIOPHANTINE [dī-ə-făn'tēn] **EQUATION,** an indeterminate equation whose solution is limited to integers. If $2x + 5y = 16$, the only solutions in terms of non-negative integers are $x = 8$, $y = 0$; and $x = 3$, $y = 2$. In terms of the full set of integers there is no limit to the number of solutions.

Diophantine equations are named after the Greek mathematician Diophantus (c.250 A.D.), who gave solutions to several kinds of these indeterminate equations. Not much was done about this type of equation until the time of the 17th-century French mathematician Pierre de Fermat. Fermat claimed that he had proved the statement that the solution to the set of Diophantine equations

$x^n + y^n = z^n$ in integers alone existed only for the case where $n = 2$. He did not disclose his proof and, as yet, it has not been established.

DIOPHANTUS [dī-ə-făn'təs] **OF ALEXANDRIA** (fl.250), Greek mathematician known as the father of algebra. Only six of the original 13 books of his chief treatise, the *Arithmetica*, have survived. The bulk of the work consists of problems leading to indeterminate quadratic equations with a few leading to equations of higher degree. Hence, the branch of the theory of numbers which deals with integral solutions of indeterminate equations has become known as Diophantine analysis.

DIOR [dē-ôr'], **CHRISTIAN** (1905–57), Paris fashion designer, born in Granville, Normandy. Originally designer for Piquet and Lelong, Dior opened his own fashion house in 1946. So great was the impact of his 1947 New Look that he dominated the fashion world until his death. Creator of the A-line, H-line, and Trapeze, he developed his *haute-couture* house into a $15,000,000 perfume, accessories, fur, and ready-to-wear enterprise, employing 1,700 in Paris, London, New York, and Venezuela.

DIOSCORIDES [dī-ŏs-kôr'ə-dēz], **PEDANIUS** (fl.1st century A.D.), Greek botanist and military surgeon who served with the Roman armies. His work, known as *Materia Medica*, or *Herbal*, described 600 plants and plant remedies, and is considered the authoritative guide on the drugs used in ancient times.

DIPHOSPHOPYRIDINE NUCLEOTIDE [dī-fŏs-fō-pĭr'ə-dēn nū'klē-ə-tīd], also known as DPN, a complex substance found in muscle, blood cells, and the retina of the eye. DPN acts in conjunction with numerous enzymes to process foods (amino acids, fats, glucose) in the body. It is found in particularly high concentrations in yeast, where it is essential for the fermentation of sugar into alcohol.

DIPHTHERIA [dĭf-thēr'ē-ə], an infectious disease caused by the diphtheria bacillus. The bacilli are sprayed from the throat of a patient or carrier of the disease to land in the throat, windpipe, or other exposed surface of a victim (usually a susceptible child). Although they tend to grow only where they have entered the body, the bacteria secrete a poison which damages the heart and nervous system.

The symptoms of diphtheria depend on where the bacillus has attacked. The most dreaded form of the disease affects the larynx (the voicebox) and the windpipe below it, both small enough to be blocked by the diphtheritic membrane which develops in response to the infection. The child may strangle unless an opening is made in its windpipe (tracheotomy).

Other major forms of diphtheria affect the tonsils and the nose. Tonsillar diphtheria causes a severe sore throat, in which the diphtheritic membrane is clearly visible. In nasal diphtheria there is less danger of obstruction to breathing, but more danger of toxin flooding the body, causing heart damage and paralysis. In rare cases the diphtheria bacillus may invade exposed areas outside the respiratory passages, such as the eye, the ear, or injured skin.

The principal means of treatment is an antitoxin which can counteract the effect of the poison given off by the diphtheria bacillus. The antitoxin cannot reverse the damage done to tissues which have been exposed to the toxin. Consequently it must be given immediately after the diagnosis is made, as even a few hours' delay may be fatal. Other treatment consists of bed rest and a humidity tent or steam room to help relieve the obstruction to breathing.

Immunization is the only known means of controlling the disease. Two or three injections of diphtheria toxoid are given at one-month intervals, usually starting at the age of three months. Booster doses are given afterward. Immunization has been so successful that it has actually increased the peril to each patient for diphtheria is now so rare that it may go unrecognized at first, resulting in a dangerous delay in treatment.

HARRY WIENER, M.D.

DIPLOCOCCUS [dĭp-lō-kŏk'əs], designation for spherical bacteria which occur in pairs, and particularly for a genus of such bacteria (*Neissera*). This genus includes organisms which cause pneumonia, gonorrhea, and epidemic meningitis. A variety of diplococci are normally present in the upper respiratory tract.
See also BACTERIA.

DIPLODOCUS. *See* DINOSAUR.

DIPLOMACY [dĭ-plō'mə-sē], art and practice of conducting international relations. While an individual may be said to have a sense of diplomacy if he is tactful in dealing with others, diplomacy in a formal sense is concerned with the form and method of conducting relations between states.

Diplomacy and Foreign Policy. Diplomacy and foreign policy are often considered identical. The foreign policy of a given state may be determined by its concept of national interest based upon an evaluation of its national strength and national goals. These may reflect the character of its geographical location, population, natural resources, economy, trade, political system, and historical relationships. Once the foreign policy of a state is formulated—be it long or short range, general or specific—the achievement of the foreign policy, short of the use of force, depends upon diplomacy. The form and method by which one state negotiates with other states can determine the degree to which its foreign policy is achieved. While all states in the international arena may desire peace and security, each has its own interpretation of what constitutes peace and security. Thus, their different foreign policy goals constantly are coming into some degree of conflict.

Diplomacy, on the other hand, is both the art and the science by which each state attempts to achieve success in its foreign policy short of forcing conclusions by armed conflict. In this sense diplomacy may be said to stop where war begins, and it starts where war ends. The word "diplomacy" is derived from *diploun*, a Greek verb meaning "to double." In Roman times persons passing along the imperial highways carried documents, or credentials, like

DIPLOMACY

passports, which consisted of wax or metal plates folded and sewn together and were called "diplomas." Later this word was extended to refer to all official documents concerning two or more parties. Thus the word "diplomacy" has, in a literal sense, a meaning of official communications between parties or states. Official communication between parties in a more realistic sense implies negotiation. The form, manner, and way in which official negotiations are carried on constitutes the art and science of diplomacy. To a state which is all-powerful in manpower, resources, and so on, the manner and mode of negotiation may not be significant in achieving its

viewpoint in international relations. On the other hand, a state limited in potentials may have to put greater reliance on its skill of diplomacy in order to give its viewpoint the necessary impact. The officials of a state principally concerned with diplomacy are called diplomats.

Early Beginning of Diplomacy. Diplomacy is as old as man. Although it has undergone continual modification, certain principles of diplomacy have become accepted as fundamental elements of its conduct. The ability to negotiate an agreement implies direct negotiation between parties. In order to have an exchange of negotiators it is necessary to give the emissaries protection. Hence one of the first principles to become firmly established was that of diplomatic immunity. Contacts between groups of Australian aborigines were made by individuals sent from one group to another who had special privileges of inviolability. These messengers, or envoys, wore a red net around their foreheads which guaranteed their right to negotiate without being subjected to personal harm. This principle of diplomatic immunity evidenced in primitive man is an accepted practice of diplomacy today.

Practices of Ancient Empires. The history of ancient Babylon, Egypt, China, and India reveals that the process of diplomacy has deep roots in the traditions of man. In 2850 B.C. the city-states of Lagash and Umma made a treaty with the Babylonian state of Shatt al-Hai on the settlement of boundary disputes. The first "international" treaty of which the full text is preserved was one drawn up between Rameses II of Egypt and Hattusilis, Prince of the Hittites. The treaty was negotiated in 1280 B.C. by Hittite envoys to Egypt who brought the treaty, written on silver tablets, back to their Prince. In the relationships of Babylon and Egypt with adjoining peoples or states certain regular features of diplomacy developed. At that time the Kings—chiefs of state—were in regular correspondence with each other. Diplomatic envoys were allowed to come and go, and there were standard practices for the reception and treatment of envoys. Varying with the period, certain languages came to be the diplomatic language used by all envoys. On more major problems, formal agreements—treaties—were decided upon between the states. Such treaties usually involved an oath to the gods, giving them a sanctity which modern treaties do not usually enjoy. This regularization of contact between states and the techniques developed for negotiating differences that were prevalent at the time of Babylon and ancient Egypt do not appear to have developed in the ancient Persian empires, but appear to have been practiced in the tribal relationships among the Hebrews when they formed more or less independent states.

In the Eastern Chou Dynasty of China (770–256 B.C.), especially after 400 B.C., not only was China divided into a series of competing states, but she was coming into contact with other parts of Asia. The Confucian and Taoist schools of thought had a considerable humane influence on negotiations between states. Envoys were appointed and received with established formalities and ceremonies. Envoys were given precise instructions on tactful procedures in building confidence in relations with others. The teachings of the Legalists, such as that of the Prince of Shang, brought an organization to the process of negotiation between governments.

Similar experiences are evident in India at about the same time. The Law of Manu (1200 B.C.) contains a series of rules for the King and ambassadors in dealing with other Indian states. There was considerable concern with the negotiating of alliances. Kautilya's *Arthasastra* (c.330 B.C.), which was a sort of handbook for rulers, has several chapters dealing with the techniques of negotiating alliances with neighboring Indian states. Treaties of alliance were recognized as solemn agreements not easily broken. While they might be negotiated by special envoys, their formal acceptance, or ratification, was effected by the sovereigns of the contracting states. The *Arthasastra* even

detailed the use of spies and various contrivances of subterfuge that might be used to influence the negotiators. While such procedures might have been used in the diplomacy of other earlier great empires, it appears to have been first formally acknowledged in ancient India.

Greek City-States. In spite of this regulation of international intercourse in the ancient world, diplomacy as we now know it traces its roots generally to the Greek city-states. In the period from 800 to 100 B.C. diplomacy evolved to a considerable degree in the atmosphere of competition of these city-states. The smallness and the lack of real strength of these city-states meant that their success in survival often depended upon the cleverness of their diplomacy. This Greek experience, which stressed the necessity of immunity for negotiators, evolved many terms in diplomacy that are used today such as alliance, conventions, and reconciliation. They often sent two ambassadors on a mission, and the envoys often presented their case to the legislative assemblies rather than to the chiefs of state. The problems of a democracy in negotiating with an authoritarian state were illustrated in instances similar to the modern world. In the direct democracies of some of the Greek city-states there was public discussion on the tactics to be used by their envoys which often revealed to their contenders the latitude of their area of negotiation.

Once the diplomats had returned from a mission they were often tried before the public assemblies on the effectiveness of their missions. This suspicion of the envoys often resulted in missions being composed of several envoys representing differing viewpoints. The more authoritarian states, on the other hand, could plan their actions in secret and achieve a greater flexibility in their negotiations. This difference in the conduct of diplomacy indirectly facilitated the advent of authoritarian states, such as Macedonia, under Philip. Nevertheless, treaties negotiated were considered sacred and were made public.

Roman Practices. It was in the days of Rome that order was brought to diplomatic process, but the fact that Rome dominated meant that diplomacy in the sense of negotiation between sovereign groups was not as evident. Thus in the Roman period the degree of ceremony and immunity that might be granted to an ambassador might well depend upon the degree to which the area he was representing was independent of Rome. The Romans, however, did view a treaty as a very solemn obligation not to be violated, though its legal implications might be subject to varying interpretations.

With the decline of Rome, the first establishment of a separate department for foreign affairs came as the Byzantine contribution to the development of diplomacy. The politically weak Byzantines used diplomacy not simply to negotiate but also to impress and undermine the states with whom they were dealing. Diplomats were trained not only in ceremonies to impress but also in the art of intrigue in order to weaken the bargaining position of other states. The type of diplomacy practiced in the Byzantine era had an impact on the nature of diplomacy as it later evolved both in the Italian city-states in the late Middle Ages and in the competition among the Russian princes. Instead of tact and subtlety, bluntness and outright insults characterized diplomacy in the 16th century

Diplomats at the Congress of Vienna (1814–15). Among those present were the Duke of Wellington *(standing far left)* from Great Britain; Metternich *(standing sixth from left)* from Austria; Wilhelm von Humboldt *(standing second from right)* from Prussia; and Talleyrand *(seated second from right)* from France. (THE BETTMANN ARCHIVE)

Cardinal Richelieu, the brilliant diplomat and statesman who became Chief Minister of Louis XIII of France in 1624. (PHOTOGRAPHIE GIRAUDON)

The signing in 1778 of a treaty of commerce and defensive alliance between France and the United States, from a mural by Charles E. Mills. Benjamin Franklin *(center)* was instrumental in concluding the agreement. (BROWN BROTHERS)

Prince Klemens von Metternich dominated Austrian diplomacy in the first half of the 19th century. (LICHTBILDWERKSTÄTTE "ALPENLAND")

Charles Maurice de Talleyrand-Perigord, French statesman with a legendary skill at diplomacy. (PHOTOGRAPHIE GIRAUDON)

in Russia. In a competitive environment of competing principalities lacking real military strength diplomacy easily succumbed to a lack of sincerity in negotiations.

Italian Principalities. The small Italian states, similar in their lack of military strength, developed the art of diplomacy in their effort to survive. Negotiations led to constant shifting of coalitions and required a very developed degree of organization and technique. Modern diplomacy owes many debts, both good and bad, to the traditions established especially by Venice and Florence. They were the first to establish a system of permanent representatives in each other's capitals, providing not only a stability to the process of negotiation but a continuity and stability to the role of the diplomat. This practice spread to Spain, Germany, France, and England which first had permanent representatives in only a few other states. By the 17th century, however, the practice became a general practice. The Italian states established a system of archives, maintaining all diplomatic documents. They stressed the importance of keeping all their diplomats aware of developments in other areas, stressed reports, and organized correspondence between the representative abroad and their home government. Although they adhered to the principles of diplomatic immunity and the right to send ambassadors, their concept of the role of the diplomat left much to be desired.

Early European Diplomacy. The Peace of Westphalia in 1648 symbolized the beginnings of change that would alter the character of diplomacy as well as increase the necessity for agreement on rules for the conduct of diplomacy. Hugo Grotius argued as early as 1625 that relationships between states could not be harmonious unless principles rather than national expediency were the basis of negotiations. His ideas were elaborated upon and developed in theory and in practice during the ministry of Cardinal Richelieu, who stressed the permanent character of diplomacy. Richelieu believed that durable negotiations were primary and that negotiations and diplomacy were a continuing process. Opportunistic gains, temporary advantages, and clever plays hindered the basic interests of a state for continuing negotiations, and Richelieu argued for the professionalism of diplomacy. He also stressed the importance of a state having a policy based on its national interest, not upon sentimentality, and upon the fact that a policy should have public opinion behind it. In a sense he argued that negotiations could not be sound and effective unless they had this realistic base. This period of French influence on diplomacy, although it did not always follow its own theory, nonetheless laid the basis for what are now accepted as fundamental principles of good diplomacy.

One of the French diplomats of this period, François de Callières, wrote a book, *De la manière de negocier avec les souverains*, first published in 1716, which remains one of the classic statements of what constitutes good diplomacy and what makes a good diplomat. De Callières felt that confidence and sincerity, not deception, were the basis of good and effective diplomacy. He said "a good negotiator will never rely for the success of his mission either on bad faith or on promises that he cannot execute." He believed the use of deceit was resorted to by those not capable of resolving a problem.

In all candor De Callières wrote, "honesty is here and everywhere the best policy; a lie always leaves behind it a drop of poison and even the most brilliant diplomatic success gained by trickery rests on an insecure foundation, since it awakes in the defeated party a sense of irritation, a desire for vengeance, and a hatred which must remain a menace to his foe." To him negotiation was not only a continuing process, based upon sincerity and honesty, but it was a process without victories or defeats. There could be no victory in negotiations without creating resentment. Therefore the whole stress had to be toward continuing efforts to harmonize the interests of the parties. He stressed the professional character of the diplomat as an individual with an observant mind, sound judgment, a discernment of the thought of others, a sense of self-control, knowing when to speak and when to be silent, and a knowledge of history and public affairs.

Today, De Callières still symbolizes the model of good diplomacy, good in the sense of effectiveness and service to a state. Although his book was written in 1716 it is still discussed in the bulletins of foreign service personnel and held up as the ideal. De Callières challenged the basic concepts of early diplomacy which stressed deception, and although the diplomats of his time, and since, have not always followed his advice, most authorities on diplomacy and diplomatic skills believe he gave the best and most complete definition of the good diplomatic method.

Diplomacy of the 18th and 19th Centuries. As the state system developed in the 18th and 19th centuries, so did the nature of diplomacy. The system of diplomacy became professionalized. Negotiations were not always bilateral but on many occasions multilateral. Stress was placed on secrecy of negotiations. While the negotiations were continuous, they were confidential. The degree of professionalism of the diplomats encouraged confidence, one with the other. At the same time if the negotiations were to be continuous, they had to be secret so that concessions might not be obvious and result in public conclusions of diplomatic victories and defeats. Such secret diplomacy was possible in the world of the 18th and 19th centuries as long as external affairs were largely in the hands of the monarch. And the professionalism of the diplomats with certain agreed standards of conduct was possible in an arena of negotiation which was largely a European club.

With the gradual ascendancy of constitutionalism and representative government, however, demands grew in protest to secret diplomacy in the hands of the heads of state or their professional diplomats. The newer and smaller states felt that secret diplomacy between the Great Powers jeopardized their existence. As the elected representatives gained power, legislatures demanded open diplomacy—"open covenants openly arrived at" in the words of President Woodrow Wilson. Thus the 20th century saw the formalization of the demand for open diplomacy come into being in the League of Nations and the United Nations. These two international organizations provided a forum for public diplomacy. In adopting the U.N. Charter it was argued that public discussion of international issues made possible the solution of problems by exposing them to world public opinion.

Ever since World War I there has been a very strong feeling among many that the problems leading to war and those involved in the peace settlement were the result of secret diplomacy. Yet if negotiations involve accommodations between points of view, a certain degree of concession and counterconcession has to be brought about in private. If one side's concessions are made public before the other side makes concessions, resulting public clamor may lead to no agreement. Thus while the practice in the 20th century, the era of representative government, has been to conduct negotiations in private, the tendency has been to condition the final conclusion of an international agreement on public legislative ratification. In other words, a treaty or agreement does not become effective until duly ratified. Even in the United Nations "quiet diplomacy" behind the scenes and before public consideration of an issue has become a matter of practice rather than the exception. The late Secretary-General of the United Nations, Dag Hammarskjöld, contended that the United Nations had a need for both types of diplomacy. On some problems the exposure to world public opinion would help in the solution of the issue, on other problems quiet negotiations might allow better adjustments of differences. Public diplomacy in the 20th century has also developed outside the United Nations. In an effort to mobilize support of other nations the Great Powers, especially since World War II, have resorted on occasion to the issuance of a public exchange of diplomatic notes.

Modern Trends. The 20th century has also seen other changes in the character of diplomacy. Instead of negotiations in a world of European states, negotiations are now conducted on a global basis, often involving more than 100 states. Furthermore, the impact of science and the industrial revolution has not only helped to speed up the process of negotiation but has also served to increase the number of problems to be negotiated. More problems are negotiated on a multilateral basis than ever before. The international conference and the institutionalization of conference diplomacy into international organizations greatly improved the process of negotiation. The Peace of Westphalia took eight years to negotiate, yet the Council of Foreign Ministers held in New York in 1946–47 was able to complete five peace treaties in six weeks. During this six weeks 855,000 pages of data were mimeographed, 143,000 maps were prepared and 44,000 volumes of documents were issued. Both the volume and speed of diplomatic activity have increased almost beyond comprehension.

The Foreign Office. As the state system has developed and the complexity of negotiations increased, the conduct of foreign affairs has become centered in a single department in each government. In the United States, for example, the State Department, headed by the Secretary of State, acting under the authority of the President, is responsible for the over-all conduct of international relations. Its responsibilities include both the planning and the execution of U.S. foreign policy. The department em-

The Potsdam Conference of 1945 attended by the leaders of the United States, Great Britain, and the Soviet Union. Foreground (to the immediate left of center) Harry S Truman, President of the United States; upper left (with cigar) Winston Churchill of Great Britain; center background (hands to chin) Clement Attlee, British Prime Minister; right (cigarette in hand) Joseph Stalin, Soviet Premier.

Wide World

ploys 35,000 to 40,000 persons, of whom about 26,000 are stationed abroad. The diplomatic missions stationed in the more than 100 countries in which the United States has diplomatic agents are concerned not only with negotiations but also with providing up-to-date information for the President and the Secretary of State to assist them in formulating policies. The department in Washington is organized both on a geographical and functional basis, in order to plan and supervise efficiently the execution of foreign policy. It is organized into divisions, each of which co-ordinates information and reports coming from a certain geographical area. Thus, there are bureaus for each of the chief geographical regions of the world—Inter-American Affairs, European Affairs, Far Eastern Affairs, Near Eastern and South Asian Affairs, and African Affairs —each headed by an assistant secretary of state. These regional bureaus, in turn, are divided into offices or desks for each country or group of countries within the region, both to deal with day-to-day details of international relations, including a vast correspondence with U.S. officials abroad, and to capitalize on the work of specialists on countries and regions. The department is also organized on a functional basis. Aside from the regional bureaus, there are a number of functional bureaus, including the bureaus for Economic Affairs, Intelligence and Research, and International Organization Affairs, each headed also by an assistant or deputy assistant secretary. These functional bureaus are concerned primarily with problems that cannot be dealt with efficiently on a regional basis.

Churchill, Roosevelt, and Stalin at the Yalta Conference in 1945.

Wide World

Foreign offices in most countries are organized on a similar pattern. A diplomatic agent deals directly with the foreign office in the country to which he is sent, and each foreign office dispatches an agent to each of the countries with which it has diplomatic relations. Of course, there may be other agencies of the government that deal with problems of foreign policy, but the foreign office is the one that co-ordinates such activities. In the U.S. government, for example, the Department of Commerce may be concerned with foreign trade, but the State Department is responsible for the negotiations on trade with other countries. Therefore in formulating foreign trade policies the President consults both the Commerce and State departments.

The Diplomatic Corps. At the capital of a state, there is a diplomatic community made up of the various diplomatic agents accredited to that state by other states of the world. The United States maintains an embassy or legation in a hundred or more states, headed by an ambassador or minister and staffed by members of the foreign service who are professionally trained and selected for this work. Foreign ambassadors and ministers to a given country are known collectively as the diplomatic corps, presided over by a senior member of the group, informally referred to as the dean.

Diplomatic Procedures. It is apparent from the scope of numbers and complexity of diplomatic problems and representatives that procedures have to be agreed upon by all the states to insure the negotiating rights of their representatives to other countries, to international conferences, and to international organizations. At least six of the eight years of negotiation for the Peace of Westphalia were concerned with reaching agreement on the procedures for negotiating the treaty. The participants had to agree on the place of the meeting, the diplomatic etiquette and ceremony to be observed, the method of summoning the conference, the means of protecting the immunity of the delegates and the examination of delegates' credentials, and the extent of their authority to negotiate on behalf of their governments. But as practices and agreements on procedures became more established and generally accepted, international conferences began to accomplish their work with greater dispatch.

By the time of the Congress of Vienna (1814–15) European states were able to reach formal agreement on a set of rules for the conduct of diplomatic relations. The treaty on diplomatic immunities formulated at the Congress of

Vienna and the Congress of Aix-la-Chapelle (1818) not only had the effect of codifying the principles of diplomatic privileges and immunities that had been in practice since the earliest times, but laid down the basis for future diplomatic intercourse. This basic instrument became the guide and source of authority for the conduct of diplomatic relations until the new Vienna Convention on Diplomatic Relations was adopted by the International Conference on Diplomatic Intercourse and Immunities in Apr., 1961. The new Vienna Convention was adopted to make such modifications and changes as were necessary in a world of many more states than existed at the time of the original Vienna Convention.

Diplomatic Agents and Missions. According to the convention, the establishment of diplomatic relations and the sending of permanent missions take place by mutual consent between the two states involved. The head of the mission must always be acceptable to the receiving state. To avoid unpleasantness arising from a refusal, it is the usual practice to submit the name of the person whom a sending state desires to appoint beforehand to the receiving state. This is known as the securing of *agréation*.

Heads of diplomatic missions are divided into three classes: (1) ambassadors or nuncios, (2) envoys, ministers, and internuncios, and (3) chargés d'affaires. With the exception of chargés d'affaires, who are accredited to the foreign minister, heads of missions are accredited to the receiving head of state. Furthermore, the foreign office of the receiving state is to be notified of all members to a diplomatic mission, and has the right to declare any of them *persona non grata* (an unacceptable person) at any time without explanation. The size of the mission is determined by the two states in consultation, and the receiving state has the obligation to assist the accredited mission in the acquisition of appropriate facilities.

The premises of a diplomatic mission are deemed inviolable and means of transportation are immune from search and seizure; it is exempt from taxation; its documents, archives, and communications are inviolable; and its couriers and dispatches are to be free from interference, inspection, or taxation. The sending state enjoys the right to fly its flag and display its emblem. Accredited diplomatic agents are immune from criminal jurisdiction in the receiving state. They are also exempted from taxation and military service. These privileges and immunities are also extended to members of the diplomat's household. In essence the purpose of the Vienna Convention is to assure that duly accredited diplomats be free to perform their diplomatic duties without harassment and interference.

The purpose of many international organizations is not simply to provide a medium for public diplomacy but also to provide a framework of previously agreed conference rules and procedures. Thus the United Nations is to a large extent a medium for continuous diplomatic conferences. Rules and procedures are previously agreed upon so that the meetings can proceed to substantive discussions with a minimum of delay. Furthermore, it has become an established practice for member nations to maintain a permanent mission at the seat of the organization so that when the occasion arises, they can participate in a U.N. meeting at a moment's notice. The existence of permanent missions at the headquarters of the United Nations has also served to make the organization a meeting ground for bilateral negotiations. Many a newly independent country has found it both convenient and economical to conduct bilateral negotiations at U.N. headquarters.

Conclusion. In a world of over a hundred states, with several hundred international organizations, all of them constantly concerned with a multitude of international relations, the role of the diplomat is an essential ingredient in the solution of problems. The caliber of the diplomats and the techniques of negotiation can have a major impact on the ability of the countries of the world to find a peaceful solution to the many problems. As long as the international community continues to be an association of sovereign independent nations, diplomacy will remain an invaluable and necessary mode in man's search for the establishment of peaceful relations.

Consult Nicolson, Harold, *Diplomacy* (1939); London, Kurt, *How Foreign Policy is Made* (1949); Elliott, W. Y., and others, *United States Foreign Policy* (1952).

THOMAS HOVET, JR.. New York University
See also CONSULAR SERVICE; INTERNATIONAL DISPUTES, PACIFIC SETTLEMENT OF; INTERNATIONAL LAW; INTERNATIONAL ORGANIZATION; UNITED NATIONS.

DIPLOMA MILL, also called degree mill, commercial enterprise that sells degrees or diplomas without giving standard and adequate instruction and without requiring the quantity and quality of learning specified by reputable educational institutions. The price may range from as low as $25 for a "bachelor's degree" to $500 or more for a "doctor's degree." Most of the instruction, if any, is by correspondence. There are, of course, reputable correspondence schools, and many universities offer home study courses. But in the United States no reputable institution of higher education confers degrees solely on the basis of correspondence study.

It is believed that there are more than 200 fraudulent degree mills in the United States, with still others operated by Americans in foreign countries and preying upon foreign nationals. There are hundreds more doing substandard work, charging excessive prices, and deceiving students and public. Sometimes the school is nothing but a post office box. Occasionally there are offices, printed catalogs, advertising—and even a few teachers. The number of students may be few or there may be thousands.

These schools are able to flourish because charters are easy to get in most of the states, and regulation of private institutions is not uniform. The federal government has no control over correspondence schools except when fraud is perpetrated through the mails. A list of recognized schools of college level is issued annually by the U.S. Office of Education and appears in its *Education Directory, Part 3, Higher Education.*

MARY IRWIN, Editor, *American Universities and Colleges*
See also CORRESPONDENCE SCHOOLS; EDUCATION: *Higher Education in the United States.*

DIPLOMATIC POUCH, official mail bags transmitted by special courier or through ordinary post to and from diplomatic missions abroad. To ensure secrecy of diplomatic dispatches, such mail pouches are granted under international law exemptions from civil and criminal jurisdiction.

DIPNOI. *See* LUNGFISH.

DIPO NEGORO [dē′pō nĕ-gōr′ō], also known as Dipa-negara (c.1785–1855), Javanese Prince, revered by Indonesians as one of the major heroes in their struggle against Dutch rule. Although the morganatic son of Hamengku Buwono III, Sultan of Jogjakarta, Dipo Negoro was promised the succession to the throne as a reward for assisting his father in his war against Sultan Sepuh in 1812. He was given only a regency, however, and retired in disappointment to Tegalredja, where he devoted himself to prayer, achieving a wide reputation as a holy man. While the heavily burdened Javanese population came to view him as their savior—the Just Prince promised by legend—the nobility, incensed by increasing Dutch political and territorial encroachments on the Javanese realms, openly began to sympathize with the anti-European feelings of Dipo Negoro and his fellow-regent, Prince Mangkubumi. Following a rumor that the Dutch were preparing to arrest them, Dipo Negoro and Mangkubumi fled, thus beginning the Java War. Dipo Negoro's resistance lasted from 1825 to 1830; but at last, deserted by his allies, he agreed to negotiate with the Dutch Gen. De Kock. In the middle of the talks De Kock had him arrested, and subsequently banished him to Manado and then to Makassar, where he died.

RUTH T. McVEY, Yale University

DIPPER, name for several birds in the dipper family, Cinclidae, also known as water ouzels. Dippers are small, grayish or brownish birds and have stocky bodies, straight bills, and short tails. They are found in many parts of the world living near cold mountain streams, and have the unique ability to walk under water. Common species include *Cinclus aquaticus*, the European dipper, and *C. mexicanus*, a native of western North America.

DIPSOMANIA. *See* ALCOHOLISM.

DIPTERA [dĭp′tər-ə], an order of insects consisting of about 85,000 species known as the true flies. The scientific name of the order means "two wings" and refers to the characteristic feature of the group—a single pair of transparent forewings. The hindwings are absent, represented by two short, knobby structures, the halteres, which function as stabilizers. The mouth parts are modified for piercing and sucking and are suited for securing

nectar, sap, or even blood. Among the many families comprising the order are Muscidae, the house flies; Culicidae, mosquitoes; Tipulidae, crane flies; Simulidae, black flies; Chironomidae, midges and gnats; Tabanidae, horse flies; Drosophilidae, pomace flies; and Oestridae, bot flies.
See also FLY; INSECT; MOSQUITO.

DIPTYCH [dĭp′tĭk], in art, a work consisting of two parts that are hinged together, like the pages in a book. Traditionally a Christian altarpiece and usually portable, the diptych may be either a painting or a piece of low-relief sculpture, such as an ivory carving. The interior of the diptych may show either one composition that fills both panels or two related compositions, as a Madonna and Child in one section and a portrait of the person who commissioned the work in the other.
See also TRIPTYCH.

DIRAC [dĭ-răk′], **PAUL ADRIEN MAURICE** (1902–   ), British mathematical physicist most widely known for his research in quantum and wave mechanics. For his contributions in the development of Heisenberg's quantum mechanics theory, he shared the 1933 Nobel Prize in physics with the Austrian physicist Erwin Schrödinger. Dirac was born in Bristol, England, and attended Bristol University and Cambridge. In 1928 Dirac proposed a new theory of the electron, which combined relativity and quantum mechanics. The nonrelativistic theory of quantum mechanics, which had been developed by Schrödinger and others, did not naturally explain a property of the electron called "spin." Dirac's new theory not only explained "spin," but also predicted the existence of the antielectron, or positron, which was later observed experimentally in 1932 by C. D. Anderson, an American physicist. Other antiparticles, such as the antiproton, predicted to exist by Dirac's theory, have been observed in recent years.

ARTHUR N. THORPE, Howard University

DIRECT CURRENT. *See* CURRENT, ELECTRIC.

DIRECTION FINDER, a radio receiver for determining direction, used primarily as an aid to navigation on aircraft and ships. The instrument consists of a receiver with a loop antenna geared to a pointer over a compass card. The received signal is strongest when the antenna is pointed toward a transmitting station. The direction, or bearing, is indicated on the compass card.

Sperry Rand Corporation

THE RADIO DIRECTION FINDER

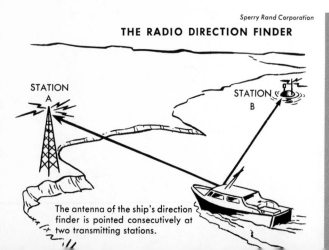

The antenna of the ship's direction finder is pointed consecutively at two transmitting stations.

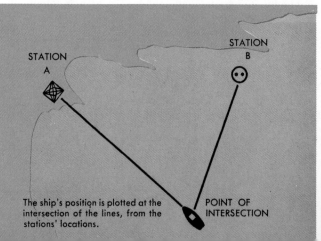

The ship's position is plotted at the intersection of the lines, from the stations' locations.

Left, Joshua Logan directs France Nuyen and William Shatner in a rehearsal of the Broadway play *The World of Suzie Wong*. Above, the director and his leading lady discuss a line in the script while playwright Paul Osborn looks on.

Friedman—Abeles

Friedman—Abeles

An aircraft or ship can obtain its position by simultaneously taking the bearing of two known transmitting stations. Then by plotting the intersection of the directional lines on a map a fix can be made. This principle is used in complex electronic navigational aids such as LORAN and TACAN, as well as by space scientists in the radio tracking systems used to follow an artificial satellite.

Conversely, a radio direction finder is used to locate an unknown radio transmitter. Two directional finders, usually mounted in separate vehicles, take simultaneous bearings of an unknown transmitter. Then, by triangulation, the exact location of the signal's origin can be mapped. In the United States this system is used by the FCC to locate unlicensed radio operators and was used extensively during the war to locate secret enemy radio transmitters.

RUFUS P. TURNER, Author, *Basic Electricity*

DIRECTOIRE [dē-rĕk-twär'] **STYLE,** French decoration style, named for the Directory, the Revolution government of 1795–99. In furniture the style, fashionable from roughly 1793 to 1800, retained some of the forms of the period of Louis XVI and foreshadowed the Empire style in its use of Greco-Roman and Egyptian motifs and forms. Characteristic pieces are slender, simple, and elegantly proportioned. The style reached England about 1795, evolving into the Regency style about 1805.

DIRECTOR, STAGE AND SCREEN, in American usage, the person responsible for determining the style of a theatrical or cinematic production as a whole, for co-ordinating the actors' interpretations, and, in general, for controlling the entire stage or film presentation. He is thus distinct from the producer, who may be either the person who finances the production and who manages its monetary side or (especially in films) a person appointed to take charge of all things connected with the production and who chooses a director to train and guide the actors.

Confusion arises from the fact that in England, the director, as he exists in American usage, is usually styled the producer; in England the American equivalent of the producer is called "manager," and the term "director" is often reserved for a person in general artistic control of a noncommercial playhouse such as the Royal Shakespeare Theatre at Stratford-on-Avon.

The office of director, in the American sense of the term, is of considerable antiquity, but until recent times it has assumed real significance and separate identity only when special theatrical styles have demanded the operation of a regulating hand. From Elizabethan times until the first part of the 19th century, the typical theater was that run by a more or less stable stock company, playing in repertory. Its performers, well acquainted with each other's skill and methods, rarely needed more than the advice of the author or of the principal player, while the stage manager took care of the scenic effects. When the stock companies began to disintegrate and when actors were engaged for runs of independent productions, it was necessary for the stage manager and actor-manager to assume greater control. Consequently the relatively novel office of director came into being and rapidly gained such prominence as to make the success or failure of a production depend largely upon his ability and sensitivity of approach. For that reason the modern playhouse has frequently been described as the "director's theater."

ALLARDYCE NICOLL, University of Birmingham, England
See also ACTING; PRODUCER.

DIRECTORY (Fr. *Directoire*), five-member executive board that, during the French Revolution, governed France between the end of the National Convention

(1795) and the seizure of power by Napoleon Bonaparte (Nov. 9, 1799). The name is also given to the styles (especially of dress) that characterized the period. Established by the constitution of Sept. 23, 1795, the Directory was elected by the Council of Ancients from a list drawn up by the lower house, the Council of Five Hundred. Terms of office were arranged so that one member was replaced each year; decisions were taken by majority vote of the Directors. The best-known members were Lazare Carnot, Emmanuel Sieyès, and Paul Barras, men of moderate or conservative tendencies. Although often opportunistic and venal, the Directory did much to stabilize and consolidate the French Revolution, repressing attempted coups by royalists and radical Jacobins in turn. During its ascendancy, austere republican ideals gave way to more luxurious and ostentatious manners, and fashions (such as the flowing gown) reflected this change of atmosphere.

RALPH H. BOWEN, Northern Illinois University
See also FRENCH REVOLUTION.

DIREDAWA [dē′rā-də-wä′], major commercial city of eastern Ethiopia, on the railroad, about halfway between Addis Ababa and the Red Sea port of Djibouti, French Somaliland. It has a cotton textile mill, a cement plant, and a very good airport. Pop., 40,000.

DISALLE [dĭ săl′], **MICHAEL VINCENT** (1908–   ), American public official. Born in New York City to Italian immigrant parents, he was reared in Toledo, Ohio, and graduated in law (1931) from Georgetown University. After launching his political career as a Democrat by election (1937) to the Ohio legislature and gaining prestige with a plan (1945) for labor-management arbitration, he was mayor of Toledo (1947–50). President Harry Truman appointed him (1950) Director of Price Stabilization. DiSalle lost his bid for the U.S. Senate in 1952 and for the Ohio governorship in 1954. He was elected Governor in 1958 but failed to win re-election four years later.

DISARMAMENT, general term used to describe the reduction, limitation, regulation, or abolition of the means by which nations wage war. The goal of eliminating war has roots deep in antiquity, but a system of controlled armaments is chiefly a 20th-century development. If the object of disarmament is peace, a basic question is whether arms are the cause of war or merely a symptom of deeper causes. While authorities differ, a common view is that arms are both a symptom and a cause of international tension in that they inevitably create an arms race. Some observers doubt, however, that an arms race must inevitably lead to war.

In modern history, various plans for disarmament have been offered. The Rush-Bagot Treaty of 1817 limited the number of ships of the United States and the United Kingdom on the Great Lakes. The Hague Conferences of 1899 and 1907, approaching the problem from the standpoint of the reduction and limitation of certain types of weapons, met with little success.

The delegates at the Paris Peace Conference following World War I found themselves faced with the failure of these earlier attempts at disarmament. Woodrow Wilson's Fourteen Points made mention of the desire for national armaments to be fixed at the lowest possible level consistent with domestic order. The representatives of the victorious nations imposed limitations on the defeated Central Powers as to the number of troops, caliber of weapons, and industrial plants which they might possess. The problem was then transferred to the League of Nations. Working from 1925 to 1932, a preparatory commission drafted a disarmament convention which the nations considered for two years. The failure to reach agreement provided Hitler with an excuse to rearm Germany. Also during this period, two international conferences were held which attempted to control naval arms. The Washington Conference (1922) limited specific arms control to capital warships, and the London Naval Conference (1930) considered a broader range of naval weapons and assigned a ratio of naval strength to the United States, Great Britain, France, Italy, and Japan. Almost all of these schemes, laboriously reached after protracted debate, failed.

Following World War II, the quest after peace and security grew more intense because of the dramatic threat of atomic weapons, the development of bacteriological and chemical warfare, and the enhanced destructiveness of conventional arms. Article 11 of the U.N. Charter empowered the organization to consider disarmament, and in June, 1946, the United States presented the Baruch Plan, named for Bernard Baruch, for the control of atomic weapons to the world body. The Security Council also established the Commission for Conventional Armaments to consider, along with the Atomic Energy Commission, the full range of weapons and the means of controlling their use. After a U.S.-Soviet deadlock on proposals, the commissions were dissolved and a single body, the Disarmament Commission, was created to examine all phases of armament control. A subcommittee of the United States, the Soviet Union, Canada, France, and the United Kingdom was also convened. Five problems characterized the subsequent negotiations: levels of strength; types of weapons to be initially controlled; time span over which disarmament was to take place; inspection, safeguards, and controls; and the relation of political questions to disarmament.

In brief, the West sought a reduction of conventional forces at the same time as atomic weapons were abolished, a full disclosure of military plans to prevent surprise attack, an agreement on inspection, an adequate international control commission to supervise disarmament, and safeguards against the secret manufacture or stockpiling of weapons. The Soviet Union attached first priority to banning the production, stockpiling, or use of atomic weapons before the reduction of conventional forces; establishment of an international control commission subject to Soviet veto; the elimination of U.S. bases encircling the Soviet Union; a neutralized Europe; and a seat for Communist China in the United Nations and at the disarmament negotiations.

In 1954, the West proposed that the following ceilings be placed on conventional forces: 1,000,000–1,500,000 men for the U.S.S.R., mainland China, and the United States; 750,000 men for France and the United Kingdom. In May, 1955, the Soviet Union, in an attempt to prevent West Germany from being rearmed, made new proposals to freeze armament levels as they were on Dec. 31, 1954, and talks were stalemated. In July, 1955, President Eisenhower proposed his "open skies" plan of aerial inspection which, while not disarmament, was calculated to ease suspicions. Five months later the Russians rejected it.

In Mar., 1956, at the U.N. Disarmament Subcommittee meeting in London, the French representative offered a compromise plan of gradual disarmament to end in a reduction of all conventional forces to agreed levels, and a moral ban on atomic weapons. The Soviet Union asked for an end to the production of atomic weapons, the liquidation of Western military bases around the Soviet Union, and a veto over the activities of the U.N. Control Commission. Throughout 1956 and 1957, the Soviet and Western positions narrowed, but no agreement could be reached on inspection. In Dec., 1957, Foreign Minister Adam Rapacki of Poland proposed that Central Europe should be made a neutral and disarmed buffer between the Cold War powers. Since West Germany would have been thus compelled to leave NATO, and because the West desired broader disarmament, the Rapacki Plan was rejected. In Nov., 1957, the Soviet Union walked out of the U.N. Disarmament Commission and forced enlargement of the commission to include all U.N. members.

The proposals offered by the U.S.S.R. after 1958 were radical and far reaching. On Sept. 14, 1959, its representatives asked for complete and general disarmament. In Mar., 1960, they demanded that rockets and nuclear weapons be abolished and claimed that inspected disarmament would be possible for conventional forces. In June, the Soviet Union asked the United States to liquidate its overseas bases, and in October they again linked world disarmament to the admission of Communist China to the United Nations.

Throughout, the West has argued for strict and effective inspection and control before disarming. The problems posed to the negotiators are identical to those faced after World War I. When international tensions are high, states will refuse to surrender their basic source of security—the ability to defend themselves.

Talks of Soviet, British, and U.S. representatives, and bilateral discussions between the United States and the U.S.S.R. continued intermittently in 1961 and 1962 but were without result. On Aug. 5, 1963, however, the United States, Britain, and the U.S.S.R. signed a treaty in Moscow banning nuclear tests in space, in the atmosphere, and under water. Within a few months many other nations acceded to the pact, France and Communist China alone among the major powers abstaining. Although the treaty left the signatories free to continue underground tests and did not halt production of atomic weapons nor restrict their use in wartime, it was widely hailed as the first major step toward international control of atomic weapons.

Shortly after the signing of the nuclear test-ban pact, a direct telegraphic circuit ("hot line") between Washington and Moscow went into operation on Aug. 30, 1963, as a result of a bilateral agreement signed at Geneva on June 20 to reduce the possibility of accidental war. A draft treaty banning the orbiting and use of mass-destruction weapons in space was unanimously approved by the U. N. General Assembly on Dec. 19, 1966.

WAYNE WILCOX, Columbia University

DISCIPLE, word used in the Bible to describe the pupils and followers of the Pharisees, John the Baptist, and Jesus (Mark 2:18). After Jesus' death it continued to be a name for Christians. A disciple was anybody who heard Jesus' call and responded to it by believing in Him and following the way of life which He taught. Such allegiance to Jesus ranked above all other loyalties (Luke 14:25–33). In some cases it demanded renunciation of a man's ordinary life to accompany Jesus on His travels. Twelve were selected for this closest companionship (Mark 3:13–19), whom He also sent forth as apostles (Mark 6:7–13; Matt. 28:19, 20).

DISCIPLES OF CHRIST. *See* CHRISTIAN CHURCHES (DISCIPLES OF CHRIST) INTERNATIONAL CONVENTION.

DISCIPLINE IN HOME AND SCHOOL. All societies have standards of conduct that must be met by their members. Any effort by authorities to encourage conformity to those standards can be regarded as a disciplinary measure. When someone says that a child "needs a little discipline," he often means that the child should be punished. But discipline has a positive as well as a negative aspect; it involves not only the prohibition of unacceptable behavior but also the encouragement of behavior which meets approved standards. Punishment is one way of controlling behavior, but it is by no means the only way.

The goals of discipline go beyond mere obedience, at least in democratic societies. As long as parents and teachers are bigger and more powerful than children, obedience is relatively easy to obtain. The major goal of discipline in a democracy is self-control on the part of the governed, and this goal is considerably more difficult to reach.

Numerous investigations are in general agreement on the following principles. Reasonable limits on child behavior are necessary for the good of others and contribute to the well-being of the child himself. Too many restraints confuse children and produce the impression that the world is an excessively forbidding place. A limited number of restraints, stated with the greatest possible clarity and coupled with an effort to channel behavior into areas of freedom, foster feelings of stability and security at a time when self-control is poorly developed.

Approval for "right" behavior has more predictably beneficial effects than punishment for "wrong" behavior. Punishment does not directly reduce the tendency to perform a forbidden act. It creates a drive, fear, and once fear is instilled forbidden behavior may be avoided, at least as long as the punisher is present. Severe punishment is often proposed as a corrective or preventive measure in the control of delinquency, but the results of research suggest that severe punishment is an ineffective way of controlling behavior. The parents of delinquents have been found to be much more prone than the parents of nondelinquents to use physical punishment in disciplining children. In a study comparing children from strict and permissive homes, those from permissive homes were more self-reliant, persistent, imaginative, spontaneous, and above all more cooperative and better adjusted socially than those from strict homes. In another study, harsh discipline by teachers led to an increase in misbehavior on the part of children who had watched the punishment being meted out to others. Severe punishment may control behavior in the situation where it is imposed, but it is likely to arouse hostility along with fear, and this can have enduring and damaging effects.

Lax and neglectful treatment, letting children do as they please, can also be damaging. Firmness and consistency are needed in the application of controls. But these are best internalized by children, so that they can control themselves, if the limits are set in an atmosphere of love and understanding.

DONALD R. PETERSON, University of Illinois
See also ADOLESCENCE; CHILD DEVELOPMENT.

DISCRIMINATION. Few words in common use carry two such diverse, even contradictory, meanings as the term "discrimination." To be a discriminating person in one sense is to draw lines of distinction based on generally accepted standards of appropriateness and excellence, that is, to know the standards of one's groups and to apply them skillfully.

In sharp contrast is the concept of discrimination as "the unequal treatment of equals," the application of an irrelevant or unfair criterion, by means of which one person or group receives an undue advantage, while another person or group, although having equal qualifications, suffers an unjustified penalty. In this context, one speaks of discrimination against, not discrimination between. Frequently, in this kind of discrimination, the members of large and heterogeneous groups are treated as if they were all substantially alike so far as the action in question is concerned. Thus we may speak also of "the equal treatment of unequals." If discrimination in the first sense means the process of making refined and subtle distinctions by the skillful application of relevant standards, discrimination in the second sense implies the inability to make such distinctions because of the use of irrelevant standards.

The explanation of the association of two such different meanings with a word seems to lie primarily in the process of social change. Since needs and values change, distinctions that were accepted in law or custom at one time and place become repugnant in a different context. For example, in a patriarchal or feudal society in which women are denied the right to vote, few people regard this as an injustice. In an equalitarian society, however, the practice becomes first unacceptable to some, then obnoxious to many, and finally inadmissible to most. "Discrimination between" has been transformed into "discrimination against."

During a process of redefinition there is often a prolonged period of controversy. Some members of a group come to believe that the application of a former line of distinction is no longer desirable, that indeed it endangers the realization of important values. Others believe the distinction is still legitimate. This does not mean that all judgments are equally valid. The use of some criteria of discrimination contradicts basic values of a society and weakens its moral unity. A democracy dedicated to equality before the law and other universalistic norms, for example, is weakened by discrimination based on race, religion, and national origin.

Discrimination is an overt act which may or may not correspond to an inner attitude. Some persons discriminate even when it violates their own beliefs about what are appropriate criteria of judgment, because they hope thereby to win some advantage.

Discrimination is not synonymous with prejudice. The latter is a rigid, emotional prejudgment, usually with negative connotations, which allows one to "know" all about a person by simple knowledge of his membership in one symbolically important group (a racial, religious, or ethnic group, for example). Prejudice disregards other group memberships and disdains any knowledge of the individual himself on the grounds that knowledge of membership in the "key" group is all that is necessary in order to predict a person's behavior. This belief may or may not be accompanied by discriminatory activity. One may be prejudiced, but have no opportunity to discriminate; or his prejudice may be offset by other values that block action; or he may fear to discriminate because of penalties involved. Conversely, one may discriminate because he believes others are prejudiced. Prejudice and discrimination very commonly occur together, each supporting the other. During periods of social change, however, they may become separated—a strategically important fact for those interested in reducing the use of an unfair criterion.

J. MILTON YINGER, Oberlin College
See also CIVIL RIGHTS AND LIBERTIES; ETHNOCENTRISM; INTEGRATION; MINORITIES.

DISCUSSION, oral or written expression of significant differences of opinion. We may sensibly discuss, for instance, "Who should be our next President?" or even "The values of modern art." But it would be better to investigate the facts than idly to discuss "What was the population of the United States recorded in the last census?"

A basic type of discussion is argumentation. This is "special pleading," the use of verbal means to win support for a particular point of view. To the extent that it is based upon emotional appeals directed to the listener's feelings, its means and aim are called persuasion. To the extent that it is based upon logical considerations and factual evidence directed to the listener's intellect, its means and aim are called conviction. But since we are influenced in matters of opinion by both our hearts and our heads, effective argumentation requires a skillful blending of both emotional and intellectual appeals in so far as each has a bearing upon the issue at stake.

It is notorious, of course, that argumentative discussion can degenerate into mere contentiousness. This is the pursuit of controversy for its own sake as a kind of exhibitionism. It has also been called "sophistry" after certain of the later Greek Sophists. In ancient times the practice of verbal trickery by these men as a deliberate device of deception was ably criticized by their own contemporaries, Plato and Aristotle. In modern times a similar exposure of questionable means of argumentation has been carried further in the fields of semantics and propaganda analysis.

At best, however, argumentation can also be the high communication skill of the true advocate—attorney, statesman, or public pleader for any special cause—presenting on behalf of his position whatever may legitimately be said for it before the forum of public opinion. This is the art which the ancients called rhetoric.

However valuable they may be under appropriate circumstances, all forms of argumentation also have their limitations. Indeed they may be positively harmful in certain situations where they serve no constructive purpose.

Impressed by the need for more detached consideration of certain problems, some specialists in the communication arts have advocated a radically different type of discussion technique. The philosopher Plato, indeed, anticipated them over 2,000 years ago, calling his method dialectic and illustrating it in his famous dialogues. But in modern terminology we can perhaps better call the method deliberation—that is, the verbal pooling of information and analytical thinking in an effort to determine the cause of a common problem and to discover the basis for a mutually satisfactory solution. Rather than debate or symposium, its commonly recommended forms are the round table or panel discussion to present issues informally for public consideration, and the open forum to permit broader audience participation.

Unquestionably there are important insights and a commendable moral tone in this deliberative approach to discussion. But we should face the possibility that not all differences of opinion can be negotiated. In some worldly situations it is entirely conceivable that the better people "understand" each other, the greater are their grounds for disagreeing. In any case, the contrasting moral attitudes of largeness or smallness of spirit need not be associated with any single concept of discussion. When considered as traits of character, these same attitudes can narrow or broaden, depress or elevate, our ways of talking things over in any form.

Consult Pellegrini, A. M., and Stirling, Brents, *Argumentation and Public Discussion* (1936); Garland, J. V., *Discussion Methods* (1951); Gondin, W. R., and Mammen, E. W., *The Art of Speaking* (1954).

WILLIAM R. GONDIN, City College of New York

See also DEBATE; PARLIAMENTARY LAW; RHETORIC; SPEECHMAKING.

DISEASE, condition of impaired health resulting from a disturbance in the structure or function of the body.

The History of Ideas Concerning Disease

Ancient man believed that disease was caused by a supernatural being or through magic practiced by another person. Treatment was administered by medicine men who achieved their results largely through the power of suggestion.

Some clear thinking concerning the origin of disease was introduced by Hippocrates, the ancient Greek physician, who is known as the "Father of Medicine," and whose oath is still sworn to by modern physicians. Hippocrates denied that diseases were punishments of the gods, but believed that they were caused by food, occupation, and climate. The physicians of this time held that there were four "humours": blood, phlegm, yellow bile,

---

DISEASE | **STUDY GUIDE**

The article on these pages is chiefly concerned with listing types of diseases. The reader whose interest is in other aspects of medicine can turn to the article MEDICINE, which covers the history of this science. A Study Guide with the medicine article directs the reader to numerous related entries, for example, PEDIATRICS, GYNECOLOGY, SURGERY, and PSYCHIATRY.

The article DISEASE names a number of disorders and a number of causes. Many of these diseases and their causes are further discussed in other articles in the **ENCYCLOPEDIA INTERNATIONAL.** As it is pointed out at the conclusion of the article, it is difficult to make a strict classification of diseases. Moreover a thorough cataloging of diseases is possible only in a technical work. Certain broad groupings are useful, however, to show the scope of coverage in this Encyclopedia.

Infectious Diseases. The reader may approach this topic through such general articles as BACTERIA, VIRUSES, and RICKETTSIAS AND RICKETTSIAL DISEASES. Another article of general importance is IMMUNITY. Specific disorders are described in many articles, of which the following are examples.

Diseases caused by bacteria: DIPHTHERIA, PLAGUE, TETANUS, TUBERCULOSIS, TYPHOID, WHOOPING COUGH.

Diseases caused by viruses: CHICKEN POX OR VARICELLA; INFLUENZA; MEASLES OR RUBEOLA; MUMPS; POLIOMYELITIS; SMALL POX OR VARIOLA; YELLOW FEVER.

Rickettsial diseases: ROCKY MOUNTAIN SPOTTED FEVER and TYPHUS FEVER.

Parasitic Diseases: MALARIA and SCHISTOSOMIASIS.

Allergic Diseases. General information is provided in the article ALLERGY and further details are in HISTAMINE, ASTHMA and HAY FEVER.

Disorders Related to Nutrition. Background for reading about this category of disease is in the article NUTRITION. Additional information is in BERIBERI, PELLAGRA, RICKETS, and SCURVY.

Metabolic Diseases. There is some material on this topic in the entry METABOLISM. There are discussions of particular metabolic disorders under the titles ARTERIOSCLEROSIS and DIABETES.

Cancer. The principal discussion of neoplastic diseases is in the entries CANCER and LEUKEMIA.

Mental Diseases. The general article is MENTAL ILLNESS, and the two major categories of mental disease are further discussed in NEUROSIS and PSYCHOSIS. Two articles related to treatment — PSYCHIATRY and PSYCHOANALYSIS — contribute to an understanding of the theories of the mechanism of mental illness. It may be noted that the discussion of neurotic behavior interrelates with the topic of psychosomatic disorders (see PSYCHOSOMATIC MEDICINE).

Disorders of some organs may have multiple causes, as noted, for example, in HEART DISEASE. Diseases of the eye are discussed in BLINDNESS, of the ear in DEAFNESS.

Many of the articles here listed comment on the prevention and treatment of disease. For further discussion the reader may consult such articles as PREVENTIVE MEDICINE, PUBLIC HEALTH, and MENTAL HEALTH.

and black bile. All diseases were thought to be caused by a disturbance of the delicate balance of these humours.

It was not until the 19th century that the role of micro-organisms as a cause of disease was firmly established. The German physician Robert Koch conclusively demonstrated that anthrax, a disease of animals and men, was caused by the *Bacillus anthracis*. Following Koch's proof of the germ theory of disease, a large number of micro-organisms were shown to be disease-producing agents. In recent years much attention has been focused on understanding the causes of noninfectious diseases, such as diabetes, gout, and arteriosclerosis. Advances in the knowledge of physiology and biochemistry have brought with them a greater understanding of those diseases which are unrelated to infection, but which are caused by disturbances in the normal functioning of the body.

The Types of Diseases

Diseases may be classified into the following major categories: infectious, allergic, congenital, deficiency, hereditary, metabolic, neoplastic, toxic, and psychosomatic and mental.

Infectious Diseases. One of the largest disease categories is the infectious group. This includes diseases caused by viruses, rickettsia, bacteria, fungi, protozoa, and worms.

The viruses are the smallest of the infectious organisms and are further distinguished by the fact that they can multiply only within living cells. Important virus diseases are the common cold, poliomyelitis, chickenpox, smallpox, and mumps. Many but not all of the virus infections are followed by long-lasting immunity.

The rickettsia are larger than viruses, but are smaller than bacteria. They share some of the characteristics of both groups. The rickettsia are almost always transmitted to man by ticks, fleas, mites, and lice. The rickettsial diseases produce fever and skin rashes and include typhus, Rocky Mountain spotted fever, Tsutsugamushi disease, and Q Fever. Like viruses, rickettsia frequently produce a long-lasting immunity after infection.

Bacteria cause disease directly by multiplying in a part of the body, or indirectly by causing an allergic reaction, or by giving off poisonous substances. Some of the diseases caused directly by bacteria are: pneumonia, caused by the pneumococcus; sore throat, caused by the streptococcus; meningitis, an infection of the central nervous system caused by the meningococcus; whooping cough, caused by the hemophilus pertussis; and tuberculosis, caused by the tubercle bacillus. Lockjaw (tetanus), diphtheria, and various types of food poisoning are caused by poisonous substances given off by bacteria.

Fungi produce skin diseases such as athlete's foot, and generalized infections of the body such as actinomycosis, blastomycosis, and histoplasmosis.

Protozoa are single-celled, primitive animals which are responsible for malaria and amebic dysentery, among other disorders.

Infestations by parasitic worms, such as ascaris, pinworm, tapeworm, and hookworm are common in warm climates where sanitary facilities are poor. The ascaris, or giant intestinal roundworm, may reach an adult length of about 14 in. in the human digestive tract.

Allergic Diseases. These diseases are caused by the interaction of antigens, foreign substances, usually proteins, with antibodies, substances produced by the body to combat antigens. The symptoms of allergic disease appear to be caused by the release of histamine, or a histaminelike substance, at the site of the allergic reaction. These chemicals cause fluid to be released into the tissues, resulting in the swellings which characterize allergic diseases. Diseases included in the allergic category are hay fever, asthma, drug reactions, and skin inflammation resulting from contact with allergic materials (contact dermatitis).

Congenital Defects. These include clubfoot, dwarfism, cleft palate, hare lip, and certain forms of heart disease. The defects result from disturbances in development while the fetus is in the womb. For the most part the causes of congenital defects are unknown, but some are inherited through the parents. The only other known causes are the occurrence of German measles in the mother during the first three months of pregnancy and exposure of the pregnant woman to high doses of X-ray treatments or to drugs.

Deficiency Diseases. The absence of certain food substances from the diet, or the failure to properly absorb them from the intestinal tract may interfere with normal body function and cause disease. Scurvy, once the plague of sailors, develops from lack of vitamin C; pellagra, a disease of the skin, gastrointestinal tract, and nervous system, results from the absence of niacin. Other vitamin deficiency diseases are rickets and beriberi. A failure to absorb vitamin B_{12} is found in pernicious anemia. In the intestinal disorder sprue there is interference with the absorption of many necessary food substances.

Hereditary Diseases. These diseases are transmitted by defective hereditary units, or genes. A classical example is hemophilia, a tendency to bleed excessively. The gene is carried by women, but the disease appears only in men. In some diseases, such as diabetes mellitus, a tendency to develop the disease may be inherited, but the disorder may not actually appear unless some stress is present.

Metabolic Diseases. This group includes those illnesses which are caused by defects in the body's ability to carry out the normal chemical activities involved in the production of energy and the building-up of body tissue. These defects may be inherited as in the case of phenylketonuria, a disease resulting in a particular form of mental deficiency. An example of a possibly nonhereditary metabolic disease is atherosclerosis, a form of hardening of the arteries in which substances deposited along the walls of arteries narrow the opening and interfere with circulation.

Neoplastic Disease. This includes cancer—a wild, uncontrolled growth of the cells of the body. Cancer may arise in any part of the body and can cause a variety of symptoms, depending upon location and type of cancer.

Toxic Diseases. This category includes those diseases which result from the consumption of, or exposure to, toxic agents, such as carbon tetrachloride, benzene, carbon monoxide, arsenic, lead, and barbiturates. Overdoses of certain vitamins may also be toxic.

Psychosomatic and Mental Diseases

Psychosomatic Diseases. In recent years it has been realized that many bodily ailments, such as peptic ulcer, high blood pressure, and asthma, may be caused or influenced by emotional disorders. A dramatic example of the ability of the mind to interfere with bodily function appears in hysteria, which may cause blindness or paralysis in the absence of any organic injury or disease. The number of diseases placed within the psychosomatic group is steadily expanding.

Mental Disease. The two broad classifications of mental disease are the psychoses and the neuroses. The psychotic individual is usually regarded as having lost contact with reality. The neurotic is aware of reality, but is the victim of powerful unconscious drives which distort his behavior. Little is known of the causes of mental diseases and a long-standing controversy in the field concerns the extent to which these diseases are of physical or mental origin.

In conclusion, it is frequently not possible to place a disease within a single classification. For example, since some metabolic diseases are inherited they could be grouped in the hereditary category. The causes of other diseases, such as rheumatoid arthritis, are not completely understood, making categorization even more difficult. One can expect that, as the knowledge of diseases and their causes becomes more extensive, the classification of diseases will change considerably.

JEROME D. WAYE, M.D.

See also MEDICINE.

DISHGARDEN, an arrangement of several plants in a small, decorative container. Dishgardening has long been practiced by the Japanese who train and dwarf trees in small, shallow containers—the art of bonsai. During the 1920's several commercial growers of house plants introduced dishgardens to the American florist trade. These so-called "Japanese rock gardens" consisted of shrubs, mosses, and plants that resembled miniature trees, all arranged in imaginative landscapes and planted in shallow

pottery containers. During World War II the oriental influence was dropped and a type of dishgarden lacking a planned landscape design became popular.

Dishgarden plants should not only have decorative value but the various plants must be chosen for their ability to grow well together. Desert plants, for example, cannot thrive in the company of rain-forest plants; for this reason it is advisable to select plants that have similar cultural requirements. A group of cacti and succulents that need full sun, dry atmosphere, and a porous soil mixture makes a satisfactory arrangement. Another planting might include tropical plants that require partial shade, high humidity, and a soil mixture rich in humus.

The choice of container depends to a great extent on individual taste. It should be from 2½ to 3 in. deep to allow the plants ample root room, and to contain enough soil and food that the plants may live for a reasonable length of time. If possible there should be drainage holes on the bottom of the dish so that surplus water can run off. It is also advisable to place a ¼ in. layer of sand and cinders at the bottom of the container for absorption of

An arrangement of tropical foliage plants accented by pieces of driftwood. The moss being placed over the soil helps retain moisture.

DISHGARDEN

This dishgarden consists of a red-berried cotoneaster and a few small evergreens. Planting implements are seen at the left.

The specimens in this cactus dishgarden are planted with the aid of wooden tongs to protect hands from sharp spines.

Walter Singer

excess moisture. The dish should then be filled with a soil mixture suitable for the type of plants used. Dishgarden plantings must be watered very carefully; overwatering will lead to damage and loss of plants. Watering should be done only when the surface of the soil becomes dry, never when the soil is moist or wet. Cactus and succulent plants do better when kept on the dry side. The beauty of a dishgarden can be enhanced by the addition of a handsome piece of driftwood or colorful pieces of rock.

WALTER SINGER, New York Botanical Garden

DISINFECTANTS, agents which kill disease-producing organisms. Most disinfectants are chemicals, such as acids, alkalis, halogens, heavy metals, formaldehyde, alcohols, phenols, dyes, and soaps. Less commonly, ultraviolet radiation and solutions of silver and copper are used as disinfectants. Disinfectants are used to destroy harmful micro-organisms found in food and water and on household surfaces and utensils. Unlike antiseptics, disinfectants can generally not be safely applied to living tissues.
See also ANTISEPTICS.

DISMAL SWAMP or GREAT DISMAL SWAMP, forested swamp in southeastern Virginia and northeastern North Carolina. Formerly almost impenetrable, it is now partially reclaimed for agriculture and lumbering. Lake Drummond is near its center and the Dismal Swamp Canal (22 mi. long), a section of the Intracoastal Waterway connecting Chesapeake Bay and Albemarle Sound, crosses the swamp. Length, 20 mi.; width 10 mi.

DISNEY [dĭz'nē], **WALTER ELIAS ("WALT")** (1901–66), American film animator and producer, born in Chicago. Disney did not create the cartoon film, but he developed it further than anyone before. He utilized the benefits from the introduction of sound and color into the medium. His first success was *Steamboat Willie* (1928), the first cartoon to use sound. It featured Mickey Mouse. Subsequent shorts introduced the now famous characters Donald Duck, Goofy, and Pluto. Disney's first full-length effort and best-known film, *Snow White and the Seven Dwarfs* (1937), was followed by other features, such as *Fantasia* (1940), *Pinocchio* (1940), and *Bambi* (1942). In these Disney explored the fantastic possibilities of cartoons in film more fully than anyone before. Later, he combined live action with animation in *The Song of the South* (1946) and produced a highly praised series of nature studies, including *The Living Desert* (1953). His animation work decreased as he began to concentrate on live-action entertainment films, the best known being *Mary Poppins* (1965).
Consult Feild, R. D., *The Art of Walt Disney* (1942).

GARY L. CAREY, Department of Film,
The Museum of Modern Art

DISNEYLAND, tourist attraction, located at Anaheim, Calif., about 25 mi. southeast of downtown Los Angeles. Opened in 1955, the vast amusement park, a creation of motion-picture producer Walt Disney, covers more than 160 acres, and is traversed by a number of novel transportation facilities, including monorails, a stagecoach, sailing ships, keel boats, canoes, and log rafts. In its first year of operation Disneyland received 3,642,597 visitors.

Electronic, aeronautical, and industrial exhibits vie for attention with fairy-tale attractions and with lavish re-creations of periods in American history.

DISORDERLY CONDUCT usually embraces actions which disturb the peace or shock the community. The vague formulation of the crime often raises the question whether the law has given sufficient warning to the actor that his conduct is illegal. Some definiteness is required by the constitutional provisions guaranteeing due process of law.

DISPENSATION (Lat. *dispensatio*, "management"), in theology, a divinely appointed order or period of time in which men are considered subject to a specific revelation of God's will, as the Jewish Dispensation and the Christian Dispensation.

In the Roman Catholic Church, dispensation is an act of competent ecclesiastical authority by which a church law is suspended, relaxed, or deprived of its penal effect in a special case. Dispensation from laws, even of general councils, was granted by early Christian Bishops; but since Innocent III (d.1216) the Roman Catholic Church has claimed this power for the Pope alone. The power to dispense from certain ecclesiastical laws is delegated by the Pope or is possessed by Bishops and pastors by reason of their office. However, some ecclesiastical laws, such as the celibacy of the Western clergy and certain matrimonial impediments are rarely, if ever, dispensed. The Pope has no authority to dispense from provisions of the divine law, but he can dispense from a personal obligation to God incurred by an individual of his own free will, as in an oath.

In 1534 Henry VIII declared the Church of England independent of this papal jurisdiction. And so in the Anglican Communion all dispensing power belongs to the Bishop.

Among the Jews a dispensation is called "giving a *heter*" ("permission") to certain laws arising from custom or rabbinic precept.

JOHN P. MARSCHALL, C.S.V., Viatorian Seminary,
Washington, D.C.

DISPERSION, in optics, the separation of a beam of light into its component colors, or wavelengths. More specifically, it is the variation in speed of light with wavelength in a transparent material. The term may also be applied to other types of radiation, such as the separation of a mixture of sound waves into its component frequencies.

Optical dispersion accounts for the brilliance of the diamond, which acts as a multiple prism dispersing the incident light into colors. Rainbows are the result of dispersion of light by drops of water.

White light is made up of many component colors, each of which corresponds to a certain wavelength. Dispersion results from nonuniform changes in the speeds of the component wavelengths as the light passes from one transparent medium into another. In vacuum, and approximately in air, the speeds of all wavelengths are identical. Because of the interaction of light with the atoms of a material medium, such as glass or water, the speeds of some wavelengths are reduced more than others. In general, the shorter wavelengths are slowed down more than the longer waves. As light enters or leaves a transparent material at an angle from the perpendicular to its surface, the changes in speed bend, or refract, the light rays. The short waves (blue, violet) are bent the most, the long (yellow, red) the least. By this means the white light is separated into its component colors of the spectrum, ranging continuously from red to violet.

Dispersion in a medium is related to the index of refraction, which is defined as the ratio of the speed of light in vacuum to its speed in a given material medium. The index of refraction therefore is different for different wavelengths, even in the same material.

The dispersion of a spectroscope or spectrograph is a quantitative expression of the power of the instrument to separate different wavelengths of light. Usually it is expressed in terms of the spatial separation of wavelengths at the eyepiece or photographic film, in angstroms per millimeter or other units. Dispersion in this general sense may be accomplished by a diffraction grating, as well as by refraction.

JOSEPH H. RUSH, National Center for Atmospheric Research

DISPLACED PERSON. *See* REFUGEE.

DISRAELI [dĭz-rā'lē], **BENJAMIN, 1ST EARL OF BEACONSFIELD** (1804–81), British statesman, one of the most brilliant figures in the history of the British Conservative party. Of Jewish descent in an age of prejudice, he was the acknowledged leader of a party of squires and churchmen. His oratorical gifts were less valuable to him than an undisputed strength of will and the confident feeling that he was a man of destiny.

Given only a fragmentary education, he first established his reputation as a man of society and a dazzling writer both of pamphlets and of novels. *Vivian Grey* appeared in 1826; his last novel, *Endymion*, was published in the last year of his life. Other novels that are still read widely are *Coningsby* (1844), a political manifesto of Toryism; *Sybil* (1845), a rewarding study of the "condition of England" question in the 1840's; and *Tancred* (1847), a book about the Jews, which shows that, although a Christian, Disraeli had by no means completely cut himself off from the faith of his fathers.

Disraeli entered Parliament in 1837. His first speech was a failure, and he only came into his own in his struggle with the Conservative Prime Minister, Sir Robert Peel, who did not give him office after the Conservative victory in 1841. Disraeli's stinging speeches in 1844, 1845, and 1846 helped to destroy Peel's hold over the Conservative party. After the split in the Conservative party occasioned by Peel's repeal of the Corn Laws in 1846, Disraeli was recognized as the cleverest, if not the most reliable, protectionist Conservative in the Commons. When the Earl of Derby formed minority Conservative governments in 1852 and 1858–59, Disraeli served on both occasions as Chancellor of the Exchequer. He worked well with Derby, who ruled the party from the Lords. On the third occasion when Derby formed a minority government, in 1866, Disraeli had the difficult but exhilarating task of piloting a Conservative Parliamentary reform bill through the Commons. The bill, which gave the vote to the urban working classes in 1867, was made much more radical

National Portrait Gallery, London

Benjamin Disraeli, as painted by Sir John Millais.

than Disraeli had intended, but he regarded it as a great triumph. In Feb., 1868, on Derby's retirement, he became Prime Minister.

The act of 1867 did not win Disraeli the general election in the autumn of 1868 as he had hoped, and he had to wait until 1874 before becoming Prime Minister again. His ministry of 1874–80 carried many notable reforms. In his novels he had urged that the Conservative party had a duty to pursue a social policy in the interests of the working classes. Some of his measures as Prime Minister realized his earlier dreams. Recognition of trade unions, public-health reform, and housing legislation were among the achievements of this ministry.

In foreign policy Disraeli was active and committed. He had little sympathy with empire in his early life, but after 1860 became increasingly attached to the idea. It was on his initiative that Queen Victoria assumed the title of Empress of India in 1876. In 1877–78 he tried, not without success, to check the predominance of Russia in Eastern Europe, and was British plenipotentiary at the Congress of Berlin in 1878 when Cyprus was annexed by Great Britain. War in Afghanistan was the last preoccupation of his ministry. All these aspects of Disraeli's foreign policy were bitterly criticized by the Liberals, especially by their leader, William E. Gladstone, and the Conservatives were defeated at the general election of 1880. Disraeli died on Apr. 19, 1881.

Disraeli married, very happily, in 1839. His wife, 12 years older than he, died in 1872. He was created Earl of Beaconsfield in 1876.

Consult Monypenny, W. F., and Buckle, G. E., *The Life of Benjamin Disraeli* (2 vols., 1929).

ASA BRIGGS, Leeds University, England

DISRAELI [*dĭz-rā′lē*], village of southern Quebec, Canada, at the northern end of Lake Aylmer, 14 mi. south of Thetford Mines. It is a summer resort and an agricultural and industrial center. Pop., 3,079.

DISSENTERS, word used since about 1639 for those in England who refused to join the worship of the established church. They were also called nonconformists (from about 1620) and free churchmen (from about 1869). Though the Roman Catholics have also dissented, the word has normally designated only Protestants. Soon after the Reformation there were a number of separated groups (Baptists, Congregationalists, Independents), but the main bodies arose in 1662 when the restored government of Charles I compelled ministers ordained under Cromwell to be reordained by a Bishop. About 1800 they were strengthened by the rise of the Methodists, who did not recognize themselves as dissenters till about 1860. The dissenters won toleration for their worship in 1689, the right to sit in Parliament in 1828, the right to conduct their marriages and attend a university in 1836, and in 1868 the right not to pay taxes to repair the established churches. In Victorian England they were sometimes a serious political force, particularly effective on behalf of the Liberal party.

W. O. CHADWICK, D.D., Selwyn College, Cambridge, England

See also BAPTISTS; CONGREGATIONALISM.

DISSOCIATION, in chemistry, the process of breaking up a molecule into component parts, not necessarily of atomic size. The most common dissociation is ionic. When a salt or other electrolyte dissolves in water, the water molecules separate the ions at a specific rate. The ions reassociate at a related rate. The resulting degree of dissociation, or the extent to which the compound exists in ionic form, can be calculated for any temperature. The ionization of an acid or base is considered to be a chemical reaction between the ions of the electrolyte and water, and not a process of simple dissociation as it once was thought to be. Nevertheless, in these and in a great many other chemical reactions, an extremely short-lived intermediary step is a dissociative one. In thermal dissociation, heat decomposes compounds whose component parts then reassemble on cooling.

DISTANCE-MEASURING EQUIPMENT (DME), aid to air navigation, designed to give a pilot his position from a ground station and his speed over the ground. It consists of a receiver and transmitter combination in the airplane, called an interrogator, and a similar set on the ground, called a transponder. The interrogator sends out a pair of pulses to the transponder, which replies with another pair. Electronic equipment measures the time lapse between interrogation and reply and translates it into a distance figure which appears on a cockpit dial. With continual knowledge of his distance from a known ground location, the pilot can readily compute ground speed.

DISTANT EARLY WARNING SYSTEM, also called the Dew Line, a series of radar stations within the Arctic Circle covering 3,000 mi. of the North American continent in a line from the Aleutian Islands to eastern Canada. Built by the United States and Canada, it went into operation in 1957. The Dew Line is continuously manned by civilian and military personnel to give the United States and Canada warning of surprise air or missile attacks over the polar region and thus provide enough time for defensive counter measures.

DISTEMPER, an acute, infectious disease of dogs, cats, and minks. Distemper is caused by a virus and most commonly affects young animals. Early symptoms include drowsiness, lack of appetite, slight fever, diarrhea, and a watery nasal discharge. As the disease progresses digestive and respiratory symptoms become more severe. Finally muscle spasms, seizures, partial paralysis, and other nervous symptoms appear. Death occurs when paralysis affects any group of vital muscles. Antibiotic therapy and careful nursing may result in cures, but about 50% of all distemper cases result in death. Effective vaccines to prevent distemper have been developed and are usually administered routinely to young animals.

DISTILLATION, production of a vapor from a liquid solution by heating, and the subsequent condensing of the vapor. The process is used to separate volatile from nonvolatile components of a mixture. The apparatus for distilling is called a still and consists of a container, in which the mixture can be heated, and of condensing apparatus attached to it to trap the vapors. Many kinds are used in industry and laboratory work, both for batch runs and continuous operation.

When a solution of solid and liquid is heated, the vapor comes off almost pure, leaving behind solid residues. The distillation of sea water purifies the water of dissolved minerals. If the minerals are the desired product, the vapors are allowed to escape and the process is one of simple evaporation.

The separation of two or more liquids is possible whenever they have different boiling points. Fractional distillation is then employed. The vapors from the still are passed upward through a fractionating column. The less volatile components in the rising vapor are condensed and flow back, and the heat so produced evaporates the more volatile components from the downward flowing liquids. The column is thus maintained at a uniform temperature gradient, decreasing in temperature from the bottom to the top. The vapor passing out of the top of the column to the condenser is the component with the lowest boiling point, or the highest volatility, whereas the liquid flowing back is rich in the component with the highest boiling point.

To prevent the decomposition of organic compounds with high boiling points, distillation can be effected under reduced pressure (vacuum distillation), which reduces the boiling point, or by the addition of steam (steam distillation).

Heat-sensitive substances, like vitamins, are separated and purified in high vacuum at relatively low temperature by molecular distillation. A refrigerated condensing surface is placed close enough to the evaporating liquid to catch the escaping molecules before they collide with one another or any other molecule.

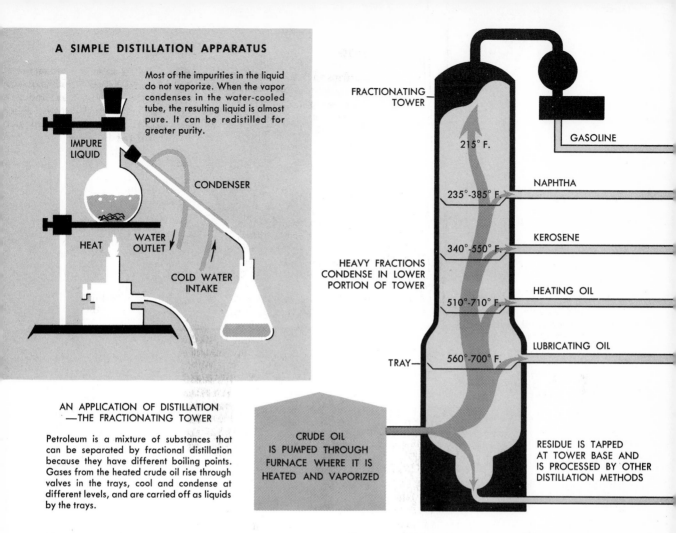

A SIMPLE DISTILLATION APPARATUS

Most of the impurities in the liquid do not vaporize. When the vapor condenses in the water-cooled tube, the resulting liquid is almost pure. It can be redistilled for greater purity.

IMPURE LIQUID

CONDENSER

HEAT

WATER OUTLET

COLD WATER INTAKE

FRACTIONATING TOWER

215° F.

235°-385° F.

340°-550° F.

510°-710° F.

560°-700° F.

TRAY

HEAVY FRACTIONS CONDENSE IN LOWER PORTION OF TOWER

GASOLINE

NAPHTHA

KEROSENE

HEATING OIL

LUBRICATING OIL

AN APPLICATION OF DISTILLATION —THE FRACTIONATING TOWER

Petroleum is a mixture of substances that can be separated by fractional distillation because they have different boiling points. Gases from the heated crude oil rise through valves in the trays, cool and condense at different levels, and are carried off as liquids by the trays.

CRUDE OIL IS PUMPED THROUGH FURNACE WHERE IT IS HEATED AND VAPORIZED

RESIDUE IS TAPPED AT TOWER BASE AND IS PROCESSED BY OTHER DISTILLATION METHODS

The oldest use of stills is in the separation of potable alcohols from fermented grain and fruit juices.

G. RAYMOND HOOD, Blackburn College

DISTILLATION, DESTRUCTIVE, also called pyrolysis, a process of converting organic substances into simpler compounds by heating them without air in a closed container. The destructive distillation of wood yields charcoal, wood alcohol (methyl alcohol), acetic acid, tar, and gases. Similarly, coal gives coke, coal gas, and coal tar. When petroleum is heated without air, its gasoline content is increased.

DISTRIBUTION. *See* STATISTICS.

DISTRIBUTOR, device used in spark-ignited internal-combustion engines to distribute high-voltage electric pulses in proper sequence to the spark plugs of the cylinders. A rotating arm receives the pulses from the ignition system through a central contact. The arm is oriented so that every time a pulse is received, it faces a terminal leading to a spark plug. It rotates at engine rpm in two-stroke engines and half-engine rpm in four-stroke cycle engines.
See also AUTOMOBILE; IGNITION SYSTEM, AUTOMOBILE.

DISTRICT HEIGHTS, city of central Maryland, east of Washington, D.C. It serves as residential suburb and com-

munity center for nearby governmental facilities. Inc., 1936; pop. (1950) 1,735; (1960) 7,524.

DISTRICT OF COLUMBIA, federal district on the Maryland bank of the Potomac River, coextensive in area with the U.S. capital, Washington. The land area is approximately 69 sq. mi. The District was created by congressional action in 1790 and 1791. The original boundaries included land on both banks of the Potomac, including Georgetown and Alexandria, ceded by Maryland and Virginia. The territory south of the Potomac was returned to Virginia in 1847. In 1967 congress enacted legislation creating a municipal government, with a commissioner and deputy comissioner as chief executive officers, to be appointed by the president. A nine-member bipartisan city council, also appointed by the president, has veto power over the budget. This replaced an earlier form of city government, established in 1878. In 1961 District residents were granted the right to vote in presidential elections, although they still have no representative in congress. Pop. (1950) 802,178; (1960) 763,956.

THEODORE R. SPEIGNER, North Carolina College at Durham
See also WASHINGTON, D.C.

DITMARS, RAYMOND LEE (1876–1942), American naturalist who specialized in the biology of snakes. He was curator of reptiles at the New York Zoological Park from

1899 to 1910, and of mammals from 1910 to 1942. He wrote a number of technical and popular books on classification and biology, especially of reptiles but also of other animals. Among his works are *The Reptile Book* (1907), *Strange Animals I Have Known* (1931), and *Snakes of the World* (1931).

DITTERSDORF, KARL DITTERS VON (1739–99), Austrian composer. Born in Vienna, he gained early fame as a violinist and later served as *Kapellmeister* to the Bishop of Breslau at Johannesberg (Silesia). A prolific composer in all media, Dittersdorf excelled in comic operas (among them the still performed *Doctor and Apothecary*, 1786), string quartets, and symphonies (approximately 150). His use of folk-derived material often produces humorous rhythmic and orchestral effects.

DIURETICS [dĭ-yŏŏ-rĕt′ĭks], compounds which reduce the amount of fluid in the body by increasing the volume of urine flow. Normally the human body consists of 45% to 70% water, which is contained in the cells, in the tissue spaces between the cells, and in the blood. In certain conditions, such as congestive heart failure, nephrosis, cirrhosis, and premenstrual edema, the fluid balance is upset and fluid accumulates in the tissue spaces, a condition known as edema. In congestive heart failure, for example, the heart does not pump enough blood, and fluid which would normally be changed into urine accumulates in the tissue spaces and the blood. This may first be noticed as a swelling in the ankles. Edema was recognized by the ancient Greeks; the Romans treated the condition by inserting a tube through the skin to drain fluid from the abdomen. In modern therapy diuretics are used to relieve edema.

Diuretics differ in the manner in which they promote urine flow. The most frequently used diuretics act directly upon the kidney (thiazides, acetazoleamide, organic mercurials, xanthines). Others may alter the acidity-alkalinity balance of the blood (ammonium or calcium chloride), or increase the fluid-holding power of the blood by raising its osmotic pressure (acacia, albumin). These drugs may occasionally cause side effects, such as skin rashes, nausea, vomiting, weakness, dizziness, muscle cramps, and acute pancreatitis. Diuretics are generally of no value when urine is not produced because of inadequate kidney function or when urine is retained in the bladder.

JAMES L. GAROFALO, M.D.

DIVER. *See* LOON.

DIVERTICULOSIS [dĭ-vər-tĭk-yə-lō′sĭs], the presence of pouches in the walls of the gastrointestinal tract. They occur most commonly in the lower portion of the large bowel. Diverticula are more common in older persons and may be associated with chronic constipation, obesity, and the tissue degeneration that occurs with age. Usually symptoms are not present unless the pouch becomes infected, with resultant abdominal pain, tenderness, and fever.

DIVERTIMENTO [dĭ-vĕr-tĭ-mĕn′tō], general name for chamber music informally combining abstract and dance

forms in two to a dozen movements. Especially popular between 1760 and 1790 among Viennese composers such as the two Haydns, Mozart, and Karl Dittersdorf, the form often consisted of five movements: Allegro, Minuet and Trio I, Andante, Minuet and Trio II, and Presto.

DIVIDE, in physiography, the line separating waters that flow into different streams or drainage basins. In rugged areas the divide is usually irregular, following the crests of ridges. In areas of low relief its position may be indefinite. Where streams are widely spaced and inter-stream areas lack through-going surface drainage, the divide may be lost in a broad topographic zone.
See also CONTINENTAL DIVIDE.

DIVINATION [dĭv-ə-nā′shən], the practice of predicting the future and revealing hidden knowledge by magical or supernatural means. Divination is based in part on the belief that supernatural forces affect the destinies of humans. The practice has been reported in all parts of the world and in many different forms, for example: haruspication (forecasting future events by inspecting the entrails of sacrificed animals), used by the ancient Etruscans; the pronouncements of the oracle of Apollo at Delphi in Greece; Babylonian astrology and dream interpretation; scapulimancy (prediction from the cracks on charred shoulder blades of animals), practiced by the North American Indians; gypsy readings of cards and tea leaves; rhabdomancy (using rods or wands to reveal water or metals underground). These various techniques may be divided into two classes. First, there are methods involving inspirational priests, seers, mediums, or shamans, who are believed to get information from gods or spirits. Other techniques make predictions from natural objects or chance events. Augury, for example, involves the flight of birds; palmistry interprets lines in the hand; ouija boards employ chance movements; and comets and eclipses have often been interpreted as omens. Some peoples, such as the Azande of the Sudan, regulate all aspects of their lives by oracles or omens; others resort to divination only when a major crisis of life is approaching. Techniques of foretelling the future often constitute a part of religion.

Divination appears to be related to basic insecurities of human life—the need for assistance in making decisions and the hope of finding explanations for mysterious events. The power of these needs and hopes is shown by the fact that astrologers, palm-readers, and fortunetellers of other kinds still do a large business in the United States, even though some of their activities are illegal. There appear to be relationships between methods of divination and games of chance, both in the methods used and in their psychological aspects. Gamblers often believe in luck or fate, and test their luck by the fall of dice or cards.

Consult Lowie, R. H., *Primitive Religion* (rev. ed., 1948); Vogt, E. Z., *Water Witching, USA* (1959).

ERIKA BOURGUIGNON, The Ohio State University
See also ORACLES.

DIVINE, FATHER. *See* FATHER DIVINE.

DIVINE COMEDY (*Divina Commedia*), name given to the great narrative poem of Dante Alighieri. The author

John R. Freeman & Co.—Illustration Research Service

Two woodcuts for the *Divine Comedy*, begun about 1306 by the Italian poet Dante Alighieri. The woodcuts, based on those of the Venetian edition of 1491, introduce cantos in the *Paradiso* canticle. Left, Michael and other angels fight Lucifer and his devil band (Canto XXIX). Right, Dante and Beatrice stand together in heavenly Paradise above a medieval town (Canto VIII).

Q UANDO AMBO & DUE i figli
di Latona,
Coperti del Montone e della Libra,
Fanno dell'orizzonte insieme zona,
Quant' è dal punto che il zenit inlibra,
Infin che l' uno & l' altro da quel cinto,

S OLEA creder lo mondo in suo periclo
Che la bella Ciprigna il folle amore
Raggiasse, volta nel terzo epiciclo;
Perchè non pure a lei facean onore
Di sacrificio e di votivo grido
Le genti antiche nell' antico errore;

called it the *Commedia*, or Comedy, because of its popular style and happy ending; later generations added the adjective. Written in Tuscan vernacular in *terza rima*, or "triple rhyme," the poem is divided into three canticles: *Inferno* (Hell), *Purgatorio* (Purgatory), and *Paradiso* (Paradise) and subdivided into 100 cantos.

Describing the poet's journey through the three realms of the other world, the poem abounds in realistic detail on the literal level. The action takes place during the 10 days from Good Friday through the Sunday after Easter in 1300. In the first part the Roman poet Vergil guides Dante through the deep pit of Hell, where many famous people undergo eternal punishments for their sins. Ascending with Vergil to the mount of Purgatory, Dante observes those who have assurance of salvation suffering temporary and less severe punishments. In the final section Dante is guided by Beatrice, his love and inspiration, through the celestial spheres of Paradise, where there is no sin or punishment.

Allegorically a portrayal of the soul's return to God, the poem is rich in symbolism. Sometimes regarded as the supreme creative accomplishment of European literature, the work has elements of the social commentary and the political tract and possesses historical, ethical, and mystical significance. So highly personal as to be definable as an extended lyric, the work also has universal meaning.

Consult Vossler, Karl, *Mediaeval Culture: an introduction to Dante and his times*, trans. by W. C. Lawton (2 vols., 1929).

THOMAS G. BERGIN, Yale University
See also DANTE ALIGHIERI; ITALY: *Italian Literature*.

DIVINE OFFICE. *See* CANONICAL HOURS.

DIVINE RIGHT, the theory that the sovereign's right to rule is based on his descent from ancestors who were divinely appointed to rule. Therefore his right does not stem from the office of King, nor from the will of the people, nor from customary law, but from birth. Furthermore, there are no grounds on which to challenge such divinely appointed rule. This theory was embraced by some of the Stuart Kings of England, most especially by James I (reigned 1603–25) in his work, *The True Laws of Free Monarchies* (1598), and supported by Sir Robert Filmer in *Patriarcha* (1680). The doctrine was also common in Asia for centuries. The last vestiges of it were extinguished in Japan when that country's defeat in World War II led to a transformation of the absolute monarchy into a constitutional monarchy.
See also ABSOLUTISM.

DIVING. *See* SWIMMING AND DIVING.

DIVINING ROD, also known as a dowsing rod, a forked twig of hazel, willow, or other wood, or a metal rod, claimed to have an occult power to locate water, oil, or minerals below the ground. Held by the operator, or dowser, so that it points straight ahead, the rod supposedly turns downward as the dowser approaches the optimum place to dig or drill. The phenomenon, sometimes called water witching, has been ascribed to the dowser's subconscious muscular movements. Some dowsers have acquired considerable knowledge of where water or minerals might be found; others succeed because water can be obtained almost anywhere in humid regions.

DIVINITY, etymologically, the quality or character of godhead. Later it came to signify the Supreme Being per se. Alternatively, it may signify, in the plural, deities or other supernatural beings as a class. Polytheistic religions accorded to each of several gods the quality of divinity, while in monotheistic creeds, divinity is the unique property of one god.

DIVORCE, legal dissolution of the marriage bond. Of all major social problems none is more persistent than divorce. And of all the problems confronting social scientists, one of the most difficult to solve in terms of cause and effect is divorce. No one can yet answer the question, "What causes divorce?" Indeed, it is doubtful whether

DIVORCE

only a single cause is involved. Sociologists have studied the problem extensively, however, and largely because of their efforts a reliable core of factual information is now available.

Historical Aspects of Divorce

Divorce is an age-old phenomenon. The first written regulations concerning it were incorporated into the Babylonian Code of Hammurabi c.1750 B.C. The ancient Hebrews, Greeks, and Romans also had provisions for divorce. Among these peoples, divorce was generally a privilege accorded the husband, rather than, as today, a legal prerogative of both sexes. All the ancient peoples, however, frowned upon divorce as a matter of social policy. The two most commonly used grounds for divorce were adultery and barrenness, or sterility, on the part of the wife.

It was not until the later Roman period, after the Punic Wars in the 2d century B.C., that women achieved the right to divorce. During this period family values declined; the birth rate in Rome fell, abortion and infanticide were common, and adultery and divorce were widespread.

With the coming of the Christian era, social policy with respect to divorce was tightened. Jesus held that divorce was not to be allowed for any reason (Mark 10:11–12; Luke 16:18), although in another Biblical passage He stated that adultery was a permissible ground (Matt. 5:32). After a long controversy, the Church ultimately affirmed the sacramental nature of marriage at the Council of Trent (1545–63) and held that the bonds of matrimony could be broken only by death. This interpretation remains the Roman Catholic view today. The Protestant reformers, Zwingli, Luther, Calvin, and Knox rejected the sacramental nature of marriage and permitted divorce for serious reasons such as desertion and adultery; although in principle they, too, opposed marital dissolutions.

The early American colonists also frowned upon divorce, and there was very little of it; in fact, the southern colonies had no provision for divorce. Even in those colonies which enacted divorce laws, such as Massachusetts, vital records suggest that three or four was the average number of divorces granted in a year.

Frequency of Divorce in the United States

Before the Civil War divorce posed no special problem in the United States, and the government did not even collect national figures. In 1867 the Census Bureau was directed to collect and publish the U.S. total for that year. The number was 9,937. In 1946, the highest divorce-rate year in the nation's history, the figure had risen to 610,000 or 4.3 per 1,000 population. In the 1950's the yearly divorce figure fluctuated between a low of 368,000 in 1958 and a high of 396,000 in 1959.

Sociologists compute divorce rates by a variety of methods: per 1,000 population, per 1,000 married females, per 100 marriages in the same year, and per 100 marriages in the preceding ten years. Technical considerations aside, all the figures indicate that the long-term trend of the U.S. divorce rate is upward.

The following figures are based on reports issued by the National Office of Vital Statistics.

U.S. Divorce Rate per 1,000 Population for Selected Years

Year	No. of Divorces	Divorces per 1,000 Population
1867	9,937	0.3
1900	55,751	0.5
1910	83,045	0.9
1920	170,505	1.6
1930	195,961	1.6
1940	264,000	2.0
1950	385,144	2.6
1959	396,000	2.2
1960	390,000	2.2

Between 1867 and the present, divorces have increased at a rate more than eight times as fast as the rate of increase of the nation's population. The United States is experiencing almost 4 million divorces per decade. It is estimated that almost one out of every four U.S. marriages ends in divorce. If desertion and other types of marital separation were included, the figure would be higher.

Why a marriage ends in divorce is still an unanswered question. Sociologists hold that the long-term increase in the divorce rate has been influenced by such factors as changing family functions, the increased number of jobs open to women, a decline in moral sanctions, accelerated urbanization, and other phenomena (such as greater mobility), which are apparently associated with an expanding industrial economy. Substantiation for this belief might be inferred from the fact that divorce rates in European countries have also increased in recent years. The divorce rates of many European countries, while not as high as that of the United States, have actually risen faster than the U.S. rate in recent years. Denmark and Germany, for instance, which formerly had divorce rates about one-third as high as the United States now have rates which are almost two-thirds that of the United States. In Roman Catholic countries such as Italy, Spain, and Eire, there is no provision for divorce.

The impression that the U.S. divorce rate is the highest in the world is incorrect. In the past, certain countries (for instance, Russia) have had divorce rates which apparently exceeded that of the United States. At present, Egypt and Zanzibar have rates which surpass U.S. figures. Divorce rates in primitive societies are notoriously high, even though in the absence of written records, it is impossible to make statistical comparisons. In the ethnologist Murdock's cross-cultural survey, "Family Stability in Non-European Cultures" (1950), it was found that in 60% of the primitive societies studied, "the divorce rate manifestly exceeds that among ourselves."

Some idea of the variation in divorce rates on a world-wide basis can be gained from the following list:

Divorce Rates per 1,000 Population, for Selected Countries

Bermuda	1.4
Canada	1.4
England and Wales	.5
France	.6
Hungary	2.2
Sweden	1.2
U.S.	2.2
U.S.S.R.	1.1
Yugoslavia	1.2
Zanzibar	4.4

Sociological Aspects of Divorce

Divorce rates are not uniform throughout the United States, but vary by region. Official figures show that the divorce rate is generally lowest in the eastern part of the country and rises as one moves toward the Pacific Coast. These regional differences are not explainable in terms of migratory divorce. It is true that Nevada has a divorce rate many times higher than the national rate, but that state accounts for only 2½% of the national total.

It has also been established that the divorce rate for Negroes is higher than for whites, and that among whites the frequency of divorce increases with decreasing socio-economic status. Thus divorce rates are lowest among the professional-managerial class and highest among the un-skilled workers, who also evidence the highest rate of desertion.

There are no national figures for divorce rates among the major religious groups in the United States. A number of regional studies, however, suggest that Catholics obtain substantially the fewest divorces in proportion to their number, Jews somewhat fewer, and Protestants more, than their proportion.

It was contended at one time that divorce was most likely to occur during the fifth year of marriage, but analysis of vital statistics figures shows rather clearly that the first and second years following marriage are the most hazardous. It is a valid generalization that the longer couples are married the less is the statistical likelihood of a divorce. There are cases on record where couples have procured a divorce after 40 or 50 years of marriage, but these instances are statistically insignificant.

Material from the U.S. Census Bureau and the National Office of Vital Statistics reveals that about two-thirds of the women and three-fourths of the men who get divorces eventually marry again, although chances of re-marrying depend on age when divorced. Moreover, they remarry rather quickly. Surprisingly enough, a divorced person has a greater probability of marriage than a single person of similar age. Available statistical evidence suggests, nevertheless, that the divorce rate is higher for divorced persons who remarry than for persons who have not been married before.

Perhaps the most widely discussed aspect of divorce relates to the effect on children. National Office of Statistics reports show, for example, that in 1922 only 34% of the divorces in the United States involved children. The same source reveals that in the 1960's more than 50% involved children. Also, in divorces involving children, the average number of children has increased. The net result of these factors within the space of a single generation is eye-catching: whereas in 1930 there were 123,376 children affected by divorce actions, by 1957 the figure had increased to 379,000.

Unfortunately, a number of technical considerations have precluded a final answer to the question of the effect of broken homes on the children. The remarriage factor complicates the picture. There is also some suggestion that children from unhappy, unbroken homes are more adversely affected than those from broken homes. In many cases the children are too young to have remembered the actual breakup of the marriage. Most studies, however, have revealed a positive relationship between juvenile de-linquency and broken homes. A final answer regarding the effect of marital instability or broken homes on the be-havioral patterns of children must await further research.

Legal Factors

There is no single divorce law in the United States, since each state has the power to decide for itself what the legal grounds should be, what the residence requirements are, and what defenses to divorce should be recognized. As a result, legal grounds and procedures vary from one state to another. New York, for instance, until a more liberal divorce law was passed in 1966, permitted but a single ground, adultery. Other states list a dozen or more grounds for divorce action.

States also vary in the wording and interpretation of the various statutes pertaining to marital dissolution. Thus it is difficult to cite an exact figure representing the number of different grounds for divorce in the United States. However, depending on terminology, the total number of grounds is probably between 35 and 40.

Several studies have been made in an effort to relate the number of legal grounds within a state to the divorce rate of that state, but no such relationship has been found to exist. One reason is that it is a simple matter for a couple to cross state lines to procure an out-of-state divorce, but if residency requirements are fulfilled by only one spouse, such divorces may not be recognized by the home state.

The only ground common to all the states is adultery. It is used as a legal ground in less than 2% of all divorce cases. Figures reported by the National Office of Vital Statistics disclose that some 90% of all divorce suits are based on two grounds: cruelty and desertion. Cruelty is the legal ground most often used in the United States. Usage of the term ranges from "inhuman treatment endangering life" to quarreling and other forms of "mental stress." Desertion, the second major ground, involves a willful absence on the part of either spouse for a continuous period as designated by statute; most states require an absence of one, two, or three years.

Legally, either spouse is entitled to bring suit for divorce, but official figures indicate that more than 70% of divorce actions involve the wife as plaintiff. This ratio is presumably a reflection of male "chivalry." Unfortunately, neither the legal grounds nor the party-to-whom-granted data reveal the real causes of divorce.

Canada

Control of divorce by the dominion Parliament was provided for in the British North America Act of 1867. Under the terms of this act all laws and civil or criminal courts existing in the various provinces before the establishment of the dominion remained in force. Nova Scotia in 1758 and New Brunswick in 1791 had enacted divorce laws and had established courts to exercise jurisdiction in divorce actions. The existing divorce legislation in British Columbia and Prince Edward Island was confirmed under the provisions of the British North America Act when these provinces joined the dominion in 1871 and 1873, respectively.

Canadian divorce law is based on the English Divorce and Matrimonial Causes Act of 1857. Pursuant to legislation enacted by the dominion parliament, this statute (and its subsequent amendments through July, 1870), became effective in British Columbia, Manitoba, Alberta, Saskatchewan, and Ontario during the period from 1858 to 1930. Since 1930 the judicial authority of the dominion Parliament in matters of divorce has been exercised only in Quebec and Newfoundland. In Quebec the provincial courts do not have jurisdiction to dissolve a valid marriage. Marriage can be dissolved only by the death of one of the partners. There is no divorce law in Newfoundland, and no provincial court has jurisdiction in divorce actions. In these two provinces suits for the dissolution of marriage must be brought before the Parliament of Canada.

Divorce may be obtained by either partner, but only if there is no evidence of collusion or condonation. With minor exceptions adultery is the sole ground admissible in the provincial courts. The adultery must be substantiated either by direct proof or by strong circumstantial evidence. Divorces obtained outside of Canada may or may not be valid, and the applicant who obtains an invalid divorce may be unable to remarry in Canada. Laws of domicile are further complicated by the fact that under Canadian law a wife's legal residence is always identical with that of her husband. Before 1900 divorce was extremely rare in Canada. During the 20th century the divorce rate has risen steadily. Although the divorce laws of most of the provinces are similar, there is no corresponding similarity among the divorce rates for the various provinces.

European Countries

Grounds for divorce in Europe are fairly similar to those used in the United States. It is usually the wife who is the plaintiff in the divorce action, but European courts are given wider latitude in interpretation. Throughout most of Europe two kinds of divorce grounds are recognized: relative and absolute. Absolute grounds are specified by statute, but relative grounds are often a matter of judicial interpretation. It should be added that, in contrast to American cases, European divorce suits are more likely to involve an official attempt by the court to effect a reconciliation of the spouses; in fact, in some countries a divorce based on relative grounds will not be granted until official reconciliation efforts have been made.

Consult Waller, W. W., *Family: A Dynamic Interpretation* (rev. ed., 1951); Doroghi, Ervin, *Grounds for Divorce in European Countries* (1955); Jacobson, P. H. and P. F., *American Marriage and Divorce* (1959).

WILLIAM M. KEPHART, University of Pennsylvania
See also FAMILY LAW.

DIX, DOROTHEA LYNDE (1802–87), American reformer. She was born in Maine. Before she had reached 20 she was conducting a school for girls in Boston, and she continued teaching until 1835, when illness forced her to suspend her work for several years. Having been shocked by conditions in a Massachusetts house of correction, she began in 1841 a campaign to improve the treatment of prisoners, the mentally retarded, and the mentally ill. She advocated the humane approach to mental illness proposed earlier by the French physician Philippe Pinel. Her efforts led to the establishment of more than 30 asylums for the mentally ill in the United States, and she extended

her influence by tours of Canada, England, and Europe. During the Civil War she was superintendent of women nurses in the Union Army. In her early years she wrote widely-known children's books; later she wrote on institutions and treatment.

DIX, DOROTHY. *See* GILMER, ELIZABETH MERIWETHER.

DIX, JOHN ADAMS (1798–1879), American statesman, born in Boscawen, N.H. He fought in the War of 1812 and in 1828 moved to New York to practice law. Active in Democratic politics and a member of the Albany Regency, he served as state adjutant general (1830–33), secretary of state (1833–39), and completed a vacated term as U.S. Senator (1845–49). President James Buchanan appointed Dix Secretary of the Treasury in 1861. During the Civil War he acted as major general of volunteers. After serving as Minister to France (1866–69), Dix was elected (1872) Governor of New York on the Republican ticket.

DIX, OTTO (1891–   ), German expressionist painter and etcher who was a bitter and morbid commentator on war and on post-World War I German society. His paintings, such as "Dr. Mayer-Hermann" (Museum of Modern Art, New York City), are dry, meticulous, unsentimental analyses of human foibles. Dix is well represented in the State Gallery in Hamburg and in the Museum of Modern Art in New York.

DIXIE, popular song associated with the American South. Written by Daniel D. Emmett, member of a minstrel troupe, in 1859, it became important as a march in the Civil War. Though used by both Union and Confederacy, it soon became an unofficial national anthem of the latter and remained the sentimental expression of Southern regional feeling for the next century.

DIXIECRATS, in American history, a political faction that walked out of the 1948 national convention of the Democratic party in protest against the inclusion of a civil rights statement in the party's platform. At a rump convention in Birmingham, Ala., the faction selected a states' rights Democratic (Dixiecrat) slate headed by Governor Strom Thurmond of South Carolina for President of the United States and Governor Fielding Wright of Mississippi for Vice-President. In the subsequent 1948 national election, the Dixiecrats' ticket received 1,169,021 popular votes and the aggregate 39 electoral votes of Alabama, Louisiana, Mississippi, South Carolina, and Tennessee.

DIXIELAND JAZZ, type of popular music stemming from the efforts of white musicians, primarily in New Orleans, to play the syncopated dance music produced by Negroes at the beginning of the 20th century. Although the playing of the Negroes was characterized by the blue tonality inherent in their singing of work songs, "hollers," and hymns, their white imitators were more affected by the brisk rhythms of ragtime. As a result, the playing of the white musicians usually had an excited, staccato feeling rather than the direct, singing quality of the Negroes. Dixieland has traditionally been a happy, tumultuous music, high-spirited, and often veering close to "corn" in its humor. Originally Dixieland was played in a syncopated variation of the two-four beat of march music, a rhythm identified as "two-beat" in which a strong beat alternates with a weak beat. During the 1920's a variant, known as "Chicago style," featured a changed rhythm of four strong beats to the bar. Since World War II "Dixieland" has often been loosely used to identify almost all prewar jazz styles of small groups, particularly anything that seems to have a New Orleans origin.

JOHN S. WILSON, Author, *Collector's Jazz: Modern*
See also CHICAGO JAZZ; JAZZ; MODERN JAZZ; NEW ORLEANS JAZZ.

DIXON, (CHARLES) DEAN (1915-), American Negro conductor. He was born in New York City and studied at the Juilliard School of Music and Columbia University. He has appeared with many symphony orchestras as guest conductor, including the New York Philharmonic and Boston Symphony orchestra. Dixon was the first American Negro to conduct the New York Philharmonic Symphony Orchestra. He is the resident conductor of the Göteborg Symphony in Sweden.

DIXON, THOMAS (1864–1946), American novelist, best known for his fictional portrayal of the South during Reconstruction. Born in Shelby, N.C., and educated at Wake Forest College, Dixon studied law and was admitted to the bar, then became a Baptist minister and a lyceum lecturer. He wrote many novels, the best-known being *The Leopard's Spots* (1902), *The Clansman* (1905), and *The Traitor* (1907), all dealing favorably with the Ku Klux Klan. His screenplay *The Birth of a Nation* based on *The Clansman*, was the basis of D. W. Griffith's famed motion picture.

DIXON, city of northwestern Illinois, and seat of Lee County. The city is a trade center serving a general farming area (dairying, beef cattle, and corn and wheat). Dixon is the site of Lincoln Monument State Memorial; Dixon State School is adjacent. Founded as a trading post in 1830, it became a city in 1859. Pop. (1950) 11,523; (1960) 19,565.

DIYARBAKIR [dē-yär-bä-kēr′], city of southeastern Turkey, and capital of the province of Diyarbakir, located on the Dicle (Tigris) River. Diyarbakir is built on flat land surrounded by ancient city walls. Most of the inhabitants are farmers and jewelry craftsmen. The local watermelons, although not exported, are the largest and heaviest in Turkey. Oil fields and refineries are 40 mi. north of the city, and a jet air base and radar station are nearby. Pop., 80,645.

DIZFUL [dĭz-fōōl′], town of southwestern Iran, crowded upon a rocky crag on the left bank of the Ab-i-Diz River, in an agricultural region. Extremely hot summers force the inhabitants to live in underground rooms below the houses. The remains of a bridge built in Sassanian times is a conspicuous point of interest. Pop., 52,121.

DJAKARTA or JAKARTA [jə-kär-tə], formerly Batavia, capital, largest city, and port of Indonesia, located on the northwestern coast of Java, on Djakarta Bay at the mouth of the Tjiliwung (Chiliwong) River. Government, transportation, and commerce are the principal activities. Most of the offices of various government agencies are located here. Djakarta is also an important industrial center, with large dry dock facilities, railroad shops, an assembly plant for motor vehicles, rubber- and cinchona-refining plants, and tea-processing, textile, chemical, soap, and margarine factories. Most of the imports of Indonesia enter through the port of Djakarta, including mainly iron and steel products, textiles, cement, paper, and canned foods. The exports from the port are considerably less and consist principally of rubber, tea, quinine, tobacco, and rice. The city maintains frequent steamship connections with all other ports in Indonesia and with many overseas countries. Railroads radiate out, leading westward to Bantam and Merak, southward to Bogor, Sukabumi, and the south coast, and eastward to Tjirebon, Semarang, Surabaya, and beyond. Roads connect Djakarta with all points in Java. The nearby Kemayoran Airport serves both domestic and international lines.

Djakarta is also an educational center. The faculties of

Three-wheel, pedaled cabs are common sights along the broad streets of Djakarta, the Indonesian capital.
(H. ARMSTRONG ROBERTS)

medicine and of law and literature of the University of Indonesia, and the National University, Krisnadwipajana University, Christian University, and the Academy of Foreign Service are located in the city. The magnetic-meteorological observatory, one of the earliest scientific institutions in the Orient, also is here. Among the interesting landmarks are the former Governor-General's palace, the Museum of the Institute for Indonesian Culture, libraries, and several 17th-century churches. Many of the government offices, consulates, hotels, and commercial offices surround the spacious Independence Square.

Djakarta is composed of four main districts: Tandjung Priok (the port), Old City, New City (formerly called Weltevreden), and Jatinegara (formerly called Meester Cornelis). The banks of the lower Tjiliwung River originally provided the port for Djakarta, but by the 1870's silting had necessitated the construction of a new port. Tandjung Priok, the artificially created port for Djakarta, six mi. northeast of the center and connected to it by rail, road, and canal, has modern docks, warehouses, and loading equipment. One of the three basins is mainly used for interisland shipping and the fishing fleet; the others are used for international shipping. Old Harbor, on the Tjiliwung and connected to the new harbor by the Antjol Canal, is seldom used; much of the silted area has been converted into fish ponds. Old City occupies the original site of Djakarta and is on swampy ground along both sides of the river at its mouth. Old City contains the main business and financial district, with banks, warehouses, commercial firms, numerous small shops, and crowded residences. New City, south of Old City on higher ground, was planned as a residential suburb, but its northern sections have become a secondary business district. Jatinegara, founded as a military camp south of the main city, is the principal residential section, and was incorporated into the urban area of Djakarta in 1935. Djakarta was laid out rectangularly around large open squares, principally the Koningsplein and the Waterlooplein. It is a modern city with wide streets, open plazas, and with many handsome cement buildings. Most of the old canals have been filled; the few remaining are spanned by numerous drawbridges.

History. Djakarta stands near the site of a 17th-century harbor town, Sunda Kelapa, chief port for the Sundanese kingdom of Padjadjaran. Although only a small settlement, the area surrounding the town was relatively densely settled. Jan Pieterszoon Coen founded a fort nearby in 1619 in order to control the peoples in the surrounding countryside and to serve as the base for the trading operations of the Dutch East India Company. The fort was called Batavia, the Latin name for the Netherlands, after the Batavi, a Belgic people. The fort was destroyed in 1620 and operations were transferred to the adjacent town, then given the name of Batavia, which became the headquarters for all company trade in Indonesia. Subsequently, with the institution of Dutch governmental control, Batavia became the center of government administration for Indonesia. The original town was patterned after a typical Dutch city. Many canals were constructed in the swampy river mouth region. However, the canals soon were filled with silt and became breeding places for insects and disease. Herman William Daendels,

who became Governor-General in 1806, razed the city, moved his headquarters to the highlands at Buitenzorg (Bogor), and then gradually rebuilt the city. The new city was captured and occupied by the British under Thomas Stamford Raffles in 1811. Batavia and all of the former Netherlands East Indies were returned to Dutch control in 1816. The city was established as the first Indonesian municipality in 1905. Japanese armed forces occupied the city on Mar. 5, 1942, controlling it until they were defeated by the Allied forces in mid-1945. With the establishment of independent Indonesia, the city was renamed Djakarta (Dec., 1949) and became the capital of the Republic of Indonesia (1950), succeeding the city of Jogjakarta.

Djakarta is a very cosmopolitan city, with a medley of ethnic groups. Indonesians are in the majority, but there are significant numbers of Chinese, Indians, Arabs, and Europeans. Many Chinese live in sections of the Old City. The population of Djakarta has grown tremendously since World War II. Pop., 2,839,900.

FREDERICK L. WERNSTEDT, *Pennsylvania State University*

DJAMBI [jäm'bē], town and capital of the province of Djambi in eastern Sumatra, Indonesia, located on the navigable Djambi River about 56 mi. above the mouth. The principal product is petroleum, which is piped to Palembang. Rubber, timber, and rattan are produced in the surrounding area. Pop., 86,419.

DJEM [jĕm], **EL-,** Arab village of Tunisia, 40 mi. south of Sousse, on the site of ancient Thysdrus. Olive and cactus plantations are in the vicinity. An enormous Roman amphitheater is preserved here from the period (first half of the 3d century A.D.) when Thysdrus flourished. Pop., about 5,000.

DJIBOUTI [jə-boo'tē], capital and largest town of French Somaliland, located on the Gulf of Tadjoura, an inlet of the Gulf of Aden. It is an important port near the southern entrance to the Red Sea and the chief outlet for exports from Ethiopia of coffee, skins, and beeswax. The port has deep-water berths, good bunkering facilities, and modern harbor equipment. Djibouti has an important slaughterhouse, a large cold-storage plant, coffee-processing mills, and extensive salt production works where seawater is evaporated. Djibouti, founded in 1888, replaced Obock as the capital of French Somaliland in 1892. It was linked by rail with Addis Ababa in 1917 and was Ethiopia's official port after 1897. It became a free port in 1949 and has an international airport. Pop., 31,300.

DJIDJELLI [jə-jĕl'ē], town of northeastern Algeria, on the Mediterranean coast, 150 mi. east of Algiers. It is a tourist center and port for local exports of wine, cork, oak, and iron ore. The town dates from Roman times and in the 16th century was the first capital of Barbarossa. Pop., 23,624.

DJILAS [jē'läs], **MILOVAN** (1911–   ), Yugoslav writer, former Vice-President of Yugoslavia, and Communist party official. An ardent leader of the then outlawed Yugoslav Communists, Djilas had been imprisoned in the 1930's. He met Tito in 1937 and became one of his closest associates. A member of the Yugoslav Communist party's policy-making councils, Djilas directed the war-time propaganda of the Partisan resistance. By 1953 he was widely regarded as Tito's successor, but soon thereafter was removed from his official posts for publishing scathing articles denouncing those in power. In Dec., 1956, after censuring Tito for his stand on the Hungarian revolt, Djilas was sentenced to three years in prison. In 1957 his book, *The New Class*, was published in the United States after the manuscript had been smuggled out of Yugoslavia. *The New Class*, which expressed Djilas' disillusionment with the Communist regime, resulted in an additional seven-year sentence for Djilas. Released conditionally in 1961, Djilas was rearrested in 1962 and convicted of divulging official secrets in his book, *Conversations with Stalin*. He was sentenced to an additional five years of imprisonment. The novel *Montenegro* (1963) and *The Leper and Other Stories* (1964) were written in prison.

DRAGOŠ D. KOSTICH, The New School for Social Research

DME. *See* DISTANCE-MEASURING EQUIPMENT (DME).

DMITRI, DIMITRI, or DEMETRIUS [də-mē′trē, də-mē-trē-əs] (1582–91), epileptic son of Ivan IV. The name was also assumed by pretenders to the Russian throne during the Time of Troubles (1604–13). Dmitri died as a boy during the reign of his half-brother Fyodor. An official commission of investigation, including some of Dmitri's relatives, determined that Dmitri committed suicide. Nonetheless, contemporary accounts blamed his uncle, Boris Godunov, who was later Tsar and main beneficiary of his death.

Because doubts arose as to whether Dmitri had really died, a pretender was able to gain acceptance, probably at the court of the Polish Prince Wysznewecki, as the rightful heir to the Russian throne. Appearing in the Ukraine at the head of a Polish-Russian army in 1604 the pretender seized the throne by capturing Moscow shortly after the death of Boris Godunov in 1605. During his year as Tsar, he favored Roman Catholics, Polish courtiers, and Russian peasants. His marriage to a Pole, Marina Mniszek, sparked the resistance of Russian nobles who put him to death in 1606 and expelled the Poles.

In 1607 a Russian ruffian in Tushino asserted that he was the true Dmitri. Recognized as such by the ambitious widow Marina, the second "False Dmitri" gained enough popular acceptance to harass the Muscovite government, thereby ultimately, but unintentionally, helping the Poles to reconquer large sections of Russia. Overthrown, he was killed by a supporter in 1610.

OSWALD P. BACKUS III, University of Kansas

DMITRI DONSKOI or DIMITRI DONSKOI [dŭn-skoi′], Duke of Muscovy (ruled 1359–89). He received the most important Russian title of the day, that of Grand Duke of Vladimir, through a Tatar charter called the *yarlyk*, after having defeated the former holder Dmitri Konstantinovich, Duke of Suzdal and Nizhni Novgorod. During a war with the Grand Duchy of Tver, Dmitri Donskoi was temporarily deprived of Tatar support and of the title of Grand Duke, which he regained after having defeated

Lithuania in 1375 and having compelled Tver to sever its links with Lithuania. Now the strongest prince in Russia, Dmitri defeated Tatar troops in Ryazan (1378). Eager for revenge, the Tatars allied themselves with Jagiello of Lithuania, who advanced east to join their forces. To prevent a junction, Dmitri attacked the Tatars and won a Pyrrhic victory, the Battle of Kulikovo, in 1380. Later Dmitri was again compelled to recognize Tatar overlordship. But though his victory of 1380 did not make Russia free, Kulikovo later became a symbol of resistance and independence for the Russians.

OSWALD P. BACKUS III, University of Kansas
See also GOLDEN HORDE; TATARS.

DNA. *See* NUCLEIC ACIDS.

DNEPRODZERZHINSK [nĕp-rō-dər-zhĭnsk′], city of the Soviet Union, in Dnepropetrovsk Oblast of the Ukrainian S.S.R. It is located on the west bank of the Dnieper River. Founded in the 19th century, it was first known as Kamenskoye; it assumed its present name in 1936. Situated at the junction of the main railroad line from Kiev to Dnepropetrovsk, it is a major transport hub and industrial center. Its chief industry, started in 1887, is the manufacturing of iron and steel products in large mills. The iron ore comes from the Krivoi Rog region to the southwest and the coking coal from the great mining area, the Donets Basin (Donbas), to the north. A large chemical industry has been developed.

Other important manufactures include machinery, railway freight cars, cement, ceramic products, and foods. From 1932 to 1955 the main source of electric power for these operations was the Dnieper hydroelectric station (Dneprogres) at Zaporozhie. A new station at Kakhovka is now a greater source. Dneprogres made possible a great expansion of the metallurgical industry during the 1930's. This resulted in a population increase from 24,000 in 1926 to 148,000 in 1939. Pop., 194,000.

ALLAN L. RODGERS, Pennsylvania State University

DNEPROPETROVSK [nĕp-rō-pə-trôfsk′], city of the Soviet Union, capital of the Dnepropetrovsk Oblast of the Ukrainian S.S.R. It is on the big eastward bend of the Dnieper River. One of the most important economic centers of the U.S.S.R., Dnepropetrovsk is a hub of rail and water communications and a key industrial city. Its industries are dominated by metallurgical works and production of machinery. The plants utilize iron ore from the Krivoi Rog district to the southwest and coking coal from the great mining region, the Donets Basin (Donbas), to the north. Electric energy is supplied by the Dnieper hydroelectric plant (Dneproges) at Zaporozhie. Other important industries include chemical production and the manufacture of construction materials, foods, and light industrial goods.

The city was founded by Prince Potemkin in 1787 in the course of the Russian conquest of the Ukraine and was first named Yekaterinoslav in honor of Catherine II. It originated on low ground subject to recurrent flooding by the Dnieper. Its later development occurred on higher ground. By the mid-19th century the city was of modest importance as a trade and administrative center. In the later part of the century the construction of a major east-west railroad through the city linking Krivoi Rog with the Donets Basin stimulated the development of the local metallurgical industry. By 1897 its population had reached 113,000. Since the beginning of the Soviet era, when the city assumed its present name, there has been a marked expansion of the metallurgical and machinery industries. The completion of Dneproges in 1932 greatly abetted this growth. By 1939 the city's population had risen to more than 500,000. During World War II, Dnepropetrovsk was occupied by the Germans (1941–43). Largely reconstructed, it stretches about 10 mi. along the Dnieper. Important monuments are the Potemkin Palace and a cathedral. Dnepropetrovsk has a large state university and many other institutions of higher learning, particularly schools specializing in the study of metallurgy, mining, construction, and other related fields. Pop., 658,000.

ALLAN L. RODGERS, Pennsylvania State University

DNEPR RIVER. *See* DNIEPER RIVER.

DNESTR RIVER. *See* DNIESTER RIVER.

DNIEPER [nē'pər] **RIVER,** second-largest river of the U.S.S.R., in the southwest, draining about 200,000 sq. mi. Rising in the Smolensk Oblast south of the Valdai Hills, it flows southwest into Belorussian S.S.R. There it turns south to enter the Ukrainian S.S.R., acting as a boundary for a short distance between the two republics. At Zaporozhie, it turns southwestward again to flow into the Dnieper Liman of the Black Sea, above Kherson. Among its tributaries are the Berezina, Pripet, Desna, Samara, and Ingulets. It is connected by canals to the Dvina, Niemen, and Vistula rivers, forming a waterway to the Baltic Sea. Several important Soviet cities are on the Dnieper. These include Smolensk, Mogilev, Kiev, Cherkassy, Dneprodzerzhinsk, Dnepropetrovsk, Zaporozhie, Nikopol, and Kherson. The Dnieper freezes for about 125 days at its source and for about three months at its mouth. Lumber, grain, oil, and coal are carried on its waters. There are two hydroelectric stations in its lower course. The largest of these is the Dnieper Dam (Dneproges) at Zaporozhie, completed in 1932. The other at Kakhovka was completed in 1955. The Dnieper was important in the settlement of Russia. During the Kievan Russia era it was a vital trade artery between the Baltic and Black Seas. Length, 1,420 mi.

ALLAN L. RODGERS, Pennsylvania State University

DNIESTER [nēs'tər] **RIVER,** major river of the western Soviet Union, draining almost 30,000 sq. mi. It rises in the Carpathian Mountains in the western Ukrainian S.S.R. at a height of about 2,950 ft. and flows generally southeastward through the Ukrainian and Moldavian S.S.R.'s. For a short distance it acts as a boundary between these two regions. The river flows into the Dniester Liman of the Black Sea, west of Odessa. It is navigable by large craft in the lower part of its course, but the traffic volume is not large. The basic commodities moving on the river are timber and grain. There are several small cities along the Dniester, the most important of which are Tiraspol, Soroki, and Sambor. Although the Dniester has high hydroelectric potential, only one medium-sized installation

has been built—at Dubossary, northeast of Kishinev. Length, about 875 mi.

DOBBS FERRY, residential village of southern New York on the east bank of the Hudson River. Masters School for girls and Children's Village for problem boys are located here. Inc., 1873; pop. (1950) 6,268; (1960) 9,260.

DÖBELN [dū'bəln], town of the northeastern German Democratic Republic (East Germany) in the district of Dresden, located on an island between two arms of the Freiberge Mulde River, southeast of Leipzig. The principal industries include the manufacture of machinery, metalwork, furniture, and sugar. The Nikolaikirche, a Gothic church erected between 1479 and 1485, contains a famous altar. A medieval town hall remains, and Döbeln has a memorial to Martin Luther. Pop., 29,410.

DOBEREINER [dū'bə-rī'nər], **JOHANN WOLFGANG** (1780–1849), German chemist. In 1829 he pointed out the existence of several groups of three elements, which he called triads. The member of a triad whose atomic weight was between the other two had physical and chemical properties midway between the other two. Dobereiner's triads were an important first step in the recognition of the periodic nature of the elements that finally led to the periodic table.

DOBERMAN PINSCHER [dō'bər-mən pĭn'shər], a handsome member of the working group of dogs that originated in Germany in the late 1800's. The Doberman is strongly built and has a long muzzle, trimmed, neat ears, and a docked tail. Adult males weigh about 80 lb. The coat is flat and sleek and usually black and tan, but may also be brownish-red. Dobermans have amazing vitality and make excellent watchdogs. A related breed, the miniature pinscher, belongs to the toy group. This pocket-size dog weighs from 6 to 10 lb. but has spirit equal to that of the Doberman.

The swift and strong Doberman pinscher is an excellent watch dog.

Percy T. Jones—Frederic Lewis

DÖBLIN [dṻ'blĕn], **ALFRED** (1878–1957), German expressionist novelist. He was a practicing physician in Berlin until 1933, when he left Germany to live in Palestine and the United States for the duration of the war. As a writer he combined a probing intellect with a fecund imagination. His most famous novel, *Berlin Alexanderplatz*, 1929, depicts life in a modern metropolis in a manner reminiscent of James Joyce.

DOBRUJA [dō'brōō-jə], Rumanian region along the Black Sea coast between the Danube River and Bulgaria. Predominantly agricultural and ethnically complex with Armenian, Jewish, Greek, Slavonic, Turkic, and Tatar minorities, Dobruja was long disputed (19th-20th centuries) between Bulgaria and Rumania. Once part of the Roman and then (4th century A.D.) of the Byzantine Empire, Dobruja went (7th century) to the Bulgarian Empire. Falling under Ottoman occupation (15th century), Dobruja was divided between Bulgaria and Rumania by the Berlin Congress (1878). Bulgaria ceded (1913) Southern Dobruja (3,000 sq. mi.) to Rumania after the Second Balkan War but reacquired it in 1940. Area, about 6,000 sq. mi.; capital, Constanţa; pop., 667,000.

DOBSON, HENRY AUSTIN (1840-1921), English essayist and poet. His interest in 18th-century literature was expressed in his light verse and in his choice of subjects for his biographical studies: Fielding (1883), Steele (1886), Goldsmith (1888), Richardson (1902), and Fanny Burney (1903). Dobson used Old French verse forms for his poetry; the best-known volumes are *Vignettes in Rhyme* (1873), *Proverbs in Porcelain* (1877), and *At the Sign of the Lyre* (1885).

DOBSON FLY. *See* HELLGRAMMITE.

DOBZHANSKY, THEODOSIUS (1900–), American geneticist. Born and educated in Russia he became an American citizen in 1936. He taught at California Institute of Technology from 1929 to 1940. Since 1940 he has been professor of zoology at Columbia University. He was influential in the development of population genetics and has been particularly interested in explaining the evolution of species in terms of modern genetic theory. Among his many published works are *Genetics and the Origin of Species* (1951), and the excellent text, *Principles of Genetics* (1925), co-authored by Edmund W. Sinnott and Leslie C. Dunn.

DOCETISM [dō-sē'tĭz-əm] (Gr. *dokein*, "to seem"), 2d-century Christian heresy which treats the humanity of Jesus as only apparent, finding it impossible that a divine being could also be truly human. This seems to be the position repudiated in I John 4:2–3, and formally attacked in the letters of St. Ignatius (c.115 A.D.). Docetism in various forms was an ingredient in most of the Gnostic systems, for which a spiritual being could not be at the same time material. The Church's reply is expressed in the emphasis in the creeds on the human birth and real suffering of Jesus. But a docetic tendency appears in various later heresies such as Apollinarianism (4th century) and even in theologians who otherwise profess orthodox doctrine.

DOCK, name for several coarse, perennial plants of the genus *Rumex*, in the buckwheat family, Polygonaceae. About 100 species are found throughout the world, and in temperate regions, dock is a common weed. The plants grow from 1 to 5 ft. tall, have oval or spear-shaped leaves, and bear clusters of small green or reddish flowers. The leaves of spinach dock, *R. patientia*, are used as a salad green in Europe.

DOCK AND WHARF, harbor structures for berthing and servicing ships. Although the terms are sometimes used interchangeably, dock refers to a ship's berth and wharf to a more general-purpose structure for loading or unloading or which can be used for fishing, car parking, or boardwalks.

Dock. The two types of docks are wet dock and dry dock. Wet docks, located in ports having a large tidal range, are berths that are either open or closed to tide. If closed, the water level in the basin is maintained by locks or gates. Repair docks, or dry docks, are for the building and repairing of ships out of water. The types are: (1) graving docks, formed of lined basins, with gates or locks, into which ships are floated before the entrance is closed and the water pumped out; (2) floating dry docks, formed of buoyant structures that lift ships out of the water; and (3) marine railways that usually consist of a ship cradle which moves on inclined tracks extending into the water. On the Great Lakes the term dock is used loosely to refer to wharves for handling bulk material and called ore docks or coal docks.

Wharf. Wharf is the general term for a quay or pier structure, including the equipment for loading and discharging ship cargo and passengers. A marginal quay wharf, or bulkhead, parallels the shoreline and offers berthing space for ships on the exposed side only. A pier is a wharf which extends outward from the shore into open water and usually provides berthing space on both sides.

The type of wharf is determined by its purpose and the site conditions of prevailing winds, waves and currents, tidal range, as well as economy of construction. The work that is to be done on the wharf influences provisions for cargo, passengers, vehicles, railroads, and lighters. Ship characteristics, such as length, beam, hatches, and capacity, determine the wharf's length, width, slip width (distance between piers), cargo handling equipment, and storage capacities. Ship draft and silting conditions set the depth of the docking basins and slips. Special wharves, such as those for fitting out and supplying ships, require special construction and equipment.

Quay wall construction for a marginal wharf includes either a retaining wall of sheet piling, stone or concrete, or stone-filled timber cribs; or a timber or concrete platform extending over the bank. Also, it can be a combination of retaining wall and platform.

Pier. A pier may be open, so that water underneath extends from one side to the other, or solid and made of solid-fill or masonry structures, to shut out water. Open piers are pile- or caisson-supported platforms constructed of timber, steel, or concrete. The platforms may provide open storage or covered storage in cargo or transit sheds. Open piers provide a minimum restriction to the flow of

59

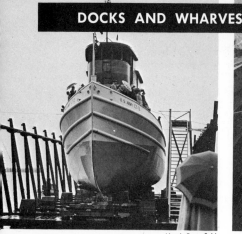

Morris Rosenfield

The marine railway is the simplest form of dry dock. It is generally used for underwater repairs on small craft.

U.S. Navy

The graving dock is an enclosed basin fitted with watertight entrance gates. Basin is pumped dry after ship enters.

Bethlehem Steel Co.

The floating dry dock can lift ships weighing up to 20,000 tons. Such docks are mobile and can be shifted to different ports.

Port of New York Authority

This modern open pier of the New York Port Authority in Brooklyn makes it possible to accommodate five freighters at one time.

Port of New York Authority

Expeditious handling of cargo reduces time freighters must spend in port. These Newark, N.J., wharves are especially designed to facilitate the quick movement of goods.

the body of water between high and mean low water levels. Solid piers may consist of cellular sheet pile construction or parallel sheet piling for retaining earth fill. Special piers for handling petroleum products or bulk cargoes usually consist of clusters of piles called dolphins.

MAURICE GRUSHKY, Tippetts-Abbett-McCarthy-Stratton, Engineers and Architects

See also HARBOR.

DOCK JUNCTION, unincorporated town of southeastern Georgia, just north of Brunswick, on the Atlantic coast. Pop. (1950) 4,160; (1960) 5,417.

DOCTOR FAUSTUS, THE TRAGICALL HISTORY OF. *See* MARLOWE, CHRISTOPHER.

DR. JEKYLL AND MR. HYDE, THE STRANGE CASE OF, English novel (1886) by Robert Louis Stevenson. In this psychological allegory of the moral duality in human nature, Jekyll, a respected doctor, discovers a drug which transforms him into the evil, grotesque dwarf Hyde. Although the drug restores him to his former self, with repeated use it begins to lose its efficacy. After Hyde commits murder, Jekyll's lawyer exposes his client's true nature, and Hyde commits suicide.

DOCTOR ZHIVAGO [zhĭ-vä′gō], Russian novel by Boris Pasternak. It was completed in 1956, but was banned in the Soviet Union; it was a best seller in Europe and America (1957–59). The novel presents a vast picture of the Russian intelligentsia in the early 20th century, and gives a vivid description of the 1917 Revolution and the early Communist regime. The book's anti-Communist, religious tendencies make it significant.

DOCUMENTARY. *See* MOTION PICTURES.

DOCUMENTATION, in early usage, a series of procedures whose limits were comparable to those of bibliography, but applied to types of materials and information presented in forms other than books. In current usage, documentation is broadly conceived to include every form or method of producing, analyzing, and delivering useful information.

Presentation and distribution of such new information involves specialized techniques of assembling, recording, and multiplying copies of the information, and developing useful patterns of distribution. Typical examples of some of these methods are microfilm, microcards, xerography, and a multitude of near-print formats.

Documentation also may involve the collection, organization, and storage of new information, whatever its form. The collection of information is complicated by the frequently unorthodox form of the material or by some special limitation on its availability. Organization is subject to similar difficulties, and the storage of all useful bits of information has given documentalists a whole field for new and ingenious devices. Some recent developments involve the use of high-speed computers and electronic brains.

These complex devices are also used in the service areas where the results of the documentalist's work reach their logical conclusion. Research into the use of systems of coding information, its reduction to minute or even microscopic form, and the numerous correlations of related bits of data are all part of documentation. The detailed subject analysis of the smallest units of information, which are then stored within any one of the devices used and finally retrieved or recovered according to patterns of need, is the essential goal of documentation.

JERROLD ORNE, University of North Carolina

See also ABSTRACTING; BIBLIOGRAPHY; LIBRARY CATALOGING AND CLASSIFICATION.

DODDER, name for about 100 species of parasitic, twining annual plants of the genus *Cuscuta,* in the Convolvulaceae, or morning glory family. Dodder is found throughout the world and in certain areas is a particularly noxious pest. The plants are leafless and bear clusters of small, white flowers. The thin stems are yellow-, red-, or orange-colored and attach to the host plant by means of rootlike suckers. Some species of dodder cause serious losses to such crops as alfalfa, clover, and flax, and also chrysanthemum, ivy, and other ornamentals. Dodder can be controlled by removing it completely from its host before the dodder has gone to seed.

DODDS, JOHNNY (1892–1940), American clarinetist and band leader. Born in New Orleans, La., he joined Kid Ory's band in 1911. Later he was with King Oliver's band for four years (1920–24), performing mostly at the Lincoln Gardens in Chicago. He then organized his own group, which played at Kelly's Stable in the same city. He is considered one of the greatest clarinetists of the New Orleans jazz style.

DODDS, WARREN ("BABY") (1898–1959), one of the greatest and most influential of the early jazz drummers. Following his lead, drummers began to play in a steadier, more integrated manner. Most frequently associated with his famous brother, clarinetist Johnny Dodds, he worked with practically all the early jazz specialists through the years. He started out with Louis Armstrong, King Oliver, and other notables on the Mississippi riverboats and in New Orleans.

DODECAHEDRON. *See* POLYHEDRON.

DODECANESE [dō-dĕk-ə-nēz′, dō-dĕk-ə-nēs′] (Gr. **DODEK-ANISOS**), group of Greek islands in the Aegean Sea, located off the southwest coast of Asia Minor between Turkey and Crete. The islands form the southern and largest part of the Southern Sporades. Geologically they are the highest points of a sunken mountain range of Anatolia (Asia Minor) of which Crete, the Cyclades, and the Greek mainland are also continuations. Although Dodecanese means "Twelve Islands," the group comprises 14 main islands plus numerous islets. Largest and most important is Rhodes (q.v.), whose main city of the same

Dorothy Hosmer—Pix

Harbor of Kastellorizo, the easternmost island of the Dodecanese group in the Aegean Sea.

name is the capital of the Dodecanese. Next in size and importance are Kos, Kalymnos, and Karpathos. The total area of the group is 1.035 sq. mi. The summers are dry and hot; the winters, when most of the rain occurs, are mild. Drought-resistant scrub covers the steeper ground of the islands. Only Rhodes and Kos have fertile soil and Rhodes has fine forests. The chief crops are cereals, olives, tobacco, grapes, and other fruits. Sheep and goats are the main livestock. Sponge fishing is also important.

The Dodecanese belonged to the Dorian Greeks in early classical times. Later they were conquered by the Romans. In the 13th century the Crusaders occupied the islands until they were captured by the Seljuk Turks. In 1310 Rhodes and other of the islands were taken by the Knights Hospitalers. The Turks again took the Dodecanese in 1522 and held them for four centuries. In 1912, during the Italo-Turkish War, they were seized by Italy and renamed the Italian Possessions in the Aegean. They were officially ceded to Italy after World War I and remained under her rule until 1943. In 1947 they were transferred to Greece by the Italian Peace Treaty. The islands' population once contained many Turks and Italians. Jews exiled from Spain went to Rhodes, and Muslims emigrated from Turkey. Today the population is largely Greek. Pop., 121,480.

NORMAN J. G. POUNDS, University of Indiana

DODGE, HENRY (1782–1867), American soldier and public official, born in Vincennes, Ind. As major-general, he fought briefly in the War of 1812 and later earned a distinguished military reputation in the Black Hawk War (1832). In 1836 he received an appointment as Governor of the new Wisconsin Territory, a post he filled until 1841 and again from 1845 to 1848. Dodge was Governor in 1848, when Wisconsin entered the Union. From 1848 to 1857 when he retired, he was one of the first U.S. Senators from the new state.

DODGE, MARY MAPES (1831–1905), influential American juvenile writer and editor, born in New York City. Her best-known story *Hans Brinker, or, The Silver Skates* (1865) was acclaimed by Netherlanders as faithful to life in their country and is considered a children's classic in the United States. In 1873 she was appointed editor of a new magazine for children which she named *St. Nicholas*, and which she used as a vehicle for her broad-minded and far-sighted ideas on what appealed to children. For over 30 years she published material by first-class writers and artists, among them Howard Pyle, Louisa M. Alcott, Mark Twain, and Rudyard Kipling.

DODGE CITY, trade center of southwestern Kansas, on the Arkansas River, and seat of Ford County. Settled in 1872 as Buffalo City, as a railhead, it was renamed in honor of nearby Fort Dodge and incorporated in 1875. From 1876 to 1886 it was the most important terminus of the cattle trails from Texas. Violence marked its early history, and William B. ("Bat") Masterson and Wyatt Earp were among the city's famous law officers. Front Street and Boot Hill Cemetery, reminders of the city's early history, and Dodge City Junior College are located here. Pop. (1950) 11,262; (1960) 13,520.

DODGSON, CHARLES LUTWIDGE. *See* CARROLL, LEWIS.

DODO [dō′dō], a large, flightless bird, *Didus ineptus*, formerly found on the island of Mauritius in the Indian Ocean, but extinct since about 1680. Two related species, *D. borbonicus* and *Pezophaps solitarius*, lived on neighboring islands and became extinct at about the same time. Dodos were about the size of a swan but had stockier bodies; short, stout legs; a ponderous hooked beak; a small tuft of curly tail feathers; and rudimentary wings. Their general appearance was preposterous and conveyed an air of stupidity; in fact their name was derived from *doudo* (Port. "silly"). Their extinction, however, was not humorous. Until the early 17th century, when their island homes were colonized, dodos had no natural enemies. The settlers not only found dodo meat to be a tasty viand, but their domesticated dogs, cats, and hogs decided that dodo eggs made a very fine meal.
See also FLIGHTLESS BIRDS.

DODOMA [dō-də′mä], town of Tanzania. Dodoma is an important market center, especially for livestock. The town is located where the main railroad crosses the Cape-Cairo highway. Pop. 13,445.

DODONA [dō-dō′nə], ancient Greek oracle of Zeus, in Epirus. The oracle was in a grove of oak trees which transmitted the divine voice through the rustling of their leaves. Probably the oldest oracle in Greece, it was second in reputation only to Delphi. It was consulted by Croesus, and Alexander left it a sizable donation. Greek excavations have partially cleared the walled acropolis, the lower city with the sanctuary, and a theater.
See also ORACLES.

DOE, JOHN, was the fictitious name of the plaintiff in the old common law action of ejectment which was brought to recover possession of land and damages for its wrongful withholding. Originally, this action could be brought only by lessees or tenants who had been ousted by someone. Later, the lease became a mere fiction allegedly granted by the plaintiff-lessor to a fictitious John Doe who was treated as the nominal plaintiff. Doe would be considered as ousted by a fictitious defendant Richard Roe, who was described as the "casual ejector." The court would then decide whether Doe's lessor had better title to the land than the actual defendant who was in possession. Statutes in most states abolished these fictions. Today, when a law suit is instituted against an unknown defendant, he is usually designated as John Doe.

DOENITZ [dö′nĭts], **KARL** (1891–   ), German naval officer, director of submarine warfare against the Allies in World War II. He became (1910) a naval cadet and during World War I commanded a submarine. An ardent follower of Adolf Hitler, Doenitz was empowered by him to construct a U-boat fleet. In 1943 he succeeded Adm. Erich Raeder as chief naval commander. Upon Hitler's death Doenitz organized a new Cabinet and accepted the unconditional surrender (May 7, 1945) for Germany. He was convicted as a war criminal in 1946 and sentenced to ten years' imprisonment.

DOG. Since prehistoric times, man and dog have been associated to their mutual benefit. Both man and dog were hunters and by pooling their talents, they found they could eat more often and with less trouble. When a kill was made, man shared the meat and bones with his hunting ally, the dog. Gradually the dog moved closer to primitive man's cave and the relation became even closer. In addition to helping in the hunt, the dog became a guardian of man's home. The affinity and association thus formed has lasted for over 10,000 years.

The domestic dog, *Canis familiaris*, is a member of the dog family, Canidae, which also includes the wolf, jackal, coyote, dingo, dhole, fox, fennec, Cape hunting dog, raccoon dog, and Colombian bush dog. The dogs constitute the most cosmopolitan family in the order Carnivora, and also the most progressive, by virtue of their adaptability to many different environments.

The Evolution of the Dog Family

The ancestor of the entire dog family is believed to have been a civetlike animal, *Miacis*, that lived about 40 or 50 million years ago. *Miacis* was a small animal with an elongated body and was arboreal, or at least seemed to have spent considerable time in the lush forests of its era. Next in the evolution of the dogs was the appearance, about 35 million years ago, of two apparently direct descendants of *Miacis*. These were *Daphaenus*, a large, heavy-boned animal with a long tail; and *Hesperocyon*, a small, slender animal who was the forerunner of the long-bodied, coyote-like "bear dogs" that eventually evolved into modern bears. *Hesperocyon* can be considered as the "grandfather" of the dog family. *Hesperocyon* retained the long body and short legs of the primitive carnivores, but unlike *Miacis*, *Hesperocyon* spent little of its time in the trees and began to hunt on the ground. Its claws were retractile, enabling it to walk on the ground and to climb trees.

From *Hesperocyon* there evolved two distinct dog types. The first, *Temnocyon*, was an important link in the evolutionary chain that led to the modern hunting dog of Africa, the Cape hunting dog. The second, *Cynodesmus*, is regarded as the ancestor of a large and diversified group of dogs that includes the modern Eurasian wolf and the American dogs, foxes, and wolves.

The animal considered to be the "father" of modern dogs, *Tomarctus*, was directly descended from *Hesperocyon*. *Tomarctus* had a body built for speed and endurance, as well as for leaping, and differed little in appearance from the modern dog. He was a hunter, an animal geared for the chase, and brought down his prey with slashing teeth. The modern dog still retains much of *Tomarctus'* anatomical structure and is surpassed in speed only by the cheetah.

As the evolutionary progress of the Canidae continued, the progeny of *Tomarctus* embarked on their development into the modern dogs, wolves, foxes, coyotes, fennecs, and jackals. At the same time, descendants of *Temnocyon* gradually emerged as the Cape hunting dog.

The Emergence of Modern Dogs

The modern dog evolved as a result of both natural selection and selective breeding. The environment selected and preserved dogs that could live under specific natural conditions. Man used selective breeding to produce dogs for a specific purpose. He wanted dogs to guard livestock, help him hunt certain game, and to guard his home and family.

Descending in a direct line from *Tomarctus*, there came four major lines of dogs: the herd dogs, the hounds and terriers, the northern and toy dogs, and the guard dogs. It is from these four lines, or groups, that modern dogs are descended. The herd dogs, a working group developed to herd sheep and cattle, were naturally rugged, had great stamina, and could withstand extremes in climate. This group, exemplified by the shepherd dogs of Germany, collies of Scotland, Briard of France, Old English sheepdog, and the Komondor, Vizsla, and Puli of Hungary, were developed through natural selection; man merely elaborated on their herding instincts.

The original members of the Northern, or Arctic, group of dogs were the Samoyed, Siberian Husky, and the chow chow and its relatives—the Pomeranian, Maltese, Pekingese, pug, and Japanese spaniel. These dogs were thick-coated, rugged, and able to stand subzero weather. The larger ones, such as the Samoyed and Husky, were powerful workers, capable of pulling heavy loads over ice and snow.

The original hounds were divided into two groups: sight hunters and scent hunters. The sight hunters, such as the saluki and Afghan, were tall, rangy, speedy dogs with keen eyesight who hunted in desert country. The scent hunters, such as the beagle and bloodhound, were short, stocky dogs that hunted with their noses to the ground. They had large earflaps that served the purpose of stirring up ground scent.

The members of the terrier group were also hunters. They were small dogs with strong forelegs, useful for digging, and powerful jaws that they used to catch rats and small animals. Their name, "terrier," is derived from the Latin word *terra*, which means earth. The spaniels, pointers, setters, and retrievers hunt with head held high to detect any airborne scent. These dogs were specially developed to hunt game birds.

The guard dogs of ancient times were large, powerful animals of considerable aggressiveness and courage. They made excellent watchdogs and were often used in war. In Greece and Rome they were used for hunting and can be considered as the forerunners of the modern war dogs. The mastiff, bulldog, boxer, and great Dane are descendants of the ancient guard dogs.

For more than a thousand years, these four groups, or lines, of dogs predominated. The dogs in any given group were considered to be types rather than breeds. The classification of dogs into breeds is an innovation of the last 100 years. From the four original types there developed the six major groups that are today recognized throughout the world.

The Sporting Group. The members of this group, the spaniels, setters, pointers, and retrievers, were developed to assist the hunter, mainly in his pursuit of feathered game. Spaniels, setters, and pointers serve mainly to locate game in the field; retrievers, and also spaniels and setters, retrieve game. Many sporting dogs are excellent swimmers and have heavy, water-repellent coats, useful when game must be retrieved from icy waters. Their long earflaps afford additional protection from cold and water. Modern breeds of sporting dogs include the wire-haired pointing griffon, German short haired pointer, weimaraner, American cocker spaniel, English cocker spaniel, Irish water spaniel, American water spaniel, Brittany spaniel, Sussex spaniel, Welsh springer spaniel, field spaniel, pointer, Irish setter, English setter, Gordon setter, Chesapeake Bay retriever, curly-coated retriever, flat-coated retriever, golden retriever, Labrador retriever, German wire-haired pointer, and the Vizsla.

The Hound Dog. Dogs in this group are active hunters who locate game by sight or by scent. The sight hunters are long-legged, coursing dogs, and number among their members the saluki, believed to be the oldest-known breed of domesticated dog. Other sight hunters are the Afghan hound, Irish wolfhound, borzoi, Norwegian elkhound, Scottish deerhound, greyhound, and whippet.

The scent hunters are short-legged, compactly-built dogs, and are generally used in packs. Members of this group are the beagle, basset, bloodhound, American foxhound, English foxhound, harrier, basenji, dachshund, black and tan coonhound, otterhound, and Rhodesian ridgeback.

The Working Group. As the name implies, dogs in this group perform a variety of useful functions. Some herd sheep and other livestock, others are draught animals, and still others are used as guide dogs or guards. Included in this utilitarian group are the Alaskan malamute, Siberian Husky, Samoyed, Belgian sheepdog, Bouvier de Flandres, boxer, Briard, smooth collie, rough collie, great Dane, Komondor, Newfoundland, Kuvasz, Old English sheepdog, Puli, mastiff, bull mastiff, German shepherd dog, Bernese Mountain dog, great Pyrenees, Rottweiler, giant schnauzer, Shetland sheepdog, Cardigan Welsh corgi, Pembroke Welsh corgi, and Saint Bernard.

The Terrier Group. The members of this diversified group hunt by digging their prey out of burrows. They are equipped with very strong forelegs and most terriers also have wiry coats as protection from the underbrush through which they must often pass. As a group, the terriers are alert and active dogs and number among their members the Scottish terrier, Sealyham terrier, Dandie Dinmont terrier, Welsh terrier, bull terrier, Lakeland terrier, Kerry blue terrier, Bedlington terrier, smooth fox terrier, wire-haired fox terrier, Cairn terrier, West Highland white terrier, border terrier, Skye terrier, Australian silky terrier, miniature schnauzer, Staffordshire terrier, Airedale terrier, Norwich terrier, and Manchester terrier.

The Toy Group. Unlike members of the four previous groups who perform some function useful to man, dogs of the toy group are kept exclusively as pets. Many are actually small versions of some larger, useful breed; others trace their ancestry to small lap dogs. The toy group includes the affenpinscher, Italian greyhound, Maltese, English toy spaniel, miniature pinscher, Chihuahua, Brussels griffon, Papillon, Pomeranian, pug, Pekingese, toy poodle, toy Manchester terrier, and the Yorkshire terrier.

The Non-sporting Group. The dogs in this final and rather diversified group were bred to perform a variety of services. The French bulldog, English bulldog, and Boston terrier are descendants of dogs bred for fighting, and have the characteristic strong jaws, teeth, and muscular neck

necessary for this cruel sport. The chow chow is the oldest of the non-sporting breeds and was used in ancient China as a hunting dog. Others are the Dalmatian, long identified as the "coach dog," and the keeshond, Lhasa terrier, standard poodle, miniature poodle, and schipperke.

The Care of Dogs

Dog management is a matter of common sense. The dog's needs are relatively few: proper housing, adequate diet, sufficient exercise, occasional grooming, and medical attention when ill. In addition to these physical necessities, all dogs need, and most dogs seem to crave the affection and approval of man. The dog is the only animal that will serve man for nothing more than a pat·on the head. Dogs should receive affection, companionship, and care in return for their loyalty and service.

Since he is basically an animal of the chase, the dog needs exercise. Large dogs require considerable exercise in order to remain in top condition. Small dogs, such as the toy breeds, can get along with little exercise. City dogs that are confined to the house during most of the day need to be taken out several times a day; each outing should be for at least a half-hour. A romp in the park or a chase after a ball should form part of the exercise period.

Dogs can be housed indoors or out. With the exception of the toy breeds, who have rather delicate constitutions, most dogs can live outdoors all year, if they are provided with a dry, draft-free house. The doghouse should be so located that it is neither exposed to winter winds nor hot summer sun. Although dogs can tolerate extremely cold weather, they are susceptible to drafts and dampness and should be protected from these in their housing. The indoor dog should be given a bed in the corner of a room, away from radiators and cracks under doors or windows.

A nutritious diet is important to the proper growth and health of the dog. The essential nutrients in a dog's diet, as in a human diet, include proteins, carbohydrates, fats, vitamins, and minerals. High-quality commercial dog

Field training. The trainer steadies a young pointer on its point. The experienced dog on the right aids in the training process.

Gaines Dog Research Center

TOY GROUP

The several breeds that compose this group are mostly of ancient and distinguished lineage. Toy breeds were developed from their standard-sized counterparts for use as house dogs or pets. Many toys were especially identified with nobility since, at the time of their development, only the ruling classes could afford to maintain dogs as pets. Because dogs of the toy group were derived from such diverse bloodlines, the different breeds have no features in common, except their smallness.

E. L. Taylor–Annan Photos

The Chihuahua was developed in Mexico during or before the 9th century A.D. The breed occurs in smooth- and long-coated varieties.

E. L. Taylor–Annan Photos

The Pekingese has been known in China since at least the 8th century A.D. In that country its ownership was reserved for the ruling aristocracy and idols were made in its image (the well-known Fu dogs).

The Italian Greyhound, a miniature version of the greyhound, originated at least 2,000 years ago in the Near East. It was popular in Greece and was the favorite house dog of the Romans.

E. L. Taylor–Annan Photos

E. L. Taylor–Annan Photos

The Papillon was probably developed in Spain during the 16th century from a larger, spaniel-type dog. The breed was named for its large, butterflylike ears (*papillon* is French for butterfly).

The Maltese has existed in its present form since at least 800 B.C. and, as its name implies, is intimately identified with the island of Malta. It was developed from spaniel bloodlines.

E. L. Taylor–Annan Photos

PLATE 1

HOUND GROUP

Hounds have been used since earliest-recorded history for hunting furred game. The first hounds (the oldest-known breeds of dogs) originated in the Near East, and from there were introduced into the Mediterranean region, and later, into northern Europe. The ancient Romans, who developed what is probably the first classification of dogs (according to their use), recognized two different kinds of hounds—sight hunters and scent hunters. This traditional division of the hound group is accepted to the present day.

SIGHT HUNTERS. This hound subgroup is sometimes referred to as the greyhound family. Sight hunters are long-legged and have lean, deep-chested bodies; sharp-pointed muzzles; and tucked-up loins. The dogs depend on their keen sight and great speed to locate and catch their prey. Sight hunters are large dogs and, despite their delicate appearance, are powerful. The Saluki, for example, has been used to hunt boars, and the Borzoi was developed to hunt wolves and to course hare.

E. L. Taylor–Annan Photos

The Saluki is the oldest-known breed of dog. Carved representations of it, dating from 7000 B.C., have been found in Near Eastern ruins.

E. L. Taylor–Annan Photos

The Irish Wolfhound, developed by the ancient Celts, was brought to Greece by them when they sacked Delphi (273 B.C.)

The Afghan Hound was developed in the Sinai Peninsula. The breed was first described in an Egyptian papyrus that is thought to date from 4000-3000 B.C.

E. L. Taylor–Annan Photos

The Borzoi, or Russian Wolfhound, was developed in the 17th century by crossing greyhounds with a native Russian dog.

Annan Photos

Camera Clix

The Greyhound is depicted in Egyptian tomb carvings that date from about 2800 B.C. A favorite of Egyptian royalty, and later of the Greek nobility, the greyhound has had a long and protected history. The breed was introduced into Britain prior to the 9th century. The Canute Laws (1016 A.D.) specified that "No meane person may keepe any greihounds, but freemen may..."

PLATE 2

SCENT HUNTERS. This subgroup of hounds includes the typical breeds identified by the term "hound." In conformation the scent hunters are distinguished by their relatively short, heavily muscled legs; broad-chested, long bodies; long skull, domed on top; wide-set eyes; and low-set, pendent ears. They are generally slower-moving than the sight hunters and rely on their well-developed sense of smell to locate game. Scent hunters are commonly hunted in packs and have distinctive barks by which they notify the hunter that the prey has been located.

Thomson–Annan Photos

The Bloodhound was used as a war dog by the Romans who greatly esteemed its scenting ability.

E. L. Taylor–Annan Photos

The Black and Tan Coonhound, a descendant of the English Talbot hound, hunts bear as well as 'coon.

The English Foxhound is perhaps bred to more rigorous standards than any other modern breed.

E. L. Taylor–Annan Photos

Annan Photos

The Beagle is the oldest indigenous British dog and one of the closest in type to the original scent hound. It has a remarkably loud, bell-like voice and a decidedly "gay" expression.

The Dachshund was once used to hunt badger and even wild boar. The modern breed occurs in short-, wire-, and long-haired varieties.

Annan Photos

The Basset Hound, an ancient breed of French origin, was derived from the St. Hubert hound and the old French bloodhound.

Annan Photos

PLATE 3

SPORTING GROUP

Sporting group breeds, like hounds, are hunting dogs. They differ from the latter in that they are used to locate and retrieve game, rather than hunt it down and kill it as most hounds do. Further, members of the sporting group are "bird dogs" and are seldom, if ever, used for hunting furred game. Several distinct types belong to the sporting group, each distinguished by its method of hunting.

POINTERS AND SETTERS. These two types of sporting dogs perform the function of locating game by pointing — freezing in position with neck and tail outstretched and one foreleg held curved and off the ground. Pointers and setters are rangy, long-limbed dogs. They differ mainly in that pointers are land hunters and are usually short-haired, while setters frequently enter the water in search of game and have long, flowing coats.

E. L. Taylor–Annan Photos

The German Shorthaired Pointer was developed early in the 20th century as an all-around dog that could point and also retrieve game.

The Irish Setter has fallen a victim to its outstanding traits — beauty and gay disposition. Its breeding is directed toward producing show dogs and it is little used for hunting.

Annan Photos

The Gordon Setter is an intelligent field dog and a loyal family pet. It is smaller but more heavily boned than other setters.

Thomson–Annan Photos

The English Setter may have been developed as long ago as the 16th century. It is thought to be one of the keenest bird dogs.

Annan Photos

The Pointer, as the simplicity of its name indicates, was the first breed developed especially for pointing game.
Annan Photos

PLATE 4

SPANIELS AND RETRIEVERS. Spaniels, although chiefly identified as retrievers of feathered game, are frequently trained as all-around gun dogs. They have broad, domed skulls; full, rounded eyes; long, pendent ears; and long, usually wavy coats. Retrievers are used principally to retrieve feathered game. They are closely related to the setters, from which the retriever breeds were probably derived.

E. L. Taylor–Annan Photos

The Labrador Retriever was developed in Newfoundland during the early 19th century. Its exceptionally heavy coat enables it to enter even icebound waters to retrieve game.

The Chesapeake Bay Retriever was developed in the United States by crossing flat- and curly-coated retrievers with rescued Newfoundlands that had been shipwrecked in transit to England.

E. L. Taylor–Annan Photos

The American Water Spaniel, which bears features of the Irish water spaniel and the curly-coated retriever, was probably developed by crossing those breeds with the English water spaniel.

Annan Photos

The English Springer Spaniel was named for its habit of "springing" from cover when flushing game.

Annan Photos

The Brittany Spaniel is very close in size and hunting style to the setters. The breed is naturally tailless.

E. L. Taylor–Annan Photos

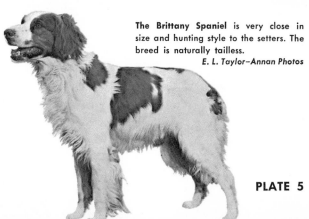

PLATE 5

NON-SPORTING GROUP

The non-sporting group is composed of several very different breeds which, with a few exceptions, are completely unrelated to one another. The group name indicates that the dogs are not used for sporting purposes. This is now generally true; but in their respective countries of origin, each of the breeds was put to some special use, and in several cases the dogs did function in some sporting capacity.

E. L. Taylor–Annan Photos

The Lhasa Apso is one of four native Tibetan dogs. Despite its small size it is extremely hardy and in its homeland was used as a guard inside dwellings. Its name means "bark lion sentinel dog."

The Boston Terrier, a cross between the English bulldog and the English terrier, was developed in the United States during the latter part of the 19th century.

E. L. Taylor–Annan Photos

E. L. Taylor–Annan Photos

The Poodle, although long the national dog of France, probably originated in Germany. It was first used as a circus performer and later to retrieve game from the water.

E. L. Taylor–Annan Photos

The Bulldog was developed in England for the cruel sport of bullbaiting. When that sport became illegal, breeders began to produce a gentle and well-mannered bulldog.

Annan Photos

The Chow Chow, the only dog with a black tongue, may be one of the basic dog breeds. It was used in China for hunting.

Annan Photos

The Dalmatian originated in the Austrian province of Dalmatia. It has been used for hunting, sheepherding, and guarding.

WORKING GROUP

Dogs of the working group are generally large, heavy-boned, and rugged. Included are some breeds of ancient origin (the great Dane, for example) and some of comparatively recent development. The members of the group may be divided into three major types: sheepdogs; fighting breeds, derived from ancient war dogs (their descendants are used as guard dogs and beasts of burden); and Eskimo dogs, breeds of extreme northern origin used for various purposes in the Arctic Regions.

Camera Clix

The St. Bernard was first mentioned as an Alpine guide and rescue dog in 1707, but the breed is known to date from at least the 10th century.

Annan Photos

The Doberman Pinscher was developed in Germany in the late 19th century. It is used primarily as a guard dog.

E. L. Taylor—Annan Photos

The Alaskan Malamute is one of the oldest Arctic sled dogs. It is powerful and has great endurance and a notably gentle disposition.

The Pembroke Welsh Corgi, a cattle herder, originated in Wales from stock brought there in 1107 A.D. by Flemish weavers.

Annan Photos

The Collie has long been identified with Scotland and sheepherding. It exists in a smooth- and in a rough-coated variety *(shown)*.

Annan Photos

PLATE 6 AND 7

TERRIER GROUP

Dogs of the terrier group were originally developed to corner foxes and badgers in their burrows. Later they were used to hunt all kinds of vermin. They are well suited to this activity by virtue of their generally small size, close-knit build, rough outer coat, and remarkable tenacity. Most terriers have longish heads, squared muzzles, and small, triangular ears.

Annan Photos
The Cairn Terrier is supposedly close in type to a terrier that once abounded on the Isle of Skye.

Annan Photos
The Smooth Fox Terrier was developed in England during the early 19th century, slightly before the familiar wire-haired variety.

E. L. Taylor–Annan Photos
The Border Terrier was developed in the English border country to track down the foxes that raided sheep herds.

The Airedale Terrier is the largest breed of its group. It is used as a guard and to hunt larger game than vermin.
E. L. Taylor–Annan Photos

The Bull Terrier, originally used in dogfighting, was developed by crossing a white English terrier with a bulldog.
Annan Photos

PLATE 8

DOG OBEDIENCE TRAINING

Teaching the dog to heel. The leash is held in the right hand and the dog walks at the trainer's left. The dog's movements are controlled by the left hand, which guides the leash.

Teaching the dog to turn left. If the dog fails to follow the trainer through a left turn, the trainer's right knee administers a gentle push to the dog's chest or neck.

Teaching the command "sit." With leash in right hand and dog at trainer's left, the dog's rump is pressed down. At the same time the vocal command "sit" is given.

Teaching the command "sit-stay." With dog in "sit" position the trainer's left hand is placed before the dog's muzzle. The vocal command "sit-stay" is then given.

Teaching "sit-stay" without the leash. When dog has mastered "sit-stay" while on the leash, this is repeated without the leash. The trainer holds leash in her right hand.

Teaching the command "stand-stay." The trainer stands facing the dog with leash held loosely. If the dog sits it is encouraged to stand by a gentle foot motion to chest.

Teaching the command "down." With the dog in the "sit" position, the trainer holds the leash in her right hand and steps on it with her right foot.

The trainer then gives the vocal command "down" and at the same time pulls the leash smoothly upward with both hands until the dog slides to the ground.

ASPCA

Advanced "down" command. When the dog has mastered the previous lesson, training is continued until the dog responds to a command "down" or to the hand signal shown.

foods provide these essential nutrients and have the added feature of being economical and easy to feed. Most dogs do well on a combination of commercial dog food and wholesome table scraps or left-overs, with added fat.

Careful grooming is another essential part of dog care. Grooming not only makes the dog look better, it also makes him feel better. Dogs should be groomed at least twice a week, and more often if practical. Too frequent bathing is not advisable since soap and water remove essential hair oils and dry out the coat. There is also the added hazard that the dog may become chilled if bathed during cold weather, and hence more susceptible to infection. During the grooming period special attention should be paid to the removal of external parasites such as fleas, lice, and ticks. Commercial preparations may also be applied to eradicate these pests which not only cause discomfort to the dog, but may also carry infection.

Diseases of Dogs. Dogs are subject to a variety of infectious and parasitic diseases. Puppies are especially susceptible to worm infestations. Hookworms enter the digestive tract and attach to the intestinal walls. Lethargy is an early symptom; later bloody diarrhea and anemia develop and, if untreated, death may ensue. Roundworms are another serious threat to young dogs. The eggs of these parasites are swallowed with contaminated food or water and hatch in the small intestine. The larval worms migrate through the intestinal walls to the lungs and are subsequently coughed up, swallowed, and return to the intestine. Symptoms include swelling of the abdomen, vomiting, and other digestive disturbances. Pneumonia often results if the lungs are massively invaded by roundworms. A variety of chemicals are available to treat roundworm, hookworm, and also tapeworm infestations. Rigid sanitary housing conditions help prevent parasitic infestations.

External parasites such as mites, ticks, fleas, and lice are a considerable nuisance to dogs. In addition to producing discomfort and causing unsightly skin lesions, some external parasites are carriers of infectious diseases. Particularly dangerous is Rocky Mountain spotted fever. This disease is transmitted by several species of ticks which are found on dogs. The dogs do not develop the disease themselves but humans may become infected by picking infected ticks from dogs. Fortunately, external parasites are fairly easy to eliminate. The dog should be treated with DDT, lindane, or rotenone insecticides, and the infested area should also be thoroughly disinfected.

Among the more serious infectious diseases affecting dogs are distemper, infectious hepatitis, rabies, and leptospirosis. Distemper is most commonly seen in dogs under one year of age who have not been immunized against the disease. It is caused by a virus organism and produces fever, loss of appetite, nasal discharge, and various digestive symptoms which appear about five days after exposure to the disease. The eyes also become light-sensitive and lymph nodes in the throat are swollen. As distemper progresses, the dog may develop nervous symptoms and a skin eruption. Death occurs within a few weeks. Very few dogs that develop distemper recover from it, although careful nursing, forced feeding, and antibiotic therapy may cure some infected animals. Several effective vaccines are available to prevent distemper and are usually administered routinely to young dogs, along with hepatitis and leptospirosis vaccines.

Canine hepatitis is a virus-caused disease of dogs. The virus is transmitted in the urine of apparently healthy dogs and may also be carried by lice infesting sick dogs. The disease attacks the liver, producing jaundice, and may also affect the tonsils and membranes of the eyes, mouth, and urinary tract. Most dogs recover from hepatitis if given supportive nursing care. Their quarters must be thoroughly disinfected to prevent spread of the disease to healthy animals. A vaccine is available to prevent canine hepatitis and is also moderately effective in treating the disease.

Rabies was once a serious threat to the dog population, but through extensive vaccination programs is no longer widespread. Unfortunately rabies has become established in many wild animal species—fox, squirrel, rabbit—where it is far more difficult to control. Rabies is caused by a virus which is transmitted by the bite of a diseased animal. Following an incubation period of from two weeks to three months an infected animal shows signs of restlessness and becomes timid or aggressively unfriendly. Paralysis and convulsions develop as the disease progresses and the animal usually dies within a week after the first symptoms appear. Because of the serious nature of rabies, dogs suspected of having the disease are usually quarantined, and if they show signs of the infection, they are destroyed.

Leptospirosis is a bacterial infection to which dogs are susceptible. The causative organisms are shed in the urine of sick animals. Early symptoms of the disease are lameness in the hind legs, constipation, loss of appetite, vomiting, and fever. Antibiotic therapy is quite effective in treating leptospirosis, particularly in its early stages. If untreated, congestion in the mucous membranes of eyes and mouth develops, the fever falls, and the animal shows signs of dehydration. In severe cases death may occur after five to ten days; in milder cases the dog may recover after a long convalescence.

Whenever a dog shows any signs of illness, prompt veterinary advice should be sought. The diagnosis and treatment of canine complaints is not a matter for the pet owner, however well-intentioned he may be. In addition, puppies should be brought to the veterinarian for a thorough examination and administration of all necessary preventive vaccines. Proper care and attention are a small price to pay for the satisfaction of owning as loving and attentive a companion as the dog.

Consult Leedham, C. G., *Care of the Dog* (1961); American Kennel Club, *Complete Dog Book* (rev. ed., 1961); McCoy, J. J., *Complete Book of Dog Training* (1962).

J. J. McCoy, Author, *The Dog Owners' Handbook*
See also articles on specific dog breeds.

DOG RACING

Dog racing is a sport in which greyhounds compete in pursuit of a mechanical rabbit. It is an outgrowth of one of the world's oldest sports, coursing. Dogs have been used for hunting and coursing since ancient times, but dog racing as it is known in the 20th century is comparatively new, dating from 1919.

Greyhounds leave the starting box at the beginning of a race at a Florida track.

Ewing Galloway

Evolution and Present Extent. In coursing, dogs pursue live game, and in early U.S. dog racing, whippets chased live rabbits. Whippets gave way to speedier greyhounds, and opposition by humane organizations to the use of live rabbits led to the evolution of the sport in its present form. An American, Oliver P. Smith, devised and first employed the mechanical rabbit, which runs along the inner or outer rail of the track and serves as an artificial lure. It was introduced at a track built by Smith in Emeryville, Calif., in 1919. Soon other tracks were built in Florida, Oklahoma, Illinois, and Kentucky. Of these pioneers, only the St. Petersburg, Fla., Kennel Club's Derby Lane was still in operation in the 1960's. At the same time, there were 32 other tracks in operation in the United States, each with legalized pari-mutuel wagering. Florida led with 17, and others were located in Massachusetts, Arkansas, South Dakota, Arizona, Montana, and Oregon.

About 6,000,000 persons attended U.S. dog races annually in the early 1960's, and wagered $250,000,000. Tax revenue in the states in which they are located amounted to approximately $20,000,000. Although privately operated, the sport is supervised by state racing commissions.

Greyhound racing also flourishes in England and Australia, and exists on a smaller scale in Ireland, Italy, Germany, France, China, Mexico, Cuba, and South Africa.

Breeding and Conduct of Sport. The average greyhound used in racing weighs 65 lb. and measures about 28 in. at the shoulders. Most are brindled or red. The dogs are bred throughout the United States, but mostly in the Midwest, where coursing is a major sport. Dogs employed in U.S. racing and coursing are registered with the National Coursing Association, which has headquarters in Abilene, Kan. In the 1960's there were about 20,000 dogs in competition, representing about 900 owners or kennels. Greyhounds usually begin to race at the age of 14–16 months; their competitive careers seldom span more than three years.

In the United States the sport is largely conducted at night. A program consists of 10 or 11 races, each involving 8 or 9 dogs. The dogs are assembled in a starting box (or "trap," as it is known in some countries), from which they are released as the mechanical rabbit passes it. Races range in length from 330 yd. to more than a mile; many are conducted over courses measuring 5/16 or 3/8 mi.

The dogs compete for purses, as in horse racing. Purses range up to $50,000 in U.S. competition. The average annual gross earnings of kennel owners is $15,000, though some owners have grossed as much as $65,000.

G. C. Moshier, St. Petersburg, Fla., Kennel Club
See also Coursing.

DOG SHOWS

Many thousands of dog owners find competition, recreation, and social outlets through dog shows, and some find profit through sales and breeding. The shows set superior dogs ahead of inferior ones in a form of competition judged not on competitive performance alone, as in field trials, but on conformation, soundness, and gait. Several hundred are held each year in most parts of the United States, usually on week ends.

There are three major kinds. The most widely attended are the all-breed shows, which range in size from 200 or 300 dogs to 3,000. The specialty show is a one-breed event held either separately or in conjunction with an all-breed show. The match show may be either all-breed or one-breed, but has no formal status and carries no championship points. It is usually a medium for introducing new dogs or new exhibitors to the ring. All the shows are conducted by clubs, usually with the help of professional superintendents.

The most important single organization in dog shows is the American Kennel Club (AKC), New York City. It conducts no shows but adopts and enforces uniform rules for them and serves as a guardian against fraud. AKC's other functions include registering dogs and maintaining a stud book. Admission of a breed to the stud book is tantamount to "recognition" in the United States, although the AKC dislikes the use of the word. In 1961 there were 115 such "recognized" breeds.

The leading American show in terms of age and prestige is that of the Westminster Kennel Club, conducted in Madison Square Garden, New York City. It was held for the first time in 1877. Limited benching space restricts entries to 2,500 dogs. The country's largest show is the International in Chicago, which in the early 1960's had entries totaling over 2,900 dogs.

Procedure in Judging. Whether an all-breed dog show is large or small, it is one of the most orderly of sports enterprises, despite an appearance of utter confusion to the first-time visitor. Every dog has an assigned role in his own

Evelyn M. Shafer

Judging entries in the working dog category during a show sponsored by the Westminster Kennel Club at Madison Square Garden in New York City.

class, and there is an inexorable progression from competition involving the smallest puppies to the award of the title "best in show." There are usually five regular classes in each sex—"puppy," "novice," "American-bred," "Bred-by-exhibitor," and "open"—and a class known as "specials" for which only champions are eligible.

When all the classes have been judged, one dog emerges as "best of breed." That dog becomes eligible to compete against all the other breed winners in his variety. There are six "variety groups": "sporting dogs," "hounds," "working dogs," "terriers," "toys," and "nonsporting dogs." When the judging of the variety groups is complete, each of the six winners is judged once more for the title "best in show."

More highly desired by many exhibitors than any single honor is the designation "champion." It is indicated by the prefix "Ch." before the dog's name, and means a dog has won out over a specified number of others of his kind in competition. To attain a championship, a dog must win 15 points under different judges and under specific conditions prescribed by the AKC. The number of dogs that must be defeated differs from breed to breed and is different in various parts of the country where shows are held. The highest number of points that can be gained in any one show is five. Some exceptional dogs win championship rating in only three major shows, but usually competition in many times that number is required.

JOHN RENDEL, New York *Times*

DOGBANE, common name for several species of herbaceous perennials of the genus *Apocynum*, in the dogbane family, Apocynaceae. Dogbane is native to North America. The plants grow to a height of about 3 ft., have oval, short-stemmed leaves, and bear bell-like white, pink, or greenish flowers. One species, *A. androsaemifolium*, is suited for garden borders. Its roots are used medicinally as are those of *A. cannabinum*, the so-called Indian hemp, whose fibrous bark is twisted into twine.

DOG DAYS, popular expression for the period of most oppressive summer weather. Its origin dates from ancient Mediterranean culture. The Egyptians and, later, the Greeks and Romans, attributed the annual return of sultry weather to the fact that the brightest star, Sirius (the Dog Star), was seen to rise with the sun during the hottest part of summer, presumably adding its heat to that of the sun. The belief that dogs are likely to go mad during dog days is a modern addition to this ancient superstition.

DOGE [dōj], title given to the highest officer of the Venetian and Genoese republics in medieval and early modern times. In Venice as early as 697 the people elected their own doge (or duke), who properly should have been appointed by the Byzantine Emperor. In medieval Venice he was elected from the nobility. The Venetian aristocracy feared tyranny and, though the doge served for life, his powers were reduced until he became little more than a government figurehead. In Genoa, the office of doge was first patterned after the Venetian model. After 1528, however, the Genoese doges were elected for only two-year terms. The French Revolution and the Napoleonic conquest of Italy brought an end (1797) to both offices.

DOGFISH, name for several small sharks of the family Squalidae, native to coastal waters of the western Atlantic and eastern Pacific oceans. The spiny dogfishes of the genus *Squalus* are named for the spinelike rays in their dorsal fins. Smooth dogfishes of the genus *Mustelus* lack these spines. Dogfishes rarely grow to more than 5 ft. in length and are not man-eaters. They feed on smaller fishes and on refuse dumped at sea. Unlike other sharks, which lay eggs encased in horny capsules, the young of dogfish develop within the mother's body, almost in the manner of mammalian young. Until the advent of synthetic vitamins dogfishes were caught in large numbers for their livers, rich in natural vitamin A. Today the dogfish is best known as a subject for dissection in comparative anatomy courses.

See also SHARK.

DOGGER BANK, an extensive shoal in the North Sea between England and Denmark. It is a fishing ground and has been the scene of several naval actions. In 1781 the English and Dutch fleets fought there and, in 1904, the Russian fleet, en route to the Far East, mistakenly fired on some English trawlers. This resulted in a diplomatic crisis. The most important naval action was the Battle of Dogger Bank, Jan. 24, 1915, during World War I, between units of the English and German fleets. The action resulted in the loss of a German cruiser, but the battle was inconclusive.

DOGMA, a Greek term originally meaning an opinion or, at times, a resolution or decree. Since the 16th century, it has been restricted to the theological sense of a doctrine revealed by God and proposed as such by the church with the guarantee of infallibility. The actuality signified is found in the New Testament, which clearly indicates that there are certain doctrines which are absolute and must be believed by all, because they come from God through Jesus Christ (for example, I Cor. 11:23ff., on the Eucharist). These make up the deposit of faith (I Tim. 6:20), which must be kept intact, since the church cannot teach another doctrine than that received (Gal. 1:8; II John 10). Dogmas are thus immutable in meaning; and a Christian is not free to accept or reject them at will, or to interpret them for himself.

IGNATIUS BRADY, O.F.M., Collegio di S. Bonaventura,
Florence, Italy

DOGON, a Western Sudanic people. They are farmers, ironworkers, and weavers. *See* AFRICA: *African Peoples.*

DOGTOOTH VIOLET, a small spring-blooming plant of the genus *Erythronium*, in the lily family, Liliaceae. Dogtooth violets are found in temperate regions throughout the world and many species are common wildflowers. The plants grow to a height of 1 ft., have long, tapering leaves, and bear nodding, lilylike flowers that may be white, pink, yellow, or lavender. Several horticultural varieties of *E. revolutum* have been developed and are well suited to garden cultivation.

DOGWOOD, common name for *Cornus*, a group of flowering trees and shrubs native to the temperate regions of North America, Europe, and Asia. Many are used in horticultural plantings for their attractive growth, brilliant autumn color, and display of flowers in the spring. There are about 26 species that are hardy in the east. *Cornus florida*, a tree with white or pink blossoms, can be seen in open woodlands and along parkways in the eastern United States. It flowers before the leaves appear. A Chinese species, *C. kousa*, flowers when the leaves are out. Cornelian cherry, *C. mas*, from Europe and Asia, is one of the earliest flowering trees. Its yellow flowers look like tiny golden bells and the scarlet fruits are edible. Red osier, *C. stolonifera*, grows to about 10 ft. The dark red stems are brilliant against the snow. It increases by underground stems and is usually found in damp places. *C. sanguinea*, from the Orient, has red-purple branches.

A dogwood tree in the spring.
(GOTTSCHO-SCHLEISNER)

Dogwood blossoms.
(GOTTSCHO-SCHLEISNER)

Leaves and fruits in the fall. (ROCHE)

The white, tan, or pink blossoms of dogwood appear in early spring, before the leaf buds have opened. By the time the leaves are fully developed, the flowers have wilted and fallen.

An extract made from the bark formerly was used to wash dogs, hence the name dogwood. The wood is very tough and is often used for tool handles.

ALYS SUTCLIFFE, Horticulturist, Brooklyn Botanic Garden

DOHA, capital and commercial center of the sheikdom of Qatar, located on the Persian Gulf. Its activities are pearling, fishing, metal working, and coastal trade. The town, surrounded by a crumbling wall, has several old forts, as well as a water distillation plant and some modern houses. Pop., about 10,000.

DOHNÁNYI [dō'nä-nyē], **ERNST VON** (1877–1960), Hungarian composer and pianist, born in Pressburg. First taught music by his father, a professor of mathematics, he studied mainly at the Royal Hungarian Academy of Music in Budapest, from which he was graduated in 1897. Thereafter he continued, throughout his life, to be engaged in a variety of musical vocations, as successful pianist, director of the Budapest Conservatory, and principal conductor of the Budapest Philharmonic. In 1949 he settled in the United States and became a member of the music faculty at Florida State University, Tallahassee. As a conservative composer, with little interest in Hungarian folk song, he represented a school of ideas in opposition to Bartók and Kodály. He is remembered today by the Suite in F♯ Minor, *Ruralia Hungarica* for orchestra, *Variations on a Nursery Song* for piano and orchestra, and some piano pieces. His works are marked by a Brahmsian romanticism and technical competence, but show little musical growth.

ALBERT WEISSER, Brooklyn College

DOISY [doi'zē], **EDWARD ADELBERT** (1893–   ), American biochemist who shared the Nobel Prize with Henrik Dam in 1943 for his work in isolating and synthesizing vitamin K, the blood-clotting vitamin. Among Doisy's other contributions are the isolation of the sex hormones theelin (1929) and dihydrotheelin (1936). His publications include *Sex Hormones* (1936) and, with Allen and Danforth, *Sex and Internal Secretions* (1939).

DOLABELLA [dŏl-ə-bĕl'ə], **PUBLIUS CORNELIUS** (c.70–43 B.C.), Roman politician. His career exemplified that of many unscrupulous and ambitious Romans of his day. He began as a follower of Pompey, but changed over to Caesar's side. He divorced his first wife and married Cicero's daughter, Tullia, in order to win Cicero's support. After Caesar's assassination he first joined the conspirators, then switched to Antony's side because it was to his advantage. After dubious activities in Syria, he was declared a public enemy by the senate, and committed suicide to escape capture.

DOLBEAU [dôl-bō'], industrial town of Quebec, Canada, located at the confluence of the Mistassini and Mistassibi rivers, in the Lake St. John region. It owes its existence to the construction of a large pulp-and-paper mill in 1926. Inc., 1926; pop., 6,052.

DOLDRUMS [dŏl'drəmz], climatic belt of calm air or of light, variable winds roughly parallel to the equator between the trade-wind belts of the Northern and Southern hemispheres. The doldrums cover about 9% of the ocean surface, but they are absent over land areas except near coasts. On the average this calm belt is centered about 5° (350 mi.) north of the equator, but it shifts with the sun as far as 20° N. lat. and 15° S. lat. Atmospheric pressure within the belt is lower than on either side, but it is about the same as the earth's average (1,013 millibars or 29.9 in. of mercury). Temperatures are warm but not extreme, usually near 80° F. Humidity is high, and tropical showers are frequent. Total annual rainfall is known only for coastal stations, where it is more than 80 in. Probably it is less over the open ocean.

FRANKLIN I. BADGLEY, University of Washington
See also HORSE LATITUDES; TRADE WINDS; WIND.

DOLE, SANFORD BALLARD (1844–1926), American lawyer and politician in Hawaii. Born in Honolulu to American missionaries, Dole attended Williams College, studied law in Boston, and returned to Hawaii to practice. After active leadership in the Hawaiian revolution of 1887 to obtain a more democratic constitution, Dole was associate justice (1887–93) of the supreme court under the resulting government. He opposed the Hawaiian revolution of 1893 that overthrew Queen Liliuokalani, but headed the resultant provisional government. He fought President Grover Cleveland's refusal to annex the islands to the United States and served (1894–98) as President of the Republic of Hawaii. Dole continued to press for annexation despite internal problems over Japanese immigration and counterrevolutionary activities. He was finally successful (1898) during President William McKinley's administration. Appointed first Governor of the Territory of Hawaii in 1900, Dole served until 1903, when he resigned to become (1904–15) U.S. district judge for Hawaii.

JAMES P. SHENTON, Columbia University

DOLIN, ANTON, original name Patrick Healey-Kay (1904–   ), English dancer and choreographer. Beginning his career with Diaghilev's Ballets Russes in 1921, he danced with it periodically until 1929. Jean Cocteau, Bronislava Nijinska, and Darius Milhaud composed *Le Train Bleu* for him in 1924. He also created roles in *Le Bal* and *Prodigal Son* by George Balanchine (1929) and the role of Satan in *Job* for the Camargo Society in London (1931). Later he was cofounder of the Markova-Dolin Ballet (1935–38). Subsequently he joined the newly founded Ballet Theater as dancer and choreographer, remaining until 1946. In 1950 he helped found the London Festival Ballet, serving as artistic director, choreographer, and dancer.

DOLL. Modern dolls are taken so for granted as a child's toy that their origins and antique usages are often forgotten. The word "doll" is derived from the Greek word *eidolon*, meaning "idol"; however, the modern usage of the word was not adopted until the middle of the 18th century. Among some societies, dolls of antiquity served a religious purpose and were thought to possess mystical powers. Archeologists have unearthed these small ancient objects of religious significance, many of which were found buried with the dead. These dolls, crude in outline,

A Japanese empress doll is fitted with an elaborately detailed costume. (BROOKLYN CHILDREN'S MUSEUM)

French lady doll (c.1870) with powdered hair. (PHILADELPHIA MUSEUM OF ART) Right, a 19th-century French Jumeau doll. (BROOKLYN CHILDREN'S MUSEUM)

were carved of stone, bone, or, less frequently, of clay. The doll has continued to hold a religious importance among certain present-day American Indian tribes and in the Orient, where annual doll festivals are held to celebrate the birthday of Buddha. Also of religious significance are the crèche dolls displayed in churches and homes at Christmas throughout the Christian world. In each case these dolls are not regarded as playthings.

Early Dolls. Dolls as toys have existed for centuries. These earliest toys, examples of which can now be found in many museums, have been discovered in the Near East and Greece. The child's imagination was exerted to its fullest, for these primitive dolls were a far cry from reality. Made of clay, stone, or bone, they rarely had any movable parts. When wood was used, it was possible to add flattened pieces for legs or arms by attaching them to the body with wooden pegs. The legless paddle doll of ancient Egypt was made from a single, flat piece of pottery or wood. These carved and painted dolls were placed in tombs to provide company for the dead.

European Dolls. An important step in dollmaking was to make the stiff wooden head with its painted features more realistic. Part of the head was hollowed out to provide narrow slits for eyes. Into these holes were inserted small pieces of opaque brown glass. The face was then covered with gesso, a plaster, and painted. Flax was used for hair, and the doll, dressed either in the brocades or cotton of the day, delighted the 18th-century child. Some of these dolls were brought from the Netherlands to colonial America. In France dolls dressed in the latest fashions were popular with the ladies of nobility as early as the 14th century. These elaborately costumed "fashion dolls" or "fashion babies" served to keep women informed of changing styles in dress.

In the 19th century other doll materials came into use: papier-mâché, wax, china, and porcelain. The first papier-mâché heads had painted features and hairdos molded in the fashion of the day. Consequently, there were dolls with the short uneven haircut of the days of the French Revolution, the highly coiffed style of the 1830's, or the severe parted center, tightly drawn with the small bun-at-the-back fashion of the 1860's. These were all lady dolls, not little girl or baby dolls. While the heads could be made of a variety of materials, the bodies were either of cloth or kid, filled with rags or sawdust, and with kid arms and legs.

Montanari, a doll manufacturer living in London in the 1840's, brought out a doll with a wax head into which he imbedded individual strands of human hair. The doll's hair could be arranged in any style. Glass eyes were inserted through an opening at the base of the head. By making more babylike features and using curved and dimpled wax arms and legs attached to the cloth-covered bodies, he achieved a more realistic baby doll than did the manufacturers of papier-mâché, china, or porcelain dolls.

German and French manufacturers were at the same time experimenting with china and bisque (unglazed clay). It was in the mid-19th century that the two well-known French dollmakers, Mme. Jumeau and Mme. Calixte Huret, created the most popular dolls. The Jumeau doll, with its delicately featured head that could be turned, was to continue as a favorite well into the 20th century. Few dolls made by Mme. Calixte Huret still exist, for the bodies of many of her creations were made of gutta-percha and completely disintegrated. Originally Mme. Huret's dolls were sold without clothes, so that the young French girls learning to sew could make dresses for their dolls. Her young public would not accept this, and, therefore, a whole new industry was born: doll-trunk makers, jewelers, bootmakers, milliners, dressmakers, umbrella makers—all creating miniature replicas of the adult world.

A great advance was made toward realism when the "pull" doll came into existence in the 1840's. This doll could be made to open or close her eyes, simply by pulling or pushing a wire which ran alongside the body (under her dress), through the neck, and into the head. Later methods made use of leaden weights attached to the back of the eyes, which forced them to open or close when the doll was moved from an upright to a prone position. Modern manufacturers have even created a winking doll.

American Dolls. By the 19th century Europe, particularly Germany, was well established as the world's dollmaking center. Up to this time American dolls had been either made by hand in the home or imported from

Europe. By mid-century, however, independent experiments had led to the development of American doll production on a commercial level. Ludwig Greiner, a German refugee who had settled in Philadelphia in the late 1840's, applied for the first U.S. patent for a doll's head of papier-mâché in 1858 and extended it in 1872. Charles Goodyear made use of his invention of hard rubber by turning out, among other things, a patented rubber doll. There quickly followed other patents for dolls' heads and bodies issued to manufacturers in and around Philadelphia. In 1862 a patent was sought for an "Autoperipatetikos, or Walking Doll." The lower part of the body held the mechanism from which protruded two metal feet to propel the doll. Fortunately hoopskirts were in fashion so that the machinery was well hidden. Not until the early 1900's was the shifting of weight of the doll's body utilized to produce a lifelike walking motion.

In 1873 Joel Ellis of Springfield, Vt., patented a jointed wooden doll. This doll was soon followed by dolls with ball joints, which gave greater motion to arms and legs. The bodies were made of composition, rather than of wood. In 1881 M. C. Lefferts and W. B. Carpenter were issued a patent for celluloid dolls.

There was still one thing lacking in all these dolls to make them realistic. Both in Europe and the United States attempts were being made to create a talking and crying doll. First, "mama" was the only uttered word; then a patent was issued for the Webber singing doll. Each body was marked with the song the doll sang. These dolls had wax faces, real hair, and kid bodies. A French doll, introduced in 1888, recited nursery rhymes in a childish voice. By the 1890's Thomas A. Edison had entered the talking doll market with his phonograph doll.

While rag dolls of grass and linen have been found in ancient Egyptian tombs, the origin of today's cloth dolls can perhaps be traced back more directly to pioneer deprivations and maternal ingenuity. Many of the dolls were crude, but others had charm enough to establish the rag doll as a permanent favorite among children. The dolls' features were greatly improved when oils for painting the face replaced stitching with different colors. Another advantage of the soft and pliable rag doll was that it could be made life-sized and yet be light enough for a child to carry.

Modern Dolls. Following World War I a radically new type of doll was created. In the 1920's the now famous German dollmaker, Kathe Kruse, began fashioning dolls so lifelike in expression and proportion that they closely resembled their human prototypes. Frau Kruse made the first of these dolls for her own children. Requests from friends followed, and eventually manufacturing of Kruse dolls was set up. Popular acceptance of these lifelike dolls came quickly and spread across Europe to the United States.

In the United States, Mrs. Grace Putnam Storey, using a real baby as a model, designed the Bye-lo baby doll. The famous German firm of J. D. Kestner made the heads for Mrs. Storey, and the dimpled arms and legs were also manufactured in Germany. Many copies were made of this popular doll, but none proved as successful as the original.

In the 1930's famous child figures were copied in the doll world—Shirley Temple, the child movie actress, and the Dionne quintuplets. In England there was the Princess Elizabeth, or Lillibet, doll.

No drastic changes were made in doll bodies until the invention of plastic, when the Dydee doll—which could drink her bottle and wet her diapers—was created. The Dydee doll was shortly followed by Tiny Tears. By using molded latex, a softer, skinlike texture was possible. Plastic filaments replaced expensive human hair. These filaments, inserted in the latex, could be washed and waved. The doll of today may also have a wardrobe which includes all the articles of feminine fashion.

Consult Fawcett, C. E., *Dolls: a Guide for Collectors* (1947); St. George, Eleanor, *The Dolls of Yesterday* (1948); Johl, Janet, *Still More About Dolls* (1950).

JANET PINNEY ARCHER, formerly Curator, Museum of the City of New York

DOLLARD DES ORMEAUX, ADAM (1635–60), French officer in Canada, hero of the battle of the Long Sault. At-

Hopi Indian religious effigy.
(TRAPHAGEN SCHOOL OF FASHION, N.Y.)

Old Susan doll of the 18th century.
(MUSEUM OF THE CITY OF NEW YORK)

A pair of ancient Peruvian dolls.
(TRAPHAGEN SCHOOL OF FASHION, N.Y.)

American rag doll.
(ESSEX INSTITUTE)

tached to the Montreal garrison soon after his arrival in Canada at the age of 23, he set out to ambush Iroquois fur trappers with 16 other Frenchmen and a few Indians. Surprised himself by a large band of Iroquois at the foot of the Long Sault, Dollard and his party, protected only by an old Indian palisade, fought off attacks for a week. All in the French party were killed, but their valiant defense is believed to have discouraged large-scale Indian attacks and thus promoted peace for the colony.

DOLLFUSS [dôl'foos], **ENGELBERT** (1892–1934), Austrian statesman. A peasant's son who had studied law and served with distinction as an officer in World War I, Dollfuss worked his way up the ladder of public administration during the postwar period until he was appointed federal Minister of Agriculture and Forestry. Dollfuss was a member of the Christian Socialist party, which represented a clerical, conservative, and nationalist point of view, but he belonged to its moderate wing. When the state elections of Apr., 1932, brought a rise of Austrian National Socialist (Nazi) strength that cut into Christian Socialist support, the ensuing government crisis was resolved with the appointment (May, 1932) of Dollfuss as Federal Chancellor. With his parliamentary support rendered ever more uncertain by pro-Germanism on one side and Socialism on the other, he had recourse to more authoritarian government. Aligning himself with Italian dictator Benito Mussolini in foreign affairs and the ultranationalists at home, Dollfuss prohibited Nazi activity, dissolved the Socialist party after its uprising of Feb., 1934, and on May 1, 1934, proclaimed a new corporative constitution—labeled "clerical-fascist" by its critics—that permitted neither Parliament nor parties except Dollfuss' own Patriotic Front organization. He was murdered by Austrian Nazis on July 25, 1934.

LEONARD KRIEGER, Yale University

DOLLIER DE CASSON [dô-lyā' də kà-sôN'], **FRANÇOIS** (1636–1701), French Sulpician priest and explorer in Canada. Born in Brittany of a noble family, he had served in the French cavalry before entering the Seminary of St. Sulpice in 1657. He went to Montreal in 1666 and that year accompanied the Marquis de Tracy's expedition against the Mohawks. He then served as chaplain at Fort Ste. Anne. In 1669 Dollier and René de Galinée voyaged through the Great Lakes, accompanied part way by the Sieur de La Salle, seeking a route to the Mississippi, knowledge of which they had from the western Indians. After enduring great hardship they returned to Montreal via Lake Nipissing and the Ottawa River. In 1671 Dollier became superior of the Sulpician seminary in Montreal. His valuable early history of Montreal was translated by Ralph Flenley (1928).

DÖLLINGER [dûl'ïng-ər], **JOHANN JOSEF IGNAZ VON** (1799–1890), church historian, theologian, and outstanding scholar. He refused to accept the dogma of papal infallibility defined by the Vatican Council and was excommunicated in 1871. Without subscribing to all their tenets, he became leader of the Old Catholic churches, among whom he worked for a reunion of the separated Christian denominations; but he was never reconciled with Rome.

DOLLIVER, JONATHAN PRENTISS (1858–1910), U.S. Senator. Dolliver was born near Kingwood, W. Va. (then in Virginia), drifted west, and sought a legal career in Iowa. Soon he was widely known as an exceptionally effective Republican orator. The party organization sent him to Congress (1889–1900) and then to the Senate (1900–10). Dolliver's last years were marked by conflict between his conservative loyalties and his awareness of need for reform. He championed railroad regulation and tariff reduction and was about to challenge conservative control of his party in Iowa when he suddenly died.

DOLL'S HOUSE, A, play (1879) by the Norwegian dramatist Henrik Ibsen. A pioneering piece in realistic social drama, it relates the ordeal of a woman who, after the resolution of a family crisis, rebels against her role as little more than that of a pampered doll. Her ultimate decision in abandoning her husband and children, to seek a fuller

The Raggedy Ann doll. (GEORGENE NOVELTIES, INC.)   Two modern lifelike dolls. **Below left,** one of the famous Kathe Kruse dolls. (TRAPHAGEN SCHOOL OF FASHION) **Right,** curly-haired Shirley Temple doll. (IDEAL TOY CORP.)   Dydee doll with her own feeding kit. (EFFANBEE DOLL CORP.)

personal identity, created a storm of protest in Ibsen's time. The play still retains an important place in the modern repertoire, though women's rise in status has blunted its original capacity for shock.

DOLOMITE [dŏl'ə-mīt], a calcium-magnesium carbonate mineral, $CaMg(CO_3)_2$. It is found occasionally in rhombohedral crystals, but commonly it is granular and massive, sometimes forming extensive beds of sedimentary rock like limestone. It is usually white, yellow, or gray. Millions of tons of dolomite are quarried annually for building stone, concrete aggregate, road stone, and railroad ballast. It also has specific uses as a fertilizer, in the manufacture of glass and paper, as a blast-furnace flux, as a refractory, and as a source of magnesium.

Properties: Crystal System, Trigonal; *Hardness* (Mohs' Scale), 3½–4; *Density*, 2.85.

See also CRYSTALLOGRAPHY; MINERALOGY; ROCKS.

DOLOMITES, Alpine mountain group in Alto Adige, Italy, between the Isarco and Piave rivers. The name is that of the rocks of which they are largely composed, and which are famous for their striking colors at sunrise and sunset. The highest peak is Marmolada (10,964 ft.). The Dolomites are favored by tourists; Cortina d'Ampezzo is the largest and most famous resort.

DOLORES [də-lôr'əs] **RIVER,** river of Colorado and Utah, in the Canyon section of the Basin and Range province. It rises in the San Miguel Mountains (a range of the southern Rocky Mountains) and flows southwest and then northwest, crossing the Colorado-Utah border to join the Colorado River a few miles inside Utah. The country it traverses is arid, but because the river flows through a gorge, 2,000 ft. deep at its mouth, it cannot be used for irrigation. Length, 250 mi.

DOLPHIN [dŏl'fĭn], name for several small whales, or cetaceans, known for their social nature and intelligence. The common dolphin, *Delphinus delphis*, reaches a length

The bottle-nosed dolphin, a small, toothed whale, was once hunted for its oil and hide.

Allan D. Cruickshank—National Audubon Society

of 9 ft. and has a tapering, 6-in. beak. It has numerous conical teeth that are very effective for catching slippery fish. Schools of dolphin often accompany ships for considerable distances, swimming at speeds of 20 knots or more. The bottle-nosed dolphin, *Tursiops truncatus*, common in Atlantic waters, often number 100 to a school. They have been exhibited in aquariums with marked success. At Marineland Studios in Florida these dolphins, at the signal of a bell, will leap high from the water to take fish from the lips of the trainer. They have also been trained to leap through a hoop held well above the water's surface. While most cetaceans are inhabitants of salt water, several species of dolphin ascend rivers for hundreds of miles, and *Sotalia*, a Nigerian dolphin, appears to be an exclusively fresh-water animal.

W. J. HAMILTON, JR., Cornell University

See also WHALE.

DOLTON [dôl'tən], suburb 18 mi. south of Chicago, Illinois. Although primarily residential, it is crossed by many railroads and contains freight yards of the Chicago and Eastern Illinois Railroad. Steel products are manufactured here. Settled, 1832; inc., 1892; pop. (1950) 5,558; (1960) 18,746.

DOMAGK [dō'mäk], **GERHARD** (1895–1964), German pathologist and bacteriologist. While director of the I. G. Farben experimental laboratory he conducted investigations on the therapeutic effects of the azo dyes and discovered the antibacterial properties of the dye prontosil red. He was awarded the Nobel Prize for this work in 1939, but declined the award because of the Nazi government's ban on acceptance. Domagk served as editor of the *Zeitschrift für Krebsforschung*, the German journal of cancer research.

DOMBEY AND SON, novel by Charles (John Huffam) Dickens (q.v.).

DOME, a roof form, generally hemispherical, that covers a circular, square, oblong, or polygonal area. Domes of varied shapes and materials have been used since prehistoric times, a traditional religious belief being that the domical shape symbolized the abode of the dead in an afterlife. This idea is associated with primitive ancestral huts of reeds and branches with roofs of pointed bulbous form, and caused these shrines to be rebuilt of permanent materials on a grander scale. The dome was not used in secular architecture until the building of the Roman baths at Pompeii, about 100 B.C.

Although the ancient Mesopotamians have been credited with the first masonry domes, this theory is unconvincing because their primitive domical structures were based on corbeling, the technique of building successive horizontal layers of brick or stone so that each projects slightly beyond the one below. The earliest true dome undoubtedly appeared first in Roman architecture. Roman domical construction culminated in the Pantheon (completed 124 A.D.), roofed by a magnificent hemispherical vault of reinforced concrete that is still intact. The largest dome in existence (142 ft. in diameter, 5 ft. greater than the dome of St. Peter's), it rests on the cylindrical

The Pantheon in Rome, as it appeared in the 18th century, by the Italian artist Giovanni Paolo Panini (below).
National Gallery of Art, Samuel H. Kress Collection

Diagram shows how pendentives are used to support a circular dome over a square structure (below).

Diagram of Hagia Sophia (below) shows the structural system that supports the 108-ft. dome. The dome is omitted to reveal the pendentives below.

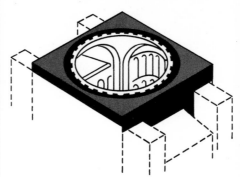

Marburg—Art Reference Bureau
Hagia Sophia in İstanbul, Turkey (above).

walls of a circular structure and, even at the time of its construction, involved no new structural principles.

The much more difficult problem of supporting a dome above a square or polygonal structure was also tackled by the Romans, who by trial and error during the next three centuries attained a partial solution, as in the Tomb of Galla Placidia at Ravenna (5th century). The next logical step was the creation of pendentives, the curved triangular pieces of masonry placed at the corners of square or polygonal structures to effect the transition to the circular dome. Achieved by Byzantine builders in Hagia Sophia (532–37 A.D.), the pendentive was passed on by them to subsequent architects. This inaugurated a new era in dome construction, determining not only the future evolution of the Byzantine style but also profoundly influencing Muslim building.

During the Renaissance the dome was popular, generally being elevated above the pendentives on a cylindrical drum pierced by windows. Brunelleschi's dome of Florence Cathedral (1420–34) was built of two concentric masonry shells, connected and strengthened by stone ribs. Michelangelo followed the same scheme for the dome of St. Peter's in Rome, which was completed toward the end of the 16th century, after his death. Christopher Wren in St. Paul's at London (completed 1710) used three concentric shells for greater strength and a more imposing external design. Although the masonry dome was introduced to the United States in the Massachusetts state capitol in 1795, the dome of the National Capitol at Washington, rebuilt during the Civil War, is of cast iron.

EMERSON H. SWIFT, Columbia University

DOME, in geology, a topographic feature shaped like an inverted cup. Half Dome in Yosemite National Park,

California, is a partially eroded granite dome, and Stone Mountain, Georgia, typifies the many granite domes of the Appalachian Mountains. A nearly circular anticline, or upwarp of layered rocks, is also called a dome. Such structural domes may not show at the surface because they have been buried by younger rocks. Structural domes are sought by geologists because many of them are traps for petroleum or natural gas.

DOMENICHINO [dō-mä-nē-kē'nō], IL, real name Domenico Zampieri (1581–1641), Italian painter. Born in Bologna, he studied there in the Carracci workshop, and soon after 1600 went to Rome to assist Annibale Carracci in the decoration of the Farnese Palace. Later he carried out many independent fresco commissions for Roman churches and other buildings. He is also known for his altarpieces ("Last Communion of St. Jerome," Vatican) and mythological paintings ("Hunt of Diana," Borghese Gallery, Rome). Domenichino in 1630 went to Naples to execute decorations in the cathedral. Despite persecution by jealous rivals, which forced him in 1634 temporarily to flee the city, he worked there until his death.

DOMENICO VENEZIANO [dō-mä'nē-kō vä-nā-tsyä'nō], real name Domenico di Bartolomeo da Venezia (fl. about 1438–61), Italian painter, who was born in Venice but worked mainly in Florence. One of the most gifted artists of an artistically rich age, he is distinguished from his Florentine contemporaries by his greater interest in color and by a lyrical quality that permeates his compositions. Notable among his few surviving works are an altarpiece "Madonna and Child with Four Saints" (Uffizi, Florence), its five panel paintings from the base now in Berlin, Cambridge, England, and Washington, D.C. (National Gallery); and a damaged fresco of the "Virgin and Child" in the National Gallery, London.

DOMESDAY [dōōmz'dā] **BOOK,** a record of lands in England compiled (1086) during the reign of William I. This survey covers all England, except the northernmost counties, the city of London, and some other cities and towns. As a detailed record of landownership, of classes of persons living on the land, of mills, livestock, and produce, the *Domesday Book* is unparalleled in the history of medieval Europe. The compilers of the book had before them the answers to standard questionnaires that royal officials had presented to juries of local men. William's object in ordering the inquiry seems to have been to make an inventory of the lands and goods available in his kingdom, to know what services his feudal tenants owed him, and to discover the prospects for further royal taxation on the wealth of the kingdom.

FREDERICK G. MARCHAM, Cornell University

DOMESTICATION OF ANIMALS. *See* FOOD; NEOLITHIC AGE.

DOMESTIC SYSTEM, also called the cottage or putting-out system, a mode of manufacture that preceded and coincided with the emerging factory system of 18th-century England and other European countries. Under it, raw materials were distributed to workmen who labored at home at piece rates. The system was advantageous for the entrepreneur: it minimized his investment and relieved him of supervisory problems. Many textile fortunes were founded by merchants who bought wool to be carded, spun, and woven by domestic workers and who then sold the finished cloth. The system was also attractive for the worker. He worked at home with his family, and although his life was regulated by the seasons and daily exigencies, his time was his own. Such a life at least had the appearance of freedom.

As the system matured, however, pressure on the worker grew. Rates of payment dropped; delivery dates advanced; and speed plus long hours, even for children, became necessary. Faulty goods brought fines instead of payment; many workers had to pay transportation charges. Market demand fluctuated, and whole families worked around the clock for days, then waited, exhausted and often ill, for another consignment. The upper class, with little understanding, drew contrasts between the "idle" and the "industrious" poor.

The domestic system declined as factories became more efficient and management developed techniques calling for total, integrated control of men, machines, material, and markets. Such control was impossible under the domestic system. In all industrial countries, including the United States, some "putting out" continues. Many marginal garment manufacturers use the system because piecework at home requires little equipment.

SAMUEL E. GLUCK, Baruch School of Business and
Public Administration, City College of New York

DOMICILE, in strict legal terminology, differs from residence. The former is a person's permanent home, whereas the latter signifies temporary presence in a place. To acquire a domicile of choice, physical presence must be coupled with an intention to remain there permanently. Mere absence does not cause a person to lose his domicile.

DOMINANCE HIERARCHY, a concept in animal behavior that refers to the tendency of group-living animals to arrange themselves into a rank order. By knowing their status in the order and accepting this organization, animals minimize aggression. Group life with very little conflict is thereby made possible.

T. Schjelderup-Ebbe made the fundamental observation that the members of a bird flock recognize each other as individuals. In a small group of hens, which have been living together without crowding, there is very little aggressive behavior. If a competitive situation is set up by providing a little pile of grain, the so-called alpha animal will come to the food and start to peck. Should another animal try to peck some of the grain, the alpha individual will threaten and eventually chase it away. If the alpha hen is removed, another hen immediately takes her place and, apparently by common consent, is allowed to dominate the source of food in the same manner. Schjelderup-Ebbe has shown that the group consists of individuals who form a hierarchy of procedure—in this case for who gets a chance to feed first. Such procedure in competition is called behavioral dominance, and it has been shown to play a role in various degrees and forms in all social behavior of animals. In chickens the hierarchy is clear-cut and linear; alpha pecks all other hens, beta pecks all hens except alpha, and so on. In other animal species the organization may be more subtle and may vary for different situations.

It is important to realize the interaction between dominance and aggression on the one hand, and dominance and territoriality on the other hand. Dominance behavior has a role in minimizing aggression, thereby preventing the waste of energy which would occur if the strongest animal at all times had to secure his part of the spoils by actually fighting off all the others. However, a subordinate individual animal sometimes needs freedom from the restraints of those higher on the totem pole, such as during reproduction. Nature has allowed for this by providing him with the urge to occupy and defend a territory. In cats, for example, the tomcats show a definite rank order for acquiring mates in the mating season, but even a low-ranked tomcat is respected by the dominants on his home ground.

Consult Schjelderup-Ebbe, T., "Social Behavior in Birds" in *Handbook of Social Psychology,* ed. by C. Murchison (1935).

ARISTIDE HENRI ESSER, M.D.
See also AGGRESSION; TERRITORIALITY.

DOMINIC [dŏm'ə-nĭk], **ST.** (1170–1221), founder of the mendicant order of preachers known as Dominicans. Born in Calarogo, Castile, he was the second son of Felix and Joanna de Guzman. Little is known of his childhood, except that it was spent in the comfort and security of a wealthy home under the counsel and direction of his saintly mother (who was herself beatified by Pope Leo XII in 1828). In 1177 his formal education began under the direction of his uncle, archpriest of Gumiel. At 14

Dominic decided on the priesthood and went to the university at Palencia, where he was well known for his keen intellect, charity, and devotion to prayer. Ordained in 1194, he was chosen by Diego de Azevelo, Bishop of Osma, to reform the canons of the Cathedral church. Under Dominic the life was well regulated, allowing time for prayer and study. In 1203 Diego and Dominic were sent on a mission for King Alfonso IX of Castile, at the conclusion of which they went to Rome to seek permission from Innocent III to go to Asia as missionaries. Permission was denied, and Innocent sent them instead to combat the Albigensian heresy in Languedoc.

Early in 1205 they arrived at Montpellier amid new successes by the heretics. The Albigensians, known for their austere lives, were much impressed by the greater asceticism of Dominic and his friends, who engaged the Albigensian doctors in public debate. In 1206, with the permission of the Bishop of Toulouse, Dominic founded a religious house for women at Prouille to accommodate converts from the heresy. Intended as a house of prayer and penance, it was the first house of the cloistered Dominican religious, called the Second Order of St. Dominic. In 1208 a religious war broke out between the heretics and Simon de Montfort. Dominic became theological adviser to de Montfort. In this capacity, he was asked merely to judge the orthodoxy of the accused.

Preaching became increasingly important to Dominic, and he saw it as his life's work. He conceived of an order of preachers who would combat the enemies of the church. In Italy St. Francis of Assisi and his followers had already shown the practicality of the religious who were not restricted to monasteries. An itinerant order of preaching friars would answer a great need of the church, especially in France. But it was not until Apr. 25, 1215, that the first religious house for men was established, at Toulouse. It was still only a local diocesan organization of preachers, so Dominic went to Rome seeking papal approbation. Innocent III refused permission to establish a new order and counseled Dominic to adopt a rule of life from among those already approved. Returning home, Dominic found his group increased by 10 new members, and he adopted the rule of St. Augustine with certain additions. These were written down and became the *Consuetudines*, the first part of the Dominican constitutions. When Innocent III died in 1216, Dominic went to Rome again and Honorius III gave official approval to the Order of Preachers on Dec. 22, 1216. Dominic remained in Rome that winter and was so eloquent in his preaching that he was made Master of the Sacred Palace, or Pope's Theologian, a post held by a Dominican ever since.

Upon returning home, Dominic resolved to disperse his 16 followers, which he did on Aug. 17, 1217. Many thought this a rash move for so young an order, but Dominic remained firm. They were to go into the cities and to the universities to combat theological error wherever they found it. During this difficult time the austerity of Dominic's life increased, for he knew that success in action was dependent on prayer and sacrifice. By 1220 the order had grown so large that Dominic called a General Chapter at Bologna in May, when the Dominican constitutions were decided upon. Dominic himself presided over a second Chapter, held in May, 1221. He was by now spent by his

St. Dominic, founder of the Dominican Order, as portrayed by the Italian artist Titian. (ALINARI—ART REFERENCE BUREAU)

tremendous labors and the austerity of his penances, but the fruits of his labors were everywhere visible. There were now 60 convents, divided into eight provinces: Spain, Toulouse, France, Lombardy, Rome, Provence, Germany, and England. Dominic died in Bologna on Aug. 6, 1221. He was canonized on July 13, 1234 by Pope Gregory IX, and his feast was set for Aug. 4.

Consult Jarrett, Bede, *Life of St. Dominic* (1924); Mandonnet, P. F., *St. Dominic and His Work* (1944); Dorcy, Sister Mary Jean, O.P., *Saint Dominic* (1959).

RICHARD J. WESTLEY, Barat College

See also DOMINICANS.

DOMINICA [dämə'nēkə], largest island of the Lesser Antilles group, in the Caribbean Sea. The island is 29 mi. long and 16 mi. wide. Of volcanic origin, it reaches 4,747 ft. in the peaks of Morne Diablotin. The land is fertile but farming is limited to the coast. Much of the interior is uninhabited and little explored. Dominica is noted for the wild beauty of its mountains. Ravines, waterfalls, craters and crater-lakes, geysers, hot springs, and torrential rivers lend the island a "lost world" atmosphere. The mostly Negro population (with a few remnant Carib Indians) cultivate tree crops. Columbus named the island for the day it was discovered, Sunday, Nov. 3, 1493 (Lat. *dies dominica*, "the Lord's Day"). Carib Indians, the French, and British struggled for control of it for 300 years. The British won out in 1805. Dominica is today a self-governing West Indian State in Association with Great Britain. Roseau is the capital and chief port. Area, 304.7 mi.; pop., 66,020.

MELVIN MORRIS, New York State University College

DOMINICAN REPUBLIC

AREA	Approx. 18,700 sq. mi.
ELEVATION	
Highest point (Pico Duarte)	10,417 ft.
Lowest point (Lake Enriquillo)	144 ft. below sea level
POPULATION	Approx. 3,014,000
PRINCIPAL LANGUAGE	Spanish
UNIT OF CURRENCY	Peso
NATIONAL ANTHEM	*Himno nacional,* words by Emilio Prud'homme, music by José Reyes
CAPITAL	Santo Domingo
PRINCIPAL PRODUCTS	Cocoa, coffee, sugar, tobacco; bauxite, iron, nickel, salt; beverages, cement, foodstuffs, textiles, tobacco products

DOMINICAN REPUBLIC [də-mĭn′ĭ-kən] (Span. **REPÚBLICA DOMINICANA**), republic occupying the eastern two-thirds of Hispaniola, the second-largest island in the Caribbean Sea. Strategically situated between Cuba and Puerto Rico, Hispaniola lies in the deep-water approaches to Panama from the Atlantic.

The Land

Physical Features. Bisected by the great east-west Cordillera Central, the Dominican Republic also has a lower mountain range to the north, the Cordillera Septentrional. Between these two ranges lies a long and extremely fertile valley, known as the Cibao. Another extensive area of plain, also noted for its agricultural activity, occupies the southeastern coastal region. The eastern edge of the country also has areas of desert. In the extreme southwest the mountains of the Sierra de Baoruco rise to more than 5,300 ft. The western part of the Dominican Republic contains both the highest mountain in the West Indies (Pico Duarte, 10,417 ft., in the Cordillera Central) and the lowest lake (Enriquillo, 144 ft. below sea level.) Many rivers rise in the Cordillera Central, the most important of which are the Yaque del Sur, the Yaque del Norte, and the Yuna.

Climate, Vegetation, and Wildlife. Although the Dominican Republic lies in the tropics, the climate of the northern coast is moderated by trade winds. Temperatures throughout the country range from 65° F. to 85° F. in winter and from 73° F. to 95° F. in summer. Frost is quite frequent in the high sierras in winter. Rainfall varies greatly; eastern regions receive an average of about 53 in. a year, but less than 20 in. fall in the west. Similarly, vegetation ranges from the desertlike growth of the inner plains near Lake Enriquillo to the rain-forest conditions of the mountain slopes. Native mahogany trees grow at middle altitudes, and in the higher mountains giant West Indian pines and thick fern beds predominate. The country's many birds include pigeons, doves, ducks, coots, flamingos, and roseate spoonbills. The rich offshore fishing grounds are visited by marlin and tuna, as well as by groupers, bonitos, and other tropical fish.

The People

Ethnology and Religion. The Dominican Republic, as the historic port of entry to the New World, represents a mingling of many races. About 60% of its population is West Indian, with traces of Amerindian as well as Caucasoid and Negroid ancestry. About 28% of the population is Caucasoid and about 11% Negroid. A striking feature of the Dominican people is the extent to which they regard themselves as a "white" nation with a European culture, in contrast to their Negro neighbors in Haiti. The language of the Dominican Republic is Spanish; near the Haitian border, however, many persons also speak French. A Spanish-French patois, mixed with African elements, is also often heard.

Roman Catholicism is the state religion, and concordats with the Holy See date back to 1884. Religious freedom prevails and there are a number of Protestant churches and Jewish synagogues.

Principal Cities and Social Conditions. The largest city is the capital, Santo Domingo. Formerly called Ciudad Trujillo, it is the administrative, commercial, and financial

ECONOMIC RESOURCES OF THE DOMINICAN REPUBLIC

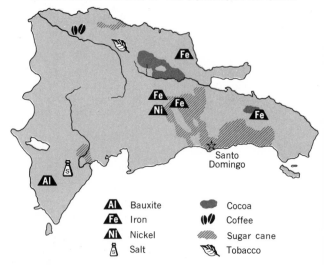

Al Bauxite		Cocoa	
Fe Iron		Coffee	
Ni Nickel		Sugar cane	
S Salt		Tobacco	

Railroad facilities on a large banana plantation ensure the rapid shipment of the fruit.

hub of the country. Santiago is the next largest city and the principal center for the interior.

Despite a gradual transition toward urbanization, about 68% of the Dominican population still lives in rural communities. Government interest in housing and resettlement has guided the urbanization trend through building and through attempts at slum clearance. Home ownership of low-cost dwellings, through government financing, is the general pattern of urban development. An important step toward social stability in rural areas was the establishment of the landless as small farmers, grouped around co-operative marketing stations called *colonias*, which also provide technical aid. Social assistance in the form of old age, maternity, disability, and sickness insurance is financed jointly by the government, employer, and employee.

Violence and political disorder have traditionally characterized Dominican national life. However, the stability achieved after 1930, despite its repressive character, produced well-educated, industrious citizens with a high level of social maturity.

Education and Cultural Life. Free and compulsory education from the age of 7 to 14 years has virtually eliminated illiteracy among the younger generation of Dominicans. The University of Santo Domingo, founded in 1538 and the oldest university in the New World, has an enrollment of about 4,000. Dominicans enjoy numerous libraries, and there are a number of national parks. There are also a National Fine Arts gallery, a theater academy, a symphony orchestra, a conservatory of music, and a school of fine arts.

Music is the favorite form of artistic expression, and the 19th and 20th centuries produced many Dominican composers, including Juan Bautista Alfonseca, José Reyes, José de Jesús Ravelo, Juan Francisco García, and Luis Emilio Mena. The 20th-century author and historian Manuel A. Peña Batlle achieved international repute. The Dominican Archives in Santo Domingo contain many fine manuscripts and studies of the country's history.

The Economy

Economic Conditions and Industry. Diversification of the economy, a policy of full employment, and strict controls imposed by President Trujillo Molina resulted in a

Market place in Santo Domingo, where produce is sold.

Transporting sugar cane to a refinery. The cane in each freight car yields about 10,000 lb. of sugar.

striking economic growth. Living standards rose, the gross national product increased, the country's heavy debt was cancelled, and a favorable balance of trade was achieved.

Increasing industrial production caters to the domestic market and includes food-processing, textiles, cement, tobacco products, beer, and tiles. Many industries are aided by both government and private investment. Mining is a small industry and produces chiefly iron, bauxite, salt, nickel, and some petroleum.

Agriculture. From the 1930's an effort was made to exploit more of the country's arable land, and a marked improvement in agriculture followed. However, much of the land is still held in large estates. Sugar is the most valuable single commodity of the economy, but its relative importance is declining. Tobacco, coffee, cocoa, and bananas are also grown in sufficient quantity for export, as are beef cattle, although the livestock industry is still young. Corn, beans, and other crops are grown for domestic use, and rice no longer has to be imported.

Transportation and Foreign Trade. The country has less than 900 mi. of railroad, most of which are privately operated by sugar mills and banana plantations. There are also about 3,000 mi. of roads. Santo Domingo is the hub of the internal transportation system, the country's major air terminal, and its principal port. San Pedro de Macorís, La Romana, Barahona, and Puerto Plata are the more important of ten other open ports. Foreign trade is conducted principally with the United States. Sugar is the principal export commodity, and machinery, foodstuffs, and fuel oils are the leading imports.

Government

Constitution. The country is a republic. Its constitution was adopted provisionally in Dec., 1961, and amended in Sept., 1962. It was replaced in July, 1963, by a new constitution, but re-adopted after a *coup d'état* two months later.

Political Parties. The only government-sanctioned political party after 1930 was the Partido Dominicano (Dominican Party), which was led by Generalissimo Rafael Leonidas Trujillo Molina and which, in fact if not in theory, was responsible for all political appointments. From time to time, however, and particularly after 1961, a number of opposition factions became prominent. These included the New National Civic Union; the Fourteenth of June Movement, which was named for an abortive revolt against Trujillo in 1959; and the Dominican Revolutionary party, founded in exile in 1939.

The Columbus House in Santo Domingo, where the famous explorer is believed to have stayed.

Charles Perry Weimer

INDEX TO DOMINICAN REPUBLIC GENERAL REFERENCE MAP   Pop. 3,014,000

DOMINICAN REPUBLIC

SCALE OF MILES

© C. S. HAMMOND & Co., Maplewood, N. J.

History

The Colonial Period. Discovered by Christopher Columbus on his first voyage in 1492, the island of Hispaniola was the site of La Isabela, the first European settlement in the New World, and of the first mint, established after the discovery of gold. The island was soon transformed into the bread basket of the Spanish New World, supplying both invasion expeditions and the intercontinental shipping trade. Production from the fields of the native Indians was supplemented by a plantation system producing cattle, cotton, sugar, and tobacco. Negro slaves were introduced in the first decade of the 16th century.

This propitious beginning was halted during the 17th and 18th centuries, however. The population became greatly depleted as settlers deserted the island for the greater wealth of the Central and South American mainland. Repeated attacks by British, Dutch, and French buccaneers also contributed to the virtual abandonment of much of the colony. In 1697, by the Treaty of Ryswick,

Spain ceded the western third of Hispaniola, now Haiti, to France, and during the following century the remaining Spanish colony, then known as Santo Domingo, became characterized by general economic and social stagnation. In 1795 the Treaty of Basel reunited the two parts of the island, but under the French flag.

Santo Domingo served as a base for the French armies during the Napoleonic Wars, and after 1804 suffered great hardship from invasions by newly independent Haiti. A Dominican revolt achieved independence in 1809, but five years later Santo Domingo was re-admitted to the status of a Spanish colony. Under the leadership of José Nuñez de Cáceres, independence from Spain was proclaimed in 1821.

Independence. The independence movement had barely achieved its goal when the Haitian army again invaded, in 1822. There followed a military occupation of 22 years, which was ended by a popular insurrection, inspired by the famous *La Trinitaria*, or triumvirate, of

DOMINICAN REPUBLIC – DOMINICANS

Juan Pablo Duarte, Francisco del Rosario Sánchez, and Ramón Mella. The new nation adopted a constitution as the Dominican Republic, but enjoyed little freedom from internecine political strife. Spain was able to restore its control from 1861 to 1865, during the U.S. Civil War, and later the United States made several attempts to obtain bases or to annex the country outright. Toward the end of the 19th century some semblance of internal order was achieved by the dictatorial methods of President Ulíses Heureáux.

Political chaos soon returned, however, and produced such events as the assassination of President Ramón Cáceres in 1911. In 1905, following an earlier political and economic crisis, the United States assumed control of the Dominican customs, and in 1916 a military occupation by the U.S. Marines was ordered by U.S. President Woodrow Wilson. This occupation was not withdrawn until 1924.

The election of 1930 brought to the presidency Rafael Leonidas Trujillo Molina, who imposed upon the Dominican Republic a military dictatorship that lasted for 31 years. Although others officially held the title of President from 1938 to 1942 and after 1952, Trujillo retained effective control of the government and economics through his Partido Dominicano. Political stability and considerable economic progress were achieved, but the Dominicans still knew few civil liberties. All opposition to the regime was suppressed by the armed forces and the secret police. In foreign affairs, Trujillo came into conflict with both the pro-Soviet regime in Cuba and the liberal government of Rómulo Betancourt in Venezuela. Charged with complicity in an attempt on Betancourt's life, the Trujillo regime was censured by the Organization of American States in Aug., 1960. Economic sanctions against the Dominican Republic followed, causing a considerable reduction in the pace of internal development. On May 30, 1961, Trujillo was assassinated. President Joaquín Balaguer, however, remained in office until Jan., 1962, when he was forced to resign. After an interim regime under Rafael Filiberto Bonnelly, the first legally elected President in 38 years, Juan Bosch, was inaugurated in Feb., 1963. His administration lasted only seven months. Charged by army leaders with pro-Communist sympathies, he was overthrown in a military *coup d'état* in Sept., and was later exiled. A three-man civilian junta then took over the government. On Apr. 25, 1965, the junta in turn was ousted by "constitutionalist rebels" calling for the return of Juan Bosch. The coup, however, collapsed, partly because of strong resistance by a military faction and partly because the United States, fearing for the lives of U.S. citizens and suspecting Communist domination of the revolution, moved in. A long stalemate ensued. With the aid of a diplomatic team under the auspices of the Organization of American States, an uneasy truce was effected on Sept. 3. Hector Garcia-Godoy, a career diplomat, was installed as provisional president. In elections held on June 1, 1966, Joaquín Balaguer won a surprise victory over Juan Bosch and Rafael Bonnelly.

Consult Johnson, P. V., *Our Neighbors the Dominicans* (1942); Rodman, Seldon, *Quisqueya: A History of the Dominican Republic* (1964); Bosch, Juan, *Unfinished Experiment: Democracy in the Dominican Republic* (1965).

Maurice de Young, University of Nevada

Jean Marquis

A Dominican friar in the Convent Sainte-Marie de la Tourette, Eveux-sur-Arbresle, France. The Dominicans became known as the "Black Friars" because of the long black mantle usually worn over the white habit seen in the picture above.

DOMINICANS, popular name of the men and women of the religious order which takes its inspiration from St. Dominic. It has three main branches: the first order of St. Dominic known formally as the Order of Friars Preachers (O.P.); the second order of St. Dominic made up of cloistered nuns; the third order of St. Dominic, composed of Third Order Regulars, who are sisters living in convents and engaged in apostolic works, and Third Order Seculars, who are lay men and women.

The Order of Friars Preachers arose from an apostolic enterprise in Languedoc, France, against the Albigensian heresy. Dominic was in Rome in 1204 offering to undertake missionary activity among the Tatars, but Pope Innocent III sent him to combat the Albigensians of Languedoc instead. The task called for intensive preaching, and because the monks assigned to the work found that they were not properly prepared or disposed for such apostolic endeavors, the work floundered. On Nov. 17, 1206, Pope Innocent III ordered the papal legates to exert their power to further apostolic preaching by men suited to the task. This was not the formal founding of the order, but it made the founding of an order of Mendicant Preachers possible and assured such an order of ecclesiastical approval. After laboring for eight years without canonical status, Dominic and his preachers were finally, in 1215, appointed the official preachers of the diocese of Toulouse, and the first house was opened there on Apr. 25. The group lived under the rule of St. Augustine with additional provisions, since technically there was no rule of St. Dominic, and received the papal approbation of Honorius III on Dec. 22, 1216. In this same year the customary practices were written down in the *Consuetudines*, which form the first part of the constitutions of the order. Members take vows of poverty, chastity, and obedience; observe perpetual abstinence; fast from Sept. 14 to Easter, and on all Fridays of the year; chant Divine

Office, but simply, without pomp; and wear a white tunic with a black cloak, whence their title "Black Friars." In May of 1220 the General Chapter of Bologna drew up the constitutions of the order, which were revised by St. Raymond of Pennafort in 1239, and have remained virtually the same since.

The ascetic elements are joined to a vocation which is primarily apostolic and clerical. The preachers are clerics, not monks, but their clericalism is subordinated to their mission of saving souls by being "champions of the Faith" and "lights of the world." Their motto is "Truth." The intellectual element of a Dominican vocation is seen in the list of illustrious scholars, artists, and mystics who were Dominicans: St. Thomas Aquinas, St. Albert the Great (Albertus Magnus), St. Vincent Ferrer, John (Meister) Eckhart, John Tauler, Thomas Cajetan, John of St. Thomas, Fra Angelico, and Fra Bartolommeo. By their vocation to defend and extend the truth, the preachers were bound to make a twofold contribution to the intellectual history of the church. They have a continuous record of constructive work admired and assimilated by the church, but they have an equally uninterrupted record of theological controversy, especially with the Jesuits and Franciscans. Far from being a source of scandal, this fact redounds to the credit of all concerned and evidences the wealth of Christian inspiration and Dominican vocation.

The Second Order of St. Dominic dates from the first years of Dominic's apostolate in Languedoc. A house was founded at Prouille in 1206 for the women who had been converted from Albigensianism. From 1212 the house took on the appearance of a monastery of the cloistered religious. In 1219 Dominic was asked by Pope Honorius III to reform some convents in Rome. He began the reform at the Monastery of St. Sixtus where the nuns were regrouped in 1221, along with some of the religious from Prouille. The rule of the second order is substantially the same as that of the first order, with proper modifications, and was declared final in 1259. The second order grew so fast that the first order asked on several occasions (1239, 1246, 1252) to be relieved of the burden of caring for them, which in each instance was granted temporarily (and partially). But finally, on Feb. 5, 1267, Pope Clement IV returned the second order monasteries to the permanent jurisdiction of the first order. Normally under pontifical cloister, the task of these nuns is continual penance and prayer for the success of all priestly activity and especially of their Dominican brothers.

The Third Order of St. Dominic is divided into regulars, who are sisters engaged actively in apostolic labors such as teaching and nursing and seculars, who are lay men and women, following a rule in their spiritual lives. St. Dominic himself did not write the rule for the tertiaries, but a group of pious laymen attracted by the Friars attached themselves to the order and asked for special spiritual direction. In reply to this request, Munio of Zamora wrote a rule for the Brothers and Sisters of Penitence of St. Dominic, their official title, in 1285. The rule is based on a similar rule of the Brothers of Penitence founded by St. Francis. The canonical existence of the Dominican tertiaries was given by Pope Honorius IV on Jan. 28, 1286.

Consult Reeves, J. B., O.P., *The Dominicans* (1930);

Foster, Paul, O.P., *The Great Society* (1958); Joret, F. D., O.P., *Dominican Life* (1958).

RICHARD J. WESTLEY, Barat College
See also DOMINIC, ST.

DOMINICAN SISTERS, members of the Third Order of St. Dominic, organized shortly after his death in 1221. Soon their white Dominican habit was common in educational and hospital work throughout Europe. Most outstanding among these tertiaries were St. Catherine of Siena (1347–1380), patroness of Italy, and St. Rose of Lima (1586–1617), the first native-born saint in the Americas. The first establishment in the United States, at St. Catherine, Ky., in 1822, has since expanded to more than 30 American mother houses, or separate congregations, with about 20,000 members active in teaching in schools and colleges, and in caring for the sick and aged. Dominican Nuns (Second Order) established a monastery in Canada in 1925, and Dominican Sisters (Third Order) opened a novitiate in Canada in 1927 and a school, in Montreal, in 1951.

WILLIAM A. DEHLER, S.J., Loyola University, Chicago

DOMINION DAY, the national holiday of Canada, celebrated on July 1. On this day in 1867 the dominion of Canada, proclaimed by Queen Victoria according to the terms of the British North America Act, came into being.

DOMINOES [dŏm'ə-nōz], game played with 28 rectangular pieces, or "bones," which have one face blank and one marked with dots. Each face is divided in half; each half of the marked faces contains from 0 to 6 dots, and there is a piece for every possible combination of dots. Pieces marked alike at each end are called doublets.

Draw Game. This most common form of dominoes is the basic game for two players. The pieces are shuffled, face down, and each player draws seven pieces, which are kept hidden from the opponent. (When three or four play, each draws five pieces.) The remaining pieces comprise the "boneyard," from which the player must draw if he is unable to play in turn from pieces in his hand.

The first piece played is called the set. Thereafter, players take alternate turns. Each turn consists in playing a piece in such a manner that it matches a piece on the table; the adjacent ends must have like numbers of dots. In any layout of pieces on the table, there are always two open areas, and it is one of these that a player must match when his turn arrives.

Each doublet is placed crosswise in matching. In the case of doublets, only the sides are considered open for matching. In the case of all other pieces, the ends are the open areas.

If a contestant is unable to play in turn, he draws pieces from the boneyard until he has a piece capable of being matched with something on the table. If he exhausts the boneyard and still cannot play, his turn expires.

The winner is the first player to dispose of all the pieces in his possession. He scores one point for each dot on his adversary's remaining pieces. If neither player goes out and the boneyard is exhausted, the winner is the player with the fewest dots on his remaining pieces; and his score is the difference between the number of dots on the

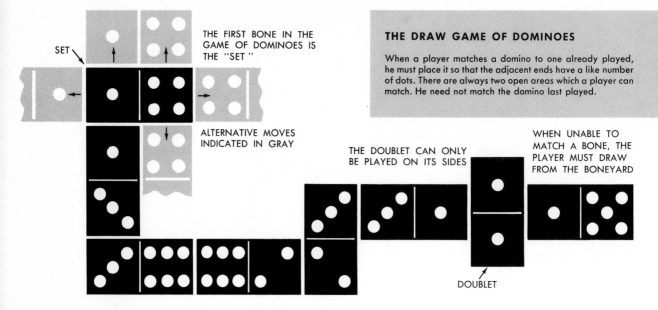

SET

THE FIRST BONE IN THE
GAME OF DOMINOES IS
THE "SET"

ALTERNATIVE MOVES
INDICATED IN GRAY

THE DOUBLET CAN ONLY
BE PLAYED ON ITS SIDES

WHEN UNABLE TO
MATCH A BONE, THE
PLAYER MUST DRAW
FROM THE BONEYARD

DOUBLET

THE DRAW GAME OF DOMINOES

When a player matches a domino to one already played, he must place it so that the adjacent ends have a like number of dots. There are always two open areas which a player can match. He need not match the domino last played.

opponent's pieces and the number on his own. The ultimate victor in the draw game is the player who scores a total of 50 or 100 points in a series of individual deals.

Muggins. This variant follows the rules of the draw game with one major difference. When, in matching pieces, a player makes the open ends of the layout total five or a multiple of five, he immediately scores that number of points in addition to the number scored otherwise in the course of play. The winner is the first player to score 200 points.

Sniff. This variant of muggins provides for making the first doublet ("sniff") matchable on four areas (ends and sides), and for making it playable either lengthwise or crosswise. Other doublets are placed only crosswise, and have two open areas for matching. The winner is the first player to score 200 points.

Both muggins and sniff may also be played by three or four contestants, in which case each draws five pieces at the outset. A variant of the draw game, called the block game, provides for the player's passing (instead of going to the boneyard) when he is unable to play in turn. It is a poor game for two contestants, but satisfactory when there are more players.

FRANK K. PERKINS, Games Columnist, Boston *Herald*

DOMITIAN [dō-mĭsh'ən], in full Titus Flavius Domitianus Augustus (51–96 A.D.), Roman Emperor (81–96). He narrowly escaped death during the troubles of the year 69, and enjoyed little real power during the reigns of his father Vespasian and his brother Titus. His own reign was autocratic and, after Saturninus' rebellion (88), positively despotic, with arbitrary arrests, treason trials, and judicial murders. Yet administration was efficient: provinces were well governed (notably Britain under Agricola), morality was enforced, and literature encouraged. Ancient calumnies notwithstanding, the Rhine frontier was strengthened. Along the Danube there were some defeats (85–92), but peace was nevertheless

signed with Decebalus, King of Dacia. A conspiracy, one of many, procured Domitian's assassination in 96. Ancient writers probably exaggerate the Domitianic terror, but their version contains much truth. By cowing the senate Domitian accelerated its decline into complete impotence, and by claiming quasi-divine honors he helped promote the absolutism of the late Empire.

E. T. SALMON, McMaster University, Hamilton, Ontario

DOM JUAN ou LE FESTIN DE PIERRE [dôn zhwän ōō lə fĕs-tăn' də pyâr], French comedy (performed 1665) by Molière. Molière's Don differs from the murderous philanderer of Spanish and Italian literature. In the play's loosely linked episodes he appears almost always at an advantage despite his evident cruelty, demonstrating the cowardice and ignorance of his retainer Sganarelle, the fickleness of the peasant girls he courts for amusement, the absurd obsequiousness of his creditor, M. Dimanche, and the credulity of his father, Dom Louis. Contemptuous of danger, he defies the animated statue of the Commander he had slain, and is dragged, unrepentant, to Hell.

DOMODOSSOLA [dō-mō-dôs'sō-lä], town of Piedmont, northern Italy. It is one of the most important railroad centers in Italy because of its location at the southern end of the Simplon Tunnel, which connects northern Italy via Switzerland with the Rhine Valley and with France. In ancient times the town was known as Oscela. The area's archeological remains attract visitors. Pop., 11,608.

DOMRÉMY-LA-PUCELLE [dôn-rä-mē'là-pü-sĕl'], village in Lorraine in eastern France, birthplace of Joan of Arc. Her parents' cottage can still be seen, as well as Joan's baptismal font in the village church. A basilica was erected on the hill where she is said to have heard her "voices." An annual play, in which the villagers take part, celebrates her story. Pop., 185.

DONALDSON, JESSE MONROE (1885–   ), U.S. Postmaster General (1947–53). He was born in Shelby, Ill., and after attending Shelbyville Normal School taught (1903–08) in one-room schools. Beginning (1908) as a letter-carrier, he advanced through various postoffice department positions to deputy second assistant postmaster general (1933), chief inspector (1943), and first assistant postmaster general (1945), before being appointed to the Cabinet by President Harry S. Truman. He raised employees' wages, increased postal rates, and sponsored improvement and expansion of air parcel post.

DONALDSON, WALTER (1893–1947), American popular songwriter, born in Brooklyn, N.Y. He began his 30-year career as a songwriter after being fired from a $15-a-week job as pianist with a music publishing firm for writing songs on company time. In the 1920's, collaborating with several lyricists, he wrote *Mammy, My Buddy, Yes, Sir, That's My Baby*, and *My Blue Heaven*. In 1930 he became president of his own publishing firm and, with *Little White Lies* and *You're Driving Me Crazy*, began writing the lyrics for many of his songs. During the 1930's and 1940's most of his songs were written for films.

DONALDSONVILLE, city of southeastern Louisiana, and seat of Ascension Parish. It is the center of a varied agricultural area. Donaldsonville was the capital of Louisiana from 1830 to 1831. Inc., 1822; pop. (1950) 4,150; (1960) 6,082.

DONAT [dō′năt], **ROBERT** (1905–58), English actor well known to American film audiences. He won an Academy Award for his performance in the title role of *Goodbye, Mr. Chips*, in 1939. His other films included *The Count of Monte Cristo* (1934), *The 39 Steps* (1935), *The Ghost Goes West* (1936), *The Citadel* (1938), and *The Winslow Boy* (1948).

DONATELLO [dŏn′ə-tĕl′ō], real name Donato di Niccolò di Betto Bardi (1386–1466), greatest sculptor of the early Renaissance and father of modern realism in art. He went directly to nature to solve the problems of

Donatello's statue of David was commissioned by Cosimo de' Medici, ruler of Florence. David rests his foot on the head of Goliath.

Alinari—Art Reference Bureau

Donatello's "Gattamelata," a monument to a Renaissance soldier of fortune whose real name was Erasmo da Narni.

Art Reference Bureau

The Annunciation Altarpiece in the Church of Santa Croce, Florence.

Alinari—Art Reference Bureau

figures at rest and in motion, of perspective and atmosphere in the backgrounds of low-relief sculptures, and he created the first equestrian statue since ancient times. His output was enormous, its variety incredible, too diversified and complex for sweeping characterization.

Born in Florence and working there most of his life, Donatello—like his friend Brunelleschi, pioneer Renaissance architect—was trained as a goldsmith. His earliest works, however, are of marble carved in traditional Gothic style, for example, the St. George for the Church of Orsanmichele (1416; now Bargello, Florence), a Christian knight incarnating the true spirit of medieval chivalry. Donatello's second period (1416–33) established in his art a fine monumental quality and a concentration on facial expression, best illustrated by his marble prophets on the famous Florence campanile, or bell tower. Most remarkable is his "Job," its face so realistically ugly that it was nicknamed Zuccone ("Pumpkinhead"). In several statues of St. John the Baptist he originated the psychological study of character, while his "Feast of Herod," a panel for the baptismal font of the Church of San Giovanni at Siena, combines expressiveness with realism. His marble "Assumption of the Virgin," sent to Naples for the tomb of Cardinal Brancaccio, solves the problem of atmospheric space and perspective in relief.

Influenced by Roman art, Donatello produced certain works (1433–43) inspired by classic ideals of beauty—for example, his Tabernacle of the Sacrament at St. Peter's in Rome; his *cantoria* (choir gallery) of Florence Cathedral, with its famous dancing cherubs that were the first to reveal the possibilities of the form of the child to modern art; the charming Annunciation Altarpiece (Church of Santa Croce, Florence); and his famous bronze "David," the first nude statue of Christian times and a landmark in Renaissance art (Bargello, Florence).

The next decade (1443–53), at Padua, witnessed Donatello's most mature work. There is renewed interest in expressing individual emotions of great depth and intensity and a further development of pictorial relief. Outstanding are his colossal "Gattamelata" (Padua), the first equestrian bronze statue since Roman times, and his bronze sculptures for the high altar of the Church of San'Antonio, including statues of saints, a great crucifix, and reliefs of St. Anthony's miracles and the Passion of Christ.

Donatello's final years (1453–66) produced such startling works as his bronze St. John the Baptist at Siena; the ugly Mary Magdalen in Florence; and panels for the two pulpits of the Church of San Lorenzo in Florence, technically audacious, but weakened by extreme emotional realism.

Consult Crutwell, Maud, *Donatello* (1911); Freeman, L. J., *Italian Sculpture of the Renaissance* (1917).

EMERSON H. SWIFT, Columbia University
See also RENAISSANCE ART.

DONATION OF CONSTANTINE, document which appeared in the Frankish Empire in mid-8th century. Universally accepted as one of the great forgeries of history, it purported to be a grant made by the Emperor Constantine to Pope Sylvester I. Relating Sylvester's role in his conversion to Christianity, the Emperor professes the faith and describes his recovery from leprosy through

baptism. He thereupon confers upon the Pope and his successors spiritual primacy over all other Patriarchs and Bishops of the world, granting him imperial honors and granting to the chief Roman clergy senatorial distinctions and honors. To supremacy in spiritual matters was added temporal dominion over Rome, Italy, and the provinces, districts, and cities of the western regions. The origin and purpose of the forgery are still obscure. It was used officially by Leo IX in 1054, and though definitely established as a forgery in the 15th century, was defended as authoritative until the 16th century.

WALTER H. TURNER, University of Detroit

DONATION OF MATILDA, bequeathal of Italian estates to the Church in 1077 by Matilda of Canossa, Countess of Tuscany. The donation was confirmed in 1102. On her death (1115) Henry V seized the properties, which controlled passage between Germany and Rome. A lengthy legal dispute ensued, which continued until 1213, when Frederick II acknowledged the Church's claim.

DONATISM [dŏn'ə-tĭz-əm], a North African schism which began in a disputed election to the see of Carthage in 311–12 A.D., but developed as a rigorist sect with strong nationalist aspects. Its formal claim was that Catholic Sacraments were vitiated by the (alleged) consecration of Caecilian of Carthage by a *traditor*, one who had surrendered sacred books during the persecution. During the 4th century the Donatist Church was predominant in much of Roman Africa. Its decline was hastened by its own divisions, the arguments of St. Augustine (who developed out of the Donatist controversy important principles on the nature of church and sacraments), and government pressure against a sect which had supported local rebels. Only a lingering fragment survived after the Vandal invasion of 429.

DONAU RIVER. *See* DANUBE RIVER.

DONBAS. *See* DONETS BASIN.

DON CARLOS [dŏn kär'lōs], opera in five acts by Giuseppe Verdi; libretto by François Joseph Méry and Camille du Locle; first performance, Mar. 11, 1867, the Opéra, Paris.

In 16th-century Spain, Philip II, wishing to marry Elizabeth of Valois, who is loved by his son Don Carlos, hands the latter over to the Inquisition. Don Carlos finally escapes to a monastery.

The opera is usually thought of as a transitional work in Verdi's career. Although it sometimes rambles and is perhaps overlong, it is basically a masterful work with many scenes that contain powerful drama. Don Carlos marks Verdi's growing search for a delineation of character in depth.

See also VERDI, (FORTUNINO) GIUSEPPE (FRANCESCO).

DONCASTER [dŏng'kəs-tər], county borough, and industrial and market town of Yorkshire, England, located on the Don River in southeastern West Riding. It has diversified industries, including locomotive and carriage works and firms manufacturing crawler tractors and farm machinery. The town is the center of the great South Yorkshire coal field. Doncaster lies along the Great North Road and along the main-line railway from London to Scotland. The town was founded by the Romans as Danum and settled by the Saxons as Donecastre. Eleven royal charters were granted between 1194 and 1688. The coming of the railway in 1848 and the establishment of a locomotive plant and carriage works in 1853 gradually transformed the market town into an industrial center.

The town is famous for horse racing, especially the St. Leger race, which has been run since 1776. The Yorkshire Residential School for the Deaf, a 14th-century grammar school, and Doncaster Technical College are located here. Pop., 86,402.

BRYAN E. COATES, *The University, Sheffield*

DONEGAL [dŏn'ĭ-gôl], county of northwestern Ireland. Almost completely separated from the rest of the Gaelic-speaking "congested western fringe" of Eire, the Donegal peninsula shares Ulster's dissected plateau of metamorphic rock, which constitutes the basin of the Foyle River system. Glaciation characterizes both the deeply serrated fjord coast between Donegal Bay and Lough Swilly and the extensively eroded interior, including broad stretches of bare stone moor interspersed with lakes and peat bogs. Climate, under Gulf Stream influence, is equable though cool, but Atlantic gales prevent tree growth while bringing over 60 in. of rainfall yearly. Moderately fertile soils in the Foyle lowlands support mixed farming (oats, potatoes, and cattle). Elsewhere, thatched, stone crofts cluster in sheltered spots, the menfolk fishing the Atlantic, quarrying granite, or spading potatoes, while the women weave soft Donegal tweed sweaters and carpets. Large tracts are uninhabited and emigration is endemic. Area, 1,865 sq. mi.; pop., 113,815.

JOHN J. HOOKER, *The Catholic University of America*

DONELSON, town of north-central Tennessee, about 7 mi. east of Nashville. It lies in the northern part of the fertile Nashville Basin agricultural region. Pop. (1950) 1,765; (1960) 17,195.

DONELSON, FORT, fortification erected in 1861 by the Confederacy in the U.S. Civil War. It was located in Stewart County, Tenn., just south of the Kentucky border, on the Cumberland River. Because of uncertainty over Kentucky's affiliation in the Civil War, the Confederates built Forts Henry and Donelson to prevent the entry of Union forces into the South by way of the Tennessee and Cumberland rivers.

Commodore Andrew H. Foote's Union gunboats appeared at Fort Henry on Feb. 6, 1862, and the garrison's undermanned forces departed and moved to Fort Donelson, 11 mi. to the east, before Gen. Ulysses S. Grant arrived with his troops. Fort Donelson was one of the best fortified positions in the Mississippi Valley and was garrisoned by 15,000 men. Foote attacked from the river on Feb. 14 without effect, while Grant surrounded the fort with 25,000 men. Gen. John B. Floyd was ready to surrender the fort, but his subordinates convinced him to attack and break open an escape route to Nashville. On Feb. 15, while Grant was absent conferring with Foote,

Gen. Gideon J. Pillow, ably supported by Gen. Simon B. Buckner and Col. Nathan B. Forrest, attacked and almost broke out, when Floyd ordered the troops back to their entrenchments. That night Floyd, Pillow, and Forrest escaped. On the 16th, Buckner surrendered to Grant. The capture of Henry and Donelson broke the South's forward defenses and gave the Union control of the Tennessee River as far south as Florence, Ala.

MARTIN BLUMENSON, *formerly, Senior Historian, Department of the Army*

DONETS BASIN, principal coal and steel producing region in the Soviet Union and a key industrial area. Known as Donbas, it encompasses about 10,000 sq. mi. and has a population of over 10 million. It is located mainly in the Ukrainian S.S.R., extending into the southern R.S.F.S.R. Much of its coal is of coking quality and has been used to develop the metallurgical and chemical industries of the region. Among its leading cities are Donetsk, Makeyevka, Gorlovka, and Lugansk.

DONETSK, city of the Soviet Union located in the Donets Basin in the southeastern part of the Ukrainian S.S.R. Aside from its administrative function, Donetsk is one of the most important transport nodes and industrial cities in the U.S.S.R. and the leading economic center of the Donets Basin. Its industries are predominantly in the heavy categories such as iron and steel, machinery, and chemicals. The largest single plant produces pig iron, steel ingots, and a variety of rolled steel products. It draws its fuel supply from local deposits of high-grade coking coals and its iron ores from the Krivoi Rog mining region, west of the Dnieper River.

Donetsk, which was known as Stalino from 1924 to 1961, is one of the oldest industrial centers in the Ukraine. It was founded as the town of Yuzovka in 1869 in connection with the building of the John Hughes Company steel mill, the forerunner of the city's present industrial complex. Coal mining, however, had been important in the area prior to that date. By 1926 the city had a population of 174,000. During the early economic planning era there was a rapid expansion of the steel and machinery industries with an associated growth of population to a level of 466,000 in 1939. During World War II Donetsk was occupied by the Germans (1941–43) and suffered massive destruction to residential sections, industrial plants, and mines, but it experienced rapid regrowth and expansion in the postwar period. The city is also an important educational and cultural center with four higher institutes in the industrial, coal, medical, and pedagogical fields. There are theaters for drama, opera, and ballet as well as a symphony hall. Pop., 699,000.

ALLAN RODGERS, *Pennsylvania State University*

DONETS [dō-nĕts'] **RIVER,** in southwestern Soviet Union, draining about 39,000 sq. mi. Rising in the uplands of central Russia above Belgorod, it flows southeastward through the Ukrainian S.S.R. to the Rostov Oblast where it empties into the Don River, of which it is the main tributary. Since the construction of the Volga-Don Canal in 1952, the Donets carries coal, oil, timber, and grain between the Donets Basin and Volga Valley.

DONGAN [dŏng'gən], **THOMAS** (1634–1715), colonial Governor of New York (1683–88). Upon his arrival in New York as Governor in Aug., 1683, Dongan ordered the election of the colony's first representative assembly. The legislature's "charter of liberties and privileges" extended the franchise to all freeholders and freemen and established proportional representation by counties. On instructions from King James II in 1685, Dongan suspended the assembly and the charter. When New York was annexed to the Dominion of New England in 1688, Dongan was replaced by Sir Edmund Andros.

DON GIOVANNI [dŏn jō-vä'nē] (Don Juan), opera in two acts by Wolfgang Amadeus Mozart; libretto by Lorenzo da Ponte; first performed at the National Theatre, Prague, Oct. 29, 1787; first American performance of English adaptation, entitled *The Libertine*, given in Philadelphia, Dec. 26, 1818; first American performance in the original Italian version at the Park Theatre, New York, May 26, 1826, with Lorenzo da Ponte present.

The original title reads *Don Giovanni, ossia il dissoluto punito* (Don Giovanni, or the dissolute one punished). Don Giovanni, pursuing Donna Anna, kills the Commendatore, her father. Later seeing the statue of the Commendatore in the cemetery, Don Giovanni invites the statue to dinner. It appears, and Don Giovanni, refusing to repent of his many romantic escapades, is dragged by demons to hell.

The original libretto designates the opera as *dramma giocoso*, a playful drama. It is a musical play in the style of the *opera buffa*, although Mozart goes beyond this style in the cemetery and dinner scenes of Act II, where supernatural elements clearly point to 19th-century romanticism. Extraordinary musical features are the simultaneous playing of three dance bands in different meters (Act I) and the quoting of airs from contemporary operas by Vicente Martín, Giuseppe Sarti, and Mozart himself (*The Marriage of Figaro*) in the dinner scene.

JOSEPH BRAUNSTEIN, Manhattan School of Music

DONIPHAN [dŏn'ə-fən], **ALEXANDER WILLIAM** (1808–87), American lawyer and soldier. Born near Maysville, Ky., he attended Augusta College, studied law, and in 1830 moved to Missouri. In his most famous legal case he defended a Mormon charged with conspiracy to murder the Governor of Missouri. Despite the bitter hostility of the Missourians against the Mormons, his client received a sentence of only five minutes in jail. Appointed as an officer of state militia to fight the Mormons, he gained fame by his moral courage in refusing to obey the order to shoot the Mormon prophet Joseph Smith.

During the Mexican War Doniphan organized the 1st Regiment of Missouri Mounted Volunteers and as their colonel led one of the most daring marches in American history. Starting at Fort Leavenworth, near the western boundary of Missouri, he proceeded to New Mexico, then west into Navajo country, then south into the Mexican province of Chihuahua, and finally east to Matamoras on the Gulf of Mexico—a journey of over 5,000 mi. in a year, punctuated by battles and skirmishes along the way.

Doniphan was elected to the Missouri legislature in 1836, 1840, and 1854, and served as Missouri delegate to the Virginia Peace Convention, which sought a compromise solution to the slavery controversy, in Washington, D.C., in Feb., 1861. He opposed the secession of Missouri in 1861, but disapproved of trying to hold the Union together by a war of one section against the other. Because of a family tragedy—the sudden death of his two sons in the early summer of 1861—Doniphan did not take a military part in the Civil War, but continued to practice law in Missouri until his death.

PHILIP S. KLEIN, Pennsylvania State University

DONIZETTI [dŏn-ĭ-zĕt'ē], **GAETANO** (1797–1848), Italian operatic composer, born in Bergamo. He studied music there and at the Liceo Filarmonico in Bologna. To avoid the teaching profession he entered the army, and while stationed in Venice in 1818 wrote his first opera. Others followed and in 1822 he was released from military service. Continuing to compose, he wrote more than 60 operas and became one of the most widely performed and phenomenally successful composers in Europe. In 1845 he was attacked with paralysis after many seizures of melancholy.

After periods of both adoration and neglect, Donizetti's position in the history of opera is now quite assured: it is slightly below Bellini's and Rossini's. He often wrote too hastily and carelessly, and his works are frequently mere vehicles for the virtuosity of singers. Still, in a few works he manages to impart real emotion, and without doubt his best comic operas still sparkle. His works of lasting value are probably *Lucia di Lammermoor* (1835), the last scene of which is one of the most moving passages he ever wrote, *La Favorita* (1840), *Linda di Chamounix* (1842), *L'Elisir d'Amore* (1832), *La Fille du Régiment* (1840), and *Don Pasquale* (1843).

ALBERT WEISSER, Brooklyn College

DON JUAN [dŏn wän], the traditional literary figure of a great lover, a central myth in Western culture who first appears in a play by Tirso de Molina, *El Burlador de Seville y convidado de piedra* (*The Playboy of Seville and the Stone Guest*), pub. 1630. Don Juan seduces several women through trickery. Despite repeated warnings he delays repenting and is punished by the statue of the Commander whom he killed in the course of seducing his daughter. In Molière's play *Dom Juan* (1665) the hero is a modern libertine, skeptical of religion, given to lengthy analyses of his fickleness. Perhaps the greatest version of the story is Mozart's opera *Don Giovanni* (1787), text by Lorenzo Da Ponte. Attended by his sarcastic servant Leporello, Giovanni is pursued by two women who love him—his neglected bride Donna Elvira, and Donna Anna, who seeks to avenge her father's murder. In Lord Byron's satiric masterpiece (1818–24) the hero is a passive innocent, but in other 19th-century versions he is a romantic rebel. Later versions include José Zorrilla's *Don Juan Tenorio* (1844) and George Bernard Shaw's *Man and Superman* (1901–03), where in a central scene, "Don Juan in Hell," Don Juan as the hero voices Shaw's theories.

Consult Weinstein, Leo, *The Metamorphoses of Don Juan* (1959); Mandel, Oscar, *The Theatre of Don Juan* (1963).

LAWRENCE GOTTHEIM, State University of N.Y. at Binghamton
See also DON GIOVANNI; MAN AND SUPERMAN.

DON JUAN OF AUSTRIA. *See* JOHN OF AUSTRIA.

DONKEY. *See* ASS.

DONNA, city of southern Texas, located in the rich irrigated lower Rio Grande valley. It is a shipping point for citrus fruits, winter vegetables, and canned goods. Pop. (1950) 7,171; (1960) 7,522.

DONNACONA, industrial town of Quebec, Canada, located at the confluence of the St. Lawrence and Jacques Cartier rivers, 25 mi. southwest of Quebec. The main industry is a newsprint mill operated since 1914. Inc., 1920; pop., 4,812.

DONNE [dŭn], **JOHN** (1572?–1631), English poet and clergyman. Born into a staunchly Catholic London family, Donne remained loyal to the old faith until well into his adult life. For this reason he was unable to take a degree from either Oxford or Cambridge, though he resided for several years at both universities. From Cambridge he turned to the study of law at the Inns of Court. There he read voraciously, although less in law than in the new Renaissance science and in foreign languages. He made a tour of the Continent in the 1590's before serving with the Earl of Essex in expeditions against the Spaniards in 1596 and 1597. He then settled in London as secretary to the influential Sir Thomas Egerton. His secret marriage to Anne More was disapproved of by the bride's father and cost him his position. Until he was ordained an Anglican clergyman in 1615, he and his family lived in poverty. After his ordination he rose to the deanship of St. Paul's Cathedral and, during the last ten years of his life, acquired great fame as a preacher.

Donne was one of the finest masters of 17th-century English prose. His highly personal, rhythmical, nervously energetic style may be best seen in his sermons and in the record of his meditations during a serious illness, *Devotions upon Emergent Occasions* (1624), from which comes the famous passage beginning "No man is an island . . ."

Portrait of John Donne, from the painting by Isaac Oliver.

and ending ". . . never send to know for whom the bell tolls; it tolls for thee." More important, however, are his poems, which were not published in a collected edition until two years after his death. In his earlier verse Donne introduces a new way of writing about love, more sensually intimate, conversational, witty, and philosophically subtle than were the more conventional lyrics of his immediate predecessors. His *Divine Poems,* in which he addresses God in a tone much like that of an impassioned lover, place him among the great religious poets. His unusual manner of writing profoundly affected both the love poetry and the devotional verse of his day. The followers in the tradition he established, including such authors as George Herbert and Henry Vaughan, are usually called by critics metaphysical poets (q.v.).

Consult Williamson, George, *The Donne Tradition* (1930); Coffin, C. M., *John Donne and the New Philosophy* (1937).

LAWRENCE V. RYAN, Stanford University

DONNELLY, IGNATIUS (1831–1901), American author, politician, and reformer. Born in Philadelphia, Donnelly read law, was admitted (1852) to the bar, and moved (1856) to Minnesota. At 28 he was elected Lieutenant Governor of Minnesota and served until his election (1863) to the U.S. House of Representatives, where he remained until 1869. A Liberal Republican, Donnelly advocated numerous radical reforms and published his views in the weekly *Anti-Monopolist,* which he edited (1874–79), as he did later (1894–1901) the Populist paper, the *Representative.* Serving almost continually in either the Minnesota senate or house from 1874 until his death, Donnelly, the Populist party's nominee for the governorship of Minnesota, wrote the party's national platform in 1892. Donnelly created a stir in literary circles with his *The Great Cryptogram* (1888) by advancing the theory that Francis Bacon wrote Shakespeare's plays; and with *Atlantis: the Antediluvian World* (1882), which placed the origin of civilization in the lost continent of Atlantis. Popular among his other writings was his novel *Caesar's Column: a Story of the Twentieth Century* (1890).

JAMES P. SHENTON, Columbia University

DONNER PASS, pass through the Sierra Nevada mountains of eastern California, 35 mi. southwest of Reno, Nev. It is traversed by U.S. Highway 40 and by the Norden Tunnel, which carries a railroad under the pass summit. Donner Pass is the site of a U.S. Weather Bureau observatory. The pass is best known for the tremendous hardships suffered by the Donner party, about 87 emigrants to California (39 of them children) who were trapped there by unusually heavy snow in Oct., 1846. Only 47 reached Sacramento in Apr., 1847; those who were not rescued either froze or starved to death. Some of those stranded had recourse to cannibalism. Donner State Historic Monument commemorates the event. Elev., 7,135 ft.

DONORA [də-nôr'ə], industrial borough of southwestern Pennsylvania, near Pittsburgh, on the Monongahela River. The chief products of Donora are iron, steel, and zinc. One of the largest wire mills in the nation is located here. Twenty persons died from a poisonous smog which covered Donora on Oct. 30–31, 1948. Inc., 1901: pop. (1950) 12,186; (1960) 11,130.

DON PASQUALE [dŏn päs-kwä′lē], opera buffa in three acts by Gaetano Donizetti; libretto by the composer and Giacomo Ruffini; first performance, Théâtre-Italien, Paris, Jan. 3, 1843.

An old bachelor, Don Pasquale, signs a marriage contract for the young Norina, but because of her extravagance begs his nephew Ernesto (who loves her) to take his place. A gay and vivacious work that retains all the elements of early 19th-century comic opera, *Don Pasquale* demonstrates Donizetti's special gift for this type of comedy. In order to be mounted with relish, it requires singers with genuine comic gifts.

DON QUIXOTE DE LA MANCHA [dŏn kē-hō′tē dā lä män′chä], Spanish novel (first part, 1605; second part, 1615) by Miguel de Cervantes Saavedra. It was begun as a parody of the popular and extravagant romances of knight-errantry, but the author's conception of his work and its characters grew as the book progressed, with the result that *Don Quixote* has become a great novel of humanity. Its chief protagonist is an hidalgo, a bottom-rung nobleman, whose mind has been so turned by his reading of romances of chivalry that he decides to become a knight-errant. Opposite him, as squire, the author has set a sharp-witted, practical-minded Spanish peasant, Sancho Panza, who follows his master in the hope of material gain. The novel's literary importance can hardly be overestimated, for in it converge all the literary currents

Cervantes' "Don Quixote," as envisioned by Honoré Daumier.
The Bettmann Archive

of the day. For the first time in the history of narrative fiction the characters cease to be mere puppets of the author and become human beings who think about themselves, discuss and analyze themselves, and are interested in their own personalities.

PAUL ROGERS, Oberlin College

See also CERVANTES SAAVEDRA, MIGUEL DE; SANCHO PANZA.

DON RIVER, major river of southwestern Soviet Union, draining almost 170,000 sq. mi. It rises in the central uplands southeast of Tula and flows southeastward to a point northwest of Volgograd, where it swerves southwest until it reaches Shakhty. There, it turns westward until it empties into the Taganrog Gulf of the Sea of Azov. The river's main port is Rostov, located near its mouth. It is navigable throughout most of its course except for about four months when it freezes. Its freight traffic consists of coal, grain, lumber, and construction materials. With the completion in 1952 of the canal linking the Volga and Don rivers, traffic on the Don increased rapidly, particularly between the Volga Valley and the Donets Basin. Length, 1,220 mi.

DOOLEY, MR. *See* DUNNE, FINLEY PETER.

DOOLITTLE, JAMES HAROLD (1896–   ), American aviator and Army officer, noted, during World War II, for the bombing of Tokyo in Apr., 1942, the first U.S. air assault on the Japanese mainland. Doolittle was born in Alameda, Calif. During World War I he served as a gunnery and flight instructor. He attained fame for a cross-country flight (Sept., 1922) from Paola Beach, Fla. to San Diego, Calif., in 21 hours and 19 minutes. He led U.S. air forces (1942) in the North African invasion and the Eighth Air Force (1944) in Europe. Doolittle retired (1946) as a lieutenant general. In 1956 he was appointed to a board of consultants that studied the operations of U.S. foreign intelligence.

DOOM PALM, a fan-leaved palm tree of the genus *Hyphaene*, native to tropical Africa. Doom palms have thick trunks that may be cylindrical or slightly pear-shaped. The fanlike fronds form a luxuriant green umbrella atop the trunk, partially concealing small, white flowers. The tree produces an edible, oval, quincelike fruit that contains a single seed. *H. crinata* is one of the handsomest species. It has bright-green foliage and is occasionally grown in conservatories in the cooler regions of North America.

DOOR, movable barrier with which an entranceway is opened or closed. Among primitive peoples it was a hanging flap or curtain of animal hide or fabric. Early in human history the door developed into a construction of wood, metal, or stone, fixed in an opening to a building, room, or passage. Doors in Egypt and other dry regions were usually made of one heavy plank, pivoted at one side into sockets in the head and sill of the doorway, while in damper locales they were often composed of several pieces of wood to prevent warping. Paneled doors of stone or marble were used in countries where wood was scarce, (for example, in some Pompeian tombs). In Rome and

THE DOPPLER EFFECT

SOUND SOURCE OF
CONSTANT FREQUENCY

AN APPROACHING SOUND SOURCE HAS A HIGHER
PITCH FOR A STATIONARY LISTENER

As the sound source approaches, the number of cycles of the wave train that reach the listener per second (the observed frequency) increases. This increase causes the rise in pitch noted by the listener.

A RECEDING SOUND SOURCE HAS A LOWER
PITCH FOR A STATIONARY LISTENER

As the sound source recedes, fewer and fewer cycles reach the listener per second. The result is the lowering of the pitch perceived by the listener. The pitch of the sound source, however, has actually remained the same in both instances.

Byzantium, bronze sheets hammered in raised designs were fastened over wood to form the remarkable doors of the Pantheon in Rome and of Hagia Sophia in Constantinople. During the 12th century pivots were replaced by hinges, usually three to a door. Medieval wooden doors were often decorated with elaborate scrolls of wrought iron or bronze extending from the hinge plates, as in the doors of the cathedral of Notre Dame in Paris. Simpler models prevailed throughout Renaissance Italy. Solid doors of cast bronze also came into use, the most noteworthy being those of the Baptistery in Florence, designed by Ghiberti. Modern doors include—besides the foregoing types—special doors designed for a variety of purposes: revolving doors, sliding doors, overhead doors, fireproof doors, accordian-folding doors, and—the latest development—doorways in which a "curtain" of air, flowing between lintel and floor, provides the only barrier between the enclosed space and the outdoors.

ROBERT RIGGS KERR, The Newark Museum

DOORNIK. *See* TOURNAI.

DOOR PENINSULA, peninsula between Green Bay and Lake Michigan, northeastern Wisconsin. It is a major cherry-growing region. French explorers and missionaries visited the peninsula in the 17th century. Sturgeon Bay is the principal community. Length, 80 mi.; width at base, 30 mi.

DOPPLER, CHRISTIAN JOHANN (1803–53), Austrian mathematician and physicist who discovered the Doppler effect; the pitch of sound from a source moving relative to an observer varies inversely with the distance between the source and the observer. Although Doppler's early writings were in mathematics, his main contributions were in physics, the Doppler effect being published in the now historic *Über das farbige Licht der Doppelsterne* (1842). Doppler was born in Salzburg, taught at the technical school in Prague, and was professor of experimental physics and director of the Physical Institute at Vienna.

DOPPLER EFFECT, a change in frequency of sound, light, or other wave phenomenon caused by motion of an observer relative to the source of the waves. It was named for the Austrian physicist C. J. Doppler (1803–53). If a fixed source of sound generates a tone of constant pitch, or frequency, the sound waves will pass a listener some distance away at the same frequency, or number of waves per second. If the listener advances toward the source of sound, he encounters more waves per second than if he were stationary. He consequently hears the sound rise in pitch (frequency) in proportion to his speed. If the listener goes away from the source of sound, the pitch drops. Motion of the source toward or away from a stationary listener has the same effect. This Doppler shift is noted in the sudden drop in pitch of an automobile horn as one meets and passes another vehicle, or in the similar change in the tone of the bell of a passing locomotive or fire truck.

Corresponding effects are observed in the behavior of radio, radar, or light waves. Movements of the electrified layers of the upper atmosphere (ionosphere) can be plotted from observations of the Doppler shift in radio signals. During World War II radars were developed that could measure the speed of a distant approaching airplane by means of the Doppler principle.

Astronomy. Optical Doppler effects are important in astronomy. A spectroscope is used to separate light into its constituent wavelengths. The spectrum of the sun or other stars includes many specific spectral lines (analogous to pitches of sound) that are characteristic of hydrogen, helium, iron, or other elements. The normal wavelengths of these lines are found from laboratory measurements. If the spectroscope shows that the wavelengths (related to frequencies) of such lines in the light of a star are shifted from their normal values, the amount of such shift is a measure of the speed of the star relative to the earth. The light is shifted toward the red or the violet end of the spectrum as the star is receding or approaching.

The wavelengths of light from all but the nearest galaxies are shifted toward the red, and the amount of this shift is proportional to the distance of each galaxy from the earth. This remarkable finding indicates—if the red shift is indeed a Doppler effect—that the galaxies are receding from us and from each other. This observation is the basis of the "expanding universe" hypothesis, which holds that the galaxies and other cosmic material are still flying outward from a vast primeval explosion.

Among other applications, the Doppler effect may be used in a speedometer for space ships. A sensitive Doppler instrument in such a craft can determine its speed relative to the sun or possibly other stars or planets. Three such measurements in different directions will give the true speed and direction of the ship's course.

JOSEPH H. BUSH, National Center for Atmospheric Research

DORADO [də-rä′dō] **or DOLPHIN,** a swift and predaceous marine fish, *Coryphaena hippurus*, the sole member of the family Coryphaenidae. The dorado, or dolphin, is found in most warm seas and should not be confused with the true dolphin, a small whale of the mammalian order Cetacea. Dorados reach a maximum length of 6 ft. and a weight of 70 lb. Their thin bodies are brilliantly colored in blue, purple, green, and gold; and a long dorsal fin extends from just behind the head to the deeply-forked tail. Males have a characteristically high, squared forehead. Dorados are among the fastest swimming fish. They have been clocked at almost 40 mph, and when in pursuit of flying fish, they often leap out of the water. Recently dorados have become a popular game fish. Their flesh is also excellent, but they are not caught in sufficient quantities to make them commercially important.

DORATI [dō-rä′tē], **ANTAL** (1906–   ), conductor, born in Budapest, Hungary. A pupil of Bartók and Kodály, he

"The Dove Sent Forth from the Ark" by Doré.   (BROWN BROTHERS)

began his career with various operatic posts in Hungary and Germany. After conducting for the Ballet Russe de Monte Carlo (1934–40), he became musical director of the Ballet Theater, New York, and then (1945) conductor of the Dallas Symphony Orchestra. He conducted the Minneapolis Symphony Orchestra from 1949 until 1960, when he resigned to devote more time to guest engagements in Europe. In 1962 he received a two-year appointment as conductor of the BBC Symphony Orchestra.

DORCAS [dôr′kəs], a member of the early Church at Joppa, noted for her charity and good works. According to the Biblical account (Acts 9:36–41), Peter was sent for when she died; and, after prayer, he restored her to life.

DORCHESTER, GUY CARLETON, 1ST BARON. *See* CARLETON, GUY, 1ST BARON DORCHESTER.

DORCHESTER [dôr′chĕs-tər], municipal borough of southwestern Dorsetshire, England, and the county town, located on the Frome River. It is an agricultural and administrative center. Called Durnovaria by the Romans, the town is the site of an ancient "amphitheater" known as Marlmbury Rings. Thomas Hardy lived here and Dorchester is the "Casterbridge" of his Wessex novels. Southwest of the town is Maiden Castle, an earthwork fortification believed to have existed about 2000 B.C. Pop., 12,266.

DORCHESTER HEIGHTS, hill on a peninsula overlooking Boston. In the American Revolution, the heights were seized on Mar. 4, 1776, by colonial forces under Gen. John Thomas. They were so speedily fortified that Gen. William Howe, commanding the British forces beleaguered in Boston, reportedly commented that the Americans had done a month's work in one night. The fortifications threatened the British navy, anchored in Boston harbor, and spurred Howe to evacuate the city, Mar. 17, 1776.

DORDRECHT [dôr′drĕкнt], port and industrial center of the west-central Netherlands, on the Oude Maas, Merwede, and Noord rivers, about 15 mi. southeast of Rotterdam. Excellent inland waterway facilities have contributed to the development of diverse industries including shipbuilding, marine engineering, metallurgy, processing of food and chemicals, and the manufacture of safes, electric and telephone equipment, and high-quality glassware. Dordrecht was the medieval seat of the Counts of Holland, and the independence of the United Provinces from Spain was proclaimed here in 1572. The town was fortified in the 13th century and remained the principal Dutch port until the 17th century, when it was surpassed by Rotterdam. The city contains many picturesque old houses and has a 14th-century Gothic church and an art museum. Dordrecht was the site of the Synod of 1618–19 which debated the Arminian-Gommarian controversy in the Dutch Reformed Church. Pop., 77,624.

JOHN F. HART, Indiana University

DORÉ [dô-rä′], **PAUL GUSTAVE** (1832–83), French graphic artist, painter, and sculptor, most famous for his book illustrations. His picturesque narrative style and romantic taste are best seen in his series of illustrations for the Bible, *The Divine Comedy*, *Paradise Lost*, La Fontaine's *Fables*, *Don Quixote*, and Balzac's *Droll Stories*. The rich chiaroscuro of his art has earned him the name "the gaslight Michelangelo."

DORGON (1612–50), Prince and Regent of the Ch'ing (Manchu) Dynasty of China. As Regent to the child Emperor Shun-chih, Dorgon was the actual founder of the dynasty. He led the Manchu army into China from Manchuria and took the capital, Peking, in 1644. His untimely death in 1650 gave rise to years of palace intrigues. But his stern demand for loyalty, coupled with his wholehearted adoption of Chinese institutions, laid the foundation for a regime that was to last for almost three centuries.

DORIA [dô'ryä], **ANDREA** (1466–1560), Italian admiral and statesman. Born into a renowned Genoese sea-faring family, he was largely responsible for maintaining Genoa's independence during the 16th-century wars between France and Spain. Early in his military career he conquered (1503–6) the island of Corsica for Genoa. Doria alternately courted the favors of France and Spain, but when convinced of Spain's superiority, ably negotiated an accord (1528) with Holy Roman Emperor Charles V (Charles I of Spain), who recognized Genoa's autonomy. Triumphantly acclaimed by his people, he assumed dictatorial rule over Genoa. Doria subsequently conducted brilliant naval operations against the French and the Turks and ruthlessly crushed conspiracies against his rule (1547, 1548).

DORIAN GRAY, THE PICTURE OF, English symbolic novel (1891) by Oscar Wilde. The image of Dorian Gray in his portrait becomes old and monstrously ugly, while the man himself, indulging in all manner of vices, remains young and handsome.

DORIANS [dôr'ē-ənz], one of the four traditional ethnic divisions of the Greeks. In historical times the most important communities of the Peloponnesus, the southern Aegean Sea, and the south coast of Asia Minor were considered Dorian settlements. These included Megara, Corinth and her many colonies, Argos, Sparta, Aegina, Melos, Thera, Halicarnassus, and many cities of Crete. The inhabitants of these communities were believed to have had a common physical and cultural heritage, and evidence for this kinship was found in their related dialects, political institutions, personality traits, and art forms. There is greater validity in the evidence adduced from the common Doric dialect than from the other similarities, since many Dorian communities differed extensively in matters of tribal divisions, political forms, social outlook, and temperament.

The traditional homeland of the Dorian peoples who migrated to the Peloponnesus and beyond was a small district in central Greece called Doris, to which they came, probably from farther north, under the leadership of Dorus, son of Hellen, the son of Deucalion. The ancient Greeks associated the movement of these Dorians into southern Greece with the conquest of most of the Peloponnesus by the descendants of Hercules, which they dated about 80 years after the Trojan War. However the "Dorian invasion" seems to have covered a considerable period of time, perhaps 100 years, and occurred in multiple stages over various routes. This movement was probably stimulated by disturbances and pressures farther north. In their search for better and safer territories the Dorians became the agents of destruction of the major sites of the Mycenaean Greeks about 1200 B.C., with the exception of Attica, which was apparently by-passed.

DONALD R. LAING, JR., University of Cincinnati

DORION [dô-ryôn'], **SIR ANTOINE AIMÉ** (1818–91), French-Canadian politician and judge. After practicing law in Montreal, he entered politics in 1854 and became one of the outstanding Reformers in Lower Canada (Quebec). Dorion formed a short-lived ministry in 1858 with George Brown, and between 1862 and 1864 he served in the ministry with John S. Macdonald. Like other Lower Canadian Reformers, he refused to join the coalition formed by John A. Macdonald and George Brown in 1864 and strenuously opposed the proposed federation of the provinces until its achievement in 1867. On the formation of Alexander Mackenzie's Liberal Cabinet in 1873, Dorion served briefly as minister of justice. From 1874 until his death he was chief justice of the Quebec Court of Queen's Bench.

DORION, residential town of Quebec, Canada, located on Lake of Two Mountains, adjacent to Vaudreuil. It is also a well-known summer resort. Inc. as town, 1916; pop., 4,996.

DORIOT [dô-ryō'], **JACQUES** (1888–1945), French politician. As leader of the fascist French Popular party, Doriot was an advocate of collaboration with Nazi Germany before and during World War II. Doriot was a prominent leader of the Communist party until his expulsion in 1934 for advocating a popular front with the socialists. He then formed his own party and devoted the rest of his life to combatting communism. During the German occupation Doriot's party actively collaborated with the Germans. In the last months of the war, Doriot formed, with German Chancellor Adolf Hitler's approval, a French government in exile. He was killed during an allied air raid on Germany.

DORKING, urban district of central Surrey, England, 18 mi. south-southwest of London. It is primarily residential and there is also some light industry. Thomas Robert Malthus, the economist, was a resident of Dorking, and George Meredith, the writer, lived and is buried here. Pop., 22,594.

DORMONT, residential suburb southwest of Pittsburgh. The name of the town comes from an inversion of the French *mont d'or*, "gold mountain." Settled, c.1790; inc., 1909; pop. (1950) 13,405; (1960) 13,098.

DORMOUSE, a rodent of the family Gliridae, native to Europe, Asia, and Africa. Dormice are like mice in size only. They bear a strong resemblance to the squirrel, sharing the latter's preference for life in the trees and a diet of fruit, nuts, and seeds. In temperate climates dormice hibernate during the winter months, as do many other rodents. Among the European species is the fat dormouse, *Glis glis*, which was regarded as a great table delicacy by the Romans.

DORNBERGER, WALTER ROBERT (1895–), German rocket engineer. He was put in charge of the German army's rocket research in 1931. In 1937 the rocket research institute at Peenemunde was founded with Col. Dornberger in command. There the V-2 ballistic missile was successfully developed. Brought to the United States in 1947, Dornberger became a guided-missile specialist for the U.S. government and for private companies.

DORR [*dôr*], **THOMAS WILSON** (1805–54), American political leader. He led the "People's party" of Rhode Island in the 1840–42 effort to obtain universal (white) male suffrage in that state, usually referred to as "Dorr's Rebellion." Son of a prosperous manufacturer of Providence, Dorr attended Phillips Exeter Academy and Harvard College. Becoming a Providence lawyer and state legislator, Dorr took the lead in the effort to extend the suffrage in Rhode Island, still governed under its old colonial charter. By the 1840's this charter disfranchised over half the state's adult males through property requirements and gave vastly disproportionate representation to rural southern Rhode Island. After futile appeals to the state legislature, Dorr's party held a referendum (with universal manhood suffrage) on its own proposed constitution, which received an overwhelming majority. The legislature then produced a compromise constitution, but the Dorrites voted it down and organized a state government of their own (May, 1842). The old government suppressed the Dorrites with relatively little violence. Dorr was immediately charged with and convicted of treason and sentenced to life imprisonment (1844). The old government was, however, forced by popular demand to grant a constitution establishing almost universal suffrage. Dorr was released in 1845; but with his health broken, he did not re-enter politics.

Consult Mowry, A. M., *The Dorr War* (1901).

ROBERT E. ROEDER, University of Chicago

DORSETSHIRE, county of southwestern England, bounded on the south by the English Channel. The land is mainly undulating, with the Purbeck Downs in the south and the Dorset Heights in the west. Bulbarrow (901 ft.), in the center, is the highest point in the county. The Chesil Bank, a shingle beach parallel to the coast and some 17 mi. long, links the Isle of Portland to the mainland. The heathlands are mainly unused, but the chalk country is mostly arable land and pastoral farming predominates in the rest of the county. Tourism is important, especially in the many coastal communities, and Weymouth is also a port for passenger traffic to the Channel Islands. Dorchester, the county town, was founded by the Romans and there are many Roman remains throughout the county. Many of Thomas Hardy's novels are set in Dorsetshire. Administrative county, area, 973 sq. mi.; pop., 309,176.

DORSEY [*dôr'sē*], **JAMES FRANCIS ("JIMMY")** (1904–57), American clarinetist, alto saxophonist, and orchestra leader. Born in Shenandoah, Pa., he became a professional musician when he was 17. In 1933, together with his brother Tommy, he formed an orchestra, but it lasted only three years. He led his own orchestra from 1935 to 1953, after which he joined his brother's band. His recordings of *Amapola*, *Green Eyes*, and *Tangerine* were very popular.

DORSEY, THOMAS FRANCIS ("TOMMY") (1905–56), American trombonist and orchestra leader, born in Mahanoy City, Pa. He first formed an orchestra in 1933 in partnership with his brother Jimmy. Three years later, he left the group to organize his own dance band, which became one of the most successful orchestras of the swing era. Among his most popular recordings were *Song of India*, *I'm Getting Sentimental Over You*, *Marie*, *I'll Never Smile Again*, and *Boogie-Woogie*. Jimmy joined Tommy's orchestra in 1953, leading it after Tommy's death.

DORT, SYNOD OF, assembly of Reformed churches at Dort (Dordrecht), the Netherlands, in 1618–19. Its chief business was to deal with an attempt by the "Remonstrants," or supporters of Arminianism, to soften the rigors of John Calvin's teaching. Adherents to the latter creed, who were in the majority, would not allow their opponents to put forward their case in public session, condemned them in five articles included in what became known as the Canons of the Synod of Dort, and had them deposed. The synod reaffirmed acceptance of the Belgic and Helvetic confessions, and thus consolidated in the Netherlands a strict Calvinism lasting two centuries.

See also ARMINIANISM; BELGIC CONFESSION, THE; HELVETIC CONFESSIONS.

DORTMUND [*dôrt'mo͝ont*], city of the German Federal Republic (West Germany), in the Ruhr industrial region, in the valley of the Emscher River and 33 mi. east of the Rhine River. In medieval times though Dortmund was a small city, it was a member of the Hanseatic League. Battles raged across it during the Thirty Years' War (1618–48). Its modern growth was spurred in the 19th century by large iron-smelting and steel-making works. This development was fostered by the rich coal deposits nearby and also by the construction of canals. Dortmund was linked both with the Rhine (Herne Canal) and with the North Sea port of Emden (Dortmund-Ems Canal). Thus the iron and steel works were supplied with local coal, and with iron ore imported mostly by canal barge. The city was severely damaged by bombing during World War II, but has been entirely rebuilt. In addition to its metallurgical works, Dortmund has oil-refining, chemical, and brewing industries. Pop., 654,551.

NORMAN J. G. POUNDS, Indiana University

DORVAL [*dôr-vàl'*], residential suburb of Quebec, Canada, west of Montreal, on Lake St. Louis of the St. Lawrence River. Located here is the largest and one of the best-equipped airports in Canada—a terminal for transatlantic and transcontinental planes and a transfer station for many air routes. Inc. as town, 1903; as city, 1956; pop., 18,592.

DOS PASSOS [*dəs păs'əs*], **JOHN RODERIGO** (1896–), American novelist, born in Chicago and graduated from Harvard in 1916. His novels *The 42nd Parallel* (1930), *1919* (1932), and *The Big Money* (1936), which were collected in 1937 in one volume entitled *U.S.A.*, are generally regarded as his major works. They constitute one of the most celebrated attempts to describe and evaluate American society in the 20th century. Dos Passos' incorporation into his fictional narrative of biographical sketches, newspaper headlines, and an autobiographic interior monologue has received widespread critical attention. Previously, he had published *Three Soldiers* (1921), the story of an aesthete's reactions to the horrors of World War I, and *Manhattan Transfer* (1925), a kaleidoscopic portrayal of New York life. Both the technical innovations and the leftist social orientation of these novels were largely abandoned in such later works as the *District of Columbia* trilogy (1952), comprising *Adventures of a Young Man* (1939), *Number One* (1943), and *The Grand Design* (1949). In these novels and in *Chosen Country* (1951) and *Midcentury* (1961), Dos Passos repudiated his earlier faith in social radicalism, deplored the increasing collectivization of American society, and favored a return to older national traditions. His growing conservatism was also reflected in such nonfictional works as *The Ground We Stand On* (1941) and *The Head and Heart of Thomas Jefferson* (1954).

SEYMOUR RUDIN, University of Massachusetts

DOSTOYEVSKY [dŏs-tŏ-yĕf'skē], **FYODOR MIKHAILOVICH** (1821–81), Russian writer, one of the world's great novelists. He was born in Moscow where his father, an impoverished nobleman, was a physician in the hospital for the poor. In 1837 he entered the School of Military Engineering in St. Petersburg. Two years later his father was murdered by his serfs, and many biographers believe that this tragic event brought on Dostoyevsky's attacks of epilepsy. After a short career as a military draftsman, he wrote his first novel, *Poor Folk* (1846), which depicted a humble government clerk who falls in love with an unhappy girl. It was hailed by the critics as a humanitarian work in the new style of Gogol's school of realism.

In 1849 Dostoyevsky was arrested as a member of the clandestine Petrashevsky Society, a radical group with socialist leanings. He was sentenced to death and put in front of a firing squad; at the last moment, however, his sentence was commuted to a prison term. Dostoyevsky spent four years as a convict in a Siberian penitentiary, which he described in 1861 in *Memories From the House of the Dead*, and another four years as a private in an Asiatic garrison. In 1857 he married Maria Isayeva, a young consumptive widow, and was allowed to return to European Russia and resume his literary activities.

The publication of the romantic novel *The Insulted and the Injured* (1861–62) marked the second period of his development as a novelist. His wife died in 1864, the year he published *Notes From the Underground*, a work that showed depth of insight into man's sadistic and masochistic drives and expressed a pessimistic philosophy of history. In the 1950's it was considered one of the first specimens of existentialist fiction.

The most fruitful period of Dostoyevsky's work opened in 1866 with the publication of *Crime and Punishment*, a masterpiece of psychological penetration and dramatic

The Bettmann Archive

Fyodor Dostoyevsky, as portrayed by W. G. Perov.

tension. In 1867 he married the stenographer to whom he dictated his novel *The Gambler* (1866); their happy marriage gave Dostoyevsky a strong feeling of security. His next works were *The Idiot* (1868); *The Possessed* (1871–72), a complex novel with strong political and antirevolutionary implications; *A Raw Youth* (1875); and finally *The Brothers Karamazov* (1879–80), which is considered the epitome of his religious and philosophical thought and his highest artistic achievement. The dramatic intensity of Dostoyevsky's narratives is often reminiscent of mystery novels, but the passions of his heroes are related with an extraordinary knowledge of the most secret recesses of the human heart. A painter of the morbid and the neurotic, Dostoyevsky is at the same time the creator of the philosophical novel. His heroes, from Raskolnikov, the murderer in *Crime and Punishment*, to Ivan Karamazov, the metaphysical rebel, build theories for self-justification and search for God or a new morality. Most of his characters are victims of their inner restlessness, and they race toward their destruction with tragic fatalism, but the problems they raise are presented by the author as living realities rather than as intellectual questions.

Dostoyevsky's influence on scores of later European and American novelists made him one of the most important figures of world literature. The novels of Dostoyevsky are all available in English translation.

Consult Gide, André, *Dostoevsky* (trans., 1926); Yarmolinsky, Avrahm, *Dostoevsky* (rev. ed., 1960); Steiner, George, *Tolstoy or Dostoevsky* (1960).

MARC SLONIM, Sarah Lawrence College

See also BROTHERS KARAMAZOV, THE; CRIME AND PUNISHMENT.

DOTHAN [dō'thən], city of southeastern Alabama, and seat of Houston County. A national Peanut Festival, sponsored by the Georgia-Florida-Alabama Peanut Association, is held here every October. Inc., 1885; pop. (1950) 21,584; (1960) 31,440.

DOU or DOW [dou], **GERARD** (1613–75), Dutch painter, best known for his portraits and genre scenes. The handling of chiaroscuro and the brushwork of his early paintings show the influence of Rembrandt, whose pupil he was. Later he turned to small scenes of everyday life executed in a polished, detailed style. Notable works include "The Evening School" (Rijksmuseum, Amsterdam) and "Woman with Dropsy" (Louvre, Paris). The Metropolitan Museum of Art in New York has a self-portrait.

DOUAI [dōō-ä'], industrial, coal-mining, and canal center of northern France, on the Scarpe River, about 20 mi. south of Lille. Coal mined in the vicinity is converted here into coke, gas, or briquettes, or shipped by barge to other areas. Coke is used in the local steel mills. After the medieval period it belonged successively to Flanders, Burgundy, and Spain, before passing to France in 1713. The university founded here in 1562 became a center of religious and political propaganda for Roman Catholics exiled from England. Here was produced the translation known as the Douay Bible, which is the basis for the modern Roman Catholic version of the Bible in English. The university was suppressed in 1793 and reopened at Lille in 1887. Douai suffered heavy damage in both world wars. Pop., 50,104.

DOUALA [dōō-ä'lə], main port, largest city, and principal economic center of the Republic of Cameroun, located on the south bank of the Wouri River estuary. The city occupies a humid site which averages about 156 in. of rainfall per year. Mount Cameroun volcano (elev., 13,350 ft.), west-northwest, can be seen on clear days. The port has about 5,700 ft. of docks. Exports include mahogany, palm oil, and cacao beans. Douala is the terminus of two railroads: a line running eastward about 190 mi. to Yaoundé, the capital, and a line, about 100 mi. long, north from the suburb of Bonaberi, across the estuary, through banana country to Nkongsamba. The city has seaplane facilities and an airport. There are Roman Catholic and Protestant missions here. Douala was claimed for Germany in 1884 and became the capital of Kamerun from 1901 until Germany lost the colony in World War I. Pop., 118,857.

DOUAY [dōō-ä'] **BIBLE,** the first Bible translation authorized for the use of English-speaking Roman Catholics. It takes its name from Douai in Flanders, where an English college for Roman Catholics was established in 1568. The New Testament appeared in 1582 (during a temporary transference of the college to Reims), the Old Testament in 1609 and 1610. The translator was Gregory Martin, a professor of the college and formerly an Oxford scholar. Despite its many fine qualities, the translation, based on the Latin Vulgate, was too full of Latinisms to be generally intelligible. It was therefore revised in 1750 by Bishop Richard Challoner.
See also BIBLE.

DOUBLEDAY, ABNER (1819–93), American army officer, born in Ballston Spa, N.Y. He served in both the Mexican and Civil wars. He has been credited with inventing baseball at Cooperstown, N.Y., in 1839, though most modern historians reject the contention.

DOUBLEDAY, FRANK NELSON (1862–1934), American publisher. Born in Brooklyn, N.Y., he went to work at Scribner's when he was 15. In 1897 he and Samuel S. McClure founded the publishing house of Doubleday, McClure & Company; this was reorganized as Doubleday, Page & Company in 1900. In 1927 the firm merged to become Doubleday, Doran & Company, Inc. Doubleday was responsible for publication of such notable authors as Joseph Conrad, O. Henry, Rudyard Kipling, Booth Tarkington, Edna Ferber, and Sinclair Lewis. Today Doubleday & Company, Inc., is one of the world's largest book publishers.

DOUBLE REFRACTION. *See* REFRACTION.

DOUBLE STAR. *See* BINARY STAR.

DOUGHERTY [dô'hər-tē], **DENNIS** (1865–1951), American Cardinal. Born in Honesville, Pa., he studied at the North American College, Rome, in 1885, and was ordained priest in 1890. He became the first American bishop in the Philippines, receiving the see of Nueva Segovia in 1903 and that of Jaro in 1908. In 1915 he was transferred to Buffalo, N.Y., and in 1918 was made Archbishop of Philadelphia. In 1921 he became the fifth American to be elected Cardinal.

DOUGHTY [dou'tē], **CHARLES MONTAGU** (1843–1926), English explorer and scholar. Between 1875 and 1878 he penetrated the almost unknown Arabian Peninsula. Striking inland from Damascus with a train of pilgrims, he encountered frequent risks and discovered important archeological remains in his adventurous wanderings, eventually emerging at the port of Jiddah. His *Travels in Arabia Deserta*, describing the desert and its people in rich Elizabethan prose, is a classic of travel literature.

DOUGLAS, Scottish noble family. The family won its fame by the exploits of Sir **WILLIAM OF DOUGLAS** (d. 1298), who fought against the English with Sir William Wallace, and Sir James Douglas, Lord of Douglas (q.v.), called "Black Douglas," who shared with Robert the Bruce the hardships of the national war against England. The descendants of this branch of the family became the earls of Douglas and were known as the "Black Douglases," while another branch, stemming from an irregular connection of the 1st Earl of Douglas, became the earls of Angus and were known as the "Red Douglases." Both branches of the family played important roles in Scottish history down through the 17th century, after which the marquessate of Douglas and the earldom of Angus, the dignities held by the Black and Red Douglases, merged in the Hamilton peerage. In addition to the dukes of Hamilton, the family is represented by the dukes of Buccleuch and Queensberry and the earls of Home and Morton.

JOHN G. SPERLING, Northern Illinois University

DOUGLAS, SIR HOWARD, 3D BART. (1776–1861), British soldier and colonial administrator. After a military career, including 10 years as commandant of the Royal Military Academy in England, he became Lieutenant-Governor and Commander in Chief of New Brunswick, 1824–31. Douglas' most conspicuous contributions to this province were the promotion of elementary and higher education and the defense of its western boundary against American freebooting expeditions. His subsequent career included the administration of the Ionian Islands, 1835–40, and participation in British politics.

DOUGLAS, SIR JAMES (1803–77), Hudson Bay factor and British colonial administrator. Born in Demerara, British Guiana, and educated in Scotland, Douglas went to British North America in 1819. He was employed by the Hudson's Bay Company (1821–58) and was governor of Vancouver Island (1851–63) and of the mainland colony of British Columbia (1858–64). Associated after 1830 on the Pacific Coast with John McLoughlin, Douglas removed the company's Pacific headquarters from Fort Vancouver (Washington) to the present site of Victoria on Vancouver Island in 1843 in anticipation of the Oregon boundary decision of 1846. When Vancouver Island was granted to the company in 1849, Douglas became its second governor in 1851. From 1858, on the creation of the colony of British Columbia and the severance of Vancouver Island from company control, he administered the government of both colonies. His most difficult assignment was that of preserving order on the mainland during the Fraser Valley gold rush precipitated in 1858. This he accomplished with eminent success, although with little regard for proper constitutional procedure. Quite out of sympathy with the growing demand for democratic institutions, Douglas returned to private life in 1864 and died in Victoria in 1877. He did much to save the infant British Pacific colonies from absorption into the United States and has aptly been called the father of British Columbia.

W. Menzies Whitelaw, *American International College*

DOUGLAS, SIR JAMES DOUGLAS, LORD OF (1286?–1330), Scottish nobleman, called the Black Douglas and Douglas the Good. Douglas fought valiantly in the Scottish wars with Robert the Bruce (Robert I) against Edward I of England, winning a knighthood at Bannockburn. On Robert I's absence in Ireland (1316), Douglas was coregent, and upon the King's death he sought to carry his heart to Palestine for burial but was killed en route fighting the Moors in Spain.

DOUGLAS, KIRK (1918–), American actor, born in Amsterdam, N.Y. He began his film career in 1946, after appearing on the New York stage. He first gained prominence in *Champion* (1949), and later starred in *Ace in the Hole* (1951), *Detective Story* (1951), *Ulysses* (1955), *Lust for Life* (1956), *Paths of Glory* (1958), and *Spartacus* (1960). He became an independent film producer in 1955.

DOUGLAS, LLOYD CASSEL (1877–1951), American author and clergyman, born in Columbia City, Ind. He served as a Lutheran minister until 1933, when he retired to devote all his time to writing. Though disapproved by the critics, such novels as *Magnificent Obsession* (1929) and *Green Light* (1935), which preached personal fulfillment through service to others, enjoyed great popularity. They were followed by *The Robe* (1942) and *The Big Fisherman* (1948), historical novels based on the New Testament which were even more successful with the public.

DOUGLAS, NORMAN (1868–1952), Scottish writer best known for his *South Wind* (1917), a novel reflecting the many years he spent in Capri. His many books include travel writings: *Fountains in the Sand* (1923), *Old Calabria* (1928); novels: *They Went* (1921), *Together* (1923), *Three of Them* (1930); and an autobiography: *Looking Back* (1933).

DOUGLAS, PAUL HOWARD (1892–), U.S. Senator. Born in Salem, Mass., and reared on a Maine farm, he graduated (1913) from Bowdoin College and received his Ph.D. degree (1921) from Columbia University. He taught economics at the University of Illinois (1916–17), at Reed College (1917–18), and at the University of Washington (1919–20), then became assistant professor of industrial relations (1920) and full professor (1925) at the University of Chicago. Douglas served (1943–1946) in the Marine Corps and was elected in 1948, 1954, and 1960, to the U.S. Senate from Illinois. A leader of the liberal Democrats, he became an authority on problems of civil rights and economics.

DOUGLAS, STEPHEN ARNOLD (1813–61), American statesman. Born in Brandon, Vt., he studied law at Canandaigua Academy in New York, moved (1833) to Jacksonville, Ill., and was admitted to the bar in 1834. Entering politics in 1835, Douglas was principally responsible for the growth and development of the Democratic party in Illinois. After serving in the state legislature (1836–37), as secretary of state (1840), and as a judge on the state supreme court (1841), he served as a Democrat in the U.S. House of Representatives (1843–47). He was elected to the U.S. Senate in 1847 and remained a prominent figure there until his death.

Appointed chairman of the Committee on Territories, Douglas was in the ideal spot to carry on his fight to give the local inhabitants of a territory or state the final decision on whether or not to allow slavery. This was the basis of the articles he drafted instituting the territorial governments of Utah and New Mexico for the Compromise of 1850. Four years later Douglas again advocated, in the Kansas-Nebraska Act (1854), his policy of "Popular Sovereignty" as a possible solution to the slavery question. It raised a storm of opposition, especially between the proslavery and the free-state forces in Kansas, and proved a contributory cause of the Civil War. When President James Buchanan gave his support to the proslavery Lecompton Constitution (1857) for Kansas, Douglas bitterly condemned both Buchanan and his administration and broke with the proslavery Democrats, preventing the constitution's approval.

In 1858 Douglas, while campaigning for re-election to the Senate, attacked the "House Divided" doctrine of his

The Bettmann Archive

Stephen Douglas, who as a U.S. Senator campaigning for re-election in 1858, engaged in a series of debates on slavery with Abraham Lincoln. Lincoln was Douglas' opponent in the election.

Republican opponent in Illinois, Abraham Lincoln. He accepted Lincoln's challenge of debate and the famous Lincoln-Douglas Debates ensued. In their second debate, at Freeport, Lincoln placed Douglas, a strong proponent of the sanctity of Supreme Court decisions, in a dilemma by asking him if he accepted the Court's Dred Scott decision, which had suggested that slavery could not be excluded anywhere in the country. Douglas replied that the inhabitants of a territory could choose to include or exclude slavery. He won re-election but was removed as chairman of the Committee on Territories by the Southern Democrats who opposed his repudiation of the Dred Scott decision.

Attending the 1860 Democratic National Convention in Charleston, S.C., Douglas secured the defeat of William L. Yancey's demands for federal protection of slavery and saw his compromise proposal of nonintervention accepted. Yancey and his followers withdrew to nominate their own presidential candidate, John C. Breckinridge. The Democratic convention removed to Baltimore and nominated Douglas for the presidency. This split in the Democratic party insured Lincoln's victory, and when he took office the defeated Douglas threw all his support and influence to the administration in a last attempt to save the Union. He died of typhoid fever during the Civil War while on a speaking tour of the North to gain support for the Union.

Consult Capers, G.M., *Stephen A. Douglas: Defender of the Union* (1959).

JAMES P. SHENTON, Columbia University

DOUGLAS, THOMAS. *See* SELKIRK, THOMAS DOUGLAS, 5TH EARL OF.

DOUGLAS, THOMAS CLEMENT (1904–), Canadian political leader. Born in Falkirk, Scotland, he went (1910) to Canada with his parents. He trained for the Baptist ministry before entering federal politics in 1935. Representing Weyburn, Saskatchewan, until 1944, Douglas promoted social-welfare measures, co-operative enterprise, and state medical aid. In 1944 he became Premier of Saskatchewan, the first Co-operative Commonwealth Federation leader to form a provincial government. His party won at the polls in 1948, 1952, 1956, and 1960, but Douglas resigned his position in 1961 to become national leader of the New Democratic party.

DOUGLAS, WILLIAM ORVILLE (1898–), American jurist. Born in Minnesota, Douglas graduated from Whitman College in 1920 and, working his way through Columbia Law School, received his law degree in 1925. After teaching law (1925–34) at both Columbia and Yale, Douglas was appointed (1934) to the Securities and Exchange Commission. As the chairman of the commission (1937–39) he instituted sweeping reforms. President Franklin Roosevelt appointed him (1939) Associate Justice of the Supreme Court. He became a leading court liberal and strongly supported Roosevelt's New Deal measures. Douglas, a Democrat, thus rose to prominence and was strongly favored as a presidential possibility in 1948 until he expressed no desire for that office. Among Douglas' numerous books are *Russian Journey* (1956) and *America Challenged* (1960).

DOUGLAS, city of southeastern Arizona, on the Mexican border. It serves as a port of entry and is adjacent to the Mexican town of Agua Prieta. The city is a center for stock raising, agriculture, and the smelting and mining of manganese, copper, and lime. Originally a cattle roundup site, the town of Douglas was founded in 1900 as a smelter location by the Phelps Dodge Corporation. Inc., 1905; pop. (1950) 9,442; (1960) 11,925.

DOUGLAS, city of south-central Georgia and seat of Coffee County. Poultry and allied products are the leading industries, augmented by the manufacture of mobile homes, clothing, and lumber. South Georgia College (estab., 1907) is here. Inc., 1897; pop. (1950) 7,428; (1960) 8,736.

DOUGLAS FIR, a tall evergreen tree, *Pseudotsuga taxifolia*, in the Pinaceae, or pine family. This handsome tree is native to western North America and is also called Douglas spruce or red fir, but is related only distantly to the spruces of genus *Abies*, and to the firs of genus *Tsuga*. Douglas firs grow to a height of 200 ft. or more, and sometimes have trunks 12 ft. in diameter. They grow rapidly in a symmetrical, pyramidal form and bear oblong, bristly

The Douglas fir has deeply furrowed, reddish-brown bark. Its flattened needles are dark yellow-green or blue-green. The light-brown cones are from 2 to 4 in. long.

cones. The lumber of Douglas firs is widely used in construction and the bark is sometimes used to tan leather. The smaller varieties are widely employed in landscaping.

DOUGLAS-HOME [dŭg'las-hūm'], **SIR ALEC,** former Earl of Home (1903–   ), British Prime Minister. He was first elected to Parliament in 1931 as a Conservative and served as parliamentary private secretary to Prime Minister Neville Chamberlain (1937–39). Swept out of the House of Commons in the Labour landslide of 1945, he returned in 1950, but succeeded to his father's title the following year and moved to the House of Lords. As Lord Home, he held the posts of Secretary of State for Commonwealth Relations (1955–60), Leader of the House of Lords (1957), and Lord President of the Council (1959–60).

He became Secretary of State for Foreign Affairs in 1960, the first peer to hold that office since 1940. The appointment aroused some criticism because Home, as a peer, could not answer for the government in the House of Commons. When Prime Minister Harold Macmillan retired for reasons of health in Oct., 1963, the Queen chose Lord Home as his successor. He then renounced his titles and won election to the House of Commons (where prime ministers traditionally sit) as Sir Alec Douglas-Home. In the general elections of Oct., 1964, Labour narrowly defeated the Conservatives, and Douglas-Home was succeeded by Harold Wilson. He retained his seat in Parliament.

JOHN G. SPERLING, San Jose State College

DOUGLASS, FREDERICK (c.1817–95), American abolitionist. Born in Maryland, the son of a Negro slave and an unknown white father, he escaped to freedom in 1838 and adopted the surname Douglass. Settling in New Bedford, Douglass was drawn into the abolitionist movement when an extemporaneous speech before the Massachusetts Anti-Slavery Society (1841) revealed his extraordinary ability as a public speaker. The story of his life as a slave, published in 1845, was a powerful antislavery document, but the publicity compelled him to leave the country and spend two years in England and Ireland until money could be raised to purchase his freedom. Once free, Douglass published (1847–64) the *North Star* in Rochester, N.Y., and spoke on behalf of the emancipation of women as well as of slaves. He became the outstand-

ing Negro abolitionist and one of the most influential members of the movement. He was forced to flee the country again after John Brown's raid at Harpers Ferry, but as public opinion changed, he returned to campaign for Abraham Lincoln. When the Civil War erupted, he helped to organize two regiments of Massachusetts Negroes. He continued to agitate for civil rights for both Negroes and women, and was appointed to several federal offices including secretary of the Santo Domingo Commission (1871), Marshal (1877–81) and Recorder of Deeds (1881–86) for the District of Columbia, and Minister to Haiti (1889–91).

HERBERT A. WISBEY, JR., Keuka College

DOUKHOBORS [dōō'kə-bôrz] (Russ. *Dukhobory,* "spirit wrestlers"), religious sect that emerged in Russia, about 1750. They believe that man, being essentially good, knows and is dutybound to follow the divinity within him, without conformity to standard religious organization or rites. They also reject civil authority, however. About 13,000 descendants of an 1899 migration to Canada now live in British Columbia and Saskatchewan as three groups, most of them peaceful and law-abiding. The Independents accepted education and private holdings. The Orthodox shifted from a communal pattern of life to that of the Independents in the 1960's. The Sons of Freedom are known for their violent protests.

The simple, democratic, Christian religion of the Doukhobors changed into a theocratic despotism from about 1775–85, mainly because of their opposition to any form of governmental restraint. This finally resulted in their banishment from the Crimea, where they had originally sought refuge, to the Caucasus, where living conditions were severe. Conflicts with the government continued until 1895, when the Russian novelist Leo Tolstoy and both the English and American Quakers sponsored a migration to Saskatchewan of about 7,000 of the then estimated 18,000 Doukhobors. In 1907 most of this group, opposed to secular education and land registration, lost their lands and civil rights, when they refused to take patriotic oaths or to register under the Homestead Act, by which they had been provided with homes. A year or so later, about 2,000 of the more extreme Doukhobors settled in British Columbia. Over a period of many years, the Sons of Freedom, as this group became known, resorted to acts of violence and nudist demonstrations, whenever they saw fit to protest governmental interference with their own social and economic principles. By 1953, however, following mass arrests, children of the group were put in government schools to receive education for the first time. Since then, with literacy increased and improved standards of living, many of the Doukhobors have assimilated fully.

SIMMA HOLT, Author,
Tenor in the Name of God: A History of the Doukhobors

DOURO [dō'rōō] **RIVER** (Span. **DUERO**), river of Portugal and Spain, which rises in the Sierra de Urbión in north-central Spain, flows west past Zamora, forms the Spanish-Portuguese boundary while flowing southwest, then flows west across Portugal to the Atlantic Ocean near Oporto. Length, 475 mi.; drainage area, 30,500 sq. mi.

Part of the white cliffs of Dover, in Kent, England, viewed from a boat in the Strait of Dover.
(J. ALLAN CASH—ILLUSTRATION RESEARCH SERVICE)

DOUROUCOULI [dōo-rōo-kōo'lē], the so-called night monkey, *Aotes*, native to tropical America. This small, furry primate has long legs, arms, and tail, and enormous round eyes set close together. The animal is solitary and strictly nocturnal. At night it becomes alert and active, prowling about for the insects on which it feeds.

DOVE [dŭv], **ARTHUR G.** (1880–1946), American painter, born in Canandaigua, N.Y. He was one of the earliest American abstractionists, beginning his experiments in this style about 1912. His paintings, though nonrepresentational, are characterized by colors and shapes suggestive of forms in nature. Dove also made collages. His works are found in the Phillips Gallery, Washington, D.C., and other museums.

DOVE [dō'və], **HEINRICH WILHELM** (1803–79), German physicist and meteorologist who formulated the law of gyration, which states that winds tend to shift in direction with the sun. He also invented the induction balance to measure the electrical conductivity of metals. Educated at Breslau and Berlin, Dove taught at the University of Berlin and conducted research on static electricity, polarized light, and various meteorological phenomena. His theory that cyclonic storms result from the interaction of tropical and polar air currents is incorporated into modern theories of cyclone development. Among his publications are *Meteorological Researches* (1837) and *The Law of Storms* (1857).

DOVE, among Christians a symbol of God's love in any of its manifestations. A dove bearing an olive leaf brought hope to Noah at the end of the flood (Gen. 8:11). At Christ's baptism the Holy Spirit appeared in the form of a dove (Matt. 3:16). A dove-shaped vessel was often suspended over ancient baptismal fonts and, as a receptacle for the Holy Eucharist, over the altar. In Christian art the dove frequently symbolizes hope, peace, martyrdom, the Holy Spirit, and the Eucharist.

DOVE, name for several birds in the pigeon family, Columbidae, found especially in tropical regions. There is no difference between doves and pigeons save that the name "dove" is generally given to the smaller members of the family.

DOVER, port city in Kent, England, on the 20-mi.-wide Strait of Dover, the narrowest part of the English Channel. The city is at the foot of high chalk cliffs in the narrow valley of the small Dover River, which has cut through the chalk.

Since the beginning of English history, Dover has been of immense commercial and strategic importance. The Romans built a lighthouse and the town of Dubris on the site. Later the Saxons fortified the cliffs above the town. Most of this structure was replaced by a much larger and stronger Norman castle. Its oldest part, Peverell's Tower, dates from shortly after 1066. In the Battle of Dover, 1217, Henry III defeated France and secured his throne. From medieval times, Dover was one of the privileged Cinque (Five) Ports. It remains the leading English port for the cross-channel traffic. During World War I, Dover was an important naval base. During World War II it was the main port in the evacuation of Dunkirk and was constantly under fire thereafter. Caves and tunnels in the cliffs were used for shelter. Pop., 35,248.

NORMAN J. G. POUNDS, Indiana University

DOVER, capital of Delaware and seat of Kent County, located in the central part of the state, 6 mi. west of the shore of Delaware Bay and about 60 mi. south of Philadelphia. The area around Dover is generally low and fertile, and the city serves as a market and distribution center. One of Dover's industries, a cooked-chicken and plum-pudding cannery founded in 1855, is known nationally. The others, producing such items as crates, fruit baskets, hosiery, and plumbing supplies, cater only to local needs.

In 1683 William Penn ordered a county seat, to be named Dover, established. A courthouse and a prison were built by 1697, but the town was not laid out until 1717. The original plan included the Green, a tree-shaded square, where fairs, markets, and militia drills were held. The Green has continued to be a focal area of Dover. The State House, built in 1792 in Georgian Colonial style, is on the Green's east side. Dover replaced New Castle as the State capital in 1777. On Dec. 7, 1787, at state convention in Dover, Delaware ratified the U.S. Constitution, making it the first state to join the Union.

Dover is an attractive city with an unusual number of buildings dating from the 18th century. Every year, on

Old Dover Day, the first Saturday in May, many historic houses are open to the public. Dover was incorporated as a city in 1929, with a council-manager form of government. The city operates its own electric generating plant, water and sewage system, and municipal incinerator. Within the city are the Kent County General Hospital, Wesley Junior College, and the Delaware State Museum. Delaware State College (estab. 1891) is nearby. Pop. (1950) 6,223; (1960) 7,250.

H. GARDINER BARNUM, The University of Vermont

DOVER, city of southeastern New Hampshire and seat of Strafford County, at the head of navigation on the Cocheco River. Electronics equipment and shoes are manufactured. Settled in 1622, it is one of the oldest communities in New Hampshire. Numerous colonial homes including the Guppy House, built in 1690, remain. Inc., 1855; pop. (1950) 15,874; (1960) 19,131.

DOVER, industrial town of northern New Jersey. Metal fabricating and the manufacture of machinery and clothing are the principal industries. Dover was formerly the center of an iron-mining district, and a forge was erected here as early as 1722. During the 19th century the town was an iron-shipping port on the Morris Canal. Picatinny Arsenal, a rocket-research center, is nearby. Inc., 1869; pop. (1950) 11,174; (1960) 13,034.

DOVER, city of east-central Ohio, on the Tuscarawas River. Chemicals, aluminum castings, and electric wire are manufactured here. Early industrial and commercial development was based on the city's canal location. Founded, 1807; pop. (1950) 9,852; (1960) 11,300.

DOVER, STRAIT OF (Fr. **PAS DE CALAIS**), narrow part of the English Channel between England and France. Connecting the main part of the Channel with the North Sea, it is 22 mi. long and 21 mi. wide at its narrowest point, between Dover and Cape Gris-Nez, near Calais. With a maximum depth of about 200 ft., it has a central shallow caused by shoals. Chalk cliffs line both sides of the strait. The most important ports are Dover and Folkestone (England), and Calais and Boulogne-sur-Mer (France); they are served by ferries. The strait has been the scene of many naval battles, including the first serious check of the Spanish Armada in 1588. Frequent fogs and shifting currents make passage through the strait difficult at times.

DOVER, TREATY OF, in English history, secret compact negotiated (1670) between Charles II of England and Louis XIV of France whereby Charles was freed from his dependence on Parliament for funds and Louis secured a military alliance and a promise that England would be restored to the Catholic Church. Charles contracted to support France in a war with the Dutch and to participate in a projected partition of the Netherlands. He likewise agreed that when the time was propitious he would restore Catholicism as the state religion. In return Louis undertook to pay him an annual subsidy and to supply troops, if needed, to force Catholicism on the English.

DOWAGIAC [dō-wŏj'ăk], city of southwestern Michigan,

in a fruit-growing and farming region. The artificial casting lure was invented here in 1898. Stoves and furnaces have been manufactured at Dowagiac for more than a century. Pop. (1950) 6,542; (1960) 7,208.

DOWER. *See* FAMILY LAW.

DOWIE [dou'ē], **JOHN ALEXANDER** (1847–1907), evangelist and founder of the Christian Catholic Church in Chicago. In 1900 he established Zion City, Ill., a religious community under theocratic rule, owning and operating its own industries and other business enterprises. He was an ardent exponent of spiritual healing.

DOWLAND [dou'lənd], **JOHN** (1563–1626), famous English composer and lutanist. While Dowland wrote some of the finest music for the lute, his greatest achievement lies in Elizabethan song. Here he combined remarkable melodic material, dramatic treatment of text, and harmonies unusual for his day. His four volumes of song (1597–1612), among the earliest examples of solo song, contain the enormously popular *Flow, my Teares* (*Lachrymae*).

DOWN, county of Northern Ireland, facing the Irish Sea between Belfast Lough and Carlingford Lough. It is hilly but fertile, and well cultivated except where the granites of the Slieve Croob hills and Mourne Mountains in the south provide open sheep-runs. The county town is Downpatrick. Area, 956 sq. mi.; pop., 267,013.

DOWNERS GROVE, residential and industrial suburb 20 mi. west of Chicago, Illinois. Chief manufactures include bearings and gears, plastic products, and electric equipment. Morton Arboretum is nearby. Downers Grove was settled in the early 1830's; inc., 1873; pop. (1950) 11,886; (1960) 21,154.

DOWNES, EDWIN OLIN (1886–1955), American music critic, born in Evanston, Ill. He received his early musical training in Boston, and in 1906 was appointed music critic of the Boston *Post*, a position he held until 1924. From then until his death he occupied the most influential single post in American musical criticism, that of music critic of the New York *Times*. An anthology of his newspaper writings appeared in 1957 under the title *Olin Downes on Music*.
See also MUSIC CRITICISM.

DOWNEY, city of southern California, located midway between Los Angeles and Long Beach. Originally a dairy and truck garden community, it now has aircraft, missile, and electronics industries and is also a sprawling commuter city. It has a symphony orchestra and a museum. A polio recuperation center is here. Pop. (1950) 29,516; (1960) 82,505.

DOWNING, JACK. *See* SMITH, SEBA.

DOWNING STREET, dead-end street in London, England, situated in Whitehall near major government offices. The house at No. 10 Downing Street is the official residence

Bobbies guard the entrance to 10 Downing Street, London official residence of the Prime Minister of England. (PICTORIAL PARADE)

of the Prime Minister; No. 11 is the residence and office of the Chancellor of the Exchequer.

DOWNINGTOWN, borough of southeastern Pennsylvania, on the east branch of Brandywine Creek. It is an industrial town manufacturing paper, textiles, and metal goods. Settled, 1739; inc., 1859; pop. (1950) 4,948; (1960) 5,598.

DOWNY MILDEW. *See* MILDEW.

DOWRY, money or goods brought by a woman to her husband when they marry. The custom of providing a dowry is of extreme antiquity and is widely distributed throughout the world. It may have originated in the mutual gift-giving of the groom's and the bride's families, a custom found among the American Indians, as well as in Asia. The conception of the dowry found in contemporary Occidental societies probably is inherited through Greco-Roman and medieval practices from Semitic traditions. In various parts of the world the husband may be required to return the dowry in case of divorce or of his wife's death while the couple is still childless.

DOWSON [dou'sən], **ERNEST CHRISTOPHER** (1867–1900), English poet. In his adult years he lived in squalor; tuberculosis and alcohol contributed to his early death. His poetry is romantic, pessimistic, and highly musical. His best-known lyric poem is "Non Sum Qualis Eram Bonae sub Regno Cynarae," with its famous refrain "I have been faithful to thee, Cynara! in my fashion." Dowson also wrote short stories, novels, a play, and translations.

DOYLE [doil], **SIR ARTHUR CONAN** (1859–1930), British writer who created Sherlock Holmes. Born in Edinburgh, he was educated in medicine at Edinburgh University, where one of his teachers was Dr. Joseph Bell, the original of Sherlock Holmes. Doyle practiced medi-

cine (1882–90) with small success; in his too-abundant leisure he began to write. *A Study in Scarlet*, embodying the first rough sketch of Holmes, was published in 1887. In 1890 came *The Sign of the Four*, and then, in the *Strand Magazine*, the stories collected as *The Adventures of Sherlock Holmes* and *Memoirs of Sherlock Holmes*, in the last of which Doyle killed off his hero. By popular demand, Holmes reappeared in the *Strand* in *The Hound of the Baskervilles* (1902), *The Return of Sherlock Holmes* (1905), and other later tales. Doyle claimed to prefer his historical romances, especially *The White Company* (1891), to his Sherlock Holmes books, but his public did not agree. Sherlock Holmes—despite careless writing, implausibilities, and even impossibilities in the stories—so captured the popular imagination that he became the folk symbol of the detective. In his later years Doyle devoted himself to spiritualism.

DeLancey Ferguson, Brooklyn College

DOYLESTOWN, borough of southeastern Pennsylvania, and seat of Bucks County. It is largely a residential community within commuting range of Philadelphia. Fonthill, the former residence of archeologist Henry C. Mercer, is now open to the public. The Bucks County Historical Society Museum is also here. Settled, 1735; inc., 1838; pop. (1950) 5,262; (1960) 5,917.

D'OYLY CARTE [doi'lē kärt'], **RICHARD** (1844–1901), English impresario, famous for his productions of Gilbert and Sullivan operas, the first of which was *Trial by Jury* (1875). In 1881 he built the Savoy Theatre in London, where all of the famous team's subsequent works were introduced. He also was responsible for the building of the Royal English Opera House (1891), now the Globe Theatre. The company that he founded to produce the Gilbert and Sullivan operas still bears his name.

DPN. *See* DIPHOSPHOPYRIDINE NUCLEOTIDE (DPN).

DRA, WADI, intermittent stream in Morocco, formed by the junction of the Dades and Imini rivers, which drain the southern slopes of the High (Grand) Atlas. Wadi Dra flows southeast through the Anti-Atlas and then, making a bend,

Sir Arthur Conan Doyle, creator of Sherlock Holmes. (CULVER PICTURES, INC.)

flows southwest to the Atlantic Ocean. The middle course of Wadi Dra forms a part of Morocco's disputed southern boundary with Algeria.

DRACO [drā′kō], first codifier of Athenian law (c.621 B.C.). Draco's assignment was simply to ascertain and write down existing laws, not to initiate modifications of any sort. He is therefore not responsible for the proverbial harshness of the code. Solon in 594 introduced more lenient penalties for crimes, except for homicide. Draco's code made it impossible for aristocratic magistrates to interpret the law in the interests of the nobility.

DRACO, also known as the Dragon, a long, serpentine constellation of spring in the Northern Hemisphere. Its head is marked by four stars about 20° south of the Little Dipper, and its tail ends north of the pointers of the Big Dipper. In Greek mythology Draco was the dragon that guarded the tree of golden apples in the Garden of the Hesperides; it was killed by Hercules. Thuban, the brightest star in Draco, marked the north celestial pole about 2800 B.C., as Polaris does today.
See also CONSTELLATION; THUBAN.

DRACULA [drăk′yə-lə], character in Bram Stoker's horror novel (1897) of the same name. The novel is a fictional embodiment of the vampire legend. It concerns the Hungarian Count Dracula, a vampire who migrates to England intent on increasing the reign of his kind. Verisimilitude is furthered by presenting the incredible story as a series of prosaic documents: letters, journals, news clippings, diaries. The novel was made into a play (1927) and a film (1931), and it inspired a whole series of additional films.

DRACUT [drā′kət], residential suburb of northeastern Massachusetts, part of the Lowell metropolitan area. Settled, 1664; inc. as town, 1702; pop. (1950) 8,666; (1960) 13,674.

DRAFT. *See* SELECTIVE SERVICE.

DRAFTING. *See* MECHANICAL DRAWING.

DRAFT RIOTS, in U.S. history, a series of protests against the Enrollment Act of Mar. 3, 1863, a national conscription law providing for Civil War military service of all able-bodied males aged 20–45. The act provided exemptions for draftees who paid $300.00 or who could furnish substitutes. It aroused considerable opposition and provoked violence throughout the North after May 25, 1863, when enlisting officers began their work. The most serious demonstration occurred in New York City, where there was a brutally destructive riot over a four-day period (July 13–16). The drawing and publication of the first draftees' names set off the rioting. The mob, largely comprised of foreign-born workmen, pro-Southern in sympathy and fearing the loss of their jobs to Negroes, burned the provost marshal's headquarters, fought the police, and plundered homes. They then assaulted and hanged Negroes, burned the Colored Orphan Asylum where there were 300 children, and set fire to the Aged Colored Women's home and prevented the fire department from extinguishing the blaze. Federal troops helped disperse the mob and restore order. Property loss was more than $1,500,000, and casualties numbered over 1,000. Governor Horatio Seymour, opposed to the draft before the riots, requested compliance with the law, and enrollments resumed on Aug. 19. The riots produced a change in the draft law that permitted only conscientious objectors to purchase exemptions.

ELSIE M. LEWIS, Howard University

DRAG. *See* AERODYNAMICS.

DRAGO [drä′gō] **DOCTRINE,** principle of international law advanced in 1902 by Argentine Foreign Minister Luis María Drago (1859–1921), affirming that force should not be used for collection of public claims and that armed occupation of territory for such purpose should not be countenanced. Drago was concerned with the considerable diplomatic and naval pressure Great Britain, Germany, and Italy were putting on the Venezuelan dictator Cipriano Castro early in the 20th century for collection of claims owed their nationals. On Dec. 29, 1902, Drago dispatched a note to the Argentine minister in Washington outlining his government's position, which was based on the Calvo Doctrine (q.v.) of many years earlier. Like the Calvo Doctrine, the Drago pronouncement was accepted only partially as a principle of international law.

DRAGON, mythical reptile of varied shape, often described as having wings and a fire-breathing head. The earliest dragon in literature is the Babylonian Tiamat, slain by the god Marduk. In the Western world dragons symbolized evil and were overcome by legendary heroes such as Hercules, St. George, Siegfried, and Arthur. In China and Japan, they are often considered benevolent, and usually symbolize fertility.

DRAGONBOAT FESTIVAL, important annual festival of China. It falls on the fifth day of the fifth month of the Chinese lunar calendar. The festival has been observed for centuries by the Chinese in memory of Ch'ü Yuan, the unhappy poet and statesman who lived in the time of the Warring States (3d century B.C.). Before drowning himself in a river, Ch'ü wrote a number of poems reflecting his sorrow over losing the favor of the King of Chu state and his deep concern for the future of his country. Features of this festival include a dragonboat race and the making of glutinous rice-cakes, which are symbolically thrown into the water, supposedly to pacify the poet's ghost.

RAMON L. Y. WOON, University of Iowa

DRAGONFLY, large-winged, harmless insect belonging to the order Odonata, closely related to damselflies. There are many species and they are found all over the world. Dragonflies are beneficial, eating large numbers of insects, especially midges and mosquitoes. The spiny legs form a scoop to catch and hold the prey while the insect is flying. Dragonflies often rest at the same spot at regular intervals, coming back repeatedly as they patrol a section of pond or stream. The wings, strong and net-veined, are held in an outstretched, horizontal position while the

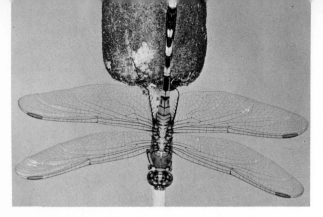

A dragonfly at rest on a cattail. (MASLOWSKI—NATIONAL AUDUBON SOCIETY)

insect rests. Females release their eggs in the water, dipping the body into the surface as they fly across it. The thick-bodied young, called nymphs, live under water, breathing by circulating water through gills located at the rear of the abdomen. Nymphs may crawl about on the bottom or shoot suddenly forward by ejecting water from the gill chambers. Their prey is usually insect larvae. It is captured by a specialized lower lip armed with pincers which is able to unhinge and dart out some distance to seize the prey. When nymphs are fully grown they climb out of the water onto a plant stalk. The skin splits along the back and the adult dragonfly emerges.

BARBARA NEILL, American Museum of Natural History

DRAGON TREE, an unusual, treelike plant, *Dracaena draco*, of the Liliaceae, or lily family, native to the Canary Islands. The genus name means "dragon" and refers to the supposed resemblance of the dried plant sap to dragon's blood. Young plants have a short, palmlike trunk topped by sword-shaped, erect or downcurved leaves. As the plant grows it branches densely and may eventually reach a height of over 60 ft. A famous dragon tree on Tenerife Island was over 70 ft. tall, and was thought to have been several thousand years old at the time (1868) it was destroyed by a storm. Dragon trees are cultivated as outdoor ornamentals in semi-tropical climates.

DRAGOON [drə-gōon'], mounted infantryman. First armed with a carbine called a "dragon" for fighting only on foot, dragoons were later trained as cavalry. After 1660 they formed a large number of the medium cavalry regiments in European armies. There were dragoon regiments in the U.S. Army until the Civil War, when cavalry assumed their double function.

DRAG RACING. *See* AUTOMOBILE RACING: *Hot Rodding.*

DRAINAGE, removal of surplus water from land by subsurface and surface facilities. Subsurface drainpipes are perforated or open-joint, installed underground and used in connection with pavements or retaining walls. For agriculture, subdrainage improves soil texture, lengthens the growing season, and permits penetration of fertilizers. Such systems preferably follow lines of natural drainage, but other common patterns are the herringbone, gridiron, and parallel systems. Drainpipes are placed from 2 to 4 ft. deep and 25 to 200 ft. apart, depending on soil permeability, and should slope at least 0.15%. Surface drainage re-

moves water promptly from improved and unimproved surfaces. Examples of surface drainage facilities are ditches, gutters, culverts, storm sewers, and the crown and side slopes of highways.

C. F. MEYER, Worcester Polytechnic Institute

DRAKE, EDWIN LAURENTINE (1819–80), American petroleum pioneer who drilled the world's first oil well, near Titusville, Pa., in 1859. A former railroad conductor, he was president and part owner of the Seneca Oil Company, formed to drill at the Titusville location. Drake's vision and determination initiated the petroleum industry, but he profited little from his accomplishment.

DRAKE, SIR FRANCIS (1541?–1596), English "sea dog" and maritime hero. He was the leader of those Elizabethan mariners who, operating out of Plymouth in Devon with somewhat ambiguous official status, paved the way for England's expansion overseas by smashing the naval strength of Spain. Born in Devon of yeoman stock, Drake was raised under the tutelage of his kinsman, the mariner John Hawkins, with whom he was present, in command of the little *Judith*, at the disastrous Spanish attack at Veracruz in 1569. He soon returned to the Spanish Main and in 1572 plundered the town of Nombre de Dios on the Isthmus of Panamá. One of Drake's most famous exploits was the second circumnavigation of the world, in 1577–80, 60 years after Ferdinand Magellan. Knowing that the whole Spanish Main was on guard against "El Draque," he decided to strike at the Spaniards' unguarded traffic on the west coast of South America. Starting out with five small vessels, he had only one, the *Golden Hind*, by the time he passed through the Strait of Magellan and entered the Pacific. As he anticipated, he caught the Spaniards entirely by surprise and captured a valuable treasure ship bound from Peru to Panamá. He continued northward to California, which he named New Albion and claimed for Elizabeth I. Then he struck across the Pacific, passed through the East Indies, and finally reached Plymouth laden with treasure. Despite Spanish protests, the Queen knighted him. In 1585, after a relatively quiet spell during which he served as mayor of Plymouth, he returned to the Caribbean, successfully raiding Cartagena, Santo Domingo, and St. Augustine.

Drake's greatest work was his leadership in the defeat of the Spanish Armada in 1588. Though Lord Howard of Effingham, because of his social rank, was titular head of the English naval forces as Lord High Admiral, the real leadership was exercised by Drake as vice admiral. In 1587, when Philip II had begun to gather his huge fleet, Drake had swooped down on Cádiz and destroyed some of the assembled vessels. He caused further serious damage by waylaying off Cape St. Vincent large numbers of vessels laden with essential supplies. In 1588, with the Spanish attack again threatening, he wanted to repeat that operation, but the Queen and her advisers objected. Consequently, he was at Plymouth, almost windbound, when the Armada approached the southwest coast. In the ensuing protracted encounter, the English employed the significant new tactic of using gunfire from a distance rather than the conventional shock action at close range. The fight continued all along the south coast; when the Span-

National Portrait Gallery, London

A portrait of Sir Francis Drake, by an unknown artist. The portrait was painted to commemorate the achievement of the "Invincible Francis Drake" in circling the globe.

iards took refuge at Calais, Drake dislodged them with fire ships and punished them terrifically in an encounter off Gravelines. By that time, the English ammunition was exhausted, but strong gales completed the destruction of the Armada.

Drake's final major action was an anticlimax. In 1595, with the war against Spain still continuing, England sent out a formidable force under Drake and the other great sea dog, Hawkins, to raid the Spanish settlements in the Caribbean. It accomplished nothing, partly because of disagreements between the leaders, both of whom died there. Drake's death took place off Nombre de Dios, which he had sacked almost a quarter-century before. Nevertheless, Spanish sea power had suffered such a deadly blow in 1588 that the English, like the Dutch, were now unchallenged in their efforts to colonize and increase trade in America and the East.

Consult Williamson, J. A., *Age of Drake* (1953).

ROBERT G. ALBION, Harvard University

DRAKENSBERG [drä′kənz-bûrg], mountain range of southeastern Africa, extending 600 mi. from Swaziland southwest through the eastern part of the Republic of South Africa and Basutoland. This massif is composed of level beds of sedimentary rocks, chiefly sandstones, above which rise a series of highly dissected basalt ridges. The range, forming a steep escarpment on its eastern slope, accounts in part for the aridity of country west of the mountains. The Orange River rises on the west slopes of the Drakensberg and flows for 1,300 mi. across the continent to the Atlantic Ocean. The Tugela River and other short streams flow east to the Indian Ocean. Elevation 3,000–10,000 ft.; highest peak, Thabantshonyana (11,425 ft.).

DRAM, unit of capacity and of weight. One fluid dram is equivalent to 60 minims and to ⅛ fl. oz.; one apothecaries′ dram, to ⅛ apothecaries′ oz. and to 60 grains; and one avoirdupois dram, to ¹⁄₁₆ avoirdupois oz.

See also WEIGHTS AND MEASURES.

DRAMA [drä′mə], town of northern Greece, in a tobacco-growing region. It was first mentioned, by Thucydides, under the name Dravesco. In the 5th century B.C. the Athenians were defeated here by the King of Macedonia. Drama was under Turkish domination until 1912, when it was occupied by Greece. It was taken over in 1917 by Bulgaria but reverted to Greece in 1918. Pop., 32,328.

DRAMA, term derived from the Greek verb meaning "act" or "do." It can apply to any mimic action, but commonly refers specifically to plays written for stage presentation. Within this wide range of meaning, at one extremity are "folk drama," often entirely wordless; "puppet drama," wherein marionettes take the place of human performers; "shadow drama," with merely the reflections of such puppets on a screen; and "dance drama," executed entirely by formal rhythmic movement. At the other extremity there is the ultimate assignment of the word "drama" not merely to any literary work cast in dialogue form, but to a particular kind of play—that in which violent action, strong passions, and bold contrasts are used to produce an often crudely thrilling effect.

In its widest sense, the drama, the exercise or art of mimetic representation, evidently satisfies an almost universal human need. Although it is true that certain peoples (the Arabs, for example) do not possess any native ceremonials or performances of this kind, the spread and variety of such activities elsewhere shows that drama was not merely the invention of a single culture but developed independently among civilizations far removed from each other in space, in time, or both. The most familiar dramatic movement is that which belongs to the European tradition, the tradition that later spread to the United States, Canada, Australia, and other countries to which the European civilization passed. The Indian drama of the 4th and 5th centuries, and the Chinese and the Japanese drama are fundamentally distinct. African tribal dances exhibit mimetic features, and among several of the American Indian tribes kindred dance dramas reached a comparatively advanced form.

Motivations of Early Drama. In the process of growth various common elements may be discerned. Undoubtedly the pleasure motive is strong, both for those taking part in the dramatic presentations and for the onlookers. At the same time, the presentations themselves nearly always are associated with religious cults and possess a kind of magical force. The primitive folk dramas, tattered remnants of which still remain in some village communities, clearly go back to a prehistoric past in their celebrations of summer's death and the mysterious rebirth of spring. At the same time, the desire to re-enact significant historical episodes—the narrative impulse—obviously also has played its part. Another part has been played by what might be called the bubbling up of a momentary spirit of irreverence and scurrility. Greek comedy, for example, ultimately seems to go back partly to burlesque farces in which the gods were treated with no ceremonious hand

Both the scope and variety of drama were given appropriate recognition in preparing the **ENCYCLOPEDIA INTERNATIONAL.** It contains articles on dramatic activity in each of its many aspects. The purpose of this guide is to acquaint the reader with the specific areas in which this material is treated. The key article, appearing on these pages, provides a broad perspective, and other articles explore specialized areas. Drama also is the basis for related activities such as opera, ballet, motion pictures, and certain forms of television and radio broadcasting, though each of these is covered under its own heading. Articles relating to drama in its most-used sense, as works with spoken dialogue created expressly for presentation on a stage, may be grouped under the following headings.

Nature and Evolution of Drama. The article DRAMA defines the term, explores its motivations (religious, social, national), and describes how dramatic activity has developed from its primitive beginnings.

Drama in Many Lands. Separate articles trace the history of drama in various ages and in specific countries and consider both literary values and practical stagecraft. CLASSICAL THEATER treats such activity in ancient Greece and Rome. MEDIEVAL THEATER discusses forms peculiar to the Middle Ages. In the articles CANADA, CHINA, FRANCE, GERMANY, INDIA, ITALY, JAPAN, SCANDINAVIA, and SPAIN, the reader can find comprehensive surveys of the theater. There also are separate articles entitled ENGLISH THEATER, LATIN-AMERICAN THEATER, RUSSIAN THEATER, UNITED STATES, THEATER OF THE (with related separate entries headed LITTLE-THEATER MOVEMENT and OFF-BROADWAY), and YIDDISH THEATER.

Friedman—Abeles

British actors Cyril Ritchard and Glynis Johns perform in George Bernard Shaw's comedy *Too True To Be Good* (1931), produced in New York in 1963. Such revivals enrich contemporary theater by presenting to the public interesting plays drawn from the varied dramatic heritages of many countries.

Types of Drama. Individual articles define and describe such basic types as COMEDY (including COMEDY OF HUMORS and COMEDY OF MANNERS), FARCE, and TRAGEDY. Separate consideration is given to other more specialized categories: COMMEDIA DELL'ARTE, MASQUE, PAGEANT, and PASSION PLAY. Articles entitled MARIONETTE and PUPPET explore another type of theater. Many other types of productions have their roots in drama, for example, BURLESQUE, CIRCUS, MINSTREL SHOW, MUSICAL COMEDY, REVUE, and VAUDEVILLE.

Dramatic Arts and Crafts. The role of the performer is treated, from both historical and analytical standpoints, in a major article titled ACTING. Related entries are CHORUS, DRAMATIC; CLOWN; and PANTOMIME. Backstage activity is treated in COSTUME DESIGN, THEATRICAL; DIRECTOR, STAGE AND SCREEN; MAKE-UP, THEATRICAL; PRODUCER; and STAGE SCENERY AND LIGHTING.

Another aspect of the theatrical world is discussed in DRAMATIC CRITICISM.

Famous Theaters. The physical aspects of theaters, from primitive origins to the present time, are described in THEATERS, HISTORY OF. Individual articles are devoted to world-famous playhouses and producing organizations: ABBEY THEATRE; AMERICAN SHAKESPEARE FESTIVAL THEATRE AND ACADEMY; COMEDIE FRANCAISE, LA; FEDERAL THEATER PROJECT; GLOBE THEATRE; GROUP THEATER; HABIMA OR HABIMAH; LINCOLN CENTER FOR THE PERFORMING ARTS; MOSCOW ART THEATER; OLD VIC THEATRE; PROVINCETOWN PLAYERS; ROYAL SHAKESPEARE THEATRE; STRATFORD SHAKESPEAREAN FESTIVAL OF CANADA; and THEATRE GUILD.

Noted Dramatic Organizations. In this category are articles titled ACTORS' STUDIO, THE; AMERICAN NATIONAL THEATRE AND ACADEMY (ANTA); FRIARS CLUB; LAMBS, THE; and PLAYERS, THE.

Great Plays. Individual plays of all periods are treated in separate articles. In most cases the works were chosen because their intrinsic worth has ensured them places in the study of drama—major plays of Shakespeare, Ibsen, Shaw, Chekhov, and O'Neill, for example. Other works—such as EAST LYNNE, OUR AMERICAN COUSIN, BLACK CROOK, THE, and TOBACCO ROAD—are included because of their historical associations.

Famous Figures in Drama. Biographic entries describe the careers and achievements of famous men and women—playwrights, actors, directors, designers, critics, and such figures of the musical theater as composers, librettists, lyricists, and choreographers. A random sample suggests the wide range of coverage: Jean ANOUILH, Brooks ATKINSON, David BELASCO, Bertolt BRECHT, BURBAGE family, Sir John GIELGUD, Oscar HAMMERSTEIN 2d, William INGE, and Jo MIELZINER.

Cross references at the ends of many articles guide the reader to related entries that provide additional information. Bibliographies at the conclusions of major articles indicate other sources of information.

Characteristics of the Field. Professional competition in the theater is formidable. Anyone preparing for a career in drama should anticipate the possibility of earning his livelihood in another field, perhaps one related to the theater. Most of the limited number of career opportunities directly connected with the stage lie in acting, directing, designing, and backstage work, such as that of the stage manager, electrician, or, for television and films, cameraman. Directly related are the professions of the playwright, producer (the business manager of theatrical enterprises), and theatrical publicity agent. For the musical stage, composers, lyricists, musicians, singers, dancers, and choreographers are also needed. Motion pictures offer opportunities for professionals in all these capacities, as does television. Radio employs people in some of them.

Acting. In the professional legitimate theater job opportunities are centered in New York, where there are Broadway and off-Broadway productions. A limited number of resident professional companies are found in large cities, such as San Francisco, Calif.; Houston and Dallas, Tex.; Washington, D.C.; and Minneapolis, Minn.; as well as Toronto and Montreal in Canada. Summer theaters provide seasonal employment to both established actors and apprentices. Television and to a lesser extent radio provide job opportunities through dramatic shows and commercials. The motion-picture industry, though not as prosperous as it once was, continues to be a goal for those with acting ambitions.

Directing. Opportunities for directors are limited. However, the growth of summer theaters and semiprofessional or amateur community theaters (little theaters) has to some extent counterbalanced the steady decline in professional stage activity in North America. Only a few of the larger little theaters employ paid directors, however. The growth of children's theaters (producing plays for juvenile audiences) and of university drama departments has also provided new openings in this area.

Designing. Opportunities for careers in scenic, costume, and lighting design have increased to a limited degree because of the growth of resident amateur or semiprofessional companies and of summer theaters. Television has also increased the potential for employment in the design field, and the motion-picture studios remain a source of possible employment.

Backstage Work. The statements concerning design are also applicable to the technicians who work behind the scenes. Television in particular has provided a substantial new area of employment.

Qualifications and Training. Among the requisites for the aspiring actor are those physical qualities that reinforce talent: a pleasing voice, good diction, correct posture, attractive or striking physical appearance, and the ability to project. An actor or actress must be able to take direction and to accept criticism. Resourcefulness and the ability to convert limitations into assets are important qualities. Equally essential is persistence in coping with the competition for employment. Experience in high school, club, and community productions often provides a barometer for judging the extent of these qualifications. Supervised training can begin in college in the classroom and in dramatic societies, many of which are supervised by professionals. Dramatic arts and crafts are an important part of many college curriculums, and the student with stage aspirations should be guided accordingly in his choice of school. In addition, many schools in the United States and Canada are devoted solely to acting. These vary widely in scope, method, and worth. Concentrated in New York and, to a lesser degree, in the Los Angeles area are a number of schools staffed by actors and directors with records of achievement in the professional theater. Another training ground is the summer theater, which makes use of apprentices as well as established actors. A few of the off-Broadway theaters in New York operate schools and successful students often graduate to small roles in their productions.

A good director must have the ability to detect the basic values of a playscript and to translate them into action on a stage or in a television or movie studio. He must be able to work well with other persons, since he holds the key to the cumulative efforts of all who are engaged in the production. Most directors begin as actors. Specialized training may be obtained in advanced theater schools. Practical experience is available in their productions and those of community theaters and professional summer theaters.

For scenic, costume, and lighting design an interest in drama must be accompanied by technical aptitude. University training in all phases of such work has become increasingly available and greatly improved since World War II. Practical experience is attainable through school productions and summer and community theater presentations.

Prospects for Employment. The major centers of employment for actors and directors are New York and Los Angeles, particularly the latter for television. In New York the actor competes with a large number of other candidates, primarily by making the rounds of producers' and casting offices and agencies that select performers for Broadway, off-Broadway, and touring productions. Once he gets his first role, he may qualify for membership in the stage actors' union, Actors' Equity Association. New York also is the principal recruiting ground for the resident professional companies in communities across the United States.

Those seeking to work in the professional theater in New York as scenic, costume, or lighting designers must request admission to the United Scenic Artists. This union conducts annual examinations for prospective members in New York. The tests are comprehensive and cover both practical and theoretical aspects of the profession—drawing, design, history of art, and history of the theater.

Young persons seeking New York careers in management and press agentry must qualify for membership in the union having sole jurisdiction in that field in the Broadway theater: the Association of Theatrical Agents & Managers. Admission follows a successful period of apprenticeship to established members.

Income. No generalization about earnings is possible, other than that the rewards for the highly successful performer or director, both in money and fame, are extremely great. The large majority of aspirants to a drama career either fail to achieve professional status or attain only modest success. Long periods of unemployment are not unusual in all areas of theatrical activity. Some in the profession supplement their incomes by teaching the various arts and crafts of the stage.

Sources of Information. Bulletins published by colleges and the drama schools are available starting points for those considering a theatrical career. The various trade unions of the theater and television also supply information to trained people. These include Actors' Equity Association, American Federation of Television & Radio Artists, Association of Theatrical Agents & Managers, and United Scenic Artists, all with headquarters in New York. Rosters of summer theaters, which are compiled annually by trade publications of the theatrical field, offer leads on employment.

The **ENCYCLOPEDIA INTERNATIONAL** article BROADCASTING, TELEVISION AND RADIO includes a Career Guide on that field. General suggestions on career planning are given in VOCATIONAL GUIDANCE.

and partly to a "Comus" procession in which derisive and licentious verses were bandied about. It might, therefore, be said that early dramatic outgrowths were animated by diverse forces—by a wish to honor and propitiate the gods, to find release in laughter, to preserve tribal memories, and to share in a pleasurable activity.

Emergence of Professionalism. A general survey of this complex impulse shows that some dramatic forces, including many folk plays and mimetic dances, continued for centuries in an arrested, fossilized state, while others exhibited development and expansion. Of the latter a few (for example, the Sanskrit plays and the Japanese No), after reaching a certain stage, either stopped growing or remained formally fixed. Others (including European and American drama) constantly evolved new features. All, however, agree in moving toward professionalism and distribution of effort. The actors tend to abandon their amateur status and concentrate on the art of interpretation. Directors take up their duties and others, such as scenic artists and technicians, apply themselves to various theatrical tasks. Architects build specially planned playhouses. And, above all, the poets contrive dialogue, which before had been either nonexistent or improvised by the performers.

The drama in this limited sense of the written play has witnessed its greatest development in Western countries. The Greek and Roman plays, which had arrived at a high level of artistry and sophistication, vanished with the breakdown of these civilizations. But the fresh start in the Middle Ages, followed by the rediscovery, during the Renaissance, of the classical models, laid the basis for a remarkable and continuous enlargement of the written drama. During the 16th and 17th centuries Shakespeare in England, Lope de Vega and Calderón in Spain, numerous Italian writers from Ariosto onward, explored the range of romantic drama. Later, Corneille, Racine, and Molière in France and the English Restoration playwrights elaborated a more "classical" style. During the 18th century a fresh impulse came from Germany, and in the century following the torch was carried to Scandinavia and Russia.

Modern Developments. Within the 20th century, despite the attractions of the newly discovered cinema and television (each of which has incorporated in its offerings material and devices borrowed from the theater), the enduring power of the stage is amply shown not only by the almost innumerable contributions of European and American authors to dramatic literature but also by the keen interest taken generally in dramatic theory. Perhaps the most noteworthy modern development in this sphere is the academic study of, and practice in, theatrical forms. Up to the present century, dramatic literature, with a few exceptions (notably Shakespeare's works), remained outside the university curriculum. Now, not only is dramatic and theatrical history a subject of scholarly investigation, but also practical stage activities are included in the work of college departments of drama.

Consult Mantzius, Karl, *History of Theatrical Art in Ancient and Modern Times* (6 vols., 1903–21); Pickard-Cambridge, A. W., *Dithyramb, Tragedy and Comedy* (1927); Gassner, John, *Masters of the Drama* (3d ed., 1954); Bieber, Margarete, *The History of the Greek and Roman Theater* (2d ed., 1961); Nicoll, Allardyce, *World Drama* (rev. ed., 1961).

ALLARDYCE NICOLL, University of Birmingham, England

See also:

ACTING	OFF-BROADWAY
BURLESQUE	PAGEANT
CLASSICAL THEATER	PANTOMIME
COMEDY	PASSION PLAY
COMMEDIA DELL'ARTE	PUPPET
DRAMATIC CRITICISM	REVUE
DIRECTOR, STAGE AND SCREEN	RUSSIAN THEATER
	SHOWBOAT
ENGLISH THEATER	STAGE SCENERY AND
FARCE	LIGHTING
LATIN-AMERICAN THEATER	THEATERS, HISTORY OF
LITTLE-THEATER MOVEMENT	TRAGEDY
	UNITED STATES, THEATER
MASK	OF THE
MASQUE	VAUDEVILLE
MEDIEVAL THEATER	YIDDISH THEATER
MELODRAMA	
MIME OR MIMUS	Articles on theater in entries
MUSICAL COMEDY	for various countries.

DRAMA CRITICS' CIRCLE AWARD, NEW YORK, presentation made annually since 1936 by the organization of drama critics for New York daily newspapers and national magazines. Awards are made to the authors of the new U.S. play, foreign play, and musical play selected as outstanding from among those produced during a Broadway season.

DRAMAMINE [drăm'ə-mēn], trade name for dimenhydrinate, an antihistaminic drug used to treat and prevent sea, air, and car sickness. It is also used to treat certain ailments of the ear and brain which cause dizziness and loss of balance. Drowsiness is a common side effect of dramamine.
See also ANTIHISTAMINES.

DRAMATIC CRITICISM. Perhaps the first official drama critics were the judges who awarded the prizes at the annual festivals of tragedy in Athens in the 5th century B.C. The first treatise on drama was the *Poetics* of Aristotle (384–322 B.C.), essentially an analytical description of Greek tragedy, which established a number of principles that have ever since been accepted, modified, or debated. These included the nature of the tragic hero, "catharsis" of pity and fear as the desired effect of tragedy, and such structural matters as the unities of time and action. Horace (65–8 B.C.), in *Epistola ad Pisones*, insisted on the didactic purpose of drama ("pleasure and profit"), the need for five acts, and the separation of dramatic types.

In the Renaissance, Italian critics rigidly followed Aristotle, while sometimes misinterpreting his observations. Lodovico Castelvetro required a third unity, only implied by Aristotle, that of place. In England, Sir Philip Sidney's *Apologie for Poetrie* (1595) approved classical "rules," and Ben Jonson, following Latin traditions in theory and practice, defined "comedy of humors." The achievement of Shakespeare, who ignored many classical rules, cast doubt on Aristotle's complete validity, and John Dryden's *Essay of Dramatic Poesy* (1668) defended Shakespeare's inspiration and art, as against the neoclassicism of Corneille and Racine.

The 19th century brought a general reaction against classical models, as shown in the works of Goethe and Victor Hugo, and the Shakespearean criticism of Hazlitt, Coleridge, and Lamb, who began to pay more attention to acting and production of particular plays. Later, in France, Zola defined and defended "naturalistic" drama, and Francisque Sarcey defined the "well-made play."

Reviews of particular productions flourished in English periodicals at the beginning of the present century, when such practitioners as George Bernard Shaw, William Archer, and Max Beerbohm gained prominence. Contemporary criticism has split into several wide streams, including reviews for newspapers and magazines in the major theatrical capitals, articles in periodicals devoted to the theater, and books and articles by teachers, professional critics, and playwrights and others employed in the theater. Outstanding 20th-century critics whose work appeared in one of these English language media include George Jean Nathan, Joseph Wood Krutch, John Mason Brown, Harold Clurman, Brooks Atkinson, Walter Kerr, Eric Bentley, and Kenneth Tynan.

JOHN GAYWOOD LINN, Queens College, New York

DRAPER, HENRY (1837–82), American astronomer noted for his pioneering work in astronomical photography. After receiving a medical degree from the University of the City of New York in 1858 he was on the staff of Bellevue Hospital until 1860, when he returned to his alma mater as professor of natural science and, later, of physiology and chemistry. An enthusiastic amateur astronomer, he built his own reflecting telescopes and adapted them for photography. In 1872 he photographed the spectrum of the star Vega, the first such photograph to be made. For his work in photographing the transit of Venus in 1874 he received a special gold medal from Congress. His widow endowed Harvard University's program of photographing and classifying the spectra of the brighter stars. The resulting Henry Draper Memorial Catalogue gives the position, magnitude, and spectrum of more than 200,000 stars.

DRAPER, JOHN WILLIAM (1811–82), American scientist and author, president from 1850 to 1873 of University of the City of New York Medical School (later New York University). Born in England and educated at the University of Pennsylvania, he did important research in radiant energy, telegraphy, photochemistry, photography, and other fields. He wrote *Human Physiology* (1856); *History of the American Civil War* (1867–70); *History of the Conflict between Religion and Science* (1874); and other books.

DRAPER, WILLIAM HENRY (1801–77), Canadian jurist and politician. He represented Toronto (1836–40) in the legislative assembly. He became a member of the executive council (1836), solicitor general (1837), attorney-general (1840–42), and a member of the legislative council (1843). From 1844 to 1847 he was virtual head of the government though not recognized as Premier. He resigned in 1847 and he was appointed puisne judge of the Queen's Bench Court (1847), chief justice of the Common Pleas Court (1858), chief justice of Upper Canada (1863), and president of the Ontario Court of Appeal (1868).

DRAVA RIVER [drä′vä] (Ger. **DRAU**), European river rising near the Carnic Alps on the border between Italy and Austria. It first flows east through southern Austria to Yugoslavia and then southeast through northern Yugoslavia until it reaches Hungary, where it receives the Mur River. It forms segments of the frontier between Yugoslavia and Hungary. Farther southeast, it joins the Danube River. Length, about 450 mi.

DRAVIDIAN [drə-vĭd′ē-ən] **LANGUAGES** are spoken chiefly in southern India. After the Indian government redrew internal political boundaries in 1956, the four major Dravidian languages were each spoken primarily in a single state. These four languages are Tamil in Madras state (26,500,000 speakers in 1951); Telugu in Andhra Pradesh (33,000,000); Kannada, or Kanarese, in Mysore state (14,500,000); and Malayalam in Kerala state (13,500,000). Tamil is also the principal language of northern Ceylon. Each of these four languages has its own writing system, and each is well established as a literary vehicle. However, the Dravidian family also includes about 15 additional languages without literatures, such as Kota and Toda, in the Madras state; Coorg and Tulu, in Mysore state; and Kolami, Naiki, Parji, Gadaba, Gondi, Konda, Kuwi, Kurukh (also called Oraon), and Malto, which extend up through central India as far north as the Ganges River. A more remote Dravidian language is Brahui, which is spoken in Baluchistan, now part of West Pakistan. The family as a whole is fairly homogeneous, and the languages differ from one another about as much as do the Romance languages in Europe.

The geographical spread of Dravidian, and in particular the location of Brahui, have led some scholars to believe that Dravidian languages were once spoken over the whole Indian subcontinent but that Dravidian speakers were subsequently driven back by the invasion of Sanskrit speakers from the northwest. It has even been suggested that the undeciphered language of the early Indus Valley culture of Harappa and Mohenjo Daro was Dravidian, but this hypothesis remains unproved.

Attempts to relate the Dravidian languages to the Finno-Ugric languages or to other languages outside India have also failed to win acceptance. It is clear, however, that Sanskrit and its modern-Indic descendants have been interacting with Dravidian languages for many centuries. The Dravidian languages have borrowed thousands of Sanskrit words, and Indic languages in turn have borrowed from Dravidian not only words, but features of pronunciation and grammar as well.

Grammatically, the Dravidian languages are of the type traditionally called agglutinative, with numerous suffixes but no prefixes. The original sound system of Dravidian is simpler than that of the Indic languages, since the contrast between voiceless and voiced consonants (such as p and b, t and d) is lacking. On the other hand, some Dravidian languages are peculiar in distinguishing three types of t-sounds made with the tip of the tongue.

WILLIAM BRIGHT, University of California at Los Angeles

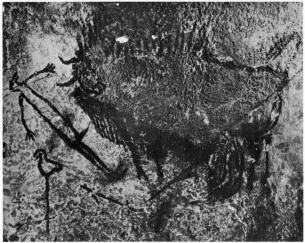

Archives—Art Reference Bureau

Bison in a cave at Lascaux, France, painted some 20,000 years ago. Colors were obtained by grinding colored earths.

The Metropolitan Museum of Art, Rogers Fund, 1923

Greek vase painting (c.470 B.C.), attributed to Douris. Two women are folding and putting away clothes.

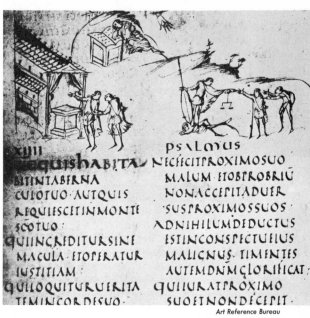

Art Reference Bureau

Detail of a page from the 9th-century Utrecht Psalter.

DRAWING. The art of drawing has been in existence since man first scratched a line on stone. Drawings may be great individual works of art in themselves; or quick sketches, exercises, and notes by an artist; or a working plan for another medium, such as painting or sculpture. One generally thinks of a drawing as a work executed in line, but it may also be composed of line combined with tonal areas, as in a typical wash or watercolor drawing, or even of tonal areas alone, as in a drawing by Georges Seurat.

The Ancient and Medieval Periods. The history of drawing extends back some 20,000 years, when Paleolithic man decorated the walls of caves in southwestern France and northern Spain with animal figures. He made such striking use of outline that these pictures still evoke awe and mystery. Like prehistoric man, the artists of ancient Egypt placed emphasis on the outline, the silhouette of figures and forms. However, developed techniques and a sense of composition can also be seen in their works. The convention for the human figure was not based on the visual image, but on an imaginative reorganization of the body, each part being shown in its most characteristic view. Thus head, arms, and legs are depicted in profile; eye, shoulders, and hands in front view. There is no indication of muscular distortion resulting from this pose. The strong contour line, which unifies and emphasizes the figure in Egyptian painting and low-relief sculpture, is still emulated by 20th-century artists.

The drawing of ancient Greece, exemplified in vase decoration, also employed outline. During the 5th century B.C. it became more curved and undulating, adding movement and a suggestion of the third dimension. The composition—that is, the arrangement of the figures in the space—is particularly beautiful in Greek art.

Drawing and calligraphy were combined to create the great manuscripts of the Middle Ages. Within the monasteries anonymous draftsmen copied testaments, psalters, and the classics on parchment, vellum, and paper. Not only the writing itself, but the complex initial letters and illustrations, sometimes heightened with color, are great works of art. The 9th-century Utrecht Psalter (Utrecht) utilizes drawings in ink as imaginative and lively illustrations of the psalms.

The Renaissance. Drawing since about 1400—approximating the close of the Middle Ages and the beginning of the Renaissance in Italy—generally has followed the styles of painting and sculpture. But within these centuries artists have created great drawings in their individual manners. Through their graphic work one catches an immediate freshness and insight into their methods of work and particular interests. As the Renaissance created new ideas of humanism and scientific method, it also brought a renewed interest in the natural world. This interest is the outstanding quality in the drawings of the Italian masters, who produced exquisite and often spontaneous notes, exercises, and sketches based on observation. Problems in three-dimensional perspective, anatomy, and light and shade were explored and re-explored in pencil, charcoal, crayon, pen, and metalpoint. The notebooks of Leonardo da Vinci are a picture encyclopedia of sketch drawings, the sheets covered with notes and studies of rocks, plants, animals, and atmospheric phenomena, as well as with drawings of his inventions. Leonardo also produced studies and cartoons for paintings. In the "Head of the Virgin" (Metropolitan Museum of Art, New York), a carefully finished drawing for the oil painting "The Virgin and Child with St. Anne" (Louvre, Paris), Leonardo used graded tones of chalk that merge into shadows and create a well-rounded representation. This manner of depicting form was used with outline by Pisanello to create drawings of great beauty. In "Studies of Monkeys" (Louvre) an expressive outline indicates the animals, but the parallel fine-line shading suggests body structure as well as the texture of the fur. Michelangelo's particular interest in three-dimensional structure is revealed in his red-chalk study (Metropolitan Museum of Art, New York) for the Libyan Sybil on the Sistine Chapel ceiling in Rome.

The graphic arts perhaps played a more important role in Germany than in any other country. The German and Dutch masters had a high regard for the bold, direct, black-and-white media. Their drawings and prints were carried throughout Europe, those of Martin Schongauer and Albrecht Dürer exerting a strong influence on artists in Italy and Spain. Dürer's "Portrait of His Mother" (Berlin State Museum) is one of the great portraits of all art. Like the Germans, Rembrandt cultivated the art of drawing for its own sake, making it a form of expression at which no other 17th-century artist approached him. "Saskia and Her Child" (Pierpont Morgan Library, New York) is a pen-and-ink sketch in which the figures are depicted with subtly varying widths of line and shades of brown ink. The washes were applied to create areas of light and dark, a technique appropriate to the baroque style.

The 18th–20th Centuries. The 18th-century court style in France, with its emphasis on portraying an elegant, pleasure-loving aristocracy, was epitomized in the work of Antoine Watteau, who mirrored the fashions, customs, and people of the court and theater with vital and realistic drawing. Watteau, whose graphic work was fundamental to his painting, is considered the master of the *trois crayons* technique. In this century landscape drawing, practiced in the earlier times by such individual stylists as Peter Bruegel the Elder, Peter Paul Rubens, Rembrandt, and Claude Lorrain, was given new emphasis. Artists like John Constable of England went into the countryside to sketch directly from nature.

The diversity of styles and schools of art in the 19th

DRAWING

Drawing is one of the most universal of mankind's activities. Examples survive from the prehistoric era, when Paleolithic man scratched pictures on the walls of caves. From the time of ancient Egypt a continuous history of drawing in the Western world exists. The most intimate and, in many ways, the most characteristic works of the great painters have been their drawings. The entry on drawing in the **ENCYCLOPEDIA INTERNATIONAL** covers the following topics.

The Ancient and Medieval Periods. Egyptian conventions of depiction; Greek vase art; and medieval manuscript illumination.

The Renaissance. The period of rebirth that produced such masters as Leonardo da Vinci, Pisanello, Michelangelo, Schongauer, and Dürer.

The 18th to 20th Centuries. The elegant court style of France; the many individual artists of the 19th century; such modern masters as Pablo Picasso, Henri Matisse, and Paul Klee.

Techniques of Drawing. The grounds, or materials, on which drawings are made; division of media into the fine and the broad; graphite, the most versatile medium.

Fine Media. Metalpoint and pen and ink; their characteristics and techniques.

Broad Media. Charcoal, chalk, crayon, pastel, wash, and water color; their attributes.

Glossary. Terms frequently used in discussions of drawings, and their technical meanings.

Illustrating this article are reproductions of drawings of the past and present. They have been selected to provide a visual survey of the history of drawing, representing the achievements of the great masters. They also offer a guide to technique and to the effects that may be achieved in the various media. Studying works of art themselves provides the surest insight into their character, the qualities of the various art styles, and those indefinable attributes that distinguish a great from a mediocre work. This visual experience is indispensable to the student who wants to draw and to the reader who wishes to develop a sensitivity to the values of art.

Readers may consult many other articles that deal with drawing. Cross references at the ends of articles provide a guide to locating the ones in which he is interested. Pertinent to the art of drawing are CALLIGRAPHY; CARICATURE; CARTOON, POLITICAL; COMICS; MANUSCRIPT ILLUMINATION; and PAINTING, HISTORY OF. Additional historical information is given in articles on countries (for example, FRANCE: *French Art*), artists (BELLINI, THE; REMBRANDT), epochs (PREHISTORIC ART), and styles (RENAISSANCE ART).

The student interested in technique may consult PASTEL, PERSPECTIVE, and WATER COLOR. The various graphic media are discussed in individual entries: AQUATINT, DRYPOINT, ENGRAVING, ETCHING, LITHOGRAPHY, MEZZOTINT, SILK SCREEN, and WOODCUT AND WOOD ENGRAVING.

Some drawings are made not for their expressive qualities but for their practical value. The reader with architectural or engineering interests may want to read BLUEPRINT and MECHANICAL DRAWING.

The reader who contemplates a career as an illustrator may be interested in COMMERCIAL ART. That article analyzes the activities of the commercial artist and provides a Career Guide, which discusses characteristics of the field, training, and salary expectations.

Those who want additional information on drawing, both its practice and its history, are referred to the bibliography at the end of DRAWING and to the other lists of books that follow many of the relevant articles. These publications have been selected for their excellent coverage of material and for their availability in schools, libraries, and bookstores.

century resulted in many modes of drawing. The pencil drawing of Ingres, a neoclassicist, is marked by cool precision and balance. In contrast, the romantics Delacroix and Géricault, and later the impressionists, utilizing a broken contour line, infused their drawings with great liveliness. In Edgar Degas both styles and attitudes meet; he emulated the strong contour line of Ingres and the warmth and spontaneity of the romantics. Two other artists from the late 19th century also have highly distinctive drawing styles: Georges Seurat composed his drawings of broad tonal areas; Vincent van Gogh created his pictures with a unique combination of short, broken lines and small circles and dots.

The political cartoonists and caricaturists of today have received a great tradition from the 19th century. Francisco Goya and Honoré Daumier created drawings and prints that expressed their feelings on current events and the conditions of their times. Goya's series of drawings "Disasters of War," actually superior to his better-known etchings bearing the same title, describe the barbarities of the Napoleonic invasion of Spain. Daumier powerfully lampooned the foibles of human nature and the injustices of poverty in France. George Grosz and Pablo Picasso have presented similar events of the 20th century, Grosz satirizing political and social injustices of the post-World War I era and the 1930's and Picasso depicting the horrors of war in innumerable sketches and studies for his large painting "Guernica" (owned by the artist, now at the Museum of Modern Art, New York), inspired by the bombing of that Spanish town.

The 20th century, like the 19th, has been characterized by diversity. In addition to Picasso, Henri Matisse and the English sculptor Henry Moore are among those whose work is both individual and aesthetically outstanding. But it is the Swiss Paul Klee who, in the Germanic tradition, has celebrated the independence of drawing. One of the great draftsmen of modern times, he has defined his art as "taking a line for a walk."

Techniques of Drawing. The materials used in drawing are simple and have changed very little in the past centuries. Paper is the usual ground, but parchment, vellum, ivory, and other materials have been used. Pencil, pen, brush, charcoal, chalk, crayon, pastel, and metalpoint are the tools. Drawings by their techniques may be divided into two broad catagories, the fine and broad media.

Graphite is the most versatile medium, the pencil now being manufactured in a number of sizes and degrees of hardness. Due to its range, it can be used for both the fine and broad techniques.

Fine Media. The fine media are metalpoint and pen and ink. A metalpoint drawing is made on a sheet of paper that has been prepared with a special opaque coating. The artist uses a stylus tipped with silver, copper, brass, lead, or gold. The metal point, which produces a very fine line, leaves an indelible mark that will not smudge. This technique, popular in the 15th and 16th centuries, was combined with pen by Pisanello when he produced his drawing "Studies of Monkeys."

The most universal technique, popular in all periods, has been pen and ink. There are three basic types of pen

"Studies of Monkeys" by Pisanello (c.1395–c.1455).

Archives—Art Reference Bureau

"Head of the Virgin" by Leonardo da Vinci (1452–1519). Black and red chalk were used in this study for one of Leonardo's most famous paintings, "The Virgin and Child with St. Anne."

The Metropolitan Museum of Art, Dick Fund, 1951

"Study for the Libyan Sybil" was executed in red chalk by Michelangelo (1475–1564).

—quill, reed, and metal. The quill was used for manuscripts in the Middle Ages as well as by later draftsmen. Reed pens, not so versatile, were popular with Van Gogh and Matisse. The metal nib, today the most common, is manufactured in a variety of sizes. It makes an extremely strong, crisp line suited for drawings to be photographically reproduced. Sepia, bistre, and India black are the principal inks.

Broad Media. The broad media are charcoal, chalk, crayon, pastel, wash (diluted ink), and water color. Used in Italy in the 15th century, charcoal and chalk later gained widespread popularity. These materials give more subtle gradations of tone and greater variation in width of line than the fine media. Charcoal is used for fast sketches as well as finished drawings, but is particularly employed for preliminary drawings on walls or canvases to be painted. The Michelangelo "Study for the Libyan Sybil" is in red chalk, the Dürer portrait of his mother in charcoal.

Crayons, which are made of clay, plumbago, and chalk, are available in a wide range of colors. Pastel is made of a gum medium and is as powdery as chalk. Both these materials may be handled as drawing materials, but with their range of color they may also be employed to produce the effects of painting.

Transparent coats of diluted ink or water color may be applied with a brush to supplement line drawings, thus modeling them with areas of light and dark or heightening them with color. Sometimes the drawing itself is executed with the tip of the brush. With ink, the term "wash drawing" is generally used; with water color, "watercolor drawing." The Rembrandt sketch, "Saskia and Her Child," is a pen and wash drawing. Gouache, an opaque water paint, is sometimes used for drawings; white gouache especially is employed for highlights.

Consult Nicolaides, Kimon, *The Natural Way to Draw* (1941); De Tolnay, Charles, *History and Techniques of Old Master Drawings* (1943); Pope, Arthur, *The Language of Drawing and Painting* (1949); Sachs, P. J., *The Pocket Book of Great Drawings* (1951); Watrous, James, *The Craft of Old-Master Drawings* (1957).

ROBERTA M. PAINE, The Metropolitan Museum of Art

Drawing Terms

The following terms are commonly used in reference to drawing:

Bistre, brown ink made from charred wood.

Calligraphy (literally, beautiful writing), elegant and beautiful line in penmanship and drawing. See separate article.

Cartoon (Ital. *cartone*, "large sheet of paper"), a full-size drawing in complete detail for a painting; in current terminology, also a satirical or humorous drawing.

Chiaroscuro (Ital., "light-dark"), use of light and shade for modeling. See separate article.

Conté, commercial name for synthetic black, red, or brown chalk; originally these chalks were individually ground by the artists.

Fixative, protective spray applied to drawings in pencil, charcoal, chalk, or pastel to keep them from smearing.

Albrecht Dürer's "Portrait of His Mother" (1514).

Bildarchiv—Art Reference Bureau

"Saskia and Her Child" by Rembrandt (1606–69). Saskia van Uylenburch was Rembrandt's wife and the mother of his son, Titus.

Pierpont Morgan Library

"Head of Le Mezzetin" by Watteau (1684–1721).

"Lady and Boy" by Ingres (1780–1867).

"Dancer with Fan" by Edgar Degas (1834–1917).

Gouache, opaque (nontransparent) water color.

Graphite, black carbon, as in the lead of a pencil; also called black lead or plumbago.

Hatching, shading by parallel lines. Cross hatching, shading by crossed lines.

Hooks and dashes, flourishes at the end of parallel hatching for increased shading; particularly used in the broad media.

Modeling, use of areas of light and shade to achieve a three-dimensional representation.

Outline, line that expresses the exterior of a form, either with or without inside detail; the edge, contour, or silhouette of a figure.

Pensiero, (Ital., "thought"), a quick or first sketch.

Plumbago, graphite, early general term for pencil drawing.

Sanguine, reddish-brown chalk.

Sepia, brown ink made from the fluid produced by the cuttlefish.

Sketch, a rough drawing or first impression put down on paper.

Squared, lined with a grid to facilitate the transfer from the drawing to a large-size surface, such as a canvas or a wall.

Stippling, modeling in light and shade by making hundreds of dots and flecks, which are then stumped.

Study, drawing of a detail for later use in a larger composition; it is more carefully detailed than a sketch.

Stump, roll of paper with a pointed end used to rub charcoal, pencil, or chalk to obtain gradations of tone.

Trois crayons, black, red, and white chalk combinations used in one drawing; **deux crayons,** red and black.

DRAYTON, MICHAEL (1563–1631), English poet. Born in Warwickshire, he became a page to Sir Henry Goodere, whose daughter Anne inspired much of Drayton's work. His sonnet sequence *Idea* (1593) is dedicated to her, and even after her marriage she remained his patroness. Drayton employed almost all the poetic forms popular in his

"Twittering Machine" (1922) by Paul Klee.

Study (1937) for "Guernica" by Pablo Picasso.

age. He achieved his greatest fame with his delightful pastorals, patriotic odes, and historical narratives in verse, and is perhaps best remembered for his sonnet, "Since there's no help, come let us kiss and part." Although not among the greatest of the Elizabethan poets, he has been called the most representative.

DREAMS, a series of images, thoughts, or emotions occurring in the mind during sleep or daydreaming. Dreams have aroused interest and reverence since the beginnings of mankind—examples of prophetic dreams and dream explanations are found throughout the Bible. In many primitive societies the dream state is considered a sojourn of the soul outside the body during sleep.

For the individual, fantasy and dreams may be considered irrational symbolic ways of dealing with reality, comparable to the use of myth and legend by societies. Sigmund Freud published *The Interpretation of Dreams* in 1900. This study of the nature of dreams shows them to be expressions of unconscious processes, such as suppressed wishes or unresolved problems.

According to Freud, the confused, illogical, and contradictory features of the dream represent the attempt of a censoring mechanism to disguise and symbolize the unconscious contents, thus allowing sleep to continue. Without this censoring mechanism, controversial thoughts and ideas might wake the dreamer, since direct confrontation with unconscious material cannot normally be tolerated and must be suppressed in the waking state. The loss of contact with reality, as experienced in the dream, resembles that occurring in psychosis, but the sane person realizes that he is dreaming, whereas the insane accepts his hallucinations as real.

Certain other aspects of the dream were elaborated by Carl Jung. These include the role of archetypes and problem-solving mechanisms, as well as the occurrence of compensatory and prospective dreams.

Dream research has acquired a physiological aspect through the discovery of periods of Rapid Eye Movement (REM) during sleep. It is during REM periods that occur the vividly detailed, unrealistic, and "hallucinatory" dreams remembered after awakening. Although rapid eye movements are the most obvious indicator of such REM periods during sleep, other changes have also been documented, such as changes in the brain-wave patterns and increases in respiratory and cardiovascular activity.

Four to five REM periods normally occur each night, lasting approximately 20 min. each. These REM periods are separated by Non Rapid Eye Movement (NREM) periods, lasting approximately 90 min. NREM periods produce realistic, though vague, dreams, which are difficult to recall upon awakening. Deprivation of REM sleep, by awakening the subject every time he shows signs of REM, leads to increasingly disturbed mental life. The significance of this observation for determining the causes of mental disease is under extensive study.

Consult Foulkes, W. D., *The Psychology of Sleep* (1966).
A. H. Esser, M.D.

See also Sleep.

DREDGE, a scow, barge, or boat equipped with machinery for removing mud, rock, silt, sand, or other material from the bottom of a body of water. The dredge is held in place by heavy posts sunk in the bottom and fastened to the hull. Some of the various operating methods used to move material are shoveling or "biting," scooping, sucking, or agitating so that the current carries material away. Dredges are used to clear and deepen channels and harbors, to dig canals, and to reclaim swamps.

DRED SCOTT CASE, U.S. Supreme Court case argued in 1856–57. The court's decision that Scott, a slave, could not sue for freedom in a federal court seemed at that time of little importance, but the accompanying obiter dictum of the court, declaring the Missouri Compromise to have been unconstitutional, created bitter sectional feelings. In 1834 Scott accompanied his owner, Dr. John Emerson, from a slave state, Missouri, to the free state of Illinois and the territory of Wisconsin where slavery was prohibited by the Missouri Compromise. After returning (1838) to Missouri, Dr. Emerson died and Scott brought suit (1846) against Mrs. Emerson, who was herself an abolitionist, for his freedom, maintaining that his residence in slave-free areas had terminated his slave status. Scott won his case in the St. Louis courts only to have the decision reversed by the Missouri Supreme Court. In order to bring Scott's petition as a test case before the federal courts, Scott had to be owned by a nonresident of Missouri. He was therefore sold to Mrs. Emerson's brother, John Sanford of New York.

Scott v. *Sanford* was appealed to the U.S. Supreme Court and argued by counsels Montgomery Blair and George T. Curtis for Scott and Reverdy Johnson for Sanford. The justices of the Supreme Court decided, in closed session, that it would be best to avoid mention of the current controversy raging around the Missouri Compromise (which was actually nullified by the Kansas-Nebraska Act of 1854) and find against Scott on the basis of the decision of the Missouri Supreme Court. However, when it was discovered that antislavery justices John McLean and Benjamin Curtis were planning to deliver opinions strongly supporting the Missouri Compromise and its constitutionality, the remaining judges decided to broaden their discussions and denounce Congress' power to prohibit slavery in the territories in hopes of settling the controversy and possibly strengthening the Union.

On Mar. 6, 1857, Chief Justice Roger B. Taney delivered the Supreme Court's finding that no Negro, slave, or person of slave ancestry was a "citizen" of the United States within the meaning of the Constitution and therefore could not bring suit in a federal court. He added that since Congress had no constitutional authority to prohibit slavery in the territories, Scott's residence in a territory covered by the Missouri Compromise had in no way affected his slave status. Rather than easing tensions, the court's decision caused further agitation between North and South and was bitterly attacked by the abolitionist press. The court's decision was later superseded by the Fourteenth Amendment.

Consult Hopkins, V. C., *Dred Scott's Case* (1951).
James P. Shenton, Columbia University

DREISER [drī'sər]**, THEODORE (HERMAN ALBERT)** (1871–1945), American writer, known especially for his naturalistic novels. Born in Terre Haute, Ind., the 12th of 13 children in a family dominated by a severe father, he was educated in several Indiana Catholic schools and one public school. After one year at the University of Indiana (1889–90), he became a newspaperman, first in Chicago (1892), then in other midwestern cities, and New York. He continued his journalistic career as a free-lance writer and magazine editor until 1910.

In 1900 Dreiser published his first novel, *Sister Carrie*, on the recommendation of Frank Norris, who was serving as a publisher's reader. But when the publisher's wife read the book, her protests led to its suppression. It was reissued in 1912. After the initial failure, 11 years passed before another novel appeared, *Jennie Gerhardt* (1911). This was followed by two novels of the Frank Cowperwood trilogy (*The Financier*, 1912, and *The Titan*, 1914), a study of the rise of an American business tycoon. (The third novel, *The Stoic*, was not published until 1947, two years after his death.) *The "Genius,"* a novel about the life of an artist, appeared in 1915.

In the ten years after the publication of *The "Genius,"* Dreiser published no novels, but tried his hand at plays, autobiography, short stories, and essays. His reputation grew steadily, and it was much enhanced by the publication in 1925 of the novel *An American Tragedy*. His best-known work, this novel is also his masterpiece. It describes the fortunes and misfortunes of a young man, Clyde Griffiths, whose impoverished and strict home life rather resembles that of Dreiser's own youth.

Dreiser's fiction is generally considered to be in the American naturalist tradition. It is usually concerned with the difficult and unconventional careers of men and women from the lower ranks of American society (the Cowperwood novels are an exception), who try to achieve some share of the "American dream" of success, but are prevented in one way or another from realizing it. In terms of this theme and of his general preoccupation with contemporary social and moral issues, Dreiser was in the center of early 20th-century literary and social affairs. He showed a sympathetic interest in labor unionism, made a visit to Russia in 1927, and before his death in 1945, applied for membership in the Communist party.

Consult Elias, R. H., *Theodore Dreiser* (1949); Matthiessen, F. O., *Theodore Dreiser* (1951).

FREDERICK J. HOFFMAN, University of California
See also AMERICAN TRAGEDY, AN.

DRESDEN [drĕz'dən], city of the German Democratic Republic (East Germany), and capital of the district of Dresden, located in a large valley on both banks of the Elbe River, 71 mi. southeast of Leipzig. Dresden has long been world famous as a cultural center, but it is also an important industrial and transportation center. The Elbe is an important waterway, and the city has large shipyards and is the focus of a major railway network. Major industries include publishing and the manufacture of machinery, optical instruments, photographic equipment, textiles, furniture, glass, cigarettes, mineral waters, beer, and chocolates.

Dresden is the seat of a Lutheran bishopric. It has a famous technical school, a commercial school, four noted high schools, a large public library, two theaters, an opera

A view of the Zwinger, Dresden. Originally intended as part of a palace, the Zwinger is today a museum. (MARBURG—ART REFERENCE BUREAU)

house, botanical and zoological gardens, and numerous museums. The city's art gallery contains a number of masterpieces by Italian, Dutch, and Flemish artists and includes Raphael's "Sistine Madonna," a Rembrandt self-portrait, Rubens' "The Judgment of Paris," Holbein's "Madonna," and Titian's "Venus." The city also has well-known collections of china, coins, armaments, and jewelry.

Dresden was founded by Slavic fishermen on the east bank of the Elbe. In the 10th century the Slavs were driven out by the Saxons. Dresden was made a town in 1216 and became the residence of the margraves of Meissen. The town was partly destroyed by a great fire in the 15th century, but it was rebuilt and fortified in the 16th century. The city's greatest glory came in the 18th century during the reigns of the electors of Saxony, Frederick Augustus I and Frederick Augustus II, when many of its baroque and rococo buildings were erected, and its art collections were founded. It was severely bombarded by Frederick the Great of Prussia in 1760 and was occupied by the Austrians and French during the Napoleonic Wars. The Battle of Dresden (Aug. 26–27, 1813) represented the last of Napoleon's victories on German soil.

The city's fortifications were dismantled in 1817 and transformed into parks and promenades which still make up a part of the city's attractive façade. Dresden's industrial capacity increased greatly after the mid-19th century, and nearby coal mines, now nearly exhausted, greatly stimulated industrial growth. During World War II Dresden was severely bombed and many of its buildings were destroyed. Among notable buildings remaining are the Zwinger, a number of buildings constructed in rococo style around a central courtyard in 1711 and rebuilt after World War II; the Taschenberg Palace (1711–15); the Japanese Palace (1715); and the Frauenkirche (1726–43). Five bridges cross the Elbe, connecting the Altstadt ("old town") and the Friedrichstadt on the western bank with the Neustadt ("new town") on the eastern bank. Pop., 491,714.

JOACHIM MARQUARDT, Commercial School for
Merchants, Berlin-Wilmersdorf

DRESS, HISTORY OF. The earliest true clothes were almost certainly made of animal skins, which Neanderthal man, using his powerful jaws, may have chewed into material sufficiently pliable to be fashioned into garments. Neanderthal man, who flourished 100,000 years ago, also had tools, some of which seem to have been used for scraping leather. Needles of bone with pierced eyes have been found in burials of the Magdalenian period (the final major phase of the Paleolithic period). It is thought that the Magdalenian culture evolved the fundamental forms of dress: the tunic, the skirt or kilt, the mantle or cape, as well as moccasins or boots. During this period a differentiation must have arisen between male and female dress, although it is far from true that trousers have always

been characteristic of the male and skirts of the female. Anthropologists distinguish rather between "arctic" (bifurcated) and "tropical" dress.

Ancient and Medieval Dress

Gradually conjecture gives place to certainty as wall paintings and statues begin to give us exact information about the clothes worn by ancient peoples. From Egyptian records it is plain that they were at first worn only by people of rank, while slaves and the lower classes generally went about naked. Men of the upper classes wore a kind of kilt, and women a sheathlike garment reaching from just below the breasts to the ankles. The materials used were cotton and flax. With these garments were worn wide collars of beads and, strangely enough, wigs, the natural hair having been shaved off.

In contrast, ancient Assyrian clothes were ample and had the appearance of being composed of a number of fringed shawls, generally of wool. The universal headdress was in the shape of a flower pot. Men wore long hair and full beards that were sometimes elaborately curled. The Medes and Persians wore trousers, garments long regarded by the Greeks and Romans as typically "barbarian." The costume of the Mycenaean culture was

---

DRESS, HISTORY OF **STUDY GUIDE**

Food, clothing, and shelter are primary needs of mankind; the history of dress deals with the changing modes of the second of these. The subject has its practical, aesthetic, anthropological, sociological, and psychological aspects. The article on these pages surveys the history of dress. The purpose of this Study Guide is to give the reader an outline of its content and to direct him to related articles in the **ENCYCLOPEDIA INTERNATIONAL.** The story of dress is told in the following manner.

Prehistoric Dress. Origin of clothing — ideas of how the first garments were made. The emergence of the fundamental forms of dress: the tunic, skirt, mantle, and moccasins or boots.

Ancient and Medieval Dress. Egyptian clothing, kilt of the men and sheathlike garment of the women. Assyrian clothing, ample garments that covered the body. Mede and Persian dress, including trousers which were regarded by the Greeks as "barbarian."

Mycenaean dress, flounced skirts of the women. Greek costume, so simple that almost any garment may be reproduced with a sheet and pins. Etruscan clothing, development of the toga. Roman costume, the toga of the aristocrat, and the tunics and cloaks of the lower classes, Byzantine dress, modeled on the Roman but enriched with jewelry and decoration.

Medieval dress, general adoption of trousers by men after the fall of the Roman Empire. The evolution of dress of the Middle Ages, tight-fitting hose and a long, full gown with tight sleeves for the men, and long, loose garments and veils for the women. The shaping of clothing to the figure in the 13th century.

The Renaissance and After. At the end of the 14th century the fashion rivalry of the courts of France, Burgundy. The evolution of dress through the 16th, 17th, and 18th centuries when men's costume became simpler.

The 19th Century. The "empire" style, inspired by contemporary concepts of ancient Greek dress. The increas-

ing width of women's skirts as the century progressed, and the introduction of the bustle. The separation of men's clothes into formal and informal.

Modern Dress. Luxuriousness of formal dress in the early 20th century and birth of the hobble skirt. The styles of the 1920's, and the increasing informality of men's dress. The World War II period. Fashions of the 1950's and early 1960's. Spread of European dress around the world.

This article features colored drawings that illustrate the information in the text, providing a comprehensive view of change in costume through the ages. After the reader has completed a study of these, he may turn to PAINTING, HISTORY OF, in which he may make a similar survey of dress by analyzing the paintings of outstanding artists from ancient Egypt to contemporary America. These works, reproduced in color, show many of the costumes of the various eras as seen by contemporaries.

Other articles of direct interest to the student of dress are FASHION, FUR, and JEWELRY, as well as the biographies of fashion designers like Christian DIOR. Also pertinent are articles on individual items of wear: BUTTON, GLOVE, HAT, SHOE, and WIG. CLOTHING treats the whole topic of dress and adornment from an anthropological and sociological viewpoint. Two small segments of the history of dress are treated in COSTUME DESIGN, THEATRICAL and REGALIA. The total effect of a person's appearance is, of course, determined by his grooming as well as his costume. The student of dress may be interested in COSMETICS, HAIRDRESSING, and MAKE-UP.

Of subsidiary interest are CLOTHING FOR THE FAMILY, DYE AND DYEING, SEWING, and TEXTILES, as well as articles on the individual cloths: COTTON, NYLON, SILK, and WOOL.

Cross references at the ends of many of the articles suggest to the reader other articles that provide information on the particular subjects in which he is interested. Lists of books selected for their excellence and availability follow most of the articles.

surprisingly elaborate especially for women, who, although they exposed the breasts, wore flounced skirts with tight waists. Classical Greek costume was, on the other hand, extremely simple, consisting of rectangular pieces of material draped over the body and kept in place by brooches or pins and a girdle. It is possible to reproduce almost any Greek garment by means of the sheet off a single bed and two safety pins. The Etruscans seem to have invented the toga, the garment that became the typical dress of the Roman aristocrats. It consisted of a large half-circle of woolen cloth draped over the body, leaving one shoulder bare. The lower classes in Rome wore tunics and cloaks and the Roman legionaries gradually took over the "barbarian" trousers, which they wore underneath a kind of short kilt. Byzantine costume is Roman costume, minus the toga, immeasurably enriched with embroidery and precious stones. Representations of the court costume of Byzantium can be seen in the mosaics at Ravenna, Italy.

In the west the collapse of the Roman Empire brought about the general use of trousers for the men. They were generally cross-gartered, that is, a thong was wound in an overlapping fashion around the leg between the ankle and knee. They were used with one or two tunics and a cloak, together with a great variety of headgear, including helmets adorned with the horns of animals. Women were clothed in a longer tunic or skirt, and wore their hair in long plaits. This costume lasted throughout the Dark Ages, and it was not until the Crusades brought knowledge of oriental luxury that the garments of Western Europe became more refined. Men's dress in the Middle Ages consisted of tight-fitting hose together with a long, full gown with tight sleeves. Younger men wore a shorter tunic. A decorated belt hung round the hips and from this were suspended the sword, dagger, and pouch. Women wore long, loose garments with veils on their heads, so that everything but the face was concealed. It was not until the end of the 13th century that clothes began to be shaped to the figure. There soon followed the cutting away of the bodice (décolletage) and the growing popularity of striking and fanciful headdresses.

The Renaissance and After

At the end of the 14th century the elaboration of women's headgear became more marked; and men, abandoning the cowl, which had long been in use, began to wear hats. The luxurious courts of France and Burgundy vied with one another in extravagant display. Shoes became excessively pointed. It was at this time that fashion introduced the necessity of perpetual change.

In the 16th century everything, shoes included, became extremely broad, as can be seen in contemporary portraits of Henry VIII. Women's hair, however, was dressed more simply and enclosed in a kind of frame. The strange habit of slashing (derived, it is thought, from the German mercenaries) was universal. Slits were cut in almost all garments to reveal an under-material of a contrasting color. The ruff which began as a mere puckering round the neck of the shirt gradually assumed larger dimensions and became a separate garment. Women wore the ruff as well as men, but it was sometimes divided to reveal the low-cut gown, and finally became the two

wings to be seen in most of the surviving portraits of Queen Elizabeth. The characteristic garment for men consisted of a doublet and trunk hose, padded over the thighs and worn with long tights. In the second half of the century women adopted the farthingale, a kind of circular hoop that kept the skirt distended. These fashions continued with only slight modification until the end of the reign of James I in 1625.

Under Charles I trunk hose gave place to breeches and the ruff became the "falling" or Vandyke collar. Puritans wore this collar plain and their hair short, hence the name Roundhead. The Cavaliers wore long curls falling onto their shoulders. Women abandoned the farthingale. A mania for ribbons seized the fashion-conscious after the Restoration of Charles II, and men wore a curious skirt-like garment instead of tight breeches. In the 1670's a fundamental change introduced the prototype of modern male garments: tight breeches and coat and waistcoat. The last two were very long and the sleeves of the coat had immense turn-back cuffs. The curious habit of wearing wigs was introduced and lasted for a century. At first they were immensely long and curly but were so inconvenient that various modifications were introduced, especially for military men who found it difficult to keep the elaborate periwigs on their heads in battle.

Women's clothes at the end of the 17th century became stiffer and more formal. The characteristic headdress was the high lace cap or "fontange," which lasted for more than a decade. Soon after the beginning of the 18th century the farthingale was revived in the form of hoops and panniers, so that women were sometimes as excessively wide as they had formerly been excessively high. Hair was dressed close to the head, but about 1770 it began to rise and ten years later the coiffure had assumed enormous proportions. Men's clothes became simpler in cut with smaller waistcoats and turn-back cuffs, but were elaborately embroidered. Ruffles of lace were worn at the wrists and sometimes a frill of lace at the throat. Wigs were made smaller but were usually powdered white or gray. The three-cornered hat was universally worn.

The 19th Century

This costume lasted almost unchanged until the French Revolution (1789–99), when men adopted what had been English country clothes of plain cloth. The three-cornered hat gave place to the top hat, originally devised as a kind of crash helmet for the hunting field. Women abandoned their elaborately embroidered dresses, their tight lacing, and their hoops, and wore what they imagined to be ancient Greek dress: a single white garment with short sleeves, low neck, and a ribbon tied round immediately beneath the breasts. This is the so-called "empire" costume, which lasted until the fall of Napoleon. Shortly afterward skirts began to swell out again and in 1820 the waist was once more in its anatomically correct location. Men's clothes showed very little change except that breeches were gradually replaced by trousers.

During the 1830's women's hats became enormous as well as their sleeves. Skirts continued to grow more ample until something had to be done to support their weight. Hoops were therefore revived and used under an improved form of the crinoline, which reached its largest di-

EGYPTIAN
Old Kingdom, c. 2600 B.C.

A 5th-Dynasty king wore a striped head-dress and a loincloth covered in front by a stiff linen triangle. Women's tunics extended from below the bosom to the feet.

ASSYRIAN
9th Century B.C.

The fringed purple robe and mantle of an Assyrian king were thrown over one shoulder.

GREEK
6th-5th Centuries B.C.

The Greek youth's linen tunic, or chiton, was short and pleated, while the girl's was long and flowing. Both sexes wore mantles fastened on one shoulder with a pin or brooch.

PERSIAN
7th-5th Centuries B.C.

The trouser-clad Persian warrior carried case for bow and arrows.

Illustrated by John Meola

PLATE 1

1st Century B.C.
1st Century A.D.

Roman aristocrats wore a plain white toga. Slaves wore a tunic girded at the waist and sandals. The women's palla was a mantle which could be draped in various ways. A legionary wore breeches under a long tunic and a leather cuirass mounted with iron.

BYZANTINE
5th Century A.D.

Byzantine costume was simple in line but luxurious in fabric and decoration. Silks and velvets, gay colors, and rich embroidery were favored.

PLATE 2

THE MIDDLE AGES

7th-9th Centuries

The Frankish nobleman wore a long-sleeved tunic and a mantle. His trousers were cross-gartered from knee to ankle. A woman's long tunic had decorated borders. Her mantle fastened on the breast. Her pointed shoes were of soft leather.

9th-12th Centuries

A Frankish noble youth wore a long gown, girdled at the waist, over tight hose. Women wore headkerchiefs and long, full gowns with wide sleeves.

14th Century

Long, tight sleeves and hose extended from under a young man's knee-length tunic. Women's cloaks had trains, and their head-dresses displayed a simple elegance.

PLATE 3

THE RENAISSANCE AND AFTER

15th Century

In the 15th century clothes became elaborate. Garments were trimmed with precious furs. Shoes had exaggerated points. Aristocratic women wore headdresses, which sometimes towered 4 ft. above their heads.

16th CENTURY

Mid-1500's

Spanish fashion was widespread in the mid-1500's, replacing the more comfortable Italian modes worn earlier in the century. A French courtier's hat, doublet, and trunk hose were Spanish. A court lady's flowing gown was in the Italian tradition.

Late 1500's

King Henry III of France, in the costume of the Order of the Holy Ghost. The lady's skirt, supported by a farthingale, the puffed and slashed bodice, and the high ruff were dictated by Spanish fashion.

PLATE 4

17th CENTURY

Late 1600's

French gentlemen during the reign of Louis XIV wore wigs, long coats over pleated breeches, and buckled shoes. Women's trailing gowns were trimmed with lace.

Mid-1600's

Spanish influence declined as the French court became the center of fashion. Women abandoned farthingales, and flat collars replaced ruffs. Men wore ribboned breeches with high-heeled boots.

18th CENTURY

1730-45

French courtiers were the fashion leaders of Europe through most of the 18th century. The styles that they initiated, including the loose, flowing dress and the gentleman's flared coat, were copied in other countries.

1760-70

Though gentlemen still wore powdered wigs and lace, their clothes were becoming simpler in cut.

1775-85

Doorways had to be enlarged because of women's enormous coiffures, which were sometimes 3 ft. high.

PLATE 5

1800-15

London became important in the 19th century as a center of male fashion. Men wore tail coats and top hats. Women, still following the French lead, wore the high-waisted "empire" style. A short coiffure and low-heeled shoes completed the costume.

1820's

Trousers permanently replaced breeches for men. Women's waistlines dropped to the natural waist. Sleeves and skirts widened.

1830's

Men wore trousers with straps fitted under the shoe. The top hat was universally worn. Women adopted dresses with billowing sleeves and skirt, balanced by an oversize bonnet.

PLATE 6

About 1860

Hoops and crinoline were used to spread the skirt; which was at its widest in the early 1860's.

Late 1860's

The bustle came into favor, accenting the back of the garment.

1870's

The cutaway coat was reserved for evening wear, and the embroidered waistcoat was abandoned. Men's clothes became more and more standardized as fashion began to assume an almost purely feminine connotation.

1890's

Balloon and leg-of-mutton sleeves were in favor. Skirts were draped, sometimes very tightly, over the hips.

PLATE 7

MODERN DRESS

1910

Women wore the hobble skirt even on long walking excursions, although it severely hindered movement.

1917

The long, narrow skirt was worn under a loose, tailored tunic. Small, high hats were popular.

1925

The waistline dropped to the hips as the hemline rose to the knee. Bobbed hair fitted under the popular cloche. Men's clothes grew more comfortable. Soft felt hats and soft collars were judged correct.

1930's

Skirts dipped in the early 1930's and the waistline regained a more normal position.

Short skirts were in vogue again in the late 1930's. By 1940 the hemline had reached the knee, where it stayed until Dior's New Look of 1947 revived the long, flared skirt for a decade. But in the late 1950's hemlines rose again, and skirts continued short in the early 1960's.

1950's

The masculine silhouette narrowed. Jackets were close-fitting with natural shoulders and slim lapels. The feminine outline was wide as women continued to wear the long, full skirts influenced by Dior's New Look.

PLATE 8

mensions in the early 1860's. Men's clothes essentially retained the lines established at the beginning of the century, except that the square cutaway coat was reserved for the evening and trousers had completely ousted knee-breeches. The top hat was universally worn by all ranks of society, though a bowler for country wear made its appearance in the 1850's. Men's clothes became very sombre, even the embroidered waistcoat being abandoned.

In the late 1860's, the crinoline lost favor and was replaced by the bustle, the material of the dress being bunched up behind. Skirts were smooth over the hips in 1880, but a new bustle appeared in the middle 1880's, sometimes made of wire netting which was considered "less heating to the spine."

In the 1890's skirts were draped very tightly over the hips, and the middle of the decade saw the revival of balloon sleeves. Men's clothes divided into the formal (frock coat and silk hat) and the informal (lounge suit and a soft felt hat). Many men began to wear knickerbockers, especially for the new sport of cycling, which modified women's clothes also, even inducing some of them to wear "bloomers." Conservative people regarded these developments with horror.

Modern Dress

Women's formal clothes became, in the early years of the 20th century, extremely luxurious. There was extensive use of lace and other expensive materials, and furs (especially Russian sable) were very fashionable. The introduction of the so-called "health" corset gave women the curious stance, with the hips pushed back and the bosom thrust forward, characteristic of the period. However, about 1910 the influence of the Russian Ballet and of the French couturier Paul Poiret brought in a new mode, softer and more oriental. This culminated in the strange hobble skirts and huge hats of the period just before World War I.

Paris continued to exert its influence on style during the war. The fashions of 1917 struck an original note, featuring a small high hat with an upright feather and a long, rather narrow skirt with a flared shorter skirt over it. By 1920 the tubular mode had made its appearance, but skirts remained long. The real transformation came in 1925, when the post-war mode established itself: short, tubular skirt with the waist round the hips, a close-fitting cloche worn over bobbed or shingled hair, and flesh-colored stockings. The universal color was beige. Men's clothes had become much less formal, the frock coat or morning coat having almost disappeared. Nearly all men wore lounge suits, soft felt hats, and soft collars. Trousers became very wide after 1924, and for golf and other sports men wore the baggy knickerbockers known as plus-fours.

In 1930 the waist resumed its normal place and skirts became long again. The cloche was abandoned in favor of a very small hat perched over one eye. Shoulders became square and wide, and evening dresses were backless. Skirts became short again shortly before the outbreak of World War II and remained so throughout the conflict. The fall of France cut England and America off from the direct influence of Paris, and shortages made it difficult to adopt new fashions. However, in 1947, Christian Dior launched the New Look, which, with its long, flared skirt

and tight waist, dominated women's fashions until the middle 1950's.

In men's clothes two opposing tendencies were seen, perhaps most clearly in England. On the one hand there was a reversion to Edwardian clothes of the early part of the century. In Savile Row, noted for its tailoring, this meant an attempt to reproduce the styles of 50 years before: narrow trousers and close-fitting jackets buttoned rather high. With these was worn a small bowler hat perched forward on the head. These modes were exaggerated and modified by the "Teddy Boys," whose trousers were even narrower than those of fashionable young men, their jackets longer and with a much more pronounced shoulder-line. They did not adopt the bowler hat; indeed they abandoned hats altogether and wore their hair rather long.

Many other men, as well as women, stopped wearing hats, and ambitious promotion campaigns were started to save the hat manufacturers from ruin. Sports clothes took on a new informality. Even plus-fours for golf were replaced by flannel or ordinary trousers, and the tweed jacket by a windbreaker. Shirts with brightly colored stripes and checks became common. In evening dress the tail coat was almost completely abandoned, the dinner jacket being worn on all but the most formal occasions.

In women's dress the New Look was succeeded in 1956 by Dior's "H-Line" and "A-Line," a frank reversion to the modes of the 1920's. This tendency had become more marked in the early 1960's, even a version of the cloche hat being found generally acceptable. Skirts in 1961 were almost as short as they had been in 1926. Many women, for shopping and work about the house, wore trousers (slacks) but, in general, unlike the tentative beach pajamas of the 1920's, these were extremely close-fitting. With them was often worn a kind of dufflecoat. Shoes for both sexes became extremely pointed, an Italian influence that had become more and more marked in all departments of fashion. American influence in Europe was reflected in the improved standard of readymade clothes, especially for the young, and also in men's clothes, which featured lighter-weight materials and brighter colors. Many Englishmen now wear tropical suits in the summer, which would have been unthinkable a generation ago.

A marked feature of recent years has been the spread of European dress to almost all parts of the world. A crowd in Tokyo is virtually indistinguishable in its dress from a crowd in New York or London; and African politicians dress like their European counterparts. Indian women have, however, retained their traditional sari even in foreign cities. In Europe peasant costume has almost entirely disappeared except during national holidays and as a tourist attraction. Paris continues to "dictate" the main lines of fashionable female dress, although these are often considerably modified before they are marketed in England and America.

Consult Planche, J. R. A., *Cyclopedia of Costume* (1876–79); Boehn, Max von, *Modes and Manners* (1925); Lester, K. M., *Historic Costume* (1925); Kelly, F. M., and Schwabe, R., *Historic Costume* (2d ed., 1929); Evans, Mary, *Costume Throughout the Ages* (1930); Wilcox, R. T., *The Mode in Costume* (1948).

JAMES LAVER, Victoria and Albert Museum

DRESSLER, MARIE, professional name of Leila Koerber (1869–1934), actress born in Cobourg, Ontario, Canada. After success on the stage in New York and London, she became an outstanding comedienne and character actress in U.S. films. She was in *Tillie's Punctured Romance* (1914); *Anna Christie* (1930); *Min and Bill,* for which she won an Academy Award in 1931; and *Tugboat Annie* (1933).

DREUX [drû], market center of northern France, on the Blaise River, about 50 mi. west of Paris. It has small factories processing local agricultural products, as well as an important piston-ring plant. The Royal Chapel of St. Louis, on a hilltop northwest of the town, was erected by Louis Philippe to hold the tombs of members of the family of Orléans. Pop., 23,494.

DREW, CHARLES RICHARD (1904–50), U.S. Negro medical researcher. Born in Washington, D.C., he graduated from McGill University Medical College. Drew did pioneer research in methods of collecting and storing blood plasma. He established a blood bank for the British government during World War II, and was then appointed director of the first U.S. Red Cross blood bank. After the war he served as chief surgeon of Howard University Medical School, and did research on fluid balances in surgery.

DREW, DANIEL (1797–1879), American railroad financier. Drew, who was born in Carmel, N.Y., was a cattle dealer before operating a Hudson River steamboat service, in which he survived his first competition with Cornelius Vanderbilt. Drawn (1844) to Wall Street, he was for ten years a broker's partner and then an independent speculator. Drew obtained a directorship from the Erie Railroad and unscrupulously manipulated its stock in the celebrated Erie War that he, Jay Gould, and James Fisk won (1866–68) over Vanderbilt. Victimized (1870) by his former associates, he went bankrupt (1876). He endowed Drew Theological Seminary, Madison, N.J., and Drew Seminary for Young Ladies, Carmel.

DREW, GEORGE ALEXANDER (1894–   ), Canadian politician. He served in World War I, practiced law in his native city of Guelph, Ontario, and became its mayor in 1925. Active in provincial politics, he was premier of Ontario from 1943 to 1948. In 1948 he was chosen national leader of the Progressive Conservative party and moved to Ottawa as a member of Parliament (1949–56). He unsuccessfully led his party in two general elections, in 1949 and in 1953. Four years later he received an appointment as Canadian high commissioner to the United Kingdom.

DREW, JOHN (1853–1927), American actor, born in Philadelphia. After early experience with the company headed by his mother, Louisa Lane Drew, he joined Augustin Daly's company in New York in 1875, where he starred with Ada Rehan in such classics as *As You Like It, The Taming of the Shrew,* and *The School for Scandal.* In 1892 he joined Charles Frohman's troupe in New York and appeared successfully in modern comedies. He was the uncle of Ethel, Lionel, and John Barrymore.

DREWRY'S BLUFF, height 8 mi. below Richmond, Va., on the south bank of the James River, scene of two engagements in the American Civil War. There, in the Peninsula Campaign, Confederate defenses checked unsupported Union gunboats on May 15, 1862. In the Wilderness Campaign, Pierre G. T. Beauregard, though his forces were considerably outnumbered, defeated Union Gen. Benjamin F. Butler and his Army of the James, May 16, 1864. Butler, driven about 12 mi. down the river, was contained until mid-June.

DREXEL [drĕk'səl], **ANTHONY JOSEPH** (1826–93), American banker. Drexel, born in Philadelphia, started his career at 13 in the bank founded by his Austrian immigrant father, Francis Martin Drexel (1792–1863). He became head of the bank and of Drexel, Morgan & Company, New York, and Drexel, Harjes & Company, Paris. He was also co-owner of the Philadelphia *Public Ledger* and founded (1892) Philadelphia's Drexel Institute of Art, Science and Industry.

DREYFUS [drā'fəs, drī'fəs] **AFFAIR,** in French history, celebrated controversy arising from the false conviction for espionage of army captain Alfred Dreyfus. In 1894 the French counterespionage service, aware that the German military attaché in Paris was obtaining military information, managed to filch from the German Embassy a memorandum written by the unknown traitor. Its contents suggested that the author was a General Staff officer with specialized technical knowledge. Dreyfus had such knowledge. Handwriting tests, moreover, seemed to confirm

Contemporary rendering of Alfred Dreyfus before the Council of War during his second trial for espionage in 1899. (CULVER PICTURES, INC.)

suspicions. Because Dreyfus was a Jew, the army regarded the charge as proved and was grateful that the betrayer was not a "real Frenchman." In the controversy that followed, it drew support from those who believed that France's regeneration was tied to the army's integrity and vitality. At Dreyfus's court-martial in 1894, handwriting experts could not agree whether the script in the memorandum was his. The prosecution thereupon introduced new documentary evidence, which the defense attorney was not allowed to see. These dubious proceedings, conducted in secret, produced a verdict of guilty. Dreyfus received a sentence of life imprisonment, was stripped of military rank, and was sent to Devil's Island.

Shortly after, the new head of the counterespionage service, Col. Georges Picquart, was nonplussed by the continued sale of military secrets to the same source and started an investigation. It led to Maj. Ferdinand Esterházy, whose handwriting matched that of the "Dreyfus" documents. Picquart informed the chief of staff that a mistake had been made and suggested that the army reopen the case. To his dismay, the army chose to let the matter rest. Picquart was soon bundled off to duty in Tunis and replaced by Maj. Hubert Henry. Henry, loyal to the army and also a friend of Esterházy, began tampering with the evidence to make the case against Dreyfus more conclusive. He did not know that Picquart had photographed the evidence before leaving for Tunis.

At this point the unorthodox procedures used in Dreyfus's trial were becoming known and arousing demands for a retrial. Esterházy, now under fire from Dreyfus's brother, asked for a court-martial to clear himself. Armed with a new document forged by Henry, he easily won acquittal. This brought the novelist Émile Zola into the fray. With his open letter to the President of the Republic, *J'accuse!* (1898), Zola charged the army with deliberately withholding evidence and protecting Esterházy. The army challenged him in court to prove his charge, something Zola could not do. To avoid jail, he took refuge in England. Meanwhile, the case against Dreyfus further dissolved when the Italian ambassador showed the French government that one of the documents used to convict Dreyfus was a forgery. The suicide of Henry assured reopening of the case. After a review by the Court of Cassation indicated Esterházy's guilt, he fled to London and there confessed. A new court-martial was ordered (1899) for Dreyfus. Its verdict against him, in spite of the new evidence, was an astounding miscarriage of justice and paved the way to political victories by the Dreyfusards. By 1906 pro-Dreyfus feeling in the country made it feasible for the Court of Cassation to set aside the verdict of 1894. Dreyfus was restored to the army, promoted to major, and decorated. Col. Picquart became a general and later War Minister. The affair, which divided France into two embittered camps, discredited elements hostile to the Third Republic.

Consult Halász, Nicholas, *Captain Dreyfus* (1955).

ROGER L. WILLIAMS, Antioch College

DRIFT, GLACIAL. *See* GLACIAL DEPOSITS.

DRIFTLESS AREA, an apparently unglaciated area of about 15,000 sq. mi. in southwestern Wisconsin and northwest-

ern Illinois. It lacks the covering of glacial drift, present elsewhere in the region, that records the existence of continental glaciers during the Ice Age. Probably the glaciers were channeled around the area via the basins of Lakes Superior and Michigan.

See also GLACIAL DEPOSITS; ICE AGE.

DRILL, a large, terrestrial monkey, *Mandrillus leucophaeus*, native to the rain forests of West Africa. The drill has a heavy body covered with dark, olive-green fur, a tiny stub for a tail, and pink buttocks. Its massive head is surrounded by a ruff of fur; its face is black. Large bands of drills roam the forest floor feeding on plants, fruit, and insects. Among themselves they are quite placid, but if molested by man, drills can be extremely dangerous. *See also* MANDRILL.

DRILLS AND DRILLING. Tools for drilling or boring holes—whether they are known as drills, drill bits, auger bits, or otherwise—have evolved from pieces of stone, flaked and chipped like extra-long arrowheads. These primitive drills were turned by hand or with the aid of straps or short bows; the upper parts were lashed to sticks. The earliest known drill formed of metal was almost as crude. It was a rod flattened and expanded at one end by hammering and used to scrape, rather than to cut, a hole. The first drill with cutting action is believed to have been developed from a gouge tool. Improvements were gradually made. The straight edge of the gouge was curved and notched to form a cutting lip. Shavings pared from the gouged hole were removed through a groove running along the length. Another type of drill, used by the Romans, was shaped like a long, narrow spoon, and called a spoon or duckbill bit.

Modern drills evolved from these boring tools. There are two principal types: the auger bits for drilling wood, and the twist drill for harder material.

Auger Bit. The auger bit, for working in wood, has a spiral groove around the shaft that carries out shavings. Two sharp cutters, or spurs, at its end sever wood fibers and two cutting lips plane away the wood. For hand boring, the bit has a threaded point, similar to a screw, to draw the bit into the wood. The auger bit is made in diameters from $\frac{3}{16}$ in. in sizes larger by $\frac{1}{16}$ in. and numbered correspondingly: a No. 5 auger bit, for example, bores a $\frac{5}{16}$ in. hole. An adjustable bit with the same type of cutting action, and called an expansive bit, bores holes up to 3 in. or even 4 in., according to the size of cutters supplied it. For power drills, a bit with a sharp center point is frequently used. Such bits can be used with interchangeable cutters.

Other wood-boring bits are (1) the centerless Forstner bit, which has a sharp rim instead of cutters and no projecting screw point, especially useful for thin wood, end-grain boring, and shallow boring; (2) the twist bit, which is pointed more sharply than the twist drill used on steel; (3) the gimlet bit with a screw point; and (4) the push-drill point for small holes, used with an automatic, or spiral, drill worked by pushing the handle.

Drills for Metal. The twist drill used on metal is a remarkable tool in respect to the skill and precision with which it is manufactured and the work it will do. In addi-

TWIST DRILLS

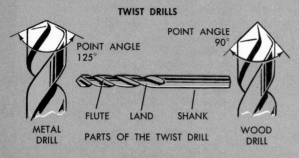

POINT ANGLE 125°

POINT ANGLE 90°

FLUTE   LAND   SHANK

METAL DRILL

PARTS OF THE TWIST DRILL

WOOD DRILL

The tapered edges of the land within the point angle do the cutting. The flute acts as a conveyor to remove drilled-out material. The shank locks into the handle through which power is supplied.

TWIST DRILL POINTS

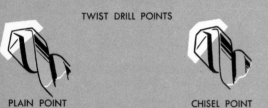

PLAIN POINT

CHISEL POINT

Whether for use on wood or metal, the plain point is used in hand drills. The chisel point is used with power drills.

COUNTERSINK BITS

COUNTERSINKING

(1)

(2)

HOLE SHAPE   SCREW INSERTED

(1) Twist drill. (2) Bit made to specific screw size. In wood, hole diameters should be slightly smaller than screw diameters so that threads anchor. In metal, threadings should match.

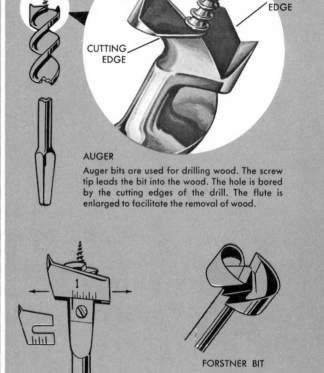

SPUR

SCREW TIP

CUTTING EDGE

CUTTING EDGE

AUGER

Auger bits are used for drilling wood. The screw tip leads the bit into the wood. The hole is bored by the cutting edges of the drill. The flute is enlarged to facilitate the removal of wood.

1

FORSTNER BIT

The sharp-rimmed, flat centerless Forstner bit, designed to bore through thin wood without splitting it.

EXPANSIVE BIT

The screwhead on the expansive bit, an auger bit, provides not only for a change of cutters but also for a range of diameters for each cutter.

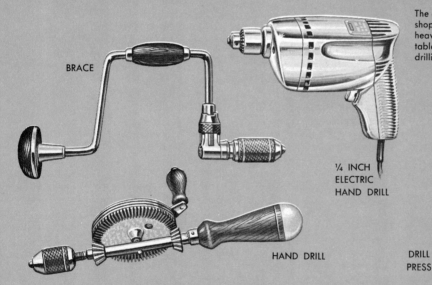

BRACE

¼ INCH ELECTRIC HAND DRILL

The electric hand drill is effective for home and light shop use. The drill press is a power installation for heavier work. Small metal pieces are clamped to the table. If necessary, the table can be moved to permit drilling on large pieces.

HAND DRILL

The brace and hand drill are used primarily in woodworking operations. The brace is better for drilling larger holes because the wide sweep of the handle gives added torque to the bit.

Rockwell Manufacturing Co.

DRILL PRESS

tion to drilling metal it is often used on wood, plastics, and relatively soft materials. Many twist drills are made of a type of steel known as carbon steel. Others are made of another kind of steel, called high-speed steel, which will withstand the strain and heat of production work at a cutting rate up to about twice that of the less expensive drills.

The twist drill point has a very short chisel edge at the center and two cutting lips of equal length which meet at an angle. The grooves carry out chips from drilled holes. Ordinarily, the shank is round and straight, but in the larger sizes, it is usually tapered. Shanks in other shapes simplify clamping in drill tools not designed for a straight or tapered shank.

For countersinking holes, combination drills and countersinks of several kinds are made, as are combination drills and reamers. Carbide-tipped drills are available for drilling masonry and other abrasive materials.

Sizes of twist drills are indicated in several ways: (1) fractional drills from $\frac{1}{64}$ in. in diameter up, by 64ths; (2) letter drills from A (.234 in.) to Z (.413 in.); (3) number drills from No. 80 (.0135 in.) to No. 1 (.228 in.); and (4) metric drills, measured in millimeters.

Hand Drilling. The tools used for hand drilling are (1) bit brace for a bit with a tapered square tang or round shank; (2) geared hand and breast drill; and (3) the automatic drill worked by pushing.

Hand drilling is done speedily and easily with portable electric power drills. The most common of these is the $\frac{1}{4}$ in. drill, which can also be used for sawing, polishing, and other workshop jobs. Various power machines also are used for heavier drilling, the principal one being the drill press.

ARTHUR WAKELING,
Consulting Editor, *Home Craftsman*
See also DRILLING MACHINES; POWER TOOLS, PORTABLE; TOOLS.

DRILLING MACHINES. Power tools for driving holes through hard surfaces are used in the machine shop to drill metal and in earth drilling to dig wells, break up rock, or drive foundation holes. In each case the work requires power—much more than that needed for hand drilling—hence the term machinery is applied to drills for these purposes.

Machine-Shop Drills. To drill holes through metal or other hard material, the required thrust force may be as high as 1,000 to 2,000 lbs. The drill press is provided with a work table, to which the work may be clamped, and a drill tool. The most generally used drill bit is the twist drill, which burrows into the metal with its rotating chisel edge, forcing chips up through its spiral flutes. The three main types of drill presses are the bench, the upright, and the radial.

The lightest work is done on the bench drill press, which is the simplest type. The work table and sometimes the drill head are adjustable. A hand lever permits manual drill feeding. Stepped pulleys allow the drill speed to be changed.

The upright drill is used for heavier work. It has a wide range of drilling speeds, the drill head is fixed in its orientation, and the work table is adjustable.

For work on large, heavy pieces of material, the radial drill press is most used. It has an adjustable drill head that can be moved along an arm that can be swung around a column. This flexibility permits complex drilling work on a wide range of sizes and shapes. These important machines are designed for very accurate performance.

When several drill heads are built into a unified machine with a common work table, the machine is called a gang drill. The work is moved from one place to another beneath the drill heads to perform step-by-step operations with different tools.

Special Drills. Multiple-spindle drill presses may have 100 or more drill spindles; they are designed for quantity production work. The spindles may be on movable arms or fixed in a single head; quite complicated drilling patterns can be performed.

When several pieces are to be drilled with uniform accuracy, a drill jig with bushings is clamped on to guide the drill. By replacing the drill bit with other tools, a drill press can do other jobs; for example, it can enlarge a hole with a bore, smooth it with a reamer, or cut a screw thread with a tapping tool.

Earth Drills. Drilling holes in rock, ground surface, or heavy roadbeds requires tools different from those used in machine shops. Instead of the rotation edges of the twist drill, a chopping action of a chisel-like tool is more common. For rock drilling, one or several chisel edges are arranged radially. They are given fractional rotations during short bursts of power to chop through the surface. Another type of drill head uses particles of hard-cutting industrial diamond on a rotating drill edge.

For deep subsurface drilling, the tool is designed to bring the material up to the surface. A core drill, or core borer, has a hollow pipe inside a cylinder to bring up core samples of earth. This is necessary in building dam foundations where the subsurface must be inspected first. In a wash borer, water under pressure is forced down through an inner pipe to carry up the material through an outer casing.

WILLARD ROGERS, University of Arizona
See also CUTTING FLUID; DRILLS AND DRILLING; MACHINE TOOLS; PETROLEUM: *Drilling for Oil.*

DRINKWATER, JOHN (1882–1937), English poet and playwright, also remembered as an actor and director. His $X = 0$ is a verse play about an episode in the Trojan War. He wrote several biographical plays: *Abraham Lincoln,* his outstanding success, and *Mary Stuart, Oliver Cromwell, Robert E. Lee,* and *Robert Burns.* His best-known comedy is *Bird in Hand.*

DRIPSTONE, general term for material deposited from solution by dripping waters, usually in caves. Most dripstone is calcite or aragonite, both calcium carbonate minerals. It forms stalactites, cylindrical or conical deposits hanging from the roof of a cavern, and stalagmites, columns or ridges rising from the cave floor, deposited by water dripping from the roof above. Excellent examples of dripstone can be seen in most limestone caves.
See also CALCITE; CAVE.

DRIVER ANT. *See* ARMY ANT OR DRIVER ANT.

DROGHEDA [drô'ə-də], municipal borough and seaport of County Louth, eastern Ireland, located where the valley of the Boyne River widens to form a tidal estuary, 30 mi. north of Dublin. In the Anglo-Norman period Drogheda was a walled town which guarded the ford and bridge along the main east-coast route. It developed as a marketing center for one of the richest farming areas in the country. The town has a cement-processing works, brewery and distillery, and factories making clothing, margarine, footwear, and chemical fertilizers. Pop., 17,071.

DRONE, in music, a long, sustained note, or chord used to accompany a melody. A single, repeated tone is called an interrupted drone. The use of the drone constitutes one of the simplest kinds of polyphony (music of many parts) and is found in Western and oriental art music as well as in the music of many primitive cultures and in European folk music. It is used in vocal and instrumental music; some instruments, such as the bagpipe, the double-flute of the Balkans, and the organ, are especially suited for it. It was used in medieval organum (music containing parallel intervals such as D-G to C-F) and in instrumental music from the Renaissance on. In Western art music it is often called organ point or pedal point because of its close association with the organ.

DRONE AIRCRAFT, a pilotless, remote-controlled aircraft used for air-to-air or ground-to-air target practice. Drone planes are launched by a catapult from the ground or the deck of a carrier, or are dropped from a mother plane. They are controlled by radio from the ground or from a guide plane, and are equipped with recovery parachutes. The attacking plane, or antiaircraft battery, fires at targets towed by the drone plane. Under special maneuvers the drone itself is destroyed.

DROPSY. See EDEMA.

DROSOPHILA [drō-sŏf'ə-lə], a genus of small insects, also known as the fruit flies, found throughout the world. The best-known is *Drosophila melanogaster*, a tiny, yellowish-brown creature who has been the subject of numerous genetic studies. This fruit fly is easily maintained in the laboratory and reproduces rapidly and in large numbers.

DROUGHT [drout], extended period of unusually dry weather resulting in a water shortage that seriously interferes with established human activity. Its seriousness depends on the degree of the unaccustomed water shortage, as well as on the duration and warmth of the dry period. Droughts result from failure to receive normal precipitation.

Most precipitation depends on water vapor carried by winds from an ocean or other source of moisture (*see* HYDROLOGIC CYCLE). If these moisture-carrying winds are replaced by winds from a dry region, or if they are modified by downward motion, as in the center of an anticyclone, the weather is abnormally dry and often persistently cloudless. Under these conditions it is impossible to end a drought by cloud seeding.

When stream flow and reservoir storage are below normal, the condition is called hydrologic drought. Agricultural drought is the lack of sufficient soil moisture for the usual plant growth. These two kinds of drought do not necessarily occur simultaneously.

Countless droughts have been recorded at irregular intervals throughout history, and nearly every nation has endured major droughts. Overpopulated areas, such as in China and India, and areas that have barely enough rainfall even in good years, are in constant danger of drought and the devastation that often accompanies it. At least a quarter of the world's population lives in such areas.

Consult Tannehill, I. R., *Drought, its Causes and Effects* (1947).

WAYNE C. PALMER, U.S. Weather Bureau
See also CLIMATOLOGY; CLOUD SEEDING; DUST STORM.

DROWNING, death from suffocation caused by water in the lungs. Ordinarily, an individual cannot be revived after five minutes of submersion in water, but in some cases life may be restored even after 15 minutes under water.

Rescuers should approach the drowning person with great caution, since the victim is usually possessed with uncontrollable fright and is hard to manage. If possible a line or plank should be extended to him or he should be approached from behind. The rescuer should turn the victim over on his back and pull him to shore either by swimming on his own back while holding the victim's head above water with both hands, or by swimming on his side with the victim slung across his hip in a back-floating position.

Once ashore the victim's clothing should be loosened. Artificial respiration should be applied immediately, and continued until the victim is breathing rhythmically on his own. The preferred method is mouth-to-mouth breathing (*see* ARTIFICIAL RESPIRATION). After he has revived, the patient should not be allowed to stand, but should be kept quiet and warmly wrapped for several hours.

The most common preventable cause of drowning is exhaustion. This is especially likely to occur when swimming in cold water. Swimmers should learn how to rest by floating in the water before attempting to swim long distances.

HERBERT BENJAMIN, M.D.

DRUG ADDICTION, an emotional and physiological dependence on drugs such that serious physical symptoms develop when the drug is withdrawn. Addiction must be distinguished from habituation, in which an individual becomes accustomed to a particular drug on a psychological rather than a physiological basis. In such cases a strong desire for the drug is present but physical symptoms do not appear if it is unavailable. Three characteristics of drug addictions are:

Tolerance. With prolonged use, increased dosages of the drug are necessary to produce the desired effect. Frequently the addict can consume quantities of the drug that would kill normal persons.

Physical Dependence and Withdrawal Syndrome. The drug must be taken at regular intervals to avoid painful symptoms. When the dosage is decreased or abolished entirely, various physical disturbances appear.

Psychological Dependence. The drug produces a sense of well-being. When deprived, the addict suffers from various degrees of mental distress.

Types of Addiction

Narcotics. These are drugs, such as heroin and morphine, that are derived from opium and synthetic opium-like compounds. Opium is obtained from the poppy plant and its juice has been used by physicians since the time of ancient Greece. Narcotics are used by present-day physicians chiefly as pain killers and, occasionally, to induce sleep.

In the United States most addicts use heroin, which is the most potent of the narcotic drugs. The addict first uses the drug to satisfy his curiosity or to "go along" with companions who are already addicted. The first experience with the drug results in a trance. Gradually greater dosages must be taken to produce the "kick," or euphoria, as the victim develops a tolerance. In the beginning the drug may be taken by inhaling the powder through the nostrils. As larger quantities become necessary the addict uses a hypodermic needle to introduce the narcotic under the skin. He may finally resort to "mainlining," or injecting the drug directly into the veins. Since the addict often uses unclean needles his body may be covered with infections that develop at the site of the injections. Diseases such as malaria, hepatitis, syphilis, and tetanus may also result from the use of contaminated needles.

Contrary to popular opinion, a narcotics addict may appear perfectly normal and may even disguise his addiction from a physician. The shabby appearance and undernourished condition that characterize many addicts is brought on, not by the effects of the drug, but by poverty. This results from their efforts to meet the exorbitant prices that they must pay for their daily supply of narcotics.

Addiction is apt to occur among physicians, nurses, and pharmacists who have easy access to narcotics. Patients who are given narcotics in the treatment of a disease may become addicts if the use of the drugs is prolonged. It has also been established that a child born of an addict mother may be addicted from birth.

If the addict cannot obtain narcotics he displays withdrawal symptoms, which vary with the particular drug used and the extent of the addiction. The first symptoms appear around the time of the next scheduled dose. The addict becomes restless and irritable. His eyes tear and his nose runs, giving the appearance of having a cold. At the height of the symptoms the patient may suffer from violent abdominal cramps, vomiting, diarrhea, muscular tremors, double vision, and occasionally delirium and mania. These symptoms usually reach their peak from 48 to 72 hours after the last dose and disappear entirely in 10 to 14 days.

The prospects for cure from narcotics addiction are not good. The first stage of treatment—hospitalizing the patient and gradually withdrawing the drug—is not difficult. The greatest failures are met in attempting to prevent a relapse. Psychotherapy and other types of guidance often prove too inadequate to enable the patient to withstand the anxieties that develop when he is once more returned to his usual surroundings. Statistics indicate that more than 75% of the addicts discharged from hospitals resume taking narcotics within a few months after their release. Estimates of a permanent cure range from 1% to 15%.

The U.S. Government maintains two hospitals for the treatment of narcotic addicts, one at Fort Worth, Tex., the other at Lexington, Ky. Local general hospitals often have to admit and treat addicts who are in the throes of withdrawal, but they are usually not equipped to handle the larger problem of the addiction itself.

Barbiturates. Barbiturates are used medically as sedatives and are commonly known as sleeping pills. While many individuals take sleeping pills without any untoward effects, some may develop a barbiturate addiction. Over a period of time tolerance to normal dosages develops and the patient must increase the amount taken in order to obtain the sedative effect. Thrill-seekers begin with larger dosages. They frequently must counter the severe depression that results by taking benzedrine (see below). Alcoholics may become barbiturate addicts when they take the drug to relieve nervousness and tremors. They soon find that the effects of alcoholic intoxication can be obtained just as easily with barbiturates. Morphine addicts may also use barbiturates when the former is not available. They thus become addicted to both drugs.

Barbiturate addiction affects the nervous system. The symptoms closely resemble those seen in chronic alcoholism and include mental changes, such as sluggishness, difficulty in thinking, poor judgment, and impaired memory. The addict may become morose, irritable, and childish. Occasionally a well developed psychosis, with confusion, fear, and delusions, results. Slurred speech, loss of balance, and double vision are commonly present.

If the barbiturate addict is suddenly deprived of the drugs, he lapses into severe and dangerous withdrawal symptoms. For 12 to 16 hours following his last dose his mental state clears. Following this, however, he becomes restless and displays anxiety and tremors. From 2 to 7 days later convulsions and delirium may occur. To treat barbiturate addiction the patient must be hospitalized and the drug withdrawn. It is essential that the drug be withdrawn gradually.

Cocaine. Cocaine is obtained from the leaves of *Erythroxylon coca* and certain other South American trees. It is applied as an anesthetic solution to the surface tissues of the eyes, nose, and throat. Cocaine addiction does not produce the severe withdrawal symptoms that characterize narcotic and barbiturate addictions. The drug produces mental stimulation and sensations of great power and well-being. Cocaine addiction is comparatively rare today, and when the drug is taken it is usually in combination with other drugs. Cocaine addicts frequently suffer from delusions of persecution and may, as a consequence, be extremely dangerous.

Benzedrine (Amphetamine). Although it is frequently misused to produce excitement and elation, addiction to benzedrine is not common. Alcoholics and barbiturate addicts often use amphetamine for a "pick-up." Characteristic withdrawal symptoms do not develop when the addict is taken off the drug. As is the case in the other addictions, benzedrine addicts usually suffer from personality defects.

Marihuana (Hashish). Marihuana is not a truly addicting drug. The social effects of marihuana consumption, however, are somewhat controversial and the drug has been placed under the Harrison Narcotic Act of 1914.

MICHAEL G. KALOGERAKIS, M.D.

See also ALCOHOLISM.

DRUGS

DRUGS, substances used in the treatment of disease. Drug therapy is one of the oldest forms of medical treatment. The Ebers Papyrus, an ancient Egyptian medical treatise, contains recipes and prescriptions for the treatment of diseases of the eyes, skin, and internal organs. In China and India "herbals," or collections of herb remedies, were compiled hundreds of years before the birth of Christ. Primitive tribes used quinine for malaria, ipecac for dysentery, and rauwolfia for a host of ailments.

Until the 20th century drugs were obtained primarily from plants. Beginning about 1900 drugs from animal sources became available. These included the hormones, such as epinephrine (adrenalin), insulin, and the male and female sex hormones. The development of organic chemistry made possible the synthesis of pure compounds to replace the crude mixtures prepared by brewing or steeping plants.

Many drugs can now be synthesized more cheaply than they can be isolated from plants and animals. In some cases new and better compounds can be synthesized.

Types of Drugs

While there is no completely satisfactory or logical method of classifying drugs, most can be grouped on the basis of their general effects on the body, or by their medical use.

Drugs used to combat infections and infestations caused by bacteria, viruses, protozoa, or worms, are known as "antiparasitic" drugs. The antibiotics are included in this group.

Drugs Which Depress the Central Nervous System. A large category includes those drugs which depress the activity of the brain and spinal cord. Some of these drugs produce a loss of sensation and consciousness and are used for general anesthesia (ether). The narcotics (opium, morphine) are important pain-relievers. Sedatives and hypnotics produce calm and sleep, respectively. The most important sedatives are the barbiturates, which are found in many sleeping potions. The "anticonvulsants" reduce or prevent the epileptic seizures seen in epilepsy. Aspirin and related compounds are termed "antipyretic analgesics," because they have the dual action of relieving pain and reducing fever. A comparatively new group of drugs are the tranquilizers, which calm anxiety and dull emotional responses without producing drowsiness.

Drugs Which Act upon the Automatic (Autonomic) Nervous System. A large group of drugs act on certain portions of the nervous system (the autonomic nervous system) that control automatic, involuntary functions such as the rate of heartbeat, blood pressure, intestinal movements, and the size of the pupils. These autonomic drugs include epinephrine, a substance normally present in the body, which helps to prepare the body for muscular exertion by increasing the blood pressure and heart rates and by stimulating the release of sugar into the blood stream. Other autonomic drugs, such as methacholine, lower the blood pressure and stimulate the movement of the digestive tract and the flow of digestive juices.

Other classifications of drugs include those which help prevent clotting of the blood (anticoagulants) and those which stimulate kidney action (diuretics). The term "digitalis" describes a group of drugs obtained from digitalis

and related species. These drugs strengthen the force of the heartbeat and are useful in treating certain types of heart disease. Hormones, such as insulin and thyroxin, may be used as drugs to meet the deficiencies which may arise from the malfunctioning of the pancreas and thyroid glands. Cortisone and hydrocortisone are hormones which are used to treat a large number of diseases involving inflammatory responses.

The Administration of Drugs

The method of giving a drug is often determined by the manner in which the body acts upon it. Many commonly used substances are readily absorbed from the stomach or intestine, and so can be taken by mouth. Examples of such drugs are aspirin, the sulfonamides, and the barbiturates. Certain drugs, however, cannot be readily absorbed from the gastrointestinal tract and so must be injected under the skin, or into muscles or veins. The hormone insulin must be injected, since it is not absorbed well from the gastrointestinal tract and it is destroyed by digestive enzymes.

Disposition in the Body. After entering the body, some drugs remain in the blood stream. Others may leave the circulatory system to penetrate the tissue fluids. Still others may gain access to particular regions, such as the brain or eye. The action of the drug will be influenced by its ability to penetrate to the target area and the manner in which the body acts upon it. The chemical activity of the body may rapidly change the drug to an inactive form. Also of importance is the rate at which the substance is removed from the body. In the case of potentially harmful drugs their rapid removal from the body may make possible their use.

Drug Action. Knowledge of the exact mechanism by which drugs produce their effects is as yet quite hazy. While it is known, for example, that when insulin is given to the diabetic the blood sugar will be lowered, the manner in which insulin achieves this effect is not clear. Similarly the ability of ether to produce stimulation in small doses and loss of sensation and consciousness and ultimately death, with increasing dosages, is familiar but poorly understood. The question remains as to exactly what changes ether causes in the cells of the brain and spinal cord.

Drug Toxicity. Since drugs are by definition chemicals that alter body function, it is clear that excess doses of any drug may produce harmful effects. The difference between the dose of a drug producing a desired effect (the therapeutic dose), and that producing a toxic effect (toxic dose), is sometimes referred to as the margin of safety. This margin varies, both for different drugs and for different individuals given the same drug. In some cases the margin is so narrow that undesired actions ("side effects") will appear. In addition to toxicity there is the possibility of an allergic sensitivity even to small doses of the substance which are quite harmless for the nonallergic subject. A well-known example is penicillin, which is normally not toxic for man at the doses needed to kill susceptible bacteria. In rare cases, however, a patient may experience a violent allergic reaction even to minute doses of penicillin.

ELIJAH ADAMS, St. Louis University School of Medicine

Drug Resistance. In the 30 years since antimicrobials were introduced, it has become increasingly clear that many bacteria develop resistance to their effect. Among the most serious problems are infections caused by staphylococci and the Enterobacteriaceae. This group includes *Escherichia coli*, the colon bacillus; *Salmonella*, which causes many ills, including typhoid; and *Shigella*, a dysentery bacillus. The staphylococci are resistant to most antibiotics, including penicillin G, the tetracyclines, chloramphenicol, streptomycin, and erythromycin. The basis of staphylococcic resistance is small, extrachromosomal elements called plasmids—minute pieces of DNA which allow the bacteria to make proteins able to interfere with antibiotic action.

The concept of antibiotic resistance originated in Japan in 1959 with the discovery of *Shigella* bacteria, able to resist six antibiotics. Some bacteria also contain a transfer factor, a small piece of DNA called an episome, which is not attached to the chromosome and not essential to the cell. When such a bacterium mates with another, it transfers this factor to the new cell, enabling it, too, to make antibiotic-resistant proteins. With the use of antibiotics in animal feeds, more and more bacteria have developed resistance factors. If a bacterium has both resistance and transfer factors, it can infect other, unrelated bacteria. Because these bacteria mate in the intestines, they are known as enteric bacteria. Enteric bacteria resistant to six or more antibiotics have been found in Japan, the United States, Britain, and Africa.

HAROLD NEU, M.D.

See also ANTIBIOTICS; SALMONELLA; STAPHYLOCOCCUS.

DRUID [droo'ĭd], member of the Celtic priestly class which together with the military composed the aristocracy of Gaul and the British Isles. The classical writers Caesar and Strabo are the earliest extant sources for modern knowledge of the Druids. Strabo describes a threefold class of Druids, bards, and prophets, which corresponds to the Druids, bards, and *filid* of ancient Ireland. If, as Caesar suggests, Druidism originated in Britain, it was perhaps pre-Celtic, but nothing certain is known.

The Druids are associated with religious beliefs which included the transmigration and immortality of souls and with ceremonies involving human sacrifice. Doctrine was preserved and transmitted in oral verse to candidates for the Druidhood. In addition to the religious role, Druids had great political, educational, and judicial influence. A chief Druid presided over an annual judicial gathering.

The Gaulish Druids were proscribed by the Roman Emperors Claudius and Tiberius for their rebellion against Roman rule in the province, but in the 4th century A.D. the Roman poet Ausonius records a family still claiming descent from the Druids. Anglesey, perhaps the Druids' British center, was sacked in 60 A.D., but the existence of British and Irish Druids was recorded as late as the 6th century. No connection has been established between Druidism and Stonehenge, or with the Welsh Eisteddfod.

JOHN MACQUEEN, Edinburgh University

See also CELTS; EISTEDDFOD.

DRUM, in general, instrument with a hollow body which is struck. Specifically, drums are members of two large groups of musical instruments. All of the membranophones—that is, instruments making use of stretched membranes or skins—which are struck are drums. Furthermore, some of the idiophones—that is, instruments whose natural, nontensed bodies are made to vibrate in order to produce sound—are conventionally called drums.

Steel drums from a band in Trinidad are made of empty oil containers, iron pots, and the like, grooved to provide tonal quality.
(BROWN BROTHERS)

A Mexican playing an ancient, rarely seen "dog" drum.
(ILLUSTRATION RESEARCH SERVICE)

In Kenya tribesmen straddle their drums to allow dance movements.
(KEN HEYMAN)

The drum is one of man's oldest and most widely used musical instruments. Found in highly developed cultures, as well as in the most primitive societies, drums are remarkably diverse in construction and tonal range.

SNARE DRUM

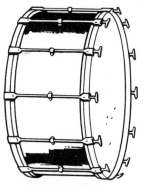

BASS DRUM

KETTLE DRUM

Such drums do not have skins. Under a different method of classification, drums are called percussion instruments because they are struck or, in a few cases, rubbed. The term "percussion" is not a very specific one, being used to indicate instruments which are struck (drums, xylophones, even the piano) as well as those which have no definite pitch (rattles, clappers, and so on). Thus all drums are percussion instruments, but not all percussion instruments are drums.

Structure and Playing Method. Drums are widespread throughout the world, and only a few of the simplest tribal cultures have none. The drums are found in many different sizes and forms and are used in many ways. Those which are membranophones may have one or two skins (drumheads), and those with one drumhead may be either open or closed at the opposite end. The skin is attached to the drum in a number of ways. The variety in size extends from instruments eight ft. tall (found in Haiti) and European kettledrums with diameter of four ft., to miniatures a few inches in diameter. The method of holding a drum varies as well; some drums are suspended from a stand or the player's body, others rest on the ground or on a stand, while others again are held under the arm or between the legs of the player. Drums are used singly or in sets, as accompanying and as solo instruments, for melodic as well as strictly rhythmic effect, and for musical as well as other purposes. They are struck with one, two, or even several sticks (several players may beat one drum, as in some American Indian tribes) with the hands, or with the individual fingers. Only a few of the most prominent drum types are described here.

Types. The most important idiophone drum is the slit drum, made of a hollowed log with a slit, found in Africa, among the Indians of Latin America, and in East Asia. The most famous variety is the *teponatzli* of the Mexican Indians, which has an H-shaped slit producing two distinct pitches. The log drums of Africa are used for signaling by reproducing the pitch patterns of spoken language. Another idiophone drum is the steel drum of the Caribbean, made of an oil container, which is grooved so that several distinct pitches and even melodies can be played on one instrument.

Among the membranophones, the kettledrums are very widespread and sophisticated in structure. Their bodies are vessels which may be filled with water; this is done in the peyote ceremonies of many North American Indian tribes. The water moistens the skin and allows adjustment of the pitch. In Western civilization the kettledrum (technically called timpanum, pl., timpani) has been the main percussion instrument of the orchestra since the 18th century. Used in groups of two to four, it can be tuned to specific pitches and is made of a copper basin which rests on a stand. The pitch is raised by tightening the drumhead with the six handles on the edge of the drum.

The two main drum types in Western military bands are the bass drum, which has two heads and a shallow body (the diameter greater than the height of the cylinder) and is beaten with a soft stick, and the snare drum or side drum. A small, shallow drum with two heads, the upper of which is beaten and the lower of which has strings tightly stretched across the middle, the snare drum has a sharp, crackling sound. Also important are the tenor drum, a large, deep type with pitch slightly lower than that of the snare drum, and the tom-tom, a single-headed drum similar in shape to the tenor drum, made in imitation of American Indian drums and used mainly in dance bands. The tambourine is a small, shallow, single-headed drum in whose body are inserted a number of metal plates, called jingles, which produce bell-like sounds when the drum is struck. Two-headed drums in the shape of hourglasses are used in the Far East.

Drums are played in groups or sets in various parts of the world. There are four drums of different types played by the drummer of a Western dance band. In African music three or four drums of the same type, but of different sizes, are played together, each having distinct rhythms. In India tuned sets of drums are also used. Drums are usually beaten with sticks in Western civilization. This is true also of American Indian drumming, while drummers of Africa and India use hands and fingers. In non-Western cultures drums frequently have symbolic and ritualistic significance quite apart from their function as musical instruments and, being intricately carved and decorated, they are often important as art objects.

Consult Coleman, S. N., *The Drum Book* (1931); Sachs, Curt, *The History of Musical Instruments* (1940); Spinney, B., *Encyclopedia of Percussion Instruments and Drumming* (1959).

BRUNO NETTL, Wayne State University
See also MUSICAL INSTRUMENTS.

DRUMFISH, common name for two marine fish, the channel bass, or red drum, *Sciaenops ocellata*, and the black drum, *Pogonias cromis;* and one fresh-water species, *Aplodinotus grunniens*, all of the croaker family, Sciaenidae. The marine species are native to western Atlantic coastal waters. The fresh-water drumfish is found in North American streams and lakes from Canada to Guatemala. Drumfish are named for their ability to make a drumming sound by vibrating the walls of their air bladder. They feed on crustaceans and mollusks, crushing the shells with powerful pharyngeal (throat) teeth. The channel bass is a well-known food fish and is also prized as a game fish.

DRUMLIN, rounded, elongate hill of glacial debris, believed to have been molded by a moving continental glacier. The average drumlin is about 100 ft. high and 3,000 ft. long, with a steeper end facing the direction from which the ice moved.

DRUMMOND [drŭm'ənd], **SIR GORDON** (1771–1854), British soldier and colonial administrator. Following military service in Europe, he went to Canada in 1813 as second-in-command to Sir George Prevost. Later in that year he became acting lieutenant-governor of Upper Canada (Ontario). For distinguished service in the War of 1812 he was knighted in 1815. He commanded the land forces that helped to capture Oswego, N.Y. (May, 1814) and stemmed the American invasion at Lundy's Lane in July of that year. In 1815 he replaced Prevost as commander-in-chief of British North America; he returned to England in 1816.

DRUMMOND, WILLIAM HENRY (1854–1907), Canadian dialect poet. Born in Ireland, he went to Canada with his parents in 1864. As a country doctor in the province of Quebec, he gained the knowledge of habitant life which he put into his books of dialect verse. Drummond's *Poetical Works* were published in 1912. His half-humorous, half-sentimental poems were praised by leading French Canadians and were very popular with English Canadians. Some critics feel that the poems give a patronizing, quaint picture of rural life in French Canada, but others argue that they did much to promote good feeling between the two groups in Canada.

DRUMMOND OF HAWTHORNDEN, WILLIAM (1585–1649), Scottish poet and essayist. A kinsman of the royal house of Scotland, he studied at Edinburgh and in France. His father died in 1610, and Drummond immediately retired to his family's estates at Hawthornden. His *Poems* (1616) are characterized by a smooth grace, although his sonnets and madrigals are often simply felicitous translations of French and Italian originals. His best prose work is *A Cypress Grove* (1623), a stylistically beautiful meditation upon death.

DRUMMONDVILLE, industrial city of Quebec, Canada, and seat of Drummond County. It is in the Eastern Townships region, 30 mi. up the St. Francis River. Founded in 1815 by veterans, heroes of the Canadian victories at Châteauguay and Chrysler's Farm, this city rapidly became an important administrative, economic, and educational center for the surrounding counties. Plants manufacturing textiles and clothing employ the greater part of the working population. Sylvania Electric (Canada), Ltd., operates an important plant here. Inc. as town, 1888; as city, 1890; pop., 27,909.

DRUMRIGHT, city of central Oklahoma. It developed from an oil-boom town in 1913 into a trade and petroleum center. Pop. (1950) 5,028; (1960) 4,190.

DRURY [drōo'rē], **ERNEST CHARLES** (1878–   ), Canadian political leader, premier of Ontario (1919–23). Born in Crown Hill, Ontario, he became a leading farmer, first secretary of the Canadian Council of Agriculture (1909), and first president of the United Farmers of Ontario. Elected to the legislature in 1919, Drury formed a "people's party" government of farmer, labor, and independent members. This administration, then considered an important break from the historic two-party system of liberals and conservatives, was largely unsuccessful.

DRURY LANE THEATRE, London's most famous theater and the oldest still in use. During its history most of the famous actors of England, including David Garrick and Mrs. Siddons, have appeared on its stage. In its early days known as the Theatre Royal (from a charter granted by King Charles II), the Drury Lane Theatre has had four buildings on its site since its opening in 1663. The present one dates from 1812. The musical *Oklahoma!* had its London run in the Drury Lane.

DRUSES or DRUZES [drōoz'sĕs] (Arab. *Duruz*), a Syrian people, mostly landholders and peasants, mainly located in the Lebanon, Anti-Lebanon, and Hauran mountains.

They have their own religion, developed in the 11th century from the Ismaili branch of Islam and based on the adoration of the Egyptian Caliph al-Hakim, who is regarded as a manifestation of God. They expect al-Hakim to return a conqueror and fill the earth with righteousness. Meanwhile the more pious of the Druses (who alone are initiated into the secrets of the faith) try to purify their souls, which are held to be reincarnated generation after generation, by disciplined and truthful living, so as to be worthy of him. The Druses have often ruled the parts of Syria in which they live. They are as famous for their brigandage and feuds as for their chivalry and hospitality. *See also* ISLAM; SHIITE ISLAM.

DRUSILLA, youngest daughter of Herod Agrippa I. In defiance of Jewish law she left her first husband, Azizus, King of Emesa, in order to marry the Roman governor of Judea, Antonius Felix (Acts 24:24).

DRUSUS [drōo'səs], **MARCUS LIVIUS** (died c.109 B.C.), Roman tribune with Gaius Gracchus in 122 B.C. He served as the agent of the senate against Gracchus, winning popularity for the senate by outbidding every democratic proposal of Gracchus with still more popular, though insincere, schemes.

DRUSUS, MARCUS LIVIUS, Roman tribune of the plebs in 91 B.C. His reform measures to help the landless urban poor, to strengthen the courts trying provincial governors for extortion, and to enfranchise the Italian allies offended both senators and equites by infringing upon their privileges, and led to the nullification of his legislation and to his assassination.

The Drury Lane Theatre as it appeared in 1776.

The Bettmann Archive

DRUSUS CAESAR JUNIOR (c.13 B.C.–23 A.D.), son of the Roman Emperor Tiberius by his first wife, Vipsania. After displaying military capacity, as well as ruthlessness, in Pannonia and Illyria (15–20), Drusus was publicly indicated in 22 as Tiberius' successor, but died the following year, allegedly poisoned by his wife Livilla, whose lover Sejanus coveted the succession for himself.

DRUSUS GERMANICUS [jər-măn′ĭ-kəs], **NERO CLAUDIUS** (38–9 B.C.), stepson of Augustus and brother of Tiberius. Before Drusus' birth his mother, Livia, divorced by Claudius Nero, had married Octavian (Augustus). Drusus himself married Augustus' niece Antonia, Mark Antony's daughter. Universally liked, Drusus was credited with republican leanings. His chief fame, however, rested on his military campaigns in unexplored lands near the upper Danube and beyond the Rhine (15–9 B.C.), which won him the surname Germanicus. He died on active service.

DRUZ, JEBEL ED-. *See* JEBEL ED-DRUZ.

DRYADS, in Greek mythology, tree nymphs, also called Hamadryads (q.v.).

DRY CELL. *See* BATTERY, ELECTRIC.

DRY CLEANING, commercial process employing chemical solvents, special soaps, and detergents, with little or no water, to clean garments and other textile products. The process is similar to washing, except that the use of solvent instead of water does not soften the fabric. When garments enter the dry cleaning plant they are separated according to fabric content, weight, and color. The actual cleaning is performed in a washer or movable drum filled with the solvent; excess solvent is then removed in a centrifuge. Next, warm air treatment takes away solvent odor. After this drying process, spots and stains are removed by a specially trained person. Then the garment is pressed.

History. The first commercial dry cleaning plant, the Jolly Belin, was established in Paris, France, around 1845. Visitors from other countries found Monsieur Belin's *nettoyage à sec* techniques practical and doubtlessly profitable, for soon dry cleaning plants were set up all over the Continent. Following publication of a booklet on French cleaning, *The Dyer and Scourer*, by an Englishman, Thomas Love, in 1862, dry cleaning was introduced in the United States.

Over the years, the dry cleaning solvents used have included carbon tetrachloride, benzine, benzol, oil of turpentine, gasoline, and naphtha. However, the danger in using these flammable solvents, particularly gasoline, provoked a joint research program to find safer solvents. Thus the National Institute of Cleaners and Dyers (which became the National Institute of Dry Cleaning), the Mellon Institute, the U.S. Department of Commerce, and the U.S. Bureau of Standards joined in developing a petroleum solvent, Stoddard. It has a minimum flash point of 100° F. and is in general use today. A similar solvent, called White Spirit, is used in Britain. Other dry cleaning fluids used are 140-F petroleum solvent (140° F. Flashpoint) and perchloroethylene, a nonflammable synthetic solvent.

National Institute of Dry Cleaning

National Portrait Gallery, London

John Dryden, Restoration poet, by Sir Godfrey Kneller.

DRYDEN [drī′dən], **JOHN** (1631–1700), greatest English poet of the Restoration period. Born into a Puritan family in Northamptonshire, Dryden was educated at Trinity College, Cambridge. He began his career as secretary to Oliver Cromwell's chamberlain, Sir Gilbert Pickering, and wrote *Heroic Stanzas* (1659) on Cromwell's death. One year later, upon the Restoration of Charles II, he composed a verse panegyric entitled *Astraea Redux*. Soon afterward he married and began to write for the theater; he continued in his career as a playwright for more than 30 years. He was elected to the Royal Society (1662), became poet laureate (1668) and historiographer royal (1670). Having joined the Catholic Church in 1685, he lost the laureateship and his other offices upon the accession of William and Mary. Again, in his old age, he had to support himself by writing.

With *The Indian Queen* (performed 1664) Dryden inaugurated the fashion for rhymed heroic drama, combining the forms of French neoclassical tragedy with Elizabethan melodrama. Attacks on this mixed genre led him to write an important critical dialogue, *Essay of Dramatic Poesy* (1668). Here and in his other essays Dryden proves himself a master of style. Modern English literary prose may be said with some fairness to have sprung from his pen. After *Aurengzebe* (performed 1675) Dryden gave up rhymed for blank verse and wrote his finest play, *All for Love* (performed 1678), which deals with the fatal affair of Antony and Cleopatra.

As a poet, Dryden achieved greatest success with the ode, apologetic religious verse, and political and literary satire. His finest odes are "A Song for St. Cecilia's Day" (1687) and "Alexander's Feast" (1697). In 1682 he defended the Anglican faith in *Religio Laici*, a philosophical discourse in verse. In 1687 he wrote *The Hind and the Panther*, an animal fable meant to justify his conversion to Catholicism. As a formal satirist, Dryden is unequaled in English before Alexander Pope. His *MacFlecknoe* (1682), which directly influenced Pope's *Dunciad*, is a devastating attack on his literary enemies. *Absalom and Achitophel* (1681), directed against the first Earl of Shaftesbury, is the masterwork in English of satiric verse portraiture.

Consult Bredvold, L. I., *The Intellectual Milieu of John Dryden* (1934); Van Doren, Mark, *John Dryden, A Study of His Poetry* (3d ed., 1946).

LAWRENCE V. RYAN, Stanford University
See also ENGLISH LITERATURE.

DRYDEN, town of northern Ontario, Canada, located midway between Lake Superior and Winnipeg. It is a summer resort center and also has a large paper mill and a paper-bag factory. Inc., 1910; pop., 5,728.

DRY DOCK. *See* DOCK AND WHARF.

DRY FARMING, an agricultural term, also called dry-land farming, referring to crop production in areas of low rainfall that also lack facilities for irrigation. Dry farming is commonly practiced in areas of the Great Plains of western United States and Canada, where the annual rainfall is approximately 20 in., and the soil is reasonably fertile. The success of dry farming is dependent on the effective conservation and use of rainfall.

Fallowing, which is the accumulation of two years' rainfall for one crop through clean cultivation in alternate seasons, is a common dry farming practice. As much as 25% of the rainfall during the fallow year is stored in the soil. Destruction of weeds by fallowing conserves the moisture otherwise used for weed growth. The chief advantage of fallowing is that in case of severe drought a crop can still be realized, whereas crops seeded in the previous year's stubble land might fail to mature. Fallowing should not be confused with dust mulch farming, an agricultural technique in which a dust mulch of finely worked soil is employed to reduce loss of soil moisture through evaporation. Dust mulching has proved to be of little value, since moisture does not migrate in soils, except above a high water table. Subsoiling and deep plowing in areas of low rainfall have also proved ineffective in additional storage of water and, in fact, may actually increase moisture loss.

Farming practices that increase rainwater absorption and reduce loss by run-off include various specialized methods of cultivation, land leveling, and field contouring. A trash mulch of disked stubble or straw is used to reduce run-off and erosion, and also cut down on wind erosion. Another common dry-farming technique is the reduction of water use by decreasing the rate of seeding or by wider spacing of row crops.

Crops associated with dry farming include corn, sorghum, and the small grains such as wheat and rye. Winter wheat is the most popular dry-farming crop because its critical growth period occurs before the summer drought. In the northern Great Plains corn is often grown in rotation with wheat instead of fallowing, since corn usually leaves enough moisture in the soil to germinate the fall wheat seeding. The individual crop yield in conservative planting is reduced compared to the yield of a crop following a fallow year, but the net return on both crops is greater. In the south and central Great Plains area, sor-

ghum is a favorite dry-farming crop. It is able to withstand the summer period of drought between the June and August months of greater rainfall.

Dry-land farming is extensive rather than intensive, relying on low acre-value return. By economic necessity field operations are reduced to a minimum, determining the pattern of shallow plowing, alternate cropping, restricted cultivation, and mulching of the crop residue.

WABUN C. KRUEGER, Rutgers University
See also FALLOW; PLOWS AND PLOWING; SOIL CONSERVATION.

DRY ICE, solid carbon dioxide, CO_2. It is prepared by compressing and cooling the purified gas to liquid, then allowing the liquid to expand into a cloth bag. Heat is absorbed by the molecules as they become gaseous, thus lowering the temperature of the remaining liquid enough to convert part of it to "snow." Usually this expansion takes place directly into presses that form the snow into blocks. Excess gas is recycled. Under normal pressure dry ice sublimes, or turns into a gas without passing through the liquid state, at $-78°$ C. ($-108.4°$ F.). It is therefore useful as a refrigerant where the formation of a liquid is undesirable. The ice cream industry is the largest consumer of dry ice.

DRYING OILS, natural oils, either vegetable or marine, which when properly treated and applied to a surface, dry to a tough, durable film by oxidation. Chemically, these oils are esters of glycerin and unsaturated fatty acids. Their speed of drying depends on the number and location of double bonds in their fatty acids. Tung oil is the fastest drying, followed by oiticica, linseed, dehydrated castor, and fish and soybean oils.

Drying oils are usually processed for industrial use. When cooked with hard, oil-soluble, resinous substances, such as rosin, these oils will form varnishes. Linseed oil is an exception, for it may be used in the raw state, as in exterior house paints.

When properly pigmented, the processed oils, varnishes, and alkyds form coatings. Drying oils are also used in printing inks, oil cloths, and related products.
See also LINSEED OIL; PAINT; TUNG OIL.

DRY MEASURE, a system for measuring the capacity of dry commodities such as fruit or grain. The units are either metric or common. In the metric system the same units are used as for fluid measurement. In the common system in the United States, the bushel is the basic unit and is equal to 2,150.42 cu. in., or 35.24 liters. The units are the dry pint, the dry quart (2 dry pints), the peck (8 dry quarts), the bushel (4 pecks), and the barrel (105 dry quarts, except for cranberries). The British quart equals 1.0320 U.S. dry quarts.
See also WEIGHTS AND MEASURES.

DRYPOINT, printing process. It produces a kind of engraving that is also called a drypoint. The metal printing plate is incised with a pen-shaped tool. This tool is usually steel, but sometimes a diamond or other hard substance is set in a holder; the base plate is usually copper. In the cutting the point throws up a ridge or burr of metal. Ink clings to the sides of the burr as well as to the incisions when the plate is inked and wiped clean. When the plate is printed, the result resembles an etching, except that the lines are softer and more velvety. The earliest known drypoints were produced by the Master of the Amsterdam Cabinet in the last quarter of the 15th century. Great artists who used the technique include Dürer, Rembrandt, and Whistler.

DRY TORTUGAS [tôr-tōō'gəz] **or TORTUGAS KEYS,** group of seven coral islets, or keys, of Florida, 68 mi. west of Key West in the Gulf of Mexico. They include Loggerhead Key, the largest (1 mi. long), with a lighthouse; Bush Key, noted for sea-bird rookeries; and Garden Key, site of old Fort Jefferson, which was occupied by federal troops during the Civil War. Fort Jefferson National Monument (87 acres) was established in 1935. Ponce de León discovered the islets in 1513 and named them for their many turtles (Span. *tortugas*); they were later called Dry Tortugas because they lack fresh water.

DUALISM [dōō'əl-ĭz-əm], as contrasted on the one hand with monism, and on the other hand with pluralism, is the name applied to philosophical theories which are based on a distinction between two fundamental things or two fundamental kinds of things. The dualism of universal and particular dominated much of ancient and medieval philosophy. But since René Descartes (1596–1650) the history of modern philosophy has revolved around the doctrine of psychophysical dualism, the metaphysical theory that the world is composed of two kinds of irreducible, particular things: (1) physical things in space, and (2) mental things which endure through time, but do not occupy space. David Hume and other empiricists have limited the scope of the mental to conscious events like images, sensations, and thoughts. Descartes and other rationalists have maintained that we must also recognize the existence of an irreducible mind or mental substance in which these events occur. Psychophysical dualism leads to the "mind-body problem" when we ask what kind of causal relationship, if any, can exist between physical events in the brain and the nonphysical images and thoughts which are correlated with them. Among the possible answers are interactionism and epiphenomenalism.

In epistemology the term "dualism" is applied to theories, like those of Descartes and John Locke, which deny that sensory data are identical with, or parts of, the external object known in perception. In this sense George Berkeley, Immanuel Kant, neorealists, and phenomenalists are not dualists but epistemological monists. In theology the term is applied to Zoroastrianism, Manichaeanism, and other doctrines which emphasize the duality of supernatural forces of good and evil.

Consult Broad, C. D., *The Mind and Its Place in Nature* (1925); Lovejoy, A. O., *The Revolt Against Dualism* (1930).

RODERICK FIRTH, Department of Philosophy, Harvard University

DUANE [dū-ān'], **JAMES** (1733–97), American Revolutionary legislator and jurist. Born in New York City, the son of a wealthy merchant, Duane prospered as a lawyer and landowner. He founded (1765) Duanesburg, N.Y., and as a land investor was embroiled in the New Hampshire Grants controversy. A conservative, Duane attempted to soften criticism of the Stamp Act and in 1768 defended a Tory politician charged with corruption. He was appointed (1774) to the Committee of Correspondence and served (1774–84) in the Continental Congress, but accepted revolution reluctantly. He supported Joseph Galloway's plan for union with Great Britain and opposed the Declaration of Independence. His conciliatory approach aroused accusations of disloyalty, but prominent revolutionists defended him. Duane was a New York state senator (1782–85; 1789–90), a member of the Governor's council (1783), and mayor of New York (1784–89), meanwhile helping to draft the state constitution and serving in the convention that ratified the federal constitution. In 1789 he became the first judge of the New York federal district court.

Consult Alexander, E. P., *Revolutionary Conservative: James Duane of New York*, (1938).

CLARENCE L. VER STEEG, Northwestern University

DUANE, WILLIAM (1760–1835), American journalist. Duane, who was born near Lake Champlain, N.Y., became a printer in Ireland in his boyhood and a publisher in India in his youth. He lost his sizable fortune and his outstanding Calcutta newspaper, the *Indian World*, when he used the journal to attack the powerful East India Company. After being expelled to England and failing to gain redress, he returned (1795) to America. There, as editor of the Philadelphia *Aurora*, he championed Thomas Jefferson's Republicans and attacked the Federalists, particularly for their passage of the Alien and Sedition Acts. He was indicted (1799) under the Alien Act and then under the Sedition Act but never prosecuted. When the capital was moved to Washington, D.C., Duane's journal lost influence, and though he remained its editor until 1822, he developed other interests, becoming adjutant general in the War of 1812. In the last years of his life, he traveled in South America and wrote extensively on military subjects.

ROBERT MIDDLEKAUFF, Yale University

DUANE, WILLIAM JOHN (1780–1865), American politician. A Democrat and Pennsylvania lawyer, he was appointed Secretary of the Treasury in May, 1833, in the expectation that he would co-operate with President Andrew Jackson's plan to remove government deposits from the Bank of the United States. When Duane refused to act before Congress convened, Jackson replaced him (Sept., 1833) with Roger B. Taney. Most of Duane's education was gained in the offices of his father's Philadelphia newspaper, the *Aurora*. He practiced law in Philadelphia between 1815 and 1833 and was influential in promoting Pennsylvania's scheme of internal improvements in the state legislature.

DUARTE [dwär'tä], foothill city in the San Gabriel Mountains, 20 mi. northeast of Los Angeles, southern California. It is best known as the home of the "City of Hope" tuberculosis and cancer medical center. Inc., 1957; pop. (1960) 13,962.

Portrait of Madame du Barry by François Drouais. (BETTMANN ARCHIVE)

DU BARRY [dūbär′ē], **MARIE JEANNE BÉCU, COMTESSE** (1743–93), Court favorite and last official mistress of Louis XV of France. An illegitimate child of humble birth, she was brought to Paris at an early age and received a convent education. In her teens she became a shopgirl but soon turned courtesan. One of her lovers, the disreputable Count Jean du Barry, took her career in hand and, after arranging her marriage to an obliging brother in 1768, had her officially presented at court in 1769. Beautiful, seductive, and clever, Du Barry made the expected impression upon the aging Louis, who raised her to royal mistress. She was showered with pensions, and the king built her the magnificent chateau Louveciennes. Unlike earlier mistresses, Du Barry had no political pretensions, though she helped oust foreign minister Choiseul, who had opposed her rise. As long as Louis lived, Du Barry was treated as unofficial queen, receiving dignitaries and holding court.

Louis' death in 1774 led to Du Barry's retirement to Louveciennes. During the French Revolution she emigrated to England (1792) but imprudently returned to France. She was condemned by the Revolutionary Tribunal and guillotined, Dec. 8, 1793, essentially for her role at court 20 years earlier.

PETER AMANN, State University of N.Y. at Binghamton

DUBINSKY [də-bǐn′skē], **DAVID** (1892–   ), American labor leader. Born in Brest Litovsk in Russian Poland, he learned the baking trade in his father's shop in Łódź. He was exiled by the Tsarist government to Siberia for ardent union activity, but escaped after two years. Reaching New York in 1911, he became a union cloak cutter and rose rapidly to become president of the International Ladies' Garment Workers' Union (1932–66). Among the first labor leaders to seize the encouragements of the New Deal of President Franklin Roosevelt, he brought the union's membership to 400,000, a ten-fold increase, by mid-century. He has been noted for improving work standards, while adding a multiplicity of social benefits, and for stabilizing a previously chaotic industry. He was a founder of the Liberal party in New York State.

See also INTERNATIONAL LADIES' GARMENT WORKERS' UNION (ILGWU).

DUBLIN, county on the east coast of Ireland, in the province of Leinster, and containing the city of Dublin. In the south it touches the Wicklow Mountains, but otherwise consists of an almost level plain in which the Liffey River valley is entrenched. Fertile soils, a relatively dry climate (less than 30 in. of rainfall per year) and the presence of Dublin city have encouraged market gardening and dairying along the coast. Hay, wheat, and pasturage and the fattening of cattle for city and export trade are the dominant farming interests. Clondalkin, Saggart, and Balbriggan are industrial and residential suburbs of Dublin city. Area, 356 sq. mi.; pop., 716,156.

DUBLIN, capital, largest city, and principal seaport of the republic of Ireland, and commercial and industrial center, located on the mouth of the Liffey River at the head of Dublin Bay, an inlet of the Irish Sea. The earliest of the attractive line of quays along the river were built in the 17th century, and since then much land has been reclaimed at the head of the bay. The breakwaters which provide the entrance to the river port were constructed in the 19th century, but constant dredging is still necessary in order to maintain a deep channel. The main export from Dublin, apart from stout and whiskey, is stock cattle, destined mostly for Birkenhead and Glasgow. Dublin imports, mainly from Great Britain, a wide variety of raw materials and manufactured goods. The growth of the city since 1922 has been rapid, and one-fifth of the country's inhabitants now live in Dublin. Half the working population is employed in commerce, administration, and transport; this is an indication of the city's metropolitan status. As a result of protectionist policy, Dublin has acquired many industries producing mainly for the home market. The commercial and shopping districts of Dublin lie for the most part within sight of O'Connell Bridge and the port and the deep-water quays. Although the Grand and the Royal canals have been abandoned, Dublin remains the great focus, on the east coast, of the country's communications network. In addition, there are regular cargo and passenger services to both Liverpool, England, and Holyhead, Wales, the latter from the outport at Dún Laoghaire (q.v.). The airport at Collinstown (5 mi. north of the city) has direct services to many British and continental cities and to New York via Shannon.

The two ancient Irish names *Dubh-linn* ("black pool") and *Áth Cliath* ("ford of the hurdles") suggest the presence of the bridgehead and harbor where the Norse or Scandinavian invaders established a town in the 9th century, on the south side of the river near the center of the modern city. In 1170 the Norsemen were ousted by the Anglo-Normans, who introduced English settlers and made Dublin the center of the Pale, an area under royal administration. The city retained this status continuously until the establishment of the independent Irish state in 1922. The appearance of the medieval walled town with its castle and two cathedrals is depicted in John Speed's plan of 1610. At this time the two leading public buildings outside the wall were St. Patrick's Cathedral (originally a Celtic church) and Trinity College (founded in 1591). Few traces survive of the medieval town and most of older Dublin does not go back further than the 18th century and the wealthy Georgian era.

Dublin: A monument to the nationalist leader Daniel O'Connell stands in the main thoroughfare in the center of the city.

Georgian Era. Dublin owes much to this era. The Wide Streets Commissioners, appointed in 1758, were responsible for designing stately highways such as Sackville Street (now O'Connell Street and the city's main thoroughfare), Westmoreland Street, and Upper Merrion Street. To these were added elegant squares and parks, especially on the Gardiner and Fitzwilliam estates, around which the tall dwelling houses of the aristocracy were erected. Some of Dublin's most impressive public buildings belong to the later 18th century. These include Parliament House in College Green (now the Bank of Ireland), the Royal Exchange (now the city hall) together with the Custom House and the Four Courts. In 1800 the Liffey River divided the city into two roughly equal parts and by this time Dublin was by far the largest Irish town and also one of the leading towns of preindustrial Europe. With the Act of Union of 1801, however, Dublin ceased to be a parliamentary capital. It is not surprising therefore to find Dublin in the forefront of the 19th-century agitation for the undoing of this union, which culminated in the Rising of 1916.

To the northwest of the Georgian section of the city lies Phoenix Park (3 sq. mi.), which contains extensive recreation grounds and zoological gardens, as well as the home of the President of the republic (the former Viceregal Lodge). To the southeast is St. Stephen's Green, one of the largest of the city parks, and nearby are the National Library, the National Museum, and the National Gallery, all built in the later 19th century. Here too are the leading educational and learned establishments, including University College (founded in 1908 as a constituent college of the National University of Ireland), the Royal Irish Acad-

emy (founded 1786), and the Institute for Advanced Studies (founded 1940). Dáil Éireann, the legislature, sits in the former residence of the Duke of Leinster in Kildare Street.

Economic Problems. The 19th century also saw the rise of a class of Roman Catholic merchants. Many notable Catholic churches in the city were built with their support. Following the Great Famine of 1845 Dublin experienced a large-scale invasion of poverty-stricken country people, and in the absence of important industrial activity this led to mass unemployment. The former mansions of the nobility became overcrowded tenements, especially on the northern and southwestern sides of the city. In 1911, for instance, the population of the city north of the Liffey amounted to 160,000 (out of a total of 386,386). Of these over a quarter (12,000 families) lived in 3,000 tenement houses. Such conditions provided the background for the plays of Sean O'Casey and the novels of Liam O'Flaherty. The rehousing of this tenement population in suburbs such as Ballyfermot, Crumlin, and Cabra on the northern and southern outskirts has been one of the main factors making for the expansion of the city since 1935. The built-up area now covers 30 sq. mi. The most favored residential quarter still lies to the southeast, along the shore of the Bay and in the direction of the foothills of the Wicklow Mountains. Pop., 535,488.

T. JONES HUGHES,
University College of Dublin

DUBLIN, city of central Georgia, and seat of Laurens County, on the Oconee River. Corn, cotton, and naval stores are economically important. Hernando de Soto is believed to have visited the area in 1540. Inc., 1812; pop. (1950) 10,232; (1960) 13,814.

DUBLIN, UNIVERSITY OF. See TRINITY COLLEGE.

DUBLIN GATE THEATRE, playhouse founded in Dublin in 1928 by Hilton Edwards and Micheál MacLiammóir, who sought to create a theater more international in its repertory than the Abbey Theatre and better equipped to encourage new styles in playwriting and production. Its skillful presentations of older plays and its support of new authors have brought it international esteem.

DUBOIS [dü-bwä'], **MARIE EUGÈNE FRANÇOIS THOMAS** (1858–1940), Dutch anatomist and paleontologist. He was educated in medicine and natural history at the University of Amsterdam, and later became professor of anatomy there. In 1887 he went to Sumatra as a military surgeon, hoping to find in the Malay Archipelago what was then conceived to be "the missing link" between man and the apes. In 1891, in the dry bed of the Solo River in Java, he discovered the fossil remains of *Pithecanthropus erectus*, sometimes called the Java ape-man. Subsequent evolutionary theory developed away from the idea that there was any single "missing link."

DU BOIS [doo bois'], **WILLIAM EDWARD BURGHARDT** (1868–1963), American author and editor. Born in Great Barrington, Mass., Du Bois studied at Fisk University, at Harvard, where he became (1895) the first Negro Ph.D., and at the University of Berlin. His study, *The Philadelphia Negro* (1899), became a sociological landmark. But it was *The Souls of Black Folk* (1903) that won him national attention and helped shape the course of Negro advancement. In this book he criticized Booker T. Washington for being willing to conform with white ideas on the subservient role of the Negro in U.S. society.

Du Bois taught at Wilberforce University, The University of Pennsylvania, and Atlanta University. He was a founder (1910) of the National Association for the Advancement of Colored People (NAACP) and editor (1910–32) of its official organ, *Crisis*. In 1961 he joined the Communist party and in 1963 he became a citizen of Ghana, where he died.

DU BOIS, WILLIAM PÈNE (1916–), American author and illustrator of children's books. He was born in Nutley, N.J., of a literary and artistic family. His first important book was *The Three Policemen* (1938, reissued 1960), a spoof on crime detection, as was his story of a horse-detective, *The Great Geppy* (1940). *Twenty-One Balloons*, a science-fantasy, won the Newbery Award in 1948. *Lion* (1956) is a magnificent picture book.

DU BOIS [doo bois'], industrial city of west-central Pennsylvania, in the Allegheny Plateau region. It is the chief railroad center between Pittsburgh and Buffalo and lies close to the big-game region of Pennsylvania. The Du Bois Undergraduate Center of Pennsylvania State College is here. The city was settled in 1812 by lumber interests and was named for an early landowner. Inc., 1881; pop. (1950) 11,497; (1960) 10,667.

DUBROVNIK [doo'brôv-nĭk], (Ital. **RAGUSA**), on the Adriatic coast of southern Yugoslavia (in Croatia). Its superb site, on a rock jutting into the Adriatic Sea from the foot of Mount Srdj, makes it one of the most attractive cities in the Mediterranean. Today the city also takes in the small port of Gruz and the peninsula of Lapad on the northwest. The city was founded in the mid-7th century by refugees from nearby Epidaurus, on the cliffs of a small island, while Slavs settled on the neighboring shore. The two settlements were joined by the end of the 13th century. The dividing waterway was filled and massive walls were created to protect the combined community. The walls and two important gates still stand. Two remaining large monasteries, Dominican and Franciscan, long were active in missionary and social work.

Until the beginning of the 13th century, Dubrovnik was under the protection of the Byzantine Empire, and thereafter came under the protection of Venice. In trade and shipping, however, Dubrovnik was a rival of Venice. Still later Dubrovnik paid tribute to Hungary, and then to the Ottoman Turks. Napoleon occupied Dubrovnik in 1806, ending its centuries of independence. From his defeat until Yugoslavia was formed after World War I, Dubrovnik was under Austrian control. Pop., 25,000.

GEORGE W. HOFFMAN, University of Texas

DUBUQUE [də-būk'], city of northeastern Iowa, and seat of Dubuque County, on the Mississippi River. Dubuque developed first as a mining, lumbering, and milling center. Its economy is based on farm-machinery manufacturing, lumbering, and meat products. The world's leading sash and door factories were located here in the 1930's. The city obtained much of its early growth from its role as a producer of lumber products.

Dubuque was named in memory of Julien Dubuque, first white man to settle in the region (1785). The first newspaper in Iowa was printed here in 1836. Among the city's educational institutions are Clarke College, University of Dubuque, and Wartburg Theological Seminary. St. Raphael's Cathedral is located here. The city was first settled in 1833 and became the county seat in 1834. Dubuque became a city in 1841. Pop. (1950) 49,671; (1960) 56,606; urb. area (1960) 59,447.

THEODORE R. SPEIGNER, North Carolina College at Durham

DUCCIO DI BUONINSEGNA [doot'chō dē bwô-nēn-sä'nyä] (c.1255–c.1318), Italian painter. The leading artist of Siena, Duccio exerted enormous influence on later painting, both inside and outside Italy, through his own work and that of his close followers Simone Martini and the Lorenzetti brothers. He is known to have been active as a painter as early as 1278. Duccio was personally a nonconformist to a degree rare among artists of his time. He was repeatedly fined for a variety of offenses that stemmed mainly from a stubbornly independent political attitude and an indifference to debts.

Little of this rebelliousness is revealed in his art. Though he was one of the great innovators who changed the direction of Italian painting toward the realism and humanism of the Renaissance, he moved away from the then current Byzantine style very gradually, preserving much of its grave and austere beauty. His "Rucellai Madonna" of

Below, "The Three Marys at the Tomb" (Siena Cathedral Museum) by Duccio.

Art Reference Bureau

Right, Duccio's "Rucellai Madonna."

Art Reference Bureau

1285 (Uffizi Gallery, Florence) is Byzantine in its figure types and flatness, but the figures are softened and made more gracious by subtly curving lines in silhouettes and draperies. In the altarpiece (1308–11) for Siena Cathedral (Siena Cathedral Museum), he used a similarly conservative style in the large panel of "Mary and Christ in Majesty," shifting in the smaller narrative scenes to a lively, spacious dramatic manner. The progressive traits of the smaller panels, along with elegance of composition and rich color, make this altarpiece one of the landmarks in Italian painting.

HOWARD DAVIS, Columbia University

DUCE, IL. *See* MUSSOLINI, BENITO.

DU CHAILLU [*dü-shȧ-yü*], **PAUL BELLONI** (1831–1903), French-American naturalist and explorer who in 1856–59 and 1863–65 thoroughly explored the equatorial rain forests of the Congo region. He published accounts of his findings, which included descriptions of such hitherto legendary phenomena as gorillas and Pygmies. These accounts were a major contribution to the knowledge of African botany, ethnology, geography, and zoology.

DUCHAMP [*dü-shäN'*], **MARCEL** (1887–   ), French painter, one of the founders of Dadaism (q.v.). While influenced by cubism he produced his painting "Nude Descending a Staircase" (Philadelphia Museum of Art), which evoked great notoriety when exhibited at the Armory Show (1913) in New York. He contributed to the development of Dadaism with his ready-mades—compositions of everyday objects juxtaposed to produce shocking effects. Most of his work is in the Philadelphia Museum of Art. He later settled in New York City and abandoned

artistic endeavor for chess. Duchamp is the brother of painter Jacques Villon and the sculptor Raymond Duchamp-Villon.

DUCHAMP-VILLON [*dü-shäN'–vē-yôN'*], **RAYMOND** (1876–1918), French sculptor who greatly influenced the development of cubist sculpture with his "Project for a Horse" (1912) and numerous versions of "Horse" (1912–14). He was the brother of Marcel Duchamp and Jacques Villon, also influential in the development of modern art. In America he is represented at the Museum of Modern Art, New York City.

DUCHESS OF MALFI [*măl'fē*], **THE,** English tragedy of revenge, written by John Webster c.1613. Remarkable for its intensity, it concerns a widowed duchess who, by remarrying beneath her rank, incurs the wrath of her brothers, Duke Ferdinand and the Cardinal. This results in her imprisonment, cruel mental torture, and strangling by Ferdinand's hirelings, as well as the destruction of all the other principal characters.

DUCHIN [*dōō'chĭn*], **EDWIN FRANK ("EDDY")** (1909–51), American popular pianist and orchestra leader. He was born in Cambridge, Mass., and joined Leo Reisman's orchestra in 1928. Three years later he formed his own dance band, which became very popular in night clubs and hotels throughout the country. During World War II he rose to the rank of lieutenant commander in the Navy. A film based on Duchin's life, *The Eddy Duchin Story*, was released in 1956.

THE SEVEN TRIBES OF DUCKS

THE SHELDUCKS (tribe Tadornini) are primitive waterfowl of the Old World. They are mostly large, boldly colored, and have rather short, thick bills.

COMMON SHELDUCK

THE DIPPING DUCKS (tribe Anatini) occur primarily in the Northern Hemisphere. They feed by "dipping" their heads into the water with tails pointed skyward.

MALLARD

wheatley

WOOD DUCK

POCHARDS (tribe Aythyini) occur throughout the world. They have short, heavy bodies and stout legs set far back beneath the body. Pochards are often called "bay ducks."

CANVASBACK

COMMON EIDER

THE EIDERS (tribe Somateriini) inhabit the colder parts of the Northern Hemisphere, breeding in large colonies along barren, rock-strewn coasts. The females line the nests with down feathers.

THE PERCHING DUCKS (tribe Cairirini) spend much of their time in trees. They have long, sharp claws and a well-developed hind toe.

THE SEA DUCKS (tribe Mergini) occur mostly in colder parts of the Northern Hemisphere. The majority of sea ducks have very narrow bills and feed exclusively on fish.

RUDDY DUCK

THE STIFF-TAILED DUCKS (tribe Oxyurini) are small, thick-necked, and swim with tail feathers cocked upright. They walk and fly clumsily, but are excellent swimmers and divers.

RED-BREASTED MERGANSER

DUCK, name for many species of aquatic birds in the waterfowl family, Anatidae, which also includes the geese, swans, and screamers. Ducks, although found throughout the world, are more abundant in northern regions, and are especially common in North America. Ducks have compact bodies supported by short legs with webbed feet, short necks, and broad, flattened beaks. Their dense plumage sheds water readily. Ducks are excellent swimmers and divers as well as powerful fliers. In most species the male, or drake, has more elaborate plumage than the female. Ducks range in size from the very large eider duck, *Somateria*, which is 24 in. long, weighs over 4 lb., and has a 41-in. wingspread, to the teal, *Anas*, and the ruddy duck, *Oxyura*, each about 14 in. long, with a wingspread of 23 in. Of intermediate size are the wood duck, *Aix*, the canvasback, *Aythya*, and the mallard, *Anas*. Ducks eat both plant foods and flesh. The gadwall, widgeon, and wood duck, are herbivorous, feeding on submerged plants, and also on seeds and tubers. The shoveler and eider ducks are chiefly carnivorous, eating snails, mussels, shrimp, sea urchins, and fish. The canvasback and mallard ducks alternate between plant foods and aquatic invertebrates, depending on seasonal availability.

Ducks can be divided into three groups. One group, known as the surface-feeding ducks—the familiar "puddle ducks" of ponds and swamps—includes the mallard, black, teal, and shoveler ducks. While feeding, they assume a bottom-up, head-down position, tipping their bodies as they seek underwater plants. A second group is known as the sea ducks, or diving ducks. They are excellent swimmers and divers, but to become air-borne, they must run over the surface of the water for a considerable distance, in contrast to the quick take-off of the pond ducks. In this group are the canvasback, eider, merganser, and harlequin ducks. The third group includes perching ducks such as the wood and muscovy ducks. Perching ducks live entirely on land, nest in trees, and have longer legs than their aquatic relatives.

All domestic ducks, with the exception of the muscovy, are descended from the mallard, which is an easily tamed species. Among the common farm ducks is the Peking, a breed especially popular in North America. It has yellowish-white plumage and walks nearly upright. The Aylesbury duck, common in Great Britain, has white plumage and holds its body more horizontally than does the Peking. The Rouen duck, popular in France, is obviously a domesticated mallard, with dark, velvety plumage similar to that of the wild bird.

CLARENCE J. HYLANDER, Author, *Feathers and Flight*

See also:

BLACK DUCK	RUDDY DUCK
CANVASBACK DUCK	SCAUP
EIDER DUCK	SCOTER
GADWALL	SHOVELER
LABRADOR DUCK	TEAL
MALLARD	WIDGEON
MUSCOVY DUCK	WOOD DUCK

DUCKBILL or PLATYPUS, a small and very unusual mammal, *Ornithorhynchus anatinus,* found in cold streams and tropical swamps of eastern Australia and Tasmania. The duckbill has webbed feet and a flat, beaverlike tail, both useful for swimming and digging burrows. Its bill-like muzzle sifts small crustaceans, mollusks, and insect larvae from the water, which are then carried in cheek pouches until swallowed. The young of duckbills are not carried within the mother's body, but are hatched from eggs. Duckbills do have some recognizable mammalian features, however: they are covered with fur, and the young "nurse" by lapping up milk secreted by mammary glands located on the mother's abdomen.

DUCKING STOOL, device for punishing scolds, gossips, and quarrelsome women in England and colonial America during the 17th and 18th centuries. The ducking stool consisted of a chair attached to one end of a long lever extending over the water from the bank of a pond or stream in the manner of a seesaw. The victim was tied in the chair or held there by an iron band. An operator manipulated the contrivance from the shore and dipped the culprit into the water, the number of duckings having been specified by the sentencing magistrate.

DUCKWEED, common name for members of a family, Lemnaceae, of minute, aquatic plants. Duckweeds form floating mats of pea-green vegetation in still ponds of all temperate and tropical regions. The plant consists of a tiny, flat leaf, beneath which hangs an unbranched root. Duckweeds of the genera *Lemna* and *Spirodela* are often introduced into artificial ponds or aquaria. In their natural habitats the plants provide food for ducks and some freshwater fish.

DUCLOS [dü-klō′], **JACQUES** (1896–), French politician. A member of the French Communist party since its foundation and, after 1931, of the party Secretariat and the Political Bureau, Duclos served as the party's parliamentary tactician. He entered Parliament in 1926 and, except for World War II, served continuously until 1958. Although he failed to win a seat in the first National Assembly of the Fifth Republic in 1958, Duclos was elected to the Senate the following year.

DUCTILITY, ability of a metal or other material to undergo permanent changes in shape without rupturing. Many forming operations such as cupping, rolling, bending, curling, drawing, and hammering depend upon the material's ductility. Ductility can be measured by a static tension test which measures the percentage of elongation and reduction in area of the fractured sample. Ductility may also be measured by the angle of bend necessary to cause fracture. Nonductile materials are brittle and fracture with little or no elongation.

DUCTLESS GLAND. *See* ENDOCRINE GLANDS.

DUDEK, LOUIS (1918–), Canadian poet, born in Montreal of Polish-Canadian parents. He was instrumental, along with Irving Layton and Raymond Souster, in establishing in Canada in the 1940's and 1950's a school of proletarian verse. His volumes of poetry include *East of the City* (1946), *The Searching Image* (1952), and *Laughing Stalks* (1958). His verse is always fairly rooted in the world about him and varies in tone from tender compassion to angry satire.

DUDEVANT, MME. *See* SAND, GEORGE.

DUDLEY, JOHN. *See* NORTHUMBERLAND, JOHN DUDLEY, DUKE OF.

DUDLEY, JOSEPH (1647–1720), English colonial Governor. The Massachusetts-born son of Thomas Dudley (1576–1653), second Governor of the Massachusetts Bay Colony, Joseph Dudley was one of the most powerful, and certainly most hated, political figures in Massachusetts after the commonwealth became a royal colony. A supporter of the King's prerogative, as against Parliamentary power and colonial autonomy, Dudley was made president of the council and Governor of Massachusetts when the Bay Colony's charter was voided Oct. 23, 1684. At the end of 1686, he was succeeded by Sir Edmund Andros, but served as Andros' most important adviser in that abortive regime. Considered a traitor by the colonists, Dudley stayed in jail for 10 months for his own safety after Andros' overthrow and then was escorted to England by British troops in 1690. Later he served briefly as head of the council of New York and returned to Massachusetts as royal Governor, Apr. 1, 1702, serving until 1715.

RICHARD M. ABRAMS, Columbia University

DUDLEY, ROBERT. *See* LEICESTER, ROBERT DUDLEY, EARL OF.

DUDLEY, historic industrial town and county borough of Worcestershire, England, within the south Staffordshire coal field, 9 mi. northwest of Birmingham. Early industrial development was based on local coal, iron ore, charcoal, and limestone. Although mining and smelting have now ceased, the town remains an important center for the manufacture of metal parts, machinery, leatherware, textiles, and clothing. A Norman castle occupies a limestone ridge overlooking the town; nearby is an ancient priory dating from 1160. Pop., 61,748.

DUDLEY, town of central Massachusetts, south of Worcester. Settled in 1714, it was a stagecoach stop on the line between Boston and Hartford. Inc., 1732; pop. (1950) 5,261; (1960) 6,510.

The famous duel between Alexander Hamilton (*left*) and Aaron Burr on July 11, 1804. During the duel the former was fatally wounded. (NEW YORK HISTORICAL SOCIETY)

DUEL, a means of settling issues between two individuals by armed contest. At the earliest dawn of civilization it was customary for men to settle disputes in this way. A later notable example of contest was the great duel between David and Goliath, as recorded in the Old Testament. In the battles for ancient Troy men fought in single, hand-to-hand combat both to prove their strength and their loyalty to and favor with the gods. So prevalent was the practice of dueling in the early centuries of Western European history that by 501 A.D. dueling had become part of the judicial process. As late as the mid-19th century gentlemen sought to settle their differences with pistols or swords.

The first duel in Anglo-North America seemed to have been fought by two serving men who came with the Pilgrims. Between 1777 and 1860 numerous duels were fought by Americans of both high and low social status. Three of the most famous contests were fought by Alexander Hamilton and Aaron Burr (1804), Stephen Decatur and James Barron (1820), and Henry Clay and John Randolph (1826). In these duels Hamilton and Decatur lost their lives.

Dueling carried with it an implication of gentility. Prominent persons most often involved were politicians, military officers, newspaper editors, and lawyers. Causes generally ranged from personal slights or hot debate exchanges in the House of Representatives and Senate to rivalries for high military rank. Lesser persons fought over women, the calling of unsavory names, and the origins of gossip. Weapons were as varied as the frequently imagined injuries. Rifles, pistols, swords, bowie knives, and even straws and a keg of whisky were specified. While duelists came from many sections of the United States, most of them originated in the South and West. Southerners in Kentucky and around New Orleans were particularly sensitive about their honor, and were ready to answer any slight by sending a challenge to combat.

By the 1840's dueling had become so offensive to much of the American public that many of the states undertook to check the practice by constitutional restrictions. Public opinion was the greatest force in bringing dueling to an end in the United States. By 1860 the duel was in both popular and legal disfavor in the United States. Most of the individual states had either incorporated antidueling clauses in their constitutions, or had adopted stern legislation against the practice.

THOMAS D. CLARK, University of Kentucky

DUE PROCESS OF LAW, a phrase used in the Constitution of the United States that illustrates both the grandeur and the variable content of constitutional law. The grandeur lies in the fact that this phrase provides assurances that the government shall not impose civil or criminal penalties by procedures that suggest unfairness, that property shall not be taken even for public purpose except upon payment of just compensation, and that unreasonable restrictions shall not be imposed, for example, on one's freedom of expression, movement, or means of livelihood.

Although the fairness aspect of the due process concept is rooted deep in man's consciousness, it did not receive specific articulation as a restraint on government until 1215. Then the Magna Carta provided that no freeman should be imprisoned, dispossessed, banished, or destroyed "except by the legal judgment of his peers or by the law of the land." This text is generally regarded as the direct antecedent of the constitutional provision that no man shall be deprived of "life, liberty, or property, without due process of law."

The expression appears in similar form in all state constitutions and twice in the Constitution of the United States—in the Fifth Amendment as a limitation upon the national government, and in the Fourteenth Amendment as a limitation upon the states. The content of the two prohibitions, as interpreted by the Supreme Court, is partly similar and partly different. To understand the differences and similarities, it is necessary to distinguish between procedural and substantive due process.

Procedural due process, which imposes similar restraints on federal and state governments, requires that the defendant, in both civil and criminal proceedings, be given adequate notice of the cause of action against him and sufficient opportunity to prepare his defense. He must be tried in a forum free of prejudice against his cause.

Substantive due process, on the other hand, restricts the federal government somewhat differently than state governments. The due process clause of the Fifth Amendment is merely supplementary to the rather specific limitations imposed upon the federal government by the Bill of Rights (the first 10 Amendments to the Constitution). These, for example, deny Congress any power to abridge freedom of speech, press, and religion, and assure the right of privacy against unreasonable search and seizure. Since the Bill of Rights restricts only the federal government, the limitation on the states must be largely found in the due process clause of the Fourteenth Amendment. Accordingly, the Supreme Court has poured into that phrase substantive content by holding that where the guarantees of the Bill of Rights state "fundamental principles of liberty and justice," such as free speech, press, and religion, and the right to be free from unreasonable search and seizure, they are absorbed into the due process clause of the Fourteenth Amendment.

Late in the 19th century the due process concept was much used in protection of alleged property interests with the consequence that the federal and state governments alike were often powerless to legislate effectively for the economic and social welfare of their citizens. Since the mid-1930's, however, wage and hour legislation, fixing of employment standards, and other regulatory legislation have been held constitutional. The only important substantive limitation of a property character now carried over from the Fifth Amendment into the due process clause of the Fourteenth is the protection against the taking of private property for public use without just compensation.

ROBERT B. McKAY, New York University School of Law

DUER [dū′ər], **WILLIAM** (1747–99), American merchant, financier, and land speculator who served as an early treasury official and helped plant one of the first settlements in Ohio. Born in England of rich parents, Duer migrated to the West Indies and in 1768 visited New York, where he made large investments in timber lands along the Hudson River. Five years later he settled permanently in New York, becoming overnight an outstanding business leader and politician. He was elected to the Continental Congress in 1777, became a member of the Board of War, and was a signer of the Articles of Confederation before resigning in 1779 to attend to his expanding business affairs.

In 1784 he helped found the Bank of New York; two years later he became secretary to the Board of the Treasury. In this advantageous position, Duer helped form the Scioto Associates, a land-speculating concern that aided the Ohio Company in securing lands in eastern Ohio and received in return the right to purchase several million acres in central Ohio. After founding the village of Gallipolis, this enterprise collapsed due to failure to attract foreign capital. Duer served briefly as assistant secretary of the treasury under Alexander Hamilton, but resigned to devote attention to his private affairs. He speculated heavily in stocks and in Maine and Vermont lands, overreaching himself until he was arrested for debt in Mar., 1792. He died in prison.

RAY A. BILLINGTON, Northwestern University

DUERO RIVER. See DOURO RIVER.

DUFAY, GUILLAUME (c.1400–74), famous Flemish composer, born probably in Chimay, Hainaut. He began his career as a choirboy in the cathedral at Cambrai and in the 1420's went to Italy, where he served the Malatesta family and sang in the Papal Choir (1428–33; 1435–37). He later served at the court of Savoy, at the Paris court, and at the court of Burgundy. In 1436 he was appointed a canon of Cambrai Cathedral, and under his direction (from 1454 and on) Cambrai became an important music center.

Dufay, the leading composer of his time, composed in all the forms—Masses, motets, Magnificats, hymns (including a cycle for the entire year), and French and Italian secular songs. Among his most popular works are the chanson *Se la face ay pale*, the Masses *Caput* and *L'Homme armé*, and the motet *Alma Redemptoris Mater*. Dufay employed all the technical resources of his time and is credited with introducing new ones on the Continent, among them, fauxbourdon (a piece including parallel sixth chords, such as C-E-A moving to B-D-G) and the application of the *cantus firmus* treatment to Masses (in which the same pre-existent melody appears in each movement of the Mass setting). His style reflected the blending of such Italian elements as flowing melodies and clear-cut phrases, Gothic emphasis on strict formal structures and contrapuntal devices, and English sonority. His music influenced not only his contemporaries but also the major composers of following generations, particularly Johannes Ockeghem and Antoine Busnois.

Consult Reese, Gustave, *Music in the Renaissance* (1954).

EILEEN SOUTHERN, Brooklyn College

See also RENAISSANCE MUSIC.

DUFF, SIR LYMAN POORE (1865–1955), Canadian jurist. Born at Meaford, Ontario, he was a law graduate of the University of Toronto (1889) and practiced in Ontario and British Columbia until his appointment (1904) to the Supreme Court of British Columbia. Duff later became a judge of the Supreme Court of Canada (1906) and a member of the Imperial Privy Council (1919). He gave his name to a famous Royal Commission on Transportation (1931) which sharply criticized both the Canadian Pacific Railway and Canadian National Railways. Duff served as chief justice of Canada from 1933 until 1944.

DUFY [dü-fē′], **RAOUL** (1877–1953), French painter. His highly individual style, which matured after World War I, utilizes line sketches that are drawn over areas of bright, flat color. His choice of subjects—fashionable resorts, racetracks, boating scenes, and parks—reflects the gaiety characteristic of his work. Dufy also created fabrics, ceramics, and other decorative art objects.

DUGAN, ALAN (1923–   ), American poet, born in New York City. A student at Queens College, he won a poetry prize while still an undergraduate. *Poetry Magazine* awarded him a prize in 1946, and the Yale Series of Younger Poets published his *Poems* in 1961. This volume received much praise, and won both the Pulitzer Prize and the National Book Award. Dugan is a painstaking craftsman, the quietness of whose language is in the service of subtlety and tight control of his verse. *Poems 2* appeared in 1963. He was awarded a Guggenheim fellowship in 1963–64.

DUGI OTOK [dōō′gē ô′tôk], island of Yugoslavia, in the Adriatic Sea off the coast of Croatia. It is reached by boat from Zadar. Sali is the main port. Area, 46 sq. mi.

DUGONG [dōō′gŏng] **or HALICORE** [hə-līk′ə-rē], a large marine mammal, *Dugong australis*, of the order Sirenia, found in shallow seas and bays from the Indian Ocean to northern Australia. This ungainly beast may reach a length of 9 ft., has paddlelike forelimbs, a broad, flattened tail, and feeds on aquatic vegetation, which it crops with its fleshy lips. A few peglike crushing teeth suffice for chewing the food. Dugongs once occurred in enormous herds, but have been greatly reduced by hunters who sought their valuable blubber.

DUHAMEL [dü-à-mĕl'], **GEORGES** (1884–1966), French writer. He was born in Paris. Duhamel belonged to the "Abbaye," a literary community at Créteil, where, with such friends as Jules Romains, he sought an ideal life in writing and manual labor (1906–8). Duhamel served as a surgeon in World War I and expressed the pity and horror of war in *La vie des martyrs*, 1917 (*The New Book of Martyrs*, 1918) and *Civilisation*, 1918 (*Civilization*, 1919). He denounced the absorption of man into a drab and overindustrialized community in the scathing pamphlet *Scènes de la vie future*, 1930 (*America: The Menace*, 1931), written after a hurried visit to the United States. Also a poet and playwright, Duhamel is known especially as the author of two novel-cycles: *Vie et aventures de Salavin*, 5 vols., 1920–32 (*Salavin*, 1936), which tells the story of a tormented little clerk who tries to grow spiritually, unaided by religion; and *La Chronique des Pasquier*, 10 vols., 1933–45 (*The Pasquier Chronicles*, 1937–46), which sketches the history of a French family from 1880 to 1920. Concern for the individual permeates his work. Although he points out the threats of modern civilization, Duhamel maintains faith in the basic goodness of human nature. He was elected to the French Academy in 1935.

BERNARD GARNIEZ, New York University

DUIKER [dī'kər] **or DUIKERBOK**, a medium-sized antelope, *Cephalophus*, native to the forest and bush country of southern and western Africa. Duikers vary in color from yellowish- to grayish-brown, are about 2 ft. high at the shoulders, have short, straight horns, and a tuft of hair atop their heads. Their name means "diver" and refers to the way duikers plunge out of sight into the underbrush.

DUISBURG [düs'bŏŏrкн], city of North Rhine-Westphalia, Federal Republic of Germany (West Germany), located at the confluence of the Rhine and Ruhr rivers, north of Düsseldorf. It is an important coal-mining center and the largest inland port of Europe. Excellent waterway communications along the Rhine-Herne and Dortmund-Ems canals connect the city with major German seaports, while Rotterdam and other Netherlands seaports are reached via the Rhine River. Iron, steel, and heavy machinery are produced at Duisburg. The site was first mentioned in the 9th century as Dispargum, a residence of the Frankish kings. It became a free imperial city in 1290 and in the 17th century belonged to Brandenburg. The city was badly damaged during World War II and most of its historic buildings were destroyed. Pop., 502,993.

DUKAS [dü-kà'], **PAUL** (1865–1935), French composer. He achieved widespread recognition with *The Sorcerer's*

Apprentice (1897), based on a ballad by Goethe and outstanding in its logical form, spirited rhythm, and sparkling orchestration. He is also remembered for his lyrical three-act opera, *Ariane et Barbe-Bleue* (1907), which has a text by Maurice Maeterlinck.

DUKE, JAMES BUCHANAN (1856–1925), American tobacco industrialist. Impoverished by the Civil War, he, his father, and brother BENJAMIN NEWTON DUKE (1855–1929) in desperation began processing tobacco on their farm near Durham, N.C., and so prospered that in 1874 they opened a factory in Durham. By aggressive price-cutting and extensive advertising, Duke forced mergers from his rivals and formed the American Tobacco Company. This colossus assimilated both retail and wholesale competitors until it was ordered dissolved (1911) into its components, which continued to prosper. With his holdings in the Southern Power Company, which he organized, Duke financed the trust that endowed Duke University.

DUKE, VERNON, original name Vladimir Dukelsky (1903–), American composer. Born in Russia, he studied there and won fame as the composer of the Diaghilev ballet *Zéphyr et Flore*. He settled in the United States in 1929. Among his songs are *April in Paris, Autumn in New York, I Can't Get Started,* and *Takin' a Chance on Love.* His most important Broadway score was written for *Cabin in the Sky* (1940).

DUKE ENDOWMENT, philanthropic fund, the major beneficiaries of which are the religious, medical, and educational institutions of North and South Carolina. Support is given in particular to hospitals serving charity patients, groups caring for orphans, Duke University, and the Methodist Church. The trust was established by James B. Duke in 1924. Headquarters are in Charlotte, N.C.

DUKE UNIVERSITY, coeducational university, privately controlled, affiliated with the Methodist Church, and located in North Carolina. Duke was founded in 1924 around the nucleus of Trinity College, a liberal arts college, whose roots extend back to 1838 in Randolph County, N.C. Between 1838 and 1892 this school was known successively as Union Institute Academy, Union Institute, Normal College, and Trinity College. Largely through the efforts of Washington Duke, Trinity was moved to Durham in 1892. His gift for that move was the first of many contributions by him and his two sons, Benjamin N. and James B. Duke, that made possible Duke University.

Today Duke University occupies two campuses. The Woman's College occupies the campus of old Trinity College, while all other schools and colleges of the university are located on the new campus, a mile and a half west. These include Trinity College (the undergraduate College of Arts and Sciences for men), the College of Engineering, the Graduate School of Arts and Sciences, the Divinity School, School of Law, School of Forestry, School of Medicine, and School of Nursing. Also on the campus are a 660-bed hospital and the library, which ranks first in the South and among the top 15 in the nation. Special facilities include the Parapsychology Laboratory, Com-

The women's college campus of Duke University. (A. DEVANEY)

monwealth-Studies Center, World Rule of Law Center, and Center for the Study of Aging (all at Durham), and the Marine Laboratory at Beaufort, N.C. For statistics, see UNIVERSITIES AND COLLEGES.

CLARENCE E. WHITEFIELD, Director, Bureau of Public Information, Duke University

DULANY [dū-lā′nē], **DANIEL** (1685–1753), English colonial official and landowner. Descended from a medieval Irish family, Dulany went to Port Tobacco, Md., with two brothers, in 1703. He launched his political career shortly after moving (1721) to Annapolis with a fight in the provincial assembly in favor of legislation to make English law the foundation for provincial law (according to the proprietary charter, Charles Calvert, 5th Baron Baltimore, 1699–1751, possessed nearly royal powers). Earlier, Dulany had made a fortune in land speculation, wheat production, and some manufacturing, which he helped to develop by encouraging the immigration of Germans into the Monocacy Valley. Until Lord Calvert appointed him to high public offices in 1733, Dulany had led the opposition to the proprietary government in Maryland. His son DANIEL DULANY (1722–97) gained public attention by opposing the Stamp Act of 1765. He argued that it was beyond Parliament's power to pass an essentially internal tax, although he upheld the Navigation Acts because they regulated only the colonies' external affairs.

RICHARD M. ABRAMS, University of California

DULCIMER [dŭl′sə-mər], string instrument (chordophone) of the zither family. It consists of a set of strings stretched

over a rectangular or trapezoidal board or box, which is usually placed on a table and struck with hammers. Various types of dulcimers have been used in the folk music of Europe and in the Middle East (where it originated in ancient times). One well-known type is the Hungarian cimbalom, used by café and dance orchestras. Best known in the United States is the plucked "Kentucky Mountain dulcimer," which has three strings, two of which sound a repeated chord while the third is used for the melody. The dulcimer is used as a solo instrument and as accompaniment for songs in British-American folk music, but it was presumably brought to America from northern Europe. *See also* CIMBALOM; PSALTERY.

DULLES [dŭl′ĭs], **ALLEN WELSH** (1893–   ), American intelligence official. Born in Watertown, N.Y., the brother of John Foster Dulles, he graduated from Princeton and entered (1916) the diplomatic service. After receiving (1926) a law degree from George Washington University, Dulles practiced privately until he joined the Office of Strategic Services in World War II. He entered the Central Intelligence Agency in 1951, became director in 1953, and retired in 1961. John A. McCone succeeded him.

DULLES, JOHN FOSTER (1888–1959), U.S. Secretary of State in the Eisenhower administration. He was born in Washington, D.C., the son of a Presbyterian pastor and the grandson of John W. Foster, U.S. Secretary of State (1892–93). His uncle, Robert Lansing, had also been secretary of state (1915–20).

Dulles graduated from Princeton University, studied at the Sorbonne in Paris, and obtained a law degree from George Washington University. He joined the law firm of Sullivan and Cromwell in New York, which specialized in international corporate law. Dulles became a legal advisor to President Woodrow Wilson and a member of the Reparations Commission at the Paris Peace Conference in 1919. He was made a senior partner in his firm in 1920.

Active as a legal consultant to the U.S. government in the World War II period, he participated in the drafting of the United Nations Charter at the San Francisco Conference in 1945. A lifelong Republican, he was ap-

John Foster Dulles, U.S. Secretary of State. (NOEL CLARK—BLACK STAR)

pointed to the U.S. Senate from New York in 1949 to fill an unexpired term. He was defeated in the ensuing election. In 1951 he helped draft the Japanese Peace Treaty. Dulles was appointed by President Dwight D. Eisenhower as the new secretary of state in 1953. He advocated an aggressive policy of "massive retaliation" against possible hostile action by the Soviet Union and China. Dulles was instrumental in the policy of isolating China from the non-Communist world. He promised to "roll back" the Soviets from Eastern Europe and proclaimed neutralism immoral. He hinted at an "agonizing reappraisal" of U.S. policy toward France and condemned the Franco-British-Israeli campaign against Nasser's Egypt in 1956.

Dulles was an active Presbyterian and devoted much of his time to important lay positions in both U.S. and international religious organizations. He played a dominant role in the shaping of U.S. foreign policy, during the Eisenhower administration. He resigned from the cabinet in Apr., 1959, after the reappearance of a malignant cancer.

SERGIO BARZANTI, Fairleigh Dickinson University

DULONG [dü-lôn'], **PIERRE LOUIS** (1785–1838), French chemist and physicist whose law, formulated in collaboration with A. L. Petit, and stating that the product of specific heat and atomic weight is a constant, made possible many atomic weight determinations. He worked as assistant to C. L. Berthollet, and taught in Paris at the École Polytechnique, where he was appointed director. His early studies were chemical, whereas his later work involved the physical properties of many substances. The Dulong-Petit law was announced in 1819.

DULSE [dŭls], a fleshy seaweed, *Rhodymenia*, in phylum Rhodophyta, the red algae. Dulse is commonly found along both seacoasts of the northern Atlantic Ocean. The fernlike plants consist of flattened branches and are a purplish-red color. Dulse is eaten either raw or cooked in Iceland, Scotland, and Ireland. In Norway it is known as sheep's weed because sheep, relishing it as food, search the beaches for it at low tide.
See also RED ALGAE.

DULUTH [də-lōōth'] or **DULHUT** [*French* dü-lüt'], **DANIEL GREYSOLON, SIEUR** (1636–1710), French explorer. He explored the Lake Superior and Minnesota regions and claimed them for France. Settling in Canada about 1674, Duluth led an expedition in 1678 to the Sioux territory around Lake Superior, establishing French claims and pacifying the Indians. The next year he founded the post that eventually became Duluth, Minn. Charged with illegal trading, he went to France in 1681 to clear himself. After his return to New France he made other expeditions, founding posts, including Fort St. Joseph on the St. Clair River (1686). He was made commandant of Fort Frontenac on Lake Ontario (1695). His reputation for fair dealing with the Indians enhances his fame as an explorer.

DULUTH [də-lōōth'], port city of northeastern Minnesota, and seat of St. Louis County, at the mouth of the St. Louis River, at the western end of Lake Superior, opposite Superior, Wis. The city is the farthest point inland on the Great Lakes–St. Lawrence Seaway and is primarily a transportation center. About two-thirds of the iron ore from the Minnesota iron ranges moves through the Duluth-Superior port, as do large quantities of wheat and feed grains from the agricultural regions to the west and south. Since the opening of the seaway, Duluth has become one of the leading grain-exporting ports of the United States. The city also has a steel mill, flour and lumber mills, canneries, cold-storage plants, and shipyards. Duluth is built on picturesque bluffs offering splendid views of the harbor and of Lake Superior. It is a popular summer resort, with nearby forest and lakelands, beaches, boating, fishing, and riding and hiking trails.

The city was named after Daniel Greysolon, Sieur Duluth, who first visited the site in 1679 in an attempt to open the area to fur trading. The first permanent settlement was in the 1850's, and the city grew as a trade and shipping port for a lumbering area.

The Duluth campus of the University of Minnesota and the College of St. Scholastica are located here. Inc., 1857. Pop. (1950) 104,511; (1960) 106,884. Duluth-Superior urb. area, pop. (1950) 143,028; (1960) 144,763.

LEVERETT HOAG, University of Minnesota

Rail and shipping facilities on the outskirts of Duluth. Huge grain elevators provide storage space for grain before shipment.
(H. ARMSTRONG ROBERTS)

DUMA

DUMA [dōō'mä], an elected national assembly introduced in Russia following the 1905 revolution. Tsar Nicholas II was led to accept concessions devised by the statesman Count Witte to appease moderate liberal elements. Before it met, however, the Tsar rendered it virtually powerless by restricting electoral rights, giving the government decree powers subject only to himself, retaining a veto on legislation, and establishing the State Council as an upper house with half of its members appointed by him. Despite these restrictions, the first Duma (Apr.–July, 1906) turned out to be dominated by the liberal Kadet (Constitutional Democratic) party and was dismissed. The second Duma (Feb.–June, 1907) was even more radical and was also dismissed. New electoral laws that reduced the popular vote still further made the last two Dumas (1907–12, 1912–17) more conservative, but the liberal minority continued to use this national forum to criticize the government. In 1917 it provided the authority for the establishment of the provisional government after the abdication of the Tsar.

GEORGE BRINKLEY, University of Notre Dame

DUMAGUETE [dōō-mä-gä'tä], port, largest city, and capital of Negros Oriental Province, southeastern Negros Island, Philippines. The city is an important interisland trading port and the commercial center for the surrounding corn- and coconut-producing area. Silliman University, established in 1901 by American missionaries, is here. Pop., 35,347.

DUMAS [dōō'mä, French dü-mä'], **ALEXANDRE** (1802–70), French playwright and novelist. He was the son of a celebrated general under Napoleon who, though of noble birth, called himself Dumas after his mother, a Haitian Negro. He is known as Dumas père to distinguish him from his son Alexandre Dumas (1824–95); the latter is known as Dumas fils.

Dumas grew up in Villers-Cotterêts and became a hulking replica of his heroic father. Going to Paris at 20, he made up for his erratic education by omnivorous reading and associated himself with the group of young romantics who were then beginning to revolutionize the arts in France. He achieved fame in 1829 with his historical drama *Henri III et sa cour* (Henry III and His Court), the first romantic play to win public acclaim. From that date forward, Dumas applied his prodigious energy and fertile imagination to the creation of torrents of writing—plays, novels, travel impressions, and even a cookery compendium—and to a high and profligate style of living. Tremendously popular, he earned a fortune many times over with his pen, but spent all of it in foolish business ventures and on a succession of mistresses who, along with his creditors, pursued him endlessly. He died in 1870, impoverished, broken in health, at his son's home in Normandy.

Both in his plays and his novels Dumas imaginatively exploited the history of France. Among his great successes in the historical novel were *Les trois mousquetaires*, 1844 (*The Three Musketeers*, 1846), *Vingt ans après*, 1845 (*Twenty Years After*, 1846), and *Le collier de la reine*, 1849–50 (*The Queen's Necklace*, 1850). But not all his successes were based on history. His play *Antony* (1831), for example, created a Byronic hero, and his novel *Le*

Alexandre Dumas père. A master of many forms of writing, Dumas père is famous for his swashbuckling novels.

Alexandre Dumas fils followed in his father's literary footsteps. He was one of the best-known French playwrights during the 19th century.

comte de Monte-Cristo, 1844–45 (*The Count of Monte-Cristo*, 1846) has become the prototype of the adventure novel. His accounts of his own travels in Spain, Italy, and Russia still make fascinating reading. His life work, consisting of over 100 volumes, could only have been written with the help of numerous collaborators. There is much truth in the witticism that Alexandre Dumas was not an author but an entire industry. Yet his was the dominant voice in all that appeared over his signature. He lacked style and a sense of form; he was unreliable about history and superficial about human character; he was incapable of profound thought. But Alexandre Dumas was a truly great natural storyteller, blessed with an inexhaustible imagination, a flair for the dramatic, and a forceful and entertaining personality that can be felt in every line he ever wrote.

Consult Bell, A. C., *Alexandre Dumas* (1950).

MURRAY SACHS, Brandeis University

DUMAS, ALEXANDRE (1824–95), French playwright and novelist. He is known as Dumas fils to distinguish him from Dumas père, whose illegitimate son he was. The unstable circumstances of his childhood made him an irresponsible playboy as a young man. But accumulating debts soon sobered him. He turned to literature and won fame with a first novel, based on personal experience, *La dame aux camélias* (1848). When he turned it into an even more successful play (1852; trans., *Camille*, 1856), his true vocation was found. A dominant figure in the French theater, he created a new kind of play (*pièce à thèse*) which consciously aimed to reform social evils. His influential dramas attacked the problems of prostitution in *Le demi-monde* (1855; trans., 1858), illegitimacy in *Le fils naturel* (The Natural Son), 1858, and the injustices inherent in the laws of marriage, adultery, and divorce of that era.

During his lifetime Dumas enjoyed greater literary prestige than did his father, for he dealt with serious ideas. But his plays were nearly all too closely dependent on the social evils they did so much to correct for interest in them to have endured, in spite of their excellent dramatic structure and their convincing dialogue. His fame now rests almost solely on his earliest and least didactic play, *Camille*. It pulses with genuine emotion, and its pathetic heroine, Marguerite Gautier, who dies of consumption, is one of the imperishable characters of world literature. The role was strikingly acted by Greta Garbo in a film version (1937). Giuseppe Verdi's opera *La traviata* (1853) is based upon the play.

MURRAY SACHS, Brandeis University

DUMAS, JEAN BAPTISTE ANDRÉ (1800–84), French chemist. His researches in organic chemistry demonstrated the process of substitution, determined the formulas of many compounds, and established the theory of types, or classes, of organic compounds. He is best known for devising a method to determine vapor densities and the molecular weights of volatile compounds.

DUMAS, JEAN DANIEL (1721–92), French soldier. He went to Canada in 1750 and served there throughout the Seven Years' War. Taking command when Liénard de Beaujeu was killed early in the Battle of the Monongahela (1755), Dumas deserves credit for defeating the English under Edward Braddock. Dumas was subsequently commandant of Fort Duquesne and inspector general of marine troops in Canada (1759). Before quitting North America, he took important part in the battles of the Plains of Abraham (1759) and Ste. Foy (1760). He continued his army career in France, becoming a field marshal in 1780.

DUMAS [dōō'məs], city of northern Texas, and seat of Moore County, located in the Panhandle plains. It is the commercial center of an extensive wheat-growing region and has natural gas fields. Petroleum refining, zinc smelting, and the manufacture of helium gas, carbon black, and fertilizers are leading industries. Pop. (1950) 6,127; (1960) 8,477.

DU MAURIER [dū mô'rē-ā], **DAPHNE** (1907–), English author, born in London. She wrote a study of her father, *Gerald, a Portrait* (1934), and of the family, *The Du Mauriers* (1937). Her widely popular novels, many of which were made into motion pictures, include *Jamaica Inn* (1931), *Rebecca* (1938), *Frenchman's Creek* (1942), *Hungry Hill* (1943), *The King's General* (1946), *My Cousin Rachel* (1952), and *Mary Anne* (1954).

DU MAURIER, GEORGE LOUIS PALMELLA BUSSON (1834–96), English author and illustrator. Born in Paris of a French father and an English mother, he studied chemistry but practiced art instead, becoming illustrator for *Punch* at 30. His three novels are extremely fanciful and, to modern taste, overly sentimental; still, all three can be read with pleasure by the sympathetic reader. *Peter Ibbetson* (1892) concerns two lovers who are separated but who live together in their dreams. *Trilby* (1894) is the story of a young woman who, although tone-deaf, is hypnotized into becoming a great singer by Svengali. *The Martian* (1897) concerns a man from Mars.

DU MAURIER, SIR GERALD (1873–1934), English actor and theater manager, son of the novelist George Du Maurier. Sir Gerald first won success in James Barrie's plays, including *Peter Pan*. In 1910 he became manager of Wyndham's Theatre in London, where he had a wide following. His style, graceful and polished, exhibited a seeming naturalness that was, in fact, the result of consummate technical skill. He was knighted in 1922.

DUMBARTON [dŭm-bär'tən], county town and Large Burgh of Scotland, 18 mi. northwest of Glasgow, located where the Leven River, flowing south from Loch Lomond, joins the Clyde River. Shipbuilding, engineering, and whisky blending are leading industries. Medieval Dumbarton was the capital of the kingdom of Strathclyde. Glencairn House, the 17th-century town house of the Dukes of Argyll, is on the High Street, which follows the curve of the Leven River. The remains of a castle stand atop Dumbarton Rock, overlooking the Leven, just outside the town. William Wallace was imprisoned here in 1305, as was Mary, Queen of Scots, before being taken secretly to France in 1548. Inc. as a Royal Burgh in 1222; pop., 26,961.

DUMBARTON [dŭm'bär-tən] **OAKS CONFERENCE,** the world security conference held at the Dumbarton Oaks estate in Washington, D.C., from Aug. 24 to Oct. 7, 1944, at which the United States, Great Britain, the Soviet Union, and China drafted the basic plan for the United Nations as an agency for the preservation of peace.

DUMBARTONSHIRE or (officially) **DUNBARTONSHIRE,** county of Scotland extending from the Highlands to the north shore of the Clyde estuary and eastward to Glasgow. A detached area, containing the town of Kirkintilloch and a small coal field, lies northeast of Glasgow. The highland section, with a maximum elevation of 3,092 ft. at Ben Vorlich, includes the greater part of Loch Lomond, source of the Leven River, which provided the soft water for the Vale of Leven's former textile industries. The industrial town of Dumbarton is still the county seat, although some of the administration is centered in Glasgow. Inland, the banks of the Clyde River are industrialized, and at Clydebank some of the world's largest ships have been built. The historic district of Lennox comprised Dumbartonshire and some adjoining areas; the shire of Dumbarton is mentioned in 1237, but it almost certainly existed earlier. Area, 244 sq. mi.; pop., 184,546.

H. A. MOISLEY, University of Glasgow

DUMBCANE, a handsome shrub, *Dieffenbachia sequina*, native to the West Indies. Its common name derives from the fact that if its stem (which contains calcium oxylate) is chewed, the tongue becomes paralyzed, or so painful that for several days one loses the power of speech. The plant has a thick, fleshy stem and large, oblong leaves. Several horticultural varieties of dumbcane have been developed and are popular as house plants.

See also DIEFFENBACHIA.

DUMFRIES [dŭm-frēs'], town and Royal Burgh of Scotland, and seat of Dumfriesshire, located on the left bank of the Nith River, 7 mi. inland from its entrance to the Solway Firth. Dumfries is the most important agricultural center in southwest Scotland. Robert Burns came to Dumfries in 1791, five years before his death, and did most of his remaining work in "Burns House." Many of his possessions have been preserved. In 1929 the town of Maxwelltown, historically in the Stewartry of Kirkcudbright, was incorporated with Dumfries. Pop., 27,780.

DUMFRIESSHIRE [dŭm-frēsh'shĭr], county of southern Scotland, one of the Border Counties, on the north shore of Solway Firth. Much of the terrain is upland, dissected by Nithsdale, Annandale, Eskdale, and many smaller valleys, and reaching a maximum elevation of 2,695 ft. at White Coomb in the Tweedsmuir Hills. The more remote dales and surrounding hills provide excellent sheep pastures; dairy farms occupy most of the lower valleys and coastlands. The towns of Dumfries (the county seat), Annan, and Lockerbie have important livestock markets; Sanquhar is the center of a small coal field. The county is strategically situated astride main routes from northwestern England to western, central, and eastern Scotland. Many castles and towers bear witness to its long, unsettled history. Gretna, a village near the English border, was formerly the favorite destination of eloping English couples who took advantage of then easy Scottish marriage customs. The county is first mentioned in the 13th century, but may be older. Area, 1,073 sq. mi.; pop., 88,423.

H. A. MOISLEY, The University, Glasgow

DUMONT [dü'mŏnt], **GABRIEL** (1838–1906), Canadian rebel leader. Born in Red River, Manitoba, of half-breed parents, he moved to Batoche, Saskatchewan, where he became leader of the new half-breed (Métis) community and organizer of the buffalo hunts. As a lieutenant of Louis Riel in the Saskatchewan rebellion (1885), he defeated a Northwest Mounted Police detachment at Duck Lake. Beaten at Batoche, where the rebellion was crushed by Gen. Frederick Middleton, he fled to the United States and remained there for several years until an amnesty permitted his return to Saskatchewan.

DUMONT, residential borough of northeastern New Jersey, 5 mi. north-northeast of Hackensack. Several dressmaking firms are located here. Inc., 1898; pop. (1950) 13,013; (1960) 18,882.

DUMONT D'URVILLE [dür-vēl'], **JULES SÉBASTIEN CÉSAR** (1790–1842), French naval officer and explorer. He had twice (1822–25; 1826–29) circumnavigated the world prior to commanding an exploratory expedition (1837–41) to Antarctica in the *Astrolabe* and *Zélée.* He explored the Straits of Magellan, encountered pack ice at 63° 29' S. lat.

and 44° 47' W. long. but failed to penetrate it. He visited South Orkney Islands, discovered Joinville Island, then, sailing westward, crossed the Pacific to Fiji and Borneo. He returned to Antarctic regions in 1840, penetrated pack ice south of New Zealand and, in Jan., 1841, discovered Adélie Coast at 143° E. long. and 66° 30' S. lat.

DUMOURIEZ [dü-mōō-ryā'], **CHARLES FRANÇOIS** (1739–1823), French general. He first saw action during the Seven Years' War and was later an agent in Louis XV's secret service. During the Revolution he joined the Girondist group, became Minister of Foreign Affairs, and engineered the declaration of war against Austria (Apr., 1792). Appointed Minister of War in June, 1792, Dumouriez soon resigned to take command vacated by Lafayette, who had been accused of treason. He defeated the Austrians at Jemappes (Nov. 6) but was beaten at Neerwinden (Mar., 1793). Under investigation after this loss, he deserted to the Austrians. Scorned by royalists and revolutionaries alike, Dumouriez lived a wandering exile until 1804, when he settled in England and advised the British government on Napoleon's strategy.

DUMPING is the sale of surplus goods in foreign markets at unusually low prices. Although consumers in the country where the goods are dumped benefit from the lower prices, the impact on the sales and the production plans of domestic businessmen may be ruinous. Serious damage may also be done to the sales of rival foreign businessmen who have business in the area where dumping occurs. Unless the country where dumping occurs is a colony, continued dumping often leads to various trade restrictions.

DUNA, DUNAJ, or DUNAV RIVER. *See* DANUBE RIVER.

DUN & BRADSTREET, INC., a gatherer and disseminator of credit information about businesses engaged in buying and selling merchandise. However, it does not supply credit ratings or information on individuals, banks, service businesses, or nonprofit organizations. In addition to confidential credit reports, it supplies subscribers with a reference book (revised six times a year) that lists geographically the names and ratings of about 3,000,000 enterprises. D & B also collects bad debts (for businesses only), and publishes two magazines: *Dun's Review and Modern Industry,* which contains general information about business, and *International Trade Review,* which specializes in marketing news.

DUNBAR, PAUL LAURENCE (1872–1906), American Negro writer. The son of former slaves, he was born in Dayton, Ohio. A high school graduate, Dunbar published his first book at the age of 20, while working as an elevator operator. Encouraged by the success of his third book, *Lyrics of Lowly Life* (published in 1896 with an introduction by William Dean Howells), Dunbar concentrated on a career as writer and public reader. Despite poor health, which caused an early death, Dunbar published six books of poetry, four novels, and four collections of stories. He also wrote lyrics for musical shows and many articles.

In the early 1900's, Dunbar was one of America's most popular poets. His reputation declined as American poetic styles changed, and he has been attacked as one who pleased his editors and readers by ridiculing Negroes and upholding myths of the plantation tradition.

Because he is famed as a writer of comic poetic monologues in Negro dialect, readers have overlooked his conscious artistry and experimentation with meter and rhyme, his skillful imitations of the dialects of Caucasian inhabitants of Ohio and Indiana, the characteristic melancholy of much of his standard-English poetry (which exceeds his dialect poetry in quantity), and his bitter, ironic social protest in many stories such as *The Strength of Gideon* (1901). It is true, however, that his talents for rhythm, narration, and satirical characterization are best revealed in his dialect poems, his major contributions to American literature.

Consult Cunningham, Virginia, *The Poet and His Song* (1951); Lawson, Victor, *Dunbar Critically Examined* (1941).

DARWIN T. TURNER, Agricultural and Technical College of North Carolina

DUNBAR, city in south central West Virginia, and part of the Charleston urban area. The chief industries are the manufacture of motorized hand plows and glass, and enameling. Inc., 1921; pop. (1950) 8,032; (1960) 11,006.

DUNCAN I (d.1040), King of Scotland (1034–40). Before his accession to the Scottish throne Duncan was already King of the Strathclyde Welsh and ruler of most of the territory south of the Firths of Forth and Clyde. Duncan was killed by Macbeth (q.v.), who took his throne.

DUNCAN, ISADORA (1878–1927), famous American dancer, born in San Francisco. Trained as a child in classic ballet, she later became a pioneer in dance forms and brought about a renaissance of the art of dancing through-

Isadora Duncan, noted American dancer. (BROWN BROTHERS)

out the entire Western world. She made her debut in Chicago (1899) and, following her Parisian debut (1900), was showered with extravagant eulogies by spectators throughout the capitals of America and Europe. She died in an unusual way when her long scarf accidentally caught in the wheel of an open car she was riding in and strangled her.

She found emotional stimulation in the music of the great masters but sought inspiration for her dance motifs in nature, believing that the Greek ideal could be realized in the 20th century through a return to free movement of the human body in harmony with movement in nature. Her pupils were taught to translate personal emotions into continuous phrases emanating from a central impulse which she located in the solar plexus. She was a visionary artist of such heroic proportions that she was able to encompass the entire gamut of human emotional experience in three simple gestures directed upward toward the universe, downward into the earth, and forward toward mankind. She created dances which were profoundly moving and essentially lyrical with a few natural movements such as walking, running, leaping, skipping. Her settings of Schubert waltzes, especially *The Three Graces*, remain today masterpieces of simplicity and pure movement.

Consult Isadora Duncan, ed. by Paul Magriel (1947).

NADIA CHILKOVSKY, Philadelphia Dance Academy
See also DANCE, MODERN.

DUNCAN, city of British Columbia, Canada, on Vancouver Island. Duncan is the distributing and administrative center of the Cowichan Valley's logging and dairying, and for the sulfate pulp mill at nearby Crofton. Inc., 1912; pop., 3,726.

DUNCAN, city of southern Oklahoma, and seat of Stephens County. It is in an oil-producing region and has refineries and other petroleum industries. Pop. (1950) 15,325; (1960) 20,009.

DUNCIAD [dŭn′sē-ăd], **THE,** English satirical poem by Alexander Pope. It first appeared in 1728 with the editor and critic Lewis Theobald as the chief "dunce." Somewhat changed and enlarged in 1729 and considerably altered in 1742, the satire achieved final form in 1743 with the playwright Colley Cibber replacing Theobald. Pope's personal animus vented itself upon dull poets, critics, textual editors, publishers, and pedants and dunces of all descriptions.

DUNDALK [dŭn-dôk′], unincorporated community of central Maryland, adjacent to eastern Baltimore, on the Patapsco River. It is a residential community and trade center for workers in nearby steel and heavy-manufacturing industries. Pop. (1960) 82,428.

DUNDAS [dŭn′dəs], town of eastern Ontario, Canada, at the western tip of Lake Ontario, 10 mi. west of Hamilton. Industries include the manufacture of machine tools and textiles. Inc., 1847; pop., 12,912.

DUNDEE [dŭn-dē′], **JOHN GRAHAM OF CLAVERHOUSE, 1ST VISCOUNT** (c.1649–89), Scottish chieftain and sol-

Sand dunes in the Sahara Desert.

dier. He was the principal hero of the Jacobites, to whose dual causes—the suppression of the Scottish Covenanters, or Presbyterians, and the restoration of the house of Stuart—he devoted himself. He was second in command of the Scottish force sent to help, unsuccessfully, the deposed James II to repel (1688) William of Orange (later William III). Returning to Scotland in 1689, Dundee raised forces and attacked William's army at the pass of Killiecrankie. Although the Jacobites were victorious, Dundee was slain. He is the subject of Sir Walter Scott's ballad *Bonnie Dundee.*

DUNDEE, seaport and industrial city of Scotland, located on the north shore of the Firth of Tay. Jute manufacture, together with that of textile machinery, has dominated the town since the mid-19th century. Other leading industries are the manufacture of marmalade and jam, office machinery, radio and electric goods, whiskies, carpets, greeting cards, leather, and linoleum.

The city's port is reached by a 10-mi. channel from the North Sea. It has a sheltered anchorage, extensive wharves and warehouses, and a fish dock, as well as grain and flour mills and timber yards. Dundee was once famous for its wooden sailing vessels, and it still has a large shipyard. There is a vehicle ferry service across the Tay to Fife.

Dundee was founded in the 12th century, and with its important trade in salt fish, raw wool, and hides, it became the second wealthiest city in Scotland, surpassed only by Edinburgh. Its modern growth dates from the 18th century, when woolen weaving gave way to linen and canvas work. The introduction of power looms was followed by the pioneering of jute as a textile raw material in place of flax and hemp.

The University College was founded at Dundee in 1883 and united with the much older University of St. Andrews in 1893. This, and other branches of the University in Dundee, are now known as Queen's College, and enjoy parity with the other half of the University in St. Andrews. The city boundaries now include, on the east, Broughty Ferry, a seaside resort and residential suburb. Pop., 182,959.

H. A. MOISLEY, *The University, Glasgow*

DUNE, mound or ridge of wind-blown sand, either bare or covered by vegetation. Dunes are found in present or past deserts, along sandy coasts, and on river plains in arid or semiarid regions. Height ranges from a few feet to more than 1,000 ft., and length from a few tens of feet to miles. Dunes may be crescentic, V-shaped, pyramidal, or irregular, and they may occur singly or in wavelike assemblages. They tend to migrate in the prevailing wind direction unless they are blocked by some topographic barrier or covered by vegetation. Moving dunes may bury forests, fields, roads, and even settlements; hence protective measures have been developed, including the planting of vegetation and the use of artificial barriers.

DUNEDIN [dŭn-ē'dən], city of New Zealand, on the southeast coast of South Island at the base of Otago Peninsula. Although the city has harbor facilities, the main port installation is at Port Chalmers, 7 mi. northeast. Dunedin is the marketing and processing center for a large agricultural region in which the main products are wool, mutton, lambs, butter, and cheese. Forestry and mining are also carried out in the interior. The city has a wide range of industries, including food processing, woolen mills, fertilizer and chemical plants, sawmills, engineering works, and machine shops.

The main commercial district is concentrated near the waterfront. Residential areas are spread over the numerous hills that rise above the harbor. The University of Otago (estab., 1869) and a teacher-training college are here.

Dunedin was surveyed in 1846 and subsequently was settled by Scottish immigrants. Its name, meaning "Edin on the hill," was the ancient name of Edinburgh. Aided by the discovery of gold in central Otago, Dunedin became the leading city of New Zealand in the 1860's and 1870's. In 1882 New Zealand's first cargo of frozen meat was shipped from Otago Harbour, beginning a new era in the country's economy. Dunedin became a city in 1878 and has since expanded to include several suburbs. Pop., 73,245.

HOWARD J. CRITCHFIELD, *Western Washington State College*

Allied troops awaiting evacuation on the beaches near Dunkerque during the spring of 1940.
(WIDE WORLD)

DUNEDIN, city of western Florida, adjoining Clearwater, on the Gulf of Mexico. It is a citrus-growing center. Pop. (1950) 3,202; (1960) 8,444.

DUNELLEN [*dŭn-ĕl'ən*], industrial borough of northeastern New Jersey. Chief industries are the manufacture of printing presses and business forms. Inc., 1887; pop. (1950) 6,291; (1960) 6,840.

DUNFERMLINE [*dŭn-fûrm'lĭn*], town and Large Burgh of Scotland, located in southwest Fife, near the Firth of Forth. It is an important center of linen manufacture, although its textile industries now also make a variety of other fabrics. The town is closely associated with the Royal Navy through the adjacent dockyard of Rosyth. It has been a Royal Burgh with a palace since the 11th century. The tomb of Robert the Bruce is in the Abbey. Andrew Carnegie was born here in 1835, amassed a huge fortune in the United States, and returned to Dunfermline in 1902. He set up the Carnegie Dunfermline Trust, which provided many gifts to the town, among them Pittencrieff Park and a library. Pop., 46,768.

DUNGENESS [*dŭnj'nĕs'*], a headland projecting into the English Channel on the southeast coast of Kent, England. The lighthouse and Lloyd's signaling station are of importance. In 1652 the Dutch defeated the English in a battle off the coast of Dungeness.

DUNHAM [*dŭn'əm*], **KATHERINE** (1914–   ), celebrated exponent of Negro dance. Born on Chicago's West Side, she earned a Master's degree in anthropology at the University of Chicago. Rockefeller and Rosenwald grants attest to her scholarship. A striking beauty, she won Broadway stardom in *Cabin in the Sky* (1940) and has appeared in several films. She toured the world with her famous dance company, including productions ranging from primitive works like *Shango* and *Rites du Passage* to dances in the ragtime and blues idioms. Her books include *Journey to Accompong* (1946), an account of her research in Jamaica, and the autobiographical *A Touch of Innocence* (1959).

DUNKERQUE [*dŭn-kĕrk*] **or DUNKIRK** [*dŭn'kûrk*], seaport and fortress of northern France, on the English Channel, about 10 mi. from the Belgian border. Dunkerque has long been fortified because of its strategic importance, and at different times has been under the control of the Counts of Flanders, the Dukes of Burgundy, and Austria, Spain, France, and England. Dunkerque was the destination of the fighting retreat of British and French troops in May, 1940. German armies surrounded 350,000 Allied troops in the area around the town, but the great majority were safely evacuated under fire by naval, fishing, and pleasure boats shuttling across the Channel. The port has a car ferry service to England and a petroleum refinery. Dunkerque is the birthplace of Jean Bart, the French naval hero. Pop., 28,388.

DUNKERS or GERMAN BAPTIST BRETHREN, a pietistic, pacifist Protestant denomination of approximately 200,000 members, today known as the Church of the Brethren. The movement was founded at Schwarzenau, Germany, in 1708, under the leadership of Alexander Mack (1679–1735), in protest against formalized established churches. The name Dunker came from the baptismal practice of triple immersion. Persecution soon drove the Brethren to flee to America, where most settled in Pennsylvania between 1719 and 1729. Democratic in government and congregational in polity, the Brethren grew slowly, spreading southward and westward. Overseas missionary work was begun in the late 19th century.

DUNKIRK (Fr.). *See* DUNKERQUE.

DUNKIRK [*dŭn'kûrk*], industrial city of extreme western New York, on Lake Erie. Dunkirk produces knit goods, tool steel, thermal products, shovels, and processed foods. Inc., as village, 1837; as city, 1880; pop. (1950) 18,007; (1960) 18,205.

DÚN LAOGHAIRE [*dŭn lâr'ə*], borough of County Dublin, Ireland, on the southeastern extremity of Dublin Bay and 8 mi. from the capital. It was a fishing village until the extensive harbor was built in the mid-19th century, and Dún

149

Laoghaire became an outport of Dublin, with frequent mail steamer service to Holyhead, Wales. Its late 19th-century development is reflected in many handsome regency houses. In the 20th century the borough became a residential suburb and resort for Dubliners. Pop., 47,803.

DUNLAP, WILLIAM (1766–1839), American playwright and painter. Born in New Jersey and raised in British-occupied New York, he studied painting in London after the American Revolution. Returning to the United States, he came to prominence as a playwright with production of *The Father* (1789), and subsequently wrote or adapted more than a score of dramas. From 1796 to 1805 he managed the Park Theater in New York. His *History of the American Theatre* (1832) and *History of the Rise and Progress of the Arts of Design in the United States* (1834) are pioneer works still consulted by scholars.

DUNMORE, JOHN MURRAY, 4TH EARL OF (1732–1809), British colonial governor in America during the Revolutionary era. A Scottish-born peer, Lord Dunmore was an appropriate governor for the manorial society of colonial Virginia, but his authoritarian temper left him little sympathy or understanding for the Virginians' aspirations for autonomy. After brief service (1770–71) in New York as Governor, Dunmore assumed the Virginia post. He blended well with the Virginians and even participated with them in western land speculation, in violation of official imperial policy. But he twice ordered the House of Burgesses dissolved for proposing a committee on correspondence for colonial grievances (1773) and a day of fasting (1774) over the Boston Port Bill. For a time he succeeded in diverting the Virginians' attention from insurgency by launching an attack against the Indians. "Lord Dunmore's War," as the colonists called it, culminated when Gen. Andrew Lewis repulsed (Oct. 10, 1774) the Shawnee at Point Pleasant. Colonial insurgency resumed early in 1775, and Dunmore cautiously removed the Williamsburg arsenal to a British ship in the harbor. Later he inflamed the southern colonies by urging the slaves to desert and by terrorizing the coastal regions with the navy. His cause lost, Dunmore fled to England in July, 1776, and resumed his place in Parliament.

RICHARD M. ABRAMS, *University of California*

DUNMORE, coal-mining borough of northeastern Pennsylvania, just east of Scranton. It was settled by Connecticut pioneers in 1783 and was called Buckstown until 1840, when it was renamed for an English nobleman who promised (but failed) to finance a local railroad. Pop. (1950) 20,305; (1960) 18,917.

DUNN, SIR JAMES HAMET, 1ST BART. (1875–1956), Canadian financier, one of North America's greatest industrialists. In 1907 he founded the international banking firm of Dunn, Fisher & Co., of London, England. Other projects included the Brazilian Traction, Light and Power Co. and the Barcelona Traction, Light and Power Co. In 1935 he became chairman and president of Algoma Steel Corp. He gave generously to universities, and upon his death the Canadian government used the succession duties on his estate to provide in large portion the $100,000,000

endowment for the Canada Council for the Encouragement of the Arts, Humanities and Social Sciences.

DUNN, LESLIE CLARENCE (1893–   ), American geneticist. He received a B.A. from Dartmouth, a D.Sc. from Harvard. After holding positions elsewhere, in 1928 he became professor of zoology at Columbia University. His most influential contributions have concerned studies of lethal mutations in mice which permitted investigation of the effects of genes in early stages of development. Among his many published works are *Heredity and Evolution in Human Populations* (1959), and *Heredity, Race, and Society* (1946), co-authored by Theodosius Dobzhansky.

DUNN, town of eastern North Carolina. It is a cotton-marketing center. Pop. (1950) 6,316; (1960) 7,566.

DUNNE, FINLEY PETER (1867–1936), American journalist, best known as the creator of Mr. Martin Dooley, Irish critic of current affairs. Born in Chicago and educated in public schools, Dunne was a professional journalist. In 1892 he began writing dialect sketches. *Mr. Dooley in Peace and War* appeared in 1898, and the last of many Dooley books in 1919. Dunne was immensely successful as a writer of nationally syndicated, humorous comment on contemporary life.

DUNNING, CHARLES AVERY (1885–1958), Canadian politician and financier. Born in Leicestershire, England, he went (1902) to Saskatchewan as an immigrant farmhand. He quickly gained prominence in the Grain Growers' Association, was elected (1912) to the provincial legislature, and became minister of agriculture (1919). After serving as provincial Premier he was Minister of Railways and Canals (1926–29) and of Finance (1929–30) in the federal government. His budget of 1930 was an able attempt to counteract the adverse effects on Canada of the U.S. Hawley-Smoot tariff act by encouraging trade with Britain. Defeated with the Liberal government in 1930, he returned to the ministry of finance in 1935 but retired in 1939 owing to poor health. He was one of the ablest Canadian politicians of his generation.

DUNNVILLE, town of southern Ontario, Canada, located on the Grand River, where it empties into Lake Erie. It is in an agricultural area and has various small industries. Inc., 1900; pop., 5,181.

DUNOON, town and Small Burgh of East Argyll, Scotland, located on the Firth of Clyde, 27 mi. west-north-west of Glasgow. It is one of the most popular yachting centers and bathing resorts in Scotland. There is a monument to Robert Burns's "Highland Mary," who was born here. The Cowal Highland Gathering is held at Dunoon each August. Pop., 8,780.

DUNSANY [dŭn-sā′nē], **EDWARD JOHN MORETON DRAX PLUNKETT, 18TH BARON** (1878–1957), prolific writer of plays, poetry, novels, and short stories. Born in London of Irish parents, he was educated at Eton and Sandhurst. Most of his work takes the reader into what he calls "the mysterious kingdoms where geography ends and fairyland begins." Ireland's Abbey Theatre brought him his first prominence with its production of *The Glittering Gate* in 1909. Thereafter he had more than 50 books published. One of his most famous plays is *A Night at an Inn* (1916). His autobiography, *Patches of Sunlight*, appeared in 1938.

DUNSINANE [dŭn-sĭ-nān'], castle where Macbeth makes his last stand in Shakespeare's play. Macbeth is made falsely secure when the witches tell him not to fear defeat "until Great Birnam wood to high Dunsinane hill shall come against him."
See also MACBETH.

DUNS SCOTUS [dŭnz skō'təs], **JOHN** (c.1265–1308), medieval theologian, often called "The Subtle Doctor" (*Doctor Subtilis*). He was born in Scotland and is an important figure in the development of Western thought, since his philosophical and theological writings were widely studied in European universities until the Renaissance.

According to tradition, Scotus studied at Paris in 1293, after entering the Franciscan Order of Friars Minor. In 1296 he went to Oxford, where he lectured on the *Sentences* of Peter Lombard. In 1302 Duns Scotus returned to Paris, but was banished shortly afterward by King Philip the Fair for having supported the papal party. The last six years of his life were spent in teaching at Oxford, Paris, and finally in Cologne, where he died.

Although his philosophy is often regarded as being excessively complicated, many distinguished writers of such disparate backgrounds and beliefs as the Jesuit poet Father Gerard Manley Hopkins and the German existentialist philosopher Martin Heidegger have praised it highly for its insights and originality. Others have seen in Scotus anticipation of the contemporary phenomenology developed by Edmund Husserl.

In the Platonic tradition, Scotus held that the present condition of the human intellect united with a body is an unnatural one, and possibly the effect of sin. The primary object of our intellect is being. Hence the desire to know God as cause of all being is basic to the human intelligence. But the intellect does not in virtue of its own constitution possess any innate knowledge of God. All human knowledge must arise from sensation; so in this life the intellect has the power of knowing God only as He is revealed through His creatures.

Scotus was convinced that unless there is a concept of being which unites God and His creatures, no knowledge of God is possible. Otherwise every argument from creatures to the existence of God would involve the fallacy of equivocation. He insisted that it is possible to form a concept of being that would be applicable to both infinite being and to finite being, without necessary reference to either.

In ethics, Scotus insisted far more upon the primacy of the divine will than most of his medieval contemporaries did. According to Scotus, only those commandments regarding reverence to God are absolutely necessary, since they alone arise from man's natural inferiority to God. The other laws expressed in the Decalogue are not based upon the intrinsic order of things, but rather on the inscrutable divine will. For this reason, Scotus' ethics has often been called voluntaristic.

His many theological writings, stressing the absolute liberty of God and His infinite love for man, have an intense and highly personal nature.

R. W. MULLIGAN, S.J., Loyola University, Chicago

DUNSTABLE [dŭn'stə-bəl], **JOHN** (c.1385–1453), eminent English composer, born probably in Dunstable, Bedfordshire. The leading English composer of his time, Dunstable was also an astronomer and a mathematician. He was musician and canon to John, Duke of Bedford and later Regent of France, as well as a canon of Hereford Cathedral and Putson Minor. More than 50 works by Dunstable are extant, including Masses, motets, and secular pieces. Among the most widely known are the motet *Veni sancte spiritus* and the chansons *Puisque m'amour* and *O rosa bella*. Vol. VIII of *Musica Britannica*, edited by Manfred Bukofzer (1953), contains a complete edition of Dunstable's works. Tinctoris, the Renaissance theorist, testified to Dunstable's great influence upon his contemporaries by hailing the composer as "chief . . . of a new art." The most influential aspects of Dunstable's style were the emphasis on sonority, a by-product of English discant style (characterized by improvised sixth-chords, such as G-B-E, A-C-F), and on a feeling for the harmonic relationships between chordal structures.

Consult Bukofzer, Manfred, "John Dunstable; a Quincentenary Report," *The Musical Quarterly* (Jan., 1954).

EILEEN SOUTHERN, Brooklyn College

See also ENGLISH MUSIC.

DUNSTABLE, municipal borough and residential town of southern Bedfordshire, England. Printing, brewing, and engineering are leading industries, replacing an ancient straw-weaving craft. It is the center of the British weather forecasting service. Dunstable stood at the crossing of two important Roman roads and possesses a fine 12th-century priory church. Whipsnade Zoo is nearby. Inc., 1864; pop., 25,618.

DUNSTAN [dŭn'stən], **ST.** (c.909–988), the most popular English saint before Thomas à Becket. He went from the household of King Athelstan of Wessex to the monastery of Glastonbury, where he became abbot (c.943). A strict reformer along Benedictine lines, he led the revival of Anglo-Saxon monasticism and scholarship. He became Bishop of Worcester and London in 957, and Archbishop of Canterbury in 959. He worked for reform in church and state, and was expert in music, metal-work, and illumination.

DUODECIMAL [dū-ō-děs'ə-məl] **SYSTEM,** in mathematics, a number system based on 12 rather than 10. The system has been suggested because of the prevalence of units of twelve in our culture. Days, hours, and minutes can be easily subdivided into units of twelve.

The numerical system 0, 1, 2, . . . 9, X, E is used to express the duodecimal system. Thus, 235X represents $(2 \times 12^3) + (3 \times 12^2) + (5 \times 12) + (10 \times 1)$ or 3,958. This system would also make it possible to express more common fractions with a finite number of digits; ⅚, which is represented in the decimal system by 0.83333 . . . , is 0.X.

DUODENAL ULCER. *See* ULCERS.

DUPLEIX [*dü-plĕks'*], **JOSEPH FRANÇOIS, MARQUIS** (1697–1763), Governor of the French possessions in India. After 20 years' service with the French East India Company, Dupleix was appointed Governor of Pondicherry in south India (1742) and given control of all French interests on the subcontinent. It was largely due to his brilliant diplomacy and hard work that the French were able to challenge British domination in India. Aware that the Mogul Empire had lost effective control, especially in the south, he reasoned that the road to power was through the courts of the various state rulers who were asserting their independence. Dupleix decided to leave the coastal strip, where the other European powers were struggling for control, and concentrate French activities in the interior, principally in the state of Hyderabad.

To accomplish his purpose, Dupleix trained Indians to fight in armies led by European officers, and found that involvement in the affairs of Indian rulers allowed him to wage war against his English rivals even when the home countries were at peace. The first great check to his power was given by Robert Clive in 1751, when the British won decisive battles from the French in south India. Dupleix was recalled by the French government in 1754 for his apparent failure to maintain the French position and for needlessly provoking war. Any real possibility of French hegemony in India was ended, for the superiority of British sea power combined with Clive's successes gave Great Britain a decisive advantage.

AINSLIE T. EMBREE, Columbia University

DUPLESSIS [*dü-plĕ-sē'*], **MAURICE LE NOBLET** (1890–1959), Canadian politician, Premier of Quebec. A lawyer, he entered politics in 1927 and in 1933 was chosen leader of the provincial Conservative party. He became premier in 1936 as head of the Union Nationale party, which he had formed earlier the same year. His party was defeated in 1939 but won the election in 1944, and he thereafter remained Premier until his death. It is said that he was more enthusiastically acclaimed by his party followers and more bitterly criticized by his many political foes than any other man in contemporary Canadian politics, especially in regard to his uncompromising stand against any encroachments on Quebec's constitutional autonomy.

DUPLICATION OF A CUBE, in mathematics, the famous classical problem: to construct a cube whose volume shall be double that of a given cube, using only compass and straight edge. Algebraic analysis has demonstrated the impossibility of performing the desired construction. When instruments other than straight edge and compass are allowed, a variety of constructions is possible.

DU PONT [*dū pŏnt'*], American family of Delaware, generally considered the most influential in American industry. The Frenchman Pierre Samuel du Pont de Nemours

E. I. du Pont de Nemours & Co.

Éleuthère Irénée du Pont, founder of E. I. du Pont de Nemours & Company, from a painting by Rembrandt Peale.

(q.v.) established (1799) the family in the United States, and his son ÉLEUTHÈRE IRÉNÉE DU PONT (1771–1834) founded (1802) the industrial dynasty when he opened a gunpowder plant near Wilmington. The founder's son HENRY DU PONT (1812–89) expanded E. I. du Pont de Nemours & Company during the Civil War and, with the aid of the closely knit family, he organized (1872) the Gunpowder Trade Association, commonly known as the Gunpowder Trust. By the 1880's it controlled more than 90% of explosives production. Henry's successor, EUGENE DU PONT (d.1902), headed the company from 1889 to 1900, a period of expansion for the firm. In 1902 ALFRED IRÉNÉE DU PONT (1864–1935) and his cousins THOMAS COLEMAN DU PONT (1863–1930) and PIERRE SAMUEL DU PONT (1870–1954) reorganized the company. They subsequently made their family pre-eminent in state journalism, politics, and public affairs. The tremendous profits amassed by the Du Ponts from World War I were invested largely in the General Motors Corporation. Through German dye trust patents seized by the United States, the Du Pont company pyramided a vast fortune and controlled the production of dyes, nitrogen, nylon, plastics, and other chemical materials.

JOHN DUNBAR, Editor and Writer

DU PONT, SAMUEL FRANCIS (1803–65), American naval officer. Du Pont established 13 blockading stations in the Civil War, but his failure to take Charleston, S.C., generated a controversy that ended in his retirement from active duty. Grandson of Pierre Samuel du Pont de Nemours, he was born in Bergen Point, N.J., became a midshipman in 1815, served in the Mediterranean, and helped to organize the United States Naval Academy in 1845. In the Mexican War, commanding the *Cyane*, he was active in securing the California coast. He was a member of the Lighthouse Board (1852–57), meanwhile being promoted to captain (1855). In Sept., 1861, Du Pont was assigned command of the South Atlantic Blockading Squadron and in November took Port Royal, S.C., for which action he was promoted to rear admiral in July, 1862. After instituting the effective blockade, he was ordered, against his wishes, to attack Charleston and was repulsed with heavy losses (Apr. 7, 1863).

DU PONT DE NEMOURS [də nə-moor'], **PIERRE SAMUEL** (1739–1817), French author, statesman, and economist of the free-trade school. After brief service as secretary of the Polish Council of Public Instruction, he returned to France (1774) to advise his friend Anne Robert Jacques Turgot, the Controller General of Finance, on economic policy. For the Foreign Minister, the Comte de Vergennes, he negotiated the recognition of the newly independent United States (1783) and supervised a trade agreement with England (1786). Elected president (1790) of the Constituent Assembly during the early part of the French Revolution, he later became unpopular because of his conservative views and was forced into hiding.

He re-entered public life after the Reign of Terror, opposing the Jacobins in the Council of Five Hundred until, disappointed, he left France for the United States (1799). Du Pont was greatly esteemed by President Thomas Jefferson for the views on education presented in his *Sur l'éducation nationale dans les États-Unis* (On National Education in the United States), 1800. Returning to France (1802), he became councilor of state after the fall of Napoleon (1814). In 1815 he went again to the United States, where he died. In America his family established the great industrial dynasty that is still influential.

RALPH H. BOWEN, Northern Illinois University
See also DU PONT.

DUPRÉ [dü-prā'], **MARCEL** (1886–   ), French organist and composer, born in Rouen. He was a brilliant student at the Paris Conservatory. In 1906 he became assistant organist to Charles Widor at the Church of St. Sulpice in Paris, and later was first organist at Notre Dame (1916–22). He achieved world-wide fame in 1920 by performing from memory the complete works of J. S. Bach in 10 recitals. Subsequently he toured London and the United States, and in 1934 succeeded Widor as organist at St. Sulpice. Excelling as musician, teacher, and composer, he has been particularly acclaimed for his rich and extensive improvisations on the organ.

DUQUESNE [doo-kān'], steel-manufacturing city of southwestern Pennsylvania, on the Monongahela River, near Pittsburgh. The city is located on the slopes overlooking the Carnegie-Illinois steel plant, which occupies the river flats. The residents of Duquesne are primarily of Slavic descent and work in the mills. Inc. as a city, 1910; pop. (1950) 17,620; (1960) 15,019.

DUQUESNE, FORT, post completed by the French in 1754 on the site of present-day Pittsburgh. In order to enforce trade monopolies that the French government had granted to Canadian traders, France sent troops into western New York, Pennsylvania, and the Ohio Valley. This challenged the claims of the Ohio Company, a Virginia land company

that included Governor Robert Dinwiddie and George Washington. In 1753 Dinwiddie had sent Washington with Virginian troops to demand French withdrawal, but the French responded by forcing them back and erecting Fort Duquesne, named after the Canadian governor. Great Britain took up Virginia's cause, sending Gen. Edward Braddock to take the Fort, but his troops were ambushed (July 9, 1755) and Braddock was killed. Fort Duquesne was crucial in the British campaign in the west during the conclusive war that followed. The British finally took the stronghold in 1758, paving the way for the capture of forts Frontenac and Niagara and the ultimate conquest of all of Canada.

RICHARD M. ABRAMS, Columbia University

DU QUOIN [doo-koin'], manufacturing and agricultural trade center of southwestern Illinois, 20 mi. north of Carbondale. In both a bituminous coal mining and an agricultural area (general farming, dairying, and fruit), Du Quoin has important manufacturing plants, which produce explosives and machinery and process agricultural goods. Inc., 1861; pop. (1950) 7,147; (1960) 6,558.

DURANCE [dü-räNs'] **RIVER,** river of southeastern France. It rises near Mount Genèvre Pass, between the Cottian and Dauphiné Alps, and flows southwest past Briançon before sweeping in a westward loop to join the Rhône near Avignon. The Durance, in its upper course, and its tributaries cut through gorges and provide hydroelectric power. The lower course of the Durance, passing through farmland, is used for irrigation canals and for the Marseilles water supply.

DURAND [dü-rănd'], **ASHER BROWN** (1796–1886), American painter and member of the Hudson River school (q.v.). He was born in Jefferson Village (now Maplewood), N.J. Durand abandoned a profitable career in engraving to become a painter. With his engraver's eye for detail and a painter's feeling for light and atmosphere, he created scenes of airy space and solitude in the style of romantic realism. His works include "Kindred Spirits" (New York City Public Library), which shows the painter Thomas Cole and William Cullen Bryant standing on a cliff that overlooks a stream in the Catskills; "The Capture of Major André" (Worcester Art Museum); and "The Wrath of Peter Stuyvesant" (New York Historical Society, New York City).

DURAND LINE, boundary line betweeen Afghanistan and Pakistan. It was decided upon in 1893 by a British commission under Sir Mortimer Durand to demarcate British India from Afghanistan. Realizing that they were unable to subdue Afghanistan, the British believed it was to their advantage to make it a buffer state between India and Russia. The problem of defining a boundary on India's northwest frontier was complicated, however, by the fiercely independent Pathan (Pushtun) tribesmen who inhabited the area and who refused allegiance to either side. War between Afghanistan and British India seemed imminent until Durand's commission worked out a line that divided the tribal area between India and Afghanistan. The Durand line later became the border between Afghanistan and Pakistan, though the tribesmen on both sides were never reconciled to separation from their kin.

DURANGO [dōo-răng′gō], interior state of northwestern Mexico. The Sierra Madre Occidental in western Durango, dissected by streams flowing to the Pacific, has temperate forests of oaks and pines. A central zone of subhumid grasslands is devoted to ranching and farming. The east is predominantly steppe and desert except for the lands irrigated from the Río Nazas. Mining is important; Durango leads the Mexican states in iron, and considerable gold, silver, and lead are also obtained. Capital, Durango; area, 47,679 sq. mi.; pop., 760,836.

DURANGO, officially **VICTORIA DE DURANGO,** capital and largest city of Durango State, Mexico. A commercial and industrial city, it is the center for an extensive agricultural, ranching, lumbering, and mining area. Silver, lead, zinc, and copper mines are nearby, and the Cerro de Mercado, the chief source of iron ore in Mexico, is situated on the city's northern outskirts. Durango is an important railroad center and the crossroads for the Matamoros-Mazatlán and Ciudad Juárez–Mexico City highways. It is also a resort city with a warm, sunny climate. Durango, founded in 1563, was for more than two centuries the capital of Nueva Vizcaya Province, which comprised much of northern New Spain. It became an episcopal city in 1623 and the seat of an Archbishop in 1891. Pop., 97,520.

DURANGO, city of southwestern Colorado, and seat of La Plata County, in rugged country of lofty peaks and farmlands. Although visited by Spaniards in early colonial years and by gold prospectors in 1859–61, the Durango-site gold finds promoted permanent occupancy only after 1872. A narrow-gauge railroad was extended into town to transport silver and gold ores from Silverton mines to the Durango smelter. Oil and gas exploration and operation in the Four Corners area (where four states adjoin), as well as uranium and vanadium mining, have

enhanced the economy of Durango. The narrow-gauge railroad still runs between Durango and Silverton, and a wagon road cut across the San Juan Mountains was developed into the present Million-Dollar Highway, linking Durango with Silverton and Ouray. Inc., 1881; pop. (1950) 7,459; (1960) 10,530.

DURANT [dū-rănt′], **WILLIAM CRAPO** (1861–1947), American automobile manufacturer, pioneer of General Motors Corporation. Durant, born in Boston, grew up in Flint, Mich., where, in 1886, he established the successful Durant-Dort Carriage Company. He founded the Buick Motor Car Company in 1905 and in 1908 the General Motors Company, into which he absorbed the Buick, the Olds, the Oakland, the Cadillac, and the Northway automobile companies. After attempting unsuccessfully to buy out Henry Ford, he organized (1915) the Chevrolet Motor Company, which was acquired (1918) by General Motors Corporation. In 1921, having sold his controlling interest in General Motors, he established Durant Motors, Inc.

DURANT, WILLIAM JAMES (1885–   ), American author and educator. Born in North Adams, Mass., he was educated at St. Peter's College in New Jersey and at Columbia University. His *Story of Philosophy* (1926) became a remarkable best seller. In 1932 he began a monumental history of civilization, and by 1965 *The Age of Voltaire*, the ninth volume of the undertaking, had appeared.

DURANT, city of southern Oklahoma, and seat of Bryan County, located in the Red River Valley. It is a trade center for a rich agricultural area. Southeastern State College is located in Durant. Pop. (1950) 10,541; (1960) 10,467.

DURAZNO [dōo-räs′nō], capital of Durazno Department, Uruguay, 105 mi. north of Montevideo. Situated on the Río Yí, a major tributary of the Río Uruguay, Durazno is a cattle and wheat center. Gen. José Fructuoso Rivera, first President of Uruguay, founded the city in 1821, hoping to make it the capital of the republic. Pop., 27,000.

DURAZZO. *See* DURRËS.

DURBAN [dûr′bən], major seaport and industrial city of the Republic of South Africa, facing the Indian Ocean, and largest city of Natal Province. Durban's southern boundary is the Bluff, a range of green hills curving around the south side of land-locked Durban Bay. The city itself has grown on the flatland north of the bay and sprawls westward and northward over hills. Along the ocean front stand most of Durban's luxury hotels and apartment houses. The Marine Parade, a 3-mi. stretch of parks, beaches, and playgrounds, has helped to make Durban the foremost winter resort of southern Africa.

Modern harbor facilities and rapid road and train connections with the Witwatersrand make Durban an important shipping center. Its port handles more tonnage than all other South African ports combined. The city is also a major railroad and internal airways terminus.

Durban lies in the center of Natal's sugar belt and has many sugar-processing plants. Large chemical plants and an oil refinery have been established here. Manufactures

View of the Marine Parade, Durban, South Africa. (OWEN—BIRNBACK)

Alte Pinacothek, Munich

"The Four Apostles" by Dürer is in the Alte Pinacothek, Munich.

National Gallery of Art, Rosenwald Collection

Dürer's "Melencolia I," a copper engraving (1514).

include fertilizers, paint, rubber, soap, footwear, textiles, and furniture. The headquarters of South Africa's whaling industry is nearby, where from May through November whales are caught and processed for commercial and industrial use.

The University of Natal has one of its two branches here with research institutions for sugar milling and for the wattle and paint industries. Durban also has a university college for Indians, a technical college, and many secondary schools. The high-domed city hall houses an art museum, natural history museum, and the city library, and is the home of the Durban Civic Orchestra.

Durban has a subtropical climate with abundant sunshine through the year. Summer is hot and humid; winter, warm and pleasant. The city is noted for the flamboyance of its vegetation, with banana, pawpaw, and mango trees, and flowers such as the poinsettia and bougainvillea, everywhere. It is a city of many colors, creeds and castes, intermingling Afrikaans- and English-speaking whites, Zulus, and many castes of Indians. The Indian Market, with its exotic oriental atmosphere, is one of the city's tourist attractions.

Durban has a municipal area of 70 sq. mi.; pop., 655,-370.

DANIEL J. VAN NIEKERK, *Information Officer for South African Government in New York*

DÜREN [dü'rən], city of North Rhine–Westphalia, Federal Republic of Germany (West Germany), situated on the Roer River, southwest of Cologne. It has steel works and iron foundries, and paper, cardboard, cloth, carpet, leather, and chemical industries. It was first mentioned in the 8th century as Duria and was an important city under

the Frankish Kings and under Charlemagne. Most of the city was destroyed during World War II but has been largely rebuilt. Pop., 49,138.

DÜRER [dü'rər], **ALBRECHT** (1471–1528), Germany's greatest painter and engraver. With Holbein and Cranach he transformed the Gothic art of North Europe in terms of Renaissance theory and practice and created one of Germany's most brilliant artistic periods. Born in Nuremberg, Dürer was at first destined to be a goldsmith like his father. However, in 1486 he began studying with two local painters, Michael Wolgemut and Wilhelm Pleydenwurf. In the 1490's he traveled through the German states, finding in Colmar a center where he could study the lovingly detailed art of Martin Schongauer and the domestic genre scenes of the so-called Housebook Master.

In 1495, and again in 1505–07, Dürer was in Venice, where he was powerfully influenced by Giovanni Bellini and other Renaissance artists. In Bellini's paintings the ample forms and logical composition formed a striking contrast to the flat, rather crowded work Dürer had known—and produced himself—in Germany. It was in Italy that the artist created his first completely Renaissance paintings: "The Feast of the Rose Garlands" (1506; Prague, National Museum), "The Madonna with the Siskin" (1506; Berlin, Deutsches Museum), and many portraits. In turn Dürer made a memorable impression on North Italian art. Back in Nuremberg in 1507, he painted the two panels of "Adam" and "Eve" now in the Prado, Madrid. Also from this period come the great new print series, for example, "The Apocalypse," and numerous commissions from his patron, Emperor Maximilian I. Among them is an enormous woodcut of a "Triumphal

Arch" and an exquisite prayer book (Munich, Staatsbibliothek), both of 1515.

About this time Dürer began to concentrate more on his graphic production, which is his supreme achievement. His finest works are probably the engravings of "St. Jerome" and "Melencolia I" (both 1514). But despite his printmaking, and a long, eventually mortal illness, in 1526 Dürer produced one of his most celebrated paintings, the two panels of "The Four Apostles" (Munich, Alte Pinacothek). Between 1513 and 1528 he also wrote several essays containing important contributions to the theories of human proportions and geometrical perspective.

While Dürer brought his Italian experience to bear on the crowded forms of Northern Gothic art, making them simpler and solider, his work retained a linear elegance and joyful German profusion of detail. This is especially true of the "Madonna with Animals" (c.1503, Vienna, Albertina), and many other delightful, lightly colored pen drawings. It was this fusion of certain tendencies in Late Gothic with the revolutionary ideas of the Renaissance that constituted Dürer's achievement. It was an achievement that gave character to vast areas of North European art in the 16th century. Prints by Dürer are in museums all over the world, the largest collections being in Germany and Austria. It is there, too, that most of the paintings are found, especially in Dresden and Vienna.

Consult Panofsky, Erwin, *The Life and Art of Albrecht Dürer* (4th ed., 1955).

GEORGE LEONARD HERSHEY, Bucknell University

DURESS [dŏŏ-rĕs', dyŏŏr'ĭs], in law, signifies unlawful coercion by which a person is forced to do an act or refrain from doing it against his own free will. Mere advice, persuasion, or annoyance do not constitute duress, since free choice, or volition, is not destroyed. Also, duress should not be confused with emotional or physical distress, which is not legal duress. There is, however, duress in any unlawful imprisonment, or in a lawful imprisonment for an unlawful purpose, such as a forced confession.

As a rule, acts performed under duress are legally null and void. If a testator makes a will under duress, often called "undue influence," it can later be voided by his next of kin. A contract executed under duress can also be rendered a nullity. An act, otherwise criminal, when committed under actual physical compulsion is excusable. In the past, a wife who committed a crime in her husband's presence was presumed to have done so by his coercion. The presumption, however, was rebuttable, and did not apply to murder and treason. Today, it has been largely abandoned. Duress of a wife by her husband, however, is still a defense if it can be shown.

ROBERT B. MAUTZ, University of Florida, College of Law

DURGA, Hindu goddess usually regarded as the wife of Shiva. The name is one of many used to represent the female or active aspect of the godhead. As Durga, the goddess is recognized in both destructive and beneficent forms. In Hindu iconography she is depicted as a ten-armed goddess in battle against the forces of evil. Today she is worshiped mainly in her beneficent form. The festival of Durga (*puja*), held annually in September or October, is the occasion for family reunions and celebrations.

DURHAM [dûr'əm], **JOHN GEORGE LAMBTON, 1ST EARL OF** (1792–1840), British statesman. A strong advocate of reform, he was known in his time as "Radical Jack." He served as a Liberal member of Parliament from 1813 to 1832. In the Whig administration of 1830–34, Durham was Lord Privy Seal and a member of the small Cabinet committee that drafted the Reform Bill of 1832, which redistributed the seats in the House of Commons and extended the franchise to include more members of the middle classes. He played a key role in the months of struggle that preceded the passage of the bill. From 1835 to 1837 Durham served as ambassador to Russia. In 1838 he was appointed high commissioner for the adjustment of constitutional questions in Canada and Governor General of the British provinces in North America. Arriving shortly after the end of the Rebellion of 1837, he attempted to conciliate the various factions but met with such bitter opposition in England that he resigned after only five months in Canada. His *Report on the Affairs of British North America*, submitted to Parliament in 1839, became a guide not only for his successors in Canada but for British statesmen dealing with questions of colonial self-government in all parts of the world. The report advocated among other changes, the development of responsible government wherein the executive would be dependent on an elected legislature.

ASA BRIGGS, University of Leeds

DURHAM, county of northeastern England, bounded on the west by the Pennine Chain and on the east by the North Sea. The northern boundary is formed by the Tyne and Derwent rivers and the southern by the Tees River. The economy is largely based on the extensive resources of coal. Mining towns, such as Houghton-le-Spring and Seaham, are characteristic of eastern Durham. Gateshead, Jarrow, South Shields, Sunderland, and West Hartlepool, all engaged in coal export, shipbuilding and ship repairing, and iron and steel manufacture, are located along the coast and navigable reaches of the Tyne and Wear rivers. In southern Durham, Billingham is the center of a great chemical industry, and Stockton and Darlington are important for their heavy industries. Durham, the county town, is located on an elevated site above a meander of the Wear River and has the status of a city. Five county boroughs are separated from the administrative county: Sunderland, South Shields, West Hartlepool, Gateshead, and Darlington.

In Roman times the area was heavily fortified and it became part of the Saxon kingdom of Northumbria in 547 A.D. After the Norman Conquest (1066), it became a county palatine under the Bishops of Durham. Durham suffered from the incursions of the Scots as late as the 17th century. Jurisdiction of the county palatine was vested in the Crown in 1836.

Coal mining and export were well established by the end of the 14th century, but great expansion came with the Industrial Revolution. The increased demand for coal, coupled with improved mining techniques and communications, led to rapid exploitation of resources. Administrative county, area, 970 sq. mi.; pop., 903,159; with county boroughs, area, 1,015 sq. mi.; pop., 1,517,039.

BRYAN E. COATES, The University, Sheffield

DURHAM, municipal borough and county town of Durham, in northern England, on the Wear River. It is an administration center and has headquarters of county government and county bodies. A rock promontory rises steeply above a loop in the river; on the narrow isthmus at its northern end, a natural defensive site, Durham's cathedral, castle, and monastery were built. The site of Durham was chosen for the shrine of St. Cuthbert in 995, and in 1070 William the Conqueror selected it for a fortress and bulwark against the Scots. A fortress with four gates and lofty embattled walls was built in the 12th century, and new walls encompassing a larger area were constructed in the 14th century. The monastic cathedral adjoins the fortress and is Durham's most magnificent edifice. It was built almost entirely between 1093 and 1133 in the Romanesque style. The streets, the buildings, the bridges, all speak of the long and eventful history of the town. In 1832 the University of Durham was founded and occupied the buildings of the castle, until then the seat of the Earl-Bishops of Durham. The ancient city is now surrounded by coal-mining settlements. Inc., 1602; pop., 20,484.

BRYAN E. COATES, The University, Sheffield

DURHAM, unincorporated village of southeastern New Hampshire, just south of Dover. The University of New Hampshire (estab., 1866) is located here. Settled in 1635, Durham suffered greatly during the Indian Wars and was destroyed by Indians in 1694. Pop. (1950) 4,172; (1960) 4,688.

DURHAM, industrial, educational, and medical center in North Carolina, and seat of Durham County. Construction of the North Carolina Railroad (1852–56) and the formation of the American Tobacco Company (1890) gave impetus to its growth. It is the nation's tobacco capital, manufacturing about one-fourth of the cigarettes in the United States. The home plant of Liggett and Myers Tobacco Company is here. Cotton textile and hosiery mills are also important. Internationally famous Duke University and its hospital, endowed by an $80,000,000 bequest of James Buchanan Duke in 1925, are an outgrowth of the earlier (1838) Trinity College. The university has two architecturally renowned campuses—the Women's, Georgian in style, and the Men's, Tudor. Durham is also the site of North Carolina College and the largest Negro-owned insurance company in the world. Pop. (1950) 71,311; (1960) 78,302; urb. area (1950) 73,368; (1960) 84,642.

BLACKWELL P. ROBINSON, Woman's College of the University of North Carolina

DURNOVARIA, ancient Roman name of Dorchester (q.v.).

DUROCHER [də-rō′shər], **LEO ERNEST ("LIPPY LEO")** (1905–), American baseball player and manager, born in West Springfield, Mass. He was a brilliant defensive shortstop for New York of the American League, and Cincinnati, St. Louis, and Brooklyn of the National League during his career as a major-league player, which began in 1925. As manager, he led Brooklyn to a pennant in 1941, and New York of the National League to championships in 1951 and 1954. He was a fiery, savagely articulate competitor. In 1961 he became a coach for Los Angeles of the National League.

DURRA. *See* SORGHUM.

DURRELL [dûrl], **LAWRENCE GEORGE** (1912–), British writer. Born in India of Irish ancestry, he served in the British Foreign Service for many years. He published his first book, *Ten Poems*, in 1933. *The Black Book* (1938) is his best-known early novel. Durrell emerged from relative obscurity to international fame with the publication of "The Alexandria Quartet." These four novels—*Justine* (1957), *Balthazar* (1958), *Mountolive* (1958), and *Clea* (1960)—are all set in exotic Alexandria and present the same characters and events from four different viewpoints.

DÜRRENMATT [dŏŏr′ən-mät], **FRIEDRICH** (1921–), Swiss playwright and novelist. His plays, chiefly tragicomedies combining the macabre and comic in expressionist forms, include *Romulus der Grosse* (Romulus the Great), 1949; *Ein Engel kommt nach Babylon* (An Angel Comes to Babylon), 1953; and *Der Besuch der alten Dame*, 1956 (*The Visit*, 1958), successfully produced in the United States. His novels, which deal mainly with crime on a philosophical level, include *Die Panne*, 1956 (*Traps*, 1960).

DÜRRES [dŏŏr′rəs] (Ital. **DURAZZO**), city of Albania, on the Adriatic coast, about 20 mi. west of Tiranë. The port was originally built by Italy, though the city is Muslim with many mosques. The city has a railroad connection with Tiranë and is the main gateway for Albanian tobacco and olive oil. Pop., 34,000.

DUR SHARRUKIN [dŏŏr shä-rŏŏ′kĭn] ("Sargon's Fort"), ancient Assyrian city, represented by modern Khorsabad, 12 mi. northeast of Mosul, Iraq. The city was founded c.710 B.C. by Sargon II as a fortified capital to protect Assyria from invasion from the north. Khorsabad was excavated in 1843 by Paul Émile Botta and in 1851–55 by Victor Place; but most of their finds were lost when the boats carrying them sank in the Tigris. The city was again excavated between 1929 and 1935 by an expedition from the Oriental Institute of Chicago.

DURYEA [dŏŏr′yā], **CHARLES EDGAR** (1861–1938) **and J. FRANK** (1870–), brothers who opened the era of the American automobile when their gasoline-fueled car drove through the streets of Springfield, Mass., in Sept., 1893. Charles, who had sold and repaired bicycles in his native Illinois, probably conceived of the design, and J. Frank, a machinist, carried out the construction, making design modifications. A bitter debate between the brothers has not clarified the question of contribution. The first car had a two-cycle gasoline engine; the 1895 model, largely of J. Frank's design, won the Chicago *Times Herald* race, with a four-cycle, water-cooled engine. The brothers separated after an unsuccessful auto manufacturing venture, with Charles becoming a writer and consultant on automobiles and J. Frank building the Stevens-Duryea car.

THOMAS P. HUGHES, Washington and Lee University

DURYEA, coal-mining borough of northeastern Pennsylvania, in the Lackawanna Valley. Textiles are also manufactured here. Settled in 1845, the town was called Babel for a time because of the many languages of the immigrant miners. Inc., 1891; pop. (1950) 6,655; (1960) 5,626.

DUSE [dōō'zā], **ELEONORA** (1859–1924), Italian actress, daughter of a theatrical family, born in a train en route between Venice and Vigevano. She first went on the stage when four years old. Her adult success came in 1878, after which the celebrated actor Ernesto Rossi made her his leading lady. She became the most admired Italian actress, appearing in a wide range of plays that included Goldoni's *The Lady of the Inn,* Dumas' *Camille,* and Sardou's *La Tosca* and *Let's Get a Divorce.* In 1885 she played in South America and in 1895 in London, acting Sudermann's *Magda* in the same week Sarah Bernhardt undertook the same role. Bernard Shaw preferred Duse, a judgment that was disputed by Max Beerbohm, his successor on the *Saturday Review,* but shared by the American critic Stark Young.

Duse was intense and darkly beautiful, less flagrantly theatrical than Bernhardt, more intellectual, more subtle, and more interested in such serious new dramatists as Ibsen. She became attached to the poet Gabriele d'Annunzio and acted in his plays, including *La Gioconda* in 1898 and *The Dead City.* Her interest in d'Annunzio's plays outlasted their popular success. In Florence in 1906, she acted in Ibsen's *Rosmersholm,* under the direction of the noted stage innovator Gordon Craig. After retiring in 1913, she went back to the stage in 1923 and died in Pittsburgh on her only American tour.

Eleonora Duse, the world-renowned Italian tragedienne.
(CULVER PICTURES, INC.)

Consult Signorelli, Olga, *Eleonora Duse* (1959); Le Gallienne, Eva, *The Mystic in the Theatre: Eleonora Duse* (1966).

HENRY POPKIN, Editor,
Concise Encyclopedia of Modern Drama

DUSHANBE [dū-shän'bĕ], city of the Soviet Union and capital of the Tadzhik S.S.R. It is located in the southern part of Soviet Central Asia, less than 90 mi. from the Afghanistan border. In addition to its administrative function, the city is a major commercial and industrial center serving a rich hinterland specializing in the production of cotton and other irrigated crops. Its industries, which are the most important in Tadzhikstan, are predominantly in the textile and food sectors. The largest establishment is an integrated cotton textile combine. Since World War II the manufacture of machinery has developed rapidly.

Dushanbe, which was known as Dyushambe until 1929 and then as Stalinabad until 1961, is essentially a Soviet creation, for it had a population of less than 5,000 in 1924 when it became the capital of the Tadzhik A.S.S.R. By 1939 its population had increased to 83,000. Its most rapid growth, however, came during World War II and the postwar period, with the development of cotton textile production and machinery fabrication. The city is the site of the Tadzhik State University; the Academy of Sciences of the Tadzhik S.S.R.; and four higher institutes, in the medical, agricultural, polytechnical, and pedagogical fields. It also has three theaters, including one for the state opera and ballet. Pop., 224,000.

ALLAN L. RODGERS, Pennsylvania State University

DÜSSELDORF [dōō'səl-dôrf], city in the Federal Republic of Germany (West Germany) and capital of North Rhine-Westphalia, on the right bank of the Rhine River, 38 mi. north of Bonn. It developed in the 12th century, though for many centuries it was overshadowed by its neighbor, Cologne. In 1511 it became the seat of the dukes of Berg and began to assume the character and appearance of a small, princely, German capital city. Later it was attached to the Palatinate and served as the residence of the Elector Palatine. The Elector Johann Wilhelm (1690–1716) laid out the planned Neustadt (New City) of Düsseldorf. It was occupied by the French in 1795. In 1806 Napoleon made it the capital of a puppet state, the Grand Duchy of Berg. At the end of the Napoleonic Wars, in 1814, it passed to Prussia. Many of the medieval buildings of Düsseldorf had been destroyed to make way for the 18th-century plans of the Electors Palatine. Their structures in turn were severely damaged by bombing during World War II. Düsseldorf has been rebuilt. Today it has an attractive, well-planned center and extensive industrial suburbs.

During the mid-19th century, Düsseldorf became an important center of heavy industry. The manufacture and fabrication of steel, in the suburbs, have remained basic to the economy, though there are large chemical, textile, and clothing industries as well. Düsseldorf is the administrative headquarters of several heavy-industry complexes and is an important Rhine port. Pop., 699,220.

NORMAN J. G. POUNDS, Indiana University

A dust storm near Springfield, Colorado, May 21, 1937.

USDA

DUST, fine-grained, solid particles easily dispersed in air. Dust is of both organic and inorganic origin, and a small amount is present in the air at all times. Refraction of light by minute dust particles produces the blue color of the sky. Were it not for dust in the air the earth's climate would be more severe, with greater extremes of temperature and less frequent rainfall, since dust particles serve as centers of condensation for droplets of moisture. Dust tends to settle out of still air, whereas rapidly moving air picks up and transports available dust. Fine particles that reach the upper atmosphere, where the air is always in motion, remain suspended indefinitely.

Dust has many sources. Some reaches the earth from outer space or from the burning of meteorites in the atmosphere, but most comes from the earth itself. The weathering of rocks yields much fine debris that is incorporated in soil. In arid and semiarid regions, especially where overgrazing or plowing has exposed the soil, high winds lift vast amounts of fine soil, often producing dust storms. Millions of tons of dust are thrown into the atmosphere by volcanic eruptions; in 1883 the explosion of Krakatoa, in Indonesia, produced a dark column 30 mi. high and it perceptibly increased the amount of atmospheric dust over most of the earth for three years. Deposits of volcanic dust, called tuff, are recognized among sedimentary rocks in all parts of the world. Organic dust particles are chiefly pollen grains, some varieties of which cause hay fever and other allergic reactions in many people. Inhaling excessive quantities of dust causes certain lung diseases, including silicosis, which affects miners and others working with siliceous rock. Dust erodes machinery, and in many industries delicate instruments must be protected by air-filtering systems.

STEPHEN E. CLABAUGH, University of Texas
See also DUST STORM.

DUST BOWL, name applied, especially in the 1930's, to a region of prevailing dust storms in the semiarid Great Plains of the United States, extending from Kansas and Colorado to middle Texas. The severe droughts of 1933, 1934 (worst ever recorded), 1935, and 1936 provided ideal conditions for dust storms in this area. Vast quantities of topsoil, transformed by drought into dust, were transported great distances by high winds. These storms destroyed crops, denuded fields of topsoil, piled dust on roads and buildings, and forced many farmers to leave the region. Rain and conservation practices helped to make the Dust Bowl productive again in the late 1930's and early 1940's. Drought conditions in the early 1950's once more caused dust storms in the Great Plains.
See also NATURAL RESOURCES, CONSERVATION OF.

DUST CLOUD HYPOTHESIS. *See* COSMOLOGY; SOLAR SYSTEM; UNIVERSE.

DUST DEVIL. *See* WHIRLWIND.

DUSTIN, HANNAH (1657–?1729), American pioneer housewife, famous Indian captive. She was born Hannah Emerson, probably in Haverhill, Mass., and there married Thomas Dustin. When Indians raided Haverhill in Mar., 1697, she was in her house with a week-old baby and a nurse, while her husband and their seven other children were nearby. The husband and children escaped, but Hannah and the nurse were taken captive; her baby was brained against a tree as she watched. After several days' march through the snow, the Indian party reached an island at the junction of the Contoocook and Merrimack rivers, where they planned to rest for a few days. Hannah immediately laid plans to escape with the nurse and an English boy. While the Indians slept, she and the boy killed ten of them, sparing only a squaw and a small child. Then, wanting proof of her exploit, she scalped all ten and made her way to Haverhill. On Apr. 21 she visited Boston to ask compensation for the property she had lost and was awarded £25 by the general court.

RAY A. BILLINGTON, Northwestern University

DUST STORM, turbulent clouds of wind-borne dust covering a large area. Dust storms occur where strong winds blow over loose, dry soil with an inadequate cover of vegetation, so that fine particles can be picked up and carried into the atmosphere. The resulting dust clouds may be several thousand feet high and the finer particles may be carried for hundreds or thousands of miles. Dust storms are frequent in semiarid areas where overgrazing or plowing has exposed the soil, as in the southern Great Plains of the United States. After a long drought in this area during the 1930's there were many severe dust storms that destroyed farm land and forced residents to seek livelihood elsewhere. A dust storm is reported by the U.S. Weather Bureau if blowing dust reduces visibility to less than ⅝ of a mile.

See also DUST; DUST BOWL; SANDSTORM.

DUSTY MILLER, the name applied to several daisylike flowering plants that have distinctly grayish or whitish leaves. Chief among them are *Lychnis coronaria* of the pink family, Caryophyllaceae, and *Artemisia stelleriana*, *Centaurea cineraria*, *C. gymnocarpa*, *Senecio cineraria*, and *S. leucostachys* of the daisy family, Compositae. Dusty millers are planted in gardens primarily for decorative foliage effects, although they also produce colorful, usually small blossoms. With the exception of *A. stelleriana*, those mentioned above will not survive cold winters and in cool climates must either be carried over the winter in greenhouses or raised each year from seed. They grow best in sunny locations in well-drained soil.

DUTCH, a West Germanic language belonging to the Germanic subfamily of the Indo-European family of languages. It is closely related to English, Low and High German, and Frisian. Dutch is spoken by more than 16 million people in the Netherlands, in northern Belgium, and in former and present overseas colonies of the Netherlands. Many dialect varieties can be observed. The dialects spoken in Belgium are usually referred to as Flemish; the northeast Dutch dialects cannot be clearly separated from the dialects of Low German. Afrikaans developed from the dialects of the Dutch settlers in South Africa. The standard written Dutch language is based on the dialect of the province of Holland and its center, Amsterdam. It developed in the 16th and 17th centuries and shows some influence from southern dialects.

The history of Dutch can be divided into three periods. The earliest period (9th to 12th centuries) is called Old Low Franconian, which represents a dialect closely akin to Old Saxon, the oldest stage of Low German. The development of a special Dutch literary language began in the Middle Dutch period (1200–1500) in the areas of Flanders and, later, of Brabant. The Modern Dutch period began in 1500.

HERBERT PENZL, University of Michigan

DUTCH ART AND ARCHITECTURE. It was not until the 17th century that a real division was made between the North and South Netherlands (Flanders) corresponding to the present-day Netherlands and Belgium respectively. But although there was no political boundary, differences in temperament of the two peoples and in their way of life were reflected in their art at least as early as the 14th century.

Painting

The 15th and 16th Centuries. Before 1400 the painting of both Holland and Flanders, like that of most of northern Europe, consisted of illuminated manuscripts and a few mural paintings, which have for the most part perished. The manuscripts, usually prayer books and occasionally secular texts, were decorated either in monasteries by monks or in the courtly circles by gifted artists who were employed to serve the royal families and nobles. These "painter-illuminators"—as contemporary documents call them—had often been trained in cosmopolitan places, especially Paris, before they were summoned to the north. The manuscripts decorated in the province of Gelderland in the northeastern part of the country, for example, show great elegance and sophistication. The influence of a polished imported style is equally evident in panel pictures, which began to appear in great numbers about the beginning of the 15th century.

By 1450, however, Holland had produced a number of painters who must be counted among the most important artists of their time, and who gave evidence in their work of a personality and spirit that is typically Dutch. One major common characteristic is a pervading directness or forthrightness, which is to be observed in the best Dutch art of all periods. It is a compound of sincerity and a realism that does not shrink from representing the commonplace or the ugly, but does so in such a way that beauty results. In the work of the early painters their sincerity of feeling makes their depiction of religious subjects deeply moving, and though their realism may at times lead them to paint crude and naive figures, the people they depict are touching in their awkwardness and seriousness and act out their roles in wonderfully convincing settings.

One of the most Dutch of the 15th-century primitives is the anonymous Master of the Virgin among Virgins, so called because of his painting "Mary with Women Saints" in Amsterdam. His style, which is easily identified in a number of works, shows a high degree of finish, strange melancholy types, and a profoundly religious mood. Dirk Bouts, who emigrated early in his life to Louvain possibly from Haarlem, never lost his solemn earnestness and his simplicity in choice of setting and costume. His powers of observation found excellent expression in a considerable number of penetrating and uncompromising portraits. Gerard David, who also went south to work in Flanders, had come from Oudewater, and unlike Bouts changed his style after he settled in Bruges. Even while retaining his sober outlook, he submitted to the elegant and refining influence of Rogier van der Weyden and the van Eycks, and the pictures he painted after he left Holland became increasingly less Dutch in spirit. Two others of the early Dutch artists are Geertgen tot Sint Jans, who made interesting and courageous experiments in lighting, and his

The Metropolitan Museum of Art, Gift of Henry G. Marquand, 1889

"Young Woman with a Water Jug" by Jan Vermeer (1632–75).

master, Albert van Ouwater of Haarlem, whose works have been largely lost but who was influential as a teacher.

During the 16th century painters of Holland, like those of other northern countries, flocked to Italy, attracted by the marvels of the Italian Renaissance. Returning to Holland, they brought back with them a new enthusiasm for architecture and ornament and an interest in the painting of the nude, which they communicated to their colleagues and pupils. Jan van Scorel, who studied painting in Haarlem and Amsterdam, visited Venice on his way to the Holy Land with a party of pilgrims. He spent several years in Rome, where he came to know the work of Raphael and Michelangelo, whose influences are evident in all the painting he did after his return to Holland and during his long and highly successful career in Utrecht and Haarlem. Cornelis Engelbrechtzen of Leyden and the great Lucas van Leyden, famous as a printmaker as well as a painter, must also be mentioned.

The 17th Century. At the beginning of the 17th century Utrecht became an important center of Dutch art. A group of Dutch admirers of the Italian innovator Caravaggio, whose dramatic effects of light and agitated compositions they followed in their own works, clustered there. Prominent were Dirk van Baburen, Hendrik Terbrugghen, Matthias Stomer, and Gerard van Honthorst, all of whom had studied in Italy.

Freed from the tyranny of Spain, Holland embarked in the 17th century on an era of economic and cultural well-being. Rembrandt van Rijn of Leyden and Jan Vermeer were only two of a host of splendid artists that the newly affluent Dutch burghers prized and sponsored. Rembrandt was a great draftsman and printmaker, as well as a painter, and the most important artist Holland ever produced. It was in the early part of his career, up to about 1642, when he painted the famous "Night Watch," that

Rembrandt was most popular and in demand as a painter of portraits. After this time, though he continued throughout his life to paint his Dutch contemporaries, his style, which had always been serious and forceful, became more complex and difficult to understand. It was also becoming richer and more meaningful, but sitters who primarily sought flattery from their portrait painter turned to the less gifted of rivals of Rembrandt, artists like Bartholomeus van der Helst.

Jan Vermeer of Delft was a contemporary of Rembrandt who gained much fame in his own time, but afterward for some reason was overlooked until his few extant and very beautiful paintings were rediscovered in the 19th century. Although we have from him two extremely fine outdoor scenes, his specialty was the representation of light and space in exquisitely serene interiors, animated by one or more very quiet, concentrating figures who seem to be utterly unaware of the presence of a spectator. Gerard Terborch and Gabriel Metsu were less intense than Vermeer, but their subject matter, like his, was drawn from everyday life as it was lived in the elegant but comfortable surroundings of the secure and wealthy Dutch. Pieter de Hooch also showed the daily life of ordinary people, but usually of a somewhat lower social and economic class.

In contrast to these painters of polite interiors, Holland produced at the same time a number of robust artists who delighted in depictions of merrymakings and life in taverns. At their head was the lusty Jan Steen, a master of drawing and color, with a fund of abundant vitality and high spirits. Frans Hals of Haarlem had a rare talent for the brilliant technical handling of oil paint and a flashing brushstroke that influenced countless subsequent painters. He created not only rowdy scenes and vigorous portraits, but some of the most sober and moving likenesses in all of Dutch art, including two impressive groups, rendered en-

"Temptation of St. Anthony" by Lucas van Leyden (1494–1533).

Musées Royaux des Beaux Arts

"A Dutch Courtyard" by Pieter de Hooch (1629–c.1683).

tirely in grays, that show the regents of the old people's home and hospital in Haarlem.

The Dutch school of landscape and marine painting that came into being in the 17th century produced works that were highly prized at the time and have been ever since. They exerted a profound influence on the English painters of landscape and on the Barbizon school, a group of 19th-century French painters. Jacob van Ruisdael and Meindert Hobbema were the giants, but their achievements were preceded by a great company of talented artists. Jacob Cuyp and his famous son Aelbert immortalized the sandy slopes and overhanging moist skies of the Dutch shorelands, as did Jan van Goyen. Van Goyen prepared for painting his more formal landscapes by traveling widely through the country, recording what he saw in countless skillful pencil drawings. Salomon van Ruysdael, the uncle of Jacob van Ruisdael, had a gift for lending interest to the simplest scenes, showing fishing boats and ferries plying between the banks of rivers and inlets. The cattle that were to be seen everywhere grazing in the meadows and pastures were naturally included in these peaceful landscapes, and certain painters, such as Paul Potter, made a specialty of painting them.

In this very creative century another branch of painting was perfected in Holland, still life. There were many different forms and variations. The flower piece, that had begun as an adjunct to religious painting, came to be painted independently. The specialists included Jacob Vosmaer, the women painters Margareta Haverman and Rachel Ruysch, and at the end of the century the baroque genius Jan van Huysum. The breakfast table laden with glass and metalware, and later with sea food and game, was developed as a popular subject, and there were also still-life painters who specialized in the huntsmen's catch of game and fowl.

The 18th-20th Centuries. With the opening of the 18th century, Holland succumbed to the dominant influence of France. Painters who were perfectly competent in the

"Self-Portrait" by Rembrandt van Rijn (1606–69) shows the artist at the age of 52.

forthright expression that suited their talents and mentalities began to emulate the graceful and mannered rococo style. They overloaded their paintings with decorations, falsified their figures by lending them foreign and unnatural airs and graces, and set them in unconvincing aristocratic interiors where they no longer seemed to feel natural and at ease. The period produced few good Dutch paintings except those of Cornelis Troost, whose conversation pieces are well managed and have entertainment and charm.

The early part of the 19th century was also a dull period. Later Johannes Bosboom based his painting on typical Dutch realism, and a school of artists, centered at the Hague, was led by Jozef Israels, Anton Mauve, and Hendrik Willem Mesdag. Jacob and Willem Maris were prominent members of this group. Holland can also claim one of the greatest painters of the postimpressionist period, Vincent van Gogh. Although van Gogh did most of his work in France, he was undeniably a Dutch artist.

In the earlier part of the 20th century the widespread general tendency toward the theoretical and abstract in painting and in architecture resulted in the founding in 1917 of a group of artists who were associated under the name of *de stijl*. Piet Mondrian was a leader who expressed the austere thinking of the movement in paintings that were divided by sharp black lines into arrangements of rectangles, often drawn on pure white backgrounds with occasional areas of bright red and yellow.

Architecture

De stijl was extremely influential in the Dutch architec-

"Wheatfields" by Jacob van Ruisdael (c.1628–1682).

The Metropolitan Museum of Art, Bequest of Benjamin Altman, 1913

tural developments of the first quarter of the 20th century, which may be said to be the most important period in Dutch architectural history. Up to the 16th century Dutch buildings followed the Gothic style, with certain definite adaptations to the climate of Holland and the not very secure foundation in the shallow soil on which they were constructed. The naves of the churches were wide in proportion to length, and there were fewer windows than in France and Belgium. The Renaissance was represented chiefly by the choice of ornament added to rather simple buildings. Hendrik de Keyser was one of the great architects of the early 17th century. This Golden Age of Holland needed elegance in architecture, and the Renaissance style suited the demand. Jacob van Campen, who built the Mauritshuis—formerly a great house, it is now the Royal Museum of Painting—in the Hague and the Royal Palace in Amsterdam made use of Renaissance design. In the 18th century, building in Holland followed that of France; the 19th century was also not very productive.

At the beginning of the 20th century Dutch architects, led by Hendrik Petrus Berlage, began to adapt their buildings to the new ideal of functionalism. Though progress was offset temporarily by a reaction stressing overly ornate forms, with the *de stijl* group Dutch architects became prominent in the development of modern architectural styles. Engineers began to work with architects, public housing became a concern of municipal governments, and building was given careful supervision and encouragement in Holland. No country in fact has contributed more to the contemporary developments in building or has illustrated better in its architecture the intention of endowing all buildings with "fitness for purpose."

Consult Bode, Wilhelm von, *Great Masters of Dutch and Flemish Painting* (1909); *The Netherlands*, ed. by Bartholomeus Landheer (1943); Metropolitan Museum of Art, New York, *A Catalogue of Early Flemish, Dutch and*

"Flower Piece" by Jan van Huysum (1682–1749).

Nelson Gallery—Atkins Museum (Nelson Fund), Kansas City, Mo.

"The Starry Night" by Vincent van Gogh (1853–90), painted in France in 1889.

Collection, The Museum of Modern Art, New York.
Acquired through the Lillie P. Bliss Bequest

German Paintings, ed. by H. B. Wehle and Margaretta Salinger (1947); Metropolitan Museum of Art, New York, *Dutch Painting: The Golden Age* (1954).

MARGARETTA SALINGER, The Metropolitan Museum of Art

DUTCH ELM DISEASE, an often fatal disease affecting elm trees, so named because it was first studied in the Netherlands. The causative organism is a fungus, *Ceratocystis ulmi,* whose spores are spread from diseased to healthy trees by the elm bark beetle. Infected elms may wilt suddenly or their leaves may yellow and fall off gradually. The disease also affects the woody parts of the tree causing internal rot. Control measures consist of immediate removal of diseased trees and spraying healthy trees with DDT solution to kill the bark beetles.
See also PLANT DISEASES.

DUTCH GUIANA. *See* SURINAM.

DUTCH HARBOR, village of Alaska, important military base during World War II, located on Unalaska Island of the Aleutian Islands. Although it is now of no military significance, it is used as a landing strip, refueling point, and weather station. Unalaska Island had a population (1960) of 219, mostly Aleut with a Russian admixture.

DUTCH LITERATURE. The Low Countries, Belgium and the Netherlands, have a common cultural heritage. Only very minor differences set off Flemish, which is spoken in northern Belgium, from the Dutch language of the Netherlands, and the same books can be read by the people of both countries.

The beginnings of Dutch literature can be traced back to the 12th century and to Hendric van Veldeke, the first poet of the Netherlands. The humorous beast epic *Van den vos Reinaerde,* the beautiful Dutch version of *Reynard the Fox,* also belongs to this early period. In the 13th century Jacob van Maerlant, a national poet who wrote didactic verse, spoke for the rising middle class. Mysticism burst forth with vigor in the ecstatic lyricism of the great woman poet Hadewijch and, in the beginning of the 14th century, in the prose of Jan van Ruusbroec (or Ruysbroeck).

The drama of the later Middle Ages arose from two streams: the mystery and miracle plays of the church and the serious plays and comedies of the secular theater. During the 15th and 16th centuries the *rederijkerskamers* (Chambers of Rhetoric), societies of burghers who wished to recite, perform, and create literature, flourished along with the guilds. Two of the greatest of the morality plays of that period are *Marieke van Nieumeghen (Mary of Nimmegen)* and *Elckerlijc;* the latter may be the source of the English *Everyman.*

Most of the great humanists of the 16th and 17th centuries, such as Desiderius Erasmus, wrote in Latin rather than Dutch, but the poetry of Jonker Jan van der Noot represents the emergence of the Renaissance in the Netherlands, which in the 17th century developed into the golden age of Dutch literature. The refined Pieter Corneliszoon Hooft wrote sonnets, plays, and historical prose. Gerbrand Adriaanszoon Bredero wrote comedies and farces. The intellectual Constantijn Huygens was a great poet, but he never achieved the extraordinary popularity of his contemporary Jacob Cats, whose homely poetry expressed the ideas of the people. The greatest of all these writers, however, was the poet and dramatist Joost van den Vondel, whose tragedies made him one of the outstanding European men of letters.

Pieter Langendijk contributed to the development of comedy during the 18th century. Later in the century two women, Betje Wolff and Aagje Deken, portrayed the middle-class society of their day in the epistolary novel.

Willem Bilderdijk (1756–1831) introduced emotion into Dutch literature in his poetry. Both the poetry and prose of A. C. W. Staring (1767–1840) show a polished style. The romantic movement entered Dutch literature with the work of Everardus Potgieter, who in 1837 founded *De Gids*, a monthly magazine which is still one of the most important magazines in the Netherlands. The novelist Nicolaas Beets is also a member of the romantic movement. Edward Douwes Dekker, writing as Multatuli, won international fame with his novels.

Modern Dutch literature began in the 1880's in a new movement which blazed forth in the lyric poetry of such writers as Willem Kloos, Albert Verwey, Frederik van Eeden, and Herman Gorter. In the years that followed, the dramas of Herman Heijermans and the novels of Louis Couperus achieved world reputation.

Since 1910 the greatest achievements in Dutch literature have been in the lyric poetry of such writers as Peter Cornelis Boutens, Jan Hendrik Leopold, Adriaan Roland Holst, Martinus Nijhoff, Hendrik Marsman, Jan Slauerhoff, Gerrit Achterberg, Bertus Aafjes, and M. Vasalis. Important novelists include Arthur van Schendel, Edgar du Perron, Simon Vestdijk, and Anna Blaman. Other important figures in the Dutch literary world include the essayist P. N. van Eyck, the critic Menno ter Braak, the poet Jan Greshoff, and the dramatist Eduard Hoornik.

SEYMOUR L. FLAXMAN, New York University

DUTCHMAN'S BREECHES, a low, stemless herb, *Dicentra cucullaria*, of the Fumariaceae, or fumitory family. The plants are native to woodlands of eastern North America and have divided, fernlike leaves. In spring the white and yellow flowers appear, drooping from arched stems. Dutchman's breeches are attractive ornamentals suitable for planting in shaded locations in humus-rich soil.

DUTCHMAN'S PIPE, a very tall, climbing vine, *Aristolochia macrophylla*, in the birthwort family, Aristolochiaceae. The species is native to eastern North America and was named for the curious shape of its tubular, curved flowers. Dutchman's pipe has large, kidney-shaped leaves. Its dense foliage makes it ideal for shade purposes.

DUTCH REFORMED CHURCH, a Protestant church of the subdivision classed as "Reformed." At the Reformation the initial influence of Ulrich Zwingli in the Netherlands soon gave way to a thoroughgoing Calvinism. Despite a challenge at the Synod of Dort (1618–19), this was the national creed till the 19th century. The liberal policies of William I's reign (1815–40) led eventually to a series of schisms which left Holland with three Reformed churches, each claiming to be the true custodian of Reformed Christianity. In 1848 the original church was disestablished, though the state still subsidizes this and most other Dutch churches.

In its four ecclesiastical courts—consistory, classis, provincial synod, and general synod—and in doctrine the Dutch Reformed Church closely resembles the Scottish

D. Jordan Wilson—Pix

The Old Dutch Reformed Church at Kingston, N.Y.

and American Presbyterian churches. In Holland itself it has a membership of 3½ million, or 35% of the population. Immigrant Dutchmen established their church in America, and in South Africa, where it is the dominant church.

Consult Lindsay, T. M., *History of the Reformation* (2 vols., 1907); McNeill, J. T., *The History and Character of Calvinism* (1954).

JAMES DIXON DOUGLAS, British Editorial Associate, *Christianity Today*

See also CALVINISM; DORT, SYNOD OF; ZWINGLI, ULRICH OR HULDREICH.

DUTCH WARS, wars (1652–54; 1665–67; 1672–78) involving the Dutch Republic, England, France, and other European powers that challenged the commercial supremacy and territorial integrity of the small Dutch Republic. The first two Dutch Wars were fought by the Dutch Republic against England, with France allied to Holland in the second; the third was a continuation of French efforts under Louis XIV to extend France's power into the Low Countries.

Anglo-Dutch Wars. In 1651 the Rump Parliament passed the first Navigation Act, a measure designed to encourage English shipping by excluding the Dutch from the carrying trade between England and third countries. Goods could only be imported in English vessels or in those of the producing country. Dutch resentment and repeated clashes at sea (including the English victory off the Downs in May, 1652, before the declaration of war) led to formal hostilities in July. The war consisted of a dozen naval engagements, mostly indecisive. The English admirals Robert Blake and George Monck were matched against the equally able Dutch commanders Michel de Ruyter (1607–76) and Maarten Tromp (1597–1653). Tromp was defeated off Portland (Feb. 18, 1653) and off the North Foreland (June 2–3). He was killed on July 31 in the battle of the Texel, won by Monck. By the Treaty of Westminster (Apr., 1654) the Dutch agreed to pay an indemnity and join England in a defensive alliance.

The second Anglo-Dutch War broke out after the Navigation Act had been stiffened and the Dutch had allied themselves with Louis XIV for protection against England. The latter seized (1664) New Netherland (later the colonies of New York and New Jersey) and some Dutch posts in Africa. The war, fought mainly at sea, went badly for the English, whose navy had been neglected and who were further weakened by the plague of 1665 and by the great London fire of 1666. The Dutch sailed up the Medway and sank (June, 1667) the British ships at their moorings within sight of London. Peace came with the Treaty of Breda (July 31, 1667), both sides having reason for anxiety about Louis XIV's invasion (1667) of the Spanish (southern) Netherlands, which opened the War of Devolution (see DEVOLUTION, WAR OF). All conquests were returned, except that England kept New Netherland in exchange for Dutch acquisition of Surinam.

France Invades. Louis XIV's attack on Holland in 1672 stemmed partly from his desire to punish it for blocking his plan to annex the Spanish Netherlands. In addition, Holland had become a threat to the mercantilist ambitions of Louis's finance minister Jean Baptiste Colbert and offered a haven for anti-French pamphleteers. In order to isolate the Dutch diplomatically from their allies, Louis concluded the secret Treaty of Dover (1670) with Charles II of England, who agreed to remain neutral in return for French subsidies sufficient to make him largely independent of Parliamentary control. Sweden was detached (1672) from the former Triple Alliance by a similar agreement.

In 1672 a French army of 100,000 led by Henri de Turenne, the Prince de Condé, and the King, easily overran the southern Netherlands and crossed the Rhine, spreading alarm among the Dutch and precipitating a wild mob outburst in which Jan De Witt and his brother Cornelis, leaders of the aristocratic republican government, were torn to pieces because they were blamed unjustly for the nation's predicament. William III of Orange became stadholder with virtually royal powers. Amsterdam and the province of Holland were saved by flooding their approaches; Spain, Brandenburg, and the Holy Roman Empire allied themselves with the Dutch. William was able, by making minor concessions, to conclude a separate peace with England in 1674. Meanwhile, French troops seized Franche-Comté, while Turenne campaigned brilliantly on the upper Rhine until killed by troops of the Elector of Brandenburg in the battle of Sasbach (July 28, 1675). Naval warfare in the Mediterranean resulted in French victories over Spanish and Dutch forces, and in 1676 the Dutch lost their best admiral, De Ruyter. Fighting in the Netherlands between Condé and William was indecisive until 1678, when the French took Ypres and Ghent by surprise.

Negotiations led to the Treaty of Nijmegen (1678–79), by which Holland recovered its freedom and declared its neutrality. Spain ceded Franche-Comté to France together with Valenciennes, Cambray, St. Omer, Ypres, Condé, Maubeuge, Bouchain, Aire, and a number of towns along the Belgian frontier. France restored Ghent, Charleroi, Oudenaarde, Courtrai, Limbourg, and several other cities to Spanish control. The Emperor yielded Freiburg-im-Breisgau to France in return for evacuation of the French garrison from Philipsburg. The Duke of Lorraine

was to be restored to his territory but refused to accept the terms offered. The Elector of Brandenburg, under French pressure, returned his Pomeranian conquests to Sweden in exchange for reversionary rights to East Friesland, which ultimately fell to Prussia in 1744 (Peace of St. Germain-en-Laye). The peace settlement reflected substantial territorial gains for France, chiefly at the expense of Spain and the Holy Roman Empire, brought Louis XIV to the highest point of his power, and encouraged him to undertake further aggressive wars that were eventually disastrous to France.

RALPH H. BOWEN, Northern Illinois University

DUTRA [dōō'trə], **EURICO G(ASPAR)** (1885–   ), Brazilian soldier and President (1946–51). Except for his excursion into the presidency, he made a lifelong career of the army. He rose steadily through officer grades after being commissioned in 1910 and in 1932 was made director of military aviation. President Getulio Vargas, whom Dutra had supported in the revolution of 1930, appointed him Minister of War in 1936. Dutra's position as war minister during World War II was complicated by a pro-German inclination within the Brazilian army and by the large number of persons of German birth or descent in Brazil. Dutra ran for the presidency in 1945 as Social Democratic party candidate and received Vargas' support, both before and after Vargas was ousted as President in October. Dutra's term as President was uneventful and moderate.

DUTT [dôt], **MICHAEL MADHU SUDAN** (1824–73), important Bengali poet. A Christian convert from a respectable Hindu family, he was determined to write in English but his poems in that language received little notice. Almost by accident he turned to writing in his mother tongue of Bengali, in which he became the greatest innovator, preparing the way for Rabindranath Tagore. He introduced Miltonic blank verse to India in his famous heroic poem *Meghanad-Badha* (The Fall of Meghanad), 1861. His *Krishna Kumari* (1861) is India's first modern tragedy. He also introduced the sonnet form and wrote brilliant social comedies. In 1862 he went to England to study law and later became a barrister in Calcutta, but ended his tragic life in utter poverty.

DUTTON, CLARENCE EDWARD (1841–1912), American geologist who in 1889 proposed the name "isostasy" for the condition of balance between high and low parts of the earth's crust. He is noted also for studies of volcanoes, earthquakes, and the geology of the plateau region of Arizona and Utah. After graduating from Yale in 1860, Dutton became a professional soldier, receiving a commission in the Ordnance Corps in 1864. He was detached for duty with the U.S. Geological Survey between 1875 and 1890.

DUUN, OLAV (1876–1939), Norwegian novelist. His main work, *Juvikfolke*, 6 vols., 1918–23 (*The People of Juvik*, 1930–35), is a massive modern saga of the transition from an agricultural to an industrial society. Also outstanding is his *Menneske og maktene*, 1938 (*Floodtide of Fate*, 1960). Duun, Knut Hamsun, and Sigrid Undset are considered the foremost 20th-century Norwegian novelists.

DUVALIER [dū-văl-yā], **FRANÇOIS** (1907–   ), Haitian politician. A physician, he was Undersecretary of Labor and later Secretary of Labor and Health during the presidency of Dunarsais Estimé. After a period of confusion and strife, Duvalier was elected president in 1957. He immediately established a terroristic, dictatorial regime. His secret police silenced opposition, and in 1961 he dissolved the congress, virtually selected the members of a new unicameral legislature, and declared himself president for another six years. In 1964 he became president for life.

DUVEEN [dū-vēn'], **JOSEPH, BARON DUVEEN OF MILBANK** (1869–1939), English art dealer and connoisseur. As an adviser to millionaires, he played an important role in the formation of outstanding collections of old masters. In the United States, the Frick, Kress, and Mellon collections attest to his abilities. Among his benefactions are the galleries in the British Museum housing the Elgin marbles. The son of an art dealer, Lord Duveen was knighted in 1919 and made a baron in 1933.

DUVERNAY [dū-vər-nā], residential suburb north of Montreal, Quebec, Canada. Inc. as town, 1958; pop., 10,939.

DUVIVIER [dū-vē-vyā'], **JULIEN** (1896–   ), French film director. Before directing his first picture, in 1919, he was an actor on the Paris stage. His major films include *Pépé le Moko*, 1936; *Un Carnet de Bal* (Dance Program), 1937; and *Le Petit Monde de Don Camillo* (*The Little World of Don Camillo*), 1952.

DUVOISIN [dū-vwä-zăn'], **ROGER ANTOINE** (1904–   ), artist and author of children's books, born in Switzerland. After working in ceramics and textile design in France, he came to the United States, where he presently began to write and illustrate children's books. In 1948 he won the Caldecott Medal for his distinguished illustrations in *White Snow, Bright Snow* by Alvin Tresselt. He is best known for his light-hearted picture books such as *One Thousand Christmas Beards* (1955), his solution to the "multiple Santa Claus" puzzle.

DUXBURY, town of eastern Massachusetts, on Plymouth Bay, south of Boston. It was founded in 1631 by Myles Standish, and was the home of Standish, William Brewster, and John and Priscilla Alden. Alden House, built in 1653, has been preserved. Standish Monument Reservation, a recreational area containing a 130-ft. tower surmounted by a statue of Myles Standish, is here. Inc., 1637; pop. (1950) 3,167; (1960) 4,727.

DVINA [dvē'nä] **RIVER**, also called Western Dvina, river of the western Soviet Union, draining almost 33,000 sq. mi. Rising in the Valdai Hills, it flows southwestward through the Belorussian S.S.R. Then it turns northwestward through the Latvian S.S.R. and empties into the Gulf of Riga. Its main ports are Riga, Daugavpils, and Vitebsk. It is almost two-thirds navigable during the ice-free months of the year, and timber is floated down in it to sawmills. It was important in the early history of Russia as part of the trade route between the Baltic and Black seas. Length, 635 mi.

Brown Brothers

Antonín Dvořák. The composer's stay in the United States influenced two of his important works, a cantata entitled *The American Flag* (1893) and the symphony *From the New World* (1893).

DVOŘÁK [dvôr'zhäk], **ANTONÍN** (1841–1904), eminent Czech composer, influenced by his country's folk music. Born in Mülhausen and destined for the butcher's trade, he left home at 16 to study at the Prague Organ School. He supported himself precariously by playing the violin in a concert band and later the viola in the Prague National Theater orchestra. In 1875 he received the Austrian State Music Prize, due to Brahms's influence. His growing fame gained him the directorship of the National Conservatory of Music in New York (1892–95). Later he was professor and then director of the Prague National Conservatory.

Dvořák, a master of instrumentation, composed nine symphonies, of which the last, *From the New World* (E Minor, Op. 95; 1893), is the most significant. He contributed to 19th century nationalism with his folklike *Slavonic Dances*, and his Slavic folksongs with piano. His cello concerto of 1895 (B Minor, Op. 104) ranks among the masterpieces in this category. Among his vocal compositions are 10 operas, choral works (unaccompanied and with orchestra), and songs. Instrumental works include two violin concertos and one piano concerto, 16 string quartets, the famous Dumky Trio (Op. 90), and piano and other chamber music.

Consult Stefan, Paul, *Anton Dvořák* (1941); Robertson, Alec, *Dvořák* (1949).

KARL GEIRINGER, Boston University
See also ROMANTIC ERA, MUSIC OF THE.

DWARF, abnormally small human being. The term "dwarf" is frequently used to mean a person of small stature born in a racial group of normal size. "Pygmy" refers to a member of a racial group in which average height is unusually small. Dwarfs are mentioned in the records of ancient Egypt, Greece, and Rome. Mark Antony is said to have had a dwarf named Sisyphus, 24 in. tall. Many European rulers of more recent

Culver Pictures, Inc.

Charles S. Stratton, known as General Tom Thumb.

times, including Charles IX of France and Peter the Great of Russia, kept dwarfs at their courts. Midgets at the court of Spain appear in paintings by Velázquez. In England, Henrietta Maria, wife of King Charles I, had two famous dwarfs: Richard Gibson was, appropriately enough, "court miniature painter"; Sir Jeffrey Hudson was a courtier who figured in two duels and the Civil War.

Probably the best known dwarf in history was General Tom Thumb (Charles Sherwood Stratton), an American circus performer whose fame was promoted by P. T. Barnum. At maturity he was about 3 ft., 4 in. tall.

In Teutonic mythology dwarfs were diminutive, ugly, clever, malevolent creatures who grew from the maggots in the body of the giant Ymir. Inhabitants of large isolated rocks and dark subterranean caverns, dwarfs were unable to bear sunlight. They were guardians of mines and metals and skillful craftsmen of weapons and ornaments. Four dwarfs—Austri, Vestri, Nordri, and Sudri—upheld the sky. The most famous dwarfs in European folk tales were the seven dwarfs in the story of Snow White.

GERRIT Y. LANSING, Writer and Editor

See also DWARFISM; ELF; PYGMY.

DWARFISM, abnormally small stature which is most commonly caused by disease of the bones or glands. Dwarfism resulting from a deficiency of the growth hormone of the pituitary gland produces a well-proportioned dwarf usually with no signs of mental deficiency or impaired sexual development. In cretinism, caused by the absence of thyroid hormone in infancy and childhood, a deformed and mentally-retarded dwarf results, with pronounced skeletal deformity. In achondroplasia, a congenital disease involving abnormal bone development, the arms and legs are short in relation to the length of the body. These individuals display a typical facial expression which is formed by the high broad forehead, the flattened nose bridge, and the prominent lower jaw. The arms and legs are often bowed. Mental and sexual development are usually nor-

mal. In rickets, a nutritional disorder caused by a deficiency of vitamin D, bone growth is interfered with, producing dwarfism with marked bowing of the legs. In inherited, or genetic, dwarfism, body proportion and sexual development are normal. Dwarfism may also result from abnormal functioning of the gonads or from malnutrition.

Tendencies to dwarfism resulting from glandular disorders can be halted in some cases by administering glandular extracts. Rickets can be treated and prevented by giving vitamin D.

PAUL CHRISTENSON, M.D.

DWARF STAR. *See* STAR.

DWARF TREES, a botanical term describing woody, perennial plants that are normal in every respect but never reach their natural height. Dwarf trees may either be naturally low-growing forms of a full-sized species, or so-called "artificial" dwarfs whose growth has been deliberately restricted. Artificial dwarfs may be produced in several ways. Perhaps the most common technique is grafting standard-sized trees to dwarfing rootstocks. The rootstock selected may be weaker and slower-growing than the top grafted to it, and therefore provides insufficient nourishment to the top growth, stunting its natural development. Other dwarfing methods include severe pruning, or cutting back; restriction of the root system; or withholding water and nutrients.

Trees are dwarfed for practical and for aesthetic reasons. Dwarf fruit trees, for example, are proportionally more productive than full-sized trees. Their small size also facilitates pruning, spraying, and harvesting. Trees dwarfed for purely ornamental purposes are particularly desirable as landscape specimens for use on small properties.

The most unusual ornamental dwarfs are produced through the Japanese art of bonsai. This exacting technique incorporates the culture of young trees in very shallow containers, under conditions in accordance with their natural environment. As the bonsai specimen grows it is carefully pruned and its branches trained into the desired

This Japanese dwarf pine is more than 100 years old.

Gottscho-Schleisner, Inc.

position. It must also be repotted at intervals to destroy old, fibrous roots. Among the trees best-suited to this type of culture are various species of pine, maple, and juniper. Bamboo, and such flowering plants as azalea, pomegranate, and ornamental fruit trees are also seen as bonsai.

JOHN P. MAHLSTEDE, Iowa State University

DWARKA [dwär'kä], town in Amreli District, Gujarat State, India. On the Arabian Sea at the western tip of Kathiawar Peninsula, it is a stop on the Bombay-Karachi sea route. It exports grain, ghee, oilseeds, and salt. Dwarka is one of India's seven sacred Hindu centers, and many pilgrims visit its Krishna temple. Pop., 10,876.

DWIGGINS, WILLIAM ADDISON (1880–1956), American illustrator and typographer. Born in Ohio, he was an accomplished illustrator and commercial artist and was the author of *Layout in Advertising* (1928; rev. ed., 1949). He first became interested in typography through the influence of the type designer Frederic Goudy, and he went on to create the Electra and Caledonia typefaces. He designed fine books up to the time of his death, becoming highly influential in the improvement of American book design.

DX, in radiotelegraphy, the abbreviation for distance, referred to only when there is a considerable separation between stations. Originally DX was one of the many time-saving abbreviations in Morse Code, but today the term is used by radiotelephone operators, as well, to designate a long-distance telephone call.

DYBBUK [dĭb'ək], **THE,** play by S. Ansky (pen name of Solomon Rappaport), first produced in 1920. Derived from Jewish folklore and rich in mysticism, it describes the tragic consequences of a ritual designed to free the soul of a girl from the spirit of her dead lover.

DYE AND DYEING. The coloring of fabrics was done in several ancient civilizations with natural dyes found in animal or vegetable matter. Indigo blue, the oldest dye, was extracted from the leaves of various species of the indigo plant in India and Java and the woad plant in Europe. Shades of Turkey red, or alizarin, were obtained from the herb root, madder, in Eurasia; fustic, a yellow, from the sumac tree; and cochineal, a reddish purple, from insects. These natural dyes were applied to fabrics with the aid of inorganic materials (mordants) which were instrumental in developing the final color and giving it a fastness to washing and to light.

Synthetic Dyes. The development of synthetic dyes supplanted the use of natural dyes and offered a wider variety of colors with improved quality.

In 1771 Woulfe prepared picric acid from indigo by treatment with nitric acid and found that the resulting product could produce yellow tints on silk and wool. Although it could not truly be called a synthetic dye, it was the first step in that direction. The first synthetic dye did not appear until the late 19th century. It was mauve, discovered by Sir William Henry Perkin in 1856. The following year he initiated commercial manufacture, thus laying the cornerstone of the dye industry.

Several other important technical discoveries followed that contributed to the evolution of the synthetic dyes. These were magenta (fuchine) by Verguin in 1859; diazonium salts by Peter Griess in 1858, which led to the diazo coupling reaction in 1864; the first brown sulfur dye by Croissant and Bretonniere in 1873; methylene blue by Heinrich Caro in 1876; synthetic indigo by Adolf von Baeyer in 1880; the first red naphthol dyes by Read, Holliday and Sons, Ltd., in 1880; indathrone, which competed with blue indigo, was the first anthraquinone vat dye by Rene Bohn in 1901; and the intense blue and green metal phthalocyanines by A. G. Dandridge in 1928. The introduction of the "fiber-reactive" dyes for cellulose by the Imperial Chemical Industries of Great Britain in 1956 was doubtless a significant contribution to the continuing development of dye technology.

Dye Properties. Among the properties desired from a dye are brightness of shade, ease of application, and color fastness that will resist washing, light, heat, bleaching, rubbing, and, in garments, perspiration. Dyes for special uses may require additional properties such as fastness to sea water in bathing suits.

In the early days of the dye industry, the main concern was with the coloring of natural fibers, primarily cotton, linen, wool, and silk. But the development of synthetic fibers greatly increased the complexity of dyeing technology and necessitated new dyes specifically tailored for the new fabrics. The various dyes can be classified by the types of fabrics they are used on.

Cotton, Linen, and Rayon Dyes. All forms of cellulose, these fabrics can be dyed readily with a numerous variety of dyes.

Direct dyes are a class of water-soluble colors that transfer directly to the fiber. They have an affinity for cellulose in an aqueous dye bath. All that is required is the immersion of the fiber in a hot solution for a short period of time, with chemicals added to promote transfer of dye molecules from water to fiber. Direct dyes are not very fast to washing, but dye bleeding can be minimized by washing in lukewarm water containing 5% to 10% sodium chloride.

Vat dyes of the anthraquinone or indigo class are water-insoluble pigments that are reduced to a water-soluble leuco form, which has an affinity for cellulose. After dyeing, the leuco derivative can be reoxidized by air or chemical agents to regenerate the insoluble pigment in the fiber. Good to excellent washing fastness is obtained.

Sulfur dye is a type of vat dye reduced by different chemical agents but used the same way.

Naphthol dyes (also known as azoic, ingrain, or ice colors) are insoluble pigments prepared directly on the fiber by the reaction of a diazonium salt and a beta-naphthol derivative. Good washing fastness is obtained. Fiber reactive dyes undergo a chemical reaction with the fiber being dyed in the presence of an alkali or at an elevated temperature. They combine good color fastness with a brightness that cannot be equaled by other dye classes.

Wool and Silk Dyes. Wool and silk are both protein fibers displaying quite similar dyeing properties.

Acid dyes which are used predominantly for coloring these fibers are water-soluble; their name derives from the fact that there is sulfuric or acetic acid in the dyeing proc-

DYES and DYEING

One of many steps in manufacture of some synthetic dyes from coal tar is addition of salt to dye solution to isolate dye from water.

Skilled dyemaker and laboratory technician check color of new batch.

Cakes of dye from filter press are placed on trays for drying.

Chemist inks engraved roll with dye paste. Fabric is roller-printed in laboratory to test color and quality of dye.

All photos: E. I. du Pont de Nemours & Co.

ess. Acid dyes are used to color the shells of "Easter eggs" with the addition of vinegar providing the necessary acid. Metal derivatives, usually chromium or cobalt, of selected acid dyes give shades with very good light fastness on the protein fibers.

Basic dyes, in the presence of a mordant, to fix the color, are sometimes used for bright shades where poor light fastness can be tolerated. Neither wool nor silk is washed under extreme conditions, so wash fastness is not an important requirement of the dyes.

Synthetic Fabric Dyes. Synthetic fibers such as cellulose acetate, nylon, polyesters, and acrylics can be dyed with disperse dyes.

Disperse dyes are manufactured as powders and have a solubility when the dye is suspended in an aqueous dye bath with the fiber. The result is that a small amount of the solid dye dissolves in the water and then transfers to the fiber. As the dye leaves the water, more of the solid dye dissolves to maintain a saturated solution. In time essentially all of the solid dye dissolves and then migrates into the fiber.

Wash fastness of the disperse dyes may vary from very good with the cellulose triacetate, polyester, and acrylic fibers to relatively poor with cellulose acetate and nylon. Improved wash fastness can be obtained on nylon through the use of direct or acid dyes. Selected basic dyes give bright shades of good light and wash fastness on acrylic fibers.

A potential negative feature of disperse dyes is their tendency to sublime or diffuse when the dyed fabric is exposed to elevated temperatures in heat-setting, pleating, or pressing operations. This problem is particularly severe where a colored yarn is adjacent to an uncolored one in a pattern. The dye subliming from the colored portion can give rise to staining the uncolored fiber. Sublimation can be minimized, by proper design of the dye molecule and by careful temperature control in the heat treatment.

Pigments. A method of coloration applicable to all textile fibers utilizes insoluble pigments rather than dyes as the coloring medium. The pigment together with a heat-setting resin is applied to the surface of a fabric, and the resin is set by the application of heat, in a process similar to the application of paint. Since the color is concentrated on the surface, it is subject to removal by the abrasive forces encountered in washing and in rubbing. The use of resin-bonded pigments is limited usually to shades of light and medium depth.

Plastic compositions in forms other than fibers usually are colored in the bulk with pigments or disperse dyes prior to shaping.

Paper, like cotton, is derived from cellulose and can be dyed in the pulp form with pigments, direct dyes, basic dyes, or acid dyes with a mordant of alum and rosin. It can be colored also by surface application of water-soluble dyes to the formed sheet.

Methods. Textiles may be dyed at any one of several

processing steps involved from producing staple or filament fibers to the final fabric. Staple fibers, as raw stock, frequently are dyed in a pressure vessel at elevated temperatures. Staple may be aligned into relatively parallel strands in a coarse bat and dyed at this stage, which is called tow dyeing. When tow is twisted into yarn, it may be dyed in the form of looped skeins. Conversely, the yarn may be wound onto cones and dyed in a way called package, or cheese, dyeing. Finally, the yarn may be woven or knitted into a fabric before dyeing is carried out as piece dyeing. Indeed, the fabric may be converted to the final garment before dyeing. This is frequently the case with knit goods, such as stockings and sweaters.

The dyer prefers to postpone dyeing until the last practical stage in the sequence from staple to fabric, since as much as 5% to 10% of the original fiber may be lost in these operations. Also, since the total sequence of fabric preparation may extend over a considerable period of time, and since the vagaries of fashion can change very suddenly, he would like to delay as long as possible the decision on the color he will use.

Dyeing Patterns. When patterns are required, it is usually necessary to dye the raw stock, the tow, or the yarn in the various shades required and ultimately weave or knit the colored yarns into the desired pattern. The selection of the specific dyeing process is largely a matter of economics. When a uniform over-all shade is required, then piece dyeing predominantly is the method of choice.

Other patterns are made by a printing, rather than a dyeing, process. Here a dye in a thickened composition containing a resin or starch is deposited on a fabric in the desired pattern. The dye is then fixed by a thermal or chemical treatment which permits it to migrate into the fiber. A vat dye print on cotton, for example, may be after-treated with a reducing agent to form the leuco derivative which has affinity for the fiber. Reoxidation then will regenerate the pigment in the desired colored pattern. Resin-bonded pigments are used extensively in printing. Thermal treatment of the printed fabric cures the resin and fixes the pattern. With any of these color types, the printing paste may be applied to the fabric from an engraved roll in roller printing or a carved block in block printing, or may be forced through a "stencil" formed by the removal of wax from selected areas of a wax-coated screen in silk screen printing.

Home Dyeing. Dyeing many types of fiber can be a task requiring complicated equipment and rigorous process control. For this reason, only the simpler processes can be operated with any degree of success in the home. The dyes for home application usually are limited to direct dyes for cotton and rayon, acid dyes for wool and nylon, and disperse dyes for cellulose acetate and nylon. Even in these instances it is very easy to obtain unsatisfactory results. The manufacturer's instructions should be followed rigorously. The material to be dyed should be washed thoroughly beforehand, since the presence of grease or other soils can produce unsightly spots in the final dyeing. Any attempt to overdye a colored fabric to another shade is risky. The risk is minimized when a light hue is converted to a much deeper or darker shade. If at all possible, the original dye should be removed with the chemical agents available for this purpose, and the white fabric should be rinsed thoroughly before redyeing is attempted. Since different fiber types respond differently to a given dye, fabrics composed of a mixture of different fibers may give unsatisfactory results in home dyeing.

S. N. Boyd, Director, Dyes and Chemicals Section,
E. I. du Pont de Nemours and Company

See also STAIN REMOVAL.

DYER [dī'ər], **MARY** (d.1660), American Quaker martyr, hanged by the Massachusetts Puritan authorities for defying several banishment decrees. Mary Dyer probably arrived in Massachusetts from England in 1635 amidst the controversy centering on Anne Hutchinson. When the latter was expelled, the Dyers moved with her to Aquidneck, in Narragansett Bay, where William Dyer soon became a man of consequence. Later Mary Dyer returned to England (1650–57), where she became a Quaker. On her way back to Aquidneck in 1657, she was arrested for preaching Quakerism almost as soon as she set foot in Boston. Banished from Boston and later from New Haven, she defied the Boston authorities three times (Sept. and Oct., 1659; and May, 1660). The death sentence was finally executed when she refused to promise never to return.

Consult Rogers, Horatio, *Mary Dyer . . . The Quaker Martyr* (1896).

DYER-BENNET, RICHARD (1913–), folk singer, born in England. He came to the United States in 1925, and began his career as a night-club entertainer in 1941. Through concert appearances and recordings, he gained fame as a singer of British, American, and Continental ballads for which he provided his own guitar accompaniment.

DYERSBURG, city of western Tennessee, and seat of Dyer County, located in the midst of a large cotton-growing area. Its manufactures consist largely of textiles, cottonseed oil, and lumber products. Vegetable processing also is important. Inc., 1836; pop. (1950) 10,885; (1960) 12,499.

DYING SWAN, THE, solo ballet choreographed by Michel Fokine for Anna Pavlova in 1905; music by Camille Saint-Saëns; first performed at a concert in St. Petersburg. Short in duration and technically extremely simple, the dance depends for its effectiveness upon the artistry of the dancer and the pathos with which she endows her portrayal of the mortally wounded bird. Probably the most famous solo ever created, it is the dance with which Pavlova, who performed it all over the world, will always be identified. More recent interpreters include Alicia Markova, Tamara Toumanova, Maria Tallchief, and Galina Ulanova.

DYKSTRA [dīk'strə], **CLARENCE ADDISON** (1883–1950), American educator, civic administrator, first national director of selective service (1940–41). Dykstra, born in Cleveland, studied municipal government at Ohio State University, did graduate work at the University of Chicago, and taught political science at the University of Kansas. Between 1918 and 1937 he served Cleveland, Los Angeles, and Cincinnati as an administrator or manager and achieved national prominence for outstanding work during the Cincinnati flood of 1937. He became president of the University of Wisconsin in 1937. In 1945 he was named provost of the University of California at Los Angeles.

DYNAMIC PRESENCE, Calvinistic doctrine of the presence of Christ in the Lord's Supper. Just as the Word of God caused the power of healing to be present in the brazen serpent (Num. 21:8), so the Word of Christ, "this is my body" (I Cor. 11:24) causes the power (dynamis) of His body to be present in the elements at the Communion service.

DYNAMICS, branch of mechanics which deals with the motion of systems, of parts of systems, or of particles. It is distinguished from statics, which is the branch of mechanics concerned with the mechanical properties of stationary systems. The term classical dynamics describes that portion of dynamics developed before about 1900, that is, previous to the introduction of quantum theory and relativity theory.

When the moving parts of a system possess electric charges, they generate magnetic fields. The study of the phenomena associated with such systems is called electrodynamics. When there are many uncharged particles involved, the study is called thermodynamics. Considerations of heat belong primarily to this subject. Thermodynamics is closely related to statistical mechanics. When liquids or fluids are involved, the study of the dynamic behavior of the system is called hydrodynamics, or if the fluid is air, aerodynamics.

Magnetohydrodynamics, sometimes called hydromagnetics, is the study of the motions and properties of systems in which some or all of the particles carry electric charges. The system undergoes repeated interactions with itself, and the motion is usually extremely complex. An example of a system exhibiting hydromagnetic properties are the plasma clouds emitted by the sun, which on arriving at the earth interact with the earth's magnetic field.

In the last half century another branch of dynamics has been developed. It is quantum electrodynamics, a portion of which is called relativistic quantum electrodynamics. Classical dynamic and electrodynamic concepts are modified by taking into account the principles of the quantum theory, quantum mechanics, and the theory of relativity. The resulting theories give formalisms which describe operations of nature when the velocities of the particles or components are sufficiently high to require relativistic equations. This frequently is the case when studying atomic phenomena.

SERGE A. KORFF, New York University
See also MECHANICS; QUANTUM THEORY; RELATIVITY, THEORY OF.

DYNAMITES, class of "high" or detonating explosives invented by Alfred Nobel and containing liquid nitroglycerin. The nitroglycerin content may vary from 5% to over 90%, depending upon the energy and speed (velocity of detonation) desired.

Nitroglycerin is a high-energy, explosive liquid more properly called glycerol trinitrate. Commercial nitroglycerin is a mixture of glycerol trinitrate and an analogous explosive liquid, ethylene glycol dinitrate (EGD), used to prevent freezing.

The solid constituents of dynamite are wood pulps or other carbonaceous combustibles, and sodium nitrate or ammonium nitrate to supply oxygen to burn the combustibles. These nitrate-combustible mixtures are used to hold the nitroglycerin and can be selected in conjunction with the nitroglycerin content to control energy, density, and velocity of detonation.

When sodium nitrate is the sole inorganic oxygen car-

National Film Board

Destruction of Ripple Rock, a navigation hazard in Seymour Narrows at Vancouver, British Columbia. Almost 3,000,000 lb. of dynamite was used to produce this blast.

rier, the explosives are called "straight" dynamites. When ammonium nitrate is used either alone or in addition to sodium nitrate, the explosives are called "extra" dynamites.

In certain cases, part of the material used to absorb the nitroglycerin may be nitrocellulose, which forms a gel with nitroglycerin. The explosives are then known as gelatin dynamites, which also may be "straight" (sodium nitrate) or "extra" (ammonium nitrate) types. Gelatin dynamites can be loaded and shot under water.

In coal-mining operations in the United States "permissible" dynamites are used. They must be approved by the U.S. Bureau of Mines, which has established a schedule of requirements that must be met to assure that the dynamite will afford maximum protection against the possibility of igniting coal mine gases and dusts.

Kieselguhr dynamite, which was the first type made by Nobel, is a simple mixture of nitroglycerin absorbed by kieselguhr. It is seldom made in the United States and is mostly of historic interest.

The uses of dynamite include quarrying, ore mining, coal mining, coal stripping, oil prospecting, road building, tunneling, dam construction, harbor improvements, and land clearing.

Eastern Laboratory, E. I. du Pont de Nemours
and Company

DYNAMO. *See* GENERATOR, ELECTRIC.

DYNAMOMETER [*dĭ-nə-mŏm′ə-tər*], device for measuring the power delivered by an engine, motor, or turbine. It consists mainly of a rotor, inside a housing, turned by the power device being measured. As the rotor turns, it tends to drag the housing around with it. The housing is mounted in bearings, and the restraining force necessary to prevent motion of the housing is measured. Horsepower can be calculated if rotor speed is also determined. The drag on the housing is caused by rubbing of the rotor on adjustable friction blocks in the housing, by electric forces, or by fluid-friction forces.

DYNAMOTOR, compact motor-generator used to raise the voltage of direct current or to change direct current to alternating current without voltage change. It is widely used in portable radio equipment and other field applications. The armature coils of the motor and the generator are wound on the same rotating core with a common field magnet supplied by the same current operating the motor. Separate commutators or slip rings are provided at opposite ends of the armature shaft.

DYNE [*dīn*], in physics, the fundamental unit of force in the centimeter-gram-second system. It is the force required to accelerate a mass of one gram one centimeter per second per second. One gram of force is the pull of the earth on one gram of mass, and it is equivalent to 980 dynes.

DYNEL [*dĭ-nĕl*], trademark name of a synthetic textile fiber made from vinyl chloride and acrilonitrile. Woven into fabrics, made from a wide range of fiber thicknesses, from soft knits to thick pile, either alone or in combination with rayon, cotton, or wool, it is made into garments, blankets, drapes, or filter cloth. Dynel resists wrinkling and because it is thermoplastic, it is easily shaped. The fiber is made by dissolving the basic powder into an acetone solution, extruding it into a tow, then cutting to staple lengths before spinning into yarn.

DYSENTERY [*dĭs′ən-tĕr-ē*] is a painful inflammation of the large intestine; it is usually accompanied by severe diarrhea. The principal types are amebic dysentery and bacillary dysentery.

Amebic Dysentery is caused by the ameba *Endamoeba histolytica*. This single-celled organism is found throughout the world, but is more common in the tropics. In the United States approximately 12 million people are estimated to be infected. In areas of the world having poor sanitation the organism may be present in half of the population.

The parasite has two forms. Outside of the body it exists as a cyst, consisting of several amebae contained within a protective wall, which enables them to resist drying and freezing. The cysts are swallowed with contaminated food. In the intestine the wall of the cyst is shed and the liberated organisms burrow into the intestinal wall. In the lower portion of the intestine, new cysts form and pass out into the feces. Infection spreads through the contaminated feces, which may pollute drinking water or be carried to food by insects or human hands. In some localities infection is spread by the practice of using human waste to fertilize crops.

The majority of persons infected with *E. histolytica* manifest no symptoms or discomfort. They are called carriers because, although not apparently ill, they may transmit the disease to others through their infected feces. Some cases may have mild indigestion and a slight fever. In severe cases diarrhea, developing over a three-to-four day period, is the most common symptom. Weakness, nausea, vomiting, and abdominal cramps are usually present. The attacks may disappear and recur at variable intervals. In rare instances the ameba may be carried by the blood stream to the liver, causing an abscess of that organ.

Severe untreated cases may be fatal. However, amebic dysentery can be treated readily through the use of various medications, including diodoquine, oxytetracycline, and carbarsone. The prevention of infection can be accomplished by sanitary disposal of human waste, control of food and water supplies, and the detection and treatment of carriers.

JEROME D. WAYE, M.D.

Bacillary Dysentery is caused by infection with bacteria of the genus *Shigella*. The most dangerous varieties of these organisms are found in the Orient. Epidemics are likely to occur where conditions are crowded and unsanitary, and for this reason the disease has played an important role in military history. The Greek historian Herodotus ascribed the defeat of the Persian armies in 480 B.C. to such an epidemic.

The infection is spread through infected feces, as in amebic dysentery. Although some persons may act as carriers, bacillary dysentery differs from the amebic form in that most cases develop rapidly and display symptoms consisting of violent, often bloody, diarrhea, fever, chills, abdominal cramps, nausea, and vomiting. Five or more bowel movements an hour are not uncommon during the first day, and severe dehydration may result.

In treating bacillary dysentery fluids must be administered to replace those that are lost. In severe cases solutions containing sodium and potassium are introduced through the veins. Treatment with antibiotic drugs, such as the tetracyclines, helps relieve the symptoms in two or three days, and usually results in complete recovery within a week. In milder infections symptoms may be limited to one or two days of mild diarrhea.

Bacillary dysentery is not ordinarily fatal. The death rate in epidemics, however, may run as high as 30% if the victims are undernourished or are otherwise in poor physical condition. The preventive techniques used in amebic dysentery also apply to the bacillary form.

ROBERT BROWN, M.D.

DYSPROSIUM [dĭs-prō'sē-əm], metal of the lanthanide series of chemical elements. It was discovered in 1886 by Lecoq de Boisbaudran who named it from the Greek word meaning "hard to get at." In a combined form it is found with the minerals associated with granite deposits. It forms a series of yellow compounds. Dysprosium oxide, Dy_2O_3, possesses strong magnetic qualities.

PROPERTIES

Symbol	Dy
Atomic number	66
Atomic weight	162.50
Density	8.56
Valence	3

DZERZHINSK [dyĕr-zhĭnsk], city of the Soviet Union and major center of Gorky Oblast, R.S.F.S.R. It is located on the Oka River in central European U.S.S.R. Dzerzhinsk lies on the main railroad line from Moscow to Gorky, 25 mi. downstream from the confluence of the Oka and Volga rivers. The city is one of the most important chemical manufacturing centers of the Soviet Union, producing nitrogen and phosphate fertilizers, toxic chemicals, caustic soda, organic chemicals, and materials for the synthetic fiber industry. Raw materials for these are apatite ores from the Kola Peninsula of northwestern European U.S.S.R. and lignite coals from the Moscow-Tula Basin. Other important industries include the production of storage tanks, gasometers, glass, and rope. The wheat output of the surrounding hinterland has led to the growth of an important flour-milling industry. Dzerzhinsk was known as Chernoye prior to the revolution; at that time its name was changed to Rastyapino. It was expanded and renamed in 1930 after the Bolshevik leader, Feliks Dzerzhinsky. Pop., 163,000.

ALLAN L. RODGERS, Pennsylvania State University

DZERZHINSKY [dyĕr-zhĭn'skə], **FELIKS EDMUNDOVICH** (1877–1926), Bolshevik leader and bureaucrat, born into the lower Polish nobility. He was arrested and imprisoned for revolutionary activity six times between 1897 and 1917. A leader of the Social Democratic party in Poland and Lithuania, Dzerzhinsky was also a member of the Central Committee of the Russian Bolshevik party from 1917 until his death. Prominent in the October Revolution, in Dec., 1917, he organized and headed the Cheka, the first Soviet secret police organization, and also directed its successors, the GPU and the OGPU, until his death. In 1921–24 he was a member of the Orgburo, the chief administrative bureau, and from 1924 to 1926 he was a candidate member of the Politburo, the policy-making body of the party. While serving as head of the secret police, Dzerzhinsky was also Commissar of Communications and Transport in 1921 and Chairman of the Supreme Council of the People's Economy in 1924. Personally honest and incorruptible, he was ruthless and fanatical, believing that revolutionary ends justified any means.

JOHN M. THOMPSON, Indiana University

DZHAMBUL [jäm-bool'], city of the Soviet Union and capital of the Dzhambul Oblast of the Kazakh S.S.R. It is located on the Talas River. Dzhambul's industries include the production of chemicals and the manufacture of leather goods, wood products, and construction materials. Situated in the sugar-beet and orchard area, it has sugar refineries and fruit-canning plants. Dzhambul was famous in the 7th century, when as a caravan trading station it was known as Taraz, or Talas. Russia acquired it in 1864. Its growth was stimulated by the Turkestan-Siberian (Turksib) railroad in 1930. Called Auliye-Ata until 1933, it then became Mirzoyan; in 1937 it was renamed Dzhambul. Pop., 67,000.

DZHUGDZHUR [joog-joor] **RANGE,** mountains in Khabarovsk Krai, Amur Oblast R.S.F.S.R. In the Soviet Far East, they extend 500 mi. northeast-southwest along the coast of the Sea of Okhotsk.

DZIERZONIÓW [jĕr-zhô'nyoof] (Ger. **REICHENBACH**), industrial city of Poland, lying at the foot of the Sudeten Mountains, in Silesia. It is the most important center for the manufacture of woolen textiles in Lower Silesia. It was settled by Germans during the Middle Ages, but became Polish in 1945. Pop., 26,800.

DZUNGARIA [zoong-gär'ē-ə], also known as the Dzungarian Basin, a vast semidesert, plateau region in north Sinkiang, northwestern China, between Tien Shan and the Altai Mountains. It is roughly triangular in shape and stretches about 700 mi. from east to west and 500 mi. from north to south at its greatest breadth. Situated at the heart of the continent and enclosed by high mountain ranges, it has a semiarid-to-arid climate. Streams generally lose themselves in sand or gravel or drain into salt lakes. The only exception is Kara Irtis River (Russ. Cherny Irtysh), which flows westward across Kazakh S.S.R. to join the Ob in western Siberia. Urumchi, Chuguchak (Tacheng), and Altai (Sharasume) are the chief communities of the basin. Known historically as Tien Shan Pei-lu (the silk route north of Tien Shan), the region passed into the hands of the Dzungars in the latter half of the 17th century and to Sinkiang in 1878.

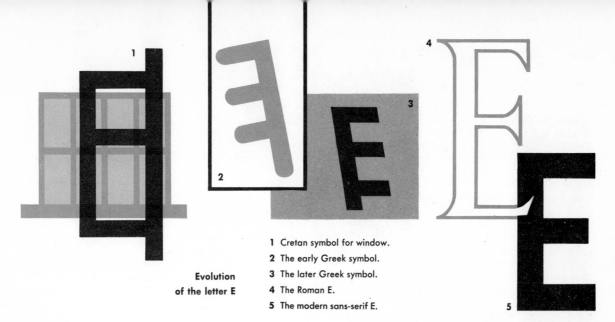

Evolution
of the letter E

1 Cretan symbol for window.
2 The early Greek symbol.
3 The later Greek symbol.
4 The Roman E.
5 The modern sans-serif E.

E, fifth letter of the English alphabet. Its North Semitic, Greek, and Latin ancestors were fifth in their alphabets. Perhaps it originally meant "a lattice window," which is what a Cretan symbol that may be compared with the letter does resemble. Called *hē* in Hebrew, the Semitic symbol denotes an initial aspirate *h*. Early Greek had an initial fricative consonant that approximates an initial *h*. When Ionic Greek lost its rough breathing, the symbol Ⴙ (*chēth*), which had come to designate an initial aspirated *e* (*he*), could be used simply for an *e* sound. But *hē* (Ⴏ), adapted from the Semitic into the Greek, meantime had come to symbolize the vocalic value *e*, a high front vowel roughly like English *e* in b*e*d or French *è*.

Nowhere in English orthography are sound and spelling more confused. Often *e* is written and not pronounced (gon*e*); the sound *e* is written *e* (b*e*d), *ea* (br*ea*d), *ie* (fr*ie*nd), *a* (*a*ny), *ai* (s*ai*d), and in other ways. Moreover, the letter itself has different values: long as in b*e*, short as in h*e*n, diphthongized as in th*e*re.

JOSHUA WHATMOUGH, Harvard University
See also ALPHABET.

EADS [ēdz], **JAMES BUCHANAN** (1820–87), American civil engineer. A man of outstanding determination, force, and character, he made a fortune as a glass manufacturer, became a leading citizen of St. Louis, and built seven Civil War ironclad river boats in 64 days. His major work was the great highway-railroad, Eads Bridge (1869–74), over the Mississippi at St. Louis, the first American work in which steel was used for its three spans. His equally famous jetties through the Mississippi Delta contributed to making New Orleans a seaport. Several of his able assistants went on to distinguished engineering careers.

EAGELS [ē′gəlz], **JEANNE** (1894–1929), American actress, born in Kansas City, Mo. A colorful, tempestuous performer, she first gained fame on the U.S. stage in *Daddies* (1918), and subsequently appeared as Sadie Thompson in *Rain* (1922), a role synonymous with her name, and in *Her Cardboard Lover* (1927).

EAGLE, name for approximately 50 species of large birds of prey in the hawk family, Accipitridae, characterized by a strongly hooked beak, powerful talons, and extremely keen vision. Eagles are carnivorous or scavenging birds of great strength and size, although both of these qualities are frequently exaggerated. The largest eagle, *Harpia*, the great harpy eagle, weighs about 12 lb., stands 3 ft. high, and has a wingspread of 7 ft. It can carry a weight of 8 to 10 lb. into the air. Ever since the Romans topped the spears of their legions with silver eagles, this bird has been a national emblem and symbol of power.

Eagles are world-wide in distribution. The true eagles, of the genus *Aquila*, are found in North America, Eurasia, and Africa. Members of this genus, which includes the golden eagle, have legs that are completely feathered, or "booted," to the toes. The genus of sea eagles, *Haliaeetus*, to which the bald eagle belongs, is characterized by unfeathered legs. Sea eagles are found living along the coasts of all continents, except South America. Harpy eagles, of the genus *Harpia*, include the largest eagles. They are found in South America, the Philippines, and New Guinea. The smaller hawk eagles, *Spizaetus*, are found in the tropical forests of Africa, Asia, and Central and South America.

CLARENCE J. HYLANDER, Author, *Feathers and Flight*
See also BALD EAGLE; GOLDEN EAGLE; HARPY EAGLE.

EAGLE PASS, city of southwestern Texas and seat of Maverick County, on the Rio Grande opposite Piedras Negras, Mexico. It is a regional trade center for an irrigated agricultural area especially noted for spinach. A U.S. radar station is here. Settled, 1849; pop. (1950) 7,276; (1960) 12,094.

EAGLETON VILLAGE, unincorporated community of eastern Tennessee, a residential suburb adjoining Maryville and Alcoa. Pop. (1960) 5,068.

EAKER [ā′kər], **IRA CLARENCE** (1896–   ), American aviator and Army officer. He was born in Field Creek, Tex. He served as a second lieutenant in the infantry during World War I and joined the Army Air Service in 1917. As chief pilot of the Army plane *Question Mark*, he set (1929) a world endurance record. In 1936 he made the first transcontinental blind flight. During World War II

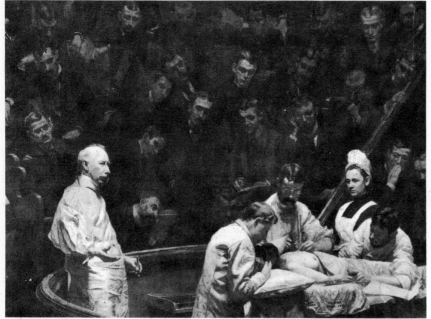

In 1889 Thomas Eakins was commissioned to do a portrait of the prominent surgeon Dr. D. Hayes Agnew, who was retiring from the University of Pennsylvania Medical School. The result was "Agnew Clinic." Dr. Agnew stands at left, explaining the operation to his students. Eakins had himself painted into the scene by his wife. His face is partially visible at the extreme right. The picture shocked the art world, and Dr. Agnew himself objected to it.

he commanded the 8th Air Force (1943) and the Mediterranean Allied Air Forces (1944). He was deputy commander of the Army Air Forces and chief of the air staff from 1945 to 1947, when he retired to enter business.

EAKINS, THOMAS (1844–1916), painter, teacher, leading American realist. Born in Philadelphia, he studied at the Pennsylvania Academy of the Fine Arts and also anatomy at Jefferson Medical College. In Paris he spent three years (1866–69) at the Académie des Beaux-Arts under Gérôme. From there he went to Spain for six months, painting in Seville and studying his favorite masters—Velázquez, Ribera, and Rembrandt—in the Prado in Madrid. He returned in 1870 to Philadelphia, his home for the rest of his life.

A complete realist in his art, Eakins was deeply interested in the sciences of anatomy, mathematics, and perspective. From the beginning his paintings were based on the everyday life of his community, its people, homes, and occupations, which he pictured with absolute realism, sure grasp of character, and reserved but deep emotional attachment. His love of outdoor activities produced many early scenes of rowing, sailing, and hunting. His absorption in medical science resulted in his early masterpiece "The Gross Clinic" (1875; Jefferson Medical College, Philadelphia), showing the famous surgeon Dr. Samuel David Gross operating before his students, and his similar "Agnew Clinic" (1889; University of Pennsylvania, Philadelphia), both of which shocked the art world.

A natural teacher, Eakins began teaching at the Pennsylvania Academy in 1876. As head of the school from 1879, he discarded the old emphasis on antique drawing and based his system on a thorough study of the nude, an innovation which had a lasting effect on American teaching methods. But conservative opposition caused him to resign in 1886. Though he continued for several years to teach at his own school, the Art Students League of Philadelphia, and elsewhere, the Academy affair was a serious blow to his career.

Probably due to this, and to lack of recognition of his own art, from the middle 1880's Eakins ceased picturing the broader contemporary scene and devoted himself almost entirely to portraiture. In this more limited field his uncompromising realism, his mastery of character and physical structure, his deep understanding of the individual man or woman, and the vitality with which he endowed them, made him the most powerful American portraitist of his time. Never a worldly success, he received few commissions, and almost all his portraits were labors of love. In the official art world he was almost entirely neglected until his last years, but his reputation has grown steadily since his death. His art has strongly influenced American realism, especially through Robert Henri and his group. The largest collection of Eakins's works is in the Philadelphia Museum. He is represented in most American museums, notably The Metropolitan Museum of Art in New York and the Addison Gallery of American Art in Andover, Mass.

LLOYD GOODRICH, Whitney Museum of American Art

EALING [ē'lǐng], municipal borough of Middlesex, England, and a residential suburb of northwestern London. It is also an important industrial center specializing in light manufacturing and consumer goods. Gunnersbury Park is on the southern boundary of the borough and was acquired from the Rothschild family by joint action of the councils of Acton, Ealing, and Brentford and Chiswick. The park contains two Regency mansions, one of which houses a museum of local history. Pop., 183,151.

EAMES [ēmz], **CHARLES** (1907–   ), American designer, best known for his furniture, especially his molded plywood and cast plastic chairs. Eames, who was born in St. Louis, also worked as an architect and as a designer and producer of industrial motion pictures. His chairs, made of pieces of molded plywood attached to a metal frame or of plastic that is formed in a mold, have greatly influenced contemporary concepts of furniture.

EAMES [āmz], **EMMA** (1865–1952), noted American operatic soprano. Born in Shanghai, she was raised in Portland, Maine. In 1889 she sang Juliette opposite the Romeo of Jean de Reszke at the Paris Opéra and made her Metropolitan Opera debut in 1891 in the same role. She remained at the Metropolitan until 1909, appearing in *Carmen, Lohengrin, Aida, The Magic Flute, Tosca,* and other works. A magnificent-looking woman gifted with a remarkable voice, she was one of the foremost sopranos of her day.

EAR, the organ of hearing and balance. The ear translates air-borne sound waves first into mechanical vibrations and then into electrical impulses which are conducted to the brain. The human ear can hear sounds ranging in loudness from a fleeting whisper to the roar of a subway train and can detect frequencies extending from the lower register of the bass fiddle to the upper notes of the trumpet. The familiar characteristics of heard sound are derived from the physical features of the sound wave. The intensity of the wave roughly corresponds to the loudness of the sound. The frequency is heard as pitch and the complexity lends timbre. How the ear faithfully transforms sound into nerve impulses and how the brain perceives tonal patterns and other complexities is not yet completely understood, but much has been learned.

STUDY GUIDE

THE EAR AND HEARING

The article on these pages deals with the structure of the ear and its functions in hearing and in balance. The topic of hearing is related to a wide range of other topics. Pertinent articles are here listed under appropriate headings.

Sound. The article SOUND discusses sound waves and their speed in air, water, and solids. This article also covers the range of frequencies audible to the human ear; the decibel, a unit for expressing intensity of sound; and the question of noise versus music.

The Ear. The article EAR discusses the organ that receives sound waves and translates them into mechanical vibrations in the middle ear and then into nerve impulses. After a description of the outer, middle, and inner ear, theories of how pitch and loudness are perceived are covered.

The Perception of Sound. Physicists and engineers know a great deal about the properties of sound waves, and medical scientists have analyzed many functions of the ear. Still unanswered are questions such as how vibrations in the air and in the ear are experienced in the mind as talk or music or the noise of an airplane. Attempts to deal with these problems are discussed in SENSATION. Two relevant articles are BRAIN and NERVOUS SYSTEM.

Deafness. The article DEAFNESS is concerned with partial as well as total lack or loss of hearing. The first section of the article deals with impaired hearing from the medical point of view. The second section covers the education and social adjustment of deaf and hard of hearing individuals. Related articles include EDUCATION: *Education of Exceptional Children* and HANDICAPPED, REHABILITATION OF THE.

The Three Parts of the Ear

The visible part of the ear is the least important from the point of view of hearing. Together with the external ear canal it comprises the external ear.

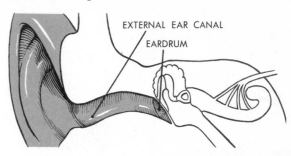

EXTERNAL EAR CANAL
EARDRUM

The middle ear begins at the eardrum which is linked to the ossicles, three delicate bones which are often picturesquely described as the hammer (malleus), anvil (incus), and stirrup (stapes). Actually, of the three, the stapes is aptly named, while the malleus looks more like a club, and the incus is nondescript.

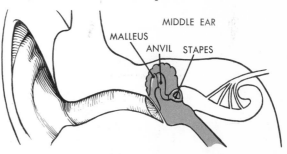

MIDDLE EAR
MALLEUS
ANVIL STAPES

Sound vibrations are transmitted by the lever system of the ossicles to the oval window. The mechanical arrangement is such that the vibrations are conducted from the eardrum to an area approximately $\frac{1}{13}$ its size at the oval window. Correspondingly the pressure at the stirrup is about 17 times greater than that at the drum.

It should also be noted that the middle ear joins the inner ear at two points, the oval window and the round window. The inner ear can be described as a fluid-filled chamber enclosed in bone.

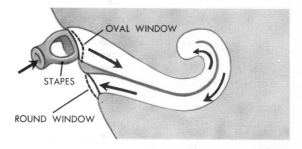

OVAL WINDOW
STAPES
ROUND WINDOW

The advantage of the round window becomes apparent from this diagram. As the stirrup moves in, the round window is pushed out. Without this flexible second window, it would be difficult to transmit energy to the fluid of the inner ear, since fluids are compressed with great difficulty and the surrounding bone is inelastic.

We do not hear sound directly. What we actually experience are nerve impulses in the brain. The diagram follows the path of two musical notes through the ear and into the brain. In the "translation" from physical sound to nerve impulse the hearing apparatus attempts to preserve the physical properties of the sound wave which cause us ultimately to experience sound as loud or soft, or as high or low in pitch. Part of this process is detailed in the "portraits of sound," presented with each of the stages, showing how the pitch of two notes is distinguished at each point along the hearing pathway.

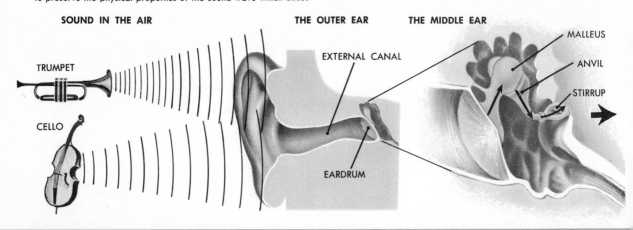

SOUND IN THE AIR **THE OUTER EAR** **THE MIDDLE EAR**

TRUMPET

CELLO

EXTERNAL CANAL

EARDRUM

MALLEUS

ANVIL

STIRRUP

In the atmosphere sound consists of vibrations of air. A snapshot of the sound moving in the air would show alternate regions of highly packed and loosely spaced molecules. The high-pitched note would show more waves per unit of time than the low-pitched note.

The funnel-shaped outer ear directs the sound waves to the eardrum. At this point the pitch of the two sounds is translated into vibrations of the eardrum. The vibration frequency is higher for the high-pitched sound and lower for the low-pitched sound.

The movements of the eardrum are transmitted through the small bones of the middle ear (hammer, anvil, and stirrup). Here the two notes are distinguished by the frequency of vibrations in the bones.

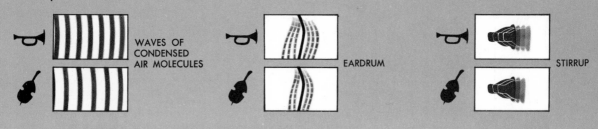

WAVES OF CONDENSED AIR MOLECULES

EARDRUM

STIRRUP

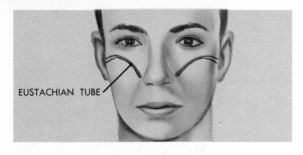

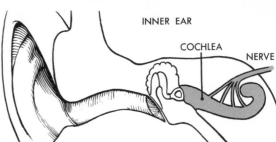

INNER EAR

COCHLEA

NERVE

EUSTACHIAN TUBE

The Eustachian Tubes—Balancing Air Pressure on the Eardrum

The unpleasant "stopped" sensation in the ears, experienced when rapidly ascending from one height to another, results from an outward bulging of the eardrum caused by inequality in air pressure. The condition is remedied by opening the mouth; this permits air to flow through the eustachian tube to the middle ear, equalizing the air pressure on either side of the eardrum.

The Inner Ear—Vibrations Into Nerve Impulses

The sound-sensing part of the inner ear is the cochlea,

a spiral structure which resembles a snail's shell. If the cochlea is examined in cross section it can be seen to be composed of a number of canals, which extend throughout its length. Each canal is subdivided into three parts. The smallest contains the organ of corti, which is actually the organ of hearing.

The hair cells of the organ of corti are thought to be the sensing elements which convert mechanical movement into nerve impulses. One of the basic problems in the study of hearing concerns how the organ of corti detects sounds of different frequency so that we are aware of differences in pitch.

SEMICIRCULAR CANALS

STIRRUP IN OVAL WINDOW

COCHLEAR DUCT

SCALA TYMPANI

SCALA VESTIBULI

ROUND WINDOW

SCALA TYMPANI

AUDITORY NERVE

AUDITORY CENTER OF BRAIN

CEREBRUM

The stirrup vibrates against the oval window, setting up waves in the fluid of the spiral cochlea. The arrows indicate the path of these waves. They originate at the oval window and then travel through the inner channel (scala vestibuli), reaching the outer chamber (scala tympani) by way of the middle section (the cochlear duct). They may also curve around the tip of the spiral. The waves terminate at the round window. Differences of pitch are preserved in the frequency of the waves.

The fluid waves of the inner chamber of the cochlea are transmitted to the middle chamber, or cochlear duct. Here the waves generate tension on hair cells, thus exciting a nerve impulse that travels from the ear in the auditory nerve. At this point pitch discrimination is no longer a question of how *often* stimulation occurs (frequency), but rather *where* in the cochlea the nerve impulses arise (with exceptions: see text). The higher the pitch of the sound the more toward the base of the cochlea the stimulation occurs.

The sound travels toward the brain, now coded in the electrochemical language of the nervous system. Sounds of specific pitch apparently travel in specific fibers. As seen in the diagram, impulses from one ear cross over to reach both halves of the brain. The nerve message ultimately reaches the auditory portion of the cerebral cortex where the pitch is recognized by virtue of which brain cells are stimulated, as the pitch of the piano depends upon which key is struck.

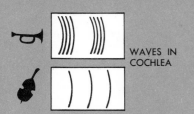

WAVES IN COCHLEA

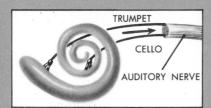

TRUMPET

CELLO

AUDITORY NERVE

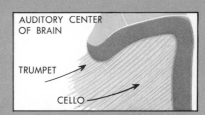

AUDITORY CENTER OF BRAIN

TRUMPET

CELLO

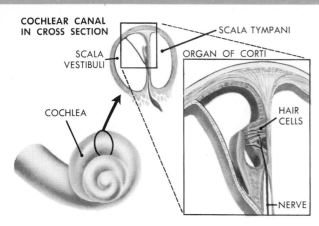

COCHLEAR CANAL IN CROSS SECTION

SCALA TYMPANI

SCALA VESTIBULI

ORGAN OF CORTI

COCHLEA

HAIR CELLS

NERVE

The "Resonance," "Telephone," and Other Theories of Pitch Perception

In 1863 the German physicist Helmholtz suggested that the cochlea might contain a special structure for each frequency of sound. Helmholtz proposed that a specific element of the cochlea resonated at a definite frequency in much the same way as a drinking glass vibrates to a particular note of a vigorous tenor—in effect, a different-sized glass for each note. This became known as the "resonance" theory. Some time later a "telephone" theory was advanced which placed the responsibility for frequency analysis with the brain. According to this view a sound impulse of say 15,000 cycles per second would be converted into a nerve message consisting of 15,000 impulses per second. The message would reach the brain which would in some way become aware of the difference between this and other frequencies.

The two theories have now been merged into the modern concept of frequency analysis. It has been demonstrated that one theory describes hearing at low frequencies and the other at high frequencies. In one case the brain "recognizes" pitch on the basis of a time factor—the interval between impulses (frequency); in the other case by a space factor—the specific part of the nerve which carries the impulse. At low frequencies the entire cochlea vibrates and pitch is analyzed on the basis of the frequency of impulses traveling in the nerve (the telephone theory). These impulses travel in fibers which are randomly distributed in the nerve. At higher frequencies a specific part of the cochlea resonates with a specific frequency—similar to the Helmholtzian notion, but not quite the same, since the entire cochlea is fused and vibrates

179

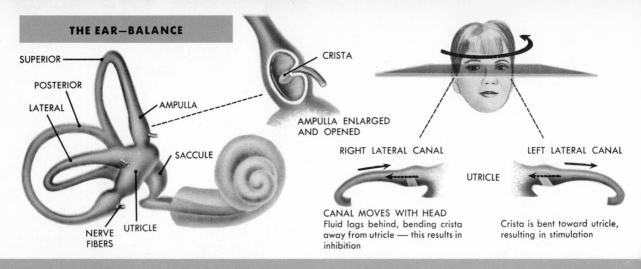

SUPERIOR

POSTERIOR

LATERAL

AMPULLA

CRISTA

SACCULE

AMPULLA ENLARGED AND OPENED

RIGHT LATERAL CANAL

LEFT LATERAL CANAL

UTRICLE

NERVE FIBERS

UTRICLE

CANAL MOVES WITH HEAD
Fluid lags behind, bending crista away from utricle — this results in inhibition

Crista is bent toward utricle, resulting in stimulation

THE SEMICIRCULAR CANALS are an important source of information concerning body movement. The three canals lie at approximately right angles to each other in the inner ear. The sensory receptors (cristae) are found in the openings (ampullae) at one end of the canal. When bent by movements of fluid within the canal, the cristae generate nerve impulses that are conducted to the brain via the vestibular nerve.

The canals are maximally activated by rotation in their own plane. When this occurs, the fluid lags behind in the canals, bending the cristae which move with the head — as a cyclist is bent by the wind when he pedals vigorously. Stimulation occurs only when the cristae are bent toward the utricle. Thus the right to left rotation above stimulates the left canal and inhibits the right canal.

as a unit, but with greater vigor at the point of resonance. The fibers, carrying impulses from a specific part of the cochlea, travel in a particular section of the nerve, so that the brain can "recognize" a frequency by the particular fibers that carry it.

The Perception of Loudness. Loudness is thought to be indicated by the total number of fibers discharging and the rate at which they discharge. The matter is not quite clear since, as observed above, the rate of fiber discharge is also supposed to indicate low-frequency sounds.

Binaural Hearing and the Localization of Sound. Sounds are heard as originating from a point in space. This localization is accomplished by the difference in time interval required for the sound to reach each ear (for lower frequencies) and by difference in intensity (for higher frequencies). "Stereophonic" sound is obtained by detecting these differences as picked up by two or more separated microphones and playing them back through separate speakers.

Hearing Tests—Audiometry

The measurement of hearing is known as audiometry. A standard procedure consists of presenting a series of pure tones (a single frequency) to the subject. In this way the sensitivity of the ear can be mapped out over the entire frequency range.

Two ingenious techniques have been devised for use with children and with those who cannot understand instructions. In the galvanic skin response (GSR) method the subject is exposed to a mild electric shock whenever he hears a tone. After a series of such shocks, presentation of an audible tone will cause an automatic reaction which lowers the electrical resistance of the skin. The operator can then test each tone by presenting successively louder impulses and noting at what level of loudness the resistance of the skin changes. In the electroencephalograph test, electrodes placed on the skull detect changes in the brain waves which occur in response to sound.

The Social-Adequacy Index (SAI) is a measure of the individual's ability to understand conversational speech. This is determined by presenting a spoken group of words at uniform intensities; the subject's ability to correctly repeat the words provides his social-adequacy index.

Bone Conduction. Sound can reach the inner ear by means of vibrations transmitted directly through the skull. This by-passing of the middle ear is useful in testing hearing in individuals suffering from middle-ear damage. A vibrator is applied to the skull for this purpose.

The Ear and Balance—the Semicircular Canals

The inner ear contains, in addition to the cochlea, a group of structures which are concerned with body balance. These structures are the three semicircular canals and the vestibule.

The sensitive elements of the canal are cone-shaped structures (cristae) found in the large open ends of the canals—the ampullae. When the head is rotated or moved in a vertical plane the fluid contained in the canals lags behind the motion of the body, deflecting the sensory structures and informing the brain of the motion. The stimulation depends upon the drag, or inertia, of the fluid against the cristae and consequently occurs only when motion begins or ceases. If the individual spins in a continuous motion, stimulation ceases after the initial acceleration and the brain receives no information as to the state of body motion. This accounts for the confusion experienced when one whirls around rapidly. Ballet dancers avoid such confusion during pirouettes by alternately increasing and decreasing their motions, stimulating the cristae with each acceleration and deceleration.

In contrast to the sensory elements of the ampullae, which detect rotary motion, other receptors (in the utricle) are stimulated principally by changes in the position of the head and by straight-line movements. These are known as "gravity" receptors.

The nerve impulses from the semicircular canals are

co-ordinated with messages from the eyes and the body muscles to maintain the normal upright position.

EDMUND S. CRELIN, Yale University School of Medicine
See also DEAFNESS; MOTION SICKNESS; SOUND.

EARHART [âr'härt], **AMELIA** (1898–1937), American aviatrix. Born in Atchison, Kan., she served as a Red Cross hospital worker in Canada during World War I, and later as a settlement worker in Boston, Mass. After that, she took a job in California to gain funds for flying lessons. On June 17, 1928, she became the first woman to fly the Atlantic, the passenger of Wilmer Stultz. Four years later, on May 20–21, 1932, she flew the same course alone from Harbor Grace, Newfoundland, to Ireland (2,026 mi.) in less than 15 hours. After flying solo from Hawaii to California, and making several record-breaking flights across the United States—one of them in a helicopter—she attempted, in 1937, a round-the-world trip in a twin-engined *Lockheed Electra* with Lt. Comdr. Fred Noonan as navigator. They had completed two-thirds of the journey and were approaching tiny Howland Island in the South Pacific when radio contact with the plane ceased. A massive search by ships and planes produced no trace of the fliers or of the Lockheed, and they were considered "lost" as of July 2, 1937. Amelia Earhart authored *The Fun of It* (1932) and *Last Flight* (1938). Her husband, publisher G. P. Putnam, wrote her biography, *Soaring Wings* (1939).

CLAYTON KNIGHT, O. B. E., Author, *The Story of Flight*

EARLY [ûr'lē], **JUBAL ANDERSON** (1816–94), Confederate army officer in the U.S. Civil War. He was born in Franklin County, Va., and graduated from West Point. Early fought briefly in Florida during the Seminole War, then resigned his commission to study and practise law at Rocky Mount, Va. After serving one term in the Virginia legislature, he volunteered for active duty in the Mexican War but saw no combat. He was opposed to secession but accepted appointment in the Confederate army. Promoted to brigadier general for his action at the first Battle of Bull Run, he fought at Chancellorsville, Gettysburg, and the Wilderness. A lieutenant general by 1864, Early was sent by Gen. Robert E. Lee at the head of an independent corps of 20,000 men to attack the Union forces in the Shenandoah Valley. After driving them westward, Early marched on Washington, D.C., crossed the Potomac and defeated Gen. Lew Wallace at the Monocacy River, near Frederick, Md., on July 9. He then moved to the outskirts of the capital. When he learned of the arrival of Union reinforcements in Washington, Early withdrew to northern Virginia.

Gen. Philip H. Sheridan's Army of Shenandoah of 50,000 men, formed to halt Early's activities, defeated him at Winchester and Fisher's Hill, Va. in September. In October, Early surprised Union troops at Cedar Creek, Va., but he was routed when Sheridan himself hastened to the battle from Winchester. Defeated by Gen. George A. Custer at Waynesboro, Va. (Mar. 2, 1865), Early was removed from command. After the war he went to Mexico and then to Canada. He returned to Virginia in 1869 and practised law.

MARTIN BLUMENSON, formerly, Senior Historian, Department of the Army

Amelia Earhart, first woman to fly the Atlantic. (BETTMANN ARCHIVE)

EARP [ûrp], **WYATT** (1848–1929), American frontier peace officer. Earp, who was more than 6 ft. tall and weighed barely 155 lb., has long been the prototype of the reticent, cold-eyed Western marshal. After working as a stagecoach driver, railroad construction hand, surveyor, and buffalo hunter, he became a policeman in the cow town of Wichita, Kans. When Dodge City became the cowboy capital of the world, Earp was sent for in May, 1876, to be chief deputy marshal at $250 a month and $2.50 for each arrest. He enforced the hitherto unenforceable ordinance against gun toting and by the following September had so quieted the "Gomorrah of the Plains" that he departed for the gold-wild town of Deadwood, S. Dak.

When in the spring of 1878 six-shooters again blazed without interference in Dodge City, Earp was sent for and once more the town was quieted. He then left for Arizona to begin a stage line, only to be asked to tame turbulent Tombstone, then in the midst of a mining boom. Arriving on Dec. 1, 1879, he rode with outbound treasure shipments to stop holdups, went after cattle rustlers, and obtained sizable fees, which he invested in real estate. Resigning as deputy sheriff, he continued to serve as a deputy federal marshal and a guard for Wells, Fargo and Company. He also served as guard for the Oriental, the town's leading gambling house, for which he received as much as $1,000 a week.

When the Clantons, a notorious group of ranchers, escaped from the Tombstone jail, a citizens' safety committee named Wyatt Earp deputy marshal again, along with his brother Morgan and John H. ("Doc") Holliday, and named Wyatt's brother, Virgil, marshal. On Oct. 25, 1881, the showdown came with the famous O.K. Corral gunfight, which resulted in the restoration of law and order in Tombstone. Argument, however, persists to this day in Arizona whether the Earps were cold-blooded killers or frontier heroes. Wyatt Earp left Arizona to live in Denver, El Paso, San Diego, and Alaska, and to care for his oil and mining interests.

JOE B. FRANTZ, University of Texas

EARTH

EARTH, third planet in order of distance from the sun. It moves about the sun in an elliptical orbit, which brings it approximately 91,000,000 mi. from the sun early in January and 94,500,000 mi. from the sun early in July. Its mean distance from the sun is slightly less than 93,000,000 mi.

Motion. The earth completes one revolution around the sun in 365 days, 5 hours, 48 minutes and 46 seconds. This is the tropical year, or year of the seasons. At the same time, every 24 hours the earth rotates upon its polar axis in relation to the sun. This rotation is in the same direction as its revolution, counterclockwise as seen from above the north pole. Thus, the earth gains slightly less than 1° on its orbit on the stars with each rotation. Its rotational period in relation to the stars is 23 hours, 56 minutes, 4 seconds of mean time. This is the *sidereal day,* or the day as determined by the stars.

The polar axis of the earth is inclined at an angle of 23° 26′ 54″ to the ecliptic—the plane of the earth's orbit around the sun. This inclination, which makes the earth present a regularly changing area of its surface to the direct rays of the sun, causes the seasons. The sun's direct rays, which produce a greater heating effect, strike the Northern Hemisphere, beginning Mar. 21 and extending to Sept. 23. The greatest altitude of the noon sun is on June 21, producing spring and summer in the Northern Hemisphere and autumn and winter south of the equator. From Sept. 23 until Mar. 21, the direct rays fall on the Southern Hemisphere, reversing the seasons.

Density. The density of the earth is 5.52 times the density of water. It is the densest of all the planets. Its mass has been calculated at 6×10^{21} metric tons (6 followed by 21 zeros). The earth is believed to have a rela-

MOTIONS OF THE EARTH

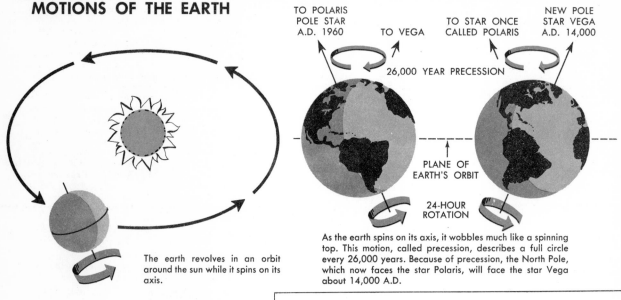

The earth revolves in an orbit around the sun while it spins on its axis.

As the earth spins on its axis, it wobbles much like a spinning top. This motion, called precession, describes a full circle every 26,000 years. Because of precession, the North Pole, which now faces the star Polaris, will face the star Vega about 14,000 A.D.

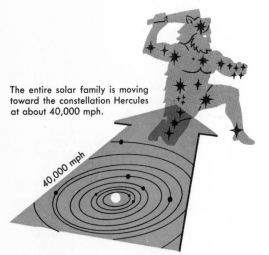

The entire solar family is moving toward the constellation Hercules at about 40,000 mph.

LONGITUDE AND LATITUDE

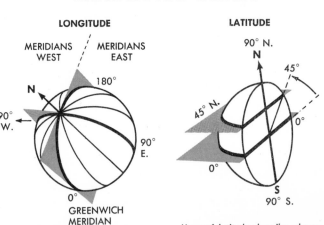

Lines of longitude are great circles, the planes of which pass through the earth's center and through the North and South poles. Halves of these circles from pole to pole are called meridians.

Lines of latitude describe planes that are parallel to the plane of the equator. Latitude is measured by the angle formed by lines drawn from the center of the earth to the equator and to the line of latitude on the earth's surface.

The article on these pages summarizes information from a number of fields of science in a brief description of the planet inhabited by man. After noting the relation of the earth to the other planets in the solar system, the article discusses the following topics.

Motions of the Earth. Revolution in orbit around the sun, rotation on its axis, and movement with the solar system through space. Explanation of the year, day and night, and the seasons.

Density. Densest of all planets. Crust and core. Amount of earth's surface covered by water.

Atmosphere. How earth retains atmosphere. Composition and layers of atmosphere. Ozone shields earth.

Magnetic Field. Concentration near poles of rotation. Formation of Van Allen Belt.

Precession and Tides. Precession of the equinoxes caused by gravitational effect of sun and moon. Tides, spring tides, neap tides. Tides generally follow the moon, varying with shore conformation.

Origin. A matter of theory. Turbulence in outer regions of nebulous cloud resulted in condensations that became planets and other small bodies. Calculation of earth's age.

Many articles provide material for further study of scientific knowledge and theories about the earth. These may be grouped in four categories. The broadest is introduced by the entry COSMOLOGY, which discusses theories of the origin and nature of the universe. SOLAR SYSTEM concentrates on one star, the sun, and its planets, presenting theories that attempt to explain their origin. Other pertinent articles include GRAVITATION, SUN, MOON, YEAR, SEASON, and CALENDAR.

A second group of articles is centered around the major entry GEOLOGY, which discusses the science that studies the earth from its beginnings. The scope of this science can be shown by citing articles on some important subdivisions and related sciences. MINERALOGY deals with natural compounds and native elements in the earth. PETROLOGY and ROCKS treat the study of rocks. GEOCHEMISTRY describes uses of the techniques of chemistry in geological studies. GEOPHYSICS takes in the study of physical properties of the whole earth — interior, surface, and atmosphere. Related articles include SEISMOGRAPH, EARTHQUAKE, and VOLCANO. GEOMORPHOLOGY discusses the study of surface features and factors that produce them, such as EROSION. The broad field of science that deals with the oceans is covered in OCEANOGRAPHY and supplementary articles. The study of fossil remains of ancient plants and animals is the topic of PALEONTOLOGY. One of the many contributions of geology to knowledge of the earth is a time scale. The four major divisions are treated in GEOLOGY and in separate entries: PRECAMBRIAN, PALEOZOIC, MESOZOIC, and CENOZOIC.

A third group of articles can be approached through METEOROLOGY, a survey of the science that deals with the atmosphere. This field is related to geophysics — an example of how the divisions of modern science interconnect. Major articles pertaining to metereology are ATMOSPHERE and CLIMATOLOGY.

A fourth group of articles centers around GEOGRAPHY. This broad area of study is concerned with the physical features of the earth's surface and therefore draws on the work of geologists. Geography extends its scope to include plant and animal life. Geographers are particularly concerned with how physical features, climates, plants, animals, and other phenomena are distributed on the earth. They study aspects of human culture such as population clusters, patterns of farming, and routes of travel and trade. Geography may thus be considered a link between the physical sciences that study the earth and the biological and social sciences that study life on earth. Articles pertinent to geography include MAP, general articles such as CONTINENT, and entries on specific continents and countries.

tively thin crust floating upon a mantle of silicates. The silicate mantle envelops a core of nickel-iron, probably molten, since the earth's central temperature has been calculated at 5,000° F. About 75% of the earth's surface is covered by water.

Atmosphere. Due to its mass and radius, the earth's surface gravity is such that a moving body must attain a velocity of 6.9 miles per second to free itself from the earth's effective gravitational pull. This is the earth's *velocity of escape*. Since the molecular motion of many gases is less than this, the earth retains about it a gaseous envelope, the atmosphere. Composition of the atmosphere is 78% nitrogen and 21% oxygen. Traces of other gases, chiefly argon and carbon dioxide, make up another 1%. Water vapor and impurities in the form of dust are in suspension in the atmosphere.

The atmosphere's pressure on the surface of the earth is sufficient to balance a column of mercury 760 mm., or 30 in. high. This pressure is reduced by 50% for every 3 mi. of distance above the earth's surface, so that 90% of the atmosphere is within 10 mi. of the surface. The layer of atmosphere closest to earth is the *troposphere*, in which most atmospheric motion and all weather phenomena occur. Above the troposphere is the *stratosphere*, extending to about 60 mi. Above that is the *ionosphere*, reaching to about 400 mi. The ionosphere is affected by forces from space, particularly from the sun, which bombard and disturb (ionize) the atoms of this part of the atmosphere.

Ionization creates a form of oxygen called *ozone*, which shields the earth from most of the lethal qualities of the sun's radiation. It also creates layers in the ionosphere, which reflect radio radiation from the earth, making radio transmission possible. Above the ionosphere is the *exosphere*, which contains the outermost traces of atmosphere and fades into space.

Magnetic Field. A magnetic field extends about the earth, concentrated at the magnetic poles which are near, but not at, the poles of rotation. The field is most extended over the earth's equatorial region. Nearly all of the particles from the sun and from space are deflected or trapped by the earth's magnetic field. They spiral about the lines of force of the magnetic field, forming the Van Allen Belt, a region of radioactive particles open at the poles but deepest above the equatorial areas.

Precession and Tides. An oblate spheroid, the earth is slightly flattened at its poles. Its polar diameter is 7,900 mi. Its diameter, measured in the plane of its equator, is 7,927 mi., giving it an oblateness of 1/297. The gravitational effect of the sun and the moon upon the slight equatorial bulge of the earth produces a third important motion of the earth. Because of the inclination of the earth's polar axis, neither the sun nor the moon is directly above the equator, except for brief periods of time. These occasions occur twice each year for the sun and twice each month for the moon. At all other times, the sun and the moon exert a gravitational pull on the earth's equatorial excess,

THE EARTH'S INTERIOR

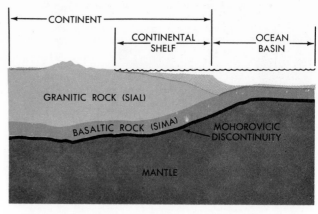

The inner core of the earth, believed to be solid, is surrounded by a molten outer core. Both are encased in a rocky layer called the mantle, which extends to the earth's crust.

Cross section of the earth's crust. Granitic rock is the dominant rock of the continents. Basaltic rock underlies both oceans and continents. The Mohorovicic discontinuity is the boundary between the crust and the underlying mantle.

PHYSICAL AND ORBITAL ELEMENTS OF THE EARTH

Size and Mass

Diameter (equatorial)	7,927 miles
Diameter (polar)	7,900 miles
Volume	2.6×10^{11} cubic miles
Mass	6×10^{21} metric tons
Specific gravity	5.52
Acceleration of gravity	32 feet per second^2
Velocity of escape	6.95 miles per second

Area

Total area	196,950,000 square miles
Land area	57,510,000 square miles
Water area	139,440,000 square miles

Elevation

Highest land elevation (Mt. Everest)	29,141 feet
Lowest land depression (Dead Sea)	1,286 feet below sea level
Average land elevation	2,700 feet
Greatest ocean depth (Mindanao Trench)	37,782 feet
Average ocean depth	12,000 feet

Temperature

Highest recorded surface temperature	136° F.
Lowest recorded surface temperature	−126.9° F.

Orbit

Mean distance from sun	92,900,000 miles
Perihelion distance from sun	91,500,000 miles
Aphelion distance from sun	94,500,000 miles
Circumference of orbit	583,400,000 miles
Revolution period (tropical year)	365 d. 5 h. 48 m. 56 s.
Anomalistic year (perihelion to perihelion)	365 d. 6 h. 13 m. 53 s.
Mean orbital velocity	18.52 miles per second
Inclination of axis to plane of orbit	23° 26′ 44.8″

Rotation

Rotational period (solar)	24 hours
Rotational period (sidereal)	23 h. 56 m. 4 sec.

trying to pull the equator into line with their positions. The earth's rapid rotation produces a gyroscopic effect, which resists this pull and produces a slow, conical swing of the polar axis about the center of the earth. Requiring 25,800 years to complete, this swing causes the earth's poles to describe circles against the star sphere. It also moves the intersections of the celestial equator and the ecliptic (the equinoxes) westward before the stars. This motion is the *precession of the equinoxes*. It produces a slow change of the celestial poles and a corresponding change in the location of the equinoxes with reference to the star sphere.

The combined gravitational effect of the sun and moon upon the earth causes the tides in the earth's oceans and a small but measureable distortion in the solid part of the earth. When the sun and the moon are generally in line with the earth, as at new moon or full moon, their gravitational forces are in the same plane and combine to cause extreme tides. These are *spring* tides, not from the name of the season, but from the verb "to spring." At first or last quarter moon, when the gravitational effects of the sun and the moon are at right angles to each other, tides are less abundant. These are *neap* tides, from an Anglo-Saxon word meaning scanty. Although gravitationally the sun is tremendously more powerful than the moon, the moon's proximity to earth gives it a tidal effect slightly greater than the sun's.

The physical effect of the gravitational pull of the sun and moon is a lifting of the waters of the earth nearest these bodies. To a lesser extent the solid body of the earth is drawn in the same direction, while the waters on the far side of the earth are left in the rear of this procession. There are, therefore, two high tides at opposite sides of the earth. The tides generally follow the moon. They show a slight daily delay due to the moon's eastward motion, which causes it to rise an average of 50 minutes later each day. If there were no land masses to act as barriers, the tides would sweep about the earth, always under the moon. As it is, the general tidal flow occurs about 50 minutes later each day, varying considerably with shore conformation.

Earth as seen by Lunar Orbiter V on Aug. 8, 1967, from 214,806 mi. away (the spacecraft was 3,640 mi. above the moon's surface). About five-sixths of the full planet is visible—14° W. long. to 135° E. long. Solar noon is over the center of the Arabian Peninsula.   (NASA)

Origin. Still a matter of theory is the earth's origin. The most widely accepted picture shows a vast, swiftly rotating, nebulous cloud, with turbulences in its outer regions, perhaps due to an uneven distribution of material there. These turbulences resulted in condensations that became the planets and other small bodies. The central region evolved into the sun. Such stages are thought to be part of the formation of all stars.

By measurement of radioactive decay, the earth's age is calculated at about 5 billion years. The earth probably took about 3 billion years to cool sufficiently for the development of life to begin. Human history covers the last 5,000 years aind a two-billion-year period of evolution, or about one millionth of the earth's age.

In about 6 billion years, according to most astronomers, the sun will expand during normal processes of stellar development. It will engulf the four small planets nearest it, including the earth.

James Pickering, Astronomer Emeritus,
Hayden Planetarium

EARTHENWARE, pottery, whether made from unrefined, refined, or blended clays, that is fired below the temperature needed for complete vitrification. The baked ware is porous and for utilitarian purposes is usually covered with a glaze that will fix at the temperature at which the ware is baked. Building bricks and flowerpots are unglazed earthenwares; faïence and most peasant pottery are glazed earthenwares.

EARTHQUAKE, a shaking of the ground caused by the sudden dislocation of material within the earth. Some earthquakes are so slight, and some occur in such remote areas, that they are barely felt. Others are so violent that they cause extensive damage.

The focus of an earthquake is the center of the region where the earthquake originates, and it is usually less than 20 mi. below the earth's surface. The greatest recorded focal depth is 450 mi. The point on the earth's surface directly above the focus is called the epicenter, near which most earthquake damage occurs.

Seismology

Causes. Most earthquakes are caused by the development of stresses below the earth's outer surface. These stresses may build up, sometimes over long periods of time, until the rocks fracture, or slip along a "fault plane." This sudden movement sets up vibrations, called seismic waves, that travel in all directions from the region of fracture. In all moderate and large earthquakes, the vibrations can be detected over the whole earth. Small earthquakes are also caused by the eruptions of volcanoes and by landslides. With some exceptions these are felt only locally, and the vibrations are relatively slight.

Nuclear explosions on or under the ground generate waves that are similar to natural seismic waves. These vibrations provide information of great value in earthquake research. The seismic energy generated in large atomic bomb explosions is about one hundred-thousandth that of the largest natural earthquake. A hydrogen bomb generates one-hundredth to one-tenth the energy of the largest earthquake.

Kinds of Waves. Seismic waves include body waves that travel through the earth's interior, and surface waves that travel only over the earth's surface. There are two types of body waves. The faster are the primary, or *P*, waves that make the earth particles vibrate back and forth in the direction of wave advance. These waves are transmitted through all parts of the earth. Slightly slower are the secondary, or *S*, waves that cause lateral vibrations. *S* waves do not travel through liquids, since liquids have only small resistance to shearing forces. *S* waves have not been detected in any part of the earth deeper than about 1,800 mi. This, together with other evidence, indicates that immediately below this depth the earth is molten or nearly molten.

Intensity and Magnitude. The intensity of an earthquake at any place is estimated in terms of its geological effects and effects on man-made structures. Several numerical intensity scales have been devised, but the one most used today is the Modified Mercalli Scale, which has been used since 1931. It is summarized in the following table:

MODIFIED MERCALLI SCALE OF EARTHQUAKE INTENSITIES

I Barefly felt by a few people.

II Felt only on upper floors of buildings; swinging of some suspended objects.

III Quite noticeable indoors, especially on upper floors; vibrations like those of a passing heaving truck.

IV Felt indoors by many, outdoors by few. At night some people are awakened. Dishes and windows rattle, doors creak; standing automobiles may rock.

V Felt by nearly all, many awakened. Some fragile objects broken, and unstable objects overturned; plaster walls may crack; trees and poles disturbed; pendulum clocks may stop.

VI Felt by all, many run outdoors; slight damage done; heavy furniture moved; some plaster falls.

VII Most people run outdoors; much damage to poorly built structures, slight damage to well-built structures; some chimneys broken.

VIII Much damage to ordinary buildings, with some collapse; slight damage to well-built structures; chimneys, monuments, stacks topple; heavy furniture overturned; water wells disturbed.

IX Much damage to nearly all buildings; frame structures thrown out of plumb; conspicuous cracks in ground; buried pipes broken.

X Some well-built wooden structures destroyed; most masonry structures destroyed; rails bent; landslides on steep slopes.

XI Few masonry structures left standing; bridges destroyed; broad cracks in ground.

XII Damage total; waves left in ground surface; roads, fences offset.

The intensity of an earthquake diminishes outward from the epicenter. If the intensities noted at various points are plotted on a map, it is possible to draw curves, called isoseismals, connecting points of equal intensity. If several isoseismals are drawn, each representing a different intensity, the result is a series of closed curves. The center of the innermost curve gives a rough guide to the epicenter, but there are sometimes considerable deviations. Isoseismal curves are not necessarily circular because various types of ground respond differently to earthquake vibrations. Buildings on filled ground, for example, generally are damaged more than structures built on solid rock even though both may be at the same distance from the epicenter.

The magnitude of a particular earthquake, in contrast with the intensities, is a single number which does not vary from place to place. Magnitude is roughly proportional to the total energy released by an earthquake at its focus. It is defined in terms of the amplitude of the trace that would be made by a standard seismograph located 100 km. (about 60 mi.) from the epicenter. The magnitude scale in common use was devised by the American seismologist C. F. Richter in 1935. The smallest earthquakes have magnitudes near zero on the Richter scale; the largest so far assigned is 8.6.

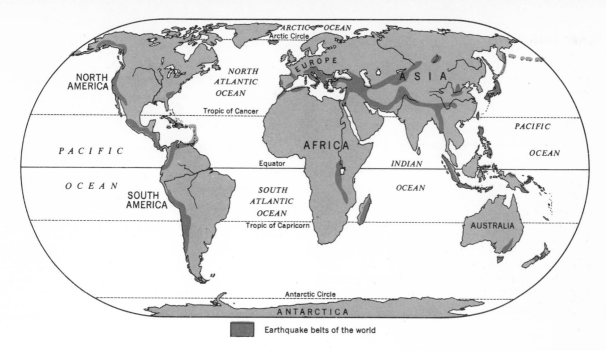

Earthquake belts of the world

The following table lists the average annual number of earthquakes of various magnitudes:

Magnitude	General Classification	Average Annual Number
8 or over	National disaster	1
7 to 8	Major earthquake	10
6 to 7	Destructive earthquake	100
5 to 6	Damaging earthquake	1,000
4 to 5	Strongly felt earthquake	10,000
3 to 4	Generally felt, small earthquake	100,000
0 to 3	Small shock, may be felt	Very many

Earthquakes of large magnitude are stronger and generally more destructive than those of small magnitude. The amount of destruction, however, depends not only on the magnitude but on the kind of ground and types of buildings thereon, and on the location of the focus in relation to heavily populated areas.

Large earthquakes are usually followed by many aftershocks, which may persist for days or months. Generally, the original shock is the most damaging, but occasionally a large earthquake is followed, perhaps days later, by an even larger aftershock. Some earthquakes are preceded by much smaller foreshocks. Sometimes "swarms" of small earthquakes persist in an area for weeks or months without being followed by a major earthquake.

EARTHQUAKES

Shock waves move in all directions from the focus of an earthquake, making the earth crack and tremble. These shock, or seismic, waves (below) are either body waves, which travel through the earth's interior, or surface waves. There are two types of body waves. Primary, or P, waves travel fastest, about 5 mi. per second. Secondary, or S, waves are about three-fifths as fast. Surface waves, called L waves, travel over the earth's surface at about 2 mi. per second.

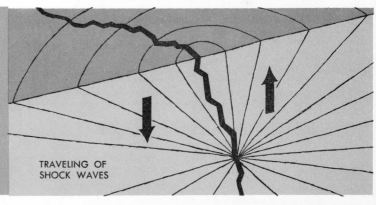

TRAVELING OF SHOCK WAVES

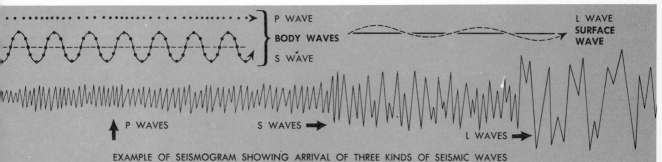

P WAVE
BODY WAVES
S WAVE

L WAVE
SURFACE WAVE

↑ P WAVES   S WAVES →   L WAVES →

EXAMPLE OF SEISMOGRAM SHOWING ARRIVAL OF THREE KINDS OF SEISMIC WAVES

Submarine Earthquakes. A ship at sea may experience a seaquake if it is close to the epicenter of a submarine earthquake. Body seismic waves pass from the focus up to the ocean floor and thence through the ocean and cause the whole ship to vibrate as though it had run aground.

More serious are the great sea waves called tsunamis (often loosely called "tidal waves") that sometimes result from a large, submarine earthquake. If the focus is just below the ocean floor, the disturbance may cause a great body of water to be suddenly raised or lowered, from which surface sea waves travel outward. The speed of these waves depends upon the ocean depth; where the ocean is 1 mi. deep, the speed is about 270 mph. Tsunamis ordinarily are too small to be noticed on the open sea. When they reach a coast line, however, the water may pile up in certain types of narrow inlets, attaining heights of 50 ft. or more in extreme cases, and causing great damage.

Distribution. Earthquakes may originate in most regions of the earth, but the predominant activity occurs in certain belts. Of all recorded seismic energy, 80% comes from a belt that roughly coincides with the borders of the Pacific Ocean. Nearly all very deep-focus earthquakes are associated with this belt and it is the site of much of the world's volcanic activity. The Pacific belt includes the Kuril Islands, Japan, the Philippine Islands, the Solomon Islands, New Guinea, New Zealand, and the west coasts of South and North America.

A second seismic belt, yielding 15% of recorded earthquake energy, branches from the Pacific belt near the East Indies and passes through southern Asia to the region of the Mediterranean Sea. The remaining 5% of seismic energy comes mainly from parts of the Arctic, Atlantic, and Indian oceans, and from eastern Africa. The least affected large land masses are Antarctica and Australia.

Prediction. It is not yet possible to predict earthquakes, apart from assigning probabilities of occurrence in particular localities, based on past frequencies. Seismologists (scientists who study earthquakes) have made some use of tiltmeters, sensitive instruments that measure the slow tilting of large rock masses, with a view to possibly obtaining warning of earthquakes. Other instruments, called strain seismographs, have been placed in mountain tunnels to measure slow movements of large geological blocks. Further work of this nature may enable seismologists to predict earthquakes in the distant future, but today the studies are still experimental.

Consult Jeffreys, Sir Harold, *Earthquakes and Mountains* (2d ed., 1950); Bullen, K. E., *Seismology* (1954); Gutenberg, Beno, and Richter, C. F., *Seismicity of the Earth* (2d ed., 1954).

K. E. BULLEN, University of Sydney, Australia
See also EARTH; FAULT, GEOLOGICAL; GEOPHYSICS; SEISMOGRAPH; VOLCANO.

Important Earthquakes

The following list summarizes some of the more important recorded earthquakes:

1755, Nov. 1, Lisbon, Portugal. 30,000 to 70,000 persons killed; 17,000 houses destroyed. Shocks felt in area of 1¼ to 1½ million sq. mi. One of most violent earthquakes in history.

1783, Feb. 5–Mar. 27, southern Italy (Calabria). Six major earthquakes killed more than 30,000 persons, destroyed more than 180 towns. Shocks felt in area of more than 88,000 sq. mi.

1811, Dec. 16–Feb. 7, 1812, New Madrid, Mo. Strongest earthquake in U.S. history. Felt in area of more than 1,000,000 sq. mi.; 30,000 to 50,000 sq. mi. of land seriously disturbed. Area sparsely populated; few casualties, little damage to buildings.

1819, June 16, Cutch, India. 1,543 persons killed; at least 10,000 houses destroyed. Shocks felt in area of more than 1,900,000 sq. mi. Ground severely disturbed.

1835, Feb. 20, Concepción, Chile. Shocks felt in area of 650,000 sq. mi. Many towns severely damaged, coastal areas uplifted.

1876, June 15, northeastern Japan. Submarine earthquake formed tsunamis up to 100 ft. high that ravaged 300 mi. of coast line; 28,321 persons killed; 6,222 houses destroyed.

1886, Aug. 31, Charleston, S.C. Strongest earthquake ever recorded along east coast of North America. Felt in area of more than 2,800,000 sq. mi. from Canada to Gulf of Mexico and from Bermuda to Arkansas. Damage not great.

1891, Oct. 28, central Honshu, Japan (near Nagoya). 7,279 persons killed; 197,530 houses destroyed. Shocks felt in area of 93,712 sq. mi.

1897, June 12, Assam, India. 1,542 persons killed, all brick and stone buildings within 3,000 sq. mi. destroyed. Shocks felt in area of 1,750,000 sq. mi. Ground faulted and warped.

1906, Apr. 18, San Francisco, Calif. 390 persons killed; 28,188 houses destroyed; most of damage caused by fire that followed earthquake. Disturbed area encompassed 373,000 sq. mi. Notable for ground displacement along San Andreas fault.

1908, Dec. 28, Messina, Sicily. 46,800 to 82,000 persons killed, 98% of houses in Messina destroyed. 170,000 sq. mi. disturbed. One of the most disastrous earthquakes of modern history.

1920, Dec. 16, Kansu Province, China. Possibly 180,000 persons killed, whole villages buried by landslides; 40,-000 sq. mi. affected.

1923, Sept. 1, Tokyo and Yokohama, Japan. 99,331 persons known dead, 43,476 missing; 500,000 to 600,000 houses destroyed in the two cities, either by shock or by ensuing fire. More than 166,000 sq. mi. disturbed.

1927, Mar. 7, southern Honshu, Japan (near Kyoto). 3,017 persons killed; 15,594 houses collapsed or burned. 200,-000 sq. mi. disturbed.

1933, Mar. 3, northeastern Japan. Submarine earthquake formed tsunamis up to 75 ft. high that devastated 300 mi. of coast line. 3,022 persons killed; 8,851 houses and 8,000 boats destroyed.

1935, May 31, Quetta, Pakistan. 20,000 persons killed in Quetta alone; all buildings destroyed. Other cities badly damaged, farmlands ruined. There were three shocks, the most violent of which lasted a full minute.

1939, Dec. 27, Erzincan, Turkey. More than 23,000 persons killed; more than 29,000 houses destroyed. City of Erzincan razed, other towns seriously damaged. Fissures up to 36 ft. wide formed in ground surface.

1950, Aug. 15, Assam, India. Second-strongest earthquake on record. 574 persons known dead; 100,000 houses destroyed. Lowlands sank, wiping out towns; rivers disappeared or changed course; 30,000 sq. mi. disturbed.

1960, Mar. 1, Agadir, Morocco. Up to 12,000 persons believed killed, 80% of Agadir destroyed.

1960, May 21–30, southern Chile. Series of earthquakes and volcanic eruptions; tsunamis swept away entire villages along coast. Islands, mountains, lakes created. Up to 5,000 persons may have been killed.

1962, Sept. 1, northwest Iran. Worst earthquake in Iranian history; over 10,000 persons killed, about 10,000 seriously injured; a 23,000-mi. area severely damaged.

1963, July 26, Skopje, Yugoslavia. Massive earthquake shattered over 80% of the city, making about 80,000 persons homeless and killing more than 1,000.

1964, Mar. 27, southern Alaska. Strongest earthquake recorded on North American continent; 31 persons known dead, 86 missing and presumed dead; some 12,000 sq. mi. of the earth's surface lifted.

1964, June 16, Niigata, Japan. More than 2,000 houses destroyed. 12,000 flooded; 90 huge oil and gas storage tanks went up in flames.

1966, Apr. 26–May 25, Tashkent, U.S.S.R. Hundreds of tremors killed 10; injured 1,000; left 300,000 homeless.

1966, Aug. 19–23, eastern Turkey. Quakes completely destroyed over 60 villages, killing 2,477 persons. About 1,500 were injured, and some 100,000 left homeless.

EARTHWORM, the common worm belonging to the phylum Annelida, class Oligochaeta. Other related annelids (segmented worms) are leeches, clam worms, and feather worms. The segments, or rings, are easily seen on the earthworm. The setae, four pairs of tiny bristles on each segment, can be felt as a roughness along the side or bottom of a large earthworm. The bristles grip the burrow as the earthworm moves along by alternately extending, then shortening, parts of its body. The anterior, or front end, is pointed and contains the nerve center and a mouth. The earthworm can regenerate a front tip and most of the rear part, but a cut through the first third of the body is fatal.

Earthworms come up to the surface at night to feed on bits of decayed leaves and other debris, often pulling food back down with them to eat later. They also swallow a good deal of soil. Undigested material, or worm castings, may be seen near their burrows. This constant burrowing aerates the soil and permits rainwater to penetrate better. Earthworms hasten the breakdown of dead vegetation into new soil. Many earthworms are seen above ground after a heavy rain, having been drowned out of their tunnels. Although their skins must be kept moist, they cannot live under water. They absorb oxygen directly through the skin by means of capillaries close to the surface. The skin is also sensitive to light and earthworms retreat from bright light.

A blood vessel can usually be seen along the earthworm's back. This is one of a number of blood vessels running lengthwise which are connected by small tubes running crosswise. Near the anterior end there are five larger muscular tubes, called aortic arches. These act like hearts, keeping the blood circulating by contracting

regularly. Earthworms lay eggs in a slime ring secreted by the clitellum, the thickened section close to the head. The slime ring with the eggs closes to form a "cocoon," when deposited on the ground. The largest earthworm is an Australian species which sometimes grows more than 10 ft. long.

BARBARA NEILL, American Museum of Natural History
See also ANNELID.

EAR WAX, or cerumen, is the protective substance secreted by skin glands in the outer ear canal. If too much is secreted the canal may become plugged up, causing hearing loss. Large accumulations of ear wax should be removed only by a physician or a specially trained nurse, because of the danger of perforation of the ear drum.

EARWIG, common name for the flat-bodied, beetlelike insects that comprise the order Dermaptera. Earwigs have four wings, the forward pair of which is poorly developed; a forcepslike tail appendage; and jointed antennae. They are nocturnal scavengers, and also prey on other insects. Many species have lost the power of flight. The European earwig, *Forficula auricularia*, is a house and garden pest, especially abundant on the Pacific coast of North America.

EASLEY, town of northwestern South Carolina, 12 mi. west of Greenville, in the upper Piedmont. Textiles and lumber are leading products. Founded, 1874; pop. (1950) 6,316; (1960) 8,283.

EAST ALTON, manufacturing town of southwestern Illinois. Part of a larger industrial area including Alton and Wood River, East Alton produces explosives, ammunition, and nonferrous metal products. Inc., 1894; pop. (1950) 7,290; (1960) 7,630.

EAST ANGLIA, Anglo-Saxon kingdom comprising the present English counties of Norfolk and Suffolk, which are still referred to as East Anglia. It was settled by the Angles in the late 5th century A.D. The kingdom had a brief ascendancy in eastern England in the early 7th century, but this was ended by the rise of Mercia, whose rulers exercised hegemony over East Anglia for long periods between 650 and 800. Between 865 and 869 East Anglia was conquered by the Danes. In 917 Edward the Elder, King of the English, defeated the Danes, and henceforth East Anglia was an earldom of England.

EAST ANGUS, small industrial town of Quebec, Canada, located on the St. Francis River east of Sherbrooke. Paper manufacture has been the key industry here since 1882. Inc., 1912; pop., 4,756.

EAST AURORA, resort village of western New York. From 1895 to 1939 East Aurora was the site of the Roycroft Shops, a community crafts project founded by Elbert Hubbard. Toys, valves, and aircraft parts are now made here. Inc., 1874; pop. (1950) 5,962; (1960) 6,791.

EASTBOURNE, county borough of southern Sussex, England, located on the English Channel, 19 mi. east of Brighton. It is an important coastal resort and residential town and has a fine, sandy beach. Beachy Head is 3 mi. southwest. Chartered, 1883; pop., 60,897.

EAST BRIDGEWATER, residential town of southeastern Massachusetts in the Brockton Metropolitan Area. A bell cast by Paul Revere hangs in the Unitarian Church here. Settled, 1649; inc., 1823; pop. (1950) 4,412; (1960) 6,139.

EAST CAPE (Russ. **CAPE DEZHNEV**), northeasternmost projection of the Chukchi Peninsula, Siberia, U.S.S.R. This cape, which has a maximum elevation of 2,430 ft., faces Alaska across the Bering Strait. It was discovered by a Russian navigator in 1648.

EAST CHICAGO, city of northwestern Indiana, situated between Chicago, Ill., and the Indiana cities of Gary, Hammond, and Whiting. East Chicago, with an area of 11 sq. mi., is the most congested industrial area of Indiana. Expansion is impossible except through the construction of man-made land in Lake Michigan. Settled in 1885 as Indiana Harbor, East Chicago is the state's largest port, with several miles of ship canal. The city contains huge oil refineries, and among its many industries are steel mills, shipyards, and meat-packing plants. Manufacturers produce chemicals, railway equipment, hardware, insulation, and other products. The Calumet Extension Center of Indiana University is located here. Pop. (1950) 54,263; (1960) 57,669.

EAST CHINA SEA (Chin. **TUNG HAI**), part of the Pacific Ocean, between the east coast of China and the Japanese Kyushu island and the Ryukyus. It merges in the north with the Yellow Sea without any definite line of demarcation, connects with the South China Sea through the Formosa Strait, and with the Sea of Japan through the Tsushima and Korea straits. Its greatest length (about 800 mi.) is between Matsu Island, off China, and Nagasaki, Japan. Its area is estimated at 485,000 sq. mi. Its average depth is 640 ft., and its extreme depth, 9,070 ft.

EAST CLEVELAND, city of northern Ohio, a manufacturing suburb adjacent to Cleveland. Electric lamps and art and cartography supplies are manufactured. Inc., 1892; pop. (1950) 40,047; (1960) 37,991.

EAST DETROIT, city of southeastern Michigan. It is a residential suburb northeast of Detroit. Pop. (1950) 21,461; (1960) 45,756.

EASTER, the feast of the Resurrection of Christ, the greatest and most ancient of the Christian festivals. Easter is celebrated on the first Sunday after the full moon following the vernal equinox. Thus, with our modern calendar, Easter may fall between March 21 and April 25.

The earliest Christians seem to have celebrated the Resurrection every Sunday; but gradually the annual feast, preceded by Lent and Holy Week, and followed by Paschaltide, developed. The origin of the name "Easter" is uncertain: Bede connects it with the Anglo-Saxon spring goddess Eostre; but it may have come from the German *ost* ("east"), the direction from which the sun rises. Christians celebrate the feast by attending church, often rising

early to greet the day, in commemoration of those who went early to the tomb "as it began to dawn toward the first day of the week" (Matt. 28:1). The services are elaborate and joyous, the churches decorated with flowers and candles, with white, the color of purity and joy, predominating. Alleluia ("Praise Yah"), the expression of joy and thankfulness, resounds. Sometime during the Easter season, Roman Catholics must make confession and receive communion.

Many of the customs associated with Easter are derived from various spring fertility rites of the pagan religions which Christianity supplanted. Eggs were a primitive symbol of fertility; but Christians saw in them a symbol of the tomb from which Christ rose, and continued the practice of coloring, giving, and eating them on Easter. The Easter rabbit, legendary producer of Easter eggs, was also a symbol of fertility and new life. The practice of wearing some new article may derive from the white garments of those newly baptized on Easter in the early church.

ELIZABETH M. DOWNIE, Director of Christian Education,
Grace Church, Mount Clemens, Mich.

EASTER, or PASCHAL, CONTROVERSY, argument in the early church as to whether the feast of redemption should be celebrated at the Jewish Passover (Gr. and Lat. *pascha*) or on the Sunday following, as the day of the Resurrection. By 180 A.D. the latter custom prevailed generally, but the churches of Asia Minor retained the Jewish date, the 14th of the lunar month, hence they were called Quartodecimans ("fourteeners"). Even at Rome, parishes of Asian Christians observed their own custom until Pope Victor I (189–198) demanded uniformity and threatened to excommunicate the churches of Asia. A number of councils supported the Roman custom, but Irenaeus and others urged Victor to take a more moderate course.

By 325 the Quartodeciman custom was extinct among orthodox Christians, and the Council of Nicaea fixed the rule still followed for the date of Easter: the Sunday after the first full moon of spring. Later controversies relate to details of calculation. In the early Middle Ages the Celtic churches used an older system, superseded elsewhere; and in modern times the Eastern churches retain the Julian calendar, which in the 20th century is 13 days behind, putting the first day of spring on Apr. 3 instead of Mar. 21.

EDWARD R. HARDY, Berkeley Divinity School,
New Haven, Conn.

EASTER ISLAND, also known by its Polynesian name, Rapa Nui, easternmost extension of Polynesia. It lies 2,230 mi. west of the South American Pacific coast and more than 1,000 mi. east of the nearest other inhabited islands. This remote, almost treeless island is triangular in shape and has a total land area of 63.9 sq. mi. Volcanic eruptions formed the island, but all craters are now extinct. Between these there are low-lying plains that were formed by lava flows. Grass covers the slopes of the volcanic cones.

A Dutch explorer, Jakob Roggeveen, discovered this lonely speck of land on Easter Sunday in 1722, and named it for this holiday. Later the island was visited by Capt. James Cook, the French explorer La Pérouse, and others.

The aboriginal way of life on Easter Island is probably as imperfectly known as that of any Pacific culture. Very little remains of the ancient customs, which were lost before they could be recorded by ethnographers. When Roggeveen visited the island it is estimated that the population numbered in the thousands. However, European epidemics and slave traders from South America reduced the number of natives to a mere 111 persons by 1872. To be maintained a culture must have continuity; the old must teach the young. For Easter Island the break between past and present was too great for the ancient culture to survive.

The Easter Islanders of today have gained in numbers slightly. They show a mixed racial heritage because of their contact with non-Polynesians although before their contact with Europeans they seem to have been clearly Polynesian with minor specialized characteristics brought about by isolation and inbreeding.

Among the most striking features of Easter Island are the stone statues, 12 to 25 ft. high, which dot the grassy volcanic slopes. Statues of this type were carved out of solid volcanic rock with crude hand tools of stone, and were finally placed erect on stone platforms near the sea. Those still imbedded in the slopes are those whose transport to the sea was interrupted. It is thought that the statues represented dead ancestors.

Experts differ concerning the significance of the so-called Easter Island script, and the puzzle may never be adequately explained. The script consists of rows of stylized figures carved on wooden tablets. The signs may represent an advanced stage of picture-writing or a higher level of development, comparable to that of Egyptian hieroglyphics. Some scholars feel that their chief function was that of memory aids in the recitation of genealogies or folk tales.

A dependency of Chile since 1888, Easter Island (Span. Isla de Pascua) is administered as part of Valparaiso Province. Pop., 809.

Consult Métraux, Alfred, *Easter Island* (1957).

ROLAND W. FORCE, Chicago Natural History Museum

EASTER LILY, common name for *Lilium longiflorum,* a bulb-bearing plant of the lily family, Liliaceae. Originally native to Asia, the Easter lily and its many horticultural varieties are now grown throughout the world for their large, trumpet-shaped and highly fragrant flowers. Although they can be grown outdoors in cold climates, in North America they are usually cultivated in greenhouses, and are forced into bloom at Easter time, hence their popular name.

See also LILY.

EASTERN ORTHODOX CHURCH, sometimes called the Eastern Church, comprising several self-governing, independent Christian churches situated in countries which once belonged to the Byzantine Empire or were evangelized by the Byzantine Church. These churches are united in doctrine and worship, and claim that they are the true church founded by Christ and His apostles. Their source of faith is holy tradition, of which the Scriptures are a part, and they accept seven ecumenical councils. The Fourth Council at Chalcedon divided them from the Monophysite churches, and the Great Schism of 1054 separated them from the Western Church.

The Orthodox Church embraces the four ancient patriarchates of Constantinople (100,000 members), Alexandria (200,000), Antioch (300,000) and Jerusalem (35,000); the churches of the Soviet Union (50,000,000), Rumania (14,000,000), Bulgaria (6,000,000), Serbia (7,500,000), and Greece (7,500,000); the independent churches in Georgian S.S.R., Cyprus, Poland, Czechoslovakia, and Finland; and others scattered throughout the world. The total membership is about 150,000,000. Each church elects its own Patriarch. The Ecumenical Patriarch of Constantinople holds "precedence of honor" and has jurisdiction over some churches (Finland, Czechoslovakia) and some dioceses in diaspora.

VESELIN KESICH, St. Vladimir's Seminary

See also GREEK CHURCH; RUSSIAN CHURCH.

EASTERN ORTHODOX LITURGY, central service of the Eastern rite, also called the Divine Liturgy, or Holy Eucharist (Thanksgiving). The term may apply generally to all church services. Divine liturgy commemorates the Last Supper and presents the life of Christ. Communion is in both bread and wine, for both priests and laymen, who also participate actively in the service.

The four liturgies in the Eastern Church are: the liturgy of St. John Chrysostom, the usual liturgy of the Eastern Church; the liturgy of St. Basil, used 10 times a year; the liturgy of the Presanctified Gifts, celebrated during Lent and the first three days of Holy Week; and the liturgy of St. James, used very rarely. The major parts of the liturgies of St. John Chrysostom and St. Basil are the preparation of the bread and wine, liturgy of the catechumens (learners), and liturgy of the faithful.

VESELIN KESICH, St. Vladimir's Seminary

EASTERN QUESTION, the complex of political problems arising from the decline of the Ottoman Empire from the 18th century to 1914.

The 18th Century. The Russian wars against Turkey between 1768 and 1774 are usually considered the opening chapter in the history of the Eastern Question, not only because they revealed the grave weakness of the Ottoman Empire but also because they demonstrated the diplomatic conflicts and tensions that divided the major European powers. Russia enjoyed in these wars the strong support of Great Britain, which saw in the rising Russia a useful counterweight against French influence in the Mediterranean. For that reason Great Britain contributed officers and provisions to the expedition of Russia's Baltic navy to the Aegean that led in 1770 to the total defeat of the Turkish fleet at Chesme (Turk. Çeşme).

In the peace of Kuchuk Kainarji (1774) Russia received most of the northern shore of the Black Sea and was recognized as the protector of the Sultan's Greek Orthodox subjects. Freedom of navigation on the Black Sea and free passage of Russian commercial vessels through the Straits (Bosporus and Dardanelles) were agreed upon. After 1780 the British grew skeptical about the wisdom of promoting Russian expansion at the expense of Turkey, particularly after Russia annexed (1783) the Crimea, from which Russian ships could reach the Straits in a two-day voyage. Austria, too, became alarmed at the possibility that Russia might gain control of the Danube principalities of Mol-

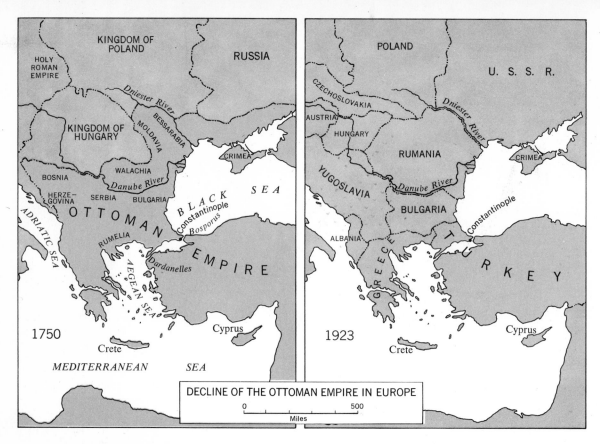

KINGDOM OF POLAND · RUSSIA · HOLY ROMAN EMPIRE · Dniester River · KINGDOM OF HUNGARY · BESSARABIA · MOLDAVIA · CRIMEA · BOSNIA · WALACHIA · Danube River · BLACK SEA · HERZE-GOVINA · SERBIA · BULGARIA · Constantinople · OTTOMAN · Bosporus · ADRIATIC SEA · RUMELIA · Dardanelles · EMPIRE · AEGEAN SEA · Cyprus · 1750 · Crete · MEDITERRANEAN SEA

POLAND · U. S. S. R. · CZECHOSLOVAKIA · Dniester River · AUSTRIA · HUNGARY · RUMANIA · CRIMEA · YUGOSLAVIA · Danube River · BULGARIA · Constantinople · ALBANIA · GREECE · T U R K E Y · 1923 · Cyprus · Crete

DECLINE OF THE OTTOMAN EMPIRE IN EUROPE

0 — 500
Miles

davia and Walachia (Rumania) and thereby block Austria's access to the Balkans. But Austria was too weak to fight Russia. Austrian Emperor Joseph II decided instead to conclude an alliance with Catherine II of Russia for the common conquest of the Turkish possessions in Europe. The war that began in 1787 did not achieve these ends. Russia advanced its frontier to the Dniester, while Austria gained only a negligible boundary correction.

Napoleon and the East. In the following period Napoleon highlighted the Eastern Question by his bold expedition to Egypt in 1798–99. Napoleon thought that French control of Egypt, added to that of Italy, would make the Mediterranean a French lake. The damage to English trade would be great. Beyond this immediate effect, Napoleon hoped to threaten the British position in India, possibly by extending the French protectorate over Egypt to all of the Turkish Empire. But the whole project failed. Turkey turned against France; and Russia, fearful of French domination of the Turkish Empire, joined the anti-French coalition.

In the years after Napoleon's return to France, the Eastern Question was completely overshadowed by the struggle among the European powers. Napoleon's defeat of Austria in 1805 and of Prussia and Russia in 1806–7 was followed by an alliance between Napoleon and Tsar Alexander I. Russia used these years to advance farther toward the Balkans. In the Peace of Bucharest (1812) Turkey ceded Bessarabia to Russia, which thereby reached the northern estuary of the Danube.

Greek Independence. The European powers continued to co-operate diplomatically for only a few years after the final defeat of Napoleon in 1815. Thereafter Great Britain followed an independent liberal policy, in which, particu-

larly after 1830, it was often supported by France. Russia, Austria, and Prussia formed a conservative bloc, usually called the Holy Alliance. Yet the ideological differences between the two groups were occasionally silenced when power interests demanded other groupings. The Eastern Question was a major cause of such regroupings, as was shown for the first time in connection with the Greek national revolution that began in 1821. Both Russia and Austria condemned the revolution in its early years, while Great Britain, wanting to preserve the Turkish Empire, gave no official support. But in 1826 Russia and England signed a protocol that envisaged the establishment of a Greek state under Turkish suzerainty. Through the accession of France the protocol became the London Treaty of 1827.

A fleet composed of British, French, and Russian ships supposed to protect the Greek shores against Turkish actions annihilated the Turkish-Egyptian fleet in the battle of Navarino on Oct. 20, 1827. In Apr., 1828, Russia went to war against Turkey. By the Treaty of Adrianople (1829) Russia imposed a large war indemnity and secured the right to occupy the Danube principalities until payment had been made. These conditions left Turkey actually under Russian domination for several years. In addition to accepting an independent Greek state, the Turks had to agree to the beginnings of autonomous administration in Serbia and the Danube principalities.

In 1833 Russia, in the Treaty of Unkiar Skelessi, imposed on Turkey the obligation to keep foreign naval vessels from passing through the Straits in time of war. The treaty was resented in Great Britain, which succeeded in 1841 in replacing the Unkiar Skelessi Treaty by a new international convention that forbade naval vessels of any nation to enter the Straits. This was the final result of Anglo-Russian co-operation against French attempts in 1840 to separate Egypt from the Turkish Empire.

The Crimean War. The Russians renewed their expansionist policies after the European revolutions of 1848–50. Some minor conflicts between Greek and Roman Christians in Palestine were used by Tsar Nicholas I to present the Sublime Porte with an ultimatum that demanded not only the correction of the local situation but also the recognition of Russia's right to intervene directly in all such cases in the future. When Turkey refused, a Russian army occupied the Danube principalities. Nicholas I expected that Britain would not go to war and that the Habsburg monarchy, which he had helped to suppress the Hungarian revolution in 1849, would actively support him. But in Great Britain the anti-Russian forces were dominant, and the new Emperor of France, Napoleon III, offered to become an ally.

In Jan., 1854, an Anglo-French fleet steamed into the Black Sea and opened the Crimean War. Austria, too, shocked the Tsar by its hostile policy. It demanded the retreat of the Russian army from the Danube principalities and forced Russia to maintain a considerable army on the Austro-Russian frontier. The Crimean War was concluded at the Congress of Paris in 1856. Russia had to cede parts of Bessarabia to the Danube principalities, which in the following decade developed into the Rumanian state. The Peace of Paris placed the principalities and Serbia under the guarantee of the Great Powers. It also guaranteed the independence and integrity of the Turkish Empire and admitted Turkey as an equal member to the concert of Europe. The treaty prohibited the building or maintenance of a Russian navy on the Black Sea.

The Crimean War had a great impact on the European history of the subsequent 15 years. Austria was isolated and proved incapable of thwarting the national unification of Italy and Germany. Russia supported Prussia in its wars against Austria in 1866 and France in 1870–71. During the latter war Russia renounced the provision of the Paris treaty that forbade Russia to keep naval forces in the Black Sea, an action condoned by a conference of the powers at London in 1871.

The Congress of Berlin. In 1875 revolts against Turkish rule broke out in Bosnia and soon spread to Serbia and Bulgaria. The cruel methods employed by the Turks in suppressing the revolts incensed Russia, and it went to war against Turkey in 1877. After the defeat of the Turkish armies, a Russian army appeared before Constantinople, and Russia imposed (Mar., 1878) the peace treaty of San Stefano (mod. Yeşilköy), which, among other things, created a large Bulgarian state. Britain and Austria-Hungary protested the virtual expulsion of Turkey from the Balkans. War was avoided by the Congress of Berlin (June 13 to July 13, 1878). Bulgaria was confined to the area between the Danube and the Balkan Mountains, and Eastern Rumelia, south of the Balkans, remained occupied by the Turks. Austria-Hungary was to occupy Bosnia and Herzegovina, and Great Britain received Cyprus from Turkey in exchange for a British guarantee of its Asiatic possessions. Russia regained Bessarabia and kept its Transcaucasian conquests. But it saw itself far removed from Constantinople.

In the subsequent years even Bulgaria slipped from Russian tutelage. Alexander von Battenberg, Prince of Bulgaria, angered the Russians, and when in 1885 a rebellion united Eastern Rumelia with Bulgaria, Russia opposed the merger and Britain supported it. A grave European crisis developed that passed only after Prince Ferdinand of Saxe-Coburg became the ruler of Bulgaria in 1887.

To World War I. Lesser crises stemming from the Eastern Question recurred during the following 20 years. But the decisive developments were the active policy of Germany in Turkey, and the strengthening of the national states in the Balkans. Whereas the first imperial German Chancellor, Otto von Bismarck, had always maintained that Germany had no interests of its own in Turkey, the Germany of Emperor William II, by building a railroad from Constantinople to Baghdad and by sending German officers to instruct the Turkish army, contributed greatly to invigorating the Turkish Empire. Russia and even Britain felt provoked by the German policy. At the same time, the Balkan states sought not only their complete liberation from all ties with Turkey but also, in the case of Serbia, the absorption of the South Slavs in Austria-Hungary. In 1912 Bulgaria, Serbia, Montenegro, and Greece formed the Balkan League and made war on Turkey. After driving the Turks from the Balkan Peninsula, Serbia and Greece could not agree with Bulgaria on the division of the spoils, and a war among the Balkan states followed. Nevertheless, all three states had by 1913 gained complete independence from Turkey.

On June 28, 1914, South Slav revolutionaries assassinated Archduke Francis Ferdinand of Austria, thus precipitating an Austro-Serbian war that at once became a general European war. In this war the Turkish Empire fought on the side of Germany and Austria-Hungary. Their defeat in 1918 led to the dissolution of the Turkish Empire in Asia as well. Thereafter the Eastern Question was superseded by a large number of new problems.

HAJO HOLBORN, Yale University

See also BALKANS; CRIMEAN WAR; OTTOMAN EMPIRE.

EASTERN STAR, ORDER OF THE, secret fraternal organization associated with the Freemasonry movement, and composed of Master Masons, their wives, daughters, mothers, widows, and sisters. The purpose of the order is to promote charity, relief, other worthwhile projects, and good will. Grants of money, in the form of Eastern Star Training Awards for Religious Leadership, are given to students needing assistance. Eastern Star membership numbers about 3,000,000 in chapters in 13 countries.

MAMIE LANDER, Right Worthy Grand Secretary, Order of the Eastern Star

EASTER REBELLION, a rebellion carried out (1916) by the Irish Republican Brotherhood against British rule in Ireland. The episode had its origins in the long history of Anglo-Irish conflict, but it grew immediately out of Britain's involvement in World War I and the opportunity given to the Irish to strike while the British were thus engaged. The Irish Volunteers, under Patrick Pearse, and the citizen army of the Irish Labor party, under James Connolly, planned for a rebellion with German aid, but this did not materialize. The rising took place on Easter

Monday. It was confined to Dublin, where about 1,000 men seized the post office and other public buildings. A large British force landed, and after four days of fighting the main body of rebels surrendered. Pearse, Connolly, and a dozen others were executed. Their deaths revived nationalist sentiment, and two years later the newly established Dáil Éireann (legislative assembly) declared *de facto* independence for Ireland. The nationalist movement Sinn Fein (q.v.) continued its efforts, which were to result (1921) in the establishment of the Irish Free State.

JOHN G. SPERLING, *Northern Illinois University*

EAST FLANDERS, province of northwestern Belgium, lying wholly within the Scheldt basin and bounded on the north by the Netherlands. Sandy soils produce abundant crops of rye, potatoes, tobacco, and flax. A network of canals connects the province with the North Sea. Ghent is the principal town and the provincial capital. Area, 1,147 sq. mi.; pop., 1,253,208.

EAST GARY, residential city of northwestern Indiana, adjoining Gary. Pop. (1950) 5,635; (1960) 9,309.

EAST GRAND FORKS, city of northwestern Minnesota. The city is a major potato market and also has a beet-sugar refinery. Inc., 1895; pop. (1950) 5,049; (1960) 6,998.

EAST GRAND RAPIDS, city of western Michigan. It is a residential suburb southeast of Grand Rapids. Pop. (1950) 6,403; (1960) 10,924.

EAST HAM, county borough and residential and industrial suburb of London, in southwestern Essex, England, on the north bank of the Thames River. Industrial enterprises include the Beckton gasworks, one of the largest of its kind in Europe, and part of the Royal Docks. Inc., 1904; pop., 105,359.

EASTHAMPTON, industrial town of western Massachusetts in the Springfield-Holyoke metropolitan area. Textiles and metal products are manufactured here. Settled, 1649; inc., 1823; pop. (1950) 10,694; (1960) 12,326.

EAST HARTFORD, town of central Connecticut, across the Connecticut River from Hartford. Propeller and jet aircraft engines, brushes, and paper goods are manufactured here. Tobacco is processed, and there are bulk oil-storage tanks. Inc., 1783; pop. (1950) 29,933; (1960) 43,977.

EAST HAVEN, town of southern Connecticut, on Long Island Sound, southeast of New Haven, in a residential, resort, and farming area. The first iron mill in Connecticut was located here. Summer cottages extend along the shore. Truck gardens supply New Haven with vegetables and fruit. Inc., 1785; pop. (1950) 12,212; (1960) 21,388.

EAST HILLS, village of southeastern New York, located on western Long Island. Cosmetics are manufactured. Inc., 1931; pop. (1950) 2,547; (1960) 7,184.

EAST INDIA COMPANY, name of a number of trading companies chartered by various European sovereigns dur-

ing the 17th century for the economic penetration of India and the Far East. Through the voyages of the 16th century, following the discovery of a sea route to India by Vasco da Gama, European merchants learned of the great wealth and new markets in the East yet to be tapped. Trade with the East, however, was a venture of such magnitude that it was far beyond the reaches of the individual merchant. To overcome the financial and technical obstacles, and with the active encouragement of their governments, European merchants formed companies, the most prominent of which were the East India companies of the British, the Dutch, and the French. Their history in the East is largely told in their struggles for power with each other and with native rulers.

East India Company. The British company was chartered by Queen Elizabeth I on Dec. 31, 1600, as part of the sudden overseas expansion made possible by the defeat of the Spanish Armada in 1588. A group of London merchants received a monopoly on all British trade and colonial administration over territories lying east of the Cape of Good Hope in return for assuming the initiative and the capital investment.

Early attempts to establish trade were bitterly opposed, at first by the Portuguese and then by the Dutch. By early in 1613 the British had received the right from the Mogul Empire to create a trading center at Surat.

Trading posts, or factories, as they were called, were also established at Madras, Bombay, and Calcutta. Although it was the spice trade that had brought the English to India, merchants found that a great market existed in Europe for other Indian products such as saltpeter, indigo, and, most significantly, cotton cloth, which was cheaper and more beautiful than European fabrics. The company also gradually built up an important trade with China through Canton for tea and silks.

During the 17th century the British established themselves by building fortified factories and obtaining grants of land from the local governments. Until the 18th century, however, the company possessed only a few square miles of territory. The French then began to try to spread their influence inland by taking advantage of the breakdown of the central Mogul power at Delhi. The British quickly adopted the same policy. The great accession of power and control of territory for the British was an outcome of the victory of Robert Clive at Plassey in Bengal (1757). As a result of this victory, the British acquired the revenue of Bengal province in 1765. However, a period of maladministration and corruption followed, and the British Parliament had to step in to regulate the provincial government by passing North's India Act (1773) and Pitt's India Act (1784). The British raj, or rule, gradually spread over the whole peninsula, with the government taking over the company's old monopoly.

Throughout the company's history there was strong opposition in Great Britain to the company's monopoly on trade with India and power to exclude all other Englishmen from settling without its permission. At the end of the 18th century the free trade advocates bitterly attacked the monopoly, and finally in 1813 trade in India was opened to all. In 1833 the company was forbidden to engage in trade, although it remained the formal government of India. By that time, the "Honourable John

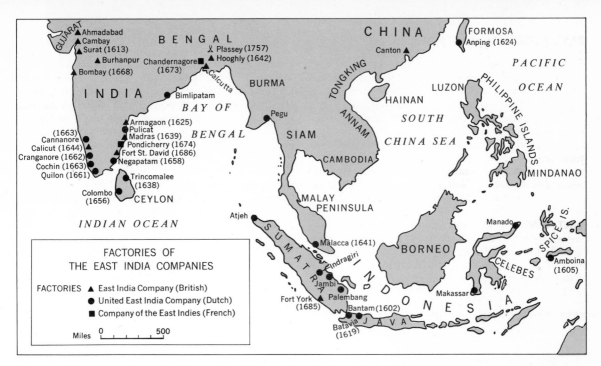

FACTORIES OF
THE EAST INDIA COMPANIES

FACTORIES ▲ East India Company (British)
● United East India Company (Dutch)
■ Company of the East Indies (French)

Miles 0 ——— 500

Company," as it was often called, was only a figurehead concerned chiefly with the patronage of lucrative jobs. The company maintained its military forces in India and also developed a remarkably effective Indian civil service, which became a model for civil service reform in Great Britain and America. As a result of the Sepoy Mutiny of 1857, the East India Company formally ended in 1858, and the rule of India passed to the crown.

ANSLIE T. EMBREE, Columbia University

Vereenigde Oostindische Compagnie (United East India Company). The Dutch company, also known as the V.O.C., established the Netherlands' commercial power in Asia and its political power in the Indonesian archipelago. Until the outbreak of the Netherlands' revolution against Spain, Dutch traders had acted as middlemen, bringing Asian goods from Spain and Portugal to northern European cities. After the break with Spain the Dutch sought to ensure their commercial position by gaining direct contact with the sources of goods in the East, particularly the spice islands of the Indonesian archipelago. In 1594 a company was formed by Amsterdam merchants to equip an expedition to Java. Led by Cornelis de Houtman, it set sail in 1595, landing in Bantam the following year. Though this attempt was only a qualified success, the Amsterdam company sent further expeditions, and rival companies soon were formed. However, to strengthen the Dutch hand against the Indonesian rulers and against Spanish and British efforts to corner the spice trade, the government forced the rival companies to combine into the V.O.C., which it chartered in 1602.

Organized somewhat like a modern corporation, the company had stockholders, issued dividends, and was operated by a board of directors, the *Heeren Zeventien* ("Seventeen Gentlemen"). In the interests of securing a monopoly on the spice trade, the company was given the right to exercise sovereign power. It was authorized, in the name of the Netherlands, to launch military expeditions, make treaties, and claim and govern territories. It first exercised these rights in 1605, claiming sovereignty over

Amboina. In 1609 Pieter Both was appointed by the company as first Governor-General of the Netherlands East Indies. In 1619 Jan Pieterszoon Coen, twice Governor-General, founded the colony's capital, Batavia, on the ruins of Jacatra. Under Coen the company strengthened its position on Java, imposed its control over the spice-producing islands of eastern Indonesia, and effectively reduced British competition for the trade of the archipelago.

In addition to its Indonesian colony, the company established an outpost in Japan. From 1639 until its demise it was the only European concern allowed to trade in that country. During the 17th century the company established forts on Formosa and seized Malacca and Ceylon from Portugal. It gained bases along the Coromandel (east) coast of India and in Gujarat on the northwest. Strongholds were established on Mauritius and the Cape of Good Hope, and commercial offices were opened in major trading ports of the Middle East and mainland Southeast Asia. Most of the trade was in luxury goods—spices from the Indies; cloth from Coromandel; gold, silver, and copper from Japan; silk from Tongking and Formosa. In spite of its original purpose, the company soon relied less on trade between Europe and the East than on traffic between various Asian ports. Changing patterns of trade, coupled with mismanagement and heavy military expenditures in the Indies, brought about the V.O.C.'s decline. Bankrupted in 1780, the company was dissolved 18 years later, its political functions in Indonesia being assumed by the Netherlands government.

RUTH T. McVEY, Yale University

Compagnie des Indes Orientales (Company of the East Indies). The French company was established by Cardinal Richelieu in 1642 and reorganized by Colbert in 1664. The French East India Company never attained the long financial success of its Dutch or British counterparts. It had a checkered career, and at first saw only partial success due to the opposition of native rulers and European rivals. However, it established its principal factories at Chandernagore (1673) and Pondicherry (1674).

At the turn of the century the schemes of John Law, a Scottish financier backed by the French government, contributed to the development of a financial bubble in the East. In 1720 the stocks of the company rapidly fell, and the bubble burst. The company's resources were nearly depleted, but in the same year it was reorganized as the Perpetual Company of the Indies. Prosperity was restored until 1744, when the French desire for power, under Marquis Joseph François Dupleix, and rivalry with the English led to war. Three years later, the so-called Carnatic wars resulted, were paralleled by wars in Europe, and finally checked French ambitions. The French were defeated by the British under Robert Clive, and in Jan., 1761, Pondicherry was surrendered. Although the company was terminated in 1769, the French maintained isolated posts and during the 19th century rose to power in Indo-China.

ROBERT G. ALBION, Harvard University

EAST KILDONAN, city of southeastern Manitoba, Canada, a residential suburb of Winnipeg. Inc., 1957; pop., 27,305.

EASTLAKE, city of northern Ohio, a residential suburb northeast of Cleveland on Lake Erie. Pop. (1950) 7,486; (1960) 12,467.

EAST LANSING, city of south-central Michigan. It is a residential suburb east of Lansing. Michigan State University is here. Pop. (1950) 20,235; (1960) 30,198.

EASTLAWN, eastern suburb of Ann Arbor, southeastern Michigan. Pop. (1950) 4,127; (1960) 17,652.

EAST LIVERPOOL, city of eastern Ohio on the Ohio River, near the Pennsylvania and West Virginia borders. It has been an important pottery center since 1840, and porcelain products, pottery supplies, and novelties are manufactured. Founded, 1798; inc., 1834; pop. (1950) 24,217; (1960) 22,306.

EAST LONDON, port and industrial city in eastern Cape Province, South Africa. Its harbor lies on the Indian Ocean, at the mouth of the Buffalo River. Exports include wool, corn, fruit, meat, and dairy products. Although wool trade is the city's prime industry, it also has confectionery, soap, footwear, and automobile assembly plants. In 1847 the site was annexed by the British government of the Cape colony to serve as a garrison and supply base. Pop., 114,584.

EAST LONGMEADOW, suburban town of western Massachusetts, in the Springfield-Holyoke metropolitan area. It was formerly an agricultural area. Settled, 1740; inc., 1894; pop. (1950) 4,881; (1960) 10,294.

EAST LOS ANGELES, east-central suburb of Los Angeles, California. Pop. (1960) 104,270.

EAST LOTHIAN or HADDINGTONSHIRE, county of southeastern Scotland, extending from the Lammermuir Hills (Lammer Law, 1,733 ft.) northward to the Firth of Forth and the North Sea. Drained mainly by the Tyne River, the low ground contains some of the best arable land in Scotland. The coast has fishing villages and resorts, North Berwick and Gullane being well known for their golf courses. Haddington, the county seat, is a small market town. The shire is mentioned in the 12th century but until the 17th century East Lothian, Midlothian, and West Lothian were under one sheriff. Area, 267 sq. mi.; pop., 52,653.

EAST LYNNE, play adapted from the English novel (1861) of the same title by Mrs. Henry Wood. In its first adaptation (1862), by Clifton Tayleure, and subsequent stage versions, it became an indestructible 19th-century repertory piece despite the implausible melodrama and unabashed sentimentality of its domestic plot.

EASTMAN, GEORGE (1854–1932), manufacturer of photographic equipment, philanthropist, and inventor, born in Waterville, N.Y. By simplifying and improving equipment, introducing mass production, and advertising, he made photography a popular pastime. He coined the word "Kodak."

When he was eight, his father died, and at 14 young George became a bank clerk and rose to a moderately well-paid position as a bank bookkeeper.

Like many aspiring young men of his era, he gave his spare time to studying and experimenting with technological contrivances—photographic equipment, in his case. Having patented (1879 in Britain; 1880 in the United States) a machine for applying the emulsion to the photographic dry plate, he formed a company with the aid of local capital to manufacture dry plates. In 1884 Eastman patented, and the company manufactured, paperbacked film, and in 1888 a simple camera for rolled strip film was marketed with the slogan "You press the button—we do the rest."

A rapidly expanding business was further stimulated by Eastman's introduction in 1885 of a celluloid material to replace the paper backing on his film, and Thomas A. Edison began using this film for his motion pictures. Eastman's success with the improved film was marred, however, by a claim of a prior invention by Episcopalian minister Hannibal W. Goodwin, who had shown Eastman the film shortly before an Eastman chemist patented a similar one. (In 1914 a U.S. Circuit Court awarded the Goodwin assignees $5,000,000.)

Through its introduction of popular-priced cameras and professional equipment, Eastman's company led in its field. Before his retirement in 1925, he was called the "Kodak King." After 1925, he gave tens of millions of dollars to the University of Rochester and Massachusetts Institute of Technology. Eastman never married and his home was without a mistress after his mother died. He took his own life, leaving a brief message: "To my friends: my work is done. Why wait?"

THOMAS HUGHES, Washington and Lee University

EASTMAN, LINDA ANNE (1867–1963), American librarian. She was head librarian (1918–38) of the Cleveland Public Library. A recognized leader of the public library movement, she received many honors, and served as president of the American Library Association in 1928.

EASTMAN, MAX (FORRESTER) (1883–   ), American author and editor, born in Canandaigua, N.Y. From 1913 to 1917 he was editor of the Socialist magazine *Masses*, which was suppressed when the U.S. entered World War I. He translated from the Russian *The History of the Russian Revolution* (1932) and *The Revolution Betrayed* (1937), both by Leon Trotsky. Increasingly critical of developments in the Soviet Union, he became a roving editor of the *Reader's Digest* in 1941. His own books include *Enjoyment of Poetry* (1913), perhaps his most influential work; *Artists in Uniform* (1934); *Enjoyment of Laughter* (1936), an important study of the psychology of humor; and *Enjoyment of Living* (1948), an autobiography.

EASTMAN, city of south-central Georgia, and seat of Dodge County. Wood products, cotton, peanuts, and livestock provide the principal industrial base. Inc., 1873; pop. (1950) 3,597; (1960) 5,118.

EAST MASSAPEQUA, residential village of southeastern New York, located on the south shore of western Long Island. Pop. (1960) 14,779.

EAST MEADOW, residential village of southeastern New York, located on western Long Island. Pop. (1960) 46,036.

EAST MOLINE, industrial town of northwestern Illinois, on the Mississippi River. Principal manufactures are farm implements. Pop. (1950) 13,913; (1960) 16,732.

EAST NORTHPORT, residential village of southeastern New York, located on the north shore of western Long Island. Pop. (1950) 3,842; (1960) 8,381.

EASTON, town on the eastern shore of Maryland, and seat of Talbot County. It is a trading center for the surrounding agricultural area. Talbot County Court House, built in 1794, is still in use. Inc., 1790; pop. (1950) 4,836; (1960) 6,337.

EASTON, industrial town of southeastern Massachusetts in the Brockton metropolitan area. Heavy industries predominate. There are numerous Indian relics at Furnace Village, part of the town. Settled, 1694; inc., 1725; pop. (1950) 6,244; (1960) 9,078.

EASTON, city of eastern Pennsylvania, and seat of Northampton County, situated at the junction of the Lehigh and Delaware rivers. Easton manufactures many products, including machinery, slate, cement, textiles, and paper. A Dixie Cup manufacturing plant is here. The city is also the home of Lafayette College. Easton was founded in 1752 by William Parsons and was important during colonial times as a key point for trade and travel. Easton was the site of many frontier conferences with the Indians. Inc. as city, 1886; pop. (1950) 35,632; (1960) 31,955.

EAST ORANGE, city of northeastern New Jersey, adjoining Newark. Located on commuter rail lines, the city is noted for its large apartment buildings and residential hotels. Upsala College (estab., 1893) is here. Inc., 1899; pop. (1950) 79,340; (1960) 77,259.

EAST PALESTINE, city of eastern Ohio, near the Pennsylvania border. Floor tile, bricks, porcelain products, furniture, and machinery are manufactured. Founded, 1828; inc., 1875; pop. (1950) 5,195; (1960) 5,232.

EAST PATERSON, borough of northeastern New Jersey, and an industrial suburb of Paterson. Important industries include the manufacture of television receivers and communications equipment. Pop. (1950) 15,386; (1960) 19,344.

EAST PEORIA, industrial town of central Illinois, on the Illinois River. A principal employment center within the Peoria urbanized area, East Peoria contains the main plant of the Caterpillar Tractor Company. Inc., 1919; pop. (1950) 8,698; (1960) 12,310.

EAST PITTSBURGH, industrial borough and southeastern suburb of Pittsburgh, Pennsylvania. The Westinghouse Electric plant here covers 185 acres. Inc., 1895; pop. (1950) 5,259; (1960) 4,122.

EAST POINT, city of northwestern Georgia, a residential suburb southwest of Atlanta. It was a key Confederate position in the defense of Atlanta during the Civil War. Inc., 1887; pop. (1950) 21,080; pop. (1960) 35,633.

EAST PROVIDENCE, city of eastern Rhode Island, located on the Providence and Seekonk rivers at the head of Narragansett Bay. The city has large petroleum docks and storage facilities. Industries include the manufacture of metal products, machinery, paper, and chemicals. Emma Pendleton Bradley Home (estab., 1930), the first neuropsychiatric hospital for children, is here. East Providence was settled about 1645 and until 1862 was considered part of Massachusetts. Inc. as a city, 1958; pop. (1950) 35,871; (1960) 41,955.

EAST PRUSSIA, former province of Prussia, now controlled by Poland and the U.S.S.R. Partly forested, the landscape is characterized by low, rolling hills and an abundance of small lakes, especially in the eastern Masurian Lakes region. The Baltic coast line is deeply indented by the Vistula and Courland lagoons, both protected by long spits of land. Because of its good harbors, important shipbuilding and fishing industries arose, but throughout its history the most important sector of its economy has been agriculture. Located there were the vast estates of the Prussian Junkers, the German landowning and military class, whose wealth depended upon the produce of potatoes and grains, especially rye.

The region, long inhabited by a people known as the Old Prussians, was conquered in the 13th century by the Teutonic Knights, who made the territory a fief of their order. The last Grand Master of the Teutonic Order, Albert of Brandenburg, secularized East Prussia and made it a fief of the house of Hohenzollern under the Polish crown. In 1618 the Elector of Brandenburg, also a Hohenzollern, inherited the duchy. But it was not until 1660, when the Peace of Oliva formally abolished the suzerainty of the Polish King, that Frederick William, the Great Elector, won full sovereignty. In 1701, as a reward for services

EAST PRUSSIA

Memel
(Klaipėda)

RETURNED
TO GERMANY
IN 1939

LITHUANIA

BALTIC SEA

DANZIG
"FREE TERRITORY"

Königsberg
(Kaliningrad)

Danzig
(Gdańsk)

GERMANY

EAST PRUSSIA

POLISH
CORRIDOR

Tannenberg
(Stębark)

Vistula River

Warsaw

POLAND

0   100   200
Miles

Germany Russia boundary in 1914 ------
German territory from 1919 to 1939
Poland-U.S.S.R. boundary in 1945 -·-·-·-

to the Emperor, the Great Elector's son was crowned King Frederick I of Prussia at the capital, Königsberg. The area was ruled by the Hohenzollerns until 1918.

During World War I East Prussia was the scene of heavy fighting—the battles of Tannenberg and Masurian Lakes. At the close of the war the area was separated from the rest of Germany by the creation of the Polish Corridor, but reunited during World War II. In 1945 the territory was again partitioned, between the Polish province of Olsztyn and the Russian S.F.S.R.

HAROLD POOR, Temple University

EAST RIDGE, town of southeastern Tennessee, and an industrial and residential suburb south of Chattanooga. Inc., 1921; pop. (1950) 9,645; (1960) 19,570.

EAST RIVER, navigable tidal strait connecting Upper New York Bay and Long Island Sound and separating the boroughs of Manhattan and Bronx from Brooklyn and Queens. It is connected with the Hudson River by the (canalized) Harlem River and Spuyten Duyvil Creek. The East River is crossed by seven highway bridges (north to south, the Throgs Neck, Bronx-Whitestone, Triborough, Queensboro, Williamsburg, Manhattan, and Brooklyn) and the Hell Gate railroad bridge; subway, railroad, and vehicular tunnels pass under it. The southern portion has many docks serving the port of New York. The New York Naval Shipyard, a federal installation, is on the Brooklyn shore. Principal islands are: Randalls, with recreational facilities; Wards, with a sewage-disposal plant; and Welfare (formerly Blackwells), the location of municipal institutions. Length, 16 mi.; width, ½–3½ mi.

EAST ROCHESTER, village of western New York, near Rochester. East Rochester has food-processing, fabricated metals, and machinery plants. Inc., 1906; pop. (1950) 7,022; (1960) 8,152.

EAST ROCKAWAY, resort and residential village of southeastern New York, on Long Island. Inc., 1900; pop. (1950) 7,970; (1960) 10,721.

EAST RUTHERFORD, industrial borough of northeastern New Jersey. Surgical instruments, ink, dyes, and roofing materials are manufactured here. Pop. (1950) 7,438; (1960) 7,769.

EAST ST. LOUIS, transportation and manufacturing center of southwestern Illinois, on the Mississippi River. With 20 entering railroads, it is a Midwest transportation center second only to Chicago. Three Mississippi River bridges cross to St. Louis. East St. Louis proper is primarily residential, for most of the main industries associated with it (meat packing, chemicals, and steel) are in adjacent small, separately incorporated industrial units. The fourth-largest city of Illinois, it is part of the St. Louis Metropolitan Area and the center of the heavily industrialized "East Side" district. Grand Marais State Park and the Southwestern Branch of Southern Illinois University are here. Settled as a ferry site, 1795; inc., 1865; pop. (1950) 82,295; (1960) 81,712.

EAST SIBERIAN SEA, sea of northeastern Siberia, covering an area of approximately 338,000 sq. mi. It lies in the Soviet Arctic between the Laptev Sea, on the west, and the Chukchi Sea, on the east.

EAST STROUDSBURG, residential borough of eastern Pennsylvania, adjoining Stroudsburg. A state teachers college that specializes in physical education is located here, and the Delaware, Lackawanna, and Western Railroad has railroad shops in the town. It is the center of a resort area. Inc., 1870; pop. (1950) 7,274; (1960) 7,674.

EASTVIEW, town of southern Ontario, Canada, a residential suburb northeast of Ottawa. Inc., 1913; pop, 24,555.

EAST WHITTIER [hwĭt′ĭ-ər], eastern suburb of Los Angeles, California. Pop. (1960) 19,884.

EAST WILMINGTON, suburb opposite Wilmington, on the Cape Fear River, southeastern North Carolina. Pop. (1950) 1,623; (1960) 5,520.

EATON [ē′tən], AMOS (1776–1842), American natural scientist and educator, born in Chatham, N. Y. He graduated from Williams College in 1799 and was admitted to the bar in 1802. Eaton practiced law in Catskill, N. Y., until convicted of forgery and imprisoned in 1811. Pardoned in 1815 he attended Yale College and studied botany, geology, and chemistry. He was strongly influenced toward these sciences and never returned to law. Beginning in 1817 he undertook a series of popular lectures on botany and geology, first at Williams College and then on tour in New England. They aroused considerable interest and are credited with leading to the establishment of the New York State Geological Survey. In 1824, sponsored by Stephen Van Rensselaer, Eaton founded the Rensselaer School, later the Rensselaer Polytechnic Institute, in Troy, N. Y. His publications include *An Index to the Geology of the Northern States* (1818), *A Manual of Botany for North America* (1833), and *Geological Notebook* (1841).

PETER FLAWN, University of Texas

EATON, JOHN HENRY (1790–1856), American politician. Born in North Carolina, Eaton migrated about 1808 to Franklin, Tenn., where he established a plantation and a legal practice. He married a ward of Gen. Andrew Jackson and, after the War of 1812, completed a laudatory biography of Tennessee's great hero. Jackson's support made him U.S. Senator (1818–29). As Senator, Eaton worked incessantly to advance Jackson's presidential candidacy. President Jackson appointed him Secretary of War in 1829. When the social boycott of Eaton's second wife, Margaret ("Peggy") O'Neale, by the wives of other Cabinet members produced an untenable situation, Eaton resigned. Jackson's plans to return him to the Senate miscarried, and he served instead as Governor of Florida (1834–36) and minister to Spain (1836–40).

EATON, THEOPHILUS (1590–1658), British merchant and colonizer, founder of New Haven. One of the original organizers of the Massachusetts Bay Company, Eaton gave up a comfortable mercantile business in London to emigrate to America with his lifelong friend John Davenport in 1637. Apparently unwilling to remain in the shadow of those who had arrived in New England before them, he and Davenport founded a separate colony at New Haven, where he exploited choice trade opportunities and served as Governor until his death. He and Davenport drew up laws in 1639 that gave church members exclusive political power and that vested in him and a few others power over admission into the church.

EATON, WALTER PRICHARD (1878–1957), American author, dramatic critic, and educator, born in Malden, Mass. His books include *Plays and Players* (1916), *The Actor's Heritage* (1924), and *The Drama in English* (1930). He taught playwriting at Yale University from 1933 to 1947.

EATON, city of southwestern Ohio and seat of Preble County. Manufactures include clothing and paperboard. Founded, 1806; pop. (1950) 4,242; (1960) 5,034.

EATONTOWN, residential borough of eastern New Jersey, 3 mi. south of Red Bank. It was named for an early resident, Thomas Eaton, who settled here prior to 1685. U.S. Army post Fort Monmouth, an important technical and scientific research base, occupies the northeast corner. Inc., 1926; pop. (1950) 3,044; (1960) 10,334.

EAU CLAIRE [ô klâr'], city of west-central Wisconsin, and seat of Eau Claire County, at the confluence of the Chippewa and Eau Claire rivers. It is a trade center in a dairying and stock-raising region. Eau Claire was settled as a trading post in the late 1700's, and the city developed as a lumbering center in the 1840's. Pulpmaking and the manufacture of paper products are still major industries. Eau Claire State College is here. Inc., 1872; pop. (1950) 36,058; (1960) 37,987.

EAU GALLIE, resort city of eastern Florida, located on Indian River lagoon. It is a citrus-growing center. Inc., 1925; pop. (1950) 1,554; (1960) 12,300.

EBAL [ē'bəl], **MOUNT,** mountain in northwestern Jordan, about 3,085 ft. above sea level. Mentioned in the Bible, it was the site of an ancient altar of Israel commemorating a divine covenant (Deut. 27:1–8). Directly south is Mount Gerizim, and in the narrow pass between them was the city of Shechem (modern Nablus).

EBAN [ē'bən], **ABBA** (1915–   ), Israel diplomat, scholar, orator, and administrator. Born in Capetown, South Africa, Eban studied and taught Middle East languages at Cambridge University in England. After wartime service with the British Army in Jerusalem, he was employed by the Jewish Agency for Palestine in 1946. He was attached to Israel's mission at the United Nations in 1947–48, becoming Israel's first permanent U.N. representative in May, 1949, and its ambassador to Washington in Sept., 1950. Eban relinquished both posts in 1959 to assume the presidency of the Weizmann Institute of Science at Rehovot and to serve as Minister without Portfolio in the Israel government. In 1960 he was appointed Minister of Education and Culture and in 1963 he became Deputy Premier. He was named Minister of Foreign Affairs in 1966.

EBBINGHAUS [ĕb'ĭng-hous], **HERMANN** (1850–1909), German experimental psychologist. His studies included color vision and techniques of measuring intelligence in children. He is most famous for his pioneering experiments with memory and the time factor in retention. Of his books the most important was *Memory: a Contribution to Experimental Psychology* (1913).

EBENEZER [ĕb-ə-nē'zər], an Old Testament place name, properly applied to a pillar erected near Mizpah by Samuel to commemorate an Israelite victory over the Philistines. The victory was attributed to Yahweh, and the name means "stone of help" (I Sam. 7:10–12).

EBENSBURG [ĕb'ənz-bûrg], residential borough of south-central Pennsylvania, and seat of Cambria County. It is largely an agricultural and shopping center for the surrounding farming and mining communities. Settled in 1800 by Welsh immigrants, the town was once a popular resort. Inc., 1825; pop. (1950) 4,086; (1960) 4,111.

EBERS [ā'bərs] **PAPYRUS,** one of the best-preserved Egyptian medical documents, which contains instructions for the treatment of virtually every disorder known to the ancient Egyptians, including headaches, heart trouble, and crocodile bites. The papyrus was discovered in Thebes in 1862 and came into the hands of the German Egyptologist Georg Ebers in 1873. It is believed to have been compiled about 1550 B.C. About one ft. wide and 68 ft. long, the document contains instructions for the preparation of salves, gargles, and inhalations, and includes a headache preparation which contains "berry-of-the-poppy-plant," apparently an Egyptian reference to opium.

EBERSWALDE [ā-bərs-väl′də], city of the northeastern German Democratic Republic (East Germany), located on the Finow Canal, in the district of Frankfurt an der Oder, northeast of Berlin. Principal industries include steelworks, sawmills, and locomotive works. It carries on a large trade in wood, coal, and agricultural products. It is the seat of an academy of forestry and also has a forestry museum. The most notable buildings are a 14th-century church, the Maria-Magdalenenkirche, and an 18th-century town hall. The city is surrounded by large wooded areas and is a summer resort, especially for residents of Berlin. Pop., 32,008.

EBERT [ā′bərt], **FRIEDRICH** (1871–1925), German statesman. As successor to Chancellor Maximilian of Baden following the collapse of the monarchy in 1918, and as first President (1919–25) of the Weimar Republic, Ebert was the chief architect of the post-World War I German state. A saddle maker by trade, he became a trade-union leader and head (1913) of the Social Democratic group in the Reichstag. Throughout World War I he promoted Socialist support of the war effort. Although personally favoring a constitutional monarchy, he found himself in 1918 heading a republican government, but he "hated revolution like sin" and effectively suppressed uprisings by both left-wing and right-wing extremists. Ebert favored co-operation of all the democratic parties and middle-of-the-road social and economic policies.

EBIONITES [ē′bē-ən-īts], early Jewish Christians who acknowledged Jesus as a human Messiah. After the fall of Jerusalem (70 A.D.) they were rejected by both church and synagogue, but lingered on, with some eccentric developments, into the 4th century. The name probably comes from their identifying themselves with the devout poor (*ebionim*) of the Psalms (for example, Psalm 72) and the Beatitudes (Matt. 5:3ff.). The Epistle of James (Jas. 2:6), while not Ebionite, illustrates the milieu out of which they arose.

EBOLI [â′bō-lē], town in Campania, southern Italy. It is small and picturesque, situated on a hilltop. Located 17 mi. from Salerno, it was the scene of heavy fighting (1943) during World War II. Places of interest are a castle and several churches. Pop., 16,315.

EBONY [ĕb′ə-nē], name for several species of large trees of the genus *Diospyros*, in the Ebenaceae, or ebony, family. Ebony trees are native to the forest of southern Asia, Africa, and tropical America and supply a heavy, almost inky-black, wood that is valued for its hardness and beauty. The most desirable lumber is obtained from *D. ebenum*, a species native to Ceylon. Important also are *D. ebenaster*, of Mexico and the West Indies, and *D. melanoxylon*, native to India. Ebony wood is used for expensive cabinet work, ornamental figures, and—until the advent of plastic—for the black piano keys.

EBRO [ā′brō] **RIVER**, river in northeast Spain, draining 33,100 sq. mi. Spain's longest river, it is the second-longest on the Iberian Peninsula. Rising in the Cantabrian Mountains, it flows southeast, emptying into the Mediterranean Sea through a delta 20 mi. below Tortosa. It is used for irrigation and also supplies half of Spain's hydroelectricity. Length, about 500 mi.

EÇA DE QUEIROZ [ā′sə thə kā-rôsh′], **JOSÉ MARIA** (1845–1900), Portugal's greatest novelist. He was educated at Coimbra and spent most of his life in the Portuguese diplomatic service in Cuba, Britain, and France. He wrote not only novels but also stories, essays, letters, and newspaper articles. He introduced realism into Portuguese fiction with *O crime do Padre Amaro* (Father Amaro's Crime), 1876 and *O primo Basílio*, 1878 (*Cousin Bazilio*, 1953), which, with *Os Maias* (The Maias), 1880, constitute a meticulous analysis of Portuguese life marked by increasingly biting irony. In *O mandarim* (The Mandarin), 1880, a new formula appears; Eça's stark realism mingles with the free flight of fantasy. *A relíquia*, 1887 (*The Relic*, 1925), *A ilustre casa de Ramires* (The Ramires Family), 1900, *A correspondència de Fradique Mendes* (Correspondence of Fradique Mendes), 1900 and *A cidade e as serras*, 1901 (*The City and the Mountains*, 1955), are written in this manner. He always strove for beauty in expression, and his style can be said to have initiated a new period in the evolution of the Portuguese language as a literary instrument. His works have been translated into 12 languages.

Ernesto Da Cal, New York University

ECAFE. *See* Economic Commission for Asia and the Far East (ECAFE).

ECBATANA, ancient name of Hamadan (q.v.) in Iran.

ECCLESIA [ĭ-klē′zē-ə], the political assembly of ancient Athens and many other Greek city-states. The Athenian ecclesia included all adult male citizens. Summoned regularly by the boule, it met on the Pnyx Hill just west of the Acropolis and Areopagus. Special meetings were also convened here and elsewhere. The ecclesia was the sovereign administrative body, controlling domestic and foreign policy as well as the selection and supervision of all elective officials. It passed decrees, but not laws in the strict sense. An agenda was prepared by the current subcommittee (prytany) of the council, or boule, and all measures were first discussed in, and recommendations made by, the council.

The president of the ecclesia was the citizen to whom the chairmanship of the current prytany had rotated on that particular day. Every member of the ecclesia had the right to debate as well as to vote on proposals. In addition, any member could propose an amendment or call for introduction of a particular topic at a subsequent meeting. Strict provisions existed for challenging proposals which contravened existing laws. A simple majority of those present was enough to carry all ordinary measures. While in principle this system was thoroughly democratic, it had weaknesses. Clever orators could persuade the voters to support unwise and even disastrous measures which took effect immediately, and even in a small state many eligible voters, particularly farmers, could not attend regularly.

WILLIAM A. McDONALD, University of Minnesota

ECCLESIASTES [ĭ-klē-zē-ăs′tēz], **BOOK OF,** book in the 3d division (the Hagiographa) of the Old Testament. It forms part of the Biblical Wisdom literature. The Hebrew title of the book is *Koheleth.* The meaning of this word is uncertain, but in the Septuagint it was translated "congregant," or "ecclesiastes," thus the title. The author identifies himself as "the son of David," and therefore the book was traditionally ascribed to King Solomon. A rabbinic tradition teaches that Solomon wrote Ecclesiastes in his old age, thus accounting for its somber and pessimistic outlook. Modern scholars, however, believe that Ecclesiastes was probably written in the 3d century B.C.

The tone of the book is pessimistic. Contemplating existence, the author says: "Vanity of vanities, all is vanity." He describes his disappointments in his search for the meaning of life. He finds injustice in the affairs of men. He counsels his readers to try to enjoy what life can offer and to avoid frustration and despair by not expecting too much. The last six verses—in contrast to the rest of the book—are optimistic in tone. Therefore, many scholars regard them as a later addition. In many Jewish congregations, Ecclesiastes is read during the Feast of Tabernacles.

Consult Gordis, Robert, *Koheleth, The Man and His World* (1951).

SEYMOUR SIEGEL, Jewish Theological Seminary of America

ECCLESIASTICAL COUNCILS. *See* COUNCILS, ECCLESIASTICAL.

ECCLESIASTICAL COURTS, tribunals organized by a church to deal with matters of ecclesiastical law. In the first three centuries of the Christian Church, controversies of all kinds were settled by the Bishop. But after the Edict of Milan (313) the areas of competence of ecclesiastical and civil courts were more clearly defined and honored. In most churches of episcopal-presbyterian polity there are systems of parish courts, diocesan courts, and often higher appellate courts. Trials include investigations of personal rights and establishment of a fact (for example, the validity of a marriage), and the infliction of an ecclesiastical penalty (in cases involving heresy or a misdemeanor). The Beth Din is a rabbinic court of law, which is operative in Israel in matters of personal rights.

ECCLESIASTICAL LAW. *See* CANON LAW.

ECCLESIASTICUS [ĭ-klē-zē-ăs′tĭ-kəs], Latin title of "the Wisdom of Jesus ben Sira," a book of the Old Testament Apocrypha. Also known as Sirach, it was translated in the 2d century B.C. into Greek by ben Sira's grandson. It exalts practical wisdom, which is sometimes personified, and identifies it with the Jewish law and a semi-Pharisaic morality expressed in proverbial language. The book was written in Hebrew and was read at Qumran, where the Dead Sea Scrolls were discovered.

ECHEGARAY Y EIZAGUIRRE [ā-chā-gä-rī′ ē ā-thä-gēr′rā], **JOSÉ** (1832–1916), Spanish dramatist. Born in Madrid, he was a successful engineer, politician, and academician before he turned to literature. His many plays, which dealt with elevated themes in an outdated, pompous, romantic style, were extremely popular, and he was awarded the Nobel Prize in 1905. Later critics have been severe with his works, which include *The Great Galeoto* (1881) and *The Madman Divine* (1900).

ECHEVERRÍA [ā-chā-vĕr-rē′ä], **ESTEBAN** (1805–51), Argentine writer. As a young man, he spent several years in Europe and was strongly influenced by French romanticism. *Rimas* (Lyrics), 1837, contains his most famous romantic poem, "La cautiva" (The Captive Maid). *El matadero,* 1838 (*The Slaughter-house,* 1959) is notable for the harsh realism of its descriptions. Echeverría felt that Latin-American literature should free itself from Spanish classical influence. In three volumes of poetry and a number of prose works he identified himself closely with the fresh environment of the New World.

ECHIDNA [ĭ-kĭd′nə], a small, egg-laying mammal, or monotreme, *Tachyglossus,* native to Australia, Tasmania, and New Guinea. The spiny anteater, as the echidna is often called, has a coat of powerful spines that almost hide its hairy body covering. Its mouth is extended into a horny beak, and its long, sticky tongue captures ants and other insects, drawing them into a toothless mouth. The mother echidna lays a single egg which she carries in an abdominal pouch. After the young hatches, it nurses from mammary glands within the pouch, and remains there until the growing spines become bothersome to the mother.

ECHINODERM [ĭ-kī′nə-dûrm], marine animals in the phylum Echinodermata, including starfish, brittle stars, sea urchins, sea cucumbers, and sea lilies. The name echinoderm comes from the Greek meaning, "hedgehog-skin," referring to the spiny skin of most echinoderms. Found in oceans nearly all over the world, they are most common in warm waters. Echinoderms are either male or female, and the young usually hatch from eggs. In most cases great numbers of eggs and sperm are simply released into the sea, and fertilization is by chance. When first hatched, the young have a bilateral pattern, but this soon changes. Typically, an echinoderm has a body with a symmetrical, five-part, radial pattern with a mouth and stomach in the center. There is no head. Around the mouth there is a nerve ring with many branches extending to all parts of the body. The tube housing the water-vascular system forms another ring. Called the ring canal, it too has branches to all parts of the body. In starfishes, sea urchins, and sea cucumbers, the branches end in tube feet which, with the help of special muscles and hydraulic action, enable the animals to move about.

Most echinoderms have a limey skeleton of jointed plates just under the skin, though in the sea cucumber these may be reduced to small nodules of lime. Echinoderms possess powers of regeneration. Starfish commonly regenerate one or more arms and the sea cucumber can even regenerate some of its internal organs.

BARBARA NEILL, American Museum of Natural History

See also BRITTLE STAR; FEATHER STAR; SAND DOLLAR; SEA CUCUMBER; SEA URCHIN; STARFISH.

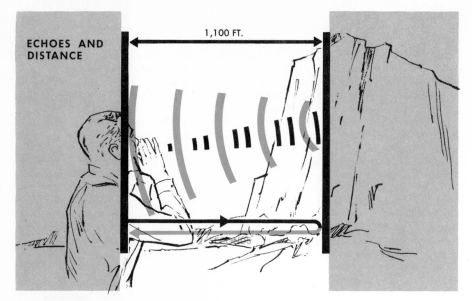

ECHOES AND DISTANCE

1,100 FT.

With an increase in temperature, the speed of sound rises beyond its standard rate of 1,088 ft. per second (at 0°C or 32°F). An echo time of 2 seconds, plus an allowance for known temperature and altitude, indicates that the cliff is 1,100 ft. away.

ECHO [ĕk′ō], in Greek mythology, a nymph deprived by Hera of the power of speech except in imitation of someone else. Echo fell hopelessly in love with Narcissus, and, rejected by him, pined away to a mere voice.

ECHO, in physics, the reflection of sound waves, radio waves, and other energy waves. The reflection occurs when the incident energy encounters a medium having a different characteristic resistance, usually a denser medium. The time interval between emission of the waves and the appearance of the echo is a measure of the distance traveled by the waves. Air-borne radar utilizes radio waves to detect the distance of an object reflecting these waves. The depth of the ocean at any point can be determined by sending sound waves through the water and measuring the time required for the echo to be reflected by the ocean floor. In the geologists' seismograph the echo produced by sound waves is used to study underground rock structures.

ECHO SOUNDER, electronic device that determines water depths by timing sound signals bounced off the bottom. Developed during World War I, partly from experiments on sonic submarine detectors, it was first used to chart depths in 1924. Although the velocity of sound in water varies according to temperature, pressure, and salinity, an average of 4,800 ft. per second is assumed. A sound head, or oscillator, emits impulses at frequent and regular intervals, and the echo is recorded either by a light flashing on a calibrated disk or by a line drawn on drum-mounted paper. The paper records are called fathograms. The precision depth recorder used by surveying vessels can detect a one-fathom (6-ft.) elevation difference on the floor of the deepest oceanic trenches.

ECHO VIRUSES, or enteric cytopathogenic human orphan viruses, a group of viruses which infect the human gastrointestinal tract. These organisms were discovered before their association with the diseases they produce was known, hence the expression "orphan." The Echo viruses primarily affect young children during the summer, producing "summer grippe," a respiratory disease with fever, "summer diarrhea," and various disorders involving fever and rashes. Some of the viruses attack the lining of the nervous system (the meninges) causing an ailment which may be mistaken for nonparalytic poliomyelitis. There is no specific treatment for Echo virus infections, but most patients recover spontaneously.
See also VIRUSES.

ECHUCA [ə-chōō′kə], city of Australia, in northern Victoria, at the junction of the Campaspe and Murray rivers. It is a trade and processing center for a region of irrigated agriculture and livestock production. Pop., 6,443.

ÉCIJA [ā′thē-hä], city of southwestern Spain, 50 mi. northeast of Seville, on the navigable Genil River. The region is noted for raising horses. Olives and cereal grains are grown. Shoemaking is important, and there are lumber mills and iron foundries. Pop., 30,303.

ECK, JOHANN MAIER (1486–1543), Roman Catholic theologian. Born in the village of Eck, Germany, Maier adopted its name as his own. He received an excellent education, and in 1510 became professor of theology at the University of Ingolstadt, where he taught until his death. His life work was the defense of Catholicism against Protestant leaders, especially Luther. Eck debated with Luther at Leipzig in 1519, promulgated the papal bull *Exsurge Domine* in 1520, headed the Catholic faction at Augsburg (1530) and at Worms and Regensburg (1540–41). Eck's major publication was entitled *Arguments against Luther and Other Enemies of the Church*, which had 45 editions during the half century following 1525.

ECKENER [ĕk′ə-nər], **HUGO** (1868–1954), German airship builder and commander. After working as publicist for the Zeppelin factory he became a pilot in 1911 and trained German naval airship pilots during World War I. In 1924 he flew the ZR-3, renamed *Los Angeles*, across the Atlantic as part of German war reparations. In 1927 he designed, and made the first of over a hundred crossings in the *Graf Zeppelin*. He is the author of *Count Zeppelin* (1938) and *My Zeppelins* (1949).

ECKERMANN [ĕk'ər-män], **JOHANN PETER** (1792–1854), German writer. In 1823 he became Goethe's private secretary and confidant and in this capacity he wrote the work on which his fame rests, the *Gespräche mit Goethe in den letzten Jahren seines Lebens 1823–1832*, 3 vols., 1836–48 (*Conversations with Goethe*, trans. by R. O. Moon, 1950).

ECKHART [ĕk'härt], **JOHN (MEISTER)** (c.1260–1327), father of German mysticism. Born in Hochheim, he entered the Dominican novitiate at Erfurt and was later sent to the *Studium* in Cologne. He was studying at Paris in 1300, and taught there as master of theology until c.1304. From this time until his death, except for a brief journey to Paris in 1311, he remained in Germany, serving from 1307 on as Vicar-General of his order. His doctrines came under heavy attack, and in 1325 he was called before a Chapter at Venice. Submitting in advance to the judgment of the Church, he sent an appeal to the Holy See in Feb., 1327. He died in Cologne that same year, and it was not until Mar. 27, 1329, that Pope John XXII condemned 17 of his theses as heretical and 11 as suspect.

As a mystic, Eckhart was bound to run into trouble with theologians concerned primarily with dogma. His mysticism was based on that of the 12th-century Victorines, and his title, "Father of German Mysticism," is justified by the renowned mystics who were his students: John Gerson, John Tauler, and Henry Suso.

RICHARD J. WESTLEY, Barat College, Lake Forest, Ill.

ECKSTINE [ĕk'stĭn], **WILLIAM CLARENCE ("BILLY")** (1914–), American jazz singer. Raised and educated in Washington, D.C., he first attracted attention as a band singer with Earl Hines (1939–43). He was partially responsible for introducing a number of modern jazz artists, including Charlie Parker, into the Hines organization. In 1944 he formed his own band composed of leading figures in the modern movement. A memorable organization, it lasted three years. Subsequently he enjoyed great success as a solo performer.

ECLAMPSIA [ek-lămp'sē-ə], convulsions and coma which may develop in late pregnancy in association with a group of disorders known as the toxemias of pregnancy. The cause of eclampsia is not known. It is immediately preceded by a rapid increase in blood pressure, swelling of the body (resulting from the retention of fluid), abdominal and stomach pains, headache, visual disturbances, and decreased output of urine. The disorder rarely appears before the sixth month of pregnancy and seems to occur more frequently in first pregnancies, in diabetic women, in women who suffered from high blood pressure before pregnancy, and in twin pregnancies.

Treatment includes terminating the pregnancy and the use of sedatives and drugs to lower the blood pressure and to stimulate kidney activity (diuretics).
See also PREGNANCY.

ECLECTICISM [ĕk-lĕk'tə-sĭz-əm], in art a more or less exact imitation of earlier styles, found particularly in architecture. Some eclecticism may be found in the Roman borrowing of Etruscan, Greek, or Egyptian forms, or in Renaissance architecture insofar as it attempted to revive Roman architecture. However, the main age of eclecticism began with the Roman, Greek, and Gothic Revivals of the late 18th century and continued through the first quarter of the 20th century. During the 18th and 19th centuries eclectic buildings might be relatively accurate imitations of the forms of past styles, but tended to be mechanical and to lack the life of their prototypes. In the 20th century, a number of architects have succeeded in recapturing not only the form but much of the vitality and spirit of their chosen styles, as in the Lincoln Memorial in Washington, D.C., and the Cathedral of Liverpool in England.

ECLECTICISM, name given to the philosophy which tries to combine compatible elements of different systems. In modern usage it refers to the doctrine which flourished in early 19th-century France. Its chief exponent was Victor Cousin, who began to expound his eclectic philosophy in 1817. He asserted that there is a "sense of truth," or human spirit, which exists firstly in the "common sense" of every man, and secondly in the history of thought, wherein successive schools represent different facets of the human spirit. Each school is incomplete, but each has its element of truth. Eclecticism did not outlive Cousin.

ECLIPSE [ē-klĭps'], in astronomy, the obscuring of one celestial object by another.

Solar Eclipses. Eclipses of the sun, which produce some of nature's greatest spectacles, occur when the moon passes between the earth and the sun. If the moon appears to be as large as the sun the eclipse is total, and the sun's atmosphere, or corona, is displayed as a beautiful, white crown around the darkened disk. If the moon appears smaller than the sun, however, only the central part of the sun's disk is obscured, so that a ring, or annulus, of light remains. Such an eclipse is termed annular. The apparent size of the moon depends on its distance from earth as the moon revolves in its elliptical orbit. Annular eclipses occur when the moon is farther from the earth, and total eclipses when it is nearer. It is a strange coincidence of nature that the sun and the moon have almost the same apparent size, so that small changes in the apparent diameter of the moon produce major effects in solar eclipses.

During total solar eclipses the belt of totality on the earth is usually no more than about 50 mi wide. This is because the darkest part of the moon's shadow, the central cone called the umbra, barely reaches the earth. In annular eclipses the umbral cone comes to an apex before reaching the earth. Outside the umbra there is a wide, partial shadow, the penumbra, within which the sun is only partly eclipsed. The zones of total and partial eclipse sweep across the earth in paths and at speeds determined by the relative positions and motions of the sun, moon, and earth. Eclipse tracks generally move from west to east with speeds on the order of 1,000 mph.

To astronomers a total solar eclipse is a truly remarkable demonstration that furnishes a wealth of information

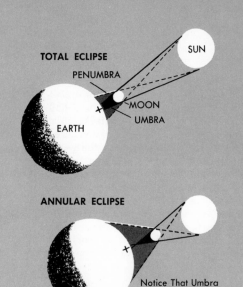

TOTAL ECLIPSE

PENUMBRA
SUN
MOON
UMBRA
EARTH

ANNULAR ECLIPSE

Notice That Umbra
Does Not Reach
Earth

SOLAR ECLIPSE

A

B

Birnback Publishing Service

The passage of the moon between the earth and the sun causes solar eclipse. When the sun is completely hidden, the eclipse is total at the point marked X on the earth *(top diagram)*. During an annular eclipse only the central part of the sun's disk is obscured *(lower diagram)*. In Fig. A above, a solar eclipse is seen developing. In Fig. B, the eclipse is total.

about the structure of the sun's outer layers. Difficulties are often encountered in using this gift of nature, however. To study eclipses astronomers often travel to remote regions of the earth, where they must set up delicate, but often ponderous, observing equipment. The eclipse lasts but a few minutes, and for many purposes but a few seconds, during which all observations must be made and all data recorded. Success or failure is determined largely by the weather, since a single cloud may obscure the view throughout the entire eclipse.

Lunar Eclipses. Eclipses of the moon occur when the earth passes between the sun and the moon. Because the earth's diameter greatly exceeds that of the moon, lunar eclipses are never annular. They may be partial, however, owing to an imperfect alignment of the earth on the line between the moon and the sun.

Since solar and lunar eclipses depend only on the geometry of the sun-earth-moon positions, they occur at fixed intervals and they are predictable. Preserved writings of ancient civilizations contain many references to eclipses, which in some cases allow the writings to be accurately dated. The ancients recognized the eclipse cycle of about 19 years, called the saros, in which the relative positions of the sun, moon, and earth are very nearly repeated. With this knowledge the Greek philosopher Thales successfully predicted an eclipse that occurred on May 28, 585 B.C. Chinese astronomers as early as 2137 B.C. tried eclipse predictions, but we do not know of their success.

Solar and lunar eclipses in early times were a source of fear and superstition to the uninformed. On more than one occasion the course of history has been changed, battles won or lost, nations freed and others conquered, as a result of superstitions about unexpected eclipses.

Other Eclipses. Another kind of eclipse important to astronomers involves binary stars (double stars) that obscure one another as they revolve around a common center of gravity. These eclipsing binaries yield valuable information on the size and atmospheric structure of stars. Sometimes with telescopes the stars can be followed visually as they periodically swing apart in their orbits, then come

back into eclipse. In other cases, if they are too faint or too distant to be seen as separate stars, their eclipsing characteristics can be studied by spectroscopic methods. A few stars are periodically eclipsed by cold, nonluminous objects that presumably are revolving planets. However, the planets must be much larger relative to the parent star than is the largest of the sun's planets; otherwise the effect of their partial eclipse would go unnoticed.

R. GRANT ATHAY, High Altitude Observatory,
Boulder, Colo.

See also BINARY STAR; CORONA, SOLAR; VARIABLE STAR.

ECLIPTIC. *See* CELESTIAL SPHERE.

ECLOGUE [ĕk′lŏg], a type of pastoral poetry in which shepherds compete with each other in songs usually dealing with their love affairs. The first known writer of the genre was Theocritus of Syracuse (3d century B.C). His *Idylls* present with some touch of realism both peasants and their natural environment. When Vergil in 37 B.C. published 10 *Eclogues*, imitations in Latin of Theocritus' *Idylls*, most of the realism disappeared. Vergil's *Eclogues* are usually set in an imaginary Arcadia, reminiscent of both Sicily and Mantua, and have a daintiness and wit which gave them considerable vogue. These *Eclogues* and *Idylls* were the principal models for all subsequent pastoral poetry.

ECOLOGY [ē-kŏl′ə-jē], a biological science that studies the interrelations of living organisms with their environment. The term "ecology" is derived from *oikos*, the Greek word for house, and was first used in 1869 by the German biologist Ernst Haeckel, who emphasized that the individual organism is a product of co-operation between its environment and its heredity. Modern ecology became established during the late 19th century with the work of Auguste Henri Forel in Switzerland, Johannes Eugenius Warming in Denmark, and the American naturalists Henry Chandler Cowles and Frederic Edward Clements. Early ecology consisted chiefly of observational studies on organisms in their natural surroundings. Later, statistical and quantitative methods were introduced which increased the scope of ecological study. As a result, its relation to other biological sciences became more significant, and also made ecology of practical value in conservation work.

Ecology, like genetics, cuts across the traditional separation of botany and zoology by studying both plant and animal communities. Ecology is concerned with the responses of living things to their environment and their relations to each other. Because of this, the science can be divided into two fields of study. One, known as autecology, is concerned with the life history of the individual organism or species and the behavior by which it becomes adapted to specific factors within its environment. The second field of ecology, known as synecology, deals with groups of living organisms. When the group consists of individuals of the same species, it is known as a population. The various populations living together in a given area form a community. All the communities occurring in a uniform climatic environment make up a biome. The basic functional unit in synecology is the ecosystem, made up of a community and its non-living environment. Synecology constitutes a large part of modern ecological research, contributing to understanding of the vital interrelations of plants and animals to each other. Major aspects of this field include the energy relations in ecosystems; the physical characteristics and behavior of populations; the interactions between different populations or species; and the characteristics of communities.

Energy Relations in Ecosystems

The life processes that occur within an ecosystem are vitally interrelated and form a continuous chain, each step of which derives its energy from the one before. The production of food, its consumption, and death and subsequent decay are actually governed by an energy-flow mechanism. Energy enters the system in the form of sunlight, some of which is converted into potential food energy by the primary producers in the ecosystem—the green plants. The energy then passes from the green plants to the primary consumers—the herbivorous animals. The secondary consumers—carnivorous animals—feed, in turn, upon the herbivores. At the final stage are the tertiary consumers—the large carnivores which feed only on smaller carnivores. Each stage in the flow of energy from one population to another is known as a trophic level. The sequence of trophic levels in any ecosystem forms a food chain. All of the food chains in a particular community constitute a food cycle. It is significant that some potential energy is lost (chiefly through respiration) at each trophic level. Because of this, the amount of energy available is greater at trophic levels closest to the primary producers—the green plants. As a result, any given community is able to support larger populations of herbivorous than carnivorous animals.

Population Characteristics

The characteristics of a population are not merely those observed in the individuals comprising the population, but are the result of interactions among those individuals, which are, in turn, dependent on the characteristics of neighboring populations. Among the significant population characteristics are population density, natality (birth

---

The article ECOLOGY deals with the science that studies the relations of plants and animals to one another and to their surroundings. Ecology is a biological science, drawing on the fields of botany and zoology. The next article — ECOLOGY, HUMAN — is concerned with a social science that studies human adaptation to the environment. Population pressure in cities is an example of the problems treated. This Study Guide first outlines the article on plant and animal ecology, then refers the reader to related entries, and finally turns to human ecology.

Fields of Ecology. (1) Autecology, the study of the individual organism in its environment. (2) Synecology, the study of groups of living organisms.

Energy Relations in Ecosystems. Energy flow: trophic levels, food chains, and food cycles.

Population Characteristics. Significant characteristics, including density, natality (birth rate), mortality (death rate), fluctuation in population density, and dispersal of populations.

Interactions Between Populations. Neutralism, competition, and symbiotic relationships: commensalism, mutualism, and parasitism.

Community Characteristics. Succession — the sequential appearance of communities as environmental conditions change.

The reader who wants additional information can find background material in the articles BIOLOGY, BOTANY, and ZOOLOGY. Other articles deal specifically with concepts used in ecology, for example, ECOSYSTEM, BIOME, COLONY, and SUCCESSION. Energy relations are described in PHOTOSYNTHESIS, FOOD CHAIN, NITROGEN CYCLE, CARBON CYCLE, and DECAY. Interactions between populations are treated in PARASITISM, SYMBIOSIS, and (more briefly) in COMMENSALISM and MUTUALISM.

A particularly relevant major article is ENVIRONMENT, which has sections on the land environment, the freshwater environment, and the marine environment. The discussion includes a note on the current problem of pollution of air and water and the resulting damage to wildlife. A discussion of variations in the natural environment as they are related to climate is presented in CLIMATOLOGY and related articles.

Other major articles include EVOLUTION. In this article under the heading *The Evidence for Evolution* there is a section on the evidence based on ecology, an example of the contributions of ecology to scientific theory. The contributions of ecology to immediate problems are evident in NATURAL RESOURCES, CONSERVATION OF.

The field of study described in ECOLOGY, HUMAN is related to plant and animal ecology. As already noted, human ecology is a social rather than a biological science. It uses concepts like those of plant and animal ecology and stresses an objective and statistical approach, but is not simply a matter of applying biological laws to human populations. As the article CULTURE points out, man's ability to do such things as make tools, use language, and develop a social organization has influenced both his evolutionary development and his history. Thus man's relation to his environment has special features of the sort discussed in URBAN PLANNING, in POPULATION and in FOOD (food supply and population growth).

The various aspects of ecology can be further explored in books available in the library. Recommended books are listed at the ends of many articles.

ECOLOGY

rate), mortality (death rate), fluctuation in populations, and dispersal of populations.

Population density is a measure of the number of individuals per unit area. Ecologists have found that there are definite limits to the size of a population, and hence, its density, including the productivity of the ecosystem, and such limiting factors within the particular environment as presence of predatory populations and geographical limits. Natality, which also influences population density, varies considerably in different populations depending upon the reproductive capabilities of the species and environmental conditions such as disease and famine. Similarly, mortality varies according to the physiological traits of the species and environmental factors. When natality is increased and mortality reduced, populations tend to reach their greatest density. In nature, this brings about sudden expansion of certain species, or it may cause their extinction by exhausting the environmental resources.

Fluctuations in population density are often periodic, depending upon the seasonal availability of food and the presence or absence of natural enemies. When population density forces organisms to seek new living areas, dispersal may take place—the emigration and immigration of plants and animal species. When the dispersal involves microorganisms that cause crop damage or human disease, it becomes a vital factor in human population density.

Interactions Between Populations

When two or more species live in the same habitat, they may or may not place similar demands upon the environment; but the populations will interact in some manner. Ecologists have discovered several possible types of interactions. If the populations do not compete for the same food, shelter, or other essentials of existence, a condition called neutralism occurs. Neutralism is coexistence without any direct interaction—harmful or beneficial—because the populations do not compete. A condition of competition takes place when two or more populations

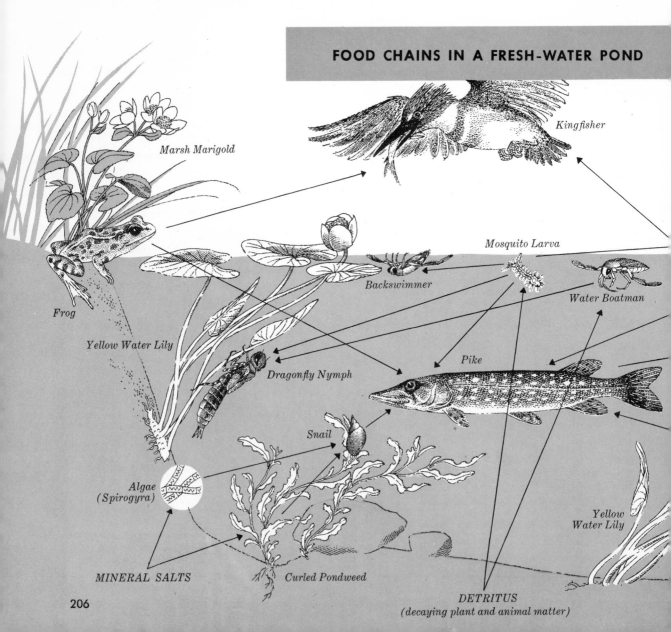

FOOD CHAINS IN A FRESH-WATER POND

Marsh Marigold

Kingfisher

Mosquito Larva

Backswimmer

Water Boatman

Frog

Yellow Water Lily

Dragonfly Nymph

Pike

Snail

Algae (Spirogyra)

Yellow Water Lily

MINERAL SALTS

Curled Pondweed

DETRITUS
(decaying plant and animal matter)

living in the same habitat place the same demands upon the environment. In the case of plants, this may be a competition for light; in the case of animals, it may involve two or more carnivorous species that feed on the same animals. Competition often results in the elimination of one population which is forced to move into another geographical area.

In the following types of interaction, the populations are vitally interrelated—a condition loosely described as symbiosis. In commensalism, only one species benefits by the relationship which, although obligatory for the commensal organism, does not affect the growth and survival of the host. Commensal crabs live in the mantle cavities of oysters, for example, but their presence has no effect on the oyster. In mutualism, the relationship is obligatory for both, and affects the survival of both species. This is the type of interaction found in lichens (algae and fungi that live together for mutual benefit).

A final and most important kind of interrelation be-

tween species is called parasitism. In a parasitic association one organism, the parasite, lives on or in another organism, the host. The parasite obtains food and shelter from the host at the expense of the host. Parasites are generally host-specific, that is, a particular species (or group of related species) of parasite lives on or in a particular species (or group of related species) of host. Parasites are also usually specially modified for their mode of existence. Parasitic roundworms, for example, may have hooks or sucker discs for holding to their hosts. A parasitic organism normally cannot survive without its host, but the host can invariably live without the parasite. Many parasites, in fact, seriously injure or may even cause the death of their hosts. Examples of such extremely harmful parasites are the specific protozoans (one-celled animals) that cause amebic dysentery and malaria in man.

Community Characteristics

A biotic community consists of the plant and animal

The ecological relationships in a particular habitat are perhaps best expressed in the feeding habits of the animals living in that habitat. The natural condition that one species preys on another and is, in turn, preyed on by still another species results in the formation of food chains. In the accompanying illustration several interrelated food chains

are shown. The arrows indicate the path of food materials from the primary source (green plants) through animal consumers. The energy transferred through the food chains (in the form of food) is initially derived from sunlight, which—together with mineral salts, water, and carbon dioxide—is utilized by green plants to manufacture food.

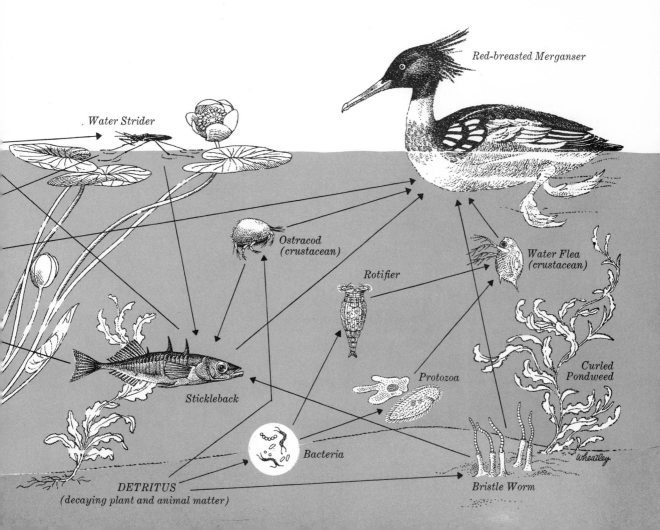

Red-breasted Merganser

Water Strider

Ostracod
(crustacean)

Rotifer

Water Flea
(crustacean)

Stickleback

Protozoa

Curled
Pondweed

Bacteria

Bristle Worm

DETRITUS
(decaying plant and animal matter)

populations that live in a particular area or habitat; it is the living part of the ecosystem. The community concept is the cornerstone of modern ecology, emphasizing that all the different populations (which comprise a series of trophic levels) form a closely interrelated group of organisms within an ecosystem. A typical farm pasture is a community: its plant and animal populations may include clover, trees, sheep, horses, and beef and dairy cattle. There may be 40 acres of bluegrass, 1 acre of clover, 12 oak trees, 50 dairy cattle, a few beef cattle and sheep, and 1 horse. Such a community would be called a bluegrass-dairy cattle community, since communities are usually named for the dominant species.

In the terrestrial environment where large plants are more in evidence than animal populations, the community is often named after the dominant vegetation which is both more stable and less mobile than animal species. In aquatic surroundings the physical nature of the habitat is often used as the name of the community; for example, a standing-water, or lentic, community. Such a community includes rooted vegetation and phytoplankton as the producers; amphibious mammals, aquatic insects, mollusks, and fish as consumers. Marine communities include mudflats, rocky shores, sand beaches, and open sea.

Succession is the appearance, in a definite sequence, of one community which replaces another as environmental conditions change. Succession is as important in ecology as Mendel's laws are in genetics. The progress of change is directed to a final, or climax, community which is in equilibrium with the environment. Knowledge of succession makes it possible to predict future changes in plant and animal populations in a given area, and is thus invaluable in planning conservation programs.

Consult Oosting, H. J., *Study of Plant Communities* (1948); Allee, W. C., and others, *Principles of Animal Ecology* (1951); Odum, E. P., *Fundamentals of Ecology* (1953); Storer, J. H., *The Web of Life* (1953).

CLARENCE J. HYLANDER, Author,
The World of Plant Life

See also:

AMENSALISM	ENVIRONMENT
BIOME	FOOD CHAIN
BIOSPHERE	MUTUALISM
CARBON CYCLE	NITROGEN CYCLE
COMMENSALISM	PARASITISM
DECAY	SYMBIOSIS
ECOSYSTEM	

ECOLOGY, HUMAN, a branch of social science dealing with the processes and organizations resulting from human efforts to develop a division of labor and specialized technologies for deriving a livelihood from the physical environment and maintaining the species through reproduction. Human ecology studies the community and the spatial and socio-economic aspects of its structure. Related to plant and animal ecology, human ecology uses many of the same concepts. Its basic premise is that each species, including man, must adapt to its total environment, which consists of all other living organisms, as well as the inanimate resources of the physical surroundings. Successful adjustment requires that the members of the species organize themselves into co-operating and inter-

acting groups so that particular members become specialized in performing specific necessary tasks and then exchange the products of their labor or service for other necessities of life. The complex system which thus develops persists and is modified by changing environmental conditions, technological advances, and population size. Thus most, if not all, human social organization and all major human social institutions are based upon the functions of survival and livelihood. In a sense human ecology is "sociological economics" very broadly defined.

This definition should not be allowed to degenerate into "social biology," however. The human species possesses mental and physical capacities unknown in quantity, if not in kind, to any other species, and efforts to analyze human livelihood behavior in terms of the lowest common denominator for quadruped mammals is incomplete, excessively abstract, and comparatively useless for understanding modern societies.

Since its formulation in the early 1920's, human ecology has had an aggressively behavioristic approach, refusing to base its analysis upon data concerning opinions, aspirations, prejudices, and emotional sets. Thus most ecological research has been statistical, consisting of the analysis of census and other enumerative data obtained from households and business establishments. Much of ecology is closely linked to the study of population pressure and adjustment. In fact population study derives much of its theory from human ecology.

DONALD J. BOGUE, University of Chicago
See also MIGRATION; POPULATION; PSYCHOLOGY: SOCIAL PSYCHOLOGY; URBAN PLANNING.

ECONOMIC ADVISERS, COUNCIL OF, body created by the U.S. Employment Act of 1946 primarily to help the President prepare the annual reports on the country's economic condition that the act requires him to make to Congress. The council is also empowered to hire specialists and others for research, to appraise government economic programs, and to make special studies in order to foster free enterprise. It consists of three economists appointed by the President.

ECONOMIC AND SOCIAL COUNCIL OF THE UNITED NATIONS, a principal organ of the United Nations. *See* UNITED NATIONS.

ECONOMIC COMMISSION FOR AFRICA (ECA), a regional economic commission of the United Nations. Operating within the framework of the Economic and Social Council of the United Nations, the commission seeks to promote the economic development of Africa through international co-operation. ECA was created on Apr. 29, 1958, to provide for Africa the same facilities for economic co-operation already existing in Europe, Asia and the Far East, and Latin America. Its mission, subject to members' approval, is to initiate and to participate in common action to develop African economies and to strengthen economic relations of the countries of the region, both among themselves and with other countries of the world. From headquarters in Addis Ababa, Ethiopia, the 31 members of the commission direct the secretariat, review projects and plans, and discuss new economic developments on the continent. The headquarters provide a forum where member states, other nations interested in sending observers, U.N. specialized agencies, intergovernmental bodies, and international nongovernmental groups may meet to consider regional economic matters.

The commission is directed by an executive secretary and is divided into a research division which undertakes economic, social, and statistical studies; a joint ECA-FAO (Food and Agricultural Organization) division; a community development branch; and a section charged with administration, conferences, and services.

WAYNE WILCOX, Columbia University

ECONOMIC COMMISSION FOR ASIA AND THE FAR EAST (ECAFE),

a regional economic commission of the United Nations. Operating within the framework of the Economic and Social Council of the United Nations, the commission seeks to promote the economic development of Asia and the Far East through international co-operation. Largely as a result of pressure from India and China, and despite Western coolness, ECAFE was established on Mar. 28, 1947. It was considered an experiment to be evaluated no later than the end of 1951, at which time it was adjudged a success and given a permanent mandate.

With the permission of interested or affected governments, ECAFE undertakes the task of initiating and of participating in common action for economic development and for raising the level of economic activity in Asia and the Far East. It also seeks to improve and to strengthen the economic relations of the countries of the region, both among themselves and with other countries of the world. The staff of the commission provides regional studies of economic and technical developments and collects, evaluates, and publishes economic and statistical information.

From its headquarters in Bangkok, Thailand, the organization co-ordinates efforts by the member states, U.N. specialized agencies, and the ECAFE staff. Both the United States and the Soviet Union are members of the commission, and cold war politics have at times played an important role in the nominally technical body. ECAFE has been so valuable that almost every country in the region holds membership in it.

WAYNE WILCOX, Columbia University

ECONOMIC COMMISSION FOR EUROPE (ECE),

regional economic commission of the United Nations. Operating within the framework of the Economic and Social Council of the United Nations, the commission seeks to initiate and participate in measures for facilitating concerted action for the economic reconstruction of Europe through international co-operation. Created on Mar. 28, 1947, the commission was initially viewed as a central forum from which European governments might contact the United States to discuss and develop policies designed to aid the reconstruction of Europe's post-World War II economies. Thus it sought to balance demand and supply, promote trade, and attain a healthy balance-of-payments situation.

In 1953, however, the commission's primary concern was shifted to raising the level of European economic activity, and maintaining and strengthening the economic relations of the European countries both among themselves and with other countries of the world. Thus its principal task became one of rationalizing distribution and production techniques and developing common European marketing and transportation practices.

The practical day-to-day work of the commission is carried out entirely through its committees and other suborgans. These organs are intergovernmental consultative and administrative bodies, and cover the following fields: agriculture, coal, electric power, energy, gas, housing, industry and materials, steel, timber, and trade. The secretariat of the commission also maintains offices of research, statistics, and public information.

The initial membership of the commission included countries in the Soviet bloc, but they declined to participate in the commission's projects. The headquarters of the commission is in Geneva, from which the secretariat circulates information pertinent to the European economy.

WAYNE WILCOX, Columbia University

ECONOMIC COMMISSION FOR LATIN AMERICA (ECLA),

a regional economic commission of the United Nations. Operating within the framework of the Economic and Social Council of the United Nations, the commission seeks to promote the economic development and growth of Latin America through international co-operation. ECLA was created on Feb. 25, 1948. Its membership includes the 20 Latin-American republics, France, the Netherlands, the United Kingdom, and the United States. Like the other U.N. commissions for economic affairs, ECLA has as a goal a healthy economic life for the region. With many developing countries in its membership, the commission has been especially active in surveying new possibilities in the Latin-American economies which have tended to be based on one commodity. Another important function has been to bring together planners from all the member countries and experts from the United Nations to review problems and to develop common programs.

The work of the commission is carried out by technical divisions dealing with economic surveys, total economic development, industry and mining, and agriculture. In particular, the foreign trade of the American republics has been an important subject for research and recommendation. Unlike the Economic Commission for Europe which dealt primarily with problems of postwar reconstruction, or that of Asia and the Far East (ECAFE) which deals largely with problems of developing economies, ECLA has found a most important sector of its work to be the co-ordination of economic activity and the promotion of co-operative ventures among countries of the region.

WAYNE WILCOX, Columbia University

ECONOMIC DEVELOPMENT,

the process whereby a country's per capita output of goods and services increases with time. It is customary to refer to the speed of development as the rate of economic growth. Both the level of economic development and the rate of growth may be measured in terms of national income per head, estimates of which are now available for all the countries of the world.

Interest in the rate of economic growth goes back at least to the 17th century, when concern over national power led the English economists Sir William Petty and

ECONOMIC DEVELOPMENT

Gregory King to prepare estimates of population and income growth. A century later Adam Smith devoted much of his great treatise, *The Wealth of Nations*, to a powerful and original analysis of the process by which national economies develop. But Smith's general optimism about the possibilities of economic growth gave way to the more pessimistic view of the classical economists of the first half of the 19th century. The Rev. Thomas Malthus, David Ricardo, and John Stuart Mill expressed the fear that a limited supply of fertile land and a rapidly growing population would eventually halt the process of economic growth. When it became apparent, by the late 19th century, that their predictions were not being fulfilled, concern over growth receded. A general resurgence of attention to the subject would have occurred earlier in the 20th century if the great depression of the 1930's had not turned the attention of economists and all men of affairs to the problems of economic recovery.

At the end of World War II, a vigorous revival of interest in economic development began. It stemmed in large part from the emergence of many colonial countries as independent nations, the division of the world into Communist and non-Communist blocs, and a cold war in which both sides used the tactic of economic assistance to underdeveloped neutral countries.

Studies reveal many significant facts about the levels of economic development in the various countries of the world. A very wide disparity in levels exists, as measured by gross national product per head. In the opinion of many authorities, this disparity has widened in recent years. Thus the gross national product per head in the United States is now nearly eight times that of the underdeveloped countries. If one takes a gross national product of $595 per head as the critical level, it appears that about 30% of the world's population lives in economically developed countries that produce more than 75% of the gross world output, while approximately 70% of the population lives in underdeveloped countries that produce less than 25% of the gross world output.

Disparities in levels of economic development have doubtless existed during all periods of human history. The present gap between the advanced and underdeveloped countries probably had its origins in the industrial revolution of the 18th century, which laid the basis for the growth of industrial economies in England and Western Europe during the 19th century. Waves of migration and the massive export of capital from Europe planted the seeds of industrialism in North America, Australia, and South Africa. Although European immigrants and capital flowed into other areas, notably South America, cultural and political conditions in those areas appear to have been unfavorable for the kind of rapid economic growth that has taken place in such new countries as the United States, Canada, and Australia.

Limiting Factors. With spreading knowledge, the historic gap in levels of economic development has increased. The sharp drop in the mortality rates of the underdeveloped countries has brought a rapid rise in population that has limited the rate of growth in output per head. Birth rates in most underdeveloped countries also tend to rise with the level of national income. But population growth is only one of a number of forces that have inhibited economic growth in the underdeveloped countries. Others are primitive agricultural techniques, low levels of educational attainment, inadequate capital facilities, and political instability.

The typical underdeveloped country has an economy dominated by technologically backward agriculture. Strongly ingrained cultural traditions and feudal systems of land tenure often constitute formidable barriers to increased productivity. As a result, many underdeveloped countries cannot produce adequate food supplies. Others suffer because the bulk of their labor force grows a single cash crop that must be sold in the unstable world commodity markets.

Low levels of literacy slow the process of social change which is a prerequisite for economic development. Widespread illiteracy tends to buttress tribal organization, the caste system, and other traditional institutions inimical to economic growth.

Another drag on economic growth in the underdeveloped countries is inadequate capital facilities such as transportation networks, sources of electric power, and water supplies. Without these facilities, which require large-scale public investments, the agricultural sector of the economy remains stagnant, and the possibilities of industrial growth are severely limited.

Unstable, inefficient central governments frequently constitute a formidable barrier to the economic progress of underdeveloped countries. Central governments that have an uncertain tenure or whose power is weakened by regional conflicts cannot take resolute steps to provide overhead capital facilities. Moreover, both native and foreign investors, whose capital could make a significant contribution to economic growth, shy away because of the uncertainty that results from political instability.

Policies. Despite the work done in constructing models of economic growth, there is as yet no generally accepted body of economic theory to serve as a policy guide for spurring economic growth in underdeveloped countries. Nevertheless, all developmental policies, whether pursued by Communist or non-Communist governments, share certain common features. All programs place emphasis on the need to raise agricultural productivity and to lay the foundations for industrial growth through the development of overhead capital facilities.

But within the Communist bloc, in China, and in the underdeveloped countries of eastern Europe, the Soviet Russian experience of the 1920's and 1930's provides a guide for policies. These newer Communist states, all with totalitarian political structures, follow the path of development by coercion, seeking to raise agricultural productivity through collectivization and to establish heavy industries by curtailing the output of consumers' goods.

In the unaligned countries of South America and Asia that have received aid from the United States and Western Europe, efforts to accelerate economic growth have generally come within the framework of democratic political institutions. Most of those countries have formulated long-range plans for the attainment of specific economic objectives, with their governments playing a leading role in virtually all such efforts.

Consult Nurkse, Ragnar, *Problems of Capital Formation in Underdeveloped Countries* (1953); Lewis, W. A.,

The Theory of Economic Growth (1955); Hirschman, A. O., *The Strategy of Economic Development* (1958); Kuznets, S. S., *Six Lectures on Economic Growth* (1959); Rostow, W. W., *The Stages of Economic Growth* (1960).

HARVEY H. SEGAL, Graduate School of Business Administration, New York University

See also EXPORT-IMPORT BANK OF WASHINGTON; GROSS NATIONAL PRODUCT; INTERNATIONAL MONETARY FUND; POPULATION.

ECONOMICS. "Economics is what economists do." This is the definition once given by Jacob Viner, a famous economist. Such a definition obviously was meant to be a bit facetious, but it underscores the difficulty of defining a discipline which has many facets. Economics may be more seriously defined as "the science dealing with the maximization of satisfactions in the face of scarcity." Economists, however, define "scarcity" differently from laymen. The economist considers something to be scarce whenever it is not available in unlimited quantities relative to the need for it. Thus, in the economists' sense of the word potatoes would be scarce, even though the average person would consider them to be readily available.

The definition of economics refers specifically to the scarcity of the basic resources, sometimes known as "factors of production." These are land, labor, and capital. Economists define "land" as "the contribution of natural resources to production." Land, therefore, includes minerals, forests, fish, and wildlife, as well as soil. The concept of "labor" includes "all contributions of human beings to productive effort." The services of the president of General Motors would therefore be included as labor, just as well as the janitor who cleans the Ford plant. "Capital" refers to tools, equipment, and inventories. All three of these resources are scarce in the sense that they are not available in unlimited quantities relative to the need for them. Furthermore, these three resources are the basic building blocks from which all goods and services are produced. Autos, for example, use aluminum and steel, but these metals may be thought of as merely combinations of land, labor, and capital.

It follows that the basic problem of economics is how to maximize our satisfactions, given the fact that our resources are limited. The housewife faces the same problem when she attempts to get the most satisfaction from a limited income. The economist examines a similar problem on the level of the entire society, rather than a particular household or a particular business. Economics, therefore, is concerned primarily with government activities and the society at large, rather than the activities of particular households or businesses.

Past Economic Thought

The Greeks (notably Plato, Aristotle, and Xenophon) and the medieval church authorities (especially Thomas Aquinas and Albertus Magnus) made many observations concerning economic matters. There was no organized school of economic thought, however, until the rise of the mercantilists in the 16th century. The mercantilists were found primarily in England, though a German branch of mercantilists, known as Kameralists, also existed. Most of the mercantilistic writers were engaged principally in commerce. Their writings were related to their principal work, and so they usually underscored the importance of commerce. Virtually all of them desired a favorable balance of trade for England. This meant that England should export more than she imported. They advocated that Britain use all methods, such as tariffs and import controls, to bring about the desired favorable balance. Many of the most naïve mercantilists desired merely a favorable balance, so that foreign nations would be forced to pay the British in gold instead of goods. Britain would thus accumulate huge stocks of gold merely for its own sake.

Some current writers believe that several of the mercantilists were more sophisticated. They desired a favorable balance of trade because the incoming gold would increase the money supply (gold was the circulating medium at the time). The more plentiful money supply would have two effects: (1) It would reduce interest rates. This would occur because the interest rate is the price for borrowing money. If money is more plentiful, it should become easier to borrow. (2) It would raise prices. With more money in existence, the value of each unit of money should fall, which means that the price level should rise. Both a lower interest rate and a higher level of prices would encourage businessmen to borrow more funds and purchase more tools and equipment. This, it was argued, would increase productive capacity and stimulate Britain's economic growth.

Unlike the Scholastic Doctors of the Middle Ages (who considered all interest to be immoral "usury"), the mercantilists felt that the charging of interest was morally and economically justified, though they desired the interest rates to be as low as possible. They also desired to lower wage rates as much as possible, for they thought this made the workers work harder. Their thoughts in these matters may be regarded as the first systematic body of economic analysis.

The Physiocrats. The mercantilistic period lasted from the 16th century until approximately 1776. During the last part of the mercantilistic period, a new school of economic thought appeared in France. This school is known as the physiocrats. Perhaps it is a bit optimistic to call it a school, for it consisted primarily of one man: François Quesnay (1694–1774), though he had several followers.

The physiocrats differed from the mercantilists in almost every particular. The mercantilists had thought that commerce was the most crucial segment of economic activity. The physiocrats believed that agriculture was the seat of all economic wealth. The mercantilists had advocated that the government take an active role in guiding the economy, while the physiocrats likened the economic system to the working of the human body. They stressed the "natural harmony" of the system, and insisted that the system would work best with a minimum degree of governmental interference. Their natural harmony was demonstrated by means of a *Tableau Economique* (Economic Table), in which the interrelationships between the various segments of the economy were demonstrated. The economy was divided into three sectors: the "productive class," the "sterile class," and the "proprietary class."

The productive class consisted of farmers, since true production could come only from natural resources, ac-

AN EXAMPLE OF ECONOMICS— FROM PRODUCTION TO CONSUMPTION

The automobile industry exemplifies basic functions of economic activity: *production*, or the manufacture of the automobile; *distribution*, getting the automobile to market outlets; and *consumption*, or the sale of the automobile to a customer. The manufacturer's mastery of these functions and of their interrelationship enables him to decide how many cars to produce, how to reach the best markets, and what design, structural improvements, and merchandising techniques may be needed to sell his automobile profitably.

PRODUCTION

Automobiles are mass-produced by means of an assembly line. Each car is assembled routinely and identically in a planned series of steps. The work done on one car at a given stage is exactly the same as that done on every car at that stage. This method of production is both economical and efficient.

(ALL PHOTOS—FORD MOTOR CO.)

The interchangeable part made to fit any car of the same model is a principle of the assembly line. Above, adding parts to a car.

Above, the body of a station wagon being added to its chassis.

Seat installation is one of the final steps on the assembly line.

cording to the physiocrats. The sterile class was composed of those engaged in molding the products produced by the productive class (manufacturing, construction). The physiocrats, contrary to modern economic thought, felt that these people did not engage in true productive activity, since they merely formed the products made by the agriculturalists. The proprietary class included the landowners, who collected rent, paid taxes, and ran the government. The *Tableau* then assumed various payments and shipments of products from one sector to the other. It is an important milestone in economic thought, because (1) it was the first major demonstration of the interdependence of the various segments of the economic system; (2) as such, it emphasized the auto-

maticity of the system and constituted the first logical defense of *laissez-faire;* (3) it was the forerunner of a powerful modern technique, known as input-output analysis.

Adam Smith. Meanwhile, the mercantilistic period in England was coming to its end with the publication in 1776 of Adam Smith's great work, *An Inquiry Into the Nature and Causes of the Wealth of Nations.* Smith's main object in writing the book was to oppose the mercantilistic views with respect to the balance of trade. "What is the true wealth of nations?" cried Smith. "It does not lie in gold, but in goods," he answered. The mercantilists had been advocating that England give up its goods in order to acquire gold, but this was wrong. A

DISTRIBUTION

Automobiles receiving a final inspection at the plant before being readied for shipment to dealers all over the world.

These automobiles, destined for consumers in a distant part of the United States, are loaded on triple-deck railway cars.

Effective distribution is as important as efficient production. Producers strive to make their products available to as large a market as possible. Swiftly and inexpensively transporting the new cars to dealers throughout the world is an important factor in the success of the enterprise.

CONSUMPTION

A buying public is as essential to the manufacturer's success as are the machinery of production and the mechanics of distribution. The consumer is the final judge of the product's marketability. His choice of an automobile depends on his standards of quality, his taste, and what he is willing or able to spend.

A new car owner is given his keys. The automotive industry is an important barometer of economic health.

A purchase is made and this car completes its movement from manufacturer to consumer. The salesman prepares the contract.

nation should be striving to accumulate goods rather than gold. Gold, according to Smith, was fundamentally useless to a nation, however useful it might be for an individual.

Smith also opposed the mercantilists' programs of government control. According to Smith, an "invisible hand" was at work, operating in such a way that even though each person was attempting to maximize his own individual welfare, the net result of his attempts to do so would be the maximization of welfare for the entire society. This "invisible hand" was none other than the market itself. Smith's work therefore was a powerful argument for *laissez-faire* and the free enterprise system.

In the process of making these arguments, Smith did

much more than defeat the mercantilists. He wrote a remarkably complete economic treatise, the principal systematic treatment of economic thought to that time. He also founded a new school of British economic thought: the classical school. Thomas Malthus, David Ricardo, and John Stuart Mill were the other principal members. He dealt in detail with such matters as the advantages of specialization, the importance of increasing market size, the determination of prices, wages, and profits, and so forth. He took an optimistic view of economic development, because he felt the growth of population would increase market size and thereby stimulate the growth of efficiency by means of specialization.

Thomas Malthus. By the end of the 18th century,

213

ECONOMICS

Smith's optimistic predictions appeared to be unwarranted. When Thomas Robert Malthus (1766–1834) looked about in 1798, he could see nothing but increased misery. The incipient Industrial Revolution had already caused crowded conditions in the cities. Men, women, and children were working up to 110 hours per week in order to gain the most meager living.

Malthus concluded that Smith's optimism was totally unjustified. The reason for the increased misery, according to Malthus, was an imbalance between the rates of growth of population and production. Malthus felt that population was growing according to a geometric progression (2, 4, 8, 16, . . .), whereas production (specifically, food) was increasing only according to an arithmetic progression (2, 4, 6, 8, . . .). The result was clear. Production per capita was falling and would continue to fall until the lowest possible per capita production on which human beings could subsist was attained. Once the subsistence level of per capita production was reached, population could no longer outstrip production because "the positive checks"—that is, famine, disease, pestilence, and so forth—would come into play to keep the population from expanding further. Moreover, any improvement in techniques, which would increase production, would simply bring about an acceleration in the rate of population growth, thereby maintaining production at the subsistence level.

Malthus saw only one way out of this dreary dilemma. It was possible that "the preventive checks," that is, birth control, could reduce the population rate of growth below the rate of growth of production. In that case, per capita production could be maintained permanently above the subsistence level. In the first edition of *Essay on the Principles of Population* (1798), Malthus believed such a possibility was most unlikely. In later editions of the *Essay* he placed somewhat more emphasis on the preventive checks, but to the end of his life he was not sanguine.

During the 19th and 20th centuries the Western world has not fallen victim to what has come to be known as "the Malthusian cycle." Population pressure has not kept per capita incomes at subsistence levels. This has been due to several factors. In the first place, the Industrial Revolution caused a huge increase in the rate of growth of production that Malthus did not foresee. Secondly, the rate of population growth decreased because of a decline in the birth rate.

Be that as it may, the "Malthusian dilemma" remains one of the most important current economic problems. In the Far East, production has never outstripped population growth by very much. The current economic problems of India, China, and Southeast Asia are inextricably bound up with the Malthusian cycle. Furthermore, with the upturns in population growth in the 20th century, it may still be that the Western world will feel the pressure of population growth.

David Ricardo. Malthus' gloomy predictions served to refocus the thought of the economists of the mid-19th century. The new topic of concern was now the distribution of income, for this was intimately connected with the subsistence problem which Malthus propounded. David Ricardo (1772–1823) was the man who codified the distribution problem into a meaningful whole. According to Ricardo, the landlords would receive an increasing rent

| STUDY GUIDE | ECONOMICS |

One indication of the importance of economics is the number of professionals active in this branch of the social sciences. Economists outnumber political scientists two to one, sociologists about three to one, and anthropologists twenty to one in the United States. Economists work in such vital areas as agriculture, business, labor, fiscal policy, and international trade and development. They also contribute to foreign policy and military intelligence. They deal with immediate problems and also try to formulate basic theories of economic behavior. The article on these pages defines the scope of economics and then examines the field in terms of the following:

Past Economic Thought. The Greeks; the mercantilists; the physiocrats; Adam Smith; Thomas Malthus; David Ricardo; John Stuart Mill; Karl Marx; and the marginalist school.

Current Economic Thought. The neoclassicists; John Maynard Keynes; modern economic thought.

The many other articles in this Encyclopedia that bear on the topic of economics can be used in several ways. The reader who is new to the subject may find it helpful to review the historical development of economic practice and thought in more detail than is possible in the main article. He can consult BARTER; FEUDALISM; GUILD; MERCANTILISM; AGRARIAN REVOLUTION; COLONIES, COLONIZATION, AND COLONIALISM; INDUSTRIAL REVOLUTION; FACTORY SYSTEM; PHYSIOCRATS; LAISSEZ FAIRE; MASS PRODUCTION; SOCIALISM; and biographic entries on such men as Adam SMITH, Thomas Robert MALTHUS, David RICARDO, John Stuart MILL, Louis BLANC, John BRIGHT, Karl MARX, and John Maynard KEYNES.

An appropriate article to climax the historical survey is ECONOMIC SYSTEMS, which describes the two chief systems of the modern world, capitalism and socialism (including communism in the U.S.S.R.), and discusses the close relationship of economic and political thought. See also ECONOMIC DEVELOPMENT.

Other major articles dealing with economic theories and policies in the 20th century include BUSINESS (which discusses the free-enterprise system and business administration), BANKS AND BANKING, ECONOMIC STABILIZATION POLICIES (treating the role of government), FEDERAL RESERVE SYSTEM, TARIFF, TAXATION, EUROPEAN COMMON MARKET, and TRADE, INTERNATIONAL.

Some articles concerned with terms and concepts used in economics have already been named. Others include CAPITAL, LABOR, LAND, COMPETITION, SUPPLY AND DEMAND, PRODUCTION, CONSUMPTION, MARKETING, COST, PROFIT, INCOME, CREDIT, INVESTMENT, INTEREST, SAVING, GROSS NATIONAL PRODUCT, COST OF LIVING, BUSINESS CYCLE, INFLATION AND DEFLATION, and EMPLOYMENT AND UNEMPLOYMENT.

Many articles suggest books for further reading. Sources such as the annual supplement to this Encyclopedia give year-by-year reports on world economic conditions.

as the population pressure on land grew. Labor would eventually receive a subsistence wage because of the constant population growth. Profits would ultimately become zero, because they would be squeezed by the ever-increasing rent. Thus, the persons who were most productive—workers and enterprisers—would lose everything to those who were least productive—the landlords. This was a sad picture, indeed. In fact, it earned for economics the opprobrious title of "the dismal science."

The Ricardian wage-rate determination (known as "The Iron Law of Wages") was but a special case of Ricardo's general theory of prices and value, wherein all reproducible goods would in the long run sell for their cost of production. This would be true because a short-run price in excess of the cost of production would provide a high profit, thereby generating an increased supply of the product, and hence a lower price and profit. On the other hand, a price below the cost of production would mean low profits, a decreased supply of the product, and a higher price. Since the cost of production of labor was its subsistence, labor was therefore doomed to a subsistence wage.

Ricardo's contribution to economic thought consisted partly in the systematic logic which he applied to his analysis. The system was welded into a logical and meaningful whole. In the course of his analysis Ricardo enunciated not only his important theories of rent, wages, profits, and value, but also the equally significant theory of comparative advantage. Here, Ricardo proved that it is advantageous for nations to trade with each other even if one nation is more efficient in the production of all goods, so long as the more efficient nation has a greater advantage in the production of one good than in the production of another.

In the process, however, Ricardo turned the thought of most economists away from problems of economic growth and employment. Because of Say's Law (discussed below) he assumed—in contrast to Malthus—that there would never be a deficiency of demand, and thus no problem of full employment of resources existed. The vast majority of economists of the period were won over to Ricardo's position on this matter.

John Stuart Mill. The culmination of the classical school of economics came with John Stuart Mill (1806–73), who summarized the development of classical economic thought in *Principles of Political Economy* (1848). Mill's primary contribution—other than the codification of current economic thought—was his insistence that the Ricardian laws of distribution need not be immutable, since society could redistribute in any way it might see fit, after the primary distribution had been made. The effect of Mill's position was to reduce the importance of distribution theory (that is, theories concerned with the distribution of incomes) in subsequent economic thought.

Karl Marx. In a sense Karl Marx (1818–83) was an offshoot of the classical economists, for his theories embodied many of the principles established by the classical writers. In the *Communist Manifesto* (1847), Marx, in collaboration with Friedrich Engels, adapted the philosophy of Georg Hegel to his concept of development. According to Marx, the development of mankind can be

European cars being unloaded on a Florida dock. International trade affects the economic well-being of every country. (LEO WITT)

viewed as a succession of economic conflicts, between the ruling class (designated by Marx as "the thesis") and the subordinate class ("the anti-thesis"), who are oppressed by the ruling class. Eventually the subordinate class defeats the ruling class, and the two classes merge into a new "synthesis," which becomes the ruling class in the next time period. At the time Marx was writing, the owners of businesses (called by Marx "capitalists" or "bourgeoisie") constituted the ruling class. They were suppressing the workers (designated as "the proletariat" by Marx). It was clear to Marx that eventually the proletariat must struggle with their oppressors and must inevitably defeat them. This time, however, the aftermath would be different. Instead of the creation of a new ruling class, the world would witness the development of a new "classless society," in which justice would prevail for all.

Marx utilized his economic theory to explain (1) how the bourgeoisie was oppressing the proletariat and (2) how the conflict would lead inevitably to the overthrow of the bourgeoisie.

Marx said that the value of any good (its "full labor value") is determined by the quantity of labor required to produce it. This is known as "the labor theory of value." Marx, in a sense, borrowed it from Ricardo, who had frequently assumed it to be true as a simplifying expository device. Marx, on the other hand, accepted it as an absolute fact. Although the capitalists charge the full labor value for their goods, they pay their workers only a subsistence wage, leaving "surplus value" (the difference between the full labor value and the subsistence wage) for the capitalists. This is an ill-gotten gain. The entire product really belongs to the workers, since they are responsible for producing all of it. The capitalists add nothing, but, like leeches, extract the surplus value from the workers. (Note that the concept of the subsistence wage is taken from the classical writers, though they considered it a simple fact, with no connotation that the capitalists were the evil exploiters of the working class.)

Marx further reasons that the downfall of the capitalists

is written in the cards, because as more and more machines replace labor, the ability of the capitalists to exploit the proletariat declines. This brings about a falling rate of profit (also a classical concept), which causes many small businessmen to go bankrupt and fall into the proletariat. The bourgeoisie, desperately attempting to maintain their profits, attempt to lower wages still more, but cannot do so because the wages are already at subsistence. At the same time they attempt to find more markets by means of a more aggressive imperialistic policy. This leads to wars and general chaos. In the midst of this, the revolt of the proletariat occurs, and the downfall of the bourgeoisie is inevitable.

Most modern economists would attack Marx's logic on several grounds. There is no satisfactory proof that the labor theory of value must hold true, nor is there absolute proof within the Marxian framework that the subsistence wage must always be paid. The majority of economists feel that the businessman is entitled to a profit, since he performs the useful economic function of taking risks and making basic decisions. Furthermore, Marx's proof of the inevitability of the falling rate of profit is weak.

Marx's hold on a large segment of the public must nevertheless be admitted. Moreover, his insights on imperialism and the downfall of small firms, with the consequent rise of large firms, seem almost prophetic. His emotional appeal, his influence on the masses, and (indirectly) his influence on world history have been immense.

The Marginalist School. At the time that Marx's collaborator, Engels, was struggling to finish Marx's work after the master's death, there arose a new group of mainstream economists. These were known as the marginalists, or the Austrians. The most prominent among them were Karl Menger (1840–1921), Friedrich von Wieser (1851–1920), Eugen von Böhm-Bawerk (1851–1914), and the Englishman, Stanley Jevons (1835–82). Vilfredo Pareto and Leon Walras are also sometimes included in this school, though they are often counted among the later neoclassical school.

The marginalist school directed its attention to a famous "paradox of value," mentioned by Adam Smith. "Why is it," said Smith, "that water, which has great 'value in use' (that is, usefulness) has such a low 'value in exchange' (price), whereas diamonds have little 'value in use' yet great 'value in exchange.'" Smith did not seem to know the answer to this conundrum, but the marginalists presented a solution. The value of a good, they said, is not determined by the total satisfaction we get from it. Rather, it is determined by the additional satisfaction ("marginal utility") that we obtain from one small unit more or less of the good in question. Water is so plentiful that an additional unit, more or less, does not change our total satisfaction very much. Diamonds, on the other hand, are sufficiently scarce, so that an additional unit alters our total satisfaction to a greater degree. The value of a good is thus determined by its marginal utility rather than its total utility.

The marginalist school was significant for several reasons. In the first place, as the name indicates, the introduction of the concept of the additional, or marginal, unit revolutionized the methodology of economics. Economists today apply the marginal concept to many areas. In analyzing a firm's behavior, they speak of marginal revenue and marginal cost. In discussing the hiring of factors of production, the concepts of marginal revenue product and marginal cost of a factor are relevant.

Secondly, the marginalists changed the focus of economic analysis from income distribution to the pricing of products. Within their analysis of the pricing of products, they altered the emphasis from supply to demand, for it was the utility of the product to the buyer which determined the price, rather than the long-run changes in supply, as the Ricardian analysis stated. In the case of the marginalists, supply was brought in "through the back door" by its effect on the marginal utility of the good.

In the third place, the marginalists emphasized the short-run, day-to-day determination of market prices, in contrast to the long-run tendencies of price movements in Ricardo's anaylsis. This concern for the short-run was to be incorporated into modern economic thought, along with the analysis of long-run price tendencies.

Lastly, it may be noted that several economists on the fringe of the marginalist school (especially Leon Walras) demonstrated the interrelationships of the various parts of the economic system by means of a general equilibrium analysis.

Current Economic Thought

The heyday of the marginalist school dates roughly from 1865 to 1895. Recent economic thought is usually said to begin with the neoclassicists. The most famous members of the school were two Englishmen, Alfred Marshall (1842–1924) and A. C. Pigou (1877–1959).

The Neoclassicists. Marshall synthesized the marginalist and classical theories of value, with their emphasis on demand and supply, respectively. Price is determined by both demand and supply, according to Marshall. The neoclassical economists (and modern economists as well) realized that the demand for a good is determined by a number of factors: tastes of buyers, their incomes, the prices of the product in question, prices of other products, expectations with respect to future prices and incomes, the size of the market, and others. Of these, the economist usually focuses on price of the product as the most important single factor. Using advanced mathematical techniques, the modern economist estimates the nature of the relationship between demand and the price of the product. He then expresses the relationship in the form of a mathematical equation, graph, or table. A similar equation or graph is determined for the supply of the good. These two relationships are then combined to determine the market price and quantity of the good which is bought and sold. The supply relationship depends greatly on the costs of production of the producer. The comparision between the costs and the market price will determine whether producers in the field will be making large profits or losses. If large profits are being made and there is freedom of entry into the field, new producers will come in, the supply will increase, and the long-run price will be below the current market price. If losses are currently being incurred, producers will leave the field, the supply will diminish, and prices will rise

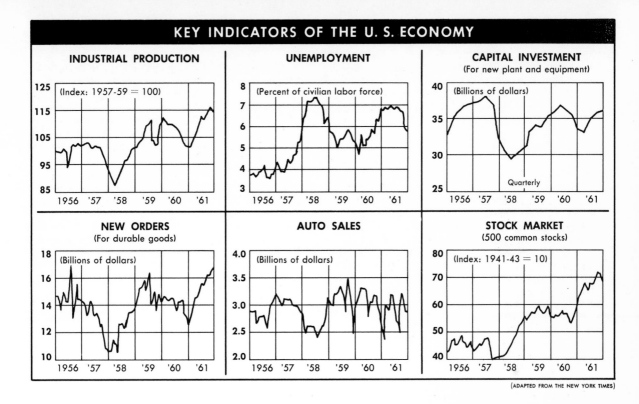

KEY INDICATORS OF THE U. S. ECONOMY

INDUSTRIAL PRODUCTION
(Index: 1957-59 = 100)

125, 115, 105, 95, 85

1956 '57 '58 '59 '60 '61

UNEMPLOYMENT
(Percent of civilian labor force)

8, 7, 6, 5, 4, 3

1956 '57 '58 '59 '60 '61

CAPITAL INVESTMENT
(For new plant and equipment)
(Billions of dollars)

40, 35, 30, 25

Quarterly

1956 '57 '58 '59 '60 '61

NEW ORDERS
(For durable goods)
(Billions of dollars)

18, 16, 14, 12, 10

1956 '57 '58 '59 '60 '61

AUTO SALES
(Billions of dollars)

4.0, 3.5, 3.0, 2.5, 2.0

1956 '57 '58 '59 '60 '61

STOCK MARKET
(500 common stocks)
(Index: 1941-43 = 10)

80, 70, 60, 50, 40

1956 '57 '58 '59 '60 '61

(ADAPTED FROM THE NEW YORK TIMES)

until they cover costs. Thus, the long-run price tends to equal costs, even though the short-run market price may not do so. Modern theory, which in this matter is identical to neoclassical theory, thereby takes into account demand and supply elements in both long- and short-run pricing.

The analysis just described is microeconomic in nature, because it analyzes small segments of the economic system—that is, specific prices of specific products. It does so, however, in order to examine the economic system's methods for allocating scarce resources—that is, channeling them into those uses which maximize our satisfactions. From this analysis most economists have concluded that if there are many producers producing a very similar product, with substantial knowledge of the market by buyers and sellers and with free entry of new sellers into the field, then allocation will be brought about efficiently and in a manner which truly maximizes our satisfactions. If, on the other hand, large elements of monopoly are present—that is, only one firm or very few firms are producing the product—the good is not standardized. Firms are then following collusive practices, knowledge is very imperfect, or freedom of entry is denied, and the allocation is liable to be less efficient and desirable from the standpoint of society. This analysis forms the social justification for the antitrust laws, which are designed to break up monopolies.

In the preceding microeconomic analysis, neoclassical and modern economists essentially agree, though the modern economists have rendered a more complete analysis by virtue of the addition of more realism and greater mathematical precision.

There is another area, however, in which the two groups differ widely. The neoclassical economists, like the marginalists and the classicists, considered the problem of full employment of resources to be solved automati-

cally by a free enterprise system. Such a belief was based on Say's Law, so named because it was first propounded by the French economist Jean Baptiste Say (1767–1832). According to Say's Law, someone receives income from every dollar spent on a product. The production of any product by the economy, therefore, will generate a sufficient income to buy the product back. Some of this income will be saved, that is, not spent on consumer goods. However, because of the workings of the interest rate, savings will be utilized for expenditures on capital goods (tools, machines). Thus, there cannot be any shortage of overall demand for goods, though particular goods might be in short demand. Furthermore, if somehow the interest-rate mechanism does not work, and a general shortage of demand should develop, the shortage could still be eliminated by a general reduction of prices. In other words, if the economy at full employment was producing $800 of product, but demand was only $700, full employment could be maintained by the simple expedient of reducing the price for the $800 total product to $700. The economy thus had double protection against a deficiency in demand: (1) Say's Law and the interest rate would cause total demand to equal total product, and (2) if Say's Law and the interest rate somehow failed to do this, price flexibility could do the job.

John Maynard Keynes. There was only one thing wrong with this analysis: it did not seem to work. It was difficult for economists to maintain that the economic system automatically guaranteed full employment when, in the mid-1930's, millions of people were unemployed throughout the world. In 1936, the British economist John Maynard Keynes (1883–1946) rocked the economic world with his *General Theory of Employment, Interest, and Money*. In the *General Theory*, Keynes attempted to refute the neoclassical argument with respect to full employment. Keynes argued that (1) the interest rate

217

does not greatly affect savings and purchases of capital goods; therefore the interest rate will not necessarily equate savings with total purchases of capital goods. In view of this, even though an $800 product generates $800 of incomes, total expenditures for goods might be less than $800. Thus, a deficiency in demand could exist. (2) If producers attempted to eliminate the demand deficiency by lowering prices, the lower prices would mean lower incomes for people and therefore a probable further reduction in demand.

Keynes's book marks the beginning of "modern" (as opposed to neoclassical) èconomic thought. Most economists today have accepted the basic Keynesian analysis. The neoclassical position, however, is still upheld by a voluble minority, led by Professor Milton Friedman of the University of Chicago. As a result of the *General Theory* a new branch of economic theory, macroeconomics, was initiated. Macroeconomics looks at large segments of the economy—total demand for all goods, total income, total expenditures, and the like—instead of at the prices of particular goods, particular wages, and so on.

Today, macroeconomic theory coexists with the older microeconomic theory. Economists have made models expressing in equation form the various major relationships within the economy. The simplest model, coming directly from Keynes, utilizes one equation to express the relationship between total consumption expenditures and total income, another equation to describe the relationship between the demand for money and the interest rate, and a third equation to express the relationship between the interest rate and the demand for investment goods. With the help of the new science of econometrics (a combination of economics, mathematics, and statistics) economists have worked out much more detailed models of the economic system with many equations. Detailed studies have been conducted to find the values of the parameters used in the equations. Such models are now being used to predict the effects of various changes (for example, an increase in the money supply) on the entire economic system.

The work of analyzing the interrelationship of the economic system has been greatly facilitated by the development of input-output analysis by Professor Vassily Leontieff of Howard University.

In addition to economic theory, econometrics, and the history of economic thought, economists are interested in several applied areas of economic thought. These include international economics, labor (including the study of wage rates, manpower problems, and organized labor movements), taxation and public control (specializing in the equity and effects of various tax plans), industrial organization (studying the effects of corporate size, antitrust policy, and so on), economic development of underdeveloped areas, and money and banking.

Consult McConnell, C. R., *Economics* (1965); Lipsey, R. G., and Steiner, P. O., *Economics* (1966); Reynolds, L. G., *Economics* (1966); Samuelson, P. A., *Economics* (1967); Heilbroner, R. L., *The Worldly Philosophers* (1968).

ALLAN B. MANDELSTAMM, Michigan State University
See also BUSINESS; COMPETITION; ECONOMIC DEVELOPMENT; ECONOMIC STABILIZATION POLICIES, U.S.; ECONOMIC SYSTEMS.

ECONOMIC STABILIZATION POLICIES, U.S., governmental methods used to avoid the extremes of depression (or recession) and inflation. As the economy becomes more complex, it seems to get out of adjustment more easily. Economic stabilizers are intended to correct these dislocations before they become serious.

In depression the problem is unemployment and low production. The solution is to raise production by encour-

ECONOMICS

Characteristics of the Field. Economics is a large field compared with other social sciences such as sociology and anthropology. It is an expanding field, both in terms of job opportunities and in terms of problems to be studied.

In the United States the greatest number of economists is employed by colleges and universities. Duties include teaching, research, writing, and consulting. Teachers not only train specialists in economics but also give courses in business schools. The federal government employs many economists to study and report on agriculture, business trends, labor, unemployment, and financial problems. Others specialize in such areas as international trade, foreign affairs, and intelligence—analyzing the economic strength of foreign powers, for example. Large private corporations, banks, brokerage houses, and other businesses employ economists to study trends and make reports that can be used to guide policy. Foundations and other nonprofit research organizations also need economists.

The nature of employment in the field determines the geographic distribution of jobs. They tend to cluster in university towns, in Washington, D. C., and in cities where large corporations have central offices—particularly New York and Chicago.

Qualifications and Training. For beginning jobs, a bachelor's degree with a major in economics may be sufficient training. In teaching, government, and industry, however, men with master's or doctor's degrees have better opportunities. In some organizations—as in leading universities—a Ph.D. is necessary for the more responsible positions. For all levels of work, training in statistics and mathematics is usually required. A knowledge of fields such as accounting, law, sociology, or psychology may be useful in some branches of economics.

Income. Highest salaries go to men with Ph.D. degrees plus experience. Many economics teachers supplement their salaries through fees for consulting work and summer teaching. In general, salaries of economists run higher than those of other social scientists.

Prospects for Employment. Qualified economists—especially with advanced degrees—are expected to find many job openings throughout the 1960's. Many new college teachers will be needed to instruct increasing numbers of students. Some economics teachers may be asked to give high school courses. Private industry is expected to rely more and more on economic research, thus creating opportunities for economists in corporations and in consulting services.

The percentage of women in the field is small, and salaries for women tend to be lower than those paid to men.

Sources of Information. ECONOMICS and related articles survey the subject matter of this field. Detailed information on the profession can be obtained from the American Economics Association, Northwestern University, Evanston, Ill. Suggestions on career planning, pertinent to all professions, are given in this Encyclopedia under the title VOCATIONAL GUIDANCE.

Wide World

During the depression of the 1930's, millions were unable to find work (*above*). The establishment of the Civilian Conservation Corps (CCC) was one of many steps taken by the U.S. government to meet the challenge of widespread unemployment. Members of the corps are shown clearing brush for a government-sponsored project (*left*).

aging consumers to buy or producers to expand their investment in factories, machinery, or inventories of goods. If private enterprise does not do this, the government may raise income directly by purchasing more supplies or by hiring more employees.

When the economy booms, the situation is reversed. As full employment of both labor and machines is reached, it becomes physically impossible to expand output substantially, and buyers with rising incomes bid up prices of scarce goods. At this point stabilization policy tries to cut down on excess demand to avoid the inequalities and distortions of a general price rise.

Monetary Policy. The traditional stabilization tool is governmental monetary policy, which attempts to control the quantity of money in circulation through regulation of the banking system. Since the largest portion of the money supply consists of checking deposits created as a result of commercial bank loans, this lending process becomes the focus of monetary policy.

Businessmen (and, to a lesser extent, consumers) borrow from commercial banks to finance their purchases. Low interest rates and ready availability of loans will induce them to borrow more and spend more. When the economy is slack, therefore, monetary policy favors low interest rates and easy money. The Federal Reserve System (q.v.), the major monetary control agency, has four basic powers to deal with recession: (1) It can lower reserve requirements, thus reducing the amount of assets that banks must tie up in their legal reserves and permitting them to lend more. (2) It can purchase government securities from banks, financial institutions, and other holders (but not from the government) to put money into the economy, increase banks' reserves, and make more loans possible. (3) It can lower the discount rate (the interest rate at which it lends to member banks) to make it easier for banks to borrow and in turn lend. (4) It can use moral suasion and pub-

licity to persuade banks to offer easier terms to borrowers in order to stimulate the economy.

In a boom the economy needs no stimulation. The problem rather is excess purchasing power, which tends to raise prices when the labor force is already fully employed. Stabilization here requires a curb on further monetary expansion, with higher interest rates and a more restrictive loan policy leading to "tight money." Under these conditions Federal Reserve policies are reversed: (1) A rise in reserve requirements will tie up more of a bank's assets in legal reserves and restrict its lending ability. This, however, is a rather drastic measure, seldom used. (2) Sales of government securities by the Federal Reserve to the public will take money out of circulation. (3) A higher discount rate will discourage banks from borrowing from the Federal Reserve, and induce them to raise interest rates on their loans to others and to lend less. (4) Moral suasion may also persuade banks to curb their loan activities.

There are also three types of selective credit controls that may be introduced to restrict lending: (1) Margin requirements, set by the Board of Governors of the Federal Reserve System, restrict the amount of money that may be borrowed to buy or hold stocks listed on the stock exchanges. Raising this margin (the percentage of a stock's cost that must be paid in cash) reduces the amount a purchaser may borrow against a stock purchase. (2) Consumer credit control, used from 1941 to 1952, restricts the amount that can be lent to consumers on installment contracts by setting minimum down payments and the maximum period for repayment of such loans. (3) Mortgage credit controls used between 1950 and 1953, specify the minimum down payment and maximum length of mortgage for real estate loans.

Frequently, particularly during depression, monetary policy alone cannot produce the desired results, for even if money is cheap, businessmen will not borrow unless they are reasonably optimistic about profit possibilities. Fiscal policy may then reinforce monetary policy.

Fiscal Policy. Fiscal policy refers to the use of the government budget to stabilize the economy. Its scope includes taxation, government spending, and government borrowing (public debt management). Generally speaking, a balanced budget (tax receipts equalling expenditures) has a neutral effect on total national output, though it may shift the composition of that output. A deficit budget (expenditures exceeding taxes) pumps more money into the economy than it takes out, which tends to raise national income. If the government operates on a surplus (taxes exceeding expenditures), it takes more money out of the economy than it puts back, and this reduces monetary demand and curbs upward pressure. Thus a deficit is an appropriate policy for putting the economy out of depression, while a surplus tends to dull the force of inflation.

A deficit can result from either a reduction in taxes or an increase in expenditures. The particular policy adopted will affect the result. A cut in personal taxes will probably increase consumer spending, while a cut in corporate taxes can encourage business expansion directly. Economists do not agree as to which helps more to boost output and employment. On the expenditure side, make-work projects—like the U.S. Works Project Administration (WPA) and Civilian Conservation Corps (CCC) during the great depression of the 1930's—put money directly into the pockets of otherwise unemployed workers and thus ease privation. Public works such as roads, dams, and schools provide assets that increase the nation's real wealth. One disadvantage of public works as a stabilizer is that they are too slow in getting under way to influence a short recession.

The method of financing a deficit also makes a difference. If the government borrows from commercial banks, the result is likely to be a net increase in the quantity of money. If, however, it borrows from individuals or savings institutions, it may restrict either consumption or the flow of funds into business investment, which would partially offset the expansive effect of the deficit.

During inflation a government surplus takes money out of circulation and eases inflationary pressure. Higher taxes and lower expenditures can create such a surplus.

Since depression and inflation tend to alternate, fiscal policy for stabilizing the economy would ideally alternate government deficits with surpluses to produce a balanced budget, not in a single year, but over the course of a business cycle. In practice the tendency has been for large deficits to alternate with smaller deficits or small surpluses, so that in the long run both the national debt and the money supply have grown. The result has been constant, though slow, inflation.

Automatic Stabilizers. Among the more effective measures for controlling the business cycle have been automatic, or built-in, stabilizers. Economic dislocation itself calls these correctives into play without action by any agency. Several such stabilizers operate through their effect on the government budget. Others are not governmental at all.

The most obvious of the automatic stabilizers is the unemployment insurance system, which works in two directions. Since the tax that finances the system comes from payrolls, any drop in employment will reduce tax payments. Simultaneously, the unemployed worker becomes eligible for unemployment compensation, which enables him to maintain some income.

The pay-as-you-go personal income tax is another stabilizer. As an individual's income falls, his tax burden lightens. Conversely, any rise in income immediately raises the recipient's tax liability and thus withdraws from circulation some of the funds that might otherwise swell the demand for scarce goods. The corporate income tax serves as a stabilizer in somewhat the same way.

To a certain extent government payments to farmers

BANK

AUTOMATIC STABILIZERS

Many factors help to bolster the American economy in time of recession. Among these are unemployment insurance and personal and corporate savings, which help to restore the purchasing power needed by a healthy economy.

PERSONAL SAVINGS

CORPORATE SAVINGS

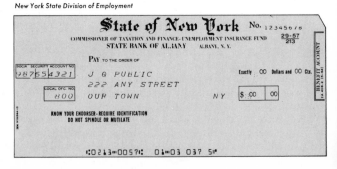

FORM 1040
U.S. Treasury Department
Internal Revenue Service

U.S. INDIVIDUAL INCOME TAX RETURN

or taxable year beginning .... 1962, ending .... 19......

Your Social Security Number

First name and initial   Last name

Occupation

(If joint return of husband and wife, use first names and middle initials of both)

Wife's Social Security Number

Home address ....
(Number and street or rural route)

Occupation

(City, town, or post office)   (Postal zone number)   (State)

Check one: □ Single; □ Unmarried "Head of Household"; □ Surviving widow or widower with dependent child; □ Married filing joint return (even if only one had income); □ Married filing separate return—If wife or husband also filing separately, give name

INCOME—(If joint return, include all income of both husband and wife)

1. Wages, salaries, tips, etc., and excess of allowances over business expenses.
   Employer's name   Where employed (city and state)   (a) Wages, etc.   (b) Federal income tax withheld

   $ $

   If either you or your wife worked for more than one employer, see page 4 of instructions

2. Totals
3. "Sick pay" if included in line 1 (attach required statement) .
4. Subtract line 3 from total wages . . . . . .
5a. Dividends (Schedule B) . . . .
  b. Interest (Schedule B or other list) . . . . .
  c. Rents, royalties, pensions, etc. (Schedule B) .
6. Business income (Schedule C) . . . . . .
7. Sale or exchange of property (Schedule D) . .
8. Farm income (Schedule F) . . . .
9. Total (add lines 4 through 8) . . . . . .

   FIGURE YOUR TAX BY USING EITHER 10 OR 11

10. Tax Table   11

THE U.S. TREASURY

The U.S. individual income tax system, primarily a source of revenue for the federal government, also has a stabilizing effect on the economy in times of recession. The percentage of tax an individual pays on his income falls if his wages fall. Thus, less money is withdrawn from circulation through the income tax in times when people are earning less.

automatically increase as farm income falls, and decrease as it rises.

Another important automatic stabilizer is corporate saving, which in good times acts as a brake on inflation. When profits fall, dividends frequently are kept where they were at the expense of corporate saving, so that even though the corporation does badly, the stockholders have as much money to spend as ever. This keeps consumption high. Personal saving may also act as a cushion against falling income. To the extent that people reduce savings rather than consumption, their purchases continue to encourage business and help maintain production.

Direct Controls. Another approach to stabilization has been to try to regulate individual prices or the production of specific industries through direct government action. The U.S. National Recovery Administration (NRA) was established in 1933 to encourage production by promoting codes of fair practice in each industry and to improve labor's income by protecting collective bargaining. It was declared unconstitutional by the Supreme Court in 1935.

During World War II the U.S. government established a number of direct controls to try to curb prices, which were then being pushed upward by a large budgetary deficit and a growing money supply. The primary tools were allocation of scarce materials, rationing, price control, and wage control. The War Production Board (WPB, 1942–45) allocated scarce materials to war industries. The Office of Price Administration (OPA, 1941–46) allocated scarce materials to consumers, primarily through a coupon rationing system, and also administered price controls covering almost all commodities as well as rents. The National War Labor Board (NWLB, 1942–45) controlled the adjustment of wages and salaries. None of these agencies was fully effective because any attempt to keep prices below equilibrium by legal restraint is likely to lead to dissatisfaction, attempts to amend the law, evasion, and black marketing. Prices edged up throughout the period, though much more slowly than they would have without

regulation. Except for rent curbs, direct controls were abandoned almost immediately after the end of the war. The Korean War brought a revival of price control under the Office of Price Stabilization (OPS, 1951–53), but this attempt was even less successful.

Administration of Policy. The primary responsibility for U.S. monetary policy rests with the Federal Reserve System, particularly its Board of Governors and the Federal Open Market Committee. The Treasury also influences the money supply and interest rates, as do a large number of government agencies that grant or guarantee credit for agricultural, real estate, and other purposes. The responsibility for fiscal policy belongs to the President and his Bureau of the Budget, and to Congress. The Treasury is concerned with debt management, which has its stabilization aspects.

Congress attempted to give direction to all of the government's stabilization programs in the Employment Act of 1946, which says that "it is the continuing policy and responsibility of the Federal Government to use all practical means . . . to coordinate and utilize all its plans, functions and resources . . . to promote maximum employment, production and purchasing power." In practice, this law did not achieve all of its objectives. But it did establish two watchdog economic agencies to evaluate programs and policies and to suggest improvements: the three-man Council of Economic Advisers, who advise the President; and the Joint Economic Committee, consisting of seven Senators and seven Representatives, which holds hearings and prepares reports for Congress as a basis for more effective stabilization legislation.

Consult Beard, C. A., and Smith, G. H., *The Old Deal and the New* (1941); Goldenweiser, E. A., *American Monetary Policy* (1951); Hart, A. G., *Defense Without Inflation* (1951); Maxwell, J. A., *Fiscal Policy* (1955); Burns, A. F., *Prosperity Without Inflation* (1958).

WALTER W. HAINES, New York University
See also INFLATION AND DEFLATION.

ECONOMIC SYSTEMS

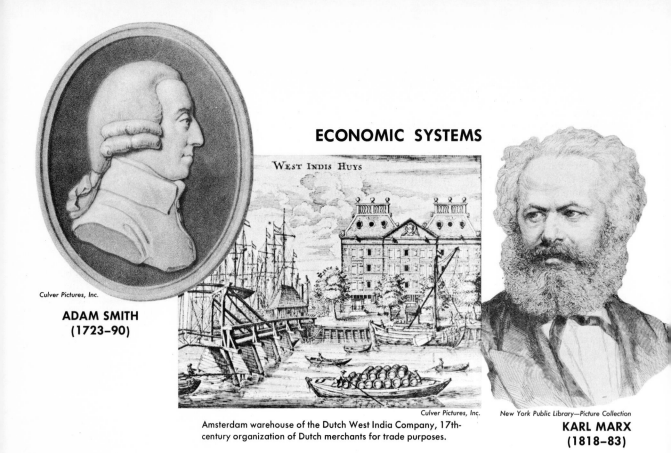

**ADAM SMITH
(1723–90)**

WEST INDIS HUYS

Amsterdam warehouse of the Dutch West India Company, 17th-
century organization of Dutch merchants for trade purposes.

**KARL MARX
(1818–83)**

ECONOMIC SYSTEMS, social arrangements for the production of goods and services and for deciding how they
shall be used (including who may enjoy them). There has
been a variety of such systems among different countries
throughout history. But their classification usually hinges
on the way they provide for the making of basic decisions
about production and distribution. The critical distinction
is this: Will the power of decision be concentrated in the
hands of the few or be widely distributed among the
many? On this basis the chief systems are capitalism, in
which decision making is widely distributed, and socialism, in which it is narrowly concentrated in a governing
group. There are also numerous economies, particularly
in underdeveloped societies, which do not fit comfortably
into this classification.

Capitalist Systems

The word "capitalism" was introduced by Karl Marx
(1818–83) to describe the economic arrangements that
replaced the feudal system of the Middle Ages. The new
system began to come into its own when changes in
methods of production came swiftly in the 18th century.
Marx picked out as the novel element in capitalism the
existence of two social classes: the property owners and
the proletariat (propertyless workers). But, without using
the name "capitalism," other writers, notably Adam
Smith in the *Inquiry into the Nature and Causes of the
Wealth of Nations* (1776), had already discussed economies in which the chief means of production—land,
labor, and capital—were subject to private control. The
maximization of goods and services in these economies,

they thought, would be attained if the government interfered as little as possible with individuals who used the
property or the labor under their control to maximize
their incomes. During much of the 19th century economists
explored the implications of these ideas.

Simple Capitalism. Property owners seeking to maximize profits were expected to use their property or to allow its use in ways which would result in the greatest
possible surplus of revenue from the sales of products over
the cost of production. As demands or methods of production changed, property would shift from less productive
(less profitable) to more productive uses. It would also
tend to gravitate to control by those who were most successful in discovering the most effective uses for resources.
In much the same way, so the assumption went, workers
would move to the places and jobs offering the highest
rewards.

Production per worker increased with the introduction
of the factory system in a social framework somewhat like
the foregoing. Much of the increase came from the economies of specialization. Enterprises and individuals concentrating on one job or on a restricted range of jobs were
likely to be more productive than those spreading their
resources over a broad variety of activities. But if people
specialized, they had to be able to exchange what they
found most profitable to produce for what they preferred
to consume (or for the investments they preferred to
make). Markets serving this function became a central
feature of capitalist economies. Markets also provided a
mechanism to guide reallocations of resources aimed at
increasing output or meeting changing preferences of

buyers. Though markets did not need to provide for a face-to-face meeting between buyer and seller, they did have to provide for an orderly flow of purchases and sales or hirings and firings.

Markets would have remained clumsy without money as a medium of exchange. But money also served as a unit of account when, for instance, a businessman compared his sales revenue and costs to measure his profit or when he sought to appraise a new and yet untried project. Finally, money was used to measure debts. The new methods of production required investments for longer periods than before, and debt became increasingly important. Thus markets and money both came to be thought indispensable to a capitalist industrial system.

Completion of the outline of a simple capitalist system called for the inclusion of a government to defend the national territory, to preserve internal order (mainly by protecting property and, to an extent, the freedom of the workers), and to provide a coinage. Otherwise individuals were to be free to act without governmental interference. The motto was *laissez faire* ("let do").

Something approximating this system developed in most of the countries of northwest Europe, the United States, Canada, Australia, and New Zealand at various dates after the middle of the 18th century. Experience, however, showed deficiencies and stirred criticism. Marx did not contemplate the possibility that property-owning groups would make concessions to meet these criticisms. He believed that they would repress protest until it found vent in a revolution that would destroy capitalism. In fact, however, the system underwent peaceful change in the above countries until by the middle of the 20th century it was difficult to say to what extent they were still capitalist.

One of the early breaches in the system occurred because businessmen outside Great Britain understandably felt the urge to follow the example of British businessmen, who were reaping rich profits out of the new methods of production. But the British, having had the advantage of being first in the field, proved hard to dislodge from countries to which they were exporting. Businessmen in these less developed countries therefore urged their governments to protect "infant industries" by taxing imports (in other words, British goods), and most of their governments complied. This was far from unfettered capitalism, but it helped countries to begin industrializing. The American steel industry, for example, grew up behind such a tariff wall.

Monopoly. The early version of capitalism could yield the promised ideal use of the means of production only if there were competition. Monopoly had always been troublesome in connection with bridges, market tolls, and the like. With the growth of industrial methods of production, however, monopoly attained a greatly increased importance because these new methods often yielded their greatest economies when production was conducted on a large scale. If only the most economical companies survived in the competitive struggle, there might be few of them, or even just one, in some markets. But the number of companies might also be seriously reduced by efforts to achieve monopoly. Whatever the reasons for the emergence of only a few companies in a market, the old kind

of competition was unlikely. Even when more than one enterprise survived, the survivors sometimes had to choose between cutthroat competition or some sort of understanding, calling, perhaps, for the acceptance of leadership by one of them.

Production could be organized in the early days of industrialism by individual entrepreneurs or partnerships. But the ever larger scale of production that was most economical in time passed beyond the capacity of the entrepreneur and the partnership to finance. The solution was the corporate method of raising money, and governments duly provided the necessary corporation laws at various times during the 19th century. But, while solving the problem of organizing mass production, the corporation modified the urge to maximum production. A corporation needs contributions of property from one group of people (stockholders and bondholders), but it hands over the management of this pooled property to another group (directors and managers). The driving force in the earlier capitalism presumably was the entrepreneur, who made economic decisions and took the consequences, good or bad. But in the large corporation the managers made the decisions, and the stockholders took the consequences.

Nationalization. A number of capitalist governments further modified their systems in the 20th century by undertaking production in some sectors. Industries like transport, electricity, and gas were nationalized because they could be economical only if run as monopolies, and governments felt frustrated in their efforts to prevent private monopolies from charging monopolistic prices. Other activities such as central banking, coal, and steel (for a time in Britain) were nationalized because they had widespread effects on economic systems as a whole. Governments that did not undertake production increasingly regulated it. After World War I they also began to regulate and to subsidize much of agriculture. Commercial banking, insurance, monopolistic practices, and the prices of public utilities all came under governmental controls where nonintervention failed to give social satisfaction.

Unions. Simple ideal capitalism required competition among free workers, as well as employers. But the freedom of workers was, in actuality, always limited. Wage earners generally owned no property and could not afford to spend much time seeking the most remunerative jobs. Moreover, the availability of jobs depended very much on decisions, in which workers took no part, as to how, and even how much, land and capital equipment were to be used. In the early stages of capitalism, when craftsmen were losing their jobs to factories, employees formed unions first to hold back the new system, then to organize it under their own control, and finally to make the best bargain they could within a system they had to accept. But out of their long struggle questions arose. Does the freedom of the worker include the freedom to unite with other workers to modify competition among them? Should the state forbear to interfere with the formation of unions? In fact, all capitalist countries have answered these questions by accepting, with varying degrees of warmth, the existence of labor unions but have often enacted legal codes to define what unions may and may not do.

Unions that only equalize the bargaining skill of workers

Standard Oil Co., N.J.

STOCKHOLDER MEETING

Stockholders, who own shares in a corporation, meet periodically to hear official reports, to vote, and to speak their minds, like the man below.

St. Louis Post Dispatch—Black Star

and employers in no way defeat the arguments about the beneficial effects of worker competition. But when they restrict entry into occupations by apprenticeship rules or other devices, or compel employers to hire more workers than they need, they are exerting monopoly power and reducing the effectiveness of the use of the labor supply.

Price Stabilization. Important deficiencies of capitalism were revealed in practice, when it came under appraisal as an ongoing system. Production had moved forward unsteadily from the beginning of capitalism. It had lurched from boom to depression and back to boom again. Resources were wasted during depressions, and the accompanying unemployment generated increasing social tension. During the 19th century there were no serious attacks on the problem of boom and bust because of fear that any such attempts would cut the heart out of capitalism by ending its reliance on the business decisions of individuals, especially about investment. Nevertheless there was growing concern regarding the ability of capitalist systems to survive many more depressions.

After World War I the need for action was obvious. Stabilization of the general level of prices seemed to provide the best line of attack. It also promised minimum interference with the economic system in general. If prices could be prevented from rising too much in times of boom, overstimulation of investment might be prevented. Excessive and temporarily unusable capacity for production might be reduced. But the near collapse of capitalist systems in the great depression of the 1930's revealed that this policy had failed. At the same time the magnitude of the depression made it more necessary than ever to take steps to ensure steadiness in the growth of production. Capitalist governments began to meet this challenge by accepting responsibility for increasing their spending to fill temporary gaps in private spending. This new policy of unbalancing government budgets to stimulate production was another basic modification of capitalism. But the fundamental problem of increasing purchasing power just fast enough but no faster than necessary to permit the absorption of the total rising output of the system remained to be solved.

All defenders of capitalism agreed that although governments should do as little as possible, they had to provide currency. Uniform and reliable coins had been essential to effective operation of markets even in early times. During the 19th century, paper currency greatly increased in importance. Later, bank deposits provided the means of settling most larger transactions as well as many small ones. But banks could influence the supply of these forms of money and, therefore, the value of the money unit (or the general level of prices). Changes in prices not only distributed windfall gains and losses but also distorted production by confusing business calculations. Furthermore, inflationary forces might gain speed and, in extreme cases, drain all purchasing power from the monetary unit. As a preventive measure, all capitalist governments have undertaken direct or indirect control of the supply of money, while recognizing that such control alone cannot do all that was expected of it in the 1920's.

By the middle of the 20th century a new influence on the price level appeared. It was claimed that labor unions in some industries and occupations could, by refusing to work, cause heavy losses to many other workers as well as to employers because of the complex interdependence of the productive organization. As a result, they might exact wage increases in excess of increases in production per worker. Either profits would fall or prices would rise. Usually prices rose, thus reducing the real incomes of those who could not thus obtain wage increases. In short, labor unions could cause inflation. Governments then faced the necessity for compromise between their policy of accepting labor unions and their policy of checking inflation.

Income Distribution. The distribution of incomes under simple capitalist systems came under criticism for its effect on production and for its lack of social acceptability. The defenders of early capitalism accepted its way of distributing income as an integral part of a system that would use resources most efficiently. But Karl Marx, taking a wider view, saw in this distribution an "inner contradiction" of capitalism that would bring the system down in ruins and make way for socialism or communism. The wages of workers tended to be just high enough to enable them and their families to survive. Employers could compel workers to produce more than was necessary to pay these wages, but annexed the "surplus value" for payment of rent and profits. The system operated in this way partly because whenever wages rose above this subsistence level, the supply of labor, and hence competition for jobs, would also rise. In addition, wages were held down by the competition of a reserve army of unemployed workers whose ranks were constantly swelled by the introduction of labor saving devices.

Businessmen, for their part, were driven by increasing competition to save and to invest in ever-improved methods of production. The result was a contradiction. There was constant effort to increase capacity for production without providing a market for all the possible product. The incomes of the mass of the population were too rigidly held down to provide much of a market.

For a number of decades in the late 18th and early 19th centuries wages did seem to follow a dismal Marxian path. Practically all gains from more economical methods of production went to profit, much of which, however, was reinvested. This phase was succeeded by one in which increased demands for labor drained the reserve army of unemployed. Moreover, birth rates began to fall. Modified capitalism now entered a period of rising wages. By this time, capitalist systems had expanded output enough to be able to pay higher wages without reducing investment in further growth.

The distribution of incomes under unreformed capitalism failed to receive social acceptance because of the coexistence of riches and poverty, apparently without adequate justification. Capitalism rested ultimately on the rational adaptation of means to ends in production. The spirit of this approach permeated society, and people began to look for rational justifications for social arrangements, especially for the distribution of incomes. Under the earlier forms of capitalism it was assumed that wages would gravitate to the level at which the demand for labor would equal the supply of it. But what governed both demand and supply? The argument that workers were paid in accordance with their contribution to production increasingly failed to carry conviction. What determined contribution to production? It was often the education, training, and other advantages that could be provided by parents. Some were fortunate in this respect, perhaps because their parents owned property, which they may have inherited. These problems presented themselves in very specific forms that not only bred discontent among the underprivileged, thus causing concern for the survival of the system, but also stimulated the social conscience. Slowly, capitalism was transformed into welfare capitalism.

Reform of Capitalism. The dislocations of the early industrial revolution had increased the number of the poor and brought them more clearly into view by concentrating them in towns. The then current theories about capitalism failed to explain how the very young, the aged, the sick, and the incapacitated would be looked after. They were left to the family or to the church, whose relation to the economic system was never rigorously explained. Governments found it necessary to increase the relief given to the poor, although fearing that this might reduce the pressure on workers to find jobs.

As the 19th century advanced, it became clear that booms and depressions were a major cause of periodic unemployment and an increasingly intolerable source of misery and social tension. Workers' organizations and local governments were impotent either to solve the problem or to ease the burden on workers able and willing to work but unable to find jobs. Not until the late 19th century did governments begin to organize compulsory systems of unemployment insurance. After each of the world wars they extended their aid to other classes in the community unable to obtain socially acceptable incomes through the workings of free markets. Thus the aged, the orphans, the sick, and the incapacitated came to receive incomes from social sources. Some governments provided for incomes adjusted to the size of the worker's family. Low-income groups also benefited increasingly from free or subsidized education for their children, medical service, improved housing, and other services regarded as socially essential. Governments undertook, too, to prescribe minimum wages where the wages set in the labor market were unacceptably low. To pay the bill, taxation took an increasingly large part of high incomes as compared with

CAPITALIST-SYSTEM FARMS

Under capitalism, farmers own and privately manage their land. Shown are a Pennsylvania tobacco crop (*below*) and Wisconsin farm land along a highway (*right*).

Philip Gendreau

Don Swenson—Gilloon

low ones, although in some countries a considerable part of the cost of helping the unemployed, the sick, and the needy children fell upon workers as a group.

Thus capitalist countries moved away from the pure capitalist principle of making incomes dependent on "contribution to production" toward the principle of an assured socially acceptable minimum for all.

Conclusion. Capitalism in its earlier, simpler form proved to be socially unacceptable. It provided an impersonal setting within which drastic changes in methods of production were introduced. But the cost of this progress was too often human misery. It had stressed competition as a spur to maximizing production, but under it competition proved all too imperfect. The striking failure of capitalism to provide steady economic growth, as well, brought governmental action of a kind that moved the system from dependence on individual to dependence on governmental decisions. Finally, capitalism's failure to satisfy the social conscience by distributing income in such a way as to create markets that would keep pace with ever-rising productive capacity also made for governmental action. Governments set socially acceptable minima, thus changing the system from one in which rewards were supposed to depend on contribution to production to one in which public authority was beginning to determine opportunities to contribute to production and the benefits to be derived from such contributions.

Socialist Systems

Socialist thinking has produced a family of closely related economic systems. Communism, strictly speaking, relates to a centrally controlled economy in which every member contributes to production according to his ability and shares in the common product according to his need. Small societies of this sort have existed from time to time, but they have neither survived for long nor made much economic progress. Anarchism relates to the elimination of the state, usually because it is regarded as an instru-

Main street in Butte, Mont., is typical of shopping areas where privately owned stores compete for patronage.

Ewing Galloway

ment for exploiting the masses. State socialism requires that the state abolish private ownership of the means of production, such as land and industrial plants, and replace them with public ownership and control. "Collectivism" is a general term often including communism, anarchism, and socialism.

Marxism. Until the 20th century these terms related mainly to proposed, but not actual, systems. They arose out of protests against poverty that went back many centuries but were much sharpened by the suffering caused by the industrial revolution. Karl Marx, writing around the middle of the 19th century, gave an apparently scientific basis and a revolutionary vigor to these protests. He prophesied that the misery of workers must inevitably increase under capitalism until capitalism collapsed and gave way to socialism or communism. But he also urged workers to help history by revolting.

Marxism had little appeal in countries where capitalism was modified in response to criticism, but it continued as an increasingly disruptive force wherever social protest was suppressed and reform was resisted. Thus the first large socialist system was established, not in Marx's own Germany or in England, the citadel of capitalism, but in backward Russia, where a revolution in 1917 established a new order. Since the Soviet Union became the archexemplar of socialism, the evolution of the system in that country offers the best case history of what the socialist way means in practice.

Marx believed that the transition to communism could not be speedy, but that there must be a period of transition under a dictatorship of the proletariat. In time, however, the state would wither away. In fact, the history of the Soviet Union provides information only about the transitional period of state socialism rather than about communism. Its dictators have been self-selected rather than chosen representatives of the proletariat. And after many years of socialist planning there was no sign of the withering away of the state.

Early Soviet Socialism. The revolutionaries of 1917 found little in the writings of Marx to help them design a socialist society. Marx had contemplated the victory of socialism in countries in the later stages of industrialism, where economic controls, by then concentrated in a few hands, could easily be transferred. But history did not take this course. The first successful socialist revolution came in a country still mainly agricultural. The new elite had, therefore, to invent a socialist framework within which to achieve an industrial revolution. They had to create a new system that would release as much labor as possible from agriculture and transfer it to industry. The new system would also have to sweep agriculture clean of the remnants of feudalism and reorganize it in such a way as to free it from the antisocialist profit motive, yet make it capable of providing enough food.

The path of transition was not easy. The Soviet Union passed through (1917–21) a phase of revolutionary communism, in which the government seized food and industrial supplies and financed itself by issues of paper money so large as to reduce the value of the monetary unit to almost zero. A far-reaching breakdown of production, plus famine and revolt, prepared the way for the second phase, in which the government adopted the New Eco-

Sovfoto

COMMUNIST COLLECTIVE FARMS

Collective farms in the U.S.S.R. are largely controlled by the state. Scenes from Soviet agriculture are pictured: (*left*) workers at a Ukrainian collective farm, and (*below*) homes and gardens of the collective farmers in Kabardino-Balkar A.S.S.R.

Sovfoto

nomic Policy (1921–27) permitting private profit in agriculture, small enterprise, and commerce. This partial retreat to capitalism was a temporary device to revive production, soften opposition, and win time to prepare a socialist system. The third phase of socialist planning began with the first Five-Year Plan (1927–32).

Industry. In industry, socialist organization borrowed from the principles underlying the capitalist corporation and the government department. Production became the function of enterprises that bought and paid for the materials, power, transport, and labor they needed and in turn were paid for the goods and services they supplied to other producing enterprises or to government departments that supplied retail stores with consumer goods. These socialist enterprises made contracts and could resort to law for their enforcement. The government, however, regulated the use of some scarce materials and services. The enterprises kept accounts of income, expenditure, and profit; compiled balance sheets; and had bank accounts like capitalist corporations. This system of organization still characterizes Soviet industry.

Production by nationalized corporations basically similar to those in industry was tried in agriculture, mostly when large estates were taken over by the government or when the chief crops were nonfood products. After World War II the proportion of seeded land operated by state farms was considerably increased, especially as part of an effort to extend the producing area eastward into semiarid lands. But the revolutionary leaders never tried to organize the whole of agriculture on this basis, partly because of the difficulty of controlling labor in agriculture and partly because of the anticipated resistance of the peasants.

Agriculture. At the time of the revolution the government seized all land without compensation. Under the New Economic Policy, individuals could grow crops for profit. But, unwilling to tolerate "capitalist exploitation" in agri-

culture, the socialist planners looked for some alternative form of organization. In 1930 they began to press the peasants to join kolkhozy (collectives). So vigorous was the resistance of the kulaks (richer peasants) that the reorganization was carried through only after imprisonments, deportations, and the slaughter of a large proportion of the livestock. Nevertheless, before World War II the majority of agricultural produce already came from co-operatives; and by 1955, 95% of the total cultivated area was operated either by collectives or by state farms.

These Soviet farm collectives are legally co-operatives leasing land from the government free of rent. They are governed by a general meeting, a managing committee, and a farm manager. But the government exercises so much control through legislation, planning, and the terms of the lease that the self-governing element in co-operative organization is largely submerged. Members may be punished if they refuse to work. They receive, in different ways at different times, credit for the work they do, based on the skills required, the harshness of the labor, the time taken, and the competence of performance. The produce is disposed of in a variety of ways. The government takes a prescribed amount, paying for it at prices it sets. In part these payments might be regarded as an equivalent of rent for the land. The remainder of the produce, after provision for seed, is either distributed in kind among the members in proportion to their credits for labor performed or is sold on village markets or to the government agency that procures food for retail distribution. The money income from sales after payment of taxes, debts, and insurance, new investments by the co-operative, rewards for exceptional work, and contributions to cultural funds goes to individual members in proportion to the labor credits they have built up.

These co-operatives evidently rely to a considerable extent on the pecuniary motive to stimulate production.

Soviet citizens convene at the Great Kremlin Palace in Moscow to participate in a virgin-soil development program—one of the many projects instituted by the government to strengthen the socialist economic system.

Sovfoto

Further, members are allowed to use small plots of land for their own gain; here they produce considerable quantities of fruits, animals, and vegetables. For a time members had to deliver to the government part of the produce of these plots, but the requirement was abolished in 1958. The government recognizes the imperfect socialist character of this agricultural organization. The capital funds it makes available to co-operatives it regards as loans, while those to nationalized industries are grants. But government authorities have rejected full communism for agriculture, believing that most people would do as little work and claim as much food as possible (a criticism in which most of those favoring capitalism could join).

Five-Year Plans. The Soviet economic system calls for some directing organization to tell the various producing units what to produce and sometimes how to produce it. In a capitalist system what is produced is the result of a number of decisions by individuals directed by considerations of profit. But a socialist society, rejecting profit as a guide, places upon its governing group the responsibility for deciding how to use the resources of the economy.

The governing elite must make certain that there is a flow of goods and services adequate not only to keep the working force alive but also reasonably co-operative. The elite must also keep in mind the resources available and the requirements of the various sectors of production. It is no good planning a given output of steel without also planning for the iron ore, coal, and transportation needed in steelmaking. Furthermore, they must plan an output of coal sufficient to meet all industrial production and other needs. Similarly the labor needed to fulfill the totality of production plans must neither exceed, nor fall short of, the supply of available labor. Without proper checks and adjustments, there will be bottlenecks in the supply of some materials or labor that will prevent enterprises from fulfilling their production plan, while other plants may not be able to dispose of their output if they use their plant to its capacity.

The basic instruments for dealing with these problems have been the Five-Year Plans, of which the Soviet Union has had a series since 1927. These plans are enacted into law but are modified at shorter intervals and are broken down into parts for each government department concerned with production and, finally (in principle), for each producing unit. The task of regulating an economy as large and as rapidly changing as that of the Soviet Union was colossal, even in 1927, and the Five-Year Plan and the organization behind it were notable economic inventions. Nevertheless, Soviet planners have themselves pointed from time to time to inefficiencies resulting from poorly informed planning, failure to mesh the various sectors of production, unexpected shortcomings of production units, and unforeseeable natural events. As might be expected, the greatest difficulties have arisen in agriculture. The great distance between the planners and the doers was a constant source of difficulty. Government departments and enterprises responsible for production underwent reorganization repeatedly. In 1957 the government established a number of regional economic councils in the hope that the bringing of planning decisions closer to operating levels would improve efficiency. But the basic economic controls remained with the central government.

Controlled Economy. The planners early abandoned the notion that a socialist economy (like a communist economy) needed no money. The government issues money and runs an elaborate banking system. Individuals receive money for labor and pay money for goods. Wage scales, however, are set by the government in accord with the degree of skill required and the arduousness of the work. These scales are designed to attract to each sector of production the labor it needs to fulfill its planned output. The government also determines prices of goods with the general object of matching the demand with the supply to be provided.

Like capitalist governments, the government of the Soviet Union has often supplied more purchasing power than was needed. The result has been inflation. For example, the cost of living rose some 400% to 600% between 1928 and 1937. After considerable price increases during World War II, the government reduced both the money supply and prices in 1947. Prices in 1952, nevertheless, were still 900% to 1,400% above the 1928 level. This inflationary trend resulted in part from the policy of using money as a spur to higher production without at the same time providing enough consumer goods to absorb the money.

Taxes are levied in money. Income taxes have yielded only about 10% of government income and have steadily declined in importance. Inequalities in income were held not serious enough to justify taxes especially suited to deal with inequality. Taxes on the profits of government enterprises have also yielded only about 10% of government tax income. The big income producer and special feature of Soviet tax policy is the "turnover tax." Turnover excises levied at different rates on different commodities yielded about 60% of tax income in peacetime.

The Soviet government spends money for military and civil purposes in much the same way as capitalist governments do. But it differs from them in that it is the main source of investment. This enables government planners to decide how the economy shall expand. In capitalist economies a large excess of price over the cost of production in some line would normally attract more private capital, raise output, and lower prices. In the Soviet Union capital is not so allocated. The excess is taken in turnover taxes and channeled as the planners choose. In the long run, capitalist economies expand in response to the choices of buyers, but socialist economies expand along lines chosen by the planning elite.

Over the first 30 years or more of the operation of this system, the total output of goods rose between 5% and 8% per year (after allowing for price changes). This expansion was considerably greater than that in capitalist countries had been. The rise was chiefly due to the investment of a large proportion of the national income in production capacity (some 25%, compared with about 17% in the United States). The high rate of investment was achieved by holding down the supply of consumer goods and holding up prices. (This amounted to compelling society as a whole to save.) The success of capitalist economies in the 19th century had been credited partly to a high rate of investment resulting from voluntary decisions. The Soviet economy outdid its capitalist predecessors, but at the expense of the workers, who were denied most of the benefits of increased production. Moreover, the Soviet government channeled some 20% of national income into military production.

The distribution of incomes presents as serious a problem in a socialist economy as in a capitalist one. It is not possible on purely economic grounds to decide how much of national resources shall be used to supply consumer goods and services, how much to invest in the expansion of production, and how much for military purposes. The planners decide as they wish, except that they must supply consumers with enough to keep them from revolting or withholding co-operation to such a degree as to impair productive efficiency. Intermittent attempts to increase allocations of consumer goods suggest that, after the first few decades of socialism, numbers of people were asking how long they would be denied. Supplies of consumer goods increased somewhat after World War II.

The defeat of Germany in World War II and the resulting political vacuum in eastern Europe provided a revolutionary opportunity that was seized by local Communist parties, backed by Soviet military power. The new socialist governments that were established borrowed heavily from the experience of the Soviet Union. The speed of conversion to the pattern of Soviet socialism varied considerably, however, from country to country according to differences in attitudes and resources. But all moved in the same direction.

Communist China. When the Chinese Communists established a central government in Peking in 1949, they brought another 550,000,000 people within the socialist form of organization. Borrowing from Soviet experience, they nationalized industry, organized collective production in agriculture, and developed a Five-Year Plan system (the first plan was for the years 1952–57). Like the Soviet Union, China received little outside economic aid. But, unlike the Soviet Union, China suffered from severe unemployment, which at least in the first decade of socialism it was unable to eliminate. Although the population began to increase fast, the government vacillated in its attitude to birth control. It concentrated on increasing the output of the labor force, which was subjected to heavy pressure.

In 1958 the government announced that the population would be reorganized into some 23,000 communes, each of which would not only absorb numbers of agricultural co-operatives but would also organize light manufacturing, process farm products, supply peasants with locally produced equipment, engage in trade, and supply credit, educational facilities, nurseries, public mess halls, and dormitories. These communes were apparently intended to squeeze still more out of the labor supply, both military and civil, even at the expense of serious inroads on family life. But peasant resistance and economic waste compelled modification of the commune system and threatened its future.

Conclusion. Just as capitalism has been modified, so has socialism, at least in the Soviet Union, the oldest socialist state. Socialists have relied considerably on pecuniary motives to stimulate production both in industry and in agriculture and to distribute workers among different lines of production. They have used money to pay workers who in turn pay money for consumer goods. Producing units have purchased and sold goods and services. Socialists have used their control of the monetary system to reduce real wages below money wages. Like capitalists, socialists have faced the problems of income distribution. Starting out with a policy of great austerity, they slowly permitted increases in the standard of living. But socialist economies stand in sharp contrast to capitalist ones in one basic respect. The allocation of the means of production is determined by the preferences of planners, with minor regard for those of the consuming population.

Underdeveloped Economies

Side by side with capitalist and socialist systems there exist societies in which economic life is dominated by tradition. In a truly traditionalist economy, economic arrangements have settled down into a pattern which changes only in response to sharp shocks from external events. Some of these survivors from precapitalist times, however, have been modified by contact with economies of more recent types.

In the earlier traditional economies, which were heavily agricultural, the population lived near the edge of survival.

Because most people produced most of what they consumed, there was little need for markets or money. The most important economic arrangements concerned the control of land. Often it was controlled by tribes, villages, or other relatively small units that allotted it to individuals and families. In western Europe during the Middle Ages, an overlord typically granted land to inferior lords in return for services and for part of the income from the land. The inferior lord in turn permitted serfs to cultivate part of the land for their own use in return for their labor on his own land. In Japan and the Middle East, the larger landowner typically obtained a share of the crop rather than a share of the labor of the cultivator.

The most important quality of these systems was that they ensured a certain economic stability at a time when most of the population lived near the survival level. Those who could command more than the means of survival typically used the surplus on more lavish consumption. It was hardly realized that investment in economic progress was possible. Concern for equity and stability, rather than progress, resulted in an organization of production so rigid as to rule out virtually all experiments with improved methods of production or different crops.

Traditionalist economies like capitalist and socialist ones have yielded to pressures for modification. After World War II, modified traditionalist societies were often referred to as "underdeveloped." These economies all had very low per capita income, derived primarily from agriculture. Land was typically privately owned but was rented out in small plots in return for a share of the crop. Craft production often survived, and there were merchants and moneylenders. The government usually protected property but did little to stimulate production or to regulate income distribution.

Most of these traditionalist, underdeveloped economies were in some way touched by the economic progress of more advanced economies. In particular, traditionalist countries with mineral deposits or special agricultural resources attracted capital and managerial resources from outside. But as wages rose, so did population, which meant that the average person still lived near the edge of survival. The introduction from more developed countries of public health measures and the suppression of internal warfare reduced death rates and further increased populations. The only well off people were the landowners and the merchants. Increases in their incomes were often spent in imitation of the wealthy of richer countries, on imported luxuries, trips abroad, or even investment abroad.

In the main, therefore, these underdeveloped societies continued to be held by tradition within a narrow daily round. Except in small areas operated by foreign enterprises, methods of production changed little, and little was invested to improve future production. While poor countries cannot save and invest much, most have some margin. But the poverty of the mass of the population provided little inducement to invest locally because there was little demand except for what might be called "survival goods." After World War II the populations of some underdeveloped societies, becoming better acquainted with the achievements of the more progressive economies, began to press for government action to break out of the vicious circle of poverty in which they were revolving. Further and serious changes in their systems seemed likely.

Consult Collectivist Economic Planning, ed. by F. A. von Hayek (1935); Smith, Adam, *An Inquiry into the Nature and Causes of the Wealth of Nations* (1937); Lange, Oscar, *On the Economic Theory of Socialism* (1938); Schumpeter, J. A., *Capitalism, Socialism, and Democracy* (3d ed., 1950); Burns, A. R., *Comparative Economic Organization* (1955); Campbell, R. W., *Soviet Economic Power* (1960); Halm, G. N., *Economic Systems* (rev. ed., 1960); Myrdal, Gunnar, *Beyond the Welfare State* (1960); Hoover, C. B., *The Economy, Liberty and the State* (1961).

ARTHUR R. BURNS, Columbia University

See also:

COMMUNISM	PRODUCTION
COMPETITION	PROFIT
CONSUMPTION	RESOURCES
COST	SOCIALISM
PRICE	TAXATION

ECONOMY, northwestern suburb of Pittsburgh, western Pennsylvania, located just east of the Ohio River. Pop. (1960) 5,925.

ECORSE [ē-kôrs′], city of southeastern Michigan, 8 mi. south of Detroit. It is a part of the great steel industrial complex along the Detroit River. Pop. (1950) 17,948; (1960) 17,328.

ECOSYSTEM, a term used in ecology to describe a living community and its nonliving environment. The ecosystem is the basic functional unit of ecology, and embraces the concept that living organisms and their environments are closely interrelated and dependent on each other. A typical ecosystem, such as a balanced aquarium, a pond, or a forest ravine, always has the following four constituents: abiotic materials, such as water and minerals; producer organisms, such as green plants, that convert the abiotic materials into organic materials; consumer organisms that ingest organic material in the form of other organisms; and decomposer organisms, such as bacteria, that break down complex organic materials into simple abiotic substances. When all four constituents are present in correct proportion, an internal balance maintains the ecosystem as a stable energy system.
See also ECOLOGY.

ECSTASY [ĕk′stə-sē] (Gr. *ekstasis,* "displacement" or "trance"), state of religious or secular exaltation. In this state, the normal mental controls are suspended, and sense of time and place are lost. Ecstasy in religious experience may be induced by participation in a rite. Soul-loss and soul-projection among Eskimos, North American Indians, and Siberian indigenes are forms of ecstasy. During these states visions are received, and healing of (primarily) psychic ills and oracular divination are practiced. The rapturous trance state is a positive and blessed occurrence. Mental aberration is not loathed but sought in these societies—and among certain subcultures of Western societies as well.

ECUADOR

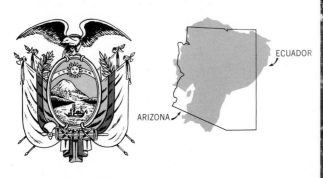

AREA	Approx. 107,500 sq. mi.
ELEVATION	
Highest point (Chimborazo)	20,561 ft.
Lowest point	Sea level
POPULATION	Approx. 4,579,000
PRINCIPAL LANGUAGE	Spanish
LIFE EXPECTANCY	52 years
PERCENTAGE OF LITERACY	56%
UNIT OF CURRENCY	Sucre
NATIONAL ANTHEM	*Salve, O Patria!* ("Hail, O Fatherland!"), words by J. L. Mera, music by A. Neumann
CAPITAL	Quito
PRINCIPAL PRODUCTS	Bananas, cacao, coffee, wheat; beverages, foodstuffs, textiles

The village of Guápulo, high in the Andes, dates from the colonial era. Its picturesque houses and its spectacular setting have made it one of Ecuador's leading tourist attractions. (CAMERA PRESS—PIX)

ECUADOR [ĕk′wə-dôr], republic on the Pacific coast of South America, on the "bulge" of the continent. It is crossed by the equator (Span. *ecuador*), for which it is named, and is the second-smallest country of South America. Bounded on three sides by Colombia and Peru, and on the fourth by the Pacific Ocean, it has an area of approximately 107,500 sq. mi. A frontier settlement with Peru, by the protocol of Rio de Janeiro in 1942, was unilaterally renounced by Ecuador in 1961. The Galápagos Islands, officially known as the Archipiélago de Colón, belong to Ecuador. These islands are principally known for their wildlife, which helped to support Charles Darwin's theory of evolution.

The Land

Physical Features. Ecuador may be divided into three major physical regions, the largest of which, the Oriente, extends from the upper reaches of the Amazon valley to the eastern slopes of the Andes. Although it thus accounts for almost half of the national territory, this region consists of tropical jungle threaded by tributaries of the Amazon, and is largely uninhabited and underdeveloped. Of much greater importance are the Highlands, or Sierra, and the Costa (Coast), which are fundamentally distinct from each other. Historical and social as well as geographical factors have combined to produce virtually two nations within a nation. The Highland region consists of the Eastern and Western cordilleras of the Andes, which form a long narrow strip from Peru in the south to Colombia in the north. Between these ranges lies a plateau extending some 390 mi. from north to south but never more than 44 mi. wide. Most of the Highland population lives in a string of 10 intermontane basins at altitudes ranging from about 7,000 ft. to 10,000 ft. Some 30 active volcanoes and many more extinct volcanic peaks surround and sometimes separate the intermontane basins, and earthquakes are a common occurrence. Among the highest peaks are Chimborazo (20,561 ft.), Cotopaxi (19,347 ft.), Cayambe (18,980 ft.) and Antisana (18,714 ft.). Many are covered with snow the year round.

The region known as the Coast lies between the Andes and the Pacific Ocean and varies in width from 100 to 12 mi. Except for a low coastal range of hills north of Guayaquil, most of this region is lowland. An important river system is formed by the Guayas and its tributaries flowing south through this region to the Pacific. The principal rivers of northern Ecuador are the Esmeraldas and its tributaries.

Natural Resources. Ecuador's principal natural resource is agricultural land, for its mineral resources are not large enough to be of commercial importance. There are deposits of copper, gold, silver, and lead, as well as petroleum on the Santa Elena peninsula. Exploration has revealed titanium and uranium, and many other minerals are thought to exist. Forest resources include lumber, balsa wood, rubber, and cinchona bark, from which quinine is extracted.

Climate, Natural Vegetation, and Wildlife. Because Ecuador straddles the equator, seasonal variations in temperature are very slight, and temperature is principally determined by altitude. The temperature in the daytime in the Highlands rarely exceeds 75° F. and at night may drop to just a few degrees above freezing. The mean annual temperature in Quito, which is fairly typical of the intermontane basins, is about 55° F. Annual rainfall in the Highlands ranges from 11 in. to 59 in. Except for the treeless plateaus (paramos) above 10,000 ft., much of the Andean region is heavily forested. However, the dense

growth of brush in the intermontane basins has been cut for fuel or cleared to provide pasture land.

The mitigating influence of the Humboldt current produces a relatively cool climate on the Coast, with average annual temperatures ranging from 70° F., to 79° F., and little seasonal variation. Although annual rainfall averages about 143 in. or more in the northern coastal region, only about 11 in. fall on the Santa Elena peninsula further south. Similarly, vegetation on the Coast ranges from dense forests in the north to desert scrub in the south. The rainy season lasts from January to May on the Coast and from October to May in the Highlands; temperatures during this season are generally somewhat higher than during the dry season. The Oriente region is wet and humid throughout the year. The more exotic wildlife of Ecuador includes the giant tortoise of the Galápagos Islands and the iguana.

The People

Population and Principal Cities. About 58% of Ecuador's population lives in the Highlands and 41% on the Coast; the Oriente region contains only 1%. The three

---

Ecuador is an agricultural country that is geographically and climatically diverse. Many articles in the **ENCYCLOPEDIA INTERNATIONAL** deal with this republic, and this Study Guide suggests how the reader may make effective use of them. The main article on these pages surveys the following topics.

The Land. Physical features (shown on one of the maps accompanying the article); natural resources; climate, natural vegetation, and wildlife.

The People. Population and principal cities; religion; education; cultural life.

The Economy. (Resources are shown on the map of physical regions.) Economic conditions; agriculture and fisheries; mining and industry; transportation; foreign trade.

Government. Structure of government; political parties.

History. The Indian and colonial eras; independence (won between 1809 and 1830); the 20th century.

For further study, the reader can turn to the article SOUTH AMERICA, which discusses the continental setting of Ecuador. LATIN AMERICA describes the social, economic, political, and cultural complex of which Ecuador is a part along with the other nations of South and Central America. Many smaller articles provide more specific information—for example, ANDES, and CHIMBORAZO, which describes the highest peak in Ecuador. The damage caused by eruptions of COTOPAXI, one of the highest active volcanoes in the world, has often been devastating. Other geographical features are discussed in HUMBOLDT CURRENT OR THE PERU CURRENT and GALAPAGOS ISLANDS (the place where Charles Darwin was impressed by giant tortoises). Cities, such as QUITO and GUAYAQUIL, are treated individually. The PAN AMERICAN HIGHWAY runs through Ecuador. The nation's literary achievements are discussed in LATIN-AMERICAN LITERATURE.

The vegetation and wildlife of Ecuador are rich. There

are many birds, small animals, and lizards, such as the IGUANA. The waters surrounding the Galápagos are known for their abundant yields of fish, especially TUNA. CINCHONA and BALSA are produced in the forest regions, CACAO and BANANA in the Coast region, and GRAIN in the Highland region. Some of the Indians of Ecuador are discussed in INDIAN TRIBES, SOUTH AMERICAN. The head-shrinking JIVARO Indians receive separate treatment.

The history of Ecuador can be traced in such articles as INCA, which describes the people who took control of the area in the 15th century. One of the important Inca rulers was ATAHUALPA OR ATABALIPA, who was defeated and executed by the Spanish CONQUISTADORS. The Spanish established a judicial-administrative body described in AUDIENCIA. After the Spanish conquest, Ecuador, Peru, and other countries composed the Viceroyalty of Peru (see PERU: *History*). During two periods Ecuador was part of the Viceroyalty of New Granada. Ecuador gained its freedom from Spain in 1822 with the aid of Antonio José de SUCRE. It was part of the federated republic of La Gran Colombia until 1830, when Juan José FLORES proclaimed independence and became the first President of Ecuador. Later Presidents include Gabriel GARCIA MORENO and, in the 20th century, José VELASCO IBARRA. Relations between nations of the Western Hemisphere are treated in PAN-AMERICANISM, PAN AMERICAN UNION, and ORGANIZATION OF AMERICAN STATES.

Ecuador has been sporadically troubled by boundary disputes since it became independent. At the beginning of the 20th century it lost parts of the Amazonian region to Colombia and Brazil. In 1942 it ceded parts of the Oriente region to Peru. A map of territorial losses is provided to help make the discussion clear.

Many articles conclude with lists of books through which the reader can extend his study of Ecuador. These and other sources may be available in the library. To keep abreast of Ecuadorian political events and economic and social developments the reader can consult such sources as the annual supplement to this Encyclopedia.

---

provinces of Guayas and Manabí on the Coast and Pichincha in the Highlands contain nearly half of the total population. Most of the principal cities are situated in the Highlands, including Quito, the capital, Cuenca, Ambato, and Riobamba. Larger than all these, however, is the coastal city of Guayaquil. The urban population of the Coast is larger than that of the Highlands. Nevertheless, Ecuador is one of the most rural nations in the world, for nearly three-quarters of its inhabitants live in rural communities. Although there is a high death rate, Ecuador also has a high rate of population increase, about 2.7% each year.

The Indians of Ecuador have never been accurately counted, but it is estimated that they constitute between 30% and 60% of the population. They live mainly in the Highlands, most of them working as laborers on the large estates of the region. Other, much smaller, Indian groups live in the tropical rain forests of the Coast and of the Oriente. Coastal tribes include the Cayapas and Colorados, and Oriente tribes include Yumbos, Jívaros, and Aucas, the last-named being one of the most hostile tribes of South America. Much of the population of both Coast and Highlands is of mixed European and Indian ancestry. Some Negroes live in the northern sections of the Coastal region, and about 10% of the total population is of European origin, chiefly Spanish. The Andean Indians, who comprise a large percentage of the Highland population, speak Quechua, although many are bilingual and speak Spanish as well. Their distinctive cultural heritage and language separate them sharply from the Spanish-speaking population, which has its cultural roots in Europe, and which constitutes virtually the entire population of the Coast (see INDIAN TRIBES, SOUTH AMERICAN).

Religion. The Roman Catholic Church has been dominant in Ecuador since early colonial days, and for a time during the later 19th century the country became virtually a theocracy. In 1895, however, state and church were separated; occasional conflict subsequently arose, especially with reference to education. Although the overwhelming majority of Ecuadorians consider themselves Roman Catholics, orthodox teachings have become intermingled with native beliefs, especially among the Andean Indians. Protestant missions, which started work in Ecuador around 1895, met with only very modest success. Freedom of worship is guaranteed by the constitution of 1946.

Education. School attendance is free and compulsory in Ecuador between the ages of 6 and 12. However, serious deficiencies in the educational system include a shortage of schools, especially in rural areas, severe overcrowding, and a lack of adequate materials. Consequently, nearly 44% of the population is illiterate. A sharp contrast in educational opportunities is reflected in a literacy rate of about 83% for the urban population but only about 46% for inhabitants of rural areas. Good private schools are found in the major cities, but few can afford them. Secondary education, too, is available only to a privileged few, and only about 1% of the population attends one or more years of college. Aside from the Central University and the Catholic University in Quito, there are universities in Cuenca, Loja, and Guayaquil, a National Polytechnic School in Quito, and the Technical University of

United Nations

Indians, carrying wares for sale, begin arriving in the Andean town of Otavalo at dawn for the Saturday fair and market.

Manabí in Portoviejo. Quito also has an International Center for Advanced Studies in Journalism, founded in 1960 under the auspices of UNESCO.

Cultural Life. A unique institution in Ecuador is the Casa de la Cultura Ecuatoriana, a semiofficial agency devoted to the development of arts and letters. Its main branches are in Quito, Guayaquil, and Cuenca. Aside from publishing, theatrical, and musical activities, it also tries to develop native arts and crafts. Ecuador has made an important contribution to South American literature through the prose of Juan Montalvo, the great writer of the romantic era, and the lyric poetry of José Joaquín de Olmedo. The outstanding literary figure of the 20th century is the novelist Jorge Icaza. Oswaldo Guayasamín Calero has achieved an international reputation as a painter, and Gerardo Guevara is one of Ecuador's leading composers (see LATIN-AMERICAN LITERATURE).

The Economy

Economic Conditions. Ecuador's per capita income of less than $200 a year reflects the general economic underdevelopment of the country. Income is almost twice as high on the Coast as it is in the Highlands. Over-all national or regional figures give a distorted picture of the real situation, however, since living standards for all but the small wealthy class are low, and frequently little above subsistence level.

Although in theory the Coast and Highland regions complement each other, allowing for the production of both tropical and temperate zone crops, in practice this

Pan American Union

Workers unload stalks of bananas at a dock in Guayaquil.

advantage has not been exploited. The geographic isolation of the Coast and the Highlands is being slowly overcome by an extensive road-building program, but the political and economic rivalry between the two regions continues to hinder the development of an integrated national economy. The Coastal region is heavily dependent upon the production of export crops and is therefore vulnerable to fluctuations in world prices, whereas Highland products are consumed domestically. Government control of the economy is limited mainly to transportation and communications and some investments. In 1954, however, a National Board of Economic Planning and Co-ordination was established, in an attempt to link regional activities in a national program.

Agriculture and Fisheries. Agriculture is the mainstay of Ecuador's economy. The principal products of the Highlands are potatoes, corn, barley, and wheat; on the Coast bananas, rice, sugar, coffee, and cacao are grown and exported. Ecuador is the world's largest exporter of bananas. The waters around the Galápagos Islands are one of the richest fishing grounds in the world, being particularly noted for tuna.

The principal deterrent to agricultural development in Ecuador is the distribution of land ownership. Although a high proportion of the rural inhabitants own land, their mountain plots are too small and unproductive to support their families. Many of these farmers seek work as laborers on the large estates that dominate the intermontane basins and the fertile coastal lowlands. About 75% of the rural population may therefore be classed as agricultural laborers who receive extremely low wages.

Mining and Industry. Mining does not play an important part in the economy, and accounts for less than 2% of the total value of exports. Small amounts of copper, lead, silver, and gold are mined. The small oil field on the Santa Elena peninsula fulfills most of the country's domestic requirements; some crude oil is exported.

Industrial development has been largely restricted to the production of clothing and foodstuffs. The expansion of the internal market is hindered by the prevailing pattern of land ownership, which prevents most Ecuadorians from achieving an income level that would enable them to buy more than the most necessary consumer goods. Small home workshops still provide many products. The textile industry is the most important single enterprise, supplying about half of the domestic market. The numerous small workshops and home industries, many belonging to the Otavalo Indians, are supplemented by 26 textile mills, 25 of which are in the Highlands. Carpets are produced as well as woolens, cottons, and rayons. Hand-woven *toquilla*, or Panama, straw hats, which Ecuador used to export in large quantities, now represent only about 1% of the value of exports. Other industries include a cement factory near Guayaquil and one near Riobamba, large breweries at both Guayaquil and Quito, and factories producing foodstuffs, shoes, furniture, cigarettes, and matches. There is also a small pharmaceutical industry.

Transportation. The development of transportation in Ecuador has been hindered by the mountainous terrain of the Andes and the torrential rainfall and floods of the Coast. The principal railway, from Guayaquil to Quito, is the main line of communication between the Coast and the Highlands. Climbing 288 mi. via numerous bridges and tunnels to an elevation of 11,841 ft., it offers one of the most spectacular rides in the world. A somewhat shorter railroad links Quito with the port of San Lorenzo near the Colombian frontier, and there are three smaller branch lines. Considerable progress has been made in road construction, particularly in the building of all-weather roads, which are essential on the Coast if transportation is to be maintained during the rainy season. The principal road is the Pan American Highway, which runs north and south through the inter-Andean valley for some 620 mi. It is cobblestoned for much of its length. More importantly economically, however, is the 224-mi.-long road from Latacunga to Manta on the Pacific Ocean. There are plans to expand Ecuador's very limited port facilities. Guayaquil, the principal port, lies some 35 mi. from the sea on the Guayas River, which, with its tributaries, serves as an important artery of communication. Manta, on the Coast northwest of Guayaquil, is the second-largest port. The Flota Mercante Grancolombiana, jointly owned by the governments of Ecuador and Colombia, has a large merchant fleet. Ecuador is served by several international and domestic airlines, the most important of the latter being Aerovías Ecuatorianas (AREA).

Foreign Trade. Ecuador's agricultural products account for 95% of the value of exports; bananas, coffee, and cacao are the most important commodities. The principal imports are machinery, vehicles, manufactured goods, and chemical and food products. The balance of trade has generally been favorable. The United States is the principal trading partner, accounting for between 50% and 60% of Ecuador's total trade.

Government

Structure of Government. Ecuador is a republic governed under its 16th constitution, adopted in 1946. The president and vice president are elected for four years and cannot stand for re-election until four years after the expiration of their terms. The president appoints his cabinet. The bicameral legislature is composed of a senate and chamber of deputies. There are two senators from each of

Rafts made of valuable hardwood glide slowly down a tributary of the Guayas River toward the seaport of Guayaquil. (CAMERA PRESS—PIX)

the 15 main provinces and one from the Galápagos Islands and each of the four Oriente provinces; all are elected for four years. In addition there are 12 "functional" senators representing specialized departments. Deputies are elected for two years on a basis of one for every 50,000 inhabitants. Voting is compulsory for all literate men over 18 years of age, but optional for women. The judicial branch of government consists of a supreme court at Quito, eight higher courts, and 15 provincial courts. There is no popular jury system, although criminal cases are heard before a specially selected jury.

The provinces are administered by governors, and are divided into cantons and parishes. The highest officials of each division are appointed by the president, but the larger cities have a popularly elected mayor.

Political Parties. After about 1870 Ecuadorian politics became dominated by the Conservative and (Radical) Liberal parties. The Conservative party draws its main strength from the Highlands and is strongly oriented toward Catholic principles. The (Radical) Liberal party, with its stronghold on the Coast, favors agrarian reform, religious tolerance, separation of church and state, and similar democratic principles. There is a small Socialist party, whose left wing controls the largest trade union in the country, the Ecuadorian Confederation of Workers; this is affiliated with the Communist-controlled World Federation of Trade Unions. There is also a Communist party and several other small groups.

History

The Indian and Colonial Eras. During the early 15th century several centers of Indian culture that had long existed in the Highlands and on the Coast were formed into the Kingdom of Quito. In 1460, however, an Inca army invaded from the south. The bloody war that ensued continued until the end of the century, when the Kingdom became part of the Inca Empire through the marriage of the Inca ruler Huayna Capac to Paccha, a Quito princess. Although the Inca Empire was divided after Huayna Capac's death, his son Atahualpa reunited it in 1532. His vast empire was short-lived, however, for in 1533 he was executed by the advancing Spaniards. Quito itself was left in ruins by the Incas in their retreat, but a year later there arose on its ashes the Villa de San Francisco de Quito founded by the Spanish conquistador Sebastián de Benalcázar. In 1535 he established Guayaquil.

In 1539 the region came under the governorship of Gonzalo Pizarro, brother of Francisco Pizarro, the conqueror of Peru. By 1563 Quito, as part of the viceroyalty of Peru, had gained importance as an economic, political, and cultural center, and was made the seat of a royal *audiencia*, a judicial-administrative body. During the 16th and 17th centuries Jesuit and Dominican missionaries were active in founding religious and educational institutions, and Quito acquired many fine examples of ecclesiastical art and architecture. In 1717 the *audiencia* was incorporated into the new Viceroyalty of New Granada. Aside from a renewed association with the Viceroyalty of Peru from 1723 to 1739, Ecuador remained part of New Granada until independence in 1822.

Independence. Dissatisfied with oppressive Spanish rule and inspired by the success of the French Revolution and Napoleon's invasion of Spain, Ecuador began its struggle for independence on Aug. 10, 1809. This Quito rebellion was ruthlessly crushed, and for more than a decade the Spaniards maintained control, although a brief two years of freedom was won in 1810. An important revolt took place in Guayaquil on Oct. 9, 1820, and on May 24, 1822, Antonio José de Sucre, the revolutionary commander in Ecuador, defeated royalist forces in a battle on the slopes of Mount Pichincha, near Quito. Ecuador was permanently freed from Spanish rule.

In accordance with the plans of "the Liberator," Simón Bolívar, Ecuador, New Granada (now Colombia), and Venezuela became a federated republic known as La Gran Colombia. Shortly before Bolívar's death in 1830 Ecuador left the federation, and on Sept. 11, a republican constitution was adopted at Riobamba, and Gen. Juan José Flores was elected President.

The recurring struggle between conservatives and liberals began at this time. The conservatives upheld the prerogatives of the army and the church, whereas the liberals, influenced mainly by French intellectuals, believed in the extension of civil liberties, the restriction of the power of the church, and secular education. Flores' harsh rule provoked a liberal revolt under the leadership of Vicente Rocafuerte, a widely traveled and highly educated man. A compromise was reached, and Rocafuerte became President in 1835, to be succeeded by Flores again four years later. Flores' attempts to retain power by unconstitutional means finally led to his exile in 1845. The ensuing period of political chaos lasted until a strong conservative leader, Gabriel García Moreno, emerged to restore national unity and order.

During García Moreno's terms as President, from 1861 to 1865 and from 1869 to 1875, considerable progress was made in education, communications, and agriculture. A staunch Roman Catholic, he signed a concordat with the Vatican in 1863, made the clergy responsible for all education, and persuaded Congress to dedicate Ecuador to the Sacred Heart of Jesus. The constitution of 1869 made membership in the Roman Catholic Church a prerequisite for citizenship. Stability and progress had been won

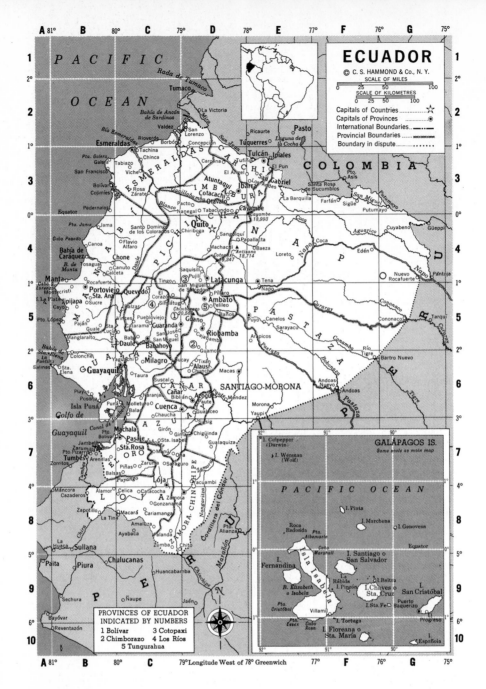

ECUADOR

© C. S. HAMMOND & Co., N. Y.

SCALE OF MILES

0   25   50   100

SCALE OF KILOMETRES

0   25   50   100

Capitals of Countries .... ☆
Capitals of Provinces .... ◉
International Boundaries .... _.._.._..
Provincial Boundaries .... _.._.._
Boundary in dispute ....

GALÁPAGOS IS.

Same scale as main map

PROVINCES OF ECUADOR
INDICATED BY NUMBERS

1 Bolívar   3 Cotopaxi
2 Chimborazo   4 Los Ríos
5 Tungurahua

by dictatorial methods, however, and in 1875 García Moreno was assassinated. There followed 20 years of turbulence and intrigue, ended, this time, by a liberal.

The 20th Century. Gen. Flavio Eloy Alfaro gained control of the government in 1895 and dominated the political scene for most of the period until 1912, although he only served as President from 1897 to 1901 and from 1906 to 1911. New constitutions in 1897 and 1906 affirmed and enacted liberal principles and divested the church of much of its power. The Guayaquil-Quito railway was completed, and general economic and social progress was made. When, in 1911, Alfaro tried to overthrow the new President, Leonidas Plaza Gutiérrez, he was imprisoned and finally lynched by a mob in Quito in 1912. Plaza Gutiérrez was able to complete this, his second, term in

1916, and the period of relative political stability continued until 1925. During those years the banking interests of the Coast dominated the national scene, and commercial and economic development was rapid. In 1925 the army, whose members were mainly from the Highlands, revolted against the government and ushered in a new era of political instability. For the next 23 years Ecuador was governed by numerous presidents, dictators, or juntas under several different constitutions and in the face of countless *coups d'état.* Boundary disputes, which had troubled Ecuador from time to time ever since independence, again flared up. Large areas of the unexplored Amazonian region had been lost to Colombia and Brazil at the beginning of the 20th century, and in 1941 vastly superior Peruvian forces invaded southeastern Ecuador. By the protocol of Rio de Janeiro in 1942, some 70,000 sq. mi. of Ecuador's Oriente region were ceded to Peru. However, the boundary between the two countries remained imperfectly defined for many years. Ecuador, which supported the Allied cause in World War II, became a member of the United Nations in Dec., 1945.

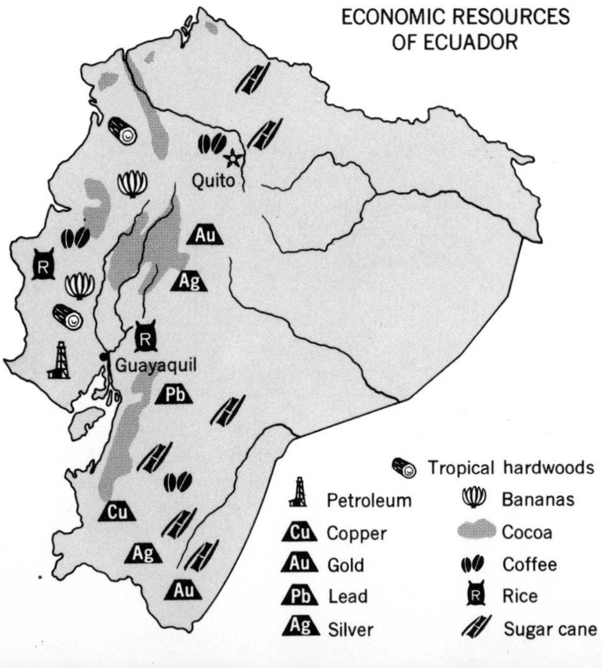

In 1948 internal stability, order, and progress returned at last to Ecuador. Galo Plaza Lasso, the son of Leonidas Plaza, was elected President and became the first since 1925 to complete his term of office. He was succeeded in 1952 by José María Velasco Ibarra, who had previously been elected and deposed twice, but who this time was also able to complete his full term. The next four years saw the administration of Camilio Ponce Enríquez, but in 1960 Velasco Ibarra was elected again. In Nov., 1961, however, after nationwide disorders in protest against his economic policies, he was deposed for the third time. His Vice President, Carlos Julio Arosemena Monroy, succeeded him as President, but was in turn ousted and exiled in July, 1963, while a military junta took over the government. The junta ruled until March, 1966, when it was forced to resign. A civilian cabinet was then sworn in, with Clemente Yerovi Indabura as provisional President.

Consult Von Hagen, V. W., Ecuador the Unknown (1940); Franklin, A. B., Ecuador: Portrait of a People (1943); Lasso, R. V., Wonderland, Ecuador (1944); Blanksten, G. I., Ecuador, Constitutions and Caudillos (1951); Ecuador, Andean Mosaic, ed. by Rolf Blomberg (1952); Linke, Lilo, Ecuador, Country of Contrasts (1960).

J. V. D. SAUNDERS, Louisiana State University

ECONOMIC RESOURCES OF ECUADOR

Quito

Au

Ag

R

Guayaquil

Pb

Cu

Ag

Au

🐚 Tropical hardwoods

🛢 Petroleum   🌼 Bananas

Cu Copper   ☁ Cocoa

Au Gold   ◖◗ Coffee

Pb Lead   R Rice

Ag Silver   🌾 Sugar cane

ECUMENICAL COUNCILS. *See* COUNCILS, ECUMENICAL.

ECUMENICAL [ĕk-ū-mĕr'ĭ-kəl] **MOVEMENT, THE,** a movement of co-operation among Christian Churches in the 20th century and an effort to develop greater unity among them throughout the world. Historically the ecumenical movement was organized along three main lines. The first was co-operation among missionary agencies, reflected in the World Missionary Conference held in Edinburgh in 1910, whose continuation committee evolved into the International Missionary Council in 1921. The second was co-operation in matters of Christian social concern, reflected on a national level in the Federal Council of the Churches of Christ in America, created in 1908, and on an international level in the Universal Christian Council on Life and Work, following a world conference in Stockholm in 1925. The third was co-operation in studying the doctrinal and ecclesiastical differences among the churches, as proposed by the Protestant Episcopal Church in 1910, which resulted in the World Conference on Faith and Order in Lausanne in 1927.

In 1937, when the second world conference on "Life and Work" was held in Oxford and the second world conference on "Faith and Order" in Edinburgh, a project for uniting their interests in a permanent World Council of Churches was approved by both. In the following year, in a consultation in Utrecht, a constitution for the proposed World Council was drafted and submitted to all interested churches for their consideration. Because of obstacles created by World War II, the process of ratification took a decade. On Aug. 22, 1948, at a great assembly of delegated representatives in Amsterdam, the World Council of Churches came into official existence. The International Missionary Council maintained a separate organizational structure, although in close co-operation, until 1961, when it became fully integrated in the World Council.

These organizational developments were the result of three clearly marked trends in the churches during a half century: a growing sense of world-wide mission, an awakening to a sense of common responsibility for the character of secular society, and a greater sensitiveness to the evils of a divided church and the spiritual necessity for greater unity.

The ecumenical movement has won sympathetic support in Protestant, Anglican, and Eastern Orthodox churches. The Roman Catholic Church has no official relation to it, but manifests a friendly interest. The genius of the movement is a concern to achieve a greater unity than is represented by the denominational patterns of the past. Its theological basis is the conviction that the Christian Churches are essentially one because of their common origin in one Lord, and that they must therefore strive to find the best way of manifesting that oneness in their life and work. Within the movement there are two different views as to its ultimate goal. One view sees enlarging and deepening fellowship among co-operating denominations as a satisfactory expression of unity. The other sees the true destiny of the ecumenical movement in the union of the separated denominations in one visible Church.

SAMUEL McCREA CAVERT, Executive Secretary (Retired),
World Council of Churches

ECZEMA [ĕk'sə-mə, ĕg'zə-mə, ĕg-zē'mə], a group of skin diseases characterized by redness, swelling, blisters, and scaling, in the severe forms, and thickening and roughening of the skin in the chronic forms. In both forms of eczema there is extreme itching. The condition may be caused by allergies, dandruff, infection, or poor circulation. Many other skin diseases, at some time in their development, display the characteristics of eczema.

In eczema, the skin frequently becomes infected as a result of the injuries inflicted by violent scratching. The severe eczemas are treated by removing the cause (in the case of allergies) or by treating the underlying condition. Wet compresses, medicated lotions, antihistamines, and drugs similar to cortisone are used. The chronic eczemas are treated similarly but instead of lotions and compresses, radiation and medicated creams are employed.

EDAM [ē'dəm], market village of the northwest Netherlands, on the western shore of the Ijsselmeer (Zuider Zee), about 15 mi. north of Amsterdam. Edam has given its name to the red-crusted cheese produced on the polder farms of North Holland. It was an important fishing center until the building of the Ijsselmeer Dam in 1932. Pop., 3,741.

EDDAS [ĕd'əz], name (probably meaning "book of Oddi") originally designating the *Prose*, or *Younger Edda*, a textbook on poetics written c.1225 by Snorri Sturluson, the Icelandic scholar and poet. This work consists of an epitome of Norse mythology, a treatise on skaldship, and an enumeration of poetic meters.

The title was applied later to the *Poetic*, or *Elder Edda*, a collection of 34 mythical and heroic poems from Iceland. In addition to the exclusively Scandinavian mythical lays, there are tragic heroic lays, including three poems whose subject matter may go back to historical events of the 2d century in the Baltic, the originally German cycle of Sigurd the Volsung (the Siegfried of the *Nibelungenlied*), and the poems of Gudrun, Brynhild, and Atli (the historical Attila). The eddic lays are strophic; the verse is alliterative. Without the *Eddas*, our knowledge of Norse mythology and Germanic heroic poetry would be scant.

PAUL SCHACH, University of Nebraska
See also MYTHOLOGY, NORSE.

EDDINGTON, SIR ARTHUR STANLEY (1882–1944), British astronomer, physicist, mathematician, and authority on the internal constitution and motion of stars. He early appreciated and propounded the importance of the theory of relativity. He was professor of astronomy and director of the observatory at Cambridge. In 1930 he endorsed and publicized Abbé Lemaître's concept of an expanding universe. He was the recipient of numerous honors, including the Order of Merit (1939), and a prolific and popular writer. His books include *The Mathematical Theory of Relativity* (1923), *The Nature of the Physical World* (1928), *The Expanding Universe* (1933).

EDDY, MARY BAKER (1821–1910), discoverer of Christian Science and founder of its church organization. She was born in Bow, N.H. Illness, bereavement, and unhap-

Culver Pictures, Inc.

Mary Baker Eddy, founder of the Church of Christ, Scientist.

piness in young womanhood caused her to reach out for a higher, more practical understanding of God as the solution to the problem of evil in human life. In 1866, after a serious accident, she turned to the Bible. While reading the account of Jesus' healing of the paralyzed man in the Gospel of Matthew, she received great spiritual illumination and was suddenly healed. The conviction came to her that God sends only good and that evil is a failure to recognize this fact.

Her healing and the illumination which accompanied it led Mrs. Eddy to spend the following three years in intensive study of the Scriptures. She searched for the absolute rules of healing through prayer, which would enable others to accomplish the works she believed Jesus expected of His followers as a natural part of Christian life. She published the results of this search in 1875, in the book which was later to become the denominational textbook of Christian Science: *Science and Health with Key to the Scriptures.* When her discovery was not readily accepted, she and a small group of those interested resolved "to organize a church designed to commemorate the word and works of our Master, which should reinstate primitive Christianity and its lost element of healing" (*Church Manual*).

Mrs. Eddy continued to be active in organizing this church and promoting its growth until her passing on Dec. 3, 1910. She had seen it become a world-wide denomination and had assured its continued orderly government by means of a *Church Manual*, administered by a board of directors. One of her most notable achievements was the founding, in her 87th year, of *The Christian Science Monitor,* now a well-known international daily newspaper.

Consult Wilbur, Sibyl, *The Life of Mary Baker Eddy* (1938); Beasley, Norman, *The Cross and the Crown* (1952).

WILL B. DAVIS, Committees on Publication,
The First Church of Christ, Scientist, Boston, Mass.

EDDY CURRENT, current induced in a metal body resting in an alternating or pulsating magnetic field or moving through a steady field. The current flows in a whirl, or eddy, hence its name. Since eddy currents heat metal, they cause a power loss and lower efficiency of electric equipment. For this reason they are regarded as a nuisance, except in such applications as induction heating, instrument damping, and electric braking.

EDELWEISS [ā'dəl-vīs], a perennial herb, *Leontopodium alpinum*, of the composite family, native to the European Alps. A related species, *L. sibiricum*, is found in the Himalayas. The edelweiss plant grows in a low tuft and is densely covered with a whitish wool. Its blossoms are star-shaped with a yellowish center surrounded by white rays. Edelweiss, long a symbol for purity, is the national flower of Switzerland. It can be grown in cool, temperate climates throughout the world, and is especially suited to rock garden planting.

EDEMA [ĭ-dē'mə], also called dropsy, a swelling of a portion of the body caused by excessive accumulation of fluid in the tissue spaces. Edema results from changes in the circulatory system that interfere with the normal exchange of fluids between the blood and the body tissues. A lowered concentration of proteins in the blood permits fluid to escape into the tissue spaces. Edema of this variety occurs in various kidney diseases, in which protein is lost through the urine; in malnutrition; and in cirrhosis of the liver.

Mechanical interference with the circulation of the blood produces increased blood pressure in the veins, and stasis, or slowing of the blood flow. The increased pressure in the veins forces fluid into the tissue spaces. This type of edema may result from heart failure, varicose veins, thrombophlebitis, and tumors that press upon the veins.

Allergic edema, or hives, and the swelling around insect bites is caused by the release of histamine from injured tissues. This substance makes the walls of the capillaries more porous and permits fluids to pass into the tissues. The treatment of edema is aimed at removing the underlying cause.

JEROME D. WAYE, M.D.

EDEN [ē'dən], **(ROBERT) ANTHONY, EARL OF AVON** (1897–   ), British statesman. Eden entered Parliament in 1923, and served as Parliamentary private secretary to Foreign Secretary Sir Austen Chamberlain from 1926 to 1929. He himself became Foreign Secretary in 1935, but resigned in 1938 because of disagreement over Prime Minister Neville Chamberlain's appeasement policy toward Nazi Germany. In 1940 Eden returned to the Foreign Office in Winston Churchill's coalition government and remained as Foreign Secretary till the Labour party took office in 1945. In 1951, when the Conservatives returned to power, Eden went back to the Foreign Office. Upon Churchill's resignation in 1955, Eden succeeded him as Prime Minister. In Nov., 1956, the Anglo-French-Israeli operation against Egypt caused Eden to lose the support of powerful opinion at home, in the Commonwealth, and in the United States. The failure of the operation made almost inevitable his resignation, which was hastened by a serious breakdown in his health. He was raised to the peerage in 1961. His books include his memoirs, *Full Circle* (1960) and *Facing the Dictators* (1962).

STEPHEN R. GRAUBARD, Harvard University

EDEN, GARDEN OF, Hebrew equivalent of "Paradise," the Biblical home of Adam and Eve, the first man and woman (Gen. 2, 3). In it were the "tree of life" and the "tree of knowledge of good and evil." This was the setting for the opening drama of history—the Fall of Man.

EDENTATES [ē-děn-tāts], name for members of an order, Edentata, of New World mammals, including the anteaters, armadillos, and sloths. The anteaters, native to semitropical and tropical America, are toothless, and secure the insects on which they feed with the aid of a long, sticky tongue. The bony-plated armadillo, found from Texas to South America, has simple, conical cheek teeth that are used to masticate vegetation and small animal life. The sloths, which are native to tropical America, have flat-crowned, molarlike teeth to chew their specialized diet of cecropia leaves. Armadillos are burrowing animals; sloths are almost entirely arboreal, and spend their time hanging upside-down from tree branches; anteaters are both arboreal and terrestrial.
See also ANTEATER; ARMADILLO; SLOTH.

EDENTON, port on Albemarle Sound in northeastern North Carolina, and historic seat of Chowan County. The town was settled before 1660, and has a number of 18th-century buildings, including St. Paul's Church (1736) and the Court House. Colonial and Revolutionary Edenton and vicinity are the subject of seven novels, known collectively as "The Carolina Series," by the adopted North Carolina novelist, Inglis Fletcher, of nearby Bandon Plantation. Fishing, farming, and the raising of jumbo peanuts are carried on. Pop. (1950) 4,468; (1960) 4,458.

EDERLE [ĕd'ər-lē], **GERTRUDE CAROLINE** (1906–), American swimmer, born in New York. She was the first woman to swim the English Channel, crossing from France to England on Aug. 6, 1926, in 14 hours, 31 minutes.

EDESSA [ē-děs'ə] (modern **URFA,** Turkey), ancient city of northwestern Mesopotamia, chiefly celebrated as the center of eastern Christianity and of Syriac language and literature in the 1st millennium A.D. From 132 B.C. Edessa was the capital of the native state of Osroene, which formed a buffer between Rome and Parthia. From 165 A.D. it was under Roman control, becoming a *colonia* in 216. Its rulers became officially Christian by the beginning of the 3d century, though worship of the sun, moon,

and planets was still practiced in the 5th century. Edessa played an important part in mediating Christianity to the Parthian Empire, Sassanian Persia, and Armenia. It fell to the Arabs in 639.

EDFU. *See* IDFU OR EDFU.

EDGEWOOD, residential borough of southwestern Pennsylvania. An eastern suburb of Pittsburgh, it is a community of middle-class homes. Inc., 1888; pop. (1950) 5,292; (1960) 5,124.

EDGEWORTH, MARIA (1767–1849), Irish writer, noted for her Irish regional stories and her accurate depictions of family life. Born in England, she went with her family to Ireland (1782), where she remained until her death. Her novels were very popular in their time; the best of them was *Castle Rackrent* (1800). Some of her stories are spoiled by moralizing, but she is important as the first writer to portray the Irish realistically.

EDICT OF TOLERATION. *See* MILAN, EDICT OF.

EDINA [ē-dī'nə], village of eastern Minnesota. It is a residential suburb southwest of Minneapolis. Inc., 1888; pop. (1950) 9,744; (1960) 28,501.

EDINBURG, city of southern Texas and seat of Hidalgo County, in the Lower Rio Grande Valley. It is in an irrigated agricultural area and has associated industries such as packing, shipping, and canning of fruits and vegetables. Cotton ginning is also important. Pan-American College (estab., 1927) is here. Pop. (1950) 12,383; (1960) 18,706.

EDINBURGH [ĕd'ən-bûrə], **THE PRINCE PHILIP, DUKE OF** (1921–), consort of Queen Elizabeth II of Great Britain. He is the son of Prince Andrew of Greece and Princess Alice of Battenberg, a great-granddaughter of Queen Victoria. (The family name Battenberg was changed to Mountbatten in 1917.) Educated at Gordonstoun, Scotland, he served in the Royal Navy and since his marriage (1947) has taken an active role in public life. He was president of the British Association for the Advancement of Science, worked enthusiastically for the National Playing Fields Association, opened the Olympic Games in Melbourne (1956), and made many tours in Commonwealth nations and British overseas possessions, both alone and with the Queen.

EDINBURGH, capital and second-largest city of Scotland, seat of Midlothian County. Situated on the southern shore of the Firth of Forth, the city is overlooked by Salisbury Crags and the hill Arthur's Seat. It is built on rocky hills and ridges, one of which rises westward 445 ft. to a precipitous rock called Castle Hill. Here since pre-Christian times when it was known as Castrum Puellarum, a castle has stood dominating the Lothian region. Along the crest of this ridge a continuous road called the Royal Mile descends eastward from Castle Hill to Canongate and Holyrood Palace, residence of Mary, Queen of Scots. Each side of the Royal Mile is flanked by the "wynds" or alleys of the Old Town. Besides the castle and palace one finds here St. Giles Church, Parliament House, Canongate Tolbooth, the Royal Exchange, and many 16th- and 17th-century dwellings, some carefully restored as museums. Seen from the southernmost street of the New Town, Princes Street, the ridge descending from Castle Hill to the Old Town, presents such a magnificent vista that Edinburgh is often called the "Athens of the North." More familiarly, it is nicknamed "Auld Reekie" because of the low-lying smoke and fog. A deep ravine north of the Old Town, formerly the Nor' Loch, was bridged so that the town could be extended onto another ridge. There, in the late 18th century the New Town was built. As the New Town grew, so much excavated debris was dumped into Nor' Loch that it was eventually made into a broad way called the Mound and today is the site of the Princes Street Gardens. Later, the port of Leith, 3 mi. north, the fishing port of Granton, the coastal town of Portobello, and other nearby villages were incorporated within the city's boundaries.

Much of the city's industry is related to its metropolitan and cultural functions. Printing, publishing, and papermaking, dating back to the 16th century, are the most important commercial industries. Edinburgh is second only to London as a center of publishing and printing in Great Britain and specializes in such work as cartography. Baking, confectionary and chocolate manufacturing, brewing, distilling, and bottling are also important. New industries include the production of rubber and electrical and marine engineering. Leith is important for shipbuilding.

History. History does not show the derivation of the name Edinburgh. Possible sources are Edwinsburgh, derived from the name of the 7th-century Northumbrian ruler, or the Gaelic name Dunedin. Others are the Latin Obsessio Etin, or Eden Oppidum, whence the Northumbrians were driven by the Picts and Scots in the 10th century. The castle mentioned earlier, commanding land and sea approaches from the west and south, gave the site particular importance. Malcolm II may have lived in the castle as early as 1018; Malcolm III did live there in 1093. During the reign of David I (12th century) people moved from within the castle walls and established a burgh around what is now High Street. Farther east, the canons of Holyrood Abbey established their own burgh, Canongate. Edinburgh was strategically valuable because it dominated land and sea routes from England, and it changed hands often during the struggles for Scottish independence. With the coronation of James II in Holyrood Abbey (1437), the city became the capital of Scotland.

The commerce of the town grew, and the government became increasingly centralized. About 1500 James IV commenced building Holyrood Palace. In 1532 the College of Justice, or supreme civil court, of Scotland was established in Edinburgh. Then, in the 1540's the English burned the town and the Abbey and Palace of Holyrood. The castle was not taken, however.

Meanwhile, John Knox, preaching the doctrines of the Protestant Reformation, gained much support in Scotland from those who saw the futility of the struggle with England and from those who resented French and papal influence. In 1560 the first General Assembly of the Reformed Church met in Edinburgh. In 1603 James VI ascended the English throne as James I and the court left Edinburgh.

The fortified Castle Hill (*left*) and Princes Street (*right*) are among Edinburgh's most famous landmarks.
William G. Froelich

However, the city continued to progress as the ecclesiastical, civil, and commercial capital of Scotland. The Royal High School had been founded in 1519 and the university in 1583. By 1640 a new Parliament House was completed. Printing had been introduced in 1507, and by the 17th century other industries included the manufacture of foundry products and glass.

Since the Act of Union (1707) uniting England and Scotland, no parliament has met in Edinburgh. Neverthe-

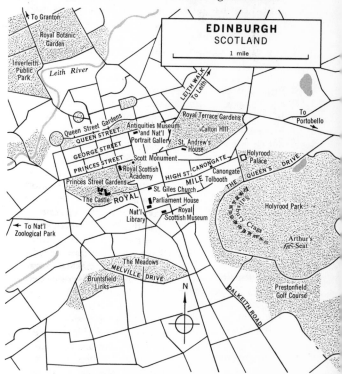

less, it has retained independent legal and educational systems. The supreme court meets in Parliament House. The Bank of Scotland and other banks issue their own notes. Despite the rise of Glasgow as an industrial city, Edinburgh is still the main center of Scottish banking and insurance. The 20th-century transfer of government departments from London has greatly increased the administrative importance of Edinburgh, as witnessed by St. Andrews House, government offices built into the steep face of Calton Hill.

Culture. Its university was founded in 1583, and Edinburgh has become an outstanding cultural center. Associated with the university are a college of agriculture, a veterinary college, a school of art, and the Heriot-Watt Technical College. Independent educational institutions and societies include the Royal College of Physicians, Royal Medical Society, Royal Physical Society, Royal College of Surgeons, Society of Antiquaries of Scotland, Royal Society of Edinburgh, and Royal Highland and Agricultural Society of Scotland. Among Edinburgh's specialized research institutes are the Royal Observatory, the Geological Survey, and the Animal Breeding Research Organization. There are also many private schools including Fettes, Donaldson's, George Watson's, Daniel Stewart's, and Merchiston Castle School.

The National Library of Scotland is located in Edinburgh. Museums include the National Gallery, National Portrait Gallery, Royal Scottish Academy of Painting, Sculpture, and Architecture, Royal Scottish Museum, and National Museum of Antiquities. The Royal Zoological Society of Scotland maintains the National Zoological Park, one of the largest in Europe. Here also is the Royal Botanic Garden and Arboretum. The establishment, in 1947, of an annual International Festival of Art, Drama, and Music has further increased Edinburgh's cultural reputation.

Many Edinburgh residents have won international renown. Among these in literature and philosophy are David Hume, Adam Smith, James Boswell, Sir Walter Scott (commemorated by an enormous memorial in Princes Street), Tobias Smollett, Robert Louis Stevenson, and Thomas Carlyle. The painter, Sir Henry Raeburn, and the architects, Robert and James Adam, also resided here. The numerous scientists from Edinburgh include Alexander Graham Bell, John Napier, Sir Robert Sibbald, Joseph Black, James Hutton, James Clerk Maxwell, and Sir Wyville Thomson. Pop., 468,378.

H. A. MOISLEY, The University, Glasgow, Scotland

EDINBURGH, UNIVERSITY OF, originally the College of Edinburgh, or The Town's College, institution of higher learning founded in 1583 by the town council of Edinburgh, under powers granted by the charter of King James VI of Scotland (James I of England), dated Apr. 14, 1582. From the first the college possessed the privilege of conferring degrees, and this privilege was ratified by the Act of Confirmation passed in 1621. This secured to the College of James VI, as it had come to be called, all the rights, immunities, and privileges enjoyed by the other universities of Scotland.

The university remained under the control and patronage of the Town Council of Edinburgh until 1858, when,

by the Universities (Scotland) Act of that year, all the universities of Scotland received new and autonomous constitutions. By the Universities (Scotland) Act of 1889 the university court became a body corporate and the chief governing body of the university. The *Senatus Academicus*, a larger body comprised of all professors and a number of other members of the academic staff, regulated, as before, the teaching and discipline of the university.

The University of Edinburgh has long enjoyed a high reputation in respect to its Faculty of Medicine, which was in the forefront of the medical revolution which took place in the 18th century, and it has been one of the outstanding international centers of medical teaching ever since. The Faculty of Divinity also holds a world position as a center of postgraduate study. The School of English Literature has a distinguished record, upheld in more modern times. David Hume, James Boswell, Thomas Carlyle, and Sir Walter Scott are among its former students. In the 20th century Edinburgh has taken a leading place in linguistic teaching, especially teaching English to those who have to teach that language in their own (non-English-speaking) countries. The university's Department of Phonetics is one of the largest and best equipped in Europe.

Its six faculties are divinity, law, medicine, arts, science, and music, each presided over by a dean. Degrees, diplomas, and certificates are awarded in each faculty after examination or upon presentation of a thesis, or both. There are several departmental museums, and of these, the instrument collection housed in the Reid School of Music is probably of greatest general interest to visitors.

In the early 1960's about 6,000 full-time students and some 1,300 part-time students attended the university.

B. S. ROBERTS, University of Edinburgh

EDINBURGH REVIEW, THE, Scottish literary and political periodical published from 1802 until 1929. It was begun at the suggestion of Sydney Smith by a group of young men at a time when magazines were little more than publishers' organs prepared by literary hacks. The critical articles of its gifted and well-paid contributors brought the new publication wide readership. It was edited from shortly after its inception until 1829 by Francis J. Jeffrey, Scottish lawyer, critic, and essayist. In 1808 when it became more obviously an advocate of the Whig reform program, Sir Walter Scott, a former contributor, joined the *Quarterly Review* in opposition. Other eminent writers who contributed to *The Edinburgh Review* included Thomas Carlyle, William Hazlitt, and Thomas Babington Macaulay.

EDIRNE [ə-dĭr′nə] **or ADRIANOPLE** [ā-drĭ-ən-ō′pl], city of European Turkey, and the capital of the province of Edirne, located on the Meriç (Maritsa) River in Thrace. It is near the Greek border and is the main port of entry into Turkey for the rail and motor traffic from Europe. Most of the inhabitants are farmers. The principal crops are wheat and barley, and Edirne is famous for its cheese. Adrianople was named after the Roman Emperor Hadrian, who founded the city in 125 A.D., on the site of ancient Usku. It was conquered by the Visigoths, Avars, and Bulgarians, and by the Crusaders. Captured by the Turks in

1361, it was the capital of the Ottoman Empire until 1453. The city was captured by Russian armies twice in the 19th century and held by the Bulgarians for a short period during the Balkan Wars. The Selim mosque, built by the architect Sinan in 1568, is a masterpiece of Turkish art. Pop., 31,865.

EDISON [ĕd′ə-sən], **THOMAS ALVA** (1847–1931), American inventor of the phonograph, the carbon telephone transmitter, the incandescent electric light, practical systems for commercial generation and distribution of electric power, the first camera to take pictures on a moving strip of film, and hundreds of other devices in electrical and mechanical fields. He also made two significant discoveries in pure science: "etheric force," the electromagnetic waves used later in wireless and radio transmission; and the "Edison Effect," a fundamental phenomenon of the electron tube.

Edison was born in Milan, Ohio, on Feb. 11, 1847, of English ancestry with possibly some Dutch. When he was seven years old his family moved to Port Huron, Mich. There the boy had his only formal schooling, limited to less than three months. The rest of his early education was ably supervised by his mother, Nancy Elliott Edison, who had been a teacher before her marriage to Samuel Edison, Jr.

At the age of ten, Edison was already interested in chemistry and had a small laboratory in the basement of his home. The year 1859 found him in "business" as a newsboy and "candy butcher" on the Grand Trunk Railway between Port Huron and Detroit. At 14 he published *The Weekly Herald*, possibly the first newspaper printed on a moving train. Earnings from these enterprises enabled him to buy books and to further his ruling passion for study and experiment.

Early Inventions. Learning telegraphy in 1862, Edison spent a few years as an operator in the Midwest, then went to Boston in 1868, where he obtained a job with the Western Union Telegraph Company. While there he developed his first patented invention, an electrical vote recorder that nobody seemed to want. This decided him to concentrate thereafter on things for which a real demand already existed or could be created.

The summer of 1869 found Edison in New York City. There his abilities attracted the attention of Marshall Lefferts, president of the Gold and Stock Telegraph Company, who assigned him to improve the stock ticker. This resulted in the Edison Universal Printer, which together with some related inventions brought Edison $40,000, his first substantial return from inventive work. He used this money to establish shops in Newark, N.J., where from 1870 to 1876 he manufactured stock tickers and improved telegraph instruments of his own invention and design.

Manufacturing as such had no serious appeal for Edison, however. He soon tired of it and determined to devote his full time to the "invention business," building a new establishment for that purpose in 1876 at Menlo Park, N.J. There he and a small staff of carefully selected assistants worked hard, day and night at times, producing scores of new inventions or improved technological developments. Before long Edison became widely known as "The Wizard of Menlo Park."

Early in the 1880's, while busily engaged on his electric light and power projects, the inventor moved to New York City. His first wife, Mary Stilwell Edison, who had borne him 3 children, died in 1884. Two years later, when he was about to remarry, Edison offered his bride-to-be, Mina Miller, her choice of a home in New York or in the country. She chose the latter, an attractive estate called Glenmont, in West Orange, N.J., where in due time a second daughter and two more sons were added to the family.

Less than a mile from Glenmont, in 1887, Edison established himself and his associates in a new laboratory constructed according to his own design, and equipped with every kind of essential machinery, scientific apparatus, and working materials stock. There, to use his own words, he would be able to "build anything from a lady's watch to a locomotive." This concept of an "invention factory" has often been considered Edison's most vital contribution to the progress of science and technology. After it were patterned many of the great research and development laboratories later established by the world's large industries. Although the inventor also built another home and a smaller laboratory at Fort Myers, Fla., and often went there in the winter months, he lived and worked mainly at West Orange for the last 44 years of his life.

World War I. In 1915, after war began, Edison became chairman of the Naval Consulting Board. In that capacity he labored hard to establish the Naval Research Laboratory for development of new weapons, conducted special experiments on more than 40 major war problems, and did a tremendous amount of other work connected with national defense of the United States. Mention should be made, too, of his "Proposed Amendment to the Federal Reserve Banking System," embodying a plan for helping farmers to finance their crops. Edison's contributions to his country's welfare in these and other respects were recognzied in 1928 by award of a special Congressional Gold Medal. He was also the first civilian to receive the Navy's Distinguished Service Medal.

Although acclaimed throughout the world as a great benefactor of mankind, Edison never rested on his laurels, but to the end of his days retained both a zest for life and a never fully satisfied urge to discover and invent new things. His last ambitious investigation, to find a practicable domestic source of natural rubber, was not yet completed when death overtook him at Glenmont on Oct. 18, 1931, at the age of 84.

Patents. Edison was granted 1,093 U.S. patents, more than any other American before or since. He also had many foreign patents. Among his most important inventions, other than those already noted, were the following: multiplex telegraph systems, an electric pen, the magnetic ore separator, the first full-sized electric railway passenger locomotive in America, radical improvements in the design and efficiency of electric motors and generators, station-to-station wireless telegraphy, various types of incandescent and fluorescent lamps, continuous nickel and copper plating, electroplating metals in a vacuum, the nickel-iron-alkaline storage battery, improved primary batteries for electric railway signals, magnetic concentration and briquetting of iron ore, long rotary kilns for cement production, electric safety lanterns which greatly reduced mine fatalities, a process for making carbolic acid

(THE BETTMANN ARCHIVE)

THE KINETOSCOPE

Edison Electric Institute

THE INCANDESCENT LAMP

Thomas Alva Edison, who had little formal education, was granted 1,093 U.S. patents for his inventions. Among them were some of the most significant inventions of modern times.

that overcame an acute shortage in World War I, the "kinetophone" (a machine to project talking motion pictures), a long-playing phonograph record, and hundreds of other improvements in the recording and reproduction of sound. Edison also invented but never patented the fluoroscope, preferring to make it available for free use to the medical profession.

Consult Dickson, W. K. L. and Antonia, *The Life and Inventions of Thomas A. Edison* (1894); Dyer, F. L., Martiń, T. C., and Meadowcroft, W. H., *Edison: His Life and Inventions* (2 vols., 1929); Simonds, W. A., *Edison: His Life, His Work, His Genius* (1934); Tate, A. O., *Edison's Open Door* (1938); Jehl, Francis, *Menlo Park Reminiscences* (3 vols., 1936–41); North, Sterling, *Young Thomas Edison* (1958); Josephson, Matthew, *Edison* (1959); Library-archives of the Edison Laboratory National Monument, West Orange, N.J., and the Henry Ford Museum and Greenfield Village, Dearborn, Mich.

MELVIN J. WEIG, Superintendent, Edison
Laboratory National Monument
See also ELECTRONICS; PHONOGRAPH; TELEGRAPH.

EDISON, formerly Raritan, a township of central New Jersey. The village of Menlo Park, where Thomas Edison established his first laboratory devoted to research and invention, is included in the township. The incandescent light bulb was invented at Menlo Park in 1879. The township has chemical and plastic industries. Pop. (1950) 16,-348; (1960) 44,799.

EDISTO [ĕd'ĭs-tō] **RIVER,** navigable river of southern

South Carolina, formed south of Orangeburg by the confluence of the North and South forks. The Edisto flows south through outer Coastal Plain swamps to the Atlantic Ocean southwest of Charleston. Before reaching the sea it separates into two channels around Edisto Island (about 80 sq. mi.). Length, 150 mi.; drainage area, 6,150 sq. mi.

EDITORIAL, article in which a publication expresses the principles and policies of the person or persons in control. In a newspaper, editorials usually appear on a special inside or back page reserved for opinion and clearly distinguished typographically from the news columns. Occasionally editorials are signed by the writer or given front-page prominence; but ordinarily they appear anonymously, representing either the individual views of an editor or the synthesized views of a group of editors.

The American colonial prototype for the "crusading" editorial was established by James Franklin when he opposed vaccination for smallpox in his New England *Courant.* Early newspapers, however, included few editorials as now identified, and the editorial function was more typically performed by pamphleteers. Horace Greeley of the New York *Tribune,* founded in 1841, is usually cited as the greatest of the 19th-century editors who implanted their own opinions in the pages of their papers. The modern editorial "we" speaks more often for a press institution or corporation than for an individual.

Editorials take many forms and perform various functions. Some inform by restating and reorganizing recognized facts; some explain, interpret, and analyze public affairs; some argue, exhort, and recommend courses of ac-

Edison making a final adjustment on the lens of the kinetoscope, an early movie projector.
(EDISON ELECTRIC INSTITUTE)

For the first phonograph, invented in 1877, Edison used cylindrical records and a large horn.
(THE BETTMANN ARCHIVE)

Chemical experiments were integral to Edison's technological work.
(EDISON ELECTRIC INSTITUTE)

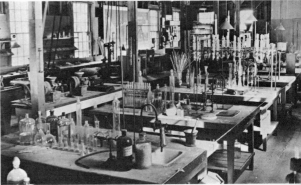

Edison's staff for the "invention business" in the Menlo Park laboratory, where the overhead incandescent bulbs had recently been invented.
(THOMAS ALVA EDISON FOUNDATION MUSEUM)

Edison's laboratory for the last 44 years of his life, in West Orange, N.J., is now a U.S. National Monument.
(EDISON ELECTRIC INSTITUTE)

tion; some provide entertainment or a change of pace in the otherwise somber columns reserved to them.

KENNETH N. STEWART, University of California

EDMOND, trade city of central Oklahoma, located in a rich farming region. Settled by homesteaders in 1889, it claims Oklahoma Territory's first church, newspaper, public school, and library. Central State College, founded there in 1890, is the oldest college in the state. Pop. (1950) 6,086; (1960) 8,577.

EDMONDS, WALTER DUMAUX (1903–   ), American novelist, born in Boonville, N.Y. He is known for his popular historical novels set in New York state. *Rome Haul* (1929), a story of the Erie Canal, was dramatized as *The Farmer Takes a Wife* (1934). Other successful fiction included *Drums Along the Mohawk* (1936) and *Chad Hanna* (1940).

EDMONDS, city of west-central Washington, located on Puget Sound, just north of Seattle. Although primarily residential it has some industries including boat building, metalworking, and the manufacture of wood products. Pop. (1950) 2,057; (1960) 8,016.

EDMONTON, capital and largest city of Alberta, Canada, 300 mi. north of the international boundary. Edmonton is cut through the center by the North Saskatchewan River. The river valley itself has been kept largely as

parkland. To the north lies the main business district. Its principal thoroughfare is Jasper Avenue. The city hall, police department, chancery hall, and public library are grouped around Sir Winston Churchill Square, near the downtown area. The provincial Legislature overlooks the river, with other government buildings nearby. South of the river is the campus of the University of Alberta. On the university grounds stands the Jubilee Auditorium, which serves as a home for the publicly supported symphony orchestra. There is also a museum of art.

Edmonton has warm summers and long, cold winters. The mean, or average, July temperature is 62° F., with extreme temperatures of over 90° F. having been recorded in each of the summer months. The mean January temperature is 6° F., but an extreme of −57° F. has been recorded. The mean duration of frost-free days is 100. Annual precipitation averages 18.0 in., most of it falling in the summer months. Mean winter snowfall is 50 in.

Edmonton is the market center for the rich grain- and livestock-producing areas of northern and central Alberta. Agriculturally based industries include slaughtering, meat packing, food processing, and fertilizer production. Since the discovery of oil and natural gas in the area in 1947, oil refining and the related production of chemicals, petrochemicals, and plastics have grown rapidly. The two largest pipelines in Canada, the Interprovincial Pipe Line and the Trans-Mountain Oil Pipe Line, terminate here. As the most northerly, major city on the continent,

The modern city hall of Edmonton, capital of Alberta. (GEORGE HUNTER)

Edmonton has long served as a warehousing and metal-fabricating center for the northern ore fields. Edmonton has two airports, from which several airlines schedule regular flights to all parts of the world. Both the C.N.R. and the C.P.R., the major Canadian railway lines, serve the city. The excellent highway system radiating from Edmonton connects it with the Trans-Canada Highway, with the Pacific Coast by the Yellowhead Route, and with the north by the Alaska Highway.

The first recorded settlement of the site dates from 1808, when trading posts were built by two rival fur companies. Fort Edmonton later became one of the main trading posts of the Hudson's Bay Company. The arrival of the railway in 1891 and the gold rush to the Yukon in 1896 hastened population growth. In 1904 Edmonton was incorporated as a city, and the following year was proclaimed capital of the newly formed province of Alberta. Pop., 389,500.

MORLEY D. ENGLISH, University of Alberta

EDMONTON, residential district and a minor industrial center in the enlarged borough of Enfield, London, England. Manufactures include furniture and clothing, and there are light industries in the eastern part of the borough. Edmonton was originally a market town that grew up on the old Roman road later named Ermine Street. It received a great influx of population with the development of public transport in the 19th century, particularly after the opening of the Eastern Counties Railway in 1872 and 1873. Formerly a separate borough, it was incorporated into Enfield in 1963.

EDMUND RICH, ST. (c.1180–1240), Archbishop of Canterbury. Born at Abingdon, Berkshire, he taught logic at Oxford and theology at Paris, before becoming treasurer of Salisbury cathedral (c.1222). Noted for his piety, preaching, and scholarship, he was elected Archbishop in 1233. After struggling unsuccessfully to defend the English church against papal and royal exploitation, he died in exile in France.

EDMUNDSTON, city of New Brunswick, Canada. It is across the St. John River from Madawaska, Maine. The population is predominantly French-speaking. A large pulp mill is the principal industrial plant in the city, which is a transportation center. Originally known as Little Falls, it was founded about 1785 as a home for Acadian refugees. The French-language University of St. Louis (estab., 1946) is here. Pop., 12,791.

EDNA, town of southern Texas and seat of Jackson County, 95 mi. southwest of Houston. It is the distribution center for a cattle-raising, oil-producing, and cotton-growing area. Inc., 1926; pop. (1950) 3,855; (1960) 5,038.

EDO. *See* TOKYO.

EDOM, alternate name for Esau (q.v.).

EDOM [ē′dəm] **or IDUMEA** [ĭd-ū-mē′ə], Palestinian kingdom southeast of the Dead Sea, also called Seir in the Bible (Gen. 32:3), and *Udumu* in Assyrian inscriptions, first established in the 13th century B.C. Its capital was on the site of the later city of Petra. Idumea was its Greek name, applied to southern Palestine west of the Dead Sea, after the destruction of the earlier kingdom by Arab invaders during the 6th century B.C.

EDOMITES [ē′dəm-īts], inhabitants of the Kingdom of Edom in ancient Palestine, traditionally descendants of Esau (Gen. 36). In the 10th century B.C., they were conquered by David, who initiated large-scale exploitation of their copper deposits. After the Babylonian destruction of Jerusalem in 587 B.C., they moved into southern Palestine and remained there in a territory later called Idumea in Greek.

EDSON, town of northwestern Alberta, Canada, adjacent to the McLeod River. It is a divisional point for the Canadian National Railways, and a timber, oil, and gas center. Pop., 3,198.

The Bettmann Archive

Relief from a Roman tomb found in Trier, Germany, depicts a teacher (*center*) instructing his pupils.

EDUCATION. In the broad sense "education" means an increase of skill or development of knowledge and understanding as a result of training, study, or experience. Education goes on in all societies for, in order to survive, a society must pass on basic skills, information, and beliefs from one generation to the next. This kind of teaching goes on even in societies that have no formal school systems. In the most highly developed and complex societies, moreover, a large part of the training of youth is done by such agencies as family, friends and associates, churches, organizations and clubs, and by books, magazines, and other means of communication. Nevertheless, organized schooling has a tremendous influence on what people know and how they develop. Also, organized programs can be described and comparisons between nations can

be made. For purposes of discussion in this article, then, "education" means formal programs of teaching, particularly those conducted by schools, colleges, and universities. This definition is not limited to "what goes on in school" but includes part-time and home study by such means as correspondence or television, under the direction of recognized institutions, as well as the in-service educational programs conducted by business, industry, and government.

The table on page 249 lists titles of sections that appear under this general heading, Education. Following each title are important related articles that will be found in other volumes. For a discussion of the coverage of education, see the Study Guide. Careers in education are discussed in a Career Guide on page 298.

HISTORY OF EDUCATION

This article will concentrate upon the development of education in Western civilization from its formal beginnings in Greece to the early 20th century. Other articles in this and other sections of the Encyclopedia will treat specific men, developments, and more recent aspects in the history of education that can only be mentioned in a survey of this scope.

Ancient Greece and Rome. The history of education in ancient Greece and Rome stretches from the foundations of those societies, the Greek story going back before 1000 B.C., the Roman to 500 B.C. The history of the two cultures becomes combined after the fall of Greece to Roman armies in 146 B.C. and terminates with the collapse of the Western Roman Empire, traditionally dated at 476 A.D. It should be noted, however, that many aspects of Hellenistic (Greco-Roman) education were maintained in Byzantium for centuries after the fall of the Western Empire. These became fused with Islamic knowledge after 620 A.D. and were reintroduced into the stream of Western culture toward the end of the Middle Ages.

As with all societies in the early phases of their development, education in Greece and Rome was originally centered in the family. There were no formal schools and

parents were responsible for the education of their children. A characteristic of Roman education was the way boys and girls learned by observing and doing as they helped their mothers and fathers in their daily duties. As societies become more complex, mounting responsibilities take the father from the home and from family duties. More highly specialized skills and knowledge are also in order, hence formal schooling is introduced by parents. A family servant or slave may be assigned to teach or a tutor may be hired. Eventually teachers, usually men, establish schoolrooms in their homes, or a group of prosperous parents may set up a school and employ a schoolmaster. In this manner formal schools eventually arose in ancient Greece and Rome. Many centuries later, on the American frontier, the first formal schooling was often provided in much the same manner.

Generally, in Greece and Rome, only the children of the citizens were schooled beyond the early years of childhood education handled by the family. Thus only a minority of the total population was literate. Most girls, except for isolated instances as in Sparta, received no formal schooling. The peasants, the landless working classes in the cities, and slaves also went without education. One of

Education is discussed in the major article beginning on these pages and in a large number of other articles in other volumes of the Encyclopedia. The table on the facing page shows, first, the scope of the main article and, second, the variety of related entries.

The main article starts with three sections that provide a background to understanding education. First, there is a summary of the history of education. Second, there is a review of theories about the extent, control, support, content, and methods of education — an introduction to educational philosophy in layman's terms. Third, the section *National Systems of Education* (drawing on the special field called comparative education) surveys theory and practice in leading countries, particularly the United Kingdom, Germany, France, and the U.S.S.R.

Next follow four sections on the educational system of the United States. *Public Education in the United States* deals with tax support, compulsory attendance, and school administration. The sections on elementary, secondary, and higher education cover history as well as modern practice and make comparisons with other nations. The features of Canadian education, including English and French influences, constitute the topic of *Education in Canada*. The balance of EDUCATION is devoted to particular topics: professional education, schooling for children who need special services, adult education, and programs of study abroad. It should be noted that *Education of Exceptional Children* deals, first, with gifted children and, second, with retarded and otherwise handicapped children.

The main article is concerned in one way or another with the major aspects of education. But, as the lists of related articles show, a more complete discussion of some topics is to be found in other volumes. Curriculum planning and major curriculum patterns are discussed in CURRICULUM. Educational psychology is grouped with the other branches of psychology (see PSYCHOLOGY: *Educational Psychology*). Additional data are presented in LEARNING, in STUDY SKILLS, IMPROVING, and in TESTING, PSYCHOLOGICAL AND EDUCATIONAL. The behavior of school-age children is discussed in CHILD DEVELOPMENT and ADOLESCENCE. Guidance services are covered in GUIDANCE AND COUNSELING, EDUCATIONAL and VOCATIONAL GUIDANCE.

A major category in education is that of methods and materials. A large number of articles deal with aspects of this subject—for example, TEACHERS AND TEACHING; TEAM TEACHING; READING, REMEDIAL; READING IMPROVEMENT; and STUDY SKILLS, IMPROVING. (The last two articles contain specific suggestions for self-help). There is also material on procedures in the sections on elementary and secondary education and education of exceptional children. Further details on methods in the early school years are found in NURSERY SCHOOL, KINDERGARTEN, and the biographic entry on Maria MONTESSORI. Another group of articles on methods and materials includes TEXTBOOKS; AUDIO-VISUAL MATERIALS IN EDUCATION; TELEVISION, EDUCATIONAL; PROGRAMMED INSTRUCTION; and TEACHING MACHINE.

A major category of education receiving special treatment is that covered in RELIGIOUS EDUCATION, PAROCHIAL SCHOOL, and RELEASED TIME.

One function of this Study Guide is to suggest the range of articles available on the principal divisions of education. This variety may be further exemplified with reference to the history of education. The numerous pertinent articles include SEVEN LIBERAL ARTS; AZHAR, UNIVERSITY OF AL-; PARIS, UNIVERSITY OF; OXFORD, UNIVERSITY OF; CAMBRIDGE, UNIVERSITY OF; HARVARD UNIVERSITY; CHAUTAUQUA; and biographies of John Amos COMENIUS, Friedrich FROEBEL, Johann PESTALOZZI, Elizabeth PEABODY, Horace MANN, Henry BARNARD, and Abraham FLEXNER, among others.

The range of articles on higher education is explained in the Study Guide with the entry COLLEGE. Particularly noteworthy is the table of accredited institutions of higher education in the United States and Canada, under the title UNIVERSITIES AND COLLEGES. Articles on countries, Canadian provinces, and U.S. states contain information on educational systems. Literacy figures, given for most countries, are one index of the scope and effectiveness of educational programs.

Major articles on education conclude with lists of books recommended for further reading. These and other sources may be available in the library. The library may also provide sources for keeping up with the progress of education around the world.

---

the continuing themes in the history of education has been the problem of extending the opportunity to attend school to those who have been unable to progress because of illiteracy.

Throughout much of the Greco-Roman period those boys who were educated usually went to the homes of their teachers. Often they were accompanied by household slaves known as pedagogues. The boys might spend time first with a grammarian for literary and writing instruction, then journey to a music or elocution teacher, and end the afternoon at a gymnasium. They had no books, just wax tablets on which they inscribed letters or words with a stylus. They counted on their fingers. Most teaching consisted of lecturing, and the ability to memorize was the prime need of the pupil.

Gradually, formal schools at various levels were established. By 150 B.C., small Roman boys would go for a few years to the elementary school, the *ludus;* then those who went on would train with a Greek or Latin grammarian who taught beyond the fundamentals previously instilled. A limited number of able upper-class boys would move on to the rhetorical school for oratorical training as well as advanced studies in other areas. This school was adopted from the Greeks, the first such school of rhetoric having been opened by Isocrates in Athens c.392 B.C. The Romans also borrowed the bulk of their curriculum, meth-

ods, and even their teachers from Greece. However, Rome had few institutions of higher education to match the apex of the Greek educational ladder, the philosophical schools such as those at Athens founded by Plato and Aristotle. Even at the height of the Empire, young Romans went abroad for their final education—to Hellenistic schools at Athens, Rhodes, Pergamum, and to the famous library and museum at Alexandria.

The Greek curriculum blended effectively emphases upon the intellectual, the aesthetic, and the physical. The traditional offerings that emerged from the Greek experience were modified and extended by the Romans. These evolved into the liberal arts—the subject matter fit for the upbringing of a young freeman. Down through the centuries in many other nations, particularly at secondary and higher levels, the content that met the needs of an elite minority in ancient Greece and Rome came to be the prototype of what was educationally proper.

Among the great Greek teachers was Socrates (469–399 B.C.), the self-styled "gadfly of Athens." For his questions and activities he was sentenced to death, thus providing one of the first examples of a problem of academic freedom, that is, of the right of the teacher and pupil to pursue the truth as they see it. Socrates' greatest pupil was Plato (429–347 B.C.). Plato's influence can be traced in educational theory from his own day to the 20th century.

Although he presented a plan for education in his own world—the emphasis being on the training of philosophers as leaders—his impact on education was even greater in other lands and times than in ancient Athens. Aristotle (384–322 B.C.), a student in Plato's Academy, became another of the world's most influential philosophers and an unequaled systematizer of scientific knowledge. His works formed the most important part of the courses of study in medieval universities a thousand years after his death.

The greatest Roman educator, Quintilian, had a renowned school of rhetoric and even taught the Emperor's nephews. He wrote the *Institutes of Oratory* (c.95 A.D.), the first practical book on the methodology of teaching. In this volume he urged such enlightened practices as group learning rather than tutorial instruction, graded materials to meet varied pupil needs, the gentle treatment of the learner, allowing all students to taste some success, and finding a place for enjoyment in learning. Unfortunately most schools and teachers of Quintilian's time did not reflect his modern viewpoints, and Roman education declined with the deterioration of the Empire from the 3d to the 5th century A.D. The Romans had done little to modify the adopted Greek education and to develop a more effective program of education for the Roman citizen. Along with the other reasons cited for the collapse of Rome should be noted the failure to maintain a satisfactory program for the general education of the masses and an effective leadership training for the elite that would have enabled them to help resolve the mounting problems challenging their society.

The Middle Ages. This period stretches from the last days of the Roman Empire into the 14th or 15th century. During the Dark Ages (about 500 to 800 A.D.) some education was maintained in a few of the town schools in France and Italy that had been established under Roman authority. Schooling was also carried on during this period by the priests and leaders of the Christian church who earlier had begun instructing youth and converts in the catacombs of Rome. As the Church grew to be the focus and force of medieval life, its educational activities expanded.

The most famous schools of this period were the monastery schools, where "the flickering lamp of learning was kept burning" by monks who copied scrolls and manuscripts and sent forth most of the educated people who were to be teachers in the years ahead. The Frankish Emperor Charlemagne (771–814) brought the scholar Alcuin from England to instruct in his palace school. They attempted to institute schools in connection with the parish churches throughout the Empire. However, it was many years before the parish or song schools emerged in towns and villages to become the most common source of formal education in Europe. These schools, when they did begin to function, were limited to a few years of mediocre instruction in reading, writing, counting, and religion.

Some of the schools attached to cathedrals in the large cities eventually extended their offerings and, by the 12th century, universities were beginning to grow out of these institutions. Centered around popular teachers, universities became important factors in late medieval society. By the end of the 15th century there were approximately 75 universities in Europe.

The Bettmann Archive
Engraving (c.1400) shows a teacher at the University of Paris leading scholars in discussion. All wear academic caps and gowns.

In the feudal period most people in the West remained illiterate. The main aim of existence being the attainment of heaven in the next life, there was limited concern for the betterment of earthly conditions. The dominant educational philosophy was scholasticism, emphasizing the development of reason and faith, which found its best-known spokesman in St. Thomas Aquinas, the great 13th-century Christian philosopher. In general, this was a period in which life followed a pattern and change came slowly. Yet, long before the end of the Middle Ages, events took place that started a process of revolutionary change. The Crusades in the 11th and 12th centuries were an epochal development in that they turned the eyes of Western men outside their own provinces and beyond Europe. As a result of the contacts between East and West that accompanied the military expeditions to recover the Holy Land for Christendom, the achievements of Near Eastern culture were introduced into Europe. The returning Crusaders had discovered a sophisticated land of Oriental and old Hellenistic culture that had maintained learning at a high level while the West had been enveloped in the Dark Ages. European scholars had already discovered, in the mosques and Islamic universities of Spain, Sicily, and North Africa, ancient Hebrew, Greek, and Roman knowledge, lost to the West in the intervening years. Here much of the ancient as well as Far Eastern learning had been gathered and was expounded by Muslim scholars.

Along with an interest in new parts of the world, there were other developments. A spirit of intellectual curiosity grew in Europe; trade developed and cities began to grow; exploration was carried on; new businesses appeared; and there was a need for and interest in more education and new kinds of education. Western man was ready for the Renaissance.

The Renaissance. The Renaissance, a development that began in the 14th century and extended into the 16th, found Western man torn between a growing interest in the worth and joy of this life (humanism) and his traditional Christian concerns. He had found infidels living better and more intelligently than he did; he had been introduced to paved roads, street lighting, sewage systems, and homes with circulating heat in a non-Christian culture. He now also knew that many of the ancient Greeks and Romans lived better than he and that much of his learning was incomplete and in error. Medieval philosophers such as Abelard (1079–1142) and, later, Roger Bacon and William of Occam had attacked the established beliefs that characterized the learning of the Middle Ages. The commercial revolution—the growth of business and industry—was another herald of a new era. Recently introduced inventions such as cheap paper and movable type, gunpowder, and the compass were other aspects of the economic, social, and political changes that were to be much more than a "rebirth" (as the Renaissance has been too narrowly defined).

Some humanists turned toward the rich life on this earth as a prime goal, and secular interests reduced the dominance of the Papacy and the Church. There was a great renewal of interest in the classics of the pagan Greeks and Romans and in the Greek and Latin languages. However, the outstanding schools and scholars of the Renaissance evidenced a worthy amalgamation of devotion to Christian beliefs and concern for promoting the welfare of mankind.

The best-known Renaissance school was the Palace school headed by Vittorino da Feltre (1378–1446) in northern Italy. In its broad and practical curriculum—its concern for a healthy, pleasant environment, for meeting individual differences, and for preparing young men for this world who were also Christian gentlemen—it personified the best of Quintilian (whose works had recently been rediscovered) as well as the best educational thinking of its own time.

Leading Renaissance educators were soon attacking "Ciceronianism," an educational malpractice that was spreading and subverting the original purposes of revitalized education. What they attacked was the slavish reading, memorization, and emulation of the ancients, particularly the Roman orator Cicero. In vain, great educational thinkers and writers of the period, such as Juan Vives (1492–1540), Desiderius Erasmus (1467–1536), and Michel de Montaigne (1533–92), fought the formalism and artificiality that appeared. These humanists deplored schooling in which the "kernel of knowledge was overlooked and lost because of superficial preoccupation with the husk." Additionally, there was a strong medieval carry-over in the dominant scholastic and religious elements in all levels of schooling that reacted against many new ideas and approaches. The door to educational improvement, set ajar at the beginning of this age, was, therefore, never fully opened. Moreover, the ensuing struggles of the Reformation further impeded educational progress.

The Reformation Era. In the 16th and 17th centuries various groups broke away from the Roman Catholic Church, and Protestantism became a force in the world. The Reformation, however, cannot be understood in merely religious terms, for it developed as part of a total pattern of economic, social, and political change that marked the thought and life of the Renaissance. Men like Martin Luther and Henry VIII were both political and religious leaders. With them appeared forces that made for educational retrogression as well as for educational progress. Luther advocated educational reforms. He wanted the masses educated so they could read for themselves his High German translation of the Bible. He urged a comprehensive curriculum and stressed the importance of proper teacher education. He favored state support and enforcement of educational attendance. This reflected his recognition that his movement would have collapsed without financial and military support from political leaders. However, most education in Europe was in Catholic hands. Schools, prime factors in inculcating new Protestant views, thus early became directly involved in the religious struggles.

A growing intolerance was evidenced by all sects. Diplomas began to be used as teaching licenses to enforce orthodoxy; viewpoints that conflicted were rejected. Books that spread contrary ideas, and even the men who wrote them, were burned. Schools were closed down by the thousands as armies crisscrossed Europe, each army suppressing the schools controlled or taught by persons of conflicting religious views. Many leaders came to seek an educational system that would primarily indoctrinate and hold the masses in line, teaching them to follow orders.

There were, of course, positive educational developments during this period. Johannes Sturm opened the prototype of the classical European secondary school at Strasbourg in 1538. His Gymnasium became a model and influenced for generations the content and conduct of secondary education in English and French schools and many other institutions modeled upon these throughout the world. Catholic orders active in the Counter Reformation—for example, the Jesuits, the Ursuline sisters, the Piarist fathers, and later the Christian brothers—made significant contributions to educating the lower classes, to women's education, to improved methodology, and to teacher education. Able teachers such as Philip Melanchthon (1479–1560) in Lutheran Germany and Richard Mulcaster (1530–1611) in England inspired others and wrote important educational reports and treatises. Mulcaster was typical of the enlightened educator far ahead of his time. He called for the education of girls, demanded instruction in the vernacular, sought the introduction of more practical subjects, crusaded for public education, urged the improvement of the profession by teacher training institutes in the universities, as well as through adequate salaries, and even advocated the forerunner of parent-and-teacher organizations.

One of the most striking educational developments of the Reformation stemmed from John Calvin and the theocratic and puritanic state he erected in Geneva. In 1559 he founded his famous Academy. Later he inaugurated an educational system for all boys that eventually sent out ministers and scholars to carry his ideas throughout Europe and to America. The French Huguenots, the Scotch Presbyterians, the Dutch Reformed Church, the American Puritans, and the later offshoot Congregationalists, Baptists, and others felt a determination to establish schools so that literate and good men would be available to serve God.

In the New World, although the Spanish had founded flourishing universities in Latin America, it was chiefly these Calvinist groups who established the school system that was to characterize education in what was to become the United States. School laws passed as early as 1642 and 1647 in Massachusetts combined public and private efforts and ordered parents to educate their children, making mandatory the establishment of elementary and Latin grammar schools. These same settlers, concerned over the leadership of their churches and their communities, founded the first colleges in New England, beginning with Harvard (1636). The Reformation conflicts served a valuable purpose in that they drove many people out of Europe to colonize North America. These emigrants brought with them their determination to be free, to better themselves, and to be educated. Their traditions and aspirations were to shape the unique destiny of education in America.

The Age of Reason. From the late 17th century to the early 19th century stretches an era of ferment and reaction known as the Enlightenment and also as the period of the rise of the common man. The great autocratic rulers of this period, men like Louis XIV and Frederick the Great, symbolized forces of absolutism and nationalism that could not stem the tides of change. Capitalism emerged as the economic system of the West; older philosophies and religious views were challenged; rigid social stratification was altered by the rise of the new middle classes; the landed aristocracy fell before peasant revolts and the growing wealth of the cities. Even absolute monarchies were swept away by the spirit of the age, identified with the Glorious Revolution in Great Britain (1688), the American Revolution (1776), and the French Revolution (1789). The victory of the forces of liberalism, coupled with the first phases of the industrial revolution, had a significant impact upon education.

Foremost among the precursors of this new era was Francis Bacon (1561–1626), English politician and writer, whose strong interest in science led him to attack current educational conditions. He opposed medieval influences and urged in his *Novum Organum* (the New Logic, meant to replace the still-flourishing authority of Aristotle) an end to the three types of learning then prevalent—the fantastical (myths and superstitions), the contentious (scholastic argumentation), and the delicate (meaningless verbalization). Bacon believed that the prime need was for man to free himself of the "idols of the past" and claimed this could best be done by applying the inductive approach to learning. Sometimes called the scientific method, this inductive approach (the observer moves from particulars to generalizations) was needed to balance the then prevalent deductive method, which fits observed particulars to predetermined principles.

By 1700 schools had not progressed materially in more than 500 years. In Europe and America large segments of the population were illiterate, education remained centered around the training of an elite for leadership, and techniques and materials were not far different from those used in Roman and medieval times. Parish schools, tied to a local church, were probably the most typical found in the Western world. Taught by a pastor or his assistant, often in Latin, children received drill in reading, writing, and arithmetic, a strong dose of Scripture, and some training in singing. In addition to these schools there were privately sponsored elementary schools and rapidly increasing numbers of town schools in the growing municipalities. All of these institutions taught approximately the same subjects, and the children who attended school usually did so for only several years—until they could be put to work. In the latter two types of elementary schools, teaching was generally conducted in the vernacular. The town schools frequently combined public and private resources. Some aspects of the school program were provided by parents or religious groups, while other parts were paid for by the community. In addition to these schools, the guilds had established in the cities reading, writing, and counting schools for their apprentices. In the rural areas there were the ineffectual dame schools (especially in Britain and the colonies) and hedge schools (on the Continent) where unprepared women and men herded children into their homes or some deserted building for a few hours of the day. At elementary levels most teachers still had no special training, held low social status, and drew starvation wages.

In both Europe and America, religious and philanthropic fervor, as well as the fact that ill-trained and indigent people were found in ever greater numbers in the manufacturing centers, led to the creation of charity and workhouse schools. Children placed in these schools attended on a boarding or day basis and were taught the four R's (reading, writing, arithmetic, and religion), frequently receiving training for a position in one of the trades or in domestic service. Often these schools were attached to a shop or a factory where the children could be put immediately to work. These were almost the only free schools; all others required a fee of some kind or, perhaps, bartered goods. This heritage of the pauper school being the free school worked for years against the success and popularity of public education. Many middle- and even lower-class persons refused to send their children to the early public schools because of the supposed taint of pauperism.

At secondary levels the classical program of the typical Latin grammar school or gymnasium served the relatively few students who were being prepared for college. Some of the private British schools were called "public" because anyone who could afford them and could pass their entrance requirements was admissible; however, these institutions were largely limited to the well-to-do. Some

schools maintained by religious orders—the early Jesuit secondary schools, for example—did provide scholarships and charged no fees. A certain number of free openings were also provided in secondary schools founded by the guilds. These schools were established in the humanist tradition and were meant to prepare the sons of tradesmen and merchants for the life of upper-class leisure that the profits of the economic revolution were bringing to the rising middle classes.

Forces in society at this time also called for a more practical secondary education. Specialized skills and new kinds of knowledge were needed which the classical schools could not provide. As has been typical in the history of education, the currently popular institution refused to modify its program to serve these needs, hence a new form of secondary school appeared. Generally called the academy, it arose in Europe and America at about the same time. Johann Hecker is credited with opening one of the first of these second-track secondary schools in Prussia in 1747. In England the Puritan academies reflected the viewpoint of John Milton's tractate, *Of Education*, which had proposed a broader and more realistic educational program. In America the academy sponsored by Benjamin Franklin opened in 1751. It had a classical division and practical divisions offering courses such as navigation and surveying. Ultimately, in the United States, the academy with its de-emphasis of classical languages was to replace the old Latin grammar school as the dominant secondary institution. As the academy matured, however, it became less responsive to new demands and after the Civil War was replaced by the public high school (first established in Boston in 1821) as the major secondary school.

The colleges and universities resisted change even more than the lower schools, remaining much like their medieval counterparts. The great scientific discoveries and technical developments of the age were arrived at by independent inventors in the new industrial establishments or through research sponsored by various scientific societies. The universities were isolated from the sweep of the industrial revolution. Therefore, to develop the necessary advanced training of engineers, for example, it was necessary to create special technical institutes. Thus, in the United States, Rensselaer Polytechnic Institute was established in 1824 for scientific and mechanical education. Such schools have continued to provide most of the advanced technical training in Europe.

The improvements in education that did appear during this era stemmed from the work and writings of a number of brilliant men. John Amos Comenius (1592–1670), a Moravian called the "grandfather of modern education," urged in his *Great Didactic* schools for all children of both sexes in a broad, practical, well-organized program of four six-year periods of education. The teaching was to be based upon 37 "natural principles of learning" and faciliated by books and materials especially prepared for children and students. One reason education had progressed so slowly through the years was that instructors had attempted to teach primarily with volumes meant for the adult reader. Comenius' most famous contribution was the development of simple, pictorial books to help teach Latin to children for whom it was a foreign tongue.

His works were translated into many languages. He served as an educational consultant in a number of European countries and inspired educational leaders who followed him.

John Locke (1632–1704) also had influence through his educational and psychological writings, as did the French romanticist Jean Jacques Rousseau (1712–78). Present-day educational historians have designated Rousseau's *Émile* as the most influential book in the history of education. Rousseau was a popularizer of worthwhile ideas, reaching back beyond Locke and Comenius to the Renaissance educators and to Quintilian. Unfortunately he incorporated many half-truths and erroneous views into his presentation, and these led well-meaning followers into some sad educational experiences. However, in his emphasis upon a child-centered education, one that is in accord with the natural development of the individual, and his attack on the coldly formal rote-memorization, adult-society focused, traditional program, Rousseau provided a needed antidote to the educational stagnation of his times. He is often called the "father" of what came to be known 150 years later as progressive education. Some of Rousseau's disciples were particularly effective in applying his valuable ideas for educational regeneration. Johann Basedow (1723–90) was a German educator whose writings and demonstration and training school at Dessau included such innovations as sex and hygiene instruction, student government, summer camps, correlated instruction, and classes in current events. Unfortunately, the enlightened emphases and techniques employed by such schools were denied the great bulk of children being educated in the 18th century. Nevertheless, the stage had been set for the developments of the 1800's and the first steps of modern education.

The Rise of Modern Education. By the early 19th century the importance of education was coming to be recognized by more and more people from all classes of society. Prussia and France developed effective national systems of education. Americans concerned with better schools and teacher training were impressed with developments in Europe, and men like Horace Mann (1796–1859) and Henry Barnard (1811–1900) devoted their lives to creating the common school (the free, public elementary school), to improving teaching conditions and salaries, improving teacher education, and building a true profession of education in the United States. Since by law and tradition educational efforts in this nation were controlled at the state and local level, these efforts were to prove piecemeal and unbelievably slow and difficult in fulfillment.

Meanwhile, European educational reformers continued to work toward long-sought educational improvements. Johann Pestalozzi (1746–1827), a Swiss teacher, after 30 years of handling orphans, opened in an old castle at Yverdon (1805) what was to become the most famous school in the history of education. He employed the psychology suggested in his *Leonard and Gertrude* and *How Gertrude Teaches Her Children* which stressed kindliness in the classroom and an activity approach with the use of field trips, models, and object lessons. Like Locke and Rousseau, he believed in the importance of sense perceptions and in learning by doing. His approaches and materials were planned to gradually lead the pupil to comprehension by moving from the simple and the concrete to the complex and abstract. His practices became very influential in teacher education in the United States, spreading from their beginnings at the training school at Oswego, New York.

The German professor Johann Herbart (1776–1841) did the most to systematize many of Pestalozzi's ideas and these became popular as a five-step process for ordering a successful lesson. Toward the end of the 19th century his enthusiastic followers in the expanding normal schools of the United States indoctrinated great numbers of teachers with Herbartian pedagogy.

Another German educator, Friedrich Froebel (1782–1852), applied the theories of Rousseau and Pestalozzi to the education of preschool children. He eventually developed the kindergarten, with its play circle, songs, pantomimes, and blocks and other building materials. Introduced into the United States by German immigrants just prior to the Civil War, the kindergarten spread rapidly, initially as a private institution. In spite of its popularity and the considerable growth of nursery schools for even younger children, in almost half of the states the kindergarten is still not recognized and supported as an integral part of the public school system.

An Italian educator, Maria Montessori (1870–1952), was also concerned with the education of little children. Working with retarded boys and girls, she came to recognize the potential for learning existing in the very young and not usually realized by elementary education. She developed clever materials that led preschoolers to read and write, and ultimately she outlined an entire elementary program. Montessori societies and schools spread around the globe and are still functioning, especially in European countries.

European viewpoints continued to have influence in America, but in the second half of the 19th century an indigenous school system was being shaped. The battle for the common school—free, public elementary school—had been won. Since increasing numbers aspired to go on to high school, the public school system was expanded above grade eight. In an important test case in 1874 the Michigan Supreme Court approved the use of local taxes to support secondary education and the future of the high school was assured. Its great growth, however, was to occur in the 20th century, for by 1900 only about 10% of eligible youth were in attendance. Meanwhile, theories about improving the structure of the educational system resulted in the beginnings of the junior high school and the junior college. At the university and college level there had also been continuing expansion. The Land-Grant Act of 1862 provided the basis upon which the American state universities rose to prominence. These multipurpose institutions, serving many educational functions, evolved as the apex of a system of universal public education unequaled in any other country of the world.

One of the most interesting aspects of the history of education is that within the American pattern educational leaders adapted, applied, and experimented with a host of the best educational ideas suggested by the great educators of the past—ideas that frequently had not found acceptance on a significant scale in other countries. Some of the foreign contributions were found wanting.

Such was the monitorial system of Joseph Lancaster (1778-1838), which had older pupils drill rooms full of younger children; it disappeared after extended trials in Eastern cities in the early 19th century. Eventually a blend of the more liberal European views found expression in the progressive education movement, which also took root around the ideas of Francis W. Parker (1837-1902) and John Dewey (1859-1952). Dewey was the most influential American educational theorist, both in his own land and abroad. Though at first centered upon the elementary school child, the progressive movement soon influenced all levels of American education, taking a variety of directions and emphases. This is not to say that all schools in the United States adopted progressive educational policies, for other philosophies of education had adherents, and many schools continued their traditional programs without drastic change. But it is certain that progressive ideas were profusely discussed by educators, and it is probable that all schools felt some influence from this new philosophy of education. In Europe and other parts of the world the New Education Fellowship promoted this needs-and-problem-centered approach; but traditions in education were stronger and times were not ripe. Where progressive ideas did take root, they were soon stamped out by totalitarian governments.

As the people of the United States examined their schools with increasingly critical eyes in the light of the impact of two world wars, a great depression, the cold war and the problems presented by sudden developments in science and technology, a reaction against progressive theories set in. Many argue that progressive education became the whipping boy for failures and weaknesses whose sources were actually far beyond the school. Others contend that the problems of the times demanded a new look at the schools. In any case, while other peoples of the world were accepting education in the United States as a model, influential Americans, looking toward goals still unreached and perhaps overlooking what had been achieved by the schools, called for changes and adjustments. These suggested alterations varied from a return to educational emphases of the past to an extended revolution in content, organization, methods, and materials of instruction. That changes would be made seemed certain, but the specific nature of these changes was hard to forecast. Nevertheless, education throughout the world has entered the most rapid and significant era of change in all of history.

Consult Cole, Luella, *A History of Education from Socrates to Montessori* (1950); Butts, R. F., *A Cultural History of Western Education* (2d ed., 1955); Meyer, A. E., *An Educational History of the American People* (1957); Mulhern, James, *A History of Education* (2d ed., 1959); Ulich, Robert, *The Education of Nations* (1961); Gross, R. E., *Heritage of American Education* (1962); Edwards, Newton, and Richey, H. G., *The School in the American Social Order* (2d ed., 1963); French, W. M., *America's Educational Tradition* (1964); Bayles, E. E., and Hood, B. L., *Growth of American Educational Thought and Practice* (1966); Brubacher, J. S., *A History of the Problems of Education* (2d ed., 1966); Sands, L. B., and Gross, R. E., *The History of Education: A Time-Line of Scope and Perspective* (1967).

RICHARD E. GROSS, Stanford University

THEORIES OF EDUCATION

Many philosophers have put forth theories of what education should aim for and how it should work toward its goals. Many writers, thinkers, and teachers have drawn on the work of philosophers to build up their own concepts of education. Plato presented a scheme for education in Greece. Hundreds of scholars since his time have used his ideas as starting points for newer philosophies of education. Thinkers from Plato and Aristotle down to William James and John Dewey have influenced the work of the schools. Yet theories are never put into practice completely. What actually goes on in the schools is usually a compromise between what people at a given period believe should be done and what their time, funds, abilities, and other resources enable them to do. A formal study of educational philosophy starts with theories and proceeds to the sort of schooling a theory calls for. Another and simpler way to approach theories of education is to take a few basic questions about education and to discuss theories bearing on them, with frequent reference to what is actually done in the schools.

Theories About the Extent of Education. A basic question is, how many people should receive education? Everyone, of course, gets education in the broad sense of training in the basic ways of society, but formal education in schools and colleges is another matter. In the early stages of history formal training was considered proper only for a small group—scribes, priests, and others who would use their special knowledge to help run a society. The government of China was for centuries staffed by an elite group of civil servants who had passed exhaustive tests of scholarship. Education for the lower classes was not considered necessary.

In Western culture, education was for a long time a privilege of the aristocracy. Gradually, however, the belief grew that boys should have at least elementary schooling. Advanced study remained something for the few. Belief in universal education—schooling for all boys and girls—is a comparatively recent idea. As democratic concepts of government grew in Europe and America, belief in the need for education grew also. Among many statements of the idea that the people of a democratic society must be educated is the following, by President James Madison: "A popular Government, without popular information or the means of acquiring it, is but a Prologue to a Farce or a Tragedy; or perhaps both. Knowledge will forever govern ignorance: And a people who mean to be their own Governors, must arm themselves with the power which knowledge gives."

In the 20th century the belief is firmly established in most of the highly developed countries that public schooling should be compulsory at least through the elementary grades and should be available to all boys and girls at least through high school. There is a growing belief, particularly in the United States, that two or four more years of education should be provided at public expense. For the rest of the world it is probably safe to state that the aim of all nations is to provide schools for all their people at least at the elementary level. An expansion of public education to the secondary and even higher levels is probably the long-range aim of many countries. For information on progress toward long-range aims, see articles on national systems of education and on elementary, secondary, and higher education.

Even in countries that have accepted the principle of universal education, there is debate on how much education and what kind of education should be provided. Some argue that schooling through the higher levels should be free to all. But others maintain the centuries-old position that advanced education should be concentrated on the elite group whose members have the capacity to become leaders in various fields. Finding and training superior students in the hope that they will make contributions to the strength and welfare of their country have become major concerns of educators in the United States, indeed in most nations. How to provide for gifted students while still carrying out the schools' obligation to educate all young people, including the handicapped, is a much-debated problem. Colleges and universities have to face the issue of trying to take in all who apply or of trying to select a limited number who can work at a high level. One theory is that all children should be given basic education, but that a selection should then be made of gifted individuals who would receive intensive higher schooling, whereas the less well-endowed would get vocational training.

Theories About the Control and Support of Education. Public education is paid for by taxes collected by government. Should it also be run by government? And should the public schools be the only schools allowed to teach? At one extreme is the belief that education should be controlled by the national government. When this theory is put into practice, as it is in many Communist countries, a major function of the schools is to teach conformity to a political doctrine. Church schools and other private schools are not tolerated. At the other extreme is the position that schools should be free of control by the national government. In the United States, church schools and other private schools operate alongside the public schools. The majority of colleges and universities are privately controlled. The public schools are regulated by state rather than federal law, and the immediate control of the schools is in the hands of local boards of education. The state governments retain considerable power over all schools, particularly through such means as certification laws, which put limits on who can be allowed to teach. It is generally believed that all schools must serve certain general purposes, such as providing courses in English and courses in history. It is not contended that schools, any more than other institutions, can be entirely free of regulation. Within broad limits, however, the schools and colleges exercise academic freedom.

Related to control is the question of support. In the United States the principle is accepted that elementary and high schools—and a growing number of colleges—are to be paid for out of taxes. Individuals retain the right to pay the tuition fees of private institutions if they want to, though they still contribute to the taxes that support the public schools. State governments and the federal government have tended to make larger and larger contributions to the support of schools. A major issue has developed over federal aid to education, since many fear that a large investment of federal funds in the schools will lead to federal control.

Theories About Content and Method. Theories about content (what is to be taught) and method (how it is to be taught) are built up from many sources. Psychology, for example, has contributed new understanding of the learning process and new proposals for teaching methods. Through studies of aptitudes and interests psychologists have also contributed to decisions about what subjects different people should study. Even more basic sources of theories are concepts of the aims of education, some of which have already been noted. Where the aim is indoctrination in the ways of a government, content and teaching are directed toward one goal. Examples of what might be called "society-centered education" can be found through history, from ancient Sparta to Fascist Italy to Communist China. The task of the schools, according to absolutist thinkers, is to train obedient fighters or workers. Truth, in their view, is what the state says is true, and facts are used or repressed according to whether or not they fit the party line. Another extreme of theory might be called "individual-centered education." This concept, advocated by Jean Jacques Rousseau but seldom put into practice, would allow the child almost complete freedom to learn whatever seemed to help his individual development. A much more workable theory, one that is exemplified in the practice of the majority of schools, has been called the "interactive position." The purposes of education, according to this concept, include the needs both of society and of the individual. He is to be helped to develop as a free man; he is also to be helped to be a useful member of his society, able to carry out his responsibilities as a citizen. This position respects the individual, whether he becomes a plain citizen or an artistic genius, but it also considers the needs of society and government.

Within this interactive position there is room for major differences of opinion about what kind of content and method will best serve the needs of the individual and his society. There are also differences as to how much individualism is to be encouraged. At the conservative end of the scale are those who believe that education should preserve and pass on the cultural heritage with as little change as possible. These people hold that the content of education should consist chiefly of traditional subjects such as history, languages, and mathematics; that learning the facts and principles established by scholars is more important for the learner than applying knowledge to specific problems; and that teachers should be experts in their subjects, should make logical presentations of subjects, and should run their classes in such a way as to ensure efficient learning. This theory of education is sometimes termed "essentialist," from its emphasis on a body of essential knowledge. Some educational philosophers who can be classed as essentialists advocate less emphasis on subject matter for its own sake and more on using it as a means to reach universally true ideas. They also encourage more spontaneity in the learner, but nevertheless wish the teacher to remain authoritative.

Another conservative approach to education is that which is founded on religious beliefs. The content of traditional Muslim education, for example, was found in one book, the Koran. In many Christian countries education is carried on by members of churches, and the content includes religious doctrine. In some countries, such as Spain, religious training is part of the curriculum of the public schools. In the United States, on the other hand, there is a strongly held belief that the public schools must not engage in religious instruction.

Still another philosophy that can be classed as conservative is that which makes training the intellect, the reasoning powers, the goal of education. Subjects are picked for their value in developing logical reasoning. Mathematics and philosophy are of greatest value for demonstrating and requiring logical thinking. Vocational courses are of comparatively minor value. A variety of teaching techniques can be used, though all must help the student sharpen his intellect. A well-known example of the content and method of this theory of education is the "Great Books" program, which builds a curriculum around a selection of classic works of philosophy, science, and literature.

All the conservative theories of education tend to focus on what is to be learned, on mastering established knowledge or on discovering ultimate truth through reason, rather than on the learner. Advocates of these theories believe, of course, that what they propose will be best for those who learn. The best guide for the present world, they maintain, is to be found in established wisdom, intellectual training, or eternal truth. A different theory, sometimes known as "experimentalism," focuses on the learner and what are considered to be his interests and needs. This theory places emphasis in the school on the process of solving problems rather than on acquiring facts and principles that can later be used as guides. It holds that subject matter should be selected for its utility in solving the problem under immediate study. The teacher, according to this theory, is more a helper and an adviser than one who directs from a superior position, though it is important that the teacher guide students to work on real problems and to reach meaningful solutions. This experimentalist theory has had its greatest importance in the United States. As a philosophic position it shows the influence of two Americans, William James and John Dewey.

Many of Dewey's educational theories were given an expression, not without distortion, in the progressive education movement, which was influential for several generations but lost force after World War II. It should be noted that this movement included numerous other influences running back to the French philosopher Rousseau. Progressives put such emphasis on the learner that they often spoke of child-centered schools.

The theories described earlier can be called conservative in that they tend to stress preserving and passing on the culture with as little change as possible. Fixed values are to be used as guides for conduct. Progressive education can be called liberal because of its belief that changing approaches are needed in a changing world. Ideas are judged by whether or not they get results rather than against a standard of ultimate truth. Progressives have

argued that the schools should have a role in making necessary changes in society.

Some modern theorists in the United States contend that it is the proper task of the schools to bring about drastic changes in society. Reconstructionism, as this position is called, sets up high ideals for improving social and political life. Critics have pointed out, however, the risk that a school setting out to remake society may become a society-centered school—in fact, an authoritarian school.

In summary, there are so many theories of education and such a gap between theory and practice that it is difficult to state which theories are of most importance in the world. Some generalizations can be made, however. One is that more people than ever before believe that some form of education is necessary for all citizens. In the nations that have become independent since World War II, notable efforts have been made to increase literacy and to teach basic skills needed in societies that are becoming industrialized. In many countries education is a powerful political tool or weapon, a means to make people loyal to a cause or party.

In the United States education is regarded as an unquestioned necessity for the citizens of a democracy, as a right open to all, and as a means to improvement of the individual and maintenance and strengthening of society. Theorists disagree on how to improve and what to maintain, but not on the importance of education. Further details on actual programs in many lands and at various levels will be found in the discussion of the history of education in earlier pages of the present article. Also pertinent are surveys of national systems of education and of elementary, secondary, and higher education and the entries listed below under *See also*.

Consult Dewey, John, *Democracy and Education* (1916) and *Experience and Education* (1938); Cunningham, W. F., *The Pivotal Problems of Education* (1940); National Society for the Study of Education, *Philosophies of Education* (41st yearbook, 1942) and *Modern Philosophies and Education* (54th yearbook, 1955); Brameld, Theodore, *Toward a Reconstructed Philosophy of Education* (1956); Butler, J. D., *Four Philosophies and Their Practice in Education and Religion* (rev. ed., 1957); *Education and Philosophy: The Year Book of Education, 1957*, ed. by G. Z. F. Bereday and J. A. Lauwerys (1957); Wegener, F. C., *The Organic Philosophy of Education* (1957); Weber, C. O., *Basic Philosophies of Education* (1960); Broudy, H. S., *Building a Philosophy of Education* (2d ed., 1961); Cremin, L. A., *The Transformation of the School: Progressivism in American Education, 1876–1957* (1961); Morris, V. C., *Philosophy and the American School* (1961).

WILLIAM R. ODELL, Stanford University

NATIONAL SYSTEMS OF EDUCATION

When studying the schools of one country and comparing them with those of other countries, certain key questions can be asked. The most basic question might seem to be: What are the aims of education in a particular country? It may be possible to find in print a statement of aims, but there may be a great gap between stated goals and observed practice. Ideas and theories cannot by themselves create educational systems. For many nations, moreover, no single, simple statement of aims can be found to stand for all the schools. Hence, it is necessary to consider practices in a country's schools in order to understand how education is controlled, who gets educated, and which courses of study are emphasized most.

How Is Education Controlled? The first question, then, concerns the control of education. In some countries many aspects of public educational policy are directed by a division of the central government, for example, the Ministry of Education and Popular Culture in Czechoslovakia, the Ministry of National Education in France, and the Ministry of Public Instruction in Italy. In the Soviet Union there is an all-Union Ministry of Higher Education, but each republic has its own ministry in charge of school budgets, curriculum, and issue of textbooks. General policy, however, is laid down in the constitution and can be set by the central government, as in the 1958 "Law on Strengthening the Ties Between School and Life and on Further Developing the Public Education System in the U.S.S.R." In the People's Republic of China there is some regional and local control of secondary and primary education, but, to quote a report by the United Nations Educational, Scientific and Cultural Organization (UNESCO), "Centralization and State control are two essential elements in the present administration." Centralized control may mean that the schools are regularly and deliberately used to foster nationalism and a particular ideology. On the other hand, the fact that schools are organized and administered by a national bureau may reflect, as in France, a tradition of central direction by which academic standards are set and the nation is kept well provided with civil servants and professional workers.

Other nations favor a more decentralized organization. The United States, Great Britain, Australia, Canada, and the Federal Republic of Germany are examples of countries in which public education is organized and administered by divisions of government below the national level. In these and many other countries, privately run schools and colleges have an important share in education. Parochial schools are part of the tradition of education in Europe and in North and South America, as are universities controlled by churches or by private bodies. In many countries the struggle between church and state for the control of education has, however, been intense.

How Many Are Educated? A second major question is: What proportion of a nation's population receives education? The most significant figures are the percentages of school-age children who are enrolled in schools. Closely related to this question are these others: Are schools compulsory? For how many years? Are girls educated on the same basis as boys? Are the schools tax supported? What is the literacy rate?

The trend seems to be to provide tuition-free, compulsory education for all boys and girls at least through the elementary grades. The rate of progress toward this goal varies enormously. Some nations give schooling to virtually all children up to the age of 14 or more, and are extending educational opportunities to older children and adults. For the whole world, however, only about 400 people out of 1,000 in the 5-to-20 age range get formal education. Thus many countries have a long way to go to reach the aim of universal education. Comparing reports over a period of ten years or so gives a measure of progress.

Related to the question of what share of a country's people gets any education is the question of what proportions progress from the elementary to the secondary level and from the secondary level to higher education. Part-time education and adult education are also important. To take world figures from UNESCO reports, about three-quarters of all those receiving education are enrolled at the first level, more than one-fifth at the level of secondary and vocational schooling, and less than one-twentieth at the university level. Several factors may determine the amount of secondary and higher study reported by a country. One is economic, that is, the ability of government and of individuals to support such education. Another factor is the degree of selectivity at the points of transfer from one level to the next. One tradition in Europe has been to make elementary schooling available to all, but to limit more advanced study, particularly at the university level, to a select minority.

In connection with levels of education, it should be noted that both terminology and standards vary from country to country; hence, comparisons must be made with care. University study in the United States, for example, may mean simply a post-secondary course but usually means study leading to an advanced degree. In Europe, university courses typically mean those leading to degrees which qualify graduates for the major professions—law, medicine, secondary school teaching, the church, and the civil service.

How Much Is Spent for Education? As noted above, the amount of education provided is related to the amount of money spent on education. The total amount may reflect what a country wants to spend, but it may also depend on what the country has available for schools and for other programs. This third basic question, then, should be posed in terms of the percentage of national income devoted to education or of how much spent per inhabitant.

What Programs Get Emphasis? A fourth question, or group of questions, involves any particular emphasis that may be observed in the curriculum. Is academic training given the highest prestige? What is the status of vocational schools? Are extracurricular activities important? Is there stress on such concepts as character building or intellectual training? The range in curricular emphasis from nation to nation is great. Some countries, as in Asia and Africa, may face a major task of teaching everyone to read and write, although, as in India, the aims of education are often broadly stated. In the highly developed nations it may be possible to plan programs that will meet a variety of needs and interests from nursery school to graduate institute.

Still other questions, requiring more detailed knowledge of a country, should be considered in order to fill out the picture of an educational system. Among them are the following: How are teachers trained? What is their status, socially and economically? What methods of teaching and testing are favored? How much attention is paid to modern audio-visual devices? What is the length of the actual school year? What standards, if any, are set for higher education? The list would have to be extended greatly to take account of the tremendous variety of schools and school systems.

General Characteristics of European Education. The answers to the questions so far stated are subject to rapid change. Thus detailed facts and figures must be sought in sources such as those listed in the bibliography at the end of this entry. A number of general observations can be made, however, on the educational systems of leading nations.

To begin with, national systems that give the mass of young people education are of fairly recent origin. It was not until the 19th century that European nations, responding to the forces of nationalism, industrialization, and political democracy, took seriously the task of providing universal and compulsory education. The systems that evolved in different nations were in some ways unique, but there were important features in common. First, shared by all the European prototypes, are the classical Greek and Judaeo-Christian traditions. From these sources two major aims can be recognized as motivating European educators: the pursuit of knowledge for its own sake and the inculcation in students of Christian virtues or morality. Second, a distinction has always been drawn between an education appropriate to the free man and the gentleman—liberal education—and that suited to the artisan—vocational education. The division between mental and intellectual work and less highly esteemed manual work has continued to find expression in the theory and practice of European education. A further belief has persisted, namely that some children are innately more capable than others of benefiting from education.

At least since the 17th century, however, traditional theories have been under attack. By the 18th century the scene was set for an educational battle drawn along sociopolitical lines. Against the classical bookish curriculum was advanced a scientific, realistic course of studies. Against an interest in words was advanced a desire to study things. Against selective education was opposed universal education. And against an education designed to provide students with a deeper and more profound knowledge of God was advanced the theory that education should enable men to maintain political democracy. A further school of thought should be mentioned, that which has its origins in socialism and communism. Karl Marx believed that all instruction if it was to be truly educative should be rooted in labor. The distinction between manual and mental work was felt to be false. Moreover, communist theory suggests that the abilities of individual children are determined more by their environment than by innate abilities. Communist educational policy thus stresses the need not only for universal educa-tion, but also for nonselective schools controlled not by the Church or by private individuals but by the communist state.

As systems of schools grew in Europe, common practices became evident. On the one hand there were the highly selective academic schools preparing able children for the universities, which provided higher education for persons entering the professions of law, medicine, the clergy, or teaching. The links between the academic schools and the universities were very close. The elementary schools, established for the mass of children, provided no access to higher education. Frequently the two systems were administered independently of each other. In some cases, the academic schools were the responsibility of the national government, the elementary schools of the local or municipal authorities. The system of teacher training for the two systems was different. Teachers intended for the academic schools were by tradition graduates of the university. Teachers for the elementary schools were either trained as apprentices or in normal schools, later to become teacher-training colleges. These schools provided an extended general education and some professional training for future teachers.

As for the curriculum, in the academic schools heavy stress was laid upon the ancient classical languages, Greek and Latin. Later, modern languages and science subjects were given more attention. The task of the elementary schools was to teach the "three R's" to as many children as possible. There grew up, to a greater or lesser degree, systems of vocational training for many of these pupils. Separate schools where special vocational skills were taught were most highly developed in the German-speaking lands. In many countries therefore, there came to exist two and sometimes three systems of education: the basic elementary, the academic secondary, and the vocational.

Compulsory attendance at school was gradually introduced during the 19th century. Until World War II a requirement of eight years of attendance, very often starting at the age of six years, was not uncommon. In England the age was five, and in Denmark and the U.S.S.R. seven. Since World War II practically all the reform movements have stressed the need to extend the period of compulsory schooling; a period of 9, 10, or even 11 years was by the early 1960's fairly common, even for children not intending to proceed to higher education.

Another feature of 20th-century reform in Europe has been an attempt to break down the sharp divisions between the academic, highly selective, secondary schools on the one hand, and the elementary and vocationally oriented schools on the other. Thus there have been movements to bring all schools under the same administrative control. Much attention has been paid to possibilities of establishing common, or comprehensive, schools at the post-primary level in place of the existing, highly differentiated organization. In the academic schools particularly, there has been pressure to reorient the curriculum so that greater attention is paid than formerly to scientific and technical subjects. Proposals have been made to bring into closer relationship the training of teachers for all types of schools. Finally, reformers have advocated an extension of higher education both in the universities and in special technological institutions.

London students use sound recording equipment in a voice and speech class. This scene is in a technical high school, of which there has been an increasing number in the United Kingdom since 1945. (A. TESSORE—UNESCO)

United Kingdom. In the United Kingdom the 1944 Education Act made education the responsibility of the Minister of Education and brought all publicly maintained schools in England and Wales under the control of local education authorities. The two distinct systems of education—secondary and elementary—were fused, and in fact three stages were established—the primary, the secondary, and further education. Each of the 146 Local Education Authorities was made responsible for these stages within its area. Administratively, the division between secondary and elementary was removed. Another feature of the act was to bring into more harmonious relationship than previously the church and local authority schools. Under the act the running expenses and a proportion of the capital costs of the church schools were to be met by funds from local authorities. Religious instruction was to be given in all local authority schools, although parents, if they wished, were allowed to withdraw their children from such lessons. Within this framework each local education authority is free to organize its schools as it thinks fit, subject to the submission of its development plans to the Minister of Education and to his approval. Consequently, in the postwar period some authorities proposed to establish so-called comprehensive, or common, secondary schools for children between the ages of 11 and the compulsory-attendance age limit of 15, and many pupils, of course, voluntarily stay on at school to prepare either for university entrance or an occupation. Children transfer from primary schools at the age of 11. After 1964 a Labour government asked local authorities to prepare plans for comprehensive education.

In other areas what is known as the tripartite system exists. On the basis of written tests pupils from primary schools are admitted by the local authority to one of three types of secondary school—the grammar, technical, or secondary modern. The grammar schools prepare students for university entrance at about the age of 18. Secondary modern schools provide a general education for the majority of children (in 1960 about 75% of the age group) up to the age of 15 or 16. Transfers between various types of school are possible, and opportunities are provided in many secondary modern schools for some students to take the General Certificate of Education examination papers (organized and administered by a number of University Examination Boards) for admission to institutes of higher education. Most grammar school students enter for this examination. In England the technical and vocational school tradition is not strong. Nevertheless,

since 1945 there has been a steady growth in the number of technical schools throughout the country. The curriculum of most schools is somewhat restricted, and in the top classes of the grammar school and in the universities it is very specialized. Great importance, however, is placed on extracurricular activities, and adult part-time facilities for education are highly developed.

France. Similar problems have faced French educators. For many years attempts were made to bring secondary and elementary education under the same administrative head. Prior to 1959 in the highly centralized French system a number of directorates existed under the Minister of Education and his cabinet—higher, secondary, elementary, technical, and youth and sports. In 1960 the direction of secondary, elementary, and technical education was co-ordinated under one director general. Considerable efforts have been made in France to raise, within a broad curriculum, the prestige of the scientific subjects in the face of the entrenched position of Greek and Latin in the academic secondary schools (*lycées* and *collèges*). A further problem has concerned the selection of students for the highly academic schools. Many reports, including that of the famous Langevin-Wallon commission, published shortly after World War II, have proposed that selection for particular courses should be postponed and that during the first years of secondary education students should be observed very carefully by their teachers, and advised, on the basis of their abilities, as to which course they should enter. The law of Jan., 1959, stated that between the ages of 11, when students usually enter the secondary school, and 13 there should be such a period of observation, after which students might be directed into long or short courses of either a general or technical nature. Later plans postponed selection.

Attempts have also been made to reform the examination system and especially the *baccalauréat*, taken by the senior students of the *lycées* and *collèges*. Success in this examination gives access to the universities; the failure rate, as in most French school examinations, is high. The French system has been said to be dominated by its examinations. Special certificates and diplomas are awarded to successful candidates in examinations taken at the conclusion of practically every type of school course. Recruitment to posts in the civil service and to some institutions of higher learning (*grandes écoles*) is on the basis of highly competitive examinations, in which the number of successful candidates is determined by the number of vacancies. Throughout the system, however, French edu-

259

cators place very great stress on the need to provide every child with a sound liberal education (*culture générale*).

Germany. In Germany and neighboring lands the reform movements have stressed the desirability of establishing common secondary schools (called *Einheitsschulen*). There, too, attempts have been made to provide a curriculum with a less heavy emphasis on the classical languages. A general feature of the school systems in the Federal Republic of Germany, Austria, and the Netherlands is that the academic schools have been, and are, rather sharply differentiated from the elementary schools, acceptance in the former taking place at about the age of ten. In most of these countries compulsory schooling lasts for at least eight years, and is being extended in many cases to nine years. A number of types of academic secondary school exist: some pay very great attention to Greek and Latin, others devote more time to modern languages and scientific subjects. Generally, the system of technical schools, some of which admit students at the age of 12, is highly developed. One feature of the Federal German system is that part-time education is compulsory to the age of 18. In these schools (*Berufsschulen*) general and vocational education is provided for students who attend school for one day a week. There are professional schools (*Fachschulen*) where highly skilled technicians are trained, and a system of technological universities exists.

Comparisons of the English, French, and German Systems. The three systems mentioned show considerable similarities of organization, and the problems educators face in the various countries of Europe are consequently rather similar. The solutions they propose depend very much, however, on the precise nature of the national theories of education which are widely held. In the United Kingdom, for example, great emphasis is placed upon character training and to achieve this end great attention is paid to games and extracurricular activities. The classical tradition, although it exists in British schools, is not so strongly held as in the Continental schools, where more emphasis is placed on the acquisition of knowledge. French educators insist that their curriculum and methods of teaching provide a liberal and general education and develop in students an ability to think logically and to express themselves clearly. The German concept of a liberal education is somewhat different. It stresses the desirability of enabling individuals to penetrate the surface of appearances to the essential nature of men and things.

Everywhere, the organization of a school system has social, political, and economic consequences. In Europe the academic schools have been used as instruments of selection. Leaders in the professions, in politics, and in industry have been drawn from the academic schools. Educational achievement is replacing the older criteria of social selection—birth and wealth. No longer is formal education reserved for a privileged minority. The schools have provided their products with the desirable occupations in society, the white-collar jobs, and have perpetuated the notion that manual labor is somehow unworthy of the gentleman. And in some cases they have reinforced a class structure previously based upon birth or wealth. In most cases the state, private, or municipal secondary schools have helped to enlarge the middle class. In weighing the various consequences of maintaining these selective schools, social reformers have seen them as conferring on a few persons special privileges. Against policies designed to abolish or reduce the influence of the selective school, it has been maintained that in any population there is an aristocracy of talent—the gifted children—which should provide the society with its leaders. The interests both of individuals and of society will, it is argued, be served best by retaining the selective schools.

The Soviet Union. Communist educational policy differs in this respect, though the U.S.S.R. undoubtedly shares many of the old European traditions. In the pre-Revolutionary era two features distinguished the Russian system from those found in most Western countries. The secondary schools included more science in their curriculum and placed less emphasis on the classical languages than was the case in most Western European countries. Secondly, in spite of the quality of the schools and universities the provision of education was not so widespread. Under the Communists a number of policy decisions were taken, dictated in most cases as much by events as by ideology. First, an attack was made on illiteracy through the provision of universal compulsory education. One feature of this program has remained throughout the changes that have occurred in Soviet policy, namely that there should be common nonselective schools for all children within the age range of compulsory attendance. For many years there was compulsory attendance for seven years and the intention was to extend this period to ten years.

Under the law of Dec., 1958, compulsory schooling was to last for eight years and a complete secondary education was to take eleven years. The law proposed that after eight years students should proceed to one of three kinds

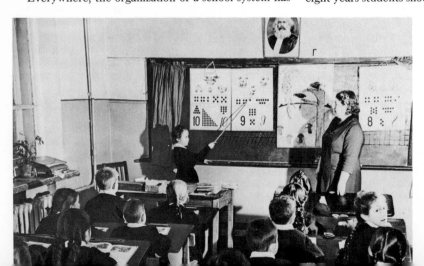

First-year students in Moscow learning their numbers. Arithmetic is basic in the educational systems of all countries. A picture of Karl Marx hangs over the illustrated charts.
(SHOLOMOVICH—UNESCO)

of school to complete their secondary education. One type would be a full-time school in which students would prepare for the universities and institutions of higher learning, but would at the same time learn something of the practical work going on in factories or on farms. The second type of school was to be a technical school working in close co-operation with a factory. In these schools students were to spend between one-third and one-half of their time in school, learning a particular skill, and the rest of the time they would be under instruction in the nearby factory. The third way of completing secondary education was for students to go into productive work in a factory or on a farm and study at school either in the evening or at times through the week made available for them by the factories. The stated object of this law was to break down the distinction between manual and mental work and to bring education, which previously had performed admirably the task of preparing students for college, nearer to life. It should be noted that the expressed objective of communist education is to develop the individual fully—morally, intellectually, physically, and aesthetically—so that he may participate effectively in the building of a truly communist society. In 1965 a decision to return to 10 years of schooling was made.

World-Wide Trends and Problems. Throughout the world today, wherever a well-developed system of formal education exists, the influence of one or other of the European prototypes can be discerned. The agencies through which these influences have spread have been many. Trading companies like those of the British and the Dutch in the East Indies took European schools to the peoples of those areas. Today the great petroleum companies and plantations have taken over their role in such widely separated areas as the remote deserts of Saudi Arabia and parts of South America. The Spanish empire left a continent and a half indelibly stamped with Spanish culture. The British in India established the first modern universities in that area (in Bombay, Madras, and Calcutta). In the Philippines, the United States attempted to build up a system of universal education. Thus educational systems were established, providing a basis on which new nations could build after becoming independent.

It should be noted that history records many instances of conscious attempts on the part of one nation to borrow from another. Peter the Great of Russia did not hesitate to copy some of the English educational institutions to which he sent observers during the 17th century. The leaders of the Meiji Restoration in Japan (1868) made a deliberate attempt to introduce Western-type schools into their backward country. Many European countries quite deliberately based their systems of examinations on the ancient practices of China. Among the European countries and North America there has been constant cross-fertilization, or cultural borrowing. The consequences of such actions are, however, always difficult to foresee. When transplanted from one social environment to another some institutions flourish, whereas others decay or are so transformed as to bear little resemblance to the originals. After World War II many institutions based on U.S. practices were introduced into Japan. School administration was decentralized, the six-three-three-four (primary-junior high-senior high-college) system of schools was put into operation, and there was a vast increase in the number of college and university students. An attempt was made to replace the traditional method of moral education by social studies. Not all these innovations took firm root in a system which was already a mixture of elements from old Japan, 19th-century Europe, and America, and during the 1950's a return was made to many traditional educational practices.

Wherever new nations are attempting to build their own national systems of education the problems that arise are in general similar, but the details differ. Everywhere, efforts are being made to marry to one another institutions that are on the one hand European and on the other indigenous. In India, for example, the government's eight-year basic education program followed by three years of high school represents an attempt to bring into organic harmony elements of the old British system and practices based upon Mahatma Gandhi's proposals that education, in its widest sense, should be craft centered.

One problem tends to dominate all others. In the second half of the 20th century, education is seen as a fundamental human right and also as contributing to economic development. It is apparent that in highly industrialized societies there is bound to be an extension of formal education and training. The provision of universal education is extremely costly, placing heavy demands on a country's resources of manpower, equipment, capital, and land. Other interests, such as defense, health services, and industrial development, compete for the same resources. National policy decisions have to be made concerning the proportion of the nation's resources to be allotted to education. Many economists are of the opinion that for too long the developed nations of the world have made too small an investment in education. For the less developed countries the choice is particularly acute. Often their real resources are tragically slender. There can be no general answer as to whether it is better to invest heavily in education rather than, for example, in the building of factories and hydroelectric works. Nor are decisions about how the available resources should be allocated within education easy to reach. The choice often lies between giving priority to secondary and higher education or to universal primary schooling. To develop secondary and higher education at the expense of universal primary education seems to deny the premise that education is a fundamental human right. When resources are limited the attempt to provide universal education might result at worst in expensive failure and at best in very considerable wastage.

The dilemma cannot be easily resolved, particularly in democratic countries. Educators have no doubt that in highly complex societies, in which industrial automation holds out the promise of vastly increased leisure, more and more formalized education will be needed if young people are to be inducted successfully into adult life. The social, political, and vocational skills they will need will make heavy demands on modern educational systems. The evident need is for a basically scientific and technological education designed to provide for all men a "complete and generous education" which will fit them "to perform justly, skilfully and magnanimously all the offices both private and public of peace and war." The great

EDUCATION AROUND THE WORLD

A main task of education today is teaching modern technology and science to the people of newly emerging nations. The scenes here illustrate the concept that education is a universal human right, and that it provides the basis for economic development and a better life.

Trainees in a metal workshop in Gagnoa, Ivory Coast. The technical center here teaches handicrafts, wood and metal work, and masonry.   (UNITED NATIONS)

The Korean Productivity Center in Seoul offers courses in business management. A class discusses research done to increase efficiency in industry.   (UNITED NATIONS)

Student nurses in Bamako, Mali, learn the anatomy of the human body. A prime benefit of modern education in new countries is the improvement of health standards and services.   (A. TESSORE—UNESCO)

Women of Cameroun study cooking in a domestic science class, one phase of a program to develop homemaking abilities. (ALMASY-VAUTHEY—UNESCO)

The government of Thailand aids in training automobile mechanics and drivers. Here, an instructor explains the internal combustion engine. (JACK LING—UNESCO)

Below, a UNESCO expert in precision mechanics demonstrates equipment for students in Cairo's National Research Center. (PHILIP BOUCAS—UNESCO)

In Niger technicians monitor a closed-circuit television broadcast of an educational program for children. (STUDIO RACCAH—UNESCO)

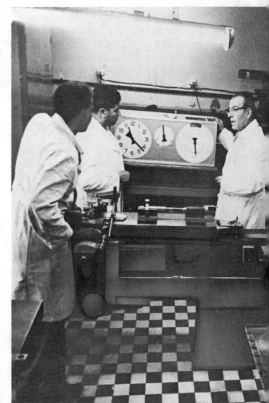

263

challenge faced by educators through the ages is well expressed in these words of John Milton, written in 1644.

Consult UNESCO World Survey of Education: General (1955), Primary Education (1958), Secondary Education (1961), Higher Education (1966); The World Book of Education, ed. by G. Z. F. Bereday and J. A. Lauwerys: The Curriculum (1958), Higher Education (1959), The Gifted Child (1962), Teacher Education (1963), The Education Explosion (1965); Mallinson, Vernon, An Introduction to the Study of Comparative Education (2d ed., 1960);

Hans, N. A., Comparative Education (3d ed., 1961); Thut, I. H., and Adams, D. K., Educational Problems in Contemporary Societies (1964); Cramer, F. J., and Brown, C. S., Contemporary Education (2d ed., 1965); U.S. Office of Education, Dept. of Health, Education, and Welfare, Digest of Educational Statistics (1965).

BRIAN HOLMES, University of London
Institute of Education

See also WOMEN, EDUCATION OF.

PUBLIC EDUCATION IN THE UNITED STATES

The term "public education" refers to instructional programs offered by government at a national, state, or local level. These programs are free in the sense that no tuition is charged, the schools being supported by taxes levied on a broad base. In the United States schooling is not only available to all children without direct cost but is also compulsory for at least the elementary years. A fourth of the total population is involved as pupils or teachers in the elementary and secondary schools. These are for the most part operated by local public school districts, though about 15% of the pupils at this age level are in private schools operated by religious or independent lay organizations. The trend is to make higher education at minimum cost available to all who want it, and universities, colleges, technical institutes, and junior colleges are operated to this end by states, cities, and local school districts.

Details on higher education and on other aspects of American school systems will be found in the entries listed at the end of this article and in the education sections of the articles on the states. This article concentrates on the public elementary and high schools, which constitute a large part of the world's most inclusive system of public education. A fact of basic importance is that the United States attempts to give increasing amounts of education to all children. This concept contrasts with the tradition of many other countries, where elementary education is free for the majority of children but more advanced schooling is restricted to a relatively small number.

Goals. Education in many nations has been the instrument of national leaders or of national movements for development and enrichment or modernization of the country. In the hands of dictators, education has been an effective tool for indoctrinating men and women to serve the dictator's purposes. In underdeveloped states that emerged after World War II, education has been regarded as a means to promote independence, self-sufficiency, and order. Education in such instances is the means by which a government maintains its position, develops its program, and screens and selects personnel. Such patterns involve teaching the dominant language, indoctrination in the beliefs and goals of the regime, and selective screening of personnel for technical and advanced education. Such education is thought of as national, and is characterized by strong central planning, control, and evaluation.

Education in the United States is regarded as a service to the individual rather than as a tool of the state. This tradition has made Americans wary of strong central con-

trol, and the United States does not have a centrally administered system of education. The federal government's role in education is limited, and schooling is the legal responsibility of the states. Thus there are 50 school systems making up the educational system of the country. The states have provided for implementation of education through local school districts. The unique feature of educational organization in the United States lies in the local school district under authority of a local, lay board of education. The principle of local citizen control of so important a matter as education is thus maintained in contrast to control through a central government agency of full-time bureaucrats, as is the case in most other countries.

Influence of the Federal Government

That education is primarily the responsibility of the individual states is implied in the Tenth Amendment: "The powers not delegated to the United States by the Constitution, nor prohibited by it to the States, are reserved to the States respectively, or to the people." The impact of the federal government on education rests on other portions of the Constitution. The preamble, stating the purposes of government—including to "insure domestic Tranquility, provide for the common defence, promote the general Welfare"—provides a broad basis for federal activity. The protection of individual civil rights of citizens stipulated in the First Amendment, and the prohibition of denying any citizen equal rights without due process of law in the Fourteenth Amendment provide further bases for federal activity. Four aspects of the impact of federal government on education are to be noted: federal financial support for education, federal court decisions, services of the Office of Education, and the array of federally operated programs of education.

Finance. Federal financial support for education antedates the Constitution. A tremendous endowment for education was made available to states and townships through federal legislation starting with the Ordinance of 1785, reaffirmed by the Northwest Territory Ordinance of 1787, and expanded by later legislation. The 16th section of each congressional township was given as endowment for education with no provision for either financial or educational accountability to the federal government. The primary national purpose was encouragement to settle the Western lands.

In 1862, during the Civil War, each state in the Union was given 30,000 acres of federal lands for each Senator and Representative then in Congress for establishment of at least one college to teach and develop agriculture and the mechanic arts and to include military tactics in the curriculum. This land grant college act spurred development of state universities and state systems of higher education. It provided for financial accountability.

In 1914 the Agricultural Extension Service was introduced. It matched federal aid with state funds for direct educational services to farmers and housewives. In 1917 Congress passed the first of several acts providing matching federal support with state aid for vocational education in agriculture, homemaking, and trade and industrial subjects to be given in local schools. These acts provided for both financial and educational accountability.

In the 1930's concern for economic stability and recovery led to aid for schoolhouse construction and for assistance to individuals. This aid was provided through the Works Progress Administration and the National Youth Administration. Contributions of surplus foods and financial support for school lunch programs were related to price parity for farm production.

With World War II began federal aid to schools impacted by military and defense plant personnel. After the war the GI Bill of Rights aided veterans attending schools and colleges. By 1958 so many aspects of education had become nationally urgent that the National Defense Education Act was passed with special emphasis on science, mathematics, foreign languages, guidance services, and technical education. The quality and availability of education reached such a point of national concern that the 1965 Congress was known as the "Education Congress" because of the number of laws passed and programs supported. Chief among the laws was the National Elementary and Secondary School Act. In all, federal aid jumped from less than 4% of total educational expenditures to about 20%.

Today the federal government has become a strong junior partner with states and local school districts. It provides money for strengthening of state departments, and to enable local school districts to relate more fully to community needs and to provide special programs for the educationally deprived. The wide availability of federal funds presents a strong incentive for states and local school districts to look at the variety of educational needs of all the people, and to seek a plan to meet these needs in cooperation with other public agencies and with private and parochial schools.

Court Decisions. A number of federal court decisions, including Supreme Court decisions, have influenced public education. Such decisions have been concerned mostly with protection of civil rights of citizens and with states rights. Most of the cases have dealt with invasion of government through public schools into the area of religious freedom, with separation of church and state, or with grievances arising because of racial discrimination. Though each of these federal court decisions was directed to the grievance of a particular individual or group in a particular situation, the legal precedent of each became a ruling that thereafter had to be considered in school operation everywhere.

The most far-reaching decisions were those in 1954 and 1955 in which the Supreme Court went beyond the separate-but-equal-facilities ruling to state that schools segregated on the basis of race denied equal opportunity, were thereby unconstitutional, and should be desegregated with all deliberate speed.

In the area of religious freedom and separation of church and state no such clearcut decision has been declared. Cases bearing on this issue include an Oregon case in 1925 in which the Supreme Court ruled that the state did not have the power to require parents to send their children to public schools, thus maintaining the right of parochial and private schools to operate. In a 1962 case the Court ruled that an official opening prayer in schools of New York State was unconstitutional.

Services. The Office of Education was set up as a Department of Education in 1867 to collect and disseminate information about the condition and progress of education, the organization and management of schools and school systems and the methods of teaching, and otherwise to promote the cause of education throughout the country. Unlike many other nations, the United States does not have an officer of Cabinet rank solely representing education. The office, headed by a commissioner of education, is a subdivision of the Department of Health, Education, and Welfare. The office serves as accountant of education in the United States through its biennial survey and other collections and reports of statistical data. Through publications, conferences, and consultative services, the office has provided stimulation, intercommunication, information, and counsel to state and local school systems and to educational agencies. It takes a leading role in stimulating educational research through contract grants and through spreading information on research problems, findings, and methods. On the crucial problem of international relations, a key service is provided in the processing and briefing of foreign students, teachers, and visiting educators for study or exchange teaching or observation in the United States, and of students and educators from the United States to study and work in other countries.

Programs. Federal agencies operate a variety of programs. These include the public schools in Washington, D.C.; the schools on Indian reservations; the educational systems of outlying territories; and school programs for dependents of military personnel stationed throughout the world, and at some installations within the country. These also include the training programs and the academies of the Army, Navy, Air Force, and Coast Guard; and training programs for employees in other governmental departments.

Common Elements in Education

There are more kinds of schools and educational programs in the United States than in any other country. There is also a great range in the quality of schools because schools are managed by local school districts under the legal authority of the states and there is no national agency to set standards. Nevertheless, American schools have enough in common so that the children of a family moving from one part of the country to another usually make a ready adjustment to a new school situation. The mass media of communication, the high mobility of population, and the broad geographic areas of operation of many business concerns tend to create similarity in ideas about education, as well as in ideas about dress, foods, homes, and other aspects of living. In addition there are unofficial influences specifically strengthening common elements in education. Textbooks, standardized tests, and audio-visual materials are sold on a nationwide scale. Voluntary associations of secondary schools and colleges for accrediting purposes have worked co-operatively on evaluative criteria for schools. There are a number of national associations concerned with the schools, for example, the National Association of Teachers of English, the National Association of Secondary School Principals, the National Education Association, and the National Congress of Parents and Teachers. The conventions and publications of these organizations spread views on the organization and operation of the schools. Thus there is an unofficial national educational policy.

The States and Education

The states have undertaken the responsibility for providing a free education for all children. The fundamental approach, as noted above, has been assignment of maintenance and operation of schools to local school districts. The state retains the power to determine the nature, size, kind, and number of such local school districts and therefore retains the power to reorganize local school districts whenever this is in the best interests of education.

Finance. As noted, public schools are paid for by taxation. The principle of supporting the schools through local taxes can be traced to the colonial period, when Massachusetts laws required towns to maintain schools. Before the modern state school systems were established, various means of support besides taxation were tried. These included lotteries, funds from license fees and the sale of land, and rate bills, that is, tuition fees based on the number of children in a family.

Practically all states now provide for financial support of the schools by assigning to school districts the power to tax local property. The manner in which such levies may be determined and assessed, upper limits for tax rates, amount of indebtedness permissible, procedure for borrowing, and procedures for receiving and expending funds are all provided through state law. Most states also allocate state revenues to local districts. Though figures vary widely from state to state, it is not uncommon for as much as half of a local school district financial support to come from state revenue sources. The balance comes chiefly from local property tax sources. Some of the funds from state sources are distributed to local districts in such a way as to equalize differences in local fiscal ability so that a minimum level of education can be provided for every child regardless of the financial ability of the school district in which he resides. Additional state support is allocated for a variety of purposes such as stimulation of special education for the handicapped, driver training programs, testing and guidance services, and provision of transportation.

Standards. The state is responsible for rules on who may be certified to teach and for some regulation of conditions affecting the employment of teachers through provisions for tenure, retirement, and minimum salary schedules. Through requiring teachers' certificates to be registered before salaries can be paid legally and through provision for revocation of certificates, the state maintains general supervision of educational personnel. This is public protection against the incompetent and undependable. It also provides a basis for designating the professionals and thus establishing a group whose careers and status involve the continuing study and practice of teaching. Local boards may select personnel, but they must select from among those who have been certified.

The state determines who may and who must attend school. The first compulsory attendance law was passed in 1852 by the Massachusetts legislature. By 1900, 32 states and the District of Columbia had laws requiring attendance, and when Mississippi enacted a law in 1918, 48 states had such statutes. Hawaii and Alaska enacted compulsory school laws in 1896 and 1929, respectively, many years before becoming states. In the aftermath of the Supreme Court's 1954 decision on desegregation of schools, Mississippi, South Carolina, and Virginia repealed their compulsory attendance laws. In 1964, however, a decision of the Supreme Court required Prince Edward County, Va., to reopen its public schools.

State law may set the age for starting school at 6, 7, or 8 and the age for leaving school at 15, 16, 17, or 18. The most common span, found in 30 states, is 7 to 16.

Exceptions to the attendance requirements are made for handicapped children, for children who attend private schools, and in some states for children who are taught by parents or tutors. Distance from school, illness, and seasonal work at home may be grounds for exemption from the laws. Most states allow children to leave school before reaching the upper compulsory attendance age limit to take lawful employment. The state also protects the safety and health of the child through requirements with respect to safety and sanitation in school buildings, school transportation, health examinations, and immunization to communicable diseases.

The states have customarily defined or prescribed some portions of subject matter to be taught in schools or have specified objectives to be served by the schools. Requirements usually include that instruction shall be in the English language, that there shall be instruction in U.S. and state history and the respective constitutions, and that there shall be attention to health and physical education. States also provide for stimulation of curriculum development through special consultative services, through special financial aids as indicated above, and through resource materials and publications. States stipulate the minimum number of school days per year and the hours of school time necessary to count as a school day.

Administration. All but two states have state boards responsible for policy and general review and regulation of education at the elementary and secondary levels. Education beyond high school may also be assigned in part to a general state board of education, though it is more customarily the responsibility of one or more special state boards for higher education in charge of specific universities or state systems of higher education. State boards vary in size, scope of responsibility, and manner in which members are elected or appointed. To repeat a key fact, the United States has 50 individual state school systems rather than one federally determined pattern of school organization and operation.

Each state has a state superintendent or commissioner of education who works under or with the state board of education. This officer and his staff comprise the state department of education with responsibility for leadership at the state level and for the regulation of education in the state. The state education department is concerned with long-range planning, with collection, analysis, and reporting of statistics, with research, with advising and consulting, with co-ordination of educational programs and activities, and with public relations. Its regulatory procedures include distribution of state financial support, enforcement of compulsory attendance laws, teacher certification, accreditation of schools on the basis of visitation and reports, and supervision of financial accounting systems. The state department of education seeks to assure an educated citizenry, provide a basic level of quality and comprehensiveness in instructional programs, guarantee responsibility and economy in the use of educational funds, encourage efficiency in school management, and protect the lives and health of children and youths. State departments also have operational responsibilities, which vary from state to state. They usually include such assignments as running trade and technical schools, providing Americanization training for foreign-born persons, operating state library and state museum services, and managing teacher retirement systems.

The Local School District

Local school districts vary in size from New York City (in which the number of pupils exceeds the total population of a number of states) to those responsible for a single classroom of children in a sparsely settled area. A distinction is to be made between the attendance unit, the geographic area from which pupils all come to school in the same building or on the same campus, and the school district, which may be a single attendance unit or may include many attendance units but which represents the whole area under one local board of education.

Organization. The basis for the organization of school districts varies over the country. Throughout most Western states school districts were initially organized in terms of distances within which all children could reasonably walk to the same school. Some of these small districts persist today but many districts have been reorganized to serve larger areas or to accommodate children of a community. In New England, where early settlement was in towns, the school started as a department of town government. School districts along town or township lines are common there as well as in Pennsylvania, New Jersey, and Indiana. Several Southeastern and Western states are organized on the basis of county-wide local school districts.

With the increasing complexity of education, the advent of faster transportation, and the growing urbanization of the population the numerous single-teacher schools or widely dispersed small schools have become outdated. There were 111,273 local school districts in 1943–44, over half of them responsible for single, one-room schools. By 1959–60 the total number of districts had been reduced through reorganization to 42,428, and still further by 1965–66 to an estimated figure of 26,802. School district reorganization to increase the efficiency of educational services has far outpaced reorganization of municipal, township, or county governments although the same factors bear upon the effectiveness of their operation.

The local school district is responsible for identifying and educating the children who may and who must attend school; for constructing, maintaining, and operating school buildings; for employing certificated teachers and other adequate staff; for approving methods and content of instruction; for financial planning and management; for reporting through appropriate officials to state education departments.

School Boards. The district's affairs are the responsibility of a board of education composed of citizens qualified as resident voters in the district. Five or seven is the most common number of members. They are most often elected at large from the district at a separate school election on a nonpartisan basis. Less than 5% of all school board members are appointed. Usually they serve overlapping three-year terms so that only a third of the terms expire each year. A most important function of the board is selection of a professionally trained superintendent or supervising principal to administer the local schools.

The board of education represents the most common and basic form of citizen participation in government in the United States. It is a representative board, which seeks to reach the wisest decision that might be made by the total citizenry if all could have the information available to board members and the same opportunity for discussion in small groups representing the community. Decisions are reached after information has been studied and alternatives have been discussed. Hence, board members can serve as board members only when the board is in session. They speak as private citizens, not as board members, when the board is not in session, except for duties related to specific roles as president or secretary of the board or in connection with specific committee work assigned.

School boards customarily hold at least one meeting each month to approve payment of bills and attend to other business. Most boards hold many additional meetings to give serious attention to the instructional program, to plan for future building needs, to discuss and approve the budget for the school year, and to fill staff positions by approval of recommendations of the chief administrator. Like other governmental units, school districts operate on the basis of a fiscal year, planning and adopting a budget which is based on estimates of income and appropriations approved for expenditures, and which provides the basis for determining the amount of taxes to be levied. At all times when the board is not in session, the chief school administrator is the agent for the district and carries on the work of the schools.

Administration. One-room school districts employ only a teacher. The chairman or other board members carry out administrative duties, under the close supervision of a county superintendent or other representative of the state education authority. Most school districts employ teachers and administrative and supervisory personnel upon nomination by the chief local school administrator. In smaller schools the superintendent may be the only professional administrator, but in very large school districts the administrative staff is large and complex.

In elementary schools, teachers are most commonly employed by grade level to teach a roomful of pupils; in high schools they are most usually employed to teach specified subjects to classes of pupils. The attendance unit in a school system is usually headed by a school principal who is responsible for such things as the instructional program, the assignment and supervision of teachers, the registration and schedules of pupils, the discipline of pupils, school activities and organizations, the day-to-day operation of the building, and conferences and co-operation with parents. In an elementary school he may have an assistant principal and clerical or secretarial assistants. In a large secondary school, organization can be elaborate with assistant principals, deans, registrars, department heads, directors of activities, counselors, and others.

The central administrative staff of a school district is responsible for managing such affairs of the whole district as the following: selection and employment of staff, coordination of the instructional program and articulation between attendance units, development and administration of the budget, purchase and distribution of school supplies and equipment, acquisition and maintenance of school buildings, collection of statistics, filing of reports, general public relations, compulsory attendance enforcement, operation of the school transportation system, and provision of health services. In addition to the superintendent there may be other personnel such as a business manager, director of instruction, director of staff personnel, and director of research and testing.

The Intermediate Unit. In most states there is some intermediate education office between the local school district and the state department of education. This has been most commonly the office of county superintendent, if the county itself is not the operating school district. The duties of such officers vary from state to state, but they include a variety of clerical and regulatory functions. Such officials most commonly operate as locally selected field representatives of the central state authority.

Consult Kimball, S. T., and McClellan, J. E., *Education and the New America* (1962); DeYoung, C. A., and Wynn, Richard, *American Education* (1964); Campbell, R. F., and others, *The Organization and Control of American Schools* (1965); Miller, Van, *The Public Administration of American School Systems* (1965).

VAN MILLER,
University of Illinois

See also:

ELEMENTARY EDUCATION IN THE UNITED STATES

Elementary, or primary, education involves far more of the world's population than any other form of schooling. According to U.N. reports on world education, for every 1,000 persons aged 5 to 19, about 400 get some formal schooling. Of these 400, slightly more than 300 are enrolled in the primary grades. There is a great range from country to country in the percentage of children who receive education. In some nations—the United States, for example—virtually all children attend elementary school. In many other countries—Canada, France, Ireland, Israel, Norway, Sweden, and the United Kingdom, for instance—the percentage of children 5 to 14 enrolled in schools ranges from 70 to above 80. In some of the underdeveloped regions, however, the percentage is frequently below 50 and may be as low as 20. The range in amount and quality of primary schooling is also extensive.

Elementary education in the United States is the first major segment of an extended system of schools. Most typically the elementary school has come to mean the first six years of formal schooling, or the first six grades of the school system. A great many children do attend kindergarten, and this is variously referred to as a preschool year or as the initial year of elementary school (which in this case runs for seven years). Many elementary schools are still organized to include the 7th and 8th grades of school, too. However, the tendency in point of view and organization is to include these as the first two years of a junior high school unit, or to organize them into a two-year unit called the intermediate school. Thus, dependent on local school district organization, children would begin their elementary school experience at age 5 or 6 in the kindergarten or first grade and would terminate it at age 12, 13, or 14, or at the end of the 6th, 7th, or 8th grade. More

recently there has been considerable interest evident in extending the elementary school downward to include all four-year-old children, and even some three-year-olds. The evidence on the effects of early stimulation on the long-term development of intellectual power provides support for this point of view. Some speculate that we may see the emergence of a new lower elementary school that will include the present nursery school and kindergarten, and grades 1 through 4, followed by a middle school that will encompass present grades 5 through 8. Whatever the details of organization, elementary education needs to be viewed as a major segment of a larger and continuing school experience that extends from kindergarten through the 12th or 14th year of school.

History of Elementary Education. As the section on History of Education notes, elementary schools can be traced back to Greece and Rome. In America, the education of young children has been required by law since the early years of the New England colonies. Massachusetts passed a law in 1642 which required town officials to compel parents to provide elementary instruction for their children. While it did not require the establishment of schools, it did require instruction in reading, in certain capital laws, and in the Catechism, and that a child be apprenticed in a trade. In 1647 another law was passed in Massachusetts requiring each town of 50 families to provide an elementary school teacher and each town of 100 families to establish a Latin grammar school. Parents were not forced to send their children to these schools, but they were required to provide instruction in some other way if they did not. Regional differences of various kinds in the Middle and Southern colonies contributed to their particular educational history.

Starting with the dame school, in which a woman in the community would gather a few children into her home for instruction, a public elementary school that taught reading, writing, and some arithmetic began to emerge in New England. It was from this beginning that the concept of the elementary school devoted to instruction in the three R's took shape in the United States. The religious motive was dominant in those early years, and reading instruction was seen as the key to understanding the Bible for one's self. It was only as the trend toward democracy became more obvious and more openly sought as a goal in America, and church and state came to be more carefully separated, that curriculum decisions came to be made with an eye to general citizenship and individual self-realization. It was in these early years, too, as the frontier expanded and as the land west of the Appalachians was opened, that "the little red school house" came to be a symbol of elementary education in the United States. One teacher, operating in a one-room school, worked with the full range of ages and grades in the elementary school. This approach to elementary education undoubtedly fitted well with the times; the one-room school was an admirable answer to the problem of providing education on the frontier. In fact, the one-room rural school is still used in some of the more remote and sparsely settled parts of the United States, though the trend is to consolidate these units into larger attendance centers.

A Quality "Common" School. From these beginnings the elementary school has been considered the very foundation of the educational system in the United States. Concern for democracy and for a republican form of government pointed to the necessity for an enlightened citizenry. As the idea of a free, tax-supported, and compulsory school system was accepted as basic to this goal, the development of elementary school education became central. The challenge was to develop a common school, common in the sense that families from all walks of life and from all religious and ethnic groups would send their children to it, and that the children would receive there a quality education. This was a departure from what had been found in the nations of Western Europe from which most of these early settlers had come. There a free school was more or less synonymous with a charity school, and attending a free school was associated with pauperism. Families who could possibly do so sent their children to private, tuition-charging elementary schools. Thus it was felt that family and child status was protected and a better quality education was insured. In the United States concern for equality of opportunity, no less in education than in any other aspect of life, pointed to the necessity to develop the public elementary school into the kind of institution that would offer an educational program equal to that found in the private school. At the present time about nine out of ten children in elementary school are in public institutions in this country, and they come from families representative of the total society. The others are enrolled in private or church-affiliated elementary schools. The nation demands that parents meet their social obligation to educate their children, but parents are free to choose whether or not they will use the public elementary school system. The extent to which it is used suggests that people have confidence in the public school.

A Neighborhood Institution. It is appropriate to refer to the elementary school as a neighborhood institution. Social scientists refer to the attendance boundaries of an individual elementary school to define a neighborhood—that is, the geographic and social area encompassed in the concept. The closeness of interests suggested by the term extends to the elementary school itself. Of course, the elementary school is that part of the larger school system to which children come for their first sustained experience outside the family group and to which parents must entrust their children. This results in a high level of parent interest in the elementary school and considerable participation by parents in school activities. Children of elementary school age, unlike the adolescent, welcome parent involvement in their school life. Additionally, in many communities parents are urged to use the elementary school plant for activities that go beyond school affairs themselves, making of the school a neighborhood center in a broader sense.

Organization of Elementary Schools. Some school districts encompass only elementary schools, and a board of education and superintendent of schools are charged with responsibilities limited to these first years of formal schooling. Other school districts, usually referred to as unified or consolidated, operate elementary school units as part of larger organizations that include secondary school

Fourth-grade students work on an anthropology project. Education no longer relies on textbooks alone.   (HELLA HAMMID—RAPHO GUILLUMETTE)

Sherwood Elementary School in Greeley, Colo., is built in four units, providing both flexibility and attractive quarters. To the right is an all-weather, domed play area.   (EDUCATIONAL FACILITIES LABORATORIES)

A school in an urban renewal area in New York City has a formal plan that blends with the monolithic apartment development nearby.

A city school in a neighborhood of small homes in New Orleans has a sheltered play area underneath the raised main building. (PERKINS & WILL, ARCHITECTS)

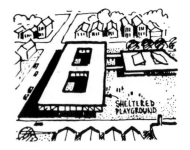

units as well. Thus a board of education and superintendent of schools are charged with responsibilities that extend over the total system.

Today's elementary school is usually headed by a principal. As a "line" officer in the administrative structure of the school system, he is given responsibility and authority to convert general district policy into an operating school program in his building. He is the educational leader in his school, and it is incumbent on him to work with his faculty and with parents and other interested lay people in his neighborhood for the realization of the best educational program possible. Increasingly, principals devote full time to administrative duties, though many still have limited teaching responsibilities also.

Each classroom in the elementary school is usually handled by one teacher, this arrangement being referred to as a self-contained classroom. The concept of self-containment is modified in some school districts by the use of special teachers in art, music, and physical education. A persistent issue in elementary education is the extent to which and the way in which subject-matter specialists should be utilized. Complete departmentalization, in

which children were instructed in each of the areas of the curriculum by a special teacher, was abandoned by almost all elementary schools in the early 1900's and replaced by an approach more consistent with understanding child growth and development and more flexible and efficient in the use of school time. More recently there have been strong challenges to the concept of the self-contained classroom. In the face of a more demanding curriculum a great number of elementary schools are turning to cooperative or teaming arrangements for teacher utilization.

The basic faculty of classroom teachers and a limited number of area specialists is frequently augmented on a full- or part-time basis by speech therapists, nurses, physicians, counselors, school psychologists, and other special personnel. Such staffing suggests both the complex nature of the educative process and the breadth of responsibility which the elementary school is asked to accept.

A full- or part-time secretary or clerk, a custodian to take care of the building and grounds, and in many instances a dietitian and staff responsible for the operation of a hot-lunch program, fill out the personnel of an elementary school.

New concepts in school design are changing the educational environment. The well-designed school harmonizes with its environment and provides the facilities that are often necessary for the successful application of new instructional techniques.

A dome-shaped elementary school in New York City. Unusual features include movable furniture, carpeting, and no interior walls. (ED LETTAU)

The Curriculum of the Elementary School. As a curriculum unit, the elementary school program is designed almost exclusively to provide certain common learnings for all normal children. There may be some variation in programming for students in the 7th and 8th grades when these are included as part of elementary education, but the rule is to have no elective courses in an elementary school program. All children are expected to come to grips with all the learning tasks included in the curriculum. The fact of individual differences keeps the school from demanding a uniform kind of accomplishment. Some will do better than others; the challenge is to try to help each child to do his best. An observer in an elementary school classroom will notice that teachers work with multiple subgroups of children in an effort to cope realistically with individual differences. There may be, for example, slow, normal, and advanced reading groups. Decisions concerning an individual child's progress must be made in relation to the ability with which the child seems to be endowed. This sort of reasoning influences policies on school promotion to a very great extent, too. There is a growing tendency to organize continuous progress sequences in non-graded elementary schools to come to grips even more with pupil differences. Such non-graded pupil groups may contain children of more than one chronological age as well. This is a further manifestation of the effort of the school to accommodate itself to the child rather than the reverse. There are even more special arrangements made for specific subgroups of pupils, as well, such as compensatory programs for so-called disadvantaged children and special provisions for gifted pupils.

Consistent with the early history of the elementary school, a primary responsibility in these first school years is to help each child to become proficient in English and mathematics. Children are helped to read with understanding, to express themselves effectively in speaking and writing, to write legibly, and to spell accurately. Increasing attention is given to the development of critical listening. It is not uncommon to find children receiving instruction in a foreign language in the elementary school, too. In the area of mathematics children are helped to understand the number system, are introduced to simple geometry and algebra, and learn to solve quantitative problems of various kinds with accuracy and reasonable speed. All children are also helped to understand their social environment, to gain insight into democratic values, processes and institutions, to sense the relationship between the culture which a people builds for itself and the alternatives which their geographic location makes available to them. Attempts are made to acquaint children with countries other than their own and with contrasting ways of life. Historical perspective is sought, too, in the social studies program. Science, as a method of inquiry, as well as an accumulated and verified body of knowledge about the natural environment, grows in importance in the elementary school program. Science as a force in the modern world, and technology as science applied to the daily affairs of man, have gained a firm place in the elementary school curriculum. The curriculum is planned to include experiences with art and music, too. The nurturing of each individual's creative power, as well as of his ability to appreciate the products of another's creative effort in the fine arts, is given due attention. Finally, the elementary curriculum embraces physical education and a program of health education. Together these areas of study constitute a broad curriculum, much broader than would have been found in the elementary school of an earlier day, but minimal in a time that requires a more inclusive definition of the fundamentals in elementary education.

Consult Reisner, E. H., *The Evolution of the Common School* (1935); *The American Elementary School, 13th Yearbook of The John Dewey Society*, ed. by H. G. Shane (1953); Caswell, H. L., and Foshay, A. W., *Education in the Elementary School* (3d ed., 1957); Ragan, W. B., and Stendler, C. B., *Modern Elementary Curriculum* (3d ed., 1966); Sowards, G. W., and Scobey, Mary-Margaret, *The Changing Curriculum and the Elementary Teacher* (2d ed., 1968).

G. WESLEY SOWARDS, Stanford University
See also CURRICULUM; KINDERGARTEN; NURSERY SCHOOL; PHYSICAL EDUCATION.

SECONDARY EDUCATION IN THE UNITED STATES

Secondary education is in a state of transition in the contemporary world. First conceived by Greek genius and later more fully developed in Western Europe, the secondary school is one of the oldest of formal educational institutions. From classic, aristocratic, and restricted beginnings it is evolving today into a more practical, democratic, and world-wide institution.

A two-track system of secondary education developed in Europe; at the conclusion of elementary school, pupils were tested and divided into two main groups. Those who passed the competitive examinations or came from influential families went to the academic high school, whereas the others went directly to work or attended a vocational school. In the United States nearly all pupils after elementary school enter public high schools. Secondary education in the United States typically takes place in a comprehensive high school, an all-purpose institution for diverse children. It is free and tax-supported, coeducational, and has a broad curriculum. America, alone in the world, has created this single, unified system of secondary education to serve all of the children of all the people. Many nations, however, are moving toward this newer, broader concept of secondary education.

In the world as a whole, secondary education still reaches only a small share of the population, according to U.N. statistics. For every 1,000 persons aged 5 to 19 only about 400 get any formal schooling at all. Of these 400, slightly more than 300 are enrolled in the primary grades and about 85 in secondary schools. There is a great range from country to country in the percentage of young people attending secondary schools. U.N. reports list more than a dozen countries in which less than 10% of high school-age children are in school. The trend in most countries is to provide more secondary schooling, but many have a long way to go. At the upper end of the scale are such highly industrialized nations as Great Britain and the United States. In the United States virtually all children go to elementary school and continue to high school. Considerable numbers drop out before completing high school; nevertheless, as an over-all figure, more than 80% of persons of high school age are in school.

Development of Secondary Education

The American public high school in the sense that is familiar today dates from 1821, when the citizens of Boston established the English Classical School in response to demands for public schools of a higher order than the elementary schools. But this institution had two predecessors, the Latin grammar school and the academy.

Latin Grammar School. In the beginning, American schools were European transplants. The curriculum was classical; a student mastered Greek and Latin and learned religious doctrine. These Latin grammar schools were college-preparatory institutions serving the wealthy and the powerful. Boys entered school at the age of seven and remained until they were capable of passing examinations for admission to college, usually a period of seven years.

Education during colonial times was considered a function of the church and of private groups, except in New England. In 1635 citizens of the Massachusetts Bay colony created the Boston Latin School and set land aside for its support. In 1647 the General Court of Massachusetts passed a law establishing a system of public elementary and secondary schools. This law set up for the first time in history a plan of compulsory, free, and tax-supported education.

The Latin grammar school, though providing the foundation for later secondary education, did not flourish long in America. A European emphasis on Latin and Greek suited few American youths. Especially in commercial centers and near the frontier, secondary schools began offering instruction in English, mathematics, and similar practical subjects. Even while the Latin school was in existence many students in New England were educated instead by private teachers. These tutors offered the rising commercial classes a wide variety of practical subjects, ranging from trigonometry and "merchants accounts" to flute playing and French.

The Academy. The academy provided the bridge whereby America advanced beyond the traditions of European education. Benjamin Franklin, in a 1749 publication entitled *Proposals Relating to the Education of the Youth in Pennsylvania*, advocated a new type of practical school, one that would "promote the welfare of its students when they should go forth to the duties of active life." Franklin suggested that the new institution be coeducational and that it have three departments—the English, the classical, and the mathematical—all equally respectable. He envisaged the English and mathematical departments as giving practical preparation for the affairs of civic and vocational life. History, geography, political science, mathematics, natural science, and other useful subjects such as surveying would be taught in the academy.

The Philadelphia Academy opened in 1751, its curriculum representing a compromise between the revolutionary proposals of Franklin and more traditional beliefs. Throughout America the academy soon replaced the Latin school to become the dominant institution for secondary education. But, as time went on, its curriculum became increasingly classical. Therefore, by the 1850's, Americans began to support a new institution, the high school, which promised a more satisfactory and practical education, and which was tax-supported and publicly controlled.

The academies were mainly private, tuition-charging institutions. High schools were founded in an effort to make available and free to all the youth of a community the same advantages of education offered by the better academies. The clamor for public high schools also reflects wider forces at work in American society during this era: a broadening concept of equality of opportunity, increased enfranchisement, immigration, and the new political power of the farmer and laborer.

The 19th-Century High School. The first public high school, Boston's English Classical School, was not college preparatory. Rather, its mandate was one of teaching practical subjects and of preparing students directly for life. This "high school," as it was soon called, probably in deference to the then famous Edinburgh High School in Scotland, began to prepare students both for life and for college. Such a pattern was followed by subsequent high schools in other cities.

Public high school advocates encountered early resistance from churches and from established academies. However, the movement flourished under the mantle of two men: Henry Barnard, secretary of the Connecticut State Board of Education, and Horace Mann, whose *Annual Reports* as secretary to the Massachusetts State Board of Education were especially influential. A general ground swell of humanitarian feeling throughout pre-Civil War America also popularized the concept of public secondary education. By 1860 the high school movement was well under way, there being more than 100 such publicly supported institutions.

During the course of the 19th century the basic idea was hammered out in heated public discussion and in such court decisions as the Kalamazoo case, that America should have free, public high schools open to all who wanted to attend. By 1900 most communities supported a local high school, but only about 10% of the youth of high school age attended these schools. The great majority of youth went directly to work before or upon completing the eighth grade, which marked the end of elementary school. The modern, more fully comprehensive high school, which the great majority of youth now attend, came into being during the first half of the 20th century.

The Modern High School

Size. Phenomenal growth in enrollment characterizes the high school of the 20th century. Although the number of youths in the 14–17 age bracket remained constant at 8,500,000 to 9,500,000 from 1930 to 1960, an increasing number of these youths attended school. Substantial growth is indicated from 1930, when 4,800,000 students were present in high school, to 1945, when 6,200,000 attended, and especially to 1960, when 8,000,000 students were enrolled in American secondary schools. By 1970 more than 12,000,000 students are expected to be in high school, a reflection of the large post-World War II birth rate and of the ever-increasing holding power of the schools. The U.S. Office of Education estimates that in 1960 there were 30,000 secondary schools in the nation, about 27,000 public and 3,000 private. Together, these schools graduated 1,500,000 seniors in 1960. Most students attend large schools. Though the majority of schools graduate classes of 100 or fewer students, only 30% of the total graduating seniors come from smaller high schools.

Attendance is compulsory in most states up to the age of 16. Some states allow students to leave at the age of 14 and others require students to remain in school until the age of 18 or graduation, whichever comes earlier. Although 99% of youths aged 12 attend school, the drop-out rate increases above this age so that by the age of 17 only 77% attend. These retention figures are much improved over 1930, when only 52% of all youth aged 14 to 17 attended school.

Objectives. A rapidly expanding American nation, the change from a rural agrarian to an urban industrial economy, developments in science and technology, great increases in national wealth, and involvement in international affairs all influenced secondary education as it developed in the late 19th century and in the 20th century.

But even more far-reaching in its effect on the objectives of secondary education was the mass infusion into high school of students "representing every conceivable shade of intelligence, background, means, interest and expectation," as a Harvard University committee expressed it in a 1945 report entitled *General Education in a Free Society*.

The objectives of secondary education have been formulated numerous times by various committees and commissions. Some statements reflect emphasis upon the needs of society, some upon the needs of students, and still others on academic or intellectual achievement.

As the high school began to grow rapidly in the latter part of the 19th century, overtaking and surpassing the academy in enrollment, the colleges and universities became concerned that high standards be maintained. Accordingly, the National Education Association appointed its now famous "Committee of Ten," headed by Charles William Eliot, then president of Harvard. This group formulated a statement of aim couched primarily in college-preparatory terms.

By 1918 the National Education Association's Committee on the Reorganization of Secondary Education, taking a broader and more functional approach to secondary education, advocated the Seven Cardinal Principles of Secondary Education: health, command of fundamental processes, worthy home membership, vocational competence, citizenship, worthy use of leisure time, and the development of ethical character. These have remained widely influential as objectives for secondary education.

In 1944 the Educational Policies Commission of the National Education Association made a major reassessment of high school education. Under the title *Education For All American Youth* the commission identified the following 10 imperative needs of youth to which education should be oriented:

1. The development of salable skills
2. The development of good health and physical fitness
3. The development of good citizenship
4. An understanding of the significance of the family
5. The knowledge of how to use goods and services wisely
6. An understanding of the methods and influence of science
7. An appreciation of the aesthetic
8. A wise use of leisure time
9. An ethical and moral understanding
10. An ability to think rationally, listen with understanding, and express thoughts clearly

Questions about the American high school arose following World War II, primarily due to evidence of low scores by some high school graduates taking military classification tests. Also, a broader segment of the American public became familiar with the rapid progress of students in selective European schools and questions arose as to whether American schools were sufficiently rigorous. The pockets of criticism became enlarged by the publication of Arthur Bestor's *The Restoration of Learning* (1955), by the speeches and articles of Adm. Hyman G. Rickover, by the formation of a Council for Basic Education, and by the Rockefeller Report, *The Pursuit of Excellence* (1958), all seeking a renewed emphasis on academic achievement.

Public concern became polarized in 1957 with the launching of *Sputnik*, signaling the strength of Soviet science. The quality of education became a national issue and James B. Conant's report *The American High School Today* (1959) achieved popular readership. Conant expressed a faith in the capability of the comprehensive high school to educate well. He suggested, however, that the academically talented student was too often working below capacity, that guidance programs be expanded, and that college-bound students study a foreign language for at least four years.

In 1961 the Educational Policies Commission of the National Education Association published a new guideline for secondary education entitled *The Central Purpose of American Education*. Acquiring the ability to think was here defined as the most essential goal of today's student. States the Commission, "The purpose which runs through and strengthens all other educational purposes—the common thread of education—is the development of the ability to think." The pamphlet advocates an education that cultivates the mind, that gives a priority to intellectual development.

As the need for talent to manage a modern society became clear, the plight of the Negro came into focus. The United States could no longer tolerate, either morally or economically, a large minority group whose education was stunted by slum schools in the North and by segregated schools in the South. In a technological world with other nations improving their educational systems, the United States could not afford to waste talent. The desegregation of schools in the South moved most quickly at the university and elementary, rather than at the secondary, level. However, the majority of states which before 1960 did segregate secondary students had by 1967 made significant progress in desegregation. In the North and West, a growing concentration of Negroes in the central cities had actually increased segregation. From 1960 to 1966 the white population in the major central cities increased by 2.5%, whereas the Negro population there rose 24.4%. Solutions to the problem include bussing Negro students out of the immediate neighborhood and the construction of large educational parks to accommodate huge areas of the city with both Negro and white neighborhoods.

The federal government has taken an active role in improving the education of educationally deprived minority groups, including passage of the Economic Opportunity Act (1964) to combat poverty, and initiation of project "Head Start" to reduce the educational handicap which young students from underprivileged areas normally have when they enter school. Thus, the major thrust of national interest in education late in the decade of the 1960's shifted from that of educational excellence for those who could afford it to educational opportunity for all youth, regardless of social class.

Administration of Secondary Schools. In the United States the 50 state legislatures are empowered to establish secondary schools and to regulate secondary education, both public and private. Most states have established boards of education as policy-making bodies. These boards often develop administrative directives to supplement and to interpret state laws dealing with education. The state in practice delegates sizable amounts of responsibility for running the schools to county and local school districts, each in the charge of a local school board, composed of lay citizens usually elected by popular vote. School superintendents are appointed directly by the school board and exercise general jurisdiction over the entire school system.

The building principals are selected with care by the superintendent and then recommended to the school board for appointment. The principal, as the chief administrative officer in immediate charge of a particular school, has many functions. He specifically recruits and supervises the teaching staff, gives leadership in developing the curriculum, makes up the budget, directs student activity programs and student discipline, plans the school year, maintains adequate records, schedules the classes, and establishes close contact with parents and with the local community. The principalship has grown in responsibility and stature with increase in school size. The headmaster of the 1700's or the principal of the 1890's taught classes daily and often worked with but five or six teachers. Today the typical urban or suburban high school employs 60 to 80 teachers, and the principal is aided by an administrative staff of full and part-time specialists—the assistant principal, deans, counselors, guidance directors, directors of student activities, and heads of academic departments. The assistant principal is usually involved in student welfare, school management, student discipline, and supervisory duties.

Secondary School Organization. Until the opening of the 20th century the school system in the United States typically consisted of an eight-year elementary school and a four-year high school, a combination known as the eight-four plan. The Committee of Ten under president Eliot challenged the efficiency of this plan, and an increasing number of educators were becoming skeptical of the eight-year elementary school requirement. By beginning a student's secondary education in the seventh grade, the schools could not only save time in preparing him for college, it was argued, but could also do a better job of teaching the subjects. In response to these ideas, Berkeley, Calif., in 1909 opened the first junior high school, an institution encompassing the 7th, 8th, and 9th grades. The Berkeley school offered an enriched curriculum, a better-prepared teaching staff, and better plant than could be provided under the traditional plan. The six-three-three movement (six years of elementary school, three years of junior high school, and three years of senior high school) gained further impetus from the recommendations of the Committee on the Reorganization of Secondary Education in 1918. Almost all states have since adopted legislation encouraging school reorganization of some type. Now, approximately three out of every four secondary school pupils are enrolled under a reorganized secondary school, either in a six-three-three or a six-six plan, or some variation other than an eight-four plan.

A significant number of large cities have established vocational high schools, and some others, notably New York City, have separate schools specializing on some other basis, such as the Bronx High School of Science and the School of Performing Arts. But even these specialized schools require a course of general studies approximating that found in the more comprehensive high schools.

School Schedule. High schools in the early part of the 20th century operated on a schedule of eight 45-minute periods a day. The conventional secondary school today operates on a daily schedule of six or seven 50-minute periods; often this includes an "activity," or nonclass period. Each pupil has classes or activities scheduled for most periods, and classes for major subjects usually meet daily at the same times. Thus schedules of teachers and students follow set patterns. This kind of schedule contrasts with the European secondary school, where students study a larger range of subjects but do not meet in classes each day to study these subjects.

American high schools are experimenting with flexible schedules in which the length of class period and the size of classes vary according to function. Instead of all periods being of equal length, there may be, for instance, a 30-minute choir rehearsal and a two-hour science laboratory; or, instead of a typical class size of 30 students, groups of 200 pupils may be assembled for a lecture, and at some later date these same students will meet in groups of 10 for discussion. Innovations such as these have been sparked by the National Association of Secondary-School Principals' Commission on the Experimental Study of the Utilization of the Staff in the Secondary School. Length of the school day varies from 4½ to 7½ hours, with a median of 7 hours including intermissions and lunch period.

Evaluation of Students' Work. Most schools use a letter grading system of A to F, and reports are issued on student achievement every six weeks or quarterly. All reports include a rating of academic progress, and some in addition carry a character rating. Automatic promotion is infrequently practiced in senior high school. Students advance from grade to grade by completing their course work with passing marks. Credit is given for each course successfully completed, and the student is graduated when sufficient credits have been accumulated. Progress of European students, in contrast, is governed less by a system of grades or credits and more by the successful passing of a series of comprehensive examinations administered by officials from outside the local school.

The Instructional Program

Curriculum. Although educational experts tend to define the curriculum as all of the experiences a learner has under the guidance of the school, the more typical view is that the curriculum consists of those courses offered by the school.

As indicated above, secondary schools have experienced a gradual broadening of their purposes and objectives. These changes are reflected in an ever-increasing array of subjects offered to meet the needs of the heterogeneous school population. In 1900 the curriculum was still largely concentrated in the areas of English, mathematics, history, science, and foreign languages. During the first half of the 20th century the subjects that grew most rapidly in popularity were the commercial courses, industrial arts, homemaking, fine arts, and other so-called nonacademic courses. Latin and foreign languages diminished in popularity, and many colleges began to accept students whose only credential was a high school diploma.

After World War II a growing interest developed in providing additional functional courses such as driver edu-

Developing marketable skills in high school. Above, potential cabinetmakers with a master craftsman. (New York Times) Below, typing class in Winston-Salem, N.C. (ROBERTS—RAPHO GUILLUMETTE)

Special audio equipment assists foreign-language students in perfecting their accents. (CARL PURCELL—NATIONAL EDUCATION ASSN.)

Learning to use an oscilloscope. (CARL PURCELL—NATIONAL EDUCATIONAL ASSN.)

Industrial arts students operate a band saw. (ROBERTS-RAPHO GUILLUMETTE)

Instruction. The selection and organization of teaching materials, the use of effective instructional procedures, the adaptation of teaching to individual differences, and the evaluation of results are all problems of instruction. In some schools the textbook is the course of study, but increasingly the teacher uses a variety of teaching materials: multiple texts, periodicals, paperbacks, audio-visual aids, tapes, overhead projectors, and *realia* (actual objects to illustrate a lesson). Teaching procedure does not usually follow the assign, study, recite routine; instead, attempts are made to adapt effective group processes to teaching, to give greater attention to problem-solving as a vehicle for instruction, and to adapt teaching to the wide variety of needs, interests, and abilities found in students.

Student Activities. The student activity, often called extracurricular, program developed rapidly in the 1930's and 1940's. Its purpose was to increase student motivation and interest, to provide opportunities for leadership, and to improve students' use of leisure time. Some problems developed when the program interfered with academic classes, when educational objectives were hazy, or when too little relationship with the regular program existed. However, despite questioning and trimming, such activities as student government, interscholastic athletics, and special-interest clubs continue as an important part of American secondary education.

Trends and Issues

In response to modern conditions, certain trends in education may be noted. These include a consolidation of the smaller school districts, renewed emphasis on all academic subjects after an initial special interest in science, mathematics, and foreign languages, expanded investigations into the nature and conditions of learning, and a modernized vocational curriculum in business and the industrial arts. Other notable trends are special programs for the educationally handicapped, particularly in low income areas, advanced placement programs for the gifted, individualized learning with students progressing at their own rate, and the increased use of electronic and mechanical teaching devices to include television, projecting equipment, and learning consoles. To be added to the list are the use of aides and clerks to help the classroom teacher, a longer school day and school year, the popularization of summer schools, and most obvious of all, a rapid growth in school enrollment. Standards for teacher certification continue to rise, with many states now requiring 30 semester hours beyond the bachelor's degree for a permanent teaching credential.

On a broader scale, the immediate issues are probably four: (1) school desegregation, (2) federal participation, (3) disparities in the quality of education from community to community, and (4) the use of technology for instruction. Prof. Patrick Suppes of Stanford University has developed one of the most sophisticated applications of technology with a complete computer-assisted classroom in daily use. Electronic and publishing firms, seeking to market educational programs integrating technology and subject matter, have established new corporations to develop and package entire educational "systems" to include content, methodology, visual and electronic aids, and examination materials.

cation, business English, and shop mathematics. Many boys and girls began spending as much as half their time after the 10th grade on courses designed to develop skills marketable upon graduation.

The curriculum in high school provides both for generalization and specialization. A certain amount of general education—usually three or four years of English, two or three years of social studies, one year of science, and one year of mathematics—is expected of everyone in the 9th through 12th grades. In addition, students may follow courses of special interest to them at the various grade levels. Those students anticipating college entrance have their program established by college admission standards and thus are able to elect only a limited number of courses.

With the passage of the Elementary and Secondary Education Act in 1965, the federal government assumed an even more active role in the direct support of secondary education to include the funding of innovative programs under Title III of the act.

But the basic educational issues remain, as in the past, the great historic questions of secondary education: selective versus universal education; practical learning versus classical academic subjects; a flexible versus a rigid curriculum; social, civic, and character development versus intellectual development; and the degrees of local, state, and federal control. Most questions concerning secondary education relate in one way or another to the capability of the comprehensive high school. A careful differentiation and specialization of student programs within the total school curriculum to provide top-flight learning for the fast, the medium, and the slow student, is necessary if the comprehensive school is to maintain its popularity.

Consult Kandel, I. L., *History of Secondary Education* (1930); Educational Policies Commission, *Education for All American Youth: A Further Look* (1952); *The High School in a New Era*, ed. by F. S. Chase and H. A. Anderson (1958); Conant, J. B., *The American High School Today* (1959); Alexander, W. M., and Saylor, J. G., *Modern Secondary Education* (1959); Scott, C. W., and others, *The Great Debate: Our Schools in Crisis* (1959); Gardner, J. W., "National Goals in Education," in the President's Commission on National Goals, *Goals for Americans* (1960); Cremin, L. A., *The Transformation of the School* (1964); Olsen, H. C., "Remaking the World of the Career Teacher": in the 1966 report of the *National Commission on Teacher Education and Professional Standards* (1966).

ROBERT N. BUSH, Stanford University
and SCOTT D. THOMSON, Principal,
Cubberley High School,
Palo Alto, Calif.

See also:

COLLEGE ENTRANCE
  REQUIREMENTS
CURRICULUM
GUIDANCE AND COUNSELING,
  EDUCATIONAL
PHYSICAL EDUCATION
PREPARATORY SCHOOL
VOCATIONAL EDUCATION
VOCATIONAL GUIDANCE

HIGHER EDUCATION IN THE UNITED STATES

Most of the formal, post-secondary education in the United States takes place in colleges and universities. These institutions are usually classified as universities, liberal arts colleges, separately organized professional schools, and junior colleges. A university includes an undergraduate college and one or more professional schools, emphasizes graduate instruction, and confers advanced degrees. A college emphasizes general undergraduate education, primarily in liberal arts and sciences, and grants baccalaureate (bachelor's) degrees. Professional schools prepare students for specialized occupations such as law and medicine. A junior (or community) college offers a two-year program, either terminal or in preparation for transfer to a university.

A college degree has long been an important status symbol, but in the new world of automated technology it has become also the ticket to opportunities for good jobs. Many students go to college because they want to enter a particular profession or vocation. Only by the college route can they become teachers, scientists, lawyers, doctors, engineers, librarians, or any of scores of specialists.

It is estimated that the college graduate during his lifetime earns from $100,000 to $200,000 more than the high school graduate. Quite aside from material benefits, college is the door to more complete development and enjoyment of an individual's intellectual, spiritual, and cultural potentials. The college experience is vital not only to what the student will do, but to what he will be. From college, he learns something of what matters in his world, and what his own relationship to it is.

Colleges and universities offer programs of study that vary widely in time required and areas of concentration. The programs may be broadly classified as undergraduate and graduate studies.

Undergraduate Programs

Many combinations of courses are offered to undergraduate students. The typical program extends over a period of four years, but some are concentrated into a shorter period, such as the two-year junior college vocational-technical program.

Liberal arts courses usually require, in the first two years, English composition, foreign language, literature, mathematics, social science, and science. Students normally take four or five subjects of study concurrently in each term. One unit of credit is allowed for each course (or semester) hour per week. Laboratory classes usually require two or three hours in the laboratory for each credit. The normal student program includes 15 or 16 hours of lecture or discussion classes each week.

Toward the end of the second year the student is expected to select his field of concentration, or "major," and with the aid of his faculty adviser to plan a suitable program of specialized study. Some colleges permit students to begin professional studies in the junior or senior year, and to receive a baccalaureate degree after the first, second, or third year of professional training.

Vocational preparation is provided in four-year curricula for professions such as agriculture, business administration, education, engineering, forestry, home economics, and nursing. There is a trend, however, toward raising the educational level of professional curricula in many fields by requiring several years of preprofessional education for admission, and a total of more than four years to obtain the first professional degree. For example, the medical degree normally requires four years beyond three or four years of undergraduate preprofessional training. Law is often 3–3; dentistry, osteopathy, and veterinary medicine frequently are 2–4. In many areas such as social work, business administration, and library science the master's degree is becoming the recognized professional degree.

Two-year courses are provided by the junior (or community) college. Transfer programs, similar to the first two years of a liberal arts curriculum, are designed for student transfer at the end of two years to a four-year

EARNED DEGREES CONFERRED BY INSTITUTIONS OF HIGHER EDUCATION IN THE UNITED STATES, 1650 to 1960.

(Associate's degree not included.)

Year	Total	Bachelor's or first professional	Master's except first professional	Doctor's
1650	9	9	0	0
1675	9	9	0	0
1700	15	15	0	0
1725	54	54	0	0
1750	42	42	0	0
1775	150	150	0	0
1800	223	223	0	0
1870	9,372	9,371	0	1
1880	13,829	12,896	879	54
1890	16,703	15,539	1,015	149
1900	29,375	27,410	1,583	382
1910	39,755	37,199	2,113	443
1920	53,516	48,622	4,279	615
1930	139,752	122,484	14,969	2,299
1940	217,454	187,396	26,768	3,290
1950	498,586	433,734	58,219	6,633
1960	479,215	394,889	74,497	9,829

1960 TOTALS

Men	315,242	255,504	50,937	8,801
Women	163,973	139,385	23,560	1,028
Per cent men	65.8	64.7	68.4	89.5
Per cent women	34.2	35.3	31.6	10.5

Sources: Three publications of U.S. Office of Education, Washington, D.C.: Eells, W. C., *Baccalaureate Degrees Conferred by American Colleges in the 17th and 18th Centuries* (1958); Badger, H. G., and Johnson, M. C., *Statistics of Higher Education, 1955-56; Faculty, Students, and Degrees* (1958); Tolliver, W. E., *Summary Report on Bachelor's and Higher Degrees Conferred During the Year 1959-60* (1961).

college. Vocational-technical programs, ending at completion of the junior college work, offer courses that provide specialized knowledge and skills for jobs demanding technical training such as electronics, shop work, and office work. Successful completion of the transfer or vocational-technical program leads to award of the associate's degree.

Special Programs

Advanced placement as freshmen is possible if able high school students take advantage of electives by studying advanced subjects, and qualify by taking tests prepared by the College Entrance Examination Board. After an acceptance by a college that subscribes to the Advanced Placement Program, the student may take the three-hour, essay type examinations in the spring. The college decides whether he is to receive college credit for the freshman subject and be permitted to go on to a more advanced course.

Cooperative (work-study) plans, available at a few institutions, permit students to spend alternate periods of several weeks in the classroom, and on the job. Institutions with such cooperative programs include Northeastern University, Antioch College, Fenn College, and The Rochester Institute of Technology.

The Reserve Officers Training Corps (ROTC) has Army, Air Force, or Navy units at many institutions, and produces a large proportion of career officers for the armed services. On most campuses the two- or four-year enrollment is voluntary. Each of the services provides a four-year "scholarship program" for about 5,000 students. In addition, there is "retainer pay" for scholarship holders during their four years, and for other ROTC students in their last two years.

Graduate and Professional Programs

The term "graduate" traditionally is used to designate those studies that are beyond the bachelor's or first professional degree and are devoted to the consideration and advancement of knowledge as well as to its utilization. Although scores of different graduate degrees are awarded, the master of arts (M.A.) and the doctor of philosophy (Ph.D.) are typical.

The master's degree has varying significance among the more than 600 U. S. institutions that confer it. Sometimes it is given upon completion of a year's work, but it may also involve a thesis, a general examination, and a language requirement. Some institutions consider the master's degree a research degree; others see it as a trial run for the Ph.D. Since some state boards of education have made the master's degree a requirement for advancement, it is increasingly associated with professional education. About half the master's degrees being granted now are estimated to be in education (usually M.Ed.). A degree rapidly growing in number of awards, especially in liberal arts institutions, is the master of arts in teaching (M.A.T.), designed for liberal arts graduates prepared for secondary school teaching.

The doctor's degree was established in the late 19th century as the highest earned degree in the American graduate school. The doctor of philosophy degree program stresses competence in research, and emphasizes a scholarly or scientific approach. Graduate schools have the dual function, however, of preparing individuals for both research and teaching. Requirements for the doctorate vary but certain steps are typical: course work, residence, foreign languages, comprehensive examination, dissertation, and final examination. This program often requires three to seven years, but a national effort is being made to reduce this time.

Professional degrees are awarded following successful completion of advanced studies whose significance is primarily vocational. For example, the professional degree of doctor of medicine (M.D.) is awarded after a schedule of courses which fits the student for practice as a physician. The curriculum for a profession typically includes instruction in the techniques and knowledge employed directly in rendering professional service and also the basic sciences or other subjects whose mastery is essential to learning and understanding the professional subjects and techniques.

Sponsored Research. Some students and teachers, particularly those in graduate schools, work on research projects related to their scholarly interests. Such research often is relevant to the needs and interests of government, industry, or other nonacademic sponsors, who thus are willing to underwrite costs. Sometimes sponsors suggest particular investigations they wish to have pursued, though usually the researcher himself originates the research proposal. Universities receive well over $1,000,-000,000 each year, mainly from the federal government, for research conducted on their campuses.

Administration and Operation

Private colleges and universities operate under state charters, and must meet standards set by state agencies. These standards vary widely, however, and are not always an assurance of institutional quality. Private institutions are financed by tuition and fees, endowment earnings, gifts from business, foundations and alumni, and in recent years by increasing federal grants.

State colleges and universities are established under state constitutions or by state law, and receive their major support from the state. They also are supported by tuition and fees, federal grants, and gifts from business, alumni, and foundations. Endowment income is negligible.

Municipal colleges are established under state law or charter. Local tax funds and student fees provide the major income, though federal support is growing.

The federal government's program of education, chiefly for national defense, includes The Military Academy (West Point), The Naval Academy (Annapolis),

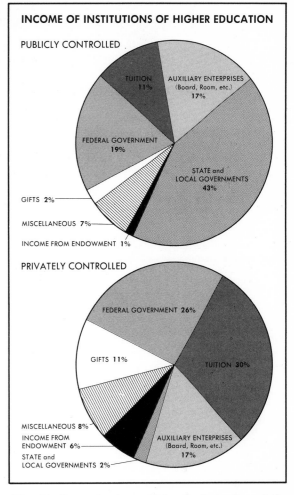

INCOME OF INSTITUTIONS OF HIGHER EDUCATION

PUBLICLY CONTROLLED

TUITION 11%
AUXILIARY ENTERPRISES (Board, Room, etc.) 17%
FEDERAL GOVERNMENT 19%
STATE and LOCAL GOVERNMENTS 43%
GIFTS 2%
MISCELLANEOUS 7%
INCOME FROM ENDOWMENT 1%

PRIVATELY CONTROLLED

FEDERAL GOVERNMENT 26%
GIFTS 11%
TUITION 30%
MISCELLANEOUS 8%
INCOME FROM ENDOWMENT 6%
STATE and LOCAL GOVERNMENTS 2%
AUXILIARY ENTERPRISES (Board, Room, etc.) 17%

The Air Force Academy (Colorado Springs), and the Coast Guard Academy (New London, Conn.). Other government institutions include the Merchant Marine Academy, Naval War College, Army War College, Air University, and Naval Postgraduate School.

Control and Administration. The control of colleges and universities is usually by a board of trustees, or board of regents. The method by which board members are selected indicates whether the institution is public or private. If a majority are elected by the people or chosen by a government official, such as the state governor, then the college is public. In some privately controlled institutions the board members choose their own successors. In others, trustees are chosen by the religious body which sponsors the college.

The board of trustees usually has the power to manage the institutions as it sees fit. In practice most boards delegate the chief executive functions to the full-time executive officers whom it selects. The principal administrative officer—usually the president, but occasionally called the chancellor—serves at the pleasure of the board, with broad powers and opportunity for initiative.

The president usually has one or more vice-presidents and several administrative assistants. Larger universities often delegate strictly educational activities to a provost or academic vice-president. In smaller institutions a dean usually is in charge of educational operations. This official is responsible to the president for faculty selection, curriculum, quality of instruction, and academic budget. Usually there are also the registrar, in charge of official records; the director of admissions, who determines the eligibility of candidates for admission; and the business officer, who manages financial affairs.

In the typical university, a liberal arts college is at the core, and graduate and professional schools (law, medicine) are at the top. The schools, headed by deans, are composed of departments under chairmen.

Faculty. A faculty member may be appointed to the rank of instructor, assistant professor, associate professor, and professor. Normally the minimum requirement for instructor or assistant professor is the master's degree, but there is increasing demand for the doctorate. Attainment of the ranks of associate professor or professor usually requires the Ph.D. or its equivalent. Individuals may be considered for promotion after stated periods of service and upon evidence of scholarly growth and teaching effectiveness. When tenure status is granted—usually after a stated period of satisfactory service—a professor's employment may be terminated only for adequate cause.

Some institutions, chiefly the larger ones, require research and publications for faculty advancement. This policy of "publish or perish" is widely believed to reduce faculty attention to teaching. The issue probably has been overstated, for studies show that in most colleges less than 10% of the faculty publishes 90% of the research.

Student Services and Physical Facilities. The importance of services to students apart from instruction is generally recognized. These include, in addition to extracurricular activities, admissions, orientation, counseling, health services, financial aid, and placement services, usually administered by a dean of students.

Campuses vary widely by reason of differences in the institution's size, wealth, setting, and architecture. For example, the value of buildings, grounds, and equipment at Harvard University is approximately $200,000,000, at Stanford University $100,000,000, and at Reed College $6,000,000. Nearly all colleges are alike, however, in having administrative offices, classrooms, laboratories, libraries, student unions, dining halls, bookstores, auditoriums, and dormitories.

The library is regarded by many educators as the single most important facility influencing the learning climate of a campus. Through it the student has access to contemporary culture as well as to the record of man's thought and action. More than 30 universities in the United States have over 1,000,000 volumes each.

Student Life

Student life varies widely in response to institutional factors such as size, urban or rural location, and type of control. Certain fairly general characteristics are discussed here.

Student Government. The chief purposes of student government, found on most campuses, are to assist the administration in maintaining effective relations with students and to give students experience in meeting the responsibilities of self-government. Student officers are chosen by the students in elections administered by their association. Student government authority ranges from control over limited student activities to a significant role in governing and disciplining students, and in some colleges even to a voice in administrative decisions. Rising student demands for larger roles in matters of faculty, curriculum, and financial management have created a major issue of the 1960–70 decade.

Student Activities. Activities beyond the regular curriculum are recognized as important in the student's educational growth. The demands of regular academic work make it necessary for most students, however, to limit their participation to two or three organized activities.

Cultural programs of student organizations serve to promote intellectual, aesthetic, religious, and social interests. Some organizations, such as a physics or French club, a drama group, or a film society, may include faculty or staff advisers. Other groups concerned with publications, intramural athletics, debating, and student government, may confine membership to students.

Athletics are the most publicized and criticized extracurricular activity. College policy on athletics varies widely, but often this activity is conducted by a highly developed division of athletics and physical education. Some sports, particularly football and basketball, tend to be commercialized and attract crowds that fill enormous stadiums and field houses. Athletic directors and coaches frequently are appointed to the faculty and accorded academic rank. A rising number of institutions, however, are reducing emphasis on intercollegiate competition.

Honor Societies. Most colleges award honors to students with outstanding grade averages. On many campuses the highest academic honor is election to Phi Beta Kappa, which has chapters at 176 institutions. Selection is based primarily on grades, though some consideration is given to other factors. Other well-known honor societies include Sigma Xi, whose members are chosen for excellence in science. Another is Phi Delta Kappa, whose members are outstanding in education. Almost every field of study has an honor society for undergraduates.

College Costs

College costs doubled from 1950 to 1965. So long as the operating costs of institutions continue to rise the financial burden upon the student and his family is likely to grow.

Student expenses vary substantially. Lowest costs are usually found at nonresidential, state, or community-supported colleges or junior colleges within commuting distance of students' homes. Annual expenses here will average $400 to $500 more than at high school. At moderately expensive institutions tuition, fees, and living expenses total $1,000 to $2,000 a year. At the most expensive institutions costs range from $2,500 to more than $3,500. Expenses everywhere vary according to the student's travel costs and living standards on campus.

Financial aid for students at college comes in loans, jobs, or scholarships. Many institutions combine two or three of these sources so as to distribute the available aid widely. The average aid per student is about $500. A limited number of on-campus jobs are available at most institutions. Students work as assistants to faculty members, as library attendants, or as buildings and grounds employees. But with both college costs and academic requirements rising, the student who can "work his way through college" without assistance is rare.

Scholarships and Fellowships. Colleges and universities are the chief sources of scholarship aid, including federal funds. Annual aid to the student ranges from a portion of tuition to complete coverage of fees and living expenses. Applications for assistance are generally made directly to the institutions. Scholastic attainment is the major basis for awards, but some scholarships are available for athletes.

The federal government gives aid to needy undergraduates and to students in special categories such as ROTC members, student nurses, Indians, and war orphans. Some states, including New York, California, Illinois, New Jersey, Virginia, and Rhode Island also award scholarships.

The National Merit Scholarship Corporation is the largest independent agency awarding scholarships. Many industries make awards on the basis of student performance in the National Merit Scholarship competition. The College Entrance Examination Board sponsors the College Scholarship Service, a cooperative effort of more than 600 participating colleges designed to make sure that funds for scholarships and other aid are wisely and fairly distributed.

Accreditation

In higher education, accreditation is the process whereby an organization or agency recognizes a college or university as having met certain qualifications or standards. These considerations include admissions policy, curriculum, faculty qualifications, faculty working conditions, physical plant, library, and finances.

Prospective enrollees should check carefully the accreditation of colleges. Graduation from an accredited institution gives the student some assurance that his diploma and credits will be recognized for admission to advanced study, for employment in positions requiring standard preparation, and for membership in learned societies. Attention to accreditation also serves as protection against fraudulent "degree mills" which deceive thousands of Americans every year.

Information on accreditation is available usually in the catalog of a college, and in *Accredited Institutions of Higher Education*, published in February and September each year by the American Council on Education.

Choosing a College

Search for the right college should begin by the junior year of high school, when there is enough evidence for a good estimate of the student's ability. After reviewing courses taken and grades achieved, he and his counselor should be able to identify several appropriate institutions. The student should then write to these colleges for detailed information.

In choosing a college the student should concentrate on three major considerations: the characteristics of institutions, the characteristics of college-bound students, and the matching of his personal characteristics to the college that will provide maximum educational development.

Characteristics of Colleges. Each college and university has characteristics that distinguish it from others. The intelligent student will make it his business to understand these differences. Also, avoiding the mistaken notion that only one college is right for him, he probably will find several institutions that suit his resources, capabilities, and aims very well.

The best size for an institution is much debated, but the answer must depend on the needs of the individual. One student may achieve most in a small college where he can know personally every student, teacher, and administrator. The small liberal arts college may offer the more personalized instruction and closer student-faculty relationships that challenge some students to greater effort.

For another student, however, greater stimulus may come from the big university, or even from a multiuniversity such as the University of California with many campuses and 100,000 students. Here the appeal is in the broad curriculum, extensive libraries, research programs, and diverse student body.

Institutional size alone is not an important consideration. A good student will usually perform equally well on a small or large campus. Coeducation also is an environmental factor of major or minor importance according to personal judgment. The proper focus of concern should be on types of programs, levels of student competition, and scholastic standards.

Whether to choose a college under public or private auspices is also a matter of preference. A few years ago two out of three students were in private institutions; today public colleges enroll two out of three. This trend continues, but most authorities believe private institutions will continue to be a substantial part of higher education in the United States.

For an adequate appraisal of his prospective campus, the student needs a firsthand impression. He should write to the college admissions office for an appointment, and take with him a summary of his record. Many colleges use such visits for interviews and appraisals, and hold the results for selection purposes.

Differences in Students. The personal history of each student reveals abilities, interests, attitudes, and styles of behavior that are peculiarly his. The student, his counselor, and the institution to which he applies should study this evidence carefully in order to assess with confidence how he will fare in the program he desires. The counselor, in estimating his student's chance of success at a particular college, must consider the great variations in the average ability of students at different institutions. Information on this is available from the College Entrance Examination Board's *Manual of Freshman Profiles*, published every two years, and from Alexander W. Astin's *Who Goes Where to College?* (1965).

Major factors in predicting a student's performance in college are the level of his high school grades, and scores on aptitude and achievement tests. Cultural background and financial resources are less important. Colleges, in making admissions decisions, consider also the student's class standing, the academic quality of courses taken, the type of school attended, and the pattern of improving or declining student performance. Assuming a satisfactory academic record, the student with a fine record of outside activities probably has a wider choice of colleges than the student with high grades and only a brief record of outside activity.

Matching of Student and Institution. The student should seek the college that seems to offer the most favorable interaction of his personality and capabilities with the environment and resources of the institution. Objective study, however, cannot explain all the successes and failures of student-college interaction.

For example, one concern should be cultural similarity or dissimilarity between the high school and college environment. If a student from a family of moderate income goes from a large city high school to a municipal college near home, he may be said to experience "cultural continuity." If he goes instead to a highly selective college far from home, where the typical students are affluent graduates of preparatory schools, he will experience "cultural discontinuity." Cultural continuity means less risk of failure, but also less opportunity for exceptional educational growth.

Applying for Admission. Early in the senior year, or preferably by the end of the junior year, a student should have a fairly definite idea of his college preferences. His strategy of making application—whether to one or several colleges—should depend largely on how he rates his qualifications against the varying admissions requirements of institutions.

Most colleges have admissions policies that are minimally selective. Students who meet minimum requirements—usually high school graduation and a minimum number of units of academic preparatory work (typically about 12)—are accepted. These colleges usually do not require entrance examinations. If there are tests, the chief purpose is to place students in courses appropriate to their aptitudes after their admission, rather than for the purpose of selection for admission. Average scores of students entering these colleges usually fall below the national average of college-bound students. These institutions often are lenient about deadlines, accept applications almost until classes begin, and offer remedial courses to students with weak preparation. Here the dropout rate of freshmen and sophomores may run high—some-

times more than 50%. It may be said that the selection process begins here after matriculation.

Selective admissions is the policy of perhaps 300 institutions. They typically expect 16 units of academic preparatory work. They may be flexible about making an exception for a student with less than 16 units provided his record is strong. Grade quality is important. The average student accepted is in the top 20% of his high school class. Entrance examinations are required. Tests of general scholastic ability in this group produce scores above average when compared with all college-bound youth.

These colleges, by trying to select students with a reasonable chance of success (likelihood of a C average or better), usually hold the dropout rate below 20%. More applicants are accepted than rejected. Here, in a sense, the selection process takes place both before and after students enter.

Competitive admissions is the policy of perhaps 100 institutions. Their definition of a qualified applicant is about the same as that of the selective institutions, but they accept only one out of five or more applicants. Achievement examinations and tests of general scholastic ability are usually required. Average scores on general ability tests are typically in the top 10% of the college-going population, and a large majority of the entering class comes from the top 20% of their high school class.

Once a competitive institution is satisfied with the intellectual qualifications of an applicant, nonintellectual factors may be determinative. These colleges often show concern for wide geographic spread, and representative skills in athletics, music, drama, and other extracurricular activities. With an academic attrition rate sometimes less than 5%, these institutions in effect select their graduates when they select their freshmen.

College Entrance Examinations. Colleges place high value on several standard tests as sources of information on students' potential success in college. These include the Scholastic Aptitude Test (SAT), the achievement tests in various subjects, and the writing sample—all administered by the Educational Testing Service (ETS) of the College Entrance Examination Board (CEEB). CEEB was founded in 1900 to provide direction, coordination,

A class of college undergraduates in a lecture course. A stimulating instructor brings his years of training and experience to his students, giving them new ideas as well as factual information. (KEN HEYMAN)

The Glee Club of the University of Virginia presents an informal outdoor concert for the students. (REED—MONKMEYER)

The mysteries of chemistry present a challenge to a student in a laboratory at Hofstra University. (HANNA W. SCHREIBER)

and research in helping students make the transition from school to college. More recently, a number of colleges have adopted the aptitude and achievement tests of the American College Testing Program.

When properly used together with school records, general ability test scores usually offer a sounder basis for student assessment than either records or scores alone. Tests are especially useful in showing how a student ranks when compared with a large representation of college-going youth. The significance of class rank in his particular school is far more limited. Many colleges consider the results of achievement tests (in English, chemistry, mathematics, and other subjects) to be an important part of the student's record not only for admissions purposes, but for placing him at specific levels of college work.

Admissions Procedures. If a student's first choice colleges are competitive institutions, he may be wise to apply also to selective or minimally selective institutions as alternatives. When his college or colleges are selected, the student should make sure he knows what each of them requires in tests, records, recommendations, applications, and timing. Some colleges require applications early in the senior year, others will not accept them until midyear.

Responses to applications are not likely to come before February, and probably not until April. If the student finds that he has over-assessed his qualifications and receives no letters of acceptance, he will need to consult his advisers and apply to less selective colleges with space available. Further inquiries may go directly to the prospective institutions, or through a college clearinghouse such as The College Admissions Center, Evanston, Ill., sponsored by the College Admissions Counselors; the College Admissions Assistance Center, New York; and the Catholic College Admissions and Information Center, Washington, D.C. These centers distribute applications to colleges with space available, the colleges write directly to the students, and the students then apply to the schools that they prefer.

History and Development

The founders of the first institution of higher learning in the United States, Harvard College (1636), were chiefly concerned with the advancement of learning and the training of clergymen. These concerns continued to dominate as eight additional colleges were founded in the United States by 1769. Thereafter emphasis on theological training steadily declined, and students began to show greatest interest in the profession of law.

While the classical curricula of Colonial colleges may seem antiquated today, these institutions were clearly effective in training leaders for the new nation. Three of the five members of the committee to draft the Declaration of Independence had been graduated from American colleges; so had four of the five members of Washington's first cabinet. These colleges, dedicated to the ideal of the gentleman scholar who knows the "best that has been said and thought in the world," remained the strongest influence in American higher education until the late 19th century.

Following the American Revolution, interest in higher education's development accelerated, and 17 institutions were founded by 1800. When the Civil War began in 1861, the number of colleges had grown to 182. Most of them retained the classically oriented curricula of the Colonial colleges, but a few separate professional schools, such as Rensselaer Polytechnic Institute (1824) and the Massachusetts Institute of Technology (1861), offered science and engineering. Meanwhile Harvard and Yale had added alternate programs emphasizing scientific training, and other established institutions soon followed their lead.

Normal schools, designed primarily to train teachers for the elementary schools, appeared in great numbers during the mid-19th century. When the growth of high schools made it evident that more comprehensive training for teachers was needed, the normal schools closed or became teachers colleges, many of which are today's state colleges.

Higher Education for Women. Many separate colleges

for women as well as the first degree-granting coeducational college (Oberlin Collegiate Institute) appeared between 1825 and 1875. By 1900, however, coeducation had become the trend. The coordinate college, separately organized for women but operating parallel with a men's college, appeared near the end of the century. Examples are Radcliffe College (Harvard) and Newcomb College (Tulane).

Rise of Universities. Demands for graduate education forced development of a new kind of higher education institution. With the founding of Johns Hopkins University in 1876 the first true university was established in the United States, and the university as an institution was on the way to its present leadership in American higher education. Many of the oldest liberal arts colleges, such as Yale, Harvard, and Columbia, soon became universities, as did some of the stronger public institutions, including Michigan, Wisconsin, and California. Possessors of great business fortunes gave generously to establish Johns Hopkins, Vanderbilt, Stanford, and the University of Chicago.

The new universities adopted a peculiarly American structure. An essentially German graduate school emphasizing research was placed structurally on top of an English college devoted to general education. Professional schools were incorporated into the university.

Land-Grant Colleges. One of the most significant events in the history of American higher education was passage of the Land-Grant College Act of 1862, often referred to by the name of its sponsor, Justin R. Morrill. The bill gave each state 30,000 acres of land (or equivalent) for each senator and representative in Congress. Proceeds from the grant were to help support one college whose principal aim should be to provide training in agriculture and the "mechanic arts." Such emphasis, however, was not to exclude "other scientific and classical studies."

The land-grant colleges and universities have been a major influence in developing the structure and curriculum of American higher education. They recognized disciplines that previously had been isolated in separate professional schools. They developed and promoted a peculiarly American concept of the university—what Ezra Cornell called "an institution where any person can find instruction in any study."

An Expanding Role. Since World War II higher education has struggled with the twin problems of an explosion of population and an explosion of knowledge. New knowledge has demanded an extraordinary increase in library books and periodicals, in laboratory and teaching equipment, and in technically qualified faculty. A growing population plus enormous demand for technically trained graduates for business, industry, and the professions has pushed enrollments steadily upward.

Colleges and universities also are being called on for assistance to government in national programs of research, social rehabilitation, and international cooperation. Increasing support from the White House and from Congress suggests that higher education is destined for still more importance in the nation's economy and culture.

Consult Rudolph, Frederick, *The American College and University* (1962); Kerr, Clark, *The Uses of the University* (1963); American Council on Education, *American Universities and Colleges*, ed. by A. M. Cartter (9th ed., 1964); Lovejoy, C. E., *Lovejoy's Complete Guide to American Colleges and Universities* (1967).

CHARLES G. DOBBINS, American Council on Education

See also:

ACADEMIC COSTUME	FRATERNITIES AND
ACADEMIC FREEDOM	SORORITIES
ACADEMIC RANK	JUNIOR COLLEGE
ACCREDITATION OF	LIBRARIES, UNITED STATES
SCHOOLS AND COLLEGES	COLLEGE AND
COLLEGE	UNIVERSITY
COLLEGE, SELECTING A	SCHOLARSHIPS
COLLEGE ENTRANCE	TEACHERS AND TEACHING
REQUIREMENTS	UNIVERSITIES AND
DEGREES, ACADEMIC	COLLEGES
FELLOWSHIPS,	WOMEN, EDUCATION OF
EDUCATIONAL	

EDUCATION IN CANADA

Canadian education can best be understood from an appreciation of its beginnings, which for the French-speaking in Quebec and Acadia date from early in the 17th century and for the English-speaking from the 18th and 19th centuries. The French settlers, of whom many had learned the observances of the Roman Catholic Church and about one-third were literate, favored continuing elementary schooling and religion. Frontiersmen, who had adopted carefree aspects of Indian life and an outlook related to life's uncertainties in the colony, caused the church authorities to be quite strict, a pattern affecting education until the quiet revolution of the 1950's.

Newfoundland, a base for European fishing ships from the 16th century on, faced towards Europe and remained Old World, little affected by the North American emphasis on economic enterprise, social democracy, and political responsibility. Many of its settlers clustered in villages and outposts and, except for those who could afford tutors, depended on charity schools and the clergy. Its education system remains denominational, under five superintendents who report to the deputy minister and operate under one School Law. Local school boards, of one faith, select teachers, pay salaries from government grants, and generally manage the schools. Newfoundland became a Canadian province in 1949.

Schools in the Maritime Provinces reflected the influence of immigrants from Britain and Europe and their American neighbors to the south. Moral and religious aims permeated the schools for many years. Ontario, influenced by European settlers and the United Empire Loyalists, moved rather rapidly from private to public schools. The Prairie Provinces, opened largely by the Hudson's Bay and North West companies, first depended on mission schools, but soon welcomed teachers from the Maritimes and Ontario who left their imprint on the early education of the West. British Columbia, separated by mountains from the rest of Canada, began its education with mission, company, and common schools separately on the island and on the mainland. Vancouver Island and the mainland colony were united in 1866. An ordinance in 1869 established the principle of public schools and the Public Schools Act of 1872 provided a basis for the present system.

Stages of Development. The colonial period fostered a variety of such schools as parish, charity, Sunday, infant, Latin grammar, community, and academic. The second stage marked the beginning of provincial systems, with strong central authorities providing support for free elementary and later secondary schools. The provincial systems provided for local school boards responsible for selecting land, constructing schools, employing teachers, and operating the schools under the School Act.

The third stage began in 1867 with Confederation of the provinces. Formal education remained the prerogative of the provincial legislatures. Provincial departments of education accepted responsibility for training and certifying teachers, issuing courses of study, authorizing text books, employing inspectors, conducting provincial examinations, and maintaining reasonably uniform, high standards. Today a departmental staff normally includes division heads for elementary, secondary, vocational, and adult education with sections for curriculum, audio-visual education, and teacher education. Also included are a registrar, accountant, subject experts, and inspectors.

The fourth stage, which represents both quantitative and qualitative revolutions, began when the surge of World War II babies entered the elementary schools, and shortages of skilled technicians, engineers, and scientists in industry made newspaper headlines. The onslaught of numbers moved upwards from elementary to secondary school to university. However, the falling birthrate of the past years indicates that Canada may soon turn attention at the lower levels to quality. Numbers at the secondary level were affected greatly by surprisingly larger percentages remaining through the secondary grades. University enrollments have skyrocketed, and are expected to double within the mid-1970's. This is in part due to increased numbers of university age, but also because a larger percentage enter universities—13% of men and 6% of women. The total is expected to double during the 1970's, with the number and percentage enrolling in graduate courses growing even greater proportionately.

Separate and Private Schools. Newfoundland has a multi-denominational system and Quebec two distinct publicly administered systems that operate under the School Act. New Brunswick and Nova Scotia have a gentlemen's agreement that schools can be basically sectarian or not, according to the wishes of the taxpayers. Ontario, Saskatchewan, and Alberta provide for publicly controlled separate schools by law. British Columbia and Manitoba provide only for public schools. All provinces allow private schools to operate.

Financing the Schools. In 1966 almost 49% of municipal, 34% of provincial, and from 4% to 5% of federal revenue went for formal education. The provinces have made flat grants or incentive and equalization grants. The trend is toward some form of foundation program under which a uniform tax is levied on an equalized assessment, the province making up any deficiencies. Universities and colleges receive about 30% of their income from student

Art class at a public elementary school in Toronto provides the opportunity for individual self-expression. (NATIONAL FILM BOARD)

fees, 44% from provincial grants, 13% from federal government grants, and the remainder from other sources.

Higher Education. Institutions of higher learning established by the Church of England, Roman Catholic, and later by other congregations, date back to the end of the 18th and first half of the 19th centuries. In the four western provinces, provincial institutions were established first, other institutions being added as needed. Many new universities have sprung up across Canada during recent years. Several provinces conducted extensive surveys to determine where these were most needed.

Teacher Education. Teacher training from the beginning has been the responsibility of provincial departments. A trend toward giving all teacher education on the university campuses continues. In the western provinces, combined education, arts, and science courses are offered; elsewhere, education is kept separate. A shortage of

High school students profit from special programs for the classroom provided by Canadian television. (ANNAN PHOTO FEATURES)

qualified teachers at all levels remains. The demand at the higher education level is most critical because of increased enrollments and rising demands on professional competence.

The Federal Government and Education. Under the British North America Act of 1867 the federal government accepted responsibility for education of the Indians, Eskimos, citizens outside the provinces, and members of the armed services. Canada has no ministry of education, but many federal departments are concerned with education. Although the federal contribution to education and related activities is some 11.6% of the total expenditure, it influences the direction of education considerably. The Department of Labour, interested in technical and professional manpower development, between 1961 and 1964 allocated some $655,000,000 for current and capital costs. This spurred efforts to add to or provide additional trade schools, institutes of technology, and vocational high school classes. From 1967 federal sums have been available for post-secondary and adult education and training, including community colleges. Grants to universities are made to the provinces on a per capita basis and paid to the universities according to their enrollments. Other contributions include grants for specific buildings and equipment, scholarships, research grants, sums for external aid, and loans for students.

With no Canadian department of education, eleven or more systems of education, and largely autonomous universities, Canadian education lacks an official spokesman. The provincial ministers of education are considering the establishment of a permanent council. At the same time the federal government is considering designating one department to coordinate federal efforts in education.

The Canadian Education Association, supported by the provincial governments, since 1892 has provided liaison among the provinces and represented Canada at certain international meetings. The Association of Universities and Colleges of Canada, the Canadian Teachers' Federation, the Canadian Council for Research in Education, and some 80 or more other national and provincial education associations contribute to cooperation and documentation in education.

The Outlook. Concomitant with current developments in the dynamic school situation are public acceptance of education as a good investment in economic growth and national welfare, and the focusing of attention on education by economists, sociologists, communication experts, engineers, and large business firms. The four-mile square, one-room, one-teacher units have generally given way to larger rural units. At the same time the trend is toward greater decentralization with increased local responsibility for curriculum, organization, examinations, research, use of audio-visual aids, and other concerns. Related innovations include ungraded classes, team teaching, independent study, and an increase in the use of electronic and other modern media.

An increased interest in a social-economic-psychological approach relates to disadvantaged youth, the physically and mentally handicapped, university selection, and pre-service and in-service training. Exciting developments are also found in the construction of buildings that are both functionally suited to the new programs and also showplaces. In Quebec, some cities have constructed academic, trade, technical, teacher-training, and other units around a common center of library, gymnasium, cafeteria, playing fields, and such.

Consult Phillips, C. E., *The Development of Education in Canada* (1957); Swift, W. H., *Trends in Canadian Education* (1958); Dominion Bureau of Statistics, *A Bibliographical Guide to Canadian Education* (1964), *The Organization and Administration of Public Schools in Canada* (3d ed., 1965), and *Canada Year Book* (annual).

FRED E. WHITWORTH, Director,
Canadian Council for Research in Education

EDUCATION FOR THE PROFESSIONS

Theology, medicine, and law have long been regarded as the classic learned professions. Many other occupations have attained professional status during the past century, and more than a score are now included in surveys of professional education. Still others will no doubt achieve professional status as the complexity of civilization and its reliance on experts increase. Definitions of "profession" vary, but the following characteristics are often found: a specific amount of training at the college or university level is required; organizations have been formed to set standards for institutions offering training and often to set up codes for the practice of the profession; some form of certification or licensing is often required.

Preparation for a profession in the 17th and 18th centuries, with the exception of the ministry, was largely of the apprenticeship type. A young man desiring to enter law or medicine, for example, worked informally with a recognized practitioner in the field. This type of professional education was followed in many fields by independently organized schools, often privately owned and run for profit, whose standards varied greatly and frequently were very low. During the present century most of these independent schools, except those of theology, have been abolished or have become constituent schools or departments of recognized universities with a vast resultant improvement in standards, equipment, and staff.

For the preparation of clergymen, separate schools have existed since the earliest times in the United States. Harvard, the oldest college in the United States (1636), was founded chiefly because the Massachusetts Puritans "dreaded to leave an illiterate Ministry to the Churches, when our present Ministers shall lie in the Dust." The same purpose was the major factor in the founding of Yale College (1701) and most of the other colonial colleges. St. Mary's Seminary and University, Baltimore, was founded in 1791, to educate Roman Catholic priests.

The first institutional instruction in medicine was given by the present University of Pennsylvania in 1765, followed by Columbia in 1767, Harvard in 1782, and Dartmouth in 1798. The first organized instruction in law was given by the Litchfield Law School, Connecticut, privately established in 1784, which continued until 1833. University instruction in law was inaugurated by the University of Maryland in 1816 and by Harvard University in 1817.

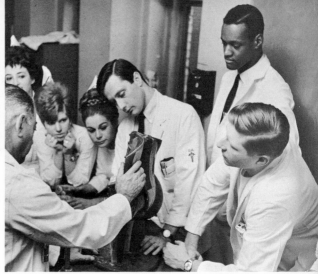

Left, future lawyers get a chance to polish their courtroom technique in a test case. (DON HINKLE) Right, medical students learn the intricacies of the human body with the aid of an anatomical model. (ESTHER BUBLEY)

A rapid increase in the number and variety of professional schools followed the Civil War. The first college-level work in architecture was given in 1865, followed by such fields as nursing (1873), business administration (1881), and librarianship (1887). Since 1900 professional education has been increasingly concentrated in the universities. Accreditation organizations have been formed in most of the professional fields, resulting in a marked improvement in standards.

There is a considerable range in the number of years of college-level study required by the professions. Four years are required for a first degree in nursing and teaching, for example. For engineering the requirement is four to five years, and the time increases to six years for law and social work and seven years for medicine.

Until modern times the professions were usually open to men only. In the 20th century, however, women have established their right to enter all fields. One recent tabulation of degrees granted in professional fields in the United States showed that 34% were awarded to women.

The American Council on Education, Washington, D.C., collects and publishes every 4 years much significant information regarding accredited schools in more than a score of professional fields. In this encyclopedia entries on major professional fields (from anthropology and architecture to zoology) include sections on the requirements for careers in those fields.

Consult Education for the Professions, ed. by G. L. Anderson (1962); *American Universities and Colleges,* ed. by Allan Cartter (1964).

WALTER CROSBY EELLS, Stanford University
See also ACCREDITATION OF SCHOOLS AND COLLEGES; VOCATIONAL GUIDANCE; and Career Guides accompanying articles on major fields.

EDUCATION OF EXCEPTIONAL CHILDREN

The term "exceptional children" has been defined by the National Society for the Study of Education as including those children "who deviate from what is supposed to be average in physical, mental, emotional, or social characteristics to such an extent that they require special educational services in order to develop their maximum capacity." The deviation from normal can be toward the higher or lower end of the scale. Hence the category of exceptional children includes the gifted as well as the handicapped. Other terms sometimes used are "atypical" and "deviant." Many sources, including publications of the United Nations Educational, Scientific and Cultural Organization (UNESCO), use "special education" to cover this area of school services.

Classification of Exceptional Children. In the United States, children may be classified as exceptional if they (1) are of high mental ability or are creative or talented, (2) are mentally retarded, (3) are on the border line of mental retardation (slow learners), (4) have visual handicaps, (5) have impaired hearing, (6) have speech problems, (7) have orthopedic handicaps (are crippled), (8) are neurologically damaged, (9) have chronic medical problems, (10) are socially and emotionally maladjusted, (11) have a cultural handicap, and (12) are educationally retarded. Further comment on these categories is given below.

A similar classification of exceptional children has been made in Canada. Under the broad heading of (1) mentally exceptional and emotionally disturbed children are grouped children who are (1a) mentally retarded, (1b) mentally gifted, and (1c) emotionally disturbed. Under (2) physically handicapped children are listed those who are (2a) blind or partially sighted, (2b) deaf or hard of hearing, (2c) speech defective, (2d) "cerebral palsied," (2e) orthopedic, (2f) hospitalized, (2g) tuberculous, in sanitoria, (2h) homebound, (2i) delicate, in open-air schools. Two additional categories are (3) delinquent and (4) orphaned and neglected. In the United Kingdom, England and Wales use similar categories except that there is no special "gifted" classification. The tendency in other countries is to make less detailed breakdowns. Italy, for example, provides special schools for three groups: mentally abnormal, blind and deaf-mutes, and physically deficient.

287

Historical Perspective. Special care of exceptional children is a comparatively new idea in history. Early civilizations exposed cripples to die and treated the mentally retarded as possessed of demons or as objects of ridicule. As late as the 19th century it was a common practice for parents to hide away chronically ill, physically handicapped, or retarded children for fear of social disgrace. Many such children were confined in institutions till they died. Some attempts at scientific care and training of the blind and deaf were made in France in the late 18th century. In the United States, Thomas Hopkins Gallaudet opened a pioneer school for the deaf at Hartford, Conn., in 1817. Special training for the mentally retarded was initiated in France and the United States in the 19th century, and around the end of that century signs of progress appeared in a number of fields. Special classes for the mentally retarded were introduced in Providence, R.I., in 1896 and Springfield, Ill., in 1897, and by 1910 more than 200 such classes had been started in the United States. The first Braille class for the blind was organized in Chicago in 1900 (other systems of teaching the blind to read had been used earlier). Programs for the gifted and for children with speech problems, for the socially and emotionally maladjusted, and for the culturally handicapped developed more slowly than programs for children with more obvious special needs. In general, large-scale educational programs for exceptional children were virtually unknown until the 20th century was well under way.

Various factors brought about changes in public attitudes toward atypical children and led to an expansion of programs. The passage of compulsory-education laws in all states by 1918 made the public schools responsible for all children. It soon became clear that children with special problems needed special services. Experience during two world wars led to increased understanding of the needs and the usefulness of handicapped persons. Organizations were formed to promote research and treatment. The growth of cities made it possible to group together enough children with similar problems to make special classes economically feasible. Progress in medicine and psychology led to earlier identification of problems. New techniques and new devices such as improved lenses and hearing aids made treatment and teaching more effective. The number of specialists in all fields increased as training programs in such fields as physiology, social work, psychology, and special education expanded.

Modern Programs in the United States. Programs for exceptional children can be discussed as follows:

(1) The public or private residential, or boarding, institution represents the oldest form of care for exceptional children. Many of these institutions used to be little more than places where children were kept in custody, in crowded conditions and with poor staffs and facilities. Modern institutions—often under such names as "state school," "industrial school," or "parental school"—have in some states improved to the point of having excellent programs, plant, and personnel. The cost for care of blind, deaf, retarded, crippled, or chronically ill children is usually paid by the state government, with parents contributing up to the limit of their ability.

(2) The special school, which serves children from a limited area and is not a full-time residential institution, provides the major portion of the education and training for certain types of exceptional children such as the blind and partially seeing and the deaf and hard of hearing.

(3) The special class, located in a regular school, was developed in an effort to overcome the most serious objections to institutions and special schools, while providing exceptional children with an effective program based upon their educational needs. Special classes have been organized for every type of exceptional child.

(4) In a further attempt to integrate exceptional children into the regular school program, educators introduced the resource room, a room in a regular school that is set aside for special programs conducted by a specially trained teacher, and the itinerant teacher, who travels from school to school to provide special programs and to help the regular class teacher.

One notable trend in programs for exceptional children is an emphasis upon keeping the child at home, in his regular school, and in a regular class if possible. When a child needs placement in a special class, the trend is to integrate this class into the regular school program and to make it as much a part of the regular school as possible. The trend toward special classes rather than special schools obtains in Sweden as well as in the United States. When a child is in need of special school placement, a determined effort is made to keep the contacts with the home as normal as possible and to give these children many of the experiences that the more normal children have. When no other placement is possible, some form of institution is called upon to provide a program for exceptional children. Local school systems are increasing their staffs of professional personnel. States have organized separate divisions of their education departments, sometimes under a director of pupil personnel and special services.

The research being carried on by universities and other agencies can be expected to improve methods of treatment and teaching and to reduce the incidence of some kinds of handicap. At the same time the total number of handicapped children can be expected to increase because of two factors, population growth and the ability to keep alive children whose handicaps would once have been fatal. Although great progress has been made in special education, the problem remains enormous. A conservative estimate for the early 1960's set the number of U.S. children needing special services at about 6,000,000. Only 15% to 20% of these children were actually enrolled in special programs.

Gifted Children

Definition of the Gifted, Talented, or Creative. Like other terms for exceptional children, "gifted" and approximate synonyms for it (talented, creative, genius, superior) are hard to define. In general, children who achieve high scores on tests of mental ability, do outstanding work in school, and show unusual talent or creative ability are considered gifted. A group of gifted children may include those who have a talent for writing, acting, art, or some other form of creative expression; children who are superior in mathematical, scientific, and mechanical work and are interested in investigation or experimentation; children who show leadership ability and are capable of planning and organizing on a high level. In the words of the National Society for the Study of Education, "The talented or gifted child is one who shows consistently remarkable performance in any worth-while line of endeavor." In the United States, gifted children are estimated to make up 2% to 3% of the school-age population.

As the scope of this definition might suggest, no single method has proved successful for identifying children with superior ability. Evidence ordinarily consists of teachers' judgments, school records, and scores on group achievement tests and on group or individual tests of mental ability. Some experts take an intelligence quotient (IQ) of 120 as the dividing point for special grouping ("normal," or "average," being between 90 and 110). Others would class as gifted those with IQ's of over 135. Aptitude tests are often used as a means of identifying children who are likely to succeed in college.

Tests have undoubted value, but their results must be used with due caution. In the first place, not all children are given the same or comparable tests. In the second place, some kinds of talent may not be revealed by the commonly employed tests of mental ability and achievement. In the third place, test results do not always show an individual's true level of ability. Teachers' judgments have also been found to be an uncertain means of identifying the gifted. Generally, teachers can recognize about half of the exceptionally able children in a classroom.

Programs. Historically, education of the gifted has received less attention than education of the handicapped. Flexible promotion (skipping grades) was tried in the 19th century, but programs for superior students did not become widespread in the United States. After World War II numerous comments on the training of gifted children were published. Some authorities pointed out that while programs were provided for the "average" person, the "superior" person was neglected. The value of superior abilities was given publicity by fears that the Soviet Union was surpassing the United States in training scientists and technicians. Bright children were seen as an important national resource. It was pointed out that a majority of the young people who had a capacity to do college work did not attend college, and that the outstanding students were relatively neglected in the high schools. Reports in the early 1960's gave the number of pupils in special programs for the gifted as less than 25% of the number of pupils in programs for the mentally retarded. Studies of the high schools by James Bryant Conant stressed the need to have academically talented students give more time to mathematics, science, and foreign languages.

Various plans have been used in an effort to provide programs for the gifted in the schools of the nation. One —acceleration, skipping, or flexible promotion—has already been mentioned. Its advantages lie in the fact that the child is challenged to work to the limits of his ability. Several studies have shown that acceleration was not particularly associated with problems in the later life of the gifted. Children who were accelerated were found to be more successful in college than those who had not been in this type of program. An increasing number of colleges are accepting carefully selected superior students for advanced placement. Nevertheless, acceleration has not been popular with many American educators. Although it is agreed that most gifted children succeed in the aca-

High school students in an advanced chemistry class learning qualitative organic analysis. (JANE LATTA)

demic areas and in social and emotional adjustment while participating in this type of program, many children break down emotionally if too severe pressure is placed on them by the school or by parents.

Special classes are another means of providing enriched programs for gifted children. Talented pupils grouped in one class can be given additional work in all subjects. Research projects, individual study in areas of special interest, and pupil-teacher conferences are features of these programs. Foreign language instruction may begin in the elementary grades.

The grouping together of superior students is most common in the high schools. Elective subjects, honors courses, and college preparatory courses have been planned to give educational opportunities to the talented. Less demanding courses are scheduled for pupils who are headed for vocational schools or who, for other reasons, are not likely to enter college.

Some studies of students in special classes indicate that they reach a high level of achievement in scholarship and are characterized by high levels of co-operation, social consciousness, leadership, and responsibility. Objections to special groupings have been made on such grounds as that these classes are undemocratic, cause some students to overwork, and are prohibitively costly. The difficulty of identifying talented students is a problem.

Another means of providing special education for the gifted is termed "enrichment." Students are left in the usual classes, not grouped according to ability. Special studies and activities are offered on an individual basis to students who can benefit from them. Favorable conditions, including small classes and teachers with versatile skills, are needed to make the program succeed.

A number of communities have experimented with providing for the gifted through part-time programs and special rooms. In these programs gifted children are members of regular classes. In the elementary school, schedules are arranged so that children are free for part of the school day. In the junior high school, special project classes or honors classes are used as part of a flexible scheduling arrangement. This program permits these children to be with their regular class for part of the day and yet to have an opportunity to move at their own pace and to explore areas of their own interest. This part-time program has been evolved in an effort to overcome unfavorable criticisms of the other types of programs.

Programs for the Handicapped

Education of Children with Retarded Mental Development. "Mental retardation" as used here includes such designations as feeble-mindedness, mental deficiency, mental handicap, amentia, oligophrenia, and the levels indicated by the terms "idiot," "imbecile," and "moron." The term "mental retardation" has been chosen as the most acceptable by the American Association on Mental Deficiency. Children who are mentally retarded usually have a combination of medical, social, maturational, physiological, and educational problems, rather than a single clinical symptom. Mental retardation is often confused with mental illness. Although mentally retarded children may also be mentally ill and mentally ill children may also be retarded, each category is conceived of as a fairly distinct area of exceptionality. The retarded must be distinguished from those who are classed as socially or emotionally maladjusted (see below). Mental retardation has been defined in terms of being below average in one or more of three areas: rate of maturation in early childhood of such skills as crawling, standing, walking, talking, and training in useful habits; learning ability, particularly in school; and social adjustment in the sense of the ability to live independently and earn a living.

For educational purposes mentally retarded children are classified in three groups, usually called educable, trainable, and custodial or severely retarded. At a conservative estimate, 2% of the U.S. school population is mentally retarded. Of this group, 85% is educable, 11.5% trainable, and 3.5% severely retarded. The term "educable mentally retarded" is applied to children of school age who will achieve no more than a maximum of 12 years in mental age at maturity. Characteristic of this group is achievement at no more than 4th or 5th grade in academic ability. However, they are capable of becoming self-sustaining, independent adults who can work in unskilled or semiskilled occupations after they have completed proper training and have been helped in finding a job. Their IQ's generally range from 50 to 75 on an individual test of mental ability.

The term "trainable mentally retarded" is applied to children of school age who will achieve no more than a maximum mental age of seven at maturity, and who for school entrance are able to walk, to have clean bodily habits, to communicate their needs, and who are responsive to simple commands. These children do not usually learn to read or compute to any usable extent, they are limited in their ability to communicate, and they will be semi-dependent or dependent as adults, needing a sheltered environment under close supervision. They often have physical disabilities. Their IQ's generally range from 25 or 30 to 50 on an individual test of mental ability.

The terms "custodial" or "severely retarded" are applied to children who are not eligible for entrance into public school because they require almost total care. Such cases usually require total care for their entire lives. Their IQ's are usually below 25 or 30 on an individual test of mental ability—if it is possible to test them at all.

Modern practice with the educable mentally retarded is to place a child who has been so identified in a special class. A majority of educators working in this field agree that special classes for the educable mentally retarded should be located in a regular school building with classes for normal children. There are a few instances, however, in which these special classes are grouped to form what is in reality a special school. When it is necessary for children to be institutionalized, an educational program is provided in a special school within the institution.

In general, the basic characteristics of the special class are as far as possible those of the regular class. Trainable and educable mentally retarded children are not grouped in the same class. In establishing special classes, major differences among pupils as to age and physical size are avoided. Every effort is made to develop a sequence of four classes so that each child will spend no more than three or four years in any one group.

The curriculum for the educable mentally retarded emphasizes the development of practical and useful knowledge, skills, and attitudes in the areas of citizenship, occupations, communication, arithmetic, health, safety, and recreation. Other areas of training and guidance are socially acceptable behavior, motor co-ordination, self-acceptance and self-confidence, vocational competence, and civic responsibility. A high school program that includes actual job experience is provided in whatever occupations are available. The school co-operates in placing these children in jobs.

Prior to 1950 there were few classes for trainable mentally retarded children in the public schools, but after the middle of the century there was a large increase in the number of these classes throughout the country, despite the fact that some educators question the responsibility

A teacher in a remedial class assists children with various reading problems. (ROBERTS—RAPHO GUILLUMETTE)

of the school for these children. Groups of parents of retarded children have been especially active in this area.

The curriculum for the trainable mentally retarded child emphasizes development of the use of the senses, good health habits, self-care and personal adequacy, motor skills, communication skills, and simple number skills. The lives of these children will usually be circumscribed by the boundaries of the home, school, immediate neighborhood, and the sheltered shop, or, as a last resort, the institution.

Education of Slow Learners. Above the level of the mentally retarded, but below the normal range of ability, are children classed as "slow learners." Such labels as "dull normal," "borderline normal," "borderline retarded," and "limited ability" are sometimes applied to this category. Children whose scores are between 75 and 90 on repeated tests of mental ability are frequently put in this group. Such pupils can achieve some degree of success in school subjects but require more time and greater effort than pupils of higher ability. About 20% of pupils in U.S. schools fall into this classification.

Besides learning at a subnormal rate, slow learners seem to differ from more normal children in ability to think abstractly, to generalize from specifics, to memorize, to think critically, and to work for long periods on school subjects. As a result of inability to be successful in school, slow learners often develop secondary personality problems and sometimes become behavior problems. It has been found that a large number of behavior problems in the school are slow learners for whom no special program has been provided.

The majority of schools attempt to care for the slow learners by nonpromotion, and many leave school as soon as they reach the upper limit of compulsory attendance. Recommendations for effective programs include early identification, smaller classes grouped according to range of ability, the employment of interested and specially trained teachers, and careful guidance.

Education of the Visually Handicapped. The visually handicapped category of exceptional children includes those who are classed as blind and those who are classed as partially sighted, or partially able to see (for definitions and statistics, *see* BLINDNESS). The partially sighted are able to use sight as their chief means of learning.

A great expansion in facilities and programs for the visually handicapped occurred during the middle decades of the 20th century. In general four types of program for the visually handicapped are in use today: (1) the state residential school; (2) the special class; (3) the integrated or co-operative program; and (4) the itinerant teacher approach. Early identification of children who need care in one of these programs is especially urgent, since corrective work during the early years can ameliorate some visual problems. Despite progress, it is estimated that eight out of nine partially sighted children do not have any type of special educational program.

The program of the residential school is similar to a regular school program. Children are grouped by age and grade and follow the same course of study as do more normal children. A number of special methods and devices are used, of course. Among these are Braille reading and writing, typewriting from the 3d or 4th grade on, "talking

With special help, a blind girl successfully attends class with children having normal vision. (BATTLE CREEK, MICH., ENQUIRER AND NEWS)

books" (recordings of books), and relief maps. Often blind students who are ready for a high school program attend a regular local high school and receive special help.

The placement of blind children in a residential school has aroused controversy among professionals working with this group. Many feel that the specialized problem of the children can best be met by a facility that is specifically geared to meet these needs. Others, however, feel that the regular public school, using a special teacher, can provide the needed help while keeping the child part of his family group. There is general agreement that the partially sighted are best served in regular schools with special services. Efforts have been made to develop educational programs in which the visually handicapped and the sighted could attend school side by side.

A number of large school systems have provided special classes for the partially sighted in regular school buildings. Complete segregation of these children is not considered desirable. On the other hand, the handicapped child must remain in the special class long enough to learn the skills he needs in order to work with the normal class. The partially seeing must not be expected to compete too soon with children having sound vision.

The co-operative plan requires a special teacher for the visually handicapped and a special room from which their program is planned and directed. Part of each day is spent in regular classrooms. Under what is called the integrated plan for the visually handicapped, these children are enrolled in regular classes. A trained teacher of the blind is available on a full-time basis to assist the regular teachers.

The use of itinerant teachers is another plan to keep the handicapped child in a regular class in his neighborhood school. In this case, the specially trained teacher

Deaf children of preschool age receive special training in a Houston, Tex., hearing clinic. Such early instruction helps avoid problems that may develop later.
(SPIEGEL—RAPHO GUILLUMETTE)

serves a number of schools, providing individual instruction and special equipment where needed and advising teachers and parents.

Services for the blind are included in the special education programs of most nations. The predominant plan is to put blind children in special schools; Austria, Bulgaria, Finland, Germany, Italy, and the Soviet Union are among the nations reporting special schools, often boarding institutions giving vocational and general training.

Education of Children with Impaired Hearing. Just as there are degrees of visual handicap there are degrees of deafness (for definitions and estimates of the numbers who suffer from impaired hearing, see DEAFNESS). From the educator's point of view, the distinction between children with moderate hearing loss and those with profound hearing loss is particularly important. The former can learn speech by ear whereas the latter cannot. Children born deaf present a problem different from that of children who lose their hearing after they have learned speech.

Three out of four children with severe loss of hearing are in residential schools. Because of the relatively low rate of incidence, it is only in the large metropolitan areas that there are enough children for the formation of day classes and special classes. Lip reading (or in some cases the manual alphabet), speech correction, auditory training, as well as the mastery of school subjects, represent the major areas of work with these children. A precision-built group hearing aid is the most essential piece of equipment for a class of deaf children.

The hard of hearing who are not, educationally, "deaf" are usually placed in special classes or in the regular classes in the public schools. However, some children with moderate hearing losses who have other problems and children with severe hearing losses need placement in a special class. The schoolwork in the special class does not differ materially from the work in the regular classroom. The classroom is usually located in a regular school building, and some general activities are shared with normal children. Every attempt is made to give the hard of hearing children enough background and training so that they may move into a regular school program. When the hard-of-hearing child is in the regular class program, the availability of a trained speech and hearing teacher is essential.

Education of Children Who Have Speech Problems. Objectively, a child may be said to have a speech defect when his speech is such that it presents a problem to him in communicating easily with a normal listener. Subjec-

tively, speech may be said to be defective if the speaker is aware of or fearful about a problem in his speech. Speech defects are frequently divided into four major types: (1) defect in articulation (sound production); (2) defects of phonation (voice production); (3) defects of rhythm (stuttering and cluttering); and (4) language dysfunctions (delayed speech or aphasia).

In current practice, children who are in need of speech help remain in the regular classroom. The speech and hearing teacher works with children who have either speech or hearing problems, dealing with them singly or in groups. Itinerant teachers are usually assigned to cover several schools; they may work with a single child or a group having similar problems.

Generally, state legislation for the physically handicapped provides for educational programs for children with speech handicaps. The number of programs is increasing in the United States. Many other countries use the old category "deaf-mutes" and place children so classified in special institutions.

Education of Children with Orthopedic Handicaps. The term "orthopedic" is used to indicate the purpose of correcting or preventing deformity. Many kinds of handicaps are included in this category, among them being crippling as a result of poliomyelitis, club foot, spinal curvature, tumors, and loss of limbs in accidents. More important than the exact nature of the crippling are such factors as the attitude of the child's family and associates, the reaction of the public, and the personality of the child.

All states now offer aid to crippled children of school age, and a majority of states have provisions for financial aid to public schools that operate programs for the orthopedically handicapped. Many areas still lack effective programs, however.

In general the programs that are provided for orthopedically handicapped children can be classed under five headings: (1) hospital schools; (2) special schools; (3) special classes; (4) home instruction; and (5) services in regular classes. Hospital schools are used to serve children who must remain in the hospital for a considerable length of time. Special techniques are used and teachers are often called upon to make major program adjustments to accommodate medical and hospital treatment. Special schools have been organized in many large cities. These facilities are usually created for children who are in need of special care or treatment that could not be given in a special class. In addition to classrooms, special schools usually have medical and health facilities, therapy rooms, rest areas, and a lunchroom. Some educators feel that such special facilities should be part of a regular school and that children should be returned to the special or regular class as soon as feasible. Special classes are organized to serve children with lesser orthopedic handicaps. These classes are usually located on the street level of a regular school building or are accessible through the use of elevators or ramps. The special classroom may have such equipment as standing tables, special chairs, parallel bars, and reading devices. Physical therapy, where needed, may be provided in the school or children may be transported to another community facility for this service.

Children who must have an extended period of rest, who are not able to travel or move around, or who can work only for a short period of time receive home instruction. The use of school-home telephones appears to have a number of advantages, and the use of educational television programs for these children is being studied.

Education of Children with Neurological Impairments. From a medical point of view, "neurological impairment" refers to damage to the brain or central nervous system. Specific problems may be diagnosed, for example, as epilepsy, cerebral palsy (which is characterized by impaired control of muscles), or aphasia (an impairment of the ability to use or comprehend language).

Since educational programs are designed to attempt to ameliorate symptoms rather than deal with causes of behavior, the types of programs vary with the nature of the particular neurological problem of each child. Children whose major symptom is motor impairment, which is evidenced by difficulty in walking or running or in using their hands, are usually placed in a program for the orthopedically handicapped as cerebral palsied. This program may be located in the hospital, special school, special class, at home, or in the regular class, depending upon the severity of the involvement. Since damage to the brain is not usually limited to a single area, children may have defects in vision, hearing, or speech in addition to motor impairment. Therapy for children who have cerebral palsy is an extremely important aspect of the program. Teaching cerebral-palsied children requires imagination and ingenuity.

Epilepsy manifests itself in seizures. It is not considered crippling from a medical point of view but rather by teachers and parents who come in contact with the child. Except for children with uncontrollable seizures, epileptic children under medical supervision can attend regular classrooms when the teacher and the children understand the problem and accept the child.

Children whose intelligence is affected by neurological impairment and who are mentally retarded are usually placed in a program with other mentally retarded children. Aphasic children are usually enrolled in special classes located in schools for the deaf. There are only a small number of such school programs in the United States.

Education of Children with Chronic Medical Problems. Conditions that may be classed as "chronic medical problems" include rheumatic fever, tuberculosis, nephrosis (kidney disease), hepatitis, allergies, diabetes, cancer, and malnutrition. Epilepsy could be put in this category. Historically, there is little evidence of attempts to provide special programs for children with such problems until modern times.

As with other exceptional children great emphasis has been placed on keeping children with chronic medical problems in the regular classroom. There are, however, instances when special classes, special schools, home instruction, and hospital programs are needed.

The teacher who works in their homes with children who have chronic medical problems needs to have specialized training in working with the handicapped. Most children receive three to five hours of instruction a week utilizing a schedule of two or three sessions of one and a half hours per day rather than several one-hour sessions. The use of closed-circuit television and the home-to-school telephone have broadened the horizons of the home instruction program.

Since the objectives of all the special programs are to enable the child to move as rapidly as possible into the main stream of a regular educational program, the special school or class may provide an intermediary step in this process. There are also some children with chronic medical problems who cannot make the adjustment to the regular classrooms and need the special school or class. Many of these children are placed in classes with children having other handicaps, where special provision to handle their problems may be made. When children with chronic medical problems can be accommodated in the regular classroom, extra care and planning by school personnel such as the school physician and nurse are required. The placement necessitates careful consideration and a sensitive teacher who accepts the child and his limitations and does not isolate the child in the classroom.

Education of Children Who Are Socially and Emotionally Maladjusted. "Social and emotional maladjustment" is manifested in one or more kinds of problem behavior: difficulties in learning that are not explained by any of the handicaps already discussed; poor relations with other children and teachers; "strange" behavior, inappropriate to the circumstances; tendencies to have depressed, unhappy moods; fears, pains, and illness associated with schoolwork. Children who have such problems may become truants or be otherwise delinquent.

Society's first reaction to children who were socially and emotionally maladjusted was to attempt to isolate the offending individuals in order to protect itself. Later it attempted to reform them, and many institutions for reformation were opened in the 19th century. In modern practice children who are socially and emotionally maladjusted are provided services in a number of settings: institutions, hospitals, special schools, special classes, and regular classes. If the problem is not too severe, and the teacher is capable, the child may remain in the regular classroom. The teacher may need assistance from staff psychologists and social workers in order to plan a program for these children. Work with the family may require the co-operation of the school with outside agencies such as a family service or child guidance clinic. The special class for the socially and emotionally handicapped is of help to children who, because of serious and continuous deviations from normal behavior, cannot profit from a program in a regular class. Large cities or a group of

A young teacher working with culturally deprived children in a special summer remedial program. (LISL STEINER)

small communities may have enough children to form a special school. The problems in these schools may be more difficult than those in a regular school because of the concentration of children who have social-emotional handicaps. Institutions and residential centers have been set up to provide for the socially and emotionally maladjusted on a total basis. A psychiatrically oriented institution can provide well-rounded services for these children.

Education of Children Who Have Cultural Handicaps. Children who have a "cultural handicap" are (1) those who have a cultural background different from that to which they are exposed in school (foreign-born, members of minority ethnic groups, and children of migrant workers); (2) those who are culturally deprived because of the lack of exposure to experiences and motivations normally brought to school by other children (children from groups low on the socioeconomic scale).

Extensive and dynamic social changes in the United States have brought to schools children who are not prepared for the ordinary program. The increase in the number of working mothers and desegregation of schools are examples of this social change. The influx of Puerto Rican children and the continued arrival of foreign-born children present a challenge for the conscientious teacher. Schools have provided programs to teach the English language to foreign-born children since early in the 20th century. Otherwise there is little that can be pointed to in the way of programs for children with cultural handicaps.

Education of Children Who Are Educationally Retarded. This category, "educationally retarded," is a broad one. Sometimes children who are not working at the level expected for pupils of their intellectual capacity are called "under-achievers." They are not in the "slow learner" or "mentally retarded" category. Their slow pace may be caused by one or more of the physical, emotional, or cultural handicaps already described or by other factors such as ineffective teaching, poor study habits, poor attendance, frequent transfer from one school to another, poor school facilities, crowded classes, lack of space to study at home, and inappropriate curriculum. Since reading is the tool most used in other subject areas, retardation in reading represents the most serious problem.

With the advent of advanced procedures for testing and appraising pupils, the specific causes of educational retardation have emerged in some school systems. Children whose educational retardation is caused by severe handicap may be helped through special programs. Thus, a child with a reading problem caused by a hearing loss would be given help in the area of speech and hearing improvement as well as remedial work in reading. As communities move toward better curricular practices, smaller classes, and better prepared teachers, the number of children who are educationally retarded is usually reduced.

Organizations. Many organizations have been formed to promote research and treatment for categories of exceptional children—the United Cerebral Palsy Association, Inc., National Association for Retarded Children, National Epilepsy League, National Society for Crippled Children and Adults, to name a few. There are organizations of professionals who work in many of the specific areas. The Council for Exceptional Children, a department of the National Education Association, includes professionals working with all categories.

Consult Genetic Studies of Genius, ed. by L. M. Terman (4 vols., 1925–47); Myklebust, H. R., *Your Deaf Child* (1950); National Society for the Study of Education, *Education of Exceptional Children. 49th Yearbook, Part II*, ed. by N. B. Henry (1950); Stern, E. M., and Castendyck, Elsa, *The Handicapped Child: A Guide for Parents* (1950); Heck, A. O., *Education of Exceptional Children* (2d ed., 1953); McMullin, M. D., *How to Help the Shut-In Child* (1954); Smith, M. F., and Burks, A. J., *Teaching the Slow Learning Child* (1954); Cohen, A. K., *Delinquent Boys* (1955); Goodenough, F. L., and Rynkiewicz, L. M., *Exceptional Children* (1956); Lowenfeld, Berthold, *Our Blind Children; Growing and Learning with Them* (1956); Cutts, N. E., and Mosley, Nicholas, *Teaching the Bright and Gifted* (1957); Woolf, M. D., and J. A., *Remedial Reading* (1957); Cruickshank, W. M., and Johnson, G. O., *Education of Exceptional Children and Youth* (1958); Magnifico, L. X., *Education for the Exceptional Child* (1958); Baker, H. J., *Introduction to Exceptional Children* (3d ed., 1959); International Society for Rehabilitation of the Disabled, *World Frontiers in Special Education:* Proceedings of the International Seminar on Special Education, 1960; Magary, J. F., and Eichorn, R. E., *The Exceptional Child* (1960); *Mental Retardation*, ed. by J. H. Rothstein (1961); UNESCO, *Manual of Educational Statistics* (1961); *Year Book of Education, 1961: Concepts of Excellence in Education*, ed. by G. Z. F.

Bereday and J. A. Lauwerys (1961); American Educational Research Association, *Education of Exceptional Children* (1966).

MILTON A. YOUNG, Connecticut State
Department of Education

See also:

ADULT EDUCATION

Adults continually learn as a result of experience, and they also acquire a great deal of information from reading newspapers and magazines, listening to the radio, and viewing television and motion-picture presentations. However, the term "adult education" is usually restricted to learning activities that include opportunities for a group of people to learn together, in which a teacher or leader is present, and which are directed toward a clearly defined learning goal, such as acquiring a new vocational skill, learning a second language, or participating in community and national affairs.

Programs. Adult education may be divided into two categories. (1) Formal adult education refers to those programs conducted by a public school, junior college, university, library, or other educational institution in which adults voluntarily participate in regularly scheduled, systematically organized classes or study groups. Frequently, programs of this kind offer credit leading to a certificate or diploma giving evidence that a designated amount of study has been completed. (2) Informal adult education includes such activities as study programs of churches and parent groups; forums, concerts, and lectures; organized educational travel; and systematic individual study involving the resources of a museum, library, televised educational program, correspondence school, or other educational facility.

The range of activities covered by adult education programs may be classified as follows: academic programs in which individuals may complete requirements for graduation from a school or college, vocational training and retraining, Americanization (preparation for U.S. citizenship), avocational and cultural programs, programs of general education, and programs designed to help individuals participate more effectively as citizens in a democracy or take a more active part in community affairs.

In recent years, many large industrial firms have undertaken to supplement the educational programs traditionally offered by schools and universities. In response to a survey of the largest American industrial corporations, nearly 85% reported carrying on educational activities requiring attendance by the participant. Many labor unions also offer educational programs for their members, both in areas closely related to union welfare and social goals, and in areas of general education. According to a study made by the National Opinion Research Center of the University of Chicago, more than 17 million adults were enrolled in 1961–62 in regularly scheduled adult education programs. Of this total, nearly 2 million were participating in programs offered by the public schools. Colleges and universities enrolled nearly 3½ million. Because much of the informal adult education activities take place outside the walls of educational institutions, it is difficult to secure precise statistics. The National Opinion Research Center study estimates that approximately 25 million adult Americans—better than one in five—were active in some educational category at the time of the study.

Development. In the early United States, formal adult education was restricted almost exclusively to vocational education and to the process of preparing new arrivals in this country to learn the language of their adopted land and to acquire the basic knowledge needed to qualify for citizenship. The first such school was established in New York state, and by 1820 many settlement houses, religious societies, and private philanthropic groups offered educational opportunities of this kind. In 1823 the principle of public support for adult education was advanced when the state of Massachusetts made the first legislative appropriation for an evening school.

Following World War I, the opportunities of adults to learn new vocational skills received emphasis as a result of legislative enactments of the U.S. Congress offering payment to the states of funds to aid in the education of adults. In 1914, the Smith-Lever Act established the Cooperative Agricultural Extension Service. This is now the largest adult education activity carried on outside of a school or university in the United States. This pattern of adult education utilizing demonstrations by county agricultural and county home demonstration agents has been introduced to many other countries of the world. In 1917, the Smith-Hughes Act, which enabled the states to set up vocational education programs for adults, as well as children, was passed.

During the depression of the 1930's the U.S. government assisted in providing adult education through a number of programs under the Works Progress Administration. Following World War II, the payment of educational benefits to veterans for a continuation of their educational opportunities represented another important recognition of adult education by the federal government.

With the enactment of the Economic Opportunity Act (1964), federal funds became available to local public schools and community groups to initiate programs designed to help undereducated adults acquire the basic skill of reading, writing, and computation.

The history of informal adult education in the United States is often traced back to the New England town meeting, where individuals of a given community had an opportunity to discuss the issues before them and then take action on the basis of understandings growing out of this kind of public consideration. From 1826 to 1835, a movement called the American Lyceum flourished. This provided a series of lectures and discussions for the gen-

An instructor in a New York City evening class for adults teaching radio and television maintenance. (WOLFF—BLACK STAR)

A class in mechanics given for adult factory workers by the University of Budapest in Hungary. (MTI—UNESCO)

eral purpose of intellectual improvement and the specific purpose of extending and improving the public school system. Another landmark in the development of informal adult education in the United States occurred in 1874 with the opening of an adult education center at Chautauqua, N.Y. In the early decades of the 20th century the Chautauqua idea extended throughout the country as traveling lectures and concerts brought opportunities for popular culture to individuals in every state.

Facilities. The use of television in adult education has widely extended educational opportunities. Commercial television stations have made available their facilities in non-prime hours, usually early morning, for teaching by television. A growing number of stations owned and operated by schools, colleges, and various community groups, and by state education departments or state educational television commissions are devoted exclusively to programs of education.

The sources of support for educational activities for adults are as varied as the activities themselves. Many programs, particularly those of men's and women's organizations, public welfare organizations, and governmental groups, are carried on as a public service out of funds not specifically earmarked for adult education. Numerous lecture series, music appreciation opportunities, and film programs are supported by admission fees. Many tax-supported schools, colleges, and libraries offer tuition courses. Other educational institutions combine their sources of public income with tuition fees collected from students as a means of financing educational opportunities for adults. The inclusion of support for programs of adult basic education (literacy education) as a part of the Economic Opportunity Act marked the advent of the federal government into participating in funding for nonvocational adult education. The program has since been transferred to the U.S. Office of Education.

Worldwide Importance. In many countries, particularly the developing nations, adult education is one of the foremost concerns of national governments. In the Soviet Union, for example, there are no tuition fees for adult courses and students are given paid vacations from work at examination time. In India, mainland China, and many of the new countries of Africa, massive educational efforts are being made by central governments to eradicate adult illiteracy, teach basic concepts of health and community living, and train men and women in basic agricultural and industrial skills.

With support from the Special Fund of the United Nations, UNESCO is now undertaking an experimental program in six developing countries, designed to show the importance of planning highly specialized and intensive programs of literacy education for selected groups.

Many European countries have strong programs of adult education. Denmark's folk high schools, for example, have been famous since the 19th century for their programs for young adults, some giving vocational training to farmers, many giving general education with stress on Danish culture. Sweden also has folk high schools, offering general education to young adults. These Swedish and Danish schools are sometimes called "people's colleges," and it is important to note that they are not high schools in the American sense of the term. The Federal Republic of Germany has established several kinds of people's schools, offering day and evening courses. The trade unions offer both vocational and general training.

Problems. With the complex and changing nature of civilization in the second half of the 20th century, continuous education on the part of every individual has now become a necessity. In reaching decisions, for example, about the peaceful uses of atomic power or their country's position in the cold war, adults in the United States are now called upon to use information and think in terms of concepts that were not known at the time they were in school. The development of a new technology, as the result of the automation of industry, makes continuous vocational retraining a priority concern of government, industry, labor, and the schools. The estimate that, by 1975, only 4% of the total labor force will be unskilled laborers, places new urgency on the efforts currently being made by state and local school systems to enable the 55 million adults in the United States with less than a high school education to have the opportunity to further upgrade their level of educational attainment.

As a means of extending and improving educational opportunities for adults, individuals engaged in adult education have formed professional associations. In the absence of an international association, much of the responsibility for the world-wide intercommunication between adult educators was assumed by UNESCO, which sponsored international conferences in Denmark in 1949 and in Canada in 1960. In 1959, an Adult Education Committee of the World Confederation of Organizations of the Teaching Profession was founded to represent the world-wide concern of public school systems for adult education.

In the United States, the Adult Education Association of the U.S.A. is a general purpose educational association. Professional groups established to represent specific occupational groups are the Association of University Evening Colleges, Council of National Organizations for Adult Education, National Association of Public School Adult Educators, and the National University Extension Association.

The recognition that learning for all should continue throughout life is rapidly increasing the educational opportunities for all adults, regardless of economic or social status or earlier attainments in formal education. The new emphasis on adult education has brought about closer agreement on a broad philosophy of adult education, the acceptance of higher professional standards for adult educators, increasing emphasis on the training of leaders and teachers, a broader curriculum to satisfy adult education needs, and increasing state and local financial aid for the development of increased educational opportunities.

Consult Kempfer, H. H., *Adult Education* (1955); Clark H. F., and Sloan, H. S., *Classrooms in the Factories* (1958); *Handbook of Adult Education in the United States,* ed. by M. S. Knowles (1960); Cook County Department of Public Aid, *A Study to Determine the Literacy Level of Able-Bodied Persons Receiving Public Assistance* (1962); National Opinion Research Center, *Volunteers for Learning Study of the Educational Pursuits of American Adults* (1965).

Robert A. Luke, Executive Secretary, National Association for Public School Adult Education

See also Chautauqua; Correspondence Schools; Extension Education; Lyceum Movement.

INTERNATIONAL EXCHANGE PROGRAMS IN EDUCATION

International exchange is the movement through which students, trainees, teachers, professors, and professional and technical experts study, train, teach, do research, and impart and share knowledge in a country other than their own for a limited period of time. International exchange can be traced to the days of the Roman Republic but has changed in motivation, aims, and functions over the centuries. Today exchanges range from the traditional "wandering scholar" pattern—the pursuit of learning for personal development and professional advancement—to the 20th-century national development pattern—the acquisition and sharing of technical and practical experience between countries for the economic and social advancement of emerging nations. There are, of course, many

shadings and variations in between. Creating international understanding and developing favorable attitudes between countries are long-range and indirect goals of international exchange.

Scope. The movement has grown rapidly since World War II because of the realization that higher education for potential leaders of other countries is one of the best avenues to building understanding between nations. The numbers of participants and the number of exchange organizations—both governmental and private—which create and facilitate exchange programs have increased. The 16th edition of UNESCO's *Study Abroad* (1966–68) lists some 170,000 individual opportunities for international study and travel offered by 1,767 agencies in 120

Chinese students talk with their American classmates in a dormitory room at Oberlin College. (BROOKS—MONKMEYER)

Exchange students in New York City hear about data processing procedures in commercial banking. (FIRST NATIONAL CITY BANK)

Characteristics of the Field. Few occupations involve and affect more people than does education. This is particularly true of countries like the United States, where teachers and students total over 25% of the population. In Canada the total is close to 25%. Where education is provided on this scale, it is the largest professional field. The number of full-time educators in the United States has passed the 2,000,000 mark. The public schools, of course, employ the largest share.

The great majority of educators at all levels are classroom teachers. At the elementary level the traditional system is to have one teacher responsible for a class, teaching the basic subjects and supervising most activities. There is a trend, however, toward having teachers in the upper grades instruct a number of classes in one subject. Special teachers are commonly employed for subjects like art and music.

In secondary schools teachers usually specialize in an area such as science, mathematics, language, or social science and teach one subject (or several related subjects) to a number of classes each day. Others concentrate on teaching art, music, home economics, business courses, or industrial arts.

At the college and university level, virtually all teachers are subject specialists. Relatively less time is spent in the classroom than is the case for elementary and secondary teachers. Research may be a major part of a professors' job.

In addition to standard classroom teaching, there are many specialized positions in the schools. Physical education, vocational training, and driver education are examples. Some schools employ specially trained consultants to supervise and assist in such areas as arithmetic and reading. Experts are also employed for remedial reading and for teaching deaf, crippled, blind and partially sighted, and other handicapped children. Television and other audio-visual devices require new specialties.

Another area of specialization, particularly important in junior and senior high schools, is counseling. Guidance counselors advise students on school courses, vocational plans, and personal problems. Guidance may be provided on a part-time basis. It may be one function of a state bureau that provides medical, psychological, and other special services.

There are many administrative positions in education. Titles and plans of organization vary, but the following titles are a sample of some of those often found in the school system of a large city: superintendent of schools, assistant superintendent for elementary schools, assistant superintendent for secondary schools, principal (each school), director of personnel, director of physical education, director of vocational education, director of audio-visual education. There are many positions in state educa-

tion departments. At the college level there are various administrative ranks—head of a department, dean of a school, and president of a university, for example.

Qualifications and Training. All U.S. states require certification of elementary and high school teachers. All but a few states require four years of college for elementary teachers. All states require at least four years of college for secondary school teaching and some require five years. Local school systems may have additional requirements. Special teaching positions and administrative jobs usually demand graduate study. At the college level the master's degree is the usual basic requirement. The doctor's degree is a prerequisite for promotion in most cases.

Income. The range of salaries in education is broad. The average for teachers in U.S. four-year colleges exceeds $8500 (for nine months' work). Elementary and secondary school teachers' average earnings are below this figure. Some public school systems, however, provide top teacher salaries above $10,000, and administrative salaries in the $20,000 range. Many professors in larger colleges and universities receive over $10,000 a year. The median for Canadian university professors is $12,000.

Prospects for Employment. Teaching is by far the largest profession for women and is among the largest for men. In the decade 1965–75 some 1,200,000 new elementary teachers, 1,000,000 secondary teachers, and 500,000 college teachers will be needed in the United States, both to replace those who leave the field and also to take care of the expanding student population. Canada expects growth of the profession at a comparable rate. In addition to these openings in full-time employment, there are certain to be thousands of part-time teaching jobs. Some Americans find teaching careers abroad, for example, in helping the people of underdeveloped regions.

Sources of Information. The article TEACHERS AND TEACHING surveys the status of the profession, its personal and educational requirements, and its prospects in the United States, Canada, and other countries. Additional information relevant to careers in schools and colleges is in EDUCATION (sections on elementary, secondary, and higher education) and in other articles such as ACADEMIC FREEDOM; ACADEMIC RANK; GUIDANCE AND COUNSELING, EDUCATIONAL; TEACHING MACHINE; VOCATIONAL EDUCATION; and VOCATIONAL GUIDANCE. Specific information can be obtained from such sources as the National Education Association, U.S. Office of Education, and American Council on Education, all in Washington, D.C., and the Canadian Teachers' Federation, in Ottawa.

countries. According to UNESCO, at least 290,000 students attended institutions of higher education in countries other than their own during 1964–65. This represents 2% of the total world enrollment in higher education, which was estimated to be 13,500,000. Exchange is, of course, heavily concentrated in highly developed countries. Eighteen countries—Australia, Austria, Belgium, Canada, France, Federal Republic of Germany, India, Ireland, Italy, Japan, Lebanon, Netherlands, Spain, Switzerland, Syria, United Arab Republic, United Kingdom, and United States—received more than 80% of all foreign students. The 74,814 foreign students in the United States in 1964–65 represented 1.7% of the total student population in that country. The 8,361 foreign

students in Switzerland in 1964 constituted 30% of the student population.

Sponsorship. Exchange students use their own funds or receive government or private grants. *Open Doors*, the Institute of International Education's annual statistical report on educational exchange, indicated that of the foreign students in the United States in 1965–66, 37.4% were self-supporting; 8.5% were supported by private organizations; 6.4% had grants from the U.S. government; and 5.4% from their own government. No accurate estimate can be made of the number of American citizens going abroad to pursue various academic interests (the Fulbright program in 1965–66 enabled about 850 American graduate students to study abroad). New opportunities are continually presenting themselves in the fields of summer study, undergraduate and graduate exchanges, and the Peace Corps.

Organizations exist to facilitate international exchange and to offer counsel about study opportunities in other countries. Emphasis is increasing on development exchange. Nations send students or trainees to other countries to acquire skills not yet available in their own country, and qualified persons from developed nations go to assist new nations to accelerate their development. Thus many new organizations have been set up. Governments, educational institutions, foundations, industry, and public and private organizations co-operate in planning and executing programs. Sponsors today must have substantial knowledge of the needs of developing countries as well as of the resources in their own country for meeting those needs. Knowledge of the foreign educational system alone no longer suffices. A country's educational system can only be understood in the light of its historical, political, religious, economic, and sociological situation. Increasing the scope and effectiveness of education, one of the most pressing needs of new nations, must be planned with full awareness of the country's long-range needs and can be successful only if the country's national concepts and aspirations are understood.

Sources of Information. A short survey cannot list all the organizations in the field, nor is there room for an extensive bibliography. The publications of the two organizations described below, which are the major clearinghouses in the field of international exchange, should be consulted.

The United Nations Educational, Scientific and Cultural Organization (UNESCO) was chartered, in 1945, as an arm of the United Nations "to contribute to peace and security by promoting collaboration among the nations through education, science and culture . . ." UNESCO's *Study Abroad*, a global work on fellowships and scholarships, lists service organizations in the field and includes extensive statistics. *Vacation Abroad* lists summer opportunities all over the world. Both are published annually. *World Survey of Education*, Vol. I, is a handbook of educational statistics. Volume II of the world survey deals with primary education.

The Institute of International Education—a private, nonprofit organization founded in 1919—administers and develops programs of educational exchange for students, teachers, leaders, and specialists between the United States and 100 other countries. It administers these programs for the U.S. government, foreign governments, universities, foundations, corporations, private organizations, and individuals. It acts as a clearinghouse on all phases of international education. The Institute's *Handbook on International Study, 1965* is a comprehensive guide to all phases of international education and contains an extensive bibliography. Volume I, *For Foreign Nationals*, describes the educational systems in the United States; U.S. institutions of higher education; study awards and special programs; summer opportunities; English language and orientation programs; U.S. government regulations affecting foreign nationals; organizations in the United States providing services to students and visitors from abroad. Volume II, *For U.S. Nationals*, covers foreign systems and institutions of higher education; study

American exchange students in Japan experience a meal served in the traditional style. (GEORGE HOLTON)

awards and special programs; summer work camps, seminars, and service programs; U.S. government regulations affecting U.S. nationals going abroad; organizations providing services to Americans going abroad; and a discussion and listing of institutions and organizations offering undergraduate programs abroad. *Open Doors* is an annual report on the population involved in international exchange, based on surveys of foreign students, scholars, and physicians studying, teaching, and training in the United States, and American students and faculty members on educational assignments abroad. A list of the Institute of International Education's publications may be obtained from the organization's New York headquarters.

Useful publications from other sources include *The Commonwealth Universities Yearbook*, published annually by the Association of Universities of the British Commonwealth in London, and the *International Handbook of Universities*, published by the International Association of Universities in Paris. These are distributed in the United States by the American Council on Education, Washington, D.C., and, together with that organization's *American Universities and Colleges*, constitute comprehensive guides to universities of the world prepared by recognized academic bodies.

KENNETH HOLLAND, President,
Institute of International Education

EDUCATION, RELIGIOUS. *See* PAROCHIAL SCHOOL; RELEASED TIME; RELIGIOUS EDUCATION.

EDUCATION, VOCATIONAL. *See* VOCATIONAL EDUCATION; VOCATIONAL GUIDANCE.

EDUCATIONAL PSYCHOLOGY. *See* PSYCHOLOGY.

EDUCATIONAL RADIO. *See* RADIO, EDUCATIONAL.

EDUCATIONAL TELEVISION. *See* TELEVISION, EDUCATIONAL.

EDWARD I (1239–1307), King of England (1272–1307); called "Longshanks" because of his tall, lithe figure. He was the son of Henry III and Eleanor of Provence. Edward married Eleanor of Castile in 1254 and, after her death, married Margaret of France. During the controversial last 15 years of Henry III's reign, the young Prince Edward was his father's principal political and military assistant. Henry ultimately turned over to Edward the government of England and his other lands. In 1270 the condition of England was peaceful enough to allow Edward to go on a Crusade. He was still abroad when Henry III died in 1272. When Llewellyn of Wales refused to do homage to him and tried to rule Wales as an independent state, Edward led three campaigns against Wales, killed Llewellyn, and reduced Wales to dependence in 1284. In 1301 Edward made his son, the future Edward II, the first Prince of Wales.

In Scotland Edward took advantage of disputes among claimants to the Scottish throne to assert (1290) his right to choose Scotland's King. Having named John de Baliol, he interfered in Scottish government and provoked resistance by Scottish nobles. He was thus drawn into a continuing struggle with the Scots. Almost yearly until the end of his reign he led armies against them, but without lasting success.

In France Edward inherited the problem of preventing the French from undermining English control of Aquitaine and Gascony. He strengthened his government there, and luckily so, for in 1295 the able French King, Philip IV, confiscated Gascony and began a war that lasted until 1297. After a long truce the two Kings agreed in 1303 to the return of Gascony to Edward.

In his government of England Edward sought to develop institutions and policies that would ensure internal order. He called on his principal subjects to show the legal authority by which they claimed the right to hold courts and exercise other feudal privileges. Those who could produce warrants, he confirmed in their privileges. At the same time, many of his actions lessened the importance of feudalism: he relied more on a mercenary army than on the required military service of feudal tenants, and he favored the division of feudal estates while limiting the practice known as subinfeudation. Edward summoned Parliaments frequently, changing their composition to suit his own needs. The most famous meeting of his councilors, the nobles and higher clergy, and elected representatives of the counties, the urban communities, and the lesser clergy, called in 1295, is known as the Model Parliament. His officials improved the administration of justice in royal courts. By statute he set new and more efficient rules for the maintenance of public order. Edward limited the jurisdiction of church courts, and, by the Statute of Mortmain (1279), required anyone who wished to give land to the church to obtain royal permission. At his death, Edward left a country whose government had been advantageously reorganized. But his vigorous assertion of royal rights had stirred much opposition and his wars had almost bankrupted England.

FREDERICK G. MARCHAM, *Cornell University*

EDWARD II (1284–1327), King of England (1307–27). He was the son of Edward I and Eleanor of Castile. Edward

The Mansell Collection

Shield of Edward I, King of England (1272–1307).

married Isabella of France in 1308. His father took Edward on campaigns with him and trained him in administration. The young Edward became Prince of Wales in 1301, the first heir to the throne to hold that title. As king, Edward II quickly showed that he was a less able and resolute ruler than his father. Because of Edward I's attempts to impose his will on nobles and clergy and to hold his own with the French and the Scots, his problems at home and abroad were immense.

Edward II's chief interests were sports and social life. Early in his reign he gave much political influence, as well as lands and social prominence, to a Gascon favorite, Piers Gaveston. From 1318 to the end of his reign he relied on the advice of Hugh Despenser and his son, English nobles. These combinations of King and favorites stirred into action the principal English nobles. In 1312 they took to arms and seized and executed Gaveston. Thomas of Lancaster, Edward's cousin, was leader in this uprising. Against Edward and the Despensers, the nobles had less success. Edward defeated them at the battle of Boroughbridge in 1322 and put Lancaster to death. Edward's struggles with the nobles caused important administrative changes. In 1312 Lancaster and his allies assumed direction of Edward's government through a committee of Lords Ordainers, so called because they had stated their program in a series of ordinances. After the defeat of the nobles in 1322, Edward issued a statement of policy at York in which he declared that henceforth important political decisions must be made in full Parliaments, not merely in meetings of nobles.

Edward's involvement in struggles with the nobles gave the Scots the opportunity to continue their fighting against England. In 1314, when Edward led a large army into Scotland in hope of reviving his influence there, Robert Bruce crushed the English at Bannockburn and won Scotland's independence. Edward II's policies during his later years suffered because of hostility between Queen Isabella and the Despensers. In 1325 she went to France, accompanied by her son, the future Edward III. With her lover Roger de Mortimer, an English noble, she organized an

Shield of Edward II, King of England (1307–27).

Shield of Edward III, King of England from 1327 to 1377.

army and in 1326 invaded England. The invaders seized and executed the Despensers and captured Edward II. Parliament met in 1327 and chose Prince Edward King, though control remained with Isabella and Mortimer. Edward II they kept a prisoner and later murdered.

FREDERICK G. MARCHAM, Cornell University

EDWARD III (1312–77), King of England (1327–77). He was the son of Edward II and Isabella of France. During the last two years of Edward II's reign, Prince Edward accompanied Queen Isabella and her lover, Roger de Mortimer, first in France, then in their successful invasion of England. Parliament deposed Edward II and chose Prince Edward as King in 1327. With the aid of English nobles, Edward III in 1330 seized and hanged Mortimer and removed Isabella from political influence. Thereafter, Edward's first concern was to reassert English influence in Scotland. He won victories at Dupplin Moor (1332) and Halidon Hill (1333), but Scotland was too difficult a country to dominate from England. Edward turned to a more hazardous enterprise, the conquest of France.

France lured him because his mother was French and because he, his father, and Edward I had suffered indignities at the hands of the French King, especially the confiscation of their Gascon lands. Edward dreamed of an empire in France, found Continental allies, and in 1337 attacked France through Flanders, thereby beginning the Hundred Years' War (q.v.). He won a naval victory at Sluys in 1340 and a military victory at Crécy in 1346. In 1355, after the Black Death had ravaged England, he struck again, and in 1356 his son, Edward the Black Prince, defeated the French at Poitiers and took John II, King of France, prisoner. The English had also been successful in fighting against the Scots, capturing the Scottish King, David II, in 1346. Edward's triumph seemed complete. For 100,000 marks he released the Scottish King. By the treaty of Bretigny (1360) he gained 3,000,000 gold crowns for releasing the French King, and title to Calais, Ponthieu, and Aquitaine.

War between Edward and the French King, Charles V,

resumed in 1369. In Edward's later years his French lands shrank to a few minor holdings, and he himself lost interest in the war. The long struggle with France, marked by striking successes and failures, deeply affected England's internal affairs. To wage war Edward needed money, and money could be had in quantity and steady supply only through Parliament. The nobles and merchants, speaking through Parliament, used the King's need to exact concessions on matters of taxation. He promised that, except for the traditional customs duties, taxation should be levied only after agreement between King and Parliament. Parliament also gained importance as a legislative body. Thus it regulated economic affairs after the Black Death in the Statute of Labourers (1351), and church affairs in the Statutes of Provisors and Praemunire (1351 and 1353).

In his last years Edward was victimized by his courtiers and his mistress, Alice Perrers. An opposition group of nobles took action against corruption at the royal court in the so-called Good Parliament of 1376. Their action was not decisive, for John of Gaunt, Edward's third son, emerged as a powerful leader of another faction. During this struggle for control of the government, in circumstances which foreshadowed the civil wars of the next century, Edward III died, neglected by all but his mistress, and she robbed him.

FREDERICK G. MARCHAM, Cornell University

EDWARD IV (1442–83), King of England (1461–83). He was the son of Richard, Duke of York, and Cecily Neville. When Richard, during the Wars of the Roses, died at the battle of Wakefield in 1460, Edward gathered an army and fought his way to London, where the citizens welcomed him, and friendly nobles declared him to be King, even though the Lancastrian Henry VI was still alive. Edward's uncle, the Earl of Warwick, supported him in these enterprises and, as "Kingmaker," stood behind him. In 1469 Warwick broke with Edward, and the two men maneuvered and fought for power. At one point Warwick fled to France; at another Edward fled to Holland. Edward returned in 1471 and defeated all his enemies at the battles of Barnet and Tewkesbury. Warwick died in battle; Prince Edward, son of Henry VI, was assassinated; Henry died, too, perhaps murdered. Edward, with the support of his brothers, George, Duke of Clarence (who had once opposed him), and Richard, Duke of Gloucester, now assumed full kingship. When Clarence became restless again in 1478, he was put to death.

After 1471 Edward IV ruled England with considerable success. He encouraged trade, made peace with Louis XI of France (who paid Edward an annual pension), and reorganized English administration. He reformed royal finance to strengthen the position of the crown and used a council consisting of men dependent on himself. The succession was his major problem, for his sons were young; Edward, the elder, having been born in 1470. When Edward IV died, his brother Richard (later Richard III), who he had hoped would be protector of his children's interests, challenged the validity of Edward's marriage to Elizabeth Woodville, disposed of Edward's sons, and himself seized the crown.

FREDERICK G. MARCHAM, Cornell University

EDWARD V (1470–83), King of England (1483). He was the son of Edward IV and Elizabeth Woodville. On Edward IV's death, Apr. 9, 1483, Richard, Duke of Gloucester, Edward IV's brother, and Richard, Earl Rivers, brother of Elizabeth Woodville, struggled for guardianship of Edward V and his younger brother, Richard, Duke of York, who were then living in the Tower of London. Richard, Duke of Gloucester, called in question the validity of Edward IV's marriage to Elizabeth Woodville on the ground that Edward had made a previous contract of marriage with another lady. Assuming that he had proved the illegitimacy of the two boys, Gloucester asserted his own claim to the throne. Meanwhile a search for Edward V and his brother in the Tower disclosed that they had been dead since Aug. or Sept., 1483. The story gained credence that they had been murdered at Gloucester's orders, a version Shakespeare presents in his play *Richard III*. Defenders of Richard dispute this story.

FREDERICK G. MARCHAM, Cornell University

EDWARD VI (1537–53), King of England (1547–53). He was the son of Henry VIII and Jane Seymour. Unlike his half sisters, Mary and Elizabeth, no question regarding his legitimacy was raised. When Henry VIII drew up his will to fix the succession to the throne of England, he gave first place to Edward, who became King on Henry's death in 1547. Henry had provided for the possibility that Edward might ascend the throne while still a child by nominating a council to govern. The council at once assumed control, but the Duke of Somerset, one of Edward's uncles and a member of the council, soon attained a dominant position, which he held for two years.

The young King had benefited from an excellent education at the hands of some of England's leading scholars and teachers. They testified that he had mastered Latin and Greek and that he had read Aristotle's *Ethics* in the original. All evidence suggests that throughout his short reign Edward maintained a lively interest in classical scholarship and in the urgent religious disputes of the day. He helped to establish new schools, notably the famous

The Mansell Collection

Portrait of Edward VI, King of England (1547–53).

schools for London boys and girls called Christ's Hospital.

While Somerset controlled the government, Parliament passed the first Act of Uniformity (1549) thereby instituting an English form of worship in the Church of England and giving to that liturgy its first Protestant character. Somerset's secular policies and his general influence provoked opposition, particularly from the Duke of Northumberland, who overthrew Somerset and later brought about his execution. Northumberland assumed control of the government in 1549 and through a second Act of Uniformity (1552) strengthened the Protestant character of worship in the Church of England and required that all Englishmen attend church. But Northumberland had more personal objectives. Aware, as all observers were, that Edward VI had only a short time to live, Northumberland arranged the marriage of his son to Lady Jane Grey, grandniece of Henry VIII, with the expectation that on Edward's death, Lady Jane would supplant Princess Mary as Queen, his son would be Prince Consort, and he himself would control England. Because Princess Mary had preserved her Catholic faith, the alignment of political forces was made to appear as a struggle to retain a Protestant Church of England on Edward's death. Edward VI had strong Protestant leanings and was ready to believe that if he executed a will in favor of Lady Jane he would strike a blow for Protestantism. Before he could sign the will, he died.

FREDERICK G. MARCHAM, Cornell University

EDWARD VII (1841–1910), King of the United Kingdom (1901–10). He was Queen Victoria and Prince Albert's eldest son. His education was inadequate, and although as Prince of Wales he expressed himself "anxious for employment," his mother excluded him from public business. Only after 1880 was he given information about cabinet decisions. In 1863 he married Princess Alexandra of Denmark. They had two sons, the elder of whom died in 1892, and three daughters. Edward, pleasure-loving and cosmopolitan, was drawn into several "scrapes." His favorite foreign country was France, which he often visited. He thus shared neither his mother's moral scruples nor her affection for Germany. He also differed sharply from her in the company he chose to keep, rich businessmen being prominent in his entourage. His popularity was not thereby diminished. Indeed, he established a reputation as a man who knew how to enjoy himself and, unlike Victoria, did not object either to pomp or to publicity. He was 60 years old when he ascended the throne in Jan., 1901. His accession was greeted with enthusiasm as the start of a new Edwardian period.

His reign falls into two halves. From 1901 to 1905 a Unionist government was in power, with Arthur James Balfour succeeding the Marquess of Salisbury as Prime Minister in July, 1902. This ministry, whose conservative outlook Edward shared, lost popularity particularly after the spring of 1903. Its Foreign Secretary, the Marquess of Lansdowne, was responsible, however, for a swing in foreign policy toward which Edward himself contributed. Edward's known pro-French views and a state visit to France in May, 1903, provided a prelude to the Entente Cordiale of 1904. Edward continued to support improvements in Franco-British relations and was not on the good terms with William II of Germany that his mother had enjoyed.

From 1905 to 1910 the Liberals were in power. They followed the same foreign policy, but their domestic policy, with its emphasis on fiscal and social reform, generated bitter Unionist opposition and a constitutional quarrel with the House of Lords. Edward was opposed to the resistance of the Lords to the Liberal budget of 1909, but he did not support Prime Minister Herbert Asquith's demand to create new peers in December of that year. He died in May, 1910, while the crisis was still in progress. The sharp social and political conflicts of his reign were as much a part of the scene as Edwardian splendor and elegance.

ASA BRIGGS, Leeds University

EDWARD VIII (1894–   ), King of Great Britain (1936) and later Duke of Windsor. Edward, who as Prince of Wales had enjoyed immense popularity at home and abroad, succeeded his father, George V, in Jan., 1936. Rumors of his connection with a twice-divorced American, Mrs. Wallis Simpson, were published outside Britain before anyone admitted the possibility at home. It was the Bishop of Bradford, in a sermon, who first broke the silence. When he called on the King to be more Christian and to model his life on that of his father, the press told the news it had previously withheld. Prime Minister Stanley Baldwin advised Edward that the Cabinet was unwilling to accept a morganatic marriage. Many in England sided with the King against his Prime Minister, but Edward saw the impossibility of the situation, and abdicated on Dec. 10. Created Duke of Windsor, he lived abroad after 1936. During World War II he served as Governor and Commander-in-Chief of the Bahama Islands.

STEPHEN R. GRAUBARD, Harvard University

EDWARD, LAKE, also called Edward Nyanza, lake of east-central Africa, in the Western Rift Valley, bordering southwestern Uganda and the northeastern part of the Republic of the Congo (Léopoldville). Its waters are carried northward by the Semliki River to Lake Albert and thence to the Nile system. Area, 830 sq. mi.; max. depth, 365 ft.

EDWARDS, EDWARD (1812–86), English librarian. He served at the British Museum (1839–49), and was the first librarian of the Manchester Free Library (1850–58). His writings include *Memoirs of Libraries* (1859), a valuable pioneer work on library history; *Libraries and Their Founders* (1865); and *Lives of the Founders of the British Museum* (1870).

EDWARDS, GUS (1879–1945), American songwriter and vaudeville performer, whose revues launched the careers of Eddie Cantor, Groucho Marx, Ray Bolger, Walter Winchell, and many others who later became stars. Born in Germany, he was brought to the United States before he was 10. His songs include *School Days*, *Sunbonnet Sue*, and *Look Out for Jimmy Valentine*.

EDWARDS, JONATHAN (1703–58), American theologian. Graduated from Yale in 1720, he became associate pastor of the Congregational church in Northampton, Mass. in 1727 and its pastor two years later. Edwards played a

Brown Brothers

Edward VII (seated third from left) surrounded by members of the British and Russian royal families. Seated left to right are the Princess of Wales (later Queen Mary), Tsar Nicholas II of Russia, the Tsarevitch (son of the Tsar), Edward VII, the Grand Duchess Anastasia (daughter of the Tsar), the Tsarina Alexandra Fyodorovna, the Prince of Wales (later George V), the Grand Duchess Maria. Standing left to right are Prince Edward (later Edward VIII), Queen Alexandra of England, Princess Mary, Princess Victoria, the Grand Duchess Olga, and the Grand Duchess Tatiana.

major role in the Great Awakening. His thoughtful defense of "true" revivalism, *Treatise on the Religious Affections* (1746), has been called the most profound exploration of religious psychology in American literature. In 1750 Edwards was dismissed from his pulpit for championing the view that only the elect should be church members in full communion. While serving as missionary to the Indians at Stockbridge, Mass., he wrote his major theological treatises. The famous *Treatise on the Will* (1754) was part of his vigorous defense of Calvinism against Arminian tendencies. Edwards went to serve as president of Princeton in 1758, but died of smallpox within a few weeks. A brilliant scholar, widely read in the science and philosophy of his time, he is today recognized as one of the ablest thinkers America has produced.

    Consult Miller, Perry, *Jonathan Edwards* (1949).

ROBERT T. HANDY, Union Theological Seminary

EDWARDS, JONATHAN, known as the Younger (1745–1801), like his famous father, Jonathan Edwards, a distinguished minister and theologian. A Princeton graduate, he served several Congregational churches in Connecticut and during the last two years of his life was president of Union College, Schenectady, N.Y. He is chiefly known for his work on the doctrine of the atonement.

EDWARDS PLATEAU, portion of the semiarid Great Plains Province, located in south-central Texas. The Balcones Escarpment separates the plateau from the Gulf Coastal Plain. The part west of the Pecos River is also called the Stockton Plateau. The Edwards Plateau is chiefly ranching country. Elev., 2,000–4,000 ft.

EDWARDS v. CALIFORNIA, U.S. Supreme Court case (1941). In Dec., 1939, Edwards, a resident of California, drove to Texas to bring his wife's indigent brother back to California with him. Edwards provided his brother-in-law with room and board in California for 10 days, at the end of which time he received assistance from the Farm Security Administration. Edwards was then sentenced to 6 months imprisonment for violating a California statute that made it a misdemeanor to bring nonresident indigents into the state. Edwards challenged the constitutionality of the act before the Supreme Court. The Court found that there was no question of Congress' power to regulate interstate commerce and no question that the transportation of persons was "commerce." The Court found, therefore, that the ban on "bringing or transportation of indigent persons into California" was not within the police power of the state and was therefore unconstitutional.

JAMES P. SHENTON, Columbia University

EDWARDSVILLE, city of southwestern Illinois, and seat of Madison County. The center of a bituminous coal-mining and agricultural area, it manufactures metal and clay products. Settled, c.1800; inc., 1837; pop. (1950) 8,776; (1960) 9,996.

EDWARDSVILLE, coal-mining borough of north-central Pennsylvania, on the Susquehanna River, opposite Wilkes-Barre. The town was named for the superintendent of a local colliery. Inc., 1884; pop. (1950) 6,686; (1960) 5,711.

The Mansell Collection

Edward the Black Prince. Panel in upper corner relates the fact that a student named Joshua Barnes, evidently an admirer of Edward, gave this portrait of the prince to his "tutor and colleagues" at Emmanuel College, Cambridge (founded, 1584).

EDWARD THE BLACK PRINCE (1330–76), English Prince, eldest son of King Edward III and Philippa of Hainault. The name Black Prince came, perhaps, from the color of his armor. His father made him Duke of Cornwall in 1333 (the first Duke to be created in England) and Prince of Wales in 1343. In 1361 Prince Edward married his cousin, Joan, Countess of Kent, known as the "Fair Maid of Kent." Their son became Richard II of England.

    Prince Edward served with his father in a campaign in France in 1345, and in 1346 had a prominent part in the great English victory at Crécy. He took part in the campaigns of the following years, and in 1355 the King gave him command of an army sent to control Gascony. After a year of skirmishing with the forces of King John of France, he defeated John at the battle of Poitiers (1356), captured the King, and brought to a successful end the first stage of the Hundred Years' War. In 1362 King Edward gave his son the title Prince of Aquitaine and put him in control of all his possessions in southern France. Prince Edward and his wife, Joan, took up residence in Gascony, where they remained for eight years. As governor of southern France he had much success, though French nobles of the region resented being governed by an Englishman.

    In 1367 Prince Edward agreed to help Peter the Cruel of Castile to regain his Spanish throne. The Prince led an army into Spain in 1367, defeated the great French soldier Bertrand du Guesclin, and assured the restoration of Peter. But the Prince's army suffered from disease and he himself became fatally ill. On returning to southern France he attempted to strengthen his position by levying heavy taxes. The nobles of southern France appealed to the French King, Charles V, for assistance, and the Hundred Years' War resumed. Prince Edward was too ill to give vigorous military leadership. He returned to England in 1371 and in 1372 gave up his career as a soldier. As an opponent of John of Gaunt, he took part in the struggle for power among the great English nobles and clergymen during the last, unhappy years of Edward III's reign.

FREDERICK G. MARCHAM, Cornell University

EDWARD THE CONFESSOR (1002?–1066), King of England (1042–66), called the Confessor because of his saintly nature. Edward was the son of Aethelred the Unready (King of the English, 978–1016) and Emma, daughter of the Duke of Normandy. Upon Aethelred's death (1016), his mother took Edward to Normandy where he was raised at the Norman Court. Emma soon returned to England to marry Aethelred's successor, the Danish conqueror Canute, and Edward gained the English kingship only because Harthacanute (son of Canute and Emma) named him as his successor.

His reign was marked by internal discords that his own defects of character helped to promote. Although affable and gracious in public and of majestic appearance (he was probably an albino and thus remarkable to his people), Edward was unfitted for kingship. His virtues were mainly spiritual, and although he desired the welfare of his people, he did very little to secure it. By nature indolent and neglectful, he was always dominated by men stronger than himself. It was due largely to the paramount influence finally achieved by the family of Godwin (Edward married the daughter of Earl Godwin) that England enjoyed any security and tranquillity during his reign.

For the first ten years of his reign Edward favored his Norman relatives and friends, but English influence was re-established by Earl Godwin and his sons, Tostig and Harold. Edward was childless, and the succession to the English throne was disputed between Harold of Norway, William of Normandy, and Harold, whom Edward designated as his successor. The matter was decided in favor of William by the Norman invasion of 1066. Edward was revered as the last of the old English Kings, and this reverence was promoted by the Norman Kings, who claimed him as a kinsman. Edward was canonized in 1161 and his sword became part of the royal regalia; its counterpart is the present sword of state.

JOHN G. SPERLING, Northern Illinois University

EEL, name for the members of about 30 families of long, slender, bony fishes that constitute the order Apodes. Eels lack spines in their fins and are frequently scaleless. Their backbones may be composed of as many as 260 separate vertebrae. Eels are found in both fresh and salt water in many parts of the world. Some species are probably entirely marine. The young eels, called leptocephalus larvae, are flat, transparent, and so unlike the adults that for many years they were not thought to be eels at all. Other species are catadromous, which means that they spend most of their life in fresh water but move downstream to the ocean for spawning.

The best-known eels belong to the genus *Anguilla*, family Anguillidae, and are common in North American and European waters. Both the American eel, *A. rostrata*, and its European relative, *A. vulgaris*, spawn near the Sargasso Sea. The larval eels, or leptocephali, follow the Gulf Stream north, transform into elvers, and then ascend the streams. Members of the family Muraenidae, the moray eels, are noted for their ferocity. They have strong jaws armed with many sharp teeth and will not hesitate to attack an unwary fisherman or diver. Moray eels are found in coral reefs and underwater caves in tropical waters around the world.

BRUCE B. COLLETTE, U.S. National Museum
See also CONGER EEL; MORAY EEL.

EEL GRASS, an aquatic plant, *Vallisneria spiralis*, in the Hydrocharitaceae, or frog's bit family. Eel grass is found growing in still, fresh waters in many parts of the world. The plants, which may grow to a height of 6 ft. or more, depending on the depth of the water, have long, sword-shaped leaves that arise from a tuftlike stalk. Curious spiral stems also arise from the stalk and bear small white flowers that are the only part of the plant to appear above the water's surface. Eel grass serves as a food for waterfowl and is also used as an aquarium plant.

EFENDI [ĕ-fĕn'dē], Turkish form of the Greek title of address *afentes*, itself a corruption of the classical *authentes*, meaning "lord," "master," and so on (cf. English "authentic"). Although in use among the Ottomans as a title of the sovereign and other important individuals, from the earliest period, about the end of the 17th century it came to be most generally applied to members of the learned

Edward the Confessor, King of England (1042–66). He was canonized by Pope Alexander III in 1161. This portrait was drawn and engraved from an altar window in Rumford Church, England.

The Mensell Collection

K. EDWARD the CONFESSOR.

class. By the 19th century the title meant no more than mister. By a law of 1934 it was replaced by *bay* in official usage, but it still remains the normal form of polite address among all classes.

EFFERVESCENCE [ĕf-ər-vĕs′əns], in chemistry, is the phenomenon of a gas escaping from a liquid, in which it has been dissolved, either because pressure is lowered or because temperature is raised. The gas will come out of solution to form bubbles at lowest pressure points and the bubbles are forced rapidly to the surface by the density difference between the gas and the liquid.

EFFICIENCY, ELECTRIC. The efficiency rating expresses how effectively a device uses the electricity required to run it. It is the ratio of the output of an electric machine or circuit to its input, expressed in per cent; the maximum theoretical value is 100%. An example is a motor generator requiring a 150-watt input, and delivering a 127.5-watt output. Its efficiency would be $100(127.5/150)$ or 85%.

EFFICIENCY, MECHANICAL, an indication of the losses caused by friction in the mechanical parts of a machine. It is the ratio of power output to power input expressed in per cent. The efficiency of machines depends in large measure on the care used in their construction, on the bearing devices employed, and on the amount and kind of lubrication.

Screws and wedges always, for example, have a low mechanical efficiency owing to large frictional forces and losses, while levers, which are almost frictionless in such machines as scales, have a high mechanical efficiency. The steam engine and the pump provide other examples of mechanical efficiency. In the steam engine, it is the ratio of the net horsepower available at the pulley to the horsepower developed by the steam in the cylinder. In the pump, it is the ratio of the power expended on the water to the power supplied to the pump.

ARON AXELROD, Bayonne Vocational and Technical
High School, Bayonne, N.J.
See also EFFICIENCY, ELECTRIC.

EFFIGY [ĕf′ə-jē], symbolic representation of a person or of a mythical or supernatural being. Sometimes the spiritual portion of a person is thought to be contained in the effigy. Thus it is believed that harming the effigy will harm the represented person through sympathetic magic. Mock killings in effigy are a remnant of such beliefs.
See also MAGIC.

EFFIGY MOUNDS, a series of prehistoric burial mounds in northeastern Iowa. Many of them are in the shape of birds and animals. They are believed to have been constructed about 1,000 years ago by the so-called "mound builders" of the Upper Mississippi. Of an estimated 100,000 mounds, many have been destroyed by modern agriculture. The state of Iowa bought the land containing the mounds and donated it to the United States. Estab. as national monument, 1949; area, 1.7 sq. mi.

EFFINGHAM, city of east-central Illinois, and seat of Effingham County. An agricultural (dairying, grain, and livestock) center, it also is the focus of a small petroleum field. Manufactures include road machinery, oil-field equipment, and prefabricated houses. Settled, 1853; inc., 1861; pop. (1950) 6,892; (1960) 8,172.

EFFLORESCENCE [ĕf-lô-rĕs′əns], in chemistry, the loss of water from a crystalline hydrate. Salts that crystallize from solution by combining in fixed proportion with water molecules have definite vapor pressures related to the temperature. If the vapor pressure of such a hydrate is higher than the partial pressure of water vapor in the air to which it is exposed, the water of crystallization will gradually be liberated, and the salt will be transformed to a hydrate of lower water content, or to the anhydrous state. The process visibly transforms shining or translucent crystals into a powder that seems to grow on the crystal's surface.

ÉGALITÉ, PHILIPPE. *See* ORLÉANS, LOUIS PHILIPPE JOSEPH, DUC D'.

EGAN, WILLIAM ALLEN (1914–   ), first governor of the state of Alaska. Born in Alaska, he was a leader of the movement that culminated in statehood in 1959. Egan, a Democrat, served in the territorial legislature, and as president of the constitutional convention of 1955–56 was principal architect of the state's charter. Following congressional approval of Alaska's admission to the Union, he was elected governor. He was re-elected in 1962.

EGER [ĕ′gĕr], city of northeastern Hungary, in Heves County, situated on the Eger River southwest of Miskolc. It was one of the first Magyar settlements in Hungary. Eger is known for its wines and food products. A bishopric was founded here by Stephen I during the 11th century. Destroyed by the Tatars (13th century), it was besieged by the Turks during the 16th century. Among its noteworthy sites are the ruins of a fortress, the 18th-century Church of the Minorites, and the County Hall. Pop., 35,375.

EGG. The egg, or ovum, is the reproductive cell of female animals. It is derived from oogonia, the dividing germ cells of the ovary. The cells produced by the final division of the oogonia, the oocytes, grow and develop to form the mature egg. After completion of this maturation process the egg is extruded from the ovary and is carried to a position where it may be fertilized by the male reproductive cell, the sperm.

The oocyte undergoes great chemical and physical changes before it becomes an egg, the most apparent of which is its change in size. In all species the mature egg is very large compared to other cells of the body. The largest eggs are found among the birds and reptiles. The oocyte of the frog, an amphibian, enlarges to 27,000 times its original size before it becomes a mature egg. Most of the egg's growth is the result of accumulation of yolk required to nourish the embryo during its initial period of development.

The process by which oocytes become mature eggs, or ova, is called gametogenesis. The resulting matured cells are called gametes. In addition to the profound change in size of the maturing oocyte, equally prominent alterations

THE EGGS OF DIFFERENT ANIMALS

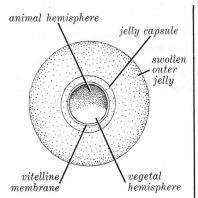

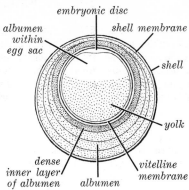

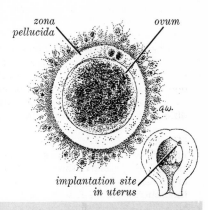

AMPHIBIAN EGG

The spherical center of the amphibian egg is roughly divided into two hemispheres: the darker animal hemisphere, in which the embryo develops; and the lighter vegetal hemisphere, which supplies nutrients to the developing embryo. The vitelline membrane and the layers of jelly protect the embryo and prevent it from becoming desiccated.

REPTILE EGG

The embryo of a reptile begins to develop on the egg's periphery at the embryonic disc. It is nourished by yolk and albumen and is surrounded by a protective membrane. Outside the vitelline membrane are additional nutrient albumen layers. The entire egg is surrounded by a shell. Because the shell prevents desiccation, the eggs of reptiles can develop on land.

MAMMALIAN EGG

The egg, or ovum, of a mammal remains inside the female's body and develops there after fertilization. The ovum is surrounded by a glassy membrane, the zona pellucida. The ovum contains virtually no nutrient material: the fertilized egg implants on the wall of the uterus, and the placenta, formed jointly by embryo and uterus, nourishes the developing embryo.

take place in the nucleus during maturation. The nucleus of an oogonium contains the same number of chromosome pairs (chromosomes are the bearers of genetic information) as all other body cells. If this oogonium merely enlarged to become the mature oocyte, then, when it was fertilized by a sperm, the resulting fertilized egg, or zygote, would have twice the number of chromosome pairs characteristic for the species. In order that the zygote have the correct number of chromosome pairs, the oogonium undergoes what is known as two meiotic divisions, with the result that the nucleus of the mature egg contains one member of each former chromosome pair—a "haploid" number of chromosomes. This is just one-half the original number. The developing sperm cell also undergoes meiotic divisions. Thus, when the sperm and egg (each contains in its nucleus one member of each pair of chromosomes) unite, the zygote has the proper number of chromosomes.

Most eggs are spherical in shape but may have enclosing membranes and outer coverings that give them a different form. Mammalian eggs are nearly spherical and are covered by membranous layers. The eggs of birds and reptiles are also spherical and are covered by protective membranes; they also have, as an additional protective feature, an exterior shell. External shells and other egg coverings are characteristically present in species in which the development of the young occurs outside the mother's body—in worms, insects, crustaceans, spiders, and lower vertebrates. .

The number of eggs produced at one time, the size of the egg, and the nature of the egg's protective covering are all determined by the environment in which the egg is fertilized and in which it subsequently develops as an embryo. Nature has provided well for the continuation of species. Lower animals usually produce many thousands of eggs, since the eggs are not only sought after by other animals for food, but the conditions under which the young animals develop (outside the mother's body) also claim many victims. Higher animal groups produce fewer eggs, but those eggs are better protected, Mammals produce the least number of eggs of any animal group—usually only one or two at a time. Mammalian young, however, are so well protected in their early developmental stages that those few eggs actually have a better chance of becoming adult individuals than does any one of the 3 or 4 million eggs produced annually by, for example, a codfish.

THOMAS H. RODERICK, Associate Staff Scientist, Roscoe B. Jackson Memorial Laboratories
See also EMBRYOLOGY; FERTILIZATION; MEIOSIS; MITOSIS.

EGGERTSVILLE, residential village of western New York, adjoining Buffalo on the northeast. Pop. (1960) 44,807.

EGGLESTON [ĕg′əl-stən], **EDWARD** (1837–1902), American novelist, born in Vevay, Ind. A member of a strict religious family, he was himself a clergyman for many years but retired in 1879 to devote his full time to writing. His best novels, *The Hoosier Schoolmaster* (1871), *The Circuit Rider* (1874), *Roxy* (1878), and *The Hoosier Schoolboy* (1883), recall experiences in backwoods country among simple people. Though his writings were unashamedly didactic, often sentimental, they were distinguished by realism in background and character portrayal.

EGGPLANT, a strong-growing perennial herb, *Solanum melongena*, of the Solanaceae, or nightshade family. Originally native to tropical Asia, eggplant is now widely grown as a garden annual in many parts of the world, and is especially prized in the Mediterranean region and the Near East. The plants are low, densely-branched shrubs and bear large, egg-shaped, shiny-skinned fruits that are usually dark purple but may also be white or yellowish. Eggplant is raised from seed and requires rich, loamy soil and a long, warm growing season. In cool climates the seedlings are usually raised indoors, then set out, in well-plowed ground, when all danger of frost has passed. Until the fruits ripen (in late summer or early fall), the plants should be protected from the variety of insect and fungus pests which attack them, by spraying with DDT and other effective insecticides.

EGG TESTING, a procedure in which eggs are examined to determine their interior quality. Eggs are inspected externally for cleanliness of shell and graded according to size. Candling is the conventional method of determining interior quality. This procedure is carried out in a darkened room by using a candler—a boxlike device with an internal light source. As the egg is held in front of an opening in the candler, light passes through the egg as it is twirled in the hand, revealing any internal imperfections such as bloodspots. Other methods of egg testing are flash candling, in which eggs are rotated under and over a lighted area; and electronic candling, in which the egg is passed before an electronic beam to detect any internal imperfections. This latter method is more accurate and faster than conventional candling and is used in commercial egg grading.

EGMONT, LAMORAL, COUNT OF (1522–68), Flemish general and statesman. Egmont distinguished himself in the service of Emperor Charles V and was a brilliant cavalry commander for Philip II of Spain. Appointed (1559) Governor-General of Flanders and Artois, Egmont attempted to negotiate a settlement of religious quarrels and, though himself a devout Catholic, sought to persuade Philip II to cease persecution of Protestants. Egmont also insisted on maintaining the Netherlands' local privileges and opposed the direct rule and centralizing policy of Spain. His firm and dignified stand encouraged resistance to Spanish rule and, though Egmont considered himself loyal to Philip and never contemplated treason, he failed to realize that his association with people thought to be plotting rebellion, including William the Silent, aroused Spanish suspicions. When Philip sent (1567) the Duke of Alba to the Netherlands to suppress the incipient rebellion, Egmont was immediately arrested. Egmont protested his innocence and asserted his continued loyalty to Philip, but Alba had him executed in an effort to frighten potential rebels. Egmont, however, had been extremely popular and his death spurred open rebellion. Egmont's life is the subject of Goethe's tragedy *Egmont*, which inspired music by Beethoven.

ARMAND PATRUCCO, Rhode Island College

EGMONT, incidental music to Goethe's tragedy, by Ludwig van Beethoven (1810, Op. 84). The overture, often played separately at concerts, is constructed in sonata form with a slow introduction leading into a dramatic allegro. The second theme recalls the opening motif (measures two and three) of the introduction. Beethoven uses four horns in the orchestra rather than the two of his *Coriolanus* overture.

EGMONT, MOUNT, extinct volcanic cone of New Zealand, near the west coast of North Island. Rising from the plains of Taranaki and isolated from any mountain range, this snow-capped peak (8,260 ft.) has been called the Fujiyama of New Zealand. Its lower slopes are densely forested.

EGO [ē′gō]. According to psychoanalytic theory, the ego is the part of the mind which deals with the real world. The infant's mind consists of the id, which is the seat of primitive desires. When the id faces the real world part of it becomes differentiated into the ego, which has the task of satisfying the id within the limitations imposed by society. The id, for example, may demand immediate satisfactions of sexual desires: the ego, recognizing the impossibility of such satisfactions, must transform the id desires into socially acceptable conduct. Later the rules of social behavior may be incorporated into the ego, forming a new structure, the superego, or conscience. The mature ego is thus charged with the responsibility of serving at least three taskmasters: the id, the superego, and the real world.

EGRET [ē′grĭt], group name of a number of members of the heron family, *Ardeidae*. This name is used chiefly for certain species whose long scapular plumes, grown during the breeding season, were formerly objects of trade for millinery purposes and called "aigrettes." All egrets are long-legged, straight-billed, wading birds, usually of white color. Best-known is the great, or common, egret, *Egretta (Casmerodius) alba*, with an enormous breeding range throughout most of the warmer parts of the world. This beautiful bird is pure white, with a yellow bill and long, straight aigrette plumes. During the period of the feather trade it became rare, but under protection it has recovered most of its range and breeds as far north as southern Canada. The much smaller snowy egret, *E. thula*, is even more graceful, with a crested head, recurved scapular plumes, black bill, and yellow toes. It breeds from New York south to Argentina. The Old World ally, the little egret, *E. garzetta*, is similar, but has straight elongated crest plumes and aigrettes, and dark color phases occur. The intermediate, or plumed, egret, *E. intermedia*, and the Chinese egret, *E. eulophotes*, are restricted to eastern Asia and the adjacent islands. The reddish egret, *Dichromanassa rufescens*, occurs as a breeder in Florida, Texas, Mexico, and the West Indies. It is normally rufous and slaty, but occasional white birds are found. The cattle egret, *Bubulcus ibis*, of the Old World tropics, has recently entered the New World, and it has rapidly increased its range. It follows grazing animals, feeding chiefly on insects that they stir up.

EUGENE EISENMANN, American Museum of Natural History

George Holton—Photo Researchers

Great Sphinx at Giza (4th Dynasty), a figure with the head of a man and the body of a lion, was carved from a rock bluff. The face is thought to represent King Khafre (26th century B.C.), whose power was symbolized by the lion's body.

EGYPT

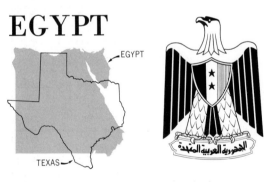

EGYPT

TEXAS

AREA	386,110 sq. mi.
POPULATION	Approx. 26,000,000
PRINCIPAL LANGUAGE	Arabic
LIFE EXPECTANCY	40 years
PERCENTAGE OF LITERACY	20%–25%
UNIT OF CURRENCY	Egyptian pound (£E)
CAPITAL	Cairo
PRINCIPAL PRODUCTS	Cotton, rice; oil; textiles, cement

EGYPT [ē′jǐpt], an historic country of Africa, now called the United Arab Republic. Its position on the Mediterranean coast has given it historical, political, and cultural links with Africa, Asia, and Europe. Its neighbors are, on the west, Libya; on the south, the Sudan; and on the northeast, Israel. The Red Sea is to the east of the country, the Mediterranean to the north. The total area of Egypt is 386,110 sq. mi., only 13,000 of which (mainly in the Nile Valley and the Nile Delta) can be cultivated by irrigation and can support a settled population. According to official estimates, the population of the country is 26,000,000.

The Land

On its way to the Mediterranean, the Nile River flows through Egyptian Nubia, Upper Egypt, and finally Lower Egypt before emptying into the sea. Egyptian Nubia above the First Cataract is a largely sterile, rocky valley, which will be wholly flooded on completion of the Aswan High Dam project. Upper Egypt lies between the First Cataract and the Delta. It consists of a ribbon of cultivated land, never more than a few miles in width, watered from the river, and enclosed between rocky hills and deserts. In Lower Egypt, north of Cairo, the landscape changes. The level and largely fertile Delta, lying between the western (Rosetta) and eastern (Damietta) branches of the Nile, is intersected by numerous streams and canals and is densely populated. The Mediterranean coast lands are low and sandy, with extensive brackish lakes and swamps at the fringes of the Delta.

The deserts to the east and west of the Nile are the home of nomadic tribes. The Western Desert is characterized by depressions, some of which contain oases with settled populations of cultivators. The largest of these is El-Faiyum, around Lake Qarun, which at one time drained

309

into the Nile. Farther south lies a series of scattered oases, in the Kharga-Dakhla and Farafra depressions. Siwa, the most remote oasis of all, lies in the west, near the Libyan border. The largest depression, that of Qattara, lies about 400 ft. below sea level, and its saline marshes support only a small population. The Eastern Desert is by contrast a highland area, sloping down to a narrow coastal plain on the Red Sea and lacking oases. It is thinly populated. Across the gulf and isthmus of Suez, now pierced by the Suez Canal, lies the Sinai peninsula, another arid and, for the most part, highland region. The geographic characteristics of Egypt that have been factors in its history are the sharp contrast between the fertile river valley and the surrounding deserts and, within the valley itself, the differentiation between the thread of Upper Egypt and the carpet of the Delta.

Climate. Climatic conditions are fairly uniform throughout Egypt. Day temperatures in summer reach 100° F.,

with a sharp drop at nightfall. The hottest season is from June to August. The winters are mild and pleasant. The Mediterranean coast lands receive a winter rainfall, which decreases sharply inland. South of Cairo, rainstorms are rare and sporadic. The prevailing wind is northwest, but during April and May a hot, southerly wind (the khamsin) carrying sandstorms frequently occurs. The late summer climate is affected by the annual Nile flood, which increases humidity between July and October.

The People

Population. The population of Egypt has increased sharply during the last 150 years. It is estimated to have been about 2,500,000 at the end of the 18th century, perhaps a third of what it had been a thousand years earlier. The first reliable census (1897) gave the figure, excluding nomads, of 9,715,000. This rose within 50 years to 19,022,000. The official estimate for the end of 1956 was

---

The Nile valley was the site of one of the first civilizations to develop on earth. Over a span of some 60 centuries Egypt has been ruled by many different powers and has been the home of several different cultures. The high civilization of the Pharaohs almost entirely disappeared after Roman and later Arab conquests of Egypt. The study of Egypt, then, is not of one continuing civilization, as in the case of China. Some students may be interested in ancient Egypt, whose culture is so much explored by archeologists. Others may be concerned with Egypt as part of the Arab-Muslim world. The article on these pages includes both topics, as the following outline indicates.

The Land. The Nile and the deserts; climate.

The People (Modern Egypt). Population; cities and towns; ethnology; religion; education; libraries, learned societies, and museums; the press; the arts.

The Economy (Modern Egypt). Agriculture; mining; manufacturing; tourism; transportation and roads; labor; the government and the economy.

National Welfare (Modern Egypt). Social legislation; public health.

History. Ancient Egypt. Chronology and historical periods from before 3000 B.C. to the Arab conquest in 642 A.D.; Predynastic Egypt; Protodynastic, or Archaic, period; Old Kingdom; First Intermediate Period; Middle Kingdom; Second Intermediate Period; New Kingdom; Late Dynasties; Ptolemaic Period; Roman and Byzantine Periods.

    People and society of ancient Egypt: economy and daily life; government; religion; temples; funerary beliefs and practices; science and learning; language and literature.

    Medieval Egypt: Ottoman Egypt (after 642 A.D.).

    Modern Egypt: Mohammed Ali (took office in 1805) and his dynasty; British occupation (1882); independent Egypt (after 1922); the 1952 revolution and republic; union with Syria in the United Arab Republic (U.A.R.); foreign relations of the U.A.R.; break in the Syrian-Egyptian union.

Egyptian Art. Archaic period (c.3000-2780 B.C.) and Old Kingdom (c.2780-2254 B.C.); Middle (1991-1778 B.C.) and New Kingdoms (1573-c.1085 B.C.).

Egyptian Dance. From ancient Egyptian to modern Arabic styles.

Egyptian Music. Musical style of ancient Egypt: musical notation and conducting; scales; harmony; vocal and instrumental styles; melody and form; professional musicians.

The reader can find many other articles on Egypt in this Encyclopedia. Of these AFRICA: *Geography*, NILE RIVER, SINAI PENINSULA, and RED SEA are relevant to ancient and modern Egypt. Other entries, however, fall into two main groups. For the understanding of ancient Egypt, a basic article is EGYPTOLOGY, which discusses the archeological studies by which the culture of early periods is known. Styles of houses, tombs, and temples are treated in EGYPTIAN ARCHITECTURE and in entries on specific structures (PYRAMIDS, SPHINX, and OBELISKS), and sites (ABYDOS, GIZA OR GIZEH, KARNAK, MEMPHIS, and THEBES, for example). Gods of the ancient Egyptians are discussed in such articles as AMON, AMEN OR AMUN; OSIRIS; and SERAPIS OR SARAPIS. Other aspects of the culture are noted in CALENDAR, HIEROGLYPHS, MUMMIFICATION, PAPYRI, and SCARAB. Side lights on history are in articles on Pharaohs such as RAMESES II and in HYKSOS, PTOLEMIES, and CLEOPATRA. Other views of history are in HITTITES, ETHIOPIA, and NUBIA; in EXODUS and JEWS, HISTORY OF THE; in ALEXANDER THE GREAT; and in ROME and Julius CAESAR.

Ancient Egyptian culture survives to a slight extent among the Copts (see COPTIC CHURCH and EGYPTIAN) and in Coptic and folk music and in the dance. Otherwise the record of Egypt since Roman times can be considered that of another civilization. Historical articles include ABBASID, AYYUBID, and FATIMID (Muslim dynasties), and MOHAMMED ALI OR MEHEMET ALI. Religious and historical background is provided by ISLAM. Aspects of 19th- and 20th-century history are treated in NAPOLEON I, SUEZ CANAL, and SUDAN (which was linked with Egypt). Articles relating to more recent times include WORLD WAR II and biographies of FARUK I, Mohammed NAGUIB, and Gamal Abdel NASSER, architect of the U.A.R.

The civilization of Muslim Egypt is treated in such articles as ALEXANDRIA and CAIRO, which also provide historical background, and PORT SAID. Religion is treated in ISLAM, SUFISM, and SHIITE ISLAM. The people are discussed in ARAB and the language in ARABIC. A famous university is covered in AZHAR, UNIVERSITY OF AL-.

The library can provide books for further study of ancient or modern Egypt. Collections of antiquities can be viewed in museums such as those listed at the conclusion of EGYPTOLOGY.

22,924,000. Both birth and death rates (41.6 and 20.6 per 1,000, respectively) are among the world's highest. The pressure of population on the land available for cultivation is thus extremely heavy, and this has lent urgency to schemes of agricultural development and industrialization. It has also promoted a drift to the towns. There are small resident alien communities, largely a development of the 19th century, composed chiefly of Syrians and Lebanese, Greeks, Italians, and Maltese. Some of these have had an economic or cultural role of far greater importance than their small numbers would suggest.

Cities and Towns. The capital, Cairo, lies on the east bank of the Nile, just above the Delta. This is an important site, strategically and commercially, for the domination of both Upper and Lower Egypt and for the handling of the internal river-borne trade of the country. Not surprisingly, therefore, modern Cairo is the successor of several ancient capitals or fortress-cities on or near this site. With a population of over 3,000,000, Cairo is the largest city of the Middle East. The other main towns have developed in consequence of maritime trade. Alexandria, a great port in ancient and medieval times, was much decayed before the 19th century, when its revival took place. It is now a leading Mediterranean port, through which pass most of Egypt's exports of cotton and rice, and it has a population of over 1,000,000. With the opening of the Suez Canal, new life came to the ancient port of Suez, at its southern end. Port Said, the northern terminus, was a creation of the canal. The inland towns of Egypt have in many cases very long histories and owe their continued importance largely to having been local administrative centers under successive regimes.

Ethnology. The modern Egyptians represent ethnically the intermingling of older stocks of the Nile valley with Arab immigrants, from the time of the Muslim conquest in the 7th century and onward. The modern Egyptians are Arabic-speaking, and preponderantly Muslim by religion. Military elites, chiefly Circassian and Turkish, which dominated Egypt at various times, left their mark, chiefly on the higher social groups and the populations of the great cities. Today the pre-Arab element is represented in its purest form by the Copts, about 1,500,000 in number out of a total population of nearly 26,000,000. The Copts retain their Christian faith, but the Coptic language, descended from Ancient Egyptian, is now used only in the Coptic liturgy. The Nubians, south of the First Cataract, are the modern representatives of stock other than that of the cultivators of the lower Nile valley. They also have been Arabized in religion and culture, but still speak a Nubian dialect. The desert nomads are for the most part composed of Arab or Arabized Berber tribes, although in the southeastern desert the Ababda and Bisharin are Arabized members of the Hamitic-speaking Beja group, otherwise found in the eastern Sudan.

Religion. Islam, which in the 7th century was the religion of the small Arab elite that had conquered Egypt, spread during the Middle Ages to all classes of the population as a result of intermarriage and conversion. Nowadays the Copts form only a small minority of the population. Although from 969 to 1171 Egypt was ruled by the heretical Muslim Fatimids, the mass of Egyptians have always remained Sunnis, attached to the majority group of

Unloading sugar cane from feluccas on the Nile at Cairo.

Muslims. One of the greatest jurists of Sunni Islam, al-Shafii, taught in Egypt, where he died and was buried in 819. His opinions on Muslim law are still generally followed in Lower Egypt.

Popular Islam, in Egypt as elsewhere, has been profoundly affected by Sufism (q.v.), systems of mystical be-

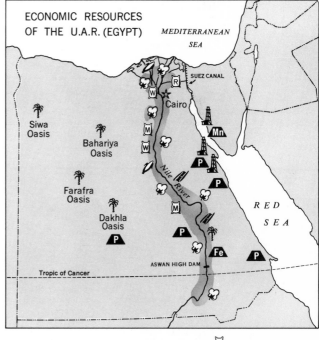

ECONOMIC RESOURCES
OF THE U.A.R. (EGYPT)

MEDITERRANEAN SEA

SUEZ CANAL

Cairo

Siwa Oasis

Bahariya Oasis

Farafra Oasis

Dakhla Oasis

Nile River

RED SEA

ASWAN HIGH DAM

Tropic of Cancer

Cultivated area:

🌿 Cotton	M Millet
🌴 Dates	Petroleum
Fe Iron	P Phosphates
Maize (corn)	R Rice
Mn Manganese	Sugar cane
	W Wheat

EGYPT
(UNITED ARAB REPUBLIC)

SCALE OF MILES

0   50   100   150   200

KILOMETRES

0   50   100   150   200

liefs which have an emotional content lacking in the more austere orthodoxy of Islam. During the Middle Ages numerous Sufi orders came into existence, each with its own forms of devotional practice leading to mystical union with God. The founders and successive teachers of these orders are believed to possess a sacred power (baraka), which can communicate itself to their disciples. They are regarded as saints, and their tombs are places of pilgrim-

age. Among the most famous of Egyptian Sufi saints is Sayyid Ahmad al-Badawi, whose tomb at Tanta (in the Delta) was a place of sanctuary. Popular celebrations are held on the annual festivals (mulids, literally "birthdays") of the Prophet Mohammed and the Sufi saints. Beginning in the 19th century the movement for religious reform in Islam has alienated many educated Muslims from the traditional Sufi beliefs and practices, which are now regarded

INDEX TO EGYPT (UNITED ARAB REPUBLIC) GENERAL REFERENCE MAP

Total Population 26,000,000

as accretions to the religion, but which still have a great hold over the poorer people and in the countryside.

Education. Egypt has for centuries been a center of traditional Muslim learning and culture. At the lowest level, religious schools (*kuttabs*) taught the elements of literacy and the Koran. These were private foundations, usually in association with mosques or other religious institutions and maintained by charitable endowments (*waqfs*). The mosque of al-Azhar, founded in the 10th century, developed from the 13th century into an Islamic university and acquired enormous prestige, which it still retains throughout the Muslim world (*see* AZHAR, UNIVERSITY OF AL-).

The beginnings of Western education in Egypt are due to Mohammed Ali, Ottoman Viceroy in Egypt from 1805–49. He established a number of schools in order to assist in his project of creating a European-style army. The Egyptians at first viewed the schools with deep mistrust because of their link with the unpopular conscript army. In Mohammed Ali's last years, Western-type education underwent a setback which continued in the reigns of Abbas I and Said. Fresh progress was made under Khedive Ismail (reigned 1863–79), who envisaged the creation of a national system of education no longer fostered for purely military purposes. A university founded at Cairo by popular subscription in 1908 was the parent of the various modern Egyptian universities.

A new period of educational development opened with the coming of independence in 1922. Progress was accelerated after World War II and still more after the revolu-

The old and the new mingle in Cairo. Domes and minarets rise above the rooftops of modern apartment buildings. (WILLIAM G. FROELICH)

Arab Information Center—Photo Researchers

The University of al-Azhar, Cairo. Al-Azhar is one of the most famous universities in the Arab world.

Birnback Publishing Service

A canal flows through the countryside in Faiyum Province, one of Egypt's most productive agricultural areas.

tion of 1952. Two general trends may be discerned in this period. The first is an attempt to establish a foundation of literacy and basic education throughout the nation. A law of 1923 made education free and compulsory between the ages of 7 and 12, but it represented the statement of an objective rather than practical legislation. Only about 41% of the children between 6 and 12 were attending school by 1951. Following the 1952 revolution the new regime attacked the problem vigorously, with the aim of providing universal primary education by 1964. In Egypt the combating of illiteracy is made particularly difficult by the peculiar nature of the Arabic script and by the wide gulf between the spoken and the written language.

The second trend is toward the integration of all scholastic institutions into a single, nationwide system, offering an educational ladder to students. Side by side with the government primary schools, which for a minority of pupils formed the bottom rung, were the elementary schools, including the traditional *kuttabs*, from which no advance was normally possible. From 1949 the curriculum of these elementary schools was expanded, and in 1951 they were amalgamated with the primary schools. In 1953 a reorganization of the postprimary schools took place.

Libraries, Learned Societies, and Museums. The Khedivial (now National) Library was established in 1870. Learned societies, such as the Khedivial Geographical Society and the Institute of Egypt, facilitated the collaboration of Egyptian and European scholars in various branches of research. The development of Egyptology was reflected in the founding of the Cairo Museum in 1863.

The Press. The greatest of Egyptian newspapers, *al-Ahram* ("The Pyramids"), was founded in 1875 by two Syrian brothers. The Egyptian press expanded and became influential throughout the Arab world at the turn of the century. It served as a meeting place for traditionalism and modernism, and as the principal vehicle for the propagation of nationalist views. However, the political vicissitudes of Egypt after World War I did not favor freedom of the press. Since the revolution of 1952, in particular, it has functioned under censorship.

The Arts. The writing of poetry, the characteristic Arabic method of literary expression, has flourished, and the novel and the drama have been adopted and naturalized as literary forms. Since Muslim art has, for theological considerations, traditionally rejected pictorial representation, modern Egyptian drawing, painting, and sculpture mark a break with the Muslim past—they have been deeply influenced both by the West and by ancient Egypt.

Egypt is the cultural center of the Arab world, and its books and periodicals circulate throughout the Middle East. In recent years it has led the way in exploiting modern methods of communication. Since 1926, when the first Egyptian film was made, an important motion picture industry has developed, which supplies other Arabic-speaking countries as well as Egypt itself. The radio, too, commands an audience far outside the Egyptian frontiers. Its established popular appeal facilitated its use by the Nasser regime for purposes of propaganda in Arabic and other languages.

The Economy

Agriculture. The economy of Egypt has depended throughout its history on agriculture, and this in turn on the control of the Nile flood. The intensively cultivated irrigable lands of Egypt have been built up throughout millennia from the fertile silt annually deposited by the Nile in flood.

The 19th century saw two revolutionary developments in Egyptian agriculture: the introduction of "perennial irrigation" by damming the river to provide water throughout the whole year; and the establishment of long-staple cotton as the principal export crop. Essential to the present system of control of the river for perennial irrigation are the Aswan Dam (begun in 1898 and twice raised) and the Jebel Aulia Dam, lying within the Sudan. The purpose of the High Dam south of Aswan, begun in 1960, was to provide long-term water storage to compensate for years of poor flood. These works not only increased the total cultivable area in Egypt, but also made possible the raising of two, three, and even four crops annually on land which had previously produced only one. The development of perennial irrigation has also brought some problems: the salinity of the soil has increased, and signs of soil exhaustion have appeared. This is due to the combination of increased cropping with a decrease in the deposition of the fertile silt in areas under perennial irrigation.

Although the Viceroy Mohammed Ali encouraged the planting of cotton, the great increase in this crop occurred in the reign of Ismail, when the American Civil War caused a boom in Egyptian cotton. The spread of perennial irrigation is closely linked with the increase of cotton-growing. Maize, another crop that flourishes under perennial irrigation, displaced wheat as the principal cereal in the 19th century, and these three crops now occupy about 70% of the cultivable land. Although the cotton exports of Egypt have been of immense value as a source of foreign exchange, the dangers of excessive dependence on this product have been very clear since the slump in the 1930's. Attempts to create a more balanced economy were frustrated by the wealthy landlords until the revolution of 1952.

Today the principal cereals are maize, wheat, rice (in the Delta), and millet (especially in Upper Egypt). Berseem (Egyptian clover) is the chief fodder crop. Sugar cane, onions, lentils, and various oilseeds are also grown, and the date palm flourishes especially in Upper Egypt. Away from the Nile and the oases, the land supports at best a sparse growth of scrub, grazed by the animals of nomadic herdsmen.

Animal Husbandry. Egypt maintains a large population of domestic animals: sheep, cattle, water buffaloes, and goats. Cattle are used for plowing as well as for milk production. The commonest transport animals are donkeys and camels, the latter being bred chiefly by the nomads. Poultry and pigeons are kept by villagers.

Mining. Egypt produces an abundance of good building stone. The Western Desert has for centuries been a source of sodium salts, which are particularly abundant in the Wadi el-Natrun ("Valley of Niter"), lying to the west of the Delta. Gold, an ancient mineral product of Egypt, is still mined in small quantities. Coal is completely lacking, but small oil fields have been tapped on the western shore of the Red Sea and in Sinai. The most productive field, that of Ras Gharib, was discovered in 1938. Egypt is now self-sufficient in petroleum, but not in paraffin (the chief

United Arab Republic Tourist Office
The Aswan Dam. Completed in 1902 and twice heightened, the dam made possible the reclamation of about 1,408,000 acres.

domestic fuel) or crude oil. Phosphate rock and manganese are mined on the Red Sea coast. A large deposit of high grade iron ore was discovered in 1937 near Aswan. The exploitation of this has been delayed by the remoteness of the site and lack of power, but steel production began on a small scale in 1950.

Manufacturing. The first attempts to introduce modern methods of manufacture into Egypt, which had a long tradition of skilled artisans and domestic craftsmanship, were made by Mohammed Ali, who imported machinery and sought to establish a textile industry. His efforts were premature, and Egyptian industrialization is mainly a development of the present century. The two world wars both provided stimuli to this development although after each there was a shrinkage in industry. Egypt has built up a small but vigorous and well-equipped industrial sector in its economy. Cotton spinning and weaving are of the greatest importance, followed by cement manufacture. The processing of agricultural products, such as sugar, tobacco, and cotton seed, is also well established.

Tourism. Egypt's wealth of historical remains from every period of its history, its mild winter climate, and the interest to foreigners of its scenery and customs have for the past century made tourism an industry of growing importance. This is to some degree precarious, being af-

Processing cotton. Since the middle of the 19th century cotton has been Egypt's most important export.

Johan M. Shoutem—Pix

In the Muqattam Hills east of Cairo, limestone slabs are cut by hand.
Birnback Publishing Service

Annan Photo Features

Gowned and turbaned longshoremen stack cotton for export on the docks of Alexandria, Egypt's major port.

fected at once by wars or signs of internal political instability, but in general, is a large and increasing source of revenue.

Transportation and Roads. Until the 19th century the Nile was Egypt's principal "highway," with Cairo as the place of transshipment for goods coming from the Mediterranean and Upper Egypt, respectively. Caravan routes across the desert linked Lower Egypt with Syria and Cyrenaica, and Upper Egypt with the Red Sea coast and the Sudan. Even today, the roads are few and poor. Egypt was, however, the first Middle Eastern country to develop a railway system, which now extends over 2,600 mi. Most railway routes run parallel to the Nile and its ancillary waterways; hence there is naturally competition between the two forms of transport. Cairo now has a great international airport, an important stage on the routes to Africa and the Far East.

Labor. The development of industrialization and the exclusion of the working class from the political elite led to the rise of a labor movement and the foundation of trade unions at the end of the 19th century. The pace of their growth quickened after the slump in the 1930's. In 1942 the trade unions received legal recognition, but state and municipal workers were forbidden to form unions. This barrier was removed after the revolution. The revolutionary regime tended to seek the collaboration of the labor movement, while keeping it under strict control.

The Government and the Economy. After the revolution of 1952, government control of the economy increased. A Permanent Council for the Development of National Production was set up, and a series of plans defined projects

for the development of agriculture, communications, and industry in the years ahead. There remained a basic problem of power; Egypt has no coal and only moderate resources of oil. Power stations connected with the Aswan Dam and the Aswan High Dam therefore occupy an important place in economic planning. Lack of capital has been another obstacle to industrialization: both local and foreign sources have tended to prefer investment in land and its adjuncts—cotton and buildings. Although the policy of the Nasser regime was to encourage foreign investment, political and international developments worked against this.

National Welfare

Social Legislation. Socially and politically, modern Egypt was dominated until the revolution of 1952 by a small class of great landowners. A great gulf existed between this Europeanized, town-dwelling aristocracy and the mass of peasantry in the countryside, ill housed, poorly fed, and living near the subsistence level. The entrenched political power of the landlord class long prevented any serious attempts to deal with this social problem. It is significant that the military *coup d'état* of 1952 was followed by the comprehensive Agrarian Law of Sept. 9, 1952, which with certain unimportant exceptions limited the total land holdings of any person to 200 feddan (approximately 200 acres). It empowered the government to seize excess holdings over a five-year period and to redistribute the land so acquired among the peasantry. The law also set up agricultural co-operative societies for peasants owning up to five feddan, and provided for the fixing of agricultural wages and the formation of agricultural workers' unions. The amount of cultivable land liable to expropriation was, however, not more than about one-tenth of the whole, and of more far-reaching importance were those clauses of the law which safeguarded the position of the agricultural tenant by fixing the level of rents and granting greater security. The law was conceived in the interests of social regeneration rather than of the technical improvement of agriculture.

Public Health. Until the 19th century Egypt suffered from recurrent epidemics of plague and other diseases, usually as a sequel to famine resulting from poor Nile floods. Although these epidemics have been eliminated through the development of sanitary control, the general standard of public health outside the large cities remains very low. Ironically, agricultural improvements have in fact produced a deterioration in the health of the peasantry since the increase of perennial irrigation has led to the spread of water-borne and mosquito-borne diseases. Although malaria has been much reduced since World War II, bilharziasis still affects about three-quarters of the village population. Tuberculosis and trachoma are prevalent in both towns and countryside. The seriousness of the public health problem has been realized by all modern governments in Egypt, and numerous measures are on hand for dealing with it. These include housing schemes, the improvement of water supplies, the building of hospitals, and the training of increased numbers of doctors.

P. M. Holt, University of London

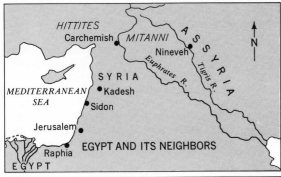

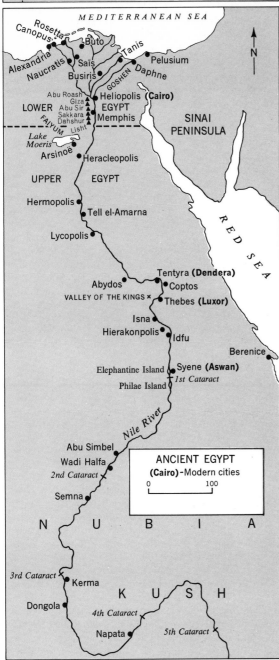

Ancient Egypt

In ancient times Egypt was called *To-meri* (Gr. Timuris) and *Kemet*, "the Black Land." The name "Egypt" itself was never used by the Egyptians, being derived from *Aigyptos*, the Greek form of *Hut-ka-Ptah*, an ancient name of Memphis. Herodotus' description of Egypt as "the gift of the Nile" accurately characterizes the country's total dependence on the great river which both formed it and nourished it and without which Egyptian civilization would not have come into being. The narrow alluvial strip along the banks of the Nile, averaging only about 2–3 mi. in width, extending 600 mi. from the Mediterranean to the First Cataract, and totaling approximately 12,000 sq. mi., in fact comprised the entirety of Egypt in earliest antiquity. By Roman times, it was made to support a population of 6,000,000. Egypt's borders were gradually pushed southward to the Fourth Cataract in Ethiopia and eastward from Sinai to the Euphrates River, although the oases of the western desert were not controlled or exploited until relatively late in Egyptian history.

Egypt's resources included limestone, sandstone, granite, gold, copper, and turquoise, but its principal wealth was the rich black silt deposited annually by the Nile, and the fertile acreage of the multibranched Delta region in the north. Egypt's confinement to a long, attenuated valley and the consequent necessity of controlling the unruly and inconstant river therefore to a remarkable degree determined the course of its history and shaped its technical and cultural development. Government itself probably originated in the need for co-operation demanded by the gigantic task of organizing the use of floodwaters. The advantages to be gained from the effective administration of large areas for the purposes of irrigation must have early encouraged centralization.

Chronology and Historical Periods. The ancient Egyptians did not use any system of era dating, nor have any complete outlines of their ancient history survived. The earliest method of dating was by naming a year after some important event, a method succeeded in the 2d Dynasty by reckoning according to the biennial cattle census. It was not until after the 6th Dynasty that dating by the regnal years of individual Kings was developed. The modern system of dynasties is due to Manetho (3d century B.C.), an Egyptian priest who lived during the reigns of Ptolemy I and II, and wrote a history of Egypt in Greek. Only a summary of this work and some fragments have survived, but, although his earlier dates are too high, his division into 31 dynasties is approximately correct and his work is a convenient and valuable aid. All those sources, however, would not have permitted the drawing up of a reliable chronology if there had not also been astronomical data. The Egyptian civil year of 365 days was supposed to begin on the traditional day of the rising of the Nile (July 19, Julian calendar), which was also the day of the heliacal rising of Sothis (the Dog Star, Sirius). The discrepancy of approximately a quarter of a day between the Egyptian civil year and the true year resulted in a cycle of 1,456 years before the two years, if not corrected, would coincide again: this is the Sothic Cycle. Egyptian references to the rising of Sothis enable us to fix certain events within a margin of four years: thus the beginning of the 12th Dynasty can be fixed at 1991 B.C., that of the 18th at 1573 B.C., and dead reckoning carries the beginning of the 11th Dynasty to about 2133 B.C. All earlier dates are subject to an increasing degree of uncertainty and modern estimates of the 1st Dynasty vary between 3400 B.C. and 2850 B.C. It is probable that 3000 B.C., or very slightly later, may ultimately prove the more realistic date.

The duration of the Predynastic Period cannot be accurately estimated, and no dates at all can be assigned to the different cultures. Even the new carbon-14 method of dating is of very limited use. For the Upper Egyptian series of cultures an ingenious system of Sequence Dates (S.D.) has been evolved in which each date represents a step in a cultural sequence, but not a date in terms of our era. According to this system, S.D. 64 is roughly contemporary with the beginning of the 1st Dynasty. It is highly improbable that any of the Predynastic cultures could have been permanently settled on the floor of the Nile Valley before 5000–4500 B.C.

As a matter of convenience the history of Egypt is now usually divided into a number of periods: Predynastic (before 3000 B.C.); Archaic, or Protodynastic (1st and 2d Dynasties, c.3000–2780 B.C.); Old Kingdom (3d to 6th Dynasties, c.2780–2254 B.C.); First Intermediate Period (7th to 11th Dynasties, c.2254–1991 B.C.); Middle Kingdom (12th Dynasty, 1991–1778 B.C.); Second Intermediate Period, including the Hyksos domination (13th to 17th Dynasties, 1778–1573 B.C.); New Kingdom (18th to 20th Dynasties, 1573–1085 B.C.); the Late Dynasties (21st to 31st Dynasties, 1085–332 B.C.); Ptolemaic Period (332–30 B.C.); and Roman and Byzantine Periods (30 B.C.–642 A.D.).

Predynastic Egypt. Men of the Old Stone Age (Paleolithic) had settled on the desert margins of the Nile Valley, but their Neolithic successors descended to Upper Egypt (southern Egypt) and developed three known Predynastic cultures. The oldest of these is the Badarian (before S.D. 30) whose settlements and cemeteries are almost exclusively confined to the district of Badari. Next is Naqada I, or Amratian (S.D. 30–38), found between Badari and the First Cataract, with its center at Naqada. Of Naqada II, or Gerzean (S.D. 38–64), cemeteries are found near the entrance to the Faiyum, and from Badari deep into Lower Nubia, with an outpost at the Second Cataract. All these groups used copper to a limited extent, and produced excellent handmade pottery, which was sometimes painted. They buried their dead in cemeteries apart from the settlements. Their graves were oval or circular, in Naqada II tending to become rectangular concurrently with the introduction of the sun-dried mud brick. The dead, accompanied by a few simple grave goods, were usually buried in a contracted position, resting on the left side, head to the south, though the attitude tends to vary in Naqada II. Walled towns or settlements built of brick are known from Naqada II at the latest. Naqada II also sees increased production of stone vessels as a consequence of easier access to copper supplies. Little is known of their religious beliefs, apart from the fact that they obviously believed in an afterlife, and that their principal deity may have been the mother goddess.

Other groups have since been found in places outside Upper Egypt proper. The earliest of these is the Faiyum A, a very primitive agricultural people who lived on an ancient lake level in the Faiyum. They did not know metal, produced some rough pottery, and had an important flint industry. Their cemeteries have never been found. Another community at Merimde-Beni Salaam, on the desert edge about 40 mi. northwest of Cairo, has often been hailed as the oldest Predynastic culture in Egypt, largely because it was exceedingly primitive and "neolithic" in type. The archeological evidence suggests that it was more likely to have been a backward group, without knowledge of copper, that existed toward the end of Naqada II. The characteristic of Merimde is of a compact village with burials in the settlement, either in the streets or houses.

Protodynastic, or Archaic, Period. Though Egypt, as a unified entity, can claim a longer recorded history than any other modern nation, its unrecorded history goes back many centuries further. It is during this so-called prehistoric period that the gradual transition from small isolated communities to ever-larger groupings took place and that the foundations of mature Egyptian civilization were laid. At the end of the Predynastic Period, Egypt was divided into two kingdoms, that of the Delta (Lower Egypt) with its capital at Buto, and that of Upper Egypt with its capital at Hierakonpolis. Also, in the final stages of the Predynastic era, a small and new racial element entered Egypt. The newcomers, though not themselves Sumerians, brought in various ideas and influences from Sumeria, including the idea of writing, the cylinder seal, a number of artistic motifs and techniques, and a new architectural style. The Upper Egyptian kingdom under Menes conquered the Delta and thus founded the united Egyptian kingdom, which was thereafter called the kingdom of "the Two Lands." The 1st Dynasty had its capital at Memphis. Practically nothing is known of the political history of the first two dynasties, though in the mid-2d Dynasty unity was temporarily disrupted by the so-called Seth Rebellion and the situation was only restored under the last King of the dynasty. Nevertheless, it is certain that these were times of very rapid growth, in which most of the permanent and characteristic features of Egyptian culture manifested themselves. Writing developed slowly; the 365-day calendar was introduced; easier access to the copper of Sinai led to a veritable copper boom, which in turn led to increased exploitation and working of stone; superb stone vases were made; and the first experiments in using stone in building were made. The royal tombs of the 1st Dynasty at Sakkara show a magnificent and exciting architecture in brick. Trade flourished, timber was imported from Syria, and trading or exploring parties penetrated at least as far south as the Second Cataract.

Old Kingdom. The preparatory work of the first two dynasties reached its fruition in the 3d Dynasty and is epitomized by the Step Pyramid of Sakkara, the tomb of Zoser, the first King of that dynasty. It was the first pyramid to be built and the first monumental building in stone. Thereafter, there was very rapid economic and cultural progress that reached its peak in the 4th Dynasty and is exemplified by the three great pyramids of Khufu, Khafre, and Menkaure and the Great Sphinx at Giza. The 5th Dynasty saw the triumph of the cult of the sun-god Ra

The first all-stone building of Egypt was the Step Pyramid of King Zoser (3d Dynasty; c.2780–c.2680 B.C.) at Sakkara. Designed by the architect Imhotep, it was the prototype of the true pyramids of the next dynasty.

Monkmeyer Press Photo Service

(or Re) of Heliopolis, but the decline in the size and quality of the pyramids testifies to changing ideas, to increasing economic stress, and to a progressive decline in the power of the crown. In the 6th Dynasty military campaigns were conducted in Asia, while trade and exploration in Nubia and the Sudan were vigorously pushed. Decentralization, however, inevitably decreased the power of the King while increasing that of the nomarchs, or provincial governors, and a combination of this with economic distress and the infiltration of Asiatics into the Delta led eventually to a social upheaval and collapse. The Old Kingdom was a time of brisk foreign trade with Africa and Asia, and the first high-water mark in architecture and in statuary and relief.

First Intermediate Period. After less than 50 years of weak rule by Kings of the 7th and 8th Dynasties during a period of confusion, control was seized by the princes of Heracleopolis, who formed the 9th and 10th Dynasties. The short-lived 9th Dynasty had at first probably lost the Delta, but eventually appears to have regained some measure of control. On the other hand, they had at least nominal rule over all Egypt as far as Aswan. But this was only of short duration and was ended by the rise to power of a family of Theban princes. In the north the 10th Dynasty succeeded in regaining the Delta, whose eastern frontier they secured with military works and colonies, and resumed trade with Syria. In the south their rule did not extend much south of Asyut and there ensued a long war of fluctuating fortune with the Theban Kings of the 11th Dynasty. In this war the Thebans were finally successful (c.2040 B.C.) and Egypt was once more united under a single ruler, Mentuhotep II. The First Intermediate Period saw a disastrous decline in art, but the production of some of the best Egyptian literary works. It saw the triumph of the cult of Osiris, god of the dead, and the partial democratization of the hereafter; that is, the privileges of eternal life were extended to the nobles. In spite of civil war and confusion, there was a considerable level of material prosperity, and wealth appears, according to

the evidence of the cemeteries, to have been more widely distributed.

Middle Kingdom. After about 40 years of peace the 11th Dynasty collapsed in renewed civil war and confusion, and the throne was seized (1991 B.C.) by Amenemhet I, formerly chief minister of Mentuhotep IV. Thereafter, for over 200 years, Egypt was ruled by an energetic and remarkable line of Kings who formed the 12th Dynasty and raised Egypt to its second period of greatness. In Syria-Palestine the political and economic influence of Egypt was dominant, and in Nubia an aggressive policy was pursued. Lower Nubia was conquered and secured by a remarkable fortress system, and a trading post was maintained at Kerma, south of the Third Cataract. The principal energies of the rulers were concentrated on internal affairs and reform. Vast irrigation schemes were carried out and the country raised to a high level of prosperity. Art, especially jewelry and statuary, flourished, and the Middle Kingdom is the classical period of Egyptian language and literature.

Second Intermediate Period. For about 100 years following the end of the 12th Dynasty, relative peace and prosperity were maintained in Upper Egypt by the 13th Dynasty, but there was a gradual decline. Gradually groups of Semites, now known collectively as the Hyksos, infiltrated into the Delta and by c.1674 B.C. they controlled to a greater or lesser degree all Egypt and Nubia. This extensive rule did not long endure. Nubia asserted its independence and the princes of Thebes (the 17th Dynasty) began a long and eventually successful war of independence. The Hyksos were by no means the barbarians that the Jewish historian Josephus and later Egyptian tradition would imply, and during their sway the horse, chariot, composite bow, and other innovations were introduced into the country.

New Kingdom. The final stages of the war against the Hyksos occupied the first few years of the reign of Ahmose I of Thebes, founder of the 18th Dynasty. After a relatively brief period to reorganize the country and to regain and extend control over Nubia, Egypt embarked on an aggressive policy in Asia. The Kassite invasions had produced a temporary vacuum in Western Asia and Egyptian policy was primarily directed toward breaking or containing its only rival, Mitanni, in northern Mesopotamia, and toward removing as far as possible any threat to its frontiers. This policy, apart from the peaceful and prosperous reign of Queen Hatshepsut, culminated in the 17 successive campaigns of Thutmose III in Asia. As a result of these campaigns, Egyptian control and influence were extended from the Euphrates to beyond the Fourth Cataract in the Sudan. This was the furthest extent of the Egyptian Empire.

In the second half of the dynasty this policy was drastically changed. The resurgence of the Hittites and the rise of Assyria threatened both Egypt and Mitanni, and the two were forced into alliance. This, however, failed to save Mitanni. Egyptian Asia was now assailed by Hittite intrigues and pressure, and by the infiltration of the Khabiri in the east. Amenhotep III, indolent, pleasure-loving, and occupied with building operations at Thebes, did not meet the threat. His son, Akhenaton (Amenhotep IV), with Akhenaton's wife, Nefertiti, was preoccupied with religious and artistic innovations and the building of a new capital at Tell el-Amarna, and neglected his imperial responsibilities. Akhenaton's attempt to introduce a form of monotheism, the worship of the Aton, or Sun's Disk, moreover, rent and weakened Egypt, and Egyptian influence in Asia sank to a new low. After the collapse of Atonism, Harmhab, the last King of the dynasty and himself a usurper, restored order at home, but was able to do little to reassert Egypt's position in Asia. In spite of internal friction and external losses, Egypt's still great wealth at this period is attested by the splendid funerary furnishings that were placed in the tomb of even a minor Pharaoh such as Tutankhamen.

The 19th Dynasty, from its capital Tanis in the northeastern Delta, attemped to regain Asia, but met with only very limited success. Seti I recaptured Palestine and Syria, but the drawn battle of Kadesh (1286 B.C.), between his son Rameses II and the Hittites, spelled the end of any larger hopes. The growing pressure of the great ethnic movement of the so-called Peoples of the Sea eventually impelled the conclusion of an Egypto-Hittite alliance (1270 B.C.). This gave Egypt a brief respite. The first attack of the Peoples of the Sea, which occurred in the reign of Merenptah, was not repulsed until it had nearly reached Memphis, but the main onslaught did not come until the reign of Rameses III, in the 20th Dynasty. A struggle that lasted six years saw the final defeat of the Sea Peoples, but also the exhaustion of Egypt and the end of its imperial power. The rest of the 20th Dynasty is the story of almost uninterrupted decline, of economic distress, internal weakness, and priestly intrigues.

Late Dynasties. Some years before the death of Rameses XI, a Prince of Tanis established a new dynasty. After Rameses' death this 21st Dynasty ruled the whole country, but it was in turn overthrown by the descendants of Libyan mercenaries who had been settled near Heracleopolis. Sheshonk I, the first King of the 22d (Libyan) Dynasty, conducted a successful campaign in Palestine, but the later years of the dynasty were contemporaneous

with the 23d Dynasty at Thebes and the 24th Dynasty in the north, and the country was rent by civil war. Thus the Ethiopian King Piankhi (25th Dynasty) had little difficulty in invading the Thebaid (730 B.C.), and eventually he and his successor, Shabaka, extended Ethiopian rule over the whole land. Egypt was now directly threatened by Assyria, but the Ethiopian Kings were torn between their homeland and Egypt. Their generalship was frequently inept, and in 664 B.C., the Assyrians finally conquered Egypt and sacked Thebes.

Under the Assyrians, control of Egypt was left in the hands of a council of Princes, whose leader, Psamtik I, in due course asserted his independence and founded the 26th, or Saite, Dynasty. Under the Saite Kings, Egypt, for 140 years, enjoyed a final era of peace, prosperity, and artificial revival. The dynasty depended primarily on a picked force of Greek mercenaries. It promoted economic revival by encouraging Greek traders at Naucratis and Daphne, and by building a strong navy and commercial fleet, while it claimed the allegiance of the Egyptians by deliberately fostering a spirit of nationalism in harking back to the glories of the past. Toward Asia the dynastic policy was one of maintaining the balance of power, and for long Egypt used its naval and economic power astutely and successfully to implement this policy. But eventually Cambyses conquered Egypt, which thus came under direct Persian rule in the 27th Dynasty (525 B.C.). The new masters were at first mild, but the increasing harshness of the later Persian Kings provoked constant native revolts, and at last the country regained its freedom (404 B.C.). For 63 years, during the 28th to 30th Dynasties, Egypt maintained an uneasy independence, due less to its inherent strength and merits than to Persian preoccupation elsewhere. Finally, in 341 B.C., under the 31st Dynasty, there came the second Persian conquest which, in turn, came to an abrupt end with the victory of Alexander the Great at Issus (333 B.C.).

Ptolemaic Period. With the victory of Alexander, the history of Egypt merges with that of the Hellenistic world. Alexander was welcomed as a liberator and in turn treated Egypt well and with imagination. He founded Alexandria, which was to become the commercial and intellectual center of the Mediterranean world. On his death (323 B.C.) the empire was divided into a number of satrapies and Egypt fell to Ptolemy, who in 304 B.C. made himself King as Ptolemy I Soter. The dynasty founded by Ptolemy lasted until 30 B.C. Though the Egyptians salved their pride by treating the Ptolemies precisely like native Pharaohs, the Ptolemies remained completely Greek, hardly entering into Egyptian life. It was not until Ptolemy V (reigned 205–180 B.C.) that one of them was crowned by Egyptian rite at Memphis, and the last of the line, the great Cleopatra, was the first to have any knowledge of the Egyptian language. The Ptolemies developed Egypt, but also exploited it for their own ends; still, the country was prosperous and at first relatively peaceful.

The victory of Ptolemy IV at Raphia in Palestine (217 B.C.), over Antiochus III of Syria, had, however, important consequences. Egyptian troops had been employed for the first time and acquitted themselves well. This in turn inspired the first of the native revolts, which thereafter were almost incessant, especially in Upper Egypt, until Ptolemy VIII destroyed Thebes in 85 B.C. The corruption and dynastic quarrels of the Ptolemies steadily weakened the regime until in 55 B.C. Ptolemy XI had to be restored by Roman legions, and it was clearly only a matter of time before Egypt fell completely into Roman hands. This duly came to pass as the result of the defeat of Antony and Cleopatra at Actium and Cleopatra's subsequent suicide (30 B.C.).

Roman and Byzantine Period. Under Rome, Egypt had a special position in, but apart from, the empire, and was governed on behalf of the Emperor by a prefect. Rome considered it judicious to follow the Ptolemaic policy toward the native religion, and at first paid the same outward attention to the old gods. But Egypt was ruinously exploited for its grain and consequently became impoverished; and as time went on it reflected the growing weakness and strains of the empire. When the capital of the empire was transferred from Rome to Constantinople (330 A.D.), Egypt entered the Byzantine Period, and became virtually Coptic, or Christian, Egypt.

Traditionally, Christianity was brought to Egypt by St. Mark, and grew rapidly, in spite of many persecutions, the most savage and notorious being those instituted under Diocletian. With the coming of Christian Emperors, the pagan cults in their turn were assailed. Theodosius I (reigned 379–95 A.D.) declared Christianity the religion of the empire and ordered the closing of the temples. But the old religion was a long time dying, especially in the more remote parts—the temple of Isis at Philae was not closed until 543 A.D., in the reign of Justinian. The Egyptian Christians, monks, priests, and patriarchs, were a turbulent people, possessed by an intensely nationalistic and bigoted spirit, and their violence and theological controversies only weakened the country still further, so that the Arabs under Amr ibn al-As had relatively little difficulty in finally conquering the country in 642 A.D.

People and Society. The Egyptians were a black-haired, dark-skinned, short and slender people of the Eastern Hamitic division of the Mediterranean branch of the Caucasoid race. Though class distinctions were not rigid in ancient Egypt, there were vast differences between the royal family, nobles, priests, scribes, and government officials, at the top of the social scale, the artisans, craftsmen, and merchants in the middle, and the workers at the bottom. In the Old Kingdom almost all men were free. Little slavery existed and there was no rigid caste system. But a kind of serfdom developed as a result of the deterioration in economic conditions toward the end of the period. In the Middle and New Kingdoms some slaves were created as a punishment. But even in the New Kingdom the vast majority of slaves were prisoners of war. It is only with the general decline in the later dynasties that the number of native slaves increased and the institution of voluntary servitude developed. At all times the rights of slaves were strictly defined by law, and slaves could even own property.

Women in ancient Egypt enjoyed an exceptionally high and respected position. They were free, unveiled, and there was no system of purdah (seclusion of women). Marriage appears to have been a legal contract rather than a religious ceremony. The rights of women and children in marriage and divorce were strictly guarded. A woman could even reign as Pharaoh. She could also own property and buy, sell, inherit, and dispose of it at will; and she could engage in commerce and trade in her own right, and testify in court. Except in the royal family, brother-sister marriages, though permissible, were rare. Monogamy prevailed except for the plural marriages contracted by Kings.

Economy and Daily Life. The peasants, who comprised the mass of the people, were engaged in agriculture—barley, flax, and emmer wheat being the chief crops. A smaller proportion of the people engaged in minor industries and crafts, and in mining, building, and quarrying (especially prisoners). Merchants sailed all over the eastern Mediterranean to exchange Egyptian copper, grain, linen, papyrus, and stone for the goods of foreign nations, especially timber, and to ports on the Red Sea and the east coast of Africa to barter for the gold, ivory, hides, ostrich feathers, and other exotic products of Somaliland. Egyptian caravans were also active in the Sudan. Under the *corvée* system, all men, unless otherwise exempted, were liable to be called upon to perform any manner of forced duties. It was men levied for the *corvée* who built the gigantic pyramids of Giza in the Old Kingdom.

The average, or poor, Egyptian lived in a small hut built of mud or sun-dried brick, covered with palm leaves or straw, with palm-trunk beams supporting the flat roof. His furnishings were minimal. Rich Egyptians, on the other hand, enjoyed more spacious homes of brick and wood construction, which were luxuriously furnished and decorated.

The diet of the poor included barley bread, fish, vegetables, and beer. The wealthy, in addition to these staples, had beef, veal, antelope and gazelle meat, fruit, and a variety of sweets.

Men's clothing at first consisted only of a loin cloth; later this developed into a pleated skirt or apron. Women wore long tight dresses attached by shoulder straps and made extensive use of cosmetics, darkening their eyebrows, outlining their eyes with black kohl and green

Model of a carpenter's chest and tools, found in a tomb at Asyut. The equipment was for a servant's use in afterlife.

Metropolitan Museum of Art, Gift of Edward S. Harkness, 1916–17

paint, applying lip rouge, and dyeing their fingernails. Wealthy Egyptian women also wore heavy black wigs made of human hair or sheep's wool both to adorn themselves and to protect themselves from the heat.

For recreation Egyptians played games, such as an ancient form of backgammon, and hunted, fished, and participated in athletic contests.

Government. The Egyptians believed that the world order was instituted at the beginning of time when the first god-king came to earth bringing the kingship with him. Their view of the cosmos was thus an essentially static one, encompassing a world made perfect once and for all by the gods, in which there was little change apart from the normal seasonal fluctuations, the change from day to night, or the annual flooding—a world of small, regular, and regulated change occurring in an immutable frame. The kingship was the keystone of Egyptian civilization. It alone explains the extraordinary stability and longevity of the Egyptian state and way of life. At the heart of the concept of kingship lay the idea of truth and justice. Maat, goddess of truth and justice, was the daughter of the sun-god Ra, the first god-king, and came to earth with him. Thereafter, gods, kings, and men were all bound by the law and could not break it. The king himself was a god. Although he differed in many ways from the gods, he was in a very real sense divine and elevated above other men. The idea of the divinity of the king was weakened seriously as time went on, but throughout Egyptian history the fiction was steadfastly maintained, for without this central, unifying, and comfortable belief, the whole fabric of society would have fallen apart. The earthly king was the living Horus, the last member of the dynasty of gods, and owed his position less to primogeniture or physical prowess than to the belief that, as Horus, he was the dutiful and legitimate son of Osiris, whose legitimacy and succession to his father's throne had been confirmed by a divine court of law. As leader and shepherd of his people, the king alone, in theory, initiated all activity. Theoretically, he owned all Egypt, though in practice individuals could own and dispose of land and property without restriction. Technically, he was the chief priest and the sole officiant in every service in every temple. He led the army in war and inspired and promoted all peaceful enterprises. He was the source of all legislation, and at the same time subservient to the law. His health and well-being were essential to the prosperity of his land and people.

A long, narrow country such as Egypt has always been difficult to hold together and rule, especially in antiquity, when communications were slow and poor, and much depended on the personal energy and drive of the ruler. In practice, of course, there had to be delegation of authority and an efficient administrative machine. In the Old Kingdom, and even in the Middle Kingdom, to a lesser extent, social organization and administration were essentially amateur. The hereditary principle began to develop only toward the end of the Old Kingdom, largely because of the need to make permanent provision for the service of funerary endowments. Earlier, any official was liable to be nominated to lead any type of undertaking, whether military, religious, economic, or administrative. Not until the New Kingdom was there a more comprehensive professional organization in the army, priesthood, and

administration, but even then one man could perform many and diverse functions. The chief minister under the King was the vizier. In the New Kingdom there were separate viziers for Upper and Lower Egypt, a practice that may already have existed at the end of the Old Kingdom. The vizier was the supreme judge and was responsible for finance, taxation, justice, agriculture, public works, custody of the archives, and the administration of the army and navy. Under him served a vast army of provincial governors and administrators, inspectors, controllers, and a multitude of subordinate officials and scribes. In the New Kingdom the rich and important province of Nubia was under a separate official, the viceroy of Nubia, answerable to the King. Throughout Pharaonic times Egypt was divided into nomes, or provinces, the standard number being 22 nomes in Upper Egypt and 20 in Lower Egypt.

Until the New Kingdom no standing army existed. Men were summoned for military service on a provincial basis. The foreign wars of the New Kingdom necessitated the formation of a professional army, which, in time of war in the field, consisted of the chariotry (the crack section of the army), the infantry, and mercenaries, and was organized into four divisions.

Religion. The ancients were profoundly impressed by the religiosity of the Egyptians, by their strange gods and sacred rites and practices. They were led to invest Egyptian religion with a far deeper mystery and significance than it really possessed—a view that has not died out even today. Egyptian religion was intensely parochial; although one may at times speak of a state cult, there was no such thing as a national religion, and a man's allegiance was primarily to his local god. This explains the immense number of gods who often differ from each other in little more than name. It was thus relatively easy for a local god to become attached to one or another of the more powerful gods.

Local loyalties were strengthened by the innate conservatism of the Egyptians which rendered them disinclined to abandon any belief or practice they had once possessed. It is the parochial nature of Egyptian religion that probably explains the family and domestic nature of the gods, their worship and festivals. This in turn accounts for the mildness of Egyptian religion, the absence of blood baths and excess in any form. Thus in matters religious the Egyptian was tolerant. His own local loyalties prevented him from seeking to impose his own local cult, whose efficacy in any event would be restricted to a particular locality, on those who lived outside its range. Hence, although there are abundant religious books in Egypt, there were no sacred books, and consequently no dogma and no heresy hunts.

Religious life in Egypt was less a matter of belief or of revealed truth than of cult, and the essential requirement was the absolutely correct performance of the ritual, accuracy of the spoken word, and the strictest ritual purity. It was only in the late period that the people in general, largely as a reaction to foreign domination, in a sense turned inward and gave passionate and exaggerated devotion to those simpler elements that were most typically Egyptian and most sharply differentiated from the beliefs and practices of foreigners.

There is good reason to believe that the earliest gods

were nature gods—birds, mammals, fish, reptiles, and so forth—worshiped because they appeared to represent forces that were feared, loved, or admired. Although in the beginning they were worshiped in their animal form, the majority were soon anthropomorphized. Probably equally primitive were certain sacred inanimate objects, whose precise origin is uncertain but is likely to be found in purely local conditions. Somewhat later were the cosmic gods who represented the great forces of nature. Inevitably such gods tended to be universal in character, but they were soon localized and were usually worshiped in human or animal form, or in a combination of the two.

From time to time certain human beings, other than Kings, were deified because of special qualities they had displayed during their lifetime. Such cults were normally short-lived and confined to a fairly restricted locality. The two most famous exceptions were Imhotep and Amenhotep. Imhotep, the chief minister and architect of Zoser, was deified and worshiped as a god of wisdom and medicine, being regarded as the son of Ptah, and later identified by the Greeks with Asclepius. Amenhotep, son of Hapu, a favorite and official of Amenhotep III, became a god of wisdom. Animal worship was always a typical feature of Egyptian religion and was particularly popular in the late period. These animal cults were on the whole local, all members of a particular species being worshiped in a specific district. Less common were the animals of which only one, distinguished by special markings, was worshiped and mummified and buried in special cemeteries. The most famous of the latter class were the bull cults, especially Apis at Memphis, Mnevis at Heliopolis, and Buchis at Armant. Also included in the Egyptian pantheon were genii, or familiar spirits, and a certain number of foreign deities that were mainly, but not exclusively, Asiatic in origin.

In order to explain their world and its creation the Egyptians elaborated three theological systems. The first and most widespread was that of Heliopolis, which from the 5th Dynasty dominated the sacred ritual. According to this system, Atum emerged out of primeval chaos and produced from himself Shu ("air") and Tefnut ("moisture"). These in turn produced Geb ("earth") and Nut ("sky"), whose children were Osiris, Isis, Seth, and Nephthys. These nine gods, with the fusion of Atum and Ra, formed the Great Ennead.

At Memphis there was formulated a different theory. Ptah at Memphis was declared to be an older god than Ra of Heliopolis, and the Memphite system seems, in part at least, to have been elaborated to combat the rising solar theology. According to this system Ptah created eight other gods who were in essence only aspects of himself. For example, Atum was his thought, Horus his heart, and Thoth his tongue. The central idea of this system was the creative Word, the world's earliest formulation of the doctrine of the Logos. As a system it was more advanced than the other theologies, but for this reason it never became popular, though it retained its appeal and force for a small minority of priests throughout the course of Egyptian history.

The third system was that of Hermopolis, which was built up around a group of eight gods, the Ogdoad. According to this system, out of the inert primeval ocean emerged four pairs of beings, four frogs (male) and four snakes (female) who represented Night, Darkness, Mystery, and Eternity. From an egg which they created at Hermopolis emerged the Sun (Atum), and it was he who created men and organized the world.

The form of solar monotheism called Atonism, associated with Akhenaton (reigned c.1369–1353 B.C.) and the Tell el-Amarna Period, is entirely distinct from the religious systems sketched above. It introduced one god only, the Aton, or Sun's Disk, more particularly the life-giving power of the sun. This system also attempted to close the temples of the old gods, to abolish all the ancient gods and cults and even the word "gods." It was exclusive and intolerant. The typical Aton temple was completely different in type from the normal cult temple. It contained no cult image and was composed of a series of courts, all of which were open to the sky. In spite of these differences, there is no justification for attempting to seek a foreign, still less a Semitic, origin for Atonism; its seeds lie solely in Egypt. It is doubtful whether the movement was purely religious. The explanation of the revolution is probably to be sought more in politics than in religion, and can be seen as an attempt to curb or break the Amon priesthood which had become too powerful, and as an attempt to establish a common religion for the whole Egyptian Empire, in Egypt, Asia, and Nubia.

Since solar worship was always somewhat remote from ordinary people, the new cult was given immediacy by linking the Aton very closely with the person of the King. Though he was the son, disciple, and high priest of the Aton, at times the King and Aton were almost identical. The movement failed. After sweeping away the old religion, including Osiris and the deeply rooted funerary beliefs of the Egyptians, as well as all the moral ideals and sanctions that were connected with them, it supplied nothing in their place and merely created a spiritual vacuum. Atonism was frankly amoral; its much vaunted "teaching" was nonexistent apart from a beautiful hymn to the Aton. Although it retained traditional funerary practices, it cast off the underlying funerary beliefs. Under it there was no celestial or underworld hereafter, no judgment of the dead. Instead, the dead, like the living, slept at night, and by day emerged from their tombs to maintain a rather forlorn existence near their former homes or in the temple of the Aton and near the King. Atonism failed to gain popular support and died with Akhenaton.

Apart from the theological system sketched above, the family triad of Osiris, Isis, and Horus enjoyed wide popularity in the funerary religion of the Egyptians. Originally a local god of Busiris, Osiris came to the fore in the First Intermediate Period and was worshiped throughout Egypt. He was therefore accounted for in the principal theologies. He was primarily the god of the dead: the human appeal of his story and the hope of eternal life in the other world that was extended to his devotees account for his great popularity.

Temples. The temple played a dominant role in Egyptian culture. More than a religious institution, it was also a center and patron of learning, and attached to it would be a "house of life," for writing and copying religious and learned books, and a staff of doctors, astronomer priests, and scribes. There were three types of temple in Egypt: (1) the normal cult temple, with its specialized subtypes, the funerary temple, and the rock-cut temple; (2) the peripteral temple, essentially a kiosk on a rectangular base, whose primary purpose was to serve as a temporary stopping place for the god at certain festivals; and (3) the solar temple, which differed from the normal cult temple in that it contained no sacred image, or idol, and that both the temple and all ceremonies performed within it were open to the sky.

Very little is known about the ordinary cult temples of the Old and Middle Kingdoms because they were destroyed to provide space and building materials for later temples, and it is only those of the New Kingdom and, still more, those of the Greco-Roman period that have been relatively well preserved. The temple was surrounded by a great brick wall, to insure both protection and privacy. In the space thus created were a sacred lake, storehouses, workshops, kitchens, administrative offices, and quarters for the priests. The temple itself was approached through a monumental doorway between massive pylons, and in the face of the latter were grooves for tall flagstaffs, and before them a pair of obelisks. The temple consisted of one or more open courts, and at least one pillared, or hypostyle, hall. Its central aisle was higher than the rest to facilitate illumination of the hall by clerestory lighting. At the rear, surrounded by a varying number of other rooms, was the sanctuary. The sanctuary and rear of the temple were devoid of any illumination. The progressive darkening from entrance to sanctuary promoted a sense of mystery and awe, an effect that was enhanced by the simple device of lowering the level of the roof and slightly raising the level of the floor the nearer one approached the sanctuary in which the god resided.

The temple was linked by processional ways to a quay on the river or canal side and to other temples in the same town. The temple was entered by priests only, and the sanctuary by a single priest, the officiant. The public was not admitted to the temple, but provision was made at the gate in the temenos wall for ordinary people to offer prayer and gifts, and to make their petitions. It is important to note that the temple and all within it were in a very real sense considered to be alive. At the dedication ceremony, repeated annually on New Year's Day, the temple as a whole—every relief on its walls and every sacred image that was kept in it—underwent the ceremony of "Opening the Mouth," which had the effect of filling the temple and its reliefs with latent life. How very real this idea was is eloquently demonstrated in both Coptic and Muslim Egypt by the care taken to "kill" the reliefs before using the rooms of the temple for purposes other than those for which it was built.

The type of temple thus briefly described was admirably designed to serve the purposes of the two types of worship: the daily service celebrated in all intimacy in the sanctuary, and the processional festivals that took place either inside or outside the temple. The ordinary daily worship consisted of services at dawn, midday, and sunset. The elaborate dawn service was in essence a dramatization, in a religious context, of daily life. The god, resting in the sanctuary, was awakened by the morning hymn

sung by the temple choir. The officiant, in theory the King, but in practice his deputy, entered the sanctuary alone, disrobed the god, performed his toilet, and offered him a meal. After all this had been completed, and after the cotemplar gods had been awakened and fed in similar but simpler fashion, the offerings were removed and a double reversion of offerings was celebrated. The first reversion was celebrated within the temple for the benefit of the royal ancestors, and was succeeded by a second reversion of offerings outside the temple to the priests. In all these ceremonies the people in general took no part. There was no congregational worship of any description.

In addition to these daily services, every temple had its own calendar of festivals which varied in length from a day to a whole month. In the 18th Dynasty the temple of Karnak had over 50 such festivals each year. The majority of these festivals were processional, some within the temple, but others outside the temple to other temples in the same town or to more distant towns. The great calendar festivals that involved processions outside the temple area, such as the Feast of Opet, were the occasions that offered the mass of the people direct contact with the official state religion. They were accompanied by popular rejoicing, free food, drink, and even side shows. Some festivals included dramatic performances somewhat akin to the medieval mystery or morality plays.

It is inevitable from the fact that almost all our knowledge of Egyptian religion, other than funerary religion, is derived from the temples, temple reliefs, and surviving temple rituals, that we should have the impression that the only religion in Egypt was that recorded on the monuments. It could hardly be otherwise, since the mass of the people were illiterate and rarely left any hint of their own beliefs. On the other hand, it would be wrong to conclude either that the people were only devotees of the state religion or that they had no religious beliefs at all. It is probable that the common man was largely unaffected by the state religion. Of course, he could participate in the excitement of a great processional festival and could, on occasion, adore or have an attachment to one of the great gods. But it seems that the religion of the mass of the simple, unlettered people was of an entirely different and more elemental order: a religion of genii, spirits, and folk-type divinities. Thus the workers of the Theban necropolis personified and worshiped as their patroness the great peak that rises at the head of the Valley of the Kings and in whose body, so to speak, their daily bread was earned.

There was no proper professional priesthood until the New Kingdom. At all times the King, in theory, was the sole officiant at all temple services. But in practice he was forced to delegate these religious duties—in the New Kingdom, to the high priest of the appropriate temple; in earlier times, to nomarchs, officials, and other laymen. Professionalism began to enter the priesthood at the end of the Old Kingdom because of the need to make permanent provision for the celebration of the funerary cult. The temple priesthood was divided into four companies, each of which served in the temple for a month at a time. Priests could fill secular posts, even the highest in the land, and could marry and engage in commerce. Appointment to, and installation of, at least the high grades was the personal act of a king; payment was in kind. Great emphasis

The gold coffin of King Tutankhamen (18th Dynasty) is painted with a likeness of the young King. The tomb was discovered in 1922 in the Valley of the Kings near Luxor by the British archeologist Howard Carter.

was laid on the strictest ritual purity. The usual role of women in the temple was as musician-priestesses, but in certain circumstances they could hold higher offices. During the New Kingdom certain priesthoods grew so rich and powerful that they became, at one time, the dominant force in the state.

Funerary Beliefs and Practices. By far the greater part of our knowledge of the ancient Egyptians is due, directly or indirectly, to their remarkable funerary beliefs and practices. So prominent do tombs, death, and preparations for death appear to be in Egyptian life, that it is easy to imagine that the Egyptians were a morbid people, with an almost pathological preoccupation with the problem of death. Such an impression is completely false. The intense interest in and preparation for death were due fundamentally to an intense passion for life. The Egyptians believed that a man only really and finally died if the last thing in which his soul, ba, could find food, drink, and shelter was destroyed. The funerary cult was therefore a vast insurance policy to avoid the ultimate disaster of dying the "second death," and its basis was the imperative need to make that permanent provision for the soul's needs on which survival depended.

From earliest times this idea of survival appears to have been linked with the preservation of the material body, or, in the last resort, some substitute for it. This idea appears to have originated in the accidental discovery in Predynastic times that the dead, when buried in shallow graves in the dry desert climate, did not necessarily decay. Thus there developed side by side with the provision for the material needs of the dead attempts to preserve the body. Mummification is attested at least as early as the 2d Dynasty, possibly even in the 1st. Mummification at first was reserved for those few who could afford it, but in the Middle Kingdom it became more widespread. The true art of mummification, however, was not acquired until the New Kingdom. Mummification at its best consisted of the dehydration of the body, after the removal of the brain and the entrails (except for the heart), and then the elaborate wrapping of the body. The vital organs were

placed in four canopic jars which accompanied the dead to the tomb. Normally, dehydration required 40 days, wrapping 30 days. The body was then buried after the Opening of the Mouth ceremony (which was supposed to restore to the dead man his vital functions) had been performed over the mummy at the entrance to the tomb. In the tomb were placed food, clothing, furniture, and even *ushabti*, or images of servants, to wait upon the deceased. The walls, bearing scenes of daily life and offerings, had a practical function, for since the Opening of the Mouth had been performed over all these as well, they were deemed capable of serving the needs of the dead man indefinitely. Magical spells and incantations, known as Pyramid Texts, were from the 5th Dynasty onward carved on the walls of certain royal pyramids to aid the dead in his journey toward the next world. In the late First Intermediate Period, Coffin Texts were inscribed inside the coffins of nonroyal people. In the 18th Dynasty a collection of spells written on papyrus, now called the Book of the Dead, was often placed inside the coffin of royalty.

In the earliest times, it can reasonably be inferred, there were two main ideas of the next world: one of an underworld in the west, and one that postulated a stellar hereafter, in which the deceased became a star, more particularly, one of the circumpolar stars. The dominance of the solar cult throughout most of the Old Kingdom had as a natural consequence the popularity of a solar hereafter. The dead supposedly ascended to the sky in one of a variety of ways and hoped to remain evermore in the company of the sun-god in his journeys across the sky and under the earth. He even had to submit to some form of trial in the presence of the sun-god. Osiris does not begin to emerge as the god of the dead until the late Old Kingdom, his rise being increasingly reflected in the Pyramid Texts. The triumph of Osiris in the First Intermediate Period meant that henceforth it was the Osirian concept of the hereafter that prevailed. The picture is not a simple one. On the one hand there were the Elysian fields where the crops grew more luxuriantly than on earth. On the other, the kingdom of Osiris was quite clearly the underworld, a dark, dismal place that could depress even Osiris himself as a passage from the Book of the Dead clearly shows. The sole comfort that the hapless dead received was the mighty passage of Ra through the 12 divisions of the underworld.

The dead man could not be admitted to the next world without passing a test to prove that he had lived a blameless and exemplary life. This test consisted of a trial before Osiris and a court of 42 assessors. The heart of the dead man was weighed against a feather, the symbol of truth, and a Denial of Sin—often, but more inaccurately, known as the Negative Confession—was made to the gods. The Osirian judgment set a moral standard and embodied a high ethical ideal. But unfortunately, magic completely nullified it, for if one could recite the Denial of Sin accurately and correctly speak or act the other prescribed measures, even the greatest sinner could avoid the consequences of his evil-doing. Failure to pass the test was annihilation, and the sinner was devoured by a monster; but, naturally, this ultimate disaster was always avoided.

Science and Learning. Life in ancient Egypt, and above all, orderly, civilized life, would have been impossible if its people had not acquired certain skills. The supreme challenge and stimulus was the river, and the problem of water. The annual inundation brought water and fertility to the land, but it also swept away landmarks and destroyed property. Administration was impossible, taxes could not be levied, or government function unless, after the floods, the land could be surveyed. On the solution of the problem of the storage, control, raising, and distribution of water, the very existence of the whole people depended. Thus the Egyptian was inevitably a practical man, who was forced to acquire a knowledge of engineering, arithmetic, geometry, surveying, and mensuration. It is typical of the Egyptian that once having acquired this knowledge and having thereby been enabled to attain his immediate end, he never felt any impulse, or stimulus, to carry this knowledge further or to develop it theoretically. The Egyptian was literal; he did not indulge in hypotheses, philosophy, or metaphysics. It was left to the Greeks, who learned much of their mathematics and medicine in the valley of the Nile, to take the forward steps that Egyptians never seemed to have envisaged.

Egyptian mathematics was essentially a decimal system, originally finger numbering, but the decimal point, the cipher zero, and positional numbering were unknown. Hence there was a cumbersome system of notation and a barbarous system of fractions that used only the numerator 1. In spite of these handicaps, Egyptian mathematics was surprisingly efficient. Any problem involving areas or volumes, contents of buildings, or arithmetical or geometrical progressions could be successfully tackled, and the Egyptian approximation to the area of the circle and the value of pi was more accurate than that of any other ancient civilization.

The Egyptians produced elementary geographical maps and star maps, and used a simple form of theodolite. They were the first to discover the 365-day year. They divided the year into 12 months, each of 30 days, or three "weeks" consisting of ten days each, and at the end of the year added five extra, or epagomenal, days. This Egyptian calendar is the direct ancestor of our modern calendar. The discovery of the 365-day year was due primarily to the Nile flood. Without any advanced knowledge or apparatus, the mean of not more than 50 years' observation of the flood would have given the true length of the year. The approximate length could have been obtained in an even shorter period.

Egyptian doctors and medical schools enjoyed a high reputation in the ancient world. Doctors were apparently attached to the court or to the temples, and included not only general practitioners but also specialists. Egyptian medicine was of two kinds: folk medicine and magic, and true scientific medicine. Medicine and magic walked hand in hand. The successful magician inevitably developed into the doctor who dealt with those cases whose cause was known or could be seen; while the magician dealt with those complaints which had no obvious cause. No operative surgery was practiced in Egypt, though one or two instances of trepanning and one case of draining an abscess by drilling a hole in the lower jaw are attested. It is noteworthy that Egyptian anatomical terms are derived from animal anatomy. In spite of practicing mummification, it is evident that they had little real knowledge of human anatomy and that that little was only derived from morbid anatomy. There must have been some taboo that prohibited the cutting of the living body or the dissection of the dead body. Yet through mummification the Egyptians were accustomed to handling and cutting corpses and hence the Greeks found in Egypt the one place in which they could dissect and study anatomy with impunity.

Language and Literature. The language of the hieroglyphic inscriptions is largely Semitic, but with some notable divergencies in grammar and, to some extent, in vocabulary; and it still preserves traces of an earlier Hamitic system, presumably the language of Predynastic Egypt. This Semitic language and the idea of writing were introduced into Egypt approximately at the end of the Predynastic Period by people who had been influenced by Sumeria, but were not themselves Sumerians. Egyptian writing was in origin picture writing and always retained some of this pictorial element. Unlike the Sumerians, the Egyptians never developed syllabic writing and never used any vowels. Hieroglyphic is purely consonantal and is a mixture of picture signs, phonograms (picture signs used for their phonetic value only), determinatives, or signs indicative of the meaning of words, and a number of uniliteral signs resulting from certain short words being reduced by normal phonetic processes to a single strong consonant. The Egyptians did not possess a true alphabet since they had no vowel signs; but all alphabetic systems of writing are ultimately derived from Egyptian. Three scripts were used: Hieroglyphic is the monumental pictorial writing carved on stone or wood. Hieratic is a cursive form of hieroglyphic, the result of drawing hieroglyphs on papyrus, linen, or other soft materials with a reed brush dipped in ink. Demotic is a still more cursive script in which the vernacular of the Late Period (from about the 5th century B.C.) was written. Finally, the latest stage of the Egyptian language, which employed Greek characters, including vowels, and seven characters borrowed from demotic, formed Coptic, the language of

Christian Egypt. Demotic continued in use until 452 A.D., and Coptic was written up to the 10th century, giving Egypt the longest continuous linguistic record in history.

The written records of Egypt cover an immense and varied field. They include history and biography, business and legal texts, letters private and official, medical and mathematical papyri, a dream book, lexicographical texts, and an immense religious literature which includes hymns, rituals, and numberless funerary papyri and texts. All these, however, are of little or no literary value. In addition to them there are many genuine literary works, both religious and secular, which may conveniently be grouped in four classes: drama, the short story, verse, and the didactic, reflective, or pessimistic literature. Some of these works were produced for political purposes, others served the ends of the official religion, but, nevertheless, the Egyptians were the first people to cultivate literature for its own sake, without thought of religion, politics, or commercial profit. The Egyptians were also the first consciously literary people in history, the first to value and appreciate style in writing.

Drama seems to have been essentially religious, though there is slight and inconclusive evidence of the existence of strolling players. The extant plays and fragments, and the stage directions that accompany them, indicate that there was no characterization, that the actors declaimed and ranted rather than acted, that very frequently a chorus played a big part, and that the dialogue was linked by continuous narrative read by a lector.

Egypt was the home of the short story, and from the Old Kingdom onward many have survived. These short stories include tales of adventure and travel, of magic and folklore, an allegory, a fragmentary detective story, and two incomplete ghost stories. The *Contendings of Horus and Seth* describes the foibles and weaknesses of the gods

in a way that is almost Homeric. The *Story of the Eloquent Peasant* is less a tale than a treatise on eloquence and a tract on social justice. As a literary form the short story may justly be claimed as an Egyptian invention. It is typically simple, direct, and factual. There is no real attempt to draw character or to set a scene, but the *Story of Sinuhe* and the *Misadventures of Wenamun* demonstrate that some Egyptians at least saw, though they never developed, the possibilities of psychological treatment.

Egyptian poetry is characterized primarily by a pronounced rhythm, or beat, a tendency to use a strophic arrangement, and the employment of such literary devices as parallelism of members. There is an enormous mass of religious verse of very little merit, marked mainly by interminable and tedious puns and endless mythological allusions. Among the few exceptions is the outstanding religious hymn, the beautiful *Hymn to the Sun* of Akhenaton, which is noteworthy for its freedom from mythological allusions and its delight in nature. In complete contrast to the state and religious poems is a considerable body of lyric poetry which includes not only snatches from the songs of the people but also many charming love poems. Many of the latter are of considerable merit and worthy of inclusion in any world anthology.

Perhaps the most characteristic of all Egyptian literary works, however, are the didactic works, or wisdom literature. These were immensely popular throughout Egyptian history. All are much of the same pattern, and most are in verse. They are strictly practical and utilitarian works of counsel on such matters as honesty, moderation, behavior at table and toward superiors—in short, how to succeed in life. One of these works, the *Teaching of Amenemopet*, has been widely accepted as the direct source of Proverbs (12:17–13:11) and some other sections of Hebrew wisdom literature.

The Metropolitan Museum of Art, Museum Excavations, 1929–30; Rogers Fund, 1930
Painted wood stele (26th Dynasty) of a priest, from Deir el-Bahri. He is shown worshiping two minor enthroned deities.

Bas-relief from the temple of Hathor at Dendera, built in the Ptolemaic Period (332–30 B.C.). Hathor, the goddess of love, mirth, and social joy, is shown at center left.

Annan Photo Features

Consult Peet, T. E., *A Comparative Study of the Literatures of Egypt, Palestine, and Mesopotamia* (1931); *The Legacy of Egypt*, ed. by S. R. K. Glanville (1942); Frankfort, Henri, *Ancient Egyptian Religion* (1948); Wilson, J. A., *The Culture of Ancient Egypt* (1951); Černý, Jaroslav, *Ancient Egyptian Religion* (1952); Hayes, W. C., *The Scepter of Egypt* (2 vols., 1953–59); Steindorff, George, and Seele, K. C., *When Egypt Ruled the East* (2d ed., rev., 1957); Montet, Pierre, *Everyday Life in Egypt in the Days of Ramesses the Great* (trans., 1958); Gardiner, A. H., *Egypt of the Pharaohs* (1961); Kees, Hermann, *Ancient Egypt: A Cultural Topography* (1961).

H. W. FAIRMAN, School of Archaeology and Oriental Studies, University of Liverpool

See also:

ABU SIMBEL	LUXOR
ABYDOS	MEMPHIS
ALEXANDRIA	MUMMIFICATION
AMON, AMEN, OR AMUN	NUBIA
ASWAN	OBELISKS
BOOK OF THE DEAD	OSIRIS
CLEOPATRA	PAPYRI
EGYPTOLOGY	PTOLEMIES
HELIOPOLIS	PYRAMIDS
HIEROGLYPHS	TELL EL-AMARNA
HYKSOS	THEBES
KARNAK	

Medieval Egypt

In Dec., 639, the Muslim general Amr ibn al-As led his Arab warriors from Syria across the frontier of the Byzantine province of Egypt. The invaders, sent by Caliph Umar I, were not resisted by the Coptic Christian population, who were antagonistic toward their Byzantine rulers, but the imperial forces put up a determined resistance at several points. The conqueror transferred the Egyptian provincial capital from Alexandria to El-Fustat ("the Camp"), a garrison city near the apex of the Delta on a site now absorbed by modern Cairo. The government of Egypt passed into the hands of the Arab Muslim military elite. The religion of the Copts, however, was tolerated by the new regime, and they continued to play an indispensable part in the bureaucracy.

Governors appointed by the Caliphs ruled Egypt for over three centuries. The earliest of these were Arabs, but after the mid-9th century, the Abbasid Caliphs sent Turks of slave origin to govern the province. Between 868 and 969 two of these set up short-lived dynasties, the Tulunids and the Ikhshidids. Egypt, with its well-marked geographical limits and great fertility, was an ideal seat for an autonomous government. In 969 the Abbasids lost the province, when it was conquered by Jawhar, the general of the Fatimid Caliphs who ruled in North Africa. The Fatimids were the heads of a heretical Muslim sect, the Ismailis, who had profited from the political and social discontent rife in the Muslim world, to organize a subversive movement against the Abbasid caliphate.

The early Fatimid period was one of prosperity for Egypt, which became the heart of an empire covering, at its widest extent, much of North Africa, southern Syria, and the Hejaz in the Arabian peninsula. Jawhar founded Cairo (El-Qahira, "the Victorious City") as the Fatimid capital, and built the mosque of Al-Azhar as a center for Ismaili propaganda. Fatimid Egypt was the center of a commercial network, linking the lands of the Indian Ocean, the Red Sea, and the Mediterranean. The wealth which flowed into the country was reflected in the magnificent palace of the dynasty and in finely worked pottery, glassware, and textiles—examples of which survive to this day. The 11th century witnessed the Fatimid decline. The later Caliphs were powerless figureheads, dominated by their ministers and soldiery, and their realm shrank to Egypt itself. In 1171 the last titular Fatimid was deposed by Saladin, the lieutenant of the paramount Muslim ruler in Syria, whose forces controlled Egypt.

Saladin, who himself shortly afterward assumed supreme power as Sultan in Muslim Syria and Egypt, was principally occupied in combating the Crusaders. After his death in 1193 his empire was partitioned among members of his family, the Ayyubids. Recurrent civil wars were the natural result of this dynastic anarchy. The last effective Ayyubid Sultan of Egypt, al-Salih (reigned 1240–49), sought to strengthen his military position by building up a highly trained guards regiment of Kipchak Turkish slaves, the Mamelukes, recruited from the steppes of Russia. During his last illness they defeated an invasion of Crusaders under King Louis IX of France at Mansura in the Delta.

After al-Salih's death the Mameluke military elite swept away the Ayyubid claimants to the throne and installed one of their own chiefs as Sultan. Although the danger to Muslim Syria and Egypt from the Crusaders was now much diminished, a very serious threat was developing with the Mongol invasion of the eastern Muslim lands. In 1258 the Mongols took Baghdad and put the Abbasid Caliph to death. A Mongol invasion of Syria was, however, repulsed by the Mamelukes at Ayn Jalut ("Goliath's Spring") in 1260. Syria was henceforward free from all but Mongol raids, while Egypt remained completely immune from their attacks.

Egypt, thus preserved from Mongol devastation, entered another phase of prosperity and cultural importance under the early Mameluke Sultans. Of these, the greatest was Baybars (reigned 1260–77), who consolidated Mameluke rule in Egypt and Syria, kept the Mongols at bay, and set up a nominal Abbasid Caliph in Cairo to legitimize his rule. A Turkish-speaking Mameluke military-political elite ruled the empire and perpetuated itself by the regular importation of fresh Mamelukes. The bureaucracy and judiciary were staffed by Arabic-speaking Copts and Muslims. In the late 14th century Circassian recruits began to supersede the original Kipchak Turkish element. The result was that, from the end of the 14th century, most of the Sultans were of Circassian origin. The 15th century was a time of slow decline. The Circassian Sultans strangled the profitable Red Sea-Mediterranean transit trade with extortionate dues and neglected the prosperity of Egypt. At the same time the Mameluke soldiery, untested in any great war and too conservative to adopt the new weapons utilizing gunpowder, lost their military effectiveness.

Ottoman Egypt. When the Ottoman Sultan Selim (I) the Grim invaded the Mameluke Empire in 1516–17, it collapsed almost without resistance. The political union between Egypt and Syria was dissolved, and Egypt sank to the position of an outlying province of a great empire. Selim's victory had been facilitated by a collaborationist Mameluke group who were prepared to assist him in order to retain their status under the new regime. Ottoman troops were stationed in Cairo, Mameluke revolts were suppressed, and an annual tribute was sent to Istanbul. Nevertheless the recruiting of Circassian Mamelukes was not stopped. Mameluke retainers formed bodies of household cavalry for the high officials, and by the 17th century the Mameluke and Ottoman elements in the dominant elite were inextricably intertwined.

Beginning in the late 16th century, a struggle for political hegemony developed within the Ottoman-Mameluke military elite. In the 18th century victory finally went to the beys, high military officers, mainly of Circassian-Mameluke origin, who absorbed the chief functions of state, and rested their power on their great households of retainers. Although divided among themselves, the beys dominated Egypt, reducing the Ottoman Viceroy to a figurehead. They ruled over a backward and impoverished country. Economic decline continued in the Ottoman period. The hierarchic and tradition-bound society of Egypt lay remote from the great historical currents of the age.

This state of affairs was abruptly ended with Napoleon Bonaparte's invasion of Egypt in 1798. Although the French failed to remain in occupation, their coming was of critical significance. Egypt became an area of importance in the conflict of European great powers. The Mameluke hegemony suffered a blow from which it never recovered. Ottoman troops were able, with British aid, to reoccupy the province, and reassert the Sultan's suzerainty. Finally, in the struggle for power which followed the French evacuation, the winner was a young Albanian officer, Mohammed Ali, who in 1805 was formally appointed by the Ottoman Sultan as Viceroy of Egypt.

Modern Egypt

Mohammed Ali and His Dynasty. Mohammed Ali's reign marks the beginning of modern Egyptian history. He organized an army on the Western model in order to consolidate his position in dealing with both internal rivals and the Ottoman Sultan. He established, in the Sultan's name, a protectorate over the Arabian region called the Hejaz, after defeating the Wahhabis, members of a Puritanical movement in the Arabian peninsula. He conquered an empire in the northern Sudan. Although he agreed in 1840 to relinquish Syria, from which he had expelled the Sultan's troops and officials nine years previously, his power in Egypt remained unshaken and the viceroyalty was made hereditary in his family. In connection with the establishment of his personal power and the creation of his new army, he reorganized the administration of Egypt and laid the foundations of a Western system of education.

The last years of Mohammed Ali's rule and the reigns of his successors Abbas I (reigned 1848–54) and Said (reigned 1854–63) were a time of retrogression and lethargy. A new impulse to development and westernization was given by the energetic viceroy Ismail Pasha (1863–79), upon whom the Ottoman Sultan conferred the title of Khedive. During his reign the Suez Canal was completed.

Ismail, however, lacked the balance and caution of Mohammed Ali. He contracted enormous debts with European financial houses, and the debts led to the intervention in Egyptian affairs of the French and British, who finally had Ismail deposed by the Sultan. He was succeeded by his more pliable son, Mohammed Tewfik who, like his father, had the title of Khedive.

Early in his reign Tewfik was confronted by a nationalist movement that had begun to develop under Ismail. It was supported by the Egyptian army officers, headed by Col. Arabi Pasha. Alarmed by this, France and Britain prepared to intervene, nominally to restore the Khedive's authority, actually to guard their own interests. Ultimately Britain alone sent troops into Egypt, defeated Arabi at Tell el-Kebir, and occupied the country in Sept., 1882. Under the occupation, originally meant to be temporary, Egypt was virtually a British protectorate. From 1883 to 1907 the real ruler of Egypt was Sir Evelyn Baring, later Lord Cromer, the British agent and consul general. Under his paternalistic control, the Egyptian government followed the instructions of British "advisers." The country received considerable material benefits: financial solvency was restored, law and order were maintained with greater humanity than in the past, and Western influence on the social and political systems was strengthened. Nevertheless the alien control was resented, both by the intelligentsia who formed new nationalist movements, and (after 1892) by the young Khedive Abbas II.

In 1907 the National party was founded by a young nationalist leader, Mustafa Kamil (1874–1908). Kamil's party represented the radical and uncompromising opposition to the British Occupation. After the death of the founder its prestige gradually declined, as the more demagogic elements seized control, and by 1914 the party was a spent force. Earlier in 1907 a more moderate group, the Umma party, which was prepared to co-operate with the British in the development of Egyptian society and resources, had come into being. The Umma party had its period of greatest success immediately before World War I.

When the Ottoman Sultan joined Germany in World War I, the British on Dec. 18, 1914, declared a protectorate over Egypt, deposed Abbas, and appointed his uncle, Husayn Kamil, as ruler with the title of Sultan. The nationalist movement, held in check during the war years, burst all bounds at the coming of peace. It found leaders in the members of a delegation (Arab., *wafd*), originally constituted to present Egypt's case for independence at the Versailles Peace Conference. In Mar., 1919, a widespread revolt broke out. This was suppressed, and the Wafd failed to secure a hearing at the Conference. The British government was nevertheless compelled, reluctantly, to realize that the maintenance of the Protectorate was impossible. On Feb. 28, 1922, a unilateral British declaration granted independence to Egypt, subject to four reserved points. Two of these were the security of British imperial communications (that is, the Suez Canal), and the status of the Sudan which, although nominally under joint Egyptian and British rule, was actually controlled by Britain.

Independent Egypt. Independent Egypt was constituted as a parliamentary monarchy under King Fuad, who had succeeded Husayn Kamil in 1917. A constitutional commission, set up in Apr., 1922, adopted the Belgian constitution as a model. The Egyptian constitution was promulgated on Apr. 19, 1923. The executive power was in the hands of the King, who could veto a bill (which, however, became law if revoted by a two-thirds majority), prorogue Parliament, or adjourn its sessions for a month, and rule in the meantime by decree. The ministers were collectively responsible to Parliament, which was composed of a Senate and a Chamber of Deputies. Two-fifths of the senators were appointed by the King on the Prime Minister's advice, the rest being elected.

The reigns of Fuad and his successor Faruk, who came to the throne in 1936, were occupied with a struggle for power between the monarch and the Wafd movement. This was now organized as a nation-wide political party and led first by Saad Zaghlul Pasha, then Mustafa al-Nahas Pasha. Britain, represented by an ambassador, and with troops still stationed in the country, sought to maintain her interests by utilizing the vicissitudes of the political struggle. The Wafd expressed Egyptian resentment at both the autocratic tendency of the monarchy and the continued British presence in Egypt. New extremist groups also sprang up to express this resentment. The most significant of these was the Muslim Brotherhood, founded in 1928 by a schoolteacher, Hasan al-Banna, to promote the strict observance of Islam. The Muslim Brotherhood thus represented a fundamentalist Muslim reaction to Western influence. It rapidly developed into a mass movement, with many supporters outside Egypt.

Mussolini's invasion of Abyssinia (1935–36) brought about a temporary rapprochement between Egypt and Britain. An Anglo-Egyptian Treaty was signed. British troops were withdrawn from Egypt, except for the Suez Canal Zone, where they might be stationed for a further 20 years. The Sudanese problem was again deferred.

During World War II Egypt remained a nonbelligerent almost to the end, but her territory was a base of vital importance to Britain and the Allies. After the war the nationalist debate with Britain was resumed with increased acerbity on both sides. Resentment at the British occupation of the Canal Zone and the control of the Sudan were the dominant themes of Egyptian nationalism. At the same time the pattern of political thought was changing. Faruk's way of life earned him much unpopularity and discredited the monarchy. The Wafd had become a party of vested political interests. Lack of success in the war against Israel in 1948 and the scandals involving the court in the supply of faulty arms to the troops completed public disillusionment with the old regime.

The 1952 Revolution and Republic. Two extremist political groups, the Muslim Brotherhood and the Communists, gained much support. But the ultimate beneficiary of the political crisis was the Free Officers Movement, an association of young, middle-class army officers, which had for some years been planning the overthrow of the regime. They seized power by a *coup d'état* on July 23, 1952, and Faruk was deposed. A Republic was proclaimed on June 18, 1953, with Gen. Mohammed Naguib as its President and Prime Minister. He was an older man, who had been brought in by the Free Officers before the revolt because of his widespread popularity. A clash was, however, developing in the ruling junta between Naguib and the Deputy Prime Minister, Col. Gamal Abdel Nasser, the founder and real director of the revolutionary movement. Naguib was anxious to restore constitutional political life; Nasser and most of his colleagues were radical reformers. The struggle occupied the early months of 1954, but by mid-April, Naguib was reduced to a figurehead. Soon afterward he was removed from politics. The attempt of a number of the Muslim Brotherhood to assassinate Nasser in Oct., 1954, was followed by a wave of arrests and suppression of the Brotherhood. With the Communists also

A ship steams through the Suez Canal, the man-made waterway that crosses the Isthmus of Suez in northeastern Egypt. The canal, opened in 1869, connects the Mediterranean and Red seas.

United Arab Republic Tourist Office

proscribed along with the Brotherhood, party political life remained in abeyance.

The military junta had some striking achievements to its credit after only a few years in power. Agrarian reform was instituted by a decree of Sept. 9, 1952. On Feb. 12, 1953, agreement was reached with Britain over the future of the Sudan. Egypt gave up her claim to sovereignty over the Sudanese, and recognized their right of self-determination. The problem of the Canal Zone proved more refractory, but on Oct. 19, 1954, an agreement was signed. The British undertook to evacuate the zone by June 18, 1956.

From this point Nasser began to assume a larger role in international affairs and to present himself as a leader of Arab, rather than purely Egyptian, nationalism. To Britain and the West, the Suez Agreement of Oct., 1954, had been a step in the direction of associating Egypt in their strategy for the containment of the U.S.S.R. To Nasser, by contrast, it was the prerequisite to the creation of a neutral group of Arab states. Moreover, the removal of the British buffer between Israel and the Nile Valley necessitated the modernization of the Egyptian army.

Nasser's development of a new policy was stimulated by two events. On Feb. 24, 1955, Turkey and Iraq signed the agreement which was the nucleus of the Baghdad Pact. Four days later Israel forces made a heavy and effective raid into the Gaza Strip. The first was a blow to Nasser's project of a neutral Arab bloc under Egyptian leadership; the second underlined Egyptian military weakness. Dissatisfied with the supply of armaments from the Western Bloc, Nasser therefore concluded an agreement with Czechoslovakia (Sept. 27, 1955). By this he obtained war equipment in exchange for rice and cotton. This opened the way to other deals with the Soviet Bloc.

Matters came to a head in a sequence of events during 1956. Nasser had pinned his hopes for the future economic development of Egypt on the construction of a High Dam above Aswan, and in Dec., 1955, he had received promises of loans from the United States and Britain, and from the International Bank in Feb., 1956. On July 19 the United States abruptly withdrew its offer; Britain followed suit, and the International Bank's offer accordingly lapsed. Nasser retaliated on July 26 by announcing the nationalization of the Suez Canal Company and the utilization of its profits to finance the High Dam. This act profoundly disturbed the British government, always sensitive for strategic and commercial reasons to matters affecting the control of the canal. Attempts to coerce or restrain Nasser however proved fruitless.

By the late autumn a highly critical situation had developed. Israel was anxious because of the backing Egypt was now receiving from the Soviet Bloc and harassed because of frequent Egyptian raids across its frontiers. France saw in Nasser, as the protagonist of Arab nationalism, a factor in the Algerian revolt. Britain wished to avert Nasser's control of the canal. An invasion of Sinai by Israel forces on Oct. 29, 1956, was followed on the next day by an Anglo-French ultimatum to both parties and, on Nov. 5, by the landing of troops at the northern end of the canal. These moves, undertaken ostensibly to prevent the spread of hostilities, were condemned by the United States, the U.S.S.R., and a majority of the member states of the United Nations. In the face of this opposition, the Anglo-French forces were halted on Nov. 6, and subsequently withdrew.

As a result of the Suez crisis, Nasser was able to win a political and diplomatic victory after a military defeat. His position as a leader of Arab nationalism was enhanced. His hold over the canal was assured. At the same time the rift between Egypt and the West generally became even deeper. Nasser now moved to solidify his leadership.

Union With Syria in the United Arab Republic (U.A.R). In Jan., 1958, talks were held between Egyptian leaders and those Syrian leaders who wished to safeguard Syria against Communist domination. On Feb. 1 the merger of the two states in the United Arab Republic was proclaimed. The proclamation provided for the vesting of executive authority in a President, who should appoint ministers responsible to himself, and for the creation of a single legislative house. The installation of Nasser as President of the new republic was approved by plebiscite on Feb. 21.

During the next two years, relations with the West, which had been at a low ebb since the Suez crisis, greatly improved. An accord was reached between the U.A.R. and the Suez Canal Company in 1958, followed by a financial agreement with France and the restoration (1959) of diplomatic relations with Britain. A technical assistance agreement with the United States was also signed in 1959, and at the end of the year loans were granted to the Suez Canal Authority by the World Bank and several private western banks. At the same time, and despite some political differences, relations with the U.S.S.R. remained amicable, and Soviet grants toward the construction of the Aswan High Dam were contracted in 1958 and 1960. On the whole, the U.A.R. appeared to be following, with some success, its chosen policy of neutralism between the power blocs.

Meanwhile, internal tensions had developed in the new state. The founding proclamation had envisaged the accession of other Arab states into the union, culminating in the eventual unification of all the Arab peoples. This hope, however, was not realized. The Syrians found themselves in a position of numerical, economic, and political inferiority, and the Syrian element in the government rapidly lost its importance. On Sept. 28, 1961, a group in Syria representing army and business interests seized the government, declared the independence of Syria, and placed Mamoun al-Kuzbari at the head of the Revolutionary Government. Syria was again recognized as independent by most of the community of nations. Nasser stated that the U.A.R., which would continue to be the name of the Egyptian part of the union, renounced all claims to Syria and would not block its entry into the United Nations. Nasser soon became occupied with other ventures.

Intervention in Yemen. On Dec. 26, 1961, Nasser broke off the U.A.R.'s federation with Yemen, thereby terminating the United Arab States. When a military revolution in Yemen overthrew the Imam in October, 1962, Nasser threw his support behind the republican government. The royal houses of Jordan and Saudi Arabia supported the Yemeni royalists, which led to the breaking of diplomatic relations between the U.A.R. and Saudi

Arabia. Inconclusive fighting continued in Yemen for three years before both intervening parties negotiated an agreement aimed at ending the war in August, 1965. But even that was not conclusive; the fighting flared up again.

New Constitution. On the home front, Nasser began (1962) to prepare the way for a new constitution to replace the one that had been discarded at the time of the union with Syria. Important in the preparations was the founding of the Arab Socialist Union, a new party and the only one permitted in the country. A popularly elected National Assembly adopted the new constitution in 1964.

Under this document the U.A.R. is designated a socialist democratic state, based on the "alliance of the forces of working people," and all the country's resources are owned by the state. The President, as chief executive, has veto powers over legislative acts and can dissolve parliament and declare a state of emergency at his own discretion, but he cannot rule by decree unless parliament is not in session. In the first presidential elections under the new constitution, held in Mar., 1965, Nasser, the only candidate, received 99.999% of the vote. His position at home had never been more secure, but the continued division of the Arab peoples still bothered him.

The Six-Day War. Ten years after the Suez crisis, U.N. troops were still patrolling the armistice line between Israel and the surrounding Arab countries. The increased frequency of raids and border skirmishes, however, indicated growing Arab impatience with the continued existence of the Jewish state. A series of such incidents during late 1966 and early 1967 prompted Nasser to seek regaining his leadership of the Arab world, which he had all but lost during the preceding years. On May 15, 1967, combat troops of the Egyptian army were placed on war footing, and from that time on events moved swiftly to a climax. On May 18, Nasser requested the United Nations to remove its emergency forces from the Israeli border. U.N. Secretary-General U Thant quickly complied. Nasser then went a step further, announcing on May 23 a blockade of the Gulf of Aqaba, which cut off Israel's access to its port at Eilat. A week later, Egypt signed a mutual defense pact with Jordan, to which Iraq soon became a party, too. Israel had already ordered a general mobilization. Efforts at mediation proved useless, and war broke out on June 5.

The Israeli army moved with lightning swiftness. After six days of fighting, when the warring parties finally heeded the call of the United Nations to cease hostilities, Israel had captured all U.A.R. territory east of the Suez Canal, all of Jordan west of the river, and a strip of Syria commanding the upper Jordan valley. The Egyptian and Jordanian air forces were completely disabled.

Upon this humiliating defeat of his armies, Nasser, on June 9, offered his resignation, but an impressive mass demonstration made him quickly change his mind. Instead, he reshuffled the army leadership and subsequently arrested a number of disgruntled officers who felt that they were being made scapegoats of political blunders.

The basic problem of Arab-Israel enmity, however, remained unsolved. In fact, the solution seemed farther away then ever. Thousands upon thousands of Arab refugees streamed out of the Israel-occupied territories into the surrounding countries, whose economies could not absorb them. Discussions at the United Nations were utterly unproductive, and the truce remained uneasy in spite of U.N. efforts at supervision.

There was, nevertheless, one major difference between the situation before and after the war. Unlike 1956, Israel now refused to remove its troops from the captured Arab territories unless some meaningful agreement on future relations were reached. But whether this position would secure peace in the area, or expose it to even further risks, was impossible to foretell.

Consult Lane, E. W., *The Modern Egyptians* (1836); Lane-Poole, Stanley, *History of Egypt in the Middle Ages* (1901); Cromer, Earl of, *Modern Egypt* (2 vols., new ed., 1916); Dodwell, Henry, *Founder of Modern Egypt* (1931); Adams, C. C., *Islam and Modernism in Egypt* (1933); Landau, J. M., *Parliaments and Parties in Egypt* (1954); Issawi, Charles, *Egypt at Mid-Century* (1954); Marlowe, John, *Anglo-Egyptian Relations, 1800–1953* (1954); *Egypt*, ed. by G. L. Harris (1957); Lacouture, Jean and Simonne, *Egypt in Transition* (1958); Little, Tom, *Egypt* (1959); Ahmed, J. M., *The Intellectual Origins of Egyptian Nationalism* (1960); Safran, Nadav, *Egypt in Search of Political Community* (1961); Vatikiotis, P. J., *The Egyptian Army in Politics* (1961); Tignor, R. L., *Modernization and British Colonial Rule in Egypt, 1882–1914* (1966); Holt, P. M., *Egypt and the Fertile Crescent, 1516–1922* (1966).

P. M. HOLT, University of London

See also AYYUBID; FATIMID; NASSER, GAMAL ABDEL; SALADIN; UNITED ARAB REPUBLIC.

EGYPTIAN ART

During a period of over 3,000 years, Egyptian art changed remarkably little in style. The Egyptians were a conservative people, living in a land of few natural features, and virtually isolated from their neighbors. Life was simple and constant, following a regular rhythm of birth, life, death, and rebirth in step with the yearly inundation of the Nile.

Statues, reliefs—either incised or standing out slightly from the ground and originally painted—and paintings were created mainly to satisfy religious needs. A statue was one guarantee of immortality, because it could house a man's spirit after death if the embalmed body were destroyed. It did not have to be an exact representation, as the name of the man was inscribed on it for identification. Therefore, most statues were idealized portraits showing their subjects as the types of men they were in their prime. A relief or painting was capable of perpetuating the actions or objects depicted. Either one could be used in a tomb to supply the man with provisions and ensure the continuance of his normal life after death, or in a temple to assist in the divine ritual.

Archaic Period and Old Kingdom. By the 1st Dynasty (c.3000–c.2980 B.C.), the relief style had developed, as in the slate palette of King Narmer (Egyptian Museum, Cairo). The decorated area is divided into registers, within each of which there is a balance of mass and movement.

The standing figures stay on the base line and are shown in typical Egyptian manner—all of the body is in profile except the shoulders and eye, which are full face. The most important figure in the scene, the King, is shown much larger than the rest, and there is the typical visual symbolism of the hawk handing over the Delta people to the King. A close relation between the scene and the written word creates the impression that the figures are really only enlarged hieroglyphs to be read as part of the inscription.

By the end of the 2d Dynasty (c.2780 B.C.), statuary had also developed along typical Egyptian style and conventions. The 2d Dynasty slate statue of King Khasekhem seated on a throne (Egyptian Museum, Cairo) and the 3d Dynasty (c.2780–c.2680 B.C.) standing statues of Sepa and his wife Neset (Louvre, Paris) show the frontality common to Egyptian, Mesopotamian, primitive Greek, and other preclassic styles. The figure faces directly to the front and the limbs are held close to the body. There is little undercutting, and where limbs protrude they are connected together or to a back pillar with bridges of stone for strength. The eyes, the eyebrows, and the anatomy of the body and limbs are treated in a conventional instead of naturalistic manner—for example, Sepa's two staffs are held in unnatural positions so that the sculptor could carve them in relief against the body instead of in the round. The impression given is of solidity and endurance, which is exactly what the Egyptians sought.

Egyptian tempera painting was at first generally employed on reliefs, but it early developed as a separate art form. The tomb of Atet in Medum, dating from the beginning of the 4th Dynasty (c.2680–c.2565 B.C.), contained painted scenes of farming, hunting, and the like, among which was the famous panel showing geese (Egyptian Museum, Cairo). In technique, style, and subject matter these paintings are in the finest Egyptian tradition and use a wide palette of colors—black, white, gray, brown, yellow, red, orange, and green.

In private tombs reliefs were at first in the form of steles, or panels of limestone, with a scene showing the deceased seated before an offering table piled high with food and other gifts. Later the walls of the offering chamber were decorated with additional scenes showing the preparation of these gifts—the butchering of the meat, growing and harvesting of the grain and grapes, and so forth—and their presentation by servants and priests. As time passed, scenes from the life of the dead man were added—hunting, playing games, or viewing cattle—and later still, scenes of the funeral.

In the temples attached to the royal pyramids and in the causeways leading to them similar scenes were represented along with religious scenes of the King worshiping various gods. The chambers of the pyramids were not decorated until the end of the 5th Dynasty (c.2565–c.2420 B.C.), and then only with inscriptions.

In private tombs statues depicting the buried man, sometimes accompanied by his wife and family, were generally hidden away for safety in an enclosed chamber, called the serdab, close to the offering chamber. Special portrait heads of the deceased were carved during the 4th Dynasty. These are known as reserve heads and served in case all other representations of the deceased were de-

Front and back views of the slate palette of King (Narmer) Menes, a ruler of Egypt during the 1st Dynasty.

A 4th Dynasty statuary group found at Giza depicts King Mycerinus (*right*) with the seated goddess Hathor and a local deity.

Marburg—Art Reference Bureau

Fresco in 18th-Dynasty King Tutankhamen's tomb portrays him embracing Osiris, god of the dead. At right, Tutankhamen is shown with Nut, goddess of the sky.

Red granite statue of the 18th-Dynasty Queen Hatshepsut, found at Deir el-Bahri.

Metropolitan Museum of Art, Rogers Fund; supplemented by a Contribution from Edward S. Harkness, 1929

stroyed. They are among the few true portraits in Egyptian art.

Royal statues stood in the funerary temples and include portraits of the King alone or with his consort, for example, the statue of Mycerinus and his Queen (Museum of Fine Arts, Boston), and groups showing the King accompanied by one or two deities under whose patronage he ruled. An example of the latter, also in Boston, is the group depicting Mycerinus with the goddess Hathor and another local goddess. These statues display a greater interest in anatomy and musculature.

In the Old Kingdom (c.2780–c.2254 B.C.) works of art were created in the royal workshops near the capital of Memphis. They have been found in the tombs and temples of Giza, Sakkara, Medum, and Abu Sir. Toward the end of the period a livelier, more naturalistic style began to develop. At the end of the Old Kingdom, when royal power waned and Egypt began to split up into separate provinces, several local art styles developed—at Aswan on the southern frontier, at Dendera and nearby Coptos, and at Thebes. These styles are more powerful, more formal, and at first cruder and less sophisticated than the northern Memphite style, which continued.

Middle and New Kingdoms. Though most Middle Kingdom (1991–c.1778 B.C.) relief was in the Memphite tradition, the statuary stayed more formal and abstract. Statues of the Kings, as those of Senusret III, have a stern, forceful expression, a broad face, high cheekbones, and thick lips. Statues of nonroyal personages also tended to follow this style of portrait, were smaller than in the Old Kingdom, and carved in hard stones instead of limestone.

The conquest of Egypt by the Hyksos, ending the Middle Kingdom, and the creation of the Empire, or New Kingdom (1573–c.1085 B.C.), brought a new outlook to Egypt. The country became wealthy from foreign tribute and was in closer contact than ever before with its neighbors in western Asia, Crete, and Nubia. The army became professional, the priesthood, which was organized under the leadership of the priests of the god Amon, grew wealthy, and a bureaucracy developed.

Art became extremely varied in character—sometimes feminine and luxurious or monumental and overpowering, sometimes spiritual and emotional or traditional and formal. Tremendous building programs were undertaken, especially in Thebes, the new capital, where many funerary temples, cult temples, and palaces were built. Hundreds of statues were also created for these temples. The funerary temple of Hatshepsut at Deir el-Bahri contained many sphinxes and standing, kneeling, and sitting statues of the queen, a selection of which can be seen in the Metropolitan Museum of Art in New York.

The rockcut tombs at Thebes were decorated with paintings rather than reliefs, and most of the finest Egyptian paintings came from these 18th- (1573–c.1349 B.C.) and 19th-Dynasty (c.1349–c.1197 B.C.) tombs. In the private tombs the artists were under less formal restraint and developed a freer, livelier, and even humorous style.

After the New Kingdom Egyptian traditions began to fall into decay, being replaced by foreign, especially Greek, modes. There were still brief periods when, by consciously imitating the past, the artists created masterpieces in the pure Egyptian style, but soon Hellenistic and later Muslim traditions prevailed.

Consult Davies, N. M., and Gardiner, A. H., *Ancient Egyptian Paintings* (1936); Smith, W. S., *History of Egyptian Sculpture and Painting in the Old Kingdom* (2d ed., 1949); Aldred, Cyril, *The Development of Ancient Egyptian Art* (1952); Smith, W. S., *Art and Architecture of Ancient Egypt* (1958).

ERIC YOUNG, The Metropolitan Museum of Art

EGYPTIAN DANCE

Six thousand years ago the Egyptians honored such gods as Hathor, Isis, and Apis with dancing. Although the Egyptian word *hbj* means both "dancing" and "to be joyful," there were mourning dances for the dead which date back to 5000 B.C. Remnants of this ceremonial are known to have survived as late as 1880 B.C. The movements were austere and mystic: the long strides of the dancers were meant to overstep death and win eternal life for the deceased.

There were many other dance-ceremonials: a folk dance of the wine press, performed 4,000 years ago; the death and resurrection of the god Osiris in the dance-play festivals at Abydos (in the Middle Kingdom during the 19th century B.C.); mimed dances, such as the feminine trio of "The Wind" dance (shown on a wall painting of the Middle Kingdom, 12th Dynasty, c.1900 B.C.); and the astral circle dances of whirling priests or women (still in existence today as the triple-circle whirling dervish dance of the Middle East).

The aristocracy had for a long time maintained a class of professional dancers; as a result, weather-charm, birth-magic, and other ritual dances became "theater." Dancers were imported; Pygmies especially were prized. By about 1500 B.C. Asian *bayaderes* had brought a new concept of feminine dance into Egypt. The long stride, the high kick, the back-bend disappeared, and the "speaking hands" (hand gestures) with quiet feet, typical of Asia, took their place.

During the centuries of Arab domination in Egypt, the broad movements and angular lines of the ancients gave place to the plastic curves of Arabia. The convulsive abdominal dance, once an austere ritual of birth, became a vehicle of sexual excitement. This *danse du ventre* (belly dance) is called by the Arabs *mesri*, a word which also means "Egyptian." It is believed that the Gaditans performed the *mesri* in ancient Rome. Toward the end of the 19th century it was believed that certain of the ancient Egyptian ritual dances still existed (for example, among the almes of Isna).

The dancing seen in Cairo, Port Said, and Alexandria today is almost purely Arabic. The feet stay close to the ground, the body moves sensuously, and the hands and face are highly expressive and generally pantomimic. There are some acrobatic movements, such as the back-bend from the knees. In the nonimitative dances, *chinchines* (finger-cymbals) are often used. Dances are improvised on the spur of the moment, and the watchers throw money to the performers.

LA MERI, Author, *Dance as an Art Form*
See also DANCE; FOLK DANCE.

EGYPTIAN MUSIC

A fairly comprehensive view of ancient Egyptian music and its millennial history can be obtained from present research and analysis of archeological, pictorial, and hieroglyphic material. The first traces of this music are revealed by prehistoric findings. Music later played an important role in the lives of Egyptians under the Pharaohs. Although it has not been possible to reconstruct ancient melodies, the indirect evidence on hand seems to certify that the strongly traditional music of ancient Egypt had developed its own characteristic traits. Notwithstanding repeated cultural importations, from the Old Kingdom on it differed from that of its Asian and African neighbors. Traces of it can still be found in the Coptic liturgy and in the folk music of modern Egypt. In the latter case this is evident in the manner of rhythmic handclapping, in the use of many of the same instruments, in the same old folk tales (the cat and the mouse), and so on.

Musical Style

Musical Notation and Conducting. Ancient Egyptians did not possess a musical notation like the modern Western one. Music was learned and passed on by purely oral tradition. However, starting with the Middle Kingdom (c.2000 B.C.) they sometimes attempted to denote musical details with the familiar means of hieroglyphic symbols, repetitions of the same letter, or other signs. Very similar means and signs were later used for the same purposes in the music of the Christian churches. Musical instruments of this time included clappers, rattles, all kinds of jingles, sistral, vessel-pipes, long flutes, double clarinets, hemispheric drums, harps, and newer instruments such as the barrel drum, castanets, and asymmetric lyre.

Another ancient method of representing music visually was used by the chironomists, as shown in the painted and sculptured music scenes from the 4th Dynasty on (c.2723–c.2563 B.C.). The chironomists were singers or special professionals communicating hand signs to the musicians. Singers and chironomists were designated by the same term in the Old Kingdom (c.2780–2254 B.C.), but from the Middle Kingdom on a distinction was made between "singers" and "singers with the hand." Chironomic signs are occasionally used in the contemporary Coptic Church.

The Egyptian signs can be classified into two series, one of rhythmic and one of melodic meaning. The rhythms have scarcely been explored, but it has been possible to interpret some of the melodic signs denoting tones and intervals.

Scales. An analysis of the instruments preserved and of the chironomic art representations seems to prove that the scales used in the Old and Middle Kingdoms had large intervals which progressively diminished during the New Kingdom (c.1573–c.1085 B.C.). The reconstructed scales show a structure in principle resembling the tetrachordal system of ancient Greece, namely, two movable notes within the frame of a fourth. The scales often contained intervals smaller than a semitone.

Harmony. Although Egyptian music was essentially a monodic (nonharmonic) art, melismatic (ornamented), and chanted, a kind of primitive polyphony (harmony) can be proved to have already existed in the music of the Old Kingdom (c.2700). Soloists were often accompanied by a vocal or instrumental drone (a continuous note or notes) which could consist of the fundamental note of the scale as well as its fifth and octave (for example C-G-C). It seems certain that heterophony (the simultaneous performance of the same melody model by several musicians with individual variants) was also practiced.

Vocal and Instrumental Styles. Singing was more highly appreciated than instrumental performances. Scientific analysis of the facial expression in art representations of singers proves that they sang with a nasal timbre resembling that of modern singers of the Near East and of the Coptic Church.

Representations of vocal and instrumental solos are rare. Singing was usually accompanied on the harp, and the male and female singers were as a rule also harpists. The accompaniment was occasionally enriched by a lute, lyre, flute, and various rhythm instruments. During the New Kingdom many new instruments were imported from Asia: double and single oboes, bronze drums, round tambourines, ladle-shaped, boat-shaped, angular, and semicircular harps of different sizes, giant lyres, and long- and short-necked lutes. Silver and gold trumpets have been found among the many relics in the relatively intact tomb of Tutankhamen.

Melody and Form. It is evident that ancient Egyptian music consisted largely of variations of traditional melody models—a practice customary in the music of the whole Orient today and in ancient Greece. Antiphonal singing (alternating choirs) in temples and accompanied solo performances are documented for the Old Kingdom. The rondeau form, consisting of solos with a refrain, became popular at least from the Middle Kingdom on. A more developed form of the rondeau, resembling the modern Arabian *dor*, which is a variation suite composed of solos and instrumental and ensemble parts, was known from the beginning of the New Kingdom. In addition, ancient Egyptians had hymns, strophic (verse form) and dance songs, and other special types of solo and ensemble music.

Professional Musicians. Musicians, particularly those attached to temples and to the court, were highly honored in ancient Egypt. The known musicians of the Old Kingdom were usually functionaries and holders of high administrative posts, or priests. They were among the confidants of the Pharaoh and were also the private music teachers of the royal family and the nobility. (The first professional musician known to music history was Khufu-Ankh, chief of the royal singers and flutists, who died c.2560).

The professional career of a gifted musician would consist of the following stages: singer in the royal choir, then assistant choir leader, later royal music director, and, at last, superintendent of court music. Music instructors were known from the Old Kingdom on, and during the New Kingdom there existed schools for temple musicians in Memphis. Specialists in the different branches of music were organized in corporations under an "overseer," who was usually one of the higher-ranking musicians at the royal court.

From the 21st Dynasty on (c.1085–c.950 B.C.) there are accounts of touring virtuosos of international reputation. The very rich documentary sources of the Saite (c.1085–332 B.C.) and of the Greco-Roman (332 B.C.–359 A.D.) periods show that musicians and other artists signed regular contracts with their employers and that a breach of contract would usually end with a lawsuit.

Finally, the existence of amateur musicians and connoisseurs should be noted, a fact documented from the beginnings of the Old Kingdom on. This is one of the striking parallels among the musical phenomena of ancient Egypt revealed to those of later cultures and of our modern civilization.

HANS HICKMANN, Hamburg University

EGYPTIAN [ĭ-jĭp′shən], the language of ancient Egypt. It constitutes a branch of the Afro-Asiatic family of languages. Egyptian was in active use from an unknown length of time before the beginning of Dynasty I (c.3200 B.C.) until the 17th century A.D. As a "dead" language it is still preserved in the liturgy of the Coptic Church. During its long life the language changed extensively, undergoing five stages: Old, Middle, and Late Egyptian, Demotic, and Coptic. All of these can now be understood, but only Coptic can be pronounced, since vowels are not expressed in the writing of the other forms.

See also AFRICA: *African Languages;* CHAMPOLLION, JEAN FRANÇOIS; HIEROGLYPHS; ROSETTA STONE.

EGYPTIAN ARCHITECTURE was simple in structure and material. The arch, though known and used in brick, was not favored by the Egyptians, who supported their roofs and doorways with posts and lintels. Materials used included wood, brick, and stone; mud was used as a mortar for brick, and a mixture of gypsum and sand for stone masonry. In the latter case the mortar served, not as a binding material, but as a lubricant in moving heavy blocks, and sheer mass was generally all that held a building together.

Houses. The house was the beginning of Egyptian architecture. The temple was the house of god; the tomb was man's eternal house. The temple and tomb were more important and generally built of stone, whereas the house for the living man was of brick and wood.

Most of what is known of Egyptian houses is derived from the city of Tell el-Amarna built during the Empire, or New Kingdom (1573–c.1085 B.C.). There the house stood in a courtyard and had a flat roof and small windows. A central living room was surrounded by an open-sided loggia and suites of rooms for masters, wives, and guests. In the courtyard also were a garden with a household shrine and a pool, kitchens, stables, storebins, and a well.

In earlier periods this style of house was often provided with a colonnaded portico overlooking the court. This portico was derived from an open-fronted tent house, the columns being derived from the tent posts. Several other types of one-room houses were also used in the earliest eras: round houses of mud and wattle, rectangular houses of mud brick or latticework with flat roofs, and wood-frame houses with low vaulted roofs. Many features of later temples, shrines, and even coffins were derived from these primitive house forms. The Egyptians were conservative and the shapes of their buildings retained in stylized form architectural elements that had long ceased to be used.

Town houses of three or four stories were built from the Middle Kingdom (1991–c.1778 B.C.) onward. Kitchens,

The Metropolitan Museum of Art

Reconstruction of the temples of King Mentuhotep (11th Dynasty) and Queen Hatshepsut (18th Dynasty) at Deir el-Bahri. The queen's temple (*foreground*) was modeled on the temple of Mentuhotep (with pyramid roof).

living rooms, and bedrooms were on the ground, second, and third floors respectively, and the flat roof was used as extra sleeping space or for storebins.

Artisans constructing the royal tombs were provided with barracks near the Great Pyramid at Giza and with walled villages at Kahun during the Middle Kingdom, and at Deir el-Medina and Tell el-Amarna during the New Kingdom. The houses were simple three- or four-room buildings laid out in rows along narrow streets, but more elaborate houses were provided for officials and overseers. Palaces differed from the better-class houses only in size and luxury.

Tombs. Abundant evidence of tomb architecture has survived from all periods. The Egyptians believed that the body must be preserved so that the soul could return to it in afterlife. The body was therefore mummified, and food and other offerings were deposited in the tomb both during and after the funeral. The tomb thus required stor-

age chambers and an offering chapel in addition to the burial chamber. The offerings attracted tomb robbers, and in time the tomb was made larger and stronger to thwart them.

The tomb began as a mere pit in the ground. As the pit became larger and deeper it was found necessary to line the sides with mud brick. As the offerings increased in quantity and variety, the pit was divided by crosswalls into an increasing number of separate chambers. The excavated material formed a mound on the surface, and this was enlarged and made rectangular with mud brick. Offerings after the funeral were at first simply placed on the ground, but soon a special niche was built to receive them. This niche became larger and more elaborate until it formed a chamber built into the superstructure.

As technology advanced, the animal skins and basketry that protected the earliest burials were replaced by rectangular coffins in the shape of houses, and the simple pit

Remains of the entrance hall to the funerary temple of King Zoser, near the Step Pyramid at Sakkara.

Marburg—Art Reference Bureau

Pillars with papyrus (*background*) and lotus motifs in the 18th Dynasty temple of Amon at Karnak.

Court built by Rameses II (13th century B.C.) in the temple of Luxor. The 80-ft.-high obelisk is covered with hieroglyphs.

became a brick tomb. Finally, by the beginning of the Old Kingdom (c.2780–c.2254 B.C.), Egyptian craftsmen had the skill and tools to make stone masonry sufficiently economical for the construction of tombs and temples.

The first all-stone building was the Step Pyramid of King Zoser, a notable King of the 3d Dynasty (c.2780–c.2680 B.C.), at Sakkara. This elaborate complex of buildings consisted of the pyramid tomb itself, plus its funerary temple and a series of special shrines for the royal ceremony held every few years for the renewing of the king's power. This is the earliest example of free-standing masonry with regular courses and fine joints, lintels and roofing blocks, decorative attached columns and false arches, all of stone. The uncertainty of the architect in his material is reflected by the employment of small-size blocks, by the columns not being free-standing, and by the constant use of decorative and structural features derived from earlier brick and wood forms.

Within four generations, by the beginning of the 4th Dynasty (c.2680–c.2565 B.C.), Egyptian stone masonry had reached its apex. Monolithic blocks were used—some weighing up to 30 tons. The casing blocks of the Great Pyramid of Khufu (Cheops) at Giza show amazingly close joints of a ten-thousandth of an inch. Even private tombs were of stone, grouped around the pyramid tombs of the Pharaohs, and consisting of a nearly solid rectangular superstructure, or mastaba, over a burial shaft. The chambers in the mastaba were decorated with painted relief scenes of daily life and the preparation and presentation of offerings. One wall in the offering chamber was in the form of a false door through which the dead man could pass to receive these offerings.

After the Old Kingdom, tombs were generally cut into the cliffs, with a concealed burial chamber, small storage chambers, and a pillared offering chamber decorated with wall paintings. In the New Kingdom, rock-cut tombs were built at Thebes, the new capital, for both royal and private burials. Many private tombs had a small brick pyramid over the entrance; others had open forecourts with decorated façades cut in the rock face. However, royal tombs with no superstructure were hidden away in some remote valley to avoid attracting robbers. The private tombs were decorated with painted scenes of daily life, but the royal tombs had religious scenes.

Temples. Egyptian architectural style is best seen in the temples. Funerary temples were a development of the offering niche in the tomb. The Old Kingdom examples, attached to the pyramids, generally had an open court with statues of the King, one or two pillared halls, and a sanctuary with a cult statue of the King and a false door. Mentuhotep I of the 11th Dynasty (c.2134–1991 B.C.) had a rock-cut tomb and a temple in the form of a dummy pyramid surrounded by a colonnade built on a terrace in front of the cliffs at Deir el-Bahri in Western Thebes.

In the New Kingdom, when royal tombs were hidden away in the Valley of the Kings, the funerary temples were built separately along the edge of the desert. That of Queen Hatshepsut at Deir el-Bahri took as its prototype the nearby terraced temple of Mentuhotep. A processional way led from a valley temple, where the mummification took place, along a causeway to a walled forecourt, and up ramps to two terraces fronted by colonnades. On the upper terrace were the sanctuary, cut into the cliff face, an open colonnaded court, and subsidiary shrines.

Sphinxes and statues of the Queen lined the way and stood in the court and sanctuary.

The cult temple housed the statue of the god, to whose daily worship and service the temple was devoted. The earliest probably consisted merely of a covered sanctuary and an open forecourt. Few traces remain until the New Kingdom. The Temple of Khons at Karnak, built by Rameses III, may be regarded as a typical temple. It is free of the usual additions and alterations of later Kings, and is thus simple in plan. A processional way lined by sphinxes leads to the pylon, a gateway flanked by two large rectangular towers. The pylon has walls that are battered, that is, they slant back slightly. They are surmounted by a concave cavetto cornice and have round torus moldings on the corners. Its form is derived from that of a primitive wall made of bound reeds that was strengthened by bundles at the corners, allowing the tops of the reeds to wave free. Behind the pylon is an open forecourt surrounded by a colonnade with capitals in the shape of papyrus buds. Next is the pillared hypostyle hall with four pairs of columns. The two center pairs have papyrus-head capitals and are higher than the outer two pairs, which have papyrus-bud capitals. This difference in height permits the hall to be lit by clerestory grill windows.

Beyond the hypostyle hall is the sanctuary, in this case open at both ends and surrounded by an ambulatory. Here rested the boat shrine containing the figure of the god. The sanctuaries in other temples sometimes had only one door and housed a small shrine containing the divine statue.

Statues of the King usually stood in the forecourt of the temple and before the pylon, in the latter case often of colossal size. A pair of monolithic stone pillars, or obelisks, stood on either side of the gateway, and tall flag staffs were fastened in grooves in front of the pylon.

The temple of Rameses II at Abu Simbel is of this type, but instead of being free-standing it is entirely carved from the solid rock of a cliff face. The great Temple of Amon at Karnak has all these features repeated several times by different kings, who added to the work of their predecessors.

A special type of temple known as the peripteral temple, consisting of a small central chamber open at both ends and surrounded by a colonnade, was used principally as a resting house for the statue of the god during religious processions.

Most Egyptian temples have been partly or completely destroyed by people seeking building material or treasure, and many were used by the Christian Egyptians, or Copts, as churches. Much damage to reliefs is due to the religious fervor of the Copts against the earlier pagan religion and to the plundering of modern Egyptians.

Consult Smith, E. B., *Egyptian Architecture as a Cultural Expression* (1938); Lange, Kurt, and Hirmer, Max, *Egypt: Architecture, Sculpture and Painting in Three Thousand Years* (1956); Smith, W. S., *The Art and Architecture of Ancient Egypt* (1958); Edwards, I. E. S., *The Pyramids of Egypt* (1961).

ERIC YOUNG, The Metropolitan Museum of Art
See also PYLON; PYRAMIDS.

Model of the hypostyle hall in the temple of Amon at Karnak. The roof is supported by 134 columns arranged in 16 rows. The central columns are 69 ft. high and are topped by capitals 11 ft. high. (THE METROPOLITAN MUSEUM OF ART, BEQUEST OF LEVI HALE WILLARD, 1883)

EGYPTOLOGY

EGYPTOLOGY [ē-jĭp-tŏl′ə-jē], the study of the archeology and culture of ancient Egypt in all its aspects, such as art, architecture, history, language, literature, and religion. In considering Egypt before the beginning of the historic period, about 3000 B.C., Egyptology naturally merges with general prehistory. Greek influences and artifacts post-dating the conquest by Alexander (332 B.C.) are usually studied as part of Hellenistic culture. The coming of Christianity, about 200 A.D., ends the period with which Egyptology is concerned. However, the Coptic language, a direct descendant of the earlier tongue, belongs to the field of Egyptian philology.

Early Egyptology. At the beginning of the Renaissance, Western knowledge of ancient Egypt was confined to the writings of a number of classical authors, including Herodotus, Diodorus Siculus, Strabo, Ptolemy, Plutarch, and Horapollon; to references in the Bible and remarks by the Jewish historian Josephus; and to ancient Egyptian monuments collected by the Romans, especially obelisks.

By the middle of the 17th century Europeans began to publish accounts of travel in Egypt. The British astronomer John Greaves (1602–52) was in Alexandria in 1637–38, traveled as far as Memphis, and in 1646 wrote *Pyramidographia*, thoroughly reviewing ancient writings and giving his own careful observations and measurements of the pyramids of Giza. Coptic manuscripts began to be brought into Europe at the beginning of this century, and Athanasius Kircher (1601–80) produced, from 1636 onward, scholarly studies of this language. In the next century many Europeans traveled in Egypt and published accounts of their journeys. But a systematic study of Egyptian antiquities really began with Napoleon. Napoleon took with him on his expedition to Egypt in 1798 a great number of scientists, scholars, and artists. One of them, Dominique Vivant Denon (1747–1825), published his own account, but the group concentrated on the publication of *Description de l'Égypte* (1809–28), including five large folios of engravings of the antiquities.

The Decipherment of Hieroglyphs. Kircher had attempted to interpret the hieroglyphic inscriptions, but had followed the lead of Horapollon in believing that the signs were wholly symbolic. In the 18th century many others followed the same course. The Danish Coptic scholar Georg Zoëga (1755–1809) and the French professor of Syriac, Joseph de Guignes (1721–1800), though wrong on other points, had guessed that the cartouches contained the names of royalty. The Swedish diplomat Johan Åkerblad (1760–1819) in 1802 identified about half the alphabet used in the demotic section of the Rosetta Stone; 12 years later the British physician and scientist Thomas Young (1773–1829) read several royal names and made other advances toward decipherment. In 1822 Jean François Champollion (1790–1832), working on the Rosetta Stone, read the name of Rameses from another monument and realized that the hieroglyphic characters and the cursive writing of the same, hieratic, were phonetic renderings of the language, and not symbolic.

Excavation. Most of the major monuments of Egyptian antiquity had never been lost to view, but many others were sites of later villages or individual dwellings, and all had to be cleared. In the ancient necropolis of Memphis and elsewhere the low structures were covered by desert sands. The expedition of Napoleon disclosed that there was an almost inexhaustible supply of antiquities, and for the rest of the century much excavation was merely the collecting of booty. Of those early engaged in such collecting, one of the most careful was Giovanni Belzoni (1778–1823). In general, records of origin were carelessly kept, if at all, and crude methods of excavation were employed. Unwanted objects were cast aside and often destroyed. Frequently the local inhabitants were the actual discoverers of antiquities, and even today some surrepti-

Excavation of the tomb of Mentemhet at Luxor. Mentemhet was a high priest and governor of Upper Egypt during the 25th Dynasty.

H. Wright—Birnback

Workers excavating the temple of Queen Hatshepsut at Deir el-Bahri use a derrick to hoist pieces of stone statuary into position.

The Metropolitan Museum of Art, Egyptian Expedition

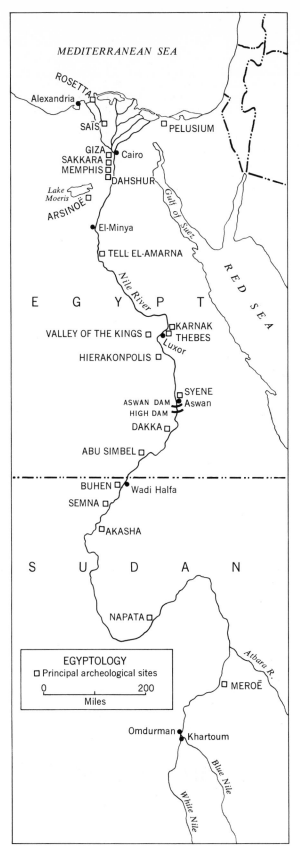

tious excavations continue. Many of the great museum collections of Egyptian antiquities were acquired through these early unscientific excavations.

In an effort to control excavation, Auguste Mariette (1821–81) was appointed Conservator of Monuments in 1858, and in 1899 the Department of Antiquities was organized under Gaston Maspero (1846–1916). Mariette also founded the first Museum of Antiquities in Cairo. At present all archeological activities in Egypt are under the control of the Department of Antiquities. Permits for excavating are given only to experienced scholars representing institutions of learning. The majority of objects found and all unique pieces are retained by the Egyptian Museum.

Mariette began excavating Sakkara in 1850, systematically exploring the Serapeum, the burial complex of the Apis bulls. Later he uncovered many mastabas (tomb superstructures) of the officials of the Old Kingdom. Just before his death in 1881 he found the inner chambers of the Sakkara pyramids, with walls covered with Pyramid Texts. These earliest religious writings are the foundation for any study of Egyptian religion. Various excavators working for the Department of Antiquities have excavated the mud-brick mastabas of the first two dynasties, the temple complex of the Step Pyramid of the 3d Dynasty, and an unfinished step pyramid.

The Giza pyramids were examined and measured by Richard Howard-Vyse and John Shae Perring in 1837–38. In 1880 Flinders Petrie (1853–1942) made more exact measurements. The tombs of the officials of this area were excavated by Selim Hassan for the Egyptian University, Hermann Junker for the Austrian Academy of Science, and George Reisner for the Boston Museum of Fine Arts and Harvard University. Reisner found in 1925 the hidden tomb of Hetepheres, mother of Khufu (Cheops). Through careful observation and removal of the disintegrated remains it was possible to reconstruct the gold-inlaid furniture. In 1954 a dismantled solar ship belonging to Khufu was found in a pit alongside the Great Pyramid, and is being reassembled.

Many tomb chapels of Tell el-Amarna were known to early travelers. The town site first came to attention in 1887, when natives offered for sale clay tablets with cuneiform writing. Wallis Budge of the British Museum purchased many. They proved to be the official correspondence of Asiatic princes with Amenhotep III and Akhenaton. Petrie excavated here in 1891–92. The best of the Amarna sculpture, including the painted head of Nefertiti, was found by Ludwig Borchardt (1863–1938) of the German Oriental Society in excavations from 1907 to 1914. From this area comes much knowledge of the Amarna religious revolution.

Most of the burials from the vicinity of ancient Thebes were robbed in ancient times, and records of the trials of the thieves are extant. In 1871 a local inhabitant discovered a cache containing mummies of some of the Kings of the 18th-20th dynasties, and ten years later these came to the attention of the authorities. No unrobbed royal tomb was known until 1922, when Howard Carter (1873–1939) found the burial chamber of Tutankhamen, which showed the splendor of the funerary equipment of even a minor Pharaoh.

Collecting the Records. When Champollion deciphered the hieroglyphs there was no body of Egyptian texts available. He sought to remedy this by his copies. Systematic recording of the monuments began with the Prussian expedition of 1842–45 under Karl Richard Lepsius (1810–84), which completed 12 giant folios. Standards of accuracy improved, and reliable copies of a great number of inscriptions are now available. The French Archaeological Institute has been copying temples of the Ptolemaic and Roman periods. The Egypt Exploration Society of London has published, in *Archaeological Survey of Egypt*, descriptions of many tomb chapels throughout Egypt. Norman de Garis Davies (1865–1941), who did much of this, also made records for the Metropolitan Museum of Art in New York. Since 1924 the Oriental Institute of the University of Chicago has produced copies of the scenes and inscriptions of the temples of Ramesses III about Luxor.

In 1897 the Prussian Academy of Science inaugurated a project for a hieroglyphic dictionary under the editorship of Adolf Erman (1854–1937). To collect material, leading Egyptologists gave their assistance for the next 15 years, copying inscriptions in museums and in Egypt. Especially able was Kurt Sethe (1869–1934), whose copies have formed the basis of many publications by himself and his pupils. The dictionary began to be published in 1926, the last volume of references appearing in 1953.

Papyri are other sources of information. On them are written stories, historical records, letters, accounts, and religious literature, including the Book of the Dead. The most important documents have been well published.

Linguistic Studies. For almost 60 years after Champollion there was no real understanding of the grammar of ancient Egyptian, but with Erman's analysis of Late Egyptian in 1880 a systematic examination was begun. As Erman continued to make advances, other scholars supported him. His methods provided a firm foundation for futher research on the structure of the language, and modern translations have a high degree of accuracy. Among the leading contemporary grammarians are Sir Alan Gardiner of England and Elmar Edel of Germany.

Centers of Egyptology. The largest collection of Egyptian antiquities, including the Tutankhamen treasure, is in the Egyptian Museum, Cairo. In Europe outstanding collections are in the museums of Berlin, Leiden, Turin, the Louvre in Paris, and the British Museum. In the United States the Museum of Fine Arts, Boston, the Metropolitan Museum of Art and the Brooklyn Museum, and the University Museum, Philadelphia, contain the largest collections; an excellent smaller one is at the Oriental Institute, Chicago.

The Department of Antiquities of Egypt is now foremost in excavation. In Cairo are the French Institute of Oriental Archaeology (founded, 1881), the German Archaeological Institute, the Swiss Archaeological Institute (a private institution), and several smaller centers. The Egypt Exploration Fund, later the Egypt Exploration Society, of London, has been working since 1882 recording inscriptions and excavating. The Oriental Institute of Chicago has permanent headquarters in Luxor.

Consult Ceram, C. W., *Gods, Graves, and Scholars* (1951); Cottrell, Leonard, *The Lost Pharaohs* (1951); Edwards, I. E. S., *The Pyramids of Egypt* (rev. ed., 1961); Gardiner, Sir Alan, *Egypt of the Pharaohs* (1961); *Journal of Egyptian Archaeology* (annually since 1914).

CHARLES FRANCIS NIMS, Oriental Institute, Chicago

EHRENBURG [ā′rən-bŏŏrKH], **ILYA GRIGORIEVICH** (1891–1967), Soviet novelist and journalist. He was born of Jewish middle-class parents, and spent most of the period 1909–41 in Paris. His work, after his early satiric novels, reflected the prevailing political currents in the Soviet

Part of the outstanding collection of Egyptian antiquities on view at the British Museum, London. In the foreground is the massive sarcophagus of an ancient scribe. (ART REFERENCE BUREAU)

The opening of the trial of Adolf Eichmann at Beit Ha'amin, Jerusalem, on April 11, 1961. Eichmann (standing in bullet-proof enclosure, left), was convicted of crimes against humanity and of war crimes, and was hanged.

Israel Office of Information

Union. He was a leading journalist and war propagandist in World War II. His best-known works include *Out of Chaos* (1933; trans., 1934), *The Fall of Paris* (1941; trans., 1942), *The Storm* (1948; trans., 1949), and *The Thaw* (1954; trans., 1955). The last of these works attracted world attention to the relaxation of literary censorship following Stalin's death.

EHRLICH [ār'lĭкн], **PAUL** (1854–1915), German bacteriologist and immunologist, who pioneered in the development of chemicals in the treatment of infectious diseases. In 1908 he shared the Nobel Prize with Élie Metchnikoff for studies on the mechanism of immunity. In 1909 Ehrlich and his coworkers succeeded in finding a potent antisyphilitic agent called salvarsan, or arsphenamine, or popularly, "606," since it was the 606th compound tested by Ehrlich and his group. Ehrlich's other contributions included the development of staining techniques for use in the laboratory and the introduction of various laboratory tests and blood-counting techniques.

EICHELBERGER [ī'kəl-bûr-gər], **ROBERT LAWRENCE** (1886–1961), American Army officer, commander of U.S. forces in the Pacific during World War II. He was born in Urbana, Ohio, and graduated (1909) from the U.S. Military Academy. He was assistant chief of staff (1918–20) to the U.S. commander in Siberia; chief of military intelligence (1920) in the Philippines; and a member (1921–24) of the military intelligence division of the general staff. After serving as adjutant general (1931–35) and as superintendent of the U.S. Military Academy (1940–42), he led (1942) the First Corps in New Guinea and New Britain. He participated (1944) in the capture of the Philippines as head of the Eighth Army and commanded (1946) Allied occupation forces in Japan under Gen. Douglas MacArthur. Eichelberger retired in 1948. He wrote *Our Jungle Road to Toyko* (1950).

EICHENDORFF [ī'кнən-dôrf], **JOSEPH, BARON VON** (1788–1857), German poet. Born of noble ancestry, he studied law at the universities of Halle and Heidelberg, eventually becoming a high government official. In his lyric poems, he has created the typical poetic landscape of German romanticism, with its rustling forests, moonlit brooks, old castles, and the distant sound of the post horn. His poetry is simple in style, imbued with a deep religious feeling, and has always enjoyed great popularity. Eichendorff's most famous prose work is *Aus dem Leben eines Taugenichts*, 1826 (*Memoirs of a Good-for-Nothing*, trans. by B. Q. Morgan, 1955), a poetic glorification of a carefree life without toil.

EICHMANN [īкн'män], **(KARL) ADOLF** (1906–62), Nazi official. Born in Germany but raised in Austria, Eichmann joined the Austrian National Socialist party in 1931. In 1933 he went to Germany as a member of the Austrian Legion and a year later was transferred to the main office of the German SD (Security Service) under the infamous Reinhard Heydrich. Eichmann's rise to prominence began in 1938 with his appointment to head the Office for Jewish Emigration in Vienna during 1938, which became, under Eichmann, the central agency for administering the extermination of the Jews. Responsible for the deportation of German and western European Jews to the extermination camps of Eastern Europe and for the policies of these camps, Eichmann persisted in this "final solution" of the Jewish problem until his disappearance in Apr., 1945. Seized by Israeli agents in Argentina in May, 1960, he was brought to trial in Israel and convicted and hanged for crimes against humanity (mass murder) and war crimes during World War II.

LEONARD KRIEGER, Yale University

EIDER [ī'dər] **DUCK,** name for several species of hardy sea ducks native to arctic and subarctic regions of the Northern Hemisphere. The common eider, *Somateria mollissima*, of northern Europe, Iceland, and northern North America grows to a length of 2 ft. The males are handsome birds with velvety black underparts, snowy white breast and back, and a black-capped head; the females are a barred, dark brown. The eider is semidomesticated in Iceland where eider down is collected. This soft down is

A common eider duck incubates her eggs in a nest lined with down feathers plucked from her breast.

plucked by the breeding female from her breast and used to line a rocky depression that serves as a crude nest. *See also* DUCK.

EIFFEL [ĕ-fĕl′], **ALEXANDRE GUSTAVE** (1832–1923), French civil engineer regarded as the father of metal construction in France. His works reflect the combination of a keen aesthetic sense with a flair for the unusual and daring which still characterize French structural design. His great arches of the "Galerie des Machines" of the Universal Exposition in Paris in 1867 were one of the first displays of metal as an architectural material. The 984-ft.-high "Tour Eiffel" of the Exposition of 1889, long the tallest structure in the world, emphasized awe-inspiring possibilities of iron.

EIFFEL [ī′fəl] **TOWER,** structure designed and erected by Alexandre Gustave Eiffel (1832–1923) to serve as the focal point of the 1889 Universal Exposition in Paris. Now a familiar part of the Paris skyline, the 984-ft.-high tower is composed of four cast-iron, latticework columns that rest on four masonry piers. The four inward-leaning columns sweep upward, joining together in one shaft at 620 ft. Elevators and staircases give access to three observation platforms.

EILAT [ā-lät′] **or ELATH** [ĕ′lăth], port of extreme southern Israel, at the head of the Gulf of Aqaba (or Eilat), an extension of the Red Sea. Eilat is Israel's gateway to the Far East and Africa. The town is at the southern end of the Arava (the Plain), enclosed by two mountain ranges: Sinai in Egypt on the west, and Edom in Jordan on the east.

Eilat is a thriving industrial center and port. New industries include diamond polishing, Red Sea fishing, building, furniture making, and tourism. The port has also become an oil-pipe terminal, from which oil is pumped to Haifa for refining and export to Europe. The Timna copper-smelting plant and mines, 20 mi. from Eilat, are on the site where King Solomon once mined copper. A marine museum and gardens are features of Eilat. In ancient times the city was an important harbor of the kingdom of Judah and for the nearby naval base of Etzion Geber, from which Solomon sailed.

The section of the Israeli coast at Eilat extends over 5 mi. Because the coast of the Gulf of Aqaba is shared by four countries (Saudi Arabia occupies the eastern shore), it is an important strategic area. Between 1949 and 1956 Egyptian gun batteries on the Sinai shore prevented ships of Israel or other countries from sailing to and from Eilat. During Israel's Sinai operation in 1956 these batteries were removed, and when the Israeli forces withdrew, a U.N. detachment occupied the site. Ships of all flags now use the gulf. Pop., 5,702.

YAAKOV MORRIS, Consul of Israel in New York City

EILSHEMIUS [īl-shē′mē-əs], **LOUIS MICHEL** (1864–1941), American painter, born at Laurel Manor, near Newark, N.J. Although his romantic landscapes were long rejected by galleries and dealers, he finally gained recognition late in his life and is now represented in many leading galleries. "Delaware Water Gap Village" is in the Metropolitan Museum of Art in New York. Eilshemius also painted figure studies.

EINAUDI [ā-nou′dē], **LUIGI** (1874–1961), Italian economist and first President of Italy (1948–55). Einaudi taught economics at the University of Turin until 1942, when his opposition to fascism forced him to flee to Switzerland. Upon returning to Italy he served (1945–48) as governor of the Bank of Italy and became (1947) Vice-Premier and Minister of the Budget in the Christian Democratic government of Alcide de Gasperi. Einaudi's policies stemmed inflation and stabilized the currency. Though holding conservative economic views, he recognized the need for social and economic reforms and was an advocate of European unity.

EINDHOVEN [īnt′hō-vən], industrial city of the south Netherlands in wooded heathland country, about 75 mi. south of Amsterdam. Eindhoven is largely a product of the age of electricity. Since 1891 it has been noted for the

The Eiffel Tower stands in a wooded park called the Champ-de-Mars.

manufacture of electric bulbs. When the industry was established here it had only 26 employees and the village had a population of less than 5,000. By 1960 the N. V. Philips Gloeilampenfabrieken employed more than 35,000 workers, and the city had become the sixth-largest in the country. The workers live in model-housing estates. Eindhoven has the only automobile factory in the Netherlands; other products include cigars, paper, radios, and textiles. The town was chartered in 1232. Vincent van Gogh lived here for many years. Eindhoven was a primary target of Allied aircraft during the German occupation in World War II. Pop., 157,621.

EINEM [ī′nəm], **GOTTFRIED VON** (1918–), Austrian composer, born in Berne, Switzerland. He is considered one of Austria's leading contemporary composers. His compositions show strong Stravinsky and jazz influences. His operas *Danton's Death* (1947) and *The Trial* (1953), the latter based on Kafka's story, have won him acclaim; his other works include ballets and orchestral pieces.

EINHARD [īn′härt] **or EGINHARD** [ā′gĭn-härt] (c.770–840), biographer of Charlemagne. Educated at the monastery of Fulda and later in Charlemagne's palace-school, he became minister of public works at the court. After the Emperor's death in 814, Einhard remained at the court until 830, when he retired to the abbey at Mulinheim, where he wrote Charlemagne's biography. The work, in 33 chapters, was written in Latin modeled on Suetonius and gives a detailed account of Charlemagne's personal habits.

EINSIEDELN [īn′zē-dəln], Benedictine abbey founded in 937 by St. Benno, on the site of a hermitage made famous by St. Meinrad, in the Canton of Schwyz, Switzerland. The abbots of Einsiedeln were made Princes of the Holy Roman Empire by Otto I in 965, and the abbey grew in reputation and power. Because of a miraculous statue of Our Lady of the Hermits set up there by St. Meinrad, the abbey is a center of pilgrimage, annually attracting 150,-000 to 200,000 pilgrims. In 1854 the abbey sent a colony of monks to America, where they founded St. Meinrad's Abbey in Indiana.

EINSTEIN [īn′stīn], **ALBERT** (1879–1955). In the recorded history of physical science, three scientists stand out: Archimedes, Newton, and Einstein. Einstein is best known for his theory of relativity, of which the celebrated formula $E = mc^2$, relating energy and mass, is a comparatively minor consequence. Yet that monumental theory was far from being his only major contribution to science. His work embraced the very large and the very small, and his ideas revolutionized scientific thought.

He was born in Ulm, Germany, but while he was still an infant, the family, suffering financial reverses, moved to Munich, and some 14 years later to Milan, Italy. The sense of wonder about the universe that inspired all of Einstein's work seems to have come to him at the age of four or five, when he became enthralled by the apparently magical behavior of a magnetic compass needle, for at the age of 70, in his autobiography, he wrote, with quaint logic, "I can still remember—or at least I believe I remem-

ber—that this experience made a deep and lasting impression on me."

As a youth, he taught himself calculus and science, and at age 17 he entered the Polytechnic Institute of Zurich. There he neglected his mathematics to perform experiments and study the writings of the great physicists, and on graduating he had to seek a job. Eventually, in 1902 he became a patent examiner in the Swiss Patent Office in Berne. Here, isolated and in scientific obscurity, he matured his ideas; and here, in 1905, his genius suddenly burst into flower. In that fabulous year he applied Planck's hypothesis of the quantum to the photoelectric effect, establishing the validity of the quantum hypothesis and extending its range; he made calculations pertaining to the Brownian movement that were instrumental in finally convincing scientists that atoms really exist; and he wrote a paper on electrodynamics and motion that presented what is now called the special theory of relativity (*see* RELATIVITY, THEORY OF), following it with a paper deducing the formula $E = mc^2$, which, at the time, like all his ideas, seemed to have little practical application.

These were dazzling discoveries—in three different branches of physics. Einstein developed them further in a quick succession of papers. Yet they were so revolutionary that few scientists immediately realized their significance, and it was not till 1909 that Einstein left the Patent Office for a professorial position at the University of Zurich. After holding professorships at the University of Prague (1911) and the Polytechnic Institute in Zurich (1912), where his potentialities had gone unrecognized when he was a student, he went to Berlin in 1914 as professor at the Royal Prussian Academy of Sciences and Director of the Kaiser Wilhelm Institute of Physics. In 1915, after 10 years of intense effort, he succeeded in generalizing his theory of relativity, creating thereby a theory of gravitation, in terms of a curved, four-dimensional world, that superseded the Newtonian theory that had held sway for more than 200 years. In 1917 he applied his theory to the problem of the shape and size of the universe and opened up a vast new field of research in cosmology. To the end of his life he strove to extend his theory still further by producing a unified field theory that would include all physical forces within one geometrical structure.

Despite prevailing scientific opinion and his own crucial contributions to the development of the quantum theory, he did not accept as final the modern probabilistic form of that theory with its denial of classical causality. He defended his views with subtle arguments and summed them up in the aphorism, "God does not play dice."

Einstein was more than a scientist. He was a courageous humanitarian in a dangerous age; a man of principle and stern conscience who was outspoken in the cause of freedom. And he was a Jew. He was not a Jew for formal religious reasons: though he was a deeply religious man, he did not feel the need for ritual, nor did he subscribe to the more pictorial aspects of formal religious belief. He believed firmly that there is a God, though not necessarily a God interested in the individual. In creating his scientific theories he sought always for simplicity and beauty, asking himself whether he would have made the universe that way had he been God. Once, irked by an irrational objection, he said, "God is deep, but he is not malicious," a re-

Albert Einstein, whose theory of relativity was a monumental contribution to science. © PHILIPPE HALSMAN

mark that is inscribed in marble, in the original German, in the mathematics building at Princeton University.

Einstein's general theory of relativity brought him world-wide fame. But it also provoked bitter opposition from anti-Semites, from nonscientists who could not forgive his active pacificism, and even from important scientists who could not accept the strange concepts of space and time that his theory entailed. Therefore, the 1921 Nobel Prize was awarded him ostensibly "for the photoelectric law and his work in the field of theoretical physics."

Rising anti-Semitism caused Einstein to identify himself ever more closely with Jewry. In 1933 the Nazis confiscated his property, and there were rumors that a price had been placed on his head. Fortunately he was not in Germany at the time, and after a brief sojourn in Belgium he went to the United States as a professor at the newly created Institute for Advanced Study in Princeton, N.J., where he remained until his death. He was tireless in his efforts to awaken the world to the dangers of nazism and to aid people to escape from Nazi persecution. In 1939, shortly before the outbreak of World War II, scientists in America tried in vain to alert the government to the frightful potentialities of the newly discovered process of nuclear fission. In desperation, they approached Einstein. And thus it came about that the former pacifist, fearful that the Nazis might make the first atomic bomb and rule the world, wrote to President Roosevelt the fateful letter that was to lead to what to Einstein must have been the supreme irony of a practical application of $E = mc^2$.

Consult Frank, P. G., *Einstein: His Life and Times* (1953); Barnett, Lincoln, *The Universe and Dr. Einstein* (rev. ed., 1957); *Albert Einstein: Philosopher-Scientist*, ed. by P. A. Schilpp (1959).

BANESH HOFFMANN, Queens College

EINSTEIN, ALFRED (1880–1952), eminent musicologist, born in Munich, Germany. A cousin of Albert Einstein, the famous physicist, he studied music at Munich University, edited several German music magazines, and was music critic of the *Berliner Tageblatt* newspaper (1927–33). He went to the United States in 1938, became a citizen in 1945, taught at Smith College (1939–50), and was visiting professor at Yale and Princeton universities (1949–50). He was a foremost Mozart scholar, and one of his most important contributions is a revised edition (1937; reprinted and corrected in 1947) of the Köchel catalog of Mozart's works.

EINSTEINIUM [īn-stĭn'ē-əm], radioactive metallic element (symbol Es; atomic number 99) of the actinide series; it is not found in nature. It was detected in 1952 among the debris of the first H-bomb explosion. In 1953 it was formed in the laboratory. Its longest-lived isotope is Es^{254}, which emits alpha particles and has a half life of 300 days.

EINTHOVEN [īnt'hō-vən], **WILLEM** (1860–1927), Dutch physiologist who was awarded the Nobel Prize in 1924 for his work on the string galvanometer, an instrument for measuring the electric activity of the heart. Although it had been known for some time that the contraction of the heart produces weak electric currents, recording and measurement of these currents first became feasible with Einthoven's galvanometer, which enabled physicians to receive electric "telegrams from the heart." For many years the string galvanometer formed the basis of the electrocardiograph used to diagnose heart disease. It was eventually superseded by more sophisticated apparatus.

EIRE. *See* IRELAND, REPUBLIC OF.

EISENACH [ī'zə-näкн], city of the west-central German Democratic Republic (East Germany), in the district of Erfurt, west of Erfurt. Located at the northern edge of the Thuringian Forest, it is surrounded by beautiful countryside and is a popular tourist center. The town is connected with the name of Martin Luther, who made his translation of the Bible there. Nearby, on a cliff 600 ft. above the town, is the Wartburg, where Luther was kept in hiding, to be protected from persecution. Eisenach has a school of forestry, a teachers' seminary, two museums, a theater, a library, a botanical garden, and a zoological garden. Industries include the manufacture of automobiles, agricultural machinery, textiles, beer, shoes, lumber, leather, and tobacco. Eisenach was founded in the 11th century. It has many historic buildings, including two 12th-century churches, of which the Nikolaikirche is the more notable; a 16th-century town hall; the birthplace of Johann Sebastian Bach; and a Luther memorial. Pop., 48,853.

JOACHIM MARQUARDT, Commercial School for Merchants, Berlin-Wilmersdorf

EISENERZ [ī'zən-ĕrts], mining community and market town of Austria, located in the province of Styria, 16 mi. northwest of Leoben, at the foot of the famous Erzberg ("ore mountain"). Iron ore has been mined here since Celtic times, and is the basis of a modern iron and steel industry. Pop., 12,759.

DWIGHT DAVID EISENHOWER

34th PRESIDENT OF THE
UNITED STATES

1953-1961

Library of Congress

Peace Negotiations, Korea

Wide World

Mamie Doud Eisenhower

Supreme Court Hears Civil Rights Case

EISENHOWER [ī′zən-hou-ər], **DWIGHT DAVID** (1890–), 34th President of the United States (1953–61). His ancestors on his father's side came from Germany and lived for many generations in Pennsylvania before moving to Kansas with a colony of the River Brethren. There, near Abilene, the Eisenhowers sank new roots into the soil. David J. and Ida Elizabeth (Stover) Eisenhower were living temporarily in Denison, Tex., when Dwight David was born to them on Oct. 14, 1890. The following spring the family returned to Abilene, where Dwight grew up—the product of a sternly religious home not far removed from the frontier.

Youth. The family was poor, and Dwight's experience selling vegetables to the more prosperous people on the other side of town gave him a lifelong hatred of snobbery. His most harrowing experience in youth was blood poisoning. The doctor pleaded with his parents for permission to amputate his swollen and blackened leg, but Dwight said he would rather die than have his leg removed. He exacted a promise from his brother Edgar to sleep by his door and protect him from any amputation after he lapsed into unconsciousness. It was his good fortune to escape surgery.

After completing his schooling at Abilene, Dwight drifted for a year before making up his mind about his future. Meanwhile he worked 12 hours a day in a creamery and, at his suggestion, lent part of his salary to Edgar to pay his tuition in law school. A friend who was preparing to attend the U.S. Naval Academy induced Dwight to take the competitive examination for a similar appointment. He passed the test for both the naval and military academies and was disappointed when he was given an appointment to West Point instead of Annapolis.

Cadet Eisenhower proved to be more outstanding in athletics than in scholarship, until he injured his knee in a football game in 1912. At graduation he stood 61st in a class of 164. His first assignment as an Infantry lieutenant took him to San Antonio in the summer of 1915. There he met Mamie Geneva Doud, daughter of a prosperous Denver family. Within a year they were married. Two sons were born to them, Dwight Doud, who died of scarlet fever in 1921, and John Sheldon Doud, who followed his father in a military career.

Military Career. During World War I Eisenhower was assigned to the training of officers. His work as commander of a tank training school was so effective that his assignment to the fighting front in Europe was postponed until Nov., 1918, and the Armistice intervened to deny him the overseas experience that he had eagerly sought. In 1922 Maj. Eisenhower was sent to the Panama Canal Zone for a tour of duty and then to the Command and General Staff School at Fort Leavenworth, Kans. He emerged first in a class of 275 that included some of the ablest younger men in the Army. An assignment with the Battle Monuments Commission then took him to Paris and gave him an opportunity to survey all the battlefields of World War I. Returning to Washington, he participated in a study of plans for conversion of the nation's industry and economy to a wartime basis in case of need.

At times during the depression years of the early 1930's Eisenhower was discouraged over his seeming lack of progress in the Army and seriously contemplated resigning his commission. In 1935, however, he was chosen by Gen. Douglas MacArthur to assist in developing a defense system for the new Philippine Commonwealth. They su-

347

Eisenhower, a cadet at West Point.

American paratroopers in England listen intently to Gen. Eisenhower on the eve of the momentous invasion of Normandy, on June 6, 1944.

pervised the founding of a Philippine military academy, the organization and training of military forces, and the development of potential war plans that both would later use. It was there that Eisenhower first acquired a reputation for diplomacy because of his skill in working with the Filipino people and in winning their confidence.

Lt. Col. Eisenhower returned from the Philippines in 1939 after the start of World War II. As executive officer of the 15th Infantry Regiment, he became known as "Alarmist Ike" because of the fears he expressed over the evolving international situation. After serving as chief of staff of the 3d Division stationed at Fort Lewis, Wash., he was advanced to be chief of staff to the 9th Army Corps. Then he earned the rank (temporary) of brigadier general in war games in Louisiana. He was working feverishly in San Antonio when the Japanese attack on Pearl Harbor brought the United States into the war on Dec. 7, 1941.

World War II and After. Eisenhower's highest ambition at this time appears to have been to command a combat division. Instead, he was summoned to Washington to assist in working out major war plans. His first responsibility was to improvise a holding operation in the Pacific until the United States could slowly gather its strength to take the initiative there. Then he turned his attention to an Allied invasion of German dictator Adolf Hitler's "Fortress Europe." This task took him to London where he worked closely with top British generals. When he had completed a detailed set of instructions for the conduct of the invasion and laid it before Chief of Staff Gen. George C. Marshall, Eisenhower was told that he himself had been chosen to direct the great invasion. Again he went to England and labored day and night to assemble an international force that would be powerful enough for a direct assault upon the Continent. The watchwords of his undertaking were unity among the Allies and tactical co-operation among the various branches of the armed forces.

Meanwhile, Soviet Premier Joseph Stalin was calling for a second front in Western Europe to relieve the pressure of Hitler's army, then fighting deep into Russia. Since many months of preparation were still essential to assure the success of a frontal attack across the English Channel, the Allies decided to invade North Africa, and the command fell to Eisenhower. His troops met with some reverses and there was much furor over the temporary political arrangements with discredited French leaders in North Africa, for which the State Department seemed to be largely responsible. The Germans were forced to withdraw, however, and the conquest was then extended to Sicily and Italy. Italian dictator Benito Mussolini's regime collapsed (July, 1943), but the Germans fought doggedly as they withdrew from the peninsula, inflicting near disaster on the Allied forces that landed at Salerno in the hope of cutting off the Nazi retreat from southern Italy.

While the fighting continued, Eisenhower met with President Franklin D. Roosevelt, British Prime Minister Winston Churchill, and other top leaders of the Allies at Quebec, Canada, and later in North Africa. Eisenhower was the unanimous choice of the Allied statesmen to command the major action of World War II—the assault upon Hitler's fortress from the west. The great invasion began on June 6, 1944, on the beaches of Normandy. Gen. "Ike," as he was affectionately known to the troops, sent 15,000 aircraft, 6,000 ships, and half a million men into action. Within a year the mighty Third Reich was crushed.

Eisenhower accepted the unconditional surrender of the Nazi high command and returned home to a hero's welcome. During the period of the country's demobilization he served as Army chief of staff for two years, giving much of his time to unification of the armed forces. In 1948 he left the Army and became president of Columbia University in the belief that he could speak more freely as a civilian about the alarming conditions that were developing in the world. The flimsy alliance of the Western powers with the Soviet Union was falling apart. The Soviet

On a visit to Korea in Dec., 1952, President-elect Eisenhower shares chow with American troops.

President Eisenhower forcefully presents his atoms-for-peace plan to the U.N. General Assembly on Dec. 8, 1953.

Union was extending its conquests and infiltrating Europe, and was soon to be in conflict with the United Nations because of the aggressive attack launched by its protégé, North Korea, against South Korea. In an effort to strengthen their defenses, nine European nations joined the United States, Canada, and Iceland in setting up the North Atlantic Treaty Organization (NATO). President Harry S. Truman called Eisenhower back into military service to lay the groundwork for this new defense system. He flew to Paris and again plunged into an enormous task of organizing inadequate national units into a common shield for the countries of the Atlantic community. Meanwhile he continued to preach the doctrine of European unity and Free World co-operation in meeting the Communist threat.

President. While Eisenhower was still in Paris, movements developed to draft him for the presidential nominations of both major parties. In a Gallup Poll, 40% of the Democrats and 30% of the Republicans responding named him as their favorite candidate. Though in 1948 he had warned against the participation of professional soldiers in politics, except in the most unusual circumstances, in Jan., 1952, he disclosed that he had a Republican voting record and later permitted his name to be entered in the New Hampshire primary. Released from his NATO assignment, he returned home in June and engaged in a spirited contest with Sen. Robert A. Taft for the Republican presidential nomination. After being nominated at Chicago, with Sen. Richard M. Nixon of California as his running mate, Eisenhower waged a vigorous and successful campaign against Governor Adlai E. Stevenson of Illinois, the Democratic candidate.

The campaign began with the slogans "I like Ike" and "It's time for a change" but ended with the Korean War as its focal point. Eisenhower announced that, if elected, he would go to Korea and try to bring the war to "an early and honorable end." After his victory (by the largest vote

ever given a presidential candidate up to that time) he flew secretly to Korea before his inauguration. The policy resulting from this visit was one of applying increasing pressure upon the North Koreans and their Chinese allies. An armistice was finally signed in July, 1953.

Foreign and Defense Policies. Along with efforts to tighten and extend the U.S. defense system, President Eisenhower made conciliatory bids for better relations with the Soviet Union. After the death of Stalin, Eisenhower called on the new leadership of Russia "to help turn the tide of history." If sincerity, peaceful purposes, and disarmament could be substituted for the cold war, he said, the United States would devote a substantial part of what could be saved "to a fund for world aid and reconstruction." In his first year he also offered his atoms-for-peace plan. This idea finally bore fruit with the creation of an international atomic pool for peaceful purposes. The broad international foundation of his policy was further illustrated by his continuous fight for U.S. aid to other independent countries and his efforts for freer international trade.

His attempt to bring about better relations with the Soviet Union came to a climax in the summit conference in Geneva in 1955, where Eisenhower unfolded his "open skies" proposal for unlimited observation of all defense preparations from the air. Nikita Khrushchev of the Soviet Union rejected this proposal, and an agreement in principle to continue working for European security, reunification of Germany, arms limitation, and freer cultural contacts brought no results, except an increase in the exchange of visitors. Failure of the "open skies" proposal caused Eisenhower to order secret espionage flights over the Soviet Union by U.S. high-flying U-2 planes to offset the Soviet Union's ready access to information about American defenses. One of these planes was shot down over Russia in 1960 on the eve of the second summit conference in Paris. The resulting uproar, which came shortly

349

President Eisenhower (with French President René Coty) arrives in Paris for the NATO summit conference of Dec., 1957.

after Khrushchev had toured the United States, led to a breakdown of the conference and to cancellation of the Soviet's invitation to Eisenhower to make a good-will tour of Russia.

Rivalry between the Communist bloc and the Free World brought the two close to war on several occasions. Eisenhower and Secretary of State John Foster Dulles offered to intervene in the fighting in Indochina, along with Britain and France, if certain conditions were met. But there was no agreement and Indochina was divided between Communist and anti-Communist factions. The struggle to save Indochina led to the organization of the Southeast Asia Treaty Organization (SEATO) as a shield against future aggression in that part of Asia. The United States also entered into a mutual-aid treaty with Nationalist China's President Chiang Kai-shek for the defense of Formosa, which Japan had ceded to China following World War II. When Communist China threatened to seize Formosa and made war on Chiang's forces on the island of Quemoy off the Chinese mainland, Eisenhower asked Congress for authority to use U.S. forces to repel any assault aimed at Formosa or the Pescadores. Congress gave its consent almost unanimously, and the Communist threats against Formosa went no further than the shelling of Quemoy.

By the "Eisenhower Doctrine," announced in 1957, the United States pledged economic and military assistance to any Middle Eastern country threatened by Communist aggression. The doctrine was first applied in 1958, when U.S. troops were sent to Lebanon at the request of its government to avert chaos and subversion. As soon as the trouble subsided, the troops were withdrawn. Eisenhower's impartiality in resisting aggression was manifested in 1956, when he opposed the British-French-Israel invasion of Egypt in connection with a dispute over the Suez Canal. This caused serious friction among the Western powers at the time, but it enhanced the prestige of the United States with the uncommitted nations, and the ties of friendship with Britain, France, and Israel weathered the storm.

Confidence in American leadership in the struggle with communism was shaken when Soviet Russia launched its first earth satellite in 1957. Eisenhower responded by speeding up the long-range ballistic missile program, bringing in new scientific advisers, and creating a new agency to explore outer space. Some of his critics demanded a more general build-up of military strength, but Eisenhower held to his moderate course. Most of the complaints about his military budgets were centered in the alleged inadequacy of forces to fight conventional wars. He relied heavily upon the United States' nuclear bombs to prevent war from breaking out, but as bombs piled up in both the United States and the Soviet Union and men increasingly realized the perils of using them, the usefulness of conventional forces was re-emphasized.

Domestic Affairs. In the domestic field also Eisenhower followed a middle-of-the-road course. He guardedly used the powers of government to counteract mild economic recessions in 1954 and 1958. He tried to liquidate the previous agricultural policy of acreage controls and high price supports, but got little co-operation from Congress. He stirred up a bitter fight with the advocates of public power when he had the Atomic Energy Commission contract with the Dixon-Yates utilities combine for construction of a power plant near Memphis to feed electricity into the Tennessee Valley Authority's system. He reformed the government's security procedures, and before the end of his administration the furor over alleged Communists in government had largely subsided.

The Democrats won control of Congress in 1954, and for the next six years the Republicans were in the minority. This gave Eisenhower a difficult problem in the enactment of his legislative program. His appeals were usually addressed to legislators of both parties, however, and he often won as much support from the Democrats as from the Republicans. His record in winning legislative support was fairly good, even though he refused to coerce members of Congress by means of patronage and political manipulations.

At the White House Eisenhower introduced a new type of organization akin to the military staff system. All major questions of policy were discussed in the Cabinet, the National Security Council, or other advisory bodies, although the President in the end made the basic decisions. Under his direction the Cabinet became a systematic policy-shaping body with a secretariat and a group of expediters to see that final policies were put into effect.

The President suffered a heart attack in Sept., 1955, and there was much speculation as to whether he would seek a second term. The outlook was further clouded when he underwent an operation in June, 1956, for removal of an intestinal obstruction. In both instances, however, his recovery was prompt and complete. The Republican National Convention in San Francisco nominated him for a second term by acclamation. Once more his Democratic opponent was Adlai Stevenson, and the campaign was a repetition of 1952, with some new issues. Eisenhower's popular vote was larger than he had received in 1952; he received 457 electoral votes, carrying 41 states, Stevenson, 74 from 7 states. His victory was largely personal, however, for the Democrats won control of both houses of Congress. This was a keen disappointment to the President. He had not been able to transfer his own popularity to his party. In part this seemed to reflect the lukewarm attitude of some Republicans toward him. Though they helped him win on election day, many of them in and out of Congress accepted his leadership reluctantly, thus tending to blight his long-range hope for the rejuvenation of his party.

After he suffered a slight stroke in 1957, Eisenhower sought an amendment to the Constitution to make clear that the Vice-President could serve temporarily in the White House, in case of inability on the part of the President, without compromising the right of the President to regain his powers upon his recovery. Congress failed to act on the proposal. The following year, therefore, Eisenhower made an agreement with Vice-President Nixon to the effect that the latter would act temporarily as President, in case of presidential inability, with the understanding that the President could regain his powers and functions at his discretion.

The elimination of racial segregation in the schools became a hot issue in the Eisenhower years. In 1954 the Supreme Court ruled (*Brown* v. *Board of Education of Topeka*) that the operation of separate schools for white and Negro children was unconstitutional. The President called in the Commissioners of the District of Columbia and asked them to take the lead in desegregating its schools as an example to the nation. Though he steadily pressed for the elimination of color lines, Eisenhower also tried to avoid inflaming racial relations. He recommended a number of civil rights laws to Congress, and some of them were enacted. One of these established the Civil Rights Commission with the duty of investigating any denial of equal rights. The Civil Rights Acts of 1957 and 1960—the first civil rights measures enacted by Congress since Reconstruction—were especially designed to protect minorities' right to vote.

In Sept., 1957, Eisenhower sent federal troops to Little Rock, Ark., to stop the rioting that followed the admission of nine Negro children to formerly all-white schools. Desegregation of the schools had been ordered by a federal court in keeping with the Supreme Court's decision. Fearing violence, Governor Orval E. Faubus called up the National Guard and excluded the Negro children from the schools. Eisenhower sought to bring the Governor into conformity with the law of the land in a personal conference, but Faubus merely withdrew the National Guard and violence ensued. When all efforts to restore order without force had failed, Eisenhower sent in federal troops. "Mob rule," he said in an address to the country, "cannot be allowed to override the decisions of the courts." His action was praised in the North, but bitterly criticized in the South, and his popularity in the latter area suffered a sharp decline. The President was deeply perturbed by the outbreak of violence and the necessity for using troops, but he felt that there was no feasible alternative.

As he approached the end of his second term, Eisenhower suffered other disappointments. The collapse of the summit conference in Paris signalized the failure of his efforts to bridge the gulf between the East and West and to reduce the danger of nuclear war. In Nov., 1960, the defeat of Vice-President Nixon in his presidential race with Sen. John F. Kennedy underlined the continued weaknesses of the Republican party. Yet Eisenhower's standing with the rank and file remained high. He retired to his farm in Gettysburg, Pa., without bitterness and continued active in public affairs.

Consult Eisenhower, D. D., *Crusade in Europe* (1948); Donovan, R. J., *Eisenhower: The Inside Story* (1956); Pusey, M. J., *Eisenhower the President* (1956); Adams, Sherman, *Firsthand Report* (1961).

MERLO J. PUSEY, Associate Editor,
The Washington Post and Times Herald

EISENHOWER, MILTON STOVER (1899–), American educator and public official. Born in Abilene, Kan., the brother of Dwight D. Eisenhower, he graduated from Kansas State College. After serving as a vice-consul in Scotland (1924–26), he became special assistant to the Secretary of Agriculture and then (1928–41) department information director. During World War II he was (1942–43) associate director of the Office of War Information, and subsequently president of Kansas State College. In 1950 he went to Pennsylvania State College as president and won the institution university status. A member of President Dwight D. Eisenhower's Commission on Government Reorganization, he was also a special ambassador (1953 and 1957–59) to South America. He became president of Johns Hopkins University in 1956.

Milton Eisenhower, university president and public servant, and a brother of Dwight D. Eisenhower.

United Press International

EISENHOWER DOCTRINE, policy offering economic aid and direct military assistance from the United States to any Middle Eastern country requesting help against "overt armed aggression from any nation controlled by international communism." The proposal, outlined (Jan., 1957) by President Dwight D. Eisenhower and supported (Mar., 1957) by an initial $200,000,000 appropriation, was attacked by the Soviet Union as an attempt to replace British and French "imperial influence" in the Middle East. Officials of Turkey, Pakistan, Iran, and Iraq immediately announced their full support of the doctrine. Its first direct military implementation occurred in the Lebanon crisis of 1958.

EISENHÜTTENSTADT, new city of the German Democratic Republic (East Germany), situated east of Berlin near the Oder River below its confluence with the Neisse River. Its economy is based on iron works capable of producing more than 1,000,000 tons annually. Founded in 1950 as Stalinstadt on the site of a Nazi prisoner of war camp, it was called "the first Socialist city of Germany" and private holdings were prohibited. In 1961 the city of Stalinstadt and the neighboring town of Fürstenberg were merged under the name Eisenhüttenstadt, meaning "iron works city." Pop., 25,000.

EISENSTADT [ī′zən-stăt], **ALFRED** (1898–   ), photojournalist who pioneered in candid photography and the sequential picture story. Born and educated in Germany, he came to the United States in 1935, joining the staff of *Life* magazine in 1936 as one of its original photographers. For *Life* he covered some 1,500 story assignments.

EISENSTADT [ī′zən-shtät], city of Austria and capital of the province of Burgenland, located on the western edge of the Pannonian Basin, near Neusiedler lake. The composer Joseph Haydn lived there from 1766 to 1778, and his home is now the Haydn Museum. State offices are housed in the nearby palace of the princes of Esterházy. Pop., 5,388.

EISENSTEIN [ī′zen-stīn], **SERGEI MIKHAILOVICH** (1898–1948), Russian film director, born in Riga. His early career was spent in the theater where his interest in crowd work led him to film. His first two pictures, *Strike* (1924) and *Battleship Potemkin* (1925), demonstrate Eisenstein's theory of editing. Shots are joined not to develop the narrative but to create a violent or intellectual shock. In *Strike*, for example, a slaughterhouse is intercut with a massacre of workers. The "Odessa Steps" sequence in *Potemkin* dramatically illustrates the medium's ability to expand an action beyond its actual time duration. Eisenstein's early work celebrated the Russian Revolution of 1905 and used the masses as protagonist rather than an individual. Later, he used Russian history. *Alexander Nevsky* (1938) and the two parts of *Ivan the Terrible* (1944–46) are directed with a tableau, almost operatic style. These films were criticized by Soviet critics as decadent and too formalistic, and his later career was marred by incompleted projects. Eisenstein is also known for his influential books on theory, *The Film Sense* (Eng. trans., 1942) and *Film Form* (Eng. trans., 1949).

Consult Seton, Marie, *Eisenstein, A Biography* (1952).
GARY L. CAREY, Department of Film,
The Museum of Modern Art

EISLEBEN [īs′lā-bən], city of the central German Democratic Republic (East Germany), located on the eastern slopes of the Harz mountains, in the district of Halle, west of Halle. The leading industries are the manufacture of small machinery and furniture. It is the center of a gardening district in which the growing of flower seeds is most important. Eisleben has some fine old churches, including the Andreaskirche, the Petri-Pauli-Kirche, the Nikolaikirche, and the Annenkirche, all built in the 15th century. In the market place stands a statue of Luther, who was born in Eisleben and died there. Pop., 29,023.

EISTEDDFOD [ā-stĕth′vŏd], Welsh contest in singing, composing, and poetry. The name has also been adopted for music contests in the United States, as well as for international music contests and festivals. Originally an institution of the bards in the Middle Ages, the eisteddfod suffered gradual decline and was discontinued about 1700, but was revived after 1800. National eisteddfods are held in Wales annually, and local ones more frequently. The contestants must show excellence in various aspects of music. Sometimes contests in arts and crafts are included. The singing is usually accompanied by small harps. An important ceremony at each contest is the "chairing" of the bards: the bard elected to preside sits in a special chair and is decorated with a silver and gold chain. The eisteddfod can be compared to the contests among troubadours, trouvères, minnesinger, and Meistersinger in medieval western Europe. In the 20th century these contests have contributed to the preservation of Welsh national feeling and of Welsh language and culture.

BRUNO NETTL, Wayne State University
See also BARD; MINSTREL; WELSH MUSIC.

EJECTMENT. *See* LAND LAWS.

EJIDOS [ā-hē′dōz], in Mexican history, communally owned properties created out of expropriated estates. A common slogan of the Mexican Revolution that began in 1910 was "land, liberty, and education." The first of these objectives was implemented by expropriating large estates (latifundia, haciendas) from both foreign and Mexican ownership and redistributing the land among the peasants in communally or village-owned parcels (*ejidos*). In a broad sense this was a revival of the pattern of land tenure prevalent in parts of Mexico in pre-Columbian times. The program began relatively slowly, gathered impetus, reached its high point during the presidency (1934–40) of Lázaro Cárdenas, and then tapered off.

Administrations after that of Cárdenas were less sympathetic to the program and took steps to restore private titles for small holdings. A major problem in establishing *ejidos* was that of providing credit and machinery for small farmers. This was partially solved by setting up *ejidal* banks, though some persons complained that abuses in the system resulted simply in substituting the banks for the former *hacendados* as proprietors of the land. In general, however, the *ejido* became a symbol of Mexico's social revolution.

RUSSELL H. FITZGIBBON, University of California

EJIMA KISEKI [ē-jē-mä kē-sä-kē] (1667–1736), Japanese writer of the Tokugawa period (1600–1868). He was associated with the famous Hachimonji publishing house in Kyoto. Having squandered the family fortune, he took up writing in order to subsist, his attention being devoted largely to Yoshiwara ("gay quarters" of Tokyo) subjects. He believed the romantic element was particularly to be found in the lives of the prostitutes, and his widely read "character books" reflect the typical psychology of the Tokugawa popular writer. He also wrote a few texts for the *joruri* (puppet theater) reciter Matsumoto Jidaiyu.

ELAGABALUS. *See* HELIOGABALUS OR ELAGABALUS.

ELASTICITY

Solids have elasticity of form. Gases and liquids, which tend to fill the same space before and after deformation, have elasticity of volume.

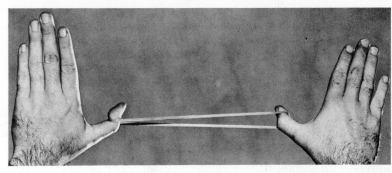

The rubber band breaks if stretched too far, but the material retains its elasticity.

The return to normal shape from the deformation caused by compression is what makes the ball bounce.

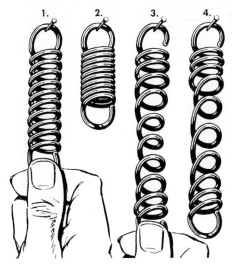

A spring subjected to tension within its elastic range (1) returns to normal size and shape (2); stretched beyond its elastic limit, (3) it breaks, or "fails" (4).

Goodyear Tire & Rubber Co.

ELAM [ē′ləm], ancient country of southwest Asia, lying at the head of the Persian Gulf east of the Tigris, now in southwestern Iran. In the 3d millennium B.C., Elam developed a state, a dynasty, and a local language written in cuneiform. Culturally related to neighboring Akkadians and Guti, the Elamites were frequently subjugated by these people during their early history. In the 2d millennium B.C., Elam was under the Kings of Anshan and Susa. Elam reached its cultural and political apogee under a new dynasty in the early 12th century B.C. The Elamite Empire then included the Tigris valley, much of the Persian Gulf shore, and the Zagros Mountains. Elam remained strong, successfully resisting Iranian and Assyrian encroachments until it fell c.642 B.C. to Ashurbanipal. In the 6th century it was dominated by Babylonia and thereafter by the Achaemenid Persians. Susa, the Elamite capital, was made a royal residence by Cyrus the Great whose ancestors had come from northern Elam. Elam was called Susiana by classical geographers.

PHYLLIS ACKERMAN, Asia Institute, New York City

ELAND [ē′lənd], name for several antelopes of the genus *Taurotragus*, distinguished by their large size, spiraled horns, and oxlike appearance. Elands, whose name is derived from the Dutch word for "elk," are found only in Africa. The common eland, *T. oryx*, stands about 5½ ft. high at the shoulder, has pale yellowish-brown fur, a loose flap of skin beneath its neck, and horns up to 40 in. long. It inhabits grassy plains from Kenya to South Africa. The giant eland, *T. derbianus*, is the largest of all antelopes. Reddish-brown in color, with vertical white stripes at the sides of its body, its massive horns may reach a length of 45 in. The giant eland frequents the forests of western, equatorial Africa.

ELASTICITY, in physics, tendency of matter to recover from deformation. The recovery is complete only if the deformation is within the elastic limit. When matter is deformed it is said to be strained, and a recovery tendency, called stress and expressed as a force per unit area, is developed. It is internal and is not to be confused with the external force per unit area producing the strain; it is equal to the external force but is oppositely directed.

Hooke's law states that within the elastic limit the stress is proportional to the strain, the proportionality factor being referred to as the modulus of elasticity. Several different moduli are recognized, depending upon the nature of the strain. If the latter is one dimensional, such as a simple stretch or compression, the modulus is known as Young's modulus. If the strain is an over-all fractional change in volume, the modulus is called the bulk modulus. The reciprocal of the bulk modulus is called the compressibility. Bodies that display shear modulus are recognized as solids; those that do not are known as fluids. Fluids comprise liquids and gases, both of which, therefore, can only resist forces that are perpendicular to their surfaces.

CLARENCE E. BENNETT, University of Maine

ELASTOMER [ĭ-lăs′tə-mər], elastic, rubber-like plastic that can return rapidly to its original shape and size after having been stretched to many times its original dimension. The initial and still greatest application for elastomers has been in the manufacture of synthetic rubber. The first commercial elastomer, "Thiokol," was produced in the United States in 1930; the following year saw the announcement of another synthetic elastomer, "Neoprene," used in the manufacture of shoe soles and heels.

Their usage was accelerated during World War II when the supply of natural elastomers (rubber) was cut off. GR-S (Government Rubber-Styrene) was first produced in Dec., 1943, and by war's end, close to a million tons had been produced. More GR-S is produced today than any other synthetic elastomer; however, it is now known under the trade name of its various manufacturers.

ELATH. *See* EILAT OR ELATH.

ELBA [ĕl′bə], Italian island in the Tyrrhenian arm of the Mediterranean Sea, largest in the Tuscan Archipelago. Located 7 mi. west of the Tuscany coast, it is governed as part of Livorno (Leghorn) Province. Its capital and main port, Portoferraio, is on the north coast. Elba's mines produce about 90% of Italy's iron ore. Other products include marble, wine, and fish. The exiled Napoleon ruled Elba briefly as a sovereign principality (1814–15). Area, 86 sq. mi.; max. elev. (Monte Capanne) 3,340 ft.; pop., 31,641.

ELBE [ĕl′bə] **RIVER** (Czech **LABE**), river of Europe, rising in the Riesengebirge range (Czech, Krkonoše) on the border of Czechoslovakia and Poland and flowing about 725 mi. generally north-northwestward through Czechoslovakia and Germany. Coursing southward from the Riesengebirge for about 50 mi., it turns westward for about 40 mi. until it reaches Kolín. There its course veers northwestward eventually to cut through the Erzgebirge mountains (Czech, Krušné Hory) and enter East Germany. It pursues its northwest course past Dresden, Dessau, and Magdeburg to the West German border. For 60 mi. it forms the boundary between East and West Germany.

In West Germany the Elbe continues northwestward toward Hamburg. Islands divide it into several channels which unite about 5 mi. below Hamburg to form the river's 60-mi. estuary emptying into the North Sea at Cuxhaven. Its tributary, the Vltava (Moldau), the longest river within Czechoslovakia, joins it in Bohemia after passing through Prague. Other tributaries are the Black Elster, Mulde, and Saale, which drain the southeast region of East Germany (Saxony), and the Havel, which drains the lake region around Berlin. The Elbe is navigable for sea-

Norderelb Bridge over the Elbe at Hamburg, West Germany. It links with autobahns connecting Hanover and Bremen.

Authenticated News International

going ships as far as Hamburg, for river boats as far as Mělník, and for barges as far as Kolín. Canal systems connect it with the Rhine and Oder rivers.

NORMAN J. G. POUNDS, University of Indiana

ELBERT, MOUNT, peak in the Sawatch Range of the southern Rocky Mountains, 12 mi. southwest of Leadville in central Colorado. It is the highest point in the state and also the highest peak in the Rocky Mountain system. Elev., 14,431 ft.

ELBERTON, city of northeastern Georgia and seat of Elbert County. It is an important granite-quarrying center, and was once a colonial tobacco and cotton market. Pop. (1950) 6,772; (1960) 7,107.

ELBLAG [ĕl′blônk] (Ger. **ELBING**), city and port of Poland, lying on the Elblag River, in the province of Gdańsk. The city was founded in the 13th century by the Teutonic Knights and became one of their chief bases for the conquest of East Prussia. It was severely damaged in 1945 but has been largely rebuilt. The port can handle only small craft, and its trade is unimportant. Pop., 74,000.

ELBRUS [ĕl′broos], **MOUNT,** highest peak (elev., 18,480) of the Caucasus Mountains, U.S.S.R. It is located in the Kabardino-Balkar Autonomous Republic in the central portion of the Greater Caucasus and is an important resort center. There are more than 50 permanent glaciers on its slopes. The Kuban River, a major stream of the region north of the Caucasus, has its source on the mountain's western slopes. Mount Elbrus was first climbed in 1829.

ELBURZ [ĕl-boorz] **RANGE** (Old Pers., **HIGH MOUNTAIN**), mountain chain in northern Iran, separating the basin of the Caspian Sea from the Iranian Plateau. It extends for 650 mi. from the western shores of the Caspian to join the Kopet-Dag range in northeastern Iran, forming an immense arc around the Caspian depression. This mountain belt is actually several parallel ranges with crests reaching 13,000 ft. or more. The highest peak is Demavend, 18,934 ft. above sea level. Teheran is located at the southern base of Elburz at an elevation of 3,810 ft.

EL CAJON [ĕl kä-hōn′], city of southern California, 12 mi. east of San Diego, in the southwesternmost corner of the United States. The city packs and ships avocados, citrus fruits, and grapes, but is primarily a residential community. Pop. (1950) 5,600; (1960) 37,618.

EL CAMPO, city of southern Texas, about 55 mi. southwest of Houston. It is a trade center for a prosperous cotton, rice, cattle, and petroleum producing area. Inc., 1905; pop. (1950) 6,237; (1960) 7,700.

EL CENTRO, city of southern California and seat of Imperial County, in the Imperial Valley near the Mexico border. The All-American Canal irrigates the area, noted for the raising and processing of cotton, and for sugarbeets, cantaloupes, tomatoes, and lettuce. The city is in the midst of a desert 45 ft. below sea level. Pop. (1950) 12,590; (1960) 16,811.

EL CERRITO [ĕl sə-rē′tō], city of western California, a residential suburb of Richmond near San Francisco Bay. Pop. (1950) 18,011; (1960) 25,437.

ELCHE [ĕl′chā], city of eastern Spain, 13 mi. southwest of Alicante. Famous for its date-palm groves, it ships palm leaves throughout Spain at Easter time. Figs and other fruits are also grown in the region. Leading industries are the making of footwear, fertilizers, cloth, and furniture. The town was founded by Iberian tribes, and became a Greek colony; the Romans called it Ilici. Under Moorish rule after the 8th century, as part of Murcia, it was acquired by Castile in the 13th century. Remains of all periods, especially Greek pottery, have been found nearby, and Elche retains aspects of the Moorish period. The bishop's palace is a historic landmark. Pop., 34,938.

ELDER, name for several shrubs and small trees of the genus *Sambucus*, in the Caprifoliaceae, or honeysuckle family. Elders are native to temperate and subtropical regions of both hemispheres and are sometimes grown as garden ornamentals. The shrubs bear clusters of small white flowers, followed by red or black, berrylike fruits. Among the better-known species are S. *nigra*, the European elder, and S. *canadensis*, the American or sweet elder. The fruit of both species is edible and is often preserved or made into wine.

ELDERS, JEWISH, the rulers in early Jewish communities and later, of the synagogue. This government of the older men (Gr. *presbyteroi*) was one of the earliest and most natural forms among all peoples, and an assembly of selected elders was probably the kernel of political government among all the early Semites. In the Bible, elders are mentioned in the Egyptian period; and during the Exodus 70 elders assist Moses in judgment of the tribes. In Canaan, elders assumed responsibility for the settlements (villages or towns) which eventually supplanted the tribes as the social and political units. Samuel instituted the monarchy on the elders' advice, and during the Babylonian Exile, the elders were the people's delegates to the prophets. Thus these elders were inevitably the model for later Rabbinic ("Sanhedrin") and Christian ("presbyters") leadership.

JAKOB J. PETUCHOWSKI, Hebrew Union College, Cincinnati

ELDON, JOHN SCOTT, 1ST EARL OF (1751–1838), English politician and jurist, leader of the reactionary wing of the Tory party in the early 19th century and a staunch opponent of every sort of change. He was the son of a Newcastle coal factor. Educated at Oxford, he became a lawyer and rapidly achieved success. As Lord Chancellor (1801–27), he proved himself a superb but dilatory equity judge. He was preoccupied with politics, vigorously opposing movements for parliamentary reform, state-supported elementary education, and Catholic Emancipation.

EL DORADO [ĕl də-rä′dō], Spanish name for a legendary land of boundless wealth somewhere in the New World. The legend originated in the Colombian (pre-Chibcha) Indian custom whereby a chief anointed with resins and covered with gold dust immersed himself in the sacred lake, Guatavita (north of present Bogotá), and became the ceremonial target of gold and gems cast by his subjects. A succession of Spanish, German, and English adventurers determinedly sought Guatavita long after the conquering Chibcha ended the custom, and several explorers actually arrived in the lake region at about the same time (c.1537). They were Gonzalo Jiménez Quesada, first on the scene, Nikolaus Federmann, and Sebastián de Benalcázar. Jiménez found substantial stores of gold and emeralds but no tremendous wealth. He went to Spain with his two rivals, and there each of the three adventurers laid individual claim to Colombia. Gonzalo Pizarro, seeking Omagua, the "Land of Cinnamon," as well as El Dorado, led (1540–41) an expedition in which his principal lieutenant, Francisco de Orellana, fortuitously explored the Amazon River to its mouth. The legend persisted during Portuguese and Brazilian colonization. Cartographers included "El Dorado" in their maps, and the expeditions of the Brazilian *bandeirantes* from São Paulo into the interior reportedly were inspired by tales of mountains of emeralds and gold-laden rivers. The German Bartholomäus Welser conducted several fruitless treasure-hunting expeditions into Venezuela after he and other creditors received the province as security for a loan to the Spanish crown. With Álvar Núñez Cabeza de Vaca's tales of the Seven Cities of Cíbola (c.1530) the search for El Dorado entered the North American Southwest and continued with Sir Walter Raleigh's quest (1595) for Manoa—the golden land—in South America.

HARRY BERNSTEIN, Brooklyn College

EL DORADO [ĕl də-rä′dō], city of southwestern Arkansas and seat of Union County. El Dorado is in the major petroleum area of Arkansas and participated in the first commercial petroleum development in the state after the discovery of oil in 1921. Petroleum products and chemicals are the dominant manufactures but poultry processing and lumber production are also of importance here. Inc., 1870; pop. (1950) 23,076; (1960) 25,292.

EL DORADO, trade center of east-central Kansas, and seat of Butler County, in an important agricultural and petroleum-producing area. Food, feed, and petroleum are the city's most important products. El Dorado Junior College is located here. Pop. (1950) 11,037; (1960) 12,523.

ELDRIDGE, DAVID ROY (1911–), American trumpeter, *Flügelhorn* player, and orchestra leader, born in Pittsburgh, Pa. He has played with various orchestras including some that he led himself. He won greatest acclaim with Gene Krupa in the early 1940's and later with Artie Shaw. Later he toured throughout the United States and Europe in jazz concerts.

ELEANOR OF AQUITAINE (c.1122–1204), Queen of France and later of England. Eleanor was the eldest daughter and only heir of William X, Duke of Aquitaine (Guienne), a large province in southwestern France. Her marriage in 1137 to Louis of France, the future Louis VII, gave the monarchs of France a claim to Guienne. She accompanied her husband on the Second Crusade, but her gaiety, frivolity, and love of art clashed with her husband's morose religiousness. Louis suspected her of adultery and in 1152 had their marriage annulled. This proved a political blunder, for Eleanor in the same year married Henry Plantagenet, Duke of Normandy and Count of Anjou, who became King of England as Henry II in 1154. As a consequence, almost all of western France came into the possession of a foreign monarch. This marriage was no happier than the first. Henry's infidelities embittered Eleanor, and in 1173 she helped her sons by this second marriage in their unsuccessful revolt against their father. For this she was held in confinement until Henry's death in 1189. The new King, Richard I, her eldest son, made her Regent during his absence on the Third Crusade. When Richard was held prisoner in Germany on his return from the Holy Land, she ransomed him in person. After Richard's death in 1199 she supported her younger son, John, against a rival claimant to the throne. Eleanor's court at Poitiers was known for its patronage of art and etiquette. She was a favorite of the troubadour poets. Still energetic at 80, she traveled to Spain to celebrate the betrothal of her granddaughter, Blanche of Castile, to Louis VIII of France.

Consult Kelly, Amy, *Eleanor of Aquitaine and the Four Kings* (1950).

ISTVAN DEAK, Columbia University

ELEATIC [ĕl-ē-ăt′ĭk] **SCHOOL,** name given to the school founded by Parmenides of Elea in South Italy and continued by his followers, Zeno and Melissus. These were the first European thinkers to rely on the power of deductive reasoning and brush aside the evidence of the senses, and their teaching made a profound and lasting impression, especially on Plato, who introduced Parmenides and Zeno into one of his most important dialogues, the *Parmenides*.

ELECAMPANE [ĕl-ĭ-kăm-pān′], common name for a hardy perennial plant, *Inula helenium*, in the composite family, native to Europe and northern Asia, and also widely grown in North America. The plants may grow to a height of 6 ft., have large, hairy leaves, and bear large, yellow blossoms; the roots are sometimes used medicinally. Elecampane is grown from seed and does well in ordinary garden soil. In eastern North America elecampane is often seen growing wild in open fields.

ELECTION, selection of officeholders by vote. It differs from other methods of choosing public officials, such as by appointment, casting lots, combat, heredity, competitive examination, seniority, and voluntary accession. Some ancient societies, including early Greece and Rome, used election, but the system did not come into general use to designate decision-makers in national governments in the West until the 19th century. Today, virtually all national and most local and provincial assemblies are designated by free elections in Western Europe, North and South America, Australia, New Zealand, Iceland, Japan, India, Israel, and a few other countries. Exceptions include the British House of Lords, which is hereditary and appointive, and the Canadian Federal Senate, which is appointive. The United States and a few other countries also elect many executive and judicial officers.

Many nations of Eastern Europe, Africa, and Asia hold pseudoelections which resemble true elections in form, but which lack the essential element of free choice. Typically, only a single, official party may nominate candidates. The voters do not choose, they only ratify official appointments.

Suffrage. When parliamentary elections first were held in England in early modern times, very few persons were eligible to vote. Only white men of material substance and religious orthodoxy were enfranchised. The granting of the right to vote for all white male citizens first occurred in the United States, in New England, early in the 17th century. By 1820 it had spread throughout the United States. France and Germany in 1871, and Switzerland in 1874 were the first countries to follow suit. The Nineteenth Amendment (1920) guaranteed women the right to vote in the United States. By 1920 almost all other Western nations had adopted universal suffrage. France, Italy, and Greece granted women the right to vote in the decade following World War II.

Most Western democracies still exclude insane persons from voting, as well as convicted criminals, noncitizens, and persons who have no permanent residence. The franchise is further restricted to men in most Swiss cantons, to property owners for Australian senatorial elections, and to members of the white race in the Republic of South Africa.

Negroes were generally excluded from the franchise in the United States before the Civil War. The Fifteenth Amendment (1870) guaranteed them the vote, but Southern whites conspired to prevent its having effect. At first they relied on intimidation and the illiteracy and political ignorance of most Southern Negroes. Then, some states adopted "grandfather clauses," which effectively denied the franchise to anyone who had not been eligible to vote before 1870, or who was not descended from persons who had been. Later the "white" primary was invented. It rested on the assumption that the Democratic party was a private association beyond the reach of the Fifteenth Amendment and, therefore, could constitutionally exclude Negroes from its primaries. As victory in the Democratic primaries was usually tantamount to election, Negroes were virtually disfranchised. Other devices to disfranchise Negroes included discriminatory application of literacy tests, poll taxes, and "good character" tests.

One by one the various exclusionary devices were stricken down by Supreme Court rulings, constitutional amendment, or congressional legislation. A series of federal statutes passed in the late 1950's and early 1960's, culminating in the Civil Rights Act of 1965, finally gave the national government effective power to enforce the Fifteenth Amendment. As a result Negro voter registration and participation increased dramatically.

Voting Participation. Universal suffrage does not, of course, mean universal electoral participation. Some qualified persons cannot vote because, by error or neglect, their names do not appear on the voter registers that most countries maintain. A lack of interest or awareness, dissatisfaction with the choices offered, or the belief that abstention is unimportant are other common reasons for voters not participating in an election. In some countries, such as Australia, Austria, Belgium, and Brazil, voluntary abstention is forbidden by law.

Statistics concerning qualified voters are not readily available, but most countries publish the number of registered voters. The percentage of registered voters casting ballots in some recent parliamentary elections in Western Europe ranged from a low of approximately 66% in Switzerland in 1963 to a high of almost 93% in Italy in 1963. Presidential elections produced percentage turnouts of about 85.3% in the United States in 1960 and 84.7% in France in 1965. Pseudoelections often draw higher turnouts than true elections. They are civic rituals in which all citizens must participate in order to demonstrate their patriotism and civic virtue. The Supreme Soviet elections, for instance, drew 99.95% of the registered votes in 1962 and 99.94% in 1966.

Indirect Elections. In most elections the voters choose directly among contending candidates for office. Sometimes, however, they choose "grand electors" who make the final choice. For instance, before 1913, U.S. senators were selected by state legislatures that had in turn been elected by the people. U.S. presidents and vice-presidents are named by an electoral college that has been elected by the people. However, the pre-1913 state legislators often cast nondiscretionary ballots, in accordance with mandatory instructions from the voters. The electoral college members almost always follow this procedure. French senators are elected by electoral colleges, composed mainly of municipal councillors, that are popularly elective. The upper legislative chambers in Austria and the Netherlands, and about one-quarter of Belgian senators are elected by provincial parliaments or councils.

Electoral Systems. The two basic forms of electoral systems are plurality and proportional representation (PR). The plurality system predominates in the United States, Canada, and Great Britain. It awards the office to the candidate receiving the largest number of votes. If more than one office is to be filled by the same contest, a number of leading candidates equal to the number of offices to be filled are declared elected.

The plurality system tends to underrepresent minorities. The voters (perhaps only 30% or less in a district) who support the winners are represented. No others are. PR was invented to correct that distortion. PR uses multi-member districts. Each political party nominates a list of candidates in each district, usually equal to the number of seats assigned to the district. Each list wins seats in proportion to its share of the vote. For instance, a list that wins 20% of the vote in a 10-member district receives two seats.

PR is widely used in Europe. The Scandinavian and Benelux countries all use it. So do West Germany, Italy, Greece, Iceland, Ireland, Israel, Belgium, Luxemburg, and Austria. So did France from 1945 to 1958. No federal or state elections in the United States have ever used PR. A number of municipalities, including New York City, Cincinnati, Toledo, and Sacramento, adopted PR early in the 20th century. Since then, all but Cambridge, Mass., have abandoned it. Usually, PR candidates receive seats in the order their names appear on the party nomination list. Some systems enable voters to indicate preferences among their party's candidates, but this rarely alters the result.

An important variant of the plurality system is the majority system, which requires that a candidate receive more than half the total number of votes cast in order to win the office. If no candidate wins a majority, a second balloting is usually held a week or two later in which a simple plurality suffices. France has used this system, with modification, for presidential and parliamentary elections since 1958. The "runoff" primary system in some southern American states is a form of the majority system.

Timing and Frequency of Elections. Some elections are held at regular, invariable intervals. A U.S. House of Representatives has been elected at precise, two-year intervals since 1788. All other government elections in the United States are similarly set, though the intervals differ. One-third of the U.S. senators are elected for six-year terms every two years. In 1967, 39 states had gubernatorial terms of four years, and 11 had two-year terms. Most other elective state-executive and administrative posts followed similar patterns. State-legislative terms were either two or four years. Annual elections are still fairly common for municipal councils and offices.

Fixed election intervals are less common in other countries. Most parliaments may be dissolved by executive order, before their terms expire. The Norwegian Storting, the French Senate, and the West German Bundesrat are important exceptions. Norwegian parliamentary elections are held invariably every four years. One-third of the French Senate is elected for a nine-year term every three years. The German Bundserat members serve indefinite terms at the will of the state government.

Even those parliaments that may be dissolved early, however, usually serve full terms. Italian parliamentary elections were held in 1948, 1953, 1958, and 1963. West German Bundestag elections were held in 1949, 1953,

Voting in 1960 in Léopoldville, the Republic of the Congo. Balloting to elect representatives to the national legislature lasted several days in the new nation. (UPI)

WHAT IS A PLURALITY OR MAJORITY VOTE?

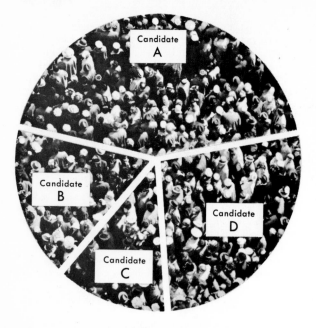

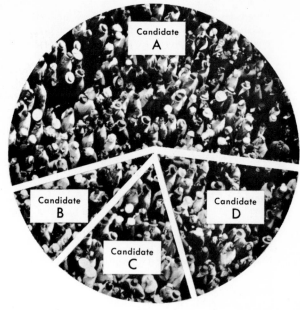

PLURALITY

Candidate A wins by a plurality when, though he has less than 51% of the total vote, he has more votes than any other opponent.

MAJORITY

Candidate A wins by a majority when he receives more than 50% of the total vote cast in the election.

1957, 1961, and 1965. Sweden, Australia, and New Zealand have invariably held their recent elections at three-year intervals. Ireland, Iceland, Finland, Belgium, Denmark, Luxemburg, the Netherlands, Israel, and Switzerland have also held elections with great regularity. On the other hand, Canada, Great Britain, France, and Austria all held early elections in recent years.

Selection of Candidates. In most political systems the nomination of candidates is an internal and largely private matter for political parties. The candidate is usually selected by a local party unit. The nomination is generally proposed by an executive committee and ratified or changed by general vote of dues-paying members. In such highly centralized parties as the British Labour party and the Communist parties of Western Europe, the national party supervises the selection process and holds a veto over the final choice. Some countries, such as West Germany, regulate the nomination process by law to insure that it proceeds democratically.

Nonparty candidates usually are permitted to put themselves forward. To discourage frivolous candidates, they often are required to post a fairly substantial deposit, which they forfeit if they do not obtain a prescribed minimum percentage of the vote.

Only in the United States is the general electorate involved in the nomination process. The direct primary is used to settle virtually all contests for major party nomination for state and congressional offices and for many local offices. Sometimes a preprimary party convention officially endorses some primary contestants. Also, presidential nominations are still made by national convention, though in about a third of the states' conventions, delegates are chosen by presidential preference primaries.

Primary elections are conducted by governments rather

than parties. Any registered voter may take part in an open primary. Only registered voters of a particular party may participate in that party's closed primary election.

Campaigns. The solicitation of voting support by the candidates is the election campaign. Most countries designate an official campaign period of two to four weeks immediately prior to the election, during which campaign activities are subsidized and regulated. The actual campaign, however, is usually much longer than the official campaign. In the United States no official campaign periods are designated, but, by custom, the period from Labor Day until election eve in November is treated as a semiofficial campaign period.

In Europe, the principal campaign device traditionally has been the candidate's open meeting. Each candidate tours the constituency, holding public meetings at all population centers, delivering short speeches, answering questions, and sometimes debating his opponent. In recent years, the development of television as a campaign medium has reduced the importance of the candidate's meetings. Television has had its greatest impact, however, in the United States, especially in contests for state and federal offices. The United States, because of commercial television, is one of the few countries where a candidate's access to the medium is limited only by his financial resources. Almost everywhere else, small time allotments on the state-owned communications systems are carefully apportioned among the contestants. Printed literature, newspaper advertisements, and outdoor posters and billboards are used almost everywhere. Door-to-door canvassing is common in English-speaking countries but little used elsewhere. Telephone canvassing is almost exclusively a U.S. campaign technique.

Campaign costs are sometimes very high if no closely

Voting in the Soviet Union. A portrait of Lenin dominates an election booth in Moscow as citizens cast votes for delegates to the Supreme Soviet and to local Deputies' Soviets. (SOVFOTO)

A citizen votes at the first presidential election of Guinea in Africa, held in 1961. Sékou Touré was elected. (BERNHEIMS-RAPHO GUILLUMETTE)

Election day in Chicago. Registration is checked to insure that only eligible voters cast a ballot. (HAYS-MONKMEYER)

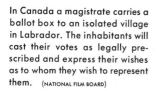

In Canada a magistrate carries a ballot box to an isolated village in Labrador. The inhabitants will cast their votes as legally prescribed and express their wishes as to whom they wish to represent them. (NATIONAL FILM BOARD)

enforced ceiling is set. In Great Britain national parties are not permitted to incur campaign expenses on behalf of their candidates. The candidates themselves may spend an average of only $3,000 each during the official three-week campaign. In the United States, at the other extreme, about $200,000,000 was spent on campaigns at all levels in 1964, $175,000,000 in 1960, and $155,000,000 in 1956. The 1964 figure included about $34,000,000 spent at the national level alone.

These expenses are covered by funds received from many sources. Most European countries provide some subsidization. Some campaign literature may be mailed postage free. Public halls are available for candidates' meetings without charge, and broadcasting time is donated. The West German government makes cash grants to political parties. So does Puerto Rico. Members' dues also help stock the campaign chests of many European parties. Some parties carry on profit-making activities, including publishing enterprises, insurance companies, and lotteries. Individuals, trade unions, agricultural associations, business corporations and associations, and cooperative societies often contribute financial support to the parties and candidates they endorse. In the United States such contributions are regulated by the Hatch Acts of 1939 and 1940 and the Taft-Hartley Act. In practice, however, their provisions have been evaded widely.

Consult Lakeman, Enid, and Lambert, J. D., *Voting in Democracies* (1955); Ranney, Austin, and Kendall, Willmoore, *Democracy and the American Party System* (1956); Mackenzie, W. J. M., *Free Elections* (1958); Duverger, Maurice, *Political Parties* (2d ed., 1959); Key, V. O., Jr., *Politics, Parties, and Pressure Groups* (5th ed., 1964).

WILLIAM G. ANDREWS, State University of N. Y., College at Brockport

See also:

APPORTIONMENT, LEGISLATIVE	POLITICAL PARTY
CONVENTION, POLITICAL	POLL TAX
ELECTORAL COLLEGE	VOTING
MACHINE, POLITICAL	WOMAN SUFFRAGE

ELECTION, DOCTRINE OF, in Christian theology, the doctrine that God from all eternity has elected some to eternal life (Eph. 1:4). This choosing by God does not exclude decision by the individual. He accepts or rejects the Gospel on the basis of his own choice; but according to this doctrine his acceptance of the Gospel ultimately depends upon the regenerating power of the Holy Spirit.

In the Old Testament, election is in the main God's election of a people, Israel. But the theme of much of prophetic teaching is that the people must not presume on the basis of this election that Israel is indispensable to God. The New Testament does not despair of the salvation of Israel (Rom. 10:1; 11:1); but the election of God is now thought of as that of the new Israel, the believers of every nation who form the church.

This doctrine was stressed particularly by John Calvin and his followers, and is especially part of the theology of the Reformed and Presbyterian churches.

IAN HENDERSON, University of Glasgow

ELECTORAL COLLEGE, in U.S. presidential elections, a system whereby independent electors choose the president and vice-president of the United States every four years. In providing for this method, the authors of the Constitution hoped to remove presidential elections from the confusion of popular voting. In the beginning of the republic most state legislatures chose their own electors, but, with the rise of political parties and the development of national conventions, popular election of the electors was provided for in all the states by 1860.

The local and state party organizations select a slate of electors numerically equal to the state's congressional delegation, as specified by the Constitution. The national party conventions nominate presidential and vice-presidential candidates to whom the party electors in the states are pledged. On election day in November, the people in the states in reality vote for the slate of electors, not the presidential and vice-presidential candidates themselves, even though in almost half the states the names of the electors are not on the ballot. (In New York, for example, each party has 43 electors.) In 10 states the electors' names appear on the ballot, rather than the names of the party nominees. The presidential and vice-presidential candidates, whose electors win a plurality of the votes cast in the state, then receive all the electoral votes of that state. This is, of course, provided that all the electors cast their ballots for their party's nominees in December in the state capital, on a date prescribed by federal law. There is no Constitutional requirement that the electors must vote for the candidates of their party. In 1948 a Tennessee Democratic elector defected from Harry S Truman, and in 1960 Alabama and Mississippi elected 14 unpledged electors who, along with one elector from Oklahoma, then proceeded to vote for Harry F. Byrd, who was not even a presidential candidate.

Following the official tallying in each state of the electors' votes, the ballots are sent to the U.S. Senate. On Jan. 6, following the election, the Senate and House meet in joint session to count the votes. The persons receiving the majority of the electoral votes for president and vice-president are then declared officially elected. In case a majority of electoral votes is not obtained, (because of the presence of third-party candidates or because of electors' defections), the election for president is decided by the House of Representatives, where each state has one vote. In the case of the vice-president, the Senate decides the election. The votes of a majority of the states are then sufficient to elect the president, and a majority of all the Senators can elect the vice-president. A president was selected this way in 1824, when the House chose John Q. Adams as president over Andrew Jackson and William H. Crawford.

The system of an entire states' electoral votes going to a candidate who receives the highest popular vote sometimes produces candidates whose share of the electoral college vote is much greater than their share of the popular vote. It is also mathematically possible for a candidate to receive an electoral college majority but not the majority of the popular vote, because of the various combinations of the states' electoral votes. In this century this happened in the elections of Presidents Woodrow Wilson (twice), Harry S Truman, and John F. Kennedy.

The will of the majority of the people can potentially be negated by electors voting for someone other than their party nominees, and by the possibility of an elector dying between the November and December balloting. Third party candidates drawing enough electoral votes to force the election into the Congress would have the same result. Numerous plans for revising the electoral method of electing the president and vice-president have been offered as amendments to the Constitution, thus far unsuccessfully.

ERWIN L. LEVINE, Skidmore College
See also ELECTION; PROPORTIONAL REPRESENTATION.

ELECTRA, in Greek legend, the daughter of Agamemnon and Clytemnestra. When Aegisthus and Clytemnestra killed her father, she sent her young brother Orestes to safety in Phocis. Aeschylus' *Libation Bearers,* Sophocles' *Electra,* and Euripides' *Electra* tell how she incited Orestes and helped him kill the murderers.

ELECTRET [ĭ-lĕk'trĭt], in physics, a body having a pair of equal and opposite permanent electric charges. It is the electric counterpart of a permanent magnet. If an electret is cut in half, two electrets result. Electrets are prepared by solidifying certain waxes or plastics in an electric field.

ELECTRICAL CODE, NATIONAL, in the United States, a set of rules and specifications to protect life and property in the use of electric equipment. It governs the size of electric conductors; the types, materials, and methods of wiring; overcurrent protection; and the grounding of circuits in both the installation and operation of equipment in homes, offices, and industry.

The code applies also to appliances, lamps, storage batteries, lightning arresters, radio and television equipment, motion-picture projectors, neon signs, X-ray machines, induction and dielectric heating equipment, motors, genera-

tors, transformers, reactors, machine tools, welders, elevators and escalators, and cranes and hoists.

Many regulatory and inspection agencies use the code to approve electrical contracting. The code is written by the National Board of Fire Underwriters, as recommended by the National Fire Protection Association, and is approved by the American Standards Association. Supplementary codes are written in many cities and towns for local use.

ELECTRICAL ENGINEERING. Electrical engineering as an independent profession dates only from the 1880's. However, it is based on fundamental principles of electricity, some of which have been studied for more than 300 years. Despite its short history, electrical engineering has had tremendous impact on the technology of today. Until the mid-1940's the electrical engineer was concerned largely with three major activities: electrical utilities and their many aspects of power generation, transmission, distribution, and utilization; the telephone and telegraph industries; and the general development of radio and the many household appliances that are electrically operated.

Electronics. Developments in electricity during World War II enlarged the domain of the electrical engineer to include work in electronics. Perhaps the most important wartime advances in electronics were those concerned with improved communications equipment, radar, and navigation devices. The development of radar led to striking advances in pulse techniques and in the generation and handling of microwave power. The earliest radar equipment operated in the 1- to 10-meter band, the band which was subsequently adopted for frequency modulation and television programming. Successive developments resulted in both improved and more sophisticated pulse systems and with the microwave wavelengths gradu-

---

ELECTRICAL ENGINEERING

Characteristics of the Field. Electrical engineers are concerned with electrical and electronic equipment. They work with it, design, develop, and manufacture it. They find employment in companies that produce electrical equipment of all kinds— electric motors and generators, communications devices, electrical appliances, and electronic apparatus, including television and computers. Companies that generate electric power or utilize electrical systems in their products or services also employ electrical engineers.

More than 200,000 electrical engineers are employed in the United States, in jobs ranging from private industry through government work to college teaching. Most find a niche in private industry, where typically they have duties such as determining how a new scientific discovery can be used to improve a piece of equipment or a process. Thus the engineer must be able to understand basic research, but also to think in such terms as size, weight, cost, and feasibility of production. Because of the enormous complexity of the electrical field, most engineers choose a particular area of interest. Electronics, equipment manufacturing, communications, and power are common specializations.

Qualifications and Training. One considering electrical engineering as a profession should have a talent for science and machinery, and a feeling for the practical utilization of scientific knowledge. He should plan on getting a bachelor's degree, involving a four- or possibly five-year course of study. The first two years of a typical program emphasize basic science—mathematics, physics, and chemistry—the last years courses pertain directly to electrical engineering. Graduate study is necessary for some specialties in the field. Many large companies provide on-the-job training to new employees, thus acquainting them with the specifics of the particular organization.

Income. The earnings of electrical engineers are in line with those of other engineers. A beginner in industry, with a bachelor's degree, may hope to start in the $7,000 to $9,000 range, though salaries vary in the many companies. The average salary for a typical engineer with 20 to 25 years of service is more than twice the beginning salary. Only a relatively small percentage of engineers achieve executive position. Beginning salaries in teaching and government are likely to be somewhat less than in industry.

Prospects for Employment. The outlook for electrical engineers is unusually good. Continued developments in automation and space exploration, the far-ranging implications of computers, and the increase in number and complexity of electrical appliances all indicate that at least through the mid-1970's electrical engineers will be in demand. In addition to the openings created by an expanding field, several thousand men leave their jobs each year for various reasons, and must be replaced. Electrical engineering is primarily a man's job, though some women do choose it for a profession.

Sources of Information. Additional information is available in the Career Guide that accompanies ENGINEERING. Also recommended are the articles on ELECTRICITY, ELECTRONICS, TELEVISION, MEDICAL ELECTRONICS, INDUSTRIAL ELECTRONICS, and the articles to which they lead. General suggestions on career planning are found in VOCATIONAL GUIDANCE. The reader may also want to contact the Institute of Electrical and Electronic Engineers, New York, or the Engineers Institute of Canada, Montreal. Information on schools and curriculums may be obtained from the Engineers' Council for Professional Development, New York.

Characteristics of the Field. Electricians may be divided into two main groups, construction and maintenance. Construction electricians work on a building that is being erected, laying out, assembling, and installing the electrical wiring, fixtures, and apparatus necessary for its operation. They also handle remodeling work and home repairs. Maintenance electricians generally work for industrial or commercial establishments, taking care of the various types of electrical equipment they use. They also sometimes modify or install the wiring, generators, or other equipment for these organizations. The fields of the construction and maintenance electricians overlap.

Qualifications. Electricians of both types need an understanding of the principles of electricity and of electrical equipment and its installation and repair. The construction electrician has to follow blueprints and specifications in his work on a building, and must know and adhere to the National Electrical Code regulations as well as local safety and other ordnances. Both types of electricians work with hand and other tools, and must be mechanically adept. They must be physically active, and able to stand for long periods or to work in cramped positions. An electrician sometimes works with wiring systems coded by color, and color blindness is therefore a handicap. He should be mentally alert, for he cannot afford the risk of dangerous mistakes.

Education and Training. An apprenticeship of about four years is the recommended training for becoming either a construction or maintenance electrician. Generally the program involves a written agreement between the apprentice and a local union-management committee, which arranges for and supervises the training. A high school degree is usually mandatory to becoming an apprentice. The training entails both on-the-job and classroom instruction.

Some electricians get their training informally, however, beginning as helpers and observing and learning from trained workmen for many years. High schools and vocational and correspondence schools offer courses of help. Electricians who have served formal apprenticeships have certain professional advantages, however, as well as a broadly based foundation of training.

Prospects for Employment. The employment outlook for electricians is good. An expanding building industry and greater use of electricity in the home combined with over-all industrial growth and the growing amount of electric and electronic equipment in factories indicates that both types of electricians will be in demand for at least a number of years. Retirements each year also create thousands of openings.

Income. Construction electricians are among the most highly paid workers in the building trades. Union hourly rates average between $4 and $5, though geographical location reflects variation in this pay rate. In general, maintenance electricians earn somewhat less, though their incomes compare favorably with other skilled workers. Also, they are less likely to lose time because of job changes and interrupted building schedules than construction electricians. Apprentices start at about 50% of the pay rate of the journeymen, and gradually increase their hourly wage until they earn 80 to 90% of his rate.

Sources of Information. The reader is referred to the article ELECTRICITY in this Encyclopedia, and to the other articles to which it leads him. General suggestions on career planning are found in VOCATIONAL GUIDANCE. Information on apprenticeships and other aspects of the profession may be obtained from an electrical contractor, a local office of the International Brotherhood of Electrical Workers (which has its central office in Washington, D.C.), or a state employment office. The National Joint Apprenticeship and Training Committee for the Electrical Industry is in Washington, D.C.

---

ally being reduced to 30 cm., 10 cm., 3 cm., and 1 cm. The shorter wavelengths are the important ones today. Moreover, microwave techniques have been extended into the millimeter wave band, which is of considerable importance in the field of radio astronomy. These developments also provided the background for microwave communication and the broad band links for carrying television signals from the place of origin to points throughout the country.

Other military electronics activities resulted in the present navigation systems for ships and aircraft. Loran, the most important long-range navigational system, and the equipment for air-traffic control were both developed in this period. These systems led to the extensive use of computers of both the analog and digital types for the handling and processing of large quantities of data.

Interesting electronic devices have modified the electronics field during these last two decades. Originally the magnetron was developed for generating large amounts of power. The klystron, first used at low power levels, mainly as part of microwave receivers, has since been developed to produce large amounts of power for radar and television applications. A large variety of new electron-beam tubes has been developed also. Perhaps the most striking developments have come with the invention of the transistor, one of the so-called solid-state semiconductor devices which have supplanted vacuum tubes in many applications. Their small size and low power demands have resulted in a reduction in the physical size of electronic devices by a factor of 10 to 100. Solid-state electronics has opened the way for microelectronic techniques, which allow miniature integrated electronic devices to be plated in successive layers. This ensures extreme reliability with very small space requirements, and may be a real boon in aircraft or spacecraft instrumentation. Likewise the importance in large-scale computers has not yet been exploited.

The development of electronic computers is having a tremendous impact on business, science, and industry. It provides the basis for data processing in both business and engineering and the means for automatically controlling and optimizing industrial operations.

Electronic equipment is vital to space programs, both in automatic and remote control of the space vehicles and in the telemetry systems for storing and transmitting upon command the data gathered by the many different satellites which have been placed in orbit around the earth and sent to other celestial bodies.

Dramatic changes in electrical engineering have taken place during the past several decades, and there is every reason to anticipate that these changes will continue. The field of electrical engineering is an expanding one, and there are rich scientific rewards for the electrical engineer. For example, links have been growing between the biological and medical sciences and the electrical engineer. With the developing complexity and sophistication of the field, the educational demands on the student become more exacting. More and more it becomes necessary for the student to have broad capabilities in mathematics, physics, the engineering sciences, and in some cases, in biology. The intellectual rewards can be as exciting as the material developments.

Engineers in the United States and Canada are served by two technical societies, the Institute of Radio Engineers, which has a world-wide membership, and the American Institute of Electrical Engineers, which also has many Canadian members. These societies publish a number of technical journals, which, together with a large number of other scientific and technical publications, provide the outlets for reporting the scientific and engineering phases of the field.

SAMUEL SEELY, National Science Foundation
See also ELECTRONICS; RADIO; TELEVISION.

ELECTRICAL WORKERS' UNIONS, in the United States, three rival labor organizations whose members work chiefly in manufacturing industries.

The International Union of Electrical, Radio and Machine Workers (AFL–CIO) has headquarters in Washington, D.C. Founded in 1949 by James B. Carey and others after the ouster from the CIO of the United Electrical, Radio and Machine Workers, the union has approximately 400,000 members. Its contracts also benefit 100,000 nonmembers.

The United Electrical, Radio and Machine Workers of America, with headquarters in New York City, has operated independently since its expulsion from the CIO in 1949 on grounds of alleged Communist domination. In 1960 it had 160,000 members.

The International Brotherhood of Electrical Workers (AFL–CIO) has headquarters in Washington, D.C. Founded in 1891, it has members in the following manufacturing industries: radio and television, electronic and electric machinery, and machine tools. It also covers nonproduction workers: radio and television broadcast engineers and telephone operators. The union's membership in 1960 was 750,000.

All three unions have educational, research, and social service programs for members and their families. Each issues publications, including a news periodical.

SAMUEL E. GLUCK, City University of New York

ELECTRIC ARC, luminous discharge between the tips of two conductors first touched together to pass current, then drawn slightly apart. The bright, intense light, in a semicircular shape, is caused by the ionization of air particles. The phenomenon is used to produce intense light in arc lamps. But it also arises elsewhere and can be potentially destructive, especially when the arc occurs on unprotected switches or relays. The term "electric arc" also denotes the luminous discharge between electrodes in gaseous tubes.

ELECTRIC-ARC FURNACE. *See* ELECTROMETALLURGY.

ELECTRIC BATTERY. *See* BATTERY, ELECTRIC.

ELECTRIC CHAIR. *See* CAPITAL PUNISHMENT; ELECTROCUTION.

ELECTRIC DISCHARGE, conduction of electricity, usually through a gas. Discharges are classified broadly as (1) the glow, a highly luminous discharge, characteristic of low pressures and low currents, and having wide applications in neon-type signs and in tubes used for voltage regulation and rectification; (2) the arc, a brilliant, hot, high-current discharge involving evaporation of the electrodes, which is used in welding, some chemical processes, and certain street lights; (3) the corona, a faint, low-current discharge occurring near sharply pointed electrodes at moderate gas pressures and high voltages, and responsible for energy losses along high-tension power lines; and (4) the spark, a short-lived discharge at high pressures and high voltages, and exemplified by lightning.
See also ELECTRICITY.

ELECTRIC EEL, an elongated, eellike fish, *Electrophorus electricus*, in the family Gymnotidae, native to the Amazon, Orinoco, and other rivers of northern South America. The electric eel is not a true eel, but is related to the carps and catfishes of order Ostariophysi. Adults are usually 3 to 5 ft. long, but 9-ft. individuals have been reported. The electric eel has powerful electric organs, composed of modified muscle cells and nerve endings, that occupy most of the latter two-thirds of its body. It can produce a discharge of over 600 volts with sufficient current to paralyze human beings and even horses. Apparently it is not injured by its own discharge or that of other eels, but uses its powers for defense and to secure the small fish and amphibians on which it feeds.

ELECTRIC EYE. *See* PHOTOELECTRIC CELL.

ELECTRIC FIELD. *See* ELECTRICITY.

ELECTRIC FISH, name for fishes of several unrelated evolutionary lines that have independently developed the ability to produce electricity. The electric rays or torpedos, of the genera *Torpedo* and *Narcine*, have two large electric organs composed of modified muscle, located on each side of their disc-shaped bodies. These organs consist of upright, hexagonal columns filled with a clear, gelatinous substance. The electric eel, *Electrophorus electricus*, has electric organs of similar structure. The electric organ of the electric catfish, *Malapterurus electricus*, is composed of a sheath of gelatinous material, located between the skin and muscles, that appears to be derived from the skin cells. The electric stargazers, of family *Uranoscopidae*, have an oval electric organ, developed from part of the eye musculature, located behind each eye. The electric discharge that many of these fishes are capable of producing is powerful enough to suggest that this ability was developed either for defensive use or for stunning prey. Large eels, flounders, and salmon that have been found intact in the stomachs of torpedos seem to indicate that the latter idea is of some merit.

It has recently been discovered that several other fishes, such as the lampreys, are able to generate electric fields. These species appear to employ electric fields in navigation, in a manner similar to the use of radar.

BRUCE B. COLLETTE, U.S. National Museum
See also ELECTRIC EEL.

ELECTRIC GENERATOR. *See* GENERATOR, ELECTRIC.

ELECTRICITY

ELECTRICITY [ĭ-lĕk-trĭs'ə-tē], one of the fundamental physical properties in nature. Only electricity at rest, that is, electrostatics, is discussed here (for a discussion of electricity in motion *see* ELECTRODYNAMICS). The basic concepts of electricity, however, are applicable to both.

Fundamentals. Electric charge, or quantity of electricity, is one of the basic attributes of matter. Most of the elementary subatomic particles such as electrons, protons, and mesons carry a characteristic electric charge which is as important to their make-up as is their mass. As fas as is known, electric charge is not resolvable into anything simpler or more fundamental. It is on an equal footing with length, time, and mass as one of the concepts that form the foundation of physics.

Electric charge is apparent through the forces associated with it: charges at rest exert electrostatic forces on each other, whereas moving charges interact through electromagnetic forces. There are known only three fundamentally different kinds of forces: gravitational, nuclear, and electric. Most forces are ultimately electric in nature. These include, for example, the forces which determine the ordinary properties of gases, liquids, and solids; the forces responsible for the chemical nature of inert and living matter; and even the force exerted by a bat on a baseball.

There are two kinds of electric charge, positive and negative, the nomenclature being arbitrary, with no mathematical connotation. The fundamental particle called the proton, usually found in an atomic nucleus, carries positive charge whereas the electron, another basic constituent particle of the atom, is negatively charged. In both cases the quantity of charge is the same, and is usually represented by e. No charge smaller than e has ever been found, and it is considered one of the fundamental constants of nature. A normal atom contains as many electrons as protons; its effective, or net, charge is zero. Such an atom is an example of a neutral body, that is, one containing as much positive as negative charge. It has never been found possible to create or destroy a net quantity of electric charge. This fact is called the conservation of charge. In certain experiments an electron with its charge of $-e$ can be created, but always simultaneously with another particle, the positron, which carries a charge of $+e$. When a positron encounters an electron there is mutual annihilation, with no charge remaining. In both of these cases the net charge before and after is zero.

One method of producing a charged body is to rub one body with a suitable dissimilar body, a process called charging by friction. This action leads to a separation of charge, one body then being positive, the other negative by the same amount. It is then found that the two bodies exert an electrostatic force of attraction on each other and tend to draw together. On the other hand, if two positively charged or two negatively charged bodies are prepared, they are found to repel one another electrostatically. The generalization of such observations is that similar charges repel, opposite charges attract.

Coulomb's law states the relation between static charges and the forces they exert on one another. If two small bodies carry positive charges in the amounts $+q_1$ and $+q_2$, respectively, and are held a distance d apart, then q_1 will repel q_2 and q_2 will repel q_1 with a force F given by

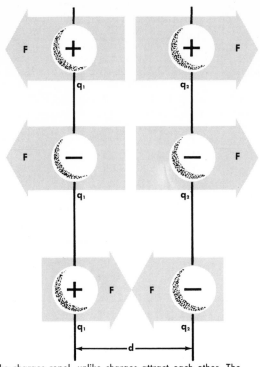

Like charges repel, unlike charges attract each other. The force (F) of the reaction depends upon the quantity of charge (q_1, q_2) and the distance (d) between charges.

Positively charged B attracts the negative particles in the metal, and repels the positive particles, which move away.

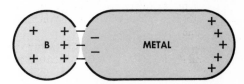

When B and the metal are brought together, some of the metal electrons flow into B and remain there.

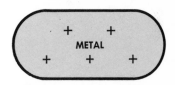

The loss of the negative particles leaves the once electrically neutral metal with a positive charge.

$F = (q_1q_2)/(kd^2)$; that is, the force is equal to the product of the charges divided by the product of a constant and the square of the distance separating the charges. The constant k has a numerical value determined by the medium in which the two charges are immersed (k for water is about 80 times k for air) and by the system of units used. If the two charges q_1 and q_2 had been negative the resultant force would have been exactly the same, but if q_1 and q_2 were of opposite sign, F, although still the same in magnitude, would be reversed in direction.

The standard unit of electric charge in the meter-kilogram-second system is the coulomb. Although this is a convenient quantity of charge in electrodynamics, it is gigantic in electrostatics. For example, if two positive charges of one coulomb each could be accumulated and held a yard apart in air, they would repel each other with a force of about 1,000,000 tons. Static charges are thus measured in small fractions of a coulomb.

Certain substances, although they may be electrically neutral, contain large numbers of charged particles that are free to move about within the material. Of such substances, called electrical conductors, the most important are the metals, especially silver and copper, with their many mobile electrons. These conduction electrons are the carriers of electric current in metals. A positively charged body B, brought near a neutral isolated piece of metal, attracts conduction electrons to the region nearest it. This leaves some locally unneutralized positive charges, contained in the immobile nuclei of the atoms of the metal, near the opposite end of the metal. If B were now touched to the metal some electrons would flow onto B,

partially neutralizing it. Finally, removing B leaves the metal with a net positive charge, acquired by contact. In conducting liquids and gases, both positive and negative particles can be moved.

Electric insulators, or nonconductors, are substances containing few mobile charged particles. An insulator used in place of the metal in the example above could contribute little charge to B. Glass, polystyrene, and dry air are excellent insulators. A good insulator such as porcelain may become a fair conductor when damp. Thus on a humid day the spark plugs of an automobile may not function properly because they are no longer well insulated from the engine. Since about 1950, semiconductors have been of growing importance in such applications as transistors. Having conductivities intermediate between those of metals and insulators, these solids depend for their special properties on their inclusion of minute, carefully controlled concentrations of impurities. Many semiconductors contain both positive and negative charge carriers. Those in which positive carriers predominate are called *P-type*, whereas *N-type* semiconductors have primarily negative carriers.

Electric Field. The fruitful concept of the electric field was developed to avoid using action-at-a-distance to explain the electrostatic force. The region of space, empty or otherwise, in the vicinity of a charged body q is assumed to be in a state different from that near a neutral body. An electric field is said to exist around the charge q_1. A second body carrying a charge q_2 placed in this field then experiences a force because of the interaction of q_2 and the field. Electrostatic forces are thus conceived as

ELECTRICITY

arising locally through the intermediary of the field, rather than by direct interaction of the two separated charges q_1 and q_2. Many advantages, conceptual and practical, accrue from this point of view, and the electric field is considered quite real. It stores energy in completely empty space and, together with the magnetic field, underlies electromagnetic radiation. Electric fields can also be produced in the absence of static charge, that is, by a changing magnetic field, which gives rise to an electric field.

The exact definition of electric field makes use of the idealized detecting device called a probe, a very small body carrying a positive charge q_p and equipped with a

MEASURING THE FIELD AROUND q

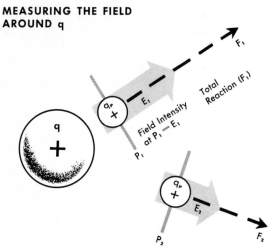

suitable force-measuring mechanism. (Whereas such a probe is possible in principle, in practice it can only be approached.) By placing this probe at some point in the field to be investigated, the magnitude and direction of the electrostatic force F experienced by q_p are noted. The ratio of F to q_p is called the electric field intensity E at that point: $E = F/q_p$. E has the same direction as F and is measured in units of newtons per coulomb (which can be shown to be equivalent to volts per meter). Thus if the probe charge q_p is placed at a point P_1, it is acted upon by force F_1, giving $E_1 = F_1/q_p$. If the probe is now moved to a point P_2, it will experience a different force, F_2, so that $E_2 = F_2/q_p$. The intensity of an electric field thus varies in general from point to point in magnitude and direction. In principle it could be measured at every point and mapped. Note that the field being investigated here is that belonging to q (not to the charge of the probe q_p), and is assumed to exist even when not being probed. It is important to realize that the field intensity E does not depend on the magnitude of the probe charge q_p since, for example, using a probe with double the charge would result in twice the force F at any given point, leaving the ratio F/q_p unchanged. If this were not so, the intensity E would be a useless concept, having no clearly defined value at any point. If q had been negative in this example, F_1 and F_2, and hence E_1 and E_2, would have been reversed in direction. Electric field intensity must not be confused with electromotive force.

The graphic constructions known as lines of force are helpful in the visualization of electric fields. These are

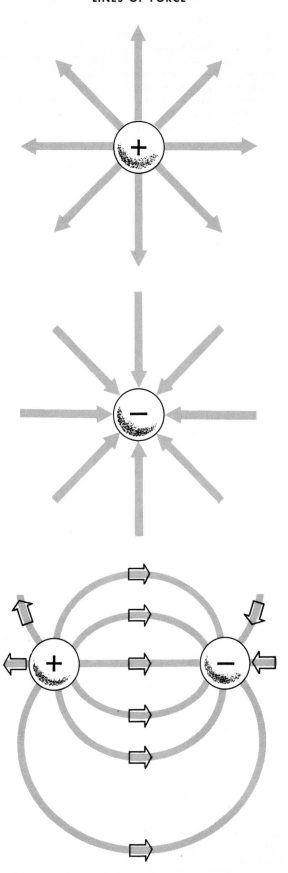

curves drawn so that their direction at any point on them, that is, the direction of the tangent to the curve at that point, is the same as the direction of the intensity E at the point. Lines of force always originate on positive charges and terminate on negative charges; they can never intersect; and they are drawn so that closer spacing indicates stronger fields.

Static Charge. Some important generalizations concerning statically charged conductors follow from the above

CONCENTRATION OF CHARGES

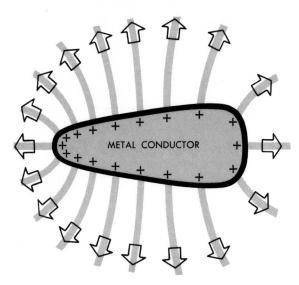

discussion. If a net charge is placed on a conductor, it quickly distributes itself and comes to rest. This final static distribution must be such that there is no electric field intensity E inside the conductor, because any electric field in the conductor would exert a force $F = Ee$ on the conduction electrons (for which $q = e$) and cause them to move. Since no charge is moving (that is what electrostatic means), there can be no field in the conductor. Thus any region of space completely surrounded by metal, no matter how thin, will be electrically undisturbed by accumulations of static charge outside of, or on, the metal. This is the basis of electrostatic shielding. One application is the enclosure of sensitive electron tubes in metal cases. In such applications, metal screens or mesh perform almost as well as solid sheets.

Similarly, it is seen that the electric field intensity E at the surface of a statically charged conductor must be perpendicular to that surface. If this were not so, there would be a component of E parallel to the surface, causing charge to move along the surface. It is necessary, therefore, that electrostatic lines of force meet the surfaces of conductors at right angles and without penetrating them.

Theory predicts and experiments confirm that *all* of the net static charge carried by a conductor is located on its outside surface. (The common argument that, since similar charges repel one another, they go to the surface to get as far apart as possible is neither convincing nor correct.) It is of interest that, if Coulomb's law were $F = (q_1q_2)/(kd)$ or $F = (q_1q_2)/(kd^3)$, or anything but the inverse-

square law, $F = (q_1q_2)/(kd^2)$, it would be possible for a conductor to have a net static charge in its interior. In the Van de Graaff high-voltage generator, charge is continuously fed by a moving belt from an external battery to the inside of a large metal sphere. Since all of this charge must move to the outside, the process can continue unhindered by charge build-up inside. The accumulating charge on the outside produces the desired high potential. When the potential becomes too high, the air around the sphere becomes somewhat conducting and charge begins to leak away. It is this action that limits the maximum voltage attainable by an electrostatic generator.

Static charge on the surface of a conductor is more closely spaced on sharp points than on blunt or flat regions, so that the lines of force, which originate and terminate on charges, are densest near points. Thus, the electric field near points may be quite intense, and can cause the surrounding air to become conducting. Lightning rods apply this effect by providing sharp points and good conducting paths. An overhead thundercloud whose lower surface has become negatively charged by friction in atmospheric turbulence induces a positive charge in the earth beneath it. This ground charge concentrates at the highest point available. The resultant conductivity of the air near the rod gives a low-resistance path for any lightning bolt in the vicinity, and the initial discharge is guided safely to the ground through a good conductor. It is also possible that leakage of the ground charge from the end of the rod neutralizes some of the cloud's charge, and thus prevents or defers some bolts.

Energy is stored in an electric field, no matter where it

GROUNDED
LIGHTNING ROD

is established. The electrostatic energy W (in joules) associated with a field of intensity E newtons per coulomb and stored in one cubic meter of empty space, such as the region between the plates of a vacuum capacitor, is given by $W = 4.4 \times 10^{-12}E^2$. If the plates of a charged capacitor are connected together with a wire, the electrostatic energy is converted to heat in the resulting electric current.

ELECTRICITY

Potential. Essential to the understanding of electric behavior are electric potential and potential difference (voltage), based upon the fundamental concepts of work and energy and having counterparts in gravitational theory. Use is again made of the idealized small probe of positive charge q_p introduced previously. Imagine such a probe in the presence of a fixed positive charge q. In order to move the probe from a point P_1 to a point P_2, some outside agency must overcome the force of electrostatic repulsion F. (Any resistive frictional forces are neglected throughout this discussion.) The agency must thus do work W.

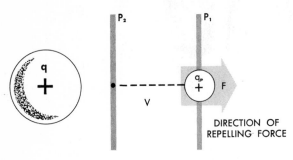

DIRECTION OF REPELLING FORCE

This work is stored as electric potential energy of the system. If the probe were released at P_2 it would accelerate toward P_1, picking up kinetic energy, at the expense of potential energy, as it went. On reaching P_1 it would have kinetic energy just equal to the work W. The electric potential difference between P_1 and P_2, represented by V, is defined as the ratio of W to q_p, or $V = W/q_p$, and is measured in volts. P_2 is said to be at a higher potential than P_1 because more energy is stored when q_p is at P_2. The natural unhindered motion of q_p would be a "fall" from P_2 to P_1. Note that if q had been negative, P_1 would have been at a higher potential than P_2. As in the case of the electric intensity E, V does *not* depend on the charge q_p: if q_p were changed, W would change in the same ratio. The work done in moving q_p between P_1 and P_2 would be the same regardless of the actual path followed by q_p. It is this fact that makes the concept of potential difference meaningful and useful. From $W = Vq_p$, the energy gained or lost by a charge q_p as it moves in an electric field can be computed simply by knowing the potential difference between the end points of its path, without knowing the details of the path shape. Furthermore, if the potential differences between any one fixed point and all other points of an electric field are known, the electric intensity E can be found by the calculus at every point in the field—a valuable analytical tool.

The term potential (rather than potential difference) used above needs some attention. As in the case of gravitational potential energy, it is convenient to select some suitable point or region for reference and to define the electric potential at any other point P as numerically equal to the potential difference between P and the reference. In the case of electrostatics the reference region of zero potential is customarily taken as infinitely distant. In circuit theory the earth is usually considered at zero (ground) potential. Since only the potential difference de-

Friction between the man's clothes and the seat covers generates static electricity. This causes the spark when his fingers (high potential) touch the door (low potential).

termines energy changes, the actual value assigned to the reference level is arbitrary (although it must not be changed, once selected for a particular problem) and is governed by convenience in computation. Any line, surface, or volume, all of whose points are at one potential is called an equipotential. It can be proved that the equipotential surface through any point must be perpendicular to the line of force at that point. From the fact that the electric field intensity E is zero inside a statically charged conductor, it follows that the interior and surface of the conductor constitute an equipotential region.

In electrostatics, very small net charges on bodies can result in the acquisition by those bodies of quite high potentials with respect to their surroundings. The spark passing between the hand and an automobile after the driver has slid out over plastic seat covers is caused by a potential difference, produced by charging by friction, which may easily be several thousand volts. The small static charge, which had been responsible for the potential difference and which flowed between the hand and the car in the spark, stored little energy and limited the current to a small value, thus constituting no personal danger. Such sparks are nevertheless a hazard near flammable vapors: although the total energy is small, very high effective temperatures are produced in small regions in the spark discharge. It must not be thought, however, that there can be no peril to life from static charge. In a high-voltage capacitor the charge and electrostatic energy stored may, on discharge, result in very dangerous current surges. The most impressive example is the lightning bolt, where the "plates" of the capacitor are the cloud and ground, and the potential difference is in millions of volts.

Consult Cornett, W. H., *Principles of Electricity* (rev. ed., 1952); Timbie, W. H., *Elements of Electricity* (4th ed., 1953); Dunsheath, Percy, *Electricity: How It Works* (1960); Sams, H. W., *Basic Electricity/Electronics* (5 vol., 1964).

LAWRENCE A. BORNSTEIN, New York University
See also ELECTRODYNAMICS; ELECTROMAGNETISM; PIEZOELECTRICITY; THERMOELECTRICITY.

ELECTRICITY, ATMOSPHERIC, continuous interchange of electric charges in the atmosphere, both to and from the earth's surface. Because electrically charged particles are concentrated in the ionosphere and, to a lesser degree, throughout other parts of the atmosphere, there is an average potential difference of several hundreds of thousands of volts between the ground and the upper atmosphere. Measured vertically, this difference varies from about 100 volts per yard near the earth to about 10 volts per yard at 20,000 ft., with positive charges directed toward the earth. As a result there is a continuous worldwide electrical current of about 1,800 amperes. Other air-to-earth currents are produced by the transport of ions through the atmosphere and from the charges carried by falling precipitation.

It is not definitely known what replenishes the positive charges in the upper atmosphere. There is strong evidence, however, that a return current is provided by the electrical discharges associated with lightning. About 100 such discharges are thought to occur each second around the earth.

JOHN R. GERHARDT, University of Texas

See also ATMOSPHERE; ELECTRICITY, TERRESTRIAL; LIGHTNING; ST. ELMO'S FIRE.

ELECTRICITY, TERRESTRIAL, natural electric currents flowing in the earth, called telluric, or earth, currents or geoelectricity. They are weak currents, first recognized in 1847 because of their effect on early attempts to transmit electric signals. Electric currents are generated by electrochemical reactions in the earth's crust. For example, the oxidation of sulfide minerals sets up electric currents, but these are local phenomena. Global electric currents that flow in sheets along the earth's surface and penetrate downward into the crust appear to be induced by electrical activity in the ionosphere. (*see* ELECTRICITY, ATMOSPHERIC). The density and flow directions can be mapped by measuring the horizontal potential gradients at the surface. This earth-current field varies with geography, time of day, and season, and is also affected by local variations in rock resistivity.

The earth's magnetic field is a product of electrical activity deep in the earth. According to one theory, the earth's nickel-iron core rotates differentially with respect to the mantle and thus acts as a dynamo that generates a magnetic field. Telluric currents, both natural and induced, are used by modern geologists to prospect for concealed mineral deposits and to decipher buried geologic structure.

PETER FLAWN, University of Texas

See also FLARE, SOLAR; MAGNETISM, TERRESTRIAL; SUNSPOT.

ELECTRIC LIGHT. *See* INCANDESCENT LAMP.

ELECTRIC LOCOMOTIVE. *See* LOCOMOTIVE.

ELECTRIC MOTOR. *See* MOTOR, ELECTRIC.

ELECTRIC POWER, energy produced by an electric generator and capable of being used by an electric motor or other electric device. The initial source of electric energy may be the blowing wind, flowing water, or heat from the combustion of such natural resources as coal and gas; or it may be produced by a conversion of the energy derived from the fission of atomic particles.

Electric power is distributed over vast areas. In the rural sections of the United States and in most of Canada, electric lines are now installed as a matter of course. Bulk transmission of electric power is feasible over a distance of 600 mi., but half that distance is considered a long line, according to present needs. Notably long power lines are located in California (the Hoover Dam–Los Angeles lines) and in Sweden (from a hydroelectric plant in the Arctic to users in Stockholm). The U.S.S.R. is planning a 1,200-mi. line. In most places in the United States, generating sites are less than 100 mi. from the load centers.

Energy and Power. In technical use the term "energy" refers to the capacity to do work, whereas "power" refers to the rate of doing work. The watt is a unit of power, and it is a rate of conversion of energy. The kilowatt (kw.) is 1,000 times as large as a watt, and is equivalent to about 1¼ hp. Thus, when the source of energy is steam, for example, the demand for a given number of kilowatts of power from an electrical distribution system necessitates the flow of a proportional number of pounds of steam per hour through the turbine driving the electric generator and a rate of fuel flow into the firebox of the steam boiler of a concomitant number of pounds of fuel per hour. The energy used by the electrical load in a specified interval of time is measured in kilowatt-hours (kw-hr), and the total amount may be correlated to the required total number of pounds of steam and of the fuel necessary for the production of the steam.

Growth of Electric Power. The production and distribution of electric power grew as the means were invented and developed, and as the demands for it increased. During the 19th century numerous attempts were made to exploit the known facts about electromagnetic phenomena. The electric telegraph was the first large-scale application of these phenomena, and the telegraph grew as the railroad systems expanded. The growth of the telegraph provided a support and focus for some of the ablest electrical experimenters and theorists, and as a result the steam-engine-driven electric generator was successfully developed in the 1870's. This machine provided the first electric power source of sufficient size, reliability, and low cost to make it suitable for industrial use. By 1880, electric lighting, in the form of arc lamps for lighthouses and incandescent lamps for exhibitions and experimentation, had been invented and developed.

The unofficial but real international race to establish a practical system of central-station generation and public distribution of electric energy was won by Thomas A. Edison, who was financially backed by several New Yorkers. At that time Edison's first task was to decide on a method of connecting the customers' appliances to the electrical source. It became clear that the only practical way to subdivide the power, so that one customer's use would not interfere with another's, was to realize a scheme of parallel distribution. This required the maintenance of constant voltage on the distribution lines, at all loads. Each customer could then connect his appliances as needed, drawing as much current as necessary. Since the voltage was

ELECTRIC POWER

The electric telegraph invented by Samuel F. B. Morse in 1835 first aroused interest in practical applications of electricity. The demand for electrical energy is now measured in billions of kilowatts a year. High tension transmission lines carry electricity from huge generating plants to central distribution stations.

Brown Brothers

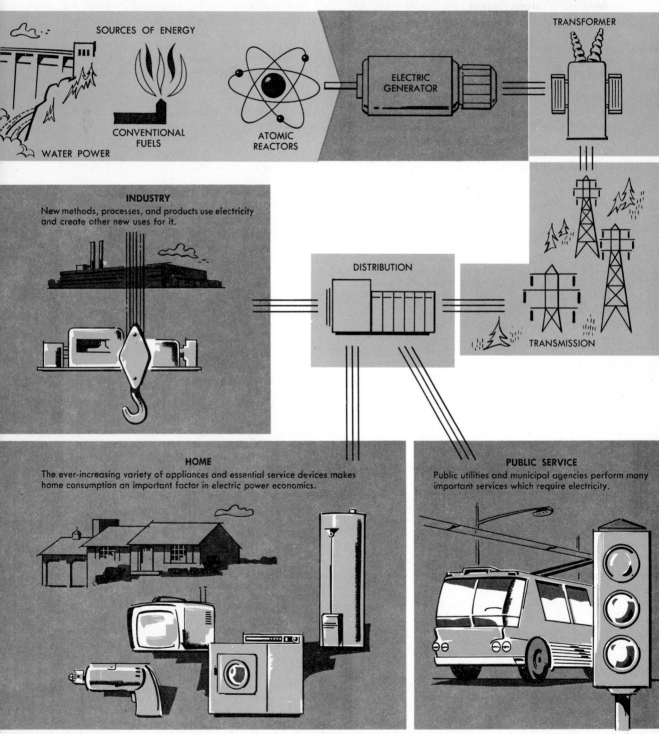

SOURCES OF ENERGY

WATER POWER

CONVENTIONAL FUELS

ATOMIC REACTORS

ELECTRIC GENERATOR

TRANSFORMER

TRANSMISSION

INDUSTRY
New methods, processes, and products use electricity and create other new uses for it.

DISTRIBUTION

HOME
The ever-increasing variety of appliances and essential service devices makes home consumption an important factor in electric power economics.

PUBLIC SERVICE
Public utilities and municipal agencies perform many important services which require electricity.

regulated by the powerhouse attendant, the operation of the appliances of the other customers would not be disturbed. The alternative would have been the use of a series connection and constant-current distribution, so that all appliances not in use would be bypassed by a closed switch instead of being disconnected by an open switch. Edison chose the 120/240-v. three-wire system, and developed a carbon filament lamp which would operate at about 120 v.

D.C. Power System. After the successful demonstration of a d.c. electric-power system at Menlo Park, N.J., a full-scale installation was planned for lower New York; but at this point political and financial forces came into play. The successful opening, in 1880, of the Pearl Street Station serving lower New York was the result of a herculean achievement which involved not only the development of the electric components (generators, and so forth) for the whole system, but also the creation of factories for their manufacture and the commercial and technical arrangements for the sale of the new electric service. Public acceptance of electric light and power was immediate. The d.c. system used by Edison had the important advantage of providing excellent mechanical power transmission because of the characteristics of the shunt motor (*see* Motor, Electric). It had the disadvantage, however, of a limited range of service. As the use of electric power grew, a more flexible system was obviously needed.

A.C. Power System. In the 1880's two inventions changed the entire prospect. William Stanley improved the transformer, an apparatus for changing alternating voltage efficiently from one value to another. This was followed by Nikola Tesla's invention of the polyphase a.c. motor and generator. George Westinghouse acquired the patent rights. The a.c. system came into use with economically proportioned voltages for generation, transmission, distribution, and utilization. When an international scientific commission recommended, in 1895, that the generators at Niagara Falls be built for polyphase a.c., it became clear that a.c. would supersede the older d.c. system.

Soon after the turn of the century, the steam turbine, with its higher efficiency and lack of reciprocating parts, came into service in the production of electric power. Since that time, the turbine design and manufacture, as well as metallurgical developments, have been carried forward, together with steam boiler and switchgear design, so that two-shaft units as large as 650,000 kw. are now in service, for example, in Tennessee Valley Authority (TVA) units in Paradise, Tenn.

The period from 1900 to 1930 was a time of increasing technical experience and insight in the field of electric-power development. Generating stations became larger. High-voltage transmission became common, isolated systems were interconnected, and homes and industrial plants were electrified in increasing numbers. In the United States, this was also a time of financial reorganization and consolidation of electric-power corporations, and it was the era when state commissions were established to regulate electric rates and service. The great holding company empires arose and collapsed during this period.

Developments After 1930. In the United States, during the 1930's, the Federal Power Commission was strengthened and was given among other duties the work of regulating interstate electric rates. The Securities and Exchange Commission was established in 1933, with the regulation of the financing of utilities as part of its responsibility. The holding companies in the electric-power field were forced to become financially realistic as well as technologically justifiable. The Rural Electrification Administration, the various federal power authorities, and the TVA were established during the decade of the 1930's. Also in the 1930's electric equipment and electric-power systems were refined to improve service and make it more reliable and more economical. Electric-power system frequency became so stable that the electric clock could be depended upon for correct time, and traffic signal systems were held in proper sequence by electric timing motors.

The standardization of electric apparatus began about the turn of the century, and the electric industry in the United States now has an extensive set of standards. There are indications that eventually world-wide standards may be set up, with beneficial commercial results. The choice of 60 cycles as the standard power frequency in the United States, made half a century ago, was a compromise between various factors. This frequency has thus far proven satisfactory.

Capacity of Equipment. As electric generation and distribution systems have increased in size, the cost has made larger individual units desirable. In the United States, two private electric utility systems (Commonwealth Edison Company and Pacific Gas and Electric Company) each now has an installed capacity in excess of 5,000,000 kw. The federal TVA system exceeds 10,000,000 kw. In Canada the Hydro-Electric Power Commission of Ontario has more than 6,000,000 kw. installed—three-fourths hydroelectric, one-fourth steam. In such large-scale operations, machines of 250,000 kw. capacity or larger may be used with safety because the output of such a unit would amount to 5% or less of system capacity.

Recent and Predicted Developments. At the end of 1960, there was a total installed generating capacity of over 165,000,000 kw. in the United States; over 750,000,000,000 kw-hr of electric energy was consumed during the year. These figures are expected to increase to over 200,000,000 installed kw. by 1965, during which year over 1,000,000,000,000 kw-hr will be consumed. By 1980 these figures might triple, and almost 10,000,000 kw. of the total installed capacity is likely to be nuclear. By the end of 1960 Canada had about 18,000,000 kw. installed. Total additions planned between 1960 and 1965 exceed 10,000,000 kw. In comparison, the Soviet Union's prediction for its consumption of electric power in 1965 is about 520,000,000,000 kw-hr, or about half that of the United States. The U.S.S.R. also boasts the largest hydroelectric plant in the world, the Volzhski, which has a capacity of over 2,500,000 kw. and is expected to generate over 11,000,000,000 kw-hr annually.

Walter A. LaPierre, Webb Institute, and Frank Yeaple, *Product Engineering*

ELECTRIC SHOCK may occur when the body becomes part of a conducting electric circuit. The consequences depend upon the wetness of the skin, the nature of the ground material, and the characteristics of the electric current. Skin resistance to current flow is lowered by

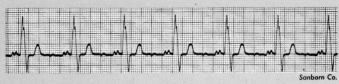

Electrodes, attached by wires to the electrocardiograph, are connected to the patient's arms, legs, and chest. Electrical impulses from the patient are transmitted to the machine, amplified, and recorded on a graph.

Frank Gordon—A. Devaney

sweating or wet clothing. If the individual is in contact with a good conductor, such as a radiator, or a water bath, he might be killed by a current which would otherwise be tolerated. Alternating currents are generally more dangerous than direct currents, particularly low-frequency currents. The shock may cause momentary or prolonged loss of consciousness, convulsions, and burns, where the current enters or leaves the body. Death may result from heart failure or paralysis of respiration. Electric-shock victims should be given immediate artificial respiration. *See also* ARTIFICIAL RESPIRATION.

ELECTRIC-SHOCK THERAPY. *See* SHOCK THERAPY.

ELECTROCARDIOGRAM [ĭ-lĕk-trō-kär′dē-ə-grăm] **(ECG)**, a record of the electric activity of the heart. Minute voltages from the auricles and ventricles of the heart are transmitted to a recording instrument (an electrocardiograph) by means of metal electrodes placed on the arms, legs, and chest. The electrocardiograph amplifies these voltages which then activate a stylus to write upon a moving paper strip.

The electric events in the chambers of the heart are reflected in characteristic fluctuations or "waves" of the ECG. Certain changes in these waves have been associated with various heart conditions and other disorders.

The ECG is extremely important in the diagnosis of coronary thrombosis, enlargement of the heart, and irregularities of the heart beat (arrhythmias). Great care is required in the interpretation of the ECG, as it has been found that many persons with severe heart conditions exhibit a normal ECG and conversely many normal persons present abnormal patterns.

HARRY JAFFE, M.D.

See also HEART.

ELECTROCHEMISTRY, that branch of chemistry dealing with chemical reactions brought about by the application of electrical energy and with chemical reactions from which electrical energy is derived. Any liquid electrolyte, or ionic compound in solution, will conduct electricity by migration of its ions to the charged electrodes. There the ions are converted to neutral atoms by accepting or giving up electrons. This method of decomposing ionic compounds is called electrolysis and is used industrially to prepare pure metals and nonmetals from their salts and to electroplate objects. Aluminum is obtained from fused bauxite and chlorine from salt solution by electrolysis.

The opposite of electrolysis occurs in any battery. The material from which the poles of a battery are made, and the electrolytes in which the poles are immersed, react chemically to produce an electromotive potential, a virtual pressure of electrons, between the poles. When they are joined by a conductor, a steady flow of electrons results.

STEPHEN G. SIMPSON, Massachusetts Institute of Technology

ELECTROCUTION, method of executing a criminal with electricity. The prisoner is fastened into the electric chair by straps pinioning the arms, legs, and torso. Electrodes are attached to the calf of one leg and to the crown of the head. After a face mask has been strapped in place, the executioner throws a switch which sends a lethal current of electricity through the victim's body. The strength of the initial single shock of 2,000 volts of alternating current is immediately reduced to about 500 volts and is followed by several shocks of lower fluctuating voltage which are reapplied at short intervals. As a rule the switch is thrown only once, but sometimes a second major shock is given if the attending physicians consider it advisable.

Electrocution was first used on Aug. 6, 1890, in the prison at Auburn, N.Y. Although it is generally believed that death is instantaneous, evidence indicates that the victim may be alive but unconscious for several minutes after the current has passed through his body. Electrocution is the method used in 24 jurisdictions in the United States to carry out sentences imposing the death penalty.

JOSEPH S. ROUCEK, University of Bridgeport

See also CAPITAL PUNISHMENT.

ELECTRODE. *See* ELECTROLYSIS.

ELECTRODYNAMICS [ĭ-lĕk-trō-dī-năm′ĭks], study of electric currents and the phenomena associated with them.

Theory. If charged particles are exposed to an electric field, the field exerts a force upon them. In electric conductors there are charges free to migrate. A field inside a conductor therefore causes charges to move, that is, it produces an electric current. Quantitatively, a steady electric current, represented by the letter I, is defined as the net positive charge q flowing through any cross-sectional area A of the conductor per unit time t, or $I = q/t$. Thus the direction of I is that in which positive charge moves. In metals the moving charges are negative electrons, therefore the current is in the direction opposite to the electron flow. The unit of current is the ampere.

Electromotive Force. A field can be maintained inside a conductor only by an external agency called a seat, or source, of electromotive force (emf), for example, a battery or generator. These devices convert, respectively, chemical and mechanical energy into electric energy, thereby sustaining an electric potential difference, or voltage, across their terminals. This terminal voltage is, in the absence of losses within the source, equal to the emf. In a battery the emf is determined by the chemical composition of the battery and remains essentially constant throughout its life. The emf of a generator, or dynamo, depends upon its construction and how fast it is driven.

When a source of emf is connected across a conductor, the potential difference across the terminals maintains a field within the conductor, and a current is established. The relationship between the potential difference, or voltage, V across an ordinary conductor and the current I in it is known as Ohm's law, which states that the current is directly proportional to the applied potential difference. However, the conductor itself has an effect. A poor conductor carries less current for the same potential difference. Taking into consideration the effect of the conductor, the complete form of Ohm's law is then: the current varies directly with the voltage and inversely with the resistance, or $I = V/R$, where R, the electrical resistance, depends upon the conductor and is measured in ohms. A good conductor thus has a low resistance. The value of R is determined by the material, temperature, and geometry of the conductor. A wire of copper has a smaller resistance than a similar wire of iron; most substances conduct better when cold; resistance is directly proportional to the length and inversely proportional to the cross-sectional area of the conductor.

Laws. Positive charge flowing through a conductor, or conventional current, moves from a higher potential to a lower, thereby giving up electric potential energy. This energy is supplied by the source of emf and is converted into heat in the conductor. Thus, on returning to the negative terminal of the battery in the circuit, the charge has lost all its electric energy. The battery replenishes this energy from its stored chemical energy and drives the charge once more through the resistor. As a battery ages its chemical energy becomes exhausted, and it can no longer sustain the current. Joule's law states the rate at which electric energy is converted into heat in the resistor: power equals the square of the current multiplied by the resistance, or $P = I^2R$, where P is the power in watts, I is the current in amperes, and R is the resistance in ohms. Ohm's law, $I = V/R$, can be written in the form $R = V/I$. If the value V/I is substituted for R in Joule's law, $P = I^2R$, the latter becomes $P = I^2V/I$, or $P = IV$. This can also be written $I = P/V$, where V is the potential difference in volts across the resistor. This last equation may be used to determine the current in a power line. For example, if a 1,200-watt broiler, an 800-watt iron, a 700-watt air conditioner, and television, lighting, and other appliances amounting to 600 watts, or a grand total of 3,300

watts, are to be simultaneously operated on a 110-volt line, the wiring must be designed to carry a current of $I = P/V = 3,300$ watts/110 volts, or 30 amperes.

If several resistors are connected in series in a circuit the current is the same in all the resistors, but the voltages across them are, in general, different. The total potential difference across the whole array is the sum of the individual voltages. In some radios the filaments of the tubes are connected in series. If one burns out or is removed, an open circuit results and all current ceases. This is characteristic of series circuits.

When circuit components are connected in parallel, however, the voltages across all of them are the same. This type of connection is used in ordinary power distribution. The components are roughly independent of one another; appliances may be turned on or off without appreciably affecting the others. If, however, too many devices are connected in parallel, or if a very low resistance (current increases as resistance decreases) were connected across the line (short circuit), the safe current-carrying capacity of the wires would be exceeded, causing overheating or even melting. To prevent this, a fuse is used in series with the main line. It is designed to melt quickly if the current becomes excessive. Clearly, a fuse with a current rating higher than the wiring it is to protect should never be used.

Meters. Ammeters are low-resistance devices for measuring current, and should always be connected in series

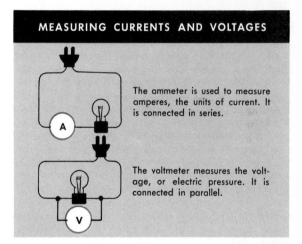

MEASURING CURRENTS AND VOLTAGES

The ammeter is used to measure amperes, the units of current. It is connected in series.

The voltmeter measures the voltage, or electric pressure. It is connected in parallel.

with the component whose current is to be determined. Voltmeters, which have high internal resistance, measure potential difference and are connected in parallel with the circuit element whose voltage is to be measured. Both of these meters usually are modifications of the basic galvanometer, a sensitive current-measuring instrument whose operation, like that of the electric motor, depends upon the force exerted by a magnetic field on a current-carrying wire. With a suitable ammeter and voltmeter, the resistance of a circuit component can be determined by using Ohm's law, $R = V/I$, and the power dissipated as heat in the component can be computed by using Joule's law, $P = VI$.

Conductors. Distilled water is a poor electric conductor. Impure water, especially that containing dissolved

THE FLOW OF ELECTRICITY

CURRENT DIRECTION

AREA A

ELECTRON MOTION
FIELD INTENSITY

ELECTRODYNAMICS

salts or acids, is a good conductor. The improved conductivity is attributed to the presence of mobile positive and negative ions, that is atoms with a deficiency or excess of electrons, contributed by the impurities. Thus, table salt in solution separates into positive sodium ions and negative chlorine ions. If a pair of metal rods, or electrodes, is inserted into a suitably prepared conducting liquid, or electrolyte, and a battery is connected across the electrodes, a current—carried by positive and negative ions— is established. With platinum electrodes and water containing a little sulfuric acid, pure hydrogen gas is liberated from the water at the negative electrode, or cathode, and oxygen appears at the positive electrode, or anode, a process called electrolysis of water. If the cathode is copper, the anode silver, and the electrolyte a silver nitrate solution, silver will be deposited on the copper, thus electroplating it. Very pure metals may be prepared in this way. Study of electrodeposition led to Faraday's law of electrolysis: the mass m of a substance released in electrolysis is given by $m = MIt/vF$, where M is the atomic weight of the substance, I is the steady current in amperes that flowed for an interval of t seconds, v is the chemical valence of the substance, and F is a fixed quantity of charge (96,519 coulombs) called the faraday. Another important electrochemical effect is the development of a potential difference across a pair of electrodes of dissimilar materials when they are dipped into a suitable electrolyte; it is this action that makes batteries possible.

Alternating Current. A device that produces across its terminals a potential difference whose polarity reverses at regular intervals is called an alternating current (a.c.) generator. If the voltage across the terminals of a 110-volt, 60 cycle per second a.c. generator is plotted against the time on a graph, a sinusoidal curve results. One full cycle of voltage is completed in 1/60 second; therefore its frequency is 60 cycles per second. The maximum V_m is 155 volts. The effective root-mean-square (RMS) voltage, based on the heating effect of the resulting current, is given by $V = V_m/\sqrt{2}$. In this example $V = 155/1.414 = 110$ volts. An a.c. circuit containing only resistors (no capacitors or inductors) follows Ohm's law as given above for direct current (d.c.) circuits, $I = V/R$. In this example, $I = 110/10 = 11$ amp. This is not a steady current, however; it has the same shape and frequency as the applied voltage, and its maximum value is given by $I_m = \sqrt{2}\,I$. In this example $I_m = (\sqrt{2})(11) = 15.5$ amp. The rate of evolution of heat in a resistor is given by Joule's law, provided the effective value of the current is used. In the present example, $P = I^2R = (11)^2(10) = 1210$ watts. Unless otherwise specified, quoted values of a.c. voltage and current are conventionally the effective values.

An important advantage of alternating current over direct current is in power distribution. Through the use of transformers alternating voltages may be increased, or stepped-up, with a resulting proportionate decrease in the current. Since the power handled is given by $P = VI$, no loss—or gain—in power results. (Small transformer heat losses are neglected here.) Most of the power lost along transmission lines goes into heat and is given by $P_{lost} = I^2R$; cutting down the current thus sharply reduces such losses. Without this transformation property of alternating currents, electric energy could not be carried economi-

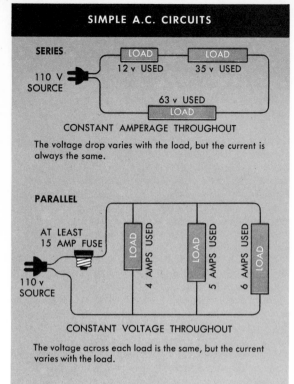

SIMPLE A.C. CIRCUITS

SERIES

110 V SOURCE — LOAD 12 v USED — LOAD 35 v USED — LOAD 63 v USED

CONSTANT AMPERAGE THROUGHOUT

The voltage drop varies with the load, but the current is always the same.

PARALLEL

110 v SOURCE — AT LEAST 15 AMP FUSE — LOAD 4 AMPS USED — LOAD 5 AMPS USED — LOAD 6 AMPS USED

CONSTANT VOLTAGE THROUGHOUT

The voltage across each load is the same, but the current varies with the load.

cally from hydroelectric generating plants to distant cities. In many applications, for example, radio and television, a.c. power cannot be used directly. These devices therefore include rectifiers, electronic or solid-state, which convert a.c. to d.c.

When a.c. flows through a coil of wire, an emf is induced across the ends of the coil. This emf opposes the flow of a.c. This opposition is called the inductive reactance, and is proportional to the frequency of the a.c. and to the inductance of the coil. A capacitor, or condenser, a device that stores electric charge, allows a.c. to flow through it. The opposition by a capacitor to a.c. is called the capacitive reactance and is inversely proportional to both the frequency of the a.c. and to the capacitance of the condenser.

In a.c. circuits containing capacitance or inductance in addition to resistance, the current is given by a modified form of Ohm's law: $I = V/Z$, where Z, the impedance, is

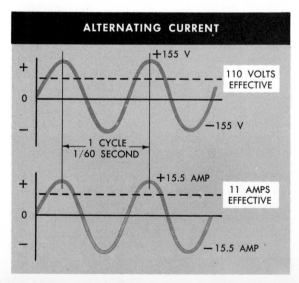

ALTERNATING CURRENT

+155 V — 110 VOLTS EFFECTIVE — −155 V

1 CYCLE 1/60 SECOND

+15.5 AMP — 11 AMPS EFFECTIVE — −15.5 AMP

measured in ohms and depends upon the inductive and capacitive reactances as well as the resistance. These reactances in turn depend upon the frequency of the current: the capacitive reactance, inversely, and the inductive reactance, directly. At a particular frequency f_0, called the resonant frequency, and given by $f_0{}^2 = \frac{1}{4}\pi^2 LC$, where L and C are the inductance and the capacitance, respectively, the two reactances will be equal. In a series a.c. circuit at resonance the resultant reactance is zero, and the current is limited only by the resistance. If the resistance is low, the current will be high and large voltages, which may easily be 10 times the generator voltage, will appear across the capacitor and across the inductor. Great care must thus be exercised in working with such circuits.

A.c. generators of frequencies above several thousand cycles per second are electronic devices, usually called oscillators. At frequencies above 100,000 cycles per second appreciable energy in the form of electromagnetic radiation is dissipated by the wires. The higher the frequency, the more efficient the radiation process.

LAWRENCE A. BORNSTEIN, New York University
See also ELECTROMAGNETISM.

ELECTROENCEPHALOGRAPH [ĭ-lĕk-trō-ĕn-sĕf'ə-lə-grăf], instrument used to record the electrical activity of the brain. Electrodes placed over the scalp detect electrical impulses from the brain (the so-called "brain waves"), which are then amplified and recorded as a continuous line on a moving paper strip.

The electroencephalograph has been used to diagnose brain tumors, epilepsy, and other types of brain disease. Neurophysiologists have made extensive use of the instrument in research. It has been found, for example, that certain regular fluctuations called alpha waves appear during light sleep and disappear in the waking state. Other distinct patterns of the electroencephalogram have been identified and have been associated with various mental states and activities.

ELECTROLUMINESCENCE [ĭ-lĕk-trō-lōō-mə-nĕs'əns], light emission caused by the excitation of phosphor in an electric field. In an electroluminescent lamp the light-producing medium, coated on a glass plate, consists of a phosphor layer embedded in a thin sheet of ceramic dielectric material between two layers of electric conduction material. The total thickness of the glass and coating is less than one-hundredth of an inch. When the two conductive layers are connected to a source of alternating current, the phosphor layer glows, usually in a greenish-blue color.

Electroluminescent lamps differ from incandescent lamps in two ways. First, they do not depend on a white-hot filament for light emission. This means that they do not get hot, and that less current is needed for the same light output, since almost all the electricity applied is converted into light. Since there is no filament to burn out, they will not fail suddenly.

The second major difference is in their shape. Incandescent and fluorescent lamps require a sealed-glass bulb or tube. Electroluminescent lamps are not sealed and emit light from the thin flat surface. Electroluminescent lamps can be constructed in strips to form letters for an illuminated sign. By energizing different combinations of these strips different letters, numbers, or shapes can be displayed. This type is used on some computers or electronic counters to display results to the operator. Electroluminescent lamps are also used as night lights and to illuminate automobiles and aircraft instrument panels.

LAURENCE D. SHERGALIS, Associate Editor, *Electronics*

ELECTROLYSIS [ĭ-lĕk-trŏl'ə-sĭs], in chemistry, defines those chemical reactions which are activated by an electric current passing through a liquid solution or a melt of the reactants. Not all substances can be electrolyzed because a necessary property of an electrolyzable substance, or electrolyte, is that it conduct electricity. It does so by liberating positive and negative ions. Acids, bases, and salts react with water to produce ions, and most salts ionize without water when they are melted, or fused.

The mechanism of electrolysis can best be explained with an illustration. If salt, sodium chloride, is heated until it melts, in a container into which electrodes are placed, the salt's Na^+ and Cl^- ions will move about freely. When the current is started, electrons from the source of the current load the cathode. Any Na^+ cations in the vicinity will accept electrons and become neutral Na^0 atoms, which then deposit on the cathode. As some of the Na^+ cations are removed, others gravitate into the field around the cathode and are neutralized. At the anode Cl^- anions give up their extra electron and become Cl^0 atoms which combine into molecules and escape as the gas Cl_2 (chlorine).

Thus the cathode is relieved of its electrons, while electrons are released to the anode. In other words the voltage difference between the electrodes causes the ions of the electrolyte to separate, and the salt is decomposed into its elements. Electrical energy has been converted into chemical energy, and the reaction can be represented by half reactions at the two electrodes:

$$\begin{array}{l} Na^+ + e^- \rightarrow Na^0 \\ \underline{Cl^- \qquad\quad \rightarrow Cl^0 + e^-} \\ Na^+ + Cl^- \rightarrow Na^0 + Cl^0 \end{array}$$

The amount of current used up is in direct proportion to the amount of substance deposited at the electrodes, according to Faraday's Law. A faraday is the number of electrons required to neutralize one gram-equivalent weight of an ion. If sodium and chlorine are allowed to react, the heat of that reaction is equivalent to the electrical energy needed to decompose the same amount of salt.

Water solutions of electrolytes follow the same pattern of conductivity and neuralization, but they show a variety of reactions at the electrodes because water itself is a very weak electrolyte, which decomposes, when pure, into hydrogen and oxygen. Therefore water and its ions will react with the neutralized elements. Electrolysis is extremely important industrially for the extraction or the purification of many metals and nonmetals, which are too difficult or too expensive to isolate chemically.

Electroplating is an adaptation of electrolysis in which the object to be plated serves as the cathode and the ions of the metal to be used for the plating are in solution.

L. VACZEK, The New School for Social Research

ELECTROLYTE. *See* ELECTROLYSIS.

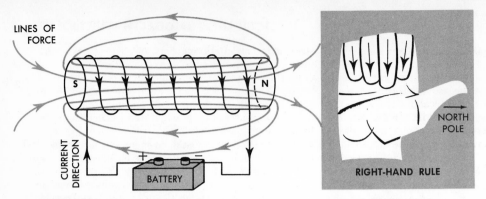

LINES OF FORCE

S   N

CURRENT DIRECTION

BATTERY

ELECTROMAGNET

Current flowing through the spiral conductor sets up a magnetic field with an axis parallel to that of the spiral. The field's lines of force follow a closed path through the core, emerging at the north magnetic pole, curving back, and re-entering at the south pole.

NORTH POLE

RIGHT-HAND RULE

ELECTROMAGNET, a magnet which, unlike the permanent magnet, requires a continuous externally produced electric current for its magnetization. Any electric current is itself an electromagnet. The straight solenoid is one of the most common practical forms. An insulated wire is wound around a solid cylindrical core, usually of iron. When a direct current is established in the winding, a steady magnetic field much like that of a bar magnet is set up, strong near the ends and within the core. If the right hand with thumb extended is wrapped around the solenoid with the fingers pointing in the direction of the current in the windings, the thumb points to the equivalent north pole.

The field of an electromagnet may be made stronger by increasing the current, by having more windings, by using cores of higher permeability, and, locally, by properly shaping the ends of the core. If the solenoid is formed into a nearly closed torus with a small air gap, the field in the gap is very much larger.

Important advantages of the electromagnet over the permanent magnet are that it can develop much stronger fields; the fields can be turned on and off conveniently; and they can be varied continuously. Electromagnets are used to produce permanent magnets and in many devices including relays, loudspeakers, and scrap-iron derricks.

LAWRENCE A. BORNSTEIN, New York University
See also ELECTROMAGNETISM; MAGNETIC MATERIALS; MAGNETISM.

ELECTROMAGNETIC INDUCTION, the production of an electromotive force (emf), and hence of electric energy, by a change in, or relative motion of, a magnetic field. It was discovered in 1831 by Michael Faraday and independently by Joseph Henry, and is the principle underlying electric generators, transformers, the induction coil, and the induction motor.

If a wire is moved through a uniform magnetic field, the magnetic lines of force are cut and an emf is induced across the ends of the wire. Reversing the motion of the wire or the field direction reverses the polarity. If the wire is moved parallel to the field, no lines of force are cut and no emf is induced (for a fine wire). If the ends of the wire are connected across a resistor, current flows through the wire and develops heat in the resistor. The energy thus dissipated comes from the work done by the agency moving the wire.

Physical motion is not essential to induce an emf. If a flat coil is inserted in the gap of an electromagnet, magnetic flux penetrates the coil when current flows in the winding of the electromagnet. A changing current will produce a changing magnetic field in the gap, which will induce an emf in the coil.

LAWRENCE A. BORNSTEIN, New York University
See also ELECTROMAGNETISM; MAGNETISM.

ELECTROMAGNETIC RADIATION. *See* ELECTROMAGNETISM.

ELECTROMAGNETIC SPECTRUM. *See* SPECTRUM.

ELECTROMAGNETIC THEORY. *See* ELECTROMAGNETISM.

ELECTROMAGNETIC WAVE, a form of energy transmission consisting of oscillations of paired electric and magnetic fields. Sometimes called a Hertzian wave (especially at low frequencies), it shares with waves of all kinds the properties of velocity, frequency, and wave length. Electromagnetic radiation travels at the speed of light, 186,000 mi. per second in a vacuum, and consists of a broad spectrum whose sections, in order of increasing frequency (decreasing wave length) are the broadcast, short-wave, television, radar, infrared, visible, ultraviolet, X-ray, and gamma-ray bands.

See also ELECTRICITY; MAGNETISM.

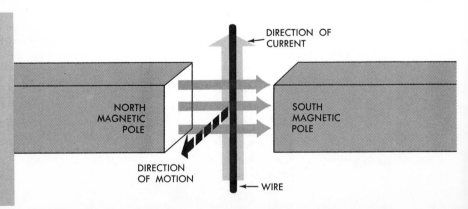

ELECTROMAGNETIC INDUCTION

As the wire cuts across the magnetic field, the interrupted lines of force initiate in it a directed movement of its electrons to produce a current. In a generator a coil of wire is rotated by steam or water power in a strong field.

DIRECTION OF CURRENT

NORTH MAGNETIC POLE

SOUTH MAGNETIC POLE

DIRECTION OF MOTION

WIRE

ELECTROMAGNETISM [ĭ-lĕk-trō-măg′nə-tĭz-əm], phenomena involving an interdependence of electric and magnetic effects. A connection between magnetism and electricity was first demonstrated by Hans Christian Oersted in 1820. This relationship can be demonstrated by allowing a compass needle to rest in its natural north-south alignment and suspending a wire horizontally above the needle with the same orientation. If an electric current is established in the wire the needle is deflected. Reversing the direction of current changes the direction of the deflection. In both cases the compass points in the direction of the resultant magnetic field, which is the sum of the earth's field (north-south) and of the field of the current.

The fundamental law has been established that all electric currents have associated magnetic fields. The conductor carrying the current is incidental to the effect. A narrow beam of electrons passing through the vacuum of a television tube has a surrounding magnetic field identical with that of an equal current in a fine copper wire. Revolving orbital electrons in atoms have associated magnetic fields that determine the magnetic properties of the substances the atoms constitute.

Lines of Force. With a small compass used as a field probe, the lines of force of the magnetic field of a long straight current are found to be circles concentric with the current. Their direction at any point is that of a compass placed at the point. The strength of this particular field is found to be directly proportional to the current and inversely proportional to the distance from the wire.

Studies of various magnetic fields have led to a fundamental generalization: lines of magnetic force are always closed, with neither beginning nor end. These are quite different from electrostatic lines of force, which originate and terminate on electric charges. It is concluded that there are no magnetic counterparts to electric charge; that is, no isolated magnetic poles exist. The exact designation for the magnetic field discussed here is magnetic induction.

Application. Magnetic fields exert no forces on electric charges at rest. A moving charge, however, constitutes an electric current and has its own magnetic field. The interaction between the magnetic field of a moving charge and the magnetic field through which the charge moves gives rise to a mechanical force whose direction may be determined by Fleming's rule and whose magnitude depends on the charge, its velocity, and the strength of the magnetic field. It is this force that keeps a proton whirling in a circular path in a cyclotron, that determines the distribution of cosmic radiation reaching the earth, and that underlies the operation of most electric motors and meters (galvanometers). In these latter devices the electromagnetic force exerted by the field of a magnet on the current in a loop of wire gives rise to a torque which causes the loop to rotate. The loop of a motor is wound on an armature and so arranged that it may rotate continuously. A meter includes a spring to exert a counter-torque that causes the loop to come to rest at an angular displacement from its equilibrium position, the displacement being proportional to the current. A motor converts electric energy into mechanical energy. The opposite—conversion of mechanical energy into electrical energy—is accomplished by a dynamo, or generator, whose principle of operation is electromagnetic induction, another fundamental phenomenon of electromagnetism.

Electromagnetic Waves. Whenever an electric charge accelerates, that is, changes its speed or direction of motion, it radiates energy in the form of electromagnetic waves. (This statement is not valid inside atoms.) Such radiation was predicted in a theory, developed by James Clerk Maxwell about 1860, based upon four fundamental partial differential equations (Maxwell's equations) concerning electric and magnetic fields. These equations express four basic laws: one is a modified formulation of Coulomb's law; a second states mathematically that free, isolated magnetic poles cannot exist; the third is Faraday's law of electromagnetic induction; and the last is a general formula for computing the magnetic fields of currents. Maxwell's main contribution was his introduction of the displacement current, a concept enabling the last equation to be applied to varying currents in circuits with capacitors. Displacement current is equivalent to the ordinary conduction current, but involves no electric charges as current carriers. Adroit manipulation of these equations led Maxwell to the prediction that electromagnetic energy can be radiated as waves which travel with the speed of light. About 1886 Heinrich Rudolph Hertz produced just such radiation, a striking confirmation of the electromagnetic theory of light and one of the outstanding achievements in classical physics.

LAWRENCE A. BORNSTEIN, New York University
See also ELECTRICITY; ELECTROMAGNETIC INDUCTION; FLEMING'S RULE; MAGNETISM.

ELECTROMETALLURGY [ĭ-lĕk-trō-mĕt′əl-ûr-jē], term covering a variety of metallurgical processes based on the use of electric current to produce either a thermal or a chemical reaction.

Electrothermal. The electrothermal processes are carried out in furnaces or by welding. The resistance furnace, for example, has a high-resistance material through which

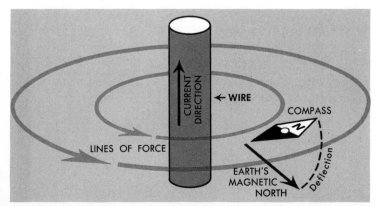

ELECTRICITY AND MAGNETISM

An electric current has a surrounding magnetic field. If a compass is placed near a charged wire, the compass needle is deflected from its natural north direction by lines of force in the magnetic field.

CURRENT DIRECTION ← WIRE
COMPASS
LINES OF FORCE
EARTH'S MAGNETIC NORTH
Deflection

377

current is passed to produce heat, which by convection and radiation, is used in annealing, normalizing, hardening, tempering, carburizing, nitriding, brazing, galvanizing, and sintering. The induction furnace has a primary coil in which the metal object is placed. When a high-frequency, alternating current is passed through the primary coil, a heavy current is induced in the metal and its resistance generates heat. Melting and heating of forgings, hardening, soldering, brazing, sintering, annealing, and other metallurgical processes are done in induction furnaces. An arc furnace is one in which heat is generated by causing the current to bridge a gap between carbon electrodes or between electrodes and the charge to be melted. Arc furnaces are widely used for refining steel and melting metals in foundry practice.

Similarly, in arc welding the current is caused to arc between the parts to be joined and an electrode or between two electrodes to produce heat. In resistance welding, heat is generated by the passage of current through the contacting faces of the parts to be joined. Spot, seam, and percussion welding are done by resistance welding.

Electrochemical. The electrochemical reaction is used to refine, form, or plate metals. It is based on the passage of direct current through an electrolyte which decomposes to produce the desired effect. In electrolytic refining this is done by placing bars of the impure metal as anodes into a tank of a salt solution of the desired metal. A thin metal sheet, as a cathode, is suspended in the solution. When a direct current passes through the solution, the electrolyte dissociates into ions. The positively charged metal ions pass to the cathode where they give up their charge and form crystals of pure metal on the cathode plate. At the same time the nonmetallic negative ions move to the anode where they give up their charge and combine with the anode metal and also regenerate the electrolyte. This process is applied to the refining of copper, gold, zinc, silver, lead, platinum, antimony, bismuth, and cadmium in an aqueous solution. High-purity aluminum, magnesium, and sodium are electrolyzed in an igneous solution by maintaining the electrolyte in a molten state. Another electrochemical process, electroforming, depends on the deposit of a metal on a graphite-impregnated wax form in order to produce such items as musical instrument components (with copper) or phonograph master records (with copper or gold). In electroplating, the electrochemical reaction is used to coat metals for protection against corrosion or resistance.

PAUL B. EATON, Purdue University
See also ANODIZING; ELECTROPLATING.

ELECTROMETER [ĭ-lĕk-trŏm′ə-tər], any one of many kinds of instruments that measure potential difference (voltage) or electric charge. In most types, operation is based on the forces of electrostatic attraction or repulsion, although modern electrometers often have special vacuum tubes as the sensing devices. Electrometers differ from ordinary voltmeters in that the former draw extremely small currents while operating and thus are essentially instruments of very high internal resistance. One of the simplest electrometers is an electroscope equipped with a scale calibrated to read voltage, or charge, directly.
See also ELECTRICITY; ELECTROSCOPE.

Radio Corporation of America

The electronic synthesizer facilitates the complex electrical processes that may be involved in the production of electronic music. The synthesizer generates basic sounds, modifies, and records, all in one sequence. Here an operator feeds coded information into the machine.

ELECTROMOTIVE FORCE (EMF), electric pressure, or voltage, that causes a current to flow through a circuit. Electromotive force is caused by the difference in potential supplied by the energy source. Generators and batteries supply this difference by effectively separating the positive and negative charges, which then, by laboring to combine, set up the stress which is emf.

ELECTROMOTIVE SERIES, classification of the elements according to their single electrode potential, a measure of the relative force with which an atom of an element changes into its ion. The metal lithium has the highest positive electrode potential and heads the list, whereas the nonmetal fluorine has the highest negative electrode potential and closes the list. The standard chosen is the hydrogen electrode, and its potential is considered zero. All the elements above hydrogen form positive ions and all below hydrogen form negative ions. Therefore any element will theoretically seize electrons from all those above it in the series.

ELECTRON [ĭ-lĕk′trŏn], fundamental unit of electricity. It is an elementary particle and a component of all atoms. The existence of the electron was established by J. J. Thomson in 1897 by experiments on cathode rays, which are streams of fast electrons, produced by the electric discharge in gases at low pressures.

The charge of an electron is a fundamental constant equal to 4.803×10^{-10} electrostatic units of charge; no smaller charge exists in nature. Its mass is 9.107×10^{-28} g., 1836.1 times smaller than the mass of a proton. The electron is not to be regarded as a geometrical point; it has finite extension, angular momentum (spin), and a magnetic moment. The ordinary electrons of matter are negatively charged. Positively charged electrons, or positrons, which are antiparticles to the ordinary electrons, also exist. When a positive and a negative electron come together they annihilate each other. In their place two gamma rays are created.

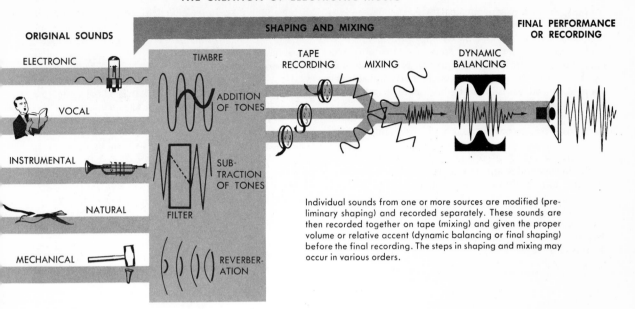

ORIGINAL SOUNDS

ELECTRONIC

VOCAL

INSTRUMENTAL

NATURAL

MECHANICAL

SHAPING AND MIXING

TIMBRE — ADDITION OF TONES

SUBTRACTION OF TONES

FILTER

REVERBERATION

TAPE RECORDING

MIXING

DYNAMIC BALANCING

FINAL PERFORMANCE OR RECORDING

Individual sounds from one or more sources are modified (preliminary shaping) and recorded separately. These sounds are then recorded together on tape (mixing) and given the proper volume or relative accent (dynamic balancing or final shaping) before the final recording. The steps in shaping and mixing may occur in various orders.

Since it is the electronic structure of atoms which determines their chemical properties, the worlds of chemistry and of biology can be regarded as manifestations of the behavior of assemblies of electrons. In good electric conductors, such as copper or aluminum, some of the electrons from the atoms composing the metal are detached and wander through the lattice of atoms which make up the crystal. When an electric field is applied to the metal, they tend to drift in one direction. This flow of electric charge constitutes an electric current. When a metal like tungsten is heated to high temperatures in a vacuum, some of the electrons escape from it and are attracted across the vacuum to an anode. This thermionic emission is the basis of the television tube.

CECIL FRANK POWELL, Nobel Prize for Physics
See also ELECTRICITY.

ELECTRONIC MUSIC, a new medium created by composers who have taken advantage of 20th-century developments in electronics by converting precise electronic tools to aesthetic purpose. The term "electronic music" applies to compositions which are created directly on magnetic tape from sound materials which are either electronically produced or developed through electronic and mechanical transformation.

The combination of machines which are used to produce electronic music may be said to constitute a new musical instrument. The composer can actually exercise, with greatly increased precision, direct control over the sound material from its raw to its finished stage. Subtleties of rhythm, timbre, and dynamics can be handled with the utmost sophistication. However, the use of the machines does not make the task of producing compositions simpler. Serious attempts in this medium are clearly derived from a tradition of musical ideas.

History

Recorded compositions produced electronically date back to the hand-written sound tracks in films made in the 1930's. To the same period belong isolated experiments such as the transformation of recorded sounds on discs by varying the speed of the turntable or by playing discs backward. After World War II systematic experimentation, first with recording and organizing sounds on discs (in France only) and then on magnetic tape, stimulated production of numerous works which came to be known by various names: in France (since 1947) as *musique concrète* (music from concrete sound); in the United States (since 1952) as "tape music." The term "electronic music" first became associated with the compositions produced at the studio of the West German Radio (since 1954) in Cologne, Germany, because the composers initially obtained their materials exclusively from electronic generators. Throughout the 1950's the kinds of sound materials used, the method of organizing these materials into compositions, and the underlying aesthetic principles constituted distinctions among the *musique concrète*, tape, and electronic music composers of France, the United States, Germany, and, subsequently, other countries. However, by 1962 the term "electronic music" came to be generally applied to all works in the tape medium with the exception of those of the *musique concrète* group. A composer like Edgar Varèse, governed by his long-existing concept of "organized sound," also found his natural expression in the realm of electronic music.

The first successful attempt to synthesize sounds by electric means must be attributed to an American, Thaddeus Cahill, whose Dynamophone, also called Telharmonium, though cumbersome and impractical, attracted the attention of the composer Ferruccio Busoni in 1906. For the next 50 years numerous attempts to achieve electric synthesis of ordinary or unusual sounds for musical purposes resulted in the development of organlike instruments, as well as several commercially successful electronic organs. None of these stimulated serious composers as did the tape recorder, which provided a more flexible means to record, modify, combine, and store sound materials and to make them available for organization into compositions on tape, thus offering composers the means for working directly in recorded sound.

In 1955 the first comprehensive apparatus for synthesis and complete programming of sound "events" was completed in the RCA laboratories by Dr. Harry Olson and Herbert Belar. Of the two existing models, the later and more advanced, called Mark II, RCA Sound Synthesizer, is located at the Columbia-Princeton Electronic Music Center at Columbia University in New York City and is being used for the composition of electronic music.

Method of Production

Production of electronic music requires the use of apparatus for a step-by-step realization of the composer's ideas: first, to generate, or create, sound material; next, to record it on tape and to modify the sound (sometimes done prior to recording); finally, to mix and shape the material to a particular form.

Source of Sound. Electronic sounds are commonly obtained from such sources as sinusoidal, square-wave, sawtooth-wave oscillators and from pulse generators. The signals which are produced on them are analogous to the single pitches of musical instruments. Sinusoidal oscillators are sources of "pure tones," that is, single pitches (frequencies, or vibrations) devoid of any overtones (harmonics). Other generators produce single pitches which are not "pure tones" (that is, tones which contain the fundamental frequency and some harmonically related frequencies). Not more than one signal can be obtained from a given position on a tuning dial of these generators. For this reason, several generators are normally required for an electronic music studio. Another commonly used source is a "white-noise generator" which produces a signal composed of all frequencies. The values of their associated amplitudes are "randomly" distributed.

Nonelectronic sound materials include sounds derived from the human voice, musical instruments, and nature, and those generated by man-made machines. Such materials have been commonly employed in *musique concrète* and tape music. Conversely, composers who had formerly restricted themselves to electronic sound materials have begun to admit the use of nonelectronic sounds into their compositions.

Shaping and Mixing of the Sound. Modification of the raw sound material is the most important stage of sound production. Raw material, obtained from any source, is modified and combined into patterns and timbres suitable as building blocks for a composition. Creation of the desired timbres can be accomplished by either an additive process (building up of a complex sound spectrum from the single frequencies), or by a subtractive process (eliminating or suppressing specific frequencies or frequency bands by filters). Additional coloration, or timbre, can be added at any stage by subjecting the sound material to artificial or natural reverberation (echo).

A succession of pitches is usually obtained by splicing together precut pieces of tape containing recorded sound material, except when the RCA Synthesizer or its less versatile European counterpart is used. This tedious process is somewhat alleviated by special devices. One of these is a multitrack tape recorder with keyboard-controlled tape speed, invented by Dr. Hugh LeCaine of the Canadian National Research Council, by which a succession of pitches from one or several timbres can be quickly obtained. A similar result can be obtained on a variable-speed tape playback device, called a phonogene, invented by the originator of *musique concrète*, Pierre Schaeffer.

Mixing of the sound material in preliminary stages can be compared to orchestration and, in the final stage, to a rehearsal of a finished composition. During mixing the final decision is made about the dynamic and the timbre relationship of the prepared patterns. These are organized in a calculated time sequence on the individual magnetic tape tracks. Final mixing produces the first performance ("rehearsal") of the finished composition. On the RCA Synthesizer, the actual performance of isolated portions of the composition is achieved much earlier because the pattern-forming and sound-shaping operations are specified on a single roll of paper in the form of a punched-out code.

Performance. Ordinarily electronic music can be performed only through loudspeakers, though several American and European works in this medium are written in such a manner that certain portions of the score are played on tape and others are performed on conventional musical instruments or sung. Electronic music also has been produced by computers, but the cost of operation and the fact that computers were designed for a very different and, in many respects, mathematically dissimilar operation, has thus far limited their use for producing electronic music.

Studios and Composers

Among the major electronic music studios are the Columbia-Princeton Electronic Music Center, New York; University of Illinois, Urbana, Ill.; University of Toronto, Canada; University of Utrecht, the Netherlands; Radio Cologne, Germany; Radio Milan, Italy; Radio Tokyo, Japan; Radio Warsaw, Poland; Siemens-Halske, Munich, Germany. Studios at Yale University, at the American Academy in Rome, and at the Television Station in Rome were under construction in 1961. A studio equipped with many keyboard electronic instruments that are used for the production of movie background electronic scores is in Moscow.

The studio for Musique Concrète continues its activity as part of the Radio Diffusion et Télévision Française, Paris, under the direction of Pierre Schaeffer and several composers.

Among the several hundred compositions of abstract or applied nature such works as *Symphonie pour un homme seul* (1950) by Pierre Schaeffer and Pierre Henry; *Rhapsodic Variations for Tape Recorder and Orchestra* (1954) by Otto Luening and Vladimir Ussachevsky; *Deserts* (1954) by Edgar Varèse; *Gesang der Jünglinge* (1955–56) by Karlheinz Stockhausen; *Hommage à Joyce* (1958) by Luciano Berio; and *Composition for Synthesizer* (1961) by Milton Babbitt have been recognized as unique contributions to the medium.

Consult Ussachevsky, Vladimir, "Notes on a Piece for Tape Recorder," *Musical Quarterly*, Vol. XXVI, No. 2 (1960).

VLADIMIR USSACHEVSKY, Columbia University
See also HARMONIC SERIES; MUSICAL ACOUSTICS.

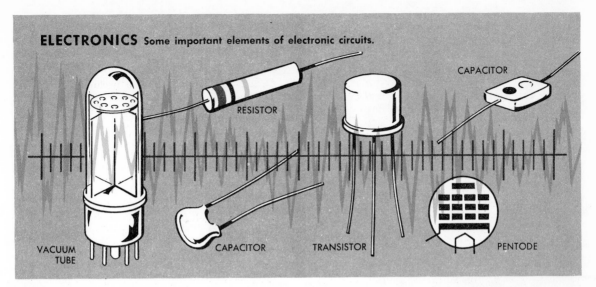

ELECTRONICS Some important elements of electronic circuits.

RESISTOR

CAPACITOR

VACUUM
TUBE

CAPACITOR

TRANSISTOR

PENTODE

ELECTRONICS [ĭ-lĕk-trŏn'ĭks] originally meant the study of electron behavior in solids, liquids, and gases, but over the years its meaning has broadened to include those pieces of equipment, such as radio and television sets, that exploit our knowledge of the electron. It is also generally used to mean the art of designing such equipment.

The concept that underlies all of the practical applications of electronics can best be described perhaps by the term "signal," that is, the way in which a changing electric current, or flow of electrons, differs from a steady, unchanging current. To illustrate, an unchanging current in a loudspeaker produces no sound. A suitably changing current, on the other hand, can produce speech, music, or even the dots and dashes of telegraph signals. From the point of view of electronics then, the signal is of paramount importance because it contains information.

An electronic signal can come about in many ways. A passing radio wave causes a corresponding current to flow in an antenna. That current varies in intensity precisely as the radio wave dictates, so we call it a signal. A light beam falling on a photoelectric cell causes a current to flow in the cell. When the light beam is stopped, the current also stops. That change in current intensity constitutes a signal, and it can be used to open doors, turn on street lights, or sound a burglar alarm.

The electronic computer is based on the fact that ordinary numbers can be translated into electronic signals, after which the signals can be added or subtracted by electron tubes or transistors. The feats accomplished by all modern electronic marvels depend on their ability to pick up signals of one sort or another and manipulate them in suitable ways in the performance of useful tasks.

The rapid development of electronics during the past half-century has touched almost every field of human endeavor. Factories, homes, and offices are becoming dependent to an ever-increasing degree on the electron. Control over its behavior has given us radio, television, tape recording, and even the sound track that permits moving pictures to talk. It is used to guide our ships at sea, our planes in the air, and our space vehicles that place scientific instruments in precise orbits around the earth

and the sun. It has given us the electric eye, or photoelectric cell, that opens doors automatically, and may one day open the way to the economical conversion of solar energy into electricity. It has done all of these marvelous things, but perhaps our greatest debt to the electron stems from its ability to do so many ordinary jobs faster and more efficiently than man can do them himself. In papermaking, for example, a long, continuous sheet comes out of the machine at great speed. Measuring the thickness of the moving paper can be a difficult task indeed. With the help of radioactive materials and simple electronic devices, the thickness can be measured continuously without physical contact with the paper. Often, the signal produced by the electronic equipment is used to make automatic corrections in the machinery whenever the thickness varies from the desired figure. Electronic devices perform thousands of similar operations in a great variety of industrial applications. Much of this versatility and competence to perform difficult tasks was born with the development of the electron tube.

How Electronics Began

The electron tube had its origin in an unexpected electric effect discovered by Thomas Edison in 1883. Edison was troubled over the blackening of the glass of his new incandescent lamps and he wondered whether charged particles from the filament might not be the cause. In order to find out, he placed a metallic plate, or anode, within the evacuated bulb, located a short distance from the filament, or cathode. (The anode and cathode are the elements of a radio tube connected to the positive and negative voltages, respectively.) The plate was connected to a wire which passed through the glass and which was connected externally to the heated filament as shown in Fig. 1 on the following page. Under these conditions Edison noticed that a current flowed from the plate through the external wire to the filament of his experimental lamp. He knew, of course, that an electric current must flow in a closed loop or path. He reasoned, therefore, that charged particles are emitted, or given off, by the hot filament and are somehow able to leap across the gap from filament to

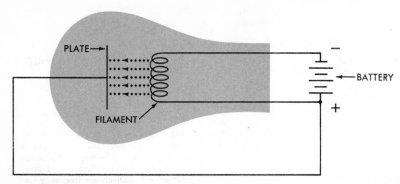

The Edison effect. Electrons are given off by the hot filament, collect on the plate, and return to the filament through the external wire.

FIGURE 1

plate in the evacuated tube. For many years the "Edison effect," as it was called, remained only a scientific curiosity. No one knew what these charged particles were or how they could be put to use. It was not until 1897 that J. J. Thomson proved that Edison's particles are really negatively charged bits of matter called electrons. This ability of hot metals to give off electrons is called thermionic emission, or commonly, emission.

A few years later, in 1904, J. A. Fleming (1849–1945), the English electrical engineer, improved on Edison's device and used it in the detection of radio signals. He called it a valve—a term still used in England—because it passed current in one direction only. Two years later, the American, Lee De Forest, took the great step that was to make electronics possible—he added a third electrode between the filament and the plate. The new elec-

trode consisted of a perforated metal or wire grid which, when a slight charge was imposed on it, controlled or changed the tiny current flowing across the gap.

Despite the existence of the new triode electron tube, as it eventually came to be called, electronics still failed to grow. No one really knew how to use the new device. Then in 1912, E. H. Armstrong (1890–1954), then a young student of electrical engineering at Columbia University, discovered the secret behind the amplification of electronic signals and a new industry was born. It had taken almost 30 years from the date of Edison's basic discovery for the first important application of electronics. With a simple radio tube circuit Armstrong was able to pick up signals from Ireland, Germany, and distant Honolulu with a clarity that had never before been possible, even with the most expensive equipment. Soon there-

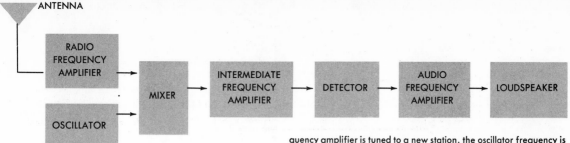

SUPERHETERODYNE RECEIVER CIRCUIT.

A signal frequency from the antenna is amplified somewhat in the radio frequency amplifier and passed into the mixer. A locally generated signal from the oscillator is also applied to the mixer. The mixer circuit then generates a new "intermediate" frequency signal whose relatively low frequency is the difference between the original signal frequency and the oscillator frequency. When the radio fre-quency amplifier is tuned to a new station, the oscillator frequency is changed in synchronism to maintain a constant frequency difference between the two. Because this difference is equal to the intermediate frequency, the intermediate frequency amplifier is tuned to the same frequency for all station frequencies. This greatly improves receiver performance because most of the required amplification and interference rejection can be achieved in a relatively low frequency amplifier where such performance is easy to obtain. The program material is then recovered in the detector circuit, amplified in the audio frequency amplifier, and applied to a loud speaker.

after, thousands of improved triodes were manufactured under the stimulus of World War I. Also during this period, Armstrong invented the superheterodyne receiver circuit which has become the heart of all modern receivers.

The Electron Tube

Diode, or Fleming Tube. As was shown by the Edison effect, electrons will flow along a conducting path furnished them in an evacuated tube and return to the filament. This flow of current depends upon the more or less random piling up of electrons on the plate, a relatively inefficient process. In fact, the accumulation of electrons on the plate soon builds up a negative charge that tends to repel other electrons that would ordinarily strike the plate. There is a method, however, of attracting many more electrons from the filament. This method is simply to create a deficiency of electrons on the plate by placing a positive charge on it. Fig. 2 indicates how this is ac-

The positive charge attracts many more negative electrons from the filament than is possible with Edison's arrangement. If the polarity of the battery is reversed, on the other hand, the plate is charged negatively and oncoming electrons are repelled back to the vicinity of the filament. Practically none of them are able to reach the plate. Instead, the electrons accumulate in a cloud around the filament, called a space charge. A condition of equilibrium is soon established, and each time an electron is emitted by the filament, another one pops back in.

Diodes are unidirectional, or one-way, devices in which the current in the plate-to-filament path—the plate current—can be controlled or even stopped altogether by the size and polarity of the plate battery that is used. This makes it possible for diodes to perform a function that is indispensable to almost all kinds of electronic equipment. This function is called rectification, the process of changing alternating currents into direct currents.

Alternating currents are those in which the direction of motion of the electrons reverses rapidly, many times each

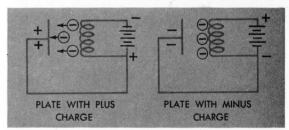

PLATE WITH PLUS CHARGE

PLATE WITH MINUS CHARGE

second. In Fig. 1, it can be shown that, by reversing the polarity of the battery very rapidly, the effect of an alternating current is produced. The same thing would happen if an alternating current source were applied between plate and filament. Whenever the plate of the diode is positive, current will flow through the plate circuit. Whenever the plate is negative, no current will flow. But whenever current does flow, it can flow only in one direction because electrons can proceed only from filament to plate, never from plate to filament. For this reason, the current is unidirectional, and it flows only during those periods in which the plate is positive. Half of the time, of course, the plate is negative and no current can flow. This means that the plate current exists in the form of short, unidirectional bursts, or pulses, separated by periods during which

FIGURE 2

Conduction of electrons in a diode. In (A) the battery E_1 places a positive charge on the plate which attracts many electrons from the filament. In (B) the plate is charged negatively and electrons are repelled by the plate. They return to the region of the filament where they build up a space charge, or cloud of electrons.

complished. A battery (E_1) is connected in the path from plate to filament forming the plate circuit of the diode. The positive terminal is connected to the plate, giving the plate a positive charge with respect to the filament.

no current flow takes place. Although this current is unidirectional, it is not identical to that from a battery because of its existence in the form of pulses. Pulsating currents of this kind can be smoothed out by devices called electric filters in much the same way that a flywheel produces constant rotation in a mechanical engine. A filter is a device that stores some of the electricity while the current is flowing in the diode, and discharges it when the diode is turned off. It makes use of electrical inertia just as a flywheel makes use of mechanical inertia. The current out of the filter is then the same as that from an ordinary dry cell or storage battery, and it can be used as such. In fact, the first rectifiers were called "battery eliminators."

In addition to rectification, diodes are also used extensively to change the high-frequency currents of radio waves to the audio-frequency currents needed to produce sound in a loudspeaker. This process, called detection, is quite similar to rectification. In a diode detector, high-frequency alternating currents are converted to a slowly varying direct current. These current variations correspond to the original sounds in the broadcasting studio.

The Triode and Amplification. The triode electron tube is similar to the two-element diode except for the addition of a third electrode, or grid, which is added between the filament and plate. The grid consists of a fine wire mesh or screen which is insulated from the other electrodes. Like the other two, it is connected to a wire passing through the tube. The grid acts as a valve which, opening and closing, controls the number of electrons passing from filament to plate. In doing this, the grid makes use of the fact that negative charges repel one another. If a large negative charge is placed on the grid, all of the electrons emitted by the filament are repelled by the grid and accumulate in a group, or cloud, around the filament. This electron cloud is identical to the space charge that develops in a diode when the plate is charged negatively. Now, if the negative charge on the grid is reduced sufficiently, a few electrons are able to find their way through the grid wires to the plate. This condition is illustrated in Fig. 3. A further reduction in the negative voltage on the grid results in a corresponding increase in plate-current

flow. In this way, varying the charge, or voltage, on the grid permits a variable, or changing, current to flow in the plate circuit. To see why this makes amplification possible, consider a signal coming from a microphone which is applied to the grid of a triode. This signal causes the charge on the grid to vary in precisely the same way that the sound pressure varies at the microphone. The charge variations are an electrical copy of the sounds to be amplified. But the amount of current that flows from filament to plate at any instant depends upon the charge on the grid at that instant. The plate current, then, is another copy of the sound variations. In an ordinary triode, however, there are large plate current variations even when the charge variations on the grid are very small. This means that a small signal on the grid can produce a similar but much larger signal on the plate.

Weak signals received in a radio antenna can therefore be amplified many times to provide the powerful signals necessary to operate the loudspeaker. It is not unusual to find signal strengths amplified 1,000,000 times or more in an ordinary radio set.

Tetrode and Pentode Electron Tubes. Once the value of the grid was discovered, it was only natural for engineers to look into further improvements that might be possible if still more electrodes were added. One of the first of these was the indirectly heated cathode, which simplifies the emission of electrons within the tube. It consists of an oxide-coated nickel cylinder which surrounds a tungsten filament that carries the heater current. The two are electrically insulated from one another and take the place of the electron-emitting filament discussed earlier. When current passes through the heater wire, the oxide-coated cylinder gets hot enough to emit a large number of electrons. Because of the oxide coating, this emission is accomplished much more efficiently than from a simple heated wire.

INDIRECTLY HEATED CATHODE

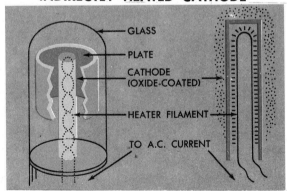

- GLASS
- PLATE
- CATHODE (OXIDE-COATED)
- HEATER FILAMENT
- TO A.C. CURRENT

The indirectly heated cathode has another important advantage—thermal stability. The temperature of the cylinder, or cathode, is extremely constant, even in the presence of current fluctuations in the heater wire. This is important, because the number of electrons given off by the cathode depends on its temperature; the higher the temperature, the greater the emission. Because of the temperature stability of the cathode, it is possible to use alternating current in the heater wire. An alternating current goes first in one direction, then in the opposite direction.

FIGURE 3

ELECTRONS GRID PLATE

FILAMENT

TO A SOURCE OF VARIABLE NEGATIVE POWER VOLTAGE

TO A SOURCE OF POSITIVE VOLTAGE

BATTERY

A triode electron tube. The grid electrode acts as a valve, controlling the number of electrons allowed to reach the plate.

At the instant that the change in direction takes place, the current must be equal to zero. At such times, an ordinary wire filament would tend to cool off and fewer electrons would be emitted. The cathode does not cool off appreciably, however, so its emission remains constant. This means that the number of emitted electrons, which depends on the temperature, will be independent of the cyclic variations of the alternating current in the heater wire. For this reason, the filament battery shown in Figures 1 and 2 can be replaced by the ordinary alternating current available in the home. In tubes using this method of emission, the oxide-coated cathode takes the place of the filament in the older tubes, and the heater wire merely serves as a source of heat.

As the radio art developed, it became desirable to operate triode electron tubes at higher and higher frequencies. When this was attempted, an inherent limitation of the triode soon became apparent. By the very nature of amplification, the signal on the plate is very much greater than the signal on the grid. In actual practice, part of the plate signal is unavoidably fed back to the grid. This transfer of signal takes place because the plate and grid are close together and a charge on the plate tends to induce a corresponding charge on the grid. This process, called feedback, gets progressively more serious as the frequency is increased. The signal that is fed back to the grid adds to the original signal and this combined signal now controls the current flowing to the plate. This causes a larger plate current to flow which, in turn, causes more feedback. The process is cumulative, and at a certain critical frequency the triode begins to oscillate, or generate its own radio-frequency signals. The tube is then useless as an amplifier. This kind of feedback in an electron tube is called regeneration.

The problem of regeneration has been solved by adding a second wire grid between the control grid and the plate.

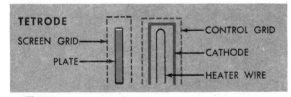

This screen grid acts as a shield which greatly minimizes the feedback radio signals from plate to control grid. Tubes containing two grids are called tetrodes and they are able to operate at extremely high frequencies.

Many tubes, called pentodes, contain a third grid located between the screen grid and the plate. Called the suppressor grid, the third grid has a rather simple function. As electrons strike the plate of a tetrode, they tend to knock out one or more additional electrons, a process

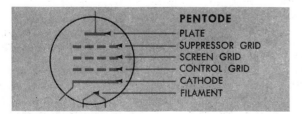

called secondary emission. Some of these secondary electrons travel to the screen grid because that grid is maintained at a relatively high positive voltage. In so doing, they subtract from the desired flow of plate current. The suppressor grid gets around this difficulty by forcing secondary electrons back into the plate.

Because of its versatility, the pentode has found wide application in electronics. It is probably the most useful of the ordinary tubes. Most of the tubes in a radio or television set are pentodes, although other types are also used. Diodes are used for rectification (changing alternating to direct current), and triodes are used in some of the circuits that control the motion of the electron beam in the picture tube.

Mercury-Vapor Tube and Thyratron. The presence of gas in an electron tube changes its characteristics drastically. In fact, a small amount of gas in an ordinary electron tube makes it just about worthless for its intended use. There are applications, however, where gas-filled tubes are extremely useful. One of these is the mercury-vapor tube, which can be used as an efficient high-power rectifier.

The mercury-vapor tube is similar to an ordinary diode except for the addition of a small amount of mercury within the tube. It uses a hot cathode to emit electrons and a positively charged plate, or anode, to collect them. These electrons do not travel unimpeded, however, because they collide with the many vaporized mercury atoms that fill the tube. If the speed of an electron is sufficiently high before collision, it will ionize the mercury atom, that is, it will knock an electron free of the atom. This produces an additional free electron and a positively charged mercury atom, or ion. Many of these collisions greatly increase the number of available electrons, and the tube is capable of providing very large currents. Furthermore, there are almost as many positive ions in the tube as electrons. Since the ions are positively charged, they flow toward the cathode and assist in attracting large numbers of electrons away from the cathode. This also helps to increase current flow. Current flow in mercury-vapor tubes is accompanied by the characteristic blue glow of mercury.

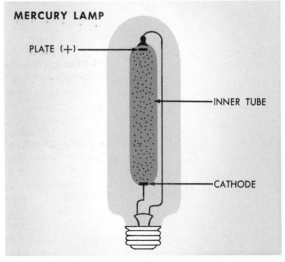

ELECTRONICS

The thyratron is a mercury-vapor tube to which has been added a control grid between plate and cathode. The grid's function is to control the flow of current to the plate, much as in a high-vacuum triode. Nevertheless, the nature of this control is considerably different in a gas tube. In the triode, the grid is able to control the magnitude of the current as well as to start and stop its flow. In the thyratron, however, the grid can only start the current; once it has begun to flow, the grid can neither stop it nor change its magnitude.

THYRATRON TUBE

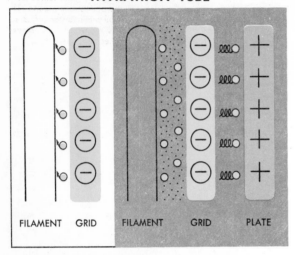

FILAMENT   GRID   FILAMENT   GRID   PLATE

To understand why this is so, imagine a thyratron—initially not ionized—which has a large negative charge on the grid and a positive charge on the plate. Because of the negative charge on the grid, electrons from the cathode are repelled and prevented from passing on to the plate. Instead, they are slowed down before they can reach the speed necessary to ionize the mercury vapor. No ionization takes place, and no plate current flows. If the negative charge on the grid is now gradually reduced, a few electrons will pass through the grid and then speed up on their way to the positively charged plate. This causes ionization of the mercury vapor just as in the mercury-vapor diode. The positive ions then neutralize the effect of the negative charge on the grid and permit unimpeded passage of electrons to the plate. The current can be stopped only by disconnecting the positive voltage from the plate.

It is apparent from the nature of the thyratron that its uses do not overlap those of the high-vacuum triode. The thyratron is essentially an electronic switch that can be turned on with the grid and off with the plate. The triode, on the other hand, is more like a valve because the magnitude of the current can be varied over a wide range. The thyratron can handle much higher currents, however, and is essentially a high-power device.

The Methods of Electronics

Thus far, a number of electron tubes have been described and their principles of operation explained. They perform a variety of electronic functions. The advent of transistors and other semiconductor devices makes it pos-

sible to perform many of these functions more easily and sometimes more economically. Electronics, however, is more than a collection of functional devices. It is a technology which combines many such devices with other components to form a consistent whole, much as a complex machine is constructed from hundreds of interrelated parts. Each has its role to play in the successful operation of the whole. In the machine, it is mechanical motion that must be controlled in the performance of a specific task; in electronic equipment it is the motion of electrons. The machine has its mechanical parts; an electronic device has its circuits.

Electronic Circuit. The electronic circuit is the subassembly, or building block, of electronics. It usually consists of a tube or two together with a number of associated parts. A radio receiver, for example, usually contains several kinds of circuits. First of all, there is the diode rectifier, which changes alternating house current into the direct current required for the plates of the various triodes and pentodes. Then there is the radio-frequency amplifier circuit. This circuit selects the desired station, amplifies the incoming signal somewhat, and applies it to the next circuit, called the converter. In the converter, the signal is changed to a lower frequency which is called the intermediate frequency. This step is desirable because amplification is simpler to achieve at lower frequencies, and also because nearby stations can be more easily rejected at these frequencies. Most of the receiver's amplification and station selectivity are accomplished in the intermediate-frequency amplifier circuit. The signal then passes into a diode-detector circuit, which abstracts the desired voice frequency currents from the signal. These currents are amplified in the audio-frequency amplifier circuit and sent to the loudspeaker. All of these sequential operations take place at speeds approaching that of light, and yet the entire process is as ordered and precise as the co-ordinated movements in a complex machine.

The arrangement of circuits described above constitutes Armstrong's superheterodyne receiver. Since its invention, electronic engineers have devised many new and specialized circuits that operate on electronic signals in hundreds of different ways. By using such circuits in suitable combinations, electronic devices can be constructed to perform almost any task. Electronics is the study of such circuits, the factors which cause them to behave as they do, and their co-ordinated utilization in useful devices.

Consult Pierce, J. R., *Electrons, Waves, and Messages* (1956); Fink, D. G., and Lutyens, D. M., *Physics of Television* (1960); Vergara, W. C., *Electronics in Everyday Things* (1961).

WILLIAM C. VERGARA, The Bendix Corporation

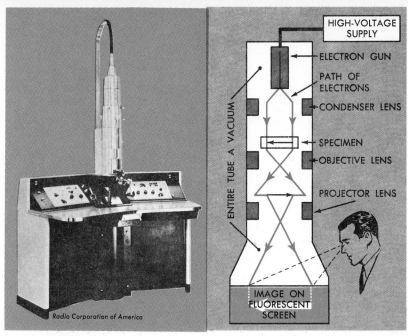

HIGH-VOLTAGE
SUPPLY

ELECTRON GUN

PATH OF
ELECTRONS

CONDENSER LENS

SPECIMEN

OBJECTIVE LENS

PROJECTOR LENS

ENTIRE TUBE A VACUUM

IMAGE ON
FLUORESCENT
SCREEN

Radio Corporation of America

ELECTRON MICROSCOPE

The electron microscope magnifies many more times than the optical microscope. It is a valuable instrument for the study of such diverse subjects as the composition of viruses and the internal structure of various kinds of materials (crystals, metals, and the like). It is comparable to an optical microscope. Electrons are the "light" and magnetized fields are the "lenses." The condenser lens and the objective lens of the electron microscope are actually magnetic fields that bend the electron rays much as glass lenses bend light rays in the optical microscope. The result is an image projected on a fluorescent screen. This image can be observed and photographed on regular film.

ELECTRONICS, INDUSTRIAL. *See* ELECTRONICS; INDUSTRIAL ELECTRONICS.

ELECTRONICS IN MEDICINE. *See* MEDICAL ELECTRONICS.

ELECTRONIC TEACHING. *See* TEACHING MACHINE

ELECTRON MICROSCOPE, powerful microscope that uses electrons instead of light to produce an image magnified up to 200,000 times and to show details as small as 10 angstrom units. The device was originally developed in Germany in 1931 by E. Ruska, who also built the first commercial instrument in 1939. About 2,000 instruments are now used all over the world.

The elements of an electron microscope are comparable to the parts of an optical microscope. However, the lenses cannot be made of a material substance such as glass, and a high vacuum must be provided for the electrons, which would otherwise be scattered by the molecules of the air. An electron gun, containing a hot filament and an accelerating electrode utilizing up to 100,000 volts corresponds to the light source. Electric or magnetic fields direct the imaging beams in a manner similar to the glass lenses in the optical microscope. A condenser concentrates the electron beam on the specimen. The objective lens immediately behind the specimen is a short-focus lens of the greatest possible precision. It produces an intermediate image usually magnified several hundred diameters. Whereas in the optical instrument this image is viewed by the eyepiece, the electron microscope uses another electron optical lens to magnify the image further. This element projects the second-stage electron image upon a fluorescent screen for observation by the electron microscopist. Some microscope designs use three stages for higher magnification. For recording the image the screen is flipped away so that the electron image falls on a photographic plate placed behind the screen.

The specimen and the photographic plates are brought into the evacuated microscope tube through vacuum locks. The microscope unit also contains the vacuum pumps and the accurately regulated power supplies which provide the high voltages and currents needed to energize the magnetic lenses.

Elaborate techniques have been developed for the preparation of the specimens, which must be very thin to allow the passage of the electron beams. Thin-sectioning microtomes are used to slice biological tissues. Metal specimens are used in the form of thin, etched foils. The surface of thick and opaque objects can be studied by making replicas with fine plastic films.

Today the electron microscope is an indispensable research tool for investigations in physics and chemistry, as well as technical production control. Its most significant contributions have been in the biological and medical sciences. Although no living matter can be observed because of the dehydrating effect of the vacuum and the intense irradiation by the electron beam, the study of cells, tissues, bacteria, viruses, protein molecules, and a multitude of other biological materials has enormously extended knowledge in the life sciences.

E. W. MUELLER, Pennsylvania State University

ELECTRON OPTICS, branch of physics concerned with the propagation of electron beams. There is great similarity between electron optics and classical light optics. The study of paths of electron beams, in geometrical electron optics, is comparable to the study of paths of rays in geometrical optics. In electron optics, as in light optics, there exist electron lenses, mirrors, and prisms having certain focal lengths, aberrations, or deflections. In physical electron optics, as in physical light optics, understanding the wave nature of the radiation is essential for understanding effects such as diffraction and interference.

An electron beam can be deflected by an electric or a magnetic field. Electron paths in electric fields are identical with light paths in a refractive medium: the square root of the potential at every point is proportional to the refractive index in the optical analog. Electrodes at different potentials, often arranged as apertures, and rings or cylinders concentric to the beam axis act as either converging or diverging lenses. A magnetic field, coaxial to the electron beam and most conveniently produced by

387

ELECTRON VOLT – ELECTROPLATING

a current flowing through a coil around the vacuum tube, can also serve as a lens. All of these lenses can be used to produce an image of a real or virtual electron source.

Focusing can be achieved by adjusting the voltage applied to electrostatic lenses or by controlling the current through the magnet coil.

The principles of electron optics are applied to the design of various electronic devices in which electron beams must be directed, for example an electron gun in a television picture tube. Other uses are in image pick-up television tubes, electronic image intensifiers, electron microscopes, velocity spectrometers, and mass spectrometers.

E. W. MUELLER, Pennsylvania State University
See also OPTICS.

ELECTRON VOLT, abbreviated ev, the amount of energy attained by an electron falling through a one-volt potential difference. It is equal to 1.60203×10^{-12} ergs and is equivalent to a temperature of approximately $11,500°$ K. This unit is convenient in atomic and nuclear physics, and is widely used in expressing the energy of moving particles. Gamma rays frequently have energies in the range of one million electron volts (Mev). One billion electron volts is abbreviated Bev.

ELECTRON WAVE, the property exhibited by an electron of behaving as a wave, as well as a particle. Under suitable conditions, electrons display diffraction effects, a quality attributed to waves. The electron microscope depends on the wave-nature of electrons for its operation.

ELECTROPHONES. *See* MUSICAL INSTRUMENTS.

ELECTROPHORESIS [ĭ-lĕk-trō-fə-rē′sĭs], the movement of colloidal particles in an electric field. Colloidal particles, such as the large protein molecules in egg white, are electrically charged. If two electrodes are placed in such a colloidal solution and a potential is applied across the electrodes, the protein molecules migrate to the electrode with a charge opposite to that of the protein. The speed of migration depends upon the charge on the particle and not upon its size. Therefore a mixture of various protein molecules may be separated according to their charge. The migration may be observed by a variety of methods, often by the changes in refraction of light by the solution. The outstanding application has been to the separation of protein mixtures. The results have been very important to our understanding of living things.

ELECTROPHORUS [ĭ-lĕk-trŏf′ər-əs], a device for producing static electricity. It consists of a slab of hard rubber and a metal disk with an insulated handle. The rubber is charged negatively by rubbing it with fur. The disk is then placed on it and grounded, allowing electrons to flow from the metal, which then has a net positive charge.

ELECTROPLATING [ĭ-lĕk′trō-plāt-ĭng], metallurgical process for depositing a thin, homogeneous coating of a metal or alloy, by electrolysis, on a metal or other conducting surface. First described in 1840, it was initially used solely

The ions of the electrolyte, silver cyanide, conduct the current between the anode and the cathode. The silver ions are deposited on the spoon. The cyanide ions react with the silver anode to form more silver cyanide, which dissolves and ionizes.

for improving the appearance of objects and, as such, was considered an art whose secrets were passed on from father to son. With increasing knowledge of its possibilities it became valuable industrially for improving surface properties of materials. Tools and other implements are electroplated for protection against corrosion, tarnishing, and chemical attack; components are given a hard surface; worn parts are built up to original dimensions; frictional effects are reduced on sliding members; light reflectors are made more efficient; and certain mechanical properties of materials are improved.

During electroplating the part to be plated becomes the cathode, or negative electrode, and the plating metal is the anode, or positive electrode. The two electrodes are suspended in a tank containing an aqueous electrolyte solution of a salt of the metal to be deposited. As a direct current passes through the electrolyte, the positively charged ions move toward the cathode while the negatively charged ions move toward the anode. The amount of metal deposited on the cathode is directly proportional to the quantity of current passing through the electrolytic cell. As the plating process proceeds the anode, in most cases, dissolves into the electrolyte.

Large parts are plated by suspending them in the plating tank but parts too small to be handled individually are barrel plated. In the latter process, a nonconducting sievelike barrel uses a number of exposed metal ribs inside that conduct current to the parts during the barrel's rotation. The process provides a burnishing action that improves the plating quality.

For corrosion resistance, plating materials are zinc, cadmium, tin, chromium, brass, nickel, and copper. For improved resistance, chromium, nickel, silver, gold, platinum, brass, copper, and rhodium are used. Chromium, nickel, and iron are used to build up worn parts and improve physical properties.

Substances other than metals, such as glass, rubber, plastics, leather, and wood, can be plated by waxing or varnishing the surfaces, then impregnating them with copper powder or graphite for conduction.

PAUL B. EATON, Purdue University

See also ANODIZING.

ELECTROSCOPE [ĭ-lĕk'trə-skōp], an instrument used to detect static electric charge. It consists essentially of one or two movable parts light enough to respond to small forces of electrostatic repulsion. An electroscope can readily be made from a wide-necked glass jar whose metal lid has been replaced by one of a good insulator, for example, clean Plexiglas or Bakelite. A metal rod about ¼ in. in diameter is tightly fitted into a hole in the lid. The rod should be smooth, project about an inch above the lid, and be spaced at least an inch from the bottom and sides. A narrow strip of very thin aluminum or gold foil is attached at its upper end to the rod (for this purpose saliva works well) so that its lower end terminates at the lower end of the rod.

When a body with a weak positive charge is brought near the projecting rod, electrons are attracted to that end, leaving positive charges on the previously neutral foil and lower rod. These charges repel one another, causing the foil to stand away from the rod. If the body is now touched to the rod, some electrons move to the body. Removal of the body then leaves the electroscope positively charged. On a dry day, this will cause the foil to stand off for some time.

LAWRENCE A. BORNSTEIN, New York University

See also ELECTRICITY.

ELECTROSTATIC [ĭ-lĕk-trō-stăt'ĭk] **GENERATOR,** machine that produces high electric potentials. It is often used to accelerate charged particles for industrial and research applications. The best-known type was developed by Robert Van de Graaff in 1931. It is an outgrowth of the Wimshurst machine, in which two disks were rotated by hand in opposite directions. Positive charges accumulated on one knob of the machine, and negative charges on the other.

In the Van de Graaff generator, a belt is driven at a high speed by an electric motor. Charge is sprayed on the belt by a small high-potential source and conveyed by the belt to an insulated electrode. As the belt continues to bring charge, the potential of the electrode rises until it reaches that voltage at which as much escapes by leakage and corona discharge as arrives per unit time on the belt. Potentials of 1,000,000 to 2,000,000 volts can be attained readily.

In various modifications, the entire assembly of belt, motor, and high-voltage electrode can be placed in a tank into which a gas of high dielectric strength, such as Freon, is added at high pressure. Such designs allow somewhat higher voltages to be attained.

The belt of a Van de Graaff generator can carry charge of either sign. In one model, one electrode is charged to a high positive potential and another similar one to a high negative potential, with respect to earth. The two electrodes then have a potential difference between themselves equal to the sum of their potentials with respect to ground. An evacuated discharge tube is then placed from the electrode to ground, or between the electrodes, and the beam to be accelerated passes through the tube. Either electrons or positive ions such as protons or alpha particles can be accelerated. Thus the device can be used to produce potentials for X-ray tubes, or proton or deuteron beams for nuclear research.

The Cockcroft-Walton electrostatic particle accelerator obtains voltages as high as 4,000,000 volts by means of a transformer and a series of condensers.

The potential produced by an electrostatic generator is steady and accurately measurable, that is, it is nearly pure direct current, a factor of great importance in research problems.

SERGE A. KORFF, New York University

See also ACCELERATORS; CYCLOTRON; SYNCHROCYCLOTRON; SYNCHROTRON.

ELECTROSTATIC PRECIPITATION, process for separating solid particles or fluid mists out of air or gas by using electric forces. The floating particles are first charged electrically; they then move through the air to a surface with an opposite electric charge, where they are deposited.

Since the principle of electric precipitation was first demonstrated, in 1906 by F. G. Cottrell, it has found many industrial uses. Factory dust and smoke can be pre-

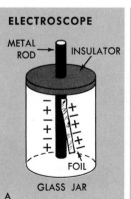

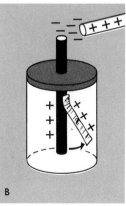

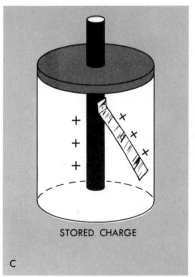

ELECTROSCOPE

METAL ROD → INSULATOR

FOIL

GLASS JAR

A

B

STORED CHARGE

C

A model of the early electroscope shows how the instrument indicates the presence of small charges of static electricity.

(A) The rod and foil are electrically neutral. (B) A positively charged body attracts negative charges from the rod and foil, leaving them with positive charges. (C) Rod and foil continue to repel each other until they are neutralized by regaining negative charges.

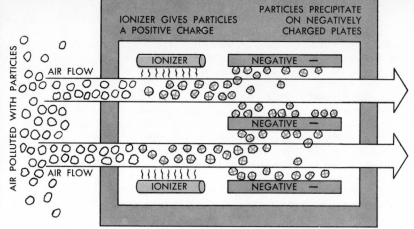

ELECTROSTATIC PRECIPITATOR

One of the most common uses of the electrostatic precipitator is to clean the air that we breathe. Factories use the precipitator to clear the air of gases and dust. The precipitator is based on a simple principle: oppositely charged particles attract each other. Polluted air is drawn into the precipitator. Ionizers charge the pollutants positively. The particles are then drawn to a series of negatively charged plates and are trapped there, leaving the air free of contamination.

cipitated onto a metallic plate to control air pollution. Paint spraying and meat smoking are other processes using this method.

ELECTROSTATICS. *See* ELECTRICITY.

ELECTROSTATIC UNIT, abbreviated e.s.u. and also known as a statcoulomb, electrostatic unit of charge. Its magnitude is such that if two equal charges 1 cm. apart in a vacuum repel each other with a force of 1 dyne, each charge is equivalent to 1 e.s.u.

ELECTROTYPE, facsimile of type matter, or halftone or line engraving used in printing. The electrotype plate, which is .154 in. thick, is more durable, easily stored, and dimensionally stable than the original. Although electrotype plates are usually flat, curved plates are made for rotary printing presses.

To form an electrotype duplicate, the original is impressed in a mold of wax, sheet lead, or vinyl. The mold is made conductive to electricity and placed in a bath of copper or nickel sulfate where electric current causes the copper or nickel in solution to deposit on the mold. After the formation of a sufficiently thick shell, the electrotype is separated from the mold. Reinforcement with molten lead gives it the proper thickness before finishing as a flat or curved plate.
See also ELECTROPLATING.

ELECTRUM, natural alloy of gold and silver. Generally the name is applied only if 20% or more of silver is present. Electrum is pale yellow to yellowish white, noticeably paler than pure gold. Otherwise it resembles gold closely, having similar chemical and physical properties. Electrum is mined in many parts of the world, usually from quartz veins. Much of the silver produced today is a by-product of the smelting of electrum.

Properties: *Crystal System,* Isometric; *Hardness* (Mohs' Scale) 2½–3; *Density,* 12–16.
See also CRYSTALLOGRAPHY; GOLD; MINERALOGY; SILVER.

ELEGY [ĕl'ə-jē], poem lamenting a death. In Greek and Roman literature the elegy expressed a variety of themes. By the Renaissance, however, the elegy was limited to poems of mourning, which frequently made use of the conventions of pastoral verse originated by Theocritus and other Greek poets. A notable example is Milton's "Lycidas," which, like Shelley's "Adonais" and Matthew Arnold's "Thyrsis," portrays the poet's friend as a shepherd. The most famous elegy in English, Thomas Gray's "Elegy Written in a Country Churchyard," makes no use of pastoral convention and mourns the death of not just one person but all men.

ELEGY WRITTEN IN A COUNTRY CHURCHYARD, poem (1751) by Thomas Gray. The *Elegy,* in which the poet muses on the inevitability of death, is one of the best-known poems in the English language. Gray spent seven years polishing his work.

ELEKTRA [ĭ-lĕk'trə], opera in one act by Richard Strauss; libretto by Hugo von Hofmannsthal (after Sophocles); first performance, Jan. 25, 1909, Dresden Hofoper; first American performance, Feb. 1, 1910, Manhattan Opera House, New York.

In the rear of the palace in Mycenae in ancient Greece Elektra mourns the murder of her father King Agamemnon by her mother Clytemnestra and her mother's lover Aegisthus. Elektra prays for revenge and vows she will one day dance on her father's grave. However, neither she nor her sister Chrysothemis can perform the violent act. Finally her brother, Orestes, who had escaped after the murder, returns and kills the Queen and Aegisthus. Elektra now dances triumphantly until she falls lifeless.

Elektra remains the powerful and haunting work that stirred its first audiences, but perhaps for different reasons. The subject matter is no longer shocking and neither does its post-Wagnerian musical language seem as dissonant and atonal as it once did. Still moving, however, are those human and startling moments—Elektra addressing the specter of the King, the recognition scene between Elektra and Orestes, and Elektra's final cathartic dance. At such moments Strauss's score stirs these characters to life and gives them extraordinary physical and emotional dimensions.

ALBERT WEISSER, Brooklyn College

ELEKTROSTAL [ĕ-lyĕk-trô-stäl'], city of the Soviet Union, important industrial center in the Moscow Oblast of the R.S.F.S.R. It is located within the Moscow metropolitan region. Its major industries are metallurgy and machine building. The Elektrostal metallurgical works, among the largest in the Soviet Union, specializes in the production of high-grade steel products. The Novo-Kramatorsk plant is a major producer of heavy machinery. The city was known as Zatishie until 1938. Pop., 97,000.

ELEMENT, CHEMICAL. In the broadest sense, elements are the fundamental substances from which the universe is made. The Greek philosopher Empedocles proposed four elements: earth, water, air, and fire; other Greek philosophers added a fifth element, ether, out of which the heavens were composed. Centuries later, alchemists considered salt, mercury, and sulfur to be elements also.

In 1661, Robert Boyle suggested that elements were simple substances which combined to form compounds, and that from these compounds the elements could be isolated again, unchanged. The elements themselves could not be decomposed into still simpler substances.

After John Dalton had advanced the atomic theory early in the 19th century, it was generally accepted that each element had its characteristic type of atom, with a specific atomic weight, and that atoms were indestructible and unchangeable.

By 1913, however, isotopes had been discovered: atoms of a particular element might differ in weight but they had the same number of protons in their nucleus. Radioactivity also proved that atoms consisted of still smaller particles. A rearrangement of these by nuclear reactions converts one element into another.

ISAAC ASIMOV, Boston University

Table

The Chemical Elements

Name	Symbol	Atomic Number	Atomic Weight°
Actinium	Ac	89	(227)
Aluminum	Al	13	26.9815
Americium	Am	95	(243)
Antimony	Sb	51	121.75
Argon	Ar	18	39.948
Arsenic	As	33	74.9216
Astatine	At	85	(210)
Barium	Ba	56	137.34
Berkelium	Bk	97	(249)
Beryllium	Be	4	9.0122
Bismuth	Bi	83	208.980
Boron	B	5	10.811
Bromine	Br	35	79.909
Cadmium	Cd	48	112.40
Calcium	Ca	20	40.08
Californium	Cf	98	(251)
Carbon	C	6	12.01115
Cerium	Ce	58	140.12
Cesium	Cs	55	132.05
Chlorine	Cl	17	35.453
Chromium	Cr	24	51.996
Cobalt	Co	27	58.9332
Columbium, *see Niobium*			
Copper	Cu	29	63.54
Curium	Cm	96	(247)
Dysprosium	Dy	66	162.50
Einsteinium	Es	99	(254)
Erbium	Er	68	167.28
Europium	Eu	63	151.96
Fermium	Fm	100	(253)
Fluorine	F	9	18.9984
Francium	Fr	87	(223)
Gadolinium	Gd	64	157.25
Gallium	Ga	31	69.72
Germanium	Ge	32	72.59
Gold	Au	79	196.967
Hafnium	Hf	72	178.49
Helium	He	2	4.0026
Holmium	Ho	67	164.930
Hydrogen	H	1	1.00797
Indium	In	49	114.82
Iodine	I	53	126.9044
Iridium	Ir	77	192.2
Iron	Fe	26	55.847
Krypton	Kr	36	83.80
Lanthanum	La	57	138.91
Lawrencium	Lw	103	(257)
Lead	Pb	82	207.19
Lithium	Li	3	6.939
Lutetium	Lu	71	174.97
Magnesium	Mg	12	24.312
Manganese	Mn	25	54.9380
Mendelevium	Md	101	(256)
Mercury	Hg	80	200.59
Molybdenum	Mo	42	95.94
Neodymium	Nd	60	144.24
Neon	Ne	10	20.183
Neptunium	Np	93	(237)
Nickel	Ni	28	58.71
Niobium (Columbium)	Nb	41	92.906
Nitrogen	N	7	14.0067
Nobelium	No	102	(254)
Osmium	Os	76	190.2
Oxygen	O	8	15.9994
Palladium	Pd	46	106.4
Phosphorus	P	15	30.9738
Platinum	Pt	78	195.09
Plutonium	Pu	94	(244)
Polonium	Po	84	(210)
Potassium	K	19	39.102
Praseodymium	Pr	59	140.907
Promethium	Pm	61	(147)
Protactinium	Pa	91	(231)
Radium	Ra	88	(226)
Radon	Rn	86	(222)
Rhenium	Re	75	186.2
Rhodium	Rh	45	102.905
Rubidium	Rb	37	85.47
Ruthenium	Ru	44	101.07
Samarium	Sm	62	150.35
Scandium	Sc	21	44.956
Selenium	Se	34	78.96
Silicon	Si	14	28.086
Silver	Ag	47	107.870
Sodium	Na	11	22.9898
Strontium	Sr	38	87.62
Sulfur	S	16	32.064
Tantalum	Ta	73	180.948
Technetium	Tc	43	(99)
Tellurium	Te	52	127.60
Terbium	Tb	65	158.924

Thallium	Tl	81	204.37
Thorium	Th	90	232.038
Thulium	Tm	69	168.934
Tin	Sn	50	118.69
Titanium	Ti	22	47.90
Tungsten	W	74	183.85
Uranium	U	92	238.03
Vanadium	V	23	50.942
Xenon	Xe	54	131.30
Ytterbium	Yb	70	173.04
Yttrium	Y	39	88.905
Zinc	Zn	30	65.37
Zirconium	Zr	40	91.22

* The figures for atomic weights are those approved by the International Union of Pure and Applied Chemistry in 1961, on the basis of Carbon = 12 having a mass of exactly 12. The figures in parenthesis represent the mass numbers of the most stable isotopes of those elements that do not occur in nature in more than traces.

ELEPHANT, the largest living land mammal, characterized by tremendous bulk, large ears, a long trunk, or proboscis, and greatly enlarged upper incisor teeth, the tusks. The Asiatic elephant, *Elephas maximus*, is found in the forests of India, Ceylon, Burma, Indochina, and the Malay Peninsula. It reaches an average shoulder height of 9 ft., may weigh 4 tons, or more, and can be distinguished from the larger, African elephant by its bulging forehead, smaller ears, and light-gray skin color. The African elephant, *Loxodonta africana*, is native to bush regions of Africa and is darker in color than the Asiatic species. It reaches a maximum shoulder height of 13 ft. and may weigh over 6 tons. Its enormous ears, which are about 3½ ft. wide, act as fans, circulating air continuously during the heat of the day. The forest elephant, *L. cyclotis*, is a smaller African species found in the woodlands of West Africa. Compared to the other species the forest elephant is small, rarely exceeding a shoulder height of 8 ft., and is often called the pygmy elephant.

Elephants are normally forest animals, although they may stray across open country to find other feeding grounds. Each elephant requires as much as ½ ton of food a day, and a large herd may wreak havoc with a plantation of trees. Food is gathered with the trunk, which has a sensitive, prehensile tip. Water is also conveyed to the mouth by the trunk, or splashed over the back when the animal bathes. If foliage is beyond the reach of the trunk, several individuals may collaborate to uproot the trees on which they feed.

Elephants become sexually mature at 12 to 14 years of age and thereafter may breed at any time during the year. Gestation lasts from 19 to 21 months in the Asiatic elephant; 22 months in the African species. The hairy young are nursed by the mother for two years. The longevity of elephants is greatly exaggerated: elephants show signs of old age at 50 years, and there are no authentic instances of 100-year-old individuals.

The elephant has been domesticated by man for more than 1,000 years. The Asiatic species are captured by being directed into a funnel-shaped opening that leads to an enclosure. There they are tied to trees and fasted for three days, after which they are led out of the enclosure by tame elephants, fed and watered. These new captives become tame in a month. Since elephants can carry 1,200-lb. loads, and can exert a pulling force equal to that of 50 men, they are widely employed in moving teak logs, hauling stones, and other arduous tasks. The African elephant can be tamed as easily as its Asiatic relative. The Carthaginians and Romans were able to break these animals to the service of war in a few weeks.

For many years elephants yielded most of the commercial ivory used in billiard balls and piano keys, and the slaughter of these great beasts was tremendous. A record tusk weighed 235 lb., although a 10-ft. tusk usually weighs about 150 lb. Sizable herds of elephants are maintained in the Kruger National Park of South Africa, where they are protected from molestation. The trained elephant of the circus ring is the smaller Asiatic species, although both forms are exhibited in zoological gardens.

W. J. HAMILTON, JR., Cornell University

Elephants have long been tamed as beasts of burden. Below, Indian elephants provide transportation on a tiger hunt.

YLLA—Rapho-Guillumette

YLLA—Rapho-Guillumette

The African elephant (above) is the largest living land mammal. It has a convex forehead and very large, rounded ears.

The Indian elephant is smaller than the African. Its ears are small, its head is prominently domed, and its forehead is concave.

New York Zoological Society

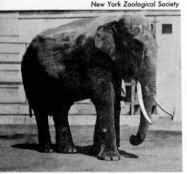

ELEPHANT BIRD, large flightless bird, *Aepyornis maximus*, once found in Madagascar, but extinct for at least 7,000 years. Fossil remains indicate that this huge bird was 9 ft. tall and weighed as much as 1,000 lb. Its eggs are the largest animal cells known. Over 1 ft. in length, they probably weighed 18 lb. when fresh and had more than 1 gal. of contents—the equivalent of 148 hen's eggs. The elephant bird was distantly related to the giant moa of New Zealand, another extinct species.
See also MOA.

ELEPHANTIASIS [ĕl-ə-fən-tī'-ə-sĭs] **or ELEPHANT DISEASE,** a term often used to describe any thickening of the skin and underlying tissues. It is most commonly caused by infection with certain tropical parasites, the filarial worms. The parasites enter the body when an infected mosquito bites into the skin. Following this male and female worms mature in the tissues where they eventually mate and release thousands of microscopic offspring into the blood stream.

Frequently the infection produces no symptoms. In a certain percentage of long-standing cases, the lymphatic vessels (the channels through which tissue fluids normally pass) in the legs, scrotum, arms, and breasts become obstructed. In such instances fluid backs up in these areas, resulting in a massive swelling. The legs may become so unwieldy as to make walking impossible. Over a period of time fibrous tissue grows in the swollen parts rendering them thick and hard.

Elephantiasis may also develop following operations in which the lymphatic vessels are disrupted. Elephantiasis of the arm occasionally appears after cancer surgery of the breast.

Elephantiasis resulting from worm infestation may be treated with hetrazan, a drug that destroys the worms. Tight bandages are applied to control the swelling, but surgical treatment may be necessary in advanced cases.
HAROLD A. TUCKER, M.D.
See also FILARIASIS.

ELEPHANTINE [ĕl-ə-făn-tī'nē], Egyptian island below the first cataract of the Nile, opposite Aswan. In antiquity it was important for red granite and as a departure point for caravans to the south. In the 26th Dynasty soldiers were garrisoned on the island to protect the frontier and in the Persian period a Jewish colony was located there. A Nilometer that had recorded especially high floods between the reigns of Augustus and Trajan was restored in 1870. The local god was ram-headed Khnum. There are ruins of a 29th-Dynasty temple with Ptolemaic and Roman additions.
See also EGYPT.

ELEPHANT SEAL, a large seal, *Mirounga augustirostris*, native to northern Pacific waters. The males are 15 ft. long and weigh 5,000 lb., more than twice the size of the females. Males have a trunklike extension of the snout, which is raised and greatly dilated when the bulls are guarding their harem. These great seals occur from Alaska to lower California; the southern elephant seal, *M. leonina*, occurs in the subantarctic islands. During breeding season huge herds of elephant seals congregate on the beaches; at other times they are solitary and live at sea. Their food consists of fish, squids, and rays.

ELEPHANT'S-EAR. *See* TARO.

ELEPHANT'S FOOT, common name for a perennial climbing plant, *Testudinaria elephantipes*, in the Dioscoreaceae, or yam family. Elephant's foot is native to South Africa and is named for its huge rootstock, often 4 ft. in diameter. The starchy root is cut into pieces, baked, and eaten by African natives.

ELEPHANT SHREW, name for the rat-size African insectivores of the family Macroscelididae, characterized by a long, mobile snout. Elephant shrews also have a long tail and kangaroolike hind limbs, adapted for leaping. These small creatures show some curious resemblances to the lower primates, particularly in their sexual physiology. They are inhabitants of the forest, feeding on insects and other small animal life.

ELEUSINIAN [ĕl-ū-sĭn'ē-ən] **MYSTERIES,** most famous of the Greek mystery cults, celebrated in honor of Demeter (q.v.) and Kore at Eleusis, near Athens. The Homeric hymn to Demeter (c.600 B.C.) recounts the mythical foundation of the cult, but its origins are much earlier, probably even Mycenaean. The rites were primarily agricultural —Demeter was the "Corn-mother," her daughter Kore (Persephone) the "Corn-daughter," the young grain. At the harvest, in late spring, the new grain was stored in underground bins; analogously, Kore was kidnaped by Pluto, god of wealth, or Hades, god of the underworld, in the myth. The Mysteries were celebrated in early autumn, when, after the parching heat of summer, the seed grain was brought up for the sowing; after four months in the underworld, Kore was reunited with her mother. Initiates in the Mysteries were promised a "happier lot" in the afterlife, but not, strictly speaking, immortality.

Initiation was open to all who spoke Greek, including slaves, and even Roman Emperors sought admission. Candidates had first to be initiated in the Lesser Mysteries, held at Agrae in spring. Some features of the Greater Mysteries were public, notably the ritual bath in the sea at Phalerum and the majestic procession from Athens to Eleusis. The nonpublic ceremonies were in three parts: Initiation, a preliminary rite performed individually; the Ritual; and the Vision; but the content of the "things done, things said, and things shown" was never divulged.
FRANCIS R. WALTON, Gennadius Library, Athens
See also MYSTERIES.

ELEUSIS [ĭ-lū'sĭs], ancient Greek town in Attica, 12 mi. northwest of Athens, site of the Eleusinian Mysteries celebrated in honor of Demeter and Kore. At first independent, Eleusis was incorporated into Attica in the 7th century B.C. The sanctuary is on a walled terrace on the east slope of the acropolis, entered by two successive gateways. The main building is the Telesterion, a square hypostyle hall, remodeled over many centuries, where the Mysteries culminated. Excavations have been carried on since 1882 by the Greek Archaeological Society. Remains of the Late Bronze Age have been found.

ELEVATOR [ĕl'ə-vā-tər], a platform or cage which moves vertically; used most commonly to convey passengers to the various levels in a building but also used to carry cargo in buildings, ships, and mines. The area in which the elevator travels is called the elevator shaft. Heavy steel cables are fastened to the top of the elevator car and extend to the top of the elevator shaft. Here the cables go over pulleys, then down the shaft where they attach to a series of counterweights. The counterweights counterbalance the elevator so that the driving motor at the top of the shaft does not have to lift the entire weight of the elevator. A motor, powerful enough to lift the difference between the coun-

THE AUTOMATIC ELEVATOR

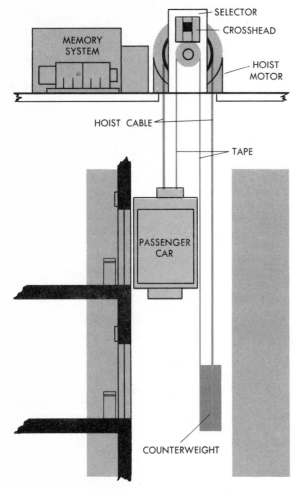

The main parts of an automatic elevator are shown above. In order that the hoist motor does not have to lift the entire weight of a loaded passenger car, a counterweight is used. Besides the hoist cable, there is a tape connected to both the car and counterweight. This tape runs around a pulley, activating a crosshead in the selector unit, moving it up or down in unison with the car. The selector records the signals from push buttons on the various floors, storing this information in its memory system. Thus, when the crosshead reaches the equivalent of a signaling floor, the elevator is stopped, and the doors open. After the passenger has entered and the doors have closed, that particular signal is erased, and the elevator moves on to answer other signals.

terweight and loaded elevator, drives the elevator from the top of the shaft. The motor usually powers a driving sheave or pulley over which the cables run. The car is guided within the elevator shaft by a pair of vertical rails.

Brakes, as well as the motor, are used to control the elevator. To stop the car so that the floor of the elevator is level with the floor of a building requires precise control. With manual adjustments this positioning may take considerable time; therefore, automatic controls are often used.

Automatic Elevators. Automatic elevators have electric storage or memory systems to record the floors chosen by passengers pressing the selector button. Thus one may enter an elevator on the twelfth floor and push a button to take him to the third floor. However, if another passenger already has pushed a button for the sixth floor, the elevator will stop at this floor on the way down. Automatic controls also prevent an elevator from becoming overloaded. Whenever an established "safe weight" is exceeded, a series of switches either sets off an alarm or automatically shuts off the elevator motor preventing its use.

In most buildings, safety codes govern the proper load an elevator may carry. These codes are established by government officials in conjunction with special engineering organizations.

Because the motor must be started and stopped quite often, special attention is given to the design of controls to assure reliable operation. In the event of power failure or other emergency, most elevators contain automatic controls to hold the elevator safely in the shaft until repairs can be made. Modern elevators are safe and serious accidents rare.

Speeds. Elevators travel at speeds ranging from less than 100 ft. per minute to more than 1,000 ft. per minute. Because of the effects of inertia upon the human body, these speeds must be attained gradually. If an elevator gains speed at a rate of 3.2 ft. per second each second, a passenger would experience a "g" force of about 1/10th his own weight. A 180-lb. man, for example, would "weigh" about 198 lb. For the safety and comfort of the passengers, these "g" forces must be kept small.

Department store elevators travel 4 to 8 mi. during an 8-hour day, making, on an average, between 300 and 400 stops per mile. In office buildings, local elevators travel 15 to 20 mi. per day, stopping 150 or more times per mile. Express elevators travel about 30 to 40 mi. per day, making only about 100 stops per mile.

An elevator can get to the top of the tallest buildings in a matter of about three minutes. If a person on foot climbed steadily at a rate of ½ vertical ft. per second, it would take him more than 40 minutes to reach the top of the 102-story Empire State Building.

Early Elevators. Although hoists of various types have been known for centuries, the first modern elevator was exhibited in the Crystal Palace at the New York World's Fair in 1853. This was a mechanical elevator able to stop automatically in the event the hoisting rope broke. The machine was designed by Elisha G. Otis. In 1859, Otis developed an independent reversible engine directly connected to the hoisting machinery. The same year, O. Tuft of Boston installed a passenger elevator in the Fifth Avenue Hotel, New York City. The elevator was raised and lowered by a vertical screw instead of ropes. In 1871 the hydraulic elevator was introduced, followed in 1889 by the first commercially successful electric elevator.

WILLARD ROGERS, University of Arizona

ELEVATOR, AIRCRAFT, a movable airfoil that controls the vertical motion of an aircraft. Conventional aircraft have two elevators, one on either side of the vertical fin, and the whole arrangement is set at the tail end of the craft. The elevators are hinged and rigged to operate together. When the control stick is pushed forward, the elevators dip downward into the slipstream, forcing the tail up and putting the plane into a glide angle which depends on the degree to which the elevators are set. When the control stick is pulled back, the elevators are raised, the slipstream presses the tail down, and the nose comes up.

ELF, in Teutonic mythology, creature having human form but of smaller size than man. Elves lived in hills and were generally benevolent, protective creatures. In Sweden, sacrificial festivals from which strangers were excluded were held in their honor in late autumn. The blood of sacrificial oxen was sometimes poured on the hills. In Norway and Iceland, these creatures still play a large role in folklore, and people are careful not to offend them since elves are thought to lead mortals into danger.

ELF OWL, a small owl, *Micrathene whitneyi*, native to the deserts of southwestern United States and northern Mexico. This sparrow-size bird is the smallest of all owls and reaches a length of no more than 6 in. Elf owls nest in holes dug in a giant cactus. They emerge at night to search for small desert rodents.

ELGAR [ĕl′gär, ĕl′gər], **SIR EDWARD WILLIAM** (1857–1934), noted English composer, born in Broadheath. He came of a musical family, and with little training became a competent violinist and organist. National recognition came in 1899 with the performance of his *Enigma Variations,* followed in 1900 by the oratorio *The Dream of Gerontius.* Other notable works are the symphonic poem *Falstaff* (1913) and the *Pomp and Circumstance* marches (1901). He received a knighthood in 1904, was appointed professor of music at Birmingham (1905–8), became Master of the King's Music in 1924, and was created a baronet in 1931. His cosmopolitan late-romantic idiom was influenced by Wagner and Strauss, but he had a strong and individual melodic gift, and there is a characteristic English quality to his romanticism. He had little influence on the English nationalists who immediately followed him, but found musical heirs two generations later in Sir Arthur Bliss and Sir William Walton.

Consult McVeagh, D. M., *Edward Elgar* (1955).

COLIN MASON, The Manchester *Guardian*
See also ENGLISH MUSIC.

ELGIN [ĕl′gĭn], **JAMES BRUCE, 8TH EARL OF** (1811–63), British colonial administrator, Governor General of British North America (Canada) (1847–54), and Viceroy of India (1862–63). His father, Thomas Bruce, 7th Earl of Elgin, was noted for acquiring the Elgin Marbles early

in the 19th century. Following a brief parliamentary career, Elgin was appointed Governor of Jamaica in 1842, where he did much to alleviate the economic unrest caused by the abolition of slavery in 1834. In 1846 he was transferred to Canada as Governor General, arriving in Montreal early in 1847. Despite intense opposition in 1849, Elgin staunchly, and at great personal danger, refused to abandon the principle of colonial autonomy for Canada. He thus assured the continuation of the new constitutional procedure of responsible government, as recommended in the 1839 report on affairs in Canada by his father-in-law, John George Lambton, 1st Earl of Durham. As a remedy for the economic distress in Canada resulting from the coming of free trade in Britain in 1846 and the abandonment of the Navigation Acts in 1849, Elgin proposed reciprocal free trade with the United States and successfully negotiated the Reciprocity Treaty of 1854. After completing difficult and dangerous assignments in China and Japan, he was appointed (1861) Viceroy of India, the first to be directly designated by the crown, and also Governor General. He died a year after arriving in India.

W. M. WHITELAW, American International College

ELGIN. *See* MORAY OR ELGIN.

ELGIN [ĕl′jĭn], industrial city of northeastern Illinois, on the Fox River. A center of diversified industry, it is well known for the Elgin Watch Company (estab., 1866) and for printing and publishing of religious materials. Elgin Academy (1856), one of the oldest boys' preparatory schools in the state, and the Elgin State (mental) Hospital are here. Settled, 1835; inc. as village, 1847; as city, 1854; pop. (1950) 44,223; (1960) 49,447.

ELGIN [ĕl′gĭn] **MARBLES,** collection of classical Greek sculpture, named after Lord Elgin. As British ambassador to Turkey he obtained permission to remove from Athens stones on which were inscriptions and figures. At that time Greece was a province of the Turkish Empire. Between 1803 and 1812, 280 cases filled with sculptures from the Parthenon, the Erechtheum, the temple of Athena Nike, and various other monuments were shipped to England and exhibited in London. Because of the boundless admiration they aroused, they were finally purchased in 1816 by act of Parliament and are now enshrined in the British Museum, where they are assembled, as far as possible, in their original groupings.

ELGON, MOUNT, extinct volcano in east-central Africa, on the Kenya-Uganda border. Mount Elgon has one of the largest crater cones in the world. It is 5 mi. in diameter and about 2,000 ft. deep. The highest point is Wagagai (14,178 ft.) on the crater rim. The lower slopes are densely populated to 7,000 ft. by the Bagishu, who grow coffee for export.

EL GRECO. *See* GRECO, EL.

ELI [ē′lī], in the Old Testament, aged priest of Shiloh and mentor of Samuel (I Sam. 1:1–4:18). When war first broke out between Israel and the Philistines, Eli's sons, Hophni and Phinehas, who were reputed to be very wicked men, were sent into battle with the Ark of the Covenant in the hope of thus securing victory. But the Philistines captured the Ark and killed Eli's sons. When Eli, 98 years old and blind, received the news, he fell over backward and died of a broken neck.

ELIA. *See* LAMB, CHARLES.

ELIAS [ĭ-lī′əs] **OF CORTONA,** known variously as Brother Elias and Elias of Assisi (c.1180–1253), companion of St. Francis of Assisi, and first vicar-general of the Franciscans. He was born in Bevilia near Assisi and studied in Bologna. In 1220 St. Francis made Elias vicar-general, and on his deathbed gave Elias his special blessing. It fell to Elias to write to the houses of the order informing them of Francis' death and of his stigmata. He immediately began building a basilica in Assisi to house the remains of his beloved Francis, temporarily interring them at the Church of San Giorgio. His campaigns for money and his desire for buildings brought him into direct conflict with other Franciscans eager to keep the spirit of holy poverty. In May, 1227, Elias was rejected as general in favor of Giovanni Parenti. He then spent himself, by order of Pope Gregory IX, in the task of building the basilica in Assisi, the lower part of which was consecrated in 1230. In 1232 he was elected general of the order, but because of his stress on education and his desire to increase the order's temporal holdings, he was opposed by Aymo of Faversham, who in 1239 convinced Gregory IX to depose Elias. When Elias backed the excommunicated Frederick II in 1240, he was himself excommunicated. He died reconciled with his church but not with his order.

RICHARD J. WESTLEY, Barat College of the Sacred Heart, Lake Forest, Ill.

ELIJAH [ĭ-lī′jə], one of the great prophets of the Old Testament, who exercised his stormy ministry in Israel during the reigns of Ahab and Ahaziah (869–849 B.C.). He is known from the record of his activity in the books of Kings (I Kings 17–19, 21; II Kings 1–2). A gaunt figure of forbidding appearance and fierce conviction, he fought for the distinctiveness of the Mosaic faith when it was threatened by the cults of Canaan (I Kings 18:17–40; II Kings 1:1–17) and for social justice when it was threatened by royal tyranny (I Kings 21). Standing in the tradition which runs from Moses to Amos, he earned the title "Troubler of Israel" (I Kings 18:17) and knew the burden of his prophetic commission (I Kings 19:4–8). His reputation became legendary in Jewish tradition. He was expected to return before the coming of the Kingdom of God (Mal. 4:5) and is regarded in the New Testament as the typical Old Testament prophet (Mark 9:4).

E. W. HEATON, Oxford University

ELIOT, CHARLES WILLIAM (1834–1926), American educator. Born in Boston, he graduated from Harvard in 1853. After teaching at Harvard he traveled in Europe (1863–65) and then taught chemistry at the Massachusetts Institute of Technology (1865–69). He became president of Harvard in 1869 and served until he retired in 1909. Under his guidance Harvard grew greatly, the student body increasing fourfold and the faculty tenfold. Eliot introduced the elective system for undergraduates, added graduate schools of arts and science, and improved medical education. In addition to editing the 50-volume Harvard Classics (known as the "five-foot shelf"), he wrote *The Happy Life* (1896), *Educational Reform* (1898), and *The Religion of the Future* (1909).

ELIOT, GEORGE, pseudonym of Mary Ann or Marian Evans (1819–80), English novelist. Born in rural Warwickshire, she was the daughter of a Tory land agent who became, in varying degrees, the prototype of all the heroic, strong, virtuously masculine figures of her books. George Eliot grew up among exactly those country classes whose peculiar piquancies she tried to catch in her novels. She was extremely intelligent, and her interests in her extensive reading were highly intellectual. At 21, with her retired father, she moved to Coventry, where she was stimulated by free-thinking friends to give up the evangelical religion of her youth. After her father died in 1849 she went to Geneva, returning to be absorbed in the London circle of the *Westminster Review*, of which she became assistant editor. From 1854 until his death in 1878 she lived, in a relationship they considered marriage, with George Henry Lewes, who was legally bound to an insane wife. It was Lewes who encouraged her to write her great novels. In 1880 she married John Walter Cross.

Although some of her earlier works—translations, essays, novellas—had appeared in print, she published her first full-length novel, *Adam Bede*, in 1859. It was an immediate popular, critical, and financial success. It was quickly followed by *The Mill on the Floss* (1860) and *Silas Marner* (1861). These early books are brooding but at times harshly humorous evocations of the countryside of

Under the pseudonym of George Eliot, Mary Ann Evans wrote *The Mill on the Floss* and other popular novels of the 19th century.

her youth. In *Romola* (1863), which is set in Savonarola's Florence, her more intellectual strain becomes evident: abstract idea replaces personal experience and treasured hearsay. In the intricately plotted *Middlemarch* (1871–72), as in no other late 19th-century English novel, a whole society is brought to life. This brilliantly imagined social history is an amazingly successful amalgamation of thought and feeling. The more intellectual *Daniel Deronda* (1876) is a plea against anti-Semitism.

The penetration of an exactly described world with exactly stated abstract, often moral, ideas lies at the heart of George Eliot's greatness. But her talents are various: no one has recreated more powerfully such aspects of ordinary life as impending financial disaster, awakening sexual attraction, and the need for social advancement.

Consult Bennett, J. F., *George Eliot: Her Mind and Her Art* (1948); Bullett, G. W., *George Eliot; Her Life and Books* (1948); Speaight, Robert, *George Eliot* (1954).

ROBERT BRENTANO, University of California at Berkeley

ELIOT, JOHN (1604–90), apostle to the Indians. A Puritan, born in England and educated at Cambridge, he migrated to Massachusetts in 1631 and settled as teacher of the church in Roxbury. In 1646 he began missionary work, gathering his "praying Indians" into 14 villages, of which Natick was the most significant. He translated many works into the Indian tongue, particularly the Bible (New Testament, 1661; Old Testament, 1663).

ELIOT, T(HOMAS) S(TEARNS) (1888–1965), poet, playwright, and critic. The seventh child in a family whose line originated in Somerset, England, and migrated to Massachusetts in the 17th century, Eliot was born in St. Louis, Mo. After private school preparation, he took his bachelor's degree at Harvard in 1910 and did graduate work there in philosophy and philology. Studying at the Sorbonne and then at Oxford, he took up what was to become permanent residence in England in 1915. He

T. S. Eliot, poet and playwright.

Brown Brothers

wrote poetry, taught at Highgate School, and worked in Lloyd's Bank before attracting notice with *Prufrock and Other Observations* (1917). He edited the *Egoist* and then, a year before assuming the editorship of the *Criterion*, created a literary sensation with the publication of *The Waste Land* (1922). This long poem explored what Eliot felt to be the spiritual decadence of the modern world, comparing it in elaborate counterpoint with previous ages which though barbaric demonstrated physical and spiritual vitality and beauty. More shocking to most readers was the poem's form, with its compression, ellipsis, "creative borrowing" from several languages and literatures, and its use of ancient myth and legend. It came to be the single most influential poem of the century thus far, giving impetus to the writing of modern "difficult" poetry.

Eliot worked for the publishing house of Faber & Faber, of which he eventually became a director. In 1927 he became a British subject, declaring himself an Anglo-Catholic, monarchist, and classicist as well. In *Ash Wednesday* (1930) he showed that orthodox Christian faith had replaced the despair of *The Waste Land*. Echoing Dante's *Divine Comedy* and the Bible, the speaker depicted the penitential course of the spirit in striving toward humility and salvation. The *Four Quartets* (1943) dealt with the twin themes of time and history. Here again Eliot drew upon familiar literary sources, as well as Christian liturgy and the Spanish mystic St. John of the Cross.

As Eliot's poetry had shown his indebtedness to the classics, the English metaphysical poets, and the French symbolists, so his critical standards were based in the great works of the past. In books such as *The Sacred Wood* (1920) he helped bring about a revaluation of English poetry, especially enhancing the reputation of Donne and other 17th-century writers. *The Idea of a Christian Society* (1939) and *Notes Toward the Definition of Culture* (1948) treated contemporary problems from a Christian point of view.

From the 1930's onward Eliot has become increasingly interested in the verse play. *The Rock* (1934) was a contemporary pageant play and *Murder in the Cathedral* (1935) dramatized the martyrdom of Thomas à Becket. *The Cocktail Party* (1949) was commercially very successful. It treated spiritual problems from the viewpoints of religion and psychiatry in witty, urbane, and poetic language. *The Confidential Clerk* (1953) and *The Elder Statesman* (1958) were serious comedies. Since about 1935 Eliot has lectured at British and American universities. His achievements were crowned in 1948 with the Order of Merit and the Nobel Prize for literature.

Consult Smith, Grover, Jr., *T. S. Eliot's Poetry and Plays: A Study in Sources and Meaning* (1956).

JOSEPH L. BLOTNER, University of Virginia

ELIS [ē′lĭs], ancient Greek province in the northwest Peloponnesus, south of Achaea, west of Arcadia, and north of Messenia. Elis includes the site of the great temple of Zeus at Olympia, and the Eleans presided over the Panhellenic Olympic games for over 1,000 years. The country is mostly flat, with low foothills inland, traversed by the two rivers Peneus and Alpheus, both of which empty into the Ionian Sea. The early inhabitants were akin to those of central Greece, and their dialect close to Aetolian. Elis was divided into three districts: Acroria, Pisatis, and Triphylia. The rustic Eleans took little interest in politics, but allied themselves with Sparta in the 5th century, though in the latter part they went over to Athens. They united with Arcadia in 369 B.C., and in the 3d century joined the Aetolian League. The city of Elis, built c.471 B.C., has been partly excavated. One of the oldest Greek inscriptions preserved is the treaty of Elis with Arcadian Heraea, dating from the early 6th century B.C. The modern capital is Pyrgos, a flourishing commercial town and center of a fertile agricultural area.

JOHN H. YOUNG, Johns Hopkins University

ELISABETH, ST. (Heb., "My God is an oath" or "faithful"), mother of John the Baptist. Of a priestly family and married to a priest, Zacharias (Luke 1:5), she was related to Mary, the mother of Jesus (Luke 1:36). Although Elisabeth and Zacharias were old and childless, an angel promised them a son, who was John the Baptist.

ELISABETHVILLE. *See* LUBUMBASHI.

ELISHA [ĭ-lī'shə], Old Testament prophet, the disciple and successor of Elijah. His prophetic ministry covered the 2d half of the 9th century B.C. (I Kings 19–II Kings 13). Despite their association, Elisha differed fundamentally from Elijah. Far from being a lonely individualist with a "double share" of Elijah's spirit (II Kings 2:9), Elisha was the head of a guild of popular prophets (II Kings 2:3; 6:1–4), living the settled life of a wonder-working holy man (II Kings 4, 13). He played a part in the blood purge of 842 B.C., by which Jehu overthrew the dynasty of Omri in Israel (II Kings 9), and then disappeared from history.

ELISIR D'AMORE, L' [ā-lē-zēr' dä-mō'rä] (The Elixir of Love), opera buffa in two acts by Gaetano Donizetti; libretto by Felice Romani, after Eugène Scribe's *Le Philtre;* first performance, May 12, 1832, Teatro della Canobbiana, Milan. Nemorino, a young farmer, secures a love potion from Dr. Dulcamara to gain the attention of Adina. She becomes jealous of the village girls, the lovers finally embrace, and all are convinced that the elixir had worked its charm. Despite some clichés, lovely tunes and a knowing wit make this gay work one of the finest of its genre. The famous tenor solo *Una furtiva lagrima* (A Furtive Tear) is sung by Nemorino in Act II.

ELISTA, city of the Soviet Union, north of the Caucasus, capital of the Kalmyk Autonomous S.S.R. It was renamed Stepnoi after 1944 when its Kalmuck (Kalmyk) population was deported for disloyalty. It reassumed the name Elista in 1957 with the reconstitution of the Kalmyk political unit. Pop., 22,000.

ELIXIR (Arab. *al-iksir*, "philosopher's stone"), in alchemy, a term applied to various solutions held to be capable of transmuting molten base metals into silver or gold. The transmuting agent, the "medicine of metals," was also called the elixir of life, because it was believed to cure human disease and prolong indefinitely the life of anyone who consumed it. In pharmacology, the term is used for

clear preparations containing flavoring substances and small amounts of medicinal agents.

ELIZABETH I (1533–1603), Queen of England and Ireland (1558–1603). She was the daughter of Henry VIII and Anne Boleyn. After her mother's execution for high treason in 1536, Princess Elizabeth lived on the fringes of the court; her legal status was uncertain because charges of immorality against her mother cast doubt on the validity of the marriage. However, when Henry defined the succession in his will (1546), he gave "our daughter Elizabeth" a place after Princess Mary. During the reign of Edward VI, Elizabeth is said to have been the object of a scheme by Thomas Seymour, brother of the Protector, the Duke of Somerset, who wished to marry her. While Mary was Queen, Elizabeth remained in the background and kept free from involvement in the cross-currents of politics, though to do so must have taxed, as well as developed, her political skill.

Elizabeth succeeded her half sister Mary in 1558, and though she was greeted with popular acclaim her task was difficult. Mary's Catholic religious policy, her marriage to Philip II of Spain, and her involvement in an unsuccessful costly war with France had shaken the security of the Tudor Dynasty. Doubts as to her legitimacy further weakened Elizabeth's position. During much of her reign the Catholic Mary, Queen of Scots was a rival for her throne. That threat partially resolved itself when Mary, in 1568, fled to England and became Elizabeth's prisoner. Nonetheless she continued to be a danger to Elizabeth as the central figure in several Catholic conspiracies. In 1570 the Pope declared Elizabeth a usurper and freed Englishmen from allegiance to her. In 1587, after Mary had been implicated in another plot, and public demand for her execution was vehement, Elizabeth signed the death warrant.

At Elizabeth's accession the need for a religious settlement was urgent. Protestant clergymen who had fled to the mainland during Mary's reign returned to England, eager to establish a rigorous form of Protestantism as the nation's only authorized religion. Elizabeth caused a compromise to be made. Her Acts of Supremacy and Uniformity (1559) declared the monarch to be supreme governor of the Church of England, retained subordinate government by Archbishops and Bishops, and required acceptance of a prayer book whose language contained both Catholic and Protestant phrases to describe controversial articles of belief. All Englishmen were required to attend church services. Elizabeth's religious settlement was a political one; it sought to avoid public disorder. She staunchly defended it throughout her reign and, as Englishmen familiarized themselves with the pattern of worship she had prescribed, a majority became devoted to it.

In foreign policy Elizabeth was at first cautious. As the moderate Protestantism of her religious policy emerged, Catholic powers turned hostile, Spain in particular. Elizabeth cautiously supported those of her subjects who tried to break Spain's monopoly of the New World by illicit trade and by voyages of discovery, such as those of Sir Francis Drake. In the middle 1580's she gave military aid to the Dutch, who had revolted against Spanish rule in the Netherlands. Her intervention there, together with the execution of Mary, Queen of Scots, moved Philip of Spain

Queen Elizabeth I, monarch of England and Ireland, depicted in a painting attributed to Marcus Gheeraerts. (NATIONAL PORTRAIT GALLERY)

to send the Armada against England in 1588 and thus to begin a war that lasted the rest of Elizabeth's reign.

Throughout her reign Elizabeth took active part in the direction of government, notably the administrative departments, the armed services, and Parliament. In the manner of her grandfather, Henry VII, she supervised the work of the council from day to day. During the relatively infrequent periods when Parliament met, she kept the House of Commons under scrutiny, intervening to prevent discussion of topics she deemed to be beyond its competence. On one occasion she spoke in full Parliament of her duties as Queen: "There will never Queen sit in my seat with more zeal to my country and care to my subjects. And though you have had and may have princes more mighty and wise sitting in this seat, yet you never had or shall have any that will be more careful and loving." All her Parliaments supported her policies.

Elizabeth was a woman of much intellectual ability. She had had an excellent education in the classics and in contemporary literature and languages. She drew to her court, and kept there under her personal supervision, many leading figures from the nobility, most persons who were prominent in public affairs, and a following of writers, artists, and musicians. The royal court became the center of the nation's cultural life as it had never been before and never has been since. She herself often traveled with her courtiers up and down the country as though to make herself known to as many of her people as possible. She chose occasions for dramatic public appearances, as in her speech to the soldiers at Tilbury during the crisis of the Spanish Armada. As an unmarried Queen, Elizabeth became the object of many marriage offers by other rulers. At first she dealt with the marriage question by evasion. Later in her reign she conducted marriage negotiations with foreign princes, notably with the French Duke of Alençon in the 1570's, though how seriously no-

body knows. Popular tales spoke of her affection for the Earl of Leicester in the 1560's and for the Earl of Essex a generation later. Though often urged by members of Parliament to marry, she remained the Virgin Queen.

Her own leadership, the enthusiasm she engendered, and the skill of her councilors in maintaining a close but benevolent supervision of central and local government, contributed to the success of Elizabethan England, a success marked by internal unity, naval enterprise, and artistic brilliance of a kind never surpassed in the history of the British Isles.

Consult Neale, J. E., *Queen Elizabeth I* (1957); Jenkins, Elizabeth, *Elizabeth the Great* (1959).

FREDERICK G. MARCHAM, Cornell University

ELIZABETH II (1926–), Queen of the United Kingdom of Great Britain and Northern Ireland and head of the Commonwealth of Nations (1952–). The first daughter of the Duke of York (later George VI), she and her sister, Margaret, were educated by governesses. During World War II the Princesses lived in Scotland and at Windsor Castle. In 1944 Princess Elizabeth was made a member of the Council of State and deputized to act for her father in his absence. She received a commission in the women's Auxiliary Territorial Service in 1945. Two years later she toured South Africa with her parents and in Nov., 1947, was married to Philip Mountbatten, the newly designated Duke of Edinburgh. In 1957 the Queen gave him the title of Prince of the United Kingdom. They are the parents of four children, Charles (b.1948), the heir apparent, Anne (b.1950), Andrew (b.1960), and Edward (b.1964). While in Kenya en route to Australia and New Zealand in 1952, the Princess and her husband received word of her father's death. She was crowned in Westminster Abbey in 1953.

The Queen's reign has been tranquil, with the Conservatives maintaining power from her accession until the victory of the Labour party in the general elections of Oct., 1964. Except for the Suez crisis in the fall of 1956,

Queen Elizabeth II at her coronation in 1953. (CECIL BEATON)

there has been no major political or diplomatic disturbance. Economic prosperity generally has characterized the period. In Commonwealth affairs, this has been a time of rapid change, with the first of the African colonies achieving Commonwealth status, and the Union of South Africa withdrawing from the association because of criticism of its racial policies. The Queen and her husband have made extensive tours both inside and outside the Commonwealth. She has given an example of selfless public service, and has enjoyed great popularity with her people.

STEPHEN GRAUBARD, Harvard University

See also WINDSOR (British royal family).

ELIZABETH, city of Australia, in South Australia, 17 mi. north of Adelaide. Founded in 1955, Elizabeth was planned to become a modern industrial and residential city. Its varied industries include an automobile factory. Pop., 23,326.

ELIZABETH, city of northeastern New Jersey and seat of Union County, on Newark Bay, bounded on the north by Newark and on the east by the Arthur Kill. Its location on major highways and railway lines and its proximity to New York City have been responsible for the city's development as an industrial port. Singer sewing machines have been manufactured here since 1873. Other industries produce mattresses, printing equipment, machinery, paper products, shirts, copper, and hardware.

Elizabeth was settled in 1664 by colonists from Long Island and was the provincial capital from 1668 to 1686. Alexander Hamilton and Aaron Burr were residents of Elizabeth and attended an academy which occupied the present site of the parish house of the First Presbyterian Church. Elizabeth was the scene of many British and Tory raids during the Revolutionary War. There are 23 pre-Revolutionary buildings, marked by plaques of George Washington, remaining in the city. The College of New Jersey (now Princeton University) was founded here in 1746, later moving to Newark and then to Princeton. Inc., 1739; pop. (1950) 112,817; (1960) 107,698.

BERTRAND BOUCHER, Montclair State College

ELIZABETHAN [ĭ-lĭz-ə-bē′thən] **STYLE,** name applied to English architecture and furniture of the 16th century. It is named after Queen Elizabeth I, though the term is not strictly limited to work created during her reign (1558–1603). The earlier phase is called more specifically Tudor —for the royal line beginning with Henry VII—and may be traced from the 15th century. The later phase yielded to the Jacobean style, named for Elizabeth's successor, James I. The three terms overlap in use.

In the earlier phase of the Elizabethan style, Gothic elements were dominant; in the later, Renaissance features, brought to England by Italian artists and also transmitted in North European versions through Flanders, prevailed. The commercial prosperity of the age encouraged domestic building, and great structures like Montacute House and Longleat were raised. Oak was the wood used in the half-timbered houses and furniture. Elizabethan architecture is characterized by a classical logic in plan, flat Tudor arches, and wood-paneled interiors. The wainscot chair, a step toward the great development of

17th- and 18th-century English furniture, is Elizabethan.

FELICIA M. STERLING DAUTERMAN,
The Cooper Union Museum for the Decorative Arts

ELIZABETH CITY, port of northeastern North Carolina, and seat of Pasquotank County. The site was settled in 1666. Its harbor on the Pasquotank River, an important link in the Intracoastal Waterway, attracts shipping and commercial and sport fishing. Yachtsmen and duck hunters use the town as a base for nearby hunting, fishing, and vacation spots. U.S. Coast Guard and Navy installations are located in or south of Elizabeth City. Pop. (1950) 12,685; (1960) 14,062.

ELIZABETH FARNESE [fär-nā′sā] (1692–1766), Queen of Spain, second wife (1714) of Philip V of Spain and for 30 years that country's evil genius. Exploiting her husband's incapacity, she controlled foreign policy and made it subservient to personal ambition; her goal was the recovery for her sons, whose half brothers barred the way to the Spanish throne, of the Italian interests Spain had forfeited at the Peace of Utrecht (1713). By a combination of open aggression and tortuous diplomacy that kept the other European powers on tenterhooks and provoked a series of hostile alliances, she won for her elder son Charles the dukedom of Parma in 1731, and in 1735, the throne of Naples and Sicily. Parma she later secured, in 1748, for her second son. She lived to see Charles succeed to the Spanish crown in 1759. Her daughter Mariana married in 1729 the future Joseph I of Portugal.

ELIZABETH PETROVNA [pǐ-trôv′nə] (1709–61), Empress of Russia (1741–61), a daughter of Peter the Great. Elizabeth was well trained in German, French, and the courtly arts, since it was Peter's hope that she would marry Louis XV of France. She became Empress in 1741 as a result of a *coup d'état* against the young Tsar Ivan VI and his German courtiers. Elizabeth's main international enterprise was her alliance with Austria against Prussia in the Seven Years' War. In domestic affairs, the main themes were gradual liberation of the landed aristocracy from state service and the spread of French cultural and intellectual influences. During Elizabeth's reign, Moscow University and an academy of fine arts were established.

ELIZABETHTON, industrial city of eastern Tennessee, and seat of Carter County, located at the confluence of the Watauga and Doe rivers. The city manufactures rayon yarn, chairs, and twine. It is known as the site of the first court held in Tennessee. Chartered, 1799; inc. as city, 1905; pop. (1950) 10,754; (1960) 10,896.

ELIZABETHTOWN, city of central Kentucky, and seat of Hardin County, in the northern Pennyroyal farming region. It is a trade center for agricultural products, and manufactures concrete blocks, men's trousers, and timing devices. Pop. (1950) 5,807; (1960) 9,641.

ELIZABETHTOWN, borough of south-central Pennsylvania. Textiles and chocolate are made here. Elizabethtown is the seat of the Masonic Homes of the Grand Lodge of Pennsylvania, a state hospital for crippled children, and Elizabethtown College. Inc., 1827; pop. (1950) 5,083; (1960) 6,780.

ELK, large, hoofed animal, *Alces alces*, in the deer family, Cervidae, found in cooler, northern regions of Europe and Asia. The elk is the largest of the Old World deer and is characterized by its heavy, much-branched antlers, grayish-brown coat, and long, broad muzzle. It has large ears and a hairy, pendulous flap of skin—the "bell"—beneath its chin. Elk commonly inhabit marshy, wooded areas and feed on the bark, buds, and leaves of trees. Full-grown males weigh up to 1,100 lb., stand about 6½ ft. at the shoulder, and may have an antler spread of over 5 ft. The name "elk" is often applied to a closely related North American species, *Cervus canadensis*, which is properly called the "wapiti," and also to the Alaskan or American moose, *Alces americana*.
See also MOOSE; WAPITI.

ELK CITY, trade city of western Oklahoma, located in an agricultural area. The petroleum-producing Elk City pool is nearby. The Sandstone Creek Project, the first trial of scientific upstream flood control in the United States, is northwest of the city. Pop. (1950) 7,962; (1960) 8,196.

ELK GROVE VILLAGE, planned residential community of Illinois, a suburb west of Chicago. Pop. (1960) 6,608.

ELKHART [ĕlk'härt], city of northern Indiana at the junction of the St. Joseph and Elkhart rivers. Elkhart has won world renown as the home of the Conn Company, manufacturers of band instruments. Medicines are produced at Miles Laboratories, and the city was a pioneer in the use of "mobile homes." Pop. (1950) 35,646; (1960) 40,274.

ELKHOUND, shortened name of the Norwegian elkhound, a member of the hound group of dogs. The breed originated in Norway and has proved its ability as a hunter of bear and elk, as well as a watchdog. This versatile animal has a long, full coat of light- or dark-gray. Adult males stand about 20 in. high at the shoulder and weigh 50 lb. The Norwegian elkhound's heavy coat suits it to life in cold climates. It is an ideal farm dog and also an excellent pet.

ELKINS, city of central West Virginia, and seat of Randolph County. Woodworking, coal mining, operation of railroad shops, and manufacture of clothing are the principal business activities. Davis and Elkins College (estab., 1903) is the site of a forest festival held each October. Elkins was known as Leadville until 1889. Inc., 1890; pop. (1950) 9,121; (1960) 8,307.

ELK ISLAND NATIONAL PARK, wildlife preserve of Alberta, Canada, 30 mi. east of Edmonton. The park, a fenced enclosure, contains more than 1,000 plains buffalo and other big-game species. Park headquarters are at Astotin Lake. Estab. as a wildlife sanctuary, 1906; as a national park, 1913; area, 75 sq. mi.

ELKO, city of northeastern Nevada, and seat of Elko County, in the Humboldt Range. It is a ranching and trade center, as well as a supply center for hunting and fishing parties in the surrounding mountains. Headquarters for the Humboldt National Forest are here. Inc., 1917; pop. (1950) 5,393; (1960) 6,298.

ELKS, BENEVOLENT AND PROTECTIVE ORDER OF (B.P.O.E.), charitable brotherhood founded in 1868 in New York by 15 members of the theatrical profession. Today the order, representing a cross section of U.S. life, has about 1,300,000 members in lodges in the 50 states and possessions. The Elks are nonpolitical and nonsectarian. The society's principles are charity, justice, brotherly love, and fidelity. It spends annually over $8,000,000 for benevolences, including rehabilitation of handicapped children, college scholarships, youth-building activities, and aid to hospitalized veterans.

The Elks National Foundation, created in 1928, is the order's principal philanthropic agency. Annual expenditures of about $300,000 finance college scholarships, training of specialists in the treatment of the cerebral palsied, and state Elk Associations' benevolent programs. More than 1,500,000 boys and girls participate in Elk-sponsored youth activities. Recreation and entertainment are provided for patients in the country's veterans hospitals by the Elks National Service Commission. Headquarters are in Chicago, in a building dedicated to members who served in World Wars I and II.

L. A. DONALDSON, Grand Secretary, Benevolent and
Protective Order of Elks

ELKTON, town of northeastern Maryland, and seat of Cecil County. The manufacture of pulp and paper, flour, fertilizer, and shirts are leading industries. Inc., 1787; pop. (1950) 5,245; (1960) 5,989.

ELLENSBURG, city of central Washington, and seat of Kittitas County. It is a market center for the irrigated Kittitas Valley and livestock district. Industries include food processing, lumbering, and meat packing. Central Washington College of Education is here. Laid out, 1875; pop. (1950) 8,430; (1960) 8,625.

ELLENVILLE, resort village of southeastern New York, in the Shawangunk Mountains. Inc., 1856; pop. (1950) 4,225; (1960) 5,003.

ELLERY, WILLIAM (1727–1820), American lawyer and signer of the Declaration of Independence. He was born in Newport, R.I., where he practiced law after graduating from Harvard College. He served in the Continental Congress from 1776 until 1781, and from 1783 to 1785. From 1790 until his death, he was the collector of customs in Newport.

ELLESMERE ISLAND, large island of North America, extending as far as 83° 7' N. lat., located west of northwestern Greenland, and administered as part of Franklin District, Northwest Territories, Canada. A United States–Canadian weather station is located here. The island is irregular in shape, mountainous (to 11,000 ft.), and mostly ice covered. Area, 77,392 sq. mi.; length, 500 mi.; width, 25–300 mi.

ELLICE [ĕl'ĭs] **ISLANDS,** atoll group in the southwest Pacific, part of the British Crown Colony of Gilbert and Ellice Islands. Ellice comprises nine inhabited atoll groups: Nanumanga, Nanumea, Niutao, Nui, Nukufetau, Nukulaelae, Nurakita, Vaitupu, and Funafuti, the capital. Pandanus fruit and coconuts are raised; copra and phosphate are exported. The English navigator John Byron discovered the islands in 1764. In 1892 they became a British protectorate and in 1915 were incorporated into the Gilbert and Ellice Islands colony. U.S. troops occupied Nanumea and Funafuti during World War II (1943) and established bases. Area, 9.5 sq. mi.; pop., 4,487.

ELLINGTON, EDWARD KENNEDY ("DUKE") (1899–), American jazz composer and pianist. Born in Washington, D.C., he began to study the piano at six, and by 1918 was leading a small orchestra. At first he played conventional dance music, but during the 1920's trombonist Joe Nanton and trumpeter James "Bubber" Miley joined him, and their work helped shape his jazz style. By late 1927 the Ellington orchestra was at the Cotton Club, New York, where he experimented with unconventional orchestrations and forms, but still within the framework of jazz. Several of his melodies became popular hits (*Solitude, Sophisticated Lady*), but his instrumental works also established him as a great jazz composer-orchestrator. By the late 1930's Ellington's talents matured in such pieces as *Ko Ko, Sepia Panorama*, and *Concerto for Cootie*. In them he integrated composition and improvisation, solo and group playing, and brought the large jazz orchestra to its fullest development. Subsequently he gave orchestral jazz recitals in Carnegie Hall, New York. In 1960 he wrote, with Billy Strayhorn, *Suite Thursday*, one of his most successful extended works.

Consult Schuller, Gunther, "The Ellington Style" in *Jazz*, ed. by Nat Hentoff and Albert McCarthy (1960).

MARTIN WILLIAMS, Editor, *The Art of Jazz*
See also JAZZ.

ELLIOT, ROBERT BROWN (1842–84), U.S. Negro Reconstruction congressman. Born in Boston, Mass., he was educated at Eton College in England, and studied law with a London barrister. At the end of the Civil War he entered Republican politics in South Carolina, and was elected to the state legislature in 1868. He was twice elected to the U.S. House of Representatives (1871 and 1874) but resigned both times in order to return to South Carolina where he could exercise more political power. In 1874 he defeated former Confederate Vice President Alexander H. Stephens in a House debate on the Civil Rights bill. He returned to South Carolina in 1874 and became speaker of the house in the state legislature.

ELLIPSE [ē-lĭps'], conic section and a closed curve such that for any point on the curve the sum of the distances to two fixed points, called the foci, is the same. The general equation for the ellipse is $\dfrac{x^2}{a^2} + \dfrac{y^2}{b^2} = 1$. The greatest diameter is the major axis; the shortest, the minor axis.

The ellipse is used extensively in architecture because of its aesthetic form. It is important in astronomy because the orbits of planets and satellites are elliptical.

An elliptic mirror reflects all rays from one focus to the other. In an elliptical room, weak sound waves produced at one focus are audible at the other focus, although the sound may be inaudible at points closer to either focus.

ELLIPSOID [ē-lĭp'soid], solid figure, symmetric about a center, such that every plane section is either an ellipse or a circle. Some common ellipsoids are generated by rotating an ellipse about one of its axes. If rotated about the major axis, the ellipsoid is called a prolate spheroid; if about the minor axis, an oblate spheroid.

ELLIS, (HENRY) HAVELOCK (1859–1939), English writer well known for his books on the medical and psychological aspects of sex. Born at Croydon, England, of a seafaring family, Ellis was sent to Australia for his health at the age of 16. Upon his return to England in 1879 he bypassed general university training and undertook medical studies. Trouble with the medical qualifying examinations led him to take a license as an apothecary. He soon became a writer for literary reviews, winning distinction as the founder of the "Mermaid" series of Elizabethan literary classics. He later became editor of the "Contemporary Science Series." Ellis is principally known for his seven-volume *Studies in the Psychology of Sex*, published between 1897 and 1928. Censorship difficulties after the publication of the first volume led him to bring out the others in the United States.

ELLIS ISLAND, small island in Upper New York Bay, about 1 mi. southwest of Manhattan Island, New York City. Sold by New York State to the federal government in 1808, it was first used as the site of an arsenal and fort. From 1892 to 1943 it was the chief immigration station of the United States, and until 1954 was used for detention of deportees and of immigrants lacking proper entry papers. The island became part of the Statue of Liberty National Monument in 1965. Area, 27 acres.

ELLISON, RALPH WALDO (1914–), Negro American novelist and essayist. Born in Oklahoma City, Okla., Ellison studied music at Tuskegee Institute, then went to New York to study sculpture. But, influenced by a poem by Richard Wright, he decided to become a writer. Although he published only two books by 1967, he is considered an outstanding writer. His one novel, *Invisible Man* (1952), won the National Book Award in 1952.

Ellison has published essays and reviews in major U.S. periodicals and has taught at Yale and Rutgers. In 1965 he published *Shadow and Act*, a collection of essays about music, literature, and life. *Invisible Man* is the odyssey of a Negro who searches for his identity. It vividly illuminates the psychological and emotional tensions of American Negroes.

DARWIN T. TURNER, North Carolina A and T State University

ELLSWORTH, ELMER EPHRAIM (1837–61), Union hero in the American Civil War. Born near Mechanicsville, N.Y., Ellsworth organized a Chicago Zouave company that won renown touring the North in 1859. He worked in the law office of Abraham Lincoln in 1860 and accompanied him to Washington in 1861. When war broke out, Ellsworth formed a Zouave regiment of firemen in New York City. In Alexandria, Va., after its occupation, Ellsworth, on May 24, 1861, removed a Confederate flag from the Marshall House and was shot dead by the proprietor, J. W. Jackson. The occurrence caused a sensation.

ELLSWORTH, LINCOLN (1880–1951), American polar explorer, born in Chicago. After a career as a railroad surveyor and mining engineer, he became a financial associate of the Norwegian explorer Roald Amundsen. In 1925 they flew from Spitsbergen to 87° 43′ N. lat. in an unsuccessful transpolar flight. The following year, joining again with Amundsen, and with the Italian explorer Umberto Nobile, he flew in the dirigible *Norge* from Spitsbergen, over the North Pole, and on to Teller, Alaska. In 1931 he was aboard the *Graf Zeppelin* as an observer on its arctic flight to Franz Josef Land. In Nov., 1935, Ellsworth and Herbert Hollick-Kenyon flew in a single-engine plane 2,300 mi. from Dundee Island, Palmer Peninsula, to the Bay of Whales, thus completing the first air crossing of the Antarctic continent. In 1939 Ellsworth flew deep into the Antarctic continent from a base in the Indian Ocean.

Consult Ellsworth, Lincoln, *Beyond Horizons* (1938).
HAROLD P. GILMOUR, Recorder-Historian,
U.S. Antarctic Service Expedition

ELLSWORTH, OLIVER (1745–1807), American statesman and jurist. He was born in Windsor, Conn., graduated (1766) from Princeton College, and practiced law in Hartford. During the American Revolution, he served in the Continental Congress. He was a member of the Connecticut governor's council (1780–85 and 1803), judge of the state supreme court (1785–89), and U.S. Senator (1789–96). At the federal Constitutional Convention of 1787, he offered the compromise that settled the dispute between large and small states over the question of representation.

A Federalist, he later wrote key provisions of the Judiciary Act of 1789, vigorously defended funding of the debt, and advocated a national bank. He was Chief Justice of the United States (1796–99) and a member of the successful peace commission (1799–1800) to France.

ELLWOOD CITY, borough of western Pennsylvania, situated on the Beaver and Lawrence county lines. It is an industrial community with tanneries, coal mines, sandstone and limestone quarries. Metal products are manufactured there. Inc., 1892; pop. (1950) 12,945; (1960) 12,413.

ELM, name for deciduous trees of the genus *Ulmus*, in the Ulmaceae, or elm family. The 18 species of elms are found throughout the temperate and colder regions of the Northern Hemisphere. Elms are usually tall trees. They have pointed, oval leaves with toothed edges and bear inconspicuous greenish flowers that often appear before the leaves. The English elm, *U. campestris*, is found in England and western and southern Europe. This stately tree grows to a height of 130 ft. and has widespread branches that form an oval head. Its tough, heavy wood is used in shipbuilding and furniture manufacture. The American, or white, elm, *U. americana*, is distributed from Newfoundland to Florida, and like all the American species, is found only east of the Rocky Mountains. It is a handsome tree with broad, spreading branches, but unfortunately is plagued by many insect pests and fungus infections. The wahoo, or winged, elm, *U. alata*, has corky "wings" growing from its branches. Less hardy than other elms, it is found most commonly in the southern United States. The slippery elm, *U. fulva*, is an interesting species, distributed from Quebec to Florida. Its gummy inner bark is used medicinally.

CLARENCE J. HYLANDER, Author, *The World of Plant Life*
See also DUTCH ELM DISEASE.

The English elm, a native of southern and western Europe, is widely planted in moist temperate regions of North America. (GOTTSCHO-SCHLEISNER)

The American elm is native to eastern North America. An excellent shade tree, it is threatened by the Dutch elm disease. (ROCHE)

The leaf of the American elm is dark green, coarsely toothed at its edges, and from 3 to 6 in. long. (ROCHE)

ELMAN, MISCHA (1891–1967), celebrated violin virtuoso, born in Talnoye, Russia. He began his violin studies at the age of six at the Royal Music School in Odessa. He later studied at the St. Petersburg Conservatory with Leopold Auer and made his debut with the Berlin Philharmonic in 1904. In his first appearance at Carnegie Hall, New York, in 1908 with the Russian Symphony Orchestra, he played the Tchaikovsky concerto, a work with which he became especially identified. He became an American citizen in 1923 and afterward gave concerts throughout the world. In 1958 he played his Golden Anniversary Concert at Carnegie Hall. He was awarded the order of Officer of the Belgian Crown. In addition to his concert career, he arranged works by Schubert, Beethoven, and Rachmaninoff and composed several violin pieces, including *In a Gondola* and *Romance.*

ELMENDORF, THERESA HUBBELL (1855–1932), American librarian, born in Pardeeville, Wis. She served the Young Men's (later Public) Library of Milwaukee as deputy librarian (1880–92) and head librarian (1892–96). She was vice-librarian of the Buffalo Public Library (1906–26). Mrs. Elmendorf was the first woman president of the American Library Association (1911-12).

ELMHURST, residential suburb 17 mi. west of Chicago, Illinois, and the site of Elmhurst College. Light industry includes the manufacture of sprinklers. Settled, 1843; inc., 1910; pop. (1950) 21,273; (1960) 36,991.

ELMIRA [ĕl-mī′rə], town of southern Ontario, Canada, 60 mi. west of Toronto. It is an industrial center producing shoes, clothing, and cattle feed. Pop., 3,337.

ELMIRA [ĕl-mī′rə], city of south-central New York, and seat of Chemung County, on the Chemung River. Lumbering, metalworking, and textiles were early industries here. Elmira's present manufactures include office machines, glass containers, greeting cards, business forms, and fabricated metals. Elmira College for Women, Elmira State Reformatory, and Arnot Art Gallery are located here, as is the grave of Mark Twain. Nearby are Newtown Battlefield Reservation and Harris Hill, scene of glider contests. Settled, 1788; inc., 1864; pop. (1950) 49,716; (1960) 46,517.

ELMIRA HEIGHTS, village of south-central New York, near Elmira. The town has automotive and clothing manufactures. Settled, 1779; inc., 1896; pop. (1950) 5,009; (1960) 5,157.

ELMIRA SOUTHEAST, suburban residential village of southern New York, adjoining Elmira. Pop. (1960) 6,698.

ELMONT, residential village of southeastern New York, on western Long Island, adjoining Queens Borough of New York City. Belmont Race Track is nearby. Pop. (1960) 30,138.

EL MONTE, suburban city of southern California, 15 mi. east of Los Angeles. Industries include the manufacture of airplane and electronic parts and metal fabrication.

Founded in 1854 as Lexington, it was the first American settlement in southern California. Its name was changed to El Monte ("The Mountain") because of its altitude of 271 ft. in the flat Los Angeles valley. Inc., 1912; pop. (1950) 8,101; (1960) 13,163.

ELMWOOD PARK, residential suburb west of Chicago, Illinois. An Indian flintworking site is marked by a monument. Inc., 1914; pop. (1950) 18,801; (1960) 23,866.

ELODEA. *See* WATERWEED.

ELOHIM [ĕl-ō-hēm′, ĕ-lō′hĭm], one of the names of God used in the Hebrew Bible. Though used with singular verbs and adjectives, its ending is plural. This is probably because the plural ending designates majesty. The origin of the word is uncertain. Scholars believe that the term "Elohim" designates deity in general, in contrast to the more specific name Yahweh. In Rabbinic literature, the term Elohim is interpreted as referring to the attribute of justice of God. "Elohim" is also used to designate idols and the gods of the nations. When used in this way, it takes plural verbs and adjectives.

EL PASO [ĕl păs′ō], city of westernmost Texas and seat of El Paso County, on the Rio Grande. It is an important port of entry connected by bridges to Ciudad Juárez, Mexico. El Paso's leading industry is copper smelting and refining, and the city also has cement works, oil refineries, cotton gins, and aircraft plants and manufactures textiles, beer, and canned foods. Many federal agencies, maintaining regional headquarters here, add to the city's economy, as does tourism. Fort Bliss army post and Biggs Air Force Base are nearby. Texas Western College (estab., 1913), El Paso Museum of Art, Texas Centennial Museum (natural history), a symphony orchestra, and two community theater groups are cultural assets.

The site of the city was settled in 1827. The area won its independence from Mexico in the Texas War of Liberation in 1836 and the town of El Paso was platted in 1859. Railroads arrived in 1881, but the dry climate remained a serious deterrent to expansion until the drilling of deep wells and the construction of Elephant Butte Dam in 1916 brought irrigation and sufficient water to the area. A longstanding U.S.-Mexican dispute over the Chamizal border zone between Ciudad Juárez and El Paso was settled in 1963 when some 435 acres were awarded to Mexico. Inc., 1873; pop. (1950) 130,485; (1960) 276,687; urb. area (1950) 136,918; (1960) 277,128.

CHARLES C. BAJZA, Texas College of Arts and Industries

EL PASO DE ROBLES. *See* PASO ROBLES.

EL RENO, commercial and transportation city in central Oklahoma, and seat of Canadian County. The city was founded soon after Apr., 1889, when the land in this area was opened to settlers. It is a Rock Island Railroad junction and has Rock Island offices and repair shops. Pop. (1950) 10,991; (1960) 11,015.

EL RIO, northern suburb of Oxnard in Ventura County, southern California. Pop. (1950) 1,376; (1960) 6,966.

EL SALVADOR

Villagers in Izalco are accustomed to the black smoke issuing from Izalco volcano. The volcano has been active since 1770.

AREA	8,259 sq. mi.
ELEVATION	
Highest point	
(Santa Ana)	7,825 ft.
Lowest point	Sea level
POPULATION	Approx. 2,612,000
PRINCIPAL LANGUAGE	Spanish
LIFE EXPECTANCY	Approx. 50 years
PERCENTAGE OF LITERACY	43%
UNIT OF CURRENCY	Colon
NATIONAL ANTHEM	*Saludemos la patria orgullosos* (Proudly hail the fatherland), words by J. J. Cañas, music by J. Aberle
CAPITAL	San Salvador
PRINCIPAL PRODUCTS	Coffee, cotton, sugar; gold, silver; beverages, textiles, wood products

EL SALVADOR [ĕl săl'və-dôr], the smallest but most densely populated republic of Central America. It is the only state of this region without an outlet to the Caribbean Sea, but it has a 160-mi. coast line on the Pacific Ocean. El Salvador is one of the few Latin-American states that has fully settled and developed its entire land area.

The Land

Physical Features. The country is predominantly mountainous, but its fertile upland regions are lower and warmer than those of its western neighbor, Guatemala. The most important region is the central plateau, where the majority of Salvadorans live, at an average altitude of about 2,000 ft. This plateau lies between two mountain ranges which cross the land from east to west, parallel to the Pacific Ocean. Many of the mountains are volcanic and have deposited fertile lava and ash, creating a soil in which coffee trees thrive. These volcanoes, however, also present a recurring threat of devastating earthquakes. The volcanic peaks San Salvador, San Miguel, and Santa Ana range from 6,000 to nearly 8,000 ft. in height and dominate the landscape. Izalco (6,300 ft.) gained fame for its eruptions at five-minute intervals and is known as the Lighthouse of the Pacific.

To the south of the plateau and mountain region lies a hot coastal plain, varying from 10 to 15 mi. in width, on which are located the two important seaports of Acajutla and La Libertad. Rocky fingers of land reach sharply down from the southernmost mountain range to the sea. To the north of the plateau is another lowland region formed by the valley of the important Lempa River, which rises in Guatemala, crosses southwestern Honduras, and flows eastward and then sharply south to the Pacific. This is a leading agricultural region; hydroelectric power is harnessed by a 200-ft.-high dam. Particularly beautiful lakes are Coatepeque in the western part of the plateau region and Ilopango on the outskirts of San Salvador. The Gulf of Fonseca to the east is one of the major bays on the Pacific Coast of Central America, with an important deepwater port at La Unión.

Climate, Vegetation, and Wildlife. The climate in central El Salvador is warm and rainy from May to October; a hotter, dry spell lasts from November to April. Temperatures vary more according to altitude than season, being considerably higher on the coast than in the highland areas. The average annual precipitation of 72 in. allows extensive coffee cultivation. The tree from which balsam is extracted (*Myroxylon pereirae*) grows in El Savador, as well as rubber trees, cedar, mahogany, and walnut, and many tropical plants. Bird life is limited, although migratory birds visit the coastal plain from about September to April, and there are many parrots. Jaguar, ocelot, coyote, tapir, and deer are frequently found, as are cayman, iguana, crocodile, and many varieties of fresh- and salt-water game fish.

The People

Ethnology and Population Distribution. Pure-blooded descendants of the original Indian peoples of El Salvador comprise only about 5% of the present population, and those of pure white ancestry total little more than 2%. The overwhelming majority of Salvadorans are of mixed Indian and European origin, due to intermarriage that occurred after the Spanish conquest. The official language is Spanish, and the Roman Catholic religion predominates. The constitution guarantees freedom of worship.

The largest cities of El Salvador are situated on the central plateau, including San Salvador, the capital, Santa Ana, San Miguel, Santa Tecla, Sonsonate, and Zacatecoluca. More than 36% of the population is classified as urban. Many Salvadorans seek seasonal employment in Guatemala and Honduras, a necessity largely due to the

405

This immense power station on the Lempa River, in full operation since 1954, supplies much of El Salvador's electric power.

A classroom scene. The government of El Salvador is waging an active campaign against illiteracy, particularly high in rural areas.

A little girl on a coffee plantation helps her mother pick coffee berries, which contain the seeds, or beans. About 1,000 berries yield a pound of coffee.

high population density of about 316 persons per square mile.

Education. One of the largest items of expenditure in the national budget is public education, which is free and compulsory. Nevertheless, some 57% of the population over ten years of age is illiterate; the problem of school enrollment and attendance is particularly great in rural areas. Primary and secondary schooling is supplemented by a number of specialized courses and schools for adult education. The autonomous National University of El Salvador was established in 1841.

Famous Salvadorans. The political leaders of El Salvador have achieved wider renown than its writers, artists, and musicians. Father José Matías Delgado became the national hero, having first sounded the cry for independence from Spain in 1811. The famed first president of the Central American Federation, Manuel José Arce, was a Salvadoran. The poet Juan José Cañas (1826–1900) was the author of the national hymn, and Claudia Lars (Carmen Brannon de Samayoa) and Salvador Salazar Arrué (called Salarrué) won international recognition in literary circles in the 20th century.

The Economy

Agriculture. Agriculture is the most important sector of the economy, accounting for over a third of the nation's production and employing three-fifths of the working population. However, the dependence on coffee, the leading crop, causes a serious disruption of the economy when international coffee prices fluctuate. The United States is the largest purchaser of Salvadoran coffee, followed by West Germany. El Salvador also exports cotton, fodder, animal and vegetable oils, and sugar. Corn and beans are grown for domestic consumption, and there is a small but developing livestock industry. A marked contrast still exists between the few wealthy landowners and the mass of rural laborers. The government is striving to solve this and other economic problems by greater diversification of crops and increased farm production.

Industry, Mining, and Transportation. El Salvador is the most industrialized country in Central America, light industry predominating. Such goods as heavy machinery and motor vehicles have to be imported, as well as petroleum products, cotton textiles, chemicals, medicines, and wheat. Manufacturing employs over 10% of the labor force and produces alcoholic drinks, cotton goods, footwear, furniture and other wood products, and processed tobacco. Small quantities of gold, silver, mercury, and lead are mined. A government plan for industrialization provides for increased hydroelectric power from the Lempa

River and the building of better roads. The most important road is the Pan American Highway. Also crossing the country from east to west are two major railroads, one foreign-owned, the other operated by the government.

Government

El Salvador is a republic governed under the constitution of 1962. The President must be a native-born son of native-born parents, and his term is for five years with no immediate re-election. There is also a Vice-President. The President has extensive powers. As chief executive he controls the armed forces, the budget, laws and international agreements, and appoints the cabinet, diplomats, military officials, and governors to administer each of the 14 national departments.

The deputies of the unicameral legislature serve for two years and are elected by universal suffrage. The judicial branch of government includes a Supreme Court, courts of first instance, chambers of second instance, and justices of the peace. Criminal trials include the use of juries, and the Supreme Court is the court of last appeal. Local government is mainly subject to national authority, but popularly elected mayors and municipal councils provide some local autonomy.

History

In 1524 the Spanish conquistador Pedro de Alvarado entered the region now known as El Salvador from Guatemala to conquer the indigenous Pipil Indians. By 1546 San Salvador had been recognized by the Spanish crown as the capital city of the area. This area included two provinces, Sonsonate and El Salvador, which remained under the Spanish captaincy general of Guatemala until independence in 1821. The region's agricultural pattern was fixed from the beginning, for it was an isolated, rural, volcano-ridden colony producing mainly sugar cane and indigo.

Independence was declared on Sept. 15, 1821, 10 years after Father José Matías Delgado had first raised the cry for liberation from Spain. True freedom was not easily achieved, however, and years of turmoil ensued. Briefly annexed to the Mexican Empire of Agustín de Iturbide (1822–23), El Salvador then became a member of the Central American Federation, which lasted until 1838. Although independence was declared in 1841, El Salvador was not formally proclaimed a republic until 1859. Political turbulence continued to be a national characteristic, and there were frequent popular uprisings and a rapid succession of leaders. For more than a century international conflicts occurred from time to time over attempts to re-establish the union of the Central American states. Agreement was at least temporarily achieved in the establishment of the Organization of Central American States (ODECA) in 1951, with its headquarters at San Salvador.

An important development in the economic history of El Salvador was the introduction of coffee in 1841, which laid the basis for the present major crop and led to a marked increase in population. Although neutral in World War I, El Salvador supported the Allied cause in World War II and became a charter member of the United Nations in 1945. At home military rule replaced the ballot as a system of government after 1932, notwithstanding the introduction of a liberal constitution in 1950. President José María Lemus was deposed by a civil-military junta in 1960, which was in turn overthrown by a second, right-wing junta three months later. A multiplicity of conflicting political parties and personalities did little to resolve the problems of political instability. A new constitution was proclaimed in Jan., 1962, and a provisional President took office. In April Julio Adalberto Rivera, running unopposed, was elected President. He assumed office in July, 1962.

Consult Martin, P. F., *Salvador of the Twentieth Century* (1911); Hoselitz, B. F., *Industrial Development of El Salvador* (1954); Osborne, Lilly de Jongh, *Four Keys to El Salvador* (1956); Martz, J. D., *Central America; The Crisis and the Challenge* (1959).

WALTER A. PAYNE, University of the Pacific

INDEX TO EL SALVADOR GENERAL REFERENCE MAP

Total Population approx. 2,612,000

EL SEGUNDO, city of southern California, on the Pacific coast. It has port facilities for oil tankers and also has oil refineries. The city has a large aircraft plant and aircraft-related industries. Pop. (1950) 8,011; (1960) 14,219.

ELSENE. *See* IXELLES.

ELSHEIMER [*ĕls'hĭ-mər*], **ADAM** (1578–1610), German painter, noted for his small landscapes that contain Biblical or mythological figures. The last ten years of his life were spent in Rome, where he produced his best work. His paintings influenced the development of landscape; both Rembrandt and Claude Lorrain were affected by them. "Tobias and the Angel" is in the National Gallery, London.

ELSIE DINSMORE, central character in 28 novels (1868–1905) for girls by the American author Martha Farquharson. Elsie was a priggish heroine whose weeping and fainting spells reformed adult sinners, and the author's melodramatic flair enchanted young readers.

ELSINORE. *See* HELSINGØR OR ELSINORE.

ELSMERE, town of northern Delaware, a residential suburb west of Wilmington. Inc., 1909; pop. (1950) 5,314; (1960) 7,319.

ELSSLER [*ĕls'lər*], **FANNY** (1810–84), famous Austrian ballerina of the romantic school, born in Vienna. She received strict classical training in Vienna and further developed her highly sensuous and dramatic style in Italy (1822–27), Berlin, and Paris. She made her London debut in 1834, toured the United States in 1840–42, and retired in 1851. Her *La Cachucha,* a Spanish character dance in the ballet *Le Diable Boiteux* (1836), and her *La Cracovienne* in *La Gitana* (1834) were great popular successes.

ELURU [*ĕ-lōō'rōō*] **or ELLORE** [*ĕ-lōōr'*], city in Andhra Pradesh, south India, situated at the junction of canals from the Godavari and Kistna rivers, close to Colair Lake. Near Eluru was the capital of the Buddhist kingdom of Vengi, which fell to a Muslim army in 1470. The ruins of this old city were used to build a fort in Eluru. A center of rice trade, Eluru is noted for carpet manufacturing. Pop., 87,213.

ELWOOD, city of central Indiana, in a choice farming area. Tomatoes are grown and canned for commercial distribution. Leading manufactures are jet engine blades, trailers, cans, and wire products. Elwood is the birthplace of Wendell L. Willkie. Pop. (1950) 11,362; (1960) 11,793.

ELY [*ē'lē*], urban district, city, and capital of the Isle of Ely, an administrative division of Cambridgeshire, England. Ely is located on the Great Ouse River in the southern Fenlands. It has a beet-sugar refinery and serves a rich farming area. The city is famed for its Norman cathedral and for remains of a great Benedictine abbey originally founded by St. Etheldreda, Queen of Northumbria, in 673. The cathedral is the third-longest in England (537 ft.) and has a unique, decorated octagon and light tower.

King's School served the monastery from the 11th century and was refounded by Henry VIII in 1541. Hereward the Wake held the last stronghold of the English against William the Conqueror here in 1071. Pop., 9,815.

ELY, city of northeastern Minnesota, on the Vermilion iron range. It is an iron-mining city and has mines within the city limits. It is also a popular resort area and is an outfitting center for wilderness canoe trips. Ely is headquarters of the Superior National Forest, a wilderness area covering 15,000 sq. mi. Inc., 1891; pop. (1950) 5,474; (1960) 5,438.

ELY, city of eastern Nevada, and seat of White Pine County. One of the world's largest open-pit copper mines is here, and the city is a trade center for the area's copper and tungsten mines. Inc., 1907; pop. (1950) 3,558; (1960) 4,018.

ELYRIA, city of northern Ohio and seat of Lorain County. Leading manufactures are automobile airbrakes, golf balls, and pipe tools. Gates Memorial Hospital for crippled children is here. Cascade Park, within the city, is noted for its many scenic caves, waterfalls, and deep forest. Pop. (1950) 30,307; (1960) 43,782.

ELYSIUM [*ĭ-lĭzh'ē-əm*] **or ELYSIAN** [*ĭ-lĭzh'ən*] **FIELDS,** in Greek mythology, originally the joyful land for departed heroes favored by the gods. This "heavenly" concept remained while the location yielded to fresh poetic and philosophical interpretations. Homer located Elysium on the farthest western edge of the world. Later poets made it a part of the lower regions, and Vergil placed it in Hades. Elysium was an area of eternal happiness for the virtuous dead. Worry was unknown, and rose-tinted celestial light radiated perpetual day.

ELZEVIR or ELZEVIER [*ĕl'zə-vĭr*] **FAMILY,** the leading publishers of the 17th century. The founder of this Dutch firm was LOUIS ELZEVIR (1540–1617), who published some 150 works, the first appearing in 1583. A number of his descendants carried on the business; his son BONAVENTURE (1583–1652) and his grandson ABRAHAM (1592–1652) were the most famous. Their small-size editions of the classics and of French scholarly authors are much admired for their beauty and clarity. The Elzevirs published at Leiden, Amsterdam, Utrecht, and The Hague. Primarily businessmen, they employed scholars and printers. Their texts, which were usually in Latin, were published especially for use by scholars, and were well edited, printed on good paper, and inexpensive. The roman type used by the Elzevirs is known in England and America as "old-style" and in Europe as "Elzevir."

EMANCIPATION PROCLAMATION, presidential decree, issued during the Civil War, by Abraham Lincoln, Sept. 22, 1862 to take effect Jan. 1, 1863, freeing all slaves in states or parts of states in rebellion against the United States.

Although President Lincoln declared in his inaugural address that he had no purpose "to interfere," directly or indirectly, with the institution of slavery where it existed, the exigencies of war forced consideration of this question. In 1861, after the firing on Fort Sumter and subsequent call for troops to suppress "combinations . . . too powerful to be suppressed by judicial proceedings," Gen. Benjamin F. Butler, commander at Fortress Monroe, Va., refused to give up three Negro slaves who came into his Union lines. The Confederate officer who, under a flag of truce, asked for the return of the fugitives revealed that the Negroes were to be sent to South Carolina to work on fortifications. Butler then declared the slaves were "contraband of war" and refused to surrender them. The news of Butler's action spread among the slaves, and within three days he had contraband valued at $60,000 in his care. In Aug., 1861, Major Gen. John Fremont proclaimed martial law in Missouri and declared free the slaves who had been confiscated from persons resisting the authority of the United States. Lincoln ordered Fremont and Butler to modify the confiscating and emancipating orders to conform to existing law. In Nov., 1861, the president drafted two bills for compensated emancipation in Delaware, but opposition in the state proved too hostile for its passage. Meanwhile, Congress had recommended and passed legislation providing that when slaves were engaged in hostile military service, the masters' claims to labor of such slaves were forfeited. Then on Nov. 7, 1861, Commodore Samuel F. DuPont's fleet captured and occupied Port Royal, S.C., where there were more than 10,000 Negroes. Deserted by their Confederate masters who fled, the Negroes remained and, under federal administration, proved they could assume the responsibilities of free men and women.

While Lincoln and Congress considered emancipation, abolitionists and philanthropists, church groups, and Negroes continued to press for the Proclamation. In his newspaper Negro leader Frederick Douglass urged the president to use Negroes as soldiers to march into the South and raise the banner of emancipation of slaves. Massachusetts Senator Charles Sumner and Daniel Payne, Negro bishop of the African Methodist Episcopal Church, pressed Lincoln to approve the bill abolishing slavery in the District of Columbia. Lincoln signed the bill on Apr. 16, 1862.

During the spring Lincoln decided to issue a proclamation freeing the slaves. In June he sought the privacy of the White House telegraph office to draft the proclamation. After several weeks he completed the draft and on July 22, 1862 he submitted it to his cabinet. The Postmaster General thought the proposed action was impolitic and would lead to the administration's defeat at the fall elections. Secretary of State Seward approved the Proclamation but questioned the expediency of issuing it when it could not be enforced. The cabinet discussed the question of the authority the government possessed to set the slaves free, and the expediency of its issuance when it could not be enforced. Lincoln believed that he had the required authority under his war powers.

The first public response to the preliminary proclamation was favorable. Negroes were elated but waited for Jan. 1, 1863. On that date a "full period of one hundred days" of grace in which no slave insurrections had occurred in the rebellious commonwealths, Lincoln issued his final proclamation. The Proclamation identified those "States and parts of states wherein the people thereof remained in rebellion against the United States," and states the memorable words that in these areas, "all persons held as slaves . . . are, and henceforward shall be free." Negroes were overjoyed. The Proclamation released from bondage those Confederate slaves where the Union army was in control (with the exception of Tennessee, and portions of Virginia and Louisiana) and opened the way for the use of Negroes as soldiers.

The Proclamation stirred the British people, especially the laboring class, and some historians claim the action had much to do with the refusal of England to recognize the Confederacy. Finally, the issuance of the Proclamation added another dimension to the civil conflict—the war was no longer one for union but for human freedom. Despite the fact that emancipation of the majority of slaves came only with the defeat of the Confederacy and the Thirteenth Amendment to the Constitution, Lincoln became the "Great Emancipator."

ELSIE M. LEWIS, Howard University

EMBALMING. *See* MUMMIFICATION.

President Abraham Lincoln reading the Emancipation Proclamation to the Cabinet. The engraving is by Alexander Hay Ritchie (1822–95), after a painting by Francis Bicknell Carpenter (1830–1900).
(CHICAGO HISTORICAL SOCIETY)

EMBARCADERO, crescent-shaped waterfront street of San Francisco, formerly called East Street. It extends 3½ mi. from the Ferry Building near the central business district to China Basin and is lined with wharves and piers. Pier No. 50 extends to Mission Rock, a deep-draught terminal.

EMBARGO [ĕm-bär′gō], in law, a term meaning the prohibition by a state of departure of vessels or goods from its ports; more broadly, prohibition of trade with another state or of exports of particular commodities. When the prohibition is laid upon ships or goods belonging to citizens of the imposing state, it is called a civil embargo; when it is laid on those belonging to the enemy, it is referred to as a hostile embargo. Under international law, however, the term refers only to the detention of foreign ships in port.

Nations have resorted to such a measure for various reasons. It was common, particularly in the 17th and 18th centuries for a state to detain the ships of another state in its ports in anticipation of war with the latter. Thus, if war did break out, these ships could be readily forfeited to the embargoing state. It was also common that foreign ships in port be detained for a specified duration for the purpose of preventing valuable military information from reaching the enemy. This is known as the *arrêt de prince*.

Furthermore, a belligerent may, under international law, requisition neutral vessels within its jurisdiction on condition of indemnification. This is known as the right of angary, and in the exercise of this right, states have often laid an embargo on all ships in their ports. Finally, by way of reprisal, nations have often detained the ships of a wrong-doing state in order to compel the latter to make reparation.

THOMAS T. CHENG, Florida Normal and Industrial Memorial College

EMBARGO ACT, in American history, a statute prohibiting commerce with foreign nations and severely restricting the import trade. It was passed by Congress in 1807 to bring economic pressure against Britain and France for violating the rights of the United States as a neutral during the Napoleonic Wars. Drastic economic losses to Americans, bitter political opposition, and the failure of the act to affect Britain led to its repeal and replacement (1809) by the milder Non-Intercourse Act.

EMBASSY, diplomatic mission presided over by an ambassador, who is regarded as the personal representative of the head of his state and is therefore entitled to special privileges. The institution of the permanent embassy came into being during the 15th century, with the Italian republics setting the example. Francesco Sforza, Duke of Milan, is credited with establishing the first permanent embassy, at the court of the Medici in Florence. Other states soon followed suit and the increased use of the embassy led to the conclusion of formal treaties dealing with the subject.

Although the ground occupied by an embassy is not the territory of the foreign state, or extraterritorial, the authorities of the host state may not interfere with the proper and legal use of the premises of the diplomatic mission. They may not impose property taxes upon it, though they may charge for public utility services. The territorial sovereign is obliged to protect the embassy from interference with its use for diplomatic purposes, and authorities of the host state may not enter the premises without the consent of the foreign state. The lawfulness or unlawfulness of acts there committed is, however, determined by the host state. Diplomatic immunity affords no justification for sheltering criminals, and in such cases the host government is justified to take measures to compel the surrender of the criminal. There has been much discussion about the right of shelter, or asylum, in diplomatic premises. Latin-American republics usually grant the right to foreign envoys to afford asylum to political refugees in time of revolution. Although no such right is officially recognized elsewhere, the European states and the United States have on occasion granted diplomatic asylum to political refugees.

GUENTER WEISSBERG, Columbia University

EMBER DAYS, three days of fasting and prayer in the Western Church occurring four times yearly. They are the Wednesday, Friday, and Saturday after the first Sunday in Lent, after Whitsunday, after Holy Cross Day (Sept. 14), and after St. Lucy's Day (Dec. 13). The name perhaps comes from the Latin *quattuor tempora,* "four seasons." Originally they were days of prayer for crops; now, in the Roman Catholic and Anglican churches they are days of prayer for the ordination of the clergy.

EMBEZZLEMENT. *See* LARCENY.

EMBOLISM, PULMONARY. *See* PULMONARY EMBOLISM.

EMBOLUS [ĕm′bə-ləs], a clot or other obstruction which is carried along in the blood stream until it becomes lodged in a blood vessel too narrow to permit its passage. Most emboli arise from blood clots, or thrombi, which form in veins or on the heart wall. Postoperative patients may develop clots in the veins of the legs and, later, emboli. A heart attack may damage the inner lining of the heart, with subsequent formation of clots, and possibly, emboli. When newly formed the clots are fragile and fragments are likely to break loose and become emboli. In decompression sickness a sudden change from high to low atmospheric pressure results in the release of nitrogen bubble emboli into the blood stream. In other cases emboli may be composed of fat, tumor cells, or atherosclerotic plaques which break loose from diseased arteries.

The symptoms resulting from the embolus depend roughly upon its size and the location of the vessel in which it lodges. Emboli which plug arteries supplying the heart and lungs are extremely dangerous. Emboli in the brain may cause a stroke.

STANLEY BLUMENTHAL, M.D.

See also THROMBOSIS.

EMBROIDERY, any decorative stitchery on a textile ground. Embroidery is extremely perishable, and lack of survivals makes it impossible to form a real account of its early history. It is undoubtedly of very ancient origin, and there are strong indications that it was practiced by the

EMBROIDERY

Victoria and Albert Museum—Illustration Research Service

David and Bathsheba, from a panel of English 17th-century stumpwork.

English 13th-century chasuble embroidered with silver-gilt and colored silks.

Victoria and Albert Museum—Illustration Research Service

Egyptians, Babylonians, and Assyrians and by the Greeks and Mycenaeans. Silk robes, banners, cloths, and hangings sumptuously embroidered in silk are part of the artistic heritage of both China and Japan, while in India, Persia, and Turkey very delicate work was done on a loosely woven cotton. Embroidery was practiced in some of the South American civilizations before the Spanish conquest. The strongly designed and colored embroideries of the Greek islands, North Africa, and the Scandinavian countries are also noteworthy.

History. Gold-embroidered garments imported from Phrygia in Asia Minor were certainly worn by the wealthier Romans in the Imperial period (29 B.C. to c.4th century A.D.), and during the same era, wool embroidery on natural-colored linen was common in Egypt, plant designs and Christian symbols being the most widely used motifs.

Byzantium is reputed to have been an important center for the fabrication and distribution of embroidered silk church vestments, pre-eminence in this art passing to Palermo in Sicily after the sack of Constantinople in 1204 by members of the Fourth Crusade. In medieval Europe embroidery was a highly regarded art, practiced not only in the monasteries and convents but also by professional embroiderers belonging to secular guilds. The English *Opus Anglicanum*—a form of silk embroidery usually depicting Christian subjects—was especially fine in the 13th and 14th centuries; examples were widely exported to religious centers on the continent. The famous Bayeux Tapestry (q.v.) is actually a wool-on-linen embroidery.

Embroidery for domestic purposes—on clothing and furnishings and for hangings—was highly developed in Europe from the 16th to mid-19th century. Notable from the 16th century are blackwork (embroidery with black silk thread) and multicolored silk embroidery, both used on linen garments, often with gold thread additions. In the 17th century there was velvet and satin applied work, as well as English stumpwork, a raised and padded embroidery on satin panels mainly used as pictures or to decorate mirror frames and the lids and sides of caskets.

The wool-on-linen embroideries of the 17th and 18th centuries, employing bold tree-and-flower motifs, were used for curtains, bed curtains, cushions, and hangings. A type of diagonal stitch, called tent stitch, was employed to cover entirely an open canvas-type material with pictorial subjects. The finished product was used for table carpets in the 17th century and for upholstery in the 18th century. In the 17th century the number of embroidery stitches greatly increased; examples are found on long, narrow linen samplers, many of which have survived. The sampler was originally a reference sheet of stitches and patterns. Most samplers in the 18th and 19th centuries were decorated with a pleasant arrangement of only a few stitches. They were primarily the productions of young girls learning to sew.

JESSIE McNAB, The Metropolitan Museum of Art
See also NEEDLEWORK.

EMBRYOLOGY is the study of the development of the individual from the egg. Since some eggs, particularly those of birds, are edible, they have long been of interest to man, and knowledge of them reaches back into antiquity. The Greek philosopher Aristotle not only made some acute observations on chick development, but also posed questions about the nature of development that still remain valid in the 20th century. He raised the question as to whether the parts of the animal are all represented in the egg at an early stage, and reach their full development consecutively, at later times; or alternatively, whether the fact that the appearance of one organ follows that of another implies a causal relationship between these events. Aristotle expressed his preference for the latter alternative.

During the Middle Ages, Albertus Magnus, among other investigators, improved slightly upon Aristotle's observations; but embryology enjoyed its next real burst of progress during or after the Renaissance. In 1600 Hieronymus Fabricius published two embryological treatises, on the chick and on the human fetus, both based on direct observation and splendidly illustrated. Fabricius' knowledge of the valves in the veins was an important influence in directing the thought of his pupil, William Harvey, toward his later discovery of the circulation of the blood. Harvey may also have gained from Fabricius some interest in development, and himself published in 1651 a large book *On the Generation of Animals*. Harvey, like Aristotle, posed the possibility of two types of development, and felt that at least in some animals development is a sequence of actions ensuing one upon another. Harvey also made a most important contribution to embryology by demonstrating that the part of the hen's egg that forms the embryo is the "cicatricula" (now called the blastodisc), the white spot of what we would call protoplasm that surmounts the yolk. Fabricius had erroneously considered the chalazae (the thick white spirals of albumen so conspicuous when a raw hen's egg is opened into a glass dish) to be the rudiment of the embryo. Development could not be studied until it was known what actually develops.

Although the whole hen's egg is very large because of its content of yolk and albumen (which provide water and nourishment for the developing embryo), the embryo itself is very small in its early stages; and the embryos of other eggs popular for study because of their accessibility (those of frogs, fishes, or insects) are also small. True understanding of developmental processes, therefore, necessitates the use of the microscope.

One influential embryological concept developed by those who began to study the egg microscopically (in the 17th century) was called *evolutio* in Latin, the language in which biological treatises were then written. In English this concept is referred to as preformation. It implies that all parts of the adult are present in the egg in miniature, and that they simply unfold as the parts of a bud unfold to form a flower. But this concept was shortly supplanted by another. In the mid-18th century, Caspar Friedrich Wolff examined the chick blastodisc more carefully and saw that no organ rudiments are present in it before incubation and that the disc appears homogeneous. His concept of development as proceeding from the homogeneous to the heterogeneous, with new organs appearing in their turn, was called epigenesis; its similarity to that of Aristotle is apparent. Wolff saw that the intestine and the nerve tube of the chick form by the folding of layers. In 1817 Christian Pander described the early development of the chick in terms of foldings of three layers, an outer, a middle, and an inner one, later called the germ layers (ectoderm, mesoderm, and endoderm). Karl Ernst von Baer (who also discovered the mammalian egg) found that these layers are present in many vertebrates, forming the same organs in each. His careful and comprehensive work established embryology as an independent science.

Embryology suffered one serious setback in its later progress when, after the publication of Darwin's *Origin of Species* (1859), Ernst Heinrich Haeckel, in a long series of popular books, went too far in postulating similarities between stages in the individual development of members of one species and adult stages in the evolutionary development of its ancestors. This idea had been held by some before the days of Von Baer, and Von Baer went to great

efforts to point out its fallacy, emphasizing that embryos of one species might resemble the embryos of another species but never the adults of another species. Nonetheless, because so persuasively presented, Haeckel's concept became influential, and its emphasis on events in adult evolution as causative of changes in the individual embryo delayed an experimental analysis of causal relationships within individual development. Finally, at the end of the 19th century, embryology became, like the rest of biology, an experimental science.

Experimental embryology has shown that if parts of some eggs, for instance those of snails or earthworms, are isolated from the whole at an early stage, they develop only what they would have formed if they had remained in place in the intact egg. This is not precisely comparable to preformation since organs are not actually present in miniature in the part, but it does imply that precursors of what an isolated part will form are contained within it, and develop without influence from other parts of the egg (a process known as independent differentiation). In other eggs, for instance those of frogs, what one part forms is determined by its relationships with other parts (a concept called dependent differentiation). One organ forms after another (as Aristotle had postulated) because of the presence of the other; differentiation is progressive. The controlling effect of one embryonic part upon another is called induction, and in 1935 Hans Spemann received a Nobel Prize for its discovery, which experimentally validated the concept of epigenesis.

In point of fact, no egg develops solely by dependent or solely by independent differentiation. The principal aim of experimental embryology has been to ascertain to what degree the development of various parts of different eggs is independent or dependent; the time at which their development becomes independent; and the nature of the factors bringing about their change. The genes, or hereditary factors, contained in the nucleus of the fertilized egg are the ultimate factors that determine how development occurs, but the methods by which they express themselves in development are not yet completely worked out and are under active investigation. What is clear is that when embryos of closely related groups resemble each other, they do so because they have inherited similar genes. The demonstration that deoxyribonucleic acid (DNA) carries genetic information that is transmitted to ribonucleic acid (RNA), and expressed in the formation of specific proteins, is of great importance for the future of embryology, since proteins are important factors in producing differences in cells. (*See* NUCLEIC ACIDS.) The solution to the problem of how molecular change is expressed in visible change of biological structure is not yet in sight. Nor is there yet an answer to the problem of what agencies regulate all the manifold and separate complicated processes of development into an orderly and organized whole.

Embryological Development

The actual sequence of events that may be observed in development is best described in several successive phases, as follows:

Gametogenesis. Each animal develops from a special cell, the female germ cell, or egg. In most species, the egg undergoes development only after fusion with a male germ cell, or spermatozoon. The male and female germ cells are known as gametes, and their formation by the body is called gametogenesis.

Oogenesis is the formation of the egg by the female reproductive organ, the ovary. An egg, no matter how large, is a single cell. Little if anything is yet known of the development of the principal feature which distinguishes the egg from other cells, namely, its capacity to form a whole new individual. It is known, however, that during the production of the egg by the ovary, a highly nutritive material, yolk, is added to the cell to provide food and energy for the developing embryo. The amount of yolk in the egg varies greatly according to the species. Eggs of mammals, which are about ¼ mm. in diameter, contain little yolk. Those of frogs are yolkier and larger; they may measure over 1 mm. in diameter. Birds' eggs are the largest of all cells. What is commonly called the yolk of a breakfast egg represents one cell with its included yolk; the albumen and shell are accessory coats added by the oviduct and uterus after the egg has left the ovary. Many eggs contain, in addition to yolk and the usual cell inclusions, other special inclusions, colored pigment granules, for instance. (*See* CELL.)

Spermatogenesis is the production of the spermatozoon by the male reproductive organ, or testis. The egg usually develops only after fusion with the spermatozoon. This latter cell is even more visibly modified, in comparison with other body cells, than is the egg. During the course of its development in the testis, the spermatozoon loses most of its cytoplasm and becomes an elaborate structure consisting principally of head and tail. It is usually extremely small. The head consists almost exclusively of the nucleus, but has at the front a special region called the acrosome that is important as the agent that perforates the egg—to permit the nucleus of the spermatozoon to enter the egg. A small middle piece connecting head and tail consists principally of mitochondria. The tail is a long filament that the electron microscope has shown to be made of 11 contractile fibers, 2 central and 9 peripheral ones. The egg has no means of movement. The spermatozoon, which is highly motile, proceeds toward it by means of vigorous lashing of its tail. Since many spermatozoa may not locate eggs to fertilize, the number of spermatozoa formed is usually far larger than the number of eggs, reaching into the millions. Some fishes, however, such as herring or cod, also produce millions of eggs each per year.

The development of the elaborate cytoplasmic structure of the gametes is not the only function of gametogenesis. Changes also take place within the nucleus. The nucleus of each body cell in most multicelled animals contains a double set of chromosomes. Provision must be made to ensure that this number does not continually redouble each time two gametes fuse. Accordingly, during gametogenesis, two special nuclear divisions occur (the maturation divisions), the reduction and equational divisions. These reduce the chromosome number of the gametic nucleus to half, so that each gamete is haploid. When the male and female gametes and their nuclei fuse, the diploid number characteristic of the species is restored. (*See* MEIOSIS.)

Fertilization. The fusion of the egg and spermatozoon is called fertilization. The process has a double significance. It furnishes to the new individual the paternal chromosomes along with their genes, and thus is of vital importance in determining the individual's inherited traits. Further, it activates the egg to begin its development. (Most eggs do not develop unless activated by the spermatozoon.)

In many organisms that shed their eggs and spermatozoa into the water in which they live, fertilization is external. In others, the spermatozoa are introduced into the reproductive tract of the female. There is a very high degree of specificity in fertilization, and usually, under normal conditions, the spermatozoa unite only with eggs of their own species. The mechanism that insures this is sometimes described as analogous to that in which antibodies combine with antigens. (*See* ANTIBODIES AND ANTIGENS.) Eggs of a few species may develop without being fertilized; such development is termed parthenogenesis, and is characteristic of aphids, bees, and even occurs in some races of turkeys. Eggs of some species that do not ordinarily develop parthenogenetically may do so after appropriate experimental treatment; frogs and, according to some authors, rabbits, are included among these.

The fertilized egg of each species contains genes different from those of the eggs of other species, and, accordingly, development differs in each species. It is not possible, therefore, to provide a description that fits all developing animals. Some generalizations, however, may be made, but to most of them there are exceptions.

Cleavage. Since the egg cell and the spermatozoon fuse at fertilization, the resulting structure—the zygote—which will form the new individual, consists of a single cell. The first conspicuous visible events of embryonic development are cleavages, or repeated mitotic divisions of the fertilized egg. As a result of these divisions, the single-celled egg becomes many-celled. The position of the cleavage planes and the specific pattern of cleavage differ in different organisms. The size of the egg and the amount of yolk it contains are among the many factors that influence cleavage types. In relatively yolkless eggs, such as those of the frog, the whole egg cleaves. In the very yolky egg of the chick, only the blastodisc cleaves.

There is no particular moment that can be designated as the time that cleavage ends; some cells (those that line the intestine in man, for example) continue to divide throughout life. In some species in which the whole egg cleaves, after a number of cells are present they produce a fluid internally, and what was formerly a solid mass of cells becomes a hollow sphere, the blastula. The blastula stage is much more conspicuous and recognizable in some forms than in others. No hollow blastula is formed in such eggs as the hen's, where cleavage involves only part of the egg. The emphasis on the blastula as a stage, found in most textbooks, is misplaced, and is simply a reminiscence of generalizations made by Haeckel that might better be forgotten. More important events occur in development than the occasional formation of a hollow sphere.

Gastrulation. Major rearrangements, called, in the aggregate, gastrulation, soon take place. Gastrulation is the process whereby cells migrate to take up their positions in the germ layers (ectoderm and endoderm in two-layered organisms such as sponges and jellyfishes; ectoderm, mesoderm, and endoderm in three-layered organisms). These are the layers mentioned earlier in this article as having been discovered by Von Baer to be relatively similar among the vertebrates. Other investigators demonstrated their existence in other many-celled animals.

It has been stated above that the precise pattern of cleavage varies among various animals; the same is true of the pattern of cell movements in gastrulation. These movements, however, always involve migration of cells into the interior of the embryo to form mesoderm and endoderm; the cells remaining on the outside are the ectoderm. In species where the blastula is a hollow sphere, one side of it may push in to form the endoderm. (Since the endoderm forms the digestive system, this is the origin of the term gastrula, which means "little stomach" in Latin.) Sometimes, as in the frog, cells roll in from the outside to the inside, over a distinct lip, to form the mesoderm and endoderm. But in many embryos, including those of the chick and the mammal, individual cells may drop inward from the surface to take up their places in the middle and inner layers. The immediate factors responsible for the co-ordination of these movements into an orderly pattern are being studied but are largely unknown at present.

Differentiation. Wolff's concept of epigenesis as a mode of development, the production of heterogeneity from homogeneity, and Von Baer's interpretation of the formation of the germ layers as a step in the embryo's attainment of heterogeneity, have been mentioned above in this article. Before gastrulation, all the cells of an embryo, barring differences in pigment and yolk or other cell inclusions, are not very different from one another. During gastrulation, as they assort themselves into layers, the cells still resemble each other. But after the completion of gastrulation, drastic alterations become apparent both within the cells themselves and in cell arrangements. These are the result of differentiation: the parts of the embryo, cells and cell aggregates, have become different from what they were, and also different from one another. Differentiation is the most essential feature of epigenesis, of homogeneity becoming heterogeneity.

Differentiation occurs at every level of the body: cell, tissue, organ, and organism as a whole. At each of these levels it involves a functional and structural specialization of the part concerned for the role it will play. Cell differentiation may be expressed by the appearance of particular visible structures within cells, such as muscle striations. It may also, however, be expressed by the production of chemical substances, such as enzymes, involved in cell function. Differentiation at the tissue level most often involves the grouping together of cells of like structure and function; at the organ level, differentiation involves grouping of cells of various types and from various tissues to form a special part that plays a vital function in the body mechanism. The brain as an organ, for example, contains not only nerve cells but also glia cells (a special type of connective tissue). It is enveloped in particular kinds of covering membranes (dura, pia, and arachnoid), and it contains a large number of blood vessels essential to its function. The orderly joining together of the parts to form the whole organ is part of the process called organogenesis. But the brain as it develops also attains a particular shape

of its own, characteristic of the species, as does every other organ of the body. The whole body, too, attains its own particular shape. The development of such changes of size and shape is sometimes called morphogenesis; but since all embryonic development entails changes in size and shape, this term is probably superfluous except as descriptive of all embryonic development. Sometimes attempts are made to contrast growth, or increase in size, with differentiation, but growth is really one component process in differentiation, and inseparable from it.

During normal embryonic development, the ectoderm usually forms the skin, the sense organs, and the nervous system. The endoderm forms the digestive system, that is, the alimentary canal and the glands associated with it, such as the liver and pancreas in vertebrates. In some organisms, including the vertebrates, the endoderm also forms the respiratory organs—gills or lungs. The mesoderm forms heart, blood vessels, skeleton, muscle, and excretory and reproductive organs and their ducts.

The specific mechanisms of organ formation are highly varied among different organisms, but they often involve the folding of layers or the pinching off of parts of layers. Wolff, as we have said, first became aware of the epigenetic nature of development when he observed the folding of layers to form the nerve tube and the intestine of the chick. Such tubular organs are not the only ones to form by folding; some parts that are solid in the adult body also form as hollow structures. The vertebrate liver, for example, is at first a hollow outgrowth of the intestinal canal; the tube representing its original connection to the intestine remains as the bile duct. The vertebrate eye is at first a hollow outgrowth of a hollow brain vesicle. The vertebrate lens and the vertebrate inner ear develop from patches of ectoderm that drop in below the surface to form hollow vesicles that only later change shape. Comparable organs are not necessarily formed, however, in the same manner in all organisms: in many fishes, the nerve cord first sinks below the surface as a solid keel and does not form by folding as it does in the chick, frog, and mammal. And many other organs, in vertebrates and invertebrates, form as solid rather than hollow ingrowths or outgrowths.

Some organs are induced to differentiate by contact with neighboring parts. In the frog, for example, the mesoderm that turns in during gastrulation induces the ectoderm above it to form the nerve tube, which would not form in the absence of contact with the underlying layer. But a number of organs form as a result of independent differentiation rather than of induction. Each organ, and each organism, develops in its own way, and the fact that organisms differ in their development is responsible for their great diversity as adults. And this diversity is the most striking attribute of the various members of the animal kingdom.

Consult Barth, L. G., *Embryology* (1953); Arey, L. B., *Developmental Anatomy* (1954); Raven, C. P., *An Outline of Developmental Physiology* (1954); Waddington, C. H., *Principles of Embryology* (1956); Balinsky, B. I., *An Introduction to Embryology* (1960).

JANE M. OPPENHEIMER, Bryn Mawr College

See also CELL; EGG; FERTILIZATION; GENETICS; NUCLEIC ACIDS; REPRODUCTION.

EMDEN, city in Lower Saxony, Federal Republic of Germany (West Germany). Located 2 mi. from the Ems estuary and connected to it by a canal, it is Germany's most westerly and third-largest North Sea port. Manufacturing, deep-sea fishing, and shipbuilding are extensive. During World War II it was heavily bombarded. Pop., 45,713.

EMERALD, bright-green, transparent, gem variety of the mineral beryl. Common beryl is usually white or pale green; the distinctive color of emerald is due to the presence of a trace of chromium. The finest emeralds come from Muzo, Colombia, where they occur in a bituminous limestone. Other famous localities are Chivor, Colombia, and the Takovaya River in the Ural Mountains, U.S.S.R. Synthetic emeralds of excellent quality have been made in Germany and in the United States. Famous emeralds include those in the Russian crown jewels and some in the British Museum (Natural History).
See also BERYL; GEM; GEM, SYNTHETIC.

EMERSON [ĕm'ər-sən], **RALPH WALDO** (1803–82), American essayist and poet, born in Boston. Descended from eight generations of New England clergymen, graduated from Harvard in 1821, he became in 1829 minister of the Second Church (Unitarian) in Boston. Shortly after the death of his wife, Ellen Tucker, he resigned in 1832, pleading inability conscientiously to administer certain Christian sacraments. After traveling for several months in Europe, where he met Wordsworth, Coleridge, and Carlyle, he returned to Boston, to enter there on his life-long career as a public lecturer. In 1835 he was married again, to Lydia Jackson, and settled in Concord, Mass., where he lived the rest of his life.

Emerson's view of the world was first set forth in a small book entitled *Nature* (1836). "Our age is retrospective," he said. It looks toward the past and conducts itself according to notions borrowed from the past. He called on contemporaries to think for themselves, to recognize truths revealed to them by the divine voice which was within every man. Nature encompassed all things, except spirit, which was shared by all. Nature existed to serve man—to provide physical necessities such as food and shelter, to offer opportunities for perception of beauty in its various forms, to supply man with language which spoke of more than physical things, and by its rigorous demands to instill a sense of duty and responsibility. Not really mystical nor idealistic nor pantheistic, Emerson's doctrine suggested each of these: truth was apprehended, not by rational means, but by intuition; spirit was more real than matter; and the spirit, which was God, was in all men and revealed itself in all things.

In an address at Harvard in 1837 on "The American Scholar," in another address the next year before the Harvard Divinity School, and in his *Essays* (1841), Emerson explained more completely his conception of the divine sufficiency of the individual, speaking most plainly in the essay on "Self-Reliance." Trust yourself, he said. Know that what is true for you in your own heart is inevitably true also for all other men, because a common spirit dwells in all men and speaks to them, when they will listen, in the same voice. The buoyant optimism of this

Culver Pictures, Inc.

Ralph Waldo Emerson, American essayist and poet.

doctrine accorded well with the spirit of Emerson's time, when America expanded westward and most Americans were increasingly likely to think of themselves as equal to all other men. Though he explained later, most clearly in the essay on "Experience" in *Essays: Second Series* (1844), that equality was only of spirit, that every man was in some respect crippled by the world, bound as much by circumstance as released toward freedom, that matter was fact as well as spirit, and that each man was relentlessly driven by demands of both, the earlier, more ebullient doctrine has to many people seemed most characteristic of Emerson.

As a poet Emerson advocated freedom in verse form. In *Poems* (1847) and *May Day and Other Pieces* (1867) he composed lines close-packed with meaning. Although disclaiming authority to speak for others, he was regarded by contemporaries as an official spokesman for transcendentalism (q.v.), and for two years (1842–44) edited its short-lived periodical the *Dial*. In *Representative Men* (1850) he developed his conception of human fallibility and human greatness as called forth by exigencies of time or place. *English Traits* (1856) was a hard-headed view of English character, exhibiting certain superiorities of the British over Americans. *The Conduct of Life* (1860) and *Society and Solitude* (1870) restated in expanded form doctrines which Emerson had set forth previously. His *Complete Works* (12 vols., 1903–4), his *Journals* (10 vols., 1909–14; re-edited in entirety, 1960–), his *Letters* (6 vols., 1939), and his *Lectures* (1959–), reveal additional facets of the man whom Matthew Arnold considered the most important writer of English prose in the 19th century.

Consult Brooks, Van Wyck, *The Life of Emerson* (1932); Rusk, R. L., *Life of Ralph Waldo Emerson* (1949); Whicher, Stephen, *Freedom and Fate: An Inner Life of Ralph Waldo Emerson* (1953).

LEWIS LEARY, Columbia University

EMERSON, suburban residential borough of northeastern New Jersey, on the western shore of Oradell Reservoir, north of Hackensack. It also has light industries. Inc., 1909; pop. (1950) 1,744; (1960) 6,849.

EMERY, rock consisting of a mixture of the minerals corundum and magnetite. Pulverized emery is used as an abrasive either in grinding wheels or glued to paper or cloth. It is used also as a polishing agent and as a nonskid element on pavements and stairways. Most emery comes from the island of Naxos in the Aegean Sea, the province of Adin, Turkey, and deposits near Peekskill, N.Y. World production is about 20,000 tons annually.
See also ABRASIVE; CORUNDUM; MAGNETITE.

EMETIC [ĭ-mĕt′ĭk], drug which produces vomiting. Emetics generally cause vomiting by stimulating the vomiting center of the brain, or by irritating the gastrointestinal tract. In the past, the principal use of these drugs was to induce vomiting to empty the stomach in cases of poisoning by foods or drugs. The use of the stomach pump has now rendered emetics obsolete for this purpose. They are used in some cases of severe asthma to help loosen plugs of mucus in the air passages. They are also used in certain cases of rapid heartbeat and in breathing difficulties in infants involving the upper airways (croup). The latter uses are based upon the stimulation of the vagus nerve which occurs during the act of vomiting: this nerve sends fibers to the heart and the upper air passages.

Among the principal emetics are apomorphine, which acts upon the vomiting center, and ipecac, copper sulfate, and mustard, which act in the stomach. Emetics should not be administered to pregnant women, or to persons suffering from high-blood pressure, or lung tuberculosis.
PAUL CHRISTENSON, M.D.

ÉMILE [ā-mēl′], celebrated French pedagogical novel (1762) by Jean-Jacques Rousseau. Holding that man's innate goodness is usually corrupted by the education society provides, Rousseau outlines for his model pupil, Émile, a new method of private education designed to shield him from contamination by society while systematically developing first, curiosity, then knowledge, intellect, and moral character. Though occasionally contradictory or impractical, *Émile* contains persuasive educational ideas which have profoundly influenced modern practices in education everywhere.

EMILIA-ROMAGNA [ā-mē′lyä-rō-mä′nyä], north Italian region, often called the granary of Italy. Southern Emilia-Romagna lies in the peaks of the northern Apennines. The northern area lies in the fertile Po Valley plain. Emilia comprises the western provinces, Romagna the eastern section. The entire region is often called simply Emilia. Bologna is the departmental capital, and the eight subsidiary provinces are Bologna, Piacenza, Reggio Emilia, Parma, and Modena in the west; Forlì, Ferrara, and Ravenna in the east.

Emilia-Romagna is one of Italy's richest farming regions. Grain, sugar beets, and vegetables are produced in abundance. Cities such as Bologna are famous for their macaroni products; Parma is noted for Parmesan cheese.

Cattle are raised in the plains and sheep in the southern mountains. The grape is grown almost everywhere. The swampy terrain along the Po near Ferrara is ideal for the growing of rice. The region showed marked industrial progress after World War II, particularly along the important railway lines. Tourists come to the sandy beaches of Romagna in the summer. Bologna is visited for its ancient university and excellent restaurants, Ferrara for its many splendid buildings erected by the Este and Borgia families.

In Roman times the region was designated as Aemilia. Romagna emerged as a separate entity by the 5th century, when the Western Roman Emperor Honorius moved his court from Rome to marsh-protected Ravenna to escape Germanic incursions. After 535 the powerful exarchate of Ravenna was established by the Eastern Roman Emperor Justinian. Byzantine influence is observable in the glittering mosaics of Ravenna's churches. By the 8th century Romagna was part of the Papal States. Western Emilia dissolved after Lombard rule into city-state factions, with centuries of struggle between Parma, Bologna, Modena, Piacenza, and Reggio Emilia. The Papacy frequently subdued Emilia, but its control was negligible until Cesare Borgia of Ferrara crushed the petty tyrants there in the early 1500's. The entire area was part of the kingdom of Italy by 1861. Emilia-Romagna is noted for its fiercely antipapal history. In the 1950's Bologna was the largest city in Italy with a Communist mayor. Area. 8,540 sq. mi.
JAMES WILHELM, Queens College, New York

EMINENT DOMAIN refers to the power of the sovereign state to take private property for a public purpose without the owner's consent. It is founded upon the idea that the common necessities and interests of the community transcend individual rights in property. Consequently, the state may appropriate private property when it is necessary or desirable to do so to promote the general welfare. Since eminent domain is inherent in sovereignty, pertinent provisions in the U.S. Constitution and in the constitutions of the states are not grants of the power, but rather limitations upon its exercise.

Eminent domain is distinguishable from other similar powers exercised by governments, such as the police power through which the state restricts the use of property in the interest of the general health, safety, morals, or welfare (for example, zoning and inspection laws), or the taxing power by which the state compels individuals to contribute to the cost of government but does not take specific property as it does under eminent domain.

Although the term "eminent domain" was first used in the early 17th century, the power was exercised by ancient societies. The Romans used it in building roads and aqueducts. Problems of eminent domain became significant in the United States during the 19th century because of the advent of railroad and highway construction and industrial development.

Eminent domain is a legislative power; but once the legislature has authorized its exercise, the executive may decide whether and to what extent the power will be invoked. The judiciary may ultimately determine in a disputed case whether the authorizing statute or its invocation violates any constitutional rights. The legislature often delegates the power of eminent domain to political subdivisions, such as cities and counties, and to private corporations, such as electric power or gas utilities. The power extends to all property, real and personal, but may be exercised only for a public use although there may be incidental private benefit. The term "public use" has been the subject of considerable litigation and there is no general agreement on its precise meaning.

The Constitution of the United States (Fifth Amendment) and the state constitutions limit the exercise of the power by providing that property may not be taken without just compensation. The government must compensate the individual not only for property actually taken, but also for interferences or disturbances with property rights resulting in injuries which are more than incidental. In awarding compensation for condemned property, the government is under a dual obligation. It must protect the rights of the individual whose property is taken by making adequate compensation, and it must also protect the interests of the public which pays for the property against excessively high awards. In some states benefits accruing to the property owner as a result of the improvement for which the property was condemned may be set off against the losses incurred by virtue of the condemnation.

Under the Fourteenth Amendment to the Constitution a state may not take property without due process of law. As a limitation on the power of eminent domain, this means that in condemnation proceedings the individual is entitled to notice and a reasonable opportunity to be heard before his property is appropriated. Although some states provide for a jury trial on the question of compensation, this is not an essential element of due process.

Consult Jahr, A. D., *Law of Eminent Domain: Valuation and Procedure* (1953).

LOUIS F. BARTELT, JR., Valparaiso University School of Law

EMINESCU [ĕm-ĭ-nĕs′kōō], **MIHAIL,** pseudonym of Mihail Eminovici (1849–89), Rumanian poet. His lyrical poems, which exhibit a masterful handling of verse and meter, are sad, romantic, and philosophical. He exerted a strong influence on Rumanian thought and literature, and is generally considered to be the greatest of all Rumanian poets.

EMMANUEL or IMMANUEL [ĭ-măn′ū-əl], Hebrew name meaning "God with us." Old Testament prophets were fond of names with religious meanings, and Isaiah uses this one twice:

"Behold, a maiden shall conceive, and bear a son, and shall call his name Immanuel" (Isa. 7:14); "And the stretching out of his wings shall fill the breadth of thy land, O Immanuel... for God is with us" (Isa. 8:8–10).

Christians early took Isa. 7:14 as a prophecy of Jesus' birth (Matt. 1:23). The famous hymn, "O come, O come, Immanuel," is ordinarily sung during Advent, the period just before Christmas.

EMMANUEL PHILIBERT (1528–80), Duke of Savoy, son of Duke Charles III. As a young man Emmanuel Philibert entered the service of Emperor Charles V and fought against the French, who were then occupying Savoy. His succession in 1553 was in name only, but in 1557 he commanded the Imperial army which defeated the French at St. Quentin, and by the Treaty of Cateau-Cambresis in 1559 he regained his largely ruined duchy. He promptly began to rebuild Savoy. He established new political institutions over which he had absolute control, reformed the administration, abolished serfdom, encouraged industry, and built up a powerful army. Over a period of years he was able to get the French, Spanish, and Swiss troops, which still occupied parts of his lands, to leave. Savoy was more French than Italian at the beginning of his reign. Emmanuel Philibert reversed the situation, making Savoy mainly Italian and creating a strong, effective state that was to become the nucleus of the future kingdom of Italy.

ROBIN S. OGGINS, State University of N.Y. at Binghamton

EMMAUS [ĕm′ē-əs], Judean town mentioned in Luke 24:13 as the destination of Cleopas and a traveling companion, who reported to the disciples a post-resurrection appearance of Jesus on their journey. Among four alleged sites west of Jerusalem, only one, El-Kubeibeh, satisfies Luke's distance of sixty stadia, or seven miles.

EMMAUS, borough of eastern Pennsylvania, near Allentown. It is chiefly a residential community with some light industries. The town was established as a preaching station by the Moravians about 1740. Inc., 1859; pop. (1950) 7,780; (1960) 10,262.

EMMET [ĕm′ĭt], **ROBERT** (1778–1803), Irish patriot. Born in Dublin, son of the physician to the Viceroy in Ireland, he imbibed his politics from his violently nationalist older brother, Thomas. Although Emmet distinguished himself at Trinity College by his brilliant oratory, his conspiratorial activities caused him to be expelled (1798); he then turned from thoughts of a professional career to becoming a professional revolutionary. Too young for an important role in the United Irish movement, he was not implicated in the "Rising of '98" and in 1800 he journeyed to the continent where he discussed with Napoleon and French Foreign Minister Charles Maurice de Talleyrand the possibility of obtaining French aid for a rebellion. He returned to Ireland in 1802 determined to organize a revolt even though he had no hope of French aid. His plans were ludicrously inadequate, his followers desperate and ignorant, and his failure certain. He escaped from Dublin the night of the rising (July 23, 1803) but returned to visit his fiancée and was captured. Leonard MacNally, the British agent, defended him at his trial. Emmet then made two brilliant speeches, one before being sentenced and one on the gallows. These romantic episodes are responsible for his sentimental importance.

JOHN G. SPERLING, Northern Illinois University

EMMETT, DANIEL DECATUR (1815–1904), American composer of popular songs. Born in Mount Vernon, Ohio, he began his career as a military drummer. He then toured extensively as a singing and banjo-playing member of minstrel units, notably The Virginia Minstrels and Bryant's Minstrels. He wrote the lyrics and music of *Dixie* (1859), which was an immediate success and later became a Southern fighting song during the Civil War.

EMOTION usually refers to mental states or processes accompanied by marked bodily reactions, which occur in anticipation or realization of frustration or satisfaction of needs. Such states also are termed "affects," since they typically are accompanied by feelings of pleasantness or unpleasantness. They were called "passions" by early Greek writers. In Latin, emotion originally meant an inner turbulence, as in a storm cloud, which discharged its forces outward. Today, the Latin terminology is accepted. Emotion, for man, connotes an inner turbulence with outward expression.

The earliest writings concerning emotion probably are in the Sanskrit literature. The Vedas (3000–1500 B.C.) and the Upanishads (800–500 B.C.) contain descriptions of pleasure, pain, and sexual enjoyment. Theories about the emotions can be found in the works of the Greek philosophers. Aristotle provided the first extensive classification of "the passions," using words that most of us continue to employ. Other Greek writers held that the passions originated in the body; they were affairs of the heart, the bowels, or the womb. The Greek Stoics decried any lack of control over the passions. To them, passion in any form was bad since it interfered with reason, which was good. The influence of such thought is still with us. One point of view in psychology today is that emotion is disruptive: it interferes with proficient thought or motor performance and should be controlled, although a few "beneficent" emotions are acknowledged.

By the 18th century man had become convinced that the brain was important in behavior, and the supposedly subservient body was largely forgotten. The passions, now called emotions, were considered mental experiences; bodily changes were secondary. In the hands of the mentalistic philosophers of the 18th and 19th centuries emotion became a "thing of the mind." Only the French psychophysiologists, from Descartes on, gave credence to possible physiological bases of the emotions.

Theories. At this time all theories of emotion take one of three forms. Theory I may be stated as follows: emotion is an indivisible mind-body reaction. Many authors disagree, and their proposals take two general forms. Theory II, the most frequently encountered, may be stated thus: emotion is a mental event which depends upon other bodily events. Less prevalent is Theory III: emotion is a bodily event which may produce mental events.

In the first half of the 20th century the second theory was dominant. It was stated most explicitly by William James in 1884: ". . . bodily changes follow directly the perception of the exciting fact, and . . . our feeling of the same changes as they occur is the emotion." For James, emotion was a mental event (feeling) dependent upon physiological events.

In 1885 Carl Lange, a Danish physiologist, published a similar but slightly different point of view. He held that changes in the circulatory system were the essentials of emotion; mental events were secondary. Perhaps because of translation difficulties, James later stated that Lange had published a view similar to his own, and many writers have erroneously referred to the "James-Lange theory of emotion." Actually, Lange's view is a circumscribed class III theory. For Lange, emotion was a bodily event which might or might not produce mental events.

The next major theory to appear was that of Walter Cannon. His physiological experiments had suggested that peripheral bodily events were unimportant in emotion but that integrated patterns of emotional behavior disappeared after destruction of the central portion of the brain (the diencephalon, which includes the thalamus and the hypothalamus). He concluded that emotion resulted from activation of these brain structures. He still believed, however, that emotion was a mental event and, like others today, ascribed most mental events to the outermost layers of the brain (the cortex). His conclusions constitute, therefore, another class II theory.

In 1927, and in 1948, international symposia were held in the United States on "Feeling and Emotion." To date none of the views presented, other than Cannon's, has had marked influence. One deserves special mention, however, since it introduced a new element—the concept that emotion is a continuous process, with ups and downs. This view, presented by an American psychologist, Knight Dunlap, in 1928, was not developed further. Basically a class III theory, it claims that emotion is the dynamic background of all behavior—it is the continuous flux and counterflux of internal bodily responses.

An extension of this view, and of Lange's, has been presented by the present writer. He subscribes to a class III theory and defines emotion as activity of the autonomic nervous system (that automatic portion of the nervous system which controls the basic functions of life such as circulation, heat control, digestion, and elimination). Since this activity is continuous in life, emotion is held to be continuous. Thus, instead of speaking of the presence or absence of emotion, one would speak of the kind of change that has occurred. In this definition the influence of skeletal muscles and endocrine (ductless) glands is minimized but not excluded. Emotional change is seen as a series of complex bodily responses which give rise to a series of different feelings, but which also may be observed in animals or in a human who cannot report his feelings. Feeling and emotion are thus conceived as separate but related phenomena.

Such a point of view questions all present classifications of the emotions. It would hold that extensive knowledge is needed of the possible changes in autonomic response patterns before classification of emotional change is possible. Meanwhile some calculated guesses may be made.

Of particular interest in this respect are attempts to classify emotional behavior in human infants. John B. Watson believed there were three primary emotions which he first called X, Y, Z. He later named them fear (elicited by loud noise or loss of support), anger (elicited by interference with activity), and lust or love (elicited by mild tactual stimulation of erogenous zones). He believed that all emotional life developed from these three behavior patterns.

Watson's views were much criticized, and the explanation advanced by K. M. B. Bridges became popular. She claimed that the primary infant emotion was excitement and that all other emotional responses became differentiated from this one response.

Behavior Patterns. The view of the present writer is that Watson's approach was appropriate but that he should have extended and modified it. He describes eight behavior patterns in infants or young children that may be regarded as distinct emotional changes:

(1) Startle, to sudden intense stimulation;

(2) Struggle, to interference with movement;

(3) Muscular arrest-tumescence, to sustained gentle stimulation of the skin;

(4) Exaggerated withdrawal, to sudden pain-producing stimuli;

(5) General activity, to sustained unpleasant internal sensations;

(6) Quiescence, to relief from unpleasant stimulation;

(7) Spitting-mouth aversion, to unpleasant tastes;

(8) Exhaustion-whimpering, to persisting and unrelieved unpleasant stimulation.

These eight patterns of behavior are believed to occur without learning and to form the bases from which develop the emotional behaviors we recognize as (1) fear, (2) anger, (3) sexual excitement, (4) pain, (5) excitement, (6) pleasure of relief, (7) disgust or revulsion, (8) disappointment or grief.

If these patterns of behavior are discrete in human infants they should be relatively discrete in adults. These views are now being tested. Few decisive experiments have been conducted, but Nina Bull has demonstrated differences in muscular attitude among some of these commonly accepted emotions, and many experimenters are attempting to determine precise differences in autonomic and endocrine responses to stressful situations. *Consult* Watson, J. B., *Psychology from the Standpoint of a Behaviorist* (1919); Lange, C. G., and James, William, *The Emotions* (1922); Cannon, W. B., *Bodily Changes in Pain, Hunger, Fear and Rage* (2d ed., 1929); Gardiner, H. M., and others, *Feeling and Emotion: A History of Theories* (1937); Bull, Nina, *The Attitude Theory of Emotion* (1951); Dunbar, H. F., *Emotions and Bodily Changes* (4th ed., 1954); Wenger, M. A., and others, *Physiological Psychology* (1956); Arnold, M. B., *Emotion and Personality*, Vol. I (1960); Young, P. T., *Motivation and Emotion* (1961).

M. A. WENGER, University of California

EMPATHY [ĕm′pə-thē], in aesthetics "feeling" or "projecting" oneself into or identifying oneself with an artistic work, object, or natural process. For example, a thin column supporting a heavy capital might arouse in an observer a feeling of straining to hold up the weight. This use of the term "empathy" is sometimes extended to cover such things as the involuntary movements spectators make while watching an athlete strain to reach his goal.

Empathy also means intellectually understanding another person's emotions without necessarily experiencing these emotions at the same time. It may be considered primarily a form of intellectual identification and is distinguished from sympathy, which implies a more intense sharing of emotions. This does not mean that affective or emotional identification is entirely excluded. A person understands and "feels" himself into the mood or attitude of another, without specifically and intensely having the same emotional experience. Thus a psychotherapist can understand a patient's anguished tears, yet not shed a tear himself. It is also possible to have empathy with a group or cause as well as with a person, object, or process. A neutral observer can appreciate and understand the attitudes or feelings of an oppressed minority group, while neither being part of the group nor aiding its cause.

LAWRENCE R. BOULTER, University of Illinois

EMPEDOCLES [ĕm-pĕd′ə-klēz] (fl. mid-5th century B.C.), Sicilian Greek philosopher, who was a unique combination of natural philosopher, poet, and mystic. In reaction to Parmenides he posited four indestructible elements (earth, water, air, and fire) which mingled and separated under the influence of two motive causes, love and strife. These prevailed alternately, causing a double cycle of evolution. Under love all four were fused indistinguishably in a sphere; under strife the same sphere exhibited them in separate concentric layers. Our world represents an intermediate stage, when neither force is in complete control, and the elements are only partly fused. The theory includes a striking description of the evolution of organic forms according to a law of the survival of the fittest.

In his religious poem, *Katharmoi* (Purifications), love and strife become moral powers, and human souls are fallen spirits condemned to undergo a cycle of reincarnations before they can win back their divine status by abjuring strife and following love.

W. K. C. GUTHRIE, Cambridge University

EMPEROR, ruler of an empire. An Emperor may be absolute in his power, or subject to constitutional provisions and limitations. The term derives from the Latin word *imperator*, or "holder of supreme power." Originally the Roman Emperor was the head of the military forces. Julius and Augustus Caesar adopted the title when they held supreme power, and it was used by all their successors. In the Christian era the elected sovereign of the Holy Roman Empire was known as Emperor. Peter the Great of Russia added the title of Emperor to his title of Tsar in 1721. Napoleon I of France adopted the title in 1804, following the example of Charlemagne. The Kings of Prussia were called Emperors of Germany after 1871. Disraeli, the British Prime Minister, persuaded Parliament to add "Empress of India" to the title of Queen Victoria in 1876.

EMPEROR CONCERTO, piano concerto in three movements (Allegro, Adagio *un poco mosso*, Rondo) in E♭ Major (Op. 73, 1809) by Ludwig van Beethoven. The last of his five piano concertos, it was dedicated to Archduke Rudolph. While the first two concertos keep something of the more restrictive style of Mozart, the last three are more broadly conceived, more orchestrally developed. The fourth (also dedicated to Archduke Rudolph) rivals the fifth in present popularity, although the latter (whose title was not Beethoven's) is the most brilliant and dramatic. It leads the way to the concertos of Liszt and his followers, in which, however, virtuosic display tends to displace expressive depth. An unusual rhythmic figuration in hemiola opens the rondo movement. Here the left hand plays the ⁶⁄₈ of the time signature, while the right plays in groups of ²⁄₈.

EMPEROR JONES, THE, play (1920) by American dramatist Eugene O'Neill. This expressionist, one-act work depicts in powerful terms the psychological disintegration of the self-created Negro ruler of a West Indian island.

EMPEROR PENGUIN. *See* PENGUIN.

EMPHYSEMA [ĕm-fə-sē'mə], **PULMONARY,** distension of the terminal air sacs (alveoli) of the lungs. A common form of emphysema (the obstructive type) is that which develops in conjunction with bronchitis. The condition results from partial obstruction of the small air passages in the lungs (the bronchioles). Air enters the alveoli more easily than it can leave them, causing the lungs to become distended with trapped air. In severe cases there is a serious interference with oxygen absorption and carbon dioxide elimination by the lungs. The disturbance in oxygen supply to the tissues often results in changes in the blood, such as an increased number of oxygen-carrying red blood cells (polycythemia) and increased blood volume. The patient may suffer from coughing, wheezing, and shortness of breath. Eventually heart failure may occur. Infections of the breathing passages are especially dangerous to the patient since they can bring on heart failure or further interfere with breathing. Treatment includes the use of antibiotics to combat infection and drugs to dilate the air passages, and to promote the coughing up of sputum. Breathing exercises and cortisone derivatives may also be of value.

STANLEY BLUMENTHAL, M.D.

EMPIRE STATE BUILDING, the world's tallest building, located on Fifth Avenue in New York City. The 1,250-ft. office building, designed by the firm of Shreve, Lamb, and Harmon, was erected 1930–31. Observation platforms on the 86th and 102d floors permit views of up to 50 mi. The building is surmounted by a 222-ft. television tower that is used by New York's eight television stations.

EMPIRE STYLE, phase of neoclassic art that prevailed in France at the time of Napoleon in the early 19th century (1804–15). It appeared also, although in modified form, in England as the Regency style and in the United States as American Empire, especially in the furniture of Duncan Phyfe.

In the reign of Louis XVI architecture, painting, and sculpture as well as furniture had shared in the swing away from the ornate forms of the mid-18th century toward a classical simplicity. The artists of the French Revolution and the Directoire carried on this neoclassical movement, providing the foundation on which Empire style is based. But in the Empire, Rome rather than Greece inspired the grandiose forms and massive members, which combined curving (though not undulating) lines with rectilinear ones. In addition to classical models, eastern Mediterranean archeology, exemplified by Egyptian collections set up in Paris by the Emperor, was carefully studied.

The Arch of Triumph in Paris is the outstanding architectural monument of the time. In furniture, dark mahogany was favored in France; gilded ornament, long in eclipse, made a reappearance. An enlarged repertoire of decorative motifs, such as the sphinx, the eagle, and the lyre shape was employed. A greater use of luxurious materials was also characteristic.

FELICIA M. STERLING DAUTERMAN,
The Cooper Union Museum for the Decorative Arts

EMPIRICAL EQUATION, in mathematics, equation formed to fit empirical data. Such equations are used in experimental science, engineering, and statistics. When numerical data are plotted on graph paper, the scattered points may seem to lie close to some known curve, such as a straight line or a parabola. By appropriate methods the coefficients of the apparent curve are obtained and its equation written. When there is more than one equation from which to choose, preference is given to the simplest one that fits the data most closely. The apparent curve is then tested for accuracy by using additional data, either interpolated or extrapolated.

For example, suppose the observed velocities of an object falling from rest are 31.9, 64.1, 96.3, 127.4, and 161.0 ft. per second at the ends of the first five seconds. One empirical equation might be $v = 32t$. The graph of this equation is a straight line, passing above the points (1, 31.9) and (4, 127.4) and below the other three points. A better straight-line fit might be found by the method of least squares in which the sum of the squares of the positive and negative errors is as small as possible.

JOHN J. KINSELLA, New York University

EMPIRICISM [ĕm-pĭr'ə-sĭz-əm] (from the Gr. term meaning "experience"), a philosophical position which emphasizes the role of experience in human knowledge and minimizes the role of reason. Empiricists have usually accepted a theory of meaning which implies that all concepts are analyzable in terms of experience. In David Hume, this was stated as the doctrine that all ideas come from impressions (including sensations, passions, and emotions). In the 20th century it has taken a form among pragmatists and logical positivists known as "the verifiability theory of meaning," the theory that statements are meaningful only to the extent that they are in principle verifiable by experience.

Essentially, however, empiricism is a theory of knowledge which denies that any of our knowledge of the actual world can be justified by reason alone. John Stuart Mill maintained that even a mathematical truth like "2 plus 2 equals 4" must ultimately be justified by observation and induction. But in general empiricists have simply denied that mathematics, of itself, gives us any knowledge of the actual world. Mathematical truths, they have argued, are, in a broad sense of the word, tautologies: they are verified by showing that they follow from definitions of their constituent terms.

RODERICK FIRTH, Harvard University

EMPLOYMENT AND UNEMPLOYMENT. The term "employment" means the state of being employed, or of "having a job." In this sense we speak of a person's seeking employment. The term is also frequently used to mean the quantity of employment, that is, the number of persons having jobs. In this sense we may speak of a 1% increase in employment. Employment and its counterpart, unemployment, are matters of major importance in modern societies. The incomes of most individuals depend on their having employment. A nation's economic health and prosperity depend on the extent to which those who wish to work can be given useful employment.

Composition of the Working Population. In the most commonly accepted usage employment refers to the state of being *gainfully* occupied, that is, of being engaged in activities contributing to the production of goods or the provision of services, in return for which pay is received. The term "employment" is broad enough to include self-employment (working for oneself), as well as the state of being employed by someone else on a contractual basis for a wage, salary, or commission. Total employment in a nation thus includes (a) employees of business firms, households, governmental bodies, and nonprofit institutions and (b) persons, such as doctors, dentists, shopkeepers, and farmers, who own and operate their own unincorporated businesses. Members of the armed services, being employees of the government, are of course included. Excluded from the ranks of the employed are students, housewives, and persons of independent means whose occupations consist of hobbies or volunteer work. Their exclusion, however, does not imply that they are not engaged in useful work.

The opposite of employment is unemployment. This latter term, however, does not include everyone who is not working, but only those who are members of the *labor force* and have no employment. A nation's labor force consists of all persons who desire to be gainfully occupied and are capable of employment. It thus excludes all who for some reason—age, physical or mental disability, or preference—are neither working nor seeking jobs. In most modern countries the labor force comprises considerably less than half of the population. In the United States it comprises about 43% of the total population, the other 57% being composed of children, students, wives who stay at home, sick persons, cripples, morons, persons with men-

tal illnesses, retired people, and a few wealthy persons who choose not to work. It is important to note the distinction between unemployed and unemployable, the latter term referring to persons who are not capable of employment.

Occupation Categories. Employment consists of work in some specific occupation. In today's world, with its myriad of products and its highly technical productive processes, there are many thousands of distinguishable occupations. These may be classified into a few broad categories. It is usual to distinguish manual labor, sometimes referred to as "blue-collar" work, from "white-collar" work—a broad category that includes clerical, technical, professional, and managerial work. Manual labor is often classified as unskilled, semiskilled, and skilled labor. Managerial work tends to be the most highly paid form of employment. This is due to the fact that superior management of an organization (or of one of its departments) can bring about sufficiently large monetary savings or gains to enable a superior manager to demand high compensation in return. Farming used to be considered a form of manual labor, and it still is, in many cases. But modern farming has become a specialized business, and many farmers today perform essentially managerial work: planning, directing operations, and making decisions regarding changes in methods of farming and the type of mechanical equipment to be used.

Changing Composition of Employment. One feature of modern societies has been the changing composition of employment. Through the years, as the economy of a nation develops more productive methods which raise its

SOME CAUSES OF UNEMPLOYMENT

Unemployment deprives the individual of purchasing power and reduces a country's national output. Much has been learned about the causes and cure of unemployment through the bitter experiences of the Great Depression of the 1930's. But since the causes of unemployment are numerous and sometimes a temporary by-product of desirable technological progress, the solutions must aim primarily at alleviating the hardships and reducing the number of jobless.

SEASONAL UNEMPLOYMENT

REGIONAL UNEMPLOYMENT

CYCLICAL UNEMPLOYMENT

TECHNOLOGICAL UNEMPLOYMENT

INDIVIDUAL UNEMPLOYMENT

The employed: workers stream from a plant at the end of a day.

standard of living, farm employment declines relative to nonfarm employment. The reason is that fewer workers are needed to produce the nation's food supply. In the United States, for example, about 73% of the nation's labor force in 1820 consisted of farmers; by 1920 only 27% worked on farms; and by the 1960's less than 8% were in agriculture. Within the growing area of nonfarm employment the percentage of workers in manufacturing industries declines, while the percentage employed in providing services (retailing, medicine, entertainment, education, and so forth) rises. The reason is that as the real incomes of people rise, they can afford to spend more and more income on services which were formerly considered a luxury. These changes often create problems for workers in those industries that experience a relative decline in employment opportunities.

Unemployment as a Social Problem. Unemployment has been a serious social problem in many countries. Unemployment is obviously undesirable, especially if it persists. From society's standpoint it is inefficient to have potential workers remain idle, since useful goods and services which might have been produced are not produced. From the individual's standpoint failure to find work means financial worries, frustration, and discouragement.

The extent of unemployment has varied considerably from year to year and from country to country. In the United States it reached its greatest magnitude in the 1930's. More than one-fifth of the labor force remained continuously idle during 1932–35. World War II reduced unemployment to less than 2%. In the postwar years unemployment varied between 2.5% in 1953 and 6.8% in 1958. For most countries of the world today unemployment stands roughly within this range, if the statistics gathered are reliable. Some European countries (Norway, Sweden, the Netherlands, France, United Kingdom) have reported unemployment of less than 1% of the labor force, but this figure is in part due to their more restricted definition of unemployment.

Unemployment: Causes and Remedies

Why Does Unemployment Exist? There is a variety of reasons:

(1) Seasonal unemployment occurs because the busi-

ness of many employers (for example, resort hotels, farming, construction) is seasonal in nature. Workers are laid off temporarily.

(2) Technological unemployment occurs when new labor-saving machines or processes replace old ones. When particular jobs and skills are made obsolete, workers must find other types of jobs and learn new skills. The growing use of automation has caused considerable technological unemployment.

(3) Continual changes in a nation's pattern of demand for products force some firms or industries to reduce production and employment, while other firms or industries (perhaps in other parts of the country) expand production and recruit new workers. The workers who lose their jobs cannot always find new jobs immediately. In some cases an entire region in which a declining industry is concentrated becomes a "depressed area." Because workers are reluctant to move from their established homes, regional unemployment can be an especially severe problem.

(4) In individual cases persons may be unable or unwilling to perform satisfactorily in their jobs and may be discharged or they may dislike their jobs and quit voluntarily. In either case the result is unemployment until a new, suitable job is found.

In these four types of unemployment joblessness is of a temporary nature and exists only because it usually takes some time to match unemployed persons with existing job vacancies. Unemployment of these sorts is often called *frictional*, or *transitional*, unemployment.

In addition there is (5) cyclical unemployment. For the past century and a half, industrial nations have experienced recurring cycles in which periods of prosperity and high rates of economic activity have been followed by slack periods, known as recessions or depressions. In these slack periods a general falling off in the demand for goods and services has caused general reductions in sales, production, and employment. The alternation of good times and bad times has come to be known as the *business cycle*. For this reason the resulting unemployment has been termed "cyclical unemployment." During the period of subnormal employment, which usually lasts a year or more, workers who lose their jobs find alternative job opportunities unusually scarce or nonexistent.

Solutions. Two kinds of solutions for the unemployment problem have been attempted. One consists of providing relief or protection from the financial hardships of unemployment. In earlier periods such measures consisted largely of local governmental assistance to the needy, together with private charitable aid. Today the United States, Britain, and other countries have fairly comprehensive schemes of compulsory unemployment insurance, in which workers and their employers contribute to a fund out of which payments are made to those who are unemployed. In the United States this system has been operating since 1935 as a joint federal-state undertaking under the Social Security Act of 1935. The employer of an insured worker is required to pay a tax, or "insurance payment," which varies with the amount of the worker's wage. Insured workers who become unemployed receive for a limited period (usually not more than six months) weekly payments which vary with the worker's previous wage or salary income and also vary with the state under whose laws the worker is insured. Unemployment insurance is an effective device for alleviating the hardships of transitional unemployment, but is less effective in coping with cyclical unemployment.

The other type of solution for the unemployment problem consists of measures aimed at creating conditions that reduce the level of unemployment. Under this heading can be mentioned the provision of (a) agencies, such as government employment services, which inform workers of job opportunities and inform employers of suitable candidates for positions; (b) programs of retraining, in order to give unemployed persons new skills that are in demand; and (c) subsidies and other incentives to encourage workers to move out of areas or occupations of labor surplus into areas or occupations in which labor is in short supply. Such measures can reduce transitional unemployment by shortening the period between loss of job and subsequent reemployment.

Remedy for Cyclical Unemployment. But these measures cannot deal effectively with cyclical unemployment. Here the problem is one of a general insufficiency of demand. The remedy for cyclical unemployment, according to modern employment theory (which owes its origin to the writings of the British economist John Maynard Keynes, later Lord Keynes), lies in measures that stimulate an increase in the nation's total expenditure on products. The most important of these measures fall under the headings of fiscal policy and monetary policy. Fiscal policy is concerned with matters of government expenditures and taxation. The government, through its power to spend more, can directly raise the total level of expenditure. Through its power to tax less (thus permitting individuals and business firms to spend more), it can indirectly raise the total level of spending and thus lift production and employment. Monetary policy is concerned with the control of the nation's banking system. By measures which permit or encourage banks to expand credit, the monetary authorities of a nation can stimulate increased amounts of business borrowing that result in increased business spending and thus increased employment. In the United States monetary policy is the province of the Board of Governors of the Federal Reserve System.

The goal of fiscal-monetary policy is "full" employment. This elusive term does not refer to a complete absence of unemployment, but to the virtual elimination of cyclical unemployment, leaving only an unavoidable amount of transitional unemployment. Under present conditions, however, even in times of "full" employment we must expect to find at least 2% to 3% of the labor force out of work on any given date.

LAWRENCE ABBOTT, Union College
See also ECONOMIC STABILIZATION POLICIES; LABOR.

EMPLOYMENT SERVICES, CANADIAN. The establishment of Canada's National Employment Service was provided for by the Unemployment Insurance Act of 1940. The nationwide free employment service has approximately 200 local offices and offers a system to provide contact between prospective employers and job-seekers from different localities. A counselling service is maintained for those entering and re-entering the job market and for handicapped persons.

EMPLOYMENT SERVICES, U.S., the nationwide federal-state system of free public employment agencies established under the Wagner-Peyser Act of 1933. Recruitment and placement are probably the most important of the many services performed by the more than 1,800 public employment offices. Job-seekers file employment applications and employers file job orders. The employment office tries to match the worker's experience and qualifications with the requirements of a particular job, and then arranges an interview between the applicant and the prospective employer. In this way the employment office serves both labor and management. The key objective of the placement program is choosing the right applicant for the right job.

The percentage of total job placements for which the public employment service is responsible varies from industry to industry and from labor market to labor market. In no case does a public employment office monopolize hiring transactions. Unions and private employment agencies also play important roles in the placement process.

Local employment offices provide special services to youth, veterans, the handicapped, older workers, clerical workers, hotel and restaurant workers, unskilled factory workers, domestic workers, and farm workers. Other services are job and aptitude testing and employment counseling.

The labor market is complex and unique. A great deal of information about its peculiarities and intricacies is necessary, therefore, if its functioning is to be understood. The collection, analysis, and dissemination of such information forms a major responsibility of the public employment service.

Currently available information includes bimonthly studies of 149 major labor market areas; data on employment, unemployment, job opportunities, and training needs; a national summary of area developments; industry manpower surveys; area-skill surveys; and local occupational guides. Such information is useful in developing national manpower policies, planning economic and industrial development, determining training needs, and evaluating skills.

O. WILLIAM ROSS, Executive Director, Manpower Utilization Council

EMPORIA [ĕm-pôr'ē-ə], trade center of east-central Kansas, and seat of Lyon County. Food processing and printing are among its important industries. The city was the home of William Allen White, author and editor of the Emporia *Gazette*, one of the nation's famous newspapers (1895–1944). Kansas State Teachers College and College of Emporia are located here. Settled, 1857; inc., 1870; pop. (1950) 15,669; (1960) 18,190.

EMPORIA, town of southern Virginia, and seat of Greenville County. It is a trade center for surrounding farming regions. A two-story brick courthouse built here in 1787 still stands in the town. Inc., 1906; pop. (1950) 5,664; (1960) 5,535.

EMPORIUM, borough of north-central Pennsylvania, and seat of Cameron County. It was an early lumber camp and is now a somewhat isolated, small, manufacturing community with a tannery and an electronic-tube plant. Inc., 1864; pop. (1950) 3,646; (1960) 3,397.

EMPSON, WILLIAM (1906–   ), English poet and critic. He was educated at Magdalene College, Cambridge. His *Seven Types of Ambiguity* (1930), first written as an assigned paper, has become a classic in modern literary criticism. His poetry, mathematically precise but sprinkled with puns and witticisms, has brought him acclaim from the New Critics. *Bacchus*, a long theological poem completed while Empson was teaching in China, is recognized as his masterpiece. His *Collected Poems* appeared in 1949.

EMU [ē′mū], large flightless bird, *Dromaeus novaehollandiae*, found in the open plains of Australia. The emu is the national bird of Australia, and is the second largest living bird; only the ostrich exceeds it in size. Adult emus average 5 ft. in height and depend on their long legs to carry them away from pursuing animals. Their plumage is a mottled gray-brown. During the breeding season female emus emit a peculiar booming call. The female lays from 7 to 12 eggs in a shallow depression in the earth and is then chased away by her mate who broods the eggs and takes care of the newly hatched young. Emus inhabit open grasslands where they feed on roots and fruit. Unlike their vicious relatives, the cassowaries, emus are easily domesticated and breed well in captivity.

EMULSION, a mixture that is formed when two liquids which do not dissolve in one another are shaken together, for example, oil and water. This emulsion separates at once into two layers; but if a third substance, such as soap, is added, the emulsion will persist. Soap is an example of an emulsifying agent. When two liquids are mixed, the system tries to adjust so that the area of contact between the liquids is as small as possible. Breaking the oil into small globules by shaking generates a vast surface area. The emulsifying agent helps to prevent the adjustment to the small area. It achieves this by forming a film at the interface of the two liquids. Part of the soap molecule is attracted to the oil and part to the water, so the molecules can "stand up" at the interface with their "heads" in the water and their "tails" in the oil.

The dispersed globules in an emulsion may usually be seen by a microscope and are generally too large to be called colloidal. Because of the great surface area, the study of emulsions comes naturally under colloid chemistry since colloid chemistry has come to mean the chemistry of surfaces. There are many common examples of emulsions. Milk is an emulsion of butterfat dispersed in water with the milk protein as emulsifying agent. Salad dressings are oil-and-water emulsions. Many cosmetics and pharmaceuticals are carefully designed emulsions.

DONALD BARTON, University of Illinois
See also COLLOIDS.

EMULSION, PHOTOGRAPHIC. *See* PHOTOGRAPHY.

EMULSION PAINT. *See* PAINT.

ENAMELS [ĭ-năm′əlz], metal objects to which a glasslike surface is fused. More specifically, enamel refers to the surface, a form of glass made of silica minium plus oxide of lead, borax, soda, and potash, with metal oxides added for color. A mixture of these ingredients is made by melting them, cooking the product and grinding it into a powder. The powder is melted at a high temperature on the metal base, to which it fuses. This surface serves as decoration and a useful protective coating.

Enamel colors must be applied separately or in separated areas to prevent their mixing during the firing. In cloisonné the colors are kept separate by wire attached to the metal base. In champlevé the powder is placed in recesses formed by hollowing out shallow areas of the metal. A variation of this method, called *basse-taille*, involves carving or etching to create a design in relief but below the surface of the metal. Transparent enamels, which al-

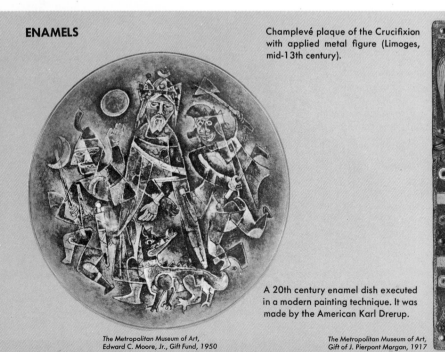

ENAMELS

Champlevé plaque of the Crucifixion with applied metal figure (Limoges, mid-13th century).

A 20th century enamel dish executed in a modern painting technique. It was made by the American Karl Drerup.

The Metropolitan Museum of Art, Edward C. Moore, Jr., Gift Fund, 1950

The Metropolitan Museum of Art, Gift of J. Pierpont Morgan, 1917

low the design to be visible, are then applied. In *plique-à-jour* the glasslike qualities of the medium are exploited, the metal being cut out after the firing to allow light to pass through the enamel. A simple flat picture area similar to a painting is achieved in Limoges enamels by applying colors in layers and firing the pieces a number of times.

History. The earliest evidence of enameling on metal dates from the 5th century B.C. in Greece, where jewelers occasionally used enamel to add a note of color. The famous statue of Zeus made by Phidias for the temple at Olympia was adorned with a golden drapery on which enamel flowers formed a pattern. Cloisonné was the favored technique of the Greeks and the Romans. As early as 240 A.D. tribes of Britain were reported working in champlevé. Enameling both in cloisonné and champlevé was practiced in northern Europe, particularly among the Celts and the Saxons from the 6th to the 9th century. Interlaced designs with fantastic figures, executed in bronze or gold, were given additional color in enamel. The rise of a new center of enameling in the Byzantine Empire late in the 9th century brought few technical advances. Cloisonné and champlevé were highly suitable to the Byzantine style, which was characterized by flat color and strong linear definition. In the 11th century the center of enamel manufacture returned to the West, in the beginning under the direction of Byzantine workmen who traveled there. The valleys of the Rhine and Meuse and the city of Cologne in particular had prominent workshops that produced enamels from the 11th to the 13th centuries. At about that time the Orient began to produce enamels using Western techniques.

In Europe, the *basse-taille* and *plique-à-jour* techniques were introduced in the 14th century as a manifestation of the elaborate late Gothic style. Late in the 15th century the technique of pictorial representation on enamels was introduced at Limoges, where the enamel industry had flourished since medieval times. Thereafter the artist was able to create an illusion of real space.

In the 18th century small objects for personal use were produced in enamel that completely covered the metal, scenes and designs in opaque colors being painted over it. The industrial revolution brought about the introduction of simple mass manufacture with designs tailored to the limitations of the machines. A revival of handcraft in the 1860's under the influence of the English theorist William Morris inspired new activity in enamels, with craftsmen relearning earlier techniques. By the end of the century new approaches to design, such as *art nouveau*, were followed by enamelists.

In the 20th century the emphasis has been on the pictorial possibilities of the medium. Several contemporary enamelists produce architectural decorations and picture plaques, employing steel as the ground instead of the more commonly used copper. Enameling has also become a medium for abstract expressionist pictures, in which new textures have been achieved by handling the materials in unorthodox ways.

Consult Bates, K. F., *Enameling: Principles and Practice* (1951).

MARVIN D. SCHWARTZ, The Brooklyn Museum
See also CLOISONNÉ.

ENAMEL PAINT. *See* PAINT.

ENCARNACIÓN [*āng-kär-nä-syōn'*], second-largest city of Paraguay, located 185 mi. southeast of Asunción. It is Paraguay's major port on the Paraná River (here called the Alto Paraná). Timber, yerba maté, cotton, tobacco, and hides are shipped downstream. The ferry that conveys the international train across the Paraná on the Asunción–Buenos Aires line crosses between Encarnación and Posadas, Argentina. Founded in 1632 as a Jesuit mission called Itapúa, it was made a town in 1843 and a city in 1907. In the early 1800's the city served for a time as the national port of entry under the dictator José Gaspar Rodríguez Francia. The oldest section of the city was entirely destroyed by a tornado in 1926. It was quickly rebuilt into a modern city. Pop., 18,783.

ENCEPHALITIS [*ĕn-sĕf-ə-lī'tĭs*], an inflammation of the brain which may be caused by bacteria, fungi, or parasites, but more commonly results from a virus infection. Most types of virus encephalitis are contagious and can cause epidemics. Although the manner in which the viruses are spread is not known in all cases, ticks, mosquitoes, and other animals are the transmitting agents for many of the infections.

Many different viruses may cause encephalitis. The names of the various virus forms of encephalitis are frequently associated with the sites at which epidemics occurred. These include: Japanese B encephalitis, St. Louis encephalitis, Australian X disease, Russian spring-summer disease, Venezuelan equine encephalitis, Eastern equine encephalitis, and Western equine encephalitis. The equine forms affect horses and various other animals, and can be transmitted to humans, producing infections of varying severity. Other forms of encephalitis may appear during or after infectious diseases such as measles, mumps, and chickenpox, or following vaccination against smallpox or rabies.

The different viruses produce diverse symptoms which include headache, fever, drowsiness, gastrointestinal disturbances, double vision, coma, tremors, convulsions, and paralyses. The infections may be fatal, although some viruses produce only mild disturbances.

There is no specific treatment for these disorders. In the case of the insect-borne viruses, spread of the disease can be controlled by screening doors and windows and attempting to eliminate the insect carrier. Vaccines have been developed which protect animals from the equine forms of encephalitis, but these have not proven practical for humans.

EDWARD PINCKNEY, M.D.

ENCINA or ENZINA [*ān-thē'nä*], **JUAN DEL** (1469?–?1529), Spanish poet, musician, and dramatist. Often called the father of the Spanish theater, Encina was responsible for the secularization of Spanish drama. Many of his plays, though written for aristocratic audiences, found their inspiration in popular types. His shepherds and shepherdesses, although comically exaggerated for the diversion of the upper classes, nevertheless act like real people and speak an authentic peasant dialect. As a poet, he wrote some of Spain's finest *villancicos* (carols). Many of these, as well as other verse, were published in his *Cancionero* (Song Book), 1496.

ENCKE [ĕng′kə], **JOHANN FRANZ** (1791–1865), German astronomer who, at the Seeberg Observatory in Switzerland, calculated the orbit of the comet that now bears his name. Born in Hamburg, he was educated there and at the University of Göttingen. From 1825 to 1863 he was director of the Berlin Observatory. Encke is noted also for determining a value of the sun's parallax that was long used to compute the earth-sun distance.
See also COMET.

ENCLOSURE MOVEMENTS, name applied in European economic history to changes involving the substitution of single, compact agricultural units, or farms, for large land units whose use was shared by a community. In Western civilization, land use by the village community was for many centuries the usual practice. The land available to the community was marked out into areas suitable for arable farming, for pasturing cattle, for gathering wood, and so forth. By custom, members of the community enjoyed the right to share in the benefits to be derived from these different areas, the shares being determined by the status of the individual.

A feature of this form of agriculture, as it applied to arable land, was the cultivation of that land in two or three large fields—open fields, as they were called in England. In these fields each individual had the right to farm one or more long, narrow strips, the location of the strips being subject to redistribution each year. A strip had as its boundaries a frame of uncultivated land, similar to a thin roadside shoulder. Where the individual had the right to cultivate more than one strip, these were scattered about in the open fields. The status of the individual also determined the number of cattle and pigs he might put out to pasture or to forage in the woods. His animals and those of his neighbors formed a common herd.

Farming on this general pattern continued in parts of Europe and Russia into the early 20th century and satisfied the wish to preserve a form of individual property right while maintaining community farming. The system had three major weaknesses: it inhibited the progressive farmer, wasted land and labor in cultivation of the strips, and caused unprofitable breeding of animals and spread disease in the common herds.

Enclosure was the practice by which the individual separated out a piece of community land, acquired a continuing use of it, and farmed it as a unit. Often he surrounded his land with a hedge or fence; sometimes he located his home on it. It became his farm. If his status were high, he would own the land; if not, he might rent it. Enclosure took place in some countries, such as France and Russia, rather suddenly and on a large scale, as an aftermath to political revolution; in others, notably England, the transition was slow.

In England enclosure began in the 13th century and from that time forward took place almost continuously until the early 19th century. At first enclosure involved only parcels of woods and waste lands called "commons." Enclosure of arable and pasture lands occurred in the 14th and 15th centuries. Then depopulation resulting from the Black Death (c.1349) and the growing practice of substituting money for labor services in landlord-tenant relationships caused landholdings to be rearranged and new lease and labor agreements to be worked out. During the 15th and early 16th centuries, the popularity of sheep farming in some districts led landowners to create enclosed farms, and in the 16th century the dissolution of the monasteries and sale of their lands to laymen encouraged reorganization of estates and enclosure. When the civil wars of the 17th century caused further redistribution of estates, some new owners sought to consolidate and enclose. By the end of the 17th century about half the cultivated land of England was enclosed.

During these centuries the encloser was almost always a member of the middle or upper class. He put pressure on lesser men, manipulated their leases, or bought up their rights. In the 18th and early 19th centuries the legal technique for carrying out enclosures changed. Rather than negotiate with the other persons concerned, sometimes taking advantage of his position as landlord, sometimes going to court for ratification of an agreement, the encloser usually obtained an individual act of Parliament to legalize his new rights. This way was open to him because the propertied classes then controlled Parliament. Almost 5,000 acts of Parliament, each authorizing a separate enclosure, completed the enclosure movement in England. By the middle of the 19th century, open-field farming was an agricultural rarity.

The enclosure movements of Europe and Russia gave a new pattern to Western agriculture, to rural society, and to the rural landscape. In England, from the 17th century onward, the enclosed farm offered the farmer opportunity to experiment and to intensify the cultivation of his land. Particularly in 18th century England the creation of substantial, compact estates made possible the investment of large amounts of capital, the use of agricultural machinery, and the production of new varieties of plants and animals.

FREDERICK G. MARCHAM, Cornell University

ENCOMIENDA [ĕn-kō-mē-ĕn′də], Spanish system of forced labor in the New World. It evolved from the earlier practice of exacting retributive toil from the defeated Moors in Spain and was introduced to Hispanic America by the conquistadors. Sometimes mistakenly compared to a land grant or to the plantation slavery system, the encomienda merely licensed the encomendero to receive tribute from the productive labor of Indians on the land. The workers in turn were assured of the landowner's protection and of the possession of their own huts, fields, and personal property. The encomienda, which was usually restricted to two generations of owners, was reluctantly sanctioned by the crown and often resisted by the colonial governors. Its abuse, and the consequent suffering of the subject Indians, caused the crown and the Dominican order to demand its abolition, but the conquistadors countervailed. The Laws of 1503, the Laws of Burgos of 1512, the Papal Bull of 1537, and the New Laws of 1542—the latter prompted by Bartolomé de las Casas—brought changes that helped to weaken the practice. The encomendero was required to convert the Indians to Christianity, to build a church, and to support its priest. Despite increased taxes and tributes levied upon the encomienda, the system prevailed, forcing the crown in the 18th century to issue more restrictive orders regarding its operation. In 1717 the viceroys' right to grant encomiendas was removed and the system was made nonhereditary. Suppressed outright by royal decree in 1785, it persisted in various forms until the period of independence.

HARRY BERNSTEIN, Brooklyn College

ENCULTURATION. *See* CULTURE.

ENCYCLOPEDIA [ĕn-sī-klə-pē′dē-ə], reference work that treats the various branches of learning or a specialized part thereof in a series of separate articles. The ancient encyclopedias of Marcus Terentius Varro (now lost) and Pliny the Elder exemplified the literal meaning of the original Greek word from which "encyclopedia" derives: instruction in the whole circle of arts and sciences. The same tradition was perpetuated in the first great medieval encyclopedia, the *Etymologiae* of Isidore of Seville (560?–636). The *Speculum majus* of Vincent of Beauvais (c.1190–c.1264) was the most famous medieval encyclopedia. Johann Heinrich Alsted's *Encyclopaedia septem tomis distincta* (1630) is the first work to bear the name "encyclopedia" and to apply it in the modern sense, and in other respects it was the best achievement in the field up to that time. Louis Moreri's *Grand dictionnaire historique* (1674) advanced the techniques of encyclopedia compilation further. But Moreri's numerous errors inspired Pierre Bayle, at least in part, to compile his *Dictionnaire historique et critique* (1697–1702), a milestone in European criticism and philosophy.

The 18th and 19th Centuries. The 18th century was the classic age of encyclopedias. The first English alphabetical encyclopedia, John Harris' *Lexicon technicum* (1704), was strong in the sciences. Ephraim Chambers' *Cyclopaedia* (1728) superseded that of Harris. Of several German encyclopedias, the largest and best was Johann Heinrich Zedler's *Grosses vollständiges Universal-Lexikon* (64 vols., 1732–50; repr., 1961). The most famous encyclopedia of all time is the great French *Encyclopédie* (1751–77). The editor, Denis Diderot, enlisted a glittering corps of contributors including Voltaire, Rousseau, Montesquieu, Buffon, Turgot, and D'Alembert. The *Encyclopédie* incorporates the basic philosophy of 18th-century French rationalism: devotion to scientific truth, hatred of superstition, and skepticism toward religion of all varieties. Although it was plagued by absurd censorship, the *Encyclopédie* nevertheless became a desk set for intellectuals of the age and went through many editions and translations.

The *Encyclopaedia Britannica* is another product of the 18th century. The first edition, "by a society of gentlemen in Scotland," appeared in Edinburgh in three volumes in 1771. It won immediate acceptance in the English-speaking world and went through two substantially enlarged editions in the 18th century. In the various editions of the 19th century some of the great names of the British intelligentsia signed *Britannica* articles: Sir Walter Scott, Sir Humphry Davy, David Ricardo, Thomas Malthus, Thomas De Quincey. By the time of the publication of the ninth edition (1875–89), the *Britannica* stood clearly in the forefront of encyclopedic scholarship and held this position

through World War I. The still widely used 11th edition (1910–11) was edited at Cambridge University, but the current revisions of the *Britannica* are edited and published in the United States.

On the Continent Brockhaus' *Konversations-Lexikon* (1796–1808) occupied a comparably prestigious position through the 19th century. The various editions (including those of the 1950's) have been copied, imitated, and even plagiarized throughout the world. In France, Pierre Larousse's *Le grand dictionnaire universal du xixᵉ siècle* (1866–76) was in the Brockhaus tradition and has been succeeded by progressively better editions, the latest in the 1960's. The Brockhaus-Larousse style of short, compact articles rather than monographic studies is the prevalent one among European encyclopedias.

The 20th Century. In the 20th century nationalism, sectarianism, political trends, and new educational theory have been factors in the production of hundreds of encyclopedias. Virtually every country either has its own national encyclopedia or has plans for one. The publishing firm of Herder in Freiburg in Breisgau, Germany, has a general encyclopedia with a Roman Catholic orientation that is a successful rival to the current Brockhaus. The remarkable *Bolshaya Sovetskaya Entsiklopedia* (2d. ed. 1949–58), sometimes ludicrously censored, reflects socialist ideology and has a powerful influence in Communist countries. On the other hand, the monumental new Yugoslav encyclopedia, in several different subject series supplementing the general one, is a completely independent work. The 80-volume *Enciclopedia universal ilustrada Europeo-Americana* (1905–33; also called "Espasa" after its publisher) and the *Enciclopedia italiana di scienza, lettere ed arti*, issued in the 1930's, enjoy enviable reputations for scholarship based on comprehensive monographic articles. A phenomenon of the 20th century has been the production of encyclopedias especially adapted for children and by experts in the children's field. *The Book of Knowledge*, *World Book Encyclopedia*, *Compton's Pictured Encyclopedia*, and *Britannica Junior* are examples.

The *Encyclopaedia Britannica* no longer holds the undisputed leadership it enjoyed in the English-speaking world through the 11th edition. In England the firm of William and Robert Chambers of Edinburgh published *Chambers's Encyclopaedia* (1859–68), and it has now superseded the *Britannica* as Britain's domestic encylopedia. The *New International Encyclopaedia*, a lineal descendant of the 1878–80 edition of Chambers's, went through two editions (2d, 1930) and earned a reputation for readability and authority by having a separate editorial staff of professional writers to revise the work of scholarly contributors. It is now out of print and out of date. The *Encyclopedia Americana* has won recognition as one of the two major English-language encyclopedias revised currently.

Guides for Evaluation. Since the 17th century the business of publishing and selling encyclopedias has been plagued by interlopers who have little respect for solid scholarship or even business ethics. Comparative studies of the relative merits of encyclopedias show that selection should be based on careful analysis of authority, scope, arrangement, format, up-to-dateness, and suitability for a specific reader or group of readers.

In ancient through early modern times the authority of an encyclopedia was simply the reputation of its individual compiler. Since the days of Diderot, encyclopedia editors have tried to select recognized authorities to write specific articles. Anyone who contemplates the purchase of an encyclopedia today should inspect the names on the editorial board and the list of contributors and their subjects.

Until editorial boards were set up in the 19th century, encyclopedias tended to be uneven and often prejudiced. Today an encyclopedia must show a proper balance among the various fields of learning; and the rapidly changing nature of modern scholarship demands that it be up-to-date. Both substantive content and bibliographies must reflect adequacy of scope.

Ancient and medieval encyclopedias were in a classified arrangement. The Franciscan Vincenzo Coronelli compiled the first great alphabetically arranged encyclopedia, *Biblioteca universale sacro-profana* (1701–6, A to Caque), and since then the great majority of general encyclopedias have been alphabetical. However, the alphabetical arrangement in no sense eliminates the need for an index, since 20 to 100 times as many index-words as entry-words are found in modern encyclopedias. The reader who seeks information only under an entry-word deprives himself of access to the great bulk of data in an encyclopedia.

Physical format of a heavily used reference work such as an encyclopedia should be a major concern of prospective purchasers. Binding, paper, typography, quality of illustrations and maps, and clarity of titles printed on the individual volumes are factors of considerable importance in selecting an encyclopedia. The physical durability of the *Encyclopédie*, many sets of which are in their original bindings, is a tribute to 18th-century book production.

Finally, a reader or a library must be sure that the encyclopedia selected is suitable for personal or institutional purposes. Not every home needs a monumental work of the size and scope of the *Americana* or the *Britannica*. Although style must always be clear and incisive, it may be pointed either at scholars or at nonacademic laymen. Illustrations, maps, and bibliographies should reflect the reader's intellectual level. The larger university and public libraries generally have samples of all types of encyclopedias; and the prospective purchaser of an encyclopedia is well advised to go to a large library, inspect the various encyclopedias, and seek advice from reference librarians with years of experience in dealing with encyclopedias.

Consult Compton, F. E., *Subscription Books* (1939); U.S. Federal Trade Commission, *Trade Practice Rules for the Subscription and Mail Order Book Publishing Industry, as Promulgated September 3, 1940* (1940); Shores, Louis, *Basic Reference Sources* (1954).

LAWRENCE S. THOMPSON, University of Kentucky

ENDECOTT [ĕn'də-kət], **JOHN** (c.1589–1665), military leader and Governor of the Massachusetts Bay Colony. To prepare the way for the major body of Puritans headed by John Winthrop, Endecott landed at Salem on Sept. 6, 1628. He proceeded to suppress independent religious thinking, set up a church organization on the lines of the Plymouth Colony, and deported two men to England for nonconformity. He organized military expeditions against the Indians. After he turned over command to Winthrop in 1630, Endecott continued a powerful figure, serving as Governor in 1644, 1649, 1651–53, and 1655–64.

ENDERS [ĕn'dərz], **JOHN FRANKLIN** (1897–   ), American bacteriologist and immunologist. After receiving his Ph.D. from Harvard University he remained there to teach, becoming a full professor at the Children's Hospital, Harvard Medical School, in 1956. In 1954, together with Thomas Weller and Frederick Robbins, he was awarded the Nobel Prize for medicine and physiology for his work on the cultivation of the poliomyelitis virus.

ENDICOTT, industrial village of south-central New York, on the Susquehanna River. Endicott, Johnson City, and Binghamton comprise the Triple Cities. Shoe manufacture, begun in 1901, heads the list of industries here. Settled, c.1795; inc., 1906; pop. (1950) 20,050; (1960) 18,775.

ENDIVE [ĕn'dīv], annual or biennial herb, *Cichorum endiva*, in the composite family, native to India but now grown in many of the world's warmer regions as a salad plant. Endive grows well in ordinary garden soil. Seeds are sown in early summer in rows 1 ft. apart. After mature leaves appear the plants are covered with pots, boards, or earth to whiten, or blanch, them. Blanching requires about three weeks, and serves the additional purpose of removing the bitter flavor from the endive heads. *See also* BLANCHING.

ENDOCRINE [ĕn'dō-krĭn] **GLANDS,** ductless glands which pour their secretions directly into the blood stream. The first scientific study of the endocrine glands was made by Berthold in 1849 when he observed that the henlike changes in body build and behavior which occurred in castrated cocks could be reversed by transplanting healthy testes into the operated animal. This effect resulted from the secretion of hormones from the transplanted tissues into the blood stream of the cock.

The endocrine system includes the pituitary gland, the thyroid, the adrenals, the ovaries, the testes, the parathyroids, the pancreas, and, in pregnancy, the placenta (the afterbirth). While the structural features of these glands are different, they are all alike in having a large number of secretory cells, a well-developed blood supply, and no ducts.

The endocrine secretions, the hormones, are often aptly described as "chemical messengers," since by their action they enable one part of the body to regulate the activity of another part. Hormones help control the pace of body activity, the rate of growth, the reproductive cycles, and the physical characteristics which distinguish men from women. The hormones are not usually stored to any great extent in the glands or the tissues and they must consequently be continuously produced. The exact mechanism of their action is not known, but it has been established that hormones alter the rate of metabolic reactions rather than initiate them. Some hormones are believed to affect enzyme reactions, while others are thought to act upon the surface of the cell, or combine with substances within the cell. Hormones are generally effective in minute

THE HORMONES

CHEMICAL ACTION AT A DISTANCE

Long-distance communication in the body can be achieved in two ways: (1) through the nervous system and (2) by chemical secretions carried in the blood. The second method is effected through hormones secreted by the endocrine glands.

PITUITARY GLAND

ANTERIOR PITUITARY HORMONES

(1) GROWTH HORMONE (STH) stimulates general growth.

(2) THYROID-STIMULATING HORMONE (TSH) stimulates the thyroid gland.

(3) ADRENOCORTICOTROPIC HORMONE (ACTH) stimulates the outer layer (cortex) of the adrenal gland.

(4) FOLLICLE-STIMULATING HORMONE (FSH) induces ripening of ovarian follicles (in females) and sperm production (in males).

(5) LUTEINIZING HORMONE (LH) stimulates ovulation (in females) and gonads (in males).

(6) PROLACTIN, OR LUTEOTROPHIC HORMONE (LTH), stimulates lactation.

POSTERIOR PITUITARY HORMONES

OXYTOCIN stimulates contractions of smooth muscle of uterus and breast.

ANTIDIURETIC HORMONE (ADH) regulates volume of urine.

ADRENALS

ADRENAL HORMONES

OUTER LAYER (cortex)

GLUCOCORTICOIDS promote conversion of protein into sugar, aid in transport of fat from storage sites to liver, and increase resistance to stress. MINERALOCORTICOIDS act on kidneys to regulate mineral composition of body fluids, increase sodium concentration, and decrease potassium concentration of body fluids. The action of the ANDROGENIC CORTICOIDS is similar to that of male sex hormones.

INNER LAYER (medulla)

ADRENALIN stimulates heart beat, inhibits gastrointestinal activity, promotes release of sugar from liver into blood, and increases blood flow to skeletal muscles. NORADRENALINE acts to constrict blood vessels throughout the body.

ADRENAL GLANDS — KIDNEYS

THYROID GLAND

THYROID HORMONES regulate metabolism and oxygen consumption of body cells and contribute to growth and development.

PARATHYROID GLANDS

PARATHORMONE regulates calcium concentration of blood.

PANCREAS

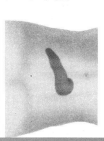

PANCREATIC HORMONES

The endocrine cells of the pancreas are contained in groups known as the Islets of Langerhans. The α cells secrete the hormone glucagon, which raises blood sugar. The β cells secrete the hormone insulin, which lowers blood sugar.

GONADS

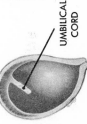

OVARY

OVARIAN HORMONES

ESTROGENS: important in regulation of menstrual cycle, stimulate uterus, and maintain female physical characteristics.

RELAXIN relaxes pelvic ligaments during pregnancy.

TESTICULAR HORMONES

ANDROGENS stimulate growth of muscle, kidneys, bone, and other tissues and influence sexual behavior.

PLACENTA

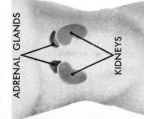

UMBILICAL CORD

During pregnancy the placenta (the afterbirth) links the circulation of the mother and child. The placenta secretes the hormone progesterone, which maintains pregnancy and prevents eggs from ripening in the ovary. Progesterone is also produced by the corpus luteum of the ovary during the normal menstrual cycle.

SOME IMPORTANT ACTIVITIES REGULATED BY HORMONES

ENERGY PRODUCTION

LIVER

BLOOD STREAM

PROTEIN → SUGAR

OXYGEN

SUGAR

CELLS

Thyroid hormone promotes utilization of oxygen by cells.

Insulin enables the cells of the body to burn sugar as fuel.

Adrenal corticosteroids promote conversion of proteins to sugar in the liver.

BODY CHEMISTRY

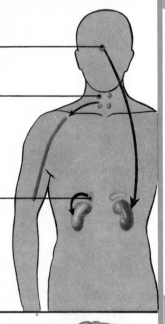

Antidiuretic hormone of the pituitary gland prevents an excessive loss of water from the body in urine.

Parathyroid hormone regulates calcium concentration of blood.

Adrenal mineralocorticoids prevent an excessive loss of sodium from the body in urine.

GROWTH

ANTERIOR PITUITARY HORMONES

INSULIN

THYROID HORMONE

ANDROGENS

MENSTRUATION

(1) Follicle-stimulating hormone (FSH) from pituitary stimulates development of egg-containing follicle in ovary.

(2) Egg ruptures from the follicle and leaves the ovary. The follicle remains behind to become the "yellow body," or corpus luteum. This occurs under the influence of the luteinizing hormone (LH) of the pituitary gland.

(3) Progesterone from the corpus luteum inhibits secretion of LH and FSH from the pituitary gland.

(4) Estrogen and progesterone from the ovary prime the lining of the uterus for the implantation of the egg. If the egg is not fertilized, the built-up uterine lining is discarded with the menstrual flow.

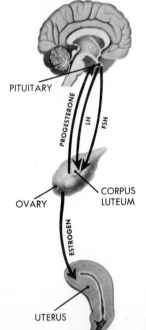

PITUITARY

PROGESTERONE

LH

FSH

OVARY

CORPUS LUTEUM

ESTROGEN

UTERUS

EMERGENCY RESPONSE TO STRESS

When the organism is threatened, the adrenal hormones help the body mobilize its resources for vigorous action. Stimulation from the brain reaches the adrenal glands (1) through direct nerve pathways to the adrenal medulla and (2) through pituitary hormones acting on the adrenal cortex.

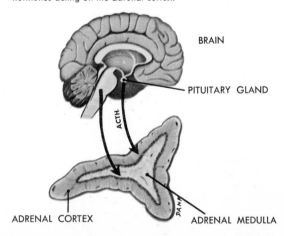

BRAIN

PITUITARY GLAND

ACTH

ADRENAL CORTEX

ADRENAL MEDULLA

Adrenal cortical hormones stimulate release of sugar from the liver and promote muscular efficiency.

Adrenalin and noradrenaline raise the blood pressure, stimulate heart action, and increase the blood flow to the skeletal muscles.

amounts. Comparatively small fluctuations in the supply of these substances can spell the difference between a normal individual and a dwarfed, deformed, or mentally retarded person.

The Regulation of Endocrine Activity

The control of endocrine output is crucial for the normal functioning of the body. The activity of the endocrine glands is governed by the direct action of the nervous system or by the concentration of hormones and certain other substances in the blood stream.

The key region in the central nervous system involved in the control of endocrine function is the hypothalamus, a structure located at the base of the brain. Nerve pathways connect the hypothalamus with the posterior pituitary and the inner part, or medulla, of the adrenal glands. The hypothalamus also controls the activity of the anterior pituitary. This latter control is particularly important since the anterior pituitary is an influential gland, which secretes hormones which in turn stimulate the activity of the ovary, testis, thyroid, and adrenal cortex. Through its control of the anterior pituitary, the hypothalamus assumes the position of the power behind the throne in endocrine affairs. Some of the endocrine glands, such as the parathyroids and the pancreas, do not seem to be influenced by the central nervous system or by anterior pituitary secretions. Their secretions are regulated instead by the blood concentration of calcium and glucose respectively.

The Pituitary or Master Gland. The pituitary gland is a small oval structure which is attached to the base of the brain by a slender stalk. It consists of two lobes: the anterior, or adenohypophysis, and the posterior, or neurohypophysis. This gland is aptly described as the master gland of the endocrine system because of the great number of functions regulated by its hormones. In addition to secreting hormones which stimulate the thyroid, adrenals, and other endocrine glands, the pituitary releases hormones which control growth, regulate the secretion of milk, and stimulate contractions of the uterus.

The rate of pituitary secretion is controlled by what has been called a feedback mechanism. A pituitary hormone, for example, stimulates the thyroid gland to secrete thyroid hormone into the blood stream. The thyroid hormone in turn inhibits the secretion of the thyroid-stimulating hormone by the pituitary. As the blood concentration of the thyroid hormone decreases, pituitary secretion increases, and so on. Evidence suggests that this feedback regulation is effected through the hypothalamus rather than directly on the pituitary itself.

The Adrenal Glands. These glands are a pair of pyramidal structures seated on the upper pole of each kidney. They are made up of two distinct parts, an inner medulla and an outer cortex. The medulla is linked by nerve fibers to the central nervous system. The medulla secretes the hormone epinephrine (adrenalin) which shunts blood from the skin to the muscles, stimulates heart action, and induces the release of sugar into the blood, thereby preparing the body for intense physical exertion. The adrenal cortex is a vital structure which exerts an important influence upon the energy-producing activities of the body, the mineral composition of the body fluid, and the sexual characteristics which distinguish men and women.

The Thyroid Gland. The thyroid gland is an H-shaped gland which straddles the trachea, or windpipe. The thyroid hormone, thyroxine, controls the pace at which various organs burn oxygen and produce energy.

The Sex Glands. The gonads, or sex glands (testis and ovary), secrete hormones which regulate reproductive functions. The chief hormone of the testis, testosterone, brings about the development of the sexual characteristics of the male, in addition to exerting important effects on body activity. The ovary secretes hormones which regulate a variety of functions in the female reproductive tract and produce the distinctive female body characteristics.

The Placenta—The Master Gland of Pregnancy. The placenta, the disclike structure through which food substances pass from the blood of the mother to the circulation of the fetus, is thought to be the major endocrine gland of pregnancy. The placenta secretes hormones which are indispensable for the maintenance of pregnancy.

The Parathyroid Glands. The parathyroid glands are pairs of small oval structures situated closely behind the thyroid. The parathyroid secretion regulates the calcium balance in the skeleton and the body fluids. A decrease in the blood calcium concentration stimulates the secretion of parathyroid hormone.

The Pancreas. The pancreas is a dual-nature gland, in that some of its secretions pass through ducts into the small intestine, while others enter the blood stream directly. The endocrine cells of the pancreas are contained in groups of cells called the Islets of Langerhans. Two different types of cells are present in the islets: α cells which probably secrete glucagon and β cells which are the source of insulin. These substances apparently work in opposite directions: Glucagon raises the blood sugar while insulin lowers it.

The Endocrine Diseases

An imbalance of hormone supply usually leads to disease. The variety of hormones and their effects is paralleled by the diversity of endocrine diseases.

The Pituitary: *Overactivity.* An excess of growth hormone during childhood may produce giants nine ft. tall. If the hormone is in oversupply after adolescence, acromegaly results, an enlargement of the hands, feet, jaw, and other body parts. An overproduction of the hormones which stimulate the outer layer (the cortex) of the adrenal glands causes Cushing's disease, which involves a distinctive type of obesity, a round face, high blood pressure, and altered sexual characteristics.

Underactivity. An undersupply of the growth hormone results in dwarfism. Pituitary dwarfs are usually well-proportioned and are not mentally retarded.

The Adrenals: *Overactivity.* Excessive secretion of male sex hormones from the cortex causes deepening of the voice and growth of a beard in women and precocious sexual maturity in boys.

Underactivity. A wasting away of the adrenal cortex causes Addison's disease, characterized by muscular weakness, loss of weight, low blood pressure, and excess pigmentation of various parts of the body.

The Thyroid: *Overactivity,* or hyperthyroidism, is marked by excessive energy, nervousness, tremors, loss of weight, rapid heart beat, and occasionally, protruding eyeballs.

Underactivity in the prenatal period, or in infancy causes cretinism, a disorder marked by stunted growth, retarded mentality, and underdevelopment of the sexual organs and the sexual characteristics. In adults undersupply of the thyroid hormone results in myxedema, characterized by puffiness of the face, dry skin and hair, diminished vigor, and slow pulse.

Goiter is a swelling of the thyroid gland which may be accompanied by either an excess of or underproduction of thyroid hormone. A common form of goiter results from a dietary deficiency of iodine, the essential constituent of the thyroid hormone. Such goiters are seen in regions where the iodine content of the water or soil is low, as in mountain villages in the Alps and the Himalayas, and in certain parts of North America near the Great Lakes. In these regions the disease is controlled by adding small quantities of iodine to the diet.

Pancreas. Diabetes, a major endocrine disease, results from inadequate supply of the pancreatic hormone—insulin. Diabetes is characterized by high blood sugar, excessive urination, and sugar in the urine. The ability of the body to burn starchy foods as a fuel is seriously impaired. The disease can be controlled, but not cured, by administering insulin.

Other endocrine diseases include disorders of the parathyroid and the sex glands. The endocrine disorders are usually treated either by supplying the missing hormone (in the case of underproduction) or by surgically removing some glandular tissue (in the case of overproduction). Advances in medical science have nowhere been more impressive or dramatic than in the field of endocrine disorders, where the isolation and commercial preparation of hormones have made possible the treatment of serious illnesses which had previously defied all treatment.

ARPAD CSAPO, M.D.

See also ADDISON'S DISEASE; ADRENAL GLANDS; DIABETES MELLITUS; GOITER; MYXEDEMA.

ENDOTHERMIC [ĕn-dō-thûr′mĭk] **and EXOTHERMIC** [ĕk-sō-thûr′mĭk] **REACTION,** in chemistry, refers to heat-absorbing and heat-liberating reactions, respectively. All reactions involve a change in the energy content of the reacting atoms. If their total energy before the reaction is greater than their total energy after, then they have liberated some energy, usually in the form of heat. An exothermic reaction has occurred. If the liberated heat is sufficiently high, an exothermic reaction may produce an explosion. The most familiar exothermic process is the burning of fuels. Once begun, it proceeds without further assistance.

In an endothermic reaction the total energy content of the products is greater than that of the reactants, and this difference must be supplied from the outside, usually in the form of heat. If the supply of heat is shut off, the reaction stops. The most important endothermic reaction is the synthesis of carbohydrates, using the energy of the sun. The total heat absorbed or developed in a reaction is the heat of reaction and is the same whatever course the reaction takes.

LOUIS VACZEK, The New School for Social Research

ENDYMION [ĕn-dĭm′ē-ən], in Greek mythology, a beautiful young shepherd. While asleep on Mt. Latmos, he was seen by the Moon, who fell in love with him and gave him eternal youth, but with it eternal sleep. The legend was used by John Lyly in his play *Endymion*, and by Keats in his famous poem of that name.

ENEMA [ĕn′ə-mə], the introduction of fluid into the rectum for the purpose of cleansing the bowel or administering sedatives, anesthetics, or other medications. Drugs may be given with retention enemas: The fluid is injected slowly and permitted to remain for several hours. Enemas of barium salts are used for X-ray examination of the gastrointestinal tract. Since barium is opaque to X rays the barium-filled intestines appear sharply outlined on the X-ray photograph. Ice-water enemas have been used to reduce fever rapidly. According to Egyptian legend, the enema was invented by the sacred bird Ibis, which injected water into its bowel by means of its beak.

ENEMY OF THE PEOPLE, AN, play published in 1882 by Norwegian dramatist Henrik Ibsen. His case for the sincere nonconformist is embodied in the story of a courageous doctor who championed a highly unpopular cause against the wishes of a cowardly and hypocritical "compact majority."

ENERGY, a basic concept in physics. It represents a measurement of the capacity to perform work. Energy may exist in different forms and can be changed from one form to another. It can neither be created nor destroyed. However, it is possible to allow it to be dissipated and become useless.

Motion. The simplest form of energy is that which a moving body possesses by reason of its motion. This energy is equal to the amount of work needed to set it moving with its particular speed, commencing from rest. By bringing the body again to rest, the energy can be recovered in the same or in another form. This can be illustrated by the energy of flowing water. In hydroelectric power stations, water is held at a high level behind a dam. If the water were allowed to overflow the dam, it would fall with a speed determined by the height of the fall. Actually, however, the water is constrained to flow down through pipes until it reaches the powerhouse below the dam. Here the flowing water enters a set of turbines and causes the blades to turn and in doing so, the water loses much of its speed of movement. With the turbines are coupled the dynamos which generate electric current. As the turbines rotate, the dynamos rotate with them. A great part of the energy which goes into the powerhouse as the energy of flowing water is thus transformed into the energy of the electric current produced by the dynamos.

A body can possess energy in two forms: potential energy, due to the position of the body; and kinetic energy, due to the motion of the body. When a heavy ball, for example, suspended by a wire from a fixed point, is pulled aside and released, it swings to and fro along the arc of a circle. Energy, as previously stated, is the ability to do work. When the ball is at one end of the arc it is momentarily at rest and possesses potential energy; that is, because of its position, it can, if released, do work. When

FORMS OF ENERGY

ENERGY IS CLASSIFIED AS MECHANICAL, ELECTRIC, CHEMICAL, RADIANT, AND ATOMIC, OR NUCLEAR. EACH FORM MAY BE CHANGED INTO ANY OF THE OTHERS.

CHEMICAL ENERGY

When wood burns, the chemical process of oxidation liberates the light and heat energy that was absorbed from the sun by the growing tree.

ATOMIC ENERGY

Physical changes in the central part, or nucleus, of an atom result in the transformation of minute quantities of matter into comparatively enormous amounts of energy. Such changes are believed to be the source of the sun's energy.

Folsom Dam and Powerplant

Energy in any form is either potential (stored and ready to do work) or kinetic (active). The water in the reservoir behind the dam has potential energy. This is transformed into kinetic energy as the water plunges down the spillway.

the ball is released it gains momentum and because it is in motion it does work against gravity and against the atmosphere. This kinetic energy can be used to drive another mechanism, as in the pendulum of a clock.

Energy may take the form of wave motion traveling through space, as for example, the sound waves emitted by a powerful siren which can be heard at a great distance. In the vibrations of the air which we perceive as sound, the energy alternates between two forms: the work needed to compress or dilate the air, and that of actual movement of the air. These alternations in the state of the air succeed one another at various points along the path of the sound. They enable the sound waves to move forward from place to place, carrying energy with them.

Heat. Another familiar form of energy is heat. Heat represents the energy of movement of the molecules of matter. This energy becomes greater when the material is heated and its temperature rises. Heat can be perceived and a rise of temperature felt by the sense of touch. That heat is a form of energy that is measurable is evident also from the operation of an electric kettle. This utensil enables us to convert specifiable quantities of electric energy into heat.

Heat can be produced directly by doing mechanical

work, as for example, by hammering a piece of lead or by vigorously stirring a sticky liquid in an enclosed vessel. Thus, heat energy has its equivalent in mechanical work. The reverse process of converting heat into mechanical work is accomplished by various types of engines, such as steam engines, diesel engines, and gasoline engines.

Light. Light also is a form of energy. Formidable quantities of energy reach the earth as a continuous unending stream of rays from the sun. The energy of the sun's rays is indeed the source of various other forms of energy that make life possible on earth.

When the sun's rays fall on the green leaves of plants, the energy of the light is absorbed by the coloring matter in the leaves. The absorbed energy is utilized for effecting chemical changes. Carbon dioxide and water vapor are taken up from the air and converted into cellulose, starch, sugar, and other plant products that serve as food for man or animal. Coal consists of the remains of plant products produced in the same manner by the energy of the sun's rays in bygone days. The energy of the winds is also derived from the energy of the sun's rays falling on and heating the surface of the earth; and it is the sun that warms the sea and evaporates its water, which is carried overland

433

as vapor by the winds, forms clouds, and finally falls on the earth as rain or snow.

Chemical Changes. When plant material is burned in air, the process by which the energy of the sun's rays built up these products in the living plant is reversed. The energy is returned as heat, while the carbon dioxide and water are reformed. This illustrates the part played by energy in chemical changes. Many of the substances found in nature are compounds of different elements. If these elements combine freely with each other, they liberate a considerable energy in the process. For example, when oxygen and hydrogen combine to form water, large quantities of energy are released as heat. The oxygen and the hydrogen thus combined to form water can only be separated from each other by supplying the same quantity of energy. A convenient way of doing this is by the use of electric energy, or electrolysis. An electric current passed through water decomposes the water into oxygen and hydrogen. A similar process is used in industry. The metal aluminum, for example, is prepared from its oxide by a process that requires large quantities of electric energy.

Mass. Energy is directly associated with matter. The energy radiated by the sun results from the continuous conversion of part of the sun's mass into energy. Einstein's famous equation, $E = mc^2$, demonstrates that energy is equal to the product of mass and the square of the velocity of light.

Sir C. V. Raman, Nobel Prize for Physics

See also Atomic Energy; Heat; Light; Mass-Energy, Conservation of.

ENERGY, CONSERVATION OF, basic law in physics which states that energy cannot be created or destroyed, but only transformed from one kind to another. For example, the electric energy flowing through a circuit is converted into light and heat in a light bulb.

Energy is the capacity to do work, which is defined as the product of force and displacement. It is called kinetic if it is due to motion, and potential, if due to position. More accurately, energy is potential only if no work is done against dissipative forces. Forces are of two kinds: conservative and dissipative. If work done is completely recoverable when the displacement is reversed, the force is conservative and is not dependent upon motion but only on the position of the body it acts upon. Friction, however, is dissipative in that reversing the direction of the displacement does not result in recovery of work, but rather in the expenditure of additional energy, which is converted into heat.

In a mechanical conservative system the sum of the kinetic and potential energy is constant. Kinetic energy can be gained only at the expense of potential energy and vice-versa. If, however, the system includes dissipative forces such as friction, heat energy must be included.

Clarence E. Bennett, University of Maine

ENERGY LEVEL, in atomic physics, a physical state of constant energy, characterized by stability for a reasonable time. The presence of energy levels is an essential characteristic of quantized systems, where a change in state between two levels gives rise to a quantum of the appropriate type. Energy levels occur both in nuclei and in the orbital electrons of atoms. The lowest state is generally called the ground state; higher ones, excited states.

ENESCO [ĕ-nĕs'kō], **GEORGES** (1881–1955), Rumanian composer, conductor, and violinist. As a child he studied violin with a gypsy and at seven entered the Vienna Conservatory. Later he studied in Paris, where in 1898 his Opus 1, *Poème Roumain*, was performed. He toured extensively as a violin virtuoso and for several years was court violinist to the Queen of Rumania. He appeared often in America and taught at the Mannes Music School in New York in 1946–47. At his farewell concert in 1950 he appeared as violinist in the Bach double concerto with his pupil, Yehudi Menuhin, played the piano in his violin sonata, and conducted the orchestra in his *Rumanian Rhapsody*. After his death, the Rumanian government renamed his native village Enescu.

Enesco was loved for his direct, sincere, and magnanimous personality. His musical interests were broad, but conservative. As a conductor he was more concerned with the large line than the details. He composed more than 35 works, many based on Rumanian folk melodies. His compositions included an opera, three symphonies, a violin concerto, chamber works, and vocal music.

Benjamin Patterson, Music Division, New York Public Library

ENFIELD, borough of Greater London, England, on the northern margin of the metropolitan area, about 12 mi. from the City of London. When Greater London was enlarged and reorganized in 1963, Enfield was taken from the county of Middlesex and joined to the boroughs of Southgate and Edmonton, the whole called Enfield. It extends from the Lea River, a tributary of the Thames, west to the low plateau that borders London on the north.

Enfield began as a market town on a Roman road, later called Ermine Street. Much of western Enfield was once the protected royal forest of Enfield Chase. Late in the 18th century the area lost its privileged status and began to develop as a residential area for London. Despite expansion in the late 19th and 20th centuries, a number of open spaces, notably Trent Park, have been preserved. Only in eastern Enfield has industry developed to any extent. Here a number of factories line the Lea valley. Among them are the government-owned works, founded in the early 1800's, that produce the world-famous Lee-Enfield rifles and other small arms. Pop., 267,660.

Norman J. G. Pounds, Indiana University

ENFIELD, town of northern Connecticut, on the east bank of the Connecticut River. Rugs and carpets, boats, greeting cards, wax paper, and tools and gauges are manufactured here. Tobacco-growing areas are being replaced by residential sites. The Shakers settled Enfield to escape religious persecution. Jonathan Edwards preached here, starting a religious revival throughout the colonies. Inc. by Massachusetts, 1683; annexed to Connecticut, 1749; pop. (1950) 15,464; (1960) 31,464.

ENGADINE [ĕng'gə-dēn], portion of the Upper Inn Valley in Switzerland, in the eastern part of Graubünden Canton.

An elevation of about 6,000 ft. and lakes, forests, glaciers, and mountain scenery have made it world famous as a resort center. St. Moritz, Zernez, Pontresina, and Schuls are the principal settlements. The Swiss National Park (area, 54 sq. mi.) is in the northeast.

EN-GEDI [ĕn-gē'dī], settlement in ancient Palestine midway along the western shore of the Dead Sea, where a copious spring creates an oasis. David took refuge there when he was pursued by Saul (I Sam. 23:29). Caves at En-gedi have in modern times yielded documents, loot, and bodies of the followers of Bar-Kokhba's revolt against Rome (132–35 A.D.).

ENGELS [ĕng'əlz], **FRIEDRICH** (1820–95), German revolutionary and socialist theoretician, best known for his long collaboration with Karl Marx, with whom he wrote the *Communist Manifesto* (1848). Born in Barmen, Prussia, Engels was the son of a textile manufacturer. In 1842 he went to England to work in a firm with which his father was associated. Involved in the struggles of the working class to raise their standard of living, and with the revolutionary movements which shook Europe in the 1840's, he was active as an agitator and organizer in Belgium, France, and Germany. His collaboration with Marx began in 1844, and in the following year Engels published his own *Condition of the Working Class in England*. A few years later he helped to found the Communist League, which issued the famous manifesto. After the failure of the revolutions of 1848 Engels returned to England, where he became a successful businessman. From this time his relationship with Marx was chiefly one of intellectual companionship, though he took part in establishing the International Workingmen's Association (1864), known as the First International. Engels assisted Marx in the collection of data for *Capital* (Vol. I, 1867) and also supported him financially. His own revolutionary thinking was embodied in such works as *Landmarks of Scientific Socialism* (1878) and *The Origin of the Family* (1884). After Marx's death in 1883, Engels was looked upon as the intellectual leader of European radical socialism and helped to found the Second International (1889). He edited the later volumes of *Capital*, which Marx had left unfinished. In general, Engels was a materialist who believed that all political and social institutions are conditioned by economic facts, that ways of life change with changing methods of production and distribution, and that the working class would eventually overthrow capitalism and establish a communist society.

STUART GERRY BROWN, Syracuse University
See also COMMUNISM; MARX, KARL.

ENGELS [ĕng'əls], city of the Soviet Union, in the Saratov Oblast of the R.S.F.S.R. It is located on the east bank of the Volga River opposite Saratov. Its most important industries are the production of transportation machinery and the manufacture of cotton cloth in an integrated textile combine. Other industries include the production of ceramics, glue, paint, and forest products, and meat processing and packing. Known as Pokrovsk until 1931, it was the capital of the former German Volga A.S.S.R. That political unit was abolished in 1941 when the German population was accused of disloyalty and deported to Siberia. Pop., 90,000.

ENGINE, term applied to machinery in which thermal energy, imparted to a working fluid, is converted into useful mechanical work. There are several kinds of engines, and as more becomes known about energy possibilities, newer fueling methods are found. The fission of nuclear fuel (uranium and plutonium) and the trapping of solar energy have been applied to produce mechanical work. The most conventional engines, however, rely on the combustion of the fossil fuels, such as coal, oil, or gas, obtained from the earth. Since there are so many different engines, the working fluid may be one of many: steam and water, air and combustion gases, or other gases such as helium. In most cases this working fluid is compressed. Thermal energy then causes it to expand and drive a piston or turbine blades or escape at high velocity through a nozzle, thus doing mechanical work.

History

The first-known engine, built by Hero of Alexandria more than 2,000 years ago, consisted of a fire-heated boiler for converting water into steam. The steam, guided into a hollow sphere through two tubes, escaped into the atmosphere and the resulting jets caused the sphere to rotate. Hero's engine was regarded as a toy and nothing important came of it until the idea of steam power was resurrected for the early steam engines in the 18th century. After several attempts by others at such engines, James Watt (1736–1819) devised the most successful one by feeding steam from a boiler into a cylinder through a sliding valve. The high pressure of the steam moved a piston and its reciprocating motion was converted into rotary motion by a connection to a rod and crankshaft. There followed the first internal-combustion engines in which thermal energy was produced inside the confines of the engine. Nikolaus Otto, of Germany, built the first successful one. The mixture of gasoline and air that it drew into the cylinder was compressed by a piston then burned; the resulting high pressure forced the piston into motion. Another famous internal-combustion engine was developed by Rudolf Diesel (1858–1913) and patented in 1892. This engine inducted air only into the cylinder and compressed it. Fuel was then injected under high pressure where it ignited in the hot air. The first gas turbine engine, built by Stolze in 1872, came almost a century after the first one had been designed, by an Englishman, John Barber, in 1791. Barber described, in a patent, an engine that used a compressor to force air into a combustion chamber where it mixed with gas and ignited. The resulting combustion gases turned a turbine wheel. In 1884 Sir Charles Parsons (1854–1931) of England obtained a patent for the first steam turbine.

Modern Engines

The engines used today in automobiles, ships, and industry can be broadly classified into two categories: internal-combustion and external-combustion. The internal-combustion engine, as mentioned above, is one in which the heat release, usually due to the combustion of gas or oil in air, occurs internally, within the confines of

SINGLE-ACTING RECIPROCATING ENGINE

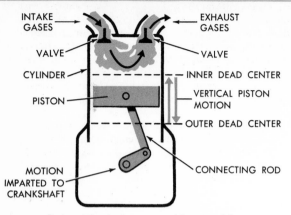

Reciprocating engines are used in automobiles.

STEAM TURBINE

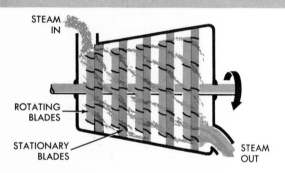

Freight locomotives often are powered by large steam turbines.

GAS TURBINE DRIVING A PROPELLER

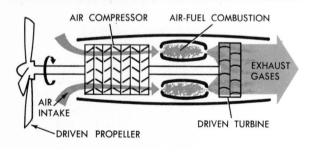

Since the gas turbine burns a mixture of compressed air and light-weight fuel, it is well suited for use in aircraft.

LIQUID FUEL ROCKET

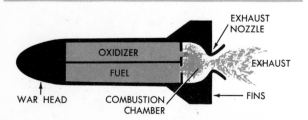

The oxidizer takes the place of oxygen from air in the combustion chamber, so the rocket can travel beyond the earth's atmosphere.

the engine. Gasoline, diesel, and gas-turbine engines belong to this category. An external combustion engine is one in which combustion occurs outside the engine, for example, in a boiler. The high-temperature, high-pressure steam is ducted to the engine which may be either a reciprocating steam engine or rotary steam turbine. Such engines are bulky, complicated, and heavy, but efficient, and have been widely used in the stationary power plant field.

Engines may also be classified as reciprocating, rotary, or reaction, each of these terms describing the method by which the engine imparts its mechanical work.

Reciprocating. Reciprocating engines may have one or more cylinder-piston arrangements. As the piston reciprocates in the cylinder between an inner dead center, and an outer dead center, this reciprocating motion is converted into rotary motion by a connecting rod and crankshaft. The gasoline engine used in automobiles is an internal-combustion, reciprocating engine.

Rotary. In rotary engines, no reciprocating parts are used. An essential part of the rotary engine is the turbine, in which the working fluid, at a high temperature, pushes against many curved blades attached to a movable disk. The disk, in turn, imparts rotary motion to a shaft, to which it is fastened.

A gas turbine engine is composed of an air compressor, a combustion chamber, or heat exchanger, in which thermal energy is added to the compressed air, and a turbine. The turbine may be sufficiently large to drive the compressor and an external load (an electric generator, the wheels of a vehicle, the propeller of an airplane, etc.), or it may be only large enough to drive the compressor. In the latter case gases leave the turbine with residual energy and are exhausted to the rear at high speed, imparting forward thrust and motion. This is the principle of the turbojet engine.

Reaction. This brings us to a class of engines that use the reaction principle of Hero's early engine. This principle is based on Newton's third law which states that "For every action there is an equal and opposite reaction." A familiar example of this principle is the recoil of a gun against one's shoulder when the bullet leaves the barrel. Reaction engines or motors may be of the turbojet types, explained above, or may be in the form of a rocket, ramjet, or pulse jet.

A rocket motor has only one opening or nozzle. Fuel and oxidizer are fed into the combustion chamber and chemically combine there. The resulting high-pressure and high-temperature gases escape to the rear out of the nozzle, thus imparting forward thrust to the rocket. Instead of fuel and oxidizer, the working fluid may be a gas, such as hydrogen, heated by nuclear fuel (nuclear propulsion), or high-speed electrical particles generated by heating a metal such as caesium (electrostatic propulsion). A rocket is the only engine that does not need atmospheric air and therefore the only suitable device for propulsion outside the earth's atmosphere.

PHILLIP S. MYERS, University of Wisconsin

See also:

ATOMIC ENERGY   HYDRAULIC TURBINE
DIESEL ENGINE   JET PROPULSION
FUEL   TURBINE
GASOLINE ENGINE

ENGINEERING embraces a family of interrelated but highly specialized professions—chemical, civil, mechanical, industrial, mining, metallurgical, and electrical. (See list at end of this article for coverage of these and other specialized fields.) With a few exceptions, these professions originated in and carry forward the interests and activities of ancient and long established practical arts.

Civilization has been defined as the process whereby a human society in search of "a good life for man," as Aristotle put it, gradually overcomes the obstacles, material and other, that stand in its way and makes man increasingly master of his environment. In this search better to meet his material needs and wants man early developed many of the skills and methods that characterize the practical arts and their modern outgrowth, engineering.

Ancient Egypt has long been known as the mother of the practical arts. As early as 3000 B.C., in the valley of the Nile, the master builder was planning and directing the construction of buildings and supervising pioneer irrigation activities. Mining and metallurgy were to remain for many centuries largely craft occupations with specialized techniques and methods passed on from worker to worker. Early man had sought flint for tools and weapons but Egyptian miners dug the ore of the first metal useful to man, copper, on the Sinai Peninsula. By 2000 B.C. the ancient metallurgist had combined this metal with tin to usher in the Bronze Age and some thousand years later iron was to come from the Hittite area to the north.

Similarly, the modern chemical engineer recalls the early maker of dyes and pigments, of glass and cement, whereas the story of many tools and mechanical devices can also be traced far back in human history. Mechanical interests, however, long remained limited primarily to hand tools, to pumping devices, and even later to the hoists used in construction and to catapults, battering rams, and other ma-

---

ENGINEERING   **STUDY GUIDE**

Traffic signals and space communication, irrigation ditches and hydroelectric plants, improved chinaware and tougher heat shields for missiles — these are a few examples of the areas in which engineers work. The contributions of engineering to modern civilization are highlighted in dozens of articles in this Encyclopedia. This Study Guide directs the reader to those that fit his interests. The general survey on these pages concentrates on the history of engineering, as the following outline shows.

Forerunners of Engineering in the Ancient World. Contributions to civilization of the practical arts, from which engineering developed. Ancient Egypt. Antecedents of all branches of engineering except electrical in construction and work with metals, tools, machines, dyes, pigments, and cement. The Assyrians. The Greeks. The Romans. The Dark Ages—master builders and military engineers.

Early Industry. Later medieval times: revival of cities and of commerce; growth of a merchant class; water wheels and other machines for industry. The Renaissance: mechanical advances; progress in military engineering; mining.

Engineering and Science. Beginnings of modern natural science. Little connection between natural science and the practical arts before the 19th century. French engineering—public and government projects. Great Britain—industrial development, use of iron, steam power.

Engineering and Industry. The industrial revolution and engineering specialization. Mechanical engineering in industry. Specialization and mass production in the modern economy. Effects of labor costs and other economic considerations on engineering.

The Power Age. Steam and electric power and the internal-combustion engine. Contributions of electrical engineering.

Recent Trends. American and European contributions to technological advancement. Greater interest in theory in Europe. Awakening of Americans during World War I to the relation of natural science to material progress. Emphasis on research to find new applications for scientific knowledge. Problem of balancing theoretical research and practical consideration.

The Engineering Profession. Professional societies. Training and licensing. Nature of the work.

The reader who wants to obtain additional data on the history of engineering may consult such articles as TOOLS AND WEAPONS, PRIMITIVE; BRONZE; BRONZE AGE; IRON AGE; RENAISSANCE; INDUSTRIAL REVOLUTION; and INVENTION. Side lights are provided in biographies of famous men, including ARCHIMEDES, LEONARDO DA VINCI, James WATT, Ferdinand de LESSEPS, Thomas A. EDISON, and George Washington GOETHALS. The early history of civil engineering can be traced in discussions of architecture — for example, ARCHITECTURE, EGYPTIAN ARCHITECTURE, PYRAMID, ARCH, GREEK ARCHITECTURE, and ROMAN ARCHITECTURE.

Modern engineering is treated in articles on major branches, as listed below. Samples of related entries show the scope of each branch.

CIVIL ENGINEERING. Related articles include BUILDING, HIGHWAY, RAILROADS, TUNNEL, BRIDGE, DAM, FLOODS AND FLOOD CONTROL, and URBAN PLANNING. Two branches of civil engineering are SANITARY ENGINEERING and HYDRAULIC ENGINEERING.

MECHANICAL ENGINEERING. Among the related articles are MACHINE, ENGINE, STEAM ENGINE, GASOLINE ENGINE, DIESEL ENGINE, TURBINE, AUTOMOBILE, and TOOLS. One branch is covered in AERONAUTICAL ENGINEERING. Another, marine engineering, is treated in SHIP AND SHIPBUILDING and NAVAL ARCHITECTURE.

INDUSTRIAL ENGINEERING. See also STEEL AND STEELMAKING, PLASTICS, PRINTING, MASS PRODUCTION, AUTOMATION, and ATOMIC POWER.

ELECTRICAL ENGINEERING. Other pertinent articles are ELECTRICITY, ELECTRIC POWER, ELECTRONICS, and INDUSTRIAL ELECTRONICS.

CHEMICAL ENGINEERING. See also CHEMISTRY, PHYSICAL CHEMISTRY, PLASTICS, and ATOMIC POWER.

METALLURGICAL ENGINEERING is treated in METALLURGY and such related entries as ALLOY.

MINING ENGINEERING — see MINES AND MINING: *Mining Engineering.*

AGRICULTURAL ENGINEERING. Among related articles are FARM MACHINERY, IRRIGATION, and NATURAL RESOURCES, CONSERVATION OF.

ENGINEERING

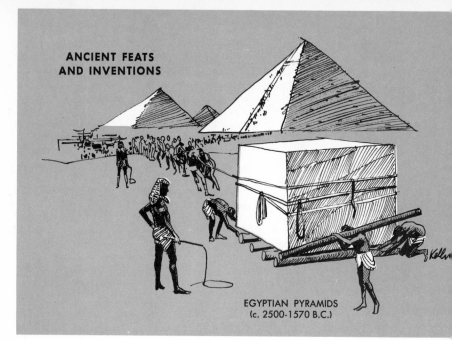

ANCIENT FEATS
AND INVENTIONS

EGYPTIAN PYRAMIDS
(c. 2500-1570 B.C.)

chines of war. Thus, among the major engineering branches only electrical engineering is a distinctly modern outgrowth, originating in scientific discoveries rather than stemming from the practical needs and wants of evolving civilization.

The Assyrians, the first to use iron on a large scale, added much to the techniques of military engineering, and by 700 B.C achieved a new level in urban development through the provision of city water supplies. This awakening interest in public works was to be carried forward by the Greeks and especially by the Romans and, together with military advances, to become the dominant factor in further engineering progress.

The Greeks turned to harbor building and urban construction. The mechanical inventions of Archimedes have

long been known and early works on engines of war, especially those of Hero of Alexandria, reflected the Greek interest in machines. They developed such mechanical devices as pulley and capstan hoists and piston pumps. It was Greek civilization also that gave to the master builder a new title of *architecton* by which he was to be known throughout ancient times.

These Greek technical advances and methods, in turn, became basic to the further progress of civilized life when the Romans took over control of the Western world.

But, through ancient times engineering remained limited in scope and interests. Industries remained almost entirely handicrafts. These were slave-civilizations and the production of consumer's goods was left to menials. Power was limited to men and oxen, for the horse was still a rid-

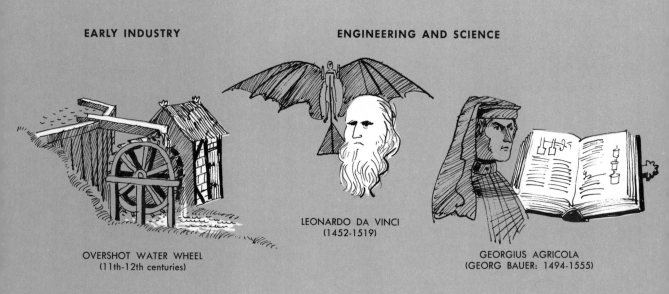

EARLY INDUSTRY

ENGINEERING AND SCIENCE

OVERSHOT WATER WHEEL
(11th-12th centuries)

LEONARDO DA VINCI
(1452-1519)

GEORGIUS AGRICOLA
(GEORG BAUER: 1494-1555)

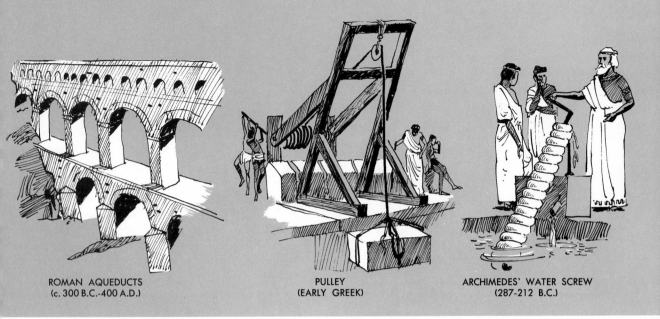

ROMAN AQUEDUCTS
(c. 300 B.C.-400 A.D.)

PULLEY
(EARLY GREEK)

ARCHIMEDES' WATER SCREW
(287-212 B.C.)

ing and pack animal—the collar needed to make him useful for draft purposes was yet to be introduced.

In the Dark Ages Roman works were allowed to fall into decay and western Europe remained more or less isolated from the rest of the Mediterranean world. As civilized life revived, however, there was a rebirth of the practical arts, and the master builder again emerged as the remarkably skilled and able craftsman of later medieval times. The collapse of Charlemagne's short-lived empire in the early 9th century led to the Age of Nobles, to an emphasis on military problems and to the first use of the title *ingeniator* (Lat., "engineer"). As early as 200 A.D. a Roman writer, Tertullian, had referred to a battering ram as an *ingenium*, and such devices became known as engines of war. By 1000 A.D. the men who designed and operated such devices and also built the massive medieval castles, the fortress-homes of the petty nobles of the day, to withstand their attack, were referred to as *ingeniatores* or *ingegnieurs*.

Early Industry. But later, medieval times also witnessed a rebirth in city life, the revival of Mediterranean commerce and trade, and the rise of a new merchant-business class and the awakening of a new economy. As serfdom declined, the possibilities of increasing the production of goods to trade for the spices and silks of the East began to be of interest. Not only were there notable innovations in machines—from spinning wheels to devices for boring logs for pipe—but water wheels came into wide use in meeting local needs such as grinding grain and sawing lumber. By the 12th century the windmill had ap-

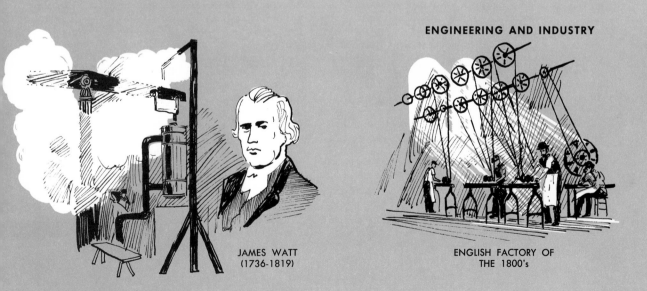

ENGINEERING AND INDUSTRY

JAMES WATT
(1736-1819)

ENGLISH FACTORY OF
THE 1800's

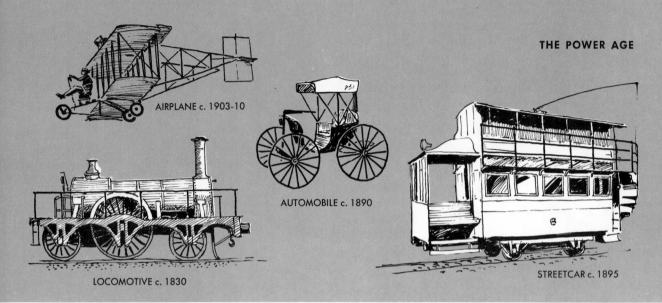

THE POWER AGE

AIRPLANE c. 1903-10

AUTOMOBILE c. 1890

LOCOMOTIVE c. 1830

STREETCAR c. 1895

peared in areas where water was not available. Early manuscript records are filled with sketches of these and other devices which were increasingly applied in furthering industrial output.

The Renaissance witnessed a continuation of these interests, as in the mechanical speculations of Leonardo da Vinci and others, and in the awakening of modern Europe which followed, engineers turned to activities other than building. In addition to mechanical advances the advent of gunpowder and cannon not only created a new era of military engineering but gave increasing impetus to surveying, to the metallurgical art, and to the provision of a new means of defense, the earthwork fort. By 1556 the growth of mining in Saxony resulted in the first great book on mining and metallurgy, Agricola's famous *De re metallica*. A number of early books were also devoted to descriptions of the new machines.

Engineering and Science. It was also in this same period that modern natural science, or natural philosophy as it was long known, was born. Agricola, for example, was a contemporary of the scientist Copernicus. There was, however, little relationship between the interests of the new science and those of the engineer. Science soon became centered in astronomical and mathematical studies little related to practical needs. Experience still remained the great engineering teacher. The remarkable metallurgical processes described by Agricola had not only been achieved through centuries of earlier trial and observation, but his work was also a pioneer treatise on mineralogy and geology. Indeed early engineering advances frequently led to scientific studies, but some two or more centuries were required to develop an effective liaison between natural science and the practical arts.

Every practical art contains the germ of a practical science and, as in medical science, engineering science is based on a development within the profession itself of more fully rationalized and quantitative techniques. Procedures are thus evolved that permit more accurate and reliable planning and design. In time decisions formerly resting solely on experience, judgment, and qualitative understandings become largely matters of mathematical analysis and quantitative computation. The parts of a machine or structure can be more accurately proportioned to meet their respective needs, "over-design" avoided, and material saved. Machines may be so designed as to produce their maximum practicable output. Safety and reliability are improved. But both more accurate scientific understandings and practical needs were essential to such development. It was not until well into the 19th century that these requirements began to result in more fully rationalized techniques in engineering design and planning.

In the 17th century France became the leading nation in Europe, and the increasing scope of engineering activities stimulated the growth of the mechanics both of structures and machines. These new understandings involved especially the testing of materials to determine safe loadings and of machines to ascertain possible output. French engineers throughout the 18th century continued to develop these new techniques and to seek what was referred to as the "perfection" of design.

After the French Revolution there was an emphasis on natural science that had little relation to the practical arts. It remained for British engineers to take further steps in the evolution of a practical science of engineering and in bridging the gap between theory and practice. Advances in the space and character of engineering endeavor stimulated this advance.

French engineering had, as in ancient times, been almost completely confined to public and governmental projects. Industries were largely limited to small local and guild-dominated city units. In Great Britain, on the other hand, foreign trade and commerce encouraged industrial interests, and major works were undertaken as private ventures. Also the advent in Great Britain of a real age of metal through the production of cast and later wrought iron in quantity and at a cost that made the use of iron possible for other than tools, weapons, and fastenings, led both to its use in bridges and to new bridge forms demanding more accurate analysis and design. The problem of reducing the fuel consumption of steam mine pumps prompted James Watt's invention of the separate condenser, and his later steam engines led to the formulation of the modern theory of heat.

Engineering and Industry. The industrial changes in Great Britain to which these advances contributed also marked the advent of a new way of life in which engineering was to play an ever-increasing role. Malthus had pointed out that unless steps were taken to limit population growth the possibilities of the prevailing agricultural-home economy to support life would ultimately be exhausted. The industrial revolution marked a change from agriculture to industry and Great Britain increasingly relied on industrial exports to secure both essential food needs and many raw materials. Further engineering specialization followed this change.

The immediate ancestor of the modern mechanical engineer was the older millwright, a carpenter-blacksmith who built the water mills and other devices of the pre-steam era. With the advent of steam, however, early British civil engineers led in the application of this new power to the evolving needs of industry. An effective linking of engineering and industry was finally achieved, and mechanical engineering emerged as a full-fledged branch of the engineering profession.

Throughout the 19th century the fundamental changes springing from this revolutionary advance began to affect vitally Western man's way of life. Engineering, long a potent and increasingly effective instrument for furthering the material life of man, was to become a major force in shaping man's relationship to man and in the evolution of modern social and political institutions and ideas.

On the one hand the advent of an age of machines and power was to relieve man of much of the physical toil that had earlier made him "brother of the ox." Productive industrial employment was created for millions who lacked the skills essential in an earlier craftsmanship economy. On the other hand, men were increasingly forced to rely on other men for many of the essentials of life from food to clothing, which were formerly produced largely in the family home. Adam Smith, the father of modern economics, in his *Wealth of Nations* of 1776, emphasized specialization as the fundamental characteristic of the changing economy of his day. Specialization and mass production have created a way of life in which man no longer stands alone but is dependent on his fellow men for the majority of his essential needs and wants. The United States was to become the leading nation in the rise and development of this interlinked and interdependent economy owing much to engineering.

In Europe engineering progressed with civilization but progress was often opposed by established interests. There was considerable resistance to the introduction of textile machines, the railroad, the electric light, and the telephone. With a plentiful supply of skilled labor, these advances were regarded as leading only to a loss of older and assured employment. The situation was different in the United States. Engineering became an integral and potent factor in creating a new nation through the exploitation of

Atomic-powered ocean liner. Nuclear reactor generates steam for conventional turbines.

the resources of a new continent. With skilled labor both scarce and costly, the urge for labor-saving machinery and rapid production became characteristic of the nation's growth. The economic element in engineering, the search to secure the desired result with the least expenditure of funds, labor, and materials had long been a guiding element in engineering planning and design. In Europe, with materials relatively costly but skilled labor available, the tendency has been to develop the more refined and accurate techniques of design that, although involving more labor in production, save materials. In the United States materials have been freely used if labor saving resulted or made possible greater speed and ease of construction or production. These basically economic considerations have affected all branches of the profession.

The Power Age. It has been estimated that by 1900 for every man, woman, and child in the United States there were available the equivalent of possibly two or three silent "slaves" created by steam power. This power use was confined largely to the piston engines that drove locomotives and pumps and turned the wheels of industry. It was the birth of electrical engineering in the later years of the 19th century that made power available not only for lighting, but also for the machines of industry as well as for home and farm equipment. Added to this distribution and utilization of electric power, the development of the internal combustion engine has created a new era of highway and air transport and a host of new farm and construction machines.

Thus electrical engineering, which originated in the observations of largely amateur scientists, and was first applied in communication, has revolutionized power use.

Recent Trends. Many of the devices involved in these and other American technological advances have been of European origin. Technical advances have not been confined by national boundaries. American workers have taken such European inventions as textile machines, the dynamo, the internal combustion engine, the motor car,

ENGINEERING

and the steam turbine, and produced and applied them to peculiarly American needs and wants on an unprecedented and unparalleled scale. With emphasis on production and use, however, American engineers have, with few exceptions, left the development of more advanced and accurate theories of analysis and design to European workers. The major contributions to engineering science and the improvement of the liaison between natural science and technology have come from Europe.

It has been said that it was due largely to the awakening of the chemical industry during World War I that the American people first began to identify the contributions of natural science with the progress of material civilization. Many earlier inventions had been developed by men who owed little to either scientific or engineering training. In the older branches of the profession, also, improvements had usually evolved through successive evolutionary rather than revolutionary advances. Major engineering devices, such as the arch and truss bridges, the canal lock,

the steam engine and locomotive, the internal combustion engine, and even the airplane, as well as copper and bronze, iron and steel, and many metallurgical and chemical processes, developed through trial and experience in response to practical needs rather than through original scientific discoveries. As noted earlier, these practical advances often stimulated scientific study. World War I made it clear, however, that many essential German chemical imports, the flow of which ceased with the advent of hostilities, were not the product of chance or inspired individual workers, but resulted from purposeful scientific research by organized research teams. Some American industries, notably in the chemical and electrical fields, had already undertaken such research and the movement spread to other engineering branches. Today both industry and government are spending billions of dollars in an organized search of the teachings of natural science, notably physics and chemistry, to uncover possible practical applications and uses. Although it is true that

Characteristics of the Field. In a sense, engineers are technical experts who translate scientific theory into industrial or governmental practice. Though their work is too complex to be easily summarized, they do deal with the results of research and with economic problems such as materials and costs. If, for example, a research chemist has discovered a new plastic, a chemical engineer may be assigned the job of designing and operating a plant that can manufacture the new product efficiently enough to make a profit. Other engineers may be brought into the project. Electrical engineers may design the plant's power supply. If the plant is to be air-conditioned, then there is a need for a mechanical engineer.

The importance of engineering is shown by the fact that there are more engineers than members of any other profession except teaching. Engineering is the largest profession for men. In the mid-1960's the number of engineers in the United States and Canada had passed the 900,000 mark and was growing.

Most engineers specialize in one of the numerous branches of the profession. The three largest are civil engineering (including sanitary engineering and hydraulic engineering), mechanical engineering, and electrical engineering. Among the other branches are aeronautical engineering, agricultural engineering, chemical engineering, industrial engineering, metallurgical engineering, and mining engineering. Some engineers combine the special knowledge and practices of engineering in their work in branches of a particular field such as nuclear power. A man with basic training in chemical or mechanical engineering, for example, may become a nuclear engineer. Some basic information and methods are useful in many branches of engineering. Thus a young man may be able to transfer from one field to another.

About 75% of all engineers are employed in private industry — notably by manufacturers of aircraft, electrical equipment, and machinery and in the construction, chemical, transportation, light and power, petroleum, and metals industries. Other important employers are agencies of federal, state, and local government; the armed forces, consulting firms; and universities and colleges.

Engineering jobs are found wherever there are industrial and governmental operations of any size. Some jobs require travel — civil engineering, for example. Jobs in many branches tend to be concentrated in centers of major industries.

Qualifications and Training. Engineering may or may not involve unusual hazards and require unusual physical exertion. Certain engineers do some field work, but others work mainly in offices. As to education, a grounding in

mathematics and the physical sciences is essential. Since many engineers work on human problems (such as housing and transporting people), courses in the social sciences and humanities are useful. The college engineering curriculum leading to a bachelor's degree may take four or five years. Graduates usually start in routine work such as drafting or laboratory testing. With experience and training they may advance to administrative and even high executive posts. Graduate degrees are often required for responsible jobs in such areas as nuclear engineering and are usually necessary for teaching careers.

All U.S. states require engineers whose work may affect life, health, or property to be licensed or registered. The majority of civil engineers are licensed (see CIVIL ENGINEERING).

Income. In the early 1960's the median salary for U.S. engineers without experience was slightly under $6,000. For engineers with 10 years' experience the median was almost $10,000. For those with 20 years' experience, about $12,400. Figures ran somewhat lower in Canada. The relatively small number of engineers who had achieved executive rank had much higher incomes.

Prospects for Employment. The prediction in the mid-1960's was for rapid growth of the engineering profession at least through the next decade. Some branches, such as aeronautical, chemical, electrical, mechanical, and metallurgical engineering, were expected to grow more rapidly than others. Industry and government foresaw a demand for more and more engineers to staff new and increasingly technical projects. Additional teachers would also be essential to train larger classes of engineering students. Women made up only a small part of the profession in the early 1960's — 1% in Canada, for example — but opportunities for women were improving.

The fact that the profession was growing did not mean that its standards would be relaxed and that anyone with technological interests should rush into it. A man who might be a first-rate technician might be only a fourth-rate engineer.

Sources of Information. See the article ENGINEERING and articles listed in the Study Guide. General suggestions on career planning are offered in VOCATIONAL GUIDANCE. Specific information on engineering can be obtained from the Engineers' Council for Professional Development and the Engineers Joint Council, both in New York, N. Y., the National Society of Professional Engineers, in Washington, D.C., the Engineering Institute of Canada in Montreal, and other professional associations.

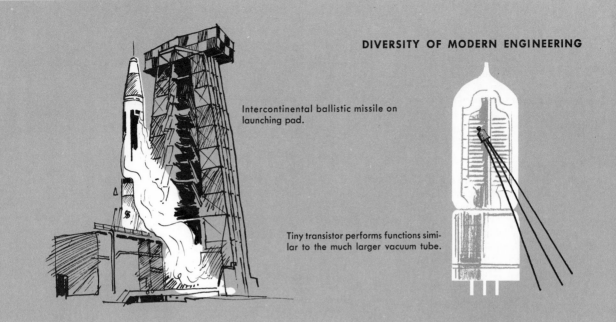

Intercontinental ballistic missile on launching pad.

Tiny transistor performs functions similar to the much larger vacuum tube.

in industry financial considerations emphasize the search for cost-quality product improvements, only time can demonstrate the effectiveness of such purposeful research in uncovering new products and revealing possible contributions to improved scientific understandings. Yet this intermediate form of scientific research has come to command almost unlimited support.

The effect of this preoccupation with science and research and the resulting neglect of the other factors which condition engineering and industrial progress pose a critical problem today, especially in engineering education. It is true that the creative ideas of the engineer are based on expert knowledge of specialized technical and scientific possibilities. But it is also true that the effective realization of these possibilities demands an unbiased appraisal of practicalities. Available materials and their relative costs, qualities, and advantages, the most effective use of available labor and equipment, as well as realistic analysis of economic and social values, of present and possible future needs and wants, are likewise basic to progressive engineering practice.

The Engineering Profession. Today various national engineering societies provide not only a means for the discussion and publication of technical methods and advances, but also of these other matters which condition engineering progress. Special groups have joined in the American Engineers Council (AEC) and the Engineers Council of Professional Development (ECPD) in the interests of professional standards and progress. In the educational field also there have been notable changes.

In earlier days engineering training was secured largely through apprenticeship. In the United States the West Point Military Academy of 1802 remained solely a military engineering post and school until shortly before the Civil War. In the civil field Norwich in Vermont began to offer engineering instruction in 1819 and Rensselaer at Troy, N.Y., followed in 1826. But the major expansion came after the Civil War. Today, more than 100 schools teach engineering. As engineering techniques become more involved, it has become increasingly difficult for young men

to acquire the essential education except through the formal processes of these schools. Furthermore a movement was initiated about 1920 to require, as in law and medicine, a license to undertake professional practice. Such laws have been enacted in all the states of the Union. Examinations, after an extended period of practice as an engineering assistant, are required.

Much of the routine work of a modern engineering office, such as surveying and many of the more or less standardized computations and details of design and the drafting of plans, are carried out by vocationally trained technical workers. The professional practice of engineering, however, is based on exacting educational and experience requirements. The modern tendency is toward increasing specialization as the scope of professional practice is extended and as special techniques are developed. Various branches of the profession from aeronautical to welding specialties as well as the older, more basic branches of the profession have been recognized. Thus, while the young man looking forward to engineering as a career today faces an exacting and challenging period of preparation, he has a wide choice of interests in which to find a challenging and promising lifework. Furthermore the profession offers opportunities for the exercise of a wide variety of aptitudes and talents, from research and the fascinating details of analysis and design to the planning and direction of construction or production, and from operation and management to distribution and sales.

Consult Kirby, R. S., and others, *Engineering in History* (1956); Usher, A. P., *History of Mechanical Inventions* (1959); Finch, J. K., *Story of Engineering* (1960).

JAMES K. FINCH, Columbia University

See also:

AERONAUTICAL ENGINEERING   HYDRAULIC ENGINEERING
AGRICULTURAL ENGINEERING   INDUSTRIAL ENGINEERING
CHEMICAL ENGINEERING   MECHANICAL ENGINEERING
CIVIL ENGINEERING   MINES AND MINING
ELECTRICAL ENGINEERING   NAVAL ARCHITECTURE

ENGINEERING DRAWING. *See* MECHANICAL DRAWING.

The Windrush River reflects the old stone houses and low bridges of Bourton-on-the-Water in the Cotswold Hills of Gloucestershire.

England

ENGLAND, the southern part of the island of Great Britain, comprising rather more than half of the entire area of the United Kingdom. The country's maximum length is nearly 360 mi. and it has a coast line of 1,835 mi. Lands End is its most westerly point, jutting into the Atlantic Ocean, and Lowestoft on the North Sea its most easterly point.

The Land

Physical Features. The coast of Cornwall and Devon, in the southwest, is fretted into numerous large rugged inlets, some of which make spectacular natural harbors. Elsewhere there are smooth sweeping bays or the long, broad tidal estuaries of the Humber, Thames, Severn, and other rivers. The relatively shallow coastal waters provide valuable offshore fishing grounds. The Isles of Scilly, the Channel Islands, and the Isle of Wight lie off the south coast, and the Isle of Man in the Irish Sea.

England has only three highland regions. In the southwest is Dartmoor, highest point of which is 2,039 ft. The rivers radiating from this and the neighboring plateaus of Bodmin Moor and Exmoor are short. In the northwest of England the Lake District, bounded on the east by the vale of Eden, includes the Cumbrian Mountains and England's highest peak, Scafell Pike (3,210 ft.). Deep valleys filled with beautiful ribbon-shaped lakes such as Windermere, Coniston Water, Ullswater, and Wastwater make a radial pattern. A third highland region is the Pennine Chain, often called the "backbone of England." Stretching south from the Tyne valley to the Peak District of north Derbyshire, its highest point, Cross Fell (2,930 ft.), is in the north. The chain is breached not only by the Tyne valley but also, further south, by the valley of the Aire.

Most of England is lowland, however, not 1,000 ft. above sea level. The very low-lying plains of Lancashire and Cheshire, in the northwest, and of Somerset in the southwest, are flat and featureless. So too is the far larger eastern plain, extending from the Vale of York in the north, across the Humber and lower Trent river basins to the Fens of East Anglia. Much of the latter region, reclaimed from the sea, is very flat and liable to flooding. North of the broad inlet of the Wash, the flat land is broken by the Lincolnshire Wolds and the Yorkshire Moors. Between the eastern plain and the Welsh border in the west lie the Midland lowlands, consisting of undulating hill country. The long, crescent-shaped ridges of the Cotswolds, the Chilterns, and other hills cross the country obliquely and alternate with the broad clay valleys of such important rivers as the Severn, the Avon, and the Trent. The Thames, however, rising in the Cotswolds, cuts across the grain of a series of such ridges and valleys as it flows eastward. Southern and southeastern England have a similar relief of ridge and vale, with chalk downs forming the dominant feature. Best known are the South Downs, which, toward the west, converge on the low chalk plateau of Salisbury Plain.

Climate. The prevailing winds from the Atlantic bring maritime conditions to the southwest of England, where winters are very mild and summers are warm. Southeast England, being more exposed to Continental influences, is cold in winter, but is the hottest part of the country in summer, with July mean temperatures exceeding 62° F. The northeast is generally cooler, while the northwest has mild winters and cool summers. The frequent passage of depressions and fronts brings cloudy, rainy, and changeable weather at all seasons, especially in the west and north. Heaviest rainfall, averaging as much as 100 in. a year, occurs in the Lake District. Over much of England, however, the mean annual rainfall is about 30 in., and in some places around the Thames estuary it falls to less than 20 in. In winter anticyclones may bring much fog to industrial and eastern England, with frosts in lowland areas. Snow seldom lies for as much as 10 mornings in southern and lowland England, but its frequency increases toward the north, particularly in the highlands.

Natural Vegetation and Wildlife. More than 2,000 years of man's occupation have left little of England's natural forest cover of oak, beech, and elm. Most of the lowlands are improved agricultural land. Some areas of woodland are conserved in the New Forest of southwest Hampshire and in Sherwood Forest, part of another ancient forest, in Nottinghamshire. In the uplands, burning and animal grazing have led to the survival of rough pasture or heather moors. The Pennine summits also have some peat bogs and cotton grass. Local reforestation is undertaken by the Forestry Commission; particularly in the Lake District and other highland areas, valuable softwoods such as larches and spruces have been planted. Little wildlife survives in England except in bird sanctuaries and reservations maintained by the Nature Conservancy Board, and in National Parks.

Natural Resources. Aside from the lowland resource of valuable agricultural soils, another of increasing significance is the distribution of water resources. In the highlands, water conservation in natural lakes and artificial reservoirs is a common feature, while the water of large rivers such as the Trent is used in the power stations of nearby industrial centers. Coal fields are located primarily on the margins of the older highland regions. Most important is the very large and rich Yorkshire-Derby-Nottinghamshire field, although smaller fields are widely distributed over northern England and the Midlands, and even as far south as Kent.

Iron ore is found extensively in the Jurassic rocks of Northamptonshire, Lincolnshire, and north Yorkshire. There are widespread limestone deposits, as well as fluorspar, salt, and other minerals, chiefly in northern England. Natural oil resources are very small. Since prehistoric times southwest England has been noted for its metal ores, including tin, copper, and lead, but these are now very limited, and china clay from south Cornwall is of greater importance.

For a bibliography see the article UNITED KINGDOM OF GREAT BRITAIN AND NORTHERN IRELAND.

ALICE GARNETT, University of Sheffield, England

The People

Ethnology and Population. The population of England in 1966 was estimated at about 46,000,000. The 1961 census gave it as 43,460,525. It is predominantly an urban population, engaged primarily in manufacturing, commerce, and service industries. No less than 18% of this population lives in the Greater London area, and there are conurbations of over a million people in the West Midland, or Birmingham, region, and in the West Yorkshire, Manchester, and Liverpool areas. Apart from London in 1966, there were 49 cities with over 100,000 inhabitants. Geographically, the population of England is concentrated in a highly industrialized belt that extends from London in the southeast to Lancashire in the northwest and the neighboring parts of Yorkshire. Within this belt lie the conurbations of the West Midlands, the East Midlands (including Leicester, Nottingham, and Derby), the West Riding of Yorkshire, and the industrial parts of south Lancashire and Greater London. Outside it there are few large cities and no extensive areas of dense population.

The concentration of population and industries in recent years has led to grave congestion in many parts of the belt. It does have excellent transportation, including England's largest ports, London and Liverpool. To combat congestion, limits have been set on the growth of large metropolitan areas by means of dispersing industries and creating "new towns." London, which presented the greatest problem, has had the most drastic treatment. Its outward growth is now checked by a "green belt." Here industrial expansion is forbidden and building development tightly restricted. Outside the "green belt" a number of new towns have been established as centers of light industries.

Today less than 30% of the total population lives in rural areas and less than 2% continues to work on the

PHYSICAL REGIONS OF ENGLAND AND WALES

The influence on the world of one small country, England, is demonstrated by the large number of articles in this Encyclopedia devoted to what Englishmen have done and thought and written. The terms "England," "English," and "British" are used so often that it is important to clarify their meanings and the scope of basic articles. BRITISH ISLES deals with the geography of the islands on which England, Wales, Scotland, Northern Ireland, and the Republic of Ireland are located. BRITAIN treats the ancient history of the largest island, whose people were called Britons, through the period of Roman occupation. ENGLAND is concerned with the southern portion of the largest island and surveys the history of the region from the end of Roman occupation to the early 18th century. WALES was joined to England in 1536 and SCOTLAND in 1707, forming the Kingdom of Great Britain. Later the term "United Kingdom" was applied to England, Wales, Scotland, and Ireland. British history beginning in 1707 is covered in UNITED KINGDOM OF GREAT BRITAIN AND NORTHERN IRELAND, while the extension of British power overseas is discussed in BRITISH EMPIRE.

The article ENGLAND deals with the English people and their culture as well as with a period of history. When applied to science, philosophy, and the arts and letters, "English" is not restricted to one part of the British Isles or one segment of history.

With the article on these pages as a background, the reader can turn to a wide range of related articles for further study. These may be grouped under six headings.

History. The reader can start his study of English history with ANGLES OR ANGLI and SAXONS and articles on the Saxon kingdoms, ESSEX, WESSEX, SUSSEX, and EAST ANGLIA, and the biography of King ALFRED. Later developments are treated in such entries as NORMAN CONQUEST; WILLIAM I OR WILLIAM THE CONQUEROR; DOMESDAY BOOK; HENRY II; HENRY III; BARONS' WAR; EDWARD III; BLACK DEATH; HENRY V; HUNDRED YEARS' WAR; ROSES WAR OF THE; RICHARD III; HENRY VII; HENRY VIII; Thomas WOLSEY; ELIZABETH I; MARY, QUEEN OF SCOTS; Sir Francis DRAKE; ARMADA, SPANISH; CHARLES I; CIVIL WAR, ENGLISH; CHARLES II; JAMES II; GLORIOUS REVOLUTION; and WILLIAM III. All English monarchs and many statesmen and other public figures are covered.

Government and Law. One of the themes in the country's history is progress toward representative government and democratic law. Development can be traced in such articles as MAGNA CARTA OR MAGNA CHARTA; PARLIAMENT, BRITISH; PETITION OF RIGHT; BILL OF RIGHTS; CONSTITUTION; CIVIL RIGHTS AND LIBERTIES; and COMMON LAW.

Language and Literature. One of the clearest demonstrations of the influence of England on the world is the spread of English to become the language of more than 250,000,000 people (see ENGLISH and, for the letters of the language, ALPHABET). English authors and playwrights have had an equally wide influence, as the articles ENGLISH LITERATURE and ENGLISH THEATER indicate. In this usage "English" includes all British writers — Sir Walter SCOTT and George Bernard SHAW as well as the whole range from John WYCLIF, Geoffrey CHAUCER, and Edmund SPENSER to Charles DICKENS and Alfred, Lord TENNYSON. The articles LITERATURE, LITERARY CRITICISM, NOVEL, POETRY, and DRAMA give appropriate attention to English figures.

Art, Architecture, and Music. The article ENGLISH ART AND ARCHITECTURE discusses artists such as Thomas GAINSBOROUGH, William HOGARTH, and Joseph TURNER and architects such as Sir Christopher WREN (whose style was influential in North America). Related articles include those on famous buildings such as ST. PAUL'S and WESTMINSTER ABBEY. ENGLISH MUSIC covers English composers and styles from the Middle Ages to the time of Sir Thomas BEECHAM and Benjamin BRITTEN.

Philosophy, Science, and Invention. The importance of Englishmen in the history of ideas is pointed out in the articles on such men as Sir Francis BACON, and John LOCKE. Sir Isaac NEWTON has been ranked with Albert Einstein. English engineers and inventors made many contributions to the progress described in INDUSTRIAL REVOLUTION.

Religion. The historical and religious significance of the Protestant church in England is discussed in ENGLAND, CHURCH OF, and in PURITANS, for instance. The translation of the Bible treated in KING JAMES VERSION is part of the literary as well as religious heritage of the English-speaking peoples.

Many articles conclude with lists of books recommended for further reading about England and English civilization. The library can provide a variety of histories, biographies, novels, poems, and plays by and about the English.

---

land. Between large and growing towns of the belt, rural areas are steadily dwindling. How to control land use and meet the needs of growing urban population for public utilities are among the most difficult problems facing English planners.

Ethnically, the English are one of the most mixed of peoples. Even before the Ice Age peoples were migrating to the British Isles from continental Europe. There was a land bridge where the Strait of Dover is now until about 5000 B.C., so that Paleolithic man was able simply to walk over. As later invaders had to come by sea, there were fewer of them at longer intervals. Little is known of the earliest migrants. At their heels came the Celts in a series of overwhelming waves during the last five centuries before the Christian era. The Celts spread across England and into Wales, penetrated the Highlands of Scotland, and crossed the sea to Ireland.

Then came the Romans. They occupied Britain (that is, England only) from 49 A.D. to the early 5th century. Roman legions camped there, Roman merchants frequented these shores, and a few settlers came from the Continent. Many cities and a network of roads were built. Yet the Roman impact on England was neither deep nor lasting. Latin was widely spoken in the south and east, while elsewhere the Celtic tongue prevailed. When the Roman armies withdrew, urban life came to an end.

Later invasions, however, altered the makeup of the future English people for all time. Not long after the Romans left, Angles, Saxons, and Jutes (north German tribes) arrived. They provided the base of the English language and in time became thoroughly blended with earlier arrivals. Next to invade Britain were the Norsemen, or Vikings (Danes and Norwegians). They too mixed in time and have descendants along the east coast. The last great invasion was that of the Normans (Norsemen who had settled in France some centuries before) in 1066. They added Latin elements to the English language. Even more important, perhaps, they brought the idea of orderly government and, for the first time in history, really united all of England.

Besides these chief elements in the English stock there was a variety of later, peaceful immigrants. Flemish weavers came in the 14th and 16th centuries, French Huguenots and Spanish Jews in the 17th century, and more recently refugees from totalitarian governments of Europe. All contributed skills and added to the richness of English life. Since World War II, as former British colonies have become independent, there have been numerous immigrants, many of them dark-skinned, from the overpopulated areas of Pakistan, India, and the Caribbean islands. Although they account for only about 2% of the population, they have formed thickly concentrated neighborhoods in some industrial cities.

Social Benefits and Education. In a flurry of legislative activity, the first Labour government after World War II created what is sometimes called a welfare state. Its purpose was to secure a more egalitarian society in which social services would be available to all, without reference to wealth and privilege. The resulting system provides scholarships and monetary grants, so that financial lacks are no bar to higher education.

By the National Health Service Act, medical, hospital and dental services became free. Today they are partly paid for by wage and salary deductions and levies on employers. Though the private practice of medicine has not been eliminated, the doctors who are paid fees for their services are now in the minority.

Similar forms of insurance provide for retirement pensions at age 65, as well as for unemployment, accident, maternity, death, and widow's pensions. These measures have eradicated cases of real destitution, though the amounts are not large, and a good deal of poverty remains.

The price of the welfare state is heavy taxation. The rates are high and more steeply graduated than in the United States, and death duties are heavy. Really high incomes are almost unknown, and inherited fortunes are being drastically reduced by taxation. Rank and privilege are thus slowly being eroded.

Education is compulsory from the age 5 to 15. Some 95% of the children are educated in free, state-supported schools, primary and secondary. These are what would be called public schools in the United States. In general, children from 5 to 11 years old attend primary schools, and those from 11 to 15 or up to 18 attend secondary schools. In the past an examination at age 11 determined whether a child would go to a secondary grammar or a secondary modern school. The grammar (or academic) schools, stressing languages, mathematics, and the sciences, up to age 18 or 19, led to university entrance. About 20% of the pupils aged 11 normally entered these schools. The rest went to secondary modern schools, in which the training was largely vocational, and there their formal education stopped.

After World War II, however, this method of dividing the "sheep" from the "goats" came under ever more severe criticism. It was seen producing an intellectual elite. Moreover, many considered age 11 too young for a child's intellectual capabilities to be so definitely graded. Today comprehensive secondary schools, not unlike American high schools, are being introduced. Such a school includes both academic and vocational courses. The change, however, requires the building of new and larger schools. If the plan continues, comprehensive secondary schools are supposed to become general by about 1990.

The public schools, led by Eton, Harrow, and Winchester, have long been regarded as preserves of the privileged and wealthy. Many are closely identified with the Church of England. They have been severely criticized as tending to preserve class distinctions, and today their future is in doubt. A few have already come in part under state control, and the rest may follow within a few years.

University education in the past has been available only to a relatively small group of England's youth, and students from the "public" schools have been favored far out of proportion to their numbers. However, change is coming in this field, too, as a number of new university and technical colleges of university status are being created. As larger public funds have become available, a university education is no longer beyond the reach of anyone considered able to benefit from it. In the late 1960's there were 36 universities largely or wholly state-supported, with about 143,000 students.

Religion. The United Kingdom, of which England is the largest part, is formally a religious country with an official state religion. In England this is the Church of England, or Anglican Church. Christianity made its appearance in England under the Roman Empire. Over much of the area this early Christianity was obliterated by the pagan Anglo-Saxons, though it survived in the Celtic lands to the west. A second wave of Christianity came with the mission of St. Augustine (597), at the same time that it was reintroduced from the Celtic lands, particularly Ireland. The two forms of Christianity differed, though ultimately they came to agreement.

Throughout the medieval period, England continued to be part of Roman Catholic Christendom. The English Reformation was brought on less by revolt against Catholic doctrines than by institutional conflicts. Its leader was the king rather than the people. There is no denying that the climate of opinion was ripe for a revolt against control by the Papacy. Yet it took the form of a legal dissolution of the bonds tying England with Rome so that the king might obtain a divorce, which the Pope had refused. The Catholic Church in England thus became the Church of England, officially created and controlled, with the monarch as its head.

A secondary modern school in Hertfordshire. Secondary modern schools offer a wide variety of academic and practical courses.
(HENRY GRANT—ILLUSTRATION RESEARCH SERVICE)

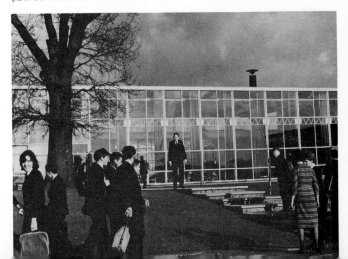

At this point the demand for reform could not be restrained. The Church of England moved away from the Catholic position in doctrine and liturgy. A number of sects appeared—predecessors of Baptists, Presbyterians, Congregationalists and others—that went even further in the direction of reform. Roman Catholics, together with the numerous nonconformist sects, continued under various legal and social disabilities until the 19th century. In several ways the state church—the Church of England—continues to enjoy a preferential status. It owns considerable land and other forms of wealth, including almost all the religious buildings of historic interest.

The Church of England claims as members somewhat more than half the total population of England. Most other religious denominations have relatively small followings. All, however, claim far more members than regularly participate in their services. The nonconformist churches claim a total membership of about 2,000,000. Of these the Methodist church, which originated in England in the 18th century as a reform movement within the established church, is the largest. Today only the Roman Catholic church appears to be growing. This is due in part to the immigration of Roman Catholic Irish. The Jewish community numbers less than half a million.

English Character and Culture. Over the long run, the most outstanding traits of the English are practical judgment and tolerance. As a people, they are extremely law-abiding, have a deep distaste for extremes, and can yield gracefully in argument without damage to their beliefs. However, in various places there can be sharp differences. The Yorkshireman is taciturn and can appear quite forbidding. In contrast, the London Cockney talks constantly to friend or stranger, and keeps a lively, knowing eye on his street. Speech, in pronunciation as well as idiom, also varies so that there are quite a few dialects. However, radio and television are slowly but certainly wiping out local differences in language. The English dearly love privacy and have great respect for "keeping oneself to oneself."

Parallel with practicality a strong streak of intellectual curiosity characterizes the English. In science, the trait led George Stephenson, for example, to apply steam power to railroads and factories. The canal system built between 1793 and 1822 in part by Thomas Telford gave another boost to the industrial revolution by providing for bulk transportation. Mass production of textiles was launched by Edmund Cartwright's invention of the power loom and James Hargreaves' invention of the spinning jenny. The process devised by Sir Henry Bessemer for the production of steel is still in use. The result of all this 19th-century work was to make Britain the first modern industrial state.

In the years since, the English have continued their record of scientific achievement. A number of Englishmen have won Nobel Prizes in science, among them Sir Alexander Fleming for the discovery of penicillin and Sir John Cockcroft for work in nuclear physics. Sir John Thomson and Lord Rutherford, among others, pioneered in the development of atomic energy. When operations began at Calder Hall, in Cumberland, in 1956 it was the first nuclear power station in the world. Englishmen have made considerable contributions to the use of gas turbines in land-, sea-, and aircraft, to the development of radar, and to the basic principles of television.

Few other countries can match and certainly none surpass England in literature, beginning with *Beowulf* 1,200 years ago. With *The Canterbury Tales*, Geoffrey Chaucer firmly established English as a literary language. Later came such giants as William Shakespeare and John Milton. The 19th century saw the flowering of the English novel at the hands of Jane Austen, Charles Dickens, William Thackeray. Any 20th-century list of outstanding writers must include D. H. Lawrence and Aldous Huxley.

Today English is the most nearly universal language in the world. Some 200,000,000 persons speak it as their first language, and its use is growing.

Though England's great artistic achievements are in its literature, it has produced some outstanding painters, especially in the 18th century: William Hogarth, Thomas Gainsborough, Sir Joshua Reynolds, and Sir Henry Raeburn. A little later came Joseph Mallord Turner. For the most part their canvases were either portraits or landscapes. In Sir Jacob Epstein and Henry Moore, England gave the 20th century two of its greatest sculptors.

England has also excelled artistically in the creation of beautiful homes and their furnishings. In the 18th century the Adam brothers, both architects and interior designers, made the Georgian style even more elegant.

Interest in art of all kinds, but especially in the theater and music, has widened in England since World War II. Many of these activities are at least partly supported by the government. The National Theatre in London, the Royal Shakespeare Theatre at Stratford-on-Avon, the Royal Opera House (Covent Garden), the Royal Ballet (formerly Sadler's Wells), and concert halls, such as the Royal Festival Hall and Albert Hall, are entertainment magnets for the English, as well as for foreign visitors.

The English have always been fond of outdoor sports, both as participants and spectators. Soccer is the big wintertime sport, followed by rugby and field hockey. Cricket comes into its own in the summer, when it seems there is a game on every village green. Racing—of horses or greyhounds—draws as huge a crowd as lawn tennis. The sports calendar includes the Cup Final (soccer), the Oxford-Cambridge Boat Race, the Derby, the Gold Cup at Ascot, the Grand National Steeplechase, the Cricket Test Matches, and the Wimbledon tennis tournaments.

Nothing is more typically English than the "pub," (public house) where beer is the usual drink. Pubs are highly respectable places that serve as gathering places not only for a drink but for talk or a game of darts.

Consult Carr-Saunders, A. M., and others, *A Survey of Social Conditions in England and Wales* (1958); Lester Smith, W. O., *Education in Great Britain* (1958); Mayfield, Guy, *The Church of England* (1958); Hall, M. P., *The Social Services of Modern England* (1959).

NORMAN J. G. POUNDS, Indiana University

See also ENGLISH ART AND ARCHITECTURE; ENGLISH LITERATURE; ENGLISH MUSIC; ENGLISH THEATER.

History

Early Britain and the Anglo-Saxons. There are traces of Paleolithic man in England. But he was superseded (c.2500–2000 B.C.) by Neolithic man, who introduced a

INDEX TO ENGLAND GENERAL REFERENCE MAP

Total Population 43,000,000

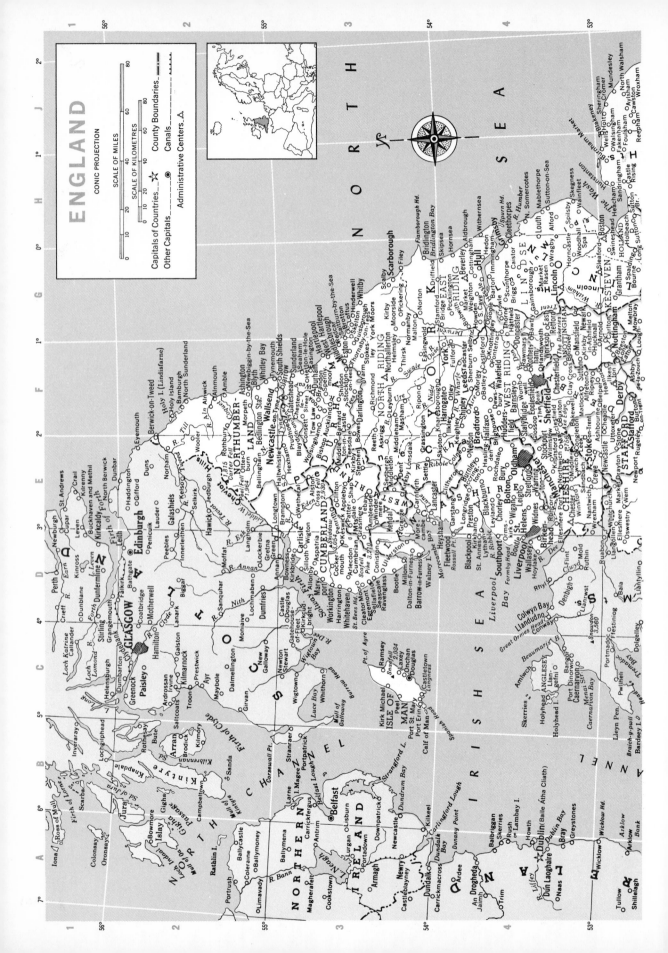

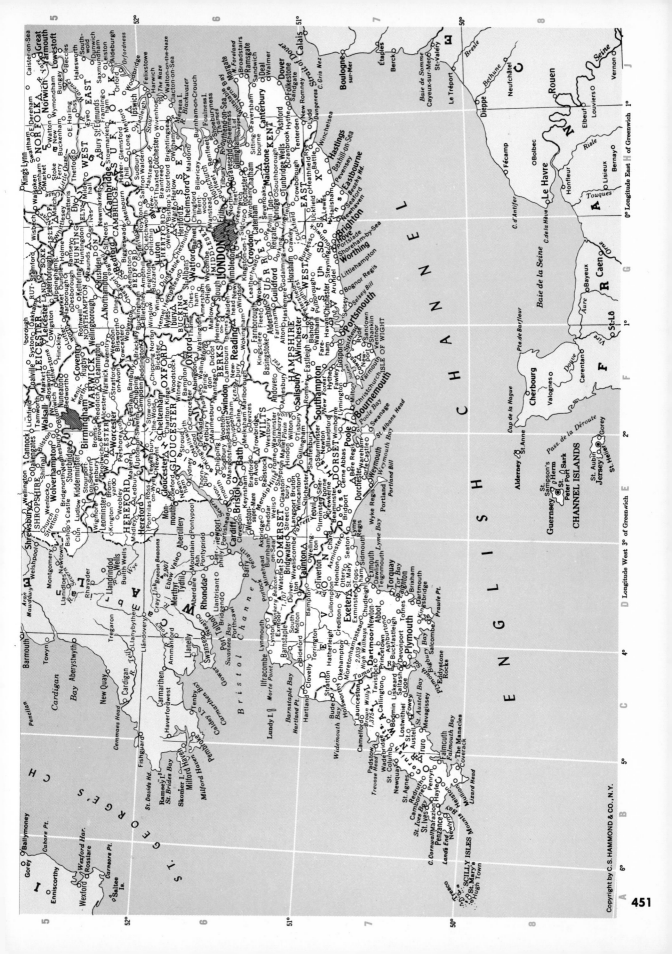

INDEX TO ENGLAND GENERAL REFERENCE MAP (Cont.)

rudimentary agriculture, mined flints for tools, built fortifications, and established well-worn lines of communication. Next to arrive were the Beaker People (so called from their distinctive pottery), who instituted the working of copper and bronze. The use of iron spread from Europe as early as the 5th century B.C. with the arrival of the Celts, whose culture soon dominated England. Little is known of contemporary tribal organization, however. "Kings" like Cunobelinus (Cymbeline), who flourished on the eve of the Roman conquest, are shadowy, legendary figures, and powerful institutions, such as the religious sect of the Druids, are little better known. For the Roman occupation of England from 43–410 A.D., see BRITAIN.

The Roman occupation left remarkably few permanent traces. Raids by German seafaring tribes of Angles, Saxons, and Jutes had begun in the 3d century, A.D., and with the retirement of the Roman legions in 410, Britain lapsed into a chaos of dissociated tribes, led by legendary figures like Vortigern, Germanus (Saint Germanus of Auxerre), and Arthur. The Saxon settlement began in the late 5th century, but not until the 7th century is it possible to distinguish the tribal kingdoms of Sussex, Wessex, Kent, and Essex in the south; of Mercia and East Anglia in the Midlands; and of Northumbria in the north.

Kent was converted to Christianity in 597 by the Roman missionary Augustine, first Archbishop of Canterbury. Northumbria was converted a generation later by Aidan and other missionaries from Iona, the center of Celtic Christianity, and the differences between the two communions were reconciled at the Synod of Whitby in 663. For two centuries Northumbria remained the center of English civilization and, in association with Ireland, had a profound influence upon contemporary European culture.

The history of the Anglo-Saxon kingdoms, meanwhile, was one of almost incessant warfare, arising largely from the fact that royal succession was only partly hereditary. Wessex in the 9th and 10th centuries was the first to establish a true hereditary dynasty, whose members were distinguished for their military and diplomatic skill. This enabled the kingdom to survive the invasion of the Vikings, or Danes, who conquered and settled Northumbria and eastern Mercia between 865 and 878. They were thrown back from Wessex in 878 by Alfred the Great and driven into Essex and East Anglia. Alfred recaptured London in 886 and became acknowledged as overlord of all England outside the Danelaw. He also strove to preserve learning and literature, and codified and supplemented the existing laws.

Alfred's son and successor, Edward the Elder, conquered the remaining Danelaw, and the Viking raids subsided after 955. When they resumed in 980, it is significant that the established Christianized settlers in the Danelaw showed no sympathy with their Scandinavian cousins. The successful levy of a national tax, the Danegeld, to purchase immunity from Danish attack, further testified to England's unity and the efficiency of its government.

Finally, however, Sweyn, King of Denmark, deposed the ineffective Ethelred the Unready in 1013. Sweyn's son, Canute, respected English law and custom, but he failed to found a dynasty, and in 1042 the House of Wessex returned to the throne in the person of Edward the Confessor. Shortly after Edward's death without direct heirs in 1066, England was invaded and conquered by William, Duke of Normandy, who was to become William I of England.

Norman England. The Norman Kings found in England a state as advanced as any in northern Europe. The country was divided into shires, or counties, and subdivided into hundreds, each with its own court of law. A royal official, the sheriff, collected taxes in each county and presided over the county court. There was even a rudimentary police organization. In 1086 William the Conqueror took advantage of this virile local government to complete, in the Domesday Book, a survey of landed property.

The Anglo-Saxon Kings had failed to exact obedience

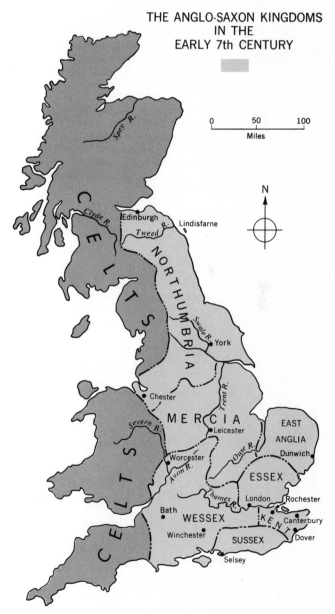

THE ANGLO-SAXON KINGDOMS
IN THE
EARLY 7th CENTURY

from the upper classes. However, the feudal system of land tenure in return for military service imported by the Normans did much to remedy this situation. As might be expected, in the absence of a professional judiciary the office of sheriff went to the powerful barons. They often abused the privilege, and hundred courts were quite commonly surrendered to private jurisdiction. Moreover, although the King exacted from all fighting men an oath of loyalty that overrode their obligations to their feudal lord, in time of rebellion this was often ignored. William and his successors were able and decisive characters, however, and the plunder of the Conquest gave them the financial means to hire mercenaries. They put down baronial rebellions with impartial severity, and administered the English judicial system with a ruthless efficiency that stamped out brigandage and petty larceny for the first time in generations.

Henry I's great Chancellor, Roger of Salisbury, founded the Exchequer as an office of receipt and account, and the first financial record, or Pipe Roll, was issued in 1131. The *Curia Regis*, originally a feudal council, began to assume broad judicial functions. Henry initiated the use of royal writs and the practice of sending out "itinerant justices" to the county courts.

But even the Anglo-Norman state could not survive the failure of male heirs, and the attempt of Henry's daughter, Matilda, to succeed him in 1135 led to a lengthy civil war, accompanied by a complete breakdown in civil government during the reign of Stephen. The Anarchy ended only with the accession in 1154 of Henry II Plantagenet, Matilda's son by Geoffrey of Anjou.

The Plantagenets. Much of Henry's reign was occupied by his quarrel with his Chancellor, Thomas à Becket, who, after he became Archbishop of Canterbury, vigorously de-

fended the Church against the authority of the state. Henry's principal achievement was to provide a machinery for determining possession of land, a machinery that was heartily endorsed by the framers of the Magna Carta half a century later. Trial by jury was established and the royal courts came to absorb an increasing amount of business at the expense of the private feudal courts. The King's income was increasing, particularly from the grant of charters to new towns. The changing nature of warfare in the 12th century reduced the military value of the heavily armored knight, and a substantial part of the royal army now consisted of mercenaries. Fiefs were now hereditary —in fact, if not in theory—and few landowners regarded themselves as professional fighting men. Agriculture was thriving; population was rising and expanding to the forests and hills; trade and industry were flourishing. War, especially in the far-flung Plantagenet dominions of Aquitaine, Gascony, or Maine, offered few profits, and the King was willing enough to let the feudal military obligation lapse. But he insisted instead on the highly unpopular scutage, or shield money.

These tensions were brought to a head by John, who succeeded to the throne in 1199 after a long struggle with his elder brother, Richard I. John's systematic abuse of feudal custom and the loss of Normandy in 1204 provoked a baronial revolt that culminated in the granting of Magna Carta in 1215. The importance of this charter has been exaggerated, and such benefits as it conferred on posterity, mainly in the establishment of legal procedure, were largely accidental. And though it was a feudal document, it failed to solve the central problem of declining feudalism; the question of military service, and to what extent it could be replaced by taxation; and the problem of incorporating the barons into a government that was growing

Surrounded by rebellious barons, King John affixes his seal to the Magna Carta at Runnymede in 1215. The painting is by Richard Caton Woodville (1856–1926).

increasingly professional. The long reign of Henry III (1216–72) was punctuated by such disputes, culminating in the rebellion led by Simon de Montfort, and civil war, which lasted from 1258 until 1265. Later Edward II had to accept the ordinances of 1311, promising the barons substantial control of the government. He was deposed and murdered in 1327.

Strong Kings were tempted to bypass domestic problems by involving the nation in almost continuous action, a temptation heightened by improvements in the army, which transferred the emphasis from cavalry to infantry armed with the longbow. Thus Edward I had spent most of his reign (1272–1307) conquering Wales and trying to place his candidate on the throne of Scotland, and in 1337, Edward III claimed the French crown and sparked the Hundred Years' War. He was brilliantly successful in battle, notably at Crécy in 1346, and at Poitiers in 1356, but the effort exhausted the nation. A further affliction was the chronic shortage of labor caused by the Black Death of 1349, which is estimated to have killed one-third of the population. The subsequent attempt of landlords to exact labor services rather than rents was one of the prime causes of the Peasants' Revolt of 1381.

But the war with France stimulated the growth of the Treasury and the Exchequer. During the 14th century, too, the central courts of law of King's Bench, Common Pleas, and Chancery became separate and distinguishable, and a legal profession, as well as a body of common law, began to rise on the foundations laid by Edward I. Parliament, to which the Commons had first been summoned in 1265, became a regular, if infrequent, part of government, and its statutes were recognized by the courts as being superior to royal edict. Edward III's constant need of money to pay his armies enabled it to seize control of taxation. The development of the House of Lords and the emergence of a hereditary peerage came too late to solve the problems attendant on the decline of feudalism, and Edward III's practice of recruiting and paying his troops through his barons turned the upper classes into so many *condottieri*.

Houses of Lancaster and York. Richard II tried to deal with opposition to his rule by establishing a despotism, but he was deposed by his cousin Henry, Duke of Lancaster, in 1399, and later murdered. Henry IV's reign also witnessed a series of conspiracies and revolts, while his son, Henry V, resorted to the usual panacea, invasion of France. He won a famous victory at Agincourt in 1415 and by 1420 had conquered Normandy, but he was succeeded in 1422 by a nine-month-old child who grew up an imbecile. During the long reign of Henry VI, England lost all her French conquests except Calais, and slid into a state of bankruptcy and disorder. This led to the Wars of the Roses, which broke out in 1455 between the houses of York and Lancaster. In 1471 Edward, Duke of York, finally eliminated all serious opposition, seized the crown, and murdered Henry VI.

Meanwhile, civil order and the administration of justice had almost entirely collapsed. The soldiers released at the end of the Hundred Years' War bound themselves by indenture to any one who would pay them. The practice of maintenance, by which a lord "maintained" the cause of his retainers, and vice versa, wrecked the jury system,

which had never been very robust. Sheriffs and assize judges, owing their appointments usually to bribery or faction politics, were corrupt or timorous, and even the central courts were paralyzed by the frequent changes in government.

The Tudors. The search for a solution to this problem fell to Edward IV and to his brother Richard III, who came to the throne in 1483 after the murder of the young Edward V and his brother in the Tower of London. Their work was continued by Henry Tudor, the principal surviving Lancastrian claimant, who defeated and killed Richard at Bosworth Field in 1485 and established a new dynasty. As Henry VII he put the finances of the crown on a firmer footing, encouraged trade, particularly in cloth and wool, and eliminated private armies. But common law was slow to re-establish itself (as late as 1504 a Parliamentary statute assumed that judges could be bribed or intimidated), and down to the end of the 16th century it was necessary to use the prerogative of the crown in the Star Chamber to suppress feuds among the upper classes and punish delinquent juries.

Henry VIII, who succeeded his father in 1509, dissipated the crown's financial reserves by an overambitious foreign policy. This left him at the mercy of Parliament, which sprang into even greater prominence after 1529, when he called upon it for assistance in coercing the Pope into sanctioning his divorce from Catherine of Aragon. The dissolution of the monasteries (1536–39) and the sale of monastic lands further strengthened the Parliamentary gentry. Henry, insisting that the Pope was in schism, rigidly maintained the orthodoxy of the English Church, but on the accession of his ten-year-old son Edward VI in 1547 it swung decisively toward Protestantism. This time Parliament was called upon to sanction a Book of Common Prayer, in English, and enforce its use. Mary I did her best to reverse this trend, but her persecution of the Protestants only injured her cause. On the accession of her half-sister Elizabeth in 1558 Parliament, now growing in authority and responsibility, was again requested to sanction a Protestant church settlement. Soon, however, the ultra-Protestants, or Puritans, were demanding extensive reforms in ritual and church government. Religious conformity was enforced by means of a high commission, and the defeat of the Spanish Armada in 1588 further strengthened the Queen's hand. But war against Spain, which lasted until 1604, and the outbreak of revolt in Ireland in 1598 only transferred the grounds of the Parliamentary quarrel from religion to war finance. In an age of steeply rising prices, the land-owning gentry were reluctant to pay increased taxation, though the income of the crown was steadily dwindling. Elizabeth's last Parliament in 1601 was openly mutinous. Nevertheless, her reign had also seen great progress. While the English navy under Sir Francis Drake and others was plundering Spanish possessions in America and the Caribbean, trade on a peaceful basis was being expanded in all directions, to Europe and the West Indies, to Africa, the Levant, and Russia. At home, economic reforms were accompanied by a marked development of industry.

The Stuarts. The quarrel with Parliament was only prolonged by the accession in 1603 of the first Stuart sovereign, James I (James VI of Scotland), who was descended from Henry VII through his mother, Mary, Queen of Scots. James's relations with Parliament were almost uniformly bad, and his son Charles I exacerbated the dispute by trying to collect taxes without Parliamentary consent and imprisoning those who refused to pay. The Petition of Right (1628) curbed his activities, but during an 11-year intermission of Parliament, from 1629 to 1640, he financed the navy by the levy of ship-money. The aggressive policy of Archbishop Laud brought about a revival of the Puritan demand for drastic church reform, and it was during Charles's reign that many Puritans left England to found Massachusetts and other colonies in North America. The Scots' rebellion of 1638 bankrupted the government, and in 1641 the Long Parliament abolished the courts of Star Chamber and high commission, and passed legislation that made taxation once and for all dependent on parliamentary consent.

Most 17th-century European monarchs were chronically short of money and hampered by the representative assemblies surviving from the Middle Ages. All except the Stuarts solved these problems, and their failure must be attributed to the tight grip that Parliament had secured on taxation in the 14th century, and to the lack of a regular army. Charles I's proposal to raise such an army, to suppress the Irish Rebellion of 1641, led directly to the first Civil War (1642–46). Parliament defeated the King, but it could find no solution to the constitutional problems now at issue. Also it was subject to considerable pressure from more radical elements, concentrated in the New Model Army led by Oliver Cromwell. When Charles proved his untrustworthiness by provoking the second Civil War in 1648, the army seized power, executed the King and proclaimed a Commonwealth (1649).

But the majority of the governing classes, even those who had fought against the King, were not ripe for republicanism, and the various constitutional experiments of the Interregnum depended for their continuance on military force. Cromwell forcibly dispersed the Long Parliament in 1653 and made himself Lord Protector. His great prestige enabled him to survive mounting difficulties, but on his death in 1658 no successor could be found. In 1660 Gen. George Monck stopped the drift toward chaos by persuading the Long Parliament to dissolve itself formally. The new Convention Parliament inevitably recalled Charles I's son from exile.

The restoration of Charles II put the clock back to 1641. The Anglican Church was re-established, and for the first time many Protestant dissenters were expelled from it. No attempt was made to restrict the royal prerogative of foreign policy and war, and Charles's alliance with France in 1670, accompanied by the conversion to Roman Catholicism of his brother, James, the heir presumptive, led to bitter quarrels with Parliament. One result of these disputes was the Test Acts of 1673 and 1678, which excluded Catholics from Parliament and public office until the 19th century. And after 1679 the opposition made a determined attempt to exclude James from the succession. But the exclusion crisis, after bringing the country to the verge of civil war, was snuffed out with surprising ease in 1681, and four years later James succeeded to the throne without incident.

But the general acceptance of James II depended upon his pursuing a conciliatory policy toward the Anglican Church. Instead, he contrived to give the appearance of extreme aggression. He might still have survived had his wife not given birth to a son in 1688. This prospect of a Catholic Dynasty led many to connive at the invasion of William of Orange, the husband of James's Protestant daughter, Mary. James fled, and in 1689 Parliament had little choice but to declare William and Mary King and Queen.

William and Mary, and Anne. Henceforward Parliament declined to vote the King a permanent income; this and war with France (1689–97) forced William III to hold a session each year. The Triennial Act of 1694 also obliged him to summon a new Parliament every three years. The effect was not as salutary as many had hoped. The land-owning classes found themselves saddled with an increasing burden of taxation, particularly the land tax, while the foundation of the Bank of England in 1694 and the creation of a national debt soon made it virtually impossible for Parliament to coerce the crown by withholding money. Frequent elections and regular Parliamentary attendance were a strain on the poorer gentry, while the growth of the armed forces and the administrative and fiscal system gave the King increasing patronage and electoral influence. These alarming trends provoked a "country" opposition cutting across the already conventional party division of Whig against Tory. This designated opposing opinions on the role of the established Church and the monarchy, and the desirability of the Glorious Revolution of 1688. Not content with cutting the army to the bone in 1698 and later impeaching five of William's ministers, the country opposition inserted in the Act of Settlement (1701) provisions which would have excluded holders of office under the crown from the Commons and suppressed the Cabinet, which was just emerging as a vital link between legislature and executive.

This opposition was checked, however, by the accession of the popular and inoffensive Queen Anne, England's entry into the War of the Spanish Succession in 1702, and by the military successes of John Churchill, Duke of Marlborough, particularly at Blenheim (1704). James II had died in 1701, and his son refused to compromise on the question of religion. Under the Act of Settlement, therefore, the crown would pass on Anne's death to the electoral house of Hanover, descended from James I's daughter Elizabeth. In 1705 the offending clauses of the Act, inserted by the country opposition, were repealed, and in 1707 union with Scotland brought to Parliament at Westminster a group of Scots members and peers who could normally be relied upon to support the King's government.

For the subsequent history of England see UNITED KINGDOM OF GREAT BRITAIN AND NORTHERN IRELAND.

Consult Jolliffe, J. E. A., *Constitutional History of Medieval England* (1947); Feiling, Keith, *History of England* (1950); Myers, A. R., *England in the Late Middle Ages* (1952); Elton, G. R., *England Under the Tudors* (1956); Barrow, G. W. S., *Feudal Britain* (1956); Hill, Christopher, *Century of Revolution 1603–1714* (1961).

JOHN P. KENYON, Christ's College, Cambridge University

See also BARONS' WAR; CLARENDON CODE; FEUDALISM; HASTINGS, BATTLE OF; PROTECTORATE, THE; ROSES, WARS OF THE; SPANISH SUCCESSION, WAR OF THE.

ENGLAND, CHURCH OF, the church established by law in England. Establishment denotes the following: (1) the King or Queen must be a member of the Church of England or abdicate; (2) the 26 senior Bishops sit and vote in the House of Lords; (3) the Archbishop of Canterbury has the right to crown the sovereign; (4) the supreme court in ecclesiastical cases is a crown court (and therefore secular), the judicial committee of the Privy Council; (5) the King or Queen nominates the Bishops for election, but in practice may only make the nomination on the advice of the Prime Minister; (6) any substantial change in the law of the church requires an act of Parliament; and (7) the parson, or priest, of the parish, feels a certain responsibility toward the whole population of the parish and not only to the confirmed members of the Church of England.

Establishment formerly meant more than this. Prior to 1868, dissenters were taxed for the upkeep of parish churches and, till 1836, had to be married in the parish church. Before 1828 dissenters could not sit as members of Parliament if they were Protestant, and not until 1829 if Roman Catholic; and prior to 1836 dissenters could not take a degree at a university. However, all these inequalities were removed during the 19th century. In the countries of the British Isles where the Church of England is a minority, it was disestablished: in Ireland in 1869, in Wales in 1920.

At present, approximately three-fourths of the English population is baptized in the Church of England, and approximately one-half of the total number of marriages are performed in the established church. The question of disestablishment has hardly been alive in England during the 20th century, though the relations between church and state give rise to epidemic discomfort—especially among churchmen who are concerned about the due independence of the church.

The official formularies of the Church of England are the Thirty-nine Articles of 1571, and the Book of Common Prayer of 1662. Although it was Henry VIII who broke with the Roman See, Protestant ideas came in under his son Edward VI. Queen Mary, who succeeded Edward, carried England back into the Roman obedience, and it was not until the reign of Queen Elizabeth I that religion was settled in a Protestant but moderate frame. It is clear that the Thirty-nine Articles were intended as the basis of a Protestant church. But they were framed widely, and within limits allowed more liberty of opinion than many of the Reformation confessions. And as time went on, a greater breadth of interpretation became customary. The original form of subscription to the Thirty-nine Articles exacted from the clergy was rigorous and detailed. But since the Clerical Subscription Act of 1865 the assent required has often been so general that it does not commit the subscriber to the truth of every phrase of the articles.

The Elizabethan Prayer Book of 1559 was an adaptation of the vernacular Prayer Book of 1552, created by the liturgical genius of Thomas Cranmer, but with small modifications designed to make it more palatable to conservatives. After the rule of Cromwell and the restoration of Charles II, this was readopted in 1662, with a few more modifications in a conservative direction. It is a liturgy of the Swiss Reformed tradition rather than the Lutheran, but having an atmosphere of liturgical tradition, and at some important points of the services retaining ancient formulas of which the Swiss reformers disapproved.

In particular, Queen Elizabeth's government took great care that the new Protestant Archbishop of Canterbury, Matthew Parker, should be consecrated by other Bishops in the old way. Hence the "apostolic succession" of the historic episcopate was retained. Though from the beginning of Elizabeth's reign there was a group of recusants who refused to conform on the ground that Catholicism must mean obedience to Rome, many conservatives felt able to use this liturgy with a clear conscience. When historical circumstances strengthened the conservative element in the Church of England, the church could find room for a wider variety of faith and practice than could be found probably anywhere else in Christendom. By the 19th century it included Calvinists at one end and Anglo-Catholics at the other.

The Reformation, while it made important changes in the doctrine and liturgy of the church, made fewer changes in the constitution, apart from the abolition of papal jurisdiction. The old assemblies of the clergy, the Convocations of Canterbury and York, continued, though they were effectively suppressed between 1717 and 1852. Since 1919, in association with a house of laity, they have been able to prepare ecclesiastical bills for Parliament; and these bills do not require Parliamentary debate unless they affect existing acts of Parliament. The old system of appointment to parishes by some lay patrons continues, and there are very few parishes in the Church of England where the congregation may select its minister. Many of the more important parish churches are medieval structures, and the cathedrals retain their medieval constitution of a dean and canons. Thus English churchmen possess a sense of historical continuity going back to the foundation of Christianity in England, and look back upon the Venerable Bede and Anglo-Saxon saints with as much

Canterbury Cathedral in 1961 as Michael Ramsey was enthroned as the 100th Archbishop of Canterbury. (PICTORIAL PARADE, INC.)

affection as they do upon the men of the Reformation. The strength of this historical sense is probably unique in Protestantism.

During the 18th and 19th centuries a devoted missionary endeavor carried the Anglican Church into the English dominions and beyond their borders, so that by 1867 the Church of England found itself the mother of a wider federation of Episcopal churches.

The Church of England has commanded the loyalty of many members because it has offered in worship a reformed Catholicism—faithful to the Bible, recognizing the insights of the Reformation, condemning the excesses of medieval Christianity, yet attempting to be Catholic in its austere traditions of ancient piety, and in its allegiance to the doctrines of the early, undivided Church. Its Elizabethan theorist, Richard Hooker, stood for the rightful place of reason in religious thought; and this tradition of reasonableness and learning has been marked among the English clergy.

In the period from 1660 to 1830 the church made signal contributions to science and philosophy, as well as to theology, and sometimes pursued learning almost at the expense of pastoral care. Consequently it was able, more easily than some churches, to make the needful adjustments before the new challenges of history and science in the age of Darwin. Especially since 1864, it has permitted a wide variety of opinion in doctrine and practice; and although these have been regretted at times as conducive to the development of ecclesiastical parties they have also been welcomed as a sign of a truly "Catholic" or "ecumenical" attitude.

Consult Ady, C. M., *The English Church and How It Works* (1940); Moorman, J. R. H., *A History of the Church in England* (1954); Neill, S. C., *Anglicanism* (1958).

W. O. Chadwick, Master of Selwyn College, Cambridge

ENGLEWOOD [ĕng′gəl-wŏŏd], city of north-central Colorado, directly south of the urban core of Denver, and within that city's metropolitan area. Manufacturing and business concerns have found advantageous locations in Englewood. It is also known as "carnation city," due to the large number of specialized greenhouses and nurseries here. Inc., 1903; pop. (1950) 16,869; (1960) 33,398.

ENGLEWOOD, city of northeastern New Jersey, 12 mi. northeast of Jersey City. It is primarily residential. Inc., 1899; pop. (1950) 23,145; (1960) 26,057.

ENGLISH [ĭng′glĭsh]. Of the more than 3,000 languages spoken in the world today, the single language which has had the most amazing, rapid, and widespread growth is unquestionably English. It is spoken as a native language by well over a quarter of a billion persons in the United States and Canada, in the British Isles, Australia, New Zealand, and South Africa, and it is also the chief language that was used by the colonizers of Asia, Africa, and Oceania. In addition, it is spoken as a second language by many more millions in countries where French or German formerly held that position.

Historical Background

The story of the English language, a West Germanic

tongue, may be begun, romantically enough, when the Romans, whose empire had included Britain, abandoned the island to self-rule under the Celts, its inhabitants, in 410 A.D. The Romans departed from Britain because Rome itself was being attacked from the north by the Goths and the Vandals.

For a while the terror of the Roman name served to protect the Celts, but as the Picts attacking from the north became ever more daring and menacing, the Celtic King Vortigern sent messengers to the hardy Germanic tribes asking them for their help. They acceded, and the chiefs Hengist and Horsa, with their followers, rowed their long boats up the English waterways in 449 A.D. When the Germans saw the richness and fertility of the land and the weakness of the Celts, they decided to take the land for themselves.

The Germanic invaders brought their separate dialects to different regions of England. The Jutes settled in Kent and spoke the Kentish dialect. Saxon tribes took over the rest of southern England. We call their dialect Saxon. In the north, above a region where the tribes were mixed and a dialect called Mercian was spoken, the speech of the tribes called Angles was Northumbrian.

It was this northern region which witnessed the beginnings of England's literary history, even though little survives from the period. After the early prominence of the northern language, Saxon was lifted into literary use by the efforts of King Alfred, who died in 901. It might well have become the standard for the whole country; but gradually trade, the court, and public interest were transferred to London, and this midland district became the cultural and linguistic center.

The history of the English language is customarily divided into three periods: Old English, Middle English, and Modern English. Old English, in comparison to Middle and Modern English, is a language of full inflections. It extends from the earliest records to about 1100—after the Norman Conquest (1066). No record of the English language exists until after the conversion of the Anglo-Saxons to Christianity, which began in 597 when St. Augustine came from Italy to convert the kingdom of Kent. Few written records have been preserved from before the late 9th century. Change in the language was constantly going on, and by 1100 many of the inflections had been leveled off. Then what is known as the Middle English period, the period of leveled inflections, began. It extended to 1500, the beginning of the Modern English period, in which inflections are lost.

Old English

In the year 800 all the dialects of England, in spite of their minor variations, were German. Indeed, Old English was more like Modern German than it is like Modern English. Names of things were masculine, feminine, or neuter. For instance, the words for *foot* and *neck* were masculine, for *hand* and *cheek* feminine, but the words for *eye* and *ear* were neuter. The word for *maiden* was also neuter, as is the cognate word in German, *Mädchen*. In like manner *wif*, "wife," and *cild*, "child," were neuter. In Modern English natural or logical gender has completely replaced grammatical gender. One no longer has to consider whether a noun is masculine, feminine, or neuter or whether it belongs to a strong or weak declension, and then inflect for number (singular and plural) and case (nominative, genitive, dative, accusative). Nouns now have only two cases—the common case and the possessive, or genitive: *boy, boy's.*

Like the noun in Old English, the adjective was highly inflected. It had five cases: those of the noun plus the instrumental. In addition it was inflected for number, gender, class, and strong and weak position. As in Modern High German, it had to agree in inflection with the number, case, and gender of the noun it modified. In Old English *eald,* "old," had the forms, *eald, ealdes, ealdne, ealdum, ealde, ealdra, ealdre, ealda, ealdan,* or *ealdena.* In Modern English all have been lost except the first. One may now say *an old man (woman) (song), the old men, the life of an old man, books for an old man, the chair is old,* or any similar expression without changing the form of the adjective and without loss of clarity in meaning. Modern English has scored two major advances in the loss of inflections in the adjective and in the loss of grammatical gender.

If one looks at the vocabulary of Old English, one finds that much of it was native English. Borrowing, however, had gone on. Words had been taken from the Latin, some of which had been borrowed before the Anglo-Saxons came to England, such as *cheese, mile, wall, kettle, wine.* Many more came into the language after Christianity was accepted, among them *priest, martyr, angel, candle.*

Later, Danes attacked the Anglo-Saxons, and the greatest influence on Old English was Scandinavian. Not only did the Scandinavians give names to more than 1,400 places in England, but they gave us several of our pronouns, *they, their, them,* and a good share of our vocabulary of short, simple words, such as *sky, give, get, egg, law, skin, skull,* and *leg.*

Middle English

The next mixture came as a result of the Norman Conquest. After 1066 the French language nearly conquered the English, but not quite. Three languages were then in use in England: French was the language of the court and the nobility; Latin of the church; and English of the common people.

English survived as the national language, but it was profoundly changed. Middle English, still a Germanic language, differed from Old English in that speakers in expressing themselves began to depend more on structure words and word order than upon inflectional devices. One of the main reasons for the leveling of inflectional endings in the Middle English period was, no doubt, the shifting of the accent to the first syllables of words. As a result, the inflectional endings were no longer heard clearly and became neutral in sound, developing into the *schwa* vowel, usually written as *ə.* The various declensions of the noun, based on the difference in vowel ending, were largely abandoned. With the leveling of the inflections under *-e,*

ENGLISH **STUDY GUIDE**

English is the language of the peoples of the British Isles, the United States, Canada, Australia, New Zealand, South Africa and other areas. More people speak it, either as a first or second language, than any other tongue, and it has become the closest approximation to an international language that has ever existed. In addition, some of the greatest literature that the world has ever known was written in English. The article on these pages deals with the development of the English language, starting with the introduction of Germanic influences into England in 449 A.D., after the departure of the Romans. The growth and change of the language are traced through Old English (to c.1100) and Middle English (c.1100-c.1500) to Modern English (beginning c.1500). Many other articles in the **ENCYCLOPEDIA INTERNATIONAL** contain additional information on English.

Relation to Other Languages. The article LANGUAGE discusses the origin and historical development of the various tongues and contains a list of world languages indicating the ones to which English is related, closely or distantly. INDO-EUROPEAN LANGUAGES surveys the history and characteristics of the family to which English belongs. Additional data are provided in GERMANIC LANGUAGES, which treats the subgroup of the Indo-European languages that includes English. DIALECT deals with variations of speech and grammar within individual languages. Also of interest is AMERICAN ENGLISH, which analyzes usage in the United States and Canada. Useful articles for comparative purposes are GERMAN and LATIN.

The English alphabet developed from North Semitic ancestors through the Phoenician, Greek, and Roman alphabets, and finally evolved into its present form. This story is told in ALPHABET and in 26 short articles, one on each of the letters.

The derivations and meanings of words and the current state of usage are recorded in reference works (see DICTIONARY and REFERENCE BOOK, which discusses the thesaurus). The article SLANG is of particular interest to the student of the current evolution of English.

Using English in Writing and Speaking. The article GRAMMAR deals with the study of words and their relationships in a sentence, and USAGE deals with choices among various correct forms of speech and writing. Additional information is provided in such articles as SENTENCE, PARTS OF SPEECH, CASE, VOICE, PUNCTUATION, and CAPITALIZATION.

Mastery of English extends beyond correctness, however, for to employ it effectively the user must develop facility. Suggestions on style are offered in WRITING, CRAFT OF. Other articles deal with particular forms of writing: RESEARCH PAPER, PRECIS WRITING, LETTER WRITING, RESUME, and OUTLINING. There are individual entries on literary forms such as the NOVEL and SHORT STORY. VERSIFICATION provides technical material on the writing of verse.

English, of course, is a spoken as well as written language. The reader concerned with the spoken words can consult PRONUNCIATION, PHONETICS, and DIACRITICAL MARKS. Those who want practical information can read SPEECHMAKING and DEBATE.

English Literature. The tradition of English literature grew around such figures as Chaucer, Shakespeare, and Milton, names that symbolize mankind's greatest achievements in the art of writing. Writers in English maintain high standards to the present day, as exemplified by the works of Shaw, Eliot, and Yeats. The reader is referred to ENGLISH LITERATURE; UNITED STATES, LITERATURE OF THE; CANADA: *Literature;* SCOTTISH LITERATURE; and IRISH LITERATURE IN ENGLISH, as well as to entries on authors and individual works.

-*es*, -*en*, the means of distinguishing grammatical gender disappeared and words began to be employed as in Modern English. During the 14th century use of -*s* for the plural ending of nouns was accepted as standard throughout England. The -*en* plural decreased in use with only a few examples remaining in Modern English, such as *oxen, brethren, children*. Along with the loss of inflections in the noun went the loss in the adjective. Other changes also occurred.

In looking at the vocabulary of Middle English one finds that throughout the whole period thousands of French words of all types and from every sphere of life poured into the English language: *government, parliament, reign, liberty, mayor, verdict, appetite, veal, beef, dinner, roast, broil, embroidery, taffeta, satin, diamond, prayer, clergy, religion, fruit, flower, soldier, guard, sergeant, cathedral, sculpture, ceiling, physician, surgeon*. The Latin influence increased. Many words relating to science, literature, theology, and law were introduced, like *allegory, scripture*, and *testimony*. English became a richer language with many synonyms as, for example, Old English *ask*, French *inquire*, and Latin *interrogate*. Nevertheless, the heart of the vocabulary remained English. Most of the words in constant use, little recurrent words like *of, at, he, you, and, will, shall*—the prepositions, conjunctions, pronouns, and auxiliaries, along with many commonly employed nouns, adjectives, and verbs—were kept along with the many loan words.

Modern English

By 1500 the English language substantially had its present structure, and all except five inflections had been lost: *s*, used in pluralizing nouns (*hat, hats*) and in forming the third person singular of most verbs (*talk, he talks*); -*ed*, employed to form the past tense of the weak verbs (*talk, talked*); -*ing* in the present participle (*talking*); the comparative -*er* (*hotter*); and the superlative -*est* (*hottest*). The language had changed from synthetic, depending chiefly upon inflections, to analytic, in which relationships are shown by means of structure words (auxiliaries, prepositions, and the like) and a more fixed word order, the usual pattern now being subject-verb-complement. This language emerged mainly from the East Midland dialect— the dialect of London and that used by the great Middle English poet Chaucer.

The two chief influences from 1500 to 1700 were the great humanistic movement of the Renaissance and the invention of printing from movable type. At this time thousands of words from Latin and Greek poured in along with many new ideas, so that today numerous words are still being formed from the classical roots, suffixes, and prefixes to supply the necessary technical terms for medicine, electronics, and the various branches of pure and applied science. To give a few examples, one might mention among the hundreds of new terms *aerospace, astronaut, cosmonaut, cybernetics, geriatrics, stratosphere, supersonic, telecast, television*.

Since the days of Shakespeare the English language has undergone relatively minor changes. A pronoun in all its forms—*thou, ye, thine, thyself, thee*—has been dropped, leaving us no way of distinguishing between *you* in the singular and *you* plural. Such constructions as "David was given a book" and "Seats were assigned them" have come into use. The subordinate clause has extended its field of usefulness. In general English has become more and more efficient, less and less logical.

And at the same time English has been steadily gaining in world-wide popularity, until today, if we have an international language, it is English. It need scarcely be added that at no time in the history of the world has any language attained such popularity.

Consult McKnight, G. H., *English Words and Their Backgrounds* (1923); Baugh, A. C., *A History of the English Language* (2d ed., 1957); Bryant, M. M., *Modern English and Its Heritage* (2d ed., 1962).

MARGARET M. BRYANT, Brooklyn College

ENGLISH ART AND ARCHITECTURE.

When in 449 A.D., the Saxons invaded England, four centuries of Roman Britain came to an end. Aside from traces of the Roman wall across northern England and parts of the baths at Bath, little remains from the Roman years. From the Dark Ages only a few churches, like those at Earls Barton in Northamptonshire or Barton-upon-Humber in Lincolnshire, are left, their towers punctuated by tiny windows and their small size testifying to the poverty of the era.

Medieval Architecture

The Normans, after their conquest of England in 1066, introduced imposing Romanesque cathedrals. The Norman style featured massive piers, round arches, and thick walls that usually supported timber roofs, although the Cathedral of Durham, the grandest Norman church, has a stone vault over both nave and aisles.

The English cathedrals grew with the fortunes of their towns, or more commonly the monasteries, that founded them. The monks and canons needed cloisters, chapter houses, refectories, and lodgings as well as the church itself. Through the centuries part after part of both church and monastery were added or rebuilt. Hence, the typical Gothic cathedral illustrates all of the three styles of English Gothic architecture: the Early English, the Decorated, and the Perpendicular.

About 1150 the Early English style appeared, probably inspired by France. The Frenchman William of Sens built the choir of Canterbury Cathedral with six-part vaults and the narrow-pointed, or lancet, windows typical of this style. Salisbury Cathedral is perhaps the most complete example of Early English architecture.

The Decorated style began about 1250. Piers and vaults became complex, and decoration profuse. The distinguishing feature of the style is the broad pointed window, its upper part filled with tracery. Until about 1300 the tracery patterns were composed of circles or segments of circles, but reversed curves appeared after that date in Exeter Cathedral.

Finally, Gloucester Cathedral introduced the Perpendicular style about 1350. Its perpendicular mullions and horizontal transoms, or crossbars, of tracery divide its large windows into repeated vertical rectangles like shelves of books. The vaults are formed into interlacing patterns; in the fan vaults the ribs spray out like those of a fan.

Beautiful as are the English cathedrals and minsters

(monasteries), set amidst lawns and trees, they are not all of English medieval architecture. The land is studded with castles and manor houses. The square Norman keep, like the 12th-century Hedingham Castle in Essex, raises its forbidding walls with few small windows to light the single living chamber on each floor. At Bodiam Castle in Sussex, of later date, towers and curtain walls, surrounded by a moat, guard a court on which the rooms open. By 1500 the Tudor peace that suppressed the private armies of feudalism made fortifications unnecessary. Compton Wynyates in Warwickshire is a manor house with large windows on the outside as well as on the court. It was built not as a castle but as a home.

Renaissance Architecture

Although the Gothic style may not have been born in England, in its English version it was so completely English art from the 12th through the 15th century that it could not readily yield in the 16th to the foreign manner of the Renaissance. Indeed, in such simplified forms as the picturesque cottages of the Cotswold Hills in Gloucestershire English Gothic persisted at least into the 18th century. Nevertheless, Henry VIII, like his French rival Francis I, admired and coveted the sophistication of the Italian Renaissance and did his best to induce Italian artists to come to England. One such, Pietro Torrigiano, designed the tomb of Henry VII in that monarch's chapel in Westminster Abbey. Small colonies of Italian craftsmen sprang up in London and Winchester to act as both teachers and producers of work in the new manner. The Italianisms could at first be only superficial. Thus in Cardinal Wolsey's palace, Hampton Court, both structure and design are fundamentally Gothic, and yet to either side of the court doorway Giovanni da Majano inserted terracotta roundels with busts of Roman emperors. From such beginnings one might expect the Renaissance to grow slowly in England, as it did in France, until a coherent local variety of the style was achieved.

In fact, it did not. England's Protestantism, dating from the reign of Henry VIII, coupled with the resulting political situation, made it inevitable that the country should find its friends in Protestant Germany and the Low Countries, and it was to them that it turned, rather than to Italy, for understanding of the Renaissance. Even the colonies of Italian craftsmen disappeared. Unfortunately Germany hardly understood Renaissance principles better than England, and German handling of Renaissance forms was peculiarly clumsy. In Burghley House in Northamptonshire, built by German craftsmen for Cecil, Lord Burghley, such absurdities as Doric columns used for chimney pots appear, and its decorative detail, if exuberant, is coarse. Nevertheless, the window area is immense, quite as large as in modern buildings. The contemporary Hardwick Hall in Derbyshire has more glass than wall. In the latter the Renaissance principle of symmetry was accepted, but the Gothic love of the vertical persisted in square towerlike forms at each corner as well as in projecting bay windows the full height of the building that balance each other on the sides of the doorways. Such vast Elizabethan mansions were the perquisite of the aristocracy and found few imitators in smaller houses. The Jacobean style, a later offshoot from the Elizabethan, perhaps was used more widely. The detail of the smaller houses, like Burton Agnes in Yorkshire, though still rich, is also less heavy and less vigorous than that of its predecessors.

During the Elizabethan and Jacobean periods, significant changes took place in the house. The enclosed court, a relic of the feudal castle, though still preserved in Burghley House, was generally abandoned, and houses were designed with projecting wings on either end of a central block, and perhaps also with a shorter protrusion in the center. The resulting plan, shaped like an E, though often

Salisbury Cathedral stands in a spacious wooded close. The cathedral was consecrated in 1258. (BRITISH TRAVEL & HOLIDAY ASSN.)

Fan vaults on the ceiling of the enclosed cloisters (built from 1351 to 1412) of Gloucester Cathedral. (GAYTON—ILLUSTRATION RESEARCH SERVICE)

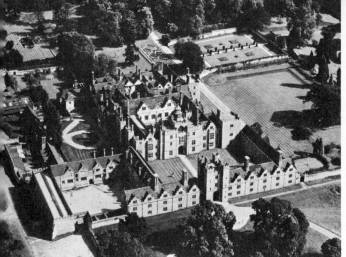

Knole House (early 17th century) in Kent is one of the largest private houses in England. The park covers several acres.

Westminster Bridge spans the Thames River beside the Houses of Parliament. Behind Big Ben (right) is Westminster Abbey.

Compton Wynyates (c.1520) in Warwickshire has the steep-pitched roofs and clustered chimneys typical of Tudor buildings (above).

The Queen's House, Greenwich (begun in 1616), by Inigo Jones, shows the influence of late Italian Renaissance architecture.

said to be a compliment to Elizabeth I, was in reality the result of changed social conditions. In the medieval manor house the entire household had converged in the hall for meals; in the Elizabethan house the hall dwindled in size and importance. When its door was set in the center, as in Aston Hall in Birmingham, it became a vestibule and not a room for living purposes. The narrow spiral stairs of medieval castles were usually set in turrets extruded from the walls. But the stairs in Knole House in Kent, built early in the 17th century, line three sides of a square room around an open well and are broad and easy of ascent. In houses of the time they had become not mere conveniences but architectural features. The largest room was a long gallery running from end to end of the house and often warmed by several large fireplaces.

During the Elizabethan and Jacobean periods English architecture had fallen out of step with advanced thought on the continent. However, one architect of the time, Inigo Jones (1573–1652), conceived an unbounded enthusiasm for Andrea Palladio, a 16th-century Italian architect and theorist, who devised rules for the Roman orders and recommended detailed proportions for their bases, columns, and entablatures. In addition to studying

his books, Jones went to examine Palladio's many buildings in Vicenza, Italy. When Jones designed the Queen's House, Greenwich, London, he discarded the lingering medievalisms of the Jacobean style, and substituted the restraint, order, and rule of Palladio's late Renaissance manner. The plan is a perfect square with no projecting turrets or bay windows. Horizontality replaces verticality. The chimney pots, scattered in the case of the Burghley House, are grouped here and are unobtrusive. The windows, sufficient in size, punctuate the walls but do not replace them.

Every element in Jones's Banqueting House, Whitehall, London, has precedent in Palladio's designs. The Ionic and Corinthian orders of pilasters and engaged columns are as correct in proportion as Palladio's rules. The balustrade on top, the corniced windows, the walls with their drafted masonry (masonry that forms a narrow groove along the edges or across the face of a stone): all is Italian in origin, and yet the design has an unaccountably English flavor. Perhaps it results from the pragmatism of the English architects, a reluctance to allow theory, however admirable, completely to dominate the building.

In his interiors, too, Jones accepted Palladian forms.

Delicate moldings enframe panels whose fields are flush with or slightly behind the wall plane. Garlands of fruit or flowers molded in stucco may accent or help to enframe doors or fireplaces. Jones's architecture is admirable in proportion, correct and restrained in detail.

Baroque and Georgian Architecture

Sir Christopher Wren (1632–1723) dominated English architecture during the Restoration. This versatile genius, a distinguished astronomer and member of the Royal Society, was appointed Royal Surveyor, or architect. His output was enormous. A few of his larger works are the buildings at Greenwich Hospital, Chelsea Hospital, extensive additions to Hampton Court Palace, and the Sheldonian Theater and the library of Queen's College at Oxford. After the great fire of London in 1666, he submitted a far-sighted plan for rebuilding the city, which, however, was not followed; he designed more than 50 churches to replace those that had been burned. These last show extraordinary imagination in adapting their plans to irregular sites. Flat ceilings, domes, and barrel or groin vaults are employed. The decorative treatment—for all its baroque license of detail—is restrained. The steeples of his churches illustrate the rich variety of his architectural vocabulary. That of St. Mary-le-Bow in London showed his sense of the silhouette as one story of different but related design rises on another, each smaller than the one below, to terminate in a slender pyramid. He even experimented with Gothic designs, as in the Church of St. Dunstan's-in-the-East, also in London.

Wren's masterpiece is, of course, St. Paul's Cathedral. St. Paul's has the distinction of being the only major cathedral to be designed and completed by a single man. Wren's style combines the boldness and freedom of the baroque and its spatial sense with the conservatism of English tradition. Occasional traces of French or Dutch influence testify to the breadth of the architect's interests.

The Georgian style of architecture, named for the English kings who ruled during the 18th century, succeeded the baroque. Under the leadership of Lord Burlington, an amateur architect and patron of a distinguished group of architects who created a series of buildings for him, the style rejected the baroque elements of Wren's buildings to return for guidance to Inigo Jones and Palladio. The archetypal Georgian mansion consists of a central block structure from which quadrants, or curved corridors, extend forward to link smaller flanking block buildings. These imposing houses trace their architectural lineage back through Inigo Jones's design of Stoke Park in Northamptonshire to Palladian villas. The smaller Georgian houses, such as those at Bath on the Queen's Square or the Circus, though less pretentious are more charming in their paneled interiors. The architect James Gibbs was somewhat independent of the Burlington group; his portico of the Church of St. Martin's-in-the-Fields, Trafalgar Square, London, may stem from Palladio, but the freedom of the steeple and the interior rivals Wren. About 1760 Robert Adam and his brother James introduced their exquisite style of interior decoration, whose motives are Roman in origin, and whose results are formal but light and elegant. Small scale supplanted the monumentality of the Georgian mansion.

Nineteenth-Century Architecture

During the 19th century the full impact of the industrial revolution, the changes in transportation, the growth of science and archeology produced a materialistic philosophy. The romanticists early in the century turned to the past as a vicarious escape from the present. John Soane copied the columns of the Roman Temple of the Sibyl at Tivoli for the Lothbury angle of the Bank of England. In some of his other work, like the Soane Museum, in London, originally his home, he was capable of brilliant nonhistorical composition of geometric masses in architecture. Others, like Robert Smirke in the British Museum, turned to Greece for inspiration.

The Roman and Greek revivals are rooted in the mid-18th century. So, too, is the Gothic Revival. But the two classic styles were at least related to the Renaissance and the Georgian, while the Gothic was antithetical. Hence Horace Walpole could insert in his 18th-century home Strawberry Hill only a collection of Gothic details valued for their sentimental associations, and with no more grasp of Gothic principles than had Chippendale's so-called Gothic designs in furniture. Not until the second quarter of the 19th century was medieval architecture understood well enough to enable Augustus Welby N. Pugin to design churches that really have much of the Gothic in form and even something in spirit. He provided the Perpendicular Gothic details for Charles Barry's Houses of Parliament, bringing them into accord with their neighbor, Westminster Abbey. In the third quarter of the century the Gothic Revival gave way to the potpourri of Victorian ostentation, as seen in George Gilbert Scott's Albert Memorial in London.

During the last quarter of the 19th century a number of designers and craftsmen, associated with the group of painters and writers known as the Pre-Raphaelites, protested the materialism of their day and the ugliness of its machine-made products. One such was William Morris, who sought to revive handicrafts. Abortive though his effort was, his own productions are fresh in design and sympathetic to their materials. The Red House at Bexley Heath was designed for him by Philip Webb, who rejected all historic styles and conceived the structure to fit its purpose and materials. As such it is an early landmark of modern architecture. Working along similar antihistorical lines, Norman Shaw did much to clear the air for a fresh approach to architecture, as did Edwin Lutyens, especially in his early work.

Foreign Influence in English Painting

Although survivals of illuminated manuscripts and stained glass from the medieval period demonstrate a long history of painting in England, the demand for portraits in court circles in the 16th and 17th centuries was mainly satisfied by foreigners. The German Hans Holbein the Younger painted Henry VIII and many other prominent figures of the second quarter of the 16th century in a precise and detailed manner with frank, pungent, and penetrating analyses of their individualities. The Flemish painter Sir Anthony Van Dyck served as court portraitist to Charles I from 1632 to 1641. Van Dyck's more decorative style, drawing heavily on Venetian Renaissance sources, is less candid and analytical than Holbein's and tends to flatter his sitters, but established the kind of society portraiture that England would follow into the early 19th century.

Sir Peter Lely, a Hollander, continued the type for the court of Charles II, and Sir Godfrey Kneller, German born, painted portraits in the same tradition in the early 18th century. The fame of these foreigners has somewhat unjustly eclipsed such forthright native portraitists as Robert Walker, who did likenesses of Oliver Cromwell and others of the 17th century. Peter Paul Rubens, the great Flemish master, executed murals on the ceiling of Jones's Banqueting House in his brilliant baroque style. The principal English decorative artist, Sir James Thornhill, painted the dome of St. Paul's Cathedral, while many of the large Georgian mansions have rooms or ceilings by the Italian Antonio Verrio or the Frenchman Louis Laguerre.

Eighteenth-Century Painting

The first great English painter, William Hogarth, had a flair for narrative. The vivid description and the cutting characterizations of his series of paintings are coupled with powerful drawing and brilliant spatial organization. Among them are "Marriage à la Mode," "The Rake's Progress," "The Harlot's Progress," and the "Election" series. In addition, Hogarth produced a number of powerful, well-characterized portraits. His "Shrimp Girl" (National Gallery, London) is remarkable for the vitality of its dashing brush work.

The late 18th century saw the flowering of the English portrait school. In general, its members followed the tradition of society portraiture introduced by Van Dyck, creating portraits that radiate aristocratic distinction. Sir Joshua Reynolds was the recognized leader. He became president of the Royal Academy on its foundation in 1768 and remained so until 1790. His painting of Mrs. Sarah Siddons (Huntington Library and Art Gallery, San Marino, Cal.) shows the celebrated Shakespearean actress as the tragic muse, enthroned like a Michelangelesque sibyl between allegorical figures. And yet Reynolds's simpler portraits of men are often more incisive than those of his women. His friend Dr. Johnson lives in his portrait (National Gallery, London) as though he were about to define a word for his dictionary or perhaps to contradict Boswell.

For sheer brilliance of painting, Thomas Gainsborough was even greater. His portrait of Mrs. Siddons (National Gallery, London) has none of the allegorical or literary overtones of Reynolds's, but it is more dashing and assured. Perhaps his most famous picture is "The Blue Boy" (Huntington Library and Art Gallery, San Marino, Cal.), erroneously said to have been painted to disprove a claim made by Reynolds that blue could not be made the dominant color in a painting. Among other members of the group were George Romney, John Hoppner, John Opie, and the Scot Henry Raeburn, who was one of the most talented. Sir Thomas Lawrence in the early 19th century carried the dashing style of this group to its glittering end, and after him the portrait school declined rapidly.

The dilettanti of the 18th century quite unjustly ranked portraiture as inherently inferior to historical painting, that is, figural compositions of moral, allegorical, mythological, or historic import. The historical themes were usually drawn from antiquity. The American-born Benjamin West served as historical painter to George III and succeeded Reynolds as president of the Royal Academy. His "histories" like "The Return of the Prodigal Son" (Metropolitan Museum of Art, New York) interest the present day less than his paintings of history, as in "The Death of Wolfe at Quebec" (National Gallery of Canada, Ottawa). In the latter he took the step, bold at the time, of depicting his characters in their contemporary uniforms. The dilettanti rated landscape below portraiture, and yet English landscape painting was born in the 18th century. Richard Wilson turned out impressive pictures of Cader Idris and other views of the Welsh mountains in a vein foretelling romanticism. Had he lived a generation later, Gainsborough would probably have been primarily a landscape painter instead of a portraitist. His "Market Wagon" (Tate Gallery, London) and other landscapes are among his finest paintings.

Nineteenth-Century Painting

It was not until the early 19th century that landscape became dominant. Then Constable and Turner achieved international importance. John Constable was determined to paint the quiet, undramatic but friendly English landscape just as he saw it. His subjects were drawn from his native Suffolk, or Salisbury and its environs, Brighton on the coast, or Hampstead Heath near London. His landscapes depicted intimate views seen close at hand with the focus relatively near the observer, instead of the panoramic ones with a distant focus of earlier painters. His fresh approach to nature, introduced to France when some of his paintings were exhibited in Paris in 1824, profoundly affected Delacroix and the painters of the Barbizon school.

Joseph M. W. Turner was more prolific and more varied. Especially in his earlier works, like "Crossing the Brook" (National Gallery, London), he was strongly influenced by the 17th century French landscapist Claude Lorrain. Its spiral composition, its concern with a distant center, and even its color prove this, and yet Turner is more natural than the man he so admired. Later, he became increasingly absorbed in color and effects of atmosphere. At their best, the swirling masses of color of these later paintings produce a powerful emotional impact but reveal little of Constable's unaffected love of nature. If Turner gave less than Constable to the French painters of his own day, he prepared the way for the impressionists.

The Pre-Raphaelite painters of the mid-Victorian age, who received their name by declaring their love for the style of Italian painting before the 16th century though they had little real understanding of it, produced work meticulous in detail, sentimental if not saccharine in spirit, and narrative or descriptive in character. Holman Hunt's "Light of the World" (Keble College, Oxford), which shows Christ holding a lantern and knocking at a closed door, is fairly typical. With the Pre-Raphaelites can be linked Dante Gabriel Rossetti, a poet as well as a painter, Edward Coley Burne-Jones, and George Frederick Watts, though each has his own individuality.

The Twentieth Century

During the 20th century England has been influenced

FAMOUS ENGLISH PAINTINGS

"Shrimp Girl," painted in the 1750's, is one of William Hogarth's finest works. Primarily known as a keen and amusing satirist, Hogarth was also a sensitive portrait painter.

"The Watering Place" (c.1775), by Thomas Gainsborough. Gainsborough often painted his poetic, idealized landscapes from memory or from landscape models set up in his studio.

"Shipping at Cowes No. 2" by J. M. Turner (1775–1851). Turner's interest in atmosphere and the transient qualities of light made him a forerunner of the impressionists.

"Lady Bamfylde" (1777), by Joshua Reynolds. The most fashionable portrait painter of his day, Reynolds employed a large workshop of journeymen assistants to help him fulfill his many commissions.

465

by the successive international styles in art and architecture, though generally English artists do not carry them to the extremes of their continental exponents. Thus modern though they are, the Daily Express Building by the firm of Herbert O. Ellis and Clarke and the Royal Festival Hall by Robert Matthew and Leslie Martin, both in London, have a certain English restraint and pragmatism that become apparent when they are compared with Le Corbusier's Chapel at Ronchamp, France.

In the 1960's a number of sculptors gained international reputations. The powerful and individual work of Henry Moore equals in quality and influence that of the leading continental sculptors. Among others doing sculpture in abstract styles are Kenneth Armitage and Reg Butler. A flourishing school of modern painting also exists, including such talents as Ben Nicholson, producer of subtly colored, restrained abstractions; Graham Sutherland, who creates evocative semiabstract landscapes filled with ominous forms and who also continues the English tradition of portraiture, though depicting his subjects with intense psychological penetration; and Francis Bacon, who renders his imaginary portraits of Cardinals and other subjects with nightmarish distortion and horror.

Consult Bond, Francis, *English Church Architecture* (2 vols., 1913); Summerson, John, *Architecture in Britain, 1530–1830* (1953); Waterhouse, E. K., *Painting in Britain, 1530 to 1790* (1953); Stone, Lawrence, *Sculpture in Britain; the Middle Ages* (1955).

EVERARD M. UPJOHN, Columbia University
See also GOTHIC ARCHITECTURE.

ENGLISH CHANNEL (Fr. LA MANCHE), a narrow arm of the Atlantic Ocean that separates England from France. Its total length is about 300 mi., and it varies in width from 140 mi. between Portland Bill and St. Malo to 21 mi. at the Strait of Dover, its narrowest point. Depth varies from 5 to 60 fathoms. The channel originated about 5,000 B.C. when the sea broke through a narrow neck of land near Dover. Until that time the area had been a large river valley with tributaries coming from both France and England. Major ports on the channel include Boulogne, Calais, Cherbourg, and Le Havre on the French coast; and Dover, Plymouth, Portsmouth, and Southampton on the English side. England and France agreed in 1964 to build a railroad tunnel under the English Channel.

The British channel steamer *Maid of Kent*, operating between Dover and Boulogne, carries both passengers and automobiles.
British Railways—Illustration Research Service

ENGLISH HORN, woodwind instrument (aerophone). It has the main characteristics of an oboe but is pitched a fifth lower. Its rich, somewhat nostalgic, alto sonority is capable of considerable expressiveness. The distinctive qualities of the instrument have been increasingly exploited by the composers of orchestral music since the middle of the 19th century. The best register of the instrument lies within the range of the two bottom octaves. Therefore, the highest notes are usually excluded in favor of the oboe, unless they are duplicated by other instruments. The dynamic capacities of the English horn are limited and do not exceed an ordinary forte.

ENGLISH LITERATURE, the literature written in England in the English language. Works in English by Irish and Scottish authors who wrote within the context of English life and letters are considered to be a part of English literature.

Old English Literature: to 1066

The Germanic tribes which settled in England brought with them reminiscences of valorous deeds performed by historical and legendary warriors during the Great Migrations. From this heroic tradition the *scops* (court bards) fashioned vernacular lays and epics, few of which have survived. Although preserved in West-Saxon manuscripts, much of this poetry was written in the Anglian dialect shortly after the introduction of Christianity by Augustine and Ine. *Widsith* contains some of the earliest Germanic verse. *Beowulf*, composed in the 8th century, is the most important Old English work and the only epic to survive in entirety. It alludes to events treated in another epic, the *Fight at Finnsburg*, of which only a short, splendid fragment remains. The locale of these three poems is Scandinavia; the characters are Scandinavians, Frisians, and Germans. The two fragments of *Waldere* show a close relationship with the German *Waltharius* of Ekkehard and the *Nibelungenlied*. Despite Christian influence, these epics extol the Germanic virtues of loyalty and bravery, and exemplify the pagan belief that only fame transcends death. Appropriate to their somberly aristocratic content is their style, based on the stately four-beat alliterating line common to all ancient Germanic poetry. Epic form and spirit characterize two late historic poems, the *Battle of Brunanburh* (937), inserted into the *Anglo-Saxon Chronicle*, and the *Battle of Maldon* (991), a tribute to the heroic defeat of the English by the Norsemen.

In addition to *The Seafarer* and *The Wanderer*, which describe a vanished greatness, and probably reflect the misfortunes caused by the Danish invasions, four noteworthy lyric poems survive: "The Wife's Lament" and "The Husband's Message," the earliest English love poems; "The Ruin," which laments a crumbling Roman stronghold; and the strophic "Deor's Lament," which shows the importance of the court bard. Surviving from this period are also pagan proverbs, riddles, and charms similar to those in Old High German.

Christian poems and epics in heroic style, some comparable to the *Heliand*, an Old Saxon epic poem on the Saviour, soon supplanted Germanic pagan poetry. Most of these works are associated with Caedmon and Cynewulf, the earliest-known English poets. Outstanding examples of such Christian writings are Cynewulf's legend of *Elene* and his imaginative, fervent vision-poem, *Dream of the Rood* in the *Vercelli Book*.

The earliest writers in Latin include the historians Gildas (died c.570) and Nennius (fl.795). Aldhelm, Bishop of Sherborne (d.709), wrote riddles, didactic and religious verse, and a treatise on metrics. The greatest scholar was Bede (d.735), author of about 40 books on theology, history, and science, whose major work is the *Ecclesiastical History of the English People* (731).

During the reign of Alfred the Great, called the "Father of English Prose," Wessex was the intellectual center of England. Alfred translated, or had translated, St. Gregory's *Pastoral Rule*, Bede's *Ecclesiastical History*, and Boethius' *Consolations of Philosophy*. To his abbreviated translation of the *Universal History* of Orosius he added descriptions of Germany. The *Anglo-Saxon Chronicle* was begun under Alfred's auspices. Two great masters of Old English prose were Aelfric and Wulfstan, Archbishop of York, both of whom wrote excellent homilies.

The most important collections of Old English manuscripts compiled in the 10th and early 11th centuries are the *Exeter Book* (Exeter Cathedral library), the *Vercelli Book* (Vercelli Cathedral library, Italy), the *Junius Manuscript* (Oxford), and the *Cotton Manuscript* which contains the only manuscript of *Beowulf* (British Museum).

PAUL SCHACH, University of Nebraska

Middle English Literature: 1066–1500

As a result of the Norman Conquest (1066), French displaced English as the language of the upper classes. Scholars continued to write in Latin. These two factors account for the absence of any memorable English literature in the first century of "the Middle English period." Although much didactic religious literature was written in various English dialects, few works deserve separate consideration. Worthy of mention, however, is *Ancren Riwle*, a set of rules for anchoresses, written toward the end of the 12th century and designed for the edification of three sisters. The treatise's charm and uniqueness derive from the variety of its unknown author's prose style and from his refreshing frankness and perceptiveness. It is only in the long poem *The Owl and the Nightingale* (c.1200) and in the first English version of King Arthur's story, Layamon's poem *Brut* (c.1205), that one meets with major secular literature of real merit.

The chief literary genres of the period from c.1200 to 1500 are the romance, a story in verse or prose dealing with chivalric adventures; the short lyric, one kind usually taking love as its theme and another kind dwelling on matters religious; the popular ballad, produced by anonymous poets and minstrels and dealing with legend, folklore, history, and incidents of contemporary interest; and religious drama, of which the two categories were mystery and morality plays. A few authors and works of importance defy simple classification into the above genres and hence are treated separately.

Romance. *Sir Gawain and the Green Knight* (c.1375), a metrical romance, is a treasure of the period. Written with a moral purpose, it nevertheless transcends this to become a compelling story; it is rich in detail about the manners, dress, and sports of the time. Much later, Sir Thomas Malory's *Morte d'Arthur* (written c.1469) brought together and preserved most of the corpus of romantic stories then available about Arthur and his knights. Malory's compilation and condensation of these tales is written in a clear, terse, and relatively unadorned style.

Lyric. Perhaps the best-known secular lyric of the period is "Sumer is icumen in," accorded in the 20th century the dubious compliment of a parody by Ezra Pound. Unfortunately, few of these fresh and charming songs have survived. More hardy, possibly because more numerous, were the religious lyrics, many of which hymned the Virgin Mary or her son Jesus. Others dealt with the terror of death or with the sacrifices and suffering of Christ, and still others expressed moral injunctions. Another body of lyric poetry, coming toward the very end of this period, concerns itself not with love, nature, and religion, but with more mundane subjects, gravitating often toward the satiric.

Ballad. The popular ballad was once thought to be of communal origin. It is now generally regarded as a conscious art form. Ballads were intended for singing; they underwent many changes as they passed from one generation to another. Some of their more remarkable features are the particularly effective use of refrain lines, shared with some of the popular lyrics; the abruptness with which many open; the incremental pattern of the slight plot structure, with information being doled out until one is brought up short by the implications of the last stanza or line; effective use of repetition; complete objectivity; striking imagery; and the absence of any attempt to suggest a lesson. The ballad *Edward*, revealing bit by bit the domestic tragedy of a son's killing his father at his mother's promptings and becoming sick with horror and hatred, is a perfect exemplar of the genre.

Drama. Medieval drama had its start in the elaboration of Holy Week church services, starting with antiphonal chanting and gradually introducing the impersonation by choir members of those present at the Resurrection. Additional dramatization of this kind later accompanied the Christmas services, and as episode after episode of Christian story was added and greater realism was sought, the newly born drama moved out of the Church and into the hands of the laity. Various guilds undertook different parts of the huge drama, and mystery cycles, which were collections of religious plays performed on wagons called pageants, came into being. The most notable of these cycles was that connected with the city of York. Surely containing more than the extant 48 plays, the cycle covers Biblical history from Creation to the Day of Judgment. Other extant cycles are those of Wakefield, Chester, and an unidentified city known as *N*. The Wakefield cycle, known as the Towneley Plays, contains the best of the plays, including the delightful *Second Shepherd's Play*.

The morality play existed for didactic purposes. It made use of allegorical characters such as Beauty, Knowledge, and Mankind, and treated allegorically such themes as the coming of Death and the struggle of the Vices and Virtues for the soul of Man. The earliest extant morality was written about 1400, but the best of the genre, the often revived *Everyman*, came about 100 years later.

Three poets remain to be considered. One is known only as the Pearl poet, from the name of one of his four alliterative poems. The other poems are *Purity*, *Patience*, and the already mentioned *Sir Gawain and the Green Knight*. *The Pearl* tells of the loss of a lovely white pearl and the dream of the bereaved owner, a dream in which he sees a fair maid, her hair adorned with pearls, whose abode is Paradise. After a glimpse of the New Jerusalem, the dreamer awakes spiritually strengthened. Obviously allegorical, the poem has lent itself to many interpretations.

The second poet, William Langland, author of the great alliterative poem of social protest commonly known as *Piers Plowman*, left three versions of his text: A (1362), B (c.1377), and C (c.1387). A long dream vision (the C text contains some 7,350 lines), it is ranked by some as second only to Chaucer's *Canterbury Tales* in this period. On "a May morning, in Malvern Hills," the author falls asleep and sees a vision of Heaven, Hell, and a "fair field, full of folk." This vision, peopled by allegorical figures such as Holy Church and Lady Meed, is succeeded by another with the introduction of the plowman and wonderful characterizations of the Seven Deadly Sins. The third and final vision involves the quest for Do-Well, Do-Bet, and Do-Best, but it is so digressive as to make discovery of an orderly plan impossible. No discussion of *Piers Plowman* would be complete, however, without praise of its author's satiric powers.

For Geoffrey Chaucer (c.1340–1400), one of the greatest poets in the English or any other language, there is much biographical material and a fixed canon of works. The best known of these are *The Book of the Duchess* (c.1369), an elegiac dream vision; *The House of Fame* (c.1380), another dream vision; the *Parliament of Fowls* (c.1382), a story of birds which doubtless represent persons now unidentifiable with any certainty; and *Troilus and Criseyde* (c.1382–86), a long retelling of this tragic love story which has been described as "the first psychological novel" in the language. *Troilus and Criseyde* contains one of Chaucer's finest comic creations, Criseyde's uncle Pandarus, whose name suggests his function. But it is *The Canterbury Tales* (c.1387–1400), with its unforgettable pilgrims exchanging stories and verbal barbs on the road to Canterbury, that is his masterpiece. Who can forget the Wife of Bath or some of the uproariously funny tales? "Here," exclaimed John Dryden, of Chaucer's *Tales* and people, "is God's plenty."

Of Chaucer's contemporaries, John Gower (1330?–1408), author of *Confessio Amantis* (c.1386–90), a collection of tales in a highly moralizing and didactic frame, deserves particular mention. A number of Scottish and English writers attempted to continue in the tradition of Chaucer, the fabulist Robert Henryson (1425?–?1500) best succeeding with his grim sequel to *Troilus and Criseyde* titled *The Testament of Cresseid*.

Renaissance Literature: 1500–1660

Dawn. With the establishment of the first printing press in England in 1476 by William Caxton (c.1422–91), literature entered a new era. The presses published chronicle histories, a notable example being Edward Hall's influential *Union of the Noble and Illustre Famelies of Lancastre and York* (1542), and translations from French and Latin. There was a new emphasis on learning, numbering among its exponents such figures as William Grocyn (c.1446–1519), Thomas Linacre (1460–1524), John Colet (1467?–1519), and William Lyly (c.1468–1522). These men were grammarians, teachers, and translators. Outstanding is the work of Sir Thomas Elyot (c.1490–1546), author of *The Book Named the Governor* (1531), a treatise on the future leaders of the nation, and of a number of other works and translations. Roger Ascham (1515–68), author of *Toxophilus* (1545) and *The Scholemaster* (1570), both educational in purpose, coupled great learning with a simple, balanced prose style. *Utopia* (1516; trans., 1551), written in Latin by Sir Thomas More (1478–1535), extols the virtues of an imaginary land and glances critically at England's shortcomings. More's *History of King Richard III* (written c.1513) influenced Shakespeare. His own life afforded William Roper (1496–1578) material for one of the best short biographies in the language. Among the important antiquarians of this period are John Leland (c.1506–52), John Stow (c.1525–1605), and William Camden (1551–1623).

The early poetry of this era was written by a group of Scottish writers. Most notable were William Dunbar's *The Golden Targe* (c.1503), a dream vision that owes something to Chaucer and Gower; the allegorical *Palace of Honour* (1501) of Gavin Douglas (1474?–1522); and various poems in different genres and meters by Sir David Lindsay (1490?–1555). The important English poets were Sir Thomas Wyatt (1503?–1542) and Henry Howard, Earl of Surrey (c.1517–?1547), transmitters of Italian and French forms and themes who also were original poets of considerable ability. Wyatt, like Surrey, wrote many sonnets in the vein of Petrarchan idolatry of women, and a number of lyrics which have seldom been surpassed. Surrey is at his best when he has something personal to write—a fragment of autobiography, a poem on Wyatt's

The knight of *The Canterbury Tales* (c.1387–1400), from a 1561 edition of Chaucer's works published by John Stow.

death. He introduced blank verse into England in his translation of Vergil's *Aeneid* (c.1554).

Although the early Scottish poets wrote some satiric verse, it was with John Skelton (c.1460–1529), Alexander Barclay (c.1475–1552), and John Heywood (c.1497–c.1580) that poetic satire came into its own. Skelton spared neither the court in general nor powerful courtiers in particular, concentrating his fire for a time on Cardinal Wolsey. He invented a meter, "Skeltonics," best exemplified in the playful *Philip Sparrow* and in the coarsely conceived and brutal *Tunning of Eleanor Rumming*. Barclay's fame rests upon his translation (1508) of Sebastian Brant's *The Ship of Fools*, in which he takes generous liberties with his original, and upon his *Eclogues* (c.1515), deriving from Italian and Latin models but often referring to English events. Heywood's nondramatic satire centers in *The Spider and the Fly* (1556), a mock-epic allegory of contemporary events, and in his epigrams and proverbs.

Heywood wrote the best of the interludes, which were the offspring of the morality plays. Prior to his work is Henry Medwall's *Fulgens and Lucrece* (performed 1497), with its humorous subplot paralleling the main action. Also before Heywood were *The Nature of the Four Elements* (printed, 1519) and *Calisto and Melebea* (performed c.1527), the first surely, and the second possibly, by John Rastell (c.1475–1536), a member of the Sir Thomas More–John Heywood circle. The wittiest of Heywood's seven interludes is undoubtedly *The Four P's*, the dénouement of which must be read to be fully savored and believed. More didactic interludes are Skelton's *Magnificence* (written c.1516), John Bale's *King John* (written before 1540), and Sir David Lindsay's *Satire of the Three Estates* (performed 1540). Hereafter, though interludes were numerous their worth declined.

Elizabethans. Prose centered about translations of the Bible and culminated in the great King James version (1611), which was the combined effort of 54 scholars working about seven years and building upon the versions of William Tyndale (c.1494–1536) and Miles Coverdale (1488–1568). Comparable in greatness was the English Book of Common Prayer by Thomas Cranmer, Archbishop of Canterbury. With the sermons and other religious works of men like Hugh Latimer (c.1485–1555); John Foxe (1516–87), author of the enormously popular *Book of Martyrs* (1563); and Richard Hooker (c.1554–1600) one comes to the end of a period in the development of English prose.

The next phase in English prose was narrative, progressing from collections of jests to collections of *novelle*, and coming to a dubious fruition in the excessively mannered work of John Lyly (1554?–1606). His *Euphues, or the Anatomy of Wit* (1578) and *Euphues and His England* (1580) both reflected and taught correct social behavior. Lyly's chief imitator was Robert Greene (1558–92), who wrote a number of euphuistic narratives and then turned to more realistic prose in works that range from exposure of swindlers to thinly concealed autobiography. Other writers in this latter tradition are Thomas Dekker, Thomas Nash, and Thomas Deloney. Still other prose writers produced translations, educational works, literary criticism, acrid controversy, abuse and defense of drama and actors, and miscellaneous efforts of every description.

Poetry in the reign (1558–1603) of Elizabeth I was strongly influenced by popular song collections, two examples of which, the famous "Tottel's Miscellany" (1557) and Francis Davison's *Poetical Rhapsody* (1602), stand at either end of the period. The writing of verse narrative was given impetus by the publication of the first edition of *A Mirror for Magistrates* (1559), a series of tragic histories taken from Lydgate's *The Fall of Princes* (written 1431–38). But it was the contributions of Thomas Sackville (1536–1608) and others to later editions of the *Mirror*, together with imitations of that work, especially those by Samuel Daniel (1562–1619) and Michael Drayton (1563–1631), which, along with Ovidian amatory verse, set the poetic tone. A few poets—Sir John Davies (1569–1626) was one—devoted themselves to the poetry of ideas.

Two boisterous comedies, Nicholas Udall's *Ralph Roister Doister* and William Stevenson's *Gammer Gurton's Needle*, and a few plays based on Italian works, preceded the plays of John Lyly, the first English dramatist with a considerable body of work to his credit. Using mythological and contemporary plots and themes and the euphuistic language of his novels, he flourished for a number of years, but gave way to a more robust wave of dramatic genius in the plays of George Peele (c.1558–97), Robert Greene, and a few others. Other important early plays were the translations of Senecan tragedy; the first English tragedy, *Gorboduc* (performed 1562), by Thomas Norton (1532–84) and Thomas Sackville (1536–1608); the work of Thomas Kyd (1558–94), who was author of the popular revenge-tragedy, *The Spanish Tragedy* (performed c.1585); chronicle history plays, often anonymous; and a number of powerful domestic tragedies, of which *Arden of Feversham* (published 1592) and *A Yorkshire Tragedy* (published 1608), both anonymous, are compelling examples. But it was Christopher Marlowe (1564–93), master of blank verse and creator of characters obsessed by the desire for power (Tamburlaine), knowledge (Doctor Faustus), or wealth (Barabas, the Jew of Malta), who prepared the way for Shakespeare.

William Shakespeare (1564–1616) began his career by imitating other dramatists such as Plautus, Lyly, and

Woodcut for a 1631 edition of Marlowe's *Doctor Faustus* depicts Faustus talking to Mephistopheles in the guise of a serpent.

Hamlet at the grave of the jester Yorick. This etching by Eugène Delacroix was inspired by Shakespeare's tragedy.

Marlowe. During Queen Elizabeth's reign he wrote all his history plays, his farces and light comedies, and *Titus Andronicus, Romeo and Juliet, Julius Caesar,* and *Hamlet.* From 1603 to his retirement (c.1610) he wrote his "dark," or "problem," comedies, *Troilus and Cressida, Measure for Measure,* and *All's Well That Ends Well;* the three great tragedies, *Othello, King Lear,* and *Macbeth;* a number of other plays; and the valedictory *The Tempest.* Shakespeare's magic is compounded of such ingredients as the quick-witted knavery of Falstaff, the verbal dexterity of his fools, the loveliness of his young heroines, the fragility of his fairies, and the stormy passions of his tragic heroes, all expressed with the versatility of his poetic genius.

Shakespeare also wrote nondramatic poetry, most notably a sonnet sequence whose most important English predecessor was Sir Philip Sidney's *Astrophel and Stella* (1591). Sidney (1554–86) was the author of a pastoral romance, *The Countess of Pembroke's Arcadia* (1590), and of a very enlightened critical work, *The Defense of Poesie* (1595). *Astrophel and Stella* made the sonnet sequence popular; it stimulated Samuel Daniel, Michael Drayton, Edmund Spenser, and others. Shakespeare's sequence, with its dark lady and rival poet, has or hints at autobiographical significance, as do the sequences of Sidney and others. Shakespeare's other poems, *The Rape of Lucrece* and *Venus and Adonis,* are conventional in subject and form.

The greatest nondramatic poet of the period, Edmund Spenser (1552?–1599), began his career with *The Shepheardes Calender* (1579), which consists of 12 eclogues which are imitative in form but original in their determination to restore English poetry to pristine vigor and simplicity. Spenser, after ten years in a secretarial post in Ireland, published in 1591 two volumes of minor poetry containing poems in various genres and stanzaic forms. It

is, however, the long allegorical romance *The Faerie Queene* (1590–96) for which he is best remembered. It is in the poet's handling of his narrative, in his characterization, in his moral purpose, and in his mastery of language —despite his often criticized use of archaisms—that the greatness of the poem is found.

Jacobeans. Playwrights in the early 17th century were many. Thomas Dekker (c.1572–1632) and Thomas Heywood (c.1570–c.1641), whose work may be exemplified by, respectively, *The Shoemaker's Holiday* (performed 1600) and *A Woman Killed With Kindness* (performed 1603), were prolific writers belonging to an older, cruder school of dramaturgy. John Webster (fl.1602–24) is not easily pigeonholed. His two great tragedies, *The White Devil* (published 1612) and *The Duchess of Malfi* (performed c.1614), ally him to Shakespeare. The quality of the poetry in his plays saves him from the accusation of being merely melodramatic. A second and larger group of playwrights adopted a satiric view of life. George Chapman (1559?–1634) introduced a "comedy of humours" based on current physiological beliefs, and Ben Jonson (1572–1637) carried it to its extremes in *Every Man in His Humour* (performed 1598) and *The Silent Woman* (performed 1609). Jonson wrote Roman tragedies also, but the comedies *Volpone* (performed c.1606) and *The Alchemist* (performed 1610) are his greatest efforts. Others prominent in this group were John Marston (1576–1634), Cyril Tourneur (c.1580–1626), and Thomas Middleton (1580–1627). Still a third group, led by the famous collaborators Francis Beaumont (1584–1616) and John Fletcher (1579–1625), concentrated on more romantic themes and subjects, often in tragicomedies.

The chief dramatists between 1625 and 1642 were Philip Massinger (1583–1640), collaborator with Fletcher and author of fine city comedies; John Ford (1586–after 1638), writer of powerful psychological tragedies; and James Shirley (1596–1666), most prolific of a group who owed much to Ben Jonson. Sir William D'Avenant (1606–68) and Thomas Killigrew (1612–83) were the most important writers of court plays prior to the closing of the theaters in 1642.

Prose of the first half of the 17th century is best exemplified by the work of a few men. The *Essays* of Francis Bacon (1561–1626), which were first published in 1597, grew in number, length, and polish by the final edition in 1625. Robert Burton (1577–1640), in his compendious *The Anatomy of Melancholy* (1621), wrote in a deliberately plain style modeled on Bacon's. "Character" writers and biographers may be represented by John Earle (c.1601–65), as in his *Microcosmography,* and Izaak Walton (1593–1683), of *Compleat Angler* fame, as in his valuable, brief *Lives.* The richly ornamented prose of this same period is found in the sermons and *Devotions upon Emergent Occasions* (1624) of John Donne (1572–1631); in Sir Thomas Browne's *Religio Medici* (1643), *Pseudodoxia Epidemica* (1646), and *Hydriotaphia, or Urn Burial* (1658); and in the works of the divine, Jeremy Taylor (1613–67).

Ben Jonson, John Donne, and John Milton were the dominant poets of the first half of the 17th century. The first was a conscious craftsman whose seemingly easy handling of the short lyric, the song, the epigram, and other forms belies the intricacy of many of his poems. Jonson sired a whole school whose members called themselves the "Tribe of Ben" and included in their number such poets as Sir John Suckling (1609–42), Richard Lovelace (1618–c.1657), and the delightful lyricist Robert Herrick (1591–1674). Donne wrote amatory and religious poetry using far-fetched comparisons and the language of various trades and professions, relying on wit to such an extent that his means often distract attention from his ends. Other notable poets in this "metaphysical" school are Abraham Cowley (1618–67) and Andrew Marvell (1621–78). Four religious poets, George Herbert (1593–1633), Richard Crashaw (c.1612–49), Henry Vaughan (1622–95), and Thomas Traherne (c.1637–74), influenced somewhat by Donne and by one another, are uneven in poetic merit but linked by a fervor that finds different outlets in their work. Prefiguring the poets of the Restoration are Edmund Waller (1606–87), exponent of smoothness and easiness in poetry; William D'Avenant; and Sir John Denham (1615–69), author of one of the first topographical poems, *Cooper's Hill* (1642).

John Milton (1608–74) straddles two eras but belongs to the first. A not uninfluential writer of political and theological prose tracts, he was first and foremost a poet, writing in Latin and English. The best known of his earlier poems are *L'Allegro* and *Il Penseroso*, the masque *Comus*, *Lycidas*, and a group of sonnets. His great work *Paradise Lost* (1667), patterned on the classical epic, essays "to justify the ways of God to man" by showing how good ultimately results from evil. *Paradise Regained* (1671) revolves about the verbal struggle between Christ and Satan, and *Samson Agonistes* (1671), a tragedy that invites comparison with the work of Aeschylus, Sophocles, and Euripides, retells the Biblical story of Samson, a figure with whom Milton surely felt himself to have much in common.

The epic battle of the angels in Milton's *Paradise Lost* (1667), illustrated by the French artist Gustave Doré in 1865.

From 1660 to 1800

John Dryden. John Dryden (1631–1700) dominated English literature from the Restoration of Charles II in 1660 to 1700. As a literary critic he easily surpassed Sir William D'Avenant and Thomas Hobbes, who concentrated on the epic, and the strict Aristotelian Thomas Rymer (1641–1713), still remembered for his caustic comments on *Othello*. Dryden's greatest critical effort was the *Essay of Dramatic Poesy* (1668), but he also wrote many excellent critical essays as prefaces to his plays and translations. Indeed, his easy conversational style and his ability to turn a phrase make him rank high as a writer of essays, along with Abraham Cowley and Sir William Temple (1628–99), who wrote on a variety of topics, many of them personal. Other essayists dealt with matters religious or political; some devoted themselves to "character" writing. George Savile, Marquess of Halifax (1633–95), and Samuel Butler (1612–80) stand out from their fellows in these areas. During this period journalism also made remarkable progress.

The two most important types of drama were comedies of manners, and heroic plays and tragedies, and Dryden wrote both. His comedies, of manners and of other kinds, are not comparable to those of Sir George Etherege (1635?–?1691), William Wycherley (1641–1716), Sir John Vanbrugh (1664–1726), and William Congreve (1670–1729), authors, respectively, of *The Man of Mode* (performed 1676), *The Country Wife* (published 1675), *The Relapse* (performed 1696), and *The Way of the World*, all brilliantly witty portrayals of fashionable society. Thomas Shadwell (c.1642–92) and a host of minor dramatists wrote in a similar vein. The emphasis on sex in many of these plays evoked the wrath of Jeremy Collier in 1698. Plays became more moral, as can be seen in the comedies —especially *The Beaux' Stratagem* (performed 1707)—of George Farquhar (1677?–1707). The heroic play, originated by Sir William D'Avenant, found its best practitioner in Dryden. His *Conquest of Granada*, in two parts (performed 1670 and 1671), and *Aurengzebe* (performed 1675), full of incredible love and valor, exotic locales, and wars and revolutions, are the outstanding examples of a highly artificial genre. Nathaniel Lee (1653?–1692), Thomas Otway (1652–85), and Thomas Southerne (1660–1746) were the chief tragedians, with Otway's "she-tragedies" *The Orphan* (performed 1680) and *Venice Preserv'd* (performed 1682) the most memorable of the achievements in tragedy.

Dryden's nondramatic poetry was largely occasional, much of it satirical, most of it in heroic couplets; it included many songs and odes. Of the last, the "Song for St. Cecilia's Day" (1687) and "Alexander's Feast" (1697) rank highest. *Absalom and Achitophel* (1681) and *Mac-Flecknoe* (1682), respectively, political and literary satire, are among the best of their kind. Dryden's religious poetry is best displayed in *Religio Laici* (1682) and *The Hind and the Panther* (1687). Dryden also distinguished himself as a translator of Vergil and others. Contemporaneous with Dryden, Samuel Butler (1612–80) wrote a highly amusing mock-heroic attack on the Puritans, *Hudibras* (1663–78), relying largely on burlesque for his effects. The period also witnessed a group of court poets writing love lyrics (often bawdy), songs, and occasional

Culver Pictures, Inc.

Among the most enduring characters in English literature are Christian (*left*), hero of Bunyan's *Pilgrim's Progress* (1678), with Hopeful (in armor), and Defoe's Robinson Crusoe (*right*), whose story (1719) is based on the experiences of a sailor.

satire. The 2d Earl of Rochester (1647–80) was the gayest and the ablest of these court poets. Often writers clubbed together to produce a miscellany of their poems.

From Dryden one goes on to the historians, the writers of memoirs and biographies, and the first novelists. Interest in the individual is manifest in the diaries of the fun-loving, excessively frank Samuel Pepys (1633–1703) and of the more sober social historian John Evelyn (1620–1706). Biographies and autobiographies by and about clergymen, noble lords and ladies, and writers; collections of brief lives; and biographical dictionaries also attest to this interest. At the same time, historians of the caliber of the 1st Earl of Clarendon (1609–74) wrote of their own times, while Bishop Gilbert Burnet (1643–1715) wrote largely of clerical history. Prose also tended in the direction of fictitious histories, chiefly embodied in long didactic romances, a plethora of epistolary narratives, and hastily written lives of famous criminals. Long short stories by such writers as Aphra Behn (1640–89) and William Congreve formed a link in the evolution of the novel. Most important in this last respect was John Bunyan (1628–88), whose *Pilgrim's Progress* (1678–84) is not only a sustained allegory but a gripping narrative as well.

Pope: An Age of Sentiment. Alexander Pope (1688–1744) occupies a position in English literature similar to Dryden's. Criticism in the period up to his death focused on the rules in drama, on imagination, on taste, and on the nature of genius. Pope's contributions were the early verse *Essay on Criticism* (1711) and the prefaces to his translation of the *Iliad* (1715–20) and to his edition of Shakespeare (1725). More important critics were John Dennis (1657–1734), the 3d Earl of Shaftesbury (1671–1713), and Joseph Addison (1672–1719). Shaftesbury's theories of taste and enthusiasm carried considerable influence with poets. Addison's periodical essays on literature and on the imagination reflect a sensitive mind at work. Many lesser figures engaged in textual criticism.

This period saw the rise of journalism, with newspapers and pamphlets, usually political, abounding. Daniel Defoe (1660–1731), political satirist and prolific hack writer,

stands out from the crowd. His *Review* (1704–13), a tri-weekly, was written almost singlehandedly. Parts of the *Review* may have influenced Addison and Richard Steele (1672–1729) in *The Tatler* (1709–11), *The Spectator* (1711–12; 1714), and their other periodical essays. These two series of essays range over a wide variety of subjects, reflect the social situation, and attempt to reconcile wit and morality. Imitations were many, but they were rarely equaled.

Drama up to 1744 was stigmatized by a self-conscious morality that eventually burgeoned into sentimentalism. Leading the movement were *Love's Last Shift* (1696) and *The Careless Husband* (published 1705) by Colley Cibber (1671–1757) and *The Conscious Lovers* (produced 1722) by Steele. The farces of Henry Fielding (1707–54) and the popular comedies of Mrs. Centlivre (1667?–1723) and a few others resisted the new direction. In tragedy *The Fair Penitent* (1703) and other she-tragedies of Nicholas Rowe (1674–1718) shared the stage with neo-classical plays such as Addison's *Cato* (performed 1713), plays based on Oriental stories and English history, and the bourgeois tragedies *The London Merchant* (performed 1731, in prose) and *Fatal Curiosity* (performed 1736) of George Lillo (1693–1739).

Defoe's *Robinson Crusoe* (1719), *Moll Flanders* (1722), and *Roxana* (1724), to mention only a few of his books, grew out of his journalistic endeavors. Episodic in nature, deceptively simple in style, sometimes primitive in characterization, rich in detail, his work leads to *Pamela* (1740), "the first English novel," by Samuel Richardson (1689–1761), and to the same author's *Clarissa* (1747–48) and *Sir Charles Grandison* (1753–54). *Clarissa*, in epistolary form, is a psychological novel of amazing depth and one of the great works of prose fiction of all time. Henry Fielding (1705–54) satirized *Pamela* fully in *Shamela* (1741) and partially in *Joseph Andrews* (1742); the latter contains the famous Parson Adams. He followed these with the sustained and ironic burlesque *Jonathan Wild* (1743), the ingeniously plotted picaresque novel *Tom Jones* (1749), and *Amelia* (1751), a less humorous, more moralistic work. Characteristic of the writings of Tobias Smollett (1721–71) is a brand of boisterous humor and

Gulliver awakes a prisoner of the Lilliputians, from an 1894 edition of Swift's classic, *Gulliver's Travels* (1726).

The Bettmann Archive

broad characterization mingled with autobiographical elements. It is best observed in *Roderick Random* (1748) and *Humphry Clinker* (1771).

Jonathan Swift (1667–1745) wrote a few essays, many pamphlets, and poems, and *Gulliver's Travels* (1726). His forte was satire, and it is present in most of what he wrote. *A Tale of a Tub* and *The Battle of the Books* (both 1704), *The Conduct of the Allies* (1711), and *A Modest Proposal* (1729) are, with *Gulliver's Travels*, his greatest prose satires. In poetry he employed many of the techniques of his prose satires, his targets being certain rigid literary genres and conventions and mankind's willingness to be deceived by externals. At the same time, other poets were writing descriptive reflective poetry, songs and ballads, hymns, and pastorals. Matthew Prior (1664–1721) wrote delightful personal lyrics as well as hilarious verse narratives and a few philosophical poems. His best poetry is witty and elegant.

Pope was surrounded by a group of poets, notably the members of the Scriblerus Club. Of these, John Gay (1685–1732) deserves special mention for his *Shepherd's Week* (1714), *Trivia; or The Art of Walking the Streets of London* (1716), and *Fables* (1727, 1738). The number and kinds of poems written by Pope are surprising. Pastorals, verse essays, odes, mock heroics, the "romantic" *Eloisa to Abelard*, descriptive poetry, Vergilian and Horatian imitations, the philosophical *Essay on Man*, *The Dunciad*, and many others seemingly flowed from his pen. He rang subtle variations on the heroic couplet; he excoriated individuals and types in his brilliant satiric pieces; and he recreated in inimitable fashion certain aspects of the society of his time. Although his followers were many, there were those who struck out in directions of their own, like James Thomson (1700–48), author of *The Seasons* (1726–30), a long poem in which natural description is mixed with reflections on all manner of subjects; Edward Young (1683–1765), who dwelt on death and immortality in his *Night Thoughts* (1742–45); the writers of graveyard poetry, exemplified in *The Grave* (1743) by Robert Blair (1699–1746); and the writers of Georgic or philosophical poems.

Johnson in the Era of Sentimentality. Samuel Johnson (1709–84), already established as a writer when Alexander Pope died, is the second dominant figure of the period 1660–1800. In his criticism—chiefly some *Rambler* essays (1750–52), the Preface and notes to his edition of Shakespeare (1765), and his *Lives* of the English poets (1779–81)—he sometimes succumbed to prejudices, his own and the century's, but more often he stated, and stated incisively, what has seldom been proved perverse. The *Discourses* of his friend Sir Joshua Reynolds (1723–92), concerned largely with painting, often parallel his views, particularly in their insistence on nature as the criterion of excellence. Other critics analyzed genius, beauty, imitation, the imagination, judgment, and taste. An important analysis of taste is *Of the Standard of Taste* (1757) by David Hume (1711–76). Another area, the sublime, was exhaustively treated by Edmund Burke (1729–97) in his *A Philosophical Inquiry into the Origin of Our Ideas on the Sublime and Beautiful* (1756). Historical criticism of Homer, Shakespeare, and Spenser was extensive.

Johnson's chief poems were *London* (1738) and *The Vanity of Human Wishes* (1749), cast as Juvenalian imitations. Contemporary with him were the Wartons, Joseph (1722–1800) and Thomas the Younger (1728–90), William Collins (1721–59), Christopher Smart (1722–71), and Thomas Gray (1716–71). With the exception of Smart, who wrote religious poetry of a high order, they were consciously revolting from the poetry of Pope and stressed fancy, melancholy, enthusiasm, the historical past, and the revival of the ode and the sonnet. Gray, with his *Elegy Written in a Country Churchyard* (1751) and Collins, with his odes, led the school. William Shenstone (1714–63) imitated Spenser. James Macpherson (1736–96) and Thomas Chatterton (1752–70) invented fictitious poets of bygone ages. Bishop Thomas Percy (1729–1811) gathered ballads and translated the older literature of other countries. Charles Churchill (1731–64) continued in the satiric tradition.

Johnson's periodical essays in *The Rambler*, *The Adventurer*, and *The Idler*, written between 1750 and 1760 and heavier in style and subject matter than *The Spectator*, were a medium for his moral, critical, and social observations. There were many other periodical essayists; the newspapers invited essays, and the century gave birth to many monthly periodicals—*The Gentleman's Magazine*, *The Monthly Review*, *The Critical Review*, and others. Oliver Goldsmith (1730?–1774) wrote his "Chinese Letters" for *The Public Ledger* and served for a time as reviewer on the *Monthly Review*. The "Chinese Letters," titled *The Citizen of the World* upon separate publication (1762), use the naïve observer as a satiric device. These, with *The Bee* (1759) and his collected *Essays* (1765), establish him as the best of the essayists after Addison and Steele.

The Gentleman's Magazine, in the 1740's, afforded Johnson a place for a number of brief biographies of men of science, naval heroes and explorers, and literary men. His life of the impecunious poet Richard Savage (1744) is a short masterpiece. His practice, and his theories as expressed in conversation and in *Rambler 60*, influenced the writing of biography, especially the great record of Johnson's own life (1791) by James Boswell (1740–95). The preoccupation with biography and autobiography found outlets in fictitious autobiography, collections of anecdotes, memoirs and diaries, and in letter writing. Learned ladies, religious leaders, noblemen, and others kept diaries or wrote their memoirs. The 4th Earl of Chesterfield (1694–1773), Gilbert White of Selborne (1720–93), Thomas Gray, Horace Walpole (1717–97), and William Cowper (1731–1800) wrote—sometimes spontaneously, sometimes very self-consciously—the best letters in the language.

Johnson's one excursion into drama, the frigid tragedy *Irene* (performed 1749), was a failure. Sentimentalism, both in comedy and in tragedy, cast a blight over the theater. Edward Moore (1712–57), Richard Cumberland (1732–1811), and Hugh Kelly (1739–77) led the movement. Ranged against them were Arthur Murphy (1727–1805), George Colman the Elder (1732–94), Oliver Goldsmith, and Richard Brinsley Sheridan (1751–1816). Goldsmith's *She Stoops to Conquer* (performed 1773) and Sheridan's *The Rivals* (performed 1775) and *The School for Scandal* (performed 1777) are classics of English

The Bettmann Archive

The rescue of Sophia Primrose, one of the most exciting episodes in Goldsmith's *The Vicar of Wakefield*, published in 1766.

comedy. Nevertheless, sentimentalism continued undeterred into the 19th century.

Sentimentalism also found its way into novels, chiefly those written by women. The comic masterpiece *Tristram Shandy* (1759–67) by Laurence Sterne (1713–68) and his only other novel, *A Sentimental Journey Through France and Italy* (1768), are touched by sentimentalism but saved by humor, often of the bawdy variety. Saved, too, was Goldsmith's *The Vicar of Wakefield* (1766), but neither Henry Mackenzie (1745–1831) nor Henry Brooke (c.1703–1783) desired such salvation. Horace Walpole's *The Castle of Otranto* (1764) began the vogue of the Gothic novel. William Beckford (1760–1844) capitalized on the Oriental tale in *Vathek* (1786); and Fanny Burney (1752–1840) wrote novels of contemporary manners, notably *Evelina* (1778).

David Hume, philosopher, historian, and essayist, with Edward Gibbon (1737–94), the historian of *The Decline and Fall of the Roman Empire* (1776–88), and Edmund Burke (1729–97), political philosopher, possessed excellent, albeit different, prose styles in which to clothe their ideas on history, philosophy, politics, religion, aesthetics, and literature.

Anticipatory of the romantic movement in poetry are William Cowper (1731–1800) and Robert Burns (1759–96), both of whom turned outward to nature and inward to themselves for inspiration. In Cowper this is seen in a few short poems and in his long blank verse essay *The Task* (1785). Burns, like Cowper a chronicler of rural life, had a greater interest in man and his social problems. His songs, many in number and varied in subject, are almost uniformly delightful.

ARTHUR SHERBO, Michigan State University

The 19th Century

Romantic Era. English literature of the early 19th century is called "romantic." A dominant literary tendency was the revolt against 18th-century neoclassicism. Poets adhered in varying degrees to an idea of the poem as an expression of the poet's being, and many revolted against the poetic diction of the previous age. The preface by William Wordsworth (1770–1850) to the second edition (1800) of the *Lyrical Ballads* suggests both tendencies in the phrases "spontaneous overflow of powerful feelings" and "a selection of the language really spoken by men."

In his long poem *The Prelude* (written 1805), Wordsworth is himself the speaker and main character, and "nature" is associated with unsullied rural life. The romantic period saw the growth of individualism and political republicanism, and the American and French revolutions greatly affected the romantic poets. George Gordon, Lord Byron (1788–1824), whose *Don Juan* (1819–24) is the greatest satire of the age, actually became involved in Italian and Greek revolutionary activity. His "Byronic heroes" are types of the isolated romantic individualist who finds reality and deity only within himself. William Godwin's *Political Justice* (1793) and Thomas Paine's *Rights of Man* (1791–92) were both influential books. Godwinian necessitarianism and romantic neoplatonism are reflected in the poetry of Percy Bysshe Shelley (1792–1822), especially in his dramatic poem *Prometheus Unbound* (1820).

Poets generally rejected overused Greek mythology, although the great lyricist John Keats (1795–1821) turned often to Greece for subject and allusion. The dominant tendency was to find inspiration in medieval romances and ballads. Samuel Taylor Coleridge (1772–1834) and Keats experimented successfully along these lines. William Blake (1757–1827), many of whose symbolic lyrics have ballad rhythms, constructed in his "prophetic books" a mythological system from sources other than the Greek alone. Blake and others created psychological or inner landscapes, as in Coleridge's "The Rime of the Ancient Mariner" (1798). Lesser poets of the period were Robert Southey (1774–1843), Walter Savage Landor (1775–1864), Thomas Moore (1779–1852), and Thomas Hood (1799–1845).

The same return to romance pervades the "Gothic" novels of Ann Radcliffe (1764–1823), *Melmoth the Wanderer* (1820) by Charles Maturin, and *Frankenstein* (1818) by Mary Wollstonecraft Shelley (1797–1851). Sir Walter Scott (1771–1832), whose Waverley novels evoke a lost Scottish past, was the major romantic novelist, and Jane Austen (1775–1817) was the supreme novelist of manners, in a period better known in prose for its literary criticism. Although Wordsworth's preface and Shelley's *Defense of Poetry* (1821) are the best-known critical documents of the age, Coleridge was its foremost critic and theorist and, in a sense, the father of modern criticism in English. His *Biographia Literaria* (1817), heavily in debt to Kant and Schelling, and his criticism of Shakespeare are among his most important writings. Other critics and practitioners of the personal essay were Charles Lamb (1775–1834), William Hazlitt (1778–1830), and Thomas De Quincey (1785–1859).

Of drama in the period the less said the better. Byron and Shelley wrote famous dramatic poems, but no considerable amount of drama has survived as literature.

Victorian Age. By 1837, when Victoria became Queen, most of the romantic writers were dead. Alfred, Lord Tennyson (1809–92), a poet of great output and impeccable technique, reflects in his *In Memoriam* (1850) the principal intellectual conflict of the new age, the warfare between science and religion. Robert Browning (1812–89), master of dramatic monologues, was the period's other major, if less popular, poet. There was much technical virtuosity in the swelling rhythms of Algernon Charles Swinburne (1837–1909), who provided a link with

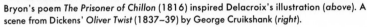
Bryon's poem *The Prisoner of Chillon* (1816) inspired Delacroix's illustration (*above*). A scene from Dickens' *Oliver Twist* (1837–39) by George Cruikshank (*right*).

French literature; the "sprung rhythm" of Gerard Manley Hopkins (1844–89), the Catholic priest, whose poems were not published until 1918; and the sonnets of Dante Gabriel Rossetti (1828–82). Religious poetry was written by Catholic poets Christina Rossetti (1830–94), Coventry Patmore (1823–96), and Francis Thompson (1859–1907), best known for his "The Hound of Heaven." Toward the end of the century A. E. Housman (1859–1936) published his poems of worldly disillusion, and Thomas Hardy (1840–1928) turned from a successful career as a novelist to the writing of ironic poems on fate and nature. The 1890's brought the "decadent" movement of English aestheticism, which found voice in *The Yellow Book* and the *Savoy*, two of its notorious literary magazines. Several *fin de siècle* poets led tragic lives, among them Ernest Dowson (1867–1900), Lionel Johnson (1867–1902), and the prominent dramatist Oscar Wilde (1854–1900). Poets who attempted to come to terms with the new scientism were George Meredith (1828–1909), Robert Bridges (1844–1930), John Davidson (1857–1909), and Hardy. The poets Rudyard Kipling (1865–1936) and William Ernest Henley (1849–1903) exalted the robust, active life.

The Victorian age might better be described, however, as one of prose. It was an age of the long novels of William Makepeace Thackery (1811–63) and Charles Dickens (1812–70). Dickens told a good story without fear of sentimentalizing his characters. These two are perhaps the best-known novelists of the period, but they are by no means the only important ones. Between the romantic novels of the Brontë sisters, Charlotte (1816–55), Emily (1818–48), and Anne (1820–49), and those novels of fate and aloof nature by Thomas Hardy, Victorian fiction flourished in the social novels of Anthony Trollope (1815–82) and the psychological works of George Eliot (1819–80) and George Meredith. There were several writers of historical novels, among them Edward Bulwer-Lytton (1803–73), Charles Reade (1814–84), and Charles Kingsley (1819–75). The satirist Samuel Butler (1835–1902) was also, with George Gissing (1857–1903), one of the first English naturalistic novelists. Among writers of romance, William Morris (1834–96), who glorified medievalism in ballad and prose, and Robert Louis Stevenson (1850–94) are the most notable of the Victorian period.

Emphasis upon the medieval was also apparent in the work of the critic John Ruskin (1819–1900), whose comments on Gothic architecture were an attack on the spiritual slavery of the English worker. Matthew Arnold (1822–88), also a considerable poet, offered his distinction between Hebraism and Hellenism, siding with Hellenic disinterestedness and the ideal of knowledge for its own sake. Walter Pater (1839–94) sounded in *The Renaissance* (1873) the first note of English aestheticism, and Arthur Symons' *The Symbolist Movement in Literature* (1899) brought the names and methods of French writers into prominence in England. There was much social criticism and polemical writing notable for distinctive style. In addition to Ruskin and Arnold, whose criticism had a social orientation, Thomas Carlyle (1795–1881) excoriated his own age. The best Victorian discursive prose centered on the great issues of the day. Among the most prominent prose writers were John Henry Newman (1801–90), a founder of the Oxford movement and later a convert to Catholicism; T. H. Huxley (1825–95), defender of the new science; John Stuart Mill (1806–73), exponent of Benthamite utilitarianism; and the historian Thomas Babington Macaulay (1800–59).

The Victorian period, like the romantic, was not distinguished for its drama. Only in the last years of the century, with George Bernard Shaw (1856–1950), Oscar Wilde, Arthur Wing Pinero (1855–1934), Henry Arthur Jones (1851–1929), and James M. Barrie (1860–1937), does the drama figure prominently in literary history.

The 20th Century

At the time of the death of Victoria the dominant movement in fiction was naturalistic and realistic, but until World War I poetry was romantic and lyrical. Novelists of this movement were George Moore (1852–1933), Arnold Bennett (1867–1931), and John Galsworthy (1867–1933), also a prominent dramatist. At the same time Joseph Conrad (1857–1924) produced his complex psychological novels. Among new poets were Walter de la Mare (1873–1956), Edward Thomas (1878–1917), and John Masefield (1878–1967). The Irish literary movement had as its center the Abbey Theatre and was dominated by William Butler Yeats (1865–1939), one of the major poets of his age and an important dramatist. Perhaps the major playwright of the Abbey, however, was John Millington Synge (1871–1909). George Bernard Shaw continued to

475

George Bernard Shaw in his study. The most successful dramatist of his day in English, Shaw was also a distinguished critic.
(OTTO SALMON—BLACK STAR)

establish himself as the most prominent dramatist in English, and Ireland produced another important playwright in Sean O'Casey (1880–1964).

The best of the poets inspired by the war was Wilfred Owen (1893–1918). Others were Rupert Brooke (1887–1915) and Siegfried Sassoon (1886–1967), the last the only one of the three to survive the fighting. The famous American literary expatriate T. S. Eliot (1888–1965) startled the literary world with his modernistic poem *The Waste Land* (1922) and continued to dominate that world with his criticism, his poetry, and later his poetic drama. Following the critic T. E. Hulme (1883–1917), Eliot attacked romanticism, finding inspiration in the 17th-century metaphysical poets and in the French symbolists. Along with Yeats, who was the greater lyricist, Eliot was generally regarded as the major poet of the period between the two world wars. In the 1930's the Spanish Civil War and Marxism attracted a group of poets, the major writer among whom was W. H. Auden (1907–   ), later to reject Marxism and embrace Anglo-Catholicism and U.S. citizenship. Other poets of the group were C. Day Lewis (1904–   ), Louis MacNeice (1907–63), and Stephen Spender (1909–   ). The major Marxist critic of the decade was Christopher Caudwell (1907–37), who was killed in the Spanish fighting. But perhaps the most influential critic after Eliot was I. A. Richards (1893–   ), psychologist and semanticist. Among other poets who began writing

Two major 20th-century literary figures, T. S. Eliot (*left*) and James Joyce, the latter painted by Jacques Émile Blanche.
(THE TIMES, LONDON)   (NATIONAL PORTRAIT GALLERY)

between the wars were Edith Sitwell (1887–1964), Robert Graves (1895–   ), Edwin Muir (1887–1959), and the Scottish poet Hugh MacDiarmid (1892–   ).

Perhaps the century's most remarkable writer was James Joyce (1882–1941), author of *Ulysses* (1922) and *Finnegans Wake* (1939). Joyce was a master of the stream-of-consciousness technique, which was developed in quite another way by the philosophical novelist Virginia Woolf (1882–1941). Mrs. Woolf and E. M. Forster (1879–   ), self-consciously symbolical writers, were influenced by other members of the "Bloomsbury group," particularly the art critic Roger Fry (1866–1934). Another major novelist, D. H. Lawrence (1885–1930), though a very different writer, became a more self-conscious symbolist as his career proceeded. Indeed, it was an age of symbolism, influenced greatly by modern psychological theories. Other novelists who began to write before World War II and continued into the 1940's and 1950's were Aldous Huxley (1894–1963), Evelyn Waugh (1903–66), Graham Greene (1904–   ), and Joyce Cary (1888–1957). After World War II, and particularly in the 1950's, a new generation of writers attacked British stratified society with comic zest. These "angry young men" had as their spokesman the dramatist John Osborne (1929–   ). Other novelists who came into prominence were C. P. Snow (1905–   ), Iris Murdoch (1919–   ), Angus Wilson (1913–   ), William Golding (1911–   ), and Samuel Beckett (1906–   ), an Irishman writing in French who was also a successful playwright. These postwar writers exhibited no common style or technique.

With the death of the Welshman Dylan Thomas (1914–53) England was bereft of its most famous young poet; he was certainly one of the most talented lyricists of the century. In the later 1950's no poet managed to capture the fancy of the literary world as had Thomas as a young man more than a decade earlier.

Consult Beach, J. W., *The Concept of Nature in Nineteenth-Century English Poetry* (1936); Chambers, E. K., *English Literature at the Close of the Middle Ages* (1945);° *A Literary History of England*, ed. by A. C. Baugh (1948); *A History of English Literature*, ed. by Hardin Craig (1950); Pinto, V. deS., *The English Renaissance, 1510–1688* (rev. ed. 1952); Allen, W. E. *The English Novel* (1954); Lewis, C. S., *English Literature in the Sixteenth Century Excluding Drama* (1954);° Fraser, G. S., *The Modern Writer and His World* (1955); Bernbaum, Ernest, *Guide Through the Romantic Movement* (rev. ed., 1956); Tindall, W. Y., *Forces in Modern British Literature, 1885–1956* (rev. ed., 1956); Daiches, David, *Critical History of English Literature* (2 vol., 1960); Dobrée, Bonamy, *English Literature in the Early Eighteenth Century, 1700–1740* (1960);° Bush, Douglas, *English Literature in the Earlier Seventeenth Century, 1600–1660* (2d rev. ed., 1962); Moody, W. V., and Lovett, R. M., *A History of English Literature* (8th ed., 1964); Legouis, E. H., *A History of English Literature* (1965).

° In *Oxford History of English Literature*, 12-volume work in progress.

HAZARD ADAMS, Michigan State University

See also DRAMA; ENGLISH THEATER; IRISH LITERATURE IN ENGLISH; LITERARY CRITICISM; NOVEL; SCOTTISH LITERATURE; WELSH LITERATURE; articles on individual writers.

ENGLISH MUSIC. The earliest classic in the history of English music is the round *Sumer is icumen in*, written at Reading Abbey, supposedly by John of Fornsete, c.1240 A.D. (although recent researchers date it about 1310 A.D.). It is an important document in the history not only of English music but of European music, since it is the earliest extant composition in six simultaneous vocal parts and is the earliest extant example of the art of canon. A leap of almost two centuries must be made to the next landmark, the work of John Dunstable (d.1453) and Leonel Power (d.1445), who were much admired abroad as well as in England. Manuscripts of their works have been found in France and Italy.

Several English kings were skilled musicians (Henry V and Henry VIII may also have been composers), and they fostered the art of music through the Chapel Royal, dating from the 12th century, in which most of the country's best musicians found employment. The music of the pre-Elizabethan era reached its height in the Masses and other choral works of John Taverner (c.1495–1545).

The Elizabethan Period. Taverner's younger contemporaries Thomas Tallis, Christopher Tye, and John Marbeck (commonly spelled Merbecke) belonged to the Elizabethan period (16th century), the so-called Golden Age of English music. Marbeck, who was a Protestant, adapted the plainsong melodies of the Roman Catholic liturgy to the accents of the English liturgical text, and Tallis was among those who harmonized Marbeck's melodies. Tallis' own Masses and other church music have been overshadowed by those of his pupil and friend, William Byrd. In 1575 Elizabeth granted the two composers jointly the sole right to print music and music paper in England. Like many musicians during that period of religious strife in England, Byrd was spared persecution because of his musical genius and was favored by Elizabeth in spite of his Roman Catholic faith (which did not prevent him from writing English as well as Latin church music).

In Byrd's time instrumental and secular vocal music became more widely cultivated. In addition to church music Byrd wrote madrigals, several large collections of pieces for virginals (harpsichord), and many pieces for viols. The last group included masterly examples of two types of work that prevailed in English music for several generations, the fantasy and the *In Nomine* (an instrumental composition based on a plainsong theme). Byrd was one of the first in the field; most of the great masters of the English madrigal, lute song, fantasy, and of music for virginals, were somewhat younger. It was only at the end of the 16th century that the first madrigals of Thomas Morley, Thomas Weelkes, and John Wilbye appeared, and Orlando Gibbons, the last of the very great madrigalists, was 40 years Byrd's junior. The supreme master of the solo song with lute accompaniment was John Dowland, and of keyboard music, John Bull.

The fantasy and the madrigal survived with diminishing importance well into the next generation, in which the outstanding figures were the brothers Henry and William Lawes, and the much younger Matthew Locke. The more important form in English music in the middle decades of the 17th century, however, was the masque. Music was second to spectacle in this art, but it paved the way for opera proper. Milton's *Comus*, with music by Henry Lawes, was one of the most famous, if not one of the most characteristic, examples of the masque. Henry Lawes also contributed, with Locke and others, to the music, unfortunately lost, of the opera *The Siege of Rhodes*, to a text by D'Avenant. The earliest surviving English opera is Locke's *Psyche* (text by Shadwell) produced in 1675.

Music Under the Restoration. The reign of the Puritans probably had the effect of slowing down, though it did not completely halt, the development of music in England, but the Restoration brought a new stimulus. Charles II started an orchestra on the French model and revived the Chapel Royal, in which the three most brilliant composers of the next generation, Pelham Humfrey, John Blow, and Henry Purcell, received their musical training under Henry (Captain) Cooke. The tremendous theatrical revival after the Restoration brought a continuous demand for incidental music, and in five works, out of a total of nearly 50, on which Purcell collaborated, the music is so extensive and impressive that they are virtually operas. Even more important than these is his short genuine opera *Dido and Aeneas*, written for a girls' school and celebrated as a triumph of English music second only to *Sumer is icumen in*. Among his other masterpieces were church anthems, secular odes and cantatas for state and ceremonial occasions, violin sonatas, harpsichord suites, and a set of fantasies for viols. The latter revived and crowned an art that had been in decline for the preceding 50 years as a consequence of the violin's gradual victory over the viol.

The Period of Handel. During Purcell's life public concerts were started in England, first by John Banister in 1672, and six years later by a coal merchant Thomas Britton. It was also during this period that the domination of English musical life by foreign musicians began, culminating in the arrival of Handel, first on a visit in 1710, and two years later as a permanent immigrant. He concentrated his attention first on Italian opera and wrote more than 45 operas in the Italian language and in the Neapolitan style. For a time this art form enjoyed a great vogue, but the public gradually tired of it, and its decline was hastened by John Gay's production of *The Beggar's Opera* (1728). This not only ridiculed the conventions of Italian opera but established a new form of entertainment, the ballad opera, which immediately became immensely popular. Handel persisted with Italian opera until 1740, although from 1720 on he also wrote secular and Biblical choral works. After the *Messiah* (1742) he abandoned opera entirely for oratorio, with far-reaching effects on English music and musical life for the next two centuries.

Several musical institutions which are still active date from Handel's time, notably the Three Choirs Festival (founded, 1724) and the Society of Musicians (founded, 1738). Native English composition, however, had begun to decline in quality. Thomas Arne had great success as an opera composer but is remembered now chiefly for a handful of Shakespearean songs. His most distinguished contemporaries, Maurice Greene and William Boyce, are little more than names known to students of music history and to church musicians through a valuable collection of earlier cathedral music (begun by Greene and completed by Boyce). Among their juniors, active after Handel's death, were Thomas Linley, Charles Dibdin, James Hook, and Stephen Storace, all of whom wrote successful works of the ballad opera type with original tunes. Another popular musical diversion of post-Handelian years, which continued throughout the first half of the 19th century, was the singing of glees (pieces for unaccompanied male chorus), for which purpose many clubs were formed.

The Classic Era. In the transition from the age of the ballad opera to the age of the piano, it was again two foreign-born musicians who were dominant in English musical life, Johann Christian Bach and the piano virtuoso Muzio Clementi, while the most gifted British composer of this time, the Irishman John Field (whose nocturnes influenced Chopin), settled in Russia. Native music was otherwise stagnant in this period, and the visits to London of the child Mozart and the elderly Haydn were the great events in English musical life during the later 18th century. In 1775 the Hanover Square Rooms were opened as a concert hall by J. C. Bach and Karl Abel, and it was here that Haydn appeared at the concerts of the impresario and violinist Johann Salomon, for whom he wrote his last 12 symphonies. The other principal concert organization of the time was the Concerts of Ancient Music, founded in 1776. In 1784 this organization established the tradition of mammoth performances of the works of Handel, with many hundreds of singers and players.

The Romantic Era. The founding in 1813 of the Philharmonic Society (since 1912, the Royal Philharmonic Society) did much to popularize the work of Beethoven. Among its first conductors and founder-members was Henry Bishop, composer of *Home, Sweet Home*, who wrote prolifically for the stage and was also responsible for some remarkably tasteless adaptations of the operas of Mozart, Rossini, and others. Light opera remained the only musical form in which native British composers produced anything of character or merit. Among Bishop's younger contemporaries two Irishmen, Michael Balfe and Vincent Wallace, were the most successful. Of the more serious composers the most gifted was Sterndale Bennett, an accomplished imitator of Mendelssohn (yet another foreign musician who played an important role in the history of English music). After a long gap another musician of talent appeared in Arthur Sullivan, who again excelled in light opera, or operetta. His first success, *Cox and Box*, was produced in 1867. Sullivan also aspired to success as a serious composer of oratorios and symphonic music, but his works in this field were quickly forgotten, like those of his worthy contemporaries Sir Charles Parry, Sir Charles Stanford, and Sir Alexander MacKenzie. Although massed choral singing had become the most widely cultivated form of music-making during the Victorian age, especially in the provinces, it inspired no native masterpiece until Sir Edward Elgar's *The Dream of Gerontius* (1900). A year earlier at the relatively late age of 42, Elgar had composed his first great orchestral work, the *Enigma Variations*. Slightly his junior was the remarkable individualist Frederick Delius, who like Elgar took a Wagnerian direction rather than the Brahmsian one favored by most of their contemporaries. He also succeeded thereby in arriving at a distinctive style of his own.

With the works of these two composers in the first decade of the 20th century English music regained a certain distinction. Outside the sphere of composition the recovery had already been under way for some time. Good concerts of orchestral and chamber music had been increasing in number ever since 1855, and in 1895 the highly successful Promenade Concerts, which are still flourishing, were started by Robert Newman under the direction of Henry Wood. During the last two decades of the 19th century several schools of music were founded, notably the Royal College of Music, London, supplementing the Royal Academy of Music, which has existed since 1822. Both are still active today. In 1879 Sir George Grove published the first volume of his great *Dictionary of Music and Musicians*, and in 1898 the English Folksong Society was founded.

The 20th Century. It was the rediscovery of folk song that inspired the outstanding composers of the next generation, Ralph Vaughan Williams and Gustav Holst. They wanted to write music that was English in character, not merely English through the nationality of its composer, as might be said of the essentially cosmopolitan music of Elgar and Delius. Vaughan Williams, particularly, identified himself with the folk song movement, the leader of which was the scholar Cecil Sharp. During his long career Vaughan Williams wrote nine symphonies (the first one with chorus). In that period popular taste inclined increasingly toward orchestral music, while choral singing declined in popularity, both in public concerts and as a form of music-making for amateurs. There are, however, still numerous large choral societies which give regular public concerts.

Among more recent composers Sir William Walton, Michael Tippett, and Benjamin Britten have written music of outstanding originality, and Britten may be considered the most successful opera composer since Richard Strauss and Giacomo Puccini. In spite of his success, native opera in England is still only precariously established. A permanent English opera company was founded at the Sadler's Wells Theater in 1931, and another at the Covent Garden Theater in 1946. This was the first in the latter theater's history, although it had served as an opera house since Handel's time. No permanent professional opera company, however, exists outside London. The Welsh National Opera and Scottish Opera, both partly amateur, function for short seasons, and the opera house at Glyndeboure provides an annual summer festival of international opera. The Sadler's Wells Opera has two full companies, one of which tours for a large part of the year.

Full-time professional symphony orchestras, on the other hand, now nationally and municipally subsidized, exist in Manchester (the Hallé Orchestra, founded by Sir Charles Hallé in 1857), Liverpool (founded in 1840), Birmingham (1920), Bournemouth (1893), and Scotland (1893). London has five main orchestras, the London Symphony, London Philharmonic, Royal Philharmonic, Philharmonia, and the BBC (British Broadcasting Corporation) Symphony Orchestra.

Other notable recent events in British musical life include the opening in 1951 of the Royal Festival Hall in London, and in 1967, adjoining it, the smaller Queen Elizabeth Hall and Purcell Room; the founding of the Edinburgh Festival (1947); and of the Cheltenham Festival of British Contemporary Music (1945).

Consult Hadow, W. H., *English Music* (1931); Blom, Eric, *Music in England* (1942); Walker, Ernest, *A History of Music in England* (3d ed., 1952).

COLIN MASON, The Manchester *Guardian*
See also IRISH MUSIC; SCOTTISH MUSIC; WELSH MUSIC.

ENGLISH SETTER, a member of the working group of dogs. The breed was established in England during the late 16th century, and was probably developed through crossing existing spaniel and pointer breeds. English setters are classic bird dogs and are used for locating and pointing feathered game. Their long, silky coats may be various colors but most commonly are white marked with shades of brown or black. Adult males weigh about 55 lb. English setters have very gentle dispositions and make excellent pets.

ENGLISH THEATER. The theater in England, as in several European countries, developed out of the church. It originated in the darkness of the 10th century when there was introduced into the Easter service a brief four-line scene in which the three Marys, impersonated by priests, spoke with the angel guarding Christ's tomb and were told of the Resurrection. Obviously the innovation was effective, since very soon this primitive Easter play was extended to include other associated episodes, such as the purchasing of perfumes at an unguent-seller's booth, while a similar dramatic development was introduced to deal with the Christmas story. Thus was established the liturgical drama performed by clerics as part of their services and chanted in Latin.

As these plays developed, the church authorities gradually became alarmed and prohibitions on performances followed. Nothing, however, could destroy the newly discovered dramatic impulse; abandoned by the priests, these plays were seized upon by the laity. They were provided with English dialogue and enlarged into great mystery cycles dealing with the chief Biblical events from the creation of the world to the Resurrection. For their production, usually on Corpus Christi day, the local trade guilds eagerly accepted responsibility.

Under this lay aegis the productions became much more "theatrical," although to the end the staging method employed derived from earliest practice. In the church, fictional localities were symbolically represented by means of "stations" (sometimes merely benches, sometimes small platforms) set up at various selected positions. Thus the Marys could first go to the unguent-seller's booth in the nave and then proceed to Christ's tomb at the altar. In this way was established the characteristic medieval simultaneous setting, wherein all or most of the localities called for in a particular drama were shown or indicated to the audience at one and the same time. For the performance of the mystery plays, the church's platforms were succeeded by tentlike "mansions" or "pageants." Generally these were grouped together in one row, with Heaven on the actors' right and Hell on the left. Sometimes they were placed dispersedly, as in the church, and sometimes they were put upon wheels and rolled from place to place.

Rise of Professionalism. Mystery plays were still being performed in Shakespeare's lifetime, but from a century before his birth records have been found of another and entirely distinct dramatic development. The performance of the mysteries always remained exclusively in the hands of amateurs. From about 1475 small groups of professionals, commonly three or four men and a boy, presented interludes—short comic or moral pieces—for the delectation either of their lords in great halls or of the public out-of-doors. These men required no scenery; consequently another staging principle was established whereby the actors localized by their words the bare stage (often simply part of a hall floor) upon which they stood. During the early 16th century, the activities of these professionals were accompanied by others—notably those of the choirboys attached to the Chapels Royal, grammar-school boys, university students, and members of the Inns of Court. In this way interest in a secular drama was increasingly fostered; the primitive styles of the early interludes were rendered more effective. Instead of the allegorical personifications of the moral plays, historical or invented characters were introduced. Gradually the forms of comedy and tragedy took shape.

ENGLISH THEATER

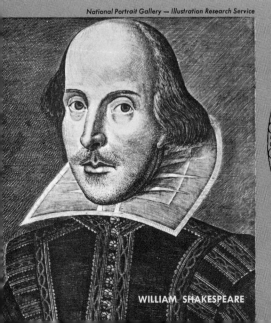

WILLIAM SHAKESPEARE

RICHARD BRINSLEY SHERIDAN

DAVID GARRICK

English dramatic tradition was enriched by Shakespeare's masterly plays, Sheridan's comedies of manners, and Garrick's advances in acting techniques.

ENGLISH THEATER

Early Permanent Theaters. By the 1560's interest in the secular theater had so far developed as to encourage the professional companies to double their numbers. Frequently they presented their plays, not on open ground, but in the great yards of city inns; and by 1576 the time had arrived for the building of London's first permanent playhouse, "The Theatre," erected in Finsbury Fields just outside the jurisdiction of the city authorities. That this met an immediate need was demonstrated by the fact that the years immediately following saw the erection of many other "public theaters," culminating in the famous Globe (1598), home of the Lord Chamberlain's Men (Shakespeare's company), and the Fortune (1600), home of their principal rivals, the Lord Admiral's Men. It should be noted here that all the companies were nominally the servants of noblemen, who offered them protection and removed from them the stigma of "rogues and vagabonds" applied to masterless entertainers. After the accession of James I in 1603, Shakespeare's company became the King's Men, and the tradition endured into the 19th century when the actors of Drury Lane Theatre were still technically called "His (or Her) Majesty's Servants."

The several theaters built between 1576 and 1600 certainly differed from each other, but they must all have been erected on similar principles. Round, hexagonal, or square, they were open to the sky, with a central yard and rows of galleries. Into the center of the yard extended a wide deep stage (the Fortune stage was 40 ft. square). At the rear was a façade broken by at least three doors of entrance, while an extension of the gallery above provided opportunity for action aloft. Clearly, in such a playhouse there could be no opportunity of introducing much scenery, so that in effect the players took over the unadorned open acting area on which the interlude players had performed, occasionally modifying this by adapting the medieval "simultaneous setting" to their own needs. Though the settings were normally indicated merely by the players' words, on occasion the entrance doors might be used to symbolize particular localities. Assuredly the equipment at the command of these men was far more extensive than anything their predecessors had enjoyed. But we must remember that often they took their plays on tour and that they could effectively perform them on any open space.

Elizabethan Dramatists. Although another type of playhouse, roofed over and capable of introducing some scenic effects, was used by boy actors associated with Paul's, the company drawn from the choristers of St. Paul's Cathedral, and Blackfriars Theatre, it was primarily the open-air public theater that welcomed and stimulated the remarkable development of the late Elizabethan and early Jacobean drama which suddenly sprang into full glory during the last 15 years of the 16th century. First came a group of young university men, of whom Christopher Marlowe was chief and who brought a vigorous poetic style, dignity, force, and strength to the stage. Then Shakespeare took command, accompanied by many others, such as Ben Jonson, Thomas Heywood, Thomas Dekker, and George Chapman, who variously exploited and expanded the resources of comedy, tragedy, and the newly developed chronicle history play. Unquestionably Shakespeare's achievements stand apart from the rest because of their consummate excellence in language and concept. Unquestionably, too, numerous dramatic writings of the time are trivial; yet, taken as a whole, this was one of the greatest periods in the entire history of the stage.

The impetus given to the drama continued on until the theaters were closed by Puritan order in 1642, but even at the beginning of that century we may discern forces at work destined to reduce its power. In the years 1600–5 there came a sudden vogue for the boy players, and the indoor theaters in which they performed came to form the model for a new type of private theater—playhouses which, largely because admission prices were higher, cultivated audiences of a more restricted kind. Through the influence of these spectators tragedy tended to lose its vigor, tragicomedy flourished, and comedy inclined toward Jonsonian realism rather than toward Shakespearean romance. Of these trends the plays included in the "Beaumont and Fletcher" folios are characteristic.

Sir Henry Irving (1838–1905), the noted actor-manager, in a painting by J. B. Lepago. (NATIONAL PORTRAIT GALLERY—ILLUSTRATION RESEARCH SERVICE)

Print of London's Drury Lane Theatre, as it appeared in 1775. The present theater dates from 1812. (THE BETTMANN ARCHIVE)

A 19th-century English theater, the stage illuminated by candlelight.
(THE BETTMANN ARCHIVE)

Modern theater design revives the Elizabethan platform stage.
(WILSON—ILLUSTRATION SERVICE)

The Restoration and Its Changes. After the theaters remained officially closed for 18 years, they reopened in 1660 on the restoration of Charles II. The audience now was even more restricted—confined largely to the small, courtly Whitehall circle. The King took active control of theatrical affairs by allowing only two "patent" companies (managed by a couple of favored courtiers) to perform plays—one under his own aegis and the other under that of his brother, the Duke of York. By royal order actresses supplanted boy actors in women's roles.

The new theaters were built in imitation of contemporary Italian and French court playhouses. Although a relic of the Elizabethan platform remained in the form of a wide "apron" jutting out into the pit and although the old stage doors remained, these houses were provided with proscenium arches and were designed for the display of scenery. This theater and its audience encouraged new styles in drama—the artificial "heroic play" penned in couplets and the witty comedy of manners cultivated by gentlemen-playwrights such as Sir George Etherege, William Wycherley, and William Congreve.

In the 1680's came still further signs of change. By that time a few wealthier citizens began to join the aristocratic courtiers in pit and boxes, and their tastes—less airy and polished, more apt to condemn moral license—gradually made themselves felt. When in 1698 Jeremy Collier issued a forthright attack upon dramatic excesses, he was expressing more than his own personal views. At about this time the sprightly though dissolute comedy of manners began to decline and first steps were taken toward the characteristic 18th-century sentimental drama.

18th-Century Developments. Throughout the 18th century, indeed as late as 1842, the "patents" still nominally held their power, but the growth in London's population, added to the increase in playgoing among the middle classes, led to the opening, often by subterfuge, of other smaller theaters. These, despite attempts to restrict or suppress them, rapidly came to exercise an important role. It was at such a house that John Gay's *The Beggar's Opera* won its great success and at another that David Garrick made his first London appearance.

In this period playhouse architecture steadily advanced toward its modern form. The apron became smaller; scenery assumed greater importance; the entrance doors

tended to lose their value; greater attention was paid to lighting. As the century advanced to its close a dual development increased the emphasis upon the theater's visual appeal: the "patent" houses, notably Drury Lane, were reconstructed in vaster proportions so that hearing became difficult, and the minor theaters, debarred by law from presenting ordinary spoken plays, sought to win favor by their scenic effects. This resulted in a change within the drama. Throughout most of the 18th century, not much of real worth was produced. Certainly the sentimental plays were laying the foundation for modern realism, but in themselves they had little intrinsic value; and outside their realm only the vivacious ballad opera and the comedies of Richard Brinsley Sheridan and Oliver Goldsmith possessed enduring quality. At the end of the period the emphasis on visual appeal, in conjunction with other trends, introduced the kind of dramatic offerings that eventually formed the characteristic repertoire of the early 19th century—melodrama, spectacle, farce, burlesque, and pantomime.

The 19th Century. The cultivation of theatrical effects was, of course, markedly aided by the introduction of gas and, later, of electric lighting. At the same time novel mechanical devices made further contributions in the same direction. It is not surprising that the mid-19th century saw the elaborate productions of Charles Kean at the

On the platform Sir Laurence Olivier (left) with Joan Greenwood in *The Broken Heart*. (ANGUS MCBEAN—ILLUSTRATION RESEARCH SERVICE)

Princess's Theater while its last years witnessed the Lyceum spectacles produced by Sir Henry Irving. Kean and Irving were men typical of their time, representative figures in the rise of the actor-managers—a movement closely associated with the advent of the director (or producer as he is known in England), the disappearance of the old stock companies, and the substitution of specially prepared shows, designed to run night after night, in place of the constantly changing repertories that had formerly been regular theatrical practice.

The theater flourished in the 19th century, but the drama had not much to offer. Many of the melodramas had verve, but their literary qualities were almost nonexistent. Men like Tom Robertson, Arthur Pinero, and Henry Arthur Jones applied themselves to the development of the realistic play, but none were of major stature. Perhaps the liveliest contributions to the drama of the time were the extravaganzas, which in Sir William Schwenck Gilbert's Savoy operas created something of enduring appeal.

Shaw and the Modern Drama. Already, however, during the last years of Victoria's reign, the star of George Bernard Shaw was shimmering on the horizon. Shaw's dramas were to prove not only the most original but also the most symbolic works of the 20th century. Among the masters of drama Shaw is distinguished by his eclecticism. In his plays the realistic drama of ideas meets with fantasy; Congreve's wit, Jonson's satire, and even Shakespeare's humor are all mingled in his writings; farce and burlesque appear alongside Ibsenian seriousness.

Precisely such eclecticism is typical of the modern theater in general. Earlier periods certainly showed changes, innovations, variety, yet in all of them dominant traditions are amply apparent. The modern theater has no such cardinal core. The proscenium-arch stage exists alongside experiments with "aprons" and performances "in the round"; naturalism in setting appears alongside conventionalism; bare-stage productions are contrasted with elaborate balletlike spectacles. In the drama, particularly during the "New Wave" which surged forward after 1956, a similar variety of forms is amply evident. Realism of a kind sometimes reminiscent of the style sponsored by the early repertory theaters coexists with attempts to establish a new form of poetic play. Relics of the "well-made" structure appear alongside revolutionary dramatic experiments that deny the value of plot and defy logic. Such variety, of course, is by no means restricted to the English stage, but is a reflection of a general dramatic movement in many countries.

Consult Chambers, E. K., *Medieval State* (2 vols., 1903) and *The Elizabethan Stage* (4 vols., 1923); Morgan, A. E., *Tendencies of Modern English Drama* (1924); Young, Karl, *Drama of the Medieval Church* (2 vols., 1933); Bentley, G. E., *Jacobean and Caroline State* (5 vols., 1941–56); Nicoll, Allardyce, *A History of English Drama, 1660–1900* (6 vols., 1952–59); Craig, Hardin, *English Religious Drama of the Middle Ages* (1955); Gascoigne, Bamber, *Twentieth-Century Drama* (1962); Taylor, J. R., *Anger and After* (1962).

ALLARDYCE NICOLL, *University of Birmingham, England*

See also COMEDY; DRAMA; FARCE; MEDIEVAL THEATER; MELODRAMA; THEATER, HISTORY OF TRAGEDY.

ENGRAVER BEETLE or BARK BEETLE, name for many small, dark-colored insects of the genera *Ips*, *Scolytus*, *Pityogenes*, and *Pityophthorus*, in the bark beetle family, Scolytidae. Engraver beetles do great harm to trees by excavating galleries beneath the bark where they lay their eggs; the larvae feed on the inner bark. In addition to direct physical damage, engraver beetles also introduce yeast and fungus spores which hinder tree growth by clogging the cells of sapwood. The European elm bark beetle, *Scolytus multisriatus*, carries the fungus which causes Dutch elm disease.

See also DUTCH ELM DISEASE.

ENGRAVING, process of incising a design in metal. It is used for such purposes as the decoration of gold and silver, but in this article it refers to the process of incising a design in a metal plate and the work of art made by printing this plate. Engraving—sometimes called line engraving—is an intaglio process, that is, the image to be printed is below the surface of the plate. The incised image is filled with ink, the plate surface wiped clean, and the image transferred to dampened paper under the heavy pressure of a press.

The word "engraving" is generically used to refer to most other types of prints, such as etchings or lithographs, though these are not true engravings. A wood engraving, or woodcut, is made by relief printing, that is, the design to be printed is raised above the surface of the wood base. In photoengraving, a branch of modern photomechanical printing, the image is etched with acid, not engraved.

Engraving is done with a tool called a burin, or graver. It is a thin bar of steel of quadrangular section, ground to an oblique angle to create a sharp, V-shaped point. The unsharpened end is set in a wooden knob. The polished metal plate, usually copper (soft steel is used for bank-note engraving), is often placed on a leather-covered pad of sand to allow the engraver flexibility in moving the plate. Holding the wooden knob in his palm, the engraver places the burin rod approximately parallel to the plate and inserts the point into the metal. He moves both the plate and the burin in the process, controlling the point, as it moves along, with thumb and forefinger. A thin ribbon of metal is removed as a groove is cut, the depth of the groove being determined by the pressure exerted.

History. Since antiquity, goldsmiths and metalworkers have engraved designs to decorate caskets, armor, and other objects. There is no proof, however, that printed impressions were made from engraved designs before the 15th century. The earliest dated engraving is "Flagellation" (1446), by the German artist known as the Master of the Berlin Passion. He has been identified as the elder Israhel van Meckenem, father of the well-known engraver of the same name. Undated engravings, however, were made earlier, in the 1430's, by the Master of the Playing Cards. Martin Schongauer and Albrecht Dürer are the most important early German workers whose names are known, Dürer generally being considered the greatest of all engravers. In the Netherlands, the most important 16th-century engraver was Lucas van Leyden.

The earliest known Italian engraver, working about 1450, was the Master of the Larger Vienna Passion. Maso Finiguerra, whose prints date from 1452, is sometimes

MAKING A METAL PLATE ENGRAVING

The burin has a sharp tip of hard metal for cutting into the soft metal of the plate. The burnisher is a blunt tool used for pressing out shallow errors. The scraper has a sharp blade for shaving away the area of a deeper error. The paper, which must be damp for printing, is soaked in the pan. The dauber and cheesecloth are used for inking the grooves and cleaning the non-printing plate surface.

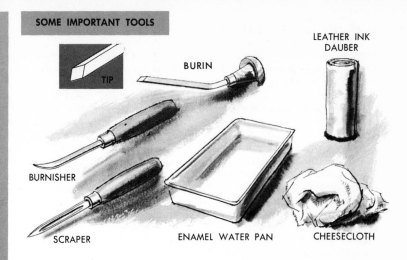

TIP
BURIN
LEATHER INK DAUBER
BURNISHER
SCRAPER
ENAMEL WATER PAN
CHEESECLOTH

SOME PRINCIPAL STEPS

The burin is held firmly in a position that affords the least opportunity for wiggling or slipping. Burins come in different sizes to give grooves of the desired width.

Pressure on the burin deepens the groove. For curved lines, the plate is turned under the moving burin. Since the design prints in reverse, it must be engraved accordingly.

When the design has been engraved, the plate is cleaned carefully. Ink is then smeared into the grooves with the dauber, which is usually made of rolled leather.

A piece of cheesecloth is used to rub the ink thoroughly into the engraved lines. This is important because it ensures the uniform inking of even the finest grooves.

Another piece of cheesecloth is used to clean the ink off the unengraved, nonprinting surface of the plate. Care must be taken not to dislodge the ink from the grooves.

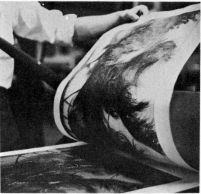

Pratt Institute, Brooklyn, N.Y.

A special press is used for printing the engraving. The pressure forces the damp paper into the inked, recessed areas of the plate and the ink is transferred onto the paper.

erroneously credited with inventing line engraving. Antonio Pollaiuolo is known for a single magnificent engraving, "The Battle of the Naked Men." Other important early Italian engravers were Andrea Mantegna and Marcantonio Raimondi, who was a major influence in turning engraving into a medium for copying the work of other artists.

Among the outstanding workers of the 16th century were Jean Duvet and Jean Gourmont in France and Hendrik Goltzius in the Netherlands. Important engravers of the 17th century included Claude Mellan and Robert Nanteuil in France. In the 18th century William Hogarth and later William Blake, in England, were especially noteworthy. Line engraving declined as an art in the 19th century after the introduction of steel plates and commercial techniques, but was revived in the 20th century by such artists as Joseph Hecht in France, Stanley William Hayter in England, and Gabor Peterdi in the United States.

Consult Peterdi, Gabor, *Printmaking: Methods Old and New* (1959).

JACOB KAINEN, Smithsonian Institution

See also AQUATINT; DRYPOINT; ETCHING; LITHOGRAPHY; MEZZOTINT; WOODCUT AND WOOD ENGRAVING.

ENID [ē′nĭd], city of northern Oklahoma, and seat of Garfield County. It is a marketing center in Oklahoma's principal wheat-producing region. Enid refines oil produced nearby and has oil-supply-and-equipment industries. Phillips University and Vance Air Force Base are in the city. Pop. (1950) 36,017; (1960) 38,859.

ENIWETOK [ĕn-ĭ-wē′tŏk], isolated atoll in the northern Marshall Islands, the scene of U.S. atomic experiments between 1947 and 1958. The 146 inhabitants were moved to Ujelang atoll and were paid $175,000.

ENLARGERS and ENLARGING, PHOTOGRAPHIC. *See* PHOTOGRAPHY.

ENLIGHTENED DESPOTISM, political doctrine supported by some writers of the Enlightenment (q.v.), including Voltaire, and applied in varying degrees by several European rulers of the period, notably Frederick II of Prussia, Joseph II of Austria, Catherine II of Russia, and Charles III of Spain. The monarch was to be "the chief servant of the state," with the duty of promoting the welfare of his people rather than his own selfish ends. Plato's "philosopher-king" was often held up as the model for such a rational, public-spirited prince, who would be independent of factions, oligarchies, or organized interests. Many important reforms, especially of military, economic, fiscal, judicial, and educational institutions, were introduced by the enlightened despots, but none of them encouraged popular initiative, none produced an equally enlightened successor, and the ideal itself was largely discredited as too authoritarian and paternalistic by the time of the French Revolution of 1789.

RALPH H. BOWEN, Northern Illinois University

ENLIGHTENMENT, THE, in European history the period just before the French Revolution of 1789, roughly coin-

ciding with the middle decades of the 18th century. The dominant preoccupation of this era was the critical examination of previously accepted principles and authorities, whether in politics, religion, or science. The more important sources of "enlightened" ideas include British empiricism and liberalism (particularly the thought of Bacon, Hobbes, Locke, and Newton), French humanism, rationalism, and skepticism (Rabelais, Montaigne, Descartes, and Bayle) and, to a degree, the ideas of Spinoza and Leibniz. Constitutionalism and efficiency in government; experimentalism in science; deism, rationalism, or skepticism in religion; and utilitarianism in ethics—were the doctrines most frequently expounded and advocated by writers and practical reformers of the Enlightenment.

Optimism, in the sense of a belief in secular progress, was widespread—its typical form being the conviction that the human race was infinitely perfectible through improved education and the amelioration of the physical and social environment. Nature, usually conceived in an idyllic sense, was often held up as the best model for imitation in all things, the implication being that all evils stemmed from man's failure, either through ignorance or through neglect of Nature's laws, to conform to the natural order. Such failure was thought to be mainly caused by prejudice and superstition, deliberately fostered in their own interests by kings, nobles, priests, and other beneficiaries of the traditional order.

Immanuel Kant, perhaps the greatest philosopher of the age, posed the question, "What is Enlightenment?" and then answered it by saying that it was man's emergence from "his self-imposed nonage"—that is, the coming to maturity of the human mind. This newly gained maturity was thought to render obsolete and harmful virtually the entire body of inherited traditions and beliefs, which were to be retained only in so far as they could pass the exacting tests of critical reason or be proven to have definite social utility. The conviction that men were not only good by nature, but fundamentally pacific and co-operative, served as the foundation for the cosmopolitanism exemplified by Benjamin Franklin's remark: "Mankind is my country; I am a citizen of the world." Benevolence and mutual help were thought to flow from the natural impulses of rational creatures who were uncorrupted by superstition.

The practical consequences of these beliefs included a successful campaign to abolish the international slave trade, as well as important reforms designed to make the criminal law less ferocious and the prisons more humane. In economics, the protectionist theories of mercantilism (based on systematic governmental control of trade and industry) were rejected in favor of the laissez-faire doctrines developed by the French physiocrats and Adam Smith in the *Wealth of Nations*. These thinkers argued that, since every individual is the best judge of his own advantage, it was in the public, as well as the private, interest that each should be left as free as possible to seek the efficiency that specialization and the division of labor made possible, thus maximizing private incomes as well as the national wealth.

The Enlightenment gave a decisive turn to the thinking of the educated classes in all countries of European civilization, including the American colonies of England and

Spain. But it had its main centers in France, England, and Germany, where characteristic local forms of the general movement appeared. The Age of Reason in England tended to complacency and support of the *status quo* in church and state that had been established by the "Glorious Revolution" of 1688–89. In Germany during the *Aufklärung*, political fragmentation and cultural stagnation discouraged practical reform movements (except those of the so-called enlightened despots—Frederick II of Prussia and Joseph II of Austria) and lent an abstract, metaphysical emphasis to most of the thought of the period.

In France, by contrast, the discussion of existing ideas and institutions was vigorous, detailed, and increasingly critical. Absolute monarchy, class privileges, censorship, legal arbitrariness and injustice, corruption and inefficiency in government, dogmatism and apriorism in science, bigotry, intolerance and persecution in religion became the main targets of the *philosophes*. The most influential of them were Voltaire, Montesquieu, Diderot, D'Alembert, Rousseau, Helvétius, Raynal, D'Holbach, and Condorcet. The views of these men were spread abroad in books, pamphlets, plays, poems, and even dictionaries, especially the great *Encyclopédie* in 35 volumes edited by Diderot between 1751 and 1772.

Despite the strong opposition of the Jesuits and other upholders of the old order, the *philosophes* were able to evade the royal and ecclesiastical censorships and by 1770 public opinion had been mostly won to the side of the "enlightened" writers. When the French Revolution attempted to reform the monarchy in and after 1789, its leaders drew their inspiration and their constitutional programs directly from the publications of the *philosophes*. In America, the same ideas were embodied in Jefferson's Declaration of Independence and in the federal Constitution and Bill of Rights.

RALPH H. BOWEN, Northern Illinois University
See also EDUCATION: *History of Education—The Age of Reason.*

ENNA [ĕn'ə], city of central Sicily, Italy; capital of Enna Province. On a hill 3,067 ft. above sea level, it is Sicily's highest city. Enna is an important agricultural market center and resort town. It was called Castrogiovanni until 1927. Pop., 25,211.

ENNIS, town of northern Texas, about 30 mi. south of Dallas, in a general farming area. The city has railway maintenance shops and publishing, clothing, and flour-milling industries. Inc., 1893; pop. (1950) 7,815; (1960) 9,347.

ENNISKILLEN, municipal borough of Northern Ireland and capital of County Fermanagh, pleasantly located between Upper and Lower Lough Erne, on a strategic site commanded by a castle built in the early 15th century. Two historic regiments of the British army take their names from the town. It has an important cattle market. Pop., 7,438.

ENNIUS [ĕn'ē-əs], **QUINTUS** (c.239–169 B.C.), early Latin poet of Greek birth, considered the father of Roman poetry. He served in the Roman army and attracted the attention of Cato. After miscellaneous productions, he wrote *The Annals*, until Vergil's day the accepted epic of Rome. In dignified, if somewhat crude, hexameters it told the story of Rome from its foundation to 171 B.C. Only fragments of Ennius' writings survive.

ENOCH [ē'nək], in Genesis 4:17, son of Cain. He is said to have been the first man to build a city. From Enoch men were born who invented arts and crafts, the skills of organized society. Tradition claimed that Enoch was pleasing to God and did not die.

ENOCH, BOOK OF, also called I Enoch, an apocalypse of the 2d century B.C., preserved as a whole only in Ethiopic, although large sections have been found in Greek and in the original Hebrew. The most interesting section describes a heavenly Son of Man, but may have been written in Christian times. An early chapter is quoted in the Epistle of Jude.

ENOCH, BOOK OF THE SECRETS OF, also called II Enoch, an apocalypse of doubtful date, preserved only in Slavonic. The calendar used in the book seems to come from the 7th century A.D., but other cosmological ideas, apparently reflected in Gnostic writings, are undoubtedly much earlier, and Origen may have known part of the work.

ENOCH PRATT FREE LIBRARY, chief public library of Baltimore, opened in 1886. Enoch Pratt, a Baltimore philanthropist, gave the central library, six branches, and an endowment. Today support is mainly by taxation. Joseph L. Wheeler, librarian (1926–45), planned a new central building, completed in 1933, that strongly influenced public library architecture.

The Enoch Pratt Free Library, Baltimore, Md.

Enoch Pratt Free Library

ENSCHEDE [ĕn-sкнǝ-dā'], town of the east Netherlands, near the West German border, about 100 mi. east of Amsterdam. Enschede is the principal city of the De Twente cotton spinning and weaving district. The city has good rail connections with the Westphalian coal fields in Germany and imports coal for its iron smelters and electrotechnical industries. Enschede has an industrial trade school. It is a modern city, well-planned with attractive buildings, and the rolling, wooded heathland countryside attracts tourists. Pop., 78,885.

ENSCHEDÉ, Dutch printing and type-founding firm now operating under the name of Johannes Enschedé Zonen. The firm was founded in Haarlem in 1703 by Isaac Enschedé (1681–1761). Printers of currency, postage stamps, books, this firm is famous for its high printing standards and for its beautiful type faces, among which are the popular Romulus and Lutetia type faces designed by J. van Krimpen.

ENSENADA [ĕn-sǝ-nä'dǝ], city of northwestern Mexico, in the state Baja California, on the Pacific coast. It has long been a fishing port on Todos Santos Bay and, with improved harbor facilities, was officially opened to international trade in 1958. Located 65 mi. southeast of San Diego, it is also a popular resort center for U.S. tourists. Pop., 42,770.

ENSILAGE. *See* SILAGE.

ENSOR [ĕn'sôr], **JAMES** (1860–1949), Belgian painter and printmaker. He produced early works that are somber images of the individual in distress, with scenes of desolate beaches and empty streets in Ostend, Belgium. Professional setbacks, disillusion, and feelings of social alienation influenced Ensor's acerb art of the late 1880's, which was climaxed by "The Triumphal Entry of Christ into Brussels" (1888). Regarding the external world as hostile to personal fulfillment, he turned inward to bitter fantasy. His dissonant color, brutal caricature, and uninhibited drawing influenced German expressionism. Ensor's Ostend home, now a museum, and the Royal Museum of Fine Arts, Antwerp, contain excellent examples of his works. He was created a baron in 1929.

ENTEBBE [ĕn-tĕb'ǝ], former capital of Uganda and a small port on the northern shores of Lake Victoria. Entebbe, founded by the British in 1893, has virtually no industry or commerce. The town has notable botanical gardens and an international airport. It is linked by highway with Kampala, now the national capital, 19 mi. northeast of Entebbe. Pop., 7,942.

ENTERITIS. *See* REGIONAL ENTERITIS.

ENTERPRISE, city of southern Alabama, and seat of Coffee County. It is famous for a monument to the boll weevil, erected in 1919 to celebrate the forced shift from cotton to peanut culture. Pop. (1950) 7,288; (1960) 11,410.

ENTERS [ĕn'tǝrs], **ANGNA** (1907–   ), choreographer and dance-mime, born in New York City. She introduced her unique dance-mime style in 1924, using for it the title Compositions in Dance Form, which she later changed to The Theatre of Angna Enters. Since 1926 she has toured the United States and Canada and has given annual seasons in London and Paris. Perhaps her greatest serious work was *The Boy Cardinal*, a Renaissance character piece. She is also a painter and sculptor, and, the author of *First Person Plural* (1937), *Silly Girl* (1944), the autobiography *Artist's Life* (1958), and other books.

ENTOMOLOGY [ĕn-tǝ-mŏl'ǝ-jē], biological science that studies insects. Insects are the most numerous animals on earth. There are over 700,000 known species, far more than all other animal species combined. Their significance to man is tremendous and their study is of equal importance. Some insects produce useful substances—honey, silk, waxes, dyes, shellac; some perform useful services—pollinating plants and eating carrion; others are eaten by fish and game birds and in this way are of indirect benefit to man. Many insects, however, are decidedly harmful, as carriers of disease, agricultural pests, and destroyers of wooden structures.

Since insects are usually very small animals, their detailed study was not possible until after the invention of the microscope, in the late 16th century. Early investigations were made by the English naturalist Robert Hooke who described the intricate details of a fly's foot, a bee's sting, and an insect's wing. Marcello Malpighi, an Italian anatomist, wrote a detailed account of the silkworm's anatomy, including a description of the structure and function of its respiratory apparatus. Systematic entomology (the classification of insects) dates from 1705 when John Ray, an English naturalist, published a work on insect taxonomy. A far more ambitious insect classification was prepared by the great Swedish taxonomist Carolus Linnaeus; and appeared in his *Systema Naturae* (1735). Among the many 18th-century naturalists who contributed to entomological knowledge were René de Réamur and P. Latreille in France, H. Burmeister in Germany, J. Westwood and W. MacLeay in England, and Thomas Say and S. Scudder in the United States.

During the 20th century emphasis has shifted from simply naming and describing insects to a number of specialized entomological subsciences. Insect physiology is concerned with the bodily functions of insects—how they breathe, what they eat, their mechanism of flight, their responses to stimuli. Investigations in this field have contributed valuable information on the control of insect

An entomologist examines grasshoppers in a sweep net. The number caught aids in estimating the degree of infestation in the area.

USDA

Accurate identification of an insect pest must be made before a means of controlling it can be decided upon (top). An entomologist dissects a housefly to determine how it has been affected by an insecticide (below).

pests by poisons; biological control of one insect species by another; and the use of insects as pollinating agents. The contributions of insect genetics, particularly the studies of the fruit fly, *Drosophila*, are well known. Medical and veterinary entomology are large and important fields in which the numerous insects transmitting diseases to man and animals are studied. Economic entomology deals with insect species which destroy crops, ornamental plants, and forests. The applications of economic entomology form the basis of national and international insect control programs. The role of entomology has been important in the past. It will be even more significant in the future as an aid in making the world's undeveloped regions suitable for agriculture and healthier as environments for man's existence.

CLARENCE J. HYLANDER, Author, *Insects on Parade*
See also INSECT.

ENTRAPMENT, a defense to a criminal charge, most frequently asserted in vice cases. It is established if the accused can show that he has been induced to commit crime because of the persuasion of law-enforcement officers. If the police merely provide the accused with an occasion for engaging in the criminal conduct which is his habit, the defense is not available.

ENTRECHAT [äN-trə-shä'] (from Ital. *capra intrecciata*, "bound or braided goat"), a complex movement in ballet during which the dancer jumps into the air and crosses and recrosses his feet. The step is reminiscent of the jumps of a goat with tied front legs.

ENTRE RÍOS [än'trə rē'ōs], province of northeastern Argentina, situated north of Buenos Aires between the Paraná and Uruguay rivers. The land is gently rolling and relatively well suited to farming and grazing. The prov-

ince is a leading producer of flaxseed, corn, wheat, cattle, and sheep. Agricultural processing is centered at Paraná, the provincial capital. Area, 29,427 sq. mi.; pop., 803,505.

ENTROPY [ĕn'trə-pē], a concept in thermodynamics. It is a measure of the unavailable energy of a system. The entropy contained in any substance is dependent directly on the total heat contained in that substance and inversely on the absolute temperature. The change in entropy which a substance may experience depends on the change in total heat energy contained in the substance divided by the absolute temperature at which the change takes place. In an adiabatic process, in which no heat enters or leaves a system, the entropy remains constant.

It is an observed fact that heat flows from hot bodies to colder ones. In this process the hot body loses entropy and the cold body gains more entropy than the hot body loses. Thus there is an increase in entropy during any such transfer. In the universe as a whole, therefore, entropy is continually increasing since hot bodies are continually giving energy, or heat, to colder ones.

Entropy is a measure of the disorganization of a system; the greater the disorganization, or randomness, the greater the entropy. A crystal, whose atoms are arranged in an orderly pattern, has very little entropy. On heating, the atoms begin to move about and become disordered: The entropy has increased.

In chemistry it is often important to determine the point at which a reaction will reach an equilibrium. When this cannot be measured directly, it can be calculated from entropy data.

SERGE A. KORFF, New York University
See also HEAT; THERMODYNAMICS.

ENUGU [ā-nōō'gōō], city of southern Nigeria, and capital of the Eastern Region. The city, on a rail line from Port Harcourt to the interior, collects palm produce, mines coal, and has railway workshops. A cement plant is at Nkalago to the east, and the University of Nigeria is at Nsukka to the north. In Enugu are a Nigerian Coal Corporation office, a Roman Catholic mission, a general hospital, and an airport. Pop., 62,764.

ENVELOPE, in mathematics, a curve which is tangent to all members of a system of curves. A circle with radius 2, for example, is the envelope of other circles with radius 1 which pass through its center. A sphere of radius 1 is the envelope of all planes one unit from its center.

ENVER PASHA [ĕn-vĕr' pä-shä'] (1881–1922), Turkish general. An early army assignment in Salonika introduced him to the Young Turk movement, and in 1908 he was one of the leaders of a successful revolt in Macedonia. By assassination and threat his party forced the Sultan to fill the government with Young Turks, Enver himself becoming Minister of War in 1914, and Turkey turned from British to German rapprochement. Enver purged the army and gradually increased his power until he was, by the end of World War I, virtually the absolute ruler of Turkey. Upon Turkey's defeat, he fled to Germany, then to Russia. He was killed while leading an insurrection against the Soviet forces in Turkestan.

ENVIRONMENT

ENVIRONMENT, term describing the aggregate of conditions and influences, both living and inanimate, that constitute surroundings of an organism. No organism can exist by itself without an environment. It is also true that every successful organism reveals a remarkable adaptation to the conditions of its environment. To some extent the environment explains the morphology, anatomy, and physiology of an organism, since structure and function are closely related to environmental factors. Environment determines whether a certain organism can survive in a given region, thereby affecting the occurrence and abundance of organisms in an area. If a new or variant species appears, the environment determines its survival, and in this way exerts a powerful influence on the evolution of life. The relative importance of environment and heredity in shaping living organisms is a controversial issue, but it is generally agreed that each has its vital role: heredity determines the potential of an organism, the environment determines whether it can exist. Among the particular environmental factors that regulate the nature of living organisms are sunlight, water, temperature, atmospheric gases, and pressure. Collectively, these factors (together with wind, tidal movement, mineral resources, and the substrate) determine the availability of food and shelter necessary to sustain life. Environment also regulates life through "biological" influences—the relations and interactions of living organisms among themselves. These physical and biological influences affect living organisms

in each of three major environments: terrestrial, fresh-water, and marine.

The Terrestrial Environment

Although land accounts for less than one-third of the earth's surface, the interaction of many environmental and geographic factors has made it possible for a far greater variety of vegetation and animal life to exist on land than is found in the oceans or in fresh water. The land environment has largely been responsible for the development of the root-leaf-stem pattern characteristic of the most successful land plants, and has also conditioned the physical form, methods of locomotion, feeding habits, and responses of land animals.

Of the many different environmental factors that have affected life on earth, water, of which living matter largely consists, is perhaps the most important. Variations in rainfall, temperature, humidity, and topography cause uneven distribution of water over the land which, in part, determines the kind of vegetation and animal life that can exist in a given region. Terrestrial life is constantly exposed to the danger of death or injury due to dehydration, and as a result many plants and animals have developed special adaptions for securing and conserving water. This can be seen in the structure and activities of such dry-land plants as the cacti, and in plants like the cattails that grow in soils of moderate moisture content. Many desert animals have developed special water-conservation mechanisms, and

The surroundings in which plants and animals live affect their survival and development. Such things as air, water, minerals, soil, and the organisms they support are the earth's natural resources. The article on these pages deals with the natural environment under three major headings.

The Terrestrial Environment. Factors affecting land plants and animals: water, temperature, sunlight, atmospheric gases (carbon dioxide, oxygen, and nitrogen), minerals (such as magnesium and calcium), the substrate (soil), air pressure, and wind. Influence of biological factors such as disease-producing organisms and predators. Man as a factor — pollution of air and water.

The Fresh-Water Environment. The dominant vegetation — rootless plants such as green algae. The dominant animals — fishes and invertebrates. Influence of variations of temperature, light, amount of gases, and supply of minerals. Biological factors — availability of food and shelter. Pollution of water by industrial works.

The Marine Environment. Conditions are more favorable to life than in fresh water or on land. Water, temperature, light, mineral supply, gas distribution, the substrate, water pressure and movement as factors. Influence of man, as in disposal of atomic wastes.

The reader who wants to continue his study of the environment can draw on many articles in the biological sciences. The description of any organism involves how it lives in its surroundings. Thus articles such as BOTANY, PLANT, ALGAE, and SEAWEED are pertinent. Animal life is treated in ZOOLOGY, ANIMAL, BIRD, FISH, REPTILE, MOLLUSK, CRUSTACEA, and other articles such as AQUATIC ANIMALS. ANIMAL includes an illustrated section headed "Where Animals Live," with pictures of desert, forest, prairie, fresh-water, and ocean animals. Several articles discuss the study of life in specific environments — MARINE BIOLOGY, for example. An entry that will help organize information from many sources is

ECOLOGY, which treats the relations of plants and animals to one another and to their environment. The influence of the environment on all of life on earth is noted in EVOLUTION, since heredity and environment are the two factors involved in the survival and development of species.

Variations in the environment are described in such articles as DESERT, ANTARCTICA, ARCTIC REGIONS, and OCEANOGRAPHY. CLIMATOLOGY introduces the subject of climatic zones and corresponding areas of vegetation and animal life.

Man is the only animal with the ability to make profound changes in the environment. This fact has influenced man's evolution as well as his way of life (see CULTURE and CIVILIZATION). Some of man's major problems in interacting with his environment (sometimes modifying it) are discussed in FOOD, CLOTHING, SHELTER, and related articles. The article on food raises the problem of intelligent use of natural resources. This topic is discussed more fully under the title NATURAL RESOURCES, CONSERVATION OF. A recent and most serious pollution problem is discussed in ATOMIC-WASTE DISPOSAL.

Since man's environment includes his culture — all of the things he has made and done — as well as his natural surroundings, man's relations to his environment are studied by the social as well as the biological sciences. CLOTHING, cited above, is a sociological article, and ECOLOGY, HUMAN suggests other examples in the field of sociology. Sociologists and psychologists have been concerned with such problems as the relative influence of heredity and environment on the characteristics of the individual (the "nature vs. nurture" controversy). Discussion of this topic may be found in CULTURE AND PERSONALITY and in PSYCHOLOGY in both the introductory section and the section *Psychology of Personality*. Another treatment of environmental and personal factors in behavior is in CRIMINOLOGY.

The various topics here introduced can be further studied in books and scientific periodicals available in the school or public library.

additionally may resort to nocturnal habits in order to avoid the heat and desiccation of daylight hours.

Temperature, like water, is a variable factor on land, with extremes at the tropical and polar regions, and great seasonal variation in areas between. Most forms of life can exist within a temperature range of 32° F. to 212° F., but will not survive upon prolonged exposure either to freezing or excessive heat. The activities of living organisms are governed by temperature changes in many ways: low temperatures inhibit growth and modify reproductive cycles; seasonal temperature changes cause deciduous trees to lose their leaves. Animals have variously responded to temperature factors by becoming warm-blooded and by developing protective coverings of feathers or fur. Some animals "avoid" the lethal effects of temperature variation through migration or hibernation.

Light, in contrast to water and temperature, is a relatively constant factor over the earth's surface. This is fortunate since light is the ultimate source of energy for the manufacture of food by plants, and animals ultimately depend on plants for their nourishment. Light also brings about special responses such as phototropism (the growing toward light seen in plants) and photoperiodism (the developmental responses of living organisms to varying lengths of exposure to light). The blind and even eyeless animals found in subterranean habitats have become that way due to an absence of light.

Atmospheric gases are also essential for life processes. Three of these are universally available to land organisms —carbon dioxide, which is essential for photosynthesis (the process by which green plants manufacture their foods in the presence of light); oxygen, necessary for respiration; and nitrogen, essential to plant protein formation.

Minerals, which are essential for the metabolic processes of both plants and animals, are distributed unevenly over the earth's surface. Green plants cannot grow without magnesium, since this is essential for the formation of chlorophyll. Similarly, calcium is vital for skeletal formation in many animals.

The substrate is important for all land plants both as a source of nutrients and water, and because it acts as a means of anchorage. The texture, porosity, amount of humus present, and existence of soil microorganisms affect plant growth. Vegetational character determines, in turn, the habits of animals seeking food and shelter.

Air pressure is a factor of minor importance to most land plants, but does affect animals, chiefly those inhabiting high altitudes. Movement of air, or wind, brings about increased water loss from plant leaves, and also "streamlines" exposed trees, whose mode of branching indicates the direction of the prevailing wind.

The biological factors of environment have a profound effect on the life of a region. The presence of disease-producing organisms can make the existence of susceptible forms impossible; for example, the fungus *Endothia parasitica* has all but wiped out the American chestnut tree. In both plants and animals competition for available food and living space alters the make-up of an environment. Predatory species also exert their influence on life. As an integral part of the animal community in a particular area, a predator may serve to regulate the population of a given species (which might otherwise overrun it) or, by elimi-

nating one group, allow the entrance of another. Man himself is a potent factor in the environment. The introduction of smog and other atmospheric pollutants, fires caused by man, and pollution of water supplies has had the effect of upsetting the delicate environmental balance established by nature through millions of years.

The Fresh-Water Environment

Although the same factors are present in the environment of streams, ponds, and lakes as in terrestrial surroundings, their roles in the two environments are far different. Water, for example, is universally available making it unnecessary for fresh-water plants to have roots and vascular systems. As a result, the dominant fresh-water vegetation consists of rootless plants such as the green algae. The dominant fresh-water animals are fishes and invertebrates; the latter, well-represented by mollusks, crustaceans, and aquatic insects. None of these need protective coverings to decrease evaporation as do land animals, and many also lack special locomotor structures, living as free-floating plankton.

Temperature within the fresh-water environment is much less variable than on land. However, the temperature variations which do exist condition reproductive cycles, the availability of food (especially by affecting the distribution of plankton), and, by forming ice on lakes and ponds, bring about seasonal migration of water fowl and the home-building activities of beavers and muskrats. Light, on the other hand, is a far more variable factor in water than on land. The wavelengths essential for photosynthesis are absorbed in the upper several hundred feet of water, limiting the vegetative zone in ponds and lakes, and its dependent herbivorous animals, to the surface layers. Gases are another variable factor in the fresh-water environment. Oxygen deficiencies are likely to occur in shallow, warm ponds where there is not sufficient vegetation. The presence of oxygen in dissolved air has been an important factor in the development of gills as respiratory structures of many aquatic animals.

Minerals accumulate in water in varying amounts depending upon the nature of the surrounding land. Lack of adequate salinity is a significant factor in preventing marine organisms from colonizing fresh-water habitats. Similarly, excessive salinity, as in salt lakes, creates an environment in which only specially adapted plants and animals can survive. The substrate of fresh waters is of little importance, since many aquatic plants and animals are not attached to the bottom. To solve the problem created by movement of the water in streams, the mosses and algae are firmly attached to the rocks; bottom-dwelling crustaceans, mollusks, and fishes often develop special hooks and suckers, or sticky undersurfaces to hold them to the bottom. Seasonal reversal of the warm upper layers and cool lower layers of water in lakes brings about a corresponding change in the plant and animal populations of those layers.

As on land, the main biological factors affecting the fresh-water environment are the availability of food and shelter, particularly the presence of algae which are the ultimate food source for fresh-water life. Additionally, the pollution of streams by human industry, with its resulting destruction of aquatic animals and plants, has had a profound effect on the fresh-water environment.

THE PHYSICAL ENVIRONMENT

The Marine Environment

Environmental conditions in the ocean are far more favorable to life than those found in fresh water or on land. As a result, although marine life is diverse, most of the sea's inhabitants have not had to develop the many special adaptations to their environment that are so essential to terrestrial organisms. Water is universally available in the marine environment, and, as in fresh water, the oceanic vegetation is dominated by rootless plants such as the green, brown, and red seaweeds. Many marine animals are simple invertebrates that need no specialized tissues to prevent water loss.

Temperature is relatively constant, but its slight variations determine reproductive cycles and the distribution of many species, especially among the plankton which, again as in fresh water, are the ultimate food source. Light penetration limits the distribution of plants, resulting in a zonation of the seaweeds: the green algae live in the uppermost, well-lighted zones; the brown algae in the intermediate zone; and the red algae at greatest depths. Below 500 ft. no plants can exist, and animals that live here must feed on materials settling from above, or on each other.

Minerals are well distributed due to ocean currents; the salinity of the ocean being the most significant feature in determining the structure of marine plants and animals. Gas distribution varies with temperature and depth, but generally does not exert a profound influence on marine life. The substrate is of importance mainly along the shore and down to the depth of light penetration. In the open seas, life consists either of plankton (floating) species of plants and animals, or free-swimming (nekton) species. Water pressure becomes important at great depths, having a marked effect on the appearance and activities of deep-sea animals. In the deepest parts of the ocean where life is found, this pressure is equivalent to over 500 atmospheres. Movement of the water often affects the type and amount of marine life. Tidal activity limits the shoreline life between tidal zones to such plants and animals as rockweeds, barnacles, and burrowing mollusks which are adapted to both an open-air and an aquatic environment.

Other biological factors affecting the marine environment, in addition to those produced by the interrelation of the various groups of oceanic organisms, have been introduced by man himself. Unwise fishing practices have altered the subtle balance of the food chain; marine construction and transportation have made certain regions unsuitable for the support of life; and industrial pollution has depopulated large coastal areas. By far the most serious factor, and one which could radically affect man's well-being, is the disposal of atomic wastes. It is rapidly becoming apparent that unless stringent measures are taken to prevent further pollution, life as we know it will find no favorable environment, on land, lake, or sea.

Consult Storer, J. H., *The Web of Life* (1953); Carson, R. L., *The Edge of the Sea* (1959).

Clarence J. Hylander, Author, *The World of Plant Life*
See also Ecology; Evolution.

SUNLIGHT

Energy derived from the sun is used directly by green plants in the manufacture of food. Transformed by the plant into carbohydrates, the energy passes to herbivorous animals (such as the grasshopper), where it is further transformed — into proteins — within the animal's body. It then passes to small carnivorous animals (such as the shrew), which feed on herbivores. From there the energy passes to large carnivores (such as the screech owl), which feed on small carnivores. In this fashion, energy derived from the sun is used by all living organisms.

TEMPERATURE

The activities of animals are affected in several ways by temperature. Because plant growth is dependent on temperature, the survival of herbivorous animals is also dependent upon it. Temperature exerts a direct influence on animals which are unable to regulate their body temperatures. Reptiles (such as the copperhead snake) and insects (such as the yellow jacket) must hibernate during very cold weather. Certain warm-blooded animals (such as the eastern chipmunk) also hibernate — not because of direct temperature effects, but because the plants on which they feed are not available during winter.

WATER

The physical characteristics of water enable aquatic animals to survive in winter. As the water beneath a frozen pond surface reaches 39.2° F., it sinks to the pond bottom causing warmer water to rise. Fishes (the pumpkinseed) can thus swim about and other animals (the pond snail and annelid worm) can overwinter by burying themselves in the bottom mud. In a desert the burning sun evaporates atmospheric moisture (humidity). By night, when cooler temperatures allow moisture to condense, the great horned owl, kangaroo rat, and gila monster can venture out without threat of becoming desiccated.

PRESSURE

Land-dwelling animals encounter the pressure factor in their environment as they move to elevations above sea level where, because the air is less dense, less oxygen is available. Marine fishes (such as the hatchetfish and viperfish) that live at great depths compensate for the tremendous pressure of the water by having a special closed organ, the swim bladder, in which a pressure equal to that of the surrounding water exists. If such a fish is brought to the surface it literally explodes since it has no way of controlling its internal pressure, which is now greater than that of its surroundings.

GASES and MINERALS

These essential substances are continuously recycled in the environment. Oxygen (O_2) is used by animals in respiration and is returned to the environment as carbon dioxide (CO_2). Green plants use CO_2 in photosynthesis and return O_2 to the environment. Atmospheric nitrogen is converted into nitrates by bacteria that live in nodules on the roots of legumes. The plant uses the nitrates to form protein. When the plant is eaten, its contained nitrogen is converted by the animal into protein, and waste nitrogen is excreted. Bacteria in soil and water act upon these wastes and eventually nitrogen is returned to the atmosphere.

The most important physical factors in an animal's environment are sunlight, temperature, water, pressure, and essential gases and minerals. Although these factors are closely interrelated, none acting independently, the effect of each can be measured. The degree to which they are present in a given environment determines how an animal lives in that environment.

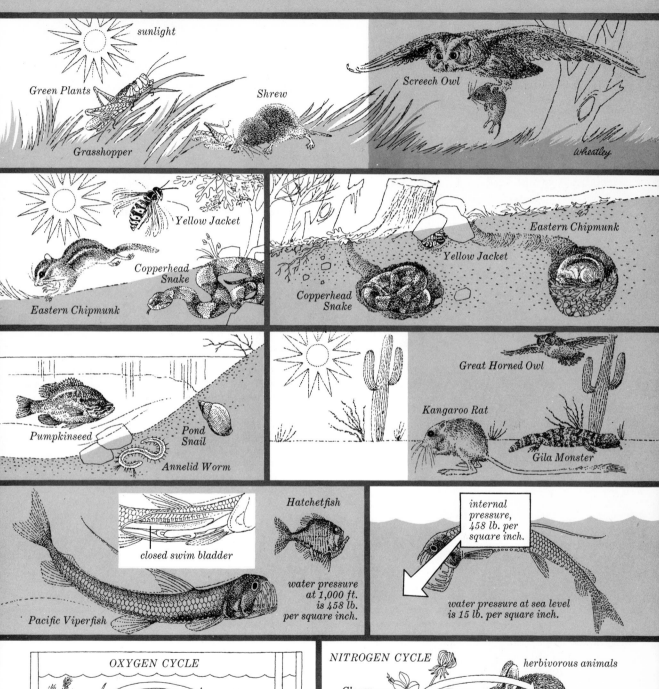

sunlight

Green Plants

Grasshopper

Shrew

Screech Owl

wheatley

Yellow Jacket

Eastern Chipmunk

Copperhead Snake

Eastern Chipmunk

Yellow Jacket

Copperhead Snake

Pumpkinseed

Pond Snail

Annelid Worm

Great Horned Owl

Kangaroo Rat

Gila Monster

Hatchetfish

closed swim bladder

water pressure at 1,000 ft. is 458 lb. per square inch.

Pacific Viperfish

internal pressure, 458 lb. per square inch.

water pressure at sea level is 15 lb. per square inch.

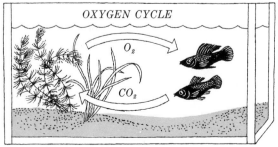

OXYGEN CYCLE

O_2

CO_2

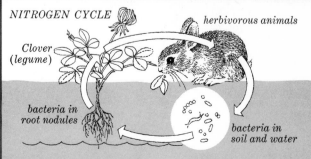

NITROGEN CYCLE

herbivorous animals

Clover (legume)

bacteria in root nodules

bacteria in soil and water

ENVIRONMENTAL SCIENCE SERVICES ADMINISTRATION, UNITED STATES, division of the Department of Commerce, established in July, 1965, by the merger of the Coast and Geodetic Survey, the Weather Bureau, and the Central Radio Propagation Laboratory (formerly a unit of the National Bureau of Standards). The administration is charged with research, description, analysis, and forecast of all aspects of the physical environment, such as earthquakes, seismic sea waves, propagation of radio waves, and general weather data. It is also responsible for astronomical observations and for the preparation of nautical and aeronautical navigation charts.

See also COAST AND GEODETIC SURVEY, UNITED STATES; WEATHER BUREAU, UNITED STATES.

ENZYMES [ĕn'zīmz], protein substances which make possible most of the chemical reactions occurring in living organisms. All living systems, from the lowest to the highest, carry out several thousand different chemical reactions which form the basis of activities such as digestion, the contraction of muscle, the beating of the heart, the secretion of urine, the processes of seeing, hearing, smelling, and thinking, and the coagulation of blood. Apart from a few exceptions, none of these reactions would take place in living things were it not for the presence of enzymes which catalyze, or speed up, these reactions. In virtually all cases the enzyme also initiates the reaction.

The Nature of Enzymatic Reactions. A simple chemical reaction can be described as the conversion of molecule A to molecule B. A few molecules of the enzyme which catalyzes this reaction would be sufficient to convert billions of molecule A to molecule B. Barring wear and tear, the enzyme could proceed indefinitely, converting more and more A into B.

An outstanding feature of the reaction is that only one thing happens: A is changed into B. In organic chemistry it is extremely rare for a reaction to have only one outcome. Usually a percentage of molecules react in some other way than that desired. In enzyme-catalyzed reactions, however, there are no side reactions of any kind.

In addition to there being only one product of the reaction, there is only one enzyme which will catalyze the reaction. This specificity derives from the fact that the enzyme and the molecule it acts upon (the substrate) have a lock and key relationship. The substrate fits perfectly into the contours of the enzyme protein and by virtue of this fit the substrate molecule becomes unstable and readily susceptible to chemical change.

The specificity of enzymes for their substrates can be very sharp. For example, certain types of molecules have two forms which are mirror images of one another. In all other respects these forms are indistinguishable chemically, yet the enzymes unerringly select the right form to act upon. Another type of specificity is based upon the size of the molecule. Enzymes will accurately distinguish three-carbon molecules from four-carbon molecules. These specificities result from the perfect fit of substrate molecules to the enzyme. They are of great biological importance because they insure that only one type of molecule and no other, regardless of how similar it might be, will undergo a given chemical change. In the laboratory of the living cell, where thousands of reactions go on at all times, the specificity of enzyme action is the safeguard against potentially dangerous reactions.

What Does the Enzyme Do to the Substrate? When the substrate molecule is seized in the chemical embrace of the enzyme it is subjected to considerable strain, which induces a high degree of chemical reactivity. The substrate molecule can be changed in a number of ways. The particular change will be determined by the area of the enzyme molecule to which the substrate becomes attached and by the distribution of electric charges over the enzyme as a whole. The part of the enzyme molecule which links with the substrate is known as the active group. The distribution of electric charges concerns the charges (positive or negative) carried by some of the amino acids which make up the enzyme molecule.

The Enzyme Team. Enzymes usually work in teams and in many parts of the cell enzymes are attached to one another like the tiles of a mosaic. Such an arrangement makes it possible for reactions to follow one another in a definite order with a minimum of lost motion. The mitochondrion of animal cells and the chloroplast of plant cells are essentially mosaics of this type. Within the mitochondrial enzyme mosaic, glucose is burned to CO_2 and water; the released chemical energy is converted into a form more useful to the cell. Within the chloroplast, light energy is changed into the chemical energy of sugar. Similarly, all energy conversions in living systems are brought about by specialized enzyme teams.

The Prosthetic Group. Many enzymes require an additional molecule, called the prosthetic group, in order to act. The prosthetic group may be a metal atom (iron, copper, zinc, molybdenum) or a complex organic molecule. Many, if not all, of the vitamins are building stones of these prosthetic groups. Consequently, if our diet is deficient in a particular vitamin, certain enzymes which contain this vitamin as part of their prosthetic group cannot function. If these enzymes do not function then certain reactions essential for life cannot go on.

The quantity of vitamins needed is minute compared to the amount of food required. The tremendous potency of small amounts of vitamins results from the extraordinary efficiency of the enzymes which they activate. The need for extremely minute, or "trace," elements of certain metals, such as copper and cobalt, is also related to the role of these metals as parts of the prosthetic groups of enzymes.

Enzymes, Poisons, and Drugs. Certain poisons and drugs are effective in minute amounts because they interfere with the action of enzymes. Some bacteria, such as the organism which produces gas gangrene in putrefying wounds, are exceedingly dangerous because of an enzyme which they release into the body. These enzymes are known as toxins and are lethal in extremely small concentrations—a few molecules are sufficient to wreak havoc in sensitive areas of the body. Drugs such as curare, and poisons such as cyanide, specifically suppress the action of certain enzymes.

Enzymes and Bacteria. Antibiotics are drugs which are able to suppress the growth of disease-producing microorganisms without harming human cells or tissues. The antibiotics paralyze the microorganism by combining with and immobilizing some key enzyme in the organism which is essential for its growth. If that particular enzyme is not present or plays a minor role in human cells, then the growth of the microorganism can be halted without damaging the body. The best antibiotics are obviously those which are potent inhibitors of enzymes, which are both unique to, and important to, the disease organisms.

The Manufacture of Enzymes. The cells of the living organism must manufacture the enzymes needed to bring about vital chemical reactions. The knowledge of enzyme manufacture is inherited by each cell and this inheritance is represented in the cell as the particular ordering of molecules which make up a substance called deoxyribose nucleic acid—the master enzyme-maker of the cell. When a particular enzyme is synthesized under the direction of deoxyribose nucleic acid, each of the enzyme molecules produced is exactly the same. The process of synthesis never slips up and all molecules are identical down to the last detail. If the molecule of deoxyribose nucleic acid, which carries the blueprint for the synthesis of an enzyme, is damaged by radiation, the blueprint could be altered, resulting in production of a modified version of that particular enzyme. Changes of this type could result in a "mutant," an organism which departs from the norm of the wild type.

The chemist can synthesize small proteins (called polypeptides) in the test tube. These substances, which include some hormones, contain only some 20 amino acids. Synthesis of larger proteins, such as enzymes containing 100 or more amino acids, is still beyond the capabilities of the chemist and will probably remain so for some years.

Consult Neilands, J. B., and Stumpf, P. K., *Outlines of Enzyme Chemistry* (rev. ed., 1958).

DAVID E. GREEN, Co-director, Institute for Enzyme
Research, University of Wisconsin

See also BIOCHEMISTRY.

EOCENE [ē'ə-sēn], second epoch of the Cenozoic Era of geologic time. The name applies also to rocks deposited during Eocene time. The Eocene Epoch began about 58 million years ago and spanned about 22 million years. It was named from Greek words meaning "early recent" in recognition of the small proportion of modern animal species that lived during the epoch. Eocene rocks are widely distributed on various continents. They include marine, swamp, and strandline sediments on coastal plains, and they also contain deposits of continental origin.

ERA	PERIOD		EPOCH
CENOZOIC	QUATERNARY		RECENT
	TERTIARY		PLEISTOCENE
MESOZOIC	CRETACEOUS		PLIOCENE
	JURASSIC		MIOCENE
	TRIASSIC		OLIGOCENE
PALEOZOIC	PERMIAN		EOCENE
	CARBON-IFEROUS	PENNSYLVANIAN	PALEOCENE
		MISSISSIPPIAN	
	DEVONIAN		
	SILURIAN		
	ORDOVICIAN		
	CAMBRIAN		
PRECAMBRIAN			

EOHIPPUS. *See* HORSE.

EOLITHIC [ē-ō-līth'ĭk], term used by prehistorians earlier in the century for the age or stage of human activity that was believed to lie before the Paleolithic, or Old Stone Age. The supposed stone artifacts of this subdivision were called eoliths or dawn stones. Some, but not all, of the specimens may actually have been utilized by very early prehistoric men. They seem not, however, to have been purposely fashioned, let alone standardized, products of human workmanship. Modern prehistorians have almost completely abandoned the use of "Eolithic" and "eoliths."

EOS [ē'ŏs], Greek goddess of dawn, the Roman Aurora, often called rosy fingered and saffron robed. She was the daughter of Hyperion and Theia. Among her many husbands and lovers were Ares, Cephalus, Orion, and Tithonus, by whom she bore Memnon.

EPAMINONDAS [ē-păm-ĭ-nŏn'dəs] (d.362 B.C.), Theban general and diplomat. His early career is obscure. He assisted in freeing Thebes from a Spartan garrison in 379 B.C., and with his close friend Pelopidas did much to restore Theban prestige. At the peace conference of 371 B.C. Epaminondas insisted on Thebes' right to act for all Boeotia in ratifying a treaty. Sparta thereupon expelled Thebes from the conference and invaded Boeotia. At Leuctra Theban forces won a stunning victory over the supposedly invincible Spartan phalanx. Credit for the victory is ascribed to Epaminondas' tactic of massing hoplites 50 deep on one wing. He followed up the advantage by a series of invasions of the Peloponnesus and twice threatened to capture Sparta itself. He freed Arcadia and Messenia, setting up new capitals at Megalopolis and Messene to counter Spartan power. In the hard-fought battle of Mantinea (362 B.C.) the Theban army won, but Epaminondas was fatally wounded. He was long remembered for moderation and diplomatic skill, as well as for military ability. Following his death Thebes' short ascendancy quickly waned.

WILLIAM A. McDONALD, University of Minnesota

ÉPERNAY [ā-pĕr-nā'], wine and market town of northern France, on the Marne River, about 85 mi. east of Paris. Épernay is one of the major centers of champagne wine production, and the surrounding limestone hills are honeycombed with more than 30 mi. of wine cellars. Other local industry is concerned primarily with making materials for the wine industry, such as corks, labels, packing material, and tinfoil. Pop., 22,799.

EPHEDRINE [ĭ-fĕd'rĭn], drug similar in action to the adrenal hormone epinephrine (adrenalin). Like adrenalin, ephedrine dilates the breathing passages, increases heart output, raises the blood pressure, and constricts blood vessels; it also dilates the pupil of the eye. Used in Chinese medicine for over 5,000 years (as the herb mahuang), ephedrine was first investigated by Western researchers in the 20th century upon the advice of a Chinese druggist. The drug has been used principally in the treatment of asthma and hay fever and other allergic disorders. Ephedrine is also used to maintain the blood pressure during spinal anesthesia and in ophthalmologic practice as a pupil dilator.

EPHEMERIS [ĭ-fĕm′ər-ĭs], tabulation of the positions at regular intervals of the sun, the planets and their satellites, of comets and asteroids, or of artificial earth satellites. Because of the rapid motions of these objects relative to the earth, and because the earth is also in motion, detailed computations are required to predict their positions among the fixed stars. After initial observations provide data on the orbit of an object, its future positions and velocity can be predicted by applying Newtonian mechanics. Both the gravitational effect of the sun and the mutual attractions of the planets and other bodies must be taken into account. *The American Ephemeris and Nautical Almanac*, published annually by the U.S. Government, gives the positions of celestial objects during the coming year.

EPHESIANS [ĭ-fē′zhənz], **EPISTLE TO THE,** New Testament book attributed to St. Paul. It begins with a long thanksgiving to God for his eternal purpose now fulfilled in Christ, who has brought all men and all things into unity in His body, the church. It continues with prayer and exhortation for the preservation of unity, for growth in knowledge, love, and Christian conduct, and for perseverance in the fight against the powers of evil. There are striking overlaps with Colossians, and neither the readers nor their circumstances are at all clear. While the theology is that of St. Paul, its Pauline authorship is questioned.

EPHESUS [ĕf′ə-səs], ancient Greek city on the west coast of Asia Minor, the richest in Ionia. It was founded by Androcles, son of Codrus, King of Athens, and, according to tradition, numbered among its pre-Greek inhabitants the Amazons. The archaic city lay near the mouth of the Cayster River in a situation to control the trade of its valley and to tap that of the Hermus and Maeander valleys, accessible by easy passes. The city escaped destruction by the Cimmerians in the 7th century; in the 6th, besieged by Croesus of Lydia, it avoided capture by dedicating itself to Artemis, stretching a rope to her sanctuary which lay seven furlongs outside. Artemis was evidently the successor of an Asiatic divinity, with whom she became contaminated. She was usually represented as many-breasted, her drapery embellished with the bees and stags which became the coin types of Ephesus. Croesus contributed columns to her new temple, the Artemisium, constructed c.550–530 B.C. Ephesus became subject in turn to Lydia, Persia, and Athens, from which it revolted c.415. In the 4th century it again became subject to Persia, governed by a local oligarchy. Alexander liberated Ephesus in 334; on the night of his birth in 356 the Artemis temple had been burned by a lunatic. A new Ionic temple with sculptured column drums was built to replace it; architectural members of both buildings have been recovered. City and temple flourished greatly in Hellenistic times, the latter, one of the Seven Wonders of the World, becoming the greatest money-lending bank of the eastern Mediterranean. In the 3d century the city became flooded through the silting of the Cayster mouth and was moved to higher ground. The site of the original town remains unknown; its successor became the chief city of the Roman province of Asia, and residence of the proconsul, with a population of 200,000. Excavation in the Roman city has revealed broad paved avenues, a theater, an elaborate library, a stadium, an odeum, and gymnasia. St. Paul visited Ephesus (55–58) when the Artemis cult still flourished, and the church he founded there prospered. Ephesus was traditionally the last home of the Virgin Mary. City and temple were destroyed by the Goths in 262 A.D. and the town declined thereafter. By the 10th century the old city was deserted. The Basilica of St. John (6th century) over the traditional tomb of St. John incorporates materials from the ancient Artemisium.

RODNEY S. YOUNG, University Museum,
University of Pennsylvania

Alfons Wotschitzky

EPHESUS

Artist's rendering of the temple of Artemis (*left*). Built in the 4th century B.C., it was one of the Seven Wonders of the World. Detail of a statue of Artemis (*below*) found at Ephesus.

Alfons Wotschitzky

EPHORS [ĕf'ôrz], chief magistrates of ancient Sparta, as well as of several other Dorian states in Greece. The origin of the Spartan institution is uncertain, but the number of members on the board (five) suggests representation from each of the five quarters comprising the town of Sparta. Elected annually, they were responsible only to the succeeding board. They supervised the activities of the Kings at home and in the field. They summoned the assemblies and presided at their meetings. They conducted negotiations on foreign policy and received embassies. They controlled all other magistrates and had wide judicial powers. With power of life and death over the perioeci and helots, they enforced on Spartan citizens the strict "Lycurgan" discipline in the education of the young and the conduct of adults. In fact, the ephors' basic function was as guardians of the monolithic Spartan state.
See also SPARTA.

EPHRAEM SYRUS [ē'frē-ĕm sĭ'rəs], **ST.** (c.306–373), Syrian commentator on Scripture and composer of prayers and hymns, known as "the bard of divine mysteries." His work includes commentaries in Syriac on the Old and New Testaments, sermons, and religious poetry. In his Scriptural interpretation he followed the historical method of the Antiochean school, while drawing on the allegorical approach of the Alexandrian school for his poetical work. His hymns represent the mystical tradition of the school of Edessa, which he probably founded. Many prayers written by him are used in the services of the Eastern Orthodox Church, and his penitential prayer said during Lent is especially well known. The Roman Catholic Church proclaimed him a "Doctor of the Church" in 1920.

EPHRAIM [ē'frē-ĭm], Israelite tribe settled in the central highlands of Palestine, named after the mountain range there. Their ancestor later came to be regarded as a son of Joseph.

EPHRATA [ĭ-frā'tə], borough of southeastern Pennsylvania. It is a small market center and industrial town, manufacturing shoes, textiles, and metal products. Ephrata was settled in 1732 as a semimonastic community by the Seventh-day Baptists under the leadership of Johann Conrad Beissel. The Cloisters, in which Beissel's followers lived and worked, is a state-maintained historical shrine. Inc., 1891; pop. (1950) 7,027; (1960) 7,688.

EPHRATA, city of central Washington, and seat of Grant County. It is the headquarters of the Columbia Basin Project and a service center for irrigated farming and livestock. Concrete pipe is manufactured. Pop. (1950) 4,589; (1960) 6,548.

EPHRATH or EPHRATHAH, name of the district of ancient Palestine in which Bethlehem (q.v.) was located.

EPIC, a long narrative poem, centered around a hero who represents the ideal of a nation or a whole cultural epoch. Unlike tragedy, which invites the reader or spectator to pity a great man in a catastrophe which he has at least partly brought upon himself, the epic invites the reader or listener to admire a national or racial hero for his great

Illustration for Dante's *Divine Comedy* by the 19th-century French artist Gustave Doré.
(ILLUSTRATIONS THIS PAGE: J. R. FREEMAN & CO.—ILLUSTRATION RESEARCH SERVICE)

A 17th-century print showing a scene from Vergil's *Aeneid* —Juno sending a storm against the ships.

A 19th-century edition of the medieval French epic *Chanson de Roland* appeared with this conception of a battle scene.

achievements. This much epics from all eras and cultures have in common; but they differ greatly in the kind of achievement that they present as admirable. The towering self-assertion which the Greeks admired in Achilles and the endless resourcefulness which they honored in Odysseus were quite different from the self-sacrificing sense of duty that the Romans honored in Aeneas. And Adam, in Milton's *Paradise Lost*, is admired for still another quality, his patient and hopeful acceptance of the consequences of his own disobedience.

Most of the characteristics of the epic as a literary type stem from this purpose of arousing admiration for the great hero whose story it tells. It begins with a formal statement of the central theme which throws the action of the hero into a very broad perspective. The statement of theme is followed by a solemn invocation of the Muse to suggest the high importance and dignity of the epic undertaking; and then the poem thrusts *in medias res*, into the very heart of the action. Details necessary for explaining the events of the story and for building up the significance of the hero are left for dramatic flashbacks. Everything possible is done to build up the stature of the hero. Epithets, pinpointing his character, are associated with his name—Aeneas, in Vergil's *Aeneid*, for example, is always *pius* ("dutiful") Aeneas. Epic similes are employed to illuminate different facets of his character; his ancestry is frequently semidivine; the gods are shown to play a very prominent place in his story; he is represented as supreme in physical prowess, intelligence, and the moral virtues which his nation or culture particularly admires; and he is given ample opportunity to build up his own stature in a series of "brag" speeches. The stature of the hero is also expanded through the formal descriptive speeches of other characters and through the heroic proportions of his own actions.

Besides these things that exalt the epic hero himself, there are features of the poem which build up an atmosphere appropriate to his serious and exalted proportions. The verse is dignified and elevated; the language is exalted and full of repetitive patterns, appropriate to a poem meant to be recited rather than merely read; there are impressive catalogues of ships, battles, and proper names freighted with rich associations from the culture which the epic reflects. Epic similes provide a pleasant relief in the many battle scenes, highlight important dramatic moments, and reflect various facets of the characters with whom they are associated; and long formal speeches by the main characters give dramatic emphasis to the main episode.

The distinction between the folk and the literary epic no longer seems admissible, but there is a recognizable difference between early epics such as the *Iliad*, the *Odyssey*, and *Beowulf*, which have actually undergone a long tradition of oral delivery, and those like the *Aeneid* and *Paradise Lost*, which were written in imitation of the earlier, more orally oriented epics.

The epic ceased to be an important literary form after the 18th century. From then on there was an ever increasing emphasis on the individual and his personal experiences. Hence the epic, concerned with the expression of a broad national or cultural ideal, ceased to be an appropriate medium of expression. For this more individual and personal interest, the novel in prose came to be the dominant narrative form.

M. B. McNamee, S.J., St. Louis University

See also:

EPICTETUS [ĕp-ĭk-tē′təs] (c.55–135 A.D.), Stoic philosopher, originally a slave at Rome. He modified the austerity of Stoicism into a creed more suited to the poor and humble—all men are brothers; everything happens through divine Providence; and freedom consists in accepting external misfortunes with fortitude, concentrating on the rectitude of one's own will.
See also Stoicism.

EPIC THEATER, dramatic theory and method of stage production propagated mainly by the dramatist Bertolt Brecht. It originated in the German theater of the 1920's, and was first applied by the director Erwin Piscator, who used film projections in staging revolutionary plays, thus combining narrative (epic) and dramatic techniques. Brecht's elaborations stressed the use of loose sequences of incidents instead of unified plots, rational argument and didacticism instead of emotional involvement, and rigidly functional staging in lieu of atmospheric settings. Later he added the so-called alienation effect, aimed at destroying theatrical illusion.

EPICUREANISM, philosophy developed by the Greek philosopher Epicurus in the late 4th century B.C. It presented "pleasure" as the highest good, but defined it as merely the absence of pain, a sort of peace of mind and body which could be achieved by avoiding the disturbing situations of life and enjoying the simple satisfactions which even the poorest life affords in some small measure. In the Hellenistic and Roman worlds it was the rival of Stoicism. Frequently today the term "Epicurean" is mistakenly used as a synonym for a gourmet or one who enjoys the satisfaction of luxurious living.
See also Epicurus.

EPICURUS [ĕp-ĭ-kū′rəs] (341–270 B.C.), Athenian philosopher. His doctrine that pleasure was the highest good gave a misleading impression of his tastes and habits. Pleasure to Epicurus meant the absence of mental turmoil, a peace of body and mind, to be attained by avoidance of all external sources of disturbance or anxiety, including public life, marriage, and the begetting of children. "To live hidden" was the ideal. He had a rare gift for friendship, lived with his disciples (including women) a retired and simple life, and died after a long and painful illness, which he bore with exemplary fortitude.

Holding that the worst enemy of spiritual peace was fear of death and of the gods, he adopted as the physical basis for his ethics the materialistic atomism of Democritus. Only sensation is infallible; all other knowledge is inference based on sensation and may be wrong. Objects are constantly giving off films of atoms which affect the sense organs by direct contact. Only atoms and the void are real. Unlike Democritus he endowed single atoms with an arbitary and incalculable power to swerve from their direct course. This accounted for their collisions and entanglements, and also provided an escape from the mechanical necessity governing the Democritean universe. Death brought dispersal of the soul-atoms and cessation of all consciousness.

Gods exist, but are material, like human souls and everything else. Space is infinite and contains innumerable worlds; and the gods dwell in the intervals between the worlds, where they enjoy a life of untroubled blessedness, unconcerned with the actions of men.

His philosophy was a natural product of the postclassical age, when Alexander's conquests had disturbed the compact unity of city-state life and religion. His school continued after his death, but made little change in the doctrine. The most famous preacher of Epicureanism was the Roman poet Lucretius, who infused intense passion into his attack on religion and the afterlife.

Consult Bailey, Cyril, *Greek Atomists and Epicurus* (1928); Festugière, A. J., *Epicurus and his Gods* (trans., 1955).

W. K. C. GUTHRIE, Cambridge University

EPIDAURUS [ĕp-ĭ-dô'rəs], ancient Greek city-state on the east coast of the Peloponnesus, on the Saronic Gulf. Politically independent throughout the history of ancient Greece, it was famed for its sanctuary of the healing god Asclepius, which lay 5 mi. outside the city. The sacred enclosure, entered by a colonnaded portico of the 4th century B.C., contains a temple of Asclepius, a fine marble tholos (rotunda) designed by the Argive Polyclitus the Younger and built c.360–330 B.C., and other buildings for patients and priests. Beyond are a beautifully preserved theater (also by Polyclitus) with remarkably fine acoustics, a stadium, gymnasium, and other buildings, all excavated by the Greek Archaeological Society. Epidaurus was at the peak of its prosperity in the 4th century B.C., but was still much frequented in Roman times.

EPIDEMICS [ĕp-ə-dĕm'ĭks] **AND EPIDEMIOLOGY** [ĕp-ə-dē-mĭ-ŏl'ə-jĭ]. An epidemic is an unusual occurrence of a disease, which affects many persons. Throughout history epidemics have been among the most dreaded of natural calamities. In the 14th century the Black Death, believed to have been bubonic plague, killed over 20,000,000 people. Smallpox epidemics took an enormous toll before the English physician Jenner developed the technique of vaccination. The great influenza epidemic of the early part of the 20th century took an estimated 21,000,000 lives.

While the term "epidemic" originally referred to these massive outbreaks of infectious diseases, it is now also applied to noninfectious conditions. Thus the prevalence of coronary heart disease, lung cancer, and automobile accidents in the United States is said to be of epidemic proportions.

Unlike the practitioner of clinical medicine who deals with an individual patient, the epidemiologist concerns

Immigrants to Singapore are examined by port health officers for infectious diseases before being permitted to debark.

Jean Manevy—World Health Organization

The effective use of DDT spray against mosquitoes is explained to Libyan school children during an antimalaria campaign.

Roche Medical Image

Bread samples, to be tested for bacteria, are removed by health officers from the public market at Zavia, Libya.

Roche Medical Image

himself with an entire community which is afflicted with an epidemic disease. His responsibility is to identify the disease and to find out how it began and how it is spread.

Investigation of Epidemics in the Field. When many cases of a similar illness appear in a community an epidemiologist must first identify the disease. This may be accomplished by studying the disease in individual patients. Often laboratory procedures are necessary. For example, culturing virus from stool specimens taken from patients is the best way of diagnosing epidemics of certain infections of the nervous system.

The sequence in which the epidemic develops may be a vital clue to its origin and manner of transmission. If most cases appear at the same time, a single common source, such as a contaminated food or water supply, might be suspected. If cases of an infectious illness appeared at different times, the epidemiologist might look for a chain of infection among patients. In the case of an infectious disease, such as smallpox, he would seek information about patient contacts with persons or places which could have been the original source of infection. When dealing with diseases such as typhoid or infectious hepatitis, which are transmitted chiefly through the gastrointestinal tract, he would also investigate food or water sources which the victims used in common, food handlers who might carry the agent, contamination of the water supply by sewage, and possible contamination of the food by flies. In the case of an insect-transmitted disease, such as yellow fever or malaria, the search would be directed to finding the type of mosquito known to carry the infectious organism.

The epidemiologist is also vitally concerned with those persons who do not contract the illness. He asks: "What common factor is shared by those who remain free of the illness as contrasted to those who succumb?" He may employ statistical techniques to determine whether the differences he finds result merely from chance variation or whether they are significant. An early example of the value of such studies was provided by John Snow, an Englishman, who in 1855 fixed the responsibility for a large cholera epidemic in London upon the water supply. Snow was able to do this by observing the very low cholera rate among groups of people who lived in the center of an epidemic area, but used a different water source.

Endemic Diseases. A disease is said to be endemic in a community if it is constantly present within the community but without causing more than a few persons to become seriously ill. A case in point is poliomyelitis, which is endemic in many areas, especially in the tropics and in underdeveloped countries. The virus circulates constantly, and is so widespread that infants are infected while still protected by the temporary immunity with which they are born. As a result, almost all children in such areas have their first infections and become immune without showing signs of illness. When living standards and hygiene improve, more children escape early infections and first encounter the polioviruses at ages when they are more likely to develop paralytic poliomyelitis. Nowadays it is possible to confer immunity on all susceptible persons by means of vaccination.

Prevention. Community health departments check food, water, and milk supplies to detect and eliminate potential disease-producing organisms. In many localities the chemical pollution of air and water is regularly investigated. An important responsibility of health departments is the maintenance of vaccination programs in non-epidemic periods to turn susceptible persons into immune persons and thus to prevent outbreaks from occurring.

JOSEPH L. MELNICK, M.D.

EPIDOTE [ĕp′ə-dōt] **MINERALS,** group of calcium, aluminum, and iron silicates comprising several species closely related in crystal structure, physical properties, and chemical composition. Commonest is epidote, which occurs in long, prismatic crystals that are yellow-green to black. Epidote is found in metamorphic rocks, commonly metamorphosed limestones. Piedmontite, a variety in which part of the aluminum is replaced by manganese, has a characteristic violet-red color. Epidote minerals with little or no iron are called clinozoisite; a similar species is zoisite. Allanite, found in granites, is an epidote in which some of the calcium is replaced by rare-earth elements.

Properties: *Crystal System*, Monoclinic (zoisite is Orthorhombic); *Hardness* (Mohs' Scale) 5½–7; *Density*, 3.3–4.2.

See also CRYSTALLOGRAPHY; MINERALOGY.

EPIGLOTTIS [ĕp-ə-glŏt′ĭs], a thin, leaf-shaped structure, composed of cartilage, which projects upward behind the root of the tongue in reptiles and mammals. The epiglottis prevents the entrance of food into the larynx, or "voice box," either by diverting it to either side, or by folding back over the entrance to the larynx.

EPIGRAM [ĕp′ə-grăm]. Among the classical writers, epigrams were brief poems on a variety of subjects. The Roman poet Martial, a renowned and witty epigrammatist, had considerable influence on many Renaissance writers of epigrams, including Ben Jonson. Since the 17th century the form has been used chiefly for satirical purpose, notably by Alexander Pope, who utilizes a two-line couplet for many of his polished epigrams, and by such later writers as Byron, Coleridge, and Lessing. The term "epigram" has since been extended to any witty, brilliantly concise statement either in prose or in verse.

EPILEPSY [ĕp′ə-lĕp-sē], a disorder of the nervous system characterized by sudden, temporary disturbances of brain function. Although epilepsy was recognized as a medical disorder as far back as the time of the ancient Greeks (who called it the "sacred disease"), it has continued to inspire dread in uninformed persons who consider the epileptic to be "possessed of the devil." In many primitive societies the epileptic was regarded as being gifted with supernatural powers.

Today epilepsy is considered to be a symptom of an underlying disease of the brain which may be caused by a tumor, infection, or injury. In some cases there is no evident disturbance and the patient is said to have "idiopathic" epilepsy. Epilepsy of this type often appears in several members of the same family. The epileptic attacks result from abnormal, uncontrolled electrical activity of the brain cells. The massive electrical discharges occurring during the attack can be recorded by the electroencephalograph, which is used to detect electrical "brain waves." This instrument is often valuable in diagnosing epilepsy.

Types of Attacks. The most familiar seizure is the *grand mal* ("great illness"). The attack is usually preceded by a warning or "aura" which may consist of hallucinatory sounds, smells, or flashes of light. The limbs stiffen briefly, after which the body jerks violently. The patient may cry or scream just before losing consciousness. During the convulsion he may foam at the mouth, bite his tongue, or, occasionally, urinate, as the bladder sphincter muscle is relaxed.

In *petit mal* (literally, "little illness"), there is usually a momentary loss of consciousness, often called "faints" or "spells." The patient sits motionless as though dazed or in a trance. He stops whatever activity he is engaged in and later resumes his work without mishap.

Psychomotor epilepsy is marked by confusion and anxiety, without loss of consciousness. The patient may perform automatic movements such as chewing and smacking the lips. The attack lasts for 1 to 2 minutes. Afterward the patient has no recollection that he has had an attack.

There is no definite evidence that the epileptic attacks produce any damaging physical effects on the organism, beyond the injuries resulting from falls that occur during seizures. Such disorders as psychosis or feeblemindedness may coexist with epilepsy, but are not caused by it.

Treatment. A number of drugs are available to control epileptic attacks; the commonest are phenobarbital, dilantin, and tridione. Patients must take medication daily, as the seizures will generally reappear if treatment is discontinued. Approximately half of all epileptic patients can be maintained completely free of seizures, while another 30% can be substantially improved. Surgery may be effective in certain cases, such as in epilepsy caused by a tumor pressing on the brain.

The frequency of epilepsy makes it a medical and social problem. It is estimated that there are between one and two million epileptics in the United States. Because of its dramatic and frequently unpredictable nature, epilepsy has often posed serious social handicaps for its victims. Epileptic children have been educated in special classes or schools and many industries will not employ epileptics, feeling that the risks of accidents are too great. The patient, aware of being a "special case," develops many psychological problems. Actually, except in cases where seizures cannot be medically controlled, most epileptics are able to lead a normal existence. Because of the importance of heredity in some types of epilepsy, marriage is still forbidden to epileptics in many states. Many authorities, however, are no longer in agreement with this policy.
MICHAEL G. KALOGERAKIS, M.D.

EPILOGUE [ĕp'ə-lôg], an address to the audience at the close of a play. At first short and direct, it was elaborated in the 17th and 18th centuries into a set of witty verses. In early drama the epilogue was generally spoken by an actor specifically assigned for the purpose; later it was often delivered by one or more of the players of regular parts. By the 19th century the epilogue had largely disappeared, though it is sometimes encountered (as in Shaw's *Saint Joan*) in the form of a short final scene, frequently separated in time or in characters from the body of the play.

EPIMETHEUS [ĕp-ĭ-mē'thē-əs] (Gr. "after thought"), in Greek mythology, the brother of Prometheus. From Zeus he received the first woman, Pandora, who let loose every human ill, although Prometheus had warned him to accept no gifts from the gods.

ÉPINAY [ā-pē-nā'], **LOUISE FLORENCE PÉTRONILLE TARDIEU D'ESCLAVELLES DE LA LIVE D'** (1726–83), French woman of letters, friend of the philosophers of the Enlightenment. Her quarrel with Jean-Jacques Rousseau (1757) is related in the latter's *Confessions* and in her own *Mémoires* (1818). Moral essays and two treatises on education are less interesting than her published letters.

EPINEPHRINE [ĕp-ə-nĕf'rĭn], also called adrenalin, is a hormone secreted by the inner portion, or medulla, of the adrenal gland. Epinephrine helps to mobilize the resources of the body for strenuous or emergency activity. It accomplishes this by shunting blood from the skin and digestive tract to the muscles of the arms, legs, and trunk, by increasing heart action and blood pressure, by widening the air passages, and by raising the sugar level of the blood.

Epinephrine is used in medicine in certain heart emergencies. It is also used in cases of bronchial asthma to relax spasms of the bronchi (the air passages) and in certain allergic conditions such as hives and severe, shocklike, serum sickness. The ability of epinephrine to constrict small blood vessels has made it useful in controlling superficial hemorrhages from the skin. For this reason the drug is frequently incorporated in anesthetic solutions. The narrowing of the blood vessels slows the rate of absorption of the anesthetic and thus prolongs its action.
PAUL CHRISTENSON, M.D.
See also ADRENAL GLANDS; ENDOCRINE GLANDS.

EPIPHANIUS [ĕp-ĭ-fā'nē-əs], **ST.** (310?–403 A.D.), Bishop of Salamis, born in Palestine. Entering the religious life, he became an ascetic, founded the monastery of Eleutheropolis, and lived a life of great sanctity. Although learned, he erroneously ascribed all heresies to the influence of Origen, thus involving himself in many unsavory conflicts. His feast day is May 12.

EPIPHANY [ĭ-pĭf'ə-nē] (Gr. *epiphaneia*), "manifestation" of Christ to the Gentiles, represented by the wise men who visited Him as an infant (Matt. 2:1–12). Their star-guided journey was early interpreted as the fulfillment of Isaiah 60:3, "the Gentiles shall come to thy light, and kings to the brightness of thy rising," whence also the wise men (actually astrologers) were taken to be kings. Its celebration as a Christian festival on Jan. 6 (Twelfth-night), which also traditionally commemorates Christ's baptism, is of greater antiquity in the Church than the observance of Christmas on Dec. 25.

EPIPHYTE. See AIR PLANT.

EPIRUS [ē-pī'rəs], historic region of northwest Greece, a portion of which serves today as an administrative district of the same name. Albania lies above the northwest boundary of modern Epirus. In ancient times Epirus was bordered on the west by the Ionian Sea, on the east by Macedonia

EPIRUS

Name of ancient city_____Nicopolis
Name of modern city_____**Ioannina**
Limits of ancient Epirus___ ▬ ▬ ▬
Limits of modern Epirus__

and Thessaly, on the south by Acarnania, and on the north by Illyria. It is mostly mountainous and travel is difficult. Husbandry is the principal occupation, as it was in antiquity. Livestock, grains, fruit, olives, and dairy products are raised. The original inhabitants were considered non-Greek by early Greek authors, and may have been a branch of the Thracians. Archeological excavation has been mostly confined to Dodona, the site of the famous oracle of Zeus, and later the capital; other cities were Ambracia, Buthrotum, Phoenice; and in Augustan times, Nicopolis. The chief tribe, the Molossians, brought Epirus into a loose federation c.400 B.C., and during the 4th century Epirus was increasingly Hellenized. Pyrrhus, who made himself King in 296, is famed for his unpredictable military exploits against Rome. After his death (272), and after a brief period as a republic c.230 B.C., Epirus sided with Macedon against Rome, but defected in 198. Epirus changed sides again; but after the defeat of Perseus of Macedon by Aemilius Paulus in 168, it became a Roman province in 146; it was later incorporated into the Eastern Roman Empire.

Barbarian invasions affected Epirus with the rest of Greece, but Slavic infiltration was surprisingly slight. In the 11th century A.D. it was a battleground for Normans against Bulgars, and after the fall of Constantinople to the Franks (1204) it became part of the eastern Latin Empire. From the end of the 13th century it was subjugated successively by Albanians, Venetians, and Serbs. Turkey occupied Epirus in the 15th century, and a prosperous period followed. Under the illustrious brigand Ali Pasha (governor of Janina, 1788–1822), Epirus achieved some independence, and Ali was host to many European notables; Byron celebrates him in *Childe Harold*. In 1877

Epirus declared itself independent. In the Second Balkan War it went to the Greeks, but the northern part was awarded to Albania in 1913. It was again a battleground in World War II. Its principal modern cities are Ioannina (the capital), Arta, and Metsovon.

Consult Cross, G. N., *Epirus* (1932).

JOHN H. YOUNG, *Johns Hopkins University*

EPISCIA [ĕ-pĭsh'ē-ə], a genus of herbaceous plants in the Gesneriaceae, or gesneria, family, to which the African violet also belongs. Episcias are native to tropical America but have been introduced into many temperate and cool regions where they are popular house plants. The hairy, succulent leaves of episcia plants are borne on trailing, vinelike stems. Their small, 5-petaled blossoms may be white, lavender, or bright red. Episcias do well in warm, shady locations and, because of their trailing growth habit, make excellent hanging basket plants. Among the many species, the horticultural varieties of *Episcia cupreata* and *E. lilacina* are especially popular, and are noted for their colorful, variegated foliage.

EPISCOPAL CHURCH. *See* PROTESTANT EPISCOPAL CHURCH.

EPISCOPATE [ĭ-pĭs'kə-pĭt], **THE,** name for the office of Bishop in the Christian Church. In the New Testament the word Bishop (Gr. *episcopos*) means "overseer" and is used as equal to the word "presbyter." But within a very short time in Asia Minor, and probably elsewhere, the name became attached to the president of the council of presbyters who governed each local church. As the original apostles died, their function of witnessing to the events of the Gospel passed into the New Testament as its canon was formed. But confronted by controversies, the leaders of the churches attributed a unique importance to the Bishop as the guarantor of the authentic Gospel in his church, and finally, by 200 A.D., as the inheritor of apostolic authority. Ignatius of Antioch, soon after 100 A.D., shows the unique status of the Bishop in Asia Minor as the center of unity; Irenaeus of Lyons, around 180 A.D., writes of "apostolic succession" in the great Christian sees as the guarantee of truth and continuity; and Cyprian of Carthage, who died in 258, uses the words "bishop" and "apostle" as interchangeable.

Cyprian laid down the classic statement of the episcopal theory of the government of the Church by councils of Bishops. After the conversion of Constantine in 313 and the end of persecution, it became possible to hold councils representative of the Church in the whole Roman Empire, and from the Council of Nicaea (325) onward, the council became the normal instrument of church government. Others besides Bishops were permitted to be present (presbyters, deacons, lay nobles) but essentially the councils were meetings of Bishops, each representative of his own see. Certain councils achieved, in subsequent thought, the special status of ecumenical. The Eastern Orthodox Church, which has maintained government by episcopal councils, recognizes seven ecumenical councils before the breach with the West. The Roman Catholic Church, disregarding the absence of the Eastern Orthodox, and later of Protestants, recognizes 21 ecumenical councils, the last two of which were held at the Vatican (1869–1870 and 1962–1965).

Among Protestants, certain churches at the Reformation retained the episcopal form of church government, but under the Catholic order a Bishop was brought into the succession by being consecrated by other Bishops, and this practice survived only in the churches of England and Sweden and, until 1884, Finland. In these churches and in the Roman Catholic and Eastern Orthodox churches the Bishop alone has the power to ordain priests and deacons, and in England and in the Roman Catholic Church the power of confirmation is restricted to him. In the Roman church the power of the Bishop has been effectively diminished, partly by the growth of papal jurisdiction and partly by the existence of exempt bodies within his diocese. In England the Bishop's prestige is very great, but his effective power is closely limited by the independent status of his clergy and by the nature of the legal establishment. The office is much valued in the Church of England, however, especially as a sign of Christian continuity through the centuries.

W. O. CHADWICK, Cambridge University

EPISTEMOLOGY [ĭ-pĭs-tə-mŏl′ə-jē] (from the Greek term meaning "knowledge"), a major branch of philosophy devoted primarily to the achievement of a better understanding of the concept of knowledge. It also concerns itself with other closely related concepts such as those of belief, truth, faith, meaning, certainty, probability, confirmation, justification, and rationality. To say that some of our true convictions are genuine knowledge (as opposed to lucky guesses or matters of faith) seems to imply that these convictions are capable of justification; and for this reason the history of epistemology is in large part an attempt to specify the conditions under which we can maintain that various kinds of convictions (scientific, ethical, religious) are warranted or justified.

A distinction has traditionally been drawn between knowledge which is justified by experience, called empirical knowledge, and knowledge which can be justified independently of experience, called a priori knowledge. One of the major problems concerning the justification of the natural sciences, and other empirical knowledge, is the problem of perception. Further philosophical problems arise when we attempt to formulate the principles of induction which allow us to infer general laws—for instance, "all or most crows are black"—from the observation of a limited number of individual cases, and especially when we ask whether it is possible to justify these principles of induction. The fame of David Hume is a result, in part, of his brilliant statement of the doctrine that induction cannot be rationally justified. Immanuel Kant's monumental *Critique of Pure Reason* was, in large part, an effort to answer Hume's argument. Further problems of justification arise with respect to what is often called our knowledge of other minds. If I see someone behaving as if he were in pain, for example, it is still possible to ask whether I have any justification for believing that he has a sensation similar to the one that I have when I behave in a similar way.

With a few notable exceptions, for example, John Stuart Mill, philosophers have generally agreed that mathematical knowledge is a priori. But the rationalists have maintained that the truths of mathematics (for instance, "2 plus 2 equals 4") are known through self-evident rational insight, whereas the empiricists have tended to maintain that such truths can be justified by showing that they follow from definitions of their constituent terms ("2," "4," "plus," "equals"). The justification of ethical and religious knowledge raises still further epistemological problems, especially if such knowledge is held to be neither empirical nor self-evident.

RODERICK FIRTH, Harvard University

EPISTLE OF THE APOSTLES or The Testament of Our Lord in Galilee, an apocryphal account, from c.150 A.D., of a revelation supposedly given the apostles by the risen Lord, who predicted the conversion of Paul, the gathering of a new Jerusalem out of Syria, and His own return after 120 years (Coptic version), or 150 (Ethiopic version).

EPITAPH [ĕp′ə-tăf], an inscription or a poem composed for a tomb or burial place. In ancient Egypt, epitaphs included the individual's name and profession with an appropriate motto characterizing him. Later, Greek inscriptions in the form of epigrams acquired some literary content. In English, epitaphs have expressed sentiments either solemn or ribald and have been employed as sections of longer poems, as in Thomas Gray's "Elegy Written in a Country Churchyard," the "Epitaph" of which begins:

"Here rests his head upon the lap of earth
A youth, to fortune and to fame unknown;
Fair science frowned not on his humble birth
And melancholy marked him for her own."

EPOXY [ĕp-ŏk′sē] **RESIN,** important class of resins with a wide variety of industrial uses as adhesives, coatings, foams, and laminates. They are outstanding bonding agents and also have flexibility, strength, and chemical and heat resistance. Epoxy and glass laminates have a flexibility strength useful in pipe, tanks, and tools and dimensional strength and impact resistance necessary for dies and small boat hulls. Epoxy foam is applied in sandwich construction reinforcement or as thermal insulation. Alloyed with other resins in coatings, epoxy becomes enamel, tube liner, or paint. As a metal-to-metal bond, epoxy resin has been used to supplement welds between inner and outer panels of automobile hoods.

Epoxy is thermosetting and is made by the reaction of bisphenol and epichlorhydrin. A typical curing operation involves adding a chemical to the resin, then applying to a moderately heated surface for 15 to 30 min. In making epoxy foam, the curing process is done in the presence of blowing agents that inject air into the plastic mass.

W. NELSON AXE, Research Division,
Phillips Petroleum Company

EPPING, urban district, and market and residential town of southwestern Essex, England, separated from Greater London by Epping Forest. The forest was the favorite hunting ground of the Norman Kings and the camp site of Dick Turpin, the 18th-century highwayman hanged at York in 1739. Pop., 9,998.

EPSOM SALT, or magnesium sulfate, consists of colorless white crystals which dissolve easily in water producing a bitter-tasting solution. It is commonly used for its laxative effect, which it achieves by causing fluids to be absorbed into the gastrointestinal tract.

EPSTEIN [ĕp'stīn], **SIR JACOB** (1880–1959), sculptor, born in New York City of Russian-Polish parents. He went to Paris in 1902 and to England in 1905, where he became a British citizen in 1906. In 1907 he received a commission to execute 18 figures for the British Medical Association building. These, like many of his later works, caused great controversy among critics and the public. In 1907 he began making bronze portraits which, because of their vigorous handling and insight into their subjects, have been highly praised. In 1931 he published *The Sculptor Speaks* and in 1940 the autobiography *Let There Be Sculpture.* Sir Jacob was knighted in 1954. His last major work was a bronze group of St. Michael triumphing over the devil, made for the new Coventry Cathedral.

EQUAL PROTECTION OF LAW. Unlike the due process of law clause which appears in the Fifth and Fourteenth Amendments to the U.S. Constitution, the equal protection clause appears only in the Fourteenth: "nor [shall any state] deny to any person within its jurisdiction the equal protection of the laws." Although the equal protection clause is thus, in terms at least, a limitation only on the power of the states, there is little doubt that an unreasonably discriminatory classification imposed by the national government would be stricken as a denial of due process.

Indeed, that is exactly what happened in the most celebrated "equal protection" case, *Brown* v. *Board of Education of Topeka* (1954), and its companion case, *Bolling* v. *Sharpe* (1954). In Brown the Supreme Court unanimously held that segregation in public education deprived the Negro plaintiffs of the equal protection of the laws guaranteed by the Fourteenth Amendment. In Bolling, which arose in the District of Columbia, where that Amendment does not apply, the court found similar protection in the due process clause of the Fifth Amendment, which limits Congress in its governance of the District of Columbia.

Ever since the Fourteenth Amendment was added to the Constitution in 1868, the equal protection clause has been most consistently used, as in the school segregation cases, to forbid discrimination in the area of human liberties, particularly in matters of race. It has played an important part in securing Negro participation in juries, extending the right of franchise, ending segregation in public facilities, outlawing state antimiscegenation statutes, and affording protection against racially restrictive covenants in connection with the sale and use of real property.

In two 1966 cases the court suggested an even wider potential sweep for the Fourteenth Amendment. In *United States* v. *Price* the Supreme Court unanimously reversed the partial dismissal of indictments against the alleged slayers of three civil rights workers in Philadelphia, Miss. In *United States* v. *Guest* the court sustained an indictment arising out of the killing of a Negro while using a state highway in Georgia. Both cases were decided on conclusions that the homicides were committed "under color of law" or that "state action" was present in sufficient degree to involve the prohibitions of the Fourteenth Amendment. More striking was the fact that a majority of the court concluded that Section 5 of the Fourteenth Amendment, giving Congress the "power to enforce, by appropriate legislation," the substance of the amendment, permits Congress to forbid private action of a discriminatory character as well as state action.

The equal protection clause was also invoked in 1964 in the important *Reapportionment Cases.* There the court held that substantial population equality is required among election districts in both houses of each bicameral state legislature.

ROBERT B. McKAY, Dean, New York University School of Law
See also BROWN V. BOARD OF EDUCATION; CONSTITUTIONAL LAW, UNITED STATES; DUE PROCESS OF LAW.

EQUATION, ALGEBRAIC, an equation involving algebraic expressions. An algebraic expression is one that can be constructed from a finite number of constants and variables connected by a finite number of additions, subtractions, multiplications, divisions, root extractions, and symbols of grouping. Some examples of algebraic equations are: $3x + 2 = 0$; $4x^3 - 2x^2 + 5x + 1 = 0$; $\sqrt{x + 2} = -3$; and $\dfrac{x}{4 - x} = \dfrac{2}{x - 4}$. Examples of equations which are not algebraic are $2 = \log x$, and $3 \sin x + \cosine x = 2^x$.

Elementary algebra stresses linear and quadratic equations. A linear equation in one variable is one of the form $ax + b = 0$, or one which can be transformed to that pattern by certain axioms. A quadratic equation is one of the form $ax^2 + bx + c = 0$. The problem in both of these is to determine what values of the variable x will produce true statements of equality when these values are combined with the constants a, b, and c. These values are called the roots. The root of $ax + b = 0$ is $\dfrac{-b}{a}$. The two roots of the quadratic are $\dfrac{-b + \sqrt{b^2 - 4ac}}{2a}$ and $\dfrac{-b - \sqrt{b^2 - 4ac}}{2a}$.

Equations such as these, in which a single variable appears with a positive integer as an exponent, are called polynomial equations. The general form of a polynomial equation is $ax^n + bx^{n-1} + \ldots k$, where k is a constant. Not until the 16th century were methods devised for finding the roots of polynomial equations of the third and fourth degrees. In the 19th century it was demonstrated that no general algebraic equation of a degree higher than the fourth could be solved in terms of algebraic operations on the coefficients. However, it has been shown that polynomial equations of the fifth and higher degrees can be solved in terms of other functions of the coefficients, such as the elliptic functions. It has also been proved that every polynomial equation of the nth degree has n roots, provided a root which is repeated is counted each time it appears, and provided that complex roots are allowed.

It is important to notice that the zeros of algebraic functions are the roots of algebraic equations. Thus, if $f(x) = x^2 - 2x - 8$, then the roots of $x^2 - 2x - 8 = 0$ are

$f(4)$ and $f(2)$. This indicates why the intersection of the graph of a function with the abscissa frequently gives good approximations to the roots of the equation $f(x) = 0$.

So far only conditional equations have been treated. An equation such as $2x + 5 = 3x + 4 - x + 1$ has as many roots as the set of permissible values of x. This kind of an equation is called an identity. The roots of a conditional equation are always a subset of the set of allowable values of x. Some conditional equations have no roots, such as $2x + 5 = 3x + 4 - x$.

JOHN J. KINSELLA, New York University

EQUATION, CHEMICAL, representation in symbolic form of the quantitative aspects of a chemical reaction. It is set up as a balanced statement, or equation, that satisfies the laws of conservation of mass and of energy. On the left side of the statement the formulas of the substances reacting are ranged with plus signs. The result of their reactions is indicated by an arrow pointing to the right at the formulas of the chemical products, which are also connected by plus signs. If the reaction is reversible, a second arrow under the first points back at the reactants. Arrows pointing up or down after a formula indicate it is a gas or a precipitate. A triangle below the arrow indicates an endothermic process. Symbols indicating heat or energy produced or absorbed can be placed on either side.

The equation is balanced with coefficients placed before the formulas so that a mathematical equating of the atoms before and after the reaction is carried out. If the equation includes separate ions, the electric charges must be balanced also. Each formula is a symbol for the molecular weight of the compound, and using their ratios the actual weight of substances used up or produced can be calculated, if the actual weight of one participant is known.

General symbols can be used instead of actual formulas, especially in organic chemistry where families of reactions are common, but then gravimetric calculations cannot be made. Equations for nuclear reactions are set up the same way with symbols that stand for nuclear notation.

LOUIS VACZEK, The New School for Social Research

EQUATOR, imaginary line, 24,897.59 mi. long, drawn around the earth at equal distances from the geographic poles. Latitudes are counted from it toward north and south. In astronomy, the equator is the intersection of the plane of the earth's equator and the celestial sphere.

EQUATORIAL COUNTERCURRENTS, currents that flow eastward (against the wind) at or near the equator. They are generally explained as a return flow in the doldrums of water that has been piled up in the west by strong trade winds. Little use has been made of them by navigators as their flow is generally too weak to be of importance to modern vessels. The strongest currents flow from $10°$ N. lat. in the west to $3°$ N. lat. in the Atlantic and from about $5°$ to $10°$ N. lat. in the Pacific.

EQUATORIAL GUINEA. *See* GUINEA, EQUATORIAL.

EQUESTRIANS [ĭ-kwĕs′trē-ənz] (from Lat. *equestris*, of or pertaining to *equites*, "cavalry"), Roman order for which some reputation for decency, and usually free birth, were

general prerequisites, and for which a minimum of 400,000 sesterces was the main requirement. An equestrian census rating goes back to the 6th century B.C. for those with sufficient wealth to afford service in the cavalry, but the history of the equestrian order as a group distinct from the senatorial order, on the one hand, and from the people, on the other, begins in 123 B.C. Then, Gaius Gracchus, who needed a counterweight to the senatorial oligarchy, proposed the bill which transferred from senators to equestrians the court where governors were tried for extortion, and excluded senators from serving as equites. Equestrian capitalists, who invested in state contracts, often resented senatorial policy in the last century of the Republic; but rivalry ended with the principate when careers in the administration of Rome, the provinces, and in the army were progressively opened to equestrians.

JAMES H. OLIVER, Johns Hopkins University

EQUIDAE [ĕk′wĭ-dē], family of hoofed animals, or ungulates, of the order Perissodactyla. The family includes the horse, zebra, ass, and onager. The hoof of these animals is a specialization of the third, or middle, toe. The other toes are reduced and lossed. The family can be traced to *Eohippus*, the dog-sized "dawn horse" of the Miocene. Although *Eohippus* was common in the New World, the modern horse, *Equus caballus*, was unknown there until introduced by the early explorers. The family also includes the African zebra, *E. zebra*, which is not widely spread; the Eurasian ass, *E. asinus*, now of worldwide range; the onager, *E. onager*, of Asia (the Biblical "wild ass"); and the kiang, *E. kiang*, of western Asia. Przewalski's horse, *E. caballus przewalskii*, a small horse of Central Asia, is also a member of the family.

EQUILIBRIUM. *See* STATICS.

EQUILIBRIUM [ē-kwə-lĭb′rē-əm], **CHEMICAL,** the condition during a reversible reaction when the rate at which the products are formed equals the rate at which the products re-form the original reactants. By rate is meant the actual weight of reactants combining in one second. A double arrow in the equation signifies that the chemical change can proceed in either direction.

The rate at which two substances, A and B, begin a reaction depends on their concentrations, on the temperature, and on the presence of a catalyst. As the reaction proceeds, the concentrations of A and B decrease and the rate of their reaction drops. The concentration of the resulting products, C and D, rises and the rate of their reaction increases. The rate of A and B reactions will eventually be equaled by the rate of C and D reactions, and a dynamic equilibrium will be established, with the two reactions continuing uninterruptedly at identical rates. This does not mean that their concentrations are equal, but that the concentrations of A, B, C, and D remain constant. Any change in the conditions will alter the equilibrium left or right to establish a new set of concentrations. Most reactions are reversible, and in industry the goal is to push the reaction toward the largest possible yield of the desired product. A rise in temperature will generally increase the rate of every reaction but there will be an optimum temperature at which the desired reaction is

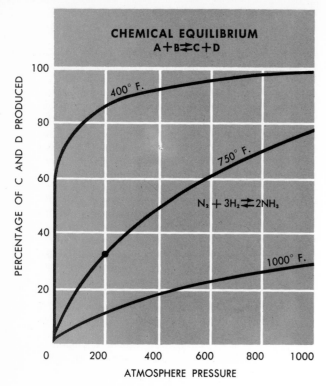

CHEMICAL EQUILIBRIUM
A + B ⇌ C + D

PERCENTAGE OF C AND D PRODUCED

400° F.

750° F.

$N_2 + 3H_2 \rightleftarrows 2NH_3$

1000° F.

ATMOSPHERE PRESSURE

At 200 atm. and 750° F., 33% of all the reactants in this reversible reaction is ammonia, NH_3. By changing the temperature and pressure, the percentage of ammonia can be increased or decreased, with a commensurate change in the percentage of N_2 and H_2.

fastest relative to its reverse. If gases are involved, pressure changes will affect the equilibrium. Intermittent or continuous removal of one of the products from the reaction area will force the reaction to completion. Some laboratory techniques, like titration, make use of the reversibility of reactions.

LOUIS VACZEK, The New School for Social Research

EQUINOX [e′kwə-noks], one of the two points on the celestial sphere where the celestial equator intersects the ecliptic. Because the earth's polar axis is inclined by 23½° to the plane of the ecliptic, the earth's path around the sun through the year, the celestial equator crosses the ecliptic at two points. At one of these, in the constellation of Pisces, the sun changes from south to north of the celestial equator. The sun appears to cross the celestial equator at this point on about Mar. 21 each year. This is the vernal equinox, meaning the "green time of equal nights and days." Because of the sun's position at this time over the earth's equator, the day is evenly divided for a brief period between sunlight and darkness. At this time, spring begins in the northern hemisphere and autumn begins south of the equator.

The opposite point of intersection is in the constellation of Virgo, where the sun appears to cross the equator from north to south. This is the autumnal equinox, and the sun reaches it each year on about Sept. 23. Autumn begins north of the equator and spring comes to the southern hemisphere.

JAMES PICKERING, Astronomer Emeritus, Hayden Planetarium
See also PRECESSION; SOLSTICE.

EQUITY [ĕk′wə-tē] is an established system of remedial justice observed in England and the United States. It has been defined as "the correction of that wherein the law by reason of its universality is deficient." The development of equity is closely associated with the origin of the Court of Chancery in England and to this day "equity" and "chancery" are interchangeable.

The early Norman Kings depended on a council of high state officials to advise them on political and judicial matters. One of these officials was the Chancellor, who was the chief law member of the council and a dignitary of the church, second in importance only to the King. As representative of the King and Keeper of the Royal Seal, the Chancellor and his College of Clerks controlled the issuance of all documents bearing the King's name, including the writs by which an action could be instituted in the common law courts. The judges of the common law courts, however, assumed exclusive jurisdiction to decide upon the validity of these writs, refusing to honor them if deemed contrary to the common law.

As long as the Chancellor was permitted to frame new writs to meet new legal situations, new legal principles could be formulated and the common law administered

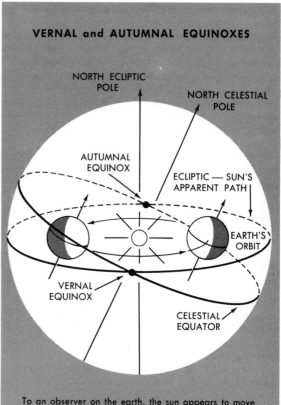

VERNAL and AUTUMNAL EQUINOXES

NORTH ECLIPTIC POLE

NORTH CELESTIAL POLE

AUTUMNAL EQUINOX

ECLIPTIC — SUN'S APPARENT PATH

EARTH'S ORBIT

VERNAL EQUINOX

CELESTIAL EQUATOR

To an observer on the earth, the sun appears to move along the ecliptic as the earth revolves. The ecliptic and the celestial equator intersect at the equinoxes. In the Northern Hemisphere spring begins at the vernal equinox when the sun appears to move north across the equator. Autumn begins at the autumnal equinox when the sun seems to move south across the equator.

in the courts was adequate for the needs of the people. In 1258, however, by the Provisions of Oxford, the Chancellor was forbidden to frame new writs without the consent of the King or his council. Although the Statute of Westminster II (1285) and subsequent statutes provided for new remedies theretofore excluded by the rules of the common law, the common law judges bound themselves by a line of precedents and refused to entertain or give relief in every case.

As this situation prevailed, it became customary for suitors to petition the King and his council, praying for relief as a matter of the King's grace, because they could not procure justice in the common law courts. Invariably these petitions were referred to the Chancellor as the keeper of the King's conscience, for he was both learned in the law and a clergyman, and hence best prepared to dispose of them. By the 14th century these petitions were presented directly to the Chancellor, who afforded relief if it could be demonstrated that the courts lacked the jurisdiction to give proper redress. It is not known exactly when the Court of Chancery became established as a separate court, but by the 15th century, it was flourishing alongside the common law courts, such as the King's Bench, Common Pleas, and the Exchequer.

Apart from meeting the requirements of justice as a matter of the King's grace, the establishment of the Court of Chancery can also be traced to another cause. In the 14th century the landowners of England conceived the idea of conveying their lands in trust to friends, who would hold them to certain uses of the grantor or some designated beneficiary. The purpose of this trust was to evade the onerous feudal burdens and restrictions on their land. The Court of Chancery as a court of conscience held itself out as prepared to enforce these trusts, or "uses," as they were called, by sending to prison the trustee who breached the trust agreement. The protection of the rights of the beneficiaries of these trusts became an important part of Chancery's jurisdiction and was highly influential in its development.

Once established as a separate court, Chancery assumed jurisdiction over matters that the common law courts refused to accept or when the relief was inadequate, such as enforcement of contracts, assignment of debts and contracts, specific performance, decedent's estates, guardianships, and accountings. The clerks of the court kept records of its decisions which eventually developed into a system of substantive and procedural law, known as "equity."

The period of modern equity begins with the Chancellorship of Nottingham in 1674. Known as the father of English equity, Nottingham systematized its principles, especially in the field of trusts. In England, the Judicature Acts (1873–75) abolished the common law courts and the High Court of Chancery and created one High Court of Justice which administers the principles of equity as well as law.

The English system of equity was transplanted to the American colonies with certain modifications. Today in most states of the United States, as well as in federal courts (since 1938), law and equity have been merged, and in the same court a single procedure is employed for both actions at law and suits in equity. The same court administers two systems of law, following the rules characteristic of each. In this sense, the distinction between legal and equitable rights is still maintained.

JULIUS J. MARKE, New York University
School of Law

ERA OF GOOD FEELING, in American history, a phrase coined (July 12, 1817) by the Boston *Columbian Centinel* to characterize President James Monroe's administration. The term had a semblance of reality by virtue of the decline of the Federalist party, Democratic-Republican sponsorship of measures formerly identified with the Federalists, and the almost unanimous support for Monroe in the electoral college in 1820. Beneath the appearance of harmony, however, there was sharp economic conflict occasioned by the panic of 1819, a heated sectional dispute (1819–21) over the admission of free and slave states, and bitter factionalism in the Cabinet.

ERASISTRATUS [ĕr-ə-sĭs′trə-təs] (c.3d century B.C.), Greek physician, anatomist, and pioneer physiologist who was one of the renowned medical teachers at the Alexandria Museum in Egypt. He traced the veins and arteries to the heart and regarded the blood as a nourishing substance. He also devised a catheter, a tubelike instrument to be introduced into body cavities, and was an early opponent of bloodletting as a therapeutic procedure.
See also MEDICINE.

ERASMUS [ĭ-răz′məs], **DESIDERIUS** (1466–1536), Renaissance humanist. Born in Rotterdam and educated by the Brethren of the Common Life, he entered (c.1487) the Augustinian monastery at Stein. Ordained a priest in 1492, he became secretary to the Bishop of Cambrai. Later, four years of theology at the Sorbonne in Paris disgusted him with decadent scholasticism, and he went to England (1499) where he became friends with John Colet and Thomas More. It was Colet who revealed to him his vocation, to rejuvenate theology by basing it on scientifically accurate documents, especially the Greek originals of the New Testament and the earliest Fathers of the Church.

In 1500 he published the *Adagia*, a collection of Latin and Greek proverbs with explanatory essays, and in 1503 the *Enchiridion* (Handbook of the Christian Soldier), a plea for interior Christianity, achieved through prayer and the knowledge of Scripture, with a minimum of devotional practices.

He was made Doctor of Divinity in Turin in 1506, and subsequently stayed in Padua, Venice, Siena, and Rome. But in 1509 he settled in England, where he wrote *The Praise of Folly*, dedicated to Thomas More, which denounced with scathing humor the manifold absurdities of mankind and Christendom.

In 1516 he published the Greek New Testament, with his own Latin version, and epoch-making prefaces and annotations, and also his edition of *Saint Jerome*, in 9 folio volumes. These two major works gave Erasmus unquestioned supremacy in the world of humanism, with correspondents all over Europe, and with Kings and Cardinals, Emperor and Pope, vying for his friendship.

As councilor to Charles V, Erasmus resided in the Low Countries from 1516 to 1521. Although the Lutheran revo-

Alinari—Art Reference Bureau

Portrait of Erasmus by Hans Holbein the Younger (Louvre, Paris).

lution disappointed his prospect of a "golden age" of peaceful learning and reform, Erasmus refused to be dragged into anti-Lutheran polemics. Leaving overconservative Louvain, he settled in the free city of Basle, where he found a printer of his own caliber, Johann Froben. His witty *Colloquies* conveyed his views on varied topics to an ever-growing public.

After long hesitation, he attacked Luther in 1524 by a vindication of free will, but remained friendly with moderate Reformers like Melanchthon, and labored to make religious toleration prevail.

When Basle became Zwinglian in 1529, Erasmus withdrew to the more congenial Catholic city of Freiburg im Breisgau, where, despite old age and failing health, he still wrote with incredible speed and energy. Revisiting Basle to supervise the printing of *Ecclesiastes*, a book on preaching, he died there in July, 1536.

Erasmus' *Complete Works*, filling 10 huge folios, were published in Basle in 1540. Erasmus was a mediocre thinker, but a peerless writer of Latin. His versatile genius and his overfluid character make it almost impossible to define and gauge him.

Consult Huizinga, Johan, *Erasmus and the Age of Reformation, with a Selection from the Letters of Erasmus* (1957); Bouyer, Louis, *Erasmus and His Times* (1959).

Abbé Germain Marc'hadour, Université Catholique, Angers, France

ERATO, one of the nine Muses (q.v.).

ERATOSTHENES [ĕr-ə-tŏs′thə-nēz] (276–194 B.C.), Greek astronomer and geographer who first determined the earth's circumference. He was born in Cyrene, Africa, and after studying in Athens he became director of the library in Alexandria. Eratosthenes computed the earth's circumference by measuring an arc of longitude between Alexandria and Syene (Aswan), Egypt (*see* Geodesy). He is noted also for finding the obliquity of the ecliptic—the angle between the planes of the earth's equator and orbit. Only fragments of his *Geographica*, containing these computations, have been preserved. Eratosthenes also developed a system of dating events from the fall of Troy, and he wrote on Greek comedy.

ERBIL [ĭr′bĭl], historic town of northeastern Iraq and capital of the province of Erbil. It is the terminal of a rail line from Baghdad. Built on an ancient fortified mound, it rises high above a vast cultivated plain; on this plain in 331 B.C. the Macedonian King Alexander the Great defeated the armies of the Persian King Darius III. Pop., 69,280.

ERBIUM [ûr′bē-əm], metallic element of the lanthanide series, first isolated in 1843 by C. G. Mosander. It forms a series of red compounds but has no important uses.

PROPERTIES

Symbol	Er
Atomic number	68
Atomic weight	167.26
Density	4.77
Valence	3

ERCILLA Y ZÚÑIGA [ĕr-thē′lyä ē thoō′nyē-gä], **ALONSO DE** (1533–94), Spanish soldier and poet. He left the Spanish royal court upon hearing of the marvels of the New World. While fighting against the Araucan Indians of Chile, he became deeply impressed by their courage and loyalty as opposed to the cruelty of the Spaniards. It was this experience which inspired him to write *La Araucana* (1569–89), possibly the greatest epic poem written in Spanish. The poem is noted for its virile style and for its emphasis on chivalry and heroic exploits. Ercilla describes the new land with remarkable facility and artistry.

ERCKMANN-CHATRIAN [ĕrk-mȧn′ shȧ-trē-än′], the name under which the French authors Émile Erckmann (1822–99) and Alexandre Chatrian (1826–90), both Alsatians, collaborated on many novels and plays. Their best-known works are *Madame Thérèse* (1863; trans., 1869), *Histoire d'un conscrit de 1813*, 1864 (*The Conscript*, 1869), *Waterloo* (1865; trans., 1869), *L'ami Fritz*, 1864 (*Friend Fritz*, 1877), and *Le blocus*, 1866 (*The Blockade of Phalsburg*, 1871). These novels, with others, form an epic of the revolutionary and Napoleonic eras in Alsace-Lorraine. Although they depict the horrors of war, their hero is really the common people, and their principal interest lies in a realistic yet poetic picture of human relations.

ERDÉLYI [ĕr′dā-lyĭ], **JÁNOS** (1814–68), Hungarian poet and writer. He is remembered for having gathered together the folk songs and folk tales of his native land. One collection was published by the Kisfaludy Society (1846–47), another the year after his death.

EREBUS [ĕr′ə-bəs], in Greek mythology, the gloomy entrance to the underworld through which departed souls had to pass. Erebus was the son of Chaos. By his sister Night he produced 20 children, all personifications of abstract concepts or basic elements, such as Air, Day, Fraud, and Envy. Erebus lived in the underworld, and his name eventually was associated with this part of it.

ERECH [ē′rĕk] **or URUK** [ōō′rōōk], ancient city of south Mesopotamia, on the Euphrates. It flourished from before 3000 B.C. to the Parthian period. It is mentioned in Genesis 10:10. It was the center of Sumerian civilization in the Protoliterate period (c.3000 B.C.), when the earliest writing (in its later stages called cuneiform) was invented there. From earliest times Erech was a center of the cults of Anu, god of the heavens, and of Ishtar, goddess of love and war. Eanna, the temple of Ishtar, owned vast estates, and in consequence Erech became in the 1st millennium B.C. virtually the administrative capital of south Babylonia. Impressive ruins at the site (modern Warka) were briefly explored by W. K. Loftus in 1854, and have been scientifically excavated by German expeditions (1912–13, 1928–39, and since 1954).

ERETRIA [ĕ-rē′trē-ə], ancient Greek city on the west coast of Euboea. It is mentioned in the Homeric Catalogue of Ships and was important in founding colonies. It early opposed Chalcis in the long Lelantine War (700–650 B.C.), but was defeated. Allied with Athens against the Persians, the city was destroyed by Darius I in 490 B.C., but quickly rebuilt; it became an Athenian colony c.445. A naval battle was fought here in 411, in which the Athenians were defeated by Sparta. Eretria again joined the Athenian League in 378 B.C. An ancient theater, the temples of Apollo Daphnephoros and Dionysus, and a shrine of Isis have been excavated, and there is an imposing fortified acropolis. The present town, Nea-Psara, was settled on its site by Greek refugees in 1821.

EREWHON, English satirical novel (1872) by Samuel Butler. The book's title is the name (anagram of "nowhere") of a country where institutions are opposite to the English ones. For instance, disease is considered a crime and crime a disease. The book is a witty satire on the England of Butler's day.

ERFURT [ĕr′fōōrt], city of south-central German Democratic Republic (East Germany), and capital of the district of Erfurt, located on the Gera River, an affluent of the Unstrut River, 65 mi. west-southwest of Leipzig. Erfurt is an important industrial center and is also noted for the culture of flower and vegetable seeds which are exported throughout the world. This branch of agriculture at first flourished in the gardens of the surrounding monasteries, among which the Augustinian monastery, in which Martin Luther lived for a time, was most successful. Industries include the manufacture of food products, shoes, metal-work, furniture, chemicals, leather, tobacco, and musical instruments. Erfurt is also a cultural center and it has an agricultural school, an academy of music, a public library, archives, a theater, and an art museum. It was the seat of one of the first universities in Europe, the University of Erfurt, chartered in 1392, but abandoned in 1816.

Erfurt was first mentioned, as Erpesfurt, in 742, when a bishopric, later abolished, was founded here. It was made a town in 1255, and in following centuries grew rapidly. Erfurt entered the Hanseatic League in the 15th century. Beginning in the 16th century it suffered from competition with Leipzig. Decay was accelerated by wars and religious struggles, especially in the Thirty Years' War (1618–48). Erfurt suffered severely when it was occupied for a time by the Swedes. From 1664 on it was ruled by the Archbishops of Mainz, and was ceded to Prussia in 1802. The Congress of Erfurt took place in 1808 and was attended by Napoleon and Alexander of Russia. The Altstadt (old town) has narrow streets and some old houses but much of it was destroyed during World War II. The more modern sections of Erfurt lie west of the central city. The most interesting building is the cathedral, a structure, partly in Romanesque and partly in Gothic style, begun in 1154 and completed in 1472. Pop., 184,819.

JOACHIM MARQUARDT, Commercial School for Merchants, Berlin-Wilmersdorf

ERG [ûrg], in physics, a unit of work or energy in the centimeter-gram-second system. It is the work done by a force of one dyne when producing a displacement of one centimeter. One joule equals 10 million ergs.

ERGOT [ûr′gət], a black fungus which grows on certain cereal grains, especially rye. Ergot contains a large number of substances which have profound effects on the body, and since ancient times it has been the cause of serious poisoning. In the Middle Ages epidemics were described in which the victims typically suffered from gangrene of the feet, hands, legs, and arms.

Before its effects were recognized by the medical profession ergot was used by midwives to shorten labor and hasten childbirth. Physicians later discovered that although ergot could be used in this way, it could cause stillbirths.

Of the many substances extracted from ergot, ergotamine and ergonovine are the most active. Ergonovine is used in the third stage of labor to help expel the afterbirth (the placenta) and to reduce blood loss. It is also used in certain cases of excessive menstrual bleeding. Ergotamine exerts a powerful constricting effect on the blood vessels and its effectiveness in relieving migraine headache is thought to be based on this action. Ergotamine can produce the symptoms of ergot poisoning, which include, in addition to gangrene of the extremities, headache, nausea, vomiting, diarrhea, and dizziness.

PAUL CHRISTENSON, M.D.

ERHARD [ĕr′härt], **LUDWIG** (1897–   ), German statesman and economist. Erhard received a doctorate in economics from the University of Frankfurt and for many years directed the Institute of Economic Affairs at Nuremberg. A financial expert with a non-Nazi past, he became head of the commission which reformed the West

Ludwig Erhard, Chancellor of the Federal Republic of Germany.
(CAMERA PRESS—PIX)

German currency after World War II. In 1949 Konrad Adenauer led the Christian Democrats to victory in the first postwar election, and Erhard joined the government as minister of economics. He advocated free enterprise and dismantled many government controls. He received great credit for the German "economic miracle," but the rapid growth of the French and Italian economies have made Erhard's wizardry seem less miraculous.

In Oct., 1963, the eighty-seven-year-old Adenauer reluctantly resigned, and despite Adenauer's opposition Erhard became leader of the Christian Democratic party and Chancellor of West Germany. In Oct., 1966, his government collapsed over a budget dispute which revealed that his colleagues had lost faith in him. In 1967 Kurt Kiesinger succeeded Erhard as party leader and chancellor and formed a coalition government with the Social Democrats.

MELVIN SHEFFTZ, State University of N.Y. at Binghamton

ERICE [ā′rē-chā] (anc. *Eryx*), town of west Sicily, Italy, on Monte San Guiliano, 2,465 ft. above sea level and 4 mi.

northeast of Trapani. The town was originally Elymian and was early a source of contention between Greeks and Carthaginians. It was captured in 278 B.C. by Pyrrhus of Epirus and destroyed by the Carthaginians in 259 and converted into a Carthaginian military base. The ruins of its temple of Aphrodite-Astarte are impressive.

ERICSON [ĕr′ik-sən], **LEIF** (fl. 985–1000), first European explorer of the New World. Born in Iceland, the son of Eric the Red, Leif went with his father to Greenland in 985 or 986. According to Icelandic sources, Bjarni Herjólfsson, an Icelandic merchant, set out for Greenland the same year. Blown off course by a northerly wind, he sighted three different lands—now identified as Newfoundland, Labrador, and Baffin Island—before he reached his destination.

In Greenland, Leif Ericson bought Bjarni's ship and set off for the new lands, but the exact year of his voyage is unknown. Finding the three countries Bjarni had seen, though in the opposite order, he named them Helluland ("Flatstoneland"), Markland ("Woodland"), and Vinland. According to Adam of Bremen (c.1070) and the Icelandic sagas, the last name means Wineland, but some scholars now believe the correct meaning to be Meadowland. Leif went ashore in all three countries and in Vinland erected a house called Leifsbúdir ("Leif's Abode"), where he wintered before returning to Greenland.

During the next few years, other explorers followed in Leif's footsteps. Among them was his brother, Thorvald, who seems to have explored the eastern part of the Gulf of St. Lawrence, and Thorfinn Karlsefni, who made an attempt at settling Vinland.

The main sources about the Vinland voyages are two medieval Icelandic books, *The Saga of the Greenlanders* (c.1200) and *The Saga of Eric the Red* (1250–1300). On the whole, the former is thought to be the more reliable. The sagas' descriptions of the new countries and their inhabitants are sufficiently clear to make it evident that these voyages actually took place. But their accounts have also been strengthened by two recent discoveries. In 1961–63 archeologists led by the Norwegian writer Helge Ingstad excavated ruins at L'Anse-aux-Meadows on the northern tip of Newfoundland. They found remains of

"The Landing of Leif Ericson" by Edward Moran depicts Ericson and his Viking crew landing on the North American continent. The painting is located at the U.S. Naval Academy, Annapolis, Md.
(BROWN BROTHERS)

iron extraction (the native Eskimos and Indians did not know how to extract iron) and coals, which were dated, by the radiocarbon method, from around 1000. In 1965 Yale University Press published the newly found Vinland map, dated by the editors c.1440. The map shows "Vinlanda Insula, discovered by the companions Bjarni and Leif."

THORHALLUR VILMUNDARSON, University of Iceland.
See also THORFINN KARLSEFNI; VINLAND.

ERICSSON, JOHN (1803–89), Swedish-American mechanical engineer remembered especially for his design of the ironclad American warship, the *Monitor*. With its revolving turrets, steam engines, and screw propulsion, it greatly strengthened the Northern naval forces in 1862 and revolutionized naval warfare. Born in Värmland, Sweden, Ericsson displayed prodigious energy and boldness of engineering concept in the Swedish military. In England he promoted his hot-air, or caloric, engine which employed a regenerator to capture the heat not utilized in driving the piston. Later, in the United States he designed the first screw-propelled warship, the USS *Princeton*. He met with several major engineering reverses resulting in part from his failure to take cognizance of advances in engineering.

THOMAS HUGHES, Washington and Lee University
See also MONITOR AND MERRIMACK.

ERIC THE RED (fl. 980–90), first European explorer and colonist of Greenland. According to the Icelandic *Landnámabók* ("Book of Settlements"), Eric was born in Norway, but migrated to Iceland with his father. From there, outlawed for manslaughter, he sailed (c.982) to Greenland, whose eastern coast had been previously visited by several Icelanders. Eric explored the east and west coasts of the country, naming it Greenland to entice immigrants. In 985 or 986 he led a fleet of 25 vessels sailing for Greenland from western Iceland. Only 14 ships reached their destination. The others turned back or perished.

Eric and his followers founded two colonies on the west coast—the Eastern Settlement, around present-day Julianehaab, and the Western Settlement, near Godthaab. Eric himself settled at Brattahlíd (now Kagssiarssuk) in the Eastern Settlement, where his wife, Thjódhild, later erected the first Christian church in North America (excavated in 1961–62). The Icelandic settlement in Greenland lasted for five centuries, but died out around 1500 for unknown reasons.

THÓRHALLUR VILMUNDARSON, University of Iceland

ERIDANUS [ĭ-rĭd′ə-nəs], known also as the River, a winter constellation consisting of an irregular stream of stars that extends from the constellation Orion, in the Northern Hemisphere, to the south circumpolar region. At the southern end of Eridanus is its brightest star, Achernar.

ERIDU [ā′rĭ-dōō], southernmost city of ancient Babylonia and, in Sumerian tradition, its first center of civilization. The city, which in antiquity lay on a lagoon of the Persian Gulf, was sacred to the god Enki (Ea). Its ruins (in modern Iraq), excavated in 1946–49 by Fuad Safar, antedate those of Al-Ubaid (c.3900–3500 B.C.).

John Ericsson, whose design of the USS *Monitor* during the Civil War radically influenced naval architecture. (CULVER PICTURES, INC.)

ERIE [ēr′ē], city of northwestern Pennsylvania, on Lake Erie, and seat of Erie County. The city is Pennsylvania's only lake port and is a diversified manufacturing center of great importance. Erie is also a marketing center for an agricultural region raising specialty crops, such as grapes and cherries. Presque Isle Peninsula encloses the city's fine harbor and offers facilities for a state park where surf bathing is enjoyed. Villa Maria College and a state soldiers' and sailors' home are located here. Originally the site of a French fort, Erie played a significant role in the War of 1812 as a base of naval operations under the command of Oliver Hazard Perry. Inc. as city, 1851; pop. (1950) 130,-803; (1960) 138,440.

ERIE, BATTLE OF LAKE, one of the most decisive battles (Sept. 10, 1813) on the Great Lakes during the War of

Oliver Hazard Perry's victory in the battle of Lake Erie, as depicted in a late 19th-century American lithograph. (CHICAGO HISTORICAL SOCIETY)

1812. The American commander, 28-year-old Capt. Oliver Hazard Perry, had 10 vessels mounting 55 guns. Six British ships (65 guns) led by Capt. Robert H. Barclay opposed him. The engagement began early in the afternoon. Each side drew its ships up in a line, Perry carefully holding a windward position. Perry's tactics were to concentrate fire on the head of the British line, but the *Niagara* failed to support his ship, the *Lawrence*, in time. The result was that British fire crippled the *Lawrence* and Perry was forced to move to the *Niagara*. Once aboard the *Niagara*, Perry maneuvered it so skillfully that its shots disabled the two strongest British ships, forcing Barclay to surrender. Perry then sent the message to Gen. William Henry Harrison telling of the victory: "We have met the enemy and they are ours." The victory placed Lake Erie firmly in American hands; the British, finding Canada vulnerable, had to evacuate Detroit and set up a line along the Niagara River.

ROBERT MIDDLEKAUFF, Yale University

ERIE, LAKE, fourth-largest and most southerly of the Great Lakes, located in northeastern United States and southeastern Canada. The lake is bordered by Ontario Province and the states of New York, Pennsylvania, Ohio, and Michigan. The international boundary approximately bisects the lake. Lake Erie is connected with Lake Huron by the Detroit River, Lake St. Clair, and the St. Clair River; with Lake Ontario by the Niagara River and Welland Canal (around Niagara Falls); and with the Hudson River by the New York State Barge Canal (enlarged Erie Canal). Islands include Bass and Kelleys (Ohio) and Pelee (Ontario). Erie is the shallowest of the Great Lakes and in perhaps 50,000 years may be drained because of the recession of Niagara Falls up the Niagara River.

Louis Jolliet is believed to have been the first European to see Lake Erie (1669), after which France claimed it. In 1763, following the French and Indian Wars, Great Britain took possession. Although the present boundaries were established in 1783 between Canada and the Northwest Territory of the United States, the region was disputed territory during the War of 1812. The Battle of Lake Erie, Commodore Oliver H. Perry's victory over the British (Sept., 1813), was one of the decisive engagements of that war.

Lake Erie is part of the Great Lakes–St. Lawrence Sea-

LAKE ERIE
AND THE
ERIE CANAL

0   50   100   150
Miles

way. Principal ports are Buffalo, N.Y.; Erie, Pa.; and Conneaut, Ashtabula, Cleveland, Lorain, Sandusky, and Toledo, Ohio. The lake usually is icebound from about Dec. 1 to Apr. 1. The principal cargo transported consists of iron ore, coal, and wheat. There is an important fruit-growing area along the lake in southeastern Ontario, western New York, northwestern Pennsylvania, and northeastern Ohio. Area, 9,940 sq. mi.; length, 241 mi.; width, 30–57 mi.; max. depth, 210 ft.; average depth, 100 ft.; surface elev., 572 ft.

PHYLLIS R. GRIESS, Pennsylvania State University

ERIE CANAL, the most successful American canal. This 363-mi. waterway, entirely in New York state, was constructed between 1817 and 1825, linking Lake Erie at Buffalo with the Hudson River at Albany. In the race among the eastern seaports to gain contact with the West, New York City thus had the great advantage of this water level route, in contrast to Boston, Philadelphia, and Baltimore. Governor DeWitt Clinton persuaded the state to undertake the construction, which cost some $7,000,000. The canal had 83 locks, each 90 ft. long. It was a success from the outset, with western wheat, flour, lumber, and whiskey finding an outlet and with imports and domestic manufactures flowing westward. Soon tolls totaled more than $1,000,000 annually and the state was reimbursed for the initial cost. The 218,000 tons of freight carried in 1825 had grown to 1,417,000 by 1840 and to 4,006,000 by 1856. Rochester, Syracuse, Utica, and other cities along the route flourished, as did Buffalo and Albany. The success of the Erie Canal encouraged much canal construction elsewhere in the country, but a combination of geography and economic conditions prevented most of the others from achieving success. Ultimately, railroad competition caused the Erie's business to dwindle away. In 1905 the enlarged New York State Barge Canal (q.v.) was commenced along the original canal's general course.

ROBERT G. ALBION, Harvard University

ERIGENA [ĕ-rĭj′ə-nə], **JOHN SCOTUS** (c.810–877), medieval philosopher. Born in Ireland and educated in Irish monasteries, Erigena was the most celebrated scholar of the 9th century. His *De Divisione Naturae*, composed probably between 862 and 866, is one of the most important works of the early Middle Ages. His basic teaching, resembling that of Plotinus, was that there is but one reality, God, from whom all things emanate. All being is divided into four classes: first, uncreated being which creates—God Himself; second, created being which also creates—the divine ideas, originating in the divine mind, the prototypes of all created beings; third, nature, which is created and does not create—that is, the world in general; fourth, that which neither creates nor is created, which is God considered as the end of all things.

Besides thus describing the cosmological process of creation as a return to God, Erigena developed as well the theme of the individual man's return to his creator, emphasizing the solidarity of mankind both in Adam's fall from grace and in Christ's resurrection from the dead. The writings of Erigena constitute a massive attempt to combine Christian theology with neoplatonic philosophy.

R. W. MULLIGAN, S.J., Loyola University, Chicago

ERIS [ēr′ĭs, ĕr′ĭs], Greek goddess of discord, the Roman Discordia, sister and companion of Ares. She tossed an apple among the guests at the wedding feast of Peleus and Thetis, inscribed to the fairest. This incident led to the Trojan War.

ERITREA [ĕr-ĭ-trē′ə], formerly an Italian colony, now a province of the Empire of Ethiopia. With a population of about 1,000,000 and an area of 45,754 sq. mi., Eritrea lies in northeast Africa on the Red Sea and is bordered by the Sudan on the west. The central Eritrean plateau (from 6,000 to 8,000 ft.) contrasts boldly with the arid Danakil depression and the desert coastal strip. There are numerous ethnic groups, the main ones being the Tigrinya-speaking Coptic Christians and the nomadic Arab-Beja and Dankali who are Muslims. The approximately 10,000 Italians are found mainly in the capital, Asmara, which is also an agricultural and commercial center, and in the ports of Massawa and Assab. The principal products are citrus fruits, hides and skins, cereals, and cotton.

Eritrea, long the possession of Ethiopia, was seized by the Ottoman Turks in the 16th century. After several Italian expeditions in the 1860's and 1870's, Assab Bay was declared an Italian possession in 1882. Control over all of Eritrea was established in 1890. The colony became the main staging point of the Italian invasion of Ethiopia in 1935. In 1952, under a resolution of the United Nations, Eritrea became an autonomous unit of the federation of Ethiopia and Eritrea. On Nov. 14, 1962, both Eritrea's legislative assembly and the Ethiopian parliament, in a joint action, decided to end Eritrea's federated status by uniting it with Ethiopia as a province of the Ethiopian Empire.

A. A. CASTAGNO, Queens College

ERIVAN. *See* YEREVAN OR ERIVAN.

ERLANGEN [ĕr′läng-ən], city in Bavaria, Federal Republic of Germany (West Germany), at the confluence of the Regnitz and Schwabach rivers. The Huguenots who fled to Erlangen after the revocation of the Edict of Nantes (1685) introduced various industries. Today the center of Germany's electromedical production, it also manufactures cotton, musical instruments, paint, paper, and beer. In 1706 a fire so destroyed the Old City that it had to be completely rebuilt. Erlangen became a possession of Bavaria in 1810. Pop., 69,552.

ERLANGER [ûr′läng-ər], JOSEPH (1874–), American physician and physiologist known for his studies of nervous function. In 1944 he shared the Nobel Prize with Herbert S. Gasser for their work *Electrical Signs of Nervous Activity*. He taught at Johns Hopkins, Wisconsin Medical School, and, since 1910, he has been at the Washington School of Medicine, where he became professor emeritus in 1946.

ERLANGER [ûr′läng-ər], town of northern Kentucky and a residential suburb, 7 mi. southwest of Covington. Pop. (1950) 3,694; (1960) 7,072.

Waagenaar—Pix

Salt flats in Eritrea. Large areas of land are flooded with sea water. After the water evaporates, salt is dug up by hand and loaded onto trucks by a series of conveyor belts.

ERLENMEYER [ĕr′lən-mī-ər], EMIL (1825–1909), German organic chemist who aided in the development of the structural theory of organic chemistry. He was at first a pharmacist, but turned to chemistry and taught at Heidelberg where he worked with F. A. Kekulé. He was one of the first to adopt and apply the Kekulé theory of the nature of carbon compounds. He also arrived at the correct structure of naphthalene, and worked on the structures of aliphatic alcohols and acids.

ERLKÖNIG [ĕrl′kû-nĭKH] (Eng., "Elf King"), ballad by Goethe inspired by Herder's translation of a Danish poem. The German *Erlkönig* is an incorrect translation of Danish *ellekonge* or "elf king." The Danish words for elf and alder (Ger. *Erle*) are identical. This fact probably contributed to the Norwegian and Danish belief that elves prefer alder trees. Goethe's poem, describing the demonic forces of nature, was set to music by Schubert in 1815.

ERMAN [ĕr′män], ADOLF (1854–1937), German Egyptologist, first to understand the structure of the ancient Egyptian language. From his first article, published in 1875, he systematically examined the morphology and syntax of the successive phases of the written language. The final edition of his works in this area were *Aegyptische Grammatik* (4th ed., 1928) and *Neuaegyptische Grammatik* (2d ed., 1933). He created and headed the group for the collection of materials for, and publication of, *Wörterbuch der aegyptischen Sprache* (11 vols., 1926–53). His popular books were translated into other languages and introduced many to ancient Egyptian culture.

ERMINE [ûr′mĭn], small, weasel-like animal, *Mustela erminea*, in the family Mustelidae of fur-bearing carnivores. The ermine, or stoat as it is also called, is found in cooler, northern and central regions of Europe and Asia. It lives mostly in wooded areas and feeds voraciously on birds, reptiles, small mammals, and eggs. Its valuable pelt, long a symbol of royalty, is white only in the winter; during the summer the ermine is brownish-red with a yellowish underside. A closely related species, *M. hibernica*, occurs in Ireland but unlike the true ermine, does not turn white in the winter.

ERNST [ĕrnst], **MAX** (1891–   ), German surrealist painter. He helped introduce the iconoclastic Dada movement in Cologne in 1919. In the 1920's in Paris he became identified with the surrealists, who sought to express the unconscious mind. His unconventional techniques have included collage (pasting together unrelated materials) and frottage (the making of rubbings by placing paper over an object, such as a wood plank, and running graphite over it).

EROICA [ĕ-rō'ĭ-kə] **SYMPHONY,** orchestral composition by Ludwig van Beethoven (No. 3, in E♭ Major, Op. 55, 1804). The symphony, an expansion rather than an alteration of 18th-century classical structure, was Beethoven's first step toward immensity (it is 47 minutes in length). The composer first dedicated the work to Napoleon Bonaparte, but removed the dedication when Napoleon proclaimed himself Emperor. The new title read *Sinfonia eroica composta per festeggiare il sovvenire d'un grand' uomo* (heroic symphony composed to celebrate a great man's memory). The substance of the work is heroism itself, eloquent in each movement; the powerful and militant opening Allegro, the deeply affecting Funeral March, the swift and incisive Scherzo, and the triumphant Finale in variation form.

EROS [ēr'ŏs, ĕr'ŏs], Greek god of love in all its manifestations, the Roman Cupid. According to Hesiod he was born from Chaos, after Gaea and Tartarus, the third being in the world. Later writers gave him various parents. Usually his mother was Aphrodite, his father Ares, Zeus, or Hermes. In art he is represented as a winged boy carrying bow and arrows. These arrows implanted the love passion in any creature they struck: even Zeus and Hades were susceptible. Eros also had an arrow that could turn against love. He had important cults at Thespiae in Boeotia and at Parium on the Hellespont. Called Cupid in the Latin text of Apuleius' *Metamorphoses*, he was the unseen bridegroom of Psyche (Soul).

EROSION [ĭ-rō'zhən], gradual but continuous wearing down of the earth's land surface. It involves the loosening and removal of rock particles and soil materials, generally carrying them from higher to lower levels. This is brought about both by chemical and by physical processes, working sometimes together, sometimes separately. The chief

Erosion can be as devastating to arable land as fire is to forests. These once rich wheat fields in the U.S. Northwest lie barren from the effects of severe erosion.

USDA—Monkmeyer

Ausable Chasm, a deep gorge carved by the Ausable River in the Adirondack Mountains in northeast New York State.
(PHILIP GENDREAU)

EROSION BY WATER, WIND, AND ICE

The wearing effect of wind has created these jutting rocks in Bryce Canyon in Utah. (RUSS KINNE)

Athabaska Glacier in Jasper National Park, Canada. The scouring action of the ice erodes the surface of the land to produce a valley with flat bottom and steep sides. (DAVID W. CROSON)

513

agents of erosion are running water, underground water, waves and currents along shores, glacial ice, and wind. Working through the hundreds of millions of years of geologic time, these seemingly weak agents have produced tremendous changes and they are still vigorously at work.

Weathering, or rock decay, is the starting point for erosion. It involves the breakdown of the hardest rocks by chemical solution and decomposition, together with mechanical splitting and disintegration by frost action and other forces. The resulting products range in size from clay and sand to cobbles and boulders, ready for pickup and removal by other processes.

Water. Running water is the most important single agent of erosion; it includes the work of rills, rivulets, and sheet flow, as well as of streams and rivers. These agents, aided by the gradual creep of the soil and more rapid landsliding on valley sides, pick up the materials prepared by weathering and carry them down river, ultimately to the sea. A measure of the rate of this process has been provided by studies of the Mississippi River, which was found to carry more than 1,000,000 tons of sediment to the Gulf of Mexico every day. At this rate the land surface of the river's entire drainage area would be lowered about one ft. in 5,000 years, on the average. Given time enough, the entire area would be reduced almost to sea level, or to an imaginary limiting surface called base-level, unless other forces intervened to raise the land surface. Thus streams continuously modify the valleys in which they flow, and, going back in time, they are found to have themselves created these valleys.

Stream erosion is fundamentally a natural process, but it can be accelerated by the work of man. The clearing of forests and the breaking of sod for cultivation, together with improper farming methods, have caused the formation of gullies and the washing away of valuable top soil, in some places making the land useless for cultivation.

Rain water seeping into and moving slowly through the ground is a less conspicuous but still important agent of erosion. It contributes to weathering, and gradually eats away soluble rocks such as limestone and gypsum, producing caves, "blind" valleys, sink holes or "swallow holes," and the generally irregular terrain called karst topography. A measure of the total importance of this process is found in river-water analyses, which indicate that some streams carry more than 100 tons of dissolved material per year for each square mile of drainage area.

The erosive attack of waves on the shore produces characteristic sea cliffs, sea caves, and other coastal features, while the material taken away is ground to sand or pebble size and deposited on beaches, bars, or spits.

Glaciers. Glacial ice is another powerful agent of erosion, both in high mountains that have or once had their own glaciers, and over great areas in northern and southern latitudes once covered by huge ice sheets, such as those of Greenland and Antarctica today. Advancing ice plowed off the original soil and scraped and sculptured the bare rock into distinctive knobs, ridges, and valleys. The material removed was later dropped in heaps, sheets, or ridges called moraines, sometimes hundreds of miles from its source.

Wind. Wind is, in general, the least important erosional agent, working mainly in desert areas. Locally its effects are spectacular, however. Desert sandstorms and dust storms can move enormous tonnages of material through the air. The erosive effects of wind-borne particles are found in distinctively grooved, fluted, and pitted rock surfaces. Wind erosion also forms undrained basins which, in regions such as North Africa, may be tens to hundreds of square miles in area and hundreds of feet deep, even extending below sea level.

Consult Cotton, C. A., *Geomorphology* (1952).

H. T. U. SMITH, University of Massachusetts
See also GEOMORPHOLOGY; NATURAL RESOURCES, CONSERVATION OF; PHYSIOGRAPHY.

ERRATIC [ĭ-răt′ĭk], in geology, a fragment of bedrock, or a boulder, that differs from the bedrock beneath it. Most erratics have been transported by glacial ice, some of them hundreds of miles. They can be any size or shape. Some are inclosed in glacial drift, and others lie free on the ground. The presence of erratics usually is considered proof of former glaciation.
See also GLACIAL DEPOSITS.

ERROR, in measurement, the range around a stated measurement within which the true measurement probably lies. Numerals are used to represent the result of a counting of objects or the result of the measurement of some object with a measuring instrument. If the numeral arises as a result of counting, it can be exact, but if it arises as a result of measuring, it is approximate. In measuring any object, for example the diameter of a piston, there are many sources of error. Some of these are physical, such as the change in size of the object and the measuring instrument due to such factors as temperature, pressure, or humidity. Others arise because someone has to make the measurement and read the measuring instrument. If it is desirable to get a measurement as accurate as possible, several competent observers make the measurement a number of times under controlled conditions and record all measurements. The arithmetic mean of the measurements is called the measurement and the greatest deviation from this is called the error. The relative error is often found by dividing the error by the measurements. This is often expressed as a percentage and is the most useful way of describing an error.

HOWARD E. WAHLERT, New York University

ERSKINE [ûr′skĭn], **JOHN** (1879–1951), American writer and educator. Born in New York City, he was educated at Columbia, where he taught English for almost 30 years. He was the author of several volumes of poetry and literary criticism and coeditor of the *Cambridge History of American Literature*. He was best known, however, for his satirical modern versions of ancient legends, in such novels as *The Private Life of Helen of Troy* (1925), *Galahad* (1926), and *Adam and Eve* (1927). In later life he became a concert pianist and was president (1928–37) of the Juilliard School of Music.

ERVINE [ûr′vĭn], **ST. JOHN GREER** (1883–   ), Irish dramatist, dramatic critic, and novelist. He is best known for his work for the stage, including the early problem plays *Mixed Marriage* (1910), *Jane Clegg* (1911), and *John*

Ferguson (1914), and a group of later comedies, including *The First Mrs. Fraser* (1928).

ERYSIPELAS [ĕr-ə-sĭp'ə-ləs] **or ST. ANTHONY'S FIRE,** an infectious skin disease caused by bacteria of the streptococcus group. In some cases the disease is preceded by an infection of the nose or throat. It may occur in persons suffering from wounds or from chronic skin diseases.

Although erysipelas can occur anywhere on the body, it usually appears on the face. After a one- or two-day incubation period, the patient develops chills and fever. The involved area appears as a sharply marked red, swollen patch of skin which may be hot and painful. If not treated a skin abscess may develop. Penicillin is effective in treating erysipelas.

ERYTHROBLASTOSIS FETALIS. *See* RH FACTOR.

ERZBERGER [ĕrts'bĕr-gər], **MATTHIAS** (1875–1921), German statesman. A liberal member of the Catholic Center Party, Erzberger was the chief architect of the Reichstag resolution of 1917 calling for a "peace without annexations." In Oct., 1918, he entered the Cabinet of Prince Maximilian of Baden as Minister without Portfolio and signed the armistice that ended the war. After the fall of the empire Erzberger entered the Cabinet of Philipp Scheidemann, but disagreed with his chief's refusal to sign the Treaty of Versailles. He became Finance Minister under Scheidemann's successor, Gustav Bauer. In this post he directed the consolidation of the German railroads and reorganized the tax system, introducing new property and income taxes.

Erzberger became known as the "best hated man in Germany"—the capitalists hated his financial policy, the Protestants his Catholicism, the militarists his role in the war, armistice, and treaty. After a libel suit in which he failed to clear his name of charges of malfeasance in office, he resigned early in 1921 and in August of that year was murdered by nationalist extremists.

Consult Epstein, Klaus, *Matthias Erzberger and the Dilemma of German Democracy* (1959).

PETER NOVICK, Columbia University

ERZGEBIRGE [ĕrts'gə-bĭr-gə], mountain range on the border of Germany and Czechoslovakia. It is about 80 mi. in length and about 25 mi. wide, with a highest elevation of 4,080 ft. The Erzgebirge is rich in minerals, especially silver, lead, copper, iron, and bismuth.

ERZURUM [ĕr-zə-rōōm'], city of eastern Turkey, and capital of the province of Erzurum, located in rugged mountainous territory at an elevation of 6,000 ft. Erzurum is on the transit route from Trabzon, on the Black Sea, to Iran. The city is a center for the production of cereals, potatoes, and sugar cane, and ranks first in Turkey's livestock breeding. It is the headquarters of the Third Army. The Atatürk University, established in 1957 with the co-operation of the University of Nebraska, is Turkey's main educational center east of Ankara. Pop., 91,196.

ESARHADDON [ē-sär-hăd'ən], Assyrian King (reigned 680–669 B.C.), son of Sennacherib. Throughout his reign he was busy fighting and enlarging the frontiers of the Assyrian Empire. He first crushed a rebellion of the Chaldaeans, then reconstructed the city and temples of Babylon, destroyed by his father. He conquered Media, broke Elam's power, and subdued Palestine and Syria. He also repelled the Cimmerians in the northwest. His greatest military achievement, however, was the conquest of Egypt, begun in 674 B.C. and completed in 671 with the taking of the Egyptian capital Memphis. Esarhaddon reorganized Egypt into 22 administrative units placed under local princes who were supervised by Assyrian officials, whose main duty was the regular collection of tribute. Esarhaddon named two of his sons to succeed him— Ashurbanipal in Assyria, and Shamash-shum-ukin in Babylonia.

ESAU [ē'sô], elder son of Isaac and Rebecca, and twin brother of Jacob (Gen. 25:21–26). A skillful hunter, Esau was the favorite of Isaac, who ate of his venison; but Rebecca loved Jacob. One time when he was weary from hunting, Esau sold his birthright to Jacob for a mess of red pottage (Gen. 25:27–34), whence he was also called Edom (Heb. for "red"); and later Rebecca and Jacob tricked Isaac into giving Jacob the blessing Isaac intended for Esau. Esau was the ancestor of the Edomites (Gen. 25:30, 36:1,8), a nation settled in Palestine in the valley south of the Dead Sea. The Israelites called them brothers, although after the Jewish exile a more hostile attitude developed. Under the Roman occupation Edom became Idumea.

ESBJERG [ĕs'byărKH], chief fishing port of Denmark, located on the west coast of Jutland. A new city, Esbjerg developed around the state-owned harbor begun in 1868. Today it ranks second only to Copenhagen in the volume of its export trade and has an important passenger transit traffic to and from England. Its industries include fish processing, the refining of herring oil, shipbuilding, flour milling, meat packing, and the manufacture of tobacco and chemical products. Pop., 55,171.

ESCALATOR [ĕs'kə-lā-tər], mechanical conveyer consisting of continuously moving steps, generally used to carry people from one floor level to another. Driven by hidden chains, drive sprockets, motors, and guides, escalators are usually inclined about 30° from the horizontal and are made to travel either up or down at a speed of about 90 ft. per minute.

The first escalator was built by the Otis Elevator Company and exhibited at the Paris Exhibition in 1900. The following year it was installed in Gimbel's Department Store in Philadelphia, where it remained in operation until 1939. The longest escalator in the world, which covers a vertical distance of 81 ft., is located in the Leicester Square station of the London subway and carries passengers to and from ground level to the train platform.

ESCANABA [ĕs-kə-nä'bə], city of northern Michigan, and leading port on the south shore of the state's Upper Peninsula. Iron ore is exported. Industries include manufacture of wood veneer, paper, hardwood products, and chemicals. Escanaba is the resort center for the surrounding hunting and fishing areas. Pop. (1950) 15,170; (1960) 15,391.

ESCAPEMENT. See CLOCK.

ESCAPE VELOCITY, velocity which an object must have in order to escape from the gravitational field of a parent body. The escape velocity v is given by the formula $v = \sqrt{2GM/r}$ where G is the Newtonian constant of gravitation; M, the mass of the parent body; and r, the radius or distance from the center of the body, at which the velocity is to be computed.

A space ship which has attained escape velocity can turn off its engines and coast without further expenditure of energy. The escape velocity from the earth is 7 mi. per second. To leave the moon, a speed of 1.2 mi. per second is needed; to leave the sun, 383 mi. per second; and to leave the solar system, starting from the earth's orbit, 26.2 mi. per second.

ESCAUT RIVER. See SCHELDT RIVER.

ESCHATOLOGY [ĕs-kə-tŏl′ə-jē], doctrine of the last things, that is, what will happen at the end of history. There is eschatology in the Old Testament in such books as Isaiah, Ezekiel, Zechariah, and Daniel; and in the New Testament some of the teachings of Jesus take an eschatological form (Matt. 24; Mark 13). In other New Testament writings, especially I and II Thessalonians, and above all the book of Revelation, the end of history is associated with a second coming of Christ.

In modern theology three treatments of eschatology should be noted. First is that of Albert Schweitzer, the famous theologian and missionary doctor, who interprets Jesus as having expected the imminent end of the world. Second is that of C. H. Dodd, the English New Testament scholar, who considers that Old Testament promises received their fulfilment at the Incarnation and that the eschatology is thus realized. Third is that of Rudolf Bultmann, the German New Testament scholar, who considers that the believer who realizes that the death of Jesus Christ, unlike, for instance, the death of Julius Caesar, is all-important for him today, has come face to face with an event which is more than merely historical and has in that sense reached the end of history.
Consult Dodd, C. H., *The Parables of the Kingdom* (1935); Bultmann, R., *History and Eschatology* (1957).

IAN HENDERSON, University of Glasgow

ESCH-SUR-ALZETTE [ĕsh′sür-àl-zĕt′], second-largest city in Luxembourg, 10 mi. southwest of the city of Luxembourg, on the Alzette River near the French border. Esch is the center of Luxembourg's important iron and steel industry. It also produces cement, tar, liquors, and fertilizers and is a market center for grains. In the Middle Ages it was a fortified city belonging at different times to Burgundy, Spain, France, Austria, and Holland. During World War I and World War II it was occupied by the Germans. Pop., 27,842.

ESCHWEILER [ĕsh′vī-lər], town in North Rhine–Westphalia, Federal Republic of Germany (West Germany),

located in a mining region. Its largest industry is the manufacture of steel products. During World War II it was captured by U.S. troops after heavy fighting (Nov., 1944). Pop., 39,590.

ESCOFFIER [ĕs-kô-fyā′], **AUGUSTE** (1847–1935), world-renowned French chef famous for his contribution to gourmet tradition and the development of modern restaurant practices. With César Ritz, Escoffier operated the Ritz in Paris, the Savoy in London, and the Grand Hotel in Monte Carlo. Author of a number of books on the art of cooking, he was made a member of the French Legion of Honor in 1920.

ESCONDIDO [ĕs-kən-dē′dō], city of western California, in the foothills northeast of San Diego. It is the center of a citrus-, avocado-, and walnut-growing area and has some light manufacturing. Several recreational lakes are nearby. Pop. (1950) 6,544; (1960) 16,377.

ESCORIAL or ESCURIAL [ĕs-kôr′ē-əl, *Spanish* ās-kō-ryäl′], more properly, San Lorenzo del Escorial, monastery, church, palace, mausoleum, and library, the most famous Renaissance structure in Spain. A complex of connected buildings in one structure, it is situated in the mountains, 31 mi. northwest of Madrid. According to tradition, it was begun in Apr., 1563, for Philip II to fulfill a vow he made for victory over the French at Saint-Quentin. This occurred on Aug. 10, 1557, a day dedicated to St. Lawrence, for whom the Escorial is named. The architect was Juan Bautista de Toledo; he was succeeded on his death in 1567 by Juan de Herrera. The work was completed Sept. 13, 1584.

The Escorial, with an area of nearly 400,000 sq. ft., is built on the plan of a rectangle. It is in the severe, unadorned architectural style popular in the period of Philip II. Underneath the altar of the church is located the royal mausoleum, in which are buried the Kings and Queens of Spain. The Escorial contains frescoes by Pellegrino Tibaldi and Luca Giordano and pictures by Titian, Tintoretto, El Greco, and Velázquez. Some of the most famous paintings have been removed to the Prado in Madrid.

WILLIAM H. GERDTS, The Newark Museum

ESCROW [ĕs′krō] is a deed, money, or chattel given to a person, the holder, by another for the purpose of delivering it to a third person upon fulfillment of a specific condition, such as the payment of the purchase price. Prior to the fulfillment of the condition, the escrow holder has the authority to deal with the subject matter in accordance with the agreement of the parties, and this power cannot be terminated without their consent. If the condition is fulfilled within a prescribed time, the escrow is to be delivered to the third party; otherwise, the escrow holder must return it to the depositor. An escrow is frequently used in transactions of real estate.

ESCUDERO [ĕs-kōō-dā′rō], **VICENTE** (1892–   ), Spanish dancer, born in Valladolid. Following his highly successful Paris debut at the Olympia Theater in 1920, flamenco dancing became the vogue in Paris. He subsequently toured Europe and made his New York debut in

The Escorial, the immense palace, monastery, and mausoleum built for Philip II of Spain. A man of austere tastes, Philip ordered that the structure be constructed in an unadorned, classic style.

J. Allen Cash—Rapho-Guillumette

1932. In 1954, together with Carmita Garcia, he formed a company which opened at the Champs-Élysées Theater in Paris. Although his specialty was flamenco dance, Escudero was an innovator. He created and used metal castanets; he used a chair for beating out rhythms which contrasted with those of his tapping feet; and he is credited with being the first stage performer to dance the flamenco Seguiriyas.

ESDAILE [ĕs'dāl], **ARUNDELL JAMES KENNEDY** (1880–1956), English bibliographer and librarian. He joined the staff of the British Museum in 1903, assisted in the preparation of its famous *Catalogue of XVth Century Books,* and was secretary of the institution (1926–40). From 1923 to 1935 he edited the *Library Association Record* and from 1939 to 1945 he was president of the Library Association. His bibliographical writings, including *Student's Manual of Bibliography* (1931), won him international fame.

ESDRAELON [ĕz-drə-ē'lən], **PLAIN OF,** name of the great plain cutting across northern Palestine, which in ancient times was the site of major Palestinian cities (Megiddo, Taanach, Beth-shan), and of many great battles. Between the 16th and 13th centuries B.C., it was a source of grain for Egypt, and beginning in the 10th century it was an Israelite province ruled from Megiddo. The name is a Greek modification of Jezreel, another of the towns within its borders.

ESDRAS [ĕz'drəs], **BOOKS OF,** two books of the Old Testament Apocrypha. I Esdras is a history of the Jewish people from 621 B.C. to the mid-5th century and is parallel to the canonical Chronicles-Ezra-Nehemiah, except for the added story of three youths at the court of Darius and the contest ending with the praise of Truth. II Esdras is a Jewish apocalypse of the 1st century A.D. with Christian additions (1–2, 15–16). Its author attempts to give a theological explanation of the fall of Jerusalem, but finally admits that he cannot do so.

ESHER, urban district of northern Surrey, England, located on the southwestern fringe of London. It is primarily a residential area, consisting of the 11 separate settlements of West Molesey, East Molesey, Thames, Long Ditton, Hinchley Wood, Esher, Claygate, Oxshott, Stoke D'Abernon, Church, and Street Cobham. Pop., 60,586.

ESHKOL [ĕsh'kōl], **LEVI,** original surname Shkolnik (1895–   ), Israeli statesman and Prime Minister. Born in the Ukraine and educated in Vilnius (now in Lithuania), he emigrated to Palestine in 1913. He worked principally in agricultural affairs and later as secretary of Histadrut, the national labor federation. Appointed Minister of Agriculture in 1951, he was Minister of Finance from 1952 to 1963, and then took office as Prime Minister. A seething intra-party conflict over the so-called Lavon affair (a bungled 1954 espionage mission in Cairo) erupted as a full-scale split in 1965, with Eshkol's predecessor, David Ben-Gurion, as his principal opponent leading a splinter party. Despite some defections, Eshkol and his government weathered the storm and won a majority of Kneset seats in the general elections of Nov., 1965.

ESKER, winding ridge of roughly stratified glacial debris. Eskers may be branching or discontinuous, but usually they extend for many miles as steep-sided ridges 20 to 100 ft. high. They are thought to have been deposited by meltwater streams flowing beneath stagnant, wasting continental glaciers, since moving ice sheets would destroy them.
See also GLACIAL DEPOSITS.

ESKILSTUNA [ā'shĭl-stoō-nä], industrial city of central Sweden, some 50 mi. west of Stockholm. The center of a diversified metal-working industry, Eskilstuna leads all other Swedish cities in the manufacture of iron and steel products. Incorporated in 1659, Eskilstuna was a major Swedish arsenal during the 17th and 18th centuries. The city's name may be traced to St. Eskil, an English missionary martyred here in the 11th century. Pop., 53,386.

517

ESKIMO [ĕs′kə-mō], aborigines living along the shores of the Arctic Ocean from eastern Greenland across North America to eastern Siberia, a territory extending about 6,000 mi. from east to west. The word "Eskimo" comes from one of the Algonkian languages, probably Abnaki, Cree, or Ojibwa, and means "eaters of raw flesh." The Eskimo call themselves *Inuit* meaning "people." They speak the Eskimo language, which together with the Aleut language (spoken primarily in the Aleutian Islands), comprises the Eskimo-Aleut linguistic family.

The Eskimo, like the other North American Indians, are classified as belonging to the Mongoloid racial stock, but their physical appearance is distinctive. They are short and muscular, with light-brown skins; broad, flat faces; high, narrow noses; and rather highly vaulted heads. The epicanthic fold in the eyelid, characteristic of Mongoloid peoples, occurs frequently. In disposition, they are usually described as peaceful, cheerful, honest, generous, and hospitable.

Just as the Eskimo are distinct from other American aborigines in language and physical type, so too are they distinct in culture. Despite regional variations in aboriginal Eskimo culture, it is substantially uniform throughout its range. The basic cultural inventory of the Eskimo includes a dependence on sea mammals for food, distinctive techniques for hunting them from ice, the use of the spear thrower, inflated sealskins as drags on harpoon lines, tailored skin clothing, skin-covered boats, the snowhouse (igloo), the stone blubber lamp, stone pots, sledges drawn by dogs, and the three- or four-pronged bird spear. These various tools and habits sharply distinguish Eskimo material culture from the cultures of the Indians living to the south on the North American continent.

Regional variations in subsistence techniques depend largely on environment. The seal is the principal source of food for most of the Eskimo. They take seals by harpooning them when they rise to breathe at their blowholes, by stalking them over ice, by harpooning them from a kayak (a skin-covered boat holding one man), or with nets. This last method is especially prominent in Alaska. The Eskimo living away from the coast in Alaska and those living inland west of Hudson Bay subsist chiefly by hunting caribou. Consequently their principal techniques of hunting are adapted to these animals and are very different from the techniques for taking sea mammals. A formerly important method of hunting caribou was to drive the animals between converging rows of posts into corrals, where hunters shot them with arrows, or into the water, where the hunters speared them from kayaks. The Eskimo living on the north coast of Alaska depend for food primarily upon whales, which are hunted from large skin-covered boats called umiaks by teams of men under a leader. In areas where whales are not hunted, the umiak is lacking or is used only for transport. The Eskimo of southern Alaska depend mainly on fish, especially salmon, which are taken in large quantities during their annual runs.

The regional differences regarding subsistence techniques affect other cultural patterns such as housing and clothing. The Eskimo who hunt sea mammals build substantial, permanent winter houses. On the west coast of Greenland, they are made of stone covered with sod; on Greenland's east coast, they have a frame of timber, a wooden roof covered with sod, and walls of stone and sod; and in northern Alaska, semisubterranean sod-covered plank houses are built. Most of the Eskimo who are primarily coastal dwellers and hunters of sea mammals move inland during the summer to hunt caribou. At such times they live in skin-covered tents which can be easily moved to follow the shifting caribou. Those Eskimo of Alaska who live permanently inland use the skin-covered tent the year round. The caribou hunters west of Hudson Bay use the skin tent in summer and make temporary winter houses of snow blocks. The snowhouse is known to all the Eskimo and is used as a temporary shelter when traveling during the winter. Clothing differences depend upon the availability of particular animal skins. Caribou is widely used if available, but where it is scarce, as on the northwest coast of Greenland, sealskins and polar bear skins provide most clothing.

When cultural elements other than those connected with subsistence are considered, it is possible to demarcate two subareas in the Eskimo culture area: a western and a central-eastern subarea, with the Mackenzie River as the dividing line. To the west, in Alaska, some Eskimo use labrets (plugs worn in holes in the lip), masks, hats, coiled basketry, and pottery. Grave monuments, mourning feasts, modest property distributions, and war parties are also part of their culture. Most of these traits were probably learned from the Tlingit Indians of the northwest coast culture area and are usually absent east of the Mackenzie.

Eskimo social structure is unelaborate. The nuclear family of husband, wife, and children is the basic social unit. Although families live together in villages for at least part of the year, each family is independent of all others. Villages have no governing bodies or headmen. Antisocial acts such as murder may be punished by death, either through the operation of the blood feud or by an informal sentence of a group.

Stanley A. Freed, American Museum of Natural History
See also Indian Tribes, North American.

ESKIMO-ALEUT [ĕs′kə-mō–ăl′ē-ōōt] **LANGUAGES,** linguistic family occupying the northern coastal areas of America. Proof is lacking for a relation between Eskimo-Aleut and any other language family of either hemisphere. The Eskimo branch of the family comprises two languages, each with several dialects: Inupik from Greenland westward through Canada to the Bering Strait region in Alaska, and Yupik in southern and southwestern Alaska and at the eastern tip of Siberia. The difference between Inupik and Yupik is comparable to that between English and German. The Aleut language, however, spoken principally in the Aleutian Islands, differs from Eskimo very markedly.

ESKIMO DOG, a recognized breed of dog of the working group. The name is also applied loosely to all Arctic dogs, as is "husky." The Eskimo dog has a broad, wedge-shaped head, sloping toward the muzzle; small, deep-set eyes; and erect, forward-pointing ears. It has heavy-boned legs with large, well-padded paws, a strong chest, bushy tail, and a coat from 3 to 6 in. long that may be white, gray, tan, bluish, or combinations of these colors. Adult males stand 23 in. at the shoulder and weigh about 65 lb. The Eskimo dog is a hardy, useful breed: It pulls sleds, sleeps in the snow,

ESKIMO LIFE

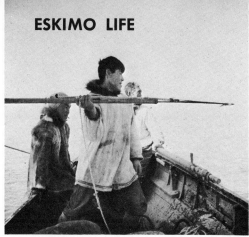

Hudson's Bay Co., Canada

An Eskimo hunter prepares to harpoon a whale. A thong on the weapon prevents it from being lost.

American Museum of Natural History

Successful whalers cutting up a catch. The men at left are standing in an open, skin-covered boat used on whaling expeditions.

Marc Riboud—Magnum

An Eskimo child wearing a warm parka fitted snugly around head and neck.

A dog team is unharnessed in northern Alaska. In the background are a sod house (*center*) and a skin-covered tent, which is used as a summer home.

Burt Glinn—Magnum

Setting a fish net under the ice. Many Eskimo live near the sea and depend largely on fish for food.

Hudson's Bay Co., Canada

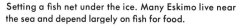

Sturdy Eskimo dogs pull a sled over the snow (*below*). The dogs have an undercoat of short, woolly hair, which keeps them warm and dry.

Hudson's Bay Co., Canada

and is a faithful worker and companion. Like other Arctic dogs, the Eskimo dog feeds mainly on fish.

ESKIMO POINT, settlement of Northwest Territories, Canada, in Keewatin District, on the west coast of Hudson Bay. A Royal Canadian Mounted Police detachment, a trading post, and a Roman Catholic mission serve the Eskimos of the region. Pop., 98.

ESKIŞEHIR [ĕs-kē-shē-hēr'], city of central Turkey, and capital of the province of Eskişehir. It is one of the main junctions of the Turkish railway system. Eskişehir is an important industrial city, with sugar, cement, and brick factories, and flour mills, airplane plants, and railway workshops. It is also famous for its meerschaum, which is carved into pipes, cigarette holders, and ornamental objects. The Eskişehir Dryfarming Experimental Station is an important research center for Turkey's agriculture. The principal Turkish Air Force installations and the Air Force War College are located here. Pop., 153,190.

ESNAULT-PELTERIE, ROBERT ALBERT CHARLES (1881–1957), French engineer and inventor who pioneered in both aviation and space travel. While still a student in Paris he tried to build a helicopter but abandoned the project. When news of the Wright brothers' experiments reached France he constructed a glider of a similar type and made soaring flights near the Channel.

Deciding that a biplane was too difficult to handle he built one of the earliest monoplanes, and flew it in 1907. He also built its engine and invented the joy stick, a movable lever, for the control of his airplane. It was the first airplane with a frame of welded steel tubing. After demonstrating it, Esnault-Pelterie received an official French pilot's license, No. 4.

In 1912 the possibility of travel into space caught his imagination, and he spent the next 15 years working out the mathematical basis. He delivered a lecture on "Exploration of the Upper Atmosphere by Rockets and the Possibility of Interplanetary Travel" to the Société Astronomique in 1927. It was later printed and then expanded into a large book called *l'Astronautique*, the title of which is the origin for the current term "astronautics" for space travel.

In 1928 Robert Esnault-Pelterie, nicknamed REP, and the banker André Hirsch established the REP-Hirsch Prize for Astronautics, to be awarded annually. In 1931 he designed his first liquid-fuel rocket motor. With support from the French Air Ministry he built the motor for a rocket designed to reach an altitude of 60 mi. This work was interrupted by the fall of Paris in 1940 and never resumed. After the war he retired to Switzerland.

WILLY LEY, Author, *Rockets, Missiles, and Space Travel*

ESOPHAGUS [ĭ-sŏf'ə-gəs], the slender, hollow tube through which food passes from the throat to the stomach. It begins in the neck as a continuation of the pharynx; descends behind the heart and in front of the spinal column; then passes through the diaphragm into the abdominal cavity where it joins the stomach. The walls of the esophagus are largely composed of muscle arranged in two layers. The rhythmic contractions and relaxations of the muscle, known as peristalsis, move food through the esophagus toward the stomach.
See also DIGESTION; PERISTALSIS.

ESP, abbreviation for Extrasensory Perception. *See* PARAPSYCHOLOGY.

ESPALIER [ĕs-păl'yər], trellis or open support on which a tree or woody perennial plant is grown. The term is also used to describe the tree or plant itself. Espalier, or wall trees as they are often called, are usually single-stemmed and are either naturally dwarfed or have been grown on stocks of dwarf plants. Espalier-training is done by tying the branches to the support, removing any unwanted growth as it appears. The trees may be trained to grow in a variety of designs—T-shaped, U-shaped, palmlike, or in the form of a candelabrum—but in all cases the effect is two-dimensional since the branches are tied flat to the support. This training permits the plant to grow with all its parts fully exposed to sunlight, which in the case of fruit trees facilitates the even ripening of fruit and allows thorough application of pesticide sprays. Espalier-training may also be employed for purely decorative effect or in gardens where there is limited planting space.

ESPANOLA [ĕs-pən-ō'lə], town of Ontario, Canada, on the Spanish River some 40 mi. southwest of Sudbury. Papermilling is the chief industry. Pop., 5,353.

ESPARTO [ĕs-pär'tō], tufted, perennial plant, *Stipa tenacissima*, in the grass family, Gramineae, native to dry, sandy, coastal areas of Spain and North Africa. The long, cylindrical leaves of the plant are gathered for use in the manufacture of mats, ropes, and especially for high-quality paper. Esparto grass is sometimes grown in warmer parts of North America as a garden ornamental.

ESPERANTO [ĕs-pə-rän'tō], international auxiliary language or interlanguage designed by Dr. Lazarus Ludwig Zamenhof (1859–1917) of Warsaw, Poland. First proposed in 1887, it has been in ever-increasing practical use since 1905, when the first World Esperanto Congress was held in France. Based on the elements of the foremost Western languages, Esperanto is so streamlined that it can be learned in one-tenth the time needed to master a national tongue. The whole grammar fits on one page, and a small basic vocabulary can be made to serve all needs by means of an ingenious system of prefixes and suffixes.

Esperanto is taught in more than 750 schools in 40 countries as well as in evening classes and over the radio. Textbooks for self-study exist in 54 languages. Teaching aids are available on records and tape, and also in Braille for the blind. Esperanto clubs exist in all major and many minor cities. Books in and about Esperanto total over 8,600, and there are approximately 145 Esperanto periodicals. Translated and original literature includes fiction, drama, and poetry as well as books on science, education, religion, the labor movement, business, travel, and world affairs.

Every year about 14,000 persons attend international conferences using Esperanto as their only or principal language. Hundreds of governments, city administrations, and chambers of commerce have published illustrated folders, books, and motion pictures using Esperanto to attract tourists or to disseminate economic, cultural, or political information. Travelers knowing the language can use the services of more than 3,000 delegates of the Universal Esperanto Association. Their addresses are listed in a *Year Book* published in Rotterdam.

Shortwave broadcasts in Esperanto originate in many countries, including Italy, France, Spain, Switzerland, Austria, Yugoslavia, Poland, Bulgaria, North Korea, Brazil, Uruguay, Venezuela, Guatemala, and the United States. When the Voice of America broadcast several series of Esperanto programs, beginning in 1960, it received 1,700 Esperanto letters from 87 countries in 15 months. Several members of the Senate and the House of Representatives as well as a number of agency heads and other government officials participated in the programs. Some of them answered questions received in Esperanto from prominent leaders abroad.

At its Montevideo Conference (1954) the United Nations Educational, Scientific, and Cultural Organization (UNESCO) passed a resolution pointing out that "the results attained by Esperanto . . . correspond with the aims and ideals of UNESCO" and that "several Member States have announced their readiness to introduce or expand the teaching of Esperanto in their schools." The resolution was adopted in response to a petition in favor of Esperanto, presented to the United Nations in 1950 and signed by 492 organizations with 15½ million members and by 895,432 individuals, including the President of France, the prime ministers of four countries, and 405 members of parliaments and legislatures.

Consult Connor, G. A., and others, *Esperanto, the World Interlanguage* (rev. ed., 1959).

WILLIAM SOLZBACHER, Past President, Esperanto
Association of North America

See also INTERNATIONAL LANGUAGES.

ESPINEL [*ās-pē-nĕl'*], **VICENTE MARTÍNEZ** (c.1551–1624), Spanish poet, musician, and novelist. He wrote the picaresque romance *Relaciones de la vida del Escudero Marcos de Obregón*, 1618 (*The History of the Life of Squire Marcos de Obregón*, 1816), which inspired parts of Lesage's *Gil Blas*. Lope de Vega attributed to him the invention of the ten-line stanza called *décima* or *espinela*.

ESPIONAGE [*ĕs'pē-ə-nĭj, ĕs'pē-ə-näzh*], use of spies, who are also called secret agents, to obtain information. This activity is part of the intelligence process. Espionage consists of two functions: (1) attempting to obtain clandestinely or under false pretenses information concerning a government, and (2) transmitting that information to another government. Transmitting the information to the government that seeks it is often more difficult than securing it, and agents use a variety of techniques, including

The Bettmann Archive

The hanging of Nathan Hale, American Revolutionary patriot. Hale was caught behind British lines on Sept. 21, 1776, and hanged as a spy the next day. Before his death Hale is said to have uttered the stirring words, "I only regret that I have but one life to lose for my country."

Pinkertons National Detective Agency, Inc.

Allan Pinkerton, organizer and leader of the Union army's espionage activities under Gen. George B. McClellan during the American Civil War.

The Bettmann Archive

The capture of Maj. John André, British spy who conspired with the American traitor Benedict Arnold to surrender West Point to the British in 1780. He concealed documents regarding the plan and defenses of West Point in his boot. In this Currier & Ives lithograph André is shown standing with his boot off, as the recovered secret documents are spread before him on the ground.

Gertrud Margarete Zelle, commonly known as Mata Hari, an exotic Dutch dancer who spied for the Germans during World War I. She was captured, tried, and executed for espionage by the French in 1917.

Col. Rudolf Ivanovich Abel, Soviet agent convicted in 1957 of conspiring to steal U.S. defense data. Sentenced to 30 years in prison, he was later exchanged, in 1962, for the American U-2 pilot Francis Gary Powers, shot down over the Soviet Union in 1960.

complicated codes, ciphers, signals, and microfilms, to deliver what they have learned. A major difficulty for those receiving agents' reports is determining the reliability of the information furnished.

Political espionage pertains to such matters as the politics, industry, commerce, agriculture, labor, and transportation of a nation. Military espionage deals with secret or classified information about the armed forces of a country. Diplomatic espionage, as it is sometimes called, is the information observed and reported by diplomatic staffs and their technical assistants.

Espionage is recognized by international law. Agents can be punished only when acting clandestinely or under false pretenses. When an agent tries to gain information in a zone of operations (combat or battle zone), he is subject, according to the practice of most nations, to the death penalty if found guilty. A trial must precede punishment. If apprehended and tried, an agent can expect neither open recognition by nor overt assistance from the government that employed him.

A great deal of what might be termed "polite" espionage is carried on by experts and technicians who confine their efforts to reading the press and published material openly available. This is closely related to strategic intelligence. But espionage in its more familiar connotation is that activity which is concerned with securing state secrets. Agents, usually disguised or operating under what is called a cover, try to gain access to classified documents or entrance to restricted areas. They may bribe or, by violence, threat, or blackmail, force nationals to divulge information that a nation seeks to safeguard from its potential or actual enemies. Nations may use agents to "plant" false information. They may employ double agents, those who are working for more than one government. Agents themselves may become double agents

without the knowledge of the government that originally employed them.

During the American Revolution, the Continentals apprehended, tried, and hanged Maj. John André of the British army as a spy. Similarly, the British put the American patriot Nathan Hale to death. After the Napoleonic Wars, the Holy Alliance (Russia, Austria, and Prussia) established and spread a tangled network of spies, informers, and *agents provocateurs* throughout Europe. During the American Civil War Allan Pinkerton organized for the Union army an intelligence system that included espionage. The Confederacy also received reports from agents, some of whom were self-appointed by virtue of their patriotism. The most famous—or notorious—spy of World War I was Mata Hari, a woman in German service who was tried by a French court and shot by a firing squad for having used her wiles to extract information from smitten Allied admirers of high rank. Earlier in that war the Germans had executed the British nurse Edith Cavell for alleged espionage activity. During World War II all the combatants had extensive espionage networks. A German agent in Turkey obtained information about the projected Allied invasion of Normandy, but his superiors were not convinced of the reliability of his report. Richard Sorge engaged in a variety of undercover work in the Far East. In the postwar period sensational trials divulged the existence in the United States, Great Britain, and Canada of Soviet spy rings particularly intent on securing knowledge of developments in nuclear weapons.

Because espionage is conducted in the greatest secrecy, it is usually impossible to know the effect such activity has on a developing political situation or on combat operations. Military espionage in a battle zone in time of war is under the direction of the staff officer charged with intelligence. The espionage agent normally employed in a theater of operations is the line-crosser, who travels across the front or parachutes into an enemy area to gain and report (by radio or other means) or bring back useful information.

MARTIN BLUMENSON, Senior Historian, Department of the Army

See also INTELLIGENCE, GOVERNMENTAL; INTELLIGENCE, MILITARY.

ESPÍRITO SANTO, coastal state of eastern Brazil, situated north of Rio de Janeiro. The coastal section is low and mostly swampy, while the remainder rises sharply to the west along the margins of the Brazilian Highlands. Tropical products are grown, including cacao, rice, sugar cane, oranges, and bananas. Industry is restricted largely to Vitória, the capital. Area, 15,780 sq. mi.; pop., 1,188,665.

ESPRONCEDA [ās-prôn-thā'thä] **Y DELGADO, JOSÉ DE** (1808–42), Spanish romantic poet. *El estudiante de Salamanca*, 1839 (*The Student of Salamanca*, 1919) was strongly influenced by Byron's *Don Juan*. The second canto of his *El diablo mundo* (This Hellish World), 1840–41, and *A Jarifa en una orgía* (To Xarifa in an Orgy) are probably the finest lyric poems of Spanish romanticism. Espronceda's verse is notable for its musicality and the purity of its language.

ESPY [ĕs'pē], **JAMES POLLARD** (1785–1860), American meteorologist who found that precipitation is caused by the rising and cooling of warm, moist air. After 1835 he devoted full time to weather studies, from which he formulated his precipitation theory. Espy was appointed chief meteorologist of the U.S. War Department in 1843, and in 1848, of the Navy Department. He organized the first daily weather-reporting service using information telegraphed from a wide area.

ESQUIMALT [ĕs-kwī'môlt], district municipality on the southeast coast of Vancouver Island, British Columbia, Canada. Discovered by the Spanish and used for years by the British navy, Esquimalt is the chief Pacific port of Canada's navy, the site of a graving dock, and a residential area for Victoria. Inc., 1912; pop., 10,384.

ESQUIROL [ĕs-kü-ē-rôl'], **JEAN ÉTIENNE DOMINIQUE** (1772–1840), French physician, called the father of French psychiatry. A student of Pinel, the man who liberated the mentally ill from their chains and other inhuman constraints, Esquirol advanced Pinel's reforms by persuading the French government to build a number of asylums for the mentally ill. He produced one of the earliest treatises on mental illness based upon scientific observation under hospital conditions.

ESSAY [ĕs'ā], prose discussion of moderate length, usually on a restricted topic. The essay is addressed to a general audience, and it attempts to communicate its idea, thesis, or information in the language of ordinary discourse, with liberal use of anecdotes, illustrations, and examples commonly drawn from general experience. There are two broad classes of essays: the formal, which is impersonal, serious of purpose, and logical in organization; and the informal, which is personal, frequently rambling in structure, free from stiffness of form or tone, and marked by gracefulness of style and gaiety of tone.

The essay has a long history, stretching back into classical literature, although the form did not acquire its present name until 1580. Then Michel de Montaigne published his witty personal observations under the name *Essais* (meaning "attempts") to suggest their tentative character. The dialogues of Plato, the "characters" of Theophrastus, the epistles of Pliny and Seneca, the disputations of Cicero, and the meditations of Marcus Aurelius are all compositions from the classical age which can accurately be called essays.

Francis Bacon's *Essays* (1597) were the earliest English attempts at the form. Where Montaigne had been graceful and conversational, Bacon was more formal and expository; but both writers relied heavily on quotations, examples, and figures of speech.

During the 18th century the essay became a widely used form. Daniel Defoe in 1704 introduced the periodical essay in *The Review*, and Joseph Addison and Richard Steele in *The Tatler* (1709–11) and *The Spectator* (1711–1712; 1714) raised the form to heights of urbanity, wit, and grace. Jonathan Swift in *A Modest Proposal* (1729) and other writings, Samuel Johnson in *The Rambler* (1750–52) and the *Idler* papers (1758–60), and Oliver Goldsmith in *The Citizen of the World* (1760–61) were other notable 18th-century essayists. Since the 18th century, as a result of these writers' work, the essay has been primarily a periodical form, although collections of essays often appear in book form.

During the 19th century both formal and informal essays appeared in profusion. Charles Lamb brought the informal essay to its highest level, although he was challenged but not surpassed by William Hazlitt, Leigh Hunt, Thomas De Quincey, and Robert Louis Stevenson. In the United States Washington Irving and Oliver Wendell Holmes practiced the informal essay with distinction, while Edgar Allan Poe, Ralph Waldo Emerson, and James Russell Lowell produced excellent formal essays. In England there were a host of fine formal essayists, including Thomas Carlyle, John Henry Newman, John Ruskin, Thomas Huxley, Matthew Arnold, and Walter Pater.

In the 20th century, G. K. Chesterton, Max Beerbohm, and E. V. Lucas in England, and Christopher Morley, H. L. Mencken, James Thurber, Agnes Repplier, and E. B. White in America, have practiced the informal essay with skill and charm. But the formal essay—usually in the form of the magazine article or the critical essay as practiced by T. S. Eliot, F. R. Leavis, and the American "New Critics"—has been a more dominant literary genre.

Consult O'Leary, R. D., *The Essay* (1928); *A Book of the Essay; From Montaigne to E. B. White,* ed. by H. C. Combs (1950); *A Century of the Essay, British and American,* ed. by David Daiches (1951); *The Essay: A Critical Anthology,* ed. by J. L. Stewart (1952); *American Essays,* ed. by C. B. Shaw (new ed., 1955); *Essays of the Masters,* ed. by Charles Neider (1956); Fiedler, Leslie, *Art of the Essay* (1958); Miles, Josephine, *Classic Essays in English* (1961); McConkey, James, *The Structure of Prose: An Introduction to Writing* (1963); *The World of Ideas,* ed. by M. W. Alssid and William Kennedy (1964).

C. HUGH HOLMAN, University of North Carolina

ESSAY ON MAN, AN, English philosophical poem (1733–34) by Alexander Pope. It is notable for the brilliant way in which Pope, who was no philosopher, phrased old ideas. His aim was to:

"Laugh where we must, be candid where we can,
But vindicate the ways of God to man."

But in the light of man's necessarily limited knowledge, he advised:

"Know then thyself, presume not God to scan,
The proper study of mankind is man."

ESSEN [ĕs′ən], city in North Rhine-Westphalia, Federal Republic of Germany (West Germany), in the heart of the Ruhr industrial region. The city grew up during the early Middle Ages around a monastic foundation, the church of which is still standing. A free city until 1803, it was incorporated into Prussia in 1815. Essen's modern importance derives from the fact that early in the 19th century Friedrich Krupp began his experiments in the manufacture of cast steel there. These led to the foundation of the Krupp Steelworks, which remained the personal possession of the Krupp family until 1967. The coal resources underlying the city were opened in the early 19th century, and contributed to the development of heavy industry. The Krupp works always specialized in high-quality steel and early acquired a reputation for the manufacture of armaments, particularly artillery. They also produced heavy machinery, especially railway locomotives. City and works were heavily bombed during World War II and largely destroyed. They were, however, rebuilt, and steel manufacture and coal mining are still the city's chief sources of employment, though the industrial pattern is more varied today with the introduction of textile manufacture, glass works, and chemical plants. South of the city pleasant hilly country extends to the Ruhr River, which is dammed to supply Essen with water. Pop., 726,550.

NORMAN J. G. POUNDS, Indiana University

ESSENCE [ĕs′əns] (Lat. *essentia*), that by which a thing is what it is. The Greek philosophers in general identified essence with substance. Thus the essence of a man was to be a rational animal. Later writers distinguished essence from substance and defined the essence of a thing as its nature considered apart from its existence. In many philosophies the essence of a thing is defined simply by its constituent elements. In others, it is held to be that immanent principle which, together with its act of existing, forms the concrete reality.

ESSENES [ĕs′ēnz], a group of Jewish ascetics who flourished from about 200 B.C. to 100 A.D. The name has been variously derived from Hebrew, Aramaic, and Syriac words covering a wide range of meanings. As described by such ancient authors as Josephus (in the *Antiquities* and *Wars*), and Philo (in the *Apology for the Jews*), they lived for the most part among, but separated from, the larger community, observing their own interpretation of the laws of ritual purity with great vigor.

"They shunned pleasures as a vice and regarded temperance and the control of the passions as a special virtue. Disdaining marriage, they adopted other men's children" (Josephus). They lived a communal existence, in which all possessions were owned jointly, and elected officers to attend to the interests of the community. The communal meal was an important function in the life of the group. They were devoted to charity and to study. Entrance into the group was preceded by a strict period of probation;

Assembly line for electric locomotives in the Krupp works at Essen. (BIRNBACK PUBLISHING SERVICE)

infringement of its rules resulted in expulsion. The doctrine of the soul's immortality was strongly affirmed.

Since the discovery of the Dead Sea Scrolls at Qumran in 1947, there has been renewed interest in the Essenes. A number of scholars have identified the community of Qumran with them, and have used the writings of that group to explain long-standing mysteries concerning the Essenes. The occurrence of the name Hasidin (see HASIDIM) in one document revived the identification of the Essenes with the Assideans of the Maccabean period.

Consult Burrows, Millar, *The Dead Sea Scrolls* (1955) and *More Light on the Dead Sea Scrolls* (1958).

LOU H. SILBERMAN, Vanderbilt University

ESSENTIAL or VOLATILE OILS, odoriferous products obtained from flowers, leaves, and roots. Their name derives from methods used for their production, methods by which the alchemists hoped to find the essence of nature. Chemically they belong to the terpenes, having carbon and hydrogen atoms in a ratio of five to eight, either arranged in open chains (rose and geranium) or in rings (pine oil, eucalyptus). Some are directly expressed, like orange oil from peel. Rose leaves are macerated with hot fat to make a pomade from which the oil can be extracted with alcohol. Some flowers, like violet, produce oil for a day after picking; they are spread on a fat layer to concentrate the oil. Costly oils, like jasmine worth $2,000 a lb., are profitably extracted with solvents to give the purest oils.

ESSEQUIBO [ĕs-ə-kwē′bō] **RIVER,** the principal river of Guyana, flowing northward across the Guiana Highlands to the Atlantic Ocean. From the Brazilian border to its mouth, near Parika, the Essequibo traverses a densely forested area of sparse population. Its navigable lower course, below Bartica, provides an outlet for gold and diamond camps along tributary streams. On one of these, the Potaro, is spectacular Kaieteur Falls. Length, 430 mi.

ESSEX [ĕs′ĭks], **ROBERT DEVEREUX, 2D EARL OF** (1566–1601), English nobleman, favorite of Elizabeth I. When his father died, his mother married the Earl of Leicester, Queen Elizabeth's favorite. Essex served with distinction under Leicester in the Netherlands and, on returning to England in 1587, soon won prominence and high office at the Queen's court by his gallantry and good looks. On Leicester's death in 1588 he became Elizabeth's chief favorite and closest companion. In 1590 Essex deeply angered Elizabeth by secretly marrying the widow of Sir Philip Sidney. But she forgave him, and at her instructions he served in military and naval expeditions, notably the assault on Cádiz in 1596. In 1599 Elizabeth appointed him her lieutenant and Governor General in Ireland to crush rebellion there. From the outset he was haughty and independent; in 1600, when his campaign failed and his dealings with the rebel leader, the Earl of Tyrone, looked suspicious, Elizabeth recalled and imprisoned him. In 1601 Essex attempted a revolution and failed in this also. In his subsequent trial and conviction for treason, Francis Bacon, once his friend, was prosecutor. After hesitation, Elizabeth signed the death warrant and Essex died on the scaffold.

FREDERICK G. MARCHAM, Cornell University

ESSEX, town of the southwestern tip of Ontario, Canada, 15 mi. southeast of Windsor. Originally a lumbering center, it now has food canneries. Inc., 1890; pop., 3,428.

ESSEX, Anglo-Saxon kingdom eventually comprising the present English counties of Essex, London, Middlesex, and most of Hertfordshire. The area was settled by Saxons in the early 6th century. The independence of the kingdom was ended by the rise of Mercia, which by 740 had taken control of London. In 825, Essex joined other eastern kingdoms in submitting to Egbert of Wessex and became an earldom. Essex was heavily settled by the Danes between 865 and 869 and became part of the Danelaw in 886. In 917, Edward the Elder, King of the English, defeated the Danes and thenceforth Essex was an earldom of England.

ESSEX, large county in southeastern England on the north side of the Thames River estuary, between London to the southwest and the North Sea to the east. The Lea and Stort rivers to the west divide it from Hertford and Middlesex counties. Its southern Thames boundary divides it from Kent. The Stour River is in part its northern boundary dividing it from Suffolk. The land reaches its highest point in the chalk hills near the Cambridgeshire border in the extreme northwest. From there the land slopes gently through rolling, wooded country to the sea. The coast is flanked by a belt of reclaimed marshes.

Away from London and the Thames, the county is mainly agricultural. Mixed farming is characteristic in the north where wheat and barley are the main produce. In the south the heavier soils are used for raising dairy cattle, poultry, and hogs, besides market vegetables and fruits. Chelmsford, the county town, and Colchester are important centers of agricultural and engineering industries. Along the Thames, forming part of Greater London, are two county boroughs, East Ham and West Ham, and eight municipal boroughs—Barking, Chingford, Dagenham, Ilford, Leyton, Romford, Walthamstow, and Wanstead and Woodford. Away from the Thames these are largely residential, but docks and industrial plants line the north bank of the estuary. At East Ham and Barking there are installations for gas and electricity generation. Oil is refined at Shellhaven near Tilbury, and automobiles are manufactured at Dagenham. Other manufactures include cement, chemicals, paper, textiles, foods, and timber products. Tilbury is the ocean terminal for London. Southend-on-Sea, at the entrance to the Thames, is the largest seaside resort. On the Stour estuary is the port of Harwich from which ferries sail to the continent.

In prehistoric times the interior of Essex was heavily wooded, but today only part of the Epping Forest remains. Although difficult of access, Essex' indented coast and proximity to the Continent attracted invaders in Iron Age and Roman times. The greatest Belgic chief of Britain, Cunobelinus (Shakespeare's Cymbeline), established his capital at Colchester (Camulodunum). Here too Emperor Claudius' legions founded the first Roman town in Britain (43 A.D.). The name Essex means "the land of the East Saxons," who invaded the land in the 5th century. Historic buildings include Waltham Abbey and fine 15th-century churches. Administrative county, area, 1,499 sq. mi.; pop.,

1,842,500; with county boroughs, area, 1,528 sq. mi.; pop., 2,286,970.

ARTHUR J. HUNT, The University, Sheffield, England

ESSEX, unincorporated residential suburb, northeast of Baltimore, Md. Pop. (1960) 35,205.

ESSEX JUNCTION, village of northwestern Vermont, adjacent to Burlington. It is the site of the annual Champlain Valley Exposition. Bricks, tile, leather gloves, electronic components, and dairy and maple products are produced. New England's largest forestry tree nursery is also here. Pop. (1950) 2,741; (1960) 5,340.

ESSEX JUNTO, in American history, derisive name originally given by John Hancock to a group of Federalists, most of them from Essex County, Mass., who supported Alexander Hamilton during the presidency of John Adams. It was later applied, during Thomas Jefferson's administration, to the Federalists led by Timothy Pickering, who sought without success to take the New England states and New York out of the federal union.

ESSLINGEN [ĕs'lĭng-ən], city in Baden-Württemberg, Federal Republic of Germany (West Germany), on the Neckar River 6 mi. southeast of Stuttgart. Railway equipment, machinery, electric products, leather goods, furniture, and textiles are manufactured here. Since the Middle Ages it has been famous for its wines. Founded in 777, it was a free imperial city from the early 13th century until 1802. It is surrounded by a medieval wall. Pop., 83,236.

ESTAING [ĕs-tăN'], **CHARLES HECTOR, COMTE D'** (1729–94), French admiral. He fought against the British in the East Indies and in India during the Seven Years' War. In the American Revolutionary War, as vice-admiral of the French fleet that supported the colonials against Great Britain, he blockaded Adm. Richard Howe at Sandy Hook (1778) and captured the islands of Grenada and St. Vincent in the West Indies, but he sustained heavy losses in the unsuccessful siege of Savannah, Ga. Elected (1787) to the French Assembly of Notables, Estaing supported the French Revolution and became an admiral in 1792, but he was convicted as a royalist and executed.

ESTATE, ADMINISTRATION OF. See WILL, in law.

ESTATES GENERAL, in French history, feudal representative body consisting of three estates or orders—clergy, nobility, and commoners. Originating as a specialized section of the royal council (*curia regis*) at about the same time and in about the same fashion as the English Parliament, the Estates General played a similar role during its early history. It was summoned for the first time as a national, tripartite assembly by Philip IV in 1302 merely to simplify negotiations for new royal revenues made necessary by wars against Flanders and England. Levies on the clergy and nobility had traditionally been consented to by local or provincial assemblies of the first two orders, and the townsmen or bourgeois (the third estate) had arranged the details of their contributions in separate dealings with royal agents; Philip's convocation of the Estates General carried with it no recognition of any right to grant or withhold new taxes. The Estates General reached the zenith of its power during the Hundred Years' War. Repeated royal exactions provoked a flat refusal (1346) by the Estates General of Langue d'Oïl (northern France) to consent to new levies. In 1355, following the Black Death, royal finances virtually collapsed, and the Estates General of both Languedoc and Langue d'Oïl (the latter led by Étienne Marcel, provost of the Paris merchants) forced the Dauphin (in the absence of John II, who was a prisoner in England) to issue an ordinance providing that he would always consult the Estates General before imposing new taxes; a commission of the Estates was to supervise collection and expenditure. But dissension in the reformers' ranks, followed by the murder of Marcel, allowed the crown to regain control. Charles V freed himself from nearly all supervision by the Estates and secured its agreement to the principle that the renewal of existing taxes did not need its approval. Lacking important powers or functions, the Estates General fell into eclipse, especially during the age of absolutism. It did not meet between 1614 and 1789, when its convocation by Louis XVI marked the start of the French Revolution.

RALPH H. BOWEN, Northern Illinois University

ESTAUNIÉ [ĕs-tō-nyā'], **ÉDOUARD** (1862–1942), French novelist. A practicing engineer for many years, he wrote novels combining a scientific spirit with an awareness of metaphysical reality. He tried to analyze the relationship in ordinary individuals between their "social" existence and their hidden spiritual suffering and emotional stress, as in *Les choses voient* (Things See), 1913.

ESTE [ĕs'tā], noble Italian family, rulers of Ferrara (1208–1598), and noted patrons of Renaissance art and literature. The founder of the family is considered to be **ALBERTO AZZO II** (996–1097), who became lord of the town of Este and adopted its name. His son **WELF IV** became Duke of Bavaria and the ancestor of the Welf dynasty and the Brunswick-Luneburg line, which in 1714 came to rule England. **AZZO IV**, of the Italian branch of the family, became lord of Ferrara in 1208. **OBIZZO II** added the lordships of Modena in 1288 and Reggio in 1289.

During the 15th century the Este became one of the foremost princely houses in Italy. **BORSO** (1413–71) became Duke of Modena and Reggio in 1452. Ferrara was made a duchy in 1470. **ALFONSO I** (1476–1534) married Lucrezia Borgia and commanded the papal forces against Venice (1508–13). The Este were noted for the brilliance of their court, to which they brought such literary and artistic figures as Alberti, Pisanello, Bellini, Piero della Francesca, Boiardo, Ariosto, and Tasso. Alfonso I's sisters **ISABELLA** and **BEATRICE D'ESTE** were among the greatest patronesses of Renaissance culture and Alfonso I's son **CARDINAL IPPOLITTO THE YOUNGER** built the famous Villa-d'Este at Tivoli. In 1597 **ALFONSO II** died, leaving his lands to his cousin Cesare, but the papacy declared Cesare illegitimate and in 1598 took over Ferrara. The Este family continued to rule Modena and Reggio until 1859, when the duchy was incorporated into the new Kingdom of Italy.

ROBIN S. OGGINS, State University of N.Y. at Binghamton

This 18th-century Flemish relief panel depicts Esther with the Persian King Ahasuerus.

Jewish Museum

ESTE, town in Padua province of Venetia in northern Italy. It lies south of the Euganean Hills and north of the Adige River. Its chief manufactures are textile machinery, ceramics, and furniture. Also located in the town is a sugar-beet refinery. Its National Museum has a fine collection of pre-Roman and Romanesque artifacts excavated from the environs. Another point of interest is a 14th-century castle erected on the ruins of an older construction.

In ancient times, when it was known as Ateste, it was a Roman military base. In 589 A.D., after a great Adige flood, the town was abandoned. It was the seat of the Este family from 1050 until they were driven out in 1275. From 1405 to 1795 Este was under the rule of the Venetian Republic. Pop., 10,640.

ESTER [ĕs′tər], one of a family of organic compounds produced when an acid reacts with an alcohol. Many esters occur in nature, the lower ones being in large part responsible for the odors of fruits and flowers. Waxes, fats, and vegetable oils are esters. The most common method of preparation is to treat the acid and alcohol with a dehydrating agent, such as sulfuric acid. Treatment of fats and oils with alkalies produces soap and glycerol. Ethyl acetate, used as a nail-polish remover, is one of the simplest esters. Esters are used for flavoring, in perfumes, as solvents, and as plasticizers. Some esters can be polymerized into commercial resins. Mineral acids and alcohols also produce esters.

ESTES [ĕs′tēz] **PARK,** resort town of north-central Colorado, in a high valley (elev., 7,525 ft.) at the foot of the Rockies. It is the eastern gateway to Rocky Mountain National Park, and thousands of visitors pass through Estes Park yearly to visit the park. Businesses in Estes Park largely serve the needs and interests of tourists. Within the town, Estes Lake marks the eastern end of the Colorado–Big Thompson water diversion system, which draws water from western slopes through a tunnel under the Continental Divide. The site of the city was first settled by Joel Estes in 1859–60. Many visitors were attracted when a toll road from the plains to the high valley was completed in 1875. The town, however, was not founded until 1905. Inc., 1917; pop. (1950) 1,617; (1960) 1,175.

ESTEVAN [ĕs′tə-văn], city of southeastern Saskatchewan, Canada. It is an oil-producing and coal-mining center and serves a mixed-farming area. Estevan has brick-and-tile plants, a creamery, a commercial nursery, and a large power-producing plant. The city is served by three railways, good highways, and an airport. Inc. as city, 1957; pop., 7,728.

ESTHER [ĕs′tər], Jewish consort of the Persian King Ahasuerus, and heroine of the Old Testament book bearing her name. An orphan of the tribe of Benjamin, and a cousin of the pious Jew Mordecai, Esther is selected in a beauty contest to succeed Queen Vashti, who had fallen from royal favor. In a time of great crisis for her people Esther, at the risk of her own life, saves the Jews from slaughter.

ESTHER, BOOK OF, one of the latest writings of the Old Testament, remarkable for its failure even to mention God. The story concerns a Jewish girl who becomes the Queen of Ahasuerus (Xerxes I?), King of Persia. When a high official, Haman, plots a pogrom against the Jews, Esther persuades the King to have Haman hanged on his own gallows, originally prepared for Esther's cousin Mordecai. She then gets permission for the Jews to reverse the pogrom and fall upon their enemies throughout the land. A new festival, Purim, was established to commemorate the event.

ESTHER, THE REST OF THE BOOK OF, part of the Old Testament Apocrypha. Since in the canonical Esther there is no mention of God it seemed advisable to add some references to Him and to revelation and to Jewish piety. Such were provided in the late 2d century B.C. and appear as Esther 10:4–16:24 in the Roman Catholic Bible.

ESTHERVILLE, city of northwestern Iowa and seat of Emmet County, on the Des Moines River. Industries include poultry processing and feed and fertilizer production. Inc., 1894; pop. (1950) 6,719; (1960) 7,927.

ESTHETICS. *See* AESTHETICS.

ESTIENNE [ĕs-tyĕn′] **or ÉTIENNE** [ā-tyĕn′], family of printers and scholars. HENRI ESTIENNE (d.1520) founded (c.1502) a printing firm in Paris. His son ROBERT (c.1503–59) edited and printed many fine editions of the classics. Attacked by the Catholics for such works as his Bible, based on critical scholarship, he moved to Geneva in 1550. HENRI (1531?–98), Robert's son, was remarkably productive as printer, editor, and author. His Greek dictionary, *Thesaurus Graecae linguae* (1572), exemplifies his prodigious scholarship.

527

ESTONIA

ESTONIA [ĕs-tō′nē-ə] (Est. **EESTI**), republic on the eastern shore of the Baltic Sea, bounded in the south by Latvia and in the east by the Russian Soviet Federated Socialist Republic (R.S.F.S.R.). An independent state after World War I, Estonia was incorporated into the Soviet Union in 1940 as the Estonian Soviet Socialist Republic. The United States and other Western countries have refused to recognize the incorporation. The Estonian S.S.R. has an area of 17,400 sq. mi. and a population of almost 2,000,000, of whom about 75% are Estonians and 20% are Russians. According to a census in 1934, 78% of the population was Lutheran and 19% belonged to the Orthodox Church.

The Country. The land is generally low, rising from northwest to southeast. Only one-tenth of the country rises over 350 ft. above sea level. The coast line has a number of good natural harbors. The rivers are generally short, and there is no river center of settlement as in Latvia or Lithuania. The major cities are Tallinn, the capital and industrial center, Tartu, a university town, Pärnu, a port, and Paldiski, a naval base. The climate is moderate continental, with precipitation of 20–25 in. annually. Temperatures range from an average of 19.4° F. to 28.4° F. in January to 60° F. to 64° F. in July.

Economy. Of the three Baltic states, Estonia is the most favored in mineral resources. The most important is oil shale, around which has developed an extracting and processing industry. Other industries include timber processing, textiles, metal working, and construction materials. Peat is the most important source of energy. Because of the poor soil, agriculture is characterized mainly by dairy farming and hog raising. Flax is the chief industrial crop.

History. The Estonians are a Finno-Ugrian people who settled in their present area some time before the Christian era. Although participating in local commerce and wars, the pagan Estonians had not achieved political unity when the German crusaders came in the 13th century. By 1227 the Germans, together with the Danes, had conquered and divided the land, the German holdings—together with Latvia—being known as Livonia. The conquerors took possession of the land, and despite repeated risings, the native Estonians were reduced to serfs by the end of the 15th century. Cities arose, populated by immigrants. (The name "Tallinn" comes from Talli linn, "Danish hill.") The crusaders brought Roman Christianity with them, but in the 16th century Lutheranism became the predominant religion of the Estonians.

When the Muscovite Tsar Ivan IV sought to break through to the Baltic Sea in the Livonian Wars (1558–83), the Livonian state collapsed. It had been weakened by internal differences and by the decline of the Hanseatic League, a league of trading cities with extensive interests in the Baltic. Northern Estonia fell to the Swedes, while the Poles occupied the southern part. The Swedes then drove the Poles out in the 17th century. (The Danes had taken the island of Saaremaa in 1559, but the Swedes took this too in 1645.) Under Swedish rule the lot of the peasantry somewhat improved, but the "good old Swedish days" of Estonian history are more tradition than fact.

In the Northern War (1700–21) Peter the Great renewed the Russian drive to the Baltic. In contrast to his predeces-

Pix, Inc.

Round towers of an ancient wall overlook the roofs of Tallinn. The wall still encloses the city's old section.

sors, he won the support of the Baltic Germans who resented the restrictions imposed upon them by the Swedish crown. Upon Estonia's formal incorporation into the Russian Empire in 1721, the Baltic nobility were guaranteed extensive privileges. In 1816–19 the Baltic provinces were the site of the first Russian experiments in peasant emancipation. Since the peasants, who were freed without land and without compensation, were not allowed to leave their villages, the reform aided only the nobility. New laws in 1849 and 1856 finally opened the way for the peasants to acquire land.

The latter 19th century saw a rapid development of national feeling among the Estonians, who, according to the Russian census of 1897, had a literacy rate of 97%. The tsarist policy of Russification under Alexander III dealt a serious blow to the Estonians. But since it was aimed particularly at the position of the Baltic Germans, the policy opened new opportunities, such as government service, to the Estonians. The development of industry had brought a new urban working class to Estonia which turned to socialist ideas. The Estonian peasantry was largely landless, but even the tenant farmers were discontent. All these factors came into play during the Russian Revolution of 1905, finding their expression in peasant risings and strikes. The government restored order only after troops had been called in, and martial law remained in force until 1909.

Independence. World War I brought great changes to Estonia. After the Russian Revolution of 1917, an Estonian Diet declared the nation's independence. In 1918 Estonia was occupied by the Germans, but with the collapse of the *Reich*, Estonia's fate hung in the balance. After a long struggle, involving invasion by Bolshevik forces, calling of German and Finnish volunteers, and subsequent conflict with German and White Russian forces, the Estonian nationalists succeeded in establishing the country's independence. A Soviet-Estonian peace treaty marked the end of the military conflict in Feb., 1920. Although the Western Allies delivered aid to the Estonians in 1919, they were hesitant to recognize the breakup of the territory of Imperial Russia, not granting *de jure* recognition to the new state until 1921.

A Constituent Assembly was convened in 1919, and it completed its work in Dec., 1920. Land reform was introduced, large estates were nationalized and designated for redistribution. The German nobles particularly suffered from this move, but the League of Nations in 1926 rejected their appeal, declaring the reform to be a social question and not one of national minority rights.

The domestic political scene in the 1920's was one of instability. In 1924 Communist conspirators succeeded in momentarily taking the telephone and telegraph exchanges in Tallinn, but government troops quickly restored order, and the Communist party was outlawed. The adoption of the system of proportional representation in the Parliament (Riigikogu) in practice prevented the establishment of a stable majority government. Instead, cabinets were repeatedly formed on a coalition basis, and discontent with this situation led in 1934 to the establishment of a new constitution and the emergence of an authoritarian regime, which banned political parties. The new government continued until 1940.

The Estonian Soviet Socialist Republic. The German-Russian nonaggression pact of Aug., 1939, had a secret protocol dividing up the Baltic area between the two powers, Estonia falling within the Soviet sphere. In the fall of 1939 the Russians forced on the Estonians a mutual security pact which provided for the stationing of Russian troops in Estonia. After the fall of Paris in 1940, the Russians presented new demands, charging that the Estonians were showing sympathies for the Western Allies

and were engaged in anti-Soviet activities. More Soviet troops entered the country, and the government fled. A new Leftist government was named, but the real director of events was Andrei Zhdanov, the Soviet spokesman of anti-Westernism in the 1940's. In July a new Parliament was elected on a one-party basis, and it declared Estonia to be a Soviet Republic. It applied for membership in the U.S.S.R., even though official sources had assured the electorate during the election campaign this would not happen. The Supreme Soviet of the U.S.S.R., announced the incorporation of Estonia in August, and by September, foreign diplomatic representatives had left the country.

The Nazi occupation from 1941 to 1944 brought the Estonians no relief, as the Nazis refused to trust any genuinely national organizations. The return of the Russians in 1944 meant the re-establishment of Communist

INDEX TO ESTONIAN S.S.R. GENERAL REFERENCE MAP
Total Population 2,000,000

An industrial plant. Oil processing, metalworking, and the production of construction materials are among Estonia's heavy industries.

Sovfoto

Sovfoto

In Pärnu, on an inlet of the Gulf of Riga, crates of fish are checked at a local fish delivery station.

government. In 1940 and 1941 the Soviet regime had carried out an extensive land reform, aimed at breaking the power of the land-holding peasantry, but it was only in 1948–49 that the farms were collectivized. At each step of Sovietization, the Communists met nationalist opposition by deporting Estonians to Siberia, especially in 1941, 1946, and 1949.

After the death of Stalin, controls were somewhat loosened—deportees were eventually allowed to return from Siberia and the country was opened to foreign visitors. The Russian census of 1959 revealed a decline in the number of Estonians in the country, while there was a sharp increase in the number of Russians as compared with figures from 1934. There were no Germans reported in the census. In 1939–40 the Baltic Germans had left the region in accordance with the terms of a Russo-German agreement. German efforts during World War II to reestablish the German position were wiped out by the Nazi defeat.

Consult Jackson, J. H., *Estonia* (1941); Uustalu, Evald, *The History of Estonian People* (1953); Page, S. W., *The Formation of the Baltic States* (1959).

ALFRED ERICH SENN, University of Wisconsin

ESTONIAN, member of the Finnic group of the Finno-Ugric branch of the Uralic language family. It was spoken by approximately 1,000,000 Estonians in 1960. Estonian is so closely related to Finnish that the two languages are in part mutually comprehensible, but it is not related to its southern neighbors, Lettish and Lithuanian, or to Russian.

ESTOPPEL [ĕs-tŏp′əl], legal doctrine. In its general sense, it is an evidentiary rule which forbids a litigant from asserting or denying a fact in issue because of his own previous allegation or conduct. Most frequently, it arises by judgment, by deed, or by conduct. The final adjudication of a fact by a court of competent jurisdiction binds the parties and estops them from raising the issue in any subsequent proceeding. A man is also estopped to contradict his own deed. Thus, a person who, without title, conveys land, but who thereafter acquires title, is estopped from asserting against the grantee the invalidity of his deed.

Estoppel by conduct presents the most far-reaching application of the term. One may not deny the truth of his earlier assertions (express or implied) to the detriment of another who has thereby been induced to act in reliance on it. For example, a retiring partner may not be permitted to deny that he is a partner as against creditors who were not given notice of his retirement.

In the law of contracts, a naked promise (that is, without consideration) is enforceable if it induced substantial action or forbearance by the promisee, which should reasonably have been expected by the promisor, and if injustice can be avoided only by enforcement of the promise. This is known as promissory estoppel.

ROBERT B. MAUTZ, University of Florida College of Law

ESTORIL, resort town of west-central Portugal, and suburb of Lisbon, situated on the Atlantic Ocean. It is noted as a refuge for Europe's displaced royalty. The town is connected to Lisbon by an electric railway. Pop., 5,545.

ESTRADA CABRERA [ãs-trä′thä kä-brä′rä], **MANUEL** (1857–1924), Guatemalan dictator. He was trained as a lawyer and later served as judge, but after 1885 he devoted himself chiefly to politics. In 1898 he succeeded an assassinated dictator and quickly became a dictator himself. He was re-elected in farcical balloting in 1905, 1911, and 1917. He required unqualified adulation from followers, and his election dates and his and his mother's birthdays were declared national holidays. Guatemala made some material progress during his rule, but civil liberties were almost entirely suppressed. He was charged with having attempted to administer a slow poison to a U.S. minister with whom he had quarreled. He was overthrown in 1920.

ESTRADA PALMA [ãs-trä′thä päl′mä], **TOMÁS** (1835–1908), Cuban independence leader and President. He fought in the Ten Years War against Spain (1868–78) and during part of that time served as president of the ("paper") provisional Cuban government. Later he operated a private school in upstate New York. When Cubans again revolted in 1895 he became the chief Cuban propagandist and supply organizer in the United States. On establishment of an independent Cuban government in 1902, Estrada Palma became President and was re-elected for a 2d term in 1906. He resigned soon afterward, however, because of a political impasse and incipient civil war. He was a man of great integrity but too "Americanized" to make him popular with many Cubans.

ESTRÊLA [ĕsh-trä′lə], **SERRA DA,** highest mountain range in Portugal. It is located in Beira Province between the Douro and Tejo rivers and is about 75 mi. long. Its highest peak, Malhão da Estrêla, rises 6,532 ft. There is a mountain range of the same name in the Brazilian state of Rio de Janeiro.

ESTREMADURA [ĕs-trā-mä-thōō'rä], region of southwest Spain, set between New Castile and Portugal and corresponding to the modern provinces of Cáceres and Badajoz. A bleak tableland cut into by the Tagus and Guadiana valleys, it suffers from prolonged droughts and is very sparsely populated. Cereals, sheep, and swine are the chief products. This "farthest," or frontier, land, that boasted in Mérida a far-famed Roman city, capital of Lusitania, and in Badajoz the center of an 11th century Muslim kingdom, has become a backwater, lacking the economic stimulus to stay emigration. Hernán Cortés, Francisco Pizarro, and other eminent conquistadors were Estremadurans. Area, 16,118 sq. mi.

ESTROGENS [ĕs'trə-jənz], the name applied to a group of compounds which stimulate the growth of the uterus and the development of the female body characteristics, and regulate the menstrual cycle. Estrogens are manufactured in the ovaries of mammals. They are widely distributed in animal and plant tissues and have been isolated from human and animal urine, from petroleum, peat, and from plants, such as the pussy willow. Synthetic estrogens have also been made.

In the human body, estrogens appear to be manufactured from cholesterol. They are deactivated by the liver. Estrogens are used to treat menopausal disturbances, certain vaginal inflammations, menstrual disorders, and cases of engorgement of the breasts following pregnancy. They have also been used with some success in the treatment of cancer of the prostate and breast.
See also ENDOCRINE GLANDS.

ESTUARY [ĕs'chōō-ĕr-ē], bay elongated approximately at right angles to the general coastal trend in contrast with lagoons, which are elongated parallel to the coast. Estu-

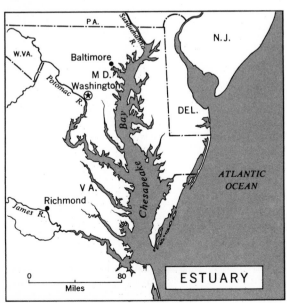

ESTUARY

aries are drowned river valleys. Most are subject to strong tides, which sometimes produce bores (advancing walls of water) during the flood tide. The water in estuaries, unlike that in glacially excavated fiords, is shallow, rarely more than 100 ft. deep. Examples of estuaries are Chesapeake Bay in the United States, the Thames River below London, and the many indentations (called rias) in the northwest coast of Spain. The lower Hudson River and the bays of the Maine coast are sometimes called estuaries, but they are more properly termed fiords as they were formed by glacial excavation.
See also COASTS AND COAST LINES; FIORD; LAGOON.

ETCHING (from Dutch *etsen*, "to eat"), a process of corroding a design into a metal plate with acid and then filling the corroded grooves with ink and printing the design onto paper by pressure; also, the work of art produced by using this process. The plate is first covered with a wax or resinous ground that is not susceptible to the acid. The artist then draws on the plate with a needle, exposing the metal without penetrating it. An acid bath eats away the exposed lines. Great subtlety of shading in the print may be obtained by taking out the plate after only a faint groove has been eaten and covering, or stopping-out, some of the lines with the ground material. The plate is reimmersed to continue eating the heavier lines. The stopping-out may be repeated a number of times.

History

In the late 15th century armorers in Augsburg, Germany, were ornamenting steel armor and weapons by coating the metal with acid-proof waxes and resins and then scratching a design for acid to eat into the exposed steel. A little after 1500 artists began to use etching to make prints. The first notable etchings were made by Albrecht Dürer from 1515 to 1518, after which he abandoned the process, probably because iron, used by all the first etchers, takes a rough line. Lucas van Leyden of Holland (1494–1533) replaced iron with copper, which the acid eats more delicately; he completed the etching with engraving, that is, by using a plough-shaped tool to dig out the metal. After 1700 practically all "engravings" were actually etchings finished by engraving small areas of delicate transitions.

But before etching could successfully imitate engraving, it needed technical refinements. Jacques Callot of France (1592-1635) grounded his copper plates with the pliant lutemaker's varnish. This enabled him to supplement the etcher's needle with an *échoppe*, a steel rod honed on an angle to an oval cutting edge, which he turned to widen or narrow a line, so that it looked like the engraver's line. It was Callot also who developed the stopping-out process.

Great Etchers. The greatest etchings are by painters. In Italy, Parmigianino (1503–40) showed student painters how to etch as freely as they sketched. Among the most individual painter-etchers are Giovanni Benedetto Castiglione (1616–70) of Genoa; the 18th-century Venetians Canaletto and Giovanni Battista Tiepolo, whose work achieved a clean sparkle of tone and launched the excellent French school of etching; and Giovanni Battista Piranesi (1720–78), perhaps best remembered for his de-

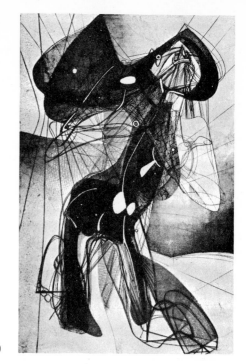

"Landscape with three gabled cottages" (1650) by Rembrandt.
(THE METROPOLITAN MUSEUM OF ART, GIFT OF FELIX M. WARBURG AND HIS FAMILY, 1941)

"Amazon" (1945) by Stanley William Hayter. (COLLECTION, THE MUSEUM OF MODERN ART, N.Y.)

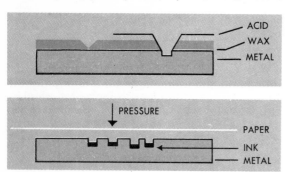

Etching is a form of engraving in which a design on a metal plate is eaten away by acid rather than cut with a pointed instrument. The plate is coated with a ground that resists the acid so that only the design cut into the ground is eaten away on the plate. The etched grooves are inked, and a press is used to force the paper firmly against the plate so that the paper draws up the ink from the grooves.

pictions of the grandeur of ancient Rome as seen in its ruins.

The most imitated etchers have been the Flemish Anthony Van Dyck (1599–1641) and the Dutch Rembrandt van Rijn (1606–69). Van Dyck, while still in his 20's, etched portraits of his famous contemporaries with deep psychological incisiveness. But it is Rembrandt who is the most varied and subtle of all etchers. The first of his 300-odd etchings were tiny portraits of his family, blatant studies of himself grimacing, and Biblical scenes. He later developed a range of tones from black to white that rival the range of color in baroque painting. In his 40's he used the needle to scratch the copper and throw up ragged metal ridges that catch the ink in rich, velvety blurs. With deepened insight into man and the Bible, he executed his last, unforgettable visions of the life of Christ, dramatized with an unrivaled power of understatement. Rembrandt dominated a Holland that produced numerous admirable etchers. One of the most individual is the 17th-century Hercules Seghers, creator of a solitary art of ruins and fractured lunar gullies.

After Rembrandt the most expressive etcher is the Spaniard Francisco Goya (1746–1828), who combined etching with aquatint (q.v.), which prints a continuous tone like an ink wash. With an 18th century delicacy of

technique, he expressed the most personal vision of the 19th century.

In France Eugène Delacroix (1798–1863) adopted Goya's etching-and-aquatint technique, and practically every later painter of the school of Paris has etched. Among the most original have been Edgar Degas; the American-born Mary Cassatt, who made the most lyrical color etchings of her era; and in our time the Spanish-born Pablo Picasso.

In England William Blake (1757–1827) exerted a strong local influence through etchings in which his sense of dramatic layout more than compensates for his copybook draftsmanship. Later artists noted for their etching include Sir Francis Seymour Haden (1818–1910); his brother-in-law, the American-born James Whistler; and the contemporary Stanley William Hayter, who in the United States and England has led many etchers to experiment with unorthodox and fruitful approaches to the copper plate.

Consult Hind, A. M., *A History of Engraving and Etching* (rev. ed., 1923); Zigrosser, Carl, *Six Centuries of Fine Prints* (1937); Hayter, S. W., *New Ways of Gravure* (1949); Peterdi, Gabor, *Printmaking* (1959).

A. HYATT MAYOR, The Metropolitan
Museum of Art

ETHANE [ĕth'ān], C_2H_6, simplest hydrocarbon after methane; it is colorless, odorless, and flammable. It comprises 9% of natural gas, and has limited use in the preparation of some substitution products. The ethyl radical $-C_2H_5$, one of the most important in organic chemistry, forms when ethane loses a hydrogen atom.

ETHENE. *See* ETHYLENE.

ETHER [ē'thər] **or DIETHYL ETHER,** an anesthetic compound first prepared in 1540, but not used in medicine until the middle of the 19th century.

Ether is prepared by heating together concentrated sulfuric acid and ethyl alcohol. It is a colorless liquid which evaporates readily and becomes highly flammable when mixed with air or oxygen.

When used as an anesthetic, ether first increases the heartbeat and breathing rates. This effect is reversed as the patient passes into a deeper anesthesia. When properly used, ether relaxes the abdominal muscles sufficiently so that the surgeon may stretch them away from the site of the operation.

Ether is a comparatively safe anesthetic, but should not be used on patients suffering from diabetes and kidney diseases. Other disadvantages associated with its use are post-operative nausea and vomiting and a tendency to stimulate mucous secretions which block the air passages. *See also* ANESTHESIA.

ETHER CONCEPT, in physics, an early theory, first held by Greek philosophers, that all space beyond the earth's atmosphere was filled with an invisible universal substance called ether that provided a medium in which waves could travel.

Nineteenth-century physicists, guided by a false analogy between light waves (electromagnetic waves) and sound waves (mechanical waves), postulated that all space was pervaded by the "ether," in order to provide a medium for transmission of light. It was thought that light waves were longitudinal, like sound waves, which would require the medium only to maintain pressure elasticity. Later scientists believed that light waves were transverse and would require a medium with the characteristics of a solid to support the wave. The ether concept could not be confirmed experimentally, and it became apparent that such a medium could not possibly exist. .

Following experiments which demonstrated that the speed of light was changed by a moving stream of water, the American physicists A. A. Michelson and E. W. Morley performed their famous interferometer experiment which brought about the abandonment of the ether concept. The devised a precise apparatus to measure the speed of the earth through the ether. From the results of their experiments it was concluded that the earth was not moving through the ether nor was the ether carried along by the earth in its motion through space.

JULIUS H. TALYOR, Morgan State College
See also MICHELSON-MORLEY EXPERIMENT.

ETHERS [ē'thərz], organic compounds having structures of the type R-O-R, where R is a hydrocarbon radical. They are chemically stable and good solvents for fats, oils, gums, and many other organic compounds. Ethers may be prepared by the dehydration of alcohols or by the reaction of sodium alkoxides with alkyl halides. This method makes possible the preparation of unsymmetrical ethers. Most of the diethyl ether and diisopropyl ether are obtained as by-products of ethyl and isopropyl alcohol manufacture from olefins. When ethers are permitted to stand in the presence of air, peroxides are formed which are highly explosive. Diethyl ether used for anesthesia must be completely free of such peroxides.

ETHICAL CULTURE, SOCIETY OF, an organization founded in New York City in 1876 by Felix Adler, on the basis of his conviction of the changeless character and absolute sovereignty of the moral law and the need of instruction in ethical principles. Societies were later founded in Chicago, Philadelphia, Boston, and other cities, each separate and autonomous, but with like aims. In 1889 the existing groups formed the American Ethical Union with the purpose of establishing new societies, the furtherance of the Ethical Culture Movement abroad, and the publication of literature interpreting the movement's principles and aims. Societies were established in England, Austria, and Germany.

The membership has never been large, but has included persons of great influence. The society allows the utmost freedom of theological thought, but always affirms its basically ethical nature. Ethical Culture meetings are conducted very much as church services, with music, meditation, the reading of Scripture or some other inspirational literature, and an address on some pertinent religious, philosophical, or moral theme. The movement has been quite active in practical efforts through education and social action to improve the level of social and individual life. Headquarters of the Ethical Union are in New York City, where the bimonthly periodical, *The Ethical Outlook*, is published.

CHARLES S. BRADEN, Northwestern University

ETHICS, the philosophical study of the nature of good, virtue, right, and other morally relevant terms. In Western culture, reflection on the nature of morality began in ancient Greece with the Sophists in the fifth century B.C. The Greeks were aware of the different moral customs of other peoples, as well as of differences existing between the Greek city-states. The awareness of diversity among customs led them to consider whether any moral practices could be regarded as better than others. Is there any possibility of disputing the correctness of opposing moral beliefs? The Sophists generally were moral skeptics because their professional posture precluded an absolutist position. They were basically teachers who sometimes advertised their talents by claiming that they could teach one to demonstrate the moral acceptability of any cause whatsoever. The teaching of success, in argument or life, was their main aim. One of the philosophical articulations of this aim is that "justice is the interest of the stronger," or, "might equals right."

The Early Greeks

Socrates (470?–399 B.C.) was the chief opponent of the Sophists. His views are presented in the early dialogues of his most famous pupil, Plato (427?–347), who portrays him as a good man in search of truth, regardless of the consequences of his pursuit. Indeed, Socrates was finally condemned to death because many believed his views were corrupting the youth of Athens. He did not have a completely defined conception of virtue, good, justice, or truth. He spent his energies in showing that those who felt they knew the truth about these subjects were really ignorant. He was willing at all times to confess his own ignorance. His wisdom consisted in showing that others were equally ignorant without knowing that they were. His most general belief was that virtue is knowledge.

Plato accepted Socrates' position on the relation of virtue and knowledge, arguing that there really must be entities rightly called "virtue" or "courage," which are distinct from individual acts of virtue or courage. These are the Ideas or Forms of the various moral qualities, and they enjoy a timeless and nonsensible existence. Through training and contemplation, a man may come to grasp the Form of the Good, enabling him actually to *be* good. Plato demonstrates the connection of justice and knowledge in his *Republic*, where he divides the soul into three parts— rational, spiritive, and passional. This division of the soul is patterned after a division of social classes, where a laboring, guardian, and governing class may be distinguished. The just society is one in which each class tends to its own business, everyone benefiting from a division of labor. Such a society must be governed by someone with a knowledge of how the labor should be divided. A state run on the basis of anything other than knowledge of the Good is bound to suffer from some defect. Similarly, a soul governed by passion is destined to suffer. The soul must be organized by reason, and this means that the just man is necessarily acquainted with truth. The great majority cannot attain knowledge and, consequently, cannot be personally just. However, by following their leaders who know the truth, they can be socially just. Plato's argument has been used to justify the subordination of subjects to their rulers.

Plato was not opposed to a life of pleasure, though he did not identify the good life with the pleasurable life. He argued that there were good and bad pleasures, and that the latter were based upon false judgment. The pleasures to be pursued are the pure ones, such as those of sight and hearing. Apprehending beautiful sights and sounds does not involve any admixture of pain. The more intense the pleasure, the greater likelihood of pain. Pleasures are rejected in accordance with their tendency to produce pain.

Aristotle (384–322 B.C.), Plato's most famous pupil, adopted many of his teacher's views, though his philosophical method was different. This difference is best illustrated in his critique of Plato's notion of the Good. Plato had argued that there must be some *one* thing which made all the individual acts which are rightly called "good," good. Aristotle rejected this argument, maintaining that there are many different ways in which the term "good" is used. Some things are good in themselves, others are good as means, and there are variations within these categories. It is wrong to suppose that some one thing makes all things good, though generally the realization of human purposes may be considered good. Building

houses, growing food, producing clothing is all good as a means to preserving and protecting man. Happiness is the only thing which is not pursued as a means but solely as an end, though it is difficult to specify exactly what happiness is.

As a keen biological observer, Aristotle was aware of the importance of functional explanation in the understanding of organic activity. Accordingly, he felt that happiness for man must consist in the realization of the function a man has insofar as he is a man, and not some unique individual. Man shares almost every function—life, nutrition, sensation—with plants and animals. Man's unique function is reason, and since every function may be exercised well or badly, it was Aristotle's contention that happiness for man involves the proper exercise of reason. It was his view that it is impossible to define any one mode of activity as virtuous. Courage, for example, is different for every man. The reckless man is easily foolhardy, the cautious man is easily cowardly. Courageousness is a mean between foolhardiness and cowardliness, but it differs for each man. Aristotle's analysis of the distinction between voluntary, involuntary, and nonvoluntary acts still stands as a deft piece of philosophical analysis, having both theoretical and practical import.

Stoics and Epicureans. The last movements in Greek ethics were Stoicism and Epicureanism, both of which manifested themselves as ways of attaining control over one's response to living conditions in the world. While the Stoics felt that a life lived in accord with the processes of nature was good, they also distinguished certain unhealthy aspects of life. They thought that dependence upon the material conditions of life was to be avoided. Through training and discipline, they believed that one could attain spiritual independence. The Epicureans dedicated their lives to the pursuit of pleasure, though in such a fashion as to minimize pain. Desire itself is depreciated because the never-ending cycle of desire, fulfillment, desire, fulfillment, produces a continuously unsettled state. The Epicureans identified pleasure more with tranquillity than with any positive emotional state.

The Rise of Modern Ethics

Hume and Kant. The direction of modern ethics has been shaped by a number of historical phenomena, most importantly the demise of church authority and the materialistic commitment generated by the growth of scientific inquiry. Philosophically, there was nothing new in the rejection of authority as a basis for morals. Nor were the problems new concerning the essential nature of human existence and the freedom of the will caused by the rising disbelief in the spirituality of the soul or mind. Both the ancients and medievalists had tangled with related problems. However, these developments tended to shake ethical inquiry loose from its religious moorings, opening new directions by making certain problems more immediate than others. The views of David Hume (1711–76) and Immanuel Kant (1724–1804) represent the two most important and contrasting approaches of the period. Hume launched a devasting attack upon naturalistic conceptions of morality. His views are reflected in the 20th-century belief that facts and values belong to separate and unrelated realms.

In his *Treatise of Human Nature*, Hume writes that "in every system of morality" he is "surprised to find, that instead of the usual copulations of propositions *is*, and *is not*, I meet with no proposition that is not connected with an *ought*, or an *ought not*." The reason Hume offers for his surprise is this: *ought* and *ought not* do not express the same relation as *is* and *is not* and, consequently, either the former cannot be deduced from the latter, or some reason must be produced showing how such a deduction is possible. Hume does not believe a reason could be produced because *is* and *is not* have to to do with truth and falsehood, whereas *ought* and *ought not* concern the passions or emotions. " 'Tis from the prospect of pain or pleasure that the aversion or propensity arises toward any object," but "a passion is an original existence," having no representative quality which could render it a copy of any possible existence or modification thereof. Truth and falsehood consist in the representative quality of ideas. If they represent reality, they are true. If not, they are false. Since a passion has no representative quality, it cannot be true or false. " 'Tis not contrary to reason to prefer the destruction of the whole world to the scratching of my finger." Consequently, one cannot point to facts or look to reason in order to support ethical beliefs.

The main thrust of the moral philosophy of Immanuel Kant was directed toward establishing a rational basis for ethical judgment. A rational judgment is one which applies to all men and to other rational creatures, if there are any, regardless of circumstance, personal inclination, desire, or purpose. Any law which serves as a basis for obligation must involve an absolute necessity. It must not be subject to conditions—that is, the judgement based upon it must be categorical and not hypothetical. The law meeting these criteria must be grounded in something that is good without qualification, namely, a good will. Other commendable qualities of mind, like courage, wit, intelligence, or perseverance, are good only if the character that possesses them is good, only if a good will governs their activities. A good will is not good because of what it effects, or for the attainment of some proposed end. It is good in itself. Most businessmen would agree that honesty is the best policy, and believing as they do, most act honestly. But the man who is honest only in policy abandons honesty if circumstances make it poor business practice. Contrast this sort of individual with the man who is honest because it is his duty: he is the man of good will. Doing the good thing *because* it is the good thing, and not because of any other reason, purpose, or motive, is the basis of all moral worth. "Duty is the necessity of acting from respect for the law." (*Fundamental Principles of the Metaphysic of Morals.*)

How does one act who acts out of respect for law? Kant maintains that "I am never to act otherwise than so that I could also will that my maxim should become a universal law." For example, if my financial circumstances are poor, it might serve my purpose to borrow money and promise to pay it back, even though I have no intention of doing so. Could I will that a lying promise become a universal law? No, since if everyone were justified in making a lying promise, it would no longer be possible to make a promise at all. No one would trust a promisor, making it impossible for him to promise. Universalizing my lying promise

would, therefore, be self-defeating. Furthermore, I could not will that someone make a lying promise to me and, consequently, I could not will that *everyone* act in the way that I wish to. A man who acts reasonably does not treat himself as an exception to law. He wills for himself only what he wills for others as well. Acting reasonably is, therefore, an end in itself, and Kant's practical imperative of all action is this: "So act as to treat humanity, whether in thine own person or in that of any other, in every case as an end withal, never as means only."

The Utilitarians

Bentham and the Mills. During the 19th century a number of philosophers attacked Kant's moral philosophy. The Utilitarian tradition, originated by Jeremy Bentham (1748–1832) and James Mill (1773–1836) and culminating in John Stuart Mill (1806–1873), was opposed to Kant's intentionalism. J. S. Mill maintained that a system of ethics is only to inform us what morality is. It is not the function of such a system to tell us what our motives or intentions should be. It does not matter whether we do the good thing *because* it is good. All that matters is that we do it. The leading principle of Utilitarianism is that actions are right in proportion as they produce happiness and wrong as they tend to cause the reverse. By happiness is meant pleasure, by unhappiness, pain. It was J. S. Mill's belief that pleasure and freedom from pain were the only things desirable as ends—not my pleasure necessarily, but that of the greatest number.

Arthur Schopenhauer (1788–1860) attacked the very basis of the Kantian ethic, maintaining that Kant confused the form of all laws with their content. It is true that a law by its very nature applies to all men, but that does not mean that one is obliged to indulge in lawlike behavior. Doing the good thing need not mean "acting from respect for the law." Furthermore, acting in a way that I would also allow others to act leaves open an egoistic determination of the good. Just because *I* would allow others some action does not mean that action is good. It was Schopenhauer's belief that the suffering and evil in the world was caused by the unrestrained action of the will, and that life is nothing but the mirror of the will. "Denial, abolition, conversion of the will, is also the abolition and the vanishing of the world, its mirror." (*The World as Will and Idea.*)

Friedrich Wilhelm Nietzsche (1844–1900) was influenced by the role Schopenhauer assigned the will in the formation of objectivity. But instead of denial of will, of self, Nietzsche found his answer in self-affirmation, in what he called the "will to power." He agreed with Schopenhauer that the creation of an objective value structure is due to will and is the cause of suffering and depravity. But Nietzsche believed that the creation of objective value structures is the product of weakness. The main purpose of such a system is to provide a lever for the weak against the strong ("the meek shall inherit the earth"), as well as a basis for them to believe in their own worth. In analyzing the genealogy of terms like "good" and "virtue," he discovered that they originally meant "noble" or "of aristocratic character," in the sense of high intelligence and strength. Those who are noble exude value from their very being. The values we assign are completely subjective, and what we have come to recognize as value is a reversal of the true position.

Max Scheler (1874–1928) developed Nietzsche's views, arguing that much of morality is the old story of the fox and the sour grapes: realizing a tension between one's lack of ability and a projected value, one is apt to ease the tension by denigrating the value and those who live up to it. Gradually, without conscious realization, one comes to adopt the values which provoke the least tension between incapacity and ideal. The weaker one is, the more the adopted values will represent a denial of life.

Existentialism

Some critics have questioned whether Existentialism has any ethics at all. The absence of an objective system of rules seems an absence of ethics. However, it is the very absence of objectivity which provides the basis for the Existentialist ethics. The recognition and acceptance of the human condition is the starting point for the Existentialist. Although there is some variation in the way the human condition is depicted by different philosophers in the movement, the core idea is always the same. It is a desire for permanence of meaning and significance of purpose, as opposed to flux, purposelessness, nothingness.

Jean-Paul Sartre (1905–). According to Sartre, the being of human reality is negativity. There are, for him, two levels of thought, reflective and pre-reflective, the latter being the constitutive precondition of the former. Consciousness, in the case of the pre-reflective *cogito* (I think), involves both a subject and object, yet when one comes to distinguish reflectively the nature of the subject, one can do so only by contrasting it to what it is *not*, the object of consciousness. Furthermore, direct reflection on a self reveals negativity also, in the sense that we can be aware of ourselves as what we *have* been and are *not* now, or as a project that we aim at, yet are *not* at present. Our past being is finished, completed, our future being is an open possibility. We are, in this sense, condemned to be free, since the heart of our being is always nothingness. The being of objects, however, is completely determinate. They are what they are and do not need to be contrasted with something else to characterize their being. A person must bear the responsibility of the freedom he possesses in the negative aspect of his being. He must avoid thinking of himself as something determinate, yet he must engage in determinate activity in order to be anything at all. This is the paradox of human existence, and there is no way out. Traditional escapes, such as God as an ultimate explanation and salvation, all come to the same sort of objectifying that Nietzsche so despised. The Existentialist hero lives a lonely existence, but he is authentic. He does not falsify his condition, and it is this which constitutes the basis of the Existentialist ethic.

Contemporary British and American Thinkers

Twentieth-century Anglo-American ethics, similar to Existentialism, has been motivated by a rebellion against traditional forms of naturalism, though it has had a negligible psychological orientation compared to Existentialism.

G. E. Moore (1873–1958) had much to do with establishing both a method and a direction for recent moral philosophy. It was his belief that "good" is a simple, nonnatural, indefinable property, and that the project of traditional ethics, insofar as it was to define the term "good," is doomed to failure. It is clear that "good" has a meaning, but equally clear that it cannot be defined. If someone asks, "Is pleasure really good?" it is evident that he is not wondering whether pleasure is really pleasant. But if "pleasure" were the definition of "good," then the one term would be a substitution for the other, and obviously no such substitution works in this case. In fact, no matter what term one attempts to use in order to define "good," it will always make sense to ask, "But is ____ really good?" The fact that this kind of question may always be meaningfully asked indicates (1) that "good" is not a meaningless term, and (2) that it cannot be defined in the way that, for example, "bachelor" may be defined as "unmarried man." One simply intuits good. Moore did not believe that ethical propositions were merely expressive of feelings because it makes sense to dispute about values. Clearly, if moral assertions were merely expressive of feeling, such disputes would be both idle and meaningless. It was this consideration which helped convince Moore that "good" must refer to a property, albeit an indefinable, nonnatural one.

A. J. Ayer (1910–) provides the clearest statement of the Positivist position in ethics. In claiming that some activity is wrong or not good, "I am merely expressing certain moral sentiments" (*Language, Truth and Logic*), and expressions of feeling cannot be classified as true or false. This being the case, there really is no disputing value. What usually passes for a value dispute is some factual question about motives or the probable consequences of some activity. But two people with completely different value systems could never meaningfully dispute a question of value. Charles L. Stevenson (1908–) gave a more refined statement of the positivistic position. He argued that ethical statements not only express feeling (whether the feeling is actually experienced or not is irrelevant), but also serve as *quasi-imperatives*, exhorting the listener to behave in a certain way.

R. M. Hare (1919–) more recently referred to the "persuasive" character of ethical statements as their prescriptivity (they prescribe behavior), in order to contrast them with descriptive statements. But Hare believes that moral statements share with descriptive ones, what he calls universalizability. If I describe my desk as brown, then I must describe other qualitatively identical objects as brown, also. Similarly, if I call a given act wrong, then under similar conditions I must call similar acts wrong as well. According to Hare, universalizability is a purely logical feature of our use of moral terms, not a substantive, moral rule itself.

M. G. Singer (1926–), among some other contemporary philosophers, views something akin to universalizability—namely, generalization—as playing a more normative role than Hare is willing to allow.

Consult Readings in Ethical Theory, ed. by W. S. Sellars and John Hospers (1952); *Ethical Theories: A Book of Readings*, ed. by A. I. Melden (1955); Warnock, Mary, *Ethics Since 1900* (1960).

EMILIO ROMA, State University of N.Y. at Binghamton
See also PHILOSOPHY.

ETHIOPIA

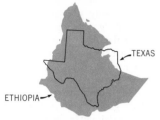

ETHIOPIA
TEXAS

country is bordered on the north by the Red Sea, on the east by Somalia and French Somaliland, on the south by Kenya, and on the west by the Sudan. Its area of approximately 457,300 sq. mi. is larger than that of California and Texas combined. Eritrea (approx. 48,000 sq. mi.), forming the northern coastal region, was federated with Ethiopia in 1952 and fully united with it in 1962.

The Land

Physical Features. Ethiopia and Eritrea have a geography bordering on the bizarre. The physical setting is marked by extreme diversity, and mountain and desert barriers isolate the population centers from the outside world. The country as a whole can be divided into five major physiographic regions. The core region and the heartland of Ethiopian culture and history is the central plateau. It has the shape of a triangle, with its longest base along a line running from the north of Eritrea to the borders of Kenya in the south. The apex of this triangle is toward the west near the Sudanese frontier, and the whole occupies slightly less than half of the total area of the country. Along the north-south edge, the plateau rises abruptly in an escarpment 3,000 to 6,000 ft. in height, both plateau and escarpment being somewhat higher to the north. The whole plateau slopes off gradually to the west and south, but it is not a level plain. Instead, altitudes may vary from 7,000 to 14,000 ft. above sea level, and the entire surface is heavily eroded. Steep-sided river valleys separate one section from another, and erosion has left many mesalike formations or flat-topped mountains (called *ambas*) above the level of the plateau. Thus, while the escarpment gives the plateau region something of the character of a natural fortress, it is a fortress with very bad intercommunication. The central plateau is, nevertheless, the most fertile and heavily populated section of the country. Most of its large rivers become a part of the vast Nile system.

The central plateau is separated from other highland regions by the rift valley, a formation produced in the geologic past when a long, narrow segment of land dropped below the level of the surrounding country along the lines of two parallel faults. As a general geographic feature, the

AREA	Approx. 457,300 sq. mi.
ELEVATION	
Highest point	
(Ras Dashan)	15,157 ft.
Lowest point	
(Danakil depression)	380 ft. below sea level
POPULATION	Approx. 22,000,000
LANGUAGES	Amharic, English, Tigre, Tigrinya, Italian
LIFE EXPECTANCY	35–40 years
PERCENTAGE OF LITERACY	1%–5%
UNIT OF CURRENCY	Ethiopian dollar
NATIONAL ANTHEM	*Ityopya hoy dass yiballish* ("Let Ethiopia be joyous")
CAPITAL	Addis Ababa
PRINCIPAL PRODUCTS	Coffee, hides and skins, oil seeds, cereals, and legumes

ETHIOPIA [ē-thē-ō′pē-ə], formally the **EMPIRE OF ETHIOPIA,** a country of East Africa, consisting of Ethiopia proper (formerly known as Abyssinia) and Eritrea (former Italian colony). Located just inland from the "horn" of Africa, the

This road winds over characteristic Ethiopian terrain, descending from plateau to plain through a valley.

Ancient and modern meanings of the term "Ethiopia" are not the same. In the ancient world Ethiopia was the name of a vaguely defined territory in the middle Nile region, called the land of the "burnt faces," and including Nubia and part of the Sudan. It was called Kush by the Hebrews. This kingdom grew powerful enough to conquer Egypt and its rulers became Egypt's 25th Dynasty. Defeated by the Assyrians, Kush moved its capital to Meroë, which was ravaged by the Aksumites in the 4th century A.D. The Aksumite Kingdom was the forerunner of what the modern world knows as Ethiopia. The country is also known unofficially by the name Abyssinia.

Ethiopia has a long record of isolation and independence. At the end of the 19th century when imperialist powers had carved up Africa only Liberia and Ethiopia remained independent. Ethiopian history and civilization are described in the article on these pages, which has the following outline.

The Land. Physical features; climate; major cities.

The People. Ethiopians; the Galla; other ethnic groupings; religion; education; cultural activities.

The Economy. Economic conditions; transportation.

Government. Structure of government: a constitutional monarchy.

History. Origins; kingdom of Aksum; introduction of Christianity; isolation of Ethiopia resulting from the rise of Islam; contacts with the Portuguese; centuries of disorder; progress in the 19th century; defeat of an Italian invasion (1896); the 20th century — Emperor Haile Selassie, conquest by Italy (1936), liberation during World War II.

For further study, the reader can turn first to the article AFRICA. Major geographic features such as GREAT RIFT VALLEY, NILE RIVER, and TANA, LAKE are covered in separate articles. ERITREA, the only coastal province, and important cities, such as ADDIS ABABA, ASMARA, MASSAWA, and HARAR, also are individually treated. Several languages are spoken in Ethiopia. They are classified in ETHIOPIC LANGUAGES, CUSHITIC LANGUAGES, and SEMITIC LANGUAGES. The conversion of Ethiopia to Christianity was probably begun by ST. FRUMENTIUS in the 4th century A.D. The reasons for its separation from Catholicism are discussed in MONOPHYSITES and COPTIC CHURCH. Another religion important in the country is treated in ISLAM and MUSLIM.

Ethiopia attracted world attention in the 19th century by its successful resistance to Italian efforts to make it a protectorate (see AFRICA: *History*, IMPERIALISM, and MENELIK II). In the 20th century Ethiopia became the focus of a world crisis. In 1935 the Fascist government of Italy attacked Ethiopia. Haile Selassie appealed to the League of Nations for help, but the League proved unable to take effective action. This failure weakened the prestige of the League of Nations, discouraged believers in peace and democracy, strengthened and encouraged the Fascist dictatorship in Italy, and may be considered a step toward World War II. This affair was part of the totalitarian challenge to the democratic nations discussed in DEMOCRACY. Other related articles are LEAGUE OF NATIONS, HAILE SELASSIE and ITALO-ETHIOPIAN WAR. Later events are included in WORLD WAR II.

Many articles conclude with lists of selected books through which the reader can extend his study of Ethiopia. These and other sources may be available in the library. The Ethiopian government is attempting to establish industry, improve education, reform administration, and in general to Westernize the country. To keep up with problems and progress, the reader can rely on such sources as the annual supplement to this Encyclopedia.

Great Rift Valley extends from the Sea of Galilee in the Palestine area far into Central Africa. Its Ethiopian segment passes through the country from north to south along the eastern base of the central plateau. The southern Ethiopian rift valley is narrow, at times less than 30 mi. wide. There are steep escarpments on either side, and a succession of small lakes occupies parts of the high valley floor. From the town of Awash northward, however, the rift valley broadens out into a lower funnel-shaped region of plains and low mountains. The northern and western part of this funnel is occupied by low, hot plains descending to 380 ft. below sea level in the Danakil depression. On the east, however, the southern Eritrean highlands extend into the rift valley along the Red Sea coast, and altitudes here may exceed 6,000 ft.

To the east of the rift valley is the eastern plateau, a second highland area much like the central plateau in elevation and geography. Again, as in the central plateau, the highest land is along the edge of the rift valley.

The two remaining physiographic regions are centered outside of the country itself, but have fringe areas extending within the frontiers of the Ethiopian state. One of these is the dry eastern plains in the corner formed by the boundaries of the Northern Region (formerly British Somaliland) and Southern Region (formerly Italian Somaliland) of Somalia. The other is a narrow strip of plain stretching along the entire length of the frontier between Ethiopia and the Sudan.

Climate. Both temperature and rainfall vary with altitude in Ethiopia, and the country is traditionally divided into three climatic zones based on altitude. The plateaus and higher mountains above 8,000 ft. are *dega*, a cool, well-watered region used mainly for grazing above 9,000 ft., and for cereals and temperate agriculture below that level. From 6,000 to 8,000 ft. is the *woin dega*—a warmer region varying from temperate to subtropical. This is the chief zone for crops such as coffee. The plateau regions and the high, southern rift valley are a combination of *dega* and *woin dega*, though the local variations of altitude are so great that the climatic map becomes a patchwork. Below 6,000 ft. is the *quolla* region, which is warm to very hot. This is mainly a land of sparse pasture, since it is generally too dry for most crops except where irrigation works are possible. Most of the northern rift valley, the Eritrean coast, and the eastern and western plains fall within this region. The well-watered regions enjoy a double rainy season, with one occurring in April and May and a second, larger rainy season, in July and August.

Major Cities. Addis Ababa is the capital and largest city. Asmara, the capital of Eritrea Province, is second in size; Massawa, on the Red Sea, is the chief port; Harar and Dessye are important provincial centers. Other cities include Dire Dawa, Gore, Jijiga, Debra Markos, Gondar, Jimma, Assab, and Keren.

The People

Ethiopians. The core area of the central plateau north of Addis Ababa is inhabited by the Tigre-Amharic people. They are the Ethiopians of history, though now outnumbered two to one by other inhabitants of the Empire. They

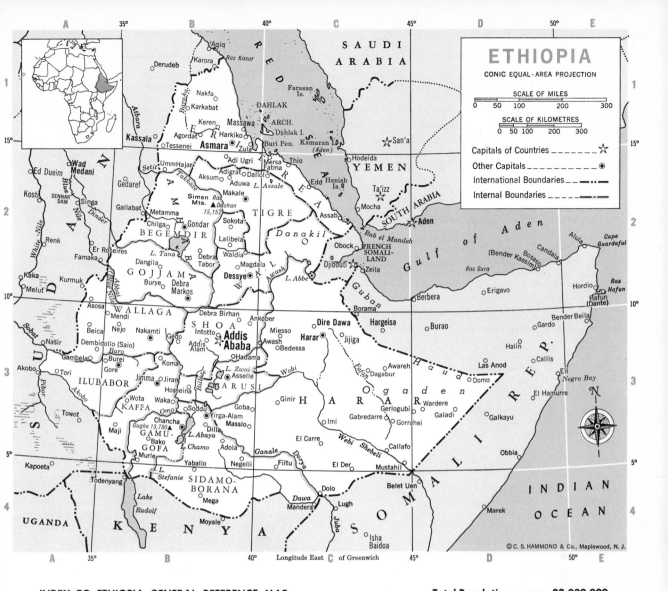

ETHIOPIA

CONIC EQUAL-AREA PROJECTION

SCALE OF MILES

0 50 100   200   300

SCALE OF KILOMETRES

0 50 100   200   300

Capitals of Countries _ _ _ _ _ _ _ ☆
Other Capitals _ _ _ _ _ _ _ _ _ ◉
International Boundaries _ _ _ _ _
Internal Boundaries _ _ _ _ _

© C. S. HAMMOND & Co., Maplewood, N. J.

INDEX TO ETHIOPIA GENERAL REFERENCE MAP

Total Population approx. 22,000,000

539

are distinguished by the fact that they practice settled agriculture, are Christian in religion, and speak languages in the Semitic subfamily of the Afro-Asiatic or Hamito-Semitic language family. There are three languages in this group—Amharic, Tigre, and Tigrinya. All three are derived from Ge'ez, a language no longer spoken, but still used as the liturgical language of the Ethiopian Church. Amharic is the most important of these and is also the national language. The Tigre-Amharic people, like most of their countrymen, were formerly classified as Hamitic in race, but the term confuses race and language. Ethiopian is a more accurate term for the stabilized racial mixture, characterized by dark skin and features resembling those of Europeans.

The Galla. The largest ethnic group in Ethiopia is the Galla people. They are racially similar to the Tigre-Amharic but are mainly non-Christian, speak a distinct language, and were nomadic tribesmen until recent times. Their original home was in the eastern plateau and the lowlands toward Somalia, but for centuries they have invaded the Tigre-Amharic lands of the central plateau. There are, therefore, scattered Galla districts in other regions, and especially to the south and southwest of Addis Ababa. The Gallas are still mainly pagan, but many have converted to Christianity or Islam. Some have assimilated Tigre-Amharic culture, though relations with the dominant minority vary greatly from province to province. The Galla language belongs to the Cushitic subfamily of the Afro-Asiatic language family, along with Somali and Dankali, spoken in the southeastern and northern plains.

Other Ethnic Groupings. In addition to the two major ethnic groups there are a number of smaller cultural groupings, of which the most important is the Negro minority of the south and southwest. These people speak one of the many languages of the Macro-Sudanic language family and make up from 5% to 10% of the population.

Religion. Religious lines in Ethiopia roughly parallel ethnic divisions. About 40% are Coptic Christians, about 40% are Muslims, and about 20% are pagan or Roman Catholic. The Tigre-Amharic minority are Christians, and Christianity is the state religion. Historically, it has been separated from Catholicism since the Council of Chalcedon, 451 A.D., when the Monophysite controversy divided the Roman and Alexandrian churches. From then onward, with few lapses, the Ethiopian Church was attached to the Coptic Patriarchate of Alexandria. The Patriarch had the right to appoint the *Abuna*, or Archbishop, of the Ethiopian Church, and this official was usually an Egyptian. Following liberation from Italy during World War II, the Church broke the administrative bond with Egypt.

Education. There is a dual system of education—traditional education provided by the religious communities, and Westernized education by government schools and foreign missions. The traditional schools, which are mainly religious, use Amharic and Ge'ez for instruction and train for the Christian priesthood, while the Muslim community has its own schools giving Koranic training in Arabic.

Under the Westernized system there are eight years of primary education, beginning in Amharic and continuing after the third grade with English, which gradually becomes the language of instruction. There are about 70,000 students in government primary schools and 8,500 in private Western schools. At the secondary level, government schools have about 2,000 students and aim at a Western standard of achievement, as represented by the London University General Certificate.

In Dec., 1961, the Haile Selassie I University was dedicated in Addis Ababa. The university college and the technical schools which were established by the government over the years were incorporated into the university system. Higher education is provided by the university and by scholarships for training abroad. There are a number of overseas scholarship students, mainly in the United Kingdom, Canada, and the United States. Meanwhile, the government is developing a more complete system of secondary and higher education at home.

Cultural Activities. Alongside the new Western learning, Ethiopia has an ancient tradition and a written literature extending back to the pre-Christian era. This literature is mostly religious in nature and mostly in Ge'ez before about the 13th century. After that period more secular works appeared, and more works in Amharic. At present books are published in both Amharic and Western languages. The Amharic press concentrates on nonfiction, but a few novels and plays have been published in recent decades. The aesthetic outlet for most Ethiopians is the traditional music, dance, painting, and folk art, though Western music and dancing have made their appearance in the cities.

Economy

Economic Condition. The only really important natural resource of Ethiopia is its land. The natural fortress of the plateaus is well watered and has fine soils for farming, although poor communication and transportation facilities have so far prevented the development of other potential forms of wealth. Exports are almost entirely agricultural products, with coffee alone accounting for more than half of the total. Hides and skins, oil seeds, cereals, and legumes are exports of lesser importance. Gold is the only mineral produced in significant quantities. Light industry produces for domestic consumption, especially in food processing and building materials. Most manufactured

Coptic priests in antique headdresses of gold and silver.

Patellani—Pix

products are imported, though the government is now attempting to encourage investment and industrialization as much as possible.

Transportation. Most goods entering and leaving the country pass through either Djibouti in French Somaliland or Massawa in Eritrea. A French-operated railway of 488 mi. connects Addis Ababa and Djibouti. In Eritrea, a government-operated railway of 189 mi. connects Massawa and Agordat, passing through Asmara. Other mechanized transportation is provided by a network of approximately 3,500 mi. of all-weather roads and almost twice that mileage of secondary roads and tracks. The main roads diverge from Addis Ababa to most of the major regions of the country. There is also the government-owned Ethiopian Air Lines, which maintains flights between more than 20 Ethiopian towns and has international services to neighboring countries, the Middle East, and Europe. In spite of these facilities, most Ethiopian transport is still nonmechanized.

United Nations

Africa Hall, in Addis Ababa, headquarters for the United Nations Economic Commission for Africa.

Government

The formal structure of the Ethiopian government is that of a constitutional monarchy under the constitution promulgated in 1955, which superseded the 1931 constitution. It contains some elements of representative government, but in general leaves real power in the hands of the emperor. The upper house (senate) of the bicameral legislature is appointed by the emperor, and the lower house (chamber of deputies) is elected directly by qualified voters. Laws may be proposed to either or both houses by the emperor or by 10 or more members of either house. The emperor maintains an absolute veto over all legislation. The executive branch is under a cabinet of 12 ministers, appointed by and responsible to the emperor. The judicial system consists of the Supreme Imperial Court (the highest court in the land), the High Court, provincial courts, and regional and communal courts. Special courts, called Kadis and Naibas Councils, have jurisdiction over the personal status of Muslims. Appointed governors are in charge of each of the 13 provinces into which the country is divided. The quality and efficiency of government vary widely from province to province.

The government is, in sum, an absolute monarchy tempered by vested interests of traditionally important families, which wield influence in the provinces, and by the emperor's desire to modernize along Western lines.

History

The history of Ethiopia is that of a country which has maintained itself for centuries in isolation, surrounded by people of alien culture and religion. The entrance of civilization into Ethiopia may date from as early as 1000 B.C., when people from the Semitic kingdom of Saba, or Sheba, in southwest Arabia migrated across the straits of Africa. Earlier migrants speaking a Cushitic language had probably already pushed the Negro peoples out of the highland regions. By the 2d century B.C. the Semitic-speaking migrants had developed the kingdom of Aksum, centered in the modern province of Tigre. The Aksumites controlled the Red Sea coast and, through their port at Adulis (near modern Massawa), they maintained commercial relations with Greco-Roman civilization. In the middle of the 4th century A.D. the Aksumite kingdom was converted to Christianity by Egyptian monks, who entered by way of Adulis; and from then onward Ethiopian Christianity was closely associated with the Christianity of Egypt.

The most important turning point in Ethiopian history was the rise of Islam in nearby Arabia, since this broke most of the cultural and commercial connections between Ethiopia and the Mediterranean world. In the 640's Egypt fell to Muslim invaders, and the Coptic Church continued only at the sufferance of an Islamic government. In the early 8th century Adulis was captured by the Arabs and the mountain kingdom was cut off from its contact with the Red Sea and the outside world. From then onward until the 13th century the Christian kingdom was very hard pressed from all sides, and there was a period of cultural sterility which may be considered the "dark ages" of Ethiopian history. In 1270, however, a new dynasty was founded, claiming descent from Solomon, and the Christian kingdom began to expand slightly at the expense of its Muslim and pagan neighbors, moving on to a new period of strength and creativity in the 15th and early 16th centuries.

Contact with the West was re-established in the late 15th century, when Portuguese travelers searching for a route to India arrived at the Ethiopian court, hoping they had discovered the kingdom of the legendary Prester John. It was not until the 1520's, however, that Francisco Alvarez came as an envoy from Portugal and returned to Europe with a description of the country. Alvarez' visit marks the beginning of a century of Portuguese missions to Ethiopia—religious, military, and diplomatic. In the end they failed in their effort to convert the Ethiopians to Catholicism. Turkey rose to new power in the Eastern Mediterranean and the Red Sea, and access to Ethiopia was only possible by passing through the Turkish blockade. One King, Susenyos (1607–32), was converted to Catholicism by Jesuit missionaries, but he was overthrown by a rising of the nobility. After 1632 Catholic missionary work was forbidden, and Ethiopia returned to its earlier isolation from the West.

At first, under Fasilidas (1632–65), there was a period

of peace and relative stability. A new capital was established at Gondar, and a brief resurgence of Ethiopian power took place; but it could not be maintained. The nobility in the provinces came to control their own affairs with increasing independence from Gondar. The nomadic Gallas from the east and south successfully raided into the very heart of the Empire, virtually separating the kingdom of Shoa (ancient kingdom which became Ethiopia's chief province) from the rest of the country.

This period of disorders lasted until 1855, when a former bandit made himself master of Gondar and then of the central plateau region. He had himself crowned Emperor under the name Theodore (1855–68), but he was not able to keep his power or pass it to a successor. The modern government of Ethiopia descends from new power which rose in the 1870's in the vicinity of Addis Ababa. The new strong man was Menelik of Shoa, who conquered much of the south for the quasi-independent kingdom of Shoa, extending his rule over the Gallas and far beyond the area of Tigre-Amharic culture. In 1899 he became Emperor of Ethiopia (see MENELIK II), defending the country during the decades when European imperialism was most active in Africa. By skillful diplomacy he fended off successive threats from Britain, France, and Italy; but in 1896 diplomacy was no longer sufficient, and he had to meet a major Italian military attack. The imperial forces, combined with the provincial forces of Tigre, defeated the Italians at Aduwa, ending the immediate European danger.

The death of Menelik in 1913 brought a new period of confusion and anarchy, which ended only in 1930, when Ras Tafari, a powerful nobleman, established himself as Emperor under the throne name of Haile Selassie (q.v.). During the first five years of his reign he endeavored to strengthen and reform the government so as to withstand possible European attack, but his government fell before the Italian invasion of 1935, and Ethiopia was governed as an Italian colony until 1941.

During World War II Haile Selassie was re-established on the throne with the aid of Great Britain and the Commonwealth. The reconquest was followed by a new period of reform and Westernization in Ethiopia. The church was separated from its Egyptian connections, and in 1952 the former Italian colony of Eritrea was united to the Empire under a federation agreement. In Nov., 1962, however, Eritrea's status was changed to that of a province.

A *coup d'état* led by intellectuals took place in Addis Ababa in Dec., 1960, while Haile Selassie was on a state visit to Brazil. The Emperor quickly returned to resume control of the government. Although the revolt was abortive, it prompted the Emperor to accelerate the pace of administrative, social, and economic reforms. In May, 1963, Ethiopia became one of the original members of the Organization of African Unity, in whose formation the Emperor played a major role.

Consult Trimingham, J. S., *Islam in Ethiopia* (1952); Talbot, D. A., *Contemporary Ethiopia* (1953); Jones, A.H.M., and Monroe, Elizabeth, *A History of Ethiopia* (1955); Howard, W. E., *Public Administration in Ethiopia* (1956); Luther, E. W., *Ethiopia Today* (1958); Doresse, Jean, *Ethiopia* (1960).

PHILIP D. CURTIN, University of Wisconsin

ETHIOPIAN WAR. *See* ITALO-ETHIOPIAN WAR.

ETHIOPIC [ē-thē-ŏp'ĭk] **LANGUAGES,** a group of languages within the southern branch of the Semitic subgroup of the Afro-Asiatic family of languages. Some time in the 1st millennium B.C. Semites from south Arabia entered Ethiopia, bringing with them a Semitic language and script which developed into the Ethiopic language.

Ge'ez, or ancient Ethiopic, is no longer spoken; it is the language of the liturgy. Tigre and Tigrinya are closely related to Ge'ez. Amharic is the national language of Ethiopia. Argobba, Harari, Gafat (now extinct), and Gurage are related to Amharic.

ETHNOCENTRISM [ĕth-nō-sĕn'trĭz-əm], according to the classical definition of William Graham Sumner, is a view of the world "in which one's own group is the center of everything, and all others are scaled and rated with reference to it." Thus to the ancient Greeks and Romans, all outsiders were "barbarians." Many tribes call themselves simply "men" or "human beings," while all others are something less. The members of many modern nations assume that their cultural patterns are right and proper, while the practices and beliefs of others are correct only in the degree to which they approximate those of one's own group.

Although ordinarily used to refer to a belief that overrates one's own society in relation to all others, ethnocentrism sometimes implies a belief in the superiority of a smaller group such as a region, a city, a religious group, a social class, or an ethnic enclave within a society. Thus in meaning it may approximate provincialism, prejudice, intolerance, and other terms connoting in-group superiority.

From the individual's point of view, ethnocentrism is simply a belief which he is taught and readily accepts because it reveals him to be a good group member, enhances his self-esteem, and facilitates his interaction with other members of the group. For the society, ethnocentrism serves to reinforce the normative system by giving it a kind of ultimate reality. The culture of a society is an elaborate and sometimes painfully acquired style of life by means of which the members have learned to struggle with problems of survival, security, and social interaction. A belief that supports this system has value under some conditions. However, when problems of security and social interaction involve continuous interdependent contact between ethnocentric groups, the belief in the superiority of a particular society may be a serious obstacle to the satisfaction of the very needs from which it originally grew.

J. MILTON YINGER, Oberlin College

See also MINORITIES.

ETHNOGRAPHY [ĕth-nŏg'rə-fē], the detailed descriptive study of the culture or way of life of individual groups of people. A modern ethnographic study attempts to record as much information about a given society as possible. It describes subsistence patterns; technology and material culture; social organization by relationship, by association, and by political structure; prestige systems; customary behavior; law; science; religion; world outlook; tradition; and the way such factors relate to each other within the life of the group to produce the fabric of daily life on the one hand and the kind of people in the society on the other. Ethnographers are also interested in the degree to which contact with other cultures and societies may have affected the group under study and in the degree of cultural conservatism, the maintenance of culture patterns despite the pressures to change.

Ethnographic studies vary in completeness, of course, according to available information, the major interests of the ethnographer, the circumstances under which he worked, and the time in which they were written. They do, however, provide the basic material for the more generalized and comparative studies of ethnology, which as a discipline attempts to uncover the laws and principles that underlie the functioning and development of culture and the course of its history. Ethnography can be regarded both as a subdivision and as a foundation of ethnology, which in turn is one of the subfields of cultural anthropology.

ROBERT W. EHRICH, Brooklyn College,
The City University of New York

See also ANTHROPOLOGY; CULTURE; ETHNOLOGY.

ETHNOLOGY [ĕth-nŏl′ə-jē], the comparative study of peoples and cultures. Although broadly concerned with the principles of cultural development and cultural functioning, the field has two main orientations: (1) the schools of ethnology that are primarily interested in cultural development and culture history and (2) those that stress the more immediate and nonhistorical inquiry into how particular cultures actually function.

In the first group we can recognize several schools of thought: (a) those that attempt to deal with general laws of culture development as they may apply to mankind as a whole; (b) what is now called historical particularism, in which ethnologists try to reconstruct either the cultural history of particular groups of people, or the origins and diffusion of particular ideas, inventions, trait complexes, and area patterns; and (c) an emerging search for cultural regularities where sets of similar conditions may restrict the number of possible variable solutions for common problems of human living.

Ethnologists of nonhistorical orientation concentrate on such problems as how various facets of culture affect each other, how cultures change, to what degree various cultural practices or pressures affect the development of personality, and how patterned behaviors and practices within societies affect relations between people.

As distinct from ethnography, which is regarded as one of its subdivisions, ethnology deals comparatively with materials from different cultures, whereas ethnography deals descriptively with cultures, one at a time, and provides much of the data with which ethnologists work.

Ethnology is one of the broad divisions of cultural anthropology, and in turn has several subfields of its own, including social anthropology, culture and personality studies, and comparative linguistics.

ROBERT W. EHRICH, Brooklyn College,
The City University of New York

See also ANTHROPOLOGY; CULTURE; CULTURE AND PERSONALITY; ETHNOGRAPHY.

ETHNOMUSICOLOGY [ĕth-nō-mū-zĭ-kŏl′ə-jē], the scientific study of music of the world's cultures, especially those outside Western civilization, in a descriptive and historical manner. Interest in music of other peoples and cultures began in the 19th century. Such music has attracted scholars from the fields of general musicology, anthropology, psychology, folklore, and linguistics. Originally known as comparative musicology, the science became generally known as ethnomusicology around 1950 because of its close association with ethnology.

Areas of Music. Traditionally, ethnomusicology comprises three broad areas of music: (1) The music of pre-literate peoples, that is, those who did not themselves develop a system of writing their own language. This is frequently called primitive music; however, the term "primitive" is possibly misleading because it implies an early stage in human development, something that cannot always be taken for granted in spite of the relatively simple style of most of this music. Examples of pre-literate cultures are those of the American Indians, African Negroes, Oceanians, Australian aborigines, among others. (2) The music of the high cultures of Asia—China, Japan, Indonesia, India, Persia, and Arabia. The cultural setting of this music is analogous to that of art music in Western civilization. (3) The folk music of the West. These three bodies of music, though not specifically related to each other, can be studied by the same methods.

Methods. Ethnomusicology has had to develop special devices for measuring intervals, scales, and rhythms, and for describing exotic musical styles. One of these devices is the cent system (invented by Alexander J. Ellis, 1890) which designates musical intervals by means of cents. Thus the octave is 1,200 cents, and each of the 12 piano semitones is 100 cents. In the scales of other cultures larger and smaller intervals (which cannot be played on the piano) are thereby readily described by their number of cents.

Ethnomusicologists are generally equally interested in the structure of exotic music and in its cultural background, that is, in the use made of music by various cultures, the role of music in the thinking of other peoples, the role of musicians, and so forth. The methods of ethnomusicology can also be applied to Western cultivated music, and after 1955 exchange of ideas and methods between this field and musicology at large increased greatly. In addition to fostering study and research, ethnomusicologists are also interested in performing the music of other cultures.

Research in ethnomusicology normally begins with field work; the raw material, which is found in cultures lacking a music notation, must be recorded on disc or tape, and its cultural background ascertained through interview and observation. The musical material is then transcribed into notation, a very time-consuming process which requires special training. Electronic machines have been invented to aid transcription. Field recordings of such music are stored in archives such as that in the Library of Congress.

Founders. Among the important early ethnomusicologists, the following must be mentioned: the Germans Carl Stumpf (1848–1936), Curt Sachs (1881–1959), and Erich Moritz von Hornbostel (1877–1935); the Americans Frances Densmore (1867–1957) and George Herzog (1901–   ); the Dutch Jaap Kunst (1891–1960); the great

Hungarian composer Béla Bartók (1881–1945); and the Englishman Alexander Ellis (1814–90). Ethnomusicology has been most strongly developed in Germany and the United States. Several societies, particularly the Society for Ethnomusicology (in the United States) and the International Folk Music Council, have been formed to promote the study.

Consult Nettl, Bruno, *Music in Primitive Culture* (1956); various issues of *Ethnomusicology, Journal of the Society for Ethnomusicology* (1957–   ); Kunst, Jaap, *Ethnomusicology* (3d ed., 1959); Sachs, Curt, *The Wellsprings of Music, An Introduction to Musicology* (1962).

BRUNO NETTL, Wayne State University

See also FOLK MUSIC; MUSICOLOGY; PRIMITIVE MUSIC; entries on the music of individual countries.

ETHOLOGY, biological study of animal behavior in its natural state. For the ethologist, all animal behavior must be analyzed not only in regard to its cause, but also for its function in furthering survival. The mechanistic views held by science around the turn of the century favored other psychological theories, notably behaviorism, which explains an animal's action on the basis of its response to a stimulus. Experimentalists are looking for "how" the animal behaves, but the ethologist first asks "why." In the last few decades, especially through the work of K. Z. Lorenz and Niko Tinbergen in Europe, the naturalistic observation of behavior has come to supplement the laboratory study of behavior which has burgeoned in the United States.

The ethologist likes to make a dossier of all the animal's behavior, called an ethogram. The units of behavior in this catalogue are subsequently analyzed, especially stereotyped behaviors that could have an instinctive background. In such behavior sequences it is possible to find motor actions that seem automated because they always proceed in the same manner—the so-called fixed action pattern (FAP). They are brought about by a "sign stimulus," or releaser. It is hypothesized that a drive makes the animal look for the specific stimulus situation needed for such actions. The predictable defensive behavior of the male European robin, when it sees another male robin while patrolling its territory, may serve as an example. The releaser for the robin's threatening actions is the orange-colored breast of the intruder, since it has been shown that a stuffed robin without the orange breast is not attacked, and a tuft of orange feathers is attacked by the irate territory-owner.

Another typical animal behavior pattern revealed by ethological studies is imprinting. Imprinting is the rapid establishment of social preferences in the young animal, which will remain in force for life without continuous reinforcement. Lorenz imprinted himself on young geese by being present at their hatching. They followed him as their mother, and when they were mature they even tried to mate with him. This type of instantaneous learning differs both from instinctual activities and from other types of learning, such as conditioning.

By careful description of the objective behavior of organisms, ethologists have revived interest in the instinctual basis of behavior and the processes by which learned and unlearned behavior merge imperceptibly. The study of ethograms provides insight into innate behavior patterns that determine social behavior, such as the phenomenon of imprinting, and the releasers and fixed action patterns which are components of complex behavior. The concept of drive, the purposiveness of many behavioral activities and their meaning for the survival of the species, have become legitimate concerns for the comparative psychologist. Laboratory research based on ethological findings has very much increased. Such research is an important supplement to the experimental findings of studies based on stimulus-response and learning theories which held the dominant position. Consequently, many new insights into the motivational aspects of animal behavior are now available for possible application in testing theories of human behavior, such as the drive theory of psychoanalysis, which hitherto could not be substantiated.

Consult Lorenz, K. L., *King Solomon's Ring* (1952); Tinbergen, Niko, *Curious Naturalists* (1958); Klopfer, P. H., and Hailman, J. P., *An Introduction to Animal Behavior* (1967).

ARISTIDE HENRI ESSER, M.D.

See also AGGRESSION; PSYCHOLOGY; TERRITORIALITY.

ETHYLENE [ĕth'ə-lēn], $CH_2 = CH_2$, an organic chemical compound. It is a stable, colorless, flammable gas, with a boiling point of $-130.9°$ C. $(-203.6°$ F.). It is economically important as a raw material in the manufacture of some 200 commercial products. Some are sold directly to the public, like ethylene glycol, an antifreeze, and others to industry, like polymers for plastics, the best known being polyethylene.

Ethylene is the first member of the olefin, or alkene, series of hydrocarbons. Its great usefulness results from its double bond which breaks open and allows a variety of addition reactions to take place. Catalysts are sometimes necessary. Ethylene can be recovered from petroleum cracking, the cracking of butane, propane, ethane, and the cracking of naphtha.

ETHYLENE GLYCOL, $HOCH_2CH_2OH$, colorless, odorless, oily liquid with a sweet taste. It is made by the addition of water to ethylene oxide. Over a billion pounds are used annually as antifreeze in automobile radiators. Alkyd resins in the paint industry, Dacron fiber, and an explosive are derivatives of ethylene glycol.

ETIQUETTE [ĕt'ə-kĕt], rules of decorum which govern or guide human social behavior. The term is derived from the French *étiquette* meaning "ticket." The word referred originally to "keep off the grass" signs at the court of Versailles, but its meaning was expanded during the reign of Louis XIV to encompass all rules of court etiquette.

Social Etiquette. Good manners form the basis of modern etiquette. Its component parts are courtesy, promptness, a sense of decorum, good taste, and—most important—consideration of and respect for others. The Golden Rule applies: "Do unto others as you would have them do unto you." These attitudes and their application are essential to the functioning of society at every level, be it social, business, or diplomatic.

Etiquette must be learned. The child, self-centered and demanding, must be taught the rudimentary social graces which will equip him for living in harmony with others.

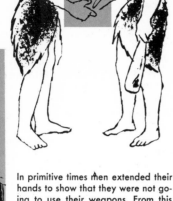

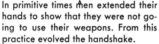

Though the rules of social conduct—etiquette—differ from age to age, many customs of today developed from practices centuries old. These rules, whether based on strictly practical considerations of primitive times or on a code of good manners of later times, have throughout history served the prime purpose of easing social intercourse.

In primitive times men extended their hands to show that they were not going to use their weapons. From this practice evolved the handshake.

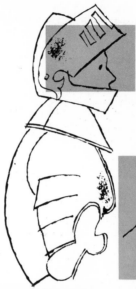

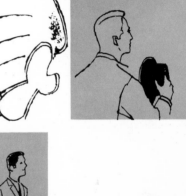

Raising the helmet visor for recognition by friendly knights is the origin of the modern acknowledgment of doffing one's hat.

Tipping, the custom of leaving gratuities for service in restaurants, hotels, and the like, was begun by early travelers who wanted to express their gratitude for free meals and lodging received at monasteries.

Among the first words a child learns are "please" and "thank you." He is taught to sit at table until others have finished eating. Thus he learns one aspect of etiquette and, however reluctantly, the meaning of patience.

As his interests expand beyond the family, the child meets with new situations outside the home and with the corresponding rules of courtesy which help him to adapt. In learning to respect the feelings, interests, and possessions of others, the child learns to look and think beyond himself and his own immediate interests. This is the basic rule of etiquette which contributes to his ability to become an adult member of society. He learns that the expression of friendship calls not only for the basic rules of politeness, but also for doing things gladly for others.

Basic Etiquette. The following rules are set forth merely as examples of the common everyday courtesies extended to others.

Introductions. The man is always introduced to the woman. (This procedure is reversed when introducing a woman to a well-known or elderly person of either sex.) Men should shake hands upon introduction. However, a man does not extend his hand to a woman, unless she first offers hers. A man rises from his chair to be introduced, whereas a woman may remain seated. Children should also stand and shake hands with an adult.

Table Manners. The napkin is reserved exclusively for the lap, with the exception that it may be tucked into a child's collar. Guests are served first, starting with the guest of honor. Once a number of the guests have been served, the hostess may suggest that they begin. The hostess serves herself next to last, and her husband last. Reaching at the table is permissible if it does not necessitate rising from the chair or interrupting others at the table. Smoking should not be indulged in until after the dessert. Children should not leave the table unless excused.

Entertaining. Invitations to an informal dinner or party may be extended by telephone or note. A guest acknowledges a written invitation as soon as possible. Guests should arrive at the time specified by the hostess. Food for a dinner party need not be elaborate; however, its selection and serving should reflect the hostess' efforts to please her guests. Often a guest brings a small hostess gift—a bottle of wine or box of candy. The hostess should acknowledge this, but in such a way as not to embarrass those who did not bring a gift. The appreciative guest thanks the hostess upon leaving and, if possible, telephones or writes her a note of appreciation within the week.

These few samples of modern manners not only illustrate the formal rules of etiquette but also reflect the desire of the individual as a social being to express his interest in and concern for others.

Changing Patterns of Social Etiquette. Many present-day social manners can be traced back to earlier times when self-preservation was a basic motivation of personal relations. The handshake, for example, was first used as a gesture of friendship and peace by primitive men who wished to show that their hands were empty of weapons. Coming-out parties have their origin in the ancient custom of secluding females until they reached the marrying age.

Other customs date from the times when chiefs or kings were in constant danger of assassination. Thus, the footmen at today's state dinners are the modern counterparts of the servants who tested their masters' food for poison. Some current customs originated in medieval times. Doffing one's hat dates back to the days of chivalry, when friendly knights in armor raised their helmet visors to be recognized. Tipping began when wayfarers wished to show their appreciation for the free food and lodging they received at monasteries and abbeys.

Inventions have caused the creation of entirely new systems of etiquette. Table manners were all but nonexistent when there were no eating utensils except a simple knife and no table appointments beyond a rude board. The development of modern methods of transportation and communication has also contributed to whole new areas of etiquette.

Etiquette in America. Early etiquette in the United States was influenced by the codes of the countries from which the settlers came. But pioneer conditions in the new land left little time for subtle, Old World elegance. In the Southern colonies gracious living was more the order of the day than in the North. A particularly interesting picture of upper-class colonial manners is presented in George Washington's *Rules of Civility and Decent Behavior in Company and Conversation*, which reflects both the crudity of early American life ("Rinse not your Mouth in the Presence of others") and the perennial need for certain warnings ("Put not another bit into your Mouth till the former be Swallowed").

The evolution of social life in the United States is clearly reflected in a series of books, both reportorial and etiquette. Mrs. Trollope's famous *Domestic Manners of the Americans* (1832), although very unpopular in the United States when it appeared, does offer a fascinating picture, from an English gentlewoman's point of view, of early 19th-century life in America. Mrs. Trollope found a "universal deficiency in good manners and graceful demeanor" in the new country. Her British restraint recoiled at the "familiarity of address" and the lack of privacy she encountered: "No one dreams of fastening a door in Western America; I was told it would be considered as an affront by the whole neighborhood. I was thus exposed to perpetual and most vexatious interruptions from people whom I had often never seen and whose names still oftener were unknown to me."

At the same time Mrs. Trollope was surprised at what she considered ultrarefinement: "It is considered indelicate for ladies and gentlemen to sit down together on the grass." When John A. Ruth published *Decorum, a Practical Treatise on Etiquette and Dress, of the Best American Society*, forty-nine years later, in 1881, the practice was still considered indelicate. Ruth advised men, "If you are walking with a woman in the country, ascending a mountain or strolling by the bank of a stream, and your companion be fatigued, should choose to sit upon the ground, on no account allow yourself to do the same, but remain rigorously standing." The rules had eased a bit by 1922, so that Emily Post in her first edition of *Etiquette, The Blue Book of Social Usage* could state that a very young girl "may motor around the country alone with a man with her father's consent, or sit with him on the rocks by the sea or on a log in the woods; but she must not sit with him in a restaurant."

Mrs. Post's writings were an excellent barometer of the changing manners and morals in the United States. Each edition of her book has reflected the increasing freedom of women in both social and business life. The trend in modern-day living has been toward the less complex in social matters. The rules still stand for such formal affairs as dances, debuts, weddings, and so forth. Today, however, less emphasis is placed on such artificial graces as calling cards, which were once considered everyday social equipment.

The increasing informality in the United States today, the continuing shortage of servants, the ever-growing amount of travel, the expanding leisure time—all have the effect of changing social etiquette. But the basic rules remain and are essential in maintaining good human relationships. As Mrs. Post maintained, "The fundamental purpose of etiquette is to make the world a more pleasant place to live in, and ourselves more pleasant to live with."

The Emily Post Institute

ETNA, industrial borough of southwestern Pennsylvania, across the Allegheny River from Pittsburgh. Iron manufacturing was begun in Etna in 1832 and is still the town's principal industry. Inc., 1868; pop. (1950) 6,750; (1960) 5,519.

ETNA [ĕt'nə], **MOUNT,** highest active volcano (elev., 10,705) in Europe, located on the southeastern coast of Sicily. It covers 460 sq. mi. and has a base circumference of 90 mi. More than 260 eruptions have beeen recorded since the descriptions by Pindar and Aeschylus in 475 B.C.; most destructive were those in 1169 and 1669. The starting point for ascending the mountain is Nicolosi.

ETON [ē′tən], urban district of southern Buckinghamshire, England, on the north bank of the Thames River opposite Windsor. It is the seat of Eton College, the great public school founded by Henry VI in 1441. The college buildings dominate the town. Its Perpendicular chapel is contemporary with King's College chapel at Cambridge. Memorials to the Duke of Wellington, Sir Robert Walpole, and many other famous Old Etonians adorn the Upper School. The old flogging block is preserved in the 15th-century Lower School. Historic buildings include the Cockpit (1420), where relics of the traditional pastime of cockfighting are displayed together with the town stocks and pillory. Pop., 3,901.

ETRURIA [ĭ-trōōr′ē-ə], in antiquity, the region of central Italy corresponding roughly to modern Tuscany, northern Lazio, and western Umbria. It was bounded on the north by the Macra River and the Apennines, on the south and east by the Tiber River, and on the west by the Tyrrhenian Sea. In ancient times it was famous for copper, iron, and apparently tin.

Apart from Falerii in the southeast corner near Mount Soracte (which contained a Latin-type population), Etruria was inhabited from 800 B.C. or later by the Etruscans, a materially advanced but mysterious people, whose origins are still uncertain. Included in the population of Etruria were numerous serfs who may have been the descendants of its pre-Etruscan inhabitants. Etruria was divided among a large number of city-states, all quite separate from, and politically independent of, one another. Mention is made of a league of 12 Etruscan cities, but these 12 cannot be certainly identified, and the league was anything but cohesive; its primary purpose may have been religious. Etruscan cities were celebrated for their architectural impressiveness, wealth, and even luxury.

From north to south the great Etruscan cities were Faesulae (modern Fiesole), traditionally the forerunner of Florence, with its Etruscan wall and Etrusco-Roman temple; Arretium (modern Arezzo), city of Maecenas and site of the bronze Chimaera, now in the Archeological Museum of Florence; Cortona, on a well-nigh impregnable site, noted for its bronzes; Volaterrae (modern Volterra), famed for its alabaster industries and its imposing Etruscan walls, gateway, and sepulchral urns; Perusia (modern Perugia), with town wall and gate built on Etruscan foundations; Clusium (modern Chiusi), in the heart of Etruria, on whose territory painted tombs have been found, including the celebrated Tomb of the Monkey; Populonia, which smelted iron ore from nearby Elba, the only Etruscan town of consequence to lie on the coast containing tombs of the archaic period; Vetulonia, which has large archaic tombs and has yielded the earliest example of the Roman emblem, the fasces; Orvieto, with temples and tombs; Volsinii, on Lake Bolsena; Vulci, which has yielded 4th-century B.C. fresco battle scenes from the François tomb, in addition to many Greek vases and bronzes; Tarquinii (modern Tarquinia), rich in tomb paintings; Caere (modern Cerveteri), with its extensive necropolis, including huge tumuli and subterranean tombs shaped like Etruscan homes, which has yielded a wealth of bronze and gold artifacts; and Veii, a near neighbor of Rome, notable for its terra-cotta statuary, particularly the Apollo of Veii.

ANCIENT ETRURIA
Blera - Ancient cities
(Chiusi) - Modern cities
0   50
Miles

Other lesser cities of Etruria were Rusellae (unexcavated), Telamon, Cosa, Pyrgi, and Graviscae on the coast, and Suana, Blera, and Sutrium inland. Outside of Etruria proper lay the Etruscan cities of Marzabotto, Felsina (modern Bologna), Spina at the mouth of the Po, and in the south of Italy, Capua.

Consult Pallottino, Massimo, *The Etruscans* (1955); MacKendrick, P. L., *The Mute Stones Speak* (1960).

E. T. Salmon, McMaster University, Hamilton, Ontario

See also:

Caere	Tarquinia
Chiusi	Veii
Cortona	Vetulonia
Etruscans	Volsinii
Fiesole	

ETRUSCAN [ĭ-trŭs′kən], language spoken by the Etruscans. It appeared in Italy (mainly in what is now Tuscany, but temporarily extending north and south of that region) around 800 B.C. Despite numerous extant inscriptions, and a knowledge of the alphabet (from which the Latin alphabet developed), the language is still largely unknown. It was gradually superseded by Latin from the 5th century B.C. onward, and has no modern descendants.

ETRUSCAN ART AND ARCHITECTURE. The art of the Etruscans, who created the highest civilization in Italy before the rise of Rome, was strongly influenced by Greece, especially after the 6th century B.C. It is nevertheless a vigorous and original creation that went through several centuries of independent development and produced works that have a distinctive character.

547

THE MYSTERIOUS ETRUSCANS
A LONG-VANISHED CULTURE

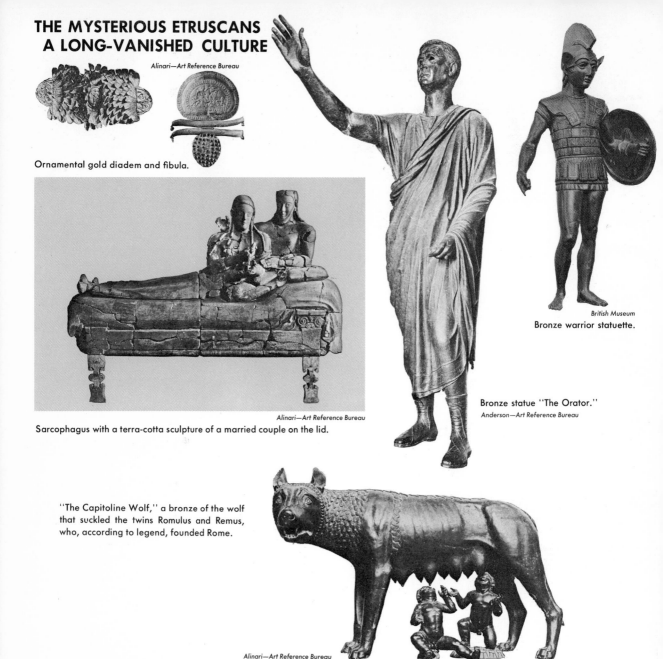

Alinari—Art Reference Bureau

Ornamental gold diadem and fibula.

Sarcophagus with a terra-cotta sculpture of a married couple on the lid.

Alinari—Art Reference Bureau

British Museum

Bronze warrior statuette.

Bronze statue "The Orator."

Anderson—Art Reference Bureau

"The Capitoline Wolf," a bronze of the wolf that suckled the twins Romulus and Remus, who, according to legend, founded Rome.

Alinari—Art Reference Bureau

Architecture. Since the Etruscans commonly employed wood and terra cotta in their buildings, very scant remains of their architecture, other than foundations, exist. The Etruscan temple, described by the Roman architect Vitruvius, was based on Greek prototypes. In some ways, however, it was unlike the Greek temple: the cella, or interior space, was often divided by interior walls into three rooms; it was set on a high platform, or podium, approached by a broad flight of steps on one end; and it had a deep porch with one or more rows of wooden columns that supported an entablature of the same material. The columns did not extend around the other three sides of the building to form a peristyle, as in Greek temples.

The few remaining examples of Etruscan architecture are works of masonry, such as city walls (notably a city gate in Perugia), fortifications, and tombs. The last were also cut into bedrock and then covered with an artificial mound of earth.

Sculpture. It was in sculpture, despite obvious Greek influence, that the Etruscans best demonstrated their originality. From earliest times there was a strong vogue for realistic portraiture, especially in figures on sarcophagus lids. This taste for the portrait carried over into Roman art. The Etruscans employed terra cotta, stone, and bronze. Survivals include portrait statues; antefixes, or works for the eaves or roofs of temples in terra cotta; sculpture for temples; and sarcophagus figures, which often were depicted reclining on a couch while propped up on an elbow. The "Apollo" from Veii (now Veio), now in Rome, a large, painted, terra-cotta work, is probably the finest surviving piece. A number of well-known bronzes have also escaped destruction: "The Mars from

548

The Metropolitan Museum of Art, Gift of J. Pierpont Morgan, 1917
Covered vase (*left*), bronze pail (*center*), and funerary urn (*right*).

Two views of the "Apollo" from Veii, a painted terra-cotta figure.

"The Chimaera from Arezzo," a bronze.

Pieces of early Etruscan pottery.

Two mural details of a dancer and musicians from the Tomb of the Triclinium at Tarquinia. Such paintings reveal the people's love of music, dance, and colorful dress.

A marble tablet showing the still undeciphered Etruscan writing.

Todi," "The Capitoline Wolf" (both Rome), "The Orator," and "The Chimaera from Arezzo" (both Florence).

Painting. The originality and creativity of the Etruscans are also revealed in their mural paintings, which have survived in tombs, particularly those at Tarquinii (now Tarquinia) and Caere (now Cerveteri). These vital works, in a flatly painted, decorative style, supply us with information on both the religious beliefs and daily life of the Etruscans. Most of the painted tombs date from the 5th century B.C. and reflect contemporary Greek painting.

Other Works. A horde of artifacts—bronze containers, urns, mirrors, tripods, candelabra, and chariots (the finest of which is in the Metropolitan Museum of Art in New York); ivories; statuettes; funerary urns; vases; and gold jewelry—have also survived. The greatest collections of Etruscan art are in Florence, Rome, and Tarquinia.

Consult Pallottino, Massimo, *Art of the Etruscans* (1955).

SIDNEY D. MARKMAN, Duke University

ETRUSCANS, a people of ancient Italy who dominated Etruria, the region corresponding to modern Tuscany, from the 8th to the 1st centuries B.C. and, for a portion of that time, Campania and the eastern plain of the Po River. The Etruscans identified themselves as Rasenna, but they were called Tusci or Etrusci by their Roman neighbors. The question of their origins, disputed in ancient and modern times, remains unsolved; their "mysterious" origins are suggested by three distinct theories. The first and most generally accepted, the "migration," or Oriental, theory, follows Herodotus, who relates that the Etruscans emigrated from Lydia in Asia Minor because of a severe

549

famine. Led by Tyrrhenus, son of the Lydian King, they eventually settled on the west coast of Italy, probably in the 8th century B.C., where they became known to the Greeks as Tyrrhenoi (hence the name Tyrrhenian Sea). In general, the second, the autochthonous, or indigenous, theory, claims that they were native to Italy, that they evolved from a mixture of the Iron-Age peoples of Italy (*see* VILLANOVAN), and that any eastern elements cited by supporters of the Oriental theory can be explained by strong influences, primarily due to commerce, from the eastern Mediterranean. The third, the northern theory, proposes an Alpine origin for the Etruscans, a hypothesis no longer upheld because early evidence for a movement from north to south has been found to be quite misleading. On the basis of chronology, Etruscan traces in the Alpine regions can be attributed to Etruscan fugitives from the Po Valley during the Gaulish invasions of the 5th century B.C.

Interest in the Etruscans has not been confined to modern times, for many of their major works of art, such as the famous bronzes—the Capitoline She-wolf, the Arezzo Chimaera, and the Trasimene Orator—were already known in the Middle Ages and the Renaissance. With increasing frequency from the 17th to the 19th centuries—at first accidentally, and later by planned exploration—numerous richly appointed tombs and monumental wall paintings were discovered. During this time it was common practice for landowners to claim as their own any antiquities discovered on their property. This practice encouraged unscientific "excavations," which led to the establishment of great private collections that, happily, later became public. Scientific archeological investigations, such as that by Zannoni at Bologna in the late 19th century, set the stage for similar campaigns throughout Etruscan territory. Recent activity, primarily under the supervision of Italian authorities, has unearthed much new data which may shed light on the true relationship between Iron-Age Italy and the Etruscans.

Government. Their political structure, as deduced from existing archeological and literary evidence, was based on a loose federation of 12 independent cities, the number of which remained constant, although the particular cities varied. Among these can be cited Caere (Cerveteri), Tarquinii (Tarquinia), Vulci, Rusellae (Roselle), Vetulonia, Populonia, Volsinii (Bolsena), Clusium (Chiusi), Arretium (Arezzo), Perusia (Perugia), Volaterrae (Volterra), Veii, Faesulae (Fiesole), and Cortona. Unity was based on religious rather than political ties, a feature which proved a serious weakness when the Etruscans were confronted with the rise of Rome. Most likely a King, or Lucumon, ruled each city, which was composed of the nobility, common people, and slaves. A supreme head, or rex, whose kingly attributes—the crown, scepter, and throne—were later appropriated by Rome, was elected annually for the federation, or "league," during the general assembly held at the still unidentified sanctuary of Voltumna.

Economy. Recognition of Etruscans as mariners is often encountered in the writings of early classical authors, who often regarded them as pirates. During the 6th century B.C., together with the Carthaginians and the Greeks, the Etruscans were numbered among the three leading maritime powers. Their fame as metalworkers has also been recorded by Greek writers of the 5th century B.C. and supported by archeological finds, not only in Italy, but also in France and Greece. It is very probable that the actual presence of the Etruscans in certain areas of Etruria was prompted by rich mineral deposits (iron ores, tin, among others). Even today, Populonia and the nearby island of Elba are active mining centers. Some insight into the Etruscan economy of the 3d century B.C., particularly agriculture, can be gleaned from the Roman historian Livy, who reports the contributions of wheat, corn, and wood made by various Etruscan cities for the outfitting of a Roman military expedition to Africa.

Rise and Fall. At the end of the 6th century B.C. the Etruscans moved north across the Apennines with comparative ease to establish such cities as Marzabotto, Felsina (modern Bologna), and others in the Po River plain. However, they were hindered in the east by rugged mountain tribes, and to the south they met with considerable opposition from the Greek colonists who had been firmly established in southern Italy and Sicily since the beginning of the 7th century B.C. Etruscan ambition clashed also with that of Carthage, which desired complete control of the western Mediterranean and possession of the islands of Corsica, Sardinia, and Sicily. An Etruscan alliance with Carthage against the threat of westward and northward expansion by the Greeks resulted in the great naval battle of 535 B.C. off the city of Alalia on the eastern coast of Corsica. Although the Greeks claimed a victory, archeological evidence indicates their defeat, for they were forced to withdraw from Corsica and to give up further thoughts of expansion. The Carthaginians, rather than the Etruscans, however, gained most from the combined victory, for the Carthaginians effectively secured their trade routes, chiefly for tin and silver, in the western Mediterranean, and at the same time limited Etruscan sea control to the Tyrrhenian Sea, a restriction which signaled the decline of Etruscan maritime power.

On land, however, the Etruscans occupied the whole of Etruria, and their presence in Latium, particularly in Rome, is supported by tradition. Livy gives a detailed account of the Etruscan dynasty of the Tarquins, who ruled Latium during the greater part of the 6th century B.C., until their expulsion c.510. The loss of dominion in Latium cut off Etruria from Campania, where the Etruscans had the prosperous city of Capua. It was through this city and through the rival Greek coastal city of Cumae that the Etruscans maintained their commercial and cultural contacts. Attacks against Cumae failed, and from the beginning of the 5th century B.C. Etruscan sway over Campania was gradually weakened, with Campania falling eventually to the wild Italic mountain tribes who descended into the plains (*see* SAMNITES).

The Gauls put an end to Etruscan power in the Po River plain about the beginning of the 4th century B.C. But it was the Romans, who, after the "Expulsion of the Kings," brought about the complete and final collapse of the Etruscans by dealing them a series of drastic military defeats and by ruthlessly destroying many of their cities (Veii in 396, Volsinii in 280, Falerii in 241). Only a few cities which had displayed good will in the past were spared and subsequently absorbed peaceably into the growing Roman state (for example, Caere in 351 B.C.). By the 3d century B.C. Rome had traded roles with the Etruscans, to become the major power in Italy. Toward the beginning of the 1st century B.C. Etruria had officially become a part of Rome. The consistent decline of Etruscan power and prestige is reflected in the known switch from a knowledge of Etruscan letters, for the educated Roman of the 4th century B.C., to Greek letters during the Empire period.

Language. A final decipherment and understanding of the Etruscan language are yet to be accomplished. Although the script is known to be derived from a very old Greek alphabet, the language, which stands quite apart from any known language, remains unintelligible. The only true parallel to the Etruscan script has been discovered on the island of Lemnos, near Turkey, and presents to those who favor the Oriental theory of Etruscan origin a forceful argument. At least 10,000 Etruscan inscriptions are known and recorded. Of these, unfortunately, only a handful are of any "serviceable" length, as the rest, engraved or painted on various works of art, consist of very few words. About 90% of these are funerary in character, merely brief epitaphs giving name, age, and lineage. From an era conscious of public decrees, it is curious that no bilingual inscription (Etruscan with a translation into another language) has yet come to light, particularly in areas where Etruscan contact with Latin- or Greek-speaking peoples existed.

Religion. Like many peoples, Etruscans believed in some aspects of life after death, to judge by the contents of their burials and the nature of their funeral urns and tomb interiors, which imitated the dwellings of the living, evidently in an attempt to recreate eternal homes for the dead. What is known of Etruscan religion suggests that they were a strongly superstitious people, surrounded by an intricate system of taboos and regulations. Unlike the Greeks, the Etruscans believed themselves to be completely dominated by the will of their deities, who were often rather vague in conception. The primitive character usually attributed to Etruscan religion, when compared with Greek religion, is very probably due to the survival of certain beliefs long relinquished by the latter. Basically, Etruscan religion can be classified as revealed. It was thought that certain occurrences could be predicted or interpreted through the art of divination, which was the practice of searching for specific signs in the livers or entrails of sacrificial animals. Well known and respected by the Romans and frequently mentioned by ancient historians (Livy and Pliny) were the haruspices, or Etruscan priests, who performed divination, a ritual whch had antecedents in ancient Babylonia. In general, the Etruscans and Greeks displayed substantially similar elements of worship: an organized priesthood, temples and sacred enclosures, and large accumulations of votive offerings. A strong Greek influence may be surmised from Etruscan equivalents for many of the major Greek divinities: Zeus, Hera, and Athena had their Etruscan counterparts in the triad of Tinia, Uni, and Menerva, later called by the Romans Jupiter, Juno, and Minerva. However, a number of Etruscan deities may have been of purely local origin, as no foreign parallels are known for them.

Legacy. The spontaneity and originality that characterize Etruscan art are perhaps most readily seen in their bronze and terra-cotta sculptures and vivid tomb paintings. The impressive tumuli surrounding numerous Etruscan cities, the multichambered tombs, sepulchral sculpture, and monumental city walls and gateways attest the material wealth and power attained by Etruscan civilization. Remains of this culture are represented in museum collections throughout the world, notably at the Louvre, the British Museum, the Metropolitan Museum of Art in New York, and the Hermitage in Leningrad. However, they can be seen in greatest quantity and to best advantage at the Archeological Museum of Florence and the Villa Giulia Museum of Rome, as well as in smaller local collections at Tarquinia, Volterra, Chiusi, and other sites of ancient Etruria.

That the Etruscan legacy to Roman civilization was large is becoming increasingly evident. The Romans early adopted the Etruscan emblems of magisterial power, including the fasces, or symbol of authority, and the triumphs permitted victorious Roman generals can be traced to the Etruscans, as can also gladiatorial combats, which are known to have originated at Capua. Early Roman military tactics and weapons were influenced by the Etruscans, and many features of Roman law, religious ritual, art, and architecture were directly derived from them. So numerous were the contributions made by the Etruscans, in fact, that it can be said that the material culture of Rome was dependent on the earlier Etruscan civilization until the 4th century B.C.

Consult Dennis, George, *The Cities and Cemeteries of Etruria* (3d ed., 1883); Randall-MacIver, David, *Villanovans and Early Etruscans* (1924) and *The Etruscans* (1927); Richter, G. M. A., *Handbook of the Etruscan Collection* (1940); Pallottino, Massimo, *Etruscan Painting* (1952); Riis, P. J., *An Introduction to Etruscan Art* (1953); Pallottino, Massimo, *The Etruscans* (1955) and *The Art of the Etruscans* (1955); Richter, G. M. A., *Ancient Italy* (1955); Von Cles-Reden, Sibylle, *The Buried People* (1955); Bloch, Raymond, *The Etruscans* (1958).

MARIO A. DEL CHIARO, University of California, Santa Barbara

See also ETRUSCAN ART AND ARCHITECTURE.

ETTERBEEK [ĕt′ər-bāk], industrial and residential suburb east of Brussels, central Belgium. It has salt works, tanning factories, and factories producing cotton thread. Etterbeek is the site of the *Parc du Cinquantenaire*, whose Royal Museum of Art and History is rich in antiquities and examples of Belgian ivories, jewelry, ceramics, tapestries, furniture, embroideries, and laces. Pop., 51,252.

ETTING, RUTH (1896–), American popular singer. Born in David City, Nebr., she first won notice singing at the Hotel Morrison in Chicago. On Broadway she appeared in the *Ziegfeld Follies* (1927, 1931), *Whoopee*, and *Simple Simon*. Songs she made famous include *Shakin' the Blues Away* and *Love Me or Leave Me*. The film *Love Me or Leave Me* was based on her life.

ÉTUDE [ā′tūd], brief musical piece which is designed for practice in mastering some particular instrumental technique. Thus the étude is intended for a student's private use rather than for public performance. However, some composers, notably Chopin, have also written concert études, which are intended both as useful study aids and as expressive compositions suitable for the recital hall.

ETYMOLOGY [ĕt-ə-mŏl′ə-jē], branch of language study concerned with the history and derivation of words. Until the 19th century etymology was limited to giving the original form of a word in the language from which the word was derived. Thus Samuel Johnson in his English dictionary (1755) traced *bread* to Saxon *breod*, *browse* to French *brouster*, and *collision* to Latin *collisio*. The American lexicographer Noah Webster invented the modern science of etymology by giving the relationships of a word to similar words in many other languages; he gave the source, the cognates in Germanic languages, and the related words in ancient languages. Thus he discovered the basic meaning of a word. About *bread* he wrote: "Saxon *breod*, German *Brot*, Dutch *brood*, Swedish *brod*, Danish *bröd*. . . . If the word signifies food in general, or that which is eaten, probably it is . . . from the Hebrew *barah*, to eat or feed." Under *collision* Webster traced each particle into which the derivative might be divided: "Latin *collisio*, from *collido*, *collisi*; *con* and *laedo*, to strike or hurt." Webster's aim was to prove the accuracy of the Biblical account of the Tower of Babel by showing that the words which God had given to Adam in the Garden of Eden had survived in modern tongues. Modern language scientists reject this theory but nevertheless seek to trace words from the many languages of the Indo-European family to a single language in the Middle East. From this study has come a more precise knowledge of the migrations of peoples and the development of the many different languages of this family. From these researches has come also a better understanding of the nature of word order, modification, tense formation, and inflection. One aspect of the history of usage is seen in the work of dialect geographers, who describe the spread of particular words and idioms in a nation or nations using a single language.

HARRY R. WARFEL, University of Florida
See also GRAMMAR; LANGUAGE.

EUBOEA [ū-bē′ə] (modern Greek EVVOIA), island just off the east coast of central Greece, 110 mi. long, 4–30 mi. wide, separated from the mainland by the channel Euripos. It was early inhabited in the north by Thessalians (Ellopians), in the center by Thracians (Abantes), and in the south by Dryopians, a mixture of Ionians and Dorians. The principal ancient cities were Chalcis and Eretria, important in trade, colonization, and art as early as the 8th century B.C. Euboea supplied neighboring Attica with timber, livestock, and marble, and though allied with Boeotia in the 6th century B.C., supported Athens in the Persian Wars and fell completely to Athens under Pericles in 446. In 411, during the Peloponnesian War, Sparta took control of the island, and at the same time Chalcis constructed a bridge linking the island with Boeotia. Euboea again became a member of the Athenian Maritime League in 378 B.C., but with the Greek defeat at Chaeronea in 338 B.C. it came under Macedon, and though liberated by the Romans in 196, became completely subject to Rome in 146. The island was of some importance in medieval times,

and in 1204 A.D. was divided by the Franks into the three baronies of Negroponte, although Venice held the ports. Subsequently it fell entirely to the Venetians (1366), then the Turks (1470); but in 1830 it became part of the newly established Greek kingdom. Pop., 163,720.

JOHN H. YOUNG, Johns Hopkins University

EUCALYPTUS [ū-kə-lĭp′təs], large and varied genus of trees in the Myrtaceae, or myrtle, family. Although native to Australia and the Malayan region, of the 300 species known, some are hardy in temperate and cool climates and have been introduced into many parts of the world. Eucalypts range in size from low, stout shrubs such as *Eucalyptus macrocarpa*, which grows from 6 to 15 ft. tall, to *E. amygdalina*, var. *regnans*, a tree often over 300 ft. in height. Most eucalypts have oval, or elongated, pointed leaves, but *E. polyanthemos* is well known for its round, grayish-green foliage. This species is hardy in cool climates and is grown as a greenhouse or outdoor ornamental in North America. Many species yield a hard, strong, and durable lumber, particularly *E. gunnii* and *E. globulus*. *E. ficifolia* and other species are planted as windbreaks in California citrus groves or used as ornamentals. *See also* GUM TREE.

EUCHARIST [ū′kə-rĭst], one of the two principal sacramental rites of the Christian churches, the other being baptism. The term is Greek, meaning "thanksgiving," and was used by the early Christians. Eastern Orthodox Christians refer to it as the Divine Liturgy. Among Roman Catholics it is generally called the Mass or Blessed Sacrament; among Protestants, the Lord's Supper or Holy Communion. Participation in the rite has, from the beginning of Christianity, been confined solely to baptized members of the church; and exclusion from the Eucharist, called excommunication, is the severest discipline with which the church may punish offending members.

The institution of this rite by Jesus Christ at the Last Supper with His disciples, on the night before His Crucifixion, is recounted in the Gospels and by St. Paul in I Corinthians 11:23–26. Because of the variant chronologies of the Gospels, it is disputed whether the Last Supper was a Jewish Passover meal or not. But the distinctive elements of the Christian rite, as defined by the words and actions of Christ, consist of bread and a cup of wine, which are blessed by a prayer of thanksgiving, then shared in common as sacred food and drink by all the disciples present. In ministering the blessed bread and wine, Christ identified them with His Body and Blood which were broken and shed upon the Cross for the salvation of mankind. And in and through these elements He promised to be present with those who believe in Him and renew this act "in remembrance" of Him as an earnest of fellowship with Him in the Kingdom of God. It is part of the New Testament witness to the Resurrection that the risen Christ made Himself known to the disciples in the "breaking of the Bread."

Thus from the first Easter Day the Eucharist has been a unique and distinctive action of the Church's corporate life, and its celebration a characteristic observance of Sundays and other holy days. In the apostolic age, the Eucharist was usually combined with a simple meal called the agape and prefaced with devotions of song, Scripture reading, prayer, and preaching of both formal and informal character. By the middle of the 2d century, however, it had become restricted to a purely ceremonial meal, and its devotional introduction formalized into a sequence of Scripture lessons, psalmody, preaching, and intercessory prayer much after the order of Jewish synagogue worship. All church members were expected to participate in it every Sunday, even at the risk of their lives during times of persecution. Those who were physically prevented from attendance shared in the "reserved" species of consecrated bread and wine taken to them from the church assembly by the deacons. The Bishop was normally the officiant, but in his absence a presbyter could preside in his place.

During the 4th and 5th centuries, after the freedom of the church from persecution, the Eucharistic celebration took on a more elaborate ceremonial, musical, and artistic splendor, and the liturgies began to crystallize, first in the East, then in the West, into their classic forms under leadership of the great metropolitan sees. The East Syrian liturgy of Edessa was adopted by the Nestorian Christians, and the liturgy of Alexandria has been preserved among the Coptic and Ethiopic Monophysites. The Antiochean tradition was developed at Constantinople in the Liturgies of St. Basil and St. John Chrysostom and became the rite of all Eastern Orthodox Churches. A variant of it is used by the Church of Armenia. In the West, two types of Latin liturgy developed: the Gallican, employed not only in Gaul, but in North Italy (Ambrosian rite), Spain (Mozarabic rite), and Celtic lands; and the Roman, to which the liturgy of North Africa was related. After Charlemagne, the Roman rite became predominant in medieval Western Churches. The liturgies of the Eucharist produced by the Protestant Reformers of the 16th century were all based upon the Roman Mass—those of the Lutherans and the Church of England being conservative revisions, those of the Reformed churches of Calvin and Zwingli more radical adaptations.

The Reformation era witnessed much controversy concerning the doctrine of the Eucharist, especially as regards the Real Presence of Christ in the consecrated bread and wine and the propriety of applying sacrificial concepts to the consecrated species. The divisions then created still remain as a major obstacle to the reunion of Christian churches. All parties appealed to the New Testament and the teaching of the early Church Fathers. Protestant theologians did not agree among themselves, but all were unanimous in rejecting the medieval scholastic interpretation of the Real Presence in terms of transubstantiation, which in the 13th century was proclaimed a dogma by the Roman see. They also rejected the doctrine that the sacrifice of Christ was mystically re-presented in the Eucharist as a propitiation for sin of the living and the dead. In general, the Reformers believed in a "spiritual" rather than a "substantial" Presence of Christ in the Eucharist, and a memorial rather than a re-presentational relation to the sacrifice of Christ on Calvary. The differences were primarily due to varying philosophical presuppositions, as well as disagreements in the method of interpreting the Scriptures.

Consult Brilioth, Yngve, *Eucharistic Faith and Practice,* *Evangelical and Catholic* (1930); Dix, Gregory, *The Shape of the Liturgy* (1945); Jungmann, J. A., *The Mass of the Roman Rite* (2 vols., 1951–55); Jeremias, Joachim, *The Eucharistic Words of Jesus* (1955).

MASSEY H. SHEPHERD, JR., The Church Divinity School of the Pacific, Berkeley, California

EUCHRE [ū′kər] **GAMES,** card games the most popular of which are euchre and five hundred.

Euchre. This is generally played by four persons in partnerships of two. The deck consists of 32 cards: in each suit, all cards from the seven through the ace. In the trump suit, the jack, or right bower, is the highest card, followed in value by the other jack, or left bower, of the same color, and then by the ace, king, queen, 10, 9, 8, and 7 of the trump suit. In the other suits, ace is high.

The deal and partnerships are decided by drawing cards. Five cards are dealt to each player in two rounds, in each of which either two or three cards are dealt. The dealer places the rest of the pack on the table, face down, and turns up the top card. This turned-up card proposes the trump suit. In the trump-making process that follows, each player, beginning with the one at the dealer's left, may accept the proposed trump suit (by declaring, "I order it up") or pass. The dealer's partner accepts by saying, "I assist." When any player, including the dealer, accepts the turned-up card for trump, the dealer discards one card from his hand by placing it crosswise under the undealt cards and takes possession of the turned-up card. If all four players pass, the dealer places the turned-up card, face up, crosswise under the undealt cards. Then the player at the dealer's left has the right to name the trump suit (which may not be that of the rejected card) or pass. If all players pass in the second round, a new dealer deals a fresh hand and the process is repeated.

The player who makes the trump has the right to play alone, without the aid of his partner's cards. In that case the partner places his cards on the table, face down.

Play begins when one player has accepted, or made, trump. If the maker of trump is playing alone, the opponent on his left makes the first lead, and other players must follow suit if possible. If the maker of trump is not playing alone, the player at the dealer's left makes the first lead.

The object of the game is to win tricks, which is accomplished by the highest trump or the highest card of the suit led. The winner of each trick leads to the next. The side making trump seeks to win at least three tricks. Failure to accomplish this means that the side is euchred.

Five points generally constitute a game, though the number may be fixed, by agreement, at 7 or 10. The side making trump scores 1 point for taking three or four tricks, and 2 points for taking five tricks (march). If the maker of trump is playing alone, he scores 4 points for winning five tricks. If the side that has made trump is euchred, the opponents score 2 points.

In three-hand euchre, the maker of trump competes against the other two players who form a temporary partnership; in scoring, he tallies 1 point for taking three or four tricks and 3 points for taking five tricks. The two-hand game is played with 24 cards (all cards from deuce through eight being excluded); otherwise the rules follow those of the four-hand game.

Five Hundred. This popular game is similar to euchre in principle. It is played most often by three persons using the 32-card euchre deck plus a joker, which ranks as high card. When four play, a 42-card deck is employed; it includes the euchre deck and the sixes and fives of each suit, plus two fours. Each player receives 10 cards; the remaining three form the widow. Trump is determined by competitive bidding; the highest bidder names trump and receives the widow, at the same time discarding three cards from his hand. In bidding each player names the number of tricks he proposes to win and the proposed trump or notrump. Each player has one bid.

In play the highest bidder is pitted against the two other contestants, who form a temporary partnership. The highest bidder makes the opening lead, and the other players must follow suit, if they are able. Tricks are won by the highest trump or by the highest card of the suit that has been led. The number of tricks bid and won governs the scoring of points, and a score of 500 points determines the winner.

FRANK K. PERKINS, Games Columnist, Boston *Herald*

EUCKEN, RUDOLPH CHRISTOPH (1846–1926), German philosopher and author. Born at Aurich and educated in universities at Göttingen and Berlin, Eucken was professor of philosophy at Basel (1871–74) and at Jena (1874–1920). His many works, among them *Life's Basis and Life's Ideal* (1907; trans. 1911) and *The Life of the Spirit* (1908; trans. 1909), won him the 1908 Nobel Prize in literature. Eucken's writings crusade against the naturalistic contention that man's life and actions are determined by environment. True human progress cannot be achieved merely by survival of the fittest. Man has a spirit as well as a body. He must use his powers of intellect and will to strive for a course of human betterment that recognizes the primacy of the spiritual element in his dual nature.

ALBERT J. DENEVE, State University of N.Y. at Binghamton

EUCLID [ū'klĭd] (fl. 2d half of the 4th century B.C.), Greek mathematician and author of a famous comprehensive treatise on geometry, the *Elements*. The material in the *Elements*, which effectively displaced all earlier textbooks in the field, was not entirely original with its author, much of it being taken from earlier work by the Pythagoreans, Hippocrates of Chios, Eudoxus, and others. The logical structure, however, is presumably due to Euclid. Although the bulk of the work is made up of geometrical propositions, there are sections on a sort of geometrical algebra and three books (VII, VIII, and IX) on the theory of numbers, including a proof that the number of primes is infinite, a formula for perfect numbers, and the "Euclidean algorithm" for finding the greatest common divisor of two magnitudes. The *Elements* is divided into 13 "books," the last of which contains the proof that there are five and only five regular solids. The so-called 14th and 15th books are spurious.

Euclid wrote many other works including the *Optics*, the *Phenomena*, the *Data*, and *On Divisions of Figures*. Among his lost works are the *Pseudaria*, the *Porisms*, a work on *Conics*, one on *Surface Loci*, and *Elements of Music*, and a *Catoptrics*.

CARL B. BOYER, Brooklyn College

EUCLID, city of northern Ohio, an industrial suburb northeast of Cleveland, on Lake Erie. Manufactured products include automobile bodies, construction machinery, machine tools, and electric wires. The National American Shrine of Our Lady of Lourdes is here. Founded 1798; inc., 1809; pop. (1950) 41,396; (1960) 62,998.

EUDOXUS [ū-dŏk'səs] (c.408–355 B.C.), Greek mathematician and astronomer who formulated the rigorous theory of proportion and who devised the system of concentric spheres which provided the basis of the Aristotelian concept of planetary motion. Most of the material in Book V of Euclid's *Elements* was originated by Eudoxus.

EUFAULA [ū-fô'lə], city of southeastern Alabama, located on the west bank of the Chattahoochee River. Founded 1813 as Irwinton, it was renamed Eufaula in 1843. The city has mainly wood-product, textile, and food industries. Pop. (1950) 6,906; (1960) 8,357.

EUGENE [ū-jēn'] **IV,** original name Gabriele Condulmaro (1383–1447), Pope (1431–1447). Born in a wealthy Venetian family, he was a nephew of Pope Gregory XII. Upon his election to the Papacy he tried unsuccessfully to dissolve the Council of Basle, and in 1439 concluded a short-lived reunion with the Greek Church at the Council of Florence.

EUGENE, city of western Oregon and seat of Lane County. Eugene is the metropolitan center of the upper Willamette Valley and the second-ranking market area of Oregon. The city is a lumber processing center as well as a trade and distribution center for a major agriculture and timber region. Eugene is the seat of the University of Oregon (estab., 1872) and headquarters of the Willamette National Forest. The city was named for Eugene Skinner, who homesteaded here in 1846. Inc., 1862; pop. (1950) 35,879; (1960) 50,977; urb. area (1960) 95,686.

EUGENE OF SAVOY (1663–1736), Austrian general and statesman. Both as the greatest general of his day and as a prudent and patient councilor, Prince Eugene was instrumental in the revival of Austria as a great power after years of defeat at the hands of the French King, Louis XIV. A younger son of a cadet line of the House of Savoy and a grandnephew of the French statesman Jules Cardinal Mazarin, Eugene was raised at the French court in Paris. When his repeated requests for an army commission were refused by Louis XIV, he entered the Austrian army, beginning his military career in 1683 against the Turks. Severe, taciturn, loyal to his Habsburg suzerains, Eugene won his greatest fame during the War of the Spanish Succession (1701–14) when, often in co-operation with the English general, the Duke of Marlborough, he defeated the French at Blenheim (1704), Turin (1706), Oudenarde (1708), and Malplaquet (1709).

Eugene served the Habsburgs also as president of the court war council (from 1703), Governor of Milan (1707–17), Governor of the Austrian Netherlands (1717–24), and vicar-general of Italy (1724–36). His victory (1717) over the Turks at Belgrade marked the high point of his career; the following years were filled with disappointments, compensated only by his patronage of the arts and his communication with the leading scholars and writers of Europe. At the age of 70 he took command of the Austrian army in the War of the Polish Succession (1733–35).

LEONARD KRIEGER, Yale University

EUGENE ONEGIN [oi'gən ō-nyĕ'gĭn], novel in verse (1823–31), the masterpiece of the Russian poet Aleksandr Pushkin. Its eight chapters are composed of 14-line stanzas rhyming in an intricate pattern related to the sonnet. Onegin, a young dandy bored with life, befriends a young idealistic poet, Vladimir Lenski, who is in love with Olga Larin. Olga's sister Tatiana acknowledges her love for Onegin in a celebrated letter, but Eugene rejects her. Lenski becomes enraged when Eugene flirts with Olga at a ball; they fight a duel and Lenski is killed. After several years of travel, Eugene again meets Tatiana, who has married a wealthy aristocrat. He falls in love with her, but now, although admitting everlasting love, she rejects him.

Both characters are conventional literary types, but Onegin became the model for a long series of "superfluous men" in Russian literature, while Tatiana established a pattern for a type of pure self-sacrificing heroine. The novel has been praised for its realism, but the narrative is full of artful literary digressions, and the language is richly stylized. Among English translations are those by Deutsch (1936), Elton (1937), Arndt (1963), and Vladimir Nabokov, whose translation includes an elaborate commentary (1964). Tchaikovsky's opera is based on the work.

LAWRENCE R. GOTTHEIM, State University of N.Y. at Binghamton

Eugénie, Spanish aristocrat who became Empress of the French after her marriage to Napoleon III. (THE BETTMANN ARCHIVE)

EUGÉNIE [û-zhā-nē'], in full **EUGÉNIE MARIE DE MONTIJO DE GUZMÁN** (1826–1920), Empress of the French (1853–70). Born in Granada, Spain, to an aristocratic family, Eugénie was brought to Paris in 1834 to be educated. A celebrated beauty, she was introduced to Louis Napoleon Bonaparte when he was President of the Second Republic. She resisted the opportunity to become his mistress, but began an intrigue to become his wife. After the proclamation of the Second Empire in 1852, Napoleon III found himself unable to secure a wife from the pre-eminent royal houses and proposed to "the Spanish woman" against the wishes of his advisers. The marriage was celebrated at Notre Dame Cathedral on Jan. 30, 1853. Eugénie never enjoyed popularity, being more conservative than the regime and devout in an irreligious age. She affected governmental policies far less than was generally believed, though in 1870 she was violently anti-Prussian and pushed hard for war. After the fall (1871) of the Second Empire, the imperial couple lived at Chislehurst in England. Eugénie moved to Farnborough after Napoleon III's death, building his mausoleum there. She and her only son, the Prince Imperial (1856–79), were also buried there.

ROGER L. WILLIAMS, Antioch College

EUGÉNIE GRANDET [grän-dĕ'], novel (1833) in the series by Honoré de Balzac called the *Comédie humaine*. Eugénie, daughter of a rich provincial miser, is the victim of her father's avarice, inheriting his wealth only after he has stifled all her hopes for love and happiness.

EUGLENA [ū-glē'nə], genus of one-celled animals in the class Mastigophora of phylum Protozoa. *Euglena*, like other members of its class, is equipped with a slender, whiplike structure, a flagellum, which it uses for food gathering, locomotion, and perhaps as a sense receptor. The single cell which comprises the body of *Euglena* is roughly oval in shape and enclosed in a thin, elastic membrane, the pellicle. Until recently there was confusion as to whether *Euglena* was plant or animal, because it contains chlorophyll and is able to manufacture its own food by photosynthesis—a characteristic of plants. The several species, such as *E. viridis* and *E. gracilis*, are found in still, fresh water throughout the warmer parts of the world.

EULACHON [ū'lə-kŏn], small marine fish, *Thaleichthys pacificus*, of the Osmeridae, or smelt, family. The eulachon, also called the candlefish, is found in the Pacific Ocean from northwestern Alaska to northern California. It lives along the coast for most of the year but enters rivers to spawn from March to May. The eulachon, which rarely exceeds a length of 12 in., is netted in large numbers for use as food. Prior to the advent of candles, eulachons were dried, fitted with a wick, and used as candles.

EULALIA [ū-lā'lē-ə], popular name for grasses of the genus *Miscanthus*, especially the varieties of *M. sinensis*, in the Gramineae, or grass, family. Native to Japan and China, this species grows from 4 to 10 ft. tall, forms a dense mass of foliage, and bears feathery clusters of white or purplish blossoms. The varieties with variegated leaves are popular ornamental grasses and are often grown in North American gardens. Eulalias are extremely hardy.

EULENSPIEGEL, TILL or TYLL, legendary German peasant prankster of the 14th century, who delighted in playing tricks on townspeople. A *Volksbuch* relating his exploits was first published in 1515 and was very widely translated, the earliest English version appearing in 1528. Richard Strauss based a tone poem on Till Eulenspiegel.

EULER [oi'lər], **LEONHARD** (1707–83), Swiss mathematician often referred to as "analysis incarnate." At Basel, where he was born, he was a student of Jean Bernoulli, and in 1727 he went to Russia to join Daniel and Nicolas Bernoulli as an associate of the Academy of Sciences. In 1733 he succeeded Daniel Bernoulli in the chair of mathematics. In 1735 he lost sight in one eye, but even this did not stay his output.

Invited by Frederick the Great, Euler went to Berlin in 1741 as a member of the Academy of Sciences and for a quarter of a century there produced a steady stream of papers. In 1766 he returned to Russia where he soon went totally blind. Nevertheless, sustained by an uncommon memory and a remarkable facility in mental computation, his productivity continued until he became the most prolific mathematician of all times.

Euler was primarily an analyst. He was responsible for the analytic treatment of the trigonometric functions as numerical ratios and for relating them to imaginary exponentials. He gave the algorithmic form of logarithms as exponents, real or imaginary. His name is associated with many branches of mathematics, from the Euler line in elementary geometry to the Eulerian integrals in advanced calculus. Through his textbooks the symbols e, π, and i came into common use; he first related them through the equation $e^{\pi i} + 1 = 0$. He also made remarkable contributions to the theory of numbers, differential geometry, and the calculus of variations.

Carl B. Boyer, Brooklyn College

EULER-CHELPIN [oi'lər-kĕl'pĭn], **HANS KARL AUGUST SIMON VON** (1873–   ), chemist who shared the Nobel Prize with Sir Arthur Harden in 1929 for his studies of sugar fermentation. Born and educated in Germany, he went in 1899 to Sweden, where he became professor of chemistry at Stockholm and director of the Vitamin Institute and the Institute for Research in Organic Chemistry. His research dealt largely with plant and enzyme chemistry.

EUMENES (c.362–316 B.C.), chief secretary of Philip of Macedon and Alexander the Great. On the death of Alexander he obtained control of Cappadocia and Paphlagonia. He supported Perdiccas in the wars of the successors. In 321 he defeated Craterus, but in 320 he was defeated by Antigonus in Asia Minor. Forced to retreat to the East, he was betrayed by his troops to Antigonus, who had him killed.

EUMENIDES [ū-mĕn'ə-dēz], underworld spirits of vengeance, usually called Erinyes by the Greeks and Furies by the Romans. The name, meaning "gracious women," is euphemistic. There were three: Allecto, Tisiphone, and Megaera. According to Hesiod, Gaea bore them after receiving the mutilated Uranus' blood. They were servants of the Fates and older than the Olympian gods. Their special duty was persecution of men who killed or otherwise wronged kinsmen. Their pursuit of the matricide Orestes is dramatized in Aeschylus' *Eumenides*. They also pursued Alcmaeon. In later times they were believed to persecute criminals of all kinds, both in life and after death. As commonly represented, they were winged, and, like the Gorgons, had snakes entwined in their hair.

EUNICE, city of southwestern Louisiana, in an agricultural area. The major industry is rice drying and milling. Gas and oil fields are nearby. Inc., 1895; pop. (1950) 8,184; (1960) 11,326.

EUNOMIUS [ū-nō'mē-əs] (c.325–395), chief theologian of the extreme Arians, often called Eunomians (Anomoeans), for whom the Son of God was a mere created being. A number of orthodox theologians replied to his *Apologia* with treatises *Against Eunomius*. A pupil of Aetius, he was briefly Bishop of Cyzicus, then lived in retirement near Constantinople until banished to his native Cappadocia after 383.

EUNUCH [ū'nək], a castrated man. The custom of castrating men was particularly widespread in the Near East, but it was also known in Greece, Rome, India, and China. Eunuchs were employed as guards, especially of the women's quarters, or harems. They also held much more important posts such as counselors to nobles and rulers, and frequently became great ministers of state in Persia, China, and the Byzantine Empire. Some men were made eunuchs as punishment for sexual crimes, but others chose this role. Eunuchism was deliberately sought by the Galli, priests of Near Eastern fertility goddesses such as the Ephesian Diana, Astarte, or Ishtar, and Cybele.

EUNUCHOIDISM [ū'nək-oid-ĭz-əm], a glandular disturbance marked by the development of female physical characteristics in men. Eunuchoidism is caused by improper functioning of the testicles, resulting in an inadequate production of the hormones that are necessary to maintain normal masculine characteristics. If the disturbance arises prior to puberty the sex organs remain small, the skin is soft, the voice is high-pitched, and the body fat is distributed in the feminine pattern. When eunuchoidism develops after puberty the changes are less dramatic, the main effects being a feminine fat distribution, decrease in the growth of the beard, and a weakening of sexual drives. Treatment consists of administering male hormones to correct the deficiency.
See also Endocrine Glands.

EUPEN [oi'pən], industrial and tourist center of the Ardennes hill country of eastern Belgium, in Liège Province, about 85 mi. east of Brussels. Tanning, brewing, and the manufacture of textiles, needles, soap, and chocolate are the principal industries. Eupen is the center of an area which was transferred from Germany to Belgium as the result of a plebiscite in 1920. Pop., 14,010.

EUPHRATES [ū-frā'tēz] **RIVER** (Arab. **Al-Furat,** "great river"; Turk. **Firat**), longest river of southwest Asia, run-

Workers loading dates into barges on the lower Euphrates, in Iraq.

Chapelle—Monkmeyer

ning about 1,800 mi. from the source of the Murad Su, one of its headwaters, in eastern Turkey, to Iraq and the Persian Gulf. The upper Euphrates, from its sources to Samsat, is a mountainous stream system, flowing alternately through rocky gorges and basin plains. It consists of two long arms: the northern or western arm (275 mi. long) is the Euphrates proper or Kara Su; the southern or eastern arm (415 mi. long) is the Murad Su. The Kara Su, although shorter, is considered the main stream. It is navigable below Erzurum for rafts.

After the junction of the headstreams, the Euphrates flows for another 115 mi. in the highlands of Turkish Armenia, receives the Tohma Su tributary, and then breaks through the Taurus Mountains in a series of cataracts and rapids. It leaves the mountain region a few miles above Samsat at an elevation of 1,500 ft.

The middle Euphrates runs from Samsat westward, then southward past Birecik in southern Turkey, crosses the Syrian desert from northwest to southeast, enters Iraq above Qaim, and flows east and then southeast for a distance of about 720 mi. until it reaches the alluvial plain near Hit. The river cuts a valley several miles wide through rocky terrain, barren and brown most of the year but covered with verdure in spring. Although some parts of the valley bottom are cultivated, the greater part of the valley is covered with tamarisk. Bedouin Arabs inhabit the region now.

The middle Euphrates was of great importance historically. For a long time it served as the boundary between the Hittites and the Assyrians and again between the eastern and western satrapies of the Persian Empire; later it was the frontier of the Roman Empire. Formerly a highway of empire and trade, the middle Euphrates is now an avenue of ruins from Samsat, ancient capital of the Seleucid Kings, to Hit, where Ezra's Biblical "river of Ahava" joins the Euphrates.

The lower Euphrates runs from Hit to the Persian Gulf, a distance of about 550 mi., including the Shatt al-Arab River, which is formed by its junction with the Tigris at Qurna, 115 mi. from the sea. At Hit, the head of a vast alluvial plain, the river has a width of 750 ft., a depth of 30 to 35 ft., and an average velocity of 4 mph. Downstream its volume decreases through the loss of water to canals and lagoons. Ancient irrigation in the Babylonian plain, lying between the Euphrates and the Tigris, rendered the land very fertile. Unfortunately the old canal system fell into disrepair in modern times. After World War II, however, efforts were made to harness the river. The Habbaniya reservoir, completed in 1956, is used for both flood control and irrigation.

Mesopotamia, the ancient area traversed by the lower Euphrates, also abounds in historical ruins and legends, bearing witness to the great civilizations that once flourished there. Ruins of famous cities of antiquity include Ur, Babylon, Lagash, Larsa, and Erech.

FREDERICK HUNG, United College, Winnipeg, Canada

EUPHROSYNE, one of the three Graces (q.v.).

EUPHUISM [ū′fū-ĭz-əm], an affected and flowery style of writing that flourished in court circles in late 16th-century England. It took its name from *Euphues: The Anatomy of Wit* (1579), by John Lyly. Among its characteristics are balanced construction, antithesis, alliteration, rhetorical questions, extended comparisons, and many examples drawn from mythology and natural history.

EURASIA [ū-rā′zhə], the land mass formed by the continents of Europe and Asia (qq.v.). If Eurasia is considered as one continent, Europe is its western peninsula.

EURASIAN, term applied to a person of mixed European

and Asian stock, in India called an Anglo-Indian. As an adjective, "Eurasian" is sometimes applied to the European-Asian land mass. *See* ANGLO-INDIAN.

EUREKA [ū-rē′kə], city of northern California and seat of Humboldt County, on Humboldt Bay. It is the state's foremost lumbering center, with several mills and an active port. Although Douglas fir and ponderosa pine furnish most of the timber, the area is still known as the Redwood (*Sequoia sempervirens*) Empire. The harbor also houses a salmon-fishing fleet. Carson Mansion, an all-wood edifice resembling a castle, is a landmark of 19th-century lumber wealth. Pop. (1950) 23,058; (1960) 28,137.

EURIPIDES [ū-rĭp′ə-dēz] (c.485–c.406 B.C.), last of the three great Athenian tragic poets, born in Athens of a re-

Culver Pictures, Inc.

Bust of Euripides, in the National Museum, Naples.

spected family. Few details of his life are known; but it seems clear that, unlike Sophocles, he was not prominent in Athenian politics. While his dramatic career was long and successful, he did not equal Aeschylus and Sophocles in public recognition; only about a fifth of his offerings were awarded first prize in the theater. After 408 B.C. he retired from Athens to the patronage of the tyrant of Macedon, possibly in disillusionment over the moral deterioration in Greece caused by the Peloponnesian War. Soon after his death, his tragedies received the highest acclaim. Throughout later antiquity he was the most popular of the tragic poets. Nineteen of his 92 plays survive.

Though he was highly conscious of, and indebted to, the tradition of the tragic art, Euripides restlessly and skillfully experimented with it, even to the point of creating new dramatic forms which cannot be wholly contained within the Aristotelian or modern definitions of tragedy. *Alcestis* (438) and *Ion* are tragi-comic, *Iphigenia in Tauris* almost pure (and superb) melodrama, and *Helen* (412) is both comic and melodramatic. Such works were to

become instrumental in shaping later Greek comedy. Yet the poet could masterfully adopt the true tragic tone, as in *Medea* (431), *Herakles*, *Hippolytus* (428), *The Trojan Women* (415), and *Bacchae* (c.405).

Among the innovations associated with Euripidean theater are the elaboration of the the melodic structure of lyrical passages, the use of stylized rhetorical debates inspired by the law courts, and the lessening of obvious relationship of the choral odes to plot. His contemporary critics charged that he often relied on pathos for effect, and lowered the dignity of tragedy by presenting certain of his "heroic" characters in shabby clothing and squalid settings.

This departure from tradition was undoubtedly a calculated element of his repeated attack on the emptiness, for his time, of the values embodied in the old heroic myths from which he drew his plots. A discerning critic, he exposed with wit and irony both the inefficacy of the lingering, outmoded aristocratic standards, and the fraudulent educational methods of the more extreme Sophists of the era. Most of all he deplored unrecognized ascendancy of the irrational, which he felt to be the ruling force in his world. This criticism of his society is adroitly conveyed through realistic psychological analysis of the complex motivations of his heroes and heroines.

Despite his preoccupation with social criticism, Euripides seldom permitted the moralist in him so to intrude into his art as to make it didactic rather than dramatic. Even his lesser plays easily demonstrate that he belongs in the small, select company of the world's great playwrights.

Consult *Euripides* (*Complete Greek Tragedies*), ed. by David Grene and Richard Lattimore (vols. I–V, 1958); Murray, Gilbert, *Euripides and His Age* (2d ed., 1946).

ROBERT D. MURRAY, JR., Princeton University

EUROPA [ū-rō′pə], in Greek mythology, the daughter of the Phoenician King Agenor, and sister of Cadmus. Zeus came in the form of a beautiful white bull to a meadow where she was gathering flowers. The gentle animal enticed her to climb upon his back and then rushed through the sea with her to Crete. There she became mother of Zeus's sons Minos and Rhadamanthus.

"The Rape of Europa" by Paolo Veronese (Ducal Palace, Venice).

Alinari—Art Reference Bureau

De Wys Inc. *Louis Goldman—Rapho-Guillumette* *Fritz Henle*

The history of Europe is a part of the culture of all of Western civilization. Much of this legacy may still be seen. Left, the Arch of Triumph, Paris; center, Palacio da Pena, Sintra, Portugal; right, town square, San Gimignano, Italy.

EUROPE [ūr'əp], the second-smallest of the continents, with a total area, including islands, of about 3,850,000 sq. mi., which is slightly greater than the area of the United States. Europe was first mentioned as a separate continent by the ancient Greeks before the 5th century B.C. It was clearly separated from Africa (which the Greeks called Libya) by the Mediterranean Sea, but establishing its exact boundary with Asia has remained a problem for geographers. The Dardanelles, Sea of Marmara, the Bosporus, and the Black Sea divide Europe from Asia Minor. Farther north, the limits generally agreed upon follow the crest of the Caucasus, the Caspian Sea, the Ural and Kama rivers, and a line approximately along the crest of the Ural Mountains to the Arctic Ocean.

Europe forms a clear westward peninsular projection from the Eurasian land mass and consists of many smaller peninsulas and islands. The Mediterranean Sea, North Atlantic Ocean, and Arctic Ocean, with their many deep penetrations (especially the Black, Aegean, Adriatic, Tyrrhenian, and Baltic seas) form its southern, western, and northern boundaries. Much of Europe consists of islands. The largest and most important are the British Isles. Important peripheral islands include the Azores, Iceland, Svalbard (Spitsbergen), and Novaya Zemlya.

The most northerly point of continental Europe is Cape Nordkyn, 71°6' N. lat., in Norway; its most southerly point is Cape Tarifa, 36°0' N. lat., in Spain; its most westerly point is Cape de Roca, 9°27' W. long., in Portugal; and its most easterly point is at the northern end of the Ural Mountains, 66°20' E. long., in the U.S.S.R.

Physical Features and Geology

Peninsular Europe extends westward from a line connecting the Finnish Baltic coast and the Vistula and Prut rivers. Europe east of this line is compact and open toward the interior of the Eurasian land mass. The coast lines of peninsular Europe are irregularly shaped, with land and sea constantly interpenetrating.

Coastal Characteristics. The configuration of the coastal lands and the adjacent submarine topography is closely related to the geological history of the land. Along the Baltic Sea, the northwest European Atlantic shores, and the northern coast of the Black Sea are flatlands with dunes, offshore sand bars, marshes, enclosed lagoons, and deep estuaries. Here the water level often changes markedly between high and low tides. The coastal lands continue seaward to form the continental shelf, a wide submarine platform between 100 and 600 ft. deep and

559

extending several hundred miles offshore. In contrast, along the Mediterranean coast the shore consists of either a very narrow flat strip or mountains sloping abruptly into the deep sea. The only exceptions are the deltas and alluvial plains built by the larger rivers. Raised coastal terraces, often several miles wide, are common. Recent geological upheavals (within the last million years), by which the Alpine mountains were formed, produced here a coast completely different from those bordering the Baltic Sea and the Atlantic from the North Sea to the Bay of Biscay. Another coastal type is the so-called cliffed coast, caused either by continuing marine erosion, as in northwestern France and southern England, or by glacial erosion and later oceanic inundations, which produced the steep fiord coasts of western Scandinavia, Scotland, and Iceland.

Land Forms. Europe's land forms are characterized by their great variety. Topographically, Europe is usually divided into four parts:

Coastal Lowlands and Plains. These form an almost continuous belt, generally under 500 ft. in elevation, from the foothills of the Pyrenees on the Atlantic side to the Baltic coast and to the Russian plains, where they widen consid-

erably. The plains of central Ireland and England are included in this division.

Central Uplands and Plateaus. These stretch, at an average elevation of from 500 to 2,000 ft., from south-central France to East Germany and northern Czechoslovakia. Some mountains extend above 6,000 ft., including Mont Doré in the Massif Central, Feldberg in the Black Forest, and Schneekoppe in the Sudeten Mountains.

Northwest Highlands. Included in this region are the mountain ranges of Scandinavia, Scotland, and Iceland. The highest elevation, 8,097 ft., is in the Jötunheimen Mountains of southern Norway. Except for their clifflike descent to the coast, most of these mountains resemble plateaus. They were affected by glacial erosion.

Southern Mountain Ranges. These comprise the ranges of the Alpine system of mountains: the Sierra Nevada, Pyrenees, Alps, Apennines, and the Carpathian, Balkan, Dinaric, and Caucasus mountains. They are characterized by high peaks, many above 10,000 ft., with incised valleys and deep canyons. The highest mountain in Europe is Elbrus (18,481 ft.) in the Caucasus.

Geology. Europe's land forms are the result of an ex-

Europe may be studied from various aspects—geographical, historical, political, economic, and cultural. The article on these pages is primarily a survey of European geography, defining the limits of the continent and describing its physical features, climate, and plant and animal life. A concluding section briefly discusses the political divisions of Europe and some aspects of its economy and its civilization. More detailed coverage of Europe is to be found in many other articles in the **ENCYCLOPEDIA INTERNATIONAL.**

Features of physical geography are described in such entries as ALPS, CAUCASUS, PYRENEES, DANUBE RIVER, LOIRE RIVER, PO RIVER, RHINE RIVER, RHONE RIVER, ELBE RIVER, VOLGA RIVER, SEINE RIVER, ATLANTIC OCEAN, MEDITERRANEAN SEA, ADRIATIC SEA, NORTH SEA, and BALTIC SEA.

All the countries of Europe, including such small states as ANDORRA and MONACO, are treated in separate articles. The reader can use the map as a check list for names and turn to articles on countries he wants to study in detail. For each country there is a survey of the land, people, government, economy, and history. Study Guides with articles on major countries direct the reader to related entries — in the case of BELGIUM, to such titles as MEUSE RIVER; ANTWERP; LOUVAIN, CATHOLIC UNIVERSITY OF; and RUBENS, PETER PAUL. In connection with articles on countries it should be noted that the Union of Soviet Socialist Republics extends over vast areas both in Europe and Asia and must be considered in studying either continent. Turkey controls a small area in Europe but is considered a Middle Eastern state and part of the continent of Asia. As a further note, two regions in which there are strong historical and cultural ties among nations are treated in special articles: BALKANS and SCANDINAVIA.

European civilization is covered in a variety of articles. For example, major art forms are discussed in ARCHITECTURE, MUSIC, DRAMA, NOVEL, SCULPTURE, and in PAINTING, HISTORY OF. National styles are included in articles on countries (FRANCE: *French Literature,* for example) and in GREEK ARCHITECTURE, DUTCH ART AND ARCHITECTURE, FLEMISH ART, ROMAN ARCHITECTURE, RUSSIAN ART AND ARCHITECTURE, RUSSIAN LITERATURE, RUSSIAN MUSIC, RUSSIAN THEATER, and ENGLISH LITERATURE. Europe is the home of TRAGEDY, of HARMONY, of OPERA, and of the psychological novel. Another view of the arts in Europe can be gained by reading entries on important periods such as BYZANTINE ART, BYZANTINE ARCHITECTURE, ROMANESQUE ART AND ARCHITECTURE, MEDIEVAL MUSIC, MEDIEVAL THEATER, GOTHIC ART, GOTHIC ARCHITECTURE, RENAISSANCE ART,

RENAISSANCE ARCHITECTURE, CLASSICAL THEATER, and CLASSIC ERA, MUSIC OF THE.

Other aspects of European culture are covered in JOURNALISM; LAW; INTERNATIONAL LAW; DIPLOMACY; PHILOSOPHY; LIBRARIES, EUROPEAN; BOOK, HISTORY OF THE; and MEDICINE. Along with artistic and literary development, scientific discovery, and educational, legal, and philosophical achievements came progress in technology as described in AGRARIAN REVOLUTION, INVENTION, INDUSTRIAL REVOLUTION, and FACTORY. The rise of the institution described in BANKS AND BANKING also occurred in Europe.

Much of the history of the Christian Church is interwoven with the history of Europe. Elaboration of this subject can be found in such articles as CHRISTIANITY, ROMAN CATHOLIC CHURCH, PAPACY, REFORMATION, and PROTESTANTISM. The influence of religion on civilization is evident in numerous articles — on art, architecture, and music, for example.

Many political theories and movements have developed or have had great influence in Europe. Pertinent articles include DEMOCRACY, NATIONALISM, SOCIALISM, COMMUNISM, FASCISM, and NATIONAL SOCIALISM OR NAZISM.

Some of the history of Europe is related in the articles named in the paragraph above. The history of each country is individually treated, as in GREECE, FRANCE, and ITALY. Other articles deal with empires: ROME; BYZANTINE EMPIRE, a potent influence on Europe even though partly Asian in location and character; HOLY ROMAN EMPIRE, an organization that once extended from Austria to the Netherlands; and BRITISH EMPIRE, a political-economic system that spread European influence around the world and at the same time affected European affairs. Still other approaches to European history are in articles on periods and movements — MIDDLE AGES, FEUDALISM, CRUSADES, and RENAISSANCE, for instance. Wars and revolutions that have altered the map and the life of Europe are described in such articles as HUNDRED YEARS' WAR; THIRTY YEARS' WAR; AUSTRIAN SUCCESSION, WAR OF THE; SPANISH SUCCESSION, WAR OF THE; FRENCH REVOLUTION; NAPOLEONIC WARS; REVOLUTIONS OF 1830; REVOLUTIONS OF 1848; FRANCO-PRUSSIAN WAR; WORLD WAR I; RUSSIAN REVOLUTION AND CIVIL WAR (1917-21); and WORLD WAR II. Postwar efforts to integrate Europe are discussed in EUROPEAN INTEGRATION and EUROPEAN COMMON MARKET. The problems and progress of Europe can be followed in sources available in the library and in the annual supplement to this Encyclopedia.

EUROPE

THE FERTILE LOWLANDS

The great European lowland extends from the English Channel to the Caspian Sea. Swept by Atlantic winds that bring abundant rainfall and moderate temperatures, this vast plain provides Europe with a greater proportion of arable land than is found on any other continent.

Louis Renault—Photo Researchers

Village in the Loir-et-Cher Department of France is surrounded by fields of wheat and clover. This wheat-growing region south of Paris, called the Beauce, is known as the breadbasket of France.

A farmer plows his fields on the Great Hungarian Plain near Eger, an area devoted chiefly to wheat and maize.

A cyclist steers along the top of a dike in the Netherlands. This land, laboriously wrung from the sea, is drained by a system of canals and ditches, bordered by dikes and windmills. The water at right is actually higher than the fields behind it.

Harrison Forman

J. P. Brouwer—Photo Researchers

PLATE 1

Barge on the Volga. The longest river in Europe, the slow-moving Volga played a leading role in the historical development of Russia and forms the backbone of the most important water-transportation system in the Soviet Union.

THE RIVERS

Many of Europe's major cities were born on the banks of its great rivers, for waterways provided relative ease of transport and communication when overland travel was still difficult and dangerous. Today, improved for navigation, the rivers are vital to European economic life.

The Rhine in Germany. The fabled beauty of the Rhine is matched by its great historic significance since the time of Caesar.

Ralph Gerstle—Photo Researchers

The Danube at Budapest (the hills of Buda are on the west bank, left; Pest is on the east). One of the longest rivers of Europe, the Danube has been an important artery of commerce and conquest since ancient times.

Aerofilms—Annan

Tower Bridge over the Thames, viewed against a portion of London's immense dock facilities. The river, which passes through the heart of London, has been vital to the city's commercial and industrial development.

The Seine flowing past the Eiffel Tower. Paris has always been closely identified with the Seine, for the city was first settled on the Ile de la Cité, an island in the river. The island formed a stronghold at the crossing of two great highways, an ancient land route and the river itself.

Dan Page

PLATE 2 and 3

EUROPE

Scale: 270 statute miles to one inch

0 100 200 300 400 500 600

Lambert Azimuthal Equal-area Projection

☆ NATIONAL CAPITAL

TUNDRA AND PERMANENT SNOW

EVERGREEN NEEDLELEAF FOREST

MID-LATITUDE MIXED FOREST

MEDITERRANEAN SCRUB WOODLAND

PRAIRIE

STEPPE

DESERT

IRRIGATED DRY LAND

CULTIVATION

ICELAND
Reykjavik

ARCTIC CIRCLE

NORWEGIAN SEA

LOFOTEN ISLANDS

FAEROE ISLANDS

SHETLAND ISLANDS

KJÖLEN

N O R W A Y

Glittertind + 8,077

Bergen

Oslo

Lake Vänern

Skagerrak Göteborg

Kattegat

ORKNEY ISLANDS

HEBRIDES IS.

SCOTLAND
Glasgow
Edinburgh
Aberdeen

NORTH SEA

NORTHERN IRELAND
Belfast

DENMARK
Copenhagen
Malmö
Kiel

IRELAND
☆ Dublin
Liverpool Manchester
Cork

Hamburg
Bremen
NORTH

EAST

WALES ENGLAND
Cardiff

NETHERLANDS
The Hague Amsterdam
Antwerp Rotterdam
WEST
Hanover
Essen
Dortmund
Berlin
Poznań

Lands End

London

English Channel
Le Havre

Brussels
BELGIUM
Cologne
Bonn
GERMANY
Leipzig
Dresden

P O

Seine
Paris
LUX.
Frankfurt
Prague

CZECHOSL

Nantes
Loire River
River
Strasbourg
Stuttgart
Brno

BAY OF

Tours

Danube
Munich
Linz
Vienna

BISCAY

F R A N C E
Rhine River
Zurich
Bern
AUSTRIA
Graz

Bordeaux
Garonne R.
AUVERGNE MTS.
Lyon
SWITZERLAND
Ljubljana
Zagreb

Cape Finisterre
Rhône River
Mt. Blanc 15,781
Milan
Venice
Trieste

N O R T H

A T L A N T I C

O C E A N

Oporto
CANTABRIAN MTS.
Bilbao
Toulouse
Turin
Po River
Genoa
Bologna

DINARIC

YUGOS

Cape St. Vincent

SPANISH
PYRENEES
Pico de Aneto 11,168
ANDORRA
Saragossa
Marseille
LIGURIAN SEA
Florence
APENNINES
ADRIATIC

PORTUGAL
SPAIN
Ebro River
CORSICA
Rome
SEA

Lisbon
PLATEAU
Tagus River
☆ **Madrid**
Barcelona
TYRRHENIAN
Naples
I T A L Y
Bari

Seville
Guadalquivir R.
Valencia
SARDINIA

Strait of Gibraltar
SA. NEVADA
BALEARIC ISLANDS
SEA
Cagliari
Palermo

Tangier
Málaga
SICILY
Catania

Casablanca Rabat
Oran
Algiers
Cape Bon

Marrakesh
Fès
Tunis

MOROCCO
A L G E R I A
TUNISIA

A F R I C A

M E D I T E R R A N E A N

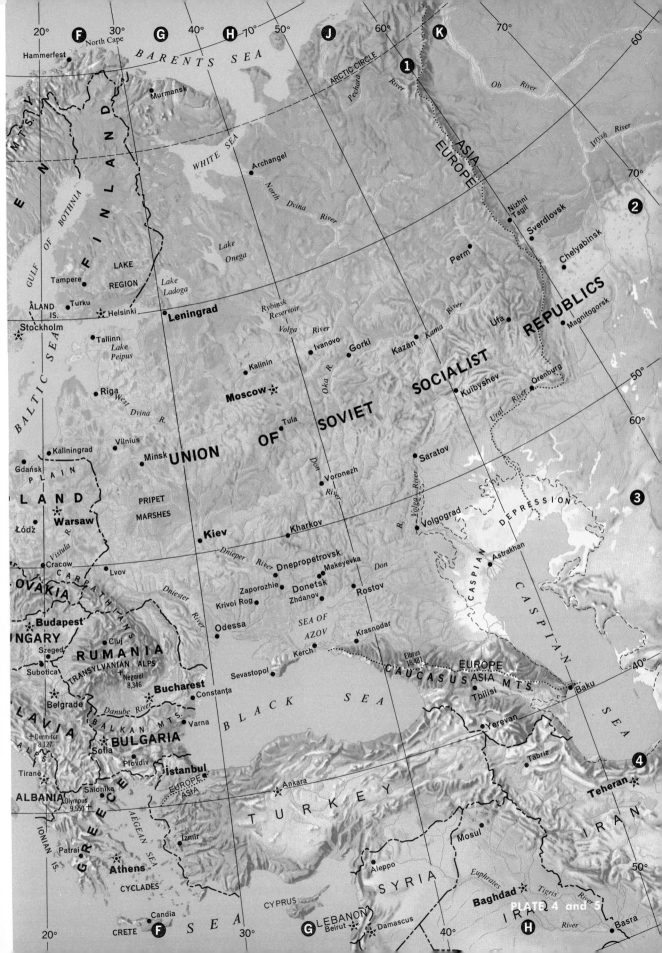

PLATE 4 and 5

INDEX TO MAP OF EUROPE

PLATE 6 and 7

THE MOUNTAINS

Despite formidable mountain barriers no part of the European continent is completely isolated. In the northwest the rocky peaks that cover much of Scandinavia and northern Britain are pierced by fingers of the sea—the fiords of Norway, the firths of Scotland. Southern Europe, below the central plain, is almost entirely mountainous, but the Alpine ranges are not impenetrable. River valleys and lofty passes cut through the ranges, assuring routes for transport and communication.

Georgia Engelhard—Camera Clix

This narrow Norwegian valley, the Naeroydalen, is an extension of the Naeroy Fiord. The most precipitous country in Scandinavia, Norway is a land of fiords and mountains.

Ewing Krainin—Annan

The Dolomites of northeast Italy form part of the Alpine massif that separates Italy from Austria. Bare peaks, snow covered much of the year, tower over forests and meadows on the lower slopes.

The fortress of Klis, dating from the Roman period, dominates a mountain landscape on the Dalmatian coast of Yugoslavia.

Robert Crone—Annan

On the lower slopes of the Spanish Pyrenees are the scattered hamlets of woodsmen, shepherds, and farmers.

Jose Ferrandiz—Camera Clix

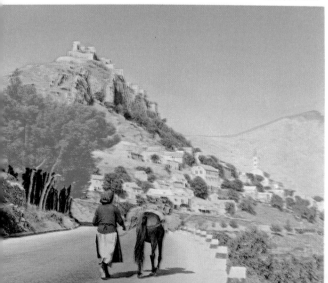

THE CITIES AND INDUSTRIES

Europe, the second-smallest of the continents, has the highest population density, with the major proportion of its peoples concentrated in sprawling cities and metropolitan areas. All European countries are industrialized to some extent, but the greatest manufacturing centers lie in a belt extending from the United Kingdom through France, Belgium, the Netherlands, West Germany, southern Poland, and into the Ukraine. Among others outside the belt are northeastern Spain, Switzerland, northern Italy, central Sweden, and the Moscow area of the U.S.S.R.

The Tower of London with post-World War II buildings rising in the background.

Blau/Bondy—

Workman tapping an iron ore blast furnace in the Ruhr valley, West Germany.

German Information Center

PLATE 8

Lessing—Magnum

A Norwegian whaling vessel docks after a successful voyage. The Norwegians send a large whaling fleet to antarctic waters.

A barefoot Portuguese boy pauses at the top of a flight of steps in the hilly Bairro Alto district of Lisbon.

Cartier-Bresson—Magnum

tremely complex geological evolution. The successive processes of mountain building and destruction have been repeated four times across Europe. Evidences of the oldest (Precambrian) mountain-building period in Europe are difficult to recognize. They are found around the Baltic Sea and toward the east in Russia, forming a large region of low relief called the Baltic, or Fenno-Scandian, Shield. Some geologists identify the Baltic Shield as part of an old northern continent (Laurasia), which also included the central Siberian Shield of Asia and the Canadian Shield of North America. These former highlands have undergone a series of erosions, inundations, uplifts, and further submersion. Much of the area was covered by thick sediment, some of which now forms the Russian plains and tablelands.

The second, or Caledonian, mountain-building period (mid-Paleozoic) followed widespread marine inundation across Europe. It is most clearly indicated in the Irish, Scottish, and Norwegian mountains, and extended southward to the English Channel. During an interval of a later (late Paleozoic) period of inundation, the last for most of the Caledonian and Baltic Shield areas, the land became overgrown with lush vegetation that later formed large coal deposits south of the Caledonian chains. This period of submersion was succeeded by the third mountain-building sequence, the Hercynian revolution, during which folded beds of coal measures were thrust over the rocks that lay to the north. Examples of these coal measures are found in Wales, Belgium, the Ruhr, Upper Silesia, and the Donets Basin. The folded and scattered Hercynian mountains consist of two arcs, a western and an eastern one, and have many parallel ridges. Hercynian structures predominate in the relief west and north of the Alps. Among the most important ranges are the Massif Central in France, the Ardennes, the Rhenish Slate Mountains, the Vosges, the Black Forest, and the Harz, Sudeten, Bohemian, and Ore mountains. The massifs of Brittany, Normandy, and the Urals are also Hercynian remnants.

The latest and youngest mountains are those of the Alpine system. A vast sea (the Tethys Sea), with arms penetrating the present Rhône valley and east into parts of the Carpathian Basin and the Hungarian plains, extended between the regions of older, more resistant rocks in the north, remnants of the Caledonian and Hercynian revolutions, and a southern continent called by some geologists Gondwanaland. Tremendous sedimentary material filled this ancient sea basin for about 100 million years. Then, starting in the mid-Miocene Period and reaching its crescendo after 10 million years, a great sequence of upheavals occurred: sediments were uplifted, folded, and overturned amid volcanic eruptions and tremendous pressures. The Tyrrhenian, Adriatic, Aegean, and Black seas were formed during this period, as were the major branches of the Alpine mountain system within Europe—the Sierra Nevada, Pyrenees, Alps, Apennines, and the Carpathian, Balkan, Dinaric, and Caucasus mountains. Many of the Hercynian massifs were uplifted and faulted, and numerous volcanic eruptions, which have not altogether ceased, testify to the strong unrest within the earth's crust. The Baltic Shield reacted to the new conditions through such adjustments as tilting, uplifts, faulting, and subsidence.

Subsequent changes in the land forms were caused by the Ice Age. Ice sheets covered all of northern Europe as far south as the Thames River, the mouth of the Rhine River, and 50° N. lat. in Poland and Russia. At the same time Alpine ice sheets affected preglacial terrain by enormously increased erosional activity—the widening of valleys, the cutting of river beds, and the depositing of sand, gravel, and loess.

Hydrography. The complex land form pattern, the deep penetration of the seas, and the distribution of precipitation were important influences on the drainage pattern. Europe's most important rivers are the Rhine, Rhône, Danube, and Volga. The first three arise in the center of peninsular Europe and flow in different directions, reach-

561

Danish children gather in front of Amalienborg Palace in Copenhagen to greet King Frederick IX of Denmark on his birthday.

referred to as "lake platforms." Lake Balaton in Hungary, the largest nonglaciated lake in Europe, occupies a structural depression.

Climate

Climatic conditions in Europe are characterized by great but gradual variations that range from the mild Mediterranean climate to the cold and harsh tundra climates of northern Scandinavia and especially northern Russia; from the moderate, marine west-coast climates to the continental climates of the Soviet Union with cold winters and hot, dry summers.

The general climatic conditions in Europe result from a number of factors. Large bodies of water penetrate the land deeply, providing access to wet west winds that significantly modify the hot summer and cold winter temperatures. The warm surface waters of the North Atlantic Current keep the ports of western and northern Scandinavia ice-free, and also heat the masses of cold air coming from the northwest. The general east-west direction of the important mountain ranges of central Europe permits the flow of oceanic and continental air masses, but excludes an interchange between tropical and polar air masses. In addition, there are various atmospheric circulations located outside the continental land mass which are responsible for the mild western European climate. Of special importance to European weather are the maritime polar and

Black derby and rolled umbrella mark this Londoner as a "City" man. The "City" is London's financial district.

ing the North, Mediterranean, and Black seas, respectively. The sources of the Rhine and Rhône are in the Swiss Alps, only 15 mi. apart. The Danube rises in the Black Forest of southern Germany. Important rivers of the Iberian Peninsula are the Duero, Tagus, and Guadiana, which easily break through the plateau (*meseta*), and the Ebro and Guadalquivir, whose courses are determined by faults. The Garonne, Loire, Seine, Meuse, Weser, Elbe, Odra, Vistula, and Thames for the most part flow through the lowlands into the Atlantic Ocean, North Sea, or Baltic Sea. Most of the Mediterranean rivers, the largest of which is the Po, are short and partially flow across flood plains. The Scandinavian rivers are also short and have numerous rapids.

The longest river of Europe is the Volga, which empties into the Caspian Sea. Other Russian rivers of importance are the Don, Dnieper, and Dniester, all flowing south into the Black Sea; the Dvina, emptying into the White Sea; the Pechora, emptying into the Barents Sea; and the Western Dvina, emptying into the Baltic Sea. The Ural Mountains represent a sharp divide between the European and the Asiatic river system.

The fresh-water bodies in Europe have a combined area of 53,000 sq. mi., with Finland's lakes accounting for nearly one-fifth of it. The lakes of Scandinavia, Scotland, and the Alpine regions are mostly of glacial origin. The North European Plains in Germany and Poland, and also central Finland with its many small lakes, are sometimes

tropical air masses, originating in the north and central Atlantic, respectively. These bring cold, moist air and warm, moist air intermittently throughout the entire year. There are also continental polar and tropical air masses originating in Asia, which bring cold, dry air in winter, and warm to hot, dry air during the summer. The meeting of warm and cold air masses is called the Polar Front. Usually the Polar Front extends across northern Europe in summer and penetrates the Mediterranean only in winter. An arctic front leaves its impact on the northernmost part of Europe only. These fronts bring about poor weather conditions in regions where they occur. Frontal precipitation is responsible for most of Europe's rainfall. The rapidly changing weather of most of central Europe is the result of constantly changing air masses.

Europe can be divided, according to basic climatic types, into four major belts in each of which certain similar conditions occur, although they do not have clear-cut boundaries except for mountainous regions. They are (1) the belt of Mediterranean or subtropical climates, characterized by rainy, cool, and moist winters and hot summers, with rainfall and dryness decreasing toward the south and east; (2) the belt of continental climates, with numerous subdivisions, depending upon the amount of rainfall, but all characterized by cold winters brought about by continental polar air and hot summers; (3) the belt of west-coast marine climates, characterized by mild winters and cool summers with a limited annual temperature range (the range increasing toward the south) and with maximum rainfall between autumn and early winter; and (4) the belt of transitional types, located between the maritime and continental climatic regions. Specific mention should be made of the Alpine mountains, which have greatly increased precipitation in higher altitudes.

Natural Vegetation and Fauna

Topographic, climatic, and human influences are mainly responsible for the present distribution of natural vegetation and of fauna. Climatic changes in Europe, especially those since the Ice Age, have left their impact on the distribution of plants and animals. Man's influence accounts for the fact that of Europe's original forested area of close to 85%, only one-third remains, much of it second growth or the scrub forest of the Mediterranean area. The extensive grasslands of the southern parts of the Soviet Union also have been intensively cultivated.

The original pattern of a clear-cut vegetation distribution from south to north is obscure; its remnants are only partly identifiable in the mountains. The distribution of Europe's natural vegetation and fauna, especially of the vegetation, is set in a zonal arrangement, closely related to present climatic zones, though earlier climatic influences still have a minor impact. The zonal arrangement is less uniform for soil distribution because its formation is determined not only by climate but also by underlying rock material, drainage conditions, vegetation, and temperature in relation to rainfall and evaporation. Following are the major European vegetation zones with their soil, flora, and fauna characteristics.

Mediterranean Zone. The most widespread vegetation is the evergreen, small scrub forest, which has various names: *maki* in Corsica, *maquis* in France, and *macchia*

in Italy. Important also are the oak (live and cork), oleander, laurel, juniper, and a great variety of thorny plants that blossom in spring and are dormant during the period of greatest heat. In higher altitudes a few stands of chestnut, beech, and conifers from former continuous stands have remained. Overpasturing and the use of wood for charcoal have destroyed most forests and make reforestation difficult. The characteristic Mediterranean soil has red color (red podsolics). When it has a deep profile it is highly productive. In Italy it is named *terra rossa* ("red earth"), but great differences exist depending on texture and on calcium or silica content. Alluvial lowlands and areas under irrigation, such as the Po plains and the *huertas* ("gardens") of Spain, are intensively cultivated. Native plants such as the olive tree (which also grows wild), citrus, fig tree, stone fruit trees, and some date palms are cultivated. Remaining animal species include mountain sheep, wild goat, wild cat, and boar. Reptiles (vipers, snakes, turtles, and lizards) are numerous.

Mixed Forest Zone. Broadleaf (deciduous) trees of this zone extend from northwestern Spain to the British Isles and southern Norway and to the western forelands of the Urals in the east. The zone is limited by excessive heat toward the south and by excessive cold toward the north. Above approximately 60° N. lat. northern (boreal) coniferous forests predominate. They also exist in higher altitudes of the Alpine mountains. The beech, elm, maple, and oak in the west, and the chestnut and pine on sandy soils, are most common. The beech, in combination with spruce and fir, predominates in central Europe, but in higher altitudes a combination of pine and larch is widespread. The oak, together with coniferous trees in the north and with grasslands in the south, is prevalent over all of eastern Europe. A variety of flora is found along the borders of the Mediterranean zone; different kinds of heather are common along the Baltic marshes. Most of the soils belong to the various podsolized subdivisions, with the color of the surface layers serving as the main characteristic. The most important are the brown and gray forest soils, which are very fertile and have been under cultivation for generations. Much of the original fauna has long been destroyed or reduced by man, including the wild ox, horse, bison, elk, and furred animals. Today the chamois, wild goat, and marmot are most widespread in the mountainous areas and the deer, fox, and badger throughout the entire zone.

Northern Forest Zone. This zone consists predominately of a spruce-fir combination with an undergrowth of mosses, and includes Europe's largest timber-growing region. The zone thins out toward the tundra in the north, where there are isolated stands of conifer and willow. The most common trees are the different species of spruce, pine, larch, and fir. Most of the soils are unproductive, heavily leached, acid, and often poorly drained and ash in color. The forests are rich in fur-bearing animals, including the bear, fox, wolf, badger, deer, and a large variety of birds.

Tundra Zone. Only a narrow strip along the Arctic Sea and in the Scandinavian highlands (fjeld) falls within this zone. It is characterized by a large number of mosses, sedges, lichens, and scattered growth of mostly dwarf birch and willow. During the summer the tundra comes to life with a variety of blossoming plants. No true soils can develop in the poorly drained surfaces and the edge of the tundra lies within the permafrost region (perennially frozen soils). Fauna is restricted to the lemming, fox, and some wolves and bears on land, and the seal, polar bear, and the occasional walrus in the arctic seas. The reindeer lives in the broad border zone to the south in winter, and uses the open tundra in summer only. The tundra is also home for numerous mosquitoes, flies, and birds.

Steppe. The transitional zone of the steppe is particularly well developed in the lower Danube region and across southern European U.S.S.R. In the north it is referred to as forest steppe because of the scattering of oak forests amid the open grasslands. Farther south the open grasslands, with characteristic black soils (Russ. *chernozem*, "black earth"), lend themselves well to the growth of cereals. Toward the southeast the grasslands become more and more scattered and turn to semidesert, with rainfall of less than 10 in. only in the extreme southeast of European U.S.S.R.

Economic, Political, and Cultural Characteristics

Europe is essentially a geographical expression. Although the continent has continuity, it lacks political, economic, and, to some extent, cultural unity.

Politically and in ideology it is divided into two contrasting groups of unequal area: the Soviet bloc, comprising part of the U.S.S.R. and seven allied states (including East Germany); and the Western bloc, comprising 15 countries (excluding the states of less than 25,000 population). A number of countries, however, are independent of the two blocs. These are Yugoslavia, Austria, Switzerland, Sweden, and Finland. In size, the 31 sovereign independent states entirely within the continent (thus excluding the U.S.S.R. and Turkey) range from France, the largest (212,736 sq. mi.), to Vatican City (109 acres). In population, the states range from West Germany (about 55,000,-000, including West Berlin) to Vatican City (about 1,000). The population of all Europe in 1960, estimated at close to 600,000,000, was one-fifth of the world's population, but in spite of its rapid increase, it is proportionally declining with regard to the other continents: Europe had one-fourth of the world's population in 1800.

In spite of the great political fragmentation, culturally there exist many similarities. The people belong chiefly to one race, the Caucasian. A very great majority professes the Christian religion in one or another of its many branches. The languages of Europe are varied, and it is not surprising that this variation has separated its peoples and fostered national consciousness. The national state and the great movements of nationalism had their origin in Europe.

Although the individual countries and peoples differ markedly in their economies, it may be said that the average Europeans have a higher standard of living than the inhabitants of other continents, except for the English-speaking peoples of North America, Australia, and New Zealand. Europe was the home of the industrial revolution, and its raw material reserves and energy resources are adequate if not abundant. The continent also has an ample labor force with technological skill; a dense, modern transportation network; and highly developed agricul-

Camera Press—Pix

On the island of Rab, off the Dalmatian coast of Yugoslavia, somberly dressed farm women offer their produce at a local market.

ture. Continuation of the existing living standards depends on imports of industrial raw materials and, to a lesser extent, of food, especially in the large urban concentrations. Exports of metallurgical goods, textiles, and chemicals pay for the needed imports. Trade within the continent and overseas therefore plays a very important role. Inasmuch as differences in the standard of living of the different peoples still exist, the need for imports and products available for export varies greatly. It is obvious that foreign trade must supply those needs and must be increased continuously. There is much economic contrast between western and eastern Europe, between the more and less advanced industrialized countries. Since World War II new emphasis has been given to increased industrialization in all countries, but especially the more backward, agricultural countries of the East. Europe's natural internal trade was hindered, reduced, and often completely stopped by the political separation between the contending blocs. Within the Western bloc a new unity is emerging in the field of commerce, with the development of a European Common Market. The economy of the Eastern bloc is geared to that of the U.S.S.R.

Overseas trade has played a vital role, especially for the countries along the Atlantic seaboard, since the age of discovery. As the limits of the known world enlarged, trade was followed by political domination, and this in turn laid the foundation for the colonial empires organized between the 16th and 19th centuries. At one time the European colonial powers held territory more than 10 times the size of their own lands, and laid claim to nearly half of the inhabited land of the world. The importance of several European countries was directly related to their important world-wide position. The United Kingdom, France, Spain, the Netherlands, Belgium, Denmark, Italy, and Portugal were the main colonial powers. However, all this began to change after World War I, and the few remaining colonial possessions now anticipate early independence. Most of the former colonial powers have already successfully adjusted to this political development. Perhaps one of Europe's greatest contributions is the imprint of its civilization on newly independent countries of other continents.

Consult Van Valkenburg, Samuel, and Held, C. C., *Europe* (2d ed., 1952); Pounds, N. J. G., *Europe and the Mediterranean* (1953); *Geography of Europe*, ed. by G. W. Hoffman and others (2d ed., 1961); Shackleton, M. R., *Europe, A Regional Geography* (7th ed., 1965).

GEORGE W. HOFFMAN, University of Texas

EUROPEAN COMMON MARKET (officially, EUROPEAN ECONOMIC COMMUNITY), economic and political association of France, West Germany, Italy, Belgium, the Netherlands, and Luxembourg. A new experiment in the relations among nations, it has already altered the shape of the world, both for its members and for outsiders.

Origins. The Common Market grew out of the powerful movement that developed in Western Europe after World War II to bring together the often warring nations into some system of peaceful co-operation. The purpose was not only to avoid war and to "bind" West Germany permanently into the Western family but also to reassert Europe's strength and influence in the world.

The first fruit of the movement was the European Coal and Steel Community, begun in 1952. After the projected European Defense Community failed in 1954, the movement revived with the signing in 1957 of the Treaty of Rome, establishing the Common Market. Members are the same as those of the Coal and Steel Community.

Why these particular six countries? Perhaps the most important reason is that they were headed by statesmen who believed in the idea of closer European union—men such as Adenauer of Germany and De Gasperi of Italy. All six countries are either overwhelmingly or at least half Catholic in religion. All had been defeated and occupied in the war. For various reasons the other nations of Continental Europe were unwilling to join a movement that meant a partial merging of national sovereignties.

Objectives. What, then, is the Common Market? It is, first, a customs union in the classic tradition. This means that the members are gradually abolishing tariffs on trade among themselves and gradually erecting a common tariff against the outside world. Tariffs on trade within the Common Market area were cut by 80% by the late 1960's and were scheduled to be eliminated altogether by 1970.

EUROPEAN COMMON MARKET

Common Market countries

Miles 0 ____ 200

OBJECTIVES

Gradual abolishment of tariffs among member nations and gradual establishment of common tariffs against nonmember nations.

Community-wide price supports for agricultural products and import levies on nonmembers' agricultural products.

TRADE ANTITRUST

LABOR SUPPLY TRANSPORTATION

CAPITAL PAY POLICIES

NEW ENTERPRISES TAXATION

Creating an economic union bound together by common policies in the fields listed above.

Against the outside world, each member moved its own tariff gradually toward the proposed common external tariff, which for most items is the arithmetical average of the national tariffs. All quantitative restrictions on trade in industrial goods have been abolished.

Trade among the members has risen spectacularly, even before tariffs have been completely eliminated. In part this rise is a continuation of a rapid growth in trade among these traditional trading partners that had started before the Common Market began. But it also reflects the effects of tariff reductions and the psychology engendered by the Common Market. Many businesses have, in effect, anticipated the day when tariffs will have been eliminated.

Second, in the field of agriculture, the Common Market is a combination of a customs union and a managed farm program. Internal trade will gradually be freed in this field, too, but to prevent severe disruption there will be a new community-wide price-support program for the main products. Against outsiders there will be either a tariff or, for the most important products, a system of variable import levies that will bring the prices of imported products, no matter how cheap, up to or above the internal prices. Such a system is deemed necessary to make the new common farm program work, but it may prove a greater threat to the trade of outsiders than the common tariff on industrial products. Much depends on the level of agricultural production within the community, which in turn depends in large measure on the price levels that will be set. If internal production remains at about present levels, there will continue to be a need for substantial imports.

The Treaty of Rome laid down only the bare outlines of the future agricultural program; the members have had to agree unanimously on all the crucial details. In a remarkable display of compromise on exceptionally difficult problems, they reached their agreement in a marathon negotiating session that ended early in the morning of Jan. 14, 1962. That date is a historic one in the construction of Europe—not so much because of the importance of the agricultural agreement itself, but because the six member countries then passed their most difficult test on the road to realizing the goals of the Common Market.

Third, and finally, the Common Market is a partial "economic union." The complex treaty of 248 articles, which is equivalent to a sort of constitution, requires of member states common policies in a host of fields besides trade: free movement of labor and capital, freedom for businessmen to establish new enterprises, a common antitrust program, a common transport policy, equal pay for men and women, and some harmonization of national legislation in fields such as taxation. Progress is slowly being made in adopting the necessary legislation in all these fields.

Operation. How does the Common Market operate in its day-to-day business? Everything starts with a nine-member international Executive Commission, sitting in Brussels. The commission's main function, besides acting as a sort of policeman to see that the treaty rules are obeyed and making certain minor decisions on its own authority, is to propose legislation to the member countries, whose representatives sit as the Council of Ministers. After lengthy debate, frequent crises, and eventual compromise, the Council of Ministers finally agrees on something that is usually quite close to the original commission proposal. The voting system within the Council of Ministers is somewhat complex. In general, any two states can block a decision, but no single state can do so. The executive bodies of the Common Market, the European Atomic Energy Community, and the European Coal and Steel Community were merged on Jan. 1, 1966.

Besides the Executive Commission and the Council of Ministers, there is a Court of Justice, sitting in Luxembourg, to rule on cases arising out of the treaty. Cases can be brought by the Executive Commission against a member state—this seems likely to be the most typical sort of case—or by a citizen or firm against the commission or a member state. So far, few cases have been brought, but a new form of international law is already in the process of being made.

Finally, there is the European Parliament which sits in Strasbourg. Made up of members appointed from the membership of the national parliaments, it has only limited powers. It debates all the current issues before the Executive Commission and the Council of Ministers and makes recommendations, but these are not binding. Various proposals have been made to expand the powers of the Assembly and even to have it elected by universal suffrage.

Consequences. What does the Common Market mean for the outside world? The answer is partly economic and, perhaps more important, partly political. The economic

	EEC	UK	USA	USSR
AREA (SQ. MI.)	449,000	94,000	3,600,000	8,600,000
POPULATION	171,000,000	52,000,000	179,000,000	218,000,000
WORKING POPULATION	74,000,000	23,000,000	72,000,000	99,000,000
STEEL PRODUCTION (TONS)	73,213,000	22,881,000	99,120,000	80,198,000
IMPORTS $ MILLIONS	40,340	13,120	17,104	7,058
EXPORTS $ MILLIONS	37,550	11,414	22,967	7,271

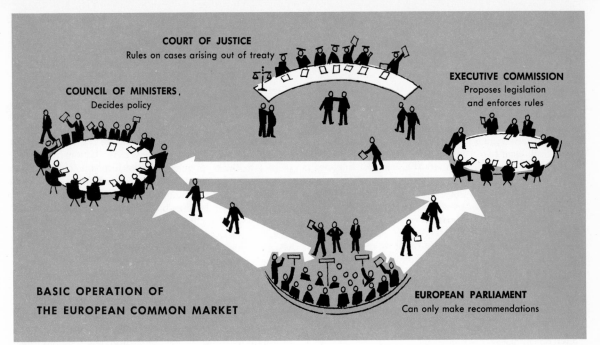

COURT OF JUSTICE
Rules on cases arising out of treaty

COUNCIL OF MINISTERS
Decides policy

EXECUTIVE COMMISSION
Proposes legislation
and enforces rules

**BASIC OPERATION OF
THE EUROPEAN COMMON MARKET**

EUROPEAN PARLIAMENT
Can only make recommendations

effects, of course, arise from the fact that the members enjoy an exclusive tariff advantage in trade among themselves. This is perfectly legal under the rules of the General Agreement on Tariffs and Trade, which governs the conduct of the world's main trading nations and which permits customs unions. But it can mean, for example, that Italian fruits will replace Israeli fruits in the German market or that French chemicals will replace American chemicals in the Belgian market.

How harmful the effects will be on outsiders remains to be seen. Probably the harm will be slight. First, the new common tariff is on the whole moderate. Second, the community has already shown a willingness to reduce it in bargains with outsiders. Finally, if the Common Market succeeds in promoting rapid economic growth among its members, as is now occurring, the community's imports from the outside world will inevitably grow. So far, the imports of the Common Market as a whole from the outside world have continued to expand, although not nearly so fast as trade among the members.

The political impact of the Common Market may, as suggested, be more important than the economic. If early successes continue, members will be drawn closer and closer together until ultimately they may become something like a single great power. There seemingly will never be a "United States of Europe" comparable to the United States of America. There is no certainty, for example, that the Common Market will have even a common currency—nothing in the treaty requires it—let alone a true federal government. Nonetheless, the constant process of contact and agreement plus the partial merging of the six economies appear likely to create a union capable of exercising considerable weight in world affairs. Already there are proposals, still hotly debated, for a new political treaty to cap the economic treaties.

This, of course, was precisely the aim of the original promoters of the idea of European union—Adenauer, De Gasperi, Monnet, Hallstein, Schuman, Spaak, and others. To what extent the new upsurge of French nationalism

during the presidency of Charles de Gaulle will slow, or perhaps reverse, the development toward European union remains to be seen.

EDWIN L. DALE, JR., The New York *Times*
See also EUROPEAN INTEGRATION.

EUROPEAN CORN BORER, the larva of a brownish moth, *Pyrausta nubilalis*, in the snout moth family, Pyralidae. The moth was originally native to Europe but is now widely distributed in North America where it is a serious agricultural pest. The adults lay their eggs on the undersides of leaves of corn, dahlia, hemp, and other plants. The larvae hatch and immediately eat their way into the stems and ears (in the case of corn). They remain in these borings over the winter and emerge as adults during the following spring. Overwintering larvae are controlled by destroying the infested plants or by the use of various insecticides.

EUROPEAN ECONOMIC COMMUNITY. *See* EUROPEAN COMMON MARKET.

EUROPEAN INTEGRATION, movements toward economic, political, military, and cultural co-operation which were undertaken by the countries of western Europe chiefly since World War II. Movements advocating closer co-operation and common institutions existed even before World War I. In the period between World Wars I and II the best known was the Pan-Europa movement, founded by the Austrian diplomat Count Coudenhove-Kalergi and backed by influential statesmen such as Aristide Briand of France. After World War II integration in Europe progressed beyond the discussion stage and contributed to the remarkable prosperity of countries which in 1945 had been starving and in ruins. The United States systematically encouraged integration in non-Communist Europe. Western Europe is now a power factor of the first order in world affairs.

Regional Arrangements Immediately After World War

II. The first large-scale supranational effort of great importance started in the closing phase of the war. Formed by 43 governments in Nov., 1943, the United Nations Relief and Rehabilitation Agency (UNRRA) carried out relief operations, as soon as hostilities had ended, from southern Italy and western France to the Urals. It distributed food, clothing, and medicine, helped to rehabilitate public services, made available essential machinery and spare parts, and repatriated or helped resettle millions of displaced persons. Simultaneously, various European governments established three specialized emergency organizations: the European Central Inland Transportation Organization (ECITO), which had the vital task of redistributing whatever rolling stock was still available; the European Coal Organization (ECO), a consultative and advisory body of European coal-importing-and-exporting countries, which worked out schemes for the equitable distribution of the meager supplies available and fostered international action to increase them; and the Emergency Economic Committee for Europe (EECE), which formulated recommendations to its member governments on general economic policies for the transition period from war to peace. The Soviet Union participated in ECITO and ECO, but not in EECE.

The "inner six"—the original members of the European Economic Community (EEC), or Common Market, established in 1957

- Belgium
- France
- West Germany
- Italy
- Luxembourg
- Netherlands

These Common Market nations are also associated with the European Coal and Steel Community (estab., 1952) and the European Atomic Energy Community (estab., 1957)

The "outer seven"—members of the European Free Trade Association (EFTA), as established in 1959

- Austria
- Denmark
- Norway
- Portugal
- Sweden
- Switzerland
- United Kingdom

Economic Commission for Europe (ECE). In 1947 UNRRA terminated its activities. At the same time, the United Nations set up, as the first of its regional economic commissions, the Economic Commission for Europe (ECE), with its headquarters in Geneva and a membership including the United Kingdom, the Soviet Union, and the United States. ECE was to promote economic co-operation on an all-European basis—"Europe" being defined to include Great Britain and the Soviet Union. ECE absorbed the three emergency organizations (ECITO, ECO, and EECE) and undertook to rehabilitate a region of 700,000,000 people. Although several European countries did not gain membership in the United Nations until 1955, they were able to participate in the ECE during the difficult early postwar years. But in view of the growing East-West tensions and the establishment of the Marshall Plan (see below), the ECE did not become the chief co-ordinator of an all-European recovery program. Nevertheless, representatives of the member countries continue to meet every spring in an assembly lasting several weeks, and various technical committees (trade, coal, electric power, gas, housing, inland transport, steel, and timber) meet throughout the year. The ECE has remained the only agency for East-West economic consultation and co-ordination.

The Marshall Plan and Organization for European Economic Cooperation (OEEC). The huge American assistance scheme known as the Marshall Plan prompted co-ordination of economic programs among the countries wishing to participate even before the plan was formalized because the United States asked that their rehabilitation plans as well as their proposals for American help come as a joint request, not as a series of separate appeals from the individual countries. The U.S. State Department also suggested that these governments establish a co-ordinating agency to implement the program. The Economic Co-operation Act, passed by the U.S. Congress in 1948, enabled the United States to participate in the scheme and was based on the promise of the European countries to set up such an agency. This resulted in the creation, also in 1948, of the Organization for European Economic Cooperation (OEEC) by 16 nations: Austria, Belgium, Denmark, France, Greece, Iceland, Ireland, Italy, Luxembourg, the Netherlands, Norway, Portugal, Sweden, Switzerland, Turkey, and the United Kingdom. Czechoslovakia, which at first wanted to join, was prevented by the Soviet Union from doing so. Subsequently, the Federal Republic of Germany (West Germany) was admitted as the 17th OEEC member. Spain, which in 1959 became a full member, was early associated with various OEEC activities, and Yugoslavia became an observer. United States relations with OEEC were in the main regulated by Congressional legislation and bilateral agreements with individual OEEC countries, but the United States and Canada became associate members in June, 1950.

OEEC was not a supranational organization; that is, the member governments did not delegate to it specific functions which the organization would then exercise by itself with binding effects on the member governments. Rather, OEEC always remained an intergovernmental organization, in which each delegate and his vote were under his government's control. Policy decisions of the OEEC's top organ, the council, even when it met at the ministerial level, required the unanimous consent of all member governments, for each member had a veto. Nevertheless, OEEC did succeed—thanks to constant consultation among the delegates and the "European outlook" of many of them. In practice, governments were often led to accept an "OEEC point of view." There also existed a permanently organized executive committee, consisting of the United States, Canada, and seven OEEC member countries, elected annually by the council. Six technical committees—fiscal, economic, trade, payments, manpower, and overseas territories—dealt with broad economic and financial problems, and 11 other committees with specialized questions or a specific industry. One of the essential rules was that recommendations on how American aid was to be divided among them were to come from OEEC. The final decision was then in the hands of the government of the United States.

The Marshall Plan contributed enormously to the recovery of the OEEC countries, and in 1952 American aid was terminated. Originally destined to be dissolved at that point, OEEC continued to function until 1961, when it was superseded by a new organization (see below). The European Payment Union (EPU), essentially a multilateral clearing house for payments among OEEC countries, which was created by OEEC in 1950, helped to facilitate trade in the OEEC area. The EPU also continued to exist until it was replaced in Dec., 1958, by the European Monetary Agreement because most OEEC currencies were by then virtually fully convertible. Apart from OEEC's over-all concern with the liberalization of trade and the harmonization of economic policies, it systematically fostered increased productivity and the modernization of agriculture.

Benelux, Brussels Treaty Organization (BTO), and Western European Union (WEU). The first customs union for the post-World War II period was agreed upon in London (Sept., 1944) by the governments in exile of Belgium, the Netherlands, and Luxembourg. This Benelux customs union, which, somewhat amended, became effective in Jan., 1948, abolished customs duties among the three countries and established a uniform tariff for imports from outside. In 1947, meanwhile, Britain and France concluded—for symbolic reasons at Dunkirk—a 50-year treaty of alliance and mutual assistance pledging common resistance to any revival of German aggression. They also agreed to consult periodically on their economic relations. In Mar., 1948, this two-power treaty was transformed into the five-nation Brussels Treaty, under which France, the United Kingdom, and the Benelux countries agreed to prepare for mutual assistance in case of "an armed attack in Europe" and to co-operate in the economic, social, and cultural fields. Italy (1954) and the Federal Republic of Germany (1955) joined the Brussels Treaty Organization (BTO), which thereupon was revised, and changed its name to Western European Union (WEU). Meanwhile, the military arrangements of the BTO had been taken over by the North Atlantic Treaty Organization (NATO).

Council of Europe. Since the mid-1940's advocates of European unity, especially Sir Winston Churchill, had propagandized for a "Council of Europe" as a first step toward a "United States of Europe." The question was

whether such a Council of Europe should consist of government ministers (as urged by Britain) or of legislators of member states (as urged by France and Belgium). Eventually, the five nations of the Brussels Treaty Organization, along with Denmark, Ireland, Italy, Norway, and Sweden reached a compromise. By treaty (May 5, 1949) they established a Council of Europe consisting of: (1) a Council of Ministers (usually the foreign ministers) of the member nations (by 1964, 17 through the addition of Austria, Cyprus, the Federal Republic of Germany, Greece, Iceland, Turkey, and Switzerland); (2) a Consultative Assembly of 144 parliamentarians from the 17 countries (18 each from Britain, France, West Germany, and Italy, and correspondingly fewer, with a minimum of 3, from the others) who are elected by their respective national legislatures. The assembly meets annually at Strasbourg, France. It cannot legislate, but it is the first international institution composed entirely of elected representatives, not of government-instructed delegates. The assembly can adopt recommendations addressed to the Council of Ministers by a two-thirds majority, and resolutions and "opinions," addressed to the Council of Ministers or to member governments, can be adopted by a simple majority.

The two main achievements of the Council of Europe are the European Convention on Human Rights (1950), which guarantees political and civil rights; and, after years of further negotiations between governments, management, and labor unions, the European Social Charter (1961). The charter guarantees social and economic rights, such as a fair wage, the right to strike, and social security, including social and medical assistance. Both instruments share a novel feature: they provide for supranational machinery to ensure the application of these rights if the signatory member states agree to such procedure. In other words, a citizen may then complain to a supranational authority—the European Court of Human Rights—that his own government violated some right guaranteed by the Convention or the Charter.

European Coal and Steel Community (ECSC). New approaches to integration in Europe—and new problems—developed in the 1950's when the three major industrial countries of western continental Europe (France, the Federal Republic of Germany, and Italy), together with the three Benelux countries (Belgium, the Netherlands, and Luxembourg), set up three new agencies: the European Coal and Steel Community (ECSC); the European Economic Community (EEC), or Common Market; and the European Atomic Energy Community (EURATOM).

In operation since 1953, the European Coal and Steel Community provides for the integration and co-ordination of the coal and steel industries of the six countries. It was based largely on the initiative of two French statesmen, Jean Monnet and Robert Schuman. The founding agreement (Aug. 10, 1952) states that the Coal and Steel Community is "to substitute for historic rivalries" (especially between Germany and France) a fusion of the "essential interests" of the six member countries.

Within a transitional period that ended in Feb., 1958, ECSC created a common market for coal, steel, iron ore, and scrap by abolishing customs duties as well as import, export, and currency restrictions. ECSC further abolished the dual pricing system, whereby export prices of those products differed from domestic prices. It also established rules for fair competition and a common tariff for imports of these products from outside the Community.

The executive organ of the ECSC is the High Authority, a nine-man body, permanently in session, whose decisions are directly binding upon the industries concerned. It may, and does, impose fines on enterprises disregarding its decisions or otherwise violating the treaty. Its members are independent of their respective governments, being guided by the interests of the Community as a whole as laid down in the treaty. The ECSC raises its own income by imposing a small levy directly on the industries it controls. This income, apart from paying ECSC's administrative expenditures, provides the funds for ECSC social services, research, and investment loans for those industries. As of Jan. 1, 1966, the High Authority was merged with the executive bodies of EEC and EURATOM.

European Economic Community (EEC), or Common Market. The Common Market is a much more ambitious scheme than ECSC. Established among the same six nations by the Treaty of Rome (1957) and in operation since Jan. 1, 1958, it aims to achieve, progressively and irreversibly, the free movement of goods, capital, and services among EEC countries, and their political, social, and cultural integration. The United Kingdom and other nations began negotiations for full or associate membership in 1961, and Greece became an associate member in 1962. Besides providing for the eventual free movement of industrial products, the member states are pledged to set up a "common organization for agricultural markets," to end transportation rate discrimination, and to evolve a common policy on international transportation and foreign trade. After the transition period, member states will no longer negotiate trade agreements individually. Under certain conditions, workers will be able to accept jobs anywhere within the Community. Social security rights acquired in any of the member countries will be honored in all others. The Community set up a European Investment Bank with a capital equivalent to $1,000,000,000 to help finance projects for underdeveloped areas in the Community, the modernization of plants, and projects of interest to several member states.

From the outset the Common Market was to include, under special arrangements, the vast African territories, which in 1957 were connected with its members (especially French and Belgian Africa). Also, a separate "development fund" was set up for them, to which the six European nations pledged $581,000,000 for the first five years. After 1960 nearly all of those territories gained independence, but the development fund continued its work and most of the new nations continued, with some changes, their association with the Common Market because it grants them preferential export possibilities and other economic benefits.

European Atomic Energy Community (EURATOM). EURATOM was established by a treaty signed in Rome (1957) simultaneously with the Common Market treaty. It includes the same six countries and is designed to develop nuclear energy for peaceful purposes. One of EURATOM's functions is, therefore, to assure through inspection and control measures that nuclear materials will not be diverted for illegal purposes. It has been estimated

that by 1980 EURATOM members' requirements for electric energy will have more than quadrupled, and that one-quarter of these needs will have to come from nuclear sources.

EURATOM also serves as a means of pooling nuclear research, training, and technical knowledge. It has a nuclear research center of its own, and the equivalent of $215,000,000 was allotted for its first five-year research program. In 1959 a "common market" for nuclear materials and equipment was set up, with a low common tariff toward nonmember countries.

Common Institutions of ECSC, EEC, and EURATOM. (a) The Council of Ministers is composed of one cabinet minister from each member state. This body is the only Community institution subject to instructions from national governments. The principal function of the council is to co-ordinate the actions of their governments and those of the Community as a whole. (b) The European Parliament (Strasbourg, France) is composed of 142 representatives from the legislatures of the member states. Eventually they are to be elected by direct popular vote. The body is advisory rather than legislative. It meets annually at Strasbourg and maintains 13 standing committees. (c) The Court of Justice, (located in Luxembourg City) is composed of seven judges. The court hears cases brought by member governments, the merged Executive Commission (of EEC, ECSC, and EURATOM), or the Council of Ministers. Associations, business firms, and even individuals may also lodge complaints. The judgments of the Court of Justice are definitive and directly binding on the parties concerned.

European Free Trade Association (EFTA). This is an organization composed of Austria, Denmark, Norway, Portugal, Sweden, Switzerland, and the United Kingdom for the gradual establishment of free trade between the members. EFTA was created by an agreement reached (1959) in Stockholm after negotiations for alignment, especially of Britain, with the Common Market had failed. The main differences between the two schemes are: (1) EFTA is only a free-trade area, not a customs union. Therefore, the members set their own import regulations and tariff barriers for outside countries. This was considered essential by Britain because of the preferential arrangements existing with the other Commonwealth countries. (2) EFTA is in essence limited to industrial goods. (3) EFTA does not aim, as does the Common Market, at increased political integration among its members. This induced three "neutrals" (Austria, Switzerland, and Sweden) to join EFTA rather than the Common Market. In 1961 Finland became an associate member of EFTA.

Although not desired by either side, considerable tension developed between the "outer seven" and the "inner six." There was some danger of western Europe being divided into competing blocs. If Britain and some other EFTA countries were to join the Common Market, EFTA would be entirely reorganized or abolished.

Organization for Economic Cooperation and Development (OECD). This is a 20-nation organization, in operation since 1961, to promote economic co-operation between North America and Europe. In order to heal the split between the Common Market and EFTA, efforts, strongly supported by the United States, were made to reform and strengthen the OEEC. They led to a convention, signed on Dec. 14, 1960, by the United States, all Common Market and EFTA nations, and six other countries, creating a successor to the OEEC, namely, the OECD. The latter's principal objective is to achieve economic growth and higher standards of living in the member countries while maintaining financial stability. It has no supranational organs or functions, but it is (apart from the U.N. Economic Commission for Europe) the only predominantly European economic agency in which the United States holds full membership.

JOHN H. E. FRIED, New York University
See also NORTH ATLANTIC TREATY ORGANIZATION.

EUROPIUM [ū-rō'pē-əm], metal of the lanthanide series, isolated in 1896 by E. Demarçay. It forms rose-colored compounds but has no important uses.

PROPERTIES

Symbol	Eu
Atomic number	63
Atomic weight	151.96
Valences	2, 3

EURYANTHE [ū-rē-ăn'thē], three-act opera by Carl Maria von Weber; libretto by Helmine von Chézy; first performed in Vienna, Oct. 25, 1823. In 12th-century France Euryanthe, falsely accused of infidelity to her fiancé, finally proves her innocence, and the pair are reunited. This is Weber's longest opera and the only one which does not have spoken dialogue, but it lacks the popular folk elements which brought success to his earlier works. The overture is often played in concert form.

EURYDICE [ū-rĭd'ə-sē], in Greek mythology the wife of Orpheus. She died from the bite of a snake, and Orpheus descended to Hades in a vain attempt to reclaim her.

EURYMEDON [ū-rĭm'ə-dŏn] **RIVER,** small river of Pamphylia in Asia Minor. At its mouth, 12 mi. west of Side, the Greeks under Cimon defeated the Persians on land and sea c.468 B.C.

EURYNOME, in Greek myth, the daughter of Oceanus, and, by Zeus, mother of the Graces (q.v.).

EURYPTERID [ū-rĭp'tər-ĭd], extinct, aquatic arthropod distantly related to scorpions and spiders. Eurypterids were among the largest arthropods, ranging from a few inches to 10 ft. long. The large, flattened head had a pair each of simple and complex eyes. Six pairs of appendages, used for crawling or swimming, were attached to the head region. The segmented abdomen ended in a flattened, spikelike tail. Eurypterids lived from the Ordovician Period through the Permian Period (from 500 million to 230 million years ago).

EUSEBIUS [ū-sē'bē-əs], **ST.** (d.380), Bishop of Samosata from 361. Theologically allied to Basil of Ancyra (Ankara),

he strongly opposed Arianism, and later became associated with St. Basil of Caesarea. His feast day is June 21.

EUSEBIUS, ST. (d.371), Bishop of Vercelli. Firm against Arian pressures at the Council of Milan (355), he refused to condemn St. Athanasius. Banished by Emperor Constantius, on his return Eusebius lived with his clergy under rule. Some modern scholars attribute the Athanasian Creed to him. His feast day is Dec. 16.

EUSEBIUS OF CAESAREA [sĕs-ə-rē'ə, sĕz-ə-rē'ə] (c.263–339), Christian scholar. Trained at Caesarea in Palestine, he suffered exile during the persecution of Diocletian, after which he became Bishop of Caesarea, about 313. The great library left by Origen gave him ample materials for his learned works, the *Chronicle* and *Church History*, and the apologetic *Praeparatio evangelica* and *Demonstratio evangelica*. Conservative in theology, he accepted the decisions of the Council of Nicaea, but in later years supported the reaction against it. A friend and admirer of Constantine, he survived him only briefly, leaving other hands to complete his eulogistic *Life* of the Emperor.

EUSTACHIAN TUBE. *See* EAR.

EUSTIS [ūs'tĭs], **WILLIAM** (1753–1825), American government official. Born in Cambridge, Mass., Eustis was an amiable, Harvard-educated Boston doctor who was successful in politics as a Jeffersonian Republican in Federalist Massachusetts. He was a member of the state legislature (1788–94) and the U.S. Congress (1801–5). President Thomas Jefferson appointed him (1807) Secretary of War, replacing another New England Republican, and President James Madison continued him in office. Without military experience beyond that of a surgeon in the Revolution, he lacked the forcefulness or skill at organization necessary for conducting the War of 1812 and had to resign (Dec., 1812). He was minister to Holland (1814–18) and again in Congress (1820–23). Finally elected Governor (1823, 1824), he died during his second term.

EUSTIS, city of central Florida, situated on Lake Eustis. It is a trading center for a citrus-growing area. Inc., 1925; pop. (1950) 4,005; (1960) 6,189.

EUSTOCHIUM [ū-stō'kē-əm], **ST. JULIA** (370–c.419), daughter of St. Paula with whom she founded a convent in Bethlehem. They assisted St. Jerome in his translation of the Vulgate. St. Julia's feast day is Sept. 28.

EUTAW [ū'tô] **SPRINGS, BATTLE OF,** engagement in the American Revolution fought (Sept. 8, 1781) about 50 mi. northwest of Charleston, S.C., between American forces under Gen. Nathanael Greene and British forces under Col. Alexander Stewart. A limited American victory, it compelled the British to withdraw from the interior of South Carolina.

EUTERPE, one of the nine Muses (q.v.).

EVAGORAS [ĭ-văg'ə-rəs] (d.374 B.C.), King of Salamis on Cyprus. In 411 B.C. he gained control of Salamis, from which his family had been displaced as rulers. Never on good terms with Persia, Evagoras maintained a strong fleet and consistently sought close contact with Greece. He gave refuge to Athenian exiles, particularly Conon. By 390 he controlled most of Cyprus, Cilicia, and Phoenicia. A massive Persian attack (382) broke his sea power, but the war dragged on and Evagoras was left in control of Salamis. He was assassinated in a palace intrigue.

EVANDER [ĭ-văn′dər], in Greco-Roman mythology, an Arcadian who began the first settlement at Rome, occupying the Palatine Hill. He brought writing, music, and crafts to Italy. He was the host of Hercules when Hercules killed Cacus.

EVANGELICAL AND REFORMED CHURCH, a union of the Evangelical Synod of North America and the Reformed Church in the United States, officially constituted in 1934 in Cleveland, Ohio. The members of the German Evangelical Church Society of the West (founded 1840), which later became the Evangelical Synod, came largely from the predominantly Lutheran sections of northern, central, and eastern Germany. The German Reformed Church, which in 1869 became the Reformed Church of the United States, was organized as an independent body in 1792. Its congregations, many of which dated back to the early 18th century and which had worked together in a coetus under Dutch Reformed auspices, were at first chiefly made up of immigrants of Reformed (Calvinist) background in western Germany. In 1922 definite steps toward the union of the two bodies were taken, and a plan of union was approved ten years later. At the time of union the total membership was 629,787; by mid-century it had increased to 735,941. In 1957 the Evangelical and Reformed Church entered into a union agreement with the Congregational Christian Churches which was ratified in 1961, forming the United Church of Christ.

Consult Dunn, David, and others, *A History of the Evangelical and Reformed Church* (1961).

ROBERT T. HANDY, Union Theological Seminary

EVANGELICAL CHURCH. *See* EVANGELICAL UNITED BRETHREN CHURCH, THE.

EVANGELICAL COVENANT CHURCH OF AMERICA, church organized by Swedish immigrants in 1885, commonly known as the Mission Covenant Church. Its headquarters in Chicago reports a membership of about 60,000 in over 500 churches.

EVANGELICALISM [ē-văn-jĕl′ĭ-kəl-ĭz-əm], theological attitude of certain Reformation churches, especially the Lutheran, based on their appeal to the Gospel (Evangel) against the hierarchy of the medieval church. In England after the 18th century it was applied to those who, like Wesley, recalled the church to Gospel truths. Wesley's successors slowly separated from the Church of England; but many evangelicals remained within the established church and have profoundly influenced its life. Evangelicals were largely instrumental in abolishing slavery in the English dominions and in forwarding the missionary endeavors of the English church. In modern times they emphasize the literal inspiration of the Bible, the importance of preaching, and the need for personal conversion.

EVANGELICAL LUTHERAN CHURCH, designation used by many Lutheran churches. Martin Luther did not wish anyone to call himself a Lutheran. "Who am I," he said, "that anyone should call himself by my insignificant name? . . . I do not want to be anyone's master, for only one is our master, even Jesus Christ." Nevertheless, his followers called themselves "Lutherans." But in accordance with Luther's suggestion (1521) that the churches of the Reformation should call themselves "evangelical" (evangel = gospel), many Lutheran churches have come to call themselves "Evangelical Lutheran."

EVANGELICAL SYNOD OF NORTH AMERICA. *See* EVANGELICAL AND REFORMED CHURCH.

EVANGELICAL UNITED BRETHREN CHURCH, THE, church formed in 1946 at Johnstown, Pa., through the union of the Evangelical Church and the Church of the United Brethren in Christ. The former had grown out of the Evangelical Association, organized in the early years of the 19th century under the leadership of Jacob Albright. The latter traced its history back to regular gatherings begun in 1800 under the leadership of Philip Otterbein and Martin Boehm. Both were originally German-speaking bodies which patterned their piety and polity after Methodism.

EVANGELINE [ĭ-văn′jə-lĭn], **A TALE OF ACADIE,** long narrative poem (1847) by Henry Wadsworth Longfellow. Religious sentiment and pictorial imagery are notable in this poignant love story of Evangeline Bellefontaine and Gabriel Lajeunesse, who were separated when the French settlers of Nova Scotia were deported in 1755.

EVANGELISM [ĭ-văn′jəl-ĭz-əm], term which in its broadest sense covers any activity designed to spread the Evangel, or the Gospel, the "Good News" of Jesus Christ. Although popularly applied to revivals, emotional services conducted by itinerant preachers, a distinction is sometimes drawn between revivals, which seek to reawaken lapsed or indifferent Christians, and evangelism, which reaches out to those who have not previously heard the Gospel. The church today makes use of many modern methods of evangelism: visitation by laymen to unchurched homes, radio and television services, newspaper advertising, direct mail messages, and rural and industrial evangelism.

EVANS [ĕv′ənz], **SIR ARTHUR JOHN** (1851–1941), British archeologist. He was keeper of the Ashmolean Museum, Oxford, from 1884 to 1908. In 1893 he began excavations in Crete, having previously worked in the Balkans. His research in Crete was capped by the excavation of the palace of Knossos (1900–08) and the discovery of a pre-Phoenician script. His discoveries forced a reinterpretation of Eastern Mediterranean history, resulting in the recognition of the importance of Minoan influences on Greek culture. His books include *The Palace of Minos* (4 vols., 1921–35) and *The Earlier Religion of Greece in the Light of Cretan Discoveries* (1931).

EVANS, DAME EDITH (1888–   ), English actress. She made her stage debut in 1912 and scored her first major success as Millamant in *The Way of the World* in London in 1924. She made her first New York appearance in 1931 and won recognition in both cities as a leading player of Shakespearean and modern roles.

EVANS, GEORGE HENRY (1805–56), American editor and agrarian reformer. The English-born radical came to the United States in 1820, learned the printing trade, and began to publish the *Working Man's Advocate* (1829–45) in New York City. Through his newspaper, the first important labor paper in the United States, Evans urged the formation of workingmen's political parties, fought such monopolies as the United States Bank, expounded his views as an atheist, and supported a number of humanitarian reforms. After 1837 he developed a program of land reform to give every man an inalienable homestead of 160 acres, resembling in its basic essentials the theories advocated by Henry George a generation later.

EVANS, MAURICE (1901–   ), stage actor and producer, born in England. He won early success in *Journey's End* (London, 1929) and in Old Vic productions of Shakespeare and Shaw (London, 1934) before making his U.S. debut in 1935 as Romeo. He produced *Hamlet* (1938) and *Macbeth* (1941) in New York and played the title roles in each. Evans also played these roles successfully in American television productions. In the U.S. theater he also appeared in *Man and Superman* (1947) and coproduced *The Teahouse of the August Moon* (1953) and *No Time for Sergeants* (1955).

EVANS, OLIVER (1755–1819), American engineer and inventor. Born in Delaware, he pioneered a number of inventive developments which later became important in mechanical engineering. His labor-saving conveying equipment, based on water power, for a flour mill, was one of the earliest examples of automation. By 1807, having proposed the first high-pressure steam engine, he had established himself as a millwright whose engines were more powerful, less complicated, and cheaper to operate than others being designed. He also devised an early form of steam dredge for underwater excavation. *See also* AUTOMATION.

EVANSDALE, town of east-central Iowa, a residential suburb southeast of Waterloo. Pop. (1950) 3,571; (1960) 5,738.

EVANSTON, residential and educational city north of Chicago, Illinois, located on Lake Michigan. Northwestern University, the National College of Education, the Seabury-Western Theological Seminary, Garrett Biblical Institute, Evanston Collegiate Institute, and Evanston Township Community College are located here. Evanston is also the headquarters of the Women's Christian Temperance Union and the site of the famous adoption agency, The Cradle. Evanston has limited but diversified manufactures, including radio and television equipment, pharmaceuticals, paint, and glass products. Settled, 1827; inc., 1892; pop. (1950) 73,641; (1960) 79,283.

EVANSVILLE, city of southwestern Indiana and seat of Vanderburgh County. Situated on the Ohio River, it is the distribution center for a densely populated area. Founded in 1812 and chartered as a city in 1847, Evansville has frequently been enlarged by annexations. It was Indiana's second-largest city from 1855 to 1915. Meat packing and the manufacture of pharmaceutical products and refrigerators are the chief industries. Industrial equipment and furniture are manufactured at Evansville. Considerable bituminous coal, gas, and oil are obtained near the city. Evansville College (estab., 1854) is located here. Pop. (1950) 128,636; (1960) 141,543; urb. area (1950) 137,573; (1960) 143,660.

EVAPORATION [ĭ-văp-ə-rā′shən], the vaporization, without visible disturbance, of a liquid at its surface. Liquids left in uncovered dishes generally disappear by this process.

METHODS TO SPEED UP EVAPORATION

1. INCREASE AIR FLOW
If air is blown over the surface of a liquid, the vaporized molecules are driven away as they escape from the surface.

2. ADD HEAT
Heating a liquid causes the molecules to move more rapidly. Hence more of them escape in a given period of time.

3. LOWER PRESSURE
If atmospheric pressure is reduced, there are fewer molecules in the atmosphere to collide with newly vaporized molecules and deflect them back into the liquid. This condition speeds evaporation.

4. INCREASE SURFACE AREA
Increasing the surface area of a liquid allows more molecules to evaporate at the same time.

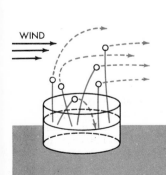

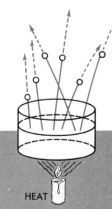

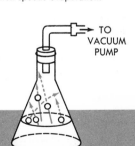

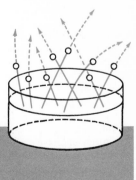

The rate of evaporation depends on the type of liquid, the temperature, the exposed surface area, the amount of ventilation, and the pressure exerted on the surface of the liquid. Evaporation is a cooling process. As the more energetic molecules escape from the liquid by evaporation, the average molecular kinetic energy of the remaining liquid is decreased. Kinetic energy is a measure of the temperature of a substance; hence, the remaining liquid is cooler. Many small domestic refrigerating units operate on this principle.

Evaporation must be distinguished from boiling. Evaporation of a liquid is a surface phenomenon and takes place at all temperatures. Boiling is the vaporization of a liquid in bubbles in the body of the liquid, as well as at the free surface. The boiling point of a liquid is a specific temperature at which the pressure of the escaping molecules, that is, the vapor pressure of the liquid, is equal to the atmospheric pressure exerted on the liquid.

Evaporation is an important aspect of hydrology, a science dealing with the occurrence and behavior of water in nature. Most atmospheric vapor is the product of evaporation from water surfaces. To a hydrologist, evaporation is the net rate at which liquid water is transferred to the atmosphere. In regions of low rainfall, evaporation rates from water surfaces are usually high and conservation of water is important. Certain chemical compounds may be spread in layers of single molecules over water surfaces and thus inhibit evaporation. This method has been effective in the control of evaporation from reservoirs.

VEN TE CHOW, University of Illinois

EVAPORIMETER [ĭ-văp-ə-rĭm′ə-tər], also called atmometer, atmidometer, or evaporation gauge, an instrument used by meteorologists to measure the rate at which water evaporates into the atmosphere. The kinds used include large tanks of water sunk into the ground, small pans of water, porous porcelain devices, and instruments using a paper wick. Evaporation should be compared only between identical instruments because the rate is influenced by both the nature of the surface and its exposure to the air.

EVAPORITE [ĭ-văp′ə-rīt], in geology, sedimentary deposit formed by the precipitation of soluble compounds from aqueous solutions as the water evaporates. The least soluble materials, including calcium and magnesium carbonates, are precipitated first, followed by calcium sulfate, rock salt (sodium chloride), and finally the highly soluble salts such as potassium chloride. Evaporites accumulate in desert basins and in restricted arms of the sea where evaporation exceeds inflow. They are economically important as sources of borax, common salt, nitrates, and potash.

EVARTS [ĕv′ərts], **WILLIAM MAXWELL** (1818–1901), American lawyer and Cabinet member. Evarts, born in Boston, graduated from Yale in 1837 and, after studying law at Harvard, became a prominent lawyer in New York City. He acted as government counsel during the Civil War in cases involving the status of captured vessels and the constitutionality of state taxes on federal bonds; and after the war he arbitrated (1871–72) the *Alabama* claims. He was chief defense counsel in the impeachment proceedings against President Andrew Johnson and then became Attorney General (1868–69) in Johnson's Cabinet. After defending Rutherford B. Hayes before the Electoral Commission on the disputed election of 1876, Evarts became Hayes's Secretary of State (1877–81). He served as U.S. Senator from 1885 to 1891.

EVATT [ĕv′ət], **HERBERT VERE** (1894–1965), Australian politician, jurist, and author. Before serving (1930–40) as a justice of the High Court of Australia, where his judgments aroused attention and respect, he was active in state politics. He entered national politics in 1940 as a Labor member of the House of Representatives. As Minister for External Affairs (1941–49), he reshaped Australian foreign policy and influenced the United Nations in its formative stages. In 1948 he was elected president of the U.N. General Assembly. As the Labor party's parliamentary leader (1951–60), he failed to win elections despite tremendous personal effort. He was closely involved in the struggle within the Labor party that led to the emergence of the separate Democratic Labor party.

Chief Justice of New South Wales from 1960 to 1962, he also became widely known for his historical and constitutional writing. His career reflects his intellectual capacity and versatility as well as his masterful and sometimes tactless disposition.

GORDON GREENWOOD, University of Queensland
(Australia)

EVE (Heb. *Hawwah*, "living one"), name of the first woman, wife of Adam, the first man, as recorded in Genesis 3:20, through whom all humanity received life. The story of her creation and life with Adam in the Garden of Eden and afterward is told in Genesis 2–4.

EVELETH, city of northeastern Minnesota on the Mesabi iron range. It is a mining center and shipping point for iron ore. Inc., 1893; pop. (1950) 5,872; (1960) 5,721.

EVELYN [ēv′lĭn], **JOHN** (1620–1706), English diarist, public servant, and amateur scientist. He studied at the Middle Temple and at Balliol College, Oxford. Evelyn served on commissions for the London streets, the mint, various hospitals, the privy seal, and for the colonies in the New World. He submitted to Robert Boyle the original plan out of which the Royal Society grew. In 1672 he became secretary to the society and submitted schemes for abating the London smoke nuisance and reforesting England. He is remembered today for his charming *Diary*, first published in 1818, which records more than half a century of London life.

EVENING PRIMROSE, name for several annual, biennial, or perennial plants of the genus *Oenothera*, in the Onagraceae, or evening primrose, family, native to Europe and North and South America. *O. biennis*, a European species, is widely grown in North America. The plants grow from 3 to 4 ft. tall and bear large, delicately scented yellow flowers that open only in the evening. Because of its bedraggled daytime appearance, evening primrose should be planted in a border with shrubs or in a wildflower garden.

Mount Everest Foundation

Camera Press—Pix

The summit of Mount Everest. Sir Edmund Hillary (*left*) and Tenzing Norkay accomplished their history-making ascent in the spring of 1953.

EVENING STAR. *See* MERCURY; VENUS.

EVEREST [ĕv′ər-ĭst], **MOUNT** (Tibet. **CHOMOLUNGMA,** "Goddess-mother of the land"), world's highest mountain, located in the eastern Himalayas on the Nepal-China (Tibet) border. Its elevation as determined by a British trigonometrical survey is 29,002 ft., or 29,141 ft. after correction for gravity anomaly. The peak's English name honors Sir George Everest, British surveyor and geographer who, in the middle of the 19th century, first determined its position and elevation. The Rongbuk Glacier descends Everest to the north, measuring 12 mi. long and falling from 22,000 ft. to 16,500 ft., transverse to the axis of the range. Tremendous curtains of nearly vertical and beautifully fluted ice encase the peak on its north face almost to its summit. The organisms living highest on the mountain are spiders that feed on bits of dead vegetation blown as high as 22,000 ft. or on each other. Beyond them lies the lifeless zone. Twelve climbing assaults on the "summit of the world" had been attempted before May 29, 1953, when Sir Edmund Hillary of New Zealand and Tenzing Norkay, a Nepalese Sherpa, finally set foot on the summit. In their ascent, which took 80 days, they climbed the southwest face from Nepal. In May, 1956, two other pairs reached the top. In May, 1960, a Chinese expedition conquered the summit by scaling the north side, an approach that had been attempted without success seven times previously. A U.S. expedition reached the summit in May, 1963: James Whittaker and a Sherpa on May 1, and four others, using different routes—two via South Col and two by the hitherto-unclimbed West Ridge—on May 23.

FREDERICK HUNG, United College

EVERETT [ĕv′ər-ĭt], **EDWARD** (1794–1865), American Unitarian clergyman, orator, and statesman. He was born in Dorchester, Mass., graduated (1811) from Harvard, and became (1814) pastor of Boston's largest congregation. After being appointed to Harvard's Chair of Greek Literature in 1815, Everett studied abroad until 1819 before assuming his duties. Elected to Congress by independent voters, Everett served five terms (1825–35) and took a moderate position on slavery at a time when many New Englanders were strongly opposing it. He served as Governor of Massachusetts (1836–39), as U.S. minister to England (1841–45), and as president of Harvard (1846–49). After four months as Secretary of State (Dec., 1852–Mar., 1853) in President Millard Fillmore's Cabinet, Everett began a six-year term in the U.S. Senate, but resigned in 1854, embarrassed by his earlier stand on slavery. He phlegmatically accepted the Constitutional Union party's nomination for Vice-President in 1860. After his defeat he spent the Civil War years lecturing to huge audiences throughout the North on the Union cause. His most famous speech was his two-hour oration preceding President Abraham Lincoln's Gettysburg Address.

JAMES SHENTON, Columbia University

EVERETT, industrial city of northeastern Massachusetts, 3 mi. north of Boston. Heavy industries predominate. Settled, 1643; inc., 1892; pop. (1950) 45,982; (1960) 43,544.

EVERETT, city and port of entry of northwestern Washington, 25 mi. north of Seattle, located at the mouth of the Snohomish River, on Everett Bay of Puget Sound. Industries include lumbering, boat building and repair, fishing, milk processing, and the manufacture of wood pulp, shingles, and plywood. The State Home for Girls is located here. Settled, c.1890; pop. (1950) 33,849; (1960) 40,304.

EVERGLADES [ĕv′ər-glādz], swampy region in southern Florida. Saw grass, open water, and isolated tree clumps characterize the low limestone plain, part of which is cov-

Florida State News Bureau

Trees rise in clumps from the waters of the Florida Everglades.

Philip Gendreau

Vacationers canoe through a forest of Everglades National Park.

ered with muck and peat to a depth of several feet. Portions of the region, which is about 100 mi. long and from 50 to 75 mi. wide, are reclaimed for truck farming and sugar-cane production and for cattle pasture. The Seminole Indian Reservation is west of the lower Everglades. The southern part, south of the Tamiami Trail (U.S. 94), was set aside for public use in 1947 as the Everglades National Park (area, 2,190 sq. mi.).

EVERGLADES NATIONAL PARK, area reserved for public use in southern Florida. The park is the meeting place of mid-latitude and tropical plants, of fresh, brackish, and salt water, and of land and sea. It is probably most noted for its tremendous assemblages of water birds. Much of its near-sea-level surface is broad sawgrass prairie, dotted by hammocks of many species of hardwoods; west and south are vast mangrove forests interlaced with waterways. The park contains virtually all of Florida Bay, haunt of the roseate spoonbill, the great white heron, and the American crocodile. The human and natural history of the park is explained at stops along the road to Flamingo, on Florida Bay. At Royal Palm Station, the Anhinga Trail takes the visitor into an Everglades slough to watch its wildlife. Gateways are at Homestead in the east and Everglades in the northwest. Estab., 1947; area, 2,190 sq. mi.

EVERGREEN, horticultural term for any plant that retains some green or live foliage throughout the year. Evergreens do not shed all of their foliage at any one time, in contrast to deciduous plants, which drop all of their leaves at the same time, usually at the end of the growing season. The term "evergreen" is popularly used as a synonym for "conifer" (a cone-bearing tree), but some of the conifers— larches and bald cypress—are deciduous, and in the tropics there are evergreens—palms and sandalwoods—that are not conifers.

Two types of evergreen plants are recognized: the

needle-leaved evergreens of class Gymnospermae, which includes spruce, fir, pine, juniper, and other conifers; and the broad-leaved evergreens of class Angiospermae, including live oak, laurel, holly, and many of the tropical hardwoods. Needle-leaved, or coniferous, evergreens make up about 35% of the forested areas of the world. These forests extend in a broad belt across North America, from Alaska through Canada and northern United States, and across northern Europe and Asia. Small coniferous forests are also found in Australia, Africa, and South America.

The broad-leaved evergreens comprise about 48% of the world's forests. They occur in Central and South America, central Africa, the Philippines, Indochina, Malaya, India, Siam, and many other parts of Asia. Typical trees include mahogany, logwood, and the rubber tree. Broad-leaved evergreens of North America are the rhododendron and laurel, found in Canada and northern United States, and magnolia, holly, and live oak, in southern United States.

CLARENCE J. HYLANDER, Author, *The World of Plant Life*
See also CONIFER; FORESTS AND FORESTRY; TREE.

EVERGREEN PARK, residential suburb southwest of Chicago, Illinois. Inc., 1893; pop. (1950) 10,531; (1960) 24,178.

EVERLASTING, floricultural term describing flowers and plants that retain their color and shape after drying. The common everlasting of European and American gardens is the yellow-flowering species, *Helichrysum bracteatum,* a member of the composite family. The French *immortelle,* or yellow everlasting, *H. arenarium,* is often bleached white or dyed in various colors. This species, and also the silvery-hued cape flower, *H. grandiflorum,* a native of South Africa, are the most commercially important everlastings. Other flowers and plants known as everlasting include the pearly-white flowering *Anaphalis margaritacea,* and various species of *Antennaria,* both native to North America.

EVERYMAN, 15th-century English morality play probably derived from the Dutch *Elckerlijc.* The play, written to teach Christians how to prepare for holy dying, portrays Everyman, who has received the summons of Death, as deserted by all companions save Knowledge (acknowledgment of his sins) and his own Good Deeds. The latter accompanies him into the grave to plead his case before the Divine Judge.

Evidence is the means by which information is presented at a trial for use in deciding issues of fact. Physical objects, called "real," or "demonstrative," evidence, must be relevant and properly authenticated.

Above, a witness identifies an object of clothing relevant as evidence.

Left, objects presented as real evidence during a trial. (THREE LIONS) **Right,** an attorney holds a wrist watch introduced as real evidence for identification by a witness. (UNITED PRESS INTERNATIONAL)

EVESHAM [ēv′shəm, ē′shəm], historic market town and municipal borough of southern Worcestershire, England, on the Avon River, 14 mi. southeast of Worcester. Its early importance is seen in the remains of Evesham Abbey, founded in 701. The town is the market center for the fertile Evesham valley with its fruit trees and truck farms. Pop., 12,608.

EVICTION. *See* LANDLORD AND TENANT.

EVIDENCE, in law, denotes all the means—for example, oral testimony, documents, physical objects—by which information is presented to courts for use in deciding factual disputes. The rules governing this process constitute the "law of evidence." Evidence law in the common law countries, such as the English-speaking countries, does not concern itself with scientific or other evaluation of the probative force (or "proof value") of different kinds of evidence, as is often done in other countries, but consists largely of rules determining when various kinds of evidence may be received and when they must be excluded. This developed from the necessities of the jury trial system and also from the adversary system of litigation, in which obtaining, selecting, and presenting evidence is left to the parties' attorneys and is not a principal concern of the court itself. Evaluation of the evidence received is then left to the common sense or experience of the trier of the facts, whether jury or judge. A basic difference in relation to the law of evidence between the two great systems of law, the common law and the civil law, is that the former focuses on questions of inadmissibility and relevancy, whereas the latter starts out from the proposition that all evidence which has value as proof should be admitted.

Evidence Terms. Some of the frequently used terms regarding evidence include direct, circumstantial, and pri-

ma facie evidence. Direct evidence is that which proves the disputed fact without the need for any inference or presumption and which, if true, establishes that fact. Circumstantial evidence is that which tends to establish the fact in dispute by proving other facts which, though true, still do not directly establish the disputed fact, but do support an inference or presumption of its existence. Prima facie evidence is that which standing alone is sufficient to prove a particular fact, unless it is contradicted or rebutted by other evidence.

Relevancy. Evidence to be admissible in court must be "relevant," that is, it must have a logical tendency to prove or disprove a fact in issue. Even if relevant, however, the evidence introduced may still be deemed inadmissible because of the numerous exclusionary rules. Evidence of minor probative importance may also be excluded if to go into it may take too much time, create prejudice or confusion, mislead the jury, or unfairly surprise a party.

Hearsay. Most evidence is presented through oral testimony of witnesses. It should ordinarily be "first-hand" evidence, that is, it must relate to matters which the witnesses themselves have seen, heard, or done. When witnesses testify to statements made by others as to what others saw, heard, or did, in order to establish as true the facts declared in those statements, the result is "second-hand" evidence, called "hearsay." Hearsay evidence is excluded because the declarants usually speak without oath, and, if not now in court, cannot be tested as to credibility by cross-examination. When a document is offered in evidence to establish facts which it declares, instead of the writer's oral testimony, it is also hearsay. Because important and probably trustworthy evidence of unavailable declarants would often be lost altogether if courts excluded hearsay completely, numerous "exceptions to the hearsay rule" have been developed. These include excep-

THE CRIME LABORATORY

The crime laboratory contributes scientific analysis of evidence tending to establish the guilt or innocence of a defendant in a criminal case. Ballistic and fingerprint identification are often crucial evidence.

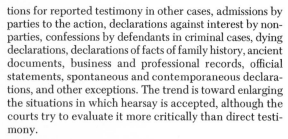

All photos—*Three Lions*

A technician fires a bullet into a tank of water. The markings left on the bullet by the gun can be compared with those of the bullet fired in the commission of the crime to identify the gun used.

A bullet used in a crime is identified by comparison with those kept in a laboratory file for such purposes.

An expert examines a set of fingerprints. His findings are accepted as scientific evidence in court.

tions for reported testimony in other cases, admissions by parties to the action, declarations against interest by nonparties, confessions by defendants in criminal cases, dying declarations, declarations of facts of family history, ancient documents, business and professional records, official statements, spontaneous and contemporaneous declarations, and other exceptions. The trend is toward enlarging the situations in which hearsay is accepted, although the courts try to evaluate it more critically than direct testimony.

Opinion. Witnesses should testify to perceived facts. Ordinary testimony as to their opinions or conclusions about the facts shown are excluded. It is for the jury or judge as trier of the facts to formulate opinions and arrive at conclusions. When matters of scientific or other specialized knowledge are involved, however, so that special training and experience are needed to form a reliable opinion, an expert's opinion is admissible when the trier of the facts can be assisted by it. The conflicting and partisan opinion evidence often given by experts, particularly in medical matters, and the elaborate hypothetical questions put to them, have impaired public confidence in such testimony. Improvement may result from the use of impartial, court-appointed medical experts.

Character. Many problems are encountered in trying to show the character of a person as having a logical bearing upon other matters in issue. Thus, the prosecution in criminal cases is forbidden to introduce initially evidence of defendant's bad character. But the accused, if he wishes, is allowed to introduce evidence of his good character, to show unlikelihood that he would have committed the crime charged. Once the accused does so, the prosecutor may show his bad character. Again, in civil and criminal cases the credibility of a witness may be attacked by

showing his bad character for truthfulness or honesty or by proving his prior conviction of crime. Only after this may his credibility be supported by proof of his good character. The character proof usually permitted is the proof of a person's reputation in his community for the character traits in question. While it is a general rule in criminal trials that proof of other crimes in which an accused has been involved may not be received, numerous exceptions are recognized when such proof serves purposes beyond merely showing that the accused is bad or a criminal type.

Competency. At common law, parties to an action and persons interested in its outcome could not testify in it. Neither could convicted felons. One spouse could not ordinarily testify for or against the other in civil or criminal cases. A religious oath and belief in a God who would punish false swearing in this life or hereafter were required of a witness. Nearly all these grounds for witness incompetency have since been removed. An important one which still remains, however, and is expressly preserved by statute, provides that surviving parties and persons interested in the outcome of the controversy may not testify to their personal transactions or communications with one since deceased in suits against the latter's estate. These "dead man statutes" were intended to protect estates of deceased persons against dishonest claims, but may just as often prevent enforcement of survivors' honest claims when other evidence is unavailable. A few states have changed this, either by admitting the survivor's testimony, but requiring some corroboration to support a judgment, or by accepting both the survivor's testimony and any writings or oral statements made by the deceased on the matter.

The incompetency of the spouse is now usually limited only to the state's inability to call one spouse as a witness against the other without the latter's consent in criminal cases, except as to crimes committed against the witness spouse. Mental defectives and children may still be incompetent, as at common law; but if they can observe, remember and recount the facts, and appreciate the duty to testify truthfully, they will be held competent. Incompetency is gradually being de-emphasized, and the grounds formerly establishing it are, instead, being considered for determining credibility and evaluating the evidence.

Privilege. As a matter of policy, the law protects against disclosure confidential communications between spouses, attorney and client, and in many jurisdictions between physician and patient, and clergyman and penitent. One may refuse to testify regarding such communications, unless the person for whose benefit this privilege exists (the other spouse, client, patient, penitent) waives the privilege. Similar privileges are recognized for secrets of state and for the identity of informers who give information to the government or, in rare jurisdictions, to newspapermen.

Writings. Before documents can be received in evidence, they must be "authenticated" by proof that they are what they are claimed to be. The ordinary exclusionary rules apply to all evidence, including writings, and certain special doctrines also apply. The "best evidence rule" requires that the original document be offered to establish its contents unless its unavailability is properly accounted for; only then may "secondary evidence" (such as copies, or oral evidence) be received. The "parol evidence rule" provides that when persons have reduced their transaction or agreement to a writing which appears complete on its face, as between such persons, no oral or extrinsic evidence of their prior or contemporaneous agreements will be received to vary or add to the terms of the instrument. Even if received without objection such evidence has no legal effect. But the rule does not bar extrinsic evidence to help interpret the writing, rather than establish additional parts of the transaction. Extrinsic evidence may also show conditional delivery, lack of consideration, fraud, and illegality. Nor does the rule exclude extrinsic evidence such as a separate collateral agreement purposely made by the parties to deal with aspects of the subject omitted from the main instrument.

Real Evidence. If practicable, physical objects which are relevant to the facts in issue may be received in evidence when properly authenticated. If they are needlessly gruesome, prejudicial, or disruptive of trial proceedings, however, a court should exclude them. The persuasive effect upon jurors of using their own senses upon physical objects is so much greater than that of mere testimony that courts must guard closely against its abuse, while recognizing the great help which relevant physical objects may give in sound fact finding. Photographs, diagrams, movies, and so on, which depict relevant objects or places, are equally admissible, if properly authenticated and shown to be accurate representations. The same principles apply to physical demonstrations and tests which are relevant to facts in issue. All these categories are "real," or "demonstrative," evidence.

Scientific Evidence. This is an expandingly important field. From fingerprint identification and analysis of questioned documents, it has broadened into the full range of techniques used by modern scientific crime laboratories, and such things as blood-grouping tests, drunkenness tests, and lie-detection methods. Especially in problems of identification by comparison, scientific proof is tellingly presented by enlarged photographs, comparison microscope, or spectroscope, so that the triers of the facts can themselves see the factual basis on which the conclusions were reached. New scientific knowledge and techniques will keep enlarging this field.

Judicial Notice. It would waste time to require evidence to prove certain kinds of obvious facts, for example, multiplication tables or the slipperiness of banana peels. They are established by taking "judicial notice" of them, instead of evidence. Even without request, courts *must* take judicial notice of specific facts and propositions of generalized knowledge so universally known as to be indisputable; and *may* judicially notice facts not so well known in their jurisdiction as to be indisputable, and specific facts and propositions of generalized knowledge capable of prompt, accurate determination from indisputably reliable reference sources. Courts *must* judicially notice the latter if a party requests, and furnishes the judge with sufficient information to comply, and also notifies adverse parties so they may be able to meet the request.

Courts also take judicial notice of the Constitutions, common and statute law of the United States and their own state, but usually not of sister states or foreign countries, or of local ordinances or administrative regulations, unless statutes so provide. Many states have adopted a uniform statute providing for judicial notice of sister-state law. Federal courts, in cases brought or removed there, judicially notice the law of every state.

Presumptions. In many situations, courts have found that proof of certain underlying facts warrants inferring the existence of other facts sought to be established and usually difficult to prove, at least until the adversary shows the contrary. The basic reason is probability, though policy considerations also enter. These legally recognized inferences are called "presumptions," and prima facie establish the presumed fact for procedural purposes. They may be permissive or mandatory, and are rebuttable. There are similar so-called "presumptions of law," which are not rebuttable, and really amount to fixed rules of substantive law.

That a person who has disappeared and been absent for seven years without tidings, despite diligent inquiry, is then presumed to be dead, or that a letter properly addressed, stamped, and mailed is presumed to have been delivered, illustrate rebuttable presumptions. That a child under seven is conclusively presumed incapable of committing a crime illustrates an irrebuttable presumption, and really means that the law does not hold him criminally responsible. The so-called "presumption of innocence" is not a presumption, but means that a higher degree of proof is required before defendant can be found guilty in a criminal case ("beyond a reasonable doubt") than is needed to prevail in a civil case ("preponderance of the evidence"). The fact that a particular rebuttable presumption exists should not itself be considered as evidence of the presumed fact, once rebuttal evidence is offered, but the question should be decided on the proven underlying facts and the evidence submitted in the rebuttal.

Burden of Proof. This term is loosely used for two different concepts. One, better called "risk of nonpersuasion," means that the party upon whom it rests will lose unless on his whole claim or defense the trier of the facts is persuaded that the facts are as he alleges. The other, better called "risk of nonproduction," means that the party upon whom it rests may have specific facts which are at issue adversely determined unless some, or further, evidence is produced to support his contention regarding them. The latter risk may shift from party to party during trial on different matters, but the risk of nonpersuasion is determined at the trial's outset (usually from the pleadings), and continues unchanged.

Recent Trends. The general trend in evidence law in recent years, except in constitutional aspects of criminal cases, has been toward more liberal admissibility and toward a larger discretion on the part of the trial judge. Two notable efforts to state modern notions of sound evidence doctrine are the American Law Institute Model Code of Evidence (1942) and the Uniform Rules of Evidence of the National Conference of Commissioners on Uniform State Laws (1953). The American Bar Association has approved the latter.

Consult Wigmore, J. H., *A Treatise on the Anglo-American Law of Evidence* (3d ed., 10 vols., 1940); McCormick, C. T., *Handbook of the Law of Evidence* (1954).

ELI M. SPARK, Catholic University of America School of Law
See also PROCEDURE, CIVIL; PROCEDURE, CRIMINAL; SEARCH AND SEIZURE; SELF-INCRIMINATION, PRIVILEGE AGAINST.

EVIL, PROBLEM OF. The problem of evil arises in connection with the alleged incompatibility of the following propositions: (1) God is omniscient (all-knowing). (2) God is omnipotent (all-powerful). (3) God is all-good. (4) God exists. (5) There is evil in the world. According to most religionists, the first three propositions are included in the definition of the concept "God." That is, it is impossible that anything could properly be called God which was not all-good, all-powerful, and all-knowing. The fourth proposition is believed true by any conventional religionist. The fifth is usually felt to be obviously true, though many religionists deny it for reasons which shall become evident presently. The incompatibility of the five propositions may be expressed in the form of a dilemma which casts doubt on the existence of any God defined with the first three attributes, and consequently on most concepts of God.

If there is evil in the world and God exists, then it must be that either He is not powerful enough to prevent it, or not aware of its existence, or did not foresee its existence at the time of creation, or He is not all-good, or all or any combination of these. In any case, if there is a God, then He does not have the attributes that most people believe God to have. Therefore, the God that most people believe exists does not exist. There may be an entity very like the one that the religionist believes in. For instance, such an entity may be all-powerful and all-good, but not all-knowing, but He cannot be *exactly* like the conventional God, or there would be no evil in the world.

There are a number of replies to this argument, most of which concern proposition (5). Some have attempted to demonstrate that what is ordinarily called evil may not be so at all. The usual account of evil connects it with pain, especially unnecessary pain, having either a human or natural origin, such as floods, earthquakes, plagues. However, why should pain be regarded as evil? Perhaps the pain endured by man is a test of his strength of character. This view seems plausible enough in cases where pain does not lead to death. But the feasibility of a test which results in death is questionable. On the other hand, pain might be a punishment for various misdeeds. This belief is widely held, but it is dubious because of the inequitable and even unjust distribution of suffering, and because of the distasteful nature of retributive accounts of justice or punishment.

A more plausible way out of the dilemma is to argue that pain, or anything customarily taken to be evil, is really conducive to the realization of some unknown end which is good. Man does not know the ways of God, and consequently what appears evil to man may not be evil. The general objection to this line of argument is that if man is ignorant of what evil really is, then why is he not ignorant of what good is, also? It may be that what men customarily regard as good is really evil. If this were true, the moral agency of man would become questionable, since one of the presuppositions of moral agency is a knowledge of good and evil.

One of the most popular ways to explain away the alleged incompatibility of God's existence and the presence of evil is to argue that God could have created a world without evil, but felt that it was more important to give man freedom of choice. He could have made man in such a way that he would always choose the good thing. But had He done so, it would not be possible to praise man for choosing rightly. Man would not be a moral agent. This sort of reply adequately accounts for evil created out of human choice, but it does not explain evil resulting from plagues, earthquakes, and other natural events. God could have given man freedom of choice and still prevented natural forms of suffering. Furthermore, many have felt that it is inconsistent to suppose that man has free choice, when God can foresee all of his actions.

Another reply of considerable interest is that evil is incomplete good. Evil represents a partial view of things as they really are. If one is judging a poem, he might suppose that a given line is poor, when considered in isolation from the rest. Yet, when he viewed it in relation to the rest of the poem, he might change his mind. The presupposition of this argument is that the universe taken as a whole is good, and this is certainly disputable. There are still other attempts to give an unassailable answer to the problem of evil, but none are beyond question.

EMILIO ROMA, State University of N.Y. at Binghamton

EVIL EYE, the supposed power of inflicting harm through looking. Belief in such a power has a wide distribution and is linked with superstitions about witchcraft. The evil influence is often thought to be provoked by jealously. A further belief is that the victim may be harmed without conscious intent. Thus a person accused of having the evil eye may not be able to prove his innocence by disclaiming any specific actions. Amulets and charms may be employed to guard against the evil eye.

EVOLUTION [ĕv-ə-lōo'shən], the natural process through which organisms have acquired their characteristic structure and function. The term is derived from the Lat. *evolvere*, "to unroll or unfold," and refers to the orderly development of species from pre-existing ones.

The past few centuries have witnessed a thorough inventory of the million or more species of plants and animals living today, as well as of the thousands of extinct species. Many biologists have studied in detail the structures, functions, habits, and distribution of these organisms. The result has been an accurate picture of the amazing variety and complexity of life. But at the same time it has spurred curiosity as to how this has all come into existence. How can the many similarities and differences among plants and animals be explained? How do new species come into being? What happens to ancestral species? Biologists believe that the evolutionary concept gives the most adequate answer to these questions. Evolution is the logical application to life of the truth that change is inevitable and universal.

The History of the Evolutionary Concept

Four theories have, at various times, been advanced to explain the origin of life. Spontaneous generation, the oldest of these theories, holds that living matter is able to arise spontaneously from nonliving. Anaximander, a Greek naturalist of the 6th century B.C., was an early proponent of this theory. Although many early naturalists were aware of the phenomenon of reproduction, the idea of spontaneous generation was not discredited until the 17th century when the Italian naturalist Francisco Redi demonstrated that maggots do not arise from dead meat, but are hatched from eggs laid on the meat by flies. Special creation is another very early attempt to explain the origin of life. This theory, which originated in pre-Biblical times, states that each species was created in its present form by an external and supernatural power. Prior to the accumulation of modern biological data, aided by such related fields as paleontology and paleobotany, many scientists as well as laymen believed in special creation. Since special creation implies that a species, once created, remains unchanged, this theory is correlated with the concept of fixity of species. Advocates of the special creation theory included such capable scientists as the Swedish botanist Linnaeus and the French zoologist Cuvier.

The other theories of the origin of life are the cosmozoic theory and the naturalistic theory. The first states that simple forms of life reached the earth from some other region of the universe. Because the extreme temperatures, radiation effects, and other factors existing in interstellar space cannot support life as it is known on earth, it is not likely that life on earth could have begun in this manner. Further, the cosmozoic theory gives no explanation as to the actual origin of life. The naturalistic concept holds that certain conditions had developed on earth that were favorable to life and that certain simple aggregates of matter that had the properties of life were then able to develop into simple living organisms, which evolved into progressively more complex forms. This very important theory was proposed in 1923 by a Russian investigator, A. I. Oparin, and has been partially supported by basic experiments performed in the early 1950's by students of the

---

All life is a continuous state of evolution — a complex and gradual process that has occurred over millions of years. The article on these pages examines some of the main evolutionary trends and also presents various theories that seek to explain this extraordinarily complex phenomenon. The article is organized in the following manner.

The History of the Evolutionary Concept. An outline of the various theories of evolution, from the ancient Greek naturalist Empedocles to Charles Darwin, whose theories form the basis of the present-day approach to the subject.

The Evidence for Evolution. Various biological sciences have provided evidence to establish the validity of the theory of evolution. These include taxonomy, anatomy, embryology, ecology, and paleontology.

The Mechanism of Evolution. A description of natural selection: how the environment, interacting with the genetic make-up of living organisms, directs the course of evolution.

The Main Patterns of Evolution. An outline of the evolution of life over a period of more than 600 million years. The three main stages of this development were the appearance of green plants, invertebrate animals, and finally vertebrate animals.

The student who wishes to further his knowledge of evolution may consult the comprehensive articles LIFE and BIOLOGY. Additional information about the various sciences that have contributed to the theory of evolution can be found in the articles ECOLOGY, EMBRYOLOGY, PALEONTOLOGY, PALEOBOTANY, and GENETICS. Another key article is ENVIRONMENT. The various stages in the long history of evolution are discussed in such articles as PLANT, ALGAE, and SPONGE for the plant world, and INVERTEBRATE, AMPHIBIAN, VERTEBRATES, and MAMMAL for the animal world. The entry ANIMAL provides a family tree of the vertebrates, a family tree of the mammals, and an illustrated animal classification.

No study of evolution is complete without a familiarity with the men who contributed its principal theories. Here, the name of Charles DARWIN stands out; the articles on Alfred Russel WALLACE and Jean Baptiste LAMARCK may also be consulted.

For a detailed study of evolution, the reader may consult books listed at the ends of many articles. As new theories are advanced and old ones discarded, and as new scientific and technological discoveries add to man's knowledge of the long history of life on this planet, it is important for the student to keep abreast of new developments in the field. Such advances are recorded in the annual supplement to the **ENCYCLOPEDIA INTERNATIONAL.** Scientific journals, available in most libraries, may also be consulted.

THE EVOLUTION OF LAND ANIMALS

Animal life began in the sea and later adapted with ease to the fresh-water environment. The land, however, was not conquered until three major evolutionary changes occurred: the development of a means of respiration in the air; the development of a limb suitable for land locomotion; the development of a land egg. The first of these requisites appeared long before it was needed: lunglike structures (in addition to gills) were present in placoderm and in lobe-finned fishes. The terrestrial limb first appeared in amphibians, but the necessary skeletal elements were present in the pectoral fins of lobe-finned fishes. An egg capable of developing on land appeared with the reptiles, the first animals to become completely adapted for life on land.

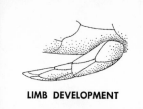

LIMB DEVELOPMENT

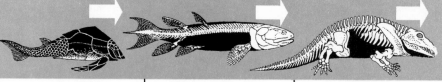

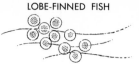
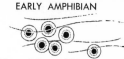

PLACODERM FISH

The placoderm, or plate-skinned, fish had jointed, flipperlike pectoral fins. Its eggs developed in the water.

LOBE-FINNED FISH

The lobe-finned fish had the skeletal rudiments of a land limb. Its eggs were released into and developed in water.

EARLY AMPHIBIAN

The adult amphibian moved on land and respired with lungs. Its eggs and young, however, had to develop in the water.

American chemist Harold C. Urey. Until this naturalistic concept is proved false, or supplanted by another theory, it remains the best available explanation of the origin of life.

The idea of evolution is almost as old as the Biblical version of special creation. It has its roots in the writings of Empedocles, an early Greek naturalist who is considered to be the father of the evolution concept. With the advent of modern biology, these early ideas of the origin of life moved from the realm of philosophy to that of science. Today, the concept of evolution is the most significant contribution of biology to human thought, and has had tremendous impact on man's outlook upon his universe.

The present-day evolutionary concept traces its origins to the studies of many 18th-century biologists. Outstanding were the French naturalists Georges Buffon, who early discarded the notion of special creation, and Jean Baptiste Lamarck, generally considered the forerunner of Charles Darwin. The British geologist Charles Lyell, who established the modern concept of earth history and its fossil record, exerted a great influence on Charles Darwin, and thus was also a contributor to the early development of the concept of evolution; as was Erasmus Darwin, the grandfather of Charles Darwin.

The contribution of Charles Darwin was so considerable that evolution is often referred to as the Darwinian theory. Darwin, however, owed much to his many predecessors and to his contemporaries, among them the British biologist Alfred Russel Wallace, who independently and almost simultaneously arrived at the idea of natural selection for which Darwin is often given sole credit. Darwin and Wallace presented their theory jointly in 1858 at a meeting of the Linnaean Society in London. Darwin's basic theory remains today a fundamental part of the evolutionary concept. However, far more information is available to modern biologists than was known to Darwin. When the laws of heredity, formulated by the Austrian monk Gregor Mendel, were rediscovered in 1900, it be-

came necessary to modify the idea of natural selection in order to emphasize the role of inheritable variation and the need for geographic isolation, in the origin of new species. Another facet to the evolutionary concept was added by the discovery of mutations by Hugo De Vries, a Dutch investigator. Also important was the concept of the continuity of the germ plasm, formulated by the German biologist August Weismann. The concept of natural selection has been modified by the idea of preadaptation—a theory which holds that many mutations may be unimportant and of little survival value to an organism in its existing environment, but can possibly become of value should the environment change.

Today the evolutionary concept is the foundation of all biological thought. It is the concept that unites all fields of biology; it explains the origin of species, their modifications, and, to some extent, the reasons for their extinction; it accounts for the variability, adaptation, and distribution of living organisms; it gives a reasonable explanation of the many peculiarities of structure and function found in organisms; it imparts scientific force to the statement that "the present is the child of the past and the parent of the future."

The Evidence for Evolution

Evolution has become established as a fact through evidence provided in many different specialized fields of biology—taxonomy, anatomy, embryology, ecology, and paleontology.

The Evidence Based on Taxonomy. This bioscience is concerned with defining, describing, and classifying species. If species possessed a haphazard and random assortment of traits, it would be impossible to arrange them in any logical classification scheme. If, for example, some birds had fur and others had feathers, some fish had feet instead of fins, some pines reproduced by juicy fruits while others had cones, then taxonomy would have little relevance to evolution. But taxonomy reveals that it is possible to group certain species together on the basis of some

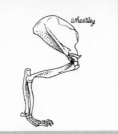

EARLY REPTILE   EARLY MAMMAL

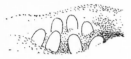

The reptile moved freely on land and respired by lungs. Most important, its shell-protected eggs could be deposited and develop on land.

The mammal's limb is finely adapted for land locomotion. Its developing young are protected within, and later nourished by, the mother's body.

features they have in common. For example, all pine trees have needlelike leaves arranged in clusters; all squirrels have certain dentition and skeletal traits in common. The categories above species—genus, family, order, class, phylum—present overwhelming evidence for descent of related species from common ancestry, the basic theme of evolution. When a number of related persons—brothers, sisters, cousins—are observed as a group, the similarities among them are the result of common ancestry. When unrelated members of a group show comparable heritable features (as do members of the cat and bear families), this is also taken as an indication of common ancestry. Charles Darwin recognized this when he stated "a community of descent—the one known cause of close similarity in organic beings—is the bond which . . . is partially revealed to us by classifications." The entire classification scheme, from algae to orchids in the plant kingdom and from protozoa to primates in the animal kingdom, forms a sequence of organisms which demonstrate relationships (and hence evolution) based on common ancestry.

The Evidence Based on Comparative Anatomy. Study of the anatomy of plants and animals reveals certain basic plans of body structure that have become established features of large groups of plants and animals. The skeleton of a frog, a lizard, a bird, and a mammal conforms to the same basic design, indicating that these animals have all inherited their skeletal pattern from a common vertebrate ancestor. The basic features of organ systems in all mammals, whether they swim, crawl, climb, or fly, are similar.

Vestigial organs—structures without any existing function—occur in many plants and animals. The whale has the remains of hip bones buried deep in its flesh even though it has no hind limbs; the limbless python has barely visible stubs of hind limbs, even though modern snakes are characterized by the absence of legs. Such vestigial organs can best be explained by assuming that they are inherited from a remote ancestor in which they were func-

tional, but have been modified through generations of disuse. Comparison of the anatomy of organisms discloses other biological puzzles to which evolution is the best answer. The wing of a bat, the flipper of a seal, and the foreleg of a horse are homologous organs—organs with similar basic structure that are modified for different uses. The presence of homologous organs is taken as further evidence for the diversification of species through evolutionary change.

The Evidence Based on Embryology. During its prebirth development, the embryo passes through stages during which it displays certain physical features of lower organisms. For example, at an early stage of its development the mammalian embryo consists of a multicellular body that resembles certain colonial aquatic invertebrates. Its digestive, circulatory, respiratory, and reproductive systems pass through developmental stages at which they display features of lower organisms. Finally a stage is reached where characteristic mammalian features appear. In the same way the embryos of other animals go through stages similar to those of species related to them but lower in the developmental scale. This is the basis of the theory of recapitulation which states that an organism, in its development from egg to adult, repeats stages that correspond to early periods in the evolution of its group. If a series of young embryos of various vertebrates is studied, it is surprising how difficult it is to tell which embryo will be a fish, which a salamander, or a rabbit. This embryological fact cannot be explained in any other way than by evolution.

The Evidence Based on Ecology. The geographic distribution of organisms exhibits many peculiarities that can best be explained as resulting from evolution. Biologists have discovered many puzzling facts about the presence or absence of certain species on various continents and islands. Adjoining oceanic islands, for example, are populated by species of birds which are slightly different from each other, but all similar to the species on the nearest mainland. Another peculiar fact about distribution is that species are often absent from regions where there are suitable habitats. Brazil has living conditions similar to those found in Africa where gorillas and elephants live, yet Brazil has neither of these animals. North America alone has opossums, turkeys, bison, and rattlesnakes; Australia has the kangaroo and platypus, found in no other region. Such anomalous patterns of distribution can be explained by assuming that each species descended from ancestors originally living on these continents, and that subsequent generations dispersed to favorable habitats until stopped by actual land barriers. In the case of aquatic animals large land masses limit dispersal; terrestrial animals are limited by large bodies of water. Eventually, a geographically isolated species, through inbreeding, gives rise to an organism especially adapted to the particular available habitat.

Another evolutionary puzzle is why all related species are not found adjacent to each other. There are only two living species of alligator, one in southeastern United States, the other in China. Their ancestors in earlier geologic periods occupied an extensive range from Asia to what is now Florida, migrating via the land bridge that at one time connected Russia and Alaska. Disappearance

583

of the land bridge isolated surviving alligators at the two extremities of their former range, eventually causing their descendants to differ slightly from each other as they adapted to their special environments. In this way evolution provides an explanation for the existence of isolated species with relatives in widely separated lands.

The Evidence Based on Fossils. By far the most dramatic evidence for evolution comes from the record which the earth itself has kept by preserving evidence of prehistoric life. Fossils reveal what kinds of plants and animals have lived and also add a time dimension by indicating when the organism lived. The dating of fossils by the decay of radioactive compounds in the earth's crust has provided a geologic time scale which establishes the sequence in which evolutionary changes have taken place. From this, we know that certain groups of plants and animals preceded other groups in time. The oldest plant fossils, for example, are those of the most primitive (in the sense of least-developed) plants. Their remains date from a time when higher forms did not yet exist. Similarly, the earliest animal remains are of simple aquatic invertebrates which antedate more advanced animal fossils. The sequential appearance of progressively higher forms of plant and animal life, as seen in the fossil record, reveals a progress of life from very simple to very complex forms. Fossils also reveal that many species became extinct, indicating that the struggle for existence results in elimination of species as well as the creation of new ones.

The Mechanism of Evolution

The fact of evolution, revealed by the foregoing evidence from many different fields of biology, is well documented. On the other hand the mechanisms of evolution, the methods by which new species are created, and by which new characteristics appear, are not as yet clearly understood. In a definition which includes a suggestion of the mechanisms involved, evolution can be described as a progression of adaptive changes in a group of organisms, brought about by natural selection which acts upon genetic differences. This emphasizes the two main forces influencing evolution: the genetic factor which is the source of change, and the environmental factor, which selects those genetic changes that are to be perpetuated.

The Genetic Factor in Evolution. Every organism, as it develops, exhibits two types of variation, or change. One is the result of environmental forces which act upon the individual, modifying its structure and function. An example of this kind of change is a tree whose growth has been stunted by growing in mineral-deficient soil. Such individual variations are not inherited, nor heritable, and do not play a role in evolution. The other type of modification is determined genetically and is passed on from one generation to the next. Heritable variation plays an important role in evolution. Since the early 1900's, when the science of genetics became established, many of the theories of the early evolutionists regarding the origin of changes have had to be revised. Modern concepts of the mechanism of evolution are largely based on the idea of mutation—spontaneous genetic change. Mutations occur at varying rates in different species and in particular genes. Estimates based on recent observations indicate that one mutation occurs per 40,000 to 500,000 cell divi-

sions. This may seem too small to account for the evolutionary changes which have taken place. But if this rate is multiplied by the number of germ cells produced, by the number of individuals in a generation, and by the number of generations during the geologic history of a species, the possible number of mutations becomes tremendous. Once mutations become established they are subjected to recombinations which make possible many new traits.

The Environment as a Factor in Evolution. The early evolutionists attempted to answer the question of the origin of variations in terms of the environment alone. In 1809 the French naturalist Jean Baptiste Lamarck proposed the theory that the environment acted as the direct stimulus to bring about the hereditary change. His now classic example was that of the long neck of a giraffe, a characteristic supposedly acquired by constant stretching to eat foliage high in the trees. Another approach was presented by Darwin and Wallace in their theory of natural selection. According to this theory the environment acts as the arbiter of evolution. Briefly stated, natural selection is based on the fact that variation is characteristic of all species, and that all organisms have an excessive natural rate of reproduction. Because of the latter, more organisms are born than can survive in the struggle for food and living space. Because of the former, some organisms will exhibit variations which give them an advantage in this struggle for survival. The result is the survival of those individuals whose variations best suit them for a particular environment or way of life. Conversely, those organisms that are least adapted to their environment will be eliminated. This idea of survival of the fittest has been called the core of natural selection. An objection to natural selection, common in Darwin's time, was that it did not explain the existence of many useless structures and functions in an organism. Later knowledge, however, has shown that many variations have no relation to survival, but are incidental effects of genetic changes. These are called nonadaptive variations.

The Main Patterns of Evolution

The Evolution of Green Plants. The divergent lines of plant and animal evolution were established over 600 million years ago, when all organisms were still in the unicellular stage of organization. Those single-celled species that possessed the unique chlorophyll-protoplasm combination, enabling them to manufacture their own food, were the ancestors of green plants. Many of these unicellular species persist to this day among the algae. As plant evolution progressed, four major milestones appeared, each initiated by a biological advance which set a precedent for a new type of plant life. The first milestone appeared with the establishment of the multicellular plant body. At first this was of the thallus type, merely an aggregate of cells with very slight tissue differentiation. The thallus body persists today in the algae.

The second milestone was the specialization of the parts of the multicellular body into organs, resulting in the root-stem-leaf pattern; this took place over 400 million years ago, and made conquest of the land by green plants possible. The first land plants were simple tracheophytes, known as psilophytes, and were probably descended from the green algae. Psilophytes were low-growing plants that lacked roots and were often leafless.

Today there are few living plants that perpetuate this primitive tracheophyte body pattern, but several lines of descent from the psilophytes led to the more complex ferns, club mosses, and horsetails. Among these were the first plants to attain tree size. The fern-type tracheophytes reached a high degree of body complexity but were handicapped by primitive reproductive habits poorly suited for terrestrial life.

The third milestone brought about a more suitable reproductive pattern—an alternation of generations involving production of seeds. This led from the psilophytes to primitive gymnosperms (plants such as the conifers, whose seeds are unprotected by a fruit), which increased in number as the formerly dominant fern plants began to wane. Modern descendants of the first seed-bearing tracheophytes are cycads, pines, redwoods, and their relatives.

The fourth milestone added another reproductive advance—the flower and the protected seed within a fruit. The first flowering plants, or angiosperms, appeared about 150 million years ago and with them was established the successful flower-fruit-seed pattern which has made flowering plants the dominant land vegetation of today. Since this innovation, no startling advance has appeared in plant evolution. However, some variations can be seen in the two large groups of flowering plants, the dicotyledons (plants whose seeds contain two cotyledons, or seed leaves) and the monocotyledons (plants whose seeds contain a single cotyledon), and among the various families of each of these main groups.

The Evolution of Invertebrate Animals. The first animals, like the first plants, were unicellular and aquatic. Their origin antedates the fossil record and is shrouded in mystery. The primitive unicellular animals established the basic animal pattern of holozoic nutrition (nutrition requiring the ingestion of organic foodstuffs). Subsequent evolution of invertebrate animals was highlighted by four major biological advances. As in plant evolution, the first milestone was the appearance of the multicellular body. The relatively small number of cells were arranged in two cell layers with some tissue differentiation but no organs. The resulting body, predominantly immobile, persists in the sponges and sea anemones, living representatives of the earliest multicellular animals which were already highly diversified 600 million years ago and thus contemporaneous with the primitive algae.

The second milestone was the development of a body with three cell layers. The middle layer, or mesoderm, formed a muscle system that made increased motility possible. Division of labor proceeded beyond tissues to the formation of organs and organ systems. Associated with these advances in complexity was the appearance of bilateral symmetry, and differentiation of anterior (head) and posterior (tail) regions—characteristics which persist in all higher groups of animals. These features first appeared in the brachiopods, or lamp shells. *Lingula*, a living brachiopod genus, has kept its present form for over 400 million years.

The third milestone was the development of a segmented body and a coelom, or body cavity. These became characteristics of the segmented worms, of which the earthworm is a living representative. Both features are fundamental to the body plan of higher invertebrates and all vertebrates.

A fourth milestone was the addition of jointed appendages and a flexible exoskeleton to the segmented, coelomate invertebrate body. These traits, which made increased motility possible, and better adapted animals to life on land, first appeared in the arthropods, or joint-footed animals. The first arthropods were the now-extinct trilobites, a primitive group that reigned as a dominant form of life for millions of years in the ancient seas. Later, another arthropod group appeared: these were the eurypterids, or sea scorpions, whose descendants were destined to be the first air-breathing animals. Last to evolve were the insects, the culmination of invertebrate evolution and today the dominant group of land invertebrates. The first insects, which appeared about 325 million years ago, were very similar to modern cockroaches. Later, the ancestors of dragonflies and beetles appeared. Butterflies and moths were the last of all insect groups to develop, timing their appearance with that of the flowering plants. The last 125 million years, or so, have seen no significant innovation in invertebrate evolution.

The Evolution of Vertebrate Animals. Vertebrates are the most highly developed of all animal groups. All the invertebrate phyla were well established when the first chordates—the armored fishes, or ostracoderms—appeared, about 500 million years ago. Structural and developmental resemblances between living lower chordates and certain groups of fossil invertebrates have given rise to several theories of chordate origin: among the groups considered are annelids (segmented worms), arachnids (spiders and allies), and echinoderms (starfish and their relatives). However, since the earliest chordates were softbodied animals, and left no fossil record, their true origin is still a matter of speculation. The novel feature which established the chordate pattern is the notochord, a solid internal supporting structure from which the skeletal system developed. Beyond this, however, many improvements were added to the basic chordate blueprint. The first innovation was the development of an internal skeletal system—first of cartilage, later of bone—to supplement the supportive function of the notochord. The earliest animals to possess a bony skeleton, as well as jaws and paired appendages, were the bony fishes of about 400 million years ago. Many of the present-day types—lungfishes, ray-finned fishes, lobe-finned fishes—date back to that time. The lobe fins are of special significance since they possessed a type of appendage which is believed to be the precursor of the terrestrial limb.

The second innovation appeared with the amphibians —the appearance of limbs and the replacement of gill breathing by lung breathing. The far-reaching result was the dispersal of backboned animals over the land. The first amphibians appeared about 380 million years ago. They were clumsy, squat, short-legged animals that crawled through the swamp forests of giant fern trees. Their bodies were somewhat adapted for terrestrial life, but their reproductive habits still depended upon water.

At this point a third innovation in vertebrate evolution appeared—the land egg, protected by a shell. This type of egg first appeared with the reptiles, giving them a great advantage over their amphibian relatives. As a result the scaly, lung-breathing reptiles, which appeared 250 million years ago, soon swarmed in great numbers and variety over the earth. Reptiles had, and still have, one great disadvantage—their cold-bloodedness. Because of this they are poorly adapted for life in cold climates.

At this stage in evolution, a fourth innovation occurred —the ability to maintain a constant body temperature. The first warm-blooded animals were descendants of two divergent reptilian stocks. One culminated in the birds, which retained the egg-laying habit of their reptile ancestors. From the other line the mammals developed. Mammals represent the culmination of vertebrate development: their young enjoy a relatively long period of embryonic development within the mother's body, and are nourished by the mother after birth. These advantages have made mammals the most successful and diversified of all animals.

Thus the story of life reaches its climax in the beginning of the Cenozoic Era, about 63 million years ago, when birds and mammals replaced reptiles as the dominant terrestrial vertebrate life, just as a few hundred million years earlier reptiles had replaced amphibians.

From the preceding summary it is obvious that the process of evolution is highly complex and presents many aspects that await separate scientific proof before they can be correlated with each other. The origin of a single species results from a great number of changes, some small and some large, sorted out of the gene "pool" every time sexual reproduction occurs. The bodily characteristics resulting from this constant change in gene make-up must then meet the test of suitability in an environment which is also constantly changing. Evolutionary change is very slow, but it must be remembered that time is of no consequence in a process which has millions of years at its disposal.

Consult Darwin, C. R., *The Origin of Species* (1859); Osborn, H. F., *From the Greeks to Darwin* (1924); Oparin, A. I., *The Origin of Life* (1938); *The New Systematics*, ed. by Julian Huxley (1940); Lack, D. L., *Darwin's Finches* (1947); Simpson, G. G., *The Meaning of Evolution* (1949); Blum, H. F., *Time's Arrow and Evolution* (1951); Dobzhansky, T. G., *Genetics and the Origin of Species* (1951); Fothergill, P. G., *Historical Aspects of Organic Evolution* (1952); Moody, P. A., *Introduction to Evolution* (1953); Eiseley, L. C., *Darwin's Century* (1958); Greene, J. C., *The Death of Adam* (1959).

CLARENCE J. HYLANDER, Author,
The World of Plant Life

See also:

ADAPTATION	GENETICS
ADAPTIVE RADIATION	HOMOLOGY
ANIMAL: *Classification*	PLANT: *Classification*
ECOLOGY	*of Plants*
EMBRYOLOGY	SELECTION
ENVIRONMENT	SPECIES

ÉVORA [â'vōō-rə], city of south-central Portugal, and capital of Alto Alentejo Province. Cork trees, olives, and grapes are grown, and there is some manufacture of cotton, flour, and metal products. Called the Museum City, its old landmarks include a Roman temple of the 2d or 3d century A.D., which is among the best-preserved Roman ruins of the Iberian Peninsula; a 12th-century cathedral; and a 16th-century university (now a high school). Pop., 25,678.

EWALD or EVALD [ī'väl], **JOHANNES** (1743–81), Danish lyric poet and dramatist. His early writings were influenced by French neoclassicism, but after a meeting with the German poet Friedrich Klopstock late in the 1760's he became deeply impressed by German literature and the *Sturm und Drang* movement. His verse tragedies include *Rolf Krage* (1770), and *Balders Død*, 1774 (trans. by George Borrow as *The Death of Balder*, 1889), but his best dramatic work is his last, *Fiskerne* (The Fishermen), 1779. One of the songs from that drama, *King Christian Stood by the Lofty Mast* (trans. by Longfellow), later became the hymn royal of Denmark. A great poet, Ewald exerted a strong influence on Danish literature—as the first to find source material in Danish legends, the first to write a tragedy, and the first to write historical drama.

EWELL [ū'əl], **RICHARD STODDERT** (1817–72), Confederate army officer in the U.S. Civil War. Born in the Georgetown section of Washington, D.C. (then an independent city), Ewell graduated from West Point. He served in the Mexican War with distinction at Contreras and Churubusco and fought Apache Indians in New Mexico in 1857. Despite his strong Union sympathies, he joined the Confederate army in May, 1861, and was appointed a major general in October. Ewell played a prominent part in the Shenandoah Valley campaign and the defense of Richmond, Va., in 1862.

At the Second Battle of Bull Run, he lost a leg but returned to active duty as a lieutenant general, even though he had to be lifted and strapped onto the saddle to ride. Ordered to clear the Shenandoah Valley, he achieved victories at Brandy Station and Winchester, then led Gen. Robert E. Lee's advance into Pennsylvania, reaching Carlisle and threatening Harrisburg. Ewell was called back to Gettysburg, occupied the town, and participated in the battle. He opposed Gen. Ulysses S. Grant successfully in the first Wilderness engagement and fought at Spottsylvania Court House, until his horse was shot from under him and he was incapacitated for further field service. He commanded the defenses of Richmond and, when the city was evacuated, was captured at Sailor's Creek and imprisoned for four months.

MARTIN BLUMENSON, formerly, Senior Historian,
Department of the Army

EWING, WILLIAM MAURICE (1906–   ), American geophysicist noted for extensive seismic and photographic exploration of the ocean floor. Educated at Rice Institute, he taught at Pittsburgh, Lehigh, and Columbia universities, and in 1949 he became director of Lamont Geological Observatory in New York. Ewing devised the SOFAR sound-ranging system for rescuing men lost at sea, and with W. L. Donn he formulated a theory to account for Ice Age climatic fluctuations.

EWING, township of western New Jersey, and a residential suburb of Trenton, on the Delaware River. It has an aircraft plant and a boatbuilding firm. Trenton State College is here. Inc., 1834; pop. (1950) 16,840; (1960) 26,628.

EXARCH [ĕks'ärk] (Gr. *exarchos*, "ruler"), a church dignitary. In the Byzantine Empire he usually held more power than metropolitans and less than patriarchs. The exarch was a Bishop with his see in the main city of a diocese, consisting of several provinces. Metropolitans might ask advice and help from the exarch of the diocese, or from the Bishop of Constantinople. An exarch may also be the head of an independent church. The primate of the Bulgarian Church was called exarch, until he assumed the title of Patriarch in 1953. A priest on a special mission abroad from a Patriarch is also often called an exarch.

EXCALIBUR, the name of the sword of Arthur (q.v.), King of the Britons.

EX CATHEDRA [ĕks kə-thē'drə] (Lat., "from the chair"), term applied to utterances of the Pope when he speaks officially as the ruler and teacher of the Church. The Vatican Council (1870) decreed that the Pope is infallible when he speaks *ex cathedra* on a matter of faith or morals.

EXCAVATOR and EXCAVATION. Excavation, or the removal of earth or rock to make way for a construction, is a job that requires the use of heavy power machinery to drive shovels and cranes.

A primary reason for excavation is to lay a foundation beneath the ground's surface. In some instances the surface soil will not bear the structure's weight, whereas the rock and earth beneath will. Also, in cold climates it is necessary to base construction deep enough so the frost cannot penetrate the entire foundation. To excavate land for highway or railway construction, large quantities of material must be moved, often by cutting through mountains. The excavated material may be used to fill in low areas along the roadway.

The most common types of excavators are power shovels and cranes, which are fitted with either clamshell or dragline buckets, but special types of excavators are made for special uses. An example is the trenching machine, or wheel excavator, once used for digging military trenches, but more commonly used to dig pipe trenches. It consists of a large wheel with its axle supported by a truck or movable frame. Buckets, attached to the rim of the wheel, dig into the earth as the wheel is turned. As the buckets fill up, their loads are dumped onto a conveyer belt or a chute near the top of the wheel. As the digging goes deeper, the wheel is lowered into the trench to the desired depth; the trench's length is extended by slowly moving the wheel apparatus forward. Special excavators for mining vary in size from walking cranes with 200-ft. beams to underground excavators which can mine coal in a shaft only a few feet high.

E. Russell Johnston, Jr., Worcester Polytechnic Institute

See also Crane; Dredge.

EXCELSIOR SPRINGS, resort city of northwestern Missouri, noted for its mineral waters. The boyhood home of the desperado Jesse James is nearby. The city was laid out as a resort center in 1880. Pop. (1950) 5,888; (1960) 6,473.

EXCEPTIONAL CHILDREN. *See* Education: *Education of Exceptional Children.*

EXCHEQUER [ĕks-chĕk'ər], **COURT OF,** in Great Britain, part of the judicial system. Early records show that this

Philip Gendreau

METHODS OF EXCAVATION

Excavating machines are as varied as the jobs they must do. Above, long-boom cranes lift steel beams for the foundations of the Time & Life Building, in New York City. Below, a trenching machine expedites a pipeline construction job near Rosetown, Saskatchewan.

Myles J. Adler

The power shovel, a familiar sight to sidewalk superintendents, can dig above the level on which it stands, as it does below left. The stripping shovel, below right, removes overburden in strip-mining operations. It weighs as much as a U. S. Navy destroyer.

A. Devaney   *St. Louis Post Dispatch—Black Star*

court had its origin in the collection of the King's revenue of taxes and debts. By the time of Henry II (1133–89), the court had begun to adjudicate disputes regarding financial relations between the monarch and his subjects. By the 14th century the revenue collection and judicial function had become separated. The Court of Exchequer served as a court of common pleas at which subjects could plead in disputes involving the royal revenue. The court also heard civil disputes between two subjects if the plaintiff claimed money owed him by the defendant was owed in turn to the crown. In 1830 the Court of Exchequer was designated as an appeal court between common law courts and the House of Lords, and in 1875 became a division of the High Court of Justice.

EXCLUSION PRINCIPLE, in atomic and nuclear physics, the principle developed by Wolfgang Pauli, Jr. in 1925 which states that in a given system having only quantized states, there can be only a limited number of particles in any one state. For example, in an atom no two electrons can exist in the same quantum state at the same time. The principle applies to fermions, including neutrons, protons, and electrons, and determines the shell structures of the orbital electrons of atoms and of atomic nuclei.
See also QUANTUM THEORY.

EXCOMMUNICATION literally means "exclusion from communion with the faithful." Such exclusion is mentioned in the New Testament (I Cor. 16:22) and it is the oldest penalty in the Roman Catholic Church. In the canon law of the Roman Catholic Church excommunication is a species of church penalty called a censure. A censure is an ecclesiastical penalty whereby a baptized person who has committed a serious sin punishable by a penalty and who scorns church authority, is deprived of certain spiritual goods until he repents and is absolved. Censures are intended to effect the conversion of the culprit. Censures are: interdicts, suspensions, and excommunication. Abortion, for example, is punished by excommunication.

The excommunicated person, while cut off from communion with the faithful, does not cease to be a Christian. He is, however, deprived of the rights and the privileges that a member of the church possesses, until he repents and is absolved. He has no right to attend divine services, but may listen to sermons. He may not receive the Sacraments while excommunicated. In certain instances he may not receive the sacraments or Christian burial. An excommunicated person does not share in the indulgences, suffrages, and public prayers of the church, but the faithful may pray for such a person privately. Many ecclesiastical acts are forbidden excommunicated persons.

EDWARD J. STOKES, S.J., St. Mary of the Lake Seminary

EXCRETORY [ĕks′krə-tôr-ē] **SYSTEM,** name for the various structures that collectively serve to remove metabolic waste from the animal body. The simplest excretory apparatus probably is the contractile vacuole, found in many one-celled animals. This spherical, fluid-filled cavity is believed to gather waste from the cell, then discharges its contents into the surrounding water. Flatworms have an excretory system consisting of a network of flame cells. Wastes are collected in tubules of this network and leave the body through surface openings. Earthworms and other segmented worms have a pair of excretory organs, the nephridia, in all but the first and last few of their body segments. The nephridia collect nitrogenous wastes from both the fluid of the body cavity (the coelom) and from the blood stream; filter out any useful proteins which are reabsorbed by the body; then transfer the urine to tube-shaped bladders where it is temporarily stored before being excreted at openings along the body surface.

In reptiles, birds, and mammals the excretory function is performed primarily by the kidneys. The kidneys collect metabolic wastes from the blood stream; filter out and reabsorb any useful material such as sugars, sodium, and calcium; and concentrate the resulting nitrogenous fluid by reabsorbing large amounts of water. The fluid waste then passes from the kidneys to the bladder by ducts (one from each kidney) known as ureters, and from the bladder through a single duct, the urethra.

Although the kidneys are the most important excretory organs of higher organisms, some excretory function is performed by other parts of the body. Carbon dioxide and water are eliminated during the respiratory process; the wastes of heavy metals and water are voided with the feces; and (especially in man) the sweat glands of the skin serve to eliminate water, salts, and traces of carbon dioxide and nitrogenous wastes.

EDWARD J. FEELEY, Loyola University of the South
See also KIDNEY; PERSPIRATION; RESPIRATION.

EXECUTION. *See* CAPITAL PUNISHMENT.

EXEGESIS [ĕk-sə-jē′sĭs], word meaning "explanation" or "interpretation," used particularly with reference to the Bible. It involves the application of the principles of hermeneutics (the science of interpretation) to the individual sections of the Biblical text, and is a basic discipline in Christian theology. Theological structures are easily overthrown unless they are securely grounded in sound exegesis. Exegesis in its turn presupposes a thorough acquaintance with the original languages (Hebrew and Aramaic in the Old Testament; Greek in the New) and the establishment of a reliable text by the methods of textual criticism. It requires also some knowledge of the historical setting and cultural environment of each Biblical writer whose work is being expounded, together with an appreciation of the variety of literary genres represented in the Bible. The capacity to enter sympathetically into the mind of the author distinguishes the best exegetes from the second-rate. This explains, for example, the abiding value of a work like B. F. Westcott's commentary on St. John's Gospel. At each stage the exegete must try to answer the question: "What did the author intend by these words?" His task, first and last, has been summed up for him in the words of Johann Albrecht Bengel: "Apply thyself wholly to the text; apply the text wholly to thyself."

F. F. BRUCE, University of Manchester

EXEKIAS [ĕk-sə-kī′əs], Greek potter and vase painter who flourished in the third quarter of the 6th century B.C. in Athens. He was one of the leading exponents of the black-figure style of vase painting. His signature, either as potter or painter or both, appears on about 10 vases that provide an idea of his individual style. One of his most famous vases is a kylix now in Munich on which is depicted the story of Dionysus bringing his gifts to mankind.

EXETER [ĕk′sə-tər], city, county borough, and county town of Devonshire, England, located on the Exe River 10 mi. above its outlet on the English Channel. Exeter is an important commercial and administrative center. The University of Exeter is here.

The original settlement, Isca Damnoniorum, was founded c.50–55 A.D. by the Romans as the administrative center for southwestern Britain. Remains of fortifications built in the 3d century can still be seen. In 1068 a castle was built, of which the great Norman gateway and Athelstan's tower survive. Exeter has been a cathedral city since 1050, but the Saxon cathedral was demolished in the 13th century. A new Norman cathedral was begun early in the 12th century; its north and south towers survive and from the former the curfew is still rung each day. The important cathedral library includes the Exeter Doomsday Book. The Guildhall, rebuilt in 1330 and reputedly the oldest municipal building in England, is one of many fine medieval buildings still existing. Pop., 80,215.

I. S. MAXWELL, The University, Sheffield, England

EXETER, town of southernmost Ontario, Canada, 31 mi. north-northwest of London. Exeter owes much of its recent development to the proximity of a Royal Canadian Air Force station at Centralia just to the south. Canning is a major industry. Pop., 3,047.

EXETER, unincorporated village of southeastern New Hampshire, on the Exeter River, 10 mi. southwest of Portsmouth. It has light manufactures. The Gilman-Clifford House (1650) and several early 18th-century houses grace the town. It was settled in 1638 and during the American Revolution was a center for patriot activities. Exeter was the capital of New Hampshire from 1774 to 1784. Phillips Exeter Academy (estab., 1783) is located here. Pop. (1950) 4,977; (1960) 5,896.

EXETER, coal-mining borough of north-central Pennsylvania, on the Susquehanna River. The town was settled about 1790 by Connecticut farmers. Inc., 1884; pop. (1950) 5,130; (1960) 4,747.

EXILE, separation from one's native land, voluntary or involuntary, for a specified time or for life. In Homeric Greece, voluntary exile was an alternative to becoming a victim of blood revenge for committing homicide. Later, with the development of systems of law in the Greek city-states, exile took on a more formal legal meaning. It became a penalty for political crimes, frequently including loss of civil rights and property. In 5th-century Athens, ostracism was a device whereby the citizens could vote a 10-year exile of persons considered "dangerous," but without loss of rights or property.

The early Roman Republic recognized voluntary exile as an alternative to punishment and, from the late second century on, compulsory exile was often used as a substitute for the death penalty. One has only to read what Cicero and Ovid wrote while in exile to appreciate how

grave a matter it was to the citizen of the classical city-state. Exiles usually had no rights in other cities and, even if allowed to remain, were always regarded as aliens. While voluntary exile is still common, compulsory exile has been comparatively rare in modern times.

GERALD E. KADISH, State University of N.Y. at Binghamton
See also DEPORTATION; OSTRACISM; REFUGEE.

EXILE, THE, also called the Babylonian Captivity, the period following Nebuchadnezzar's conquest of Judah in the 6th century B.C., during which the leaders of the Jewish community were exiled in Babylon. The first deportation occurred after the devastation of Judaean towns in 597 (II Kings 24) and the second deportation after the destruction of the Temple and city of Jerusalem in 587 (II Kings 25). The return of the exiles began fitfully after Cyrus the Persian conquered Babylon in 539 and issued his edict of religious toleration (Ezra 6:3–5). He appointed Sheshbazzar to restore the sacred vessels to Jerusalem and lay the foundations of the Second Temple (Ezra 1:7–11; 5:14–16). A larger number of Jews returned home with Zerubbabel, a Davidic prince appointed Governor of Judah, some time before 522, and in conditions of great difficulty (Hag. 1:1–11) the new Temple was completed in the spring of 515 (Ezra 6:13–18). The Jews in Babylon during the "Captivity," so far from being prisoners, lived in their own communities (Ezek. 3:15; 33:30–33) and were free to develop such distinctive religious observances as the Sabbath and Circumcision. Many families settled and prospered in their new surroundings (Jer. 29:5–13) and never returned to Palestine. Although Jewish religious life was maintained amid the ruins of Jerusalem throughout this period (Jer. 41:5), the Exile was the most decisive turning point in Old Testament history. It brought to an end Israel's existence as an independent state, and with it the institution of the Davidic monarchy. It inaugurated the priestly and scribal community of postexilic Judaism.

Consult Noth, Martin, *A History of Israel* (1958); Bright, John, *A History of Israel* (1959).

E. W. HEATON, Oxford University

EXISTENTIALISM [ĕg-zĭs-tĕn′shəl-ĭz-əm], term first coined after World War I to designate the philosophies of Karl Jaspers and Martin Heidegger. Both were indebted to Søren Kierkegaard. But it was mainly through the writings of Jean-Paul Sartre that existentialism came to attract attention in the English-speaking world after World War II. When Sartre called his own philosophy existentialism, Jaspers and Heidegger repudiated the label. They considered their disagreements more important than any common elements. None of them accepted the Christian beliefs that mattered most to Kierkegaard.

Existentialism is not one particular philosophy, nor a school of thought. Rather, the name is a convenient label for a tradition that differs markedly from British empiricism and philosophic idealism. The existentialists share the conviction that most academic philosophy is too remote from life—and death. Instead of concentrating on logic or science, existentialism is primarily concerned with human existence, especially with man's most extreme experiences: the confrontation with death, anguish and anxiety, despair and guilt. Generally, man tries to escape from himself; but in these experiences the individual is roused from his inauthenticity (his failure to be himself), in which he submits to the dominion of the public "they." Existentialism seeks authentic existence rather than certain knowledge.

These tendencies are not confined to the four men mentioned so far. Albert Camus and Gabriel Marcel, Martin Buber and Friedrich Nietzsche, Blaise Pascal and St. Augustine, among others, have also sometimes been called existentialists. It would be idle to insist either that they were or that they were not existentialists; one can point out what each writer has in common with some of the others and what sets him apart. Sartre's attempt in a published lecture to define existentialism as the doctrine that existence precedes essence prompted Heidegger's initial declaration that he was not an existentialist, and the definition has since been abandoned by Sartre himself.

Consult Kaufmann, Walter, *Existentialism from Dostoevsky to Sartre* (1956) and *From Shakespeare to Existentialism* (rev. ed., 1960).

WALTER KAUFMANN, Princeton University

EXMOOR, plateau of Somerset and Devonshire, England, bordering the Bristol channel on the north. The highest point is Dunkery Beacon, 1,707 ft. There are prehistoric earthworks here. Area, 265 sq. mi.

EXODUS [ĕk'sə-dəs] (Gr., "departure"), second book in the Old Testament, so called from its title in the Greek version. It is the second book of the Pentateuch, the five books of the law at the beginning of the Bible. It begins with the oppression of Israel in Egypt, when they were no longer a family, but a nation. Moses was called by God, who revealed His name as Yahweh, to deliver Israel. After a succession of plagues and the introduction of the feast of Passover, Israel escaped and crossed the Sea of Reeds (often translated "Red Sea"). Then follow stories of the stay in the desert in the region of Kadesh, under the leadership of Moses. The last part of the book (chaps. 19–40) is the story of the revelation on Mount Sinai. God revealed His presence on the mountain before the assembled people and gave them the Ten Commandments (20:1–17). To this is added an old code of laws, the Book of the Covenant (20:22–23:33), and in chap. 24 God makes a covenant with the people. The instructions for the making of a Tabernacle (25–31) and the account of how this was carried out (35–40) are from the last (Priestly Code) part of the book.

RONALD E. CLEMENTS, University of Edinburgh

EXOPHTHALMOS [ĕk-sŏf-thăl'məs], protrusion of the eyeball which may result from inflammations, fluid swellings, or tumors developing behind the eyeball and pushing it forward. Overactivity of the thyroid gland (hyperthyroidism) is a common cause. Some cases of congenital enlargement of the eyeball may simulate exophthalmos.

EXORCISM [ĕk'sôr-sĭz-əm], ritual practice of driving out evil spirits from a person, an animal, an object, or a given locality. It is clearly associated with belief in spirit possession and demonology and is widely distributed in Asia, Africa, and Europe. Where physical or mental illness is attributed to spirit possession, exorcism may be employed as a means of treatment. Exorcism is mentioned in the New Testament and was widely practiced in the early Christian Church. The Roman Catholic Church has a ritual of exorcism. This rite can be used only with the permission of a bishop and is now rarely employed. "Driving out of devils" is practiced in the curing rites of various Pentecostal churches in the United States as well as in their missionary activities, which may involve exorcism of native deities. Exorcism may involve both spiritual and physical methods—for example, prayer, scourging the victim, or the use of incense.

ERIKA BOURGUIGNON, Ohio State University

EXORCIST (Gr. *eksorkidzein*, "to cast out by adjuration"), in the early Christian Church anyone who drove out evil spirits from persons, places, or things. The exorcist's office was established for clerics in the 3d century, but gradually his duties were assumed by the priest. In the Roman Catholic Church the office of Exorcist is the 3d minor order or step to the priesthood.

EXOTHERMIC REACTION. *See* ENDOTHERMIC AND EXOTHERMIC REACTION.

EXPANDING UNIVERSE. *See* ASTRONOMY; COSMOLOGY; UNIVERSE.

EXPANSION, in physics, increase in length or volume, usually as the result of an increase in temperature. The majority of solids and liquids expand when heated. The amount of such expansion is measured by the expansion coefficient of each substance, a number representing the change in length per unit length (or change in volume per unit volume) for each degree rise in temperature. The expansion coefficient is a characteristic of each substance; for example, for platinum it is 0.0000089, and for copper, 0.000014. Expansion may also result from the application or removal of a mechanical force; the change is then called compressibility.

EX PARTE MILLIGAN, U.S. Supreme Court case (1866). This was the first test of the President's power to authorize trial for civilians by military tribunals rather than in the civil courts. In 1863 President Abraham Lincoln suspended the writ of habeas corpus in cases where persons were to be tried for acts against the military. Lambdin P. Milligan was arrested in Indiana by military authorities, tried by the military for inciting rebellion and other treasonable acts, convicted, and sentenced to be hanged on May 19, 1865. When the sentence was approved by President Andrew Johnson, Milligan filed a writ of habeas corpus with the U.S. circuit court in Indiana claiming that his constitutional right of trial by jury had been violated. The Supreme Court found that even though the United States had been at war, no civilian could be tried by military tribunal as long as the civil courts were functioning properly. Milligan was released.

JAMES P. SHENTON, Columbia University

EXPATRIATION [ĕks-pā-trē-ā'shən], as a legal term, means the breaking of the bond of allegiance to a state. This may be either voluntary, that is, an individual may renounce his citizenship in one country in order to take up citizenship in another, or it may be by an act of the state. For example, totalitarian states, particularly Nazi Germany, expatriated many persons as a means of depriving them of rights as citizens. Sometimes states use expatriation to punish citizens for not fulfilling their various obligations as citizens.

The right of an individual to renounce citizenship has been in some dispute. According to traditional European practice, the consent of the state was necessary for an individual to renounce citizenship. It was on the basis of this position that Great Britain seized U.S. sailors after the American Revolution, the British doctrine being "once an Englishman, always an Englishman." The continuation of such practices by the English helped precipitate the War of 1812. Young men threatened with military service during the 18th and 19th centuries often attempted to use expatriation as a means of escape. Thus European states insisted on state consent for voluntary expatriation.

The rule in the United States has been that an individual has an inherent right to renounce citizenship with or without the state's consent. Since the early population of the United States was made up of voluntary expatriates, this position was adopted and was enacted into law by Congress in 1868. James Buchanan, first as Secretary of State and then as President, was instrumental in developing a U.S. policy of expatriation without consent of the state.

STUART GERRY BROWN, Syracuse University
See also CITIZENSHIP; DEPORTATION; NATURALIZATION; REFUGEE.

EXPECTATION OF LIFE. See LIFE, EXPECTATION OF.

EXPECTORANT [ĕk-spĕk'tər-ənt], drug or agent which aids in the removal of secretions from the breathing passages. The expectorants may accomplish this by stimulating the flow of secretions, thus making the sputum thinner. They are most frequently used to relieve inflammations of the respiratory tract. Among the expectorant drugs are ammonium chloride, ipecac, and ammonium carbonate. Steam and carbon dioxide inhalations are also excellent expectorant agents.

EXPERIMENT, a procedure designed to discover some truth, to confirm or disprove something doubtful, or to illustrate a known or suggested truth. In the last sense, an experiment to test an established law (for example, Boyle's law) is a useful technique in demonstrating the scientific method and a valuable asset for the educational process.

Experimentation is distinctive of the scientist; it rests on the difference between recording bare observations of natural phenomena and recording observations made under controlled conditions. It is a method of questioning nature in a specific way to obtain a particular answer.

Plan. Since inferences that can be drawn from results of an experiment depend upon the way it is conducted, the plan of every experiment must be clearly defined:
(1) What hypothesis is being tested?
(2) What particular question is being asked?

	DAY 1		2		3		4		5		6	
	L	R	L	R	L	R	L	R	L	R	L	R
ATTRACTANT CAGE I COUNT	6	4	1	3	5	2	3	5	2	6	4	1
ATTRACTANT CAGE II COUNT	6	5	1	2	4	3	2	4	3	6	5	1
ATTRACTANT CAGE III COUNT	1	5	3	6	4	2	6	1	5	4	2	3
ATTRACTANT CAGE IV COUNT	2	3	4	5	6	1	3	4	1	2	5	6
ATTRACTANT CAGE V COUNT	4	1	2	6	3	5	5	2	1	3	6	4

Chart of scheduled Drosophila preferential feeding experiment with space for recording each day's total count.

(3) To what extent will the results of this experiment contribute to proving or disproving the hypothesis?
(4) To what extent will the method of asking the question influence the results?

In general, results of an experiment are measurements, and are recorded numerically. They must be set down in organized, concise form so as to yield accurate and valid conclusions and a measurement of the imperfections of the results. These imperfections constitute the experimental errors. Primarily, the results of an experiment are influenced (1) by the procedures whose effects are being observed and compared, and (2) by external variations which tend to mask these effects. To illustrate: (1) The errors may be due to a lack of uniformity in the conduct of the experiment; thus treatment of an ore sample by hot acid may yield a higher iron content than treatment of an identical sample by cold acid. (2) The errors may be due to an inherent quality of the material being investigated; thus a dozen bits of iron ore, picked up at random in a mine pit, may yield 12 quite different percentages of iron content ranging from 0% to 40%.

The plan for an experiment requires: (1) that extraneous errors may be made minimal by careful sampling of the material of whatever sort; (2) that uniformity of measurements be secured through standardized techniques; and (3) that the procedures adopted be such that their effects on the results can be evaluated. The researcher selects or designs procedures, and he needs to recognize how these influence the objectives of his experiment. Hence preliminary testing of procedures is often desirable or necessary. Such tests should be planned so that the various factors present in the designed experiment may be investigated to decide if certain of them have any effect, and to discover possible interactions among the factors. The results of the preliminary testing may indicate that the proposed experiment is practicable; they may suggest improved techniques; or they may lead to a change in techniques or the adoption of a quite different method of experimentation. The design of efficient experimental procedures is the basic essential to successful research.

An Example. As an illustration of an experiment, suppose that in a biology class the question is raised as to what flavors, or odors, are most attractive to fruit flies (Drosophila). The design of the experiment must be adapted to the problem being investigated so as to yield maximum information; its plan must be clearly defined.

591

In the example given, the hypothesis tested is essentially: "Are Drosophila flies attracted to foods by odor preferentially?" The particular question asked is, "Will they prefer certain of five chosen odors over others?" The experimental design attempts to take into account extraneous factors, so that the extent to which the method of asking the question influences the results can be estimated; the experimental errors are thus controlled or evaluated. The proposal adopted might take the following form:

(1) Five attractant flavors are selected to be tested, preferably after appropriate library research; such pungent odoriferous chemicals as methyl acetate, ethyl acetate, and amyl acetate (pears, apples, bananas), suggest themselves.

(2) Five similar glass-walled "cages" are set up, and each is provided with a fairly large population of Drosophila in essentially equal numbers. These cages are kept under the same temperature and lighting conditions. The cages are provided with slots covered by fly-tight slides, so that petri dishes containing agar preparations may be introduced and removed without loss of the inmates.

(3) A nutrient agar preparation is made up and divided into six batches; each of five batches is flavored with a different attractant odor. One batch is left unflavored, except for the odor of the nutrient agar, as a control. Samples of these six batches are plated onto petri dishes for each experiment.

(4) Five students are chosen as observers: one is assigned to each cage. Each observer introduces into his cage two petri dishes having different odors. The dishes are placed side by side and positioned uniformly in each cage. The observer then counts, at uniform time intervals, the number of fruit flies then present on each dish, alternately counting the left and right dishes. Suppose 10 counts on each dish can be made during one laboratory period; the sum of 10 counts on each dish then constitutes the recorded entries for that day.

(5) The experiment is carried out during, say, six days. The temperature, relative humidity, and atmospheric pressure are recorded each day. The schedule of measurements to be made by each student is drawn up beforehand; it must be adhered to strictly. An open-block diagram of the scheduled counts is shown below:

The diagram shows that observer No. I counts the number of flies attracted by preparations 6 and 4 in cage I on the first day, the number of flies attracted by preparations 1 and 3 on the second day, and so on. The sums of the 10 counts made on each preparation are entered in the appropriate spaces provided.

During the first three days, every possible pair of attractants is compared; each student compares three of the 15 possible combinations. During the six days, every possible pair of attractants has been compared by two observers. Every student has made two counts for each attractant; on a left-hand dish and on a right-hand dish; and every student has compared six of the possible 15 combinations of attractants. Thus the sum of all the counts made during the first three days, compared with the sum of all the counts made during the last three days, affords a measure of the experimental error arising from a combination of all factors.

The sum of all the counts made by observer No. I during the six days compared with the sum of all the counts made by observer No. V, affords a measure of the errors arising from inequality of population densities of the flies in the several cages and from counting inaccuracies, since environmental factors have in effect been canceled out.

Every attractant has been tested at least once every day. If environmental factors—temperature, humidity, and atmospheric pressure—had varied considerably over the testing period, comparison of the counts for each day would have yielded some information about the effect of environment on the activity and feeding habits of Drosophila flies. However, even if these environmental factors were essentially the same throughout the test period, the possibility of their affecting the outcome of the experiment has not been eliminated. Their effect could be determined by additional, separate tests conducted under a wide range of temperature, pressure, and so forth, either naturally occurring or laboratory-produced.

The total number of flies counted on each preparation gives a measure of its attractant power in competition with every other attractant.

The arrangement of the measurements into a block design permits the maximum of information to be gained through a relatively limited number of observations; it recognizes that the six attractants can be combined two-by-two in 15 different ways, and organizes the comparisons among these combinations effectively. Without recourse to sophisticated mathematics, a reasonably thorough statistical analysis of the 60 entries in this block of experimental measurements can be obtained.

As to what extent the findings of this experiment contribute to proving or disproving the hypothesis, the result may be a plausibly valid arrangement of the six preparations in the order of their attractant power for Drosophila flies. Negative or inconclusive results may be as valuable to the researcher as positive results. They may indicate, in this case, that the flies are not influenced by the odors tested, or they may indicate that nature has been asked the wrong question, or asked the right question in the wrong way.

In either event, well-planned classroom experimentation frequently illustrates the serendipity of science.

In experimentation, as in theory, the principle of parsimony applies. A simple direct experiment, uncluttered by confusing details and designed to answer one specific question, is always to be preferred. The researcher must never forget that a great variety of causes may contribute to what he conceives to be a single effect; and that a great variety of effects may arise from what he conceives to be a single cause. The results of experiments are determined solely by the questions asked of nature and by the methods of asking; the interpretation of the results is the measure of man's understanding of the nature of the world.

G. RAYMOND HOOD, Blackburn College, Illinois

EXPERIMENTAL PSYCHOLOGY. *See* PSYCHOLOGY: *Experimental Psychology.*

EXPERIMENT STATION. *See* AGRICULTURAL EXPERIMENT STATION.

EXPLORATION. For more than 3,000 years, explorers by land, sea, and air have extended Western civilization's knowledge of the rest of the world. By far the most significant "unrolling of the map" occurred during the 35 years from 1487 through 1522, with the voyages in particular of Bartholomeu Dias, Christopher Columbus, Vasco da Gama, and Ferdinand Magellan, augmented by the findings of John and Sebastian Cabot, Amerigo Vespucci, Vasco Núñez de Balboa, and others. For the first time Europeans learned of the route around Africa, the existence of the Americas, and the existence and extent of the Pacific Ocean. Before that time discovery had been spasmodic; after that it tended to be fairly localized, as in the Pacific in the late 18th century, in Central Africa in the mid-19th, and in the Antarctic in the 20th.

Of the various motives for exploration, commerce has probably been the most frequent, but conquest and missionary zeal have also played their part. In modern times geographical and scientific curiosity have loomed large. Normally, an exploring expedition has been too expensive for the explorer's individual resources. Financing has come most often from governments, from trading companies, from missionary organizations, and from geographical societies.

Ancient and Medieval Explorers

Much of the earliest exploration is unrecorded or, at the most, a matter of hazy legend. This is particularly true of the Far East, southern Asia, and the Pacific. Even in the Mediterranean, the center of early Western civilization and maritime activity, the gradual extension of knowledge by Egyptians, Cretans, Phoenicians, and Greeks is too complicated and too little known to follow in detail. Several early ventures outside the Mediterranean area are, however, matters of fairly definite record. It seems that around 1750 B.C. an Egyptian nobleman named Hannu was sent from the Nile to the Red Sea and down to "Punt," somewhere in East Africa. A similar expedition was sent thither by Queen Hatshepsut around 1500 B.C. and the Upper Nile was explored. Historians are skeptical of the tale told by Herodotus about a Phoenician expedition sent out around 600 B.C. by the Pharaoh Necho, which started from the Red Sea, circumnavigated Africa, and returned by way of Gibraltar. There is more cause to credit the tale that the Carthaginian Hanno around 500 B.C. took 60 vessels out through Gibraltar and down the west coast of Africa to the Guinea Coast, where the crew encountered gorillas.

New Sea Routes. In 325 B.C. two Greeks opened up new sea routes, one in the northwest and the other in the southeast corner of the known world. The Phoenicians had already ventured outside the Mediterranean to establish trade with the tin miners of southern England. Then at one sweep a Greek from Marseille named Pytheas apparently extended the knowledge of the western waters as far north as the Arctic Circle. After visiting Britain he continued on to a region he called "Thule," apparently the Shetlands, Norway, or even Iceland, and finally reached a frozen sea. On the same or a second trip, he seems to have reached northwest Germany and perhaps the Baltic. That same year Alexander the Great, having proceeded overland to northern India, sent the

EXPLORATION — THE WORLD AS KNOWN TO EUROPEANS

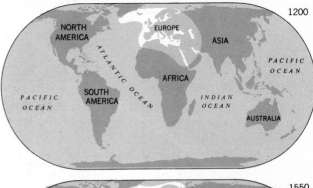
1200

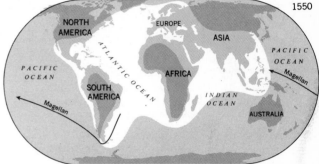
1550

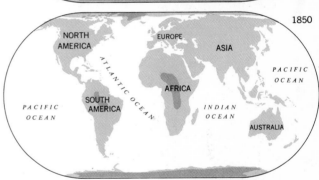
1850

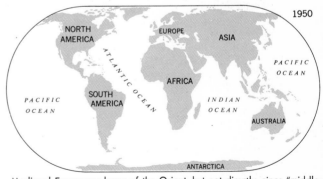
1950

Medieval Europeans knew of the Orient, but not directly, since "middlemen" conducted the intermittent trade between Europe and the Far East. After 1200, personal reports by travelers—notably Marco Polo—stimulated European interest in the East. The Vikings visited the North American mainland before 1200, but this region nonetheless remained generally unknown to Europeans until the 15th century. The most spectacular period of geographical discovery occurred between 1487 and 1522. Subsequent exploration efforts focused on the Pacific (18th century), Africa (19th century), and the polar regions (20th century). In the mid-20th century man actively took on the long-standing challenge of space exploration.

On the threshold of space exploration, 20th-century man is in a position comparable to that of late 15th-century man as he began a period of great discoveries. For both, breakthroughs in knowledge opened up new frontiers, thus the story of exploration has a particular timeliness today. The basic article in the **ENCYCLOPEDIA INTERNATIONAL** on the history of exploration is found on these pages. It starts with a summary of the character of exploration before, during, and after, its most significant period (from 1487 through 1522). The body of the article covers explorations from ancient times to the 20th century. Many other articles provide further information.

One chapter of the history of exploration is covered in detail in the separate article POLAR EXPLORATION. The new venture of the 20th century is the subject of SPACE EXPLORATION. The entries MAP and COMPASS include pertinent general information.

Specific data on discovery and exploration are given in entries on areas and countries: ASIA, NORTH AMERICA, SOUTH AMERICA, AFRICA, AUSTRALIA, ARCTIC REGIONS, and ANTARCTICA as well as EGYPT, PHOENICIA, CRETE, CHINA, ITALY, SPAIN, ENGLAND, VINLAND or WINELAND, and UNITED STATES. Related to these is COLONIES, COLONIZATION, AND COLONIALISM, an entry that gives the history of one of the great motivations for exploration. BRITISH EMPIRE surveys the history of a colonial system that extended around the world. Also pertinent are the entries on geographical features that were pathways or goals for exploration, for example, ATLANTIC OCEAN, PACIFIC OCEAN, MEDITERRANEAN SEA, NILE RIVER, and NORTHWEST PASSAGE.

Historical articles on eras, events, and organizations provide additional insights, for example, MIDDLE AGES; RENAISSANCE; ARMADA, SPANISH; LEWIS AND CLARK EXPEDITION; HUDSON'S BAY COMPANY; and NORTH WEST COMPANY.

Records of the great explorers are an excellent source of information on the history of exploration. The table entitled World Explorers lists men and their achievements over a time span from the travels of Herodotus to the conquest of Mount Everest by Sir Edmund Hillary. Many of the famous discoverers are also treated in biographic entries. A list of the achievements of polar explorers accompanies POLAR EXPLORATION.

One of the notable explorations of the 19th century is the cruise of the *Beagle*, an expedition motivated by scientific curiosity (see the article on Charles DARWIN). Another manifestation of man's continuing efforts to know his world is described in INTERNATIONAL GEOPHYSICAL YEAR. A 20th-century traverse of the Northwest Passage was made by the USS NAUTILUS. Among the most recent names to be added to the roster of famous explorers are Alan Bartlett SHEPARD, Jr., John Herschel GLENN, Jr., and Yuri Alekseyevich GAGARIN.

Cross references at the end of many articles direct the reader to other entries in the **ENCYCLOPEDIA INTERNATIONAL** and suggest related subjects of study, for example, the civilization of the Aztecs, the early colonies of North America, or the primitive art of the Pacific islands. If he wants more complete information, he may consult the bibliographies that follow many of the articles.

---

mariner Nearchus back by sea from the site of present-day Karachi to the Persian Gulf.

Asia. Further contacts with Asia had been made by the time the Roman Empire was at its height, though they remain fairly anonymous. Vessels were proceeding from the Red Sea or Persian Gulf around India and Southeast Asia all the way to China. There was also trade with China by the overland "silk routes," which, after traversing the desolate reaches of Central Asia, reached the Mediterranean either through Syria or by way of the Black Sea and Constantinople. That lengthy caravan traffic had a strange "off and on" story. Active in Roman times, it was shut off after the spread of Arab power in the 7th century but came to life again briefly during the Mongol-Tatar period in the later Middle Ages, only to be closed down once more when the Turks blocked one end of it and the Mings the other. Those changing conditions on the routes to China, by sea as well as by land, brought into the exploration story a group who were technically travelers rather than explorers because others had long before discovered most of the places they visited. A number of Arabs fell into this category, notably Suleyman the Merchant, who voyaged from the Persian Gulf to Canton around 850 A.D. and the tireless Ibn Battuta, who traveled some 75,000 mi. in the course of 30 years during the mid-14th century, visiting all Islamic and other regions.

However, by that time several Europeans had distinguished themselves along the old overland silk routes. Following the amazing conquests of the Mongol-Tatars under Genghis Khan, his descendants, particularly his grandson Kublai Khan, built up by the mid-13th century an empire that stretched from China through much of Asia into eastern Europe. The Khans had a far less negative attitude toward Europeans than the Arabs had had. To take advantage of this, Pope Innocent IV sent a Franciscan friar, Giovanni de Carpini, to the Great Khan at Karakorum in 1245. Several years later another Franciscan, Guillaume Rubruquis (William of Rubruck), was sent thither by the French King Louis IX. Both described their experiences, but their accounts were overshadowed by that of Marco Polo, a Venetian who spent almost a quarter century in Asia. Around 1260, his father and uncle, on a jewel-trading trip, had happened to reach the court of Kublai Khan at Peking; the Khan asked them to have the Pope send out a hundred missionaries. They were not forthcoming, but the Polos set out again in 1271 with young Marco by the overland route. The Great Khan liked him so well that from 1275 to 1292 he utilized him for diplomatic missions around China and even Burma. The Polos finally returned by sea through the Straits of Malacca and around India to the Persian Gulf and home by way of Constantinople. Captured three years later by the Genoese in a sea fight, Marco Polo dictated his lengthy story to a fellow prisoner. It aroused great interest and afterward, when the overland route to the East was blocked, it helped to stimulate the quest for a sea route.

Vikings. The voyage of Pytheas was followed by more than a thousand years without significant exploration in the Atlantic. There were vague rumors about an island of Atlantis or Antilla, of a seagoing Irish monk named St. Brendan and so on, but the first definite record of pre-Columbian discoveries came from the far-flung achievements of the Scandinavian Northmen, or Vikings. In addition to plundering the settled coasts of western Europe and developing an overland trade route through Russia, they pushed boldly out into the North Atlantic.

WORLD EXPLORERS

Aguilar, Martín de, *Spanish.* Explored coast of California to about 43° N. lat. Discovered, with Sebastián Vizcaíno, Monterey Bay. Exploration Period: 1602-3.

Alarcón, Hernando de, *Spanish.* Explored Gulf of California, discovered the Colorado River. Exploration Period: 1540.

Albuquerque, Affonso de, *Portuguese.* Founder of the Portuguese Empire in the East. Journeyed (1503) to India. Explored (1506) coasts of Madagascar and eastern Africa. Captured Hormuz (1507) and Goa (1510). His capture (1511) of Malacca completed Portuguese control of southeastern Asia. Exploration Period: 1503-11.

Alexander the Great, *Macedonian.* King of Macedon. Explored and conquered much of southwestern Asia. Crossed the Hellespont and conquered (334 B.C.) most of Asia Minor. Entered Egypt (332) and the Persian Empire (330). Continued his conquest through Afghanistan to the Indus and its delta. Exploration Period: 334–323 B.C.

Almagro, Diego de, *Spanish.* Conquistador. Participated in the first (1524) and second (1526–28) expeditions of Francisco Pizarro against Peru. Marched (1535-36) south through Chile; returned over the Atacama Desert. Exploration Period: 1524-36.

Alvarez, Francisco, *Portuguese.* Explored Ethiopia and gave a detailed description of the land in his later writings. Exploration Period: 1520-27.

Andrews, Roy Chapman, *American.* Explored (1911-12) northern Korea. Visited (1913) Alaska and (1916) southwestern China and borders of Burma and Tibet. Visited (1919) Mongolia and later explored the Gobi Desert. His expeditions resulted in the discovery of some of the world's greatest fossil fields. Exploration Period: 1908-30.

Baker, Sir Samuel White, *English.* Explored (1861-62) Upper Nile River and its tributaries in Ethiopia. Discovered Lake Albert on the Belgian Congo-Uganda border. Returned (1869) to Egypt and opened up lake areas to commerce. Exploration Period: 1861-69.

Balboa, Vasco Núñez de, *Spanish.* Conquistador. Sailed (1501) with Rodrigo de Bastidas to mouth of the Magdalena River. Sailed (1510) with Martín Fernández de Encisco to Panama. Crossed the Isthmus of Panama and discovered (1513) the Pacific Ocean. Exploration Period: 1501-13.

Baptista, Pedro, *Portuguese.* Made first recorded crossing of the African continent eastward from Angola. Exploration Period: 1802-6.

Barth, Heinrich, *German.* Explored (1845-47) North Africa and the Levant. Crossed (1849-55) the Sahara and explored the kingdom of West Sudan (for British government). Exploration Period: 1845-55.

Bass, George, *English.* Discovered Bass Strait, separating Tasmania from Australia, and circumnavigated Tasmania. Exploration Period: 1795-98.

Bastidas, Rodrigo de, *Spanish.* Conquistador in Colombia. With Balboa and Juan de la Cosa, discovered (1501) the mouths of the Magdalena River. Founded (1525) Santa Marta, Colombia. Exploration Period: 1501-25.

Becknell, William, *American.* Opened up the Santa Fe trade route between Franklin, on the Missouri River, and Santa Fe. Exploration Period: 1821.

BALBOA

Around 850, they discovered Iceland and soon settled there in large numbers. In 985, Eric the Red sailed from Iceland to discover Greenland, where a Norse colony survived for almost four centuries. In 1002 his son Leif reached the mainland of North America, proceeding southward to a still unidentified region which he named Vineland; several other Norse expeditions reached there during the next few years. The knowledge of those discoveries, however, barely spread beyond Scandinavia, and the settlement of Iceland was the only permanent result. Mariners from various countries apparently reached the Canaries and Madeira after 1350 but their voyaging led to no immediate follow-up.

The Age of Discovery

Prince Henry. In contrast to the spasmodic findings through the centuries, exploration and subsequent overseas empire have had a continuous development ever since a young Portuguese prince decided around 1415 to promote systematically the finding of new sea routes. Known to history as Prince Henry the Navigator, though he never actually navigated at sea, he was the third son of King John I of Portugal and his English Queen, Philippa, daughter of John of Gaunt. Henry conceived the idea of sending ship after ship down the west coast of Africa. This process was eventually to lead the Portuguese around the Cape of Good Hope to India, though Henry may not have envisioned that much at the start. His father made him head of a military crusading order with a well-filled treasury, and Henry established at Sagres near Cape St. Vincent, the southwest corner of Portugal, a remarkable headquarters for exploration knowledge and techniques, gathering all the writings he could, and attracting experts thither to discuss various problems. There was also a need to train mariners, for the Portuguese had done little but fishing and coastal trade.

BURTON

Beckwourth, James Pierson, *American.* Explored the Rocky Mountains (1824-25). Lived among the Crow Indians for six years. Credited as one of the founders (1842) of Pueblo, Colo. Exploration Period: 1823-42.

Bell, Gertrude Margaret Lowthian, *English.* Journeyed extensively in Persia, Palestine, Mesopotamia, Anatolia, and Syria. Reached (1914) Hail in the Arabian Desert. Exploration Period: 1892-1914.

Benalcázar or Belalcázar, Sebastián de, *Spanish.* Served in Darién and Nicaragua. Joined (1532) Francisco Pizarro in conquest of Peru. Entered Ecuador and founded (1533) Guayaquil. Marched (1535) through southwestern Colombia in search of fabled El Dorado. Exploration Period: 1520-39.

Bienville, Jean Baptiste Lemoyne, Sieur de, *French.* Accompanied (1698-99) Iberville on colonizing expedition to mouth of the Mississippi River. Explored Mississippi north to mouth of the Red River. Founded (1718) New Orleans. Exploration Period: 1698-1720.

Boone, Daniel, *American.* Explored (1767-71) the Kentucky region, blazed (1775) the Wilderness Road, and founded Boonesboro on the Kentucky River. Exploration Period: 1767-79.

Bougainville, Louis Antoine de, *French.* Led first French expedition on voyage around the world. Explored South Pacific islands, including Tahiti, Samoa, and the New Hebrides. Exploration Period: 1766-69.

Brazza, Pierre Paul François Camille Savorgnan de, *French-Italian.* Explored (1873-74) the Gabon in West Africa and discovered (1875) affluents of the Congo. Reached (1880) Stanley Pool on the Congo and later in the same year founded Brazzaville. Exploration Period: 1873-83.

Bridger, James, *American.* Fur trapper and guide. Explored much of the country north of Spanish New Mexico and east of California. Probably the first white man to visit (1824) Great Salt Lake. Exploration Period: 1822-45.

Bruce, James, *Scottish.* Traveled (1768) down Red Sea as far as Straits of Bab el Mandeb. Explored Ethiopia and rediscovered (1770) the source of the Blue Nile, which he explored to its confluence with the White Nile. Exploration Period: 1768-73.

Burckhardt, Johann Ludwig, *Swiss.* Explored the Nile River and crossed Africa to the Red Sea. Later explored in Syria and Egypt. Rediscovered (1812) Petra, ancient rock city of Jordan. Exploration Period: 1809-14.

Burke, Robert O'Hara, *Irish.* With William Wills, succeeded in crossing the Australian continent from Menindee on the Darling River to the Gulf of Carpentaria. Both died on return journey. Exploration Period: 1860-61.

Burton, Sir Richard Francis, *English.* Journeyed (1853) in Muslim disguise to Mecca and Medina. With John Speke, led exploring expedition into Somaliland and later, again with Speke, explored (1856) east-central Africa and found (1858) Lake Tanganyika. Alone, he explored Ethiopia and the Bight of Biafra. He visited the Gold Coast (1881-82). Exploration Period: 1842-82.

Cabeza de Vaca, Álvar Núñez, *Spanish.* Reached Florida (1528) with expedition commanded by Pánfilo de Narváez, but expedition dissolved. For next nine years, explored coast of Gulf of Mexico and probably reached California. Exploration Period: 1527-37.

Cabot, John, *Italian* (sailed for England). Discovered North American coast and explored shore lines of Nova Scotia and Newfoundland. British claims to North America based on his discovery. Exploration Period: 1497-98.

For a while superstition and navigational difficulties slowed the progress down the coast; sailors believed the tales of the terrors lying beyond Cape Bojador in Morocco. The first real triumph for the Age of Exploration came in 1434, when one of Henry's captains, Gil Eannes, pushed his ship beyond Bojador, demonstrating that these rumors were unfounded. Then, advancing down the coast toward Senegal, the Portuguese began to pick up gold and slaves, whereupon the merchants of Lisbon decided that Henry's project was not as idly visionary as it had seemed. In the meantime, out in the Atlantic, Henry's captains had rediscovered Madeira in 1420 and visited some of the Azores in 1427-31. Both were soon colonized under Henry's direction. The Portuguese also reached the Canaries, which later went to Spain, and the Cape Verde Islands. In 1445, Cape Verde was discovered. By Henry's death in 1460, exploration had extended along the Guinea Coast to Sierra Leone or beyond.

Cam and Dias. Henry's exploration policy was revived by his great-nephew, who came to the throne as John II in 1481. To serve as a center of trade and control on the Gold Coast, a prefabricated castle was built at Elmina ("The Mine") in 1482. That same year saw the start of a remarkable southward push which in seven years, under Diogo Cam (Cão) and Bartholomeu Dias, extended the knowledge of the African coast some 2,700 mi. from near the equator to the far side of the Cape of Good Hope. On his first voyage (1482–84), Cam discovered the Congo River and planted one of the stone crosses he had brought with him. On his second voyage (1485–87), in addition to proceeding up the Congo River to its head of navigation, he pushed southward along the bleak coast of Southwest Africa to the vicinity of Walvis Bay. In Aug., 1487, a more significant expedition left Lisbon under Bartholomeu Dias.

Proceeding beyond Cam's outer limit in Southwest Africa, Dias headed southward in increasing gales for 13

Cabot, Sebastian, *Italian* (sailed for Spain). Son of John Cabot. Led expedition to west coast of South America. Explored extensively in the Río de la Plata country and along the Paraná River. Exploration Period: 1526-30.

Cabral, Pedro Álvares, *Portuguese.* Explored east coast of Brazil and claimed the land for Portugal. Continued voyage around Africa to Madagascar, Mozambique, and India. Exploration Period: 1500-01.

Cabrillo, Jaun Rodríguez, *Spanish.* Conquistador. Participated in conquests of Mexico and Guatemala. Later, sailed up west coast of Mexico, discovered San Diego Bay, and explored California coast to north of San Francisco Bay. Exploration Period: 1520-43.

Cadamosto, Alvise da, *Italian* (sailed for Portugal). Sailed for Prince Henry the Navigator of Portugal. Explored African coast to Gambia River. Reached (1456) Cape Verde Islands. Exploration Period: 1455-57.

Cadillac, Antoine de la Mothe, *French.* Arrived (1683) in Nova Scotia. Later, explored upper Mississippi valley. Founded (1701) Detroit. Appointed (1711) Governor of Louisiana territory. Exploration Period: 1683-1716.

Caesar, Julius, *Roman.* Visited Asia (81 B.C. and 74 B.C.). Warred (62-60) in Farther Spain. Waged (58-49) the Gallic Wars, during which he investigated and invaded (55-54) Britain. Between 49 and 45, traveled in Egypt, Syria, Africa, and Spain. Recorded information that added greatly to then current geographical knowledge. Exploration Period: 81-44 B.C.

Caillié, René, *French.* Explored Africa. Traveled from Guinea Coast to Fès and Tangier. First white man to visit Timbuktu (and survive). Traveled disguised as a Muslim trader. Exploration Period: 1827-28.

Cam or Cão, Diogo, *Portuguese.* On voyage to Africa, discovered mouth of Congo River. Reached (1486) Cape Negro. Exploration Period: 1482-87.

Cano, Juan Sebastián del, *Spanish.* First to complete a circumnavigation of the globe. Sailed (1519) under Magellan. After Magellan's death in the Philippines, took command of the expedition and arrived (Sept. 6, 1522) in Spain with the *Victoria.* Exploration Period: 1519-26.

Cárdenas, García López de, *Spanish.* A member of Francisco Coronado's expedition (1540), he explored in southwest United States. Discovered (1540) the Grand Canyon of the Colorado. Exploration Period: 1540-42.

Carpini, Giovanni de Piano, *Italian.* A Franciscan monk, he traveled to Kiev, crossed the Dnieper, and went on to the Don and Volga. Reached (1246) Karakorum, Mongolia. He traveled as a legate of Pope Innocent IV. Exploration Period: 1245-47.

Carson, ("Kit") Christopher, *American.* Joined (1826) caravan bound for Santa Fe. From then until 1846, served as guide to many overland expeditions into the American Southwest, the Rocky Mountain regions, and California. Exploration Period: 1826-46.

Cartier, Jacques, *French.* Made three voyages (1534; 1535-36; 1541-42) to North America. Explored the Gulf of St. Lawrence and discovered St. Lawrence River. Discovered Prince Edward Island and the Magdalen Islands. Took possession of the Gaspé Peninsula in the name of France. Exploration Period: 1534-42.

Carver, Jonathan, *American.* Explored the upper Mississippi River region. Crossed overland to Lake Superior and followed its coast to the Grand Portage in search for the "western ocean." Exploration Period: 1766-69.

CARTIER

days, coming back to land on the far side of the tip of Africa in Feb., 1488. Prevented by his storm-worn crews from going farther, he sighted on his return the spectacular point which he is said to have named the Cape of Storms, only to have it changed to the Cape of Good Hope by the King, who now saw the way clear to India.

Da Gama. Then followed a strange lapse of almost nine years in reaching India, during which Columbus made his famous voyage for Spain. For one thing the King sent out by way of the Mediterranean Pedro de Covilhão, who scouted the west coast of India and also Ethiopia. Henry's dream of the route around Africa finally came to fruition in the voyage (1497–99) of Vasco da Gama. With bold navigational innovation, he struck down across the South Atlantic almost to Brazil—the next voyage, under Pedro Álvares Cabral, did in fact reach Brazil on its way to India in 1500. Then he headed back southeastward—a route which sailing vessels were to follow for centuries to come—rounded Good Hope and then proceeded up the coast of East Africa, where he met with varied treatment from the Arabs at different ports. Finally, in the spring of 1498, Da Gama's squadron arrived at Calicut on the Malabar coast, laying the foundation of a century of highly profitable spice trade for Portugal. He reached Lisbon with a cargo of spices early in 1499.

By the time Da Gama returned from India, exploration was in full swing on several distant routes, mainly under Italian initiative. Most of the progress on the Lisbon-Guinea-Good Hope-India route had been made by Portuguese mariners; the one prominent exception was the Italian Alvise da Cadamosto. The relationship of Italy to the Age of Discovery was an interesting one. Once the new sea lanes were established, the highly profitable trade of Venice and Genoa—picking up silks, spices, and other Eastern wares brought overland to the Mediterranean and then distributing them throughout Europe—withered.

COLUMBUS

Champlain, Samuel de, *French.* Voyaged (1603) to New France. Explored and mapped St. Lawrence River to the rapids at Lachine. Explored (1604-7) the New England coast to Martha's Vineyard. Discovered (1609) Lake Champlain and explored (1615) lakes Huron and Ontario. Exploration Period: 1603-15.

Charlevoix, Pierre, *French.* Arrived (1705) in New France. Visited (1720-22) French settlements in North America from Quebec to New Orleans. Exploration Period: 1705-22.

Clapperton, Hugh, *Scottish.* With Dixon Denham, explored (1822-25) in Africa from Tripoli to Lake Chad. Explored (1825-27), with Richard Lander, the lower Niger River. Exploration Period: 1822-27.

Clark, William, *American.* One of the leaders of the Lewis and Clark Expedition across the Rocky Mountains to the Pacific Ocean. Exploration Period: 1804-6.

Colter, John, *American.* Joined (1803) Lewis and Clark Expedition to California. Served as guide for expedition (1807) led by Manuel Lisa to mouth of Bighorn River. Later explored Wind River Range and Teton Range. Believed to be first white man to travel through region now included in Yellowstone National Park. Exploration Period: 1803-10.

Columbus, Christopher, *Italian* (sailed for Spain). Made four voyages across Atlantic to the Americas. Discovered (1492) West Indies. Discovered (1493-94) Virgin Islands, St. Kitts, Leeward Islands, and Puerto Rico. Discovered (1498) mouth of the Orinoco River in Venezuela. On fourth voyage (1502), explored Central America to the Gulf of Darien. Exploration Period: 1492-1502.

Cook, James, *English.* Made three voyages into the Pacific. Explored (1769-70) coasts of New Zealand and eastern Australia and completed (1771) a circumnavigation of the globe. Commanded expedition (1772-75) to South Pacific, proved nonexistence of continental land reaching north of the Antarctic Circle into the South Pacific. Made exploratory voyage (1776-79), discovered Hawaiian Islands, and searched for passage from Pacific to Atlantic Ocean along the northwest coast of North America. Exploration Period: 1769-79.

Coronado, Francisco Vásquez de, *Spanish.* Commanded expedition into southwest United States. Crossed Arkansas plains region and went northward into Kansas. Garcí López de Cárdenas, member of the expedition, discovered Grand Canyon. Exploration Period: 1540-42.

Cortés, Hernán, *Spanish.* Led expedition (1518) into Mexico. Completed conquest of Aztec Empire with the capture (1521) of Tenochtitlán. Extended conquest over most of Mexico and into northern Central America. Exploration Period: 1518-26.

Cosa, Juan de la, *Spanish.* Sailed with Columbus in 1492 as pilot of the *Santa María*, and again in 1498. With Alonso de Ojeda, explored (1499-1500) northern coast of South America. Exploration Period: 1492-1509.

Covilhão, Pedro de, *Portuguese.* Traveled through Egypt and Arabia. Explored west coast of India and east coast of Africa south to Zambezi River. Exploration Period: 1487.

Cunha, Tristão da, *Portuguese.* Sailed (1506) with 15 ships for India. Discoveries included several islands (including Tristan de Cunha) in the South

Nevertheless, Italian mariners, the most competent professionals afloat, played active parts in the development of new sea routes. Already three of them—Christopher Columbus, John Cabot, and Amerigo Vespucci—had achieved voyages of significance. Throughout this whole period of exploration the benefits of discovery went not to the native region of the explorer but rather to those who sponsored him.

Columbus. Columbus was the most important of all explorers. Born in Genoa, he developed contacts with Portugal, where his father-in-law was a colonial governor; he voyaged into the north and visited Elmina in its early stages. Then he conceived the idea of reaching the Indies by sailing west into the Atlantic. Seriously underestimating the size of the earth, and believing that Asia extended much farther eastward than it actually did, he reckoned that Japan was only 2,400 mi. from the Canaries instead of the actual 10,600. The King of Portugal, with the around-Africa success in sight, refused to support such a project. Columbus thereupon turned to Spain, finally receiving the backing of Queen Isabella. On Aug. 3, 1492, he sailed from Palos on the first and most significant of his four expeditions. Going by way of the Canaries with his three small vessels, he made his landfall on Oct. 12 off the coast of America. Then, and until his death, he believed that he had reached the Indies. After discovering Cuba and Hispaniola, he returned to Palos on Mar. 15, 1493. The King and Queen were delighted, and Pope Alexander VI, a Spaniard, decreed that the newly discovered lands in the west would go to Spain. Columbus made three more voyages, complicated by unhappy colonial experiments in Hispaniola. On his second voyage (Sept., 1493, to June, 1496) he discovered the whole string of the Lesser Antilles. On the third (May, 1498, to Oct., 1500) he discovered the big island of Trinidad and visited the nearby Venezuelan mainland

Atlantic. Captured Socotra on the Arabian Sea, then continued voyage to India. Exploration Period: 1506.

Dampier, William, *English.* Participated in buccaneering expedition (1679-81) against Spanish America. Engaged in voyage (1683) of piracy along coast of Africa; crossed Atlantic and rounded Cape Horn. Explored (1699-1701) west and northwest coasts of Australia; discovered Dampier Archipelago and Dampier Strait. Commanded privateering expedition (1703-7) to Pacific and completed voyage around the world (1708-11). Exploration Period: 1679-1711.

Daniel of Kiev, *Russian.* Explored the Holy Land, visiting Jaffa, Jerusalem, Jordan, and Damascus. Exploration Period: 1106.

Darwin, Charles, *English.* A naturalist, he made extensive explorations during world cruise (1831-36) of the *Beagle.* Exploration Period: 1831-36.

Denham, Dixon, *English.* With Hugh Clapperton, explored (1822-25) central Sudan and Lake Chad regions in Africa. Exploration Period: 1822-25.

Desideri, Ipolito or Ippolito, *Italian.* Explored central Asia; reached Tibetan city of Lhasa from Kashmir. Exploration Period: 1714-21.

De Soto, Hernando or Fernando, *Spanish.* Served under Francisco Pizarro in Peru. Led expedition (1538-39) to coast of Florida. Explored through Georgia, the Carolinas, and Tennessee. Continued westward advance and discovered (1541) the Mississippi River. Exploration Period: 1538-42.

Dias, Bartholomeu, *Portuguese.* First European to round (1488) Cape of Good Hope. Accompanied Pedro Álvares Cabral on voyage (1500-01) that resulted in discovery of Brazil. Exploration Period: 1488-1501.

Diaz, Diniz, *Portuguese.* Explored west coast of Africa to Cape Verde Islands. Exploration Period: 1445.

Drake, Sir Francis, *English.* First Englishman to circumnavigate (1577-80) the world. Commanded (1585) fleet of 25 vessels in voyage of conquest across the Atlantic; captured Santo Domingo and Cartagena and raided the Florida coast. Exploration Period: 1567-86.

Du Chaillu, Paul Belloni, *French-American.* Led two expeditions to Africa; explored the Gabon country and brought back the first gorillas to be seen in the United States. Exploration Period: 1856-65.

Duluth, Daniel Greysolon, *French.* Explored west Canada and the Lake Superior region. Founded (1686) Fort St. Joseph on the St. Clair River. Exploration Period: 1672-88.

Dupuis, Jean, *French.* Led expedition into China. Explored the Tongking route and opened up the Red River to French trade. Exploration Period: 1873-82.

Eannes, Gil, *Portuguese.* Sailing for Prince Henry the Navigator, he rounded Cape Bojador in 1434. Exploration Period: 1433-35.

Emin Pasha (original name, Eduard Schnitzer), *German.* Traveled in Albania and Egypt. Made extensive explorations in central Africa. Searched for by Sir Henry Stanley and rescued (1888) by him. Later, returned to region of Lake Tanganyika, where he was murdered. Exploration Period: 1876-91.

Enciso, Martín Fernández de, *Spanish.* Conquistador. Founded (1510) new colony in Darien, on the Isthmus of Panama. Original colony, established (1509) by Diego de Nicuesa, failed. Exploration Period: 1509-14.

DRAKE

in South America. On the fourth (Apr., 1502, to Nov., 1504) he sailed up and down the coast of Central America, hoping to find a strait into the Indian Ocean.

Cabot. On May 2, 1497, two months before Da Gama began his voyage, John Cabot set sail from Bristol, England, on a voyage in which he was to discover North America. Born in Genoa but naturalized in Venice, he had become interested in the Eastern trade. Like Columbus, he believed that the East could be reached by sailing west. He received support in the English port of Bristol and the official backing of Henry VII, the first Tudor, who was not deterred by the exclusive claims of Spain and Portugal. On June 24, he apparently reached Cape Breton Island and took possession in the name of Henry VII, giving England a valid claim for its later settlements in North America. He also discovered Newfoundland and the Grand Banks, teeming with cod, which would soon attract fishermen of various nations. On a sec-

ond voyage, in 1498, he seems to have explored the coasts of Greenland, Baffin Land, Labrador, Newfoundland, and part of the American coast down to 38° N. lat. His son Sebastian, who probably accompanied him, later saw service with Spain.

Vespucci. Even greater uncertainty surrounds the voyaging of Amerigo Vespucci, the versatile Florentine businessman, navigator, cartographer, and publicity expert, who was lucky enough to have his name permanently attached to the two continents of the New World. As representative of the Medici financial interests at Seville, he became involved in procuring shipping for the Columbus expeditions. There seems good evidence that he explored in 1499–1500 for Spain and in 1501–2 for Portugal, but there is skepticism about claims of a 1497–98 voyage for Spain to the Gulf of Mexico, reaching the mainland ahead of Columbus, and of a 1503–4 voyage for Portugal to Brazil. On Mar. 18, 1499, two days be-

GAMA

Estevanico, *Moroccan*. Penetrated deep into the American Southwest as guide for Spanish expedition (1538) in search of the Seven Cities of Cibola. Killed by Indians. Paved the way to Spanish conquests in the Southwest. Exploration Period: 1527-38.

Eyre, Edward John, *English*. Explored interior Australia. Discovered Lake Torrens. Crossed continent from Spencer Gulf to King George Sound. Exploration Period: 1832-45.

Federmann, Nikolaus, *German*. An adventurer in Venezuela, Colombia, and Bolivia, he searched for fabled El Dorado. Exploration Period: 1530-39.

Fernández de Córdoba, Franciso de, *Spanish*. Sailed from Cuba on slave hunt. Discovered Yucatán and uncovered evidence of Mayan culture. Exploration Period: 1514-26.

Ferrer, Jayme, *Catalonian*. 14th-century maps indicate that he rounded Cape Bojador on west coast of Africa. Exploration Period: 1346.

Fitzpatrick, Thomas, *American*. Conducted trading expedition (1823) up Missouri River. Served as guide on several important overland expeditions. Exploration Period: 1823-46.

Flinders, Matthew, *English*. Naval captain and hydrographer. Circumnavigated (1795-99; again, 1801-3) Australia and Tasmania, mapping and charting coastal waters. Exploration Period: 1795-1803.

Forrest, John Forrest, 1st Baron, *Australian*. Led expedition (1869) into interior Australia to search for the missing Friedrich Leichhardt. Reversing Edward Eyre's route, he crossed continent from Perth to Adelaide. Exploration Period: 1869-74.

Frémont, John Charles, *American*. Extensively explored western United States. Exploration Period: 1838-45.

Gama, Vasco da, *Portuguese*. Discovered sea route to India by way of Cape of Good Hope. Voyage (1497-99) most significant, for out of it grew the Portuguese Empire. Commanded (1502) second voyage of 20 ships to India. Exploration Period: 1497-1503.

Gilbert, Sir Humphrey, *English*. Failed in first attempt (1578) to establish colony in North America. Second expedition (1583) reached Newfoundland, where he established himself as Governor. Exploration Period: 1578-83.

Giles, Ernest, *English*. Crossed the Australian desert from Port Augusta to Perth and made return. Exploration Period: 1875-76.

Gist, Christopher, *American*. Noted frontiersman, he descended (1750) Ohio River, explored Kentucky, and crossed to North Carolina. Served (1753-54) with George Washington on journey to Ohio valley. Served (1755) as guide to Gen. Edward Braddock on expedition against Fort Duquesne. Exploration Period: 1750-55.

Goes, Bento de, *Portuguese*. Made first exploratory overland journey into China after Marco Polo. Exploration Period: 1603-5.

Gómez, Estéban, *Portuguese*. Commanded voyage to North America; explored coast from Nova Scotia to Florida. Exploration Period: 1524-25.

Gosnold, Bartholomew, *English*. Explored (1602) North American coast from Maine to Narragansett Bay; discovered Cape Cod. Second voyage (1606) brought settlers to Virginia, where they founded Jamestown. Exploration Period: 1602-7.

---

fore Da Gama returned from his great voyage, Vespucci sailed as commercial representative and astronomer in an expedition under Alonzo de Ojeda, a former captain under Columbus. This expedition explored some 3,000 mi. of coast from Venezuela down to Brazil, and discovered the Amazon. By 1501, Brazil was receiving ample attention. Cabral, commanding the second Portuguese expedition to India, touched there as did Vicente Yáñez Pinzon, a veteran of the first Columbus voyage, and Vespucci, who continued far down the coast. He is credited with recognizing, as Columbus did not, that this was really a "new world" and a continuous continent. On the strength of that, Martin Waldseemuller, a geographer who was recording the new discoveries on a map, applied the name America to part of South America; before long it spread to both continents. Returning to Spain, Vespucci received over-all charge of charts and exploration, a post soon afterward held by Sebastian Cabot.

Balboa and Magellan. An important discovery came in 1513, while the Spaniards were beginning to establish themselves in Central America. Then, Vasco Núñez de Balboa, temporary head of the turbulent settlement on the isthmus of Panama, crossed it and from a peak got the first glimpse of the Pacific, or "Great South Sea" as it was first called. He waded out and took possession of it for the King of Spain. The news of that event may have helped to prompt the exploration of that new-found sea in one of the great voyages of history. Ferdinand Magellan, a Portuguese sailing for Spain, had spent seven years (1505–12) in the Indies while the Portuguese were establishing their empire, participating in several expeditions and visiting the Spice Islands. Returning home, he encountered royal disfavor at Lisbon and shifted his allegiance to Spain. He won the support of Charles V for his project of finding a passage through South America to the Pacific as a new approach to the Orient.

Goyer, Pieter van, *Dutch.* Journeyed through China. Reached Peking via overland route from Canton. Exploration Period: 1656.

Gray, Robert, *American.* First American to circumnavigate (1787-90) the globe. Explored northwest coast of the United States; discovered (1792) and sailed up the Columbia River. Exploration Period: 1787-93.

Gregory, John Walter, *English.* Made extensive explorations in Tibet. Exploration Period: 1922.

Grijalva, Juan de, *Spanish.* Commanded (1518) expedition to Yucatán; explored coast of Mexico to Veracruz. Participated (1523) in conquest of Nicaragua. Exploration Period: 1518-23.

Groseilliers, Médard Chouart, Sieur de, *French.* Explored with Pierre Radisson upper Mississippi River and Lake Superior regions of North America. Exploration Period: 1658-59.

Halévy, Joseph, *French.* Explored interior of southwestern Arabia. Exploration Period: 1869-70.

Hanno, *Carthaginian.* Led fleet of 60 vessels down west coast of Africa; explored Guinea coast and probably reached Sierra Leone. Exploration Period: 500 B.C.

Hartog, Dirk, *Dutch.* Commanded exploratory voyage to South Pacific regions; explored Australian coast. Exploration Period: 1616.

Heceta, Bruno, *Spanish.* Explored northwest coast of North America to 55° N. lat. Entered mouth of the Columbia River and sailed through Nootka Sound. Exploration Period: 1774-75.

Hedin, Sven Anders, *Swedish.* Traveled extensively in Persia, Turkestan, and Tibet. Discovered sources of the Brahmaputra and the Indus rivers. Exploration Period: 1885-1908.

Hennepin, Louis, *French.* Sailed (1679) with Sieur de La Salle (on first ship to sail Great Lakes) from Fort Frontenac to Green Bay. Explored upper Mississippi River from Illinois River to Minnesota. Exploration Period: 1675-82.

Herodotus, *Greek.* Traveled the coast of Asia Minor to the Black Sea. Visited Mesopotamia, Babylon, and Egypt. Helped found Athenian colony in southern Italy. Exploration Period: 484-425 B.C.

Heyerdahl, Thor, *Norwegian.* Led *Kon-Tiki* expedition. Drifted on balsa raft for 101 days from Peru to Polynesia. Proved that Peruvian Indians could have made similar voyages centuries before. Exploration Period: 1947.

Hillary, Sir Edmund Percival, *New Zealander.* Led several expeditions to investigate the Himalayas. He and the Nepalese mountain climber Tensing Norkay were the first to reach (1953) the summit of Mount Everest. Exploration Period: 1951-55.

Himilco, *Carthaginian.* Believed to have sailed up the west coast of Europe; possibly crossed to Britain. Exploration Period: 5th century B.C.

Hovell, William, *English.* With Hamilton Hume, led expedition into interior of southeastern Australia. Exploration Period: 1824-25.

Huc, Évariste Régis, *French.* Catholic missionary. Traveled through China, Mongolia, and Tibet; reached (1846) Lhasa. Exploration Period: 1839-46.

Hudson, Henry, *English* (sailed for Holland). Discovered (1609) Hudson River and ascended it to site of present-day Albany. Voyage gave Dutch their claim to region. Exploration Period: 1609.

HEYERDAHL

Sailing with five ships and 280 men on Sept. 20, 1519, he reached the bulge of Brazil and skirted the coast looking for a passage. He wintered in Patagonia and suppressed a serious mutiny. Between Oct. 21 and Nov. 28, 1520, he traversed the straits which would later bear his name and set out across the Pacific. The men almost starved on the lengthy crossing, for they missed almost all the islands. On Mar. 6, 1521, he reached Guam and then moved on to the Philippines, where he was killed on Apr. 27, 1521, in a scuffle with the natives. The expedition continued on to the Moluccas and secured a cargo of cloves at Tidore. One ship had been wrecked, one had deserted, and two more were too worn out to continue. The little *Victoria*, of barely 90 tons, went on alone under Sebastián del Cano. On Sept. 6, 1522, after almost three years out, the ship limped into the harbor of Seville, having completed the first circumnavigation of the world.

Magellan's voyage brought to a climax the great Age of Discovery. Ranking with the voyages of Columbus and Da Gama as one of the most significant in history, it at last gave Europe a fair idea of the size of the earth and its major geographical divisions. From that time on, the nature of exploration underwent a change. There were, to be sure, still plenty of areas to be investigated by sea—the eastern and western coasts of North America; the western coast of South America; the whole of Australasia; and finally, the frozen wastes of the Arctic and Antarctic.

Later Exploration of the Americas

Inland America. Exploration, however, tended to go inland, with persistent investigation of the interior of the Americas, chiefly by the Spaniards. This was linked in places with the spectacular work of the conquistadors. Whereas the Portuguese in the East were content with

LA SALLE

Hume, Hamilton, *English.* Explored interior of southeastern Australia. Exploration Period: 1824–25.

Hunt, Wilson Price, *American.* Pioneered Snake-Columbia River route to Pacific—later known as the Oregon Trail. Exploration Period: 1811-12.

Huntington, Ellsworth, *American.* Explored the upper Euphrates River and Chinese Turkestan. Exploration Period: 1901-6.

Iberville, Pierre Lemoyne, Sieur d', *French.* Made five expeditions (1686; 1689; 1691; 1694; 1697) against British posts in Hudson Bay. Captured (1696) St. John's, Newfoundland. Founded (1699) Old Biloxi, Miss. Explored Mississippi River delta. Exploration Period: 1686-1706.

Ibn Battuta, *Arabian.* Visited every Muslim nation from Spain to India. Traveled extensively in Far East, western Africa, and Arabia. Exploration Period: 1325-55.

Idrisi, al-, *Arabian.* Traveled through Europe, Asia Minor, and North Africa. Completed (1154) a description and map of world compiled from his observations. Exploration Period: 1117-34.

Johnson, Martin Elmer and Osa Helen Leighty, *American.* Together made several expeditions to many parts of Africa, photographing wildlife. Exploration. Period: 1921-35.

Jolliet or Joliet, Louis, *French.* With Father Jacques Marquette, led expedition to the upper Mississippi River and descended it to south of mouth of Arkansas River. Exploration Period: 1672-74.

Kämpfer, Engelbert, *German.* Made journey to Far East; explored and described Siam and Japan. Exploration Period: 1683-93.

Kennedy, Edmund, *Australian.* Led expedition to explore course of Victoria River. Exploration Period: 1847.

Kino or Chini, Eusebio Francisco, *Spanish.* Arrived (1681) as missionary in New Spain. Explored Gila and Colorado rivers. Reached head of Gulf of California and proved that California is not an island. Exploration Period: 1681-1702.

Lahontan, Louis de, *French.* Led French expedition into upper Mississippi River region; circulated erroneous report of "long river" leading to the "western sea." Exploration Period: 1688.

Laing, Alexander, *Scottish.* Explored (1824) West African coast and Niger River basin. Journeyed (1825-26) from Tripoli to Timbuktu, but was murdered on return trip. Exploration Period: 1824-26.

Lander, Richard Lemon, *English.* Accompanied (1825) Hugh Clapperton on African expedition to lower Niger River. Made two subsequent Niger expeditions. Exploration Period: 1825-34.

La Pérouse, Jean François de Galaup, Comte de, *French.* Explored coasts of northwest North America (in search of northwest passage), Siberia, and China. Continued voyage into the South Seas; discovered (1787) La Pérouse Strait. Sailed (1788) from Botany Bay and was lost at sea. Exploration Period: 1785-88.

La Salle, René Robert Cavelier, Sieur de, *French.* Explored (1669) upper Ohio River. Sailed (1679) in the *Griffon* (first sailing vessel on the Great Lakes) across Great Lakes to head of Lake Michigan. Descended (1681-82) the Mississippi River to its delta. Failed to locate mouth of the Mississippi from the Gulf of Mexico. Killed by mutinous crew on Texas coast. Exploration Period: 1666-87.

coastal forts and trading posts, the Spaniards sought with varying success to spread their authority over vast areas, the most striking episodes being the conquest of Mexico (1518–21) and of Peru (1532). Within the boundaries of the later United States, several expeditions explored the southeastern and southwestern regions. Ponce de León, harsh governor of Puerto Rico, was seeking a "Fountain of Youth" when he explored both coasts of Florida in 1513. Most of the others were seeking a rumored "El Dorado" rich in gold; trudging hundreds or even thousands of miles through the wilderness, they found much that was profitable to geography but not to themselves. Two big expeditions, going on almost simultaneously around 1540, explored the continent from Georgia across to southern California. Fernando, or Hernando, de Soto, a veteran of the conquest of Peru, set out from Tampa Bay in 1539, pushed up through Georgia to the Carolinas, came back through Alabama, crossed the Missis-

sippi (already discovered by another Spaniard), reached the Ozarks in Arkansas, and died on his return to the Mississippi; the survivors found their way down the river and then to Mexico. In the meantime Francisco de Coronado moved up from Mexico into what would be Arizona and New Mexico, and then, following a false rumor of gold, even up to Kansas.

In South America the conquistadors spread out from Peru, also in quest of further "El Dorado's." In exploration proper, as distinct from conquest, two significant expeditions were undertaken in the early 1540's, while De Soto and Coronado were exploring in North America. Pedro de Valdivia thoroughly explored coastal Chile, after an abortive attempt by Diego de Almagro a few years earlier. Valdivia established Valparaiso and Santiago, then, 500 mi. to the south, a city named for himself; he then sent ships to the Straits of Magellan. At the same time, Francisco de Orellana, starting in Ecuador, reached

Laudonnière, René Goulaine de, *French.* Sailed (1562) with Jean Ribault on expedition to Florida. Attempted (1564-65) second unsuccessful French effort to establish permanent colony on the coast of South Carolina. Exploration Period: 1562-65.

La Vérendrye, Pierre Gaultier de Varennes, Sieur de, *French.* Searched (1727-28) for an overland northwest passage to "western sea." Explored (1729-34) regions northwest of Lake Superior. Discovered (1739) Lake Manitoba. Led (1742-43) expedition that possibly reached as far west as the Rocky Mountains. Exploration Period: 1727-43.

Liechhardt, Friedrich Wilhelm Ludwig, *German.* Explored coast line of Australia from Queensland to Arnhem Land. Disappeared in attempt to cross the continent from east to west. Exploration Period: 1844-48.

Lewis, Meriwether, *American.* Coleader of the Lewis and Clark Expedition. Explored the Missouri River to its source, crossed the Rocky Mountains, and descended the Columbia to the Pacific. Exploration Period: 1804-6.

Lisa, Manuel, *American.* Explored upper Mississippi region and the northern Rocky Mountains. Led expedition, with John Colter as guide, to mouth of Bighorn River. Exploration Period: 1807-8.

Livingstone, David, *Scottish.* Greatest of African explorers. Crossed the Kalahari Desert and reached (1849) Lake Ngami. Discovered (1851) the Zambezi River. Traveled (1853) to Luanda. Discovered (1855) Victoria Falls and reached (1856) Portuguese East Africa. Commanded exploratory expedition (1857-63) to Zambezi River region. Explored upper Congo River tributaries and discovered (1859) Lake Nyasa. Reached (1871) the Lualaba tributary of the Congo. Believed lost, he was located (1871) by Sir Henry Stanley at Lake Tanganyika. Exploration Period: 1849-71.

Long, Stephen, *American.* Explored the plains region between the Platte and Arkansas rivers. Exploration Period: 1819-20.

Magellan, Ferdinand, *Portuguese.* Sailed (1519) with five ships and 270 men; reached (1520) Rio de la Plata, discovered and sailed through Strait of Magellan. Crossed Pacific and reached Philippines, where he was killed on Apr. 27, 1521. The *Victoria*, only remaining ship, under command of Juan Sebastián del Cano, completed (Sept. 6, 1522) first circumnavigation of the earth. Exploration Period: 1519-21.

Marquette, Jacques, *French.* With Louis Jolliet, discovered and explored (1672-74) the Mississippi River from the Wisconsin River to the Arkansas; returned to the Great Lakes region by way of the Illinois-Chicago portage. Exploration Period: 1666-74.

Meares, John, *English.* Explored (1786) coast of Alaska. Established (1788) trading post at Nootka Sound and built the *Northwest America,* first ship launched in British Columbia. Exploration Period: 1786-88.

Mendaña, Álvaro de, *Spanish.* Commanded voyage to South Pacific and discovered (1567) the Solomón Islands. On a later voyage, discovered (1595) the southern group of the Marquesas Islands. Exploration Period: 1567-95.

Narváez, Pánfilo de, *Spanish.* Conquistador. With Diego Velázquez, participated (1511) in conquest of Cuba. Made (1520) unsuccessful attempt to force Hernán Cortés out of Mexico. Sailed (1527) from Spain with five ships and 600 men to conquer and settle Florida. Landed (1528), but was turned back by Indians. Exploration Period: 1511-28.

MAGELLAN

the headwaters of the Amazon and sailed down its whole length to the sea.

France. By that time France had begun the exploration of the coast of North America. In 1524, Giovanni da Verrazano, a Florentine sailing for France, skirted the coast from North Carolina up to Maine, apparently being the first to sight New York harbor, where a great bridge would one day be named for him; he recorded clearly all he saw. Following Verrazano's voyage came those of a native Frenchman, Jacques Cartier, in 1534 and again the next year. Ascending the St. Lawrence to Quebec and Montreal, he established the French claim to that area. Like Cabot and others before them, Verrazano and Cartier had been looking for a route to the Pacific and the East.

Arctic. With the "southeast" passage around the Cape of Good Hope held by the Portuguese and the "southwest" through the Straits of Magellan controlled by the Spaniards, the nations of northern Europe were beginning to search for a "northeast" passage over the top of Europe and Asia or a "northwest" passage through or over North America. Thereby a stimulus was given to Arctic exploration. In 1553 an English expedition promoted by old Sebastian Cabot was sent in search of a northeast passage; one ship, under Richard Chancellor, reached Archangel in the White Sea and established a valuable commerce with Russia. Later the Dutch came into the picture, with Willem Barents the leading figure in three attempts between 1594 and 1597, discovering Spitsbergen with its valuable whale fishery. In the meantime, two Elizabethan "sea dogs" had penetrated the Arctic in quest of a northwest passage; Martin Frobisher made three voyages in 1576–78 and the skillful navigator John Davys three more in 1585–87. Both left their names on the Arctic map, as did William Baffin in 1615–16. After that, Arctic exploration died down for almost 200 years.

603

PIKE

Nearchus, *Macedonian.* Commanded fleet built by Alexander the Great on the Indus on voyage up the unknown Persian coast to rejoin Alexander at Susa. Exploration Period: 325-324 B.C.

Nicolet, Jean, *French.* Searched for northwest passage via the Great Lakes; explored Lake Huron to the Straits of Mackinac, Green Bay, and the Fox River. Exploration Period: 1618-34.

Nicuesa, Diego de, *Spanish.* Failed in attempt to establish a permanent colony at Darien on the Isthmus of Panama. Exploration Period: 1508-9.

Niebuhr, Karsten, *German* (explored for Denmark). Led expedition to Arabia; explored Yemen and reached cities of Sana and Mocha. Sailed for India from Mocha, returning by way of Persian Gulf and Tigris River to Turkey. Exploration Period: 1761-67.

Oderico, Friar, or Oderic of Pordenone, *Italian.* Traveled the southern Asiatic coast and went into central Asia. Exploration Period: 1318-31.

Ogden, Peter Skene, *Canadian.* Led expedition from Fort Spokane, Wash., to Snake River; explored northern Great Basin; discovered Humboldt River and explored shores of Great Salt Lake. Exploration Period: 1818-28.

Ojeda, Alonso de, *Spanish.* Conquistador. Sailed with Columbus on his second voyage (1493-94) to America. Joined briefly with Amerigo Vespucci in discovery and exploration of northern coast of South America. Appointed (1508) Governor of Nueva Andalucía (now northwest Colombia and the Isthmus of Panama). Exploration Period: 1493-1508.

Oñate, Juan de, *Spanish.* Explored (1598) New Mexico and took possession in the name of Spain. Led (1601) expedition into Oklahoma and Kansas; explored westward to the Colorado River and south to the Gulf of Mexico. Exploration Period: 1598-1601.

Orellana, Francisco de, *Spanish.* Participated in conquest of Peru. Crossed Andes and descended Amazon River to its mouth. Exploration Period: 1538-41.

Páez, Pedro, *Spanish.* A Jesuit missionary, he first traveled to Goa, India. He reached (1603) Ethiopia and visited (1613) source of the Blue Nile. Exploration Period: 1603-22.

Park, Mungo, *Scottish.* Explored the Gambia River. Drowned while attempting to trace course of Niger River. Exploration Period: 1795-1805.

Perez, Juan, *Spanish.* Explored northwest coast of North America from Monterey to 55° N. lat. Discovered (1774) Nootka Sound. Exploration Period: 1774-75.

Phoenician Sailors. Sailed Mediterranean west to edge of known world as early as 1200 B.C. Made trading voyages along the Iberian Peninsula to Dardanelles. May have sailed as far west as the British Isles. Reported by Herodotus to have sailed (c.600 B.C.) around Africa under orders of King Necho. Phoenician sailors may have reached East Indies. Exploration Period: 1200-600 B.C.

Pigafetta, Antonio, *Italian.* Accompanied Ferdinand Magellan; completed voyage (with Juan Sebastián del Cano) after Magellan's death and wrote famous account of the journey. Exploration Period: 1519-22.

Pike, Zebulon Montgomery, *American.* Led expedition (1805) to map upper Mississippi River. Explored (1806-7) newly acquired Louisiana Territory. Discovered (1806) Pikes Peak. Exploration Period: 1805-7.

After 1588. The defeat of the Spanish Armada in 1588 broke the Spanish-Portuguese monopoly of distant sea routes. The Dutch, English, and French were then able to go directly around the Cape of Good Hope to the East and also to settle in America north of Florida. Holland, on the threshold of a remarkable half-century of maritime effort, explored in all directions, mostly along routes already known, but occasionally engaging in new discovery. Outstanding as explorers were Willem Cornelis Schouten, who in 1616 discovered stormy Cape Horn as an alternative to the tortuous Straits of Magellan, and Abel Tasman, who in 1642 discovered Tasmania and New Zealand and in 1644 visited the northern coast of Australia. The Englishman Henry Hudson was sailing for Holland when he discovered the Hudson River in 1609 but for England a year later, when he found Hudson Bay. Under Samuel de Champlain, the French returned to the St. Lawrence, this time to stay. Between 1604 and 1615 Champlain explored the present-day Maritime Provinces, named Mount Desert on the Maine coast, and proceeded up the St. Lawrence above Montreal, discovering Lake Champlain and Lake Ontario. Later Frenchmen penetrated still farther into the interior. Among others, Jean Nicolet in 1634 discovered Lake Huron, Lake Michigan, and the upper Mississippi. Between 1678 and 1682, Sieur de La Salle discovered Niagara Falls, sailed the Great Lakes to the south end of Lake Michigan, and then went down the Mississippi.

Exploration of the Pacific

The latter half of the 18th century saw a sudden burst of interest in exploring the Pacific Ocean. Since Magellan's great voyage, discovery had been spasmodic. In 1577–80, Francis Drake, greatest of the English "sea dogs," made the second circumnavigation of the world, varying the Magellan pattern by sailing up the whole

Piñeda, Alonso Alvárez de, *Spanish.* Explored Gulf of Mexico; may have discovered mouth of the Mississippi River. Exploration Period: 1519.

Pinto, Fernám Mendes, *Portuguese.* Traveled and explored extensively in India, China, and Africa. First European to land (1546) on Japanese soil. Exploration Period: 1537-58.

Pinto, Serpa, *Portuguese.* Headed expedition across Africa from Angola to Mozambique. Exploration Period: 1877-79.

Pinzón, Vicente Yáñez, *Spanish.* Commanded the *Niña* on first expedition (1492-93) of Columbus. Commanded (1499-1500) expedition to Brazil; discovered mouth of the Amazon River. Explored (1508-9) coasts of Yucatán, Honduras, and Venezuela. Exploration Period: 1492-1509.

Pizarro, Francisco, *Spanish.* Conquistador. Explored northwestern South America. Conquered Peru. Exploration Period: 1510-41.

Pizarro, Gonzalo, *Spanish.* Conquistador, half brother of Francisco. Commanded (1540-42) expedition down Napo River to the Amazon. Exploration Period: 1536-42.

Pizarro, Hernando, *Spanish.* Conquistador, half brother of Francisco. Participated in conquest of Peru. Fought (1537) against Diego de Almagro and defeated (1538) and executed him. Exploration Period: 1530-38.

Pizarro, Juan, *Spanish.* Conquistador, half brother of Francisco. Assisted in conquest of Peru and fought with his brothers against the Inca Manco Capac during siege (1536-37) of Cuzo. Exploration Period: 1530-36.

Polo, Marco, *Italian.* Journeyed (1271) with father, Niccolò Polo, and uncle, Maffeo Polo, to China by way of central Asia and to the court of Kublai Khan at Kaifeng. Reached (1275) Peking. Traveled in the service of the Khan for next 17 years throughout central Asia, northern China, India, and southeastern Asia. Returned to Europe by sea by way of Sumatra, Ceylon, and Persia. Exploration Period: 1271-95.

Ponce de León, Juan, *Spanish.* Discovered and explored (1513) the coasts of Florida. Accompanied (1493) Columbus on second voyage. Participated in conquest of Higüey (Dominican Republic) and conquered (1508) Puerto Rico. Led (1521) second expedition to Florida, but was repulsed by the Indians. Exploration Period: 1493-1521.

Przhevalsky, Nikolai Mikhailovich, *Russian.* Explored central Asia and Mongolia. Crossed the Gobi Desert and entered Tibet. Credited with discovery of Lop Nor in southeastern Sinkiang Province, China, and of the Astin Tagh range. Exploration Period: 1867-88.

Pumpelly, Raphael, *American.* Conducted (1861-63) geological surveys in Japan and China. Made (1865) first extensive geological survey of the Gobi Desert. Conducted (1881-84) northern transcontinental survey and made (1903-4) explorations in Turkestan. Exploration Period: 1861-1904.

Queiros, Pedro Fernandes de, *Portuguese.* Sailed (1595) on expedition to Pacific; discovered northern group of the Marquesas Islands. On later expedition, discovered (1606) the New Hebrides islands. Exploration Period: 1595-1606.

Quesada, Gonzalo Jiménez de, *Spanish.* Conquistador. Explored the Magdalena River in search of El Dorado. Conquered (1538) New Granada and founded Bogotá. Led (1569) expedition to the confluence of the Guaviare and Orinoco rivers. Exploration Period: 1536-69.

POLO

west coast of the Americas as far as Vancouver and discovering San Francisco Bay. Around that same time, some of the islands Magellan had missed were discovered by Spanish expeditions; one of these led in 1606 to the finding by Luis Vaez de Torres of the strait between Australia and New Guinea. Tasman's discovery of Tasmania and New Zealand in 1642 has already been mentioned. At the end of that century, William Dampier, a wide-ranging English freebooter, prowled through those seas, twice reaching Australia. But there was no effective follow-up until the series of important naval voyages, partly scientific, after 1763. Some of these were French, under Louis Antoine de Bougainville, the Comte de La Pérouse, and others, but they were overshadowed by the three British voyages of Capt. James Cook in 1768, 1772, and 1776.

Capt. Cook's Three Voyages. On his first voyage, after observing the transit of Venus at Tahiti, Cook rediscovered New Zealand and visited the southeast coast of Australia, which he named New South Wales. On the second, he secured negative results by cruising widely in the Pacific to disprove the existence of a great southern continent north of Antarctica. On the third, he discovered the Hawaiian Islands and proceeded to the American northwest coast—to Alaska, to the Aleutians, and through the strait between America and Asia named for Vitus Bering, a Dane sailing for Russia, who had found it in 1728. Returning to Hawaii, Cook was killed in a fight with the natives. His voyages led to immediate results in opposite corners of the Pacific. In 1788, England established a penal colony in New South Wales and soon extended its settlements to other parts of Australia and then New Zealand. On the northwest coast of America, Cook's discovery of the sea otters led to a four-nation scramble for their valuable furs. Spain, in its last burst of colonial energy, moved north from California to Nootka Sound on the island later named for Capt. George Vancouver. Aided by

RALEIGH

Radisson, Pierre Esprit, *French.* With Médard de Groseilliers, explored Lake Superior and upper regions of Mississippi River—perhaps the first white men to enter region. Exploration Period: 1658-59.

Raleigh or Ralegh, Sir Walter, *English.* Sent out colonizing expeditions from England under Sir Richard Grenville and Sir Ralph Lane (1585) and under John White (1587), which ended tragically with the "lost colony" of Roanoke Island. Later led (1595-96) expedition up the Orinoco River in search of El Dorado. Exploration Period: 1585-1618.

Ribault, Jean, *French.* With René Laudonnière, sailed (1562) from France with 150 colonists. Landed near St. Johns River, Fla. Claimed region for France. Established colony on coast of South Carolina, but it was later abandoned. Second attempt (1564-65) to establish permanent colony also failed. Exploration Period: 1562-65.

Ricci, Matteo, *Italian.* Established first Christian missions in China. Exploration Period: 1578-1610.

Richthofen, Ferdinand, Baron von, *German.* Participated (1860-62) in German expedition to east Asia. A geographer and geologist, he made (1867-72) several exploratory journeys to China and Japan. Exploration Period: 1860-72.

Roggeveen, Jakob, *Dutch.* On exploratory voyage to South Pacific, discovered Samoa and visited and named Easter Island. Exploration Period: 1721-22.

Rubruquis, Guillaume, *Flemish.* Traveled to Mongolia by way of southern Russia and Turkestan. Exploration Period: 1253-55.

Schouten, Willem Cornelis, *Dutch.* Commanded (1615-16) expedition to Pacific, rounded Cape Horn (named for his birthplace, Hoorn), and discovered the Bismarck Archipelago. Exploration Period: 1615-16.

Schweinfurth, Georg August, *German.* An ethnologist, he explored extensively in eastern and equatorial Africa and in Arabia. Discovered (1870) the Uele River, and on a later journey established the existence of African Pygmies. Exploration Period: 1863-88.

Sevilha or Seville, Diogo de, *Portuguese.* On exploratory voyage into the Atlantic, discovered, and later may have settled, some of the Azores. Exploration Period: 1427-31.

Smith, Jedediah Strong, *American.* Guided party of 17 men from Missouri to the Rocky Mountains over the famous South Pass. Crossed (1825) from Great Salt Lake, reached the Colorado River, and continued across the Mojave Desert to California. Traveled north to the Columbia River and on to Fort Vancouver. Explored (1831) the Cimarron River, where he was killed by Comanche Indians. Exploration Period: 1822-31.

Smith, John, *English.* Explored and mapped much of the area in the vicinity of Jamestown, Va. (1607), and the coastal area of New England (1614). Exploration Period: 1606-14.

Solís, Juan Diaz de, *Spanish.* With Vicente Yáñez Pinzón, explored (1508-9) Yucatán, Honduras, and Venezuela. On later voyage (1515-16), explored mouth of the Rio de la Plata. Exploration Period: 1508-16.

Speke, John Hanning, *English.* Joined (1854) Sir Richard Burton's expedition to Somaliland. With Burton, explored (1856) east-central Africa and, exploring alone, discovered Lake Victoria. Exploration Period: 1854-63.

Peter Puget, Vancouver made detailed hydrographic studies in 1792–94; an American merchant captain, Robert Gray, was just ahead of him in discovering the Columbia River in 1792. That same year, a hardy Scottish fur trader, Alexander Mackenzie, was pushing across the Rockies to reach that same area in 1793; he had already discovered in 1789 the Mackenzie River, which flows into the Arctic. An American expedition, coming overland from Missouri under Meriwether Lewis and William Clark, reached the mouth of the Columbia in 1805. In the meantime the Russians had also entered the picture, gradually pushing down from Alaska, which they had been penetrating ever since Bering discovered it.

19th and 20th Centuries

The early 19th century produced a further crop of scientific exploring expeditions, the most celebrated of which was the voyage (1831–36) of H.M.S. *Beagle* in South American and Australian waters with Charles Darwin aboard as naturalist. In 1838–42, the "United States Exploring Expedition" conducted extensive scientific work in the Pacific and on the edge of Antarctica. These ventures blended into the complicated story of Arctic and Antarctic exploration, dormant during the two centuries since Baffin and Hudson, but now fully revived under the Russian, Fabian von Bellingshausen, and the Britons, James Weddell, John Ross, James C. Ross, George Back, William E. Parry, and Sir John Franklin.

Inland Africa. One of the greatest achievements of latter-day exploration was the revealing of the interior of Africa during the mid-19th century. Its coasts had been known since the early days of the Portuguese, but the rest of it was the "Dark Continent." Mungo Park, a Scot, had discovered part of the upper Niger in 1796 and 1806, but the great discoveries began in the 1840's, when David Livingstone, a Scottish medical missionary, began

Stanley, Sir Henry Morton, *Welsh.* Searched for and found (1871) explorer David Livingstone at Lake Tanganyika in Africa. On three subsequent expeditions (1874-77; 1879-84; and 1887-89), explored equatorial Africa, descended the Congo to the Atlantic Ocean, discovered Stanley Pool and Lake Edward, and explored the Ruwenzori Mountains. Exploration Period: 1871-90.

Strabo, *Greek.* Traveled widely through Asia Minor, western Asia, and the Mediterranean lands. Produced the most complete geography of ancient times. Exploration Period: c.20- c.15 B.C.

Stuart, John McDouall, *Scottish.* With Charles Sturt, explored (1844-45) central Australia. Led (1858-62) six expeditions into the interior. Made (1860) unsuccessful attempt to cross continent but succeeded (1862) on second attempt. Exploration Period: 1844-62.

Sturt, Charles, *English.* Commanded (1828-29) expedition to Australia to find source of the Macquarie River. Discovered (1828) the Darling River and explored the Murray River to its mouth. With John M. Stuart, explored (1844-45) southern Australia, and penetrated to center of the continent. Exploration Period: 1828-45.

Tasman, Abel Janszoon, *Dutch.* Made (1632-53) exploratory voyages to the Pacific and Indian oceans. Discovered (1642-43) Tasmania (named Van Diemen's Land) and New Zealand. Circumnavigated Australia. Exploration Period: 1632-53.

Teleki, Samuel, Count, *Hungarian.* Explored Africa; discovered lakes Rudolf and Stephanie. Exploration Period: 1888.

Thompson, David, *Canadian.* Surveyed (1797-98) source of the Mississippi River and crossed (1807) the Rocky Mountains to the Columbia River. Later explored entire Columbia River system. Exploration Period: 1787-1811.

Thomson, Joseph, *Scottish.* Led four expeditions to Africa. Reached (1879) Lake Tanganyika. Explored (1892-93) new areas in Kenya and Uganda and explored (1885) the Sudan. Traveled (1890) to southeast Africa and explored the Zambezi River. Exploration Period: 1879-90.

Tonti or Tonty, Henri de, *French.* Accompanied (1678) La Salle to Canada. Constructed first sailing vessel, *Griffon,* to sail the Great Lakes. Voyaged with La Salle to the mouth of the Mississippi River. Descended Mississippi again (1686) in search of La Salle. Exploration Period: 1678-86.

Torres, Luis Vaez de, *Spanish.* On voyage of exploration, sailed through, and possibly discovered, Torres Strait, between New Guinea and Cape York Peninsula, Australia. Exploration Period: 1606.

Tristam, Nuno, *Portuguese.* Explored the west coast of Africa; reached the Senegal River. Exploration Period: 1441-46.

Ulloa, Francisco de, *Spanish.* Explored (1538-39) Gulf of California; reached head of gulf and proved Lower California a peninsula. Exploration Period: 1538-39.

Valdivia, Pedro de, *Spanish.* Conquistador. Explored and conquered Chile. Participated with Pizarro in the conquest of Peru. Moved (1540) south over the Chilean Atacama Desert and founded Santiago and Valparaiso. Continued in Chile until 1547, when he returned to Peru. Appointed (1549) Governor of Chile. Killed (1554) in revolt of Araucanian Indians under Lautara. Exploration Period: 1535-52.

STANLEY

to explore the Zambezi region. During the 1850's he discovered Victoria Falls and Lake Nyasa. By the late 1860's, he was extending his solitary travels into the Tanganyika region. That part of East Africa had just been explored, between 1857 and 1864, by a series of expeditions under Richard F. Burton, John H. Speke, James A. Grant, and Samuel W. Baker; they had discovered lakes Tanganyika, Victoria, and Albert, and had identified the source of the White Nile. Some of this exploration had been sponsored by the Royal Geographical Society, which had been established in 1830 following similar organizations in France and Germany. In 1869, James Gordon Bennett, proprietor of the New York *Herald,* sent Henry M. Stanley, a Welsh-born journalist, to locate Livingstone who had disappeared from sight. They met at Ujiji on Lake Tanganyika in 1871. Soon afterward, Stanley traced the whole course of the Congo from East Africa to its mouth. The attendant publicity did much to precipitate the sudden "scramble for Africa" which quickly divided up the continent among various European powers.

Other Countries. Exploration was going on in other continents from the early 19th century, but none of it led to the striking results of those African discoveries. Many of the mysteries of Central Asia were unveiled by Nikolai M. Przhevalsky, Khrishna Pandit, Francis E. Younghusband, Sven A. Hedin, and Aurel Stein; Percy Sykes made extensive explorations in Western Asia and Charles M. Doughty penetrated the Arabian peninsula. The first major trip into the interior of Australia was made by John M. Stuart. Later the continent was traversed from south to north by Charles Sturt and by Robert O'Hara Burke and William Wills, both of whom died on the way back. In South America George C. Musters explored the interior of Patagonia; the wild jungles of the upper Amazon were explored by P. H. Fawcett, who disappeared mysteriously.

The early years of the 20th century saw spectacular

VERRAZANO

Vancouver, George, *English.* Sailed with Capt. James Cook on his second (1772-75) and third (1776-79) voyages around the world. Later embarked on voyage (1792-94) to northwestern coast of North America; explored and mapped Puget Sound. Exploration Period: 1772-94.

Varthema, Lodovico or Ludovici di, *Italian.* Traveled extensively in Arabia, Persia, India, and the East Indies. Exploration Period: 1502-7.

Velázquez, Diego, *Spanish.* Sailed with Columbus on second voyage (1493-94) to Hispaniola. Assisted by Pánfilo de Narváez, he invaded and conquered (1511-14) Cuba. Exploration Period: 1493-1514.

Verrazano, Giovanni da, *Italian* (sailed for France). Explored (1524) northeast coast of North America in search of Northwest Passage. Possibly the first European to enter New York Bay. Explored (1526) the West Indies, where he was attacked and killed by natives. Exploration Period: 1524-26.

Vespucci, Amerigo, *Italian* (sailed for Spain and Portugal). Accompanied (1499) Alonso de Ojeda on voyage to West Indies. Crossed to northern shore of South America; discovered and explored the mouths of Amazon River. In service of the Portuguese, explored (1501-2) the southern coast of South America, possibly to 50° S. lat.; discovered mouth of the Río de la Plata. Exploration Period: 1499-1502.

Vizcaíno, Sebastián, *Spanish.* Sailed up coast of California to about 43° N. lat. Discovered (1602) Monterey Bay. Exploration Period: 1602-3.

Walker, Joseph, *American.* Explored western United States; crossed the Great Basin between Great Salt Lake and California. Exploration Period: 1833-34.

Warburton, Peter Egerton, *English.* Used camels to cross western Australia from Alice Springs to Roebourne. Exploration Period: 1873.

Wilkes, Charles, *American.* Commanded U.S. naval exploring expedition to the Pacific Ocean. Explored (1840-41) Fiji and the Hawaiian Islands and the Pacific Northwest to the Juan de Fuca Strait. Completed (1842) a circumnavigation of the globe. Exploration Period: 1838-42.

Wills, William, *English.* With Robert Burke, made first crossing of the Australian continent from north to south. Both men perished on return journey. Exploration Period: 1860-61.

Wyeth, Nathaniel Jarvis, *American.* Led (1832-33) expedition over the Oregon Trail to the Columbia River. On second expedition (1834-36) founded Fort Hall and Fort William on the Columbia River. Exploration Period: 1832-36.

Xavier, St. Francis, *Basque.* Jesuit missionary in Goa (1541). Traveled to west India and explored coast from Ceylon northward. Visited Malacca (1545) and the Moluccas (1546). Introduced (1549-51) Christianity into Japan. Exploration Period: 1541-52.

Young, Ewing, *American.* With Kit Carson as guide, opened up the Spanish Trail between Santa Fe and Los Angeles. Exploration Period: 1829-31.

Younghusband, Sir Francis Edward, *English.* Explored and surveyed in Kashmir, central Asia, and Tibet. First European to cross the Muztagh Pass into India. His military expedition (1904) opened Tibet to Western trade. Exploration Period: 1886-1904.

---

achievements in the Arctic and Antarctic (*see* POLAR EXPLORATION). It is enough to mention here that the North Pole was discovered by Robert E. Peary on Apr. 6, 1909, and the South Pole by Roald Amundsen on Dec. 14, 1911, just one month before Robert F. Scott, who perished on the way out. Amundsen was also the first to traverse the long-sought Northwest Passage between 1903 and 1906; he later also traveled the Northeast Passage, first explored in 1879 by Baron Nils A. E. Nordenskjöld. Finally, in the course of one month, two atomic submarines of the U.S. Navy traversed the Arctic by way of the North Pole in 1959, and the observance of the International Geophysical Year (1959–60) led to intensive investigations in Antarctica and elsewhere around the world.

Consult Leithäuser, Joachim, *Worlds Beyond the Horizon* (1955); Herrmann, Paul, *Great Age of Discovery* (1958); Bettex, Albert, *Discovery of the World* (1960).

ROBERT G. ALBION, Harvard University

EXPLORER SATELLITE, first U.S. earth satellite, orbited on Feb. 1, 1958, by the U.S. Army, using a modified Redstone missile. Instrumentation was primarily a Geiger counter to measure radiation and a microphone to record collisions with micrometeorites.

EXPLOSION, any sudden or violent expansion process. The source is usually a chemical reaction in which huge volumes of hot gas are produced from very small volumes of solid or liquid reactants, with shattering effect on their environment. Explosives manufactured for the purpose allow precalculation of the effect. Explosions also occur when flammable gases, or combustible dust, such as gasoline vapor or flour dust, mix with air. Though such a mixture has a large volume, when ignited it expands enormously. Explosions which are not chemical occur when gases under pressure demolish their containers. *See also* EXPLOSIVES.

ENCYCLOPEDIA INTERNATIONAL

GUIDE TO FULL USE OF YOUR ENCYCLOPEDIA

GUIDE TO PRONUNCIATION

This pronunciation key was expressly designed by the late Irving Lorge, Ph.D., Teachers College, Columbia University, to present clear and accurate phonetic transcriptions of all entry words and names that might prove difficult for the average user of this work. Since many terms are derived from languages other than English, the reader will find these pronunciations, which appear immediately after the entry word, of considerable value. The pronunciations themselves were prepared by Ramona R. Michaelis, supervising editor of the Funk & Wagnalls Standard College Dictionary.

ă	pat, sad, snack, gas
ā	stay, sail, feign, tape
ä	father, psalm, arch, stark
â	air, fare, heir, where
à	French ami
b	boy, sob, abbot, bear
ch	chew, church, teacher, child
d	dandy, dog, date, ended
ĕ	men, said, fell, bury
e	seed, field, meat, meter
f	far, safe, graph, tough
g	guess, log, ghost, gone
h	hurl, harm, who, head
hw	when, why, whale, wheat

ENCYCLOPEDIA INTERNATIONAL is easy to use. It has five built-in aids for readers.

To get the most from your encyclopedia, use all the aids available to you.

- ■ Alphabetical plan for articles, as in most dictionaries
- ● Study and Career Guides with major articles
- ● Cross references to related terms ("See") and related topics ("See also")
- ● Suggestions of books for additional reading
- ■ Complete Index in Volume 20

SOLAR SYSTEM

- ■ Main Article
- ● Study Guide
- ● See also Astronomy, Mars, Moon, Sun
- ● Book Suggestions
- ■ Index Entries

INTERIOR DECORATION

- ■ Main Article
- ● Study and Career Guides
- ○
- ● Book Suggestions
- ■ Index Entries